THE CAMBRIDGE HISTORY
OF THE BRITISH EMPIRE

VOLUME TWO

CAMBRIDGE
UNIVERSITY PRESS
LONDON: BENTLEY HOUSE
NEW YORK, TORONTO, BOMBAY
CALCUTTA, MADRAS: MACMILLAN
TOKYO: MARUZEN COMPANY LTD

THE
CAMBRIDGE HISTORY
OF THE
BRITISH EMPIRE

General Editors

J. HOLLAND ROSE, M.A., Litt.D., F.B.A.
*Fellow of Christ's College; formerly Vere
Harmsworth Professor of Naval
History in the University
of Cambridge*

A. P. NEWTON, M.A., D.Lit., B.Sc., F.S.A.
*Emeritus Professor of Imperial
History in the University
of London*

E. A. BENIANS, M.A.
*Master of St John's College,
Cambridge*

VOLUME II
THE GROWTH OF THE NEW EMPIRE
1783–1870

CAMBRIDGE
AT THE UNIVERSITY PRESS
1940

PRINTED IN GREAT BRITAIN

PREFACE

THE Old Empire consisted for the most part of contiguous territory in North America which had been settled and peopled from the British Isles. Though not the product of a plan of State building, its natural and historical ties with the mother land seemed to promise a lasting union. But British statesmen lacked the imagination and sympathy equal to their opportunity, and the opportunity passed. The foundations of the Second Empire, the rise and development of which are now our theme, were laid with more deliberation. So far as there was a definite policy in its foundation, that policy was not the expansion of the nation, which in the late eighteenth century seemed to have halted, but the traditional policy of enlarging our maritime and commercial power. In favouring circumstances, Great Britain, in the thirty years following the loss of her American colonies, added to the remnants of her older Empire dominion in India and a circle of small possessions, scattered round the world, and necessary to her object. Thus the new Empire, as it took shape in 1815, was made up of many different communities—real English colonies in Canada and the West Indies; penal settlements, growing into colonies, in the Southern Pacific; conquered European colonies in Canada, South Africa and the West Indies; kingdoms annexed in India, Ceylon and the Malay Archipelago; some footholds in tropical Africa, and strategic posts guarding the routes of trade in the Mediterranean, the Caribbean Sea, the South Atlantic and the Indian Ocean—a vast diversity of race and region.

The object of this expansion of power was not, as Adam Smith had said of the First Empire, to raise up a people of customers, but to secure to Great Britain the freedom to sell all over the world the products of her growing industries. The stimulus of the industrial revolution created the motive of imperial policy. Little conscious of the manifold problems in which their activity entangled us, our merchants and statesmen, seeking new markets, were binding up our fortunes with a quarter of the human race.

As English colonists had been left to govern themselves, a commercial policy had sufficed for an imperial policy in the Old Empire, but English statesmen were now setting themselves a larger task, and had to learn the art of government in a great variety of climes and circumstances and over a great variety of peoples. And this not in a stationary world, but in a world awakened to a new energy with the discoveries and stimulus of industrial and political revolution. And not in a stationary empire, but in one which grew and changed before their embarrassed eyes.

In earlier centuries our colonial policy was not affected to any appreciable extent by religious and humanitarian movements at home. But in the years when the Second Empire was taking shape the impulses of evangelical religion were powerful forces in English politics, missionary societies exerted an important influence, and the Humanitarian movement was pursuing its eager and tumultuous course. Public attention in England was increasingly directed to the issues of slavery and the slave trade and our relations with aboriginal races, which were bound up with problems of colonial government and imperial expansion.

In the Old Empire, too, there had been little movement of population from the mother country to the colonies, once the colonies had been planted. But the New Empire took shape in an age when economic changes at home and improved means of communication stimulated and facilitated emigration. Population was growing apace and seemed redundant, and, with the end of the Napoleonic Wars, the outflow overseas, checked for so long, began again and swelled in volume. It was not the statesmen and merchants who wished to change the character of the Empire; it was the emigrants spreading over the new lands, transforming trading places and penal stations, who built up again colonies of settlement. There was a second dispersion of population, wider and more continuous than the great emigration of the seventeenth century. In England reform was in the air, the tide of British freedom was flowing again, and the emigrants carried with them English ideas of political liberty to our colonies in the New World, to South Africa and the Pacific.

Thus, in the generation after the great wars, opinion was slowly turning against some of the main principles of our colonial system—against slavery, on which the economic life of some colonies was based, against the penal system which had supplied the original nucleus of labour in them, against the restriction of colonial trade and against the control of the executive government of the colonies from home. Criticism of our colonial system came from all sides—religious, humanitarian, political and economic—and after 1830 was reinforced by the Colonial Reformers with their ideas of systematic colonisation and their ideal of reviving the ancient glory of British expansion. While Colonial Secretaries, following one another in rapid succession, sought to solve colonial problems in relation to Parliamentary exigencies, one steadfast and penetrating mind was interpreting imperial policy in ethical terms. The intellect and purpose of James Stephen raised colonial government to a higher political plane and contributed greatly to the attempts to solve its new problems. The Canadian rebellion brought to a head the question of the centralisation of colonial government. Durham poured a flood of light on imperial relations and bade ministers cut the Gordian knot in which their government of the greater colonies was entangled. Thus, in swift succession, a series of great changes revolutionised our imperial system. Slavery was abolished, transportation was abolished, the restrictions on colonial trade were loosened, and responsible government was introduced. There was a new birth of colonial freedom.

Historians have done justice to the restoration of colonial self-government, which was the great contribution of early and mid-Victorian statesmen to the government of the Empire. But to the colonial policy of the half century which preceded this development, and to the parallel organisation of the Crown Colony system by the side of semi-independent communities, they have given less attention. It has been one of our objects to bring this part of British colonial policy into a truer perspective.

In the mid-Victorian age the new principles of colonial government were being steadily applied, tested and extended in the light of experience, and our colonial system was being adapted to the changed conditions created by the emancipation of the slaves, the flow of emigration, the adoption of free trade by the mother country and the spread of responsible government. Britain, strong in her expanding trade, lost little by her economic concessions, and on the political side was relieved, to the immense gain of herself and the colonies, of responsibilities she could never properly discharge. She faithfully pursued the policy of endowing her greater colonies with the advantages and, as far as she could, the duties of self-government, self-development and local defence. The Crown Colonies—many of them small in size and with historic problems of mixed populations, local clashes of interests, and financial difficulties—could not be assimilated in their political system to the young self-governing nations, and the dual character of the Empire, as an association of dependent and semi-independent communities, became more apparent. For foreign policy and imperial defence the Home Government was solely responsible, and it regulated the relations of the members of the Empire and, in the case of Crown Colonies, their principal domestic affairs.

The unity in this vast diversity was to be seen in the influence of English law, language and literature, English political conceptions and the methods of English industry and finance, which, in varying degrees, and with little official pressure or deliberate policy, was permeating this vast association of human groups. Peace, order and the rule of law came as benefits to many troubled lands; hopes and ideals were stirred, a spirit of freedom roused, and there was set a pattern of material and intellectual progress. At the same time the enterprise of English traders and capitalists—building up commercial, industrial and agricultural undertakings in countries oversea—enriched the mother country, brought settlement and industry to empty lands, and, with good and ill results, multiplied the contacts of ancient and primitive civilisations with the life of the West. The growth of the Empire was acting as a slow but powerful agent in the awakening of the world by Western progress to a new unity.

Meantime, English opinion was adjusting itself to the loss of the supposed advantages of controlling colonial trade and governing distant possessions. To some minds the uselessness of colonial appendages was now convincingly demonstrated, but others had a vision of an empire that grew stronger as it grew more free, and already sensed the beginnings of a British Commonwealth of nations, with the Crown as the symbol of its unity. A new conception of the Empire dawned faintly on the horizon.

Throughout these years the expansion of the Empire proceeded— by natural growth in new lands, by agreement with rival colonial powers, and by occasional war, conquest and annexation. Our Government watched with jealous eyes the security of our communications and the interests of our overseas subjects, yet sought to avoid new commitments, which missionaries, traders and our colonists themselves often pressed upon them. In the New World our aim was peacefully to settle our territorial disputes with the United States and to secure our South American trade; in the Pacific to avoid expansion; in China to press our trade; in India to extend our sovereignty within the limits of the natural frontiers of the land; in Africa to limit expansion, while opening up by exploration new commercial opportunities; in Europe to avoid conflict, but to maintain unchallenged the security of the routes of trade. It was a period of expansion, and yet the impression conveyed by our policy, except in India, is of an obstinate reluctance to extend the responsibilities of the Empire. In India our attitude was different. Down to the Mutiny there was no pause in the extension of British power, and no doubt in the British mind of the necessity for our supremacy in India and of the superiority of our government over that of the Indian princes.

The cardinal fact in this phase of British expansion was the relative absence of competition with other colonising powers. The strenuous colonial rivalry of earlier centuries was abated; England and France, turning for the most part in different directions, could peacefully settle their occasional collisions; Spain, Portugal and Holland were no longer active and were left in the peaceful possession of what remained of their colonial empires; Russia was occupied in her great task of colonising northern and central Asia; and no new rivalries arose, for neither Italy nor Germany as yet aspired to colonial power. To a great extent Great Britain was free to choose whether and where and when she would seek further expansion. No colonising power ever took or refused so many opportunities, and no great empire was ever built with so little show or use of force. This part of our subject is treated partly in two separate chapters, and, partly woven of necessity into the general story. So far as concerns the Dominions, it has already been dealt with in other volumes.

If less is said of British sea power in this volume than in our first, it is not that it was less important, but because, after Trafalgar, it was virtually unchallenged. Sea power remained the condition of British expansion, of Britain's influence for peace and order in the world, and of Britain's existence as a great power. The great routes of trade which she guarded were not mere roads, but the arteries of her life.

For the rest our plan is sufficiently indicated in the list of chapters. Our task has been to set out in its continuity and unity a story which has many aspects and runs into many separated incidents. It is the story of the overflowing activity of a growing people, who, by their maritime proclivities, and in the absence of much competition, carried their enterprise to many parts of the world and dragged their reluctant Government into the military and political problems of an imperial State. In the flux of human change a great State may fulfil other purposes than those its founders designed or foresaw, and the historian may draw the moral from the heterogeneous character of our Second Empire that diversity of race and geography need be no obstacle to a union of states and nations in free and peaceful co-operation.

It remains to express our thanks to all our contributors and, on their behalf and our own, to the many other scholars who have helped our work with their advice on various questions, and, in particular, to Dr A. D. McNair, Vice-Chancellor of the University of Liverpool, who read the proofs of the chapter contributed by the late Professor A. Pearce Higgins, to Admiral Sir Herbert Richmond for assisting us with the chapter on imperial defence, to the late Professor Harold Temperley, Professor J. H. Clapham, Professor Paul Knaplund, Dr A. G. Doughty, Professor D. A. McArthur, Professor J. L. Morison, Dr W. P. Morrell, Dr A. C. V. Melbourne and Dr J. C. Beaglehole.

For his work on the Bibliography we are particularly indebted to Mr A. T. Milne, who, in addition to his own contributions to both Parts, has arranged and supplemented the material submitted by some of our contributors.

We also gratefully acknowledge once more the help so readily given by Mr S. C. Roberts, Secretary to the Syndics, and by the Staff of the University Press.

J. H. R.
A. P. N.
E. A. B.

30 *June* 1939

ABBREVIATIONS OF TITLES OF WORKS AND
SOURCES QUOTED IN THIS VOLUME

Adm.	Admiralty Records in P.R.O., London.
B.M. Add. MSS.	British Museum, Additional MSS.
B.F.S.P.	British and Foreign State Papers.
B.T.	Board of Trade Records in P.R.O., London.
Cal. St. Pap. Col. Cal. St. Pap. Dom. Cal. St. Pap. For.	Calendars of State Papers, Colonial, Domestic, Foreign, in P.R.O., London.
C.H.B.E.	Cambridge History of the British Empire.
C.H.B.F.P.	Cambridge History of British Foreign Policy.
C.J.	Journals of the House of Commons.
C.M.H.	Cambridge Modern History.
Chatham MSS.	MSS. of Earl of Chatham and the younger Pitt in P.R.O., London.
C.O.	Colonial Office Records in P.R.O., London.
D.N.B.	Dictionary of National Biography.
E.H.R.	English Historical Review.
F.O.	Foreign Office Records in P.R.O., London.
Hansard	Hansard's Parliamentary Debates.
Hist. MSS. Comm.	Reports of the Historical Manuscripts Commission, London.
H.O.	Home Office Records in P.R.O., London.
L.J.	Journals of the House of Lords.
N.R.S.	Publications of the Navy Records Society, London.
Parl. Pap.	Great Britain, Parliament, House of Commons, Parliamentary Papers.
P.R.O.	Public Record Office, London.
St. Pap. Col. St. Pap. Dom. St. Pap. For.	MSS. Documents of State Papers, Colonial, Domestic, Foreign, in P.R.O., London.

TABLE OF CONTENTS

CHAPTER I

THE BEGINNINGS OF THE NEW EMPIRE
1783–1793

BEFORE the Peace of Versailles ended the long and unpopular war England had become reconciled to the loss of her American colonies. The idea that she could reconquer them vanished in the disappointment of successive failures; the idea that their loss would be the ruin of England was vanishing too, as sober opinion took stock of facts and the country recovered stability of mind after the shock it had sustained. France had indeed, as Cowper wrote, "picked the jewel out of England's crown", with consequences too vast to be measured. And peace was bought with other sacrifices too, of which ministers offered the best defence they could.[1] As they were surrendering what their predecessors had won they naturally depreciated what their predecessors had praised, and the necessity of self-defence so sharpened their vision that they prophesied as great a trade with America under conditions of freedom as of monopoly. Our retention of Canada, Gibraltar and nearly all our East and West Indies, showed that the victors had not dictated terms, and, though it was not to be expected that Spain would rest content or that the ceaseless friction about her colonial trade would end, with France the settlement had been comprehensive and removed for the time being all questions in dispute between the two countries. However good a face was put upon the matter, there had been a loss of valuable islands and places of trade, and Parliament had to be reminded that a nation cannot emerge scatheless from an unsuccessful war. But though in the years of depression in which the war ended gloomy doubts prevailed and Parliament abolished (1782) the Third Secretary of State (for the Colonies) and the Board of Trade, the country turned in characteristic fashion from vain regrets to the urgent problems of the hour. In the East Indies, in the West Indies, in Canada and at home difficulties multiplied and unforeseen complications appeared.

There was indeed little time for chastening reflections; for the wave that submerged the old empire was uncovering a new. Out of the disastrous war were coming dominion in Asia, with responsibilities too large to be welcomed or refused, and new settlements in Canada and Nova Scotia with their incalculable future; and in the wake of the war, but no less its product, followed new ventures in the Pacific and in tropical Africa which were to lay broad again the foundations of our imperial power. "It appeared a madness", Shelburne said a few years later, "to think of colonies after what had passed in North America."[2] But the new empire was not based on deliberate policy

[1] See *C.H.B.E.* I, 775–83. Parl. Hist. xxviii, 946.

and had no formal beginning. Who would have proposed to found
a new empire with the exiles from the old colonies, the escaped
negroes, the convicts now excluded from the New World? Yet in
providing for them the new beginnings were made. Far less than the
first empire was the second the product of a desire for expansion;
it sprang again shoot by shoot from the old stock and was sustained
by the same vitality of maritime power and commercial enterprise.
Though England in 1783 certainly hoped to recover her lost influence
in Europe and to maintain her greatness as a seafaring and trading
nation, the majority of Englishmen probably neither contemplated
nor desired that she should become again a great colonial power.
Those who like Adam Smith reflected on the history of her Empire,
while they did justice to the wonderful feats of the explorers, merchants
and captains who had staked out her great claims, and recognised
in her the least ungenerous of mother countries, yet believed that her
whole policy had been a mistaken one, that her Empire had added
little to her strength and that all the labour of generations of statesmen had conjured up nothing but a golden dream which was as well
dissipated. On the mercantile spirit of our policy was laid the blame
for this disastrous illusion. "A great Empire", wrote Adam Smith,
"has been established for the sole purpose of raising up a nation of
customers."[1] Such an Empire could not be preserved and was not
worth preserving. And, too late to influence the destiny of America,
he put forward the alternative idea of mother country and colonies
bound together on a footing of equality, sharing in due proportion
the burden and opportunities of the Empire and sending representatives to a common Parliament.[2] Whatever the cause, whether the
selfish mercantilism or the natural growth of human societies, the
plain fact stood out that English statesmanship in the eighteenth
century had not been equal to the task of uniting her noblest colonies
to the motherland, and no desire was felt to repeat an effort which
after so much exertion and expense had collapsed so ignominiously.

But the sense of failure was a mood rather than a conviction. We
did not give up Canada and Nova Scotia, or any West India island
we could keep, and we did not hesitate to embark on the government
of Indian provinces or relax our activities in any sea. In December
1781 Horace Walpole was writing of "the moment of the fall of an
Empire", but he was soon taking comfort: "I did not much expect
to live to see peace, without far more extensive ruin than has fallen
on us."[3] It was soon clear that Great Britain was not mortally
wounded by the sacrifices of the Peace. She did not feel herself
beaten. The faces that look down on us to-day from the canvases
of Gainsborough show little consciousness of national ruin. Even in
her great loss, that of America, she had not received the "fatal blow"

[1] Smith, Adam, *Wealth of Nations* (ed. J. S. Nicholson), p. 274.
[2] *Ibid.* pp. 257–9.   [3] *Letters of Horace Walpole* (ed. 1840), VI, 151, 192.

of which Shelburne spoke in July 1782. The grievous truth proclaimed by Adam Smith, that she had so governed her Empire as to gain little from it, carried this consoling consequence that its diminution was the less severely felt. She still held those great advantages from which her oversea power had sprung. She had her commanding geographical position, her contact with the Old World and her outlook to the New, a position which grew ever more central for trade and communication as the world progressed. She had recovered her sea power. Disastrous as the war had been, at its conclusion she enjoyed an unquestioned maritime superiority and an undiminished trade. To the unexplored and unoccupied continents, islands and coasts of the Pacific she had an open road, and for the growth of her Eastern power she retained the essential instrument. Her mercantile community was ready for new enterprises. And heavy as was the debt under which she laboured, the country was not bankrupt. Solvency and prosperity could soon be restored by prudent management. The decade that followed the American war was a time of great commercial activity. As Shelburne said, "This seems to be the era of protestantism in trade. All Europe appear enlightened, and eager to throw off the vile shackles of oppressive ignorant monopoly".[1] Great Britain was not likely to lag behind in an age of commercial enterprise and increasing freedom. New pioneers of expansion were pointing the way to new spheres of action and touching the imagination of the young. At Oxford Richard Wellesley had just won a prize for a Latin poem on Cook.[2] "The latest Discoveries", remarks a contemporary writer, "appear to engross conversation from the politest circles and throughout every class in the Kingdom."[3] Though we were not eager for new colonies, we cultivated assiduously every possibility of trade and encouraged exploration—"an object", says the same writer, "worthy the prosecution of a commercial people". In the new circumstances of the age and the coming men lay the promise of the future: "the rising generation does give one some hopes", wrote Horace Walpole.[4]

Nor was the effect of the war on other powers immaterial to our prospects. If Great Britain had suffered much, her opponents had suffered more. "Of all the European powers concerned in the war, Great Britain suffered the least in the event of it, especially in a commercial view."[5] France and Spain had achieved a costly revenge, and Great Britain could more easily pay for her defeat than they for their victory. If American independence was a cruel blow to the British Empire, it was also a notable example to the colonies of other powers, more pleasing to the philosopher than the statesman. Long

---

[1] Parl. Hist. XXIII, 409.
[2] Mallet, Sir C., History of the University of Oxford, p. 150.
[3] Bankes, T., Universal Geography (? 1787), pp. 1, 9.
[4] Letters, VI, 126.   [5] Macpherson, D., Annals of Commerce, IV, 9.

a favourite prophecy of French writers, it was not so satisfactory a prospect to the other member of the Family Compact. Spain indeed was slow to recognise what she had helped to achieve, and France did not welcome the large concessions with which Great Britain sought to conciliate the feelings of her late colonists. The reverberations of the event were heard in other continents. The colonial world moved nearer the verge of revolution, and Louis XVI found that the liberty necessary for Americans might be asked for nearer home. It was soon apparent that our neighbours had humiliated more than they had weakened us, and weakened rather than exalted themselves. The Peace left France, Spain, the United States and Holland at variance with each other and freed us for a time from fear of their joint pressure. Though little dreamed of in England at the moment, the possibility of a new expansion was opening before her. The same men who saw her power sink beyond the Atlantic hailed in the East its second dawn, and were soon scanning the horizon of the world for new scenes of action and gain.

For her rapid recovery after the Peace of Versailles the country owed much to the wisdom and firmness which inspired the conduct of her affairs. We need not here follow in detail the fluctuating course of domestic politics which had brought the younger Pitt to power. It is enough to say that the Marquis of Rockingham had taken North's place in March 1782, and that when he died in July Shelburne became head of the administration and negotiated the preliminaries of the Peace. In February 1783 a coalition between Fox and North censured the proposed terms of peace and put the Government in a minority in the House of Commons. In April the King was forced to give them office, and in November they accepted almost unchanged the Peace they had condemned. Thurlow told Pitt that the King "had *gone through the worst*, in the struggle which ended in bringing them in", and "could never forgive their conduct".[1] Certainly he showed little scruple in getting them out, dismissing them after he had contributed to the defeat of Fox's India Bill in the Lords. Pitt assumed office in December and carried on the Government for a few weeks in a minority. In March, he wrote to Rutland, he had the enemy "on their backs", and after the dissolution he gained power as the undoubted choice of the nation. An imperial question had been the occasion of the Coalition's downfall, but the country, in rejecting them, judged between the antagonists, not on the merits of their Indian policies, but as custodians of the public interest. On the one hand was the son of the great statesman who had raised the country to its highest renown in his "immortal war", the memory of whose victories was still ringing in the ears of Englishmen; on the other, joined now in unholy alliance, were the old foes, of whom one had borne the responsibility for the war which had sunk the British

---

[1] Pitt to Temple, 22 July 1783. *Dropmore Papers* (Hist. MSS. Comm.), I, 216.

name and power so low and the other had rejoiced in his failure and the collapse of British arms. With the victory of Pitt the King escaped Whig domination, but at the price of an independent Prime Minister. His personal government ended. It was the King's policy which had lost America, but now it was made clear that no succeeding King would have a similar opportunity. The relations of Great Britain with the outer Empire would be determined henceforward by a Ministry responsible to Parliament.

In ten years Pitt did for Great Britain what Frederick the Great had predicted, though, apparently, not expected. He restored her "to the importance which she had formerly held in the scale of Europe".[1] He did also what no one either predicted or expected; he made the beginnings of a new empire. Partly as the consequence of historic accident and good fortune, but none the less on foundations laid (though not all happily) in this decade, Great Britain's second empire was constructed. Pitt was not, like his father, a great imperial statesman, with words on his lips which could touch the heart alike of America and Bengal. But he brought to the problems of the Empire a constructive talent, by which India benefited, and a generous breadth of view, which might have transformed our relations with Ireland. He regarded India as "an object of the greatest consideration to the Empire". Perhaps he remembered his father's words: "the hearts and good affections of the people of Bengal are of more worth than all the profits of ruinous and odious monopolies." He would have made great concessions to reconcile Ireland. He would have given her equal commercial privileges in return for a proper contribution towards the burden of the Empire, raised her from a state of subordination to a real partnership, provided only "that *her strength and riches will be our benefit*".[2] His humanity shone out in his support of the movement to abolish the slave trade, and his desire for justice in his vote for the impeachment of Hastings. Of imperial defence he wrote: "There can be but *one navy* for the Empire at large and it must be administered by the executive power in this country."[3] If no imagination appears in his dealings with Australia, he was a far-sighted and vigilant guardian of our imperial interests and was only too ready to vindicate them with all the might of Britain. Three times during the decade of peace he ran the risk of war, with France in 1787, with Spain in 1790, with Russia in 1791, in defence of our trade and Empire. Pitt had not the authority to realise all his ideas of imperial reconstruction. He had not, it is said, a close understanding of the policy of Continental States. The times were not propitious, and his Government was for long too much of a one man affair. In the circumstances of his advent to power he

[1] *C.H.B.F.P.* I, 143.
[2] Pitt to Rutland, 7 Oct. 1784. *Pitt-Rutland Correspondence*, 1781–7, p. 43.
[3] Pitt to Rutland, 6 Jan. 1785. *Op. cit.* p. 73.

could not form a strong Cabinet, and like many able men he seems not to have desired colleagues of the first rank. "The country", wrote Gibbon in 1786, "seems to be governed by a set of most respectable boys."[1] "When I have finished the portrait of the minister", wrote Wraxall in 1787, "I may be said in it to have comprehended almost the whole administration."[2] Save for one other, Wraxall sees "only a vast vacuity". There could be no mistaking the great abilities of the Lord Chancellor Thurlow, more apt though he was to display them in criticising than in collaborating with his colleagues. In the "vast vacuity" that remained, which Pitt's fine talents could not wholly illumine, Lord Sydney shone, a minor constellation, but "a most practicable, punctual, and good humoured correspondent".[3] The kindly fates and not a genius for empire prepared for him the honour of founding another England in the Southern Seas. Time was to bring Pitt more support at home, but greater difficulties abroad.

Against the ministers were powerful opponents in the Commons and the Lords, and in the problems of imperial, foreign and domestic policy which confronted them was a maze in which the ablest might go astray. "Ireland", wrote Rutland, "is not a land of tranquillity."[4] It might imitate America. The state of Europe was a cause of constant anxiety. Our position on the morrow of the Peace was low indeed. We had lost our influence on the Continent. France and Spain were leagued against us. Holland, our traditional ally, was under French influence and soon bound to France by an alliance (1785). Austria and Russia were attached to our enemies. Prussia would not take the risks of an alliance. Frederick the Great told Cornwallis in September 1785 that "he considered England as his ally", but that no further treaty could be contemplated for the present.[5] The assertion of our interests oversea was in such circumstances hazardous and difficult. But Pitt was fearless in policy at home and abroad. He had a clear conception of the basis of England's strength—her wealth, her maritime power, her commercial activity—he saw her interest was peace, but she must be ready for war. To be strong again she must recover her financial stability. Hence those financial measures which occupy the chief place in the early years of his administration —the funding of debt, the suppression of smuggling,[6] the reduction of duties, the additional taxes, the consolidation of customs and excise, and those larger measures for the extension of commerce—the commercial treaty with France and the reconstruction of the Board of Trade. Pitt was an apt pupil of Adam Smith, and it was not his

[1] Prothero, R. E., *Letters of Edward Gibbon*, II, 143.
[2] Wraxall, Sir N., *A Short Review of the Political State of Great Britain*, 1787.
[3] Rutland to Pitt, 16 June 1784. *Pitt-Rutland Correspondence*, p. 20.
[4] Rutland to Pitt, 16 June 1784. *Ibid.* p. 19.   [5] *Cornwallis Corresp.* I, 209.
[6] "His restraints on the smuggling of tea have already ruined the East India Companies of Antwerp and Sweden,...even the Dutch will scarcely find it worth their while to send any ships to China." Gibbon to Lord Sheffield, 13 March 1785. Prothero, *Gibbon*, II, 127.

fault that free trade and commercial equality between England and Ireland and commercial reciprocity with America were not established. But in the years of peace the debt was reduced by ten millions, the revenue expanded, and English trade greatly increased. The value of our exports and imports rose from under twenty millions in 1782 to nearly forty in 1790.[1] Nor did his economies involve parsimonious treatment of army and navy.[2] Our forces in the East Indies and the Mediterranean were strengthened, and a scheme of fortifications was carried through in the West Indies in order that the islands might hold out till a relieving force could reach them. These measures made England formidable again: she became a desirable ally and could take up any challenge to her interests oversea.

While Pitt was making it his first business at home to restore order to our finances and prosperity to our commerce, and in Europe to recover the lost alliance with the Dutch and rescue the country from the isolation in which the late war had left her, oversea it was necessary to face the consequences of the war and to adjust our policy to the new circumstances of the Empire. Relations with America, the future of Canada, the needs of the West Indies, the struggle raging in the East, were among the urgent problems which the war had bequeathed, and our imperial politics moved accordingly for some years in the wake of that great catastrophe until, with another and greater war, new tides of circumstance obliterated the force of the old.

The thirteen colonies were gone irrecoverably—that was the fundamental fact, and with them went the vast interior of the continent, so recently conquered from the French. And Florida had gone back to Spain. On the continent we retained only Nova Scotia, with its population of fishermen and farmers, Quebec, with its compact French settlement and its two ports, and the vast tract of land to north and west where the agents of the Hudson's Bay Company carried on a valuable fur trade. Off the mainland we had the islands in the Gulf of St Lawrence and Newfoundland, that nursery of sailors. The great maritime dominion on either side of the North Atlantic which had been envisaged in 1763 had passed from the horizon. Unless new developments strengthened our position, we were left with but a precarious hold on the skirts of the New World.

But what were to be our future relations with the young Republic to which we had now given both birth and recognition? It did not perhaps require much imagination to realise the importance of this question, and our Government at once displayed a genuine intention to secure the friendship of America. The large concessions of territory, the access to the British North American fisheries which the Peace

---

[1] Buxton, S., *Finance and Politics*, i, p. 4 n.
[2] Rose, J. H., *Short Life of William Pitt*, pp. 44–5.

granted were in proportion to the magnitude of this object. In defending them ministers frankly explained in Parliament that they had tried to avoid harsh discussions with America and to lay the foundations of future amity. In the past we had counted on the resources of America to strengthen us in our long struggle with France. We could not count on them in the future, but we might prevent them from being thrown into the scale against us. It was not to our interest that the two Powers, either of which might with good reason covet our remaining possessions on the continent, should remain bound in alliance. Policy as well as sentiment pointed to the wisdom of friendship with the United States. Our experience both in attacking the Canadian frontier before 1763 and in defending it since made us desire peace in America. But to end a civil war so that it leaves no wounds, to reconcile on a new basis a revolted colony and its motherland (the more embittered, and the more disposed to expect much of each other, because of their former ties), is a problem to baffle the resources of statesmanship.

The Peace made a good beginning, but it did not promise the Americans one thing they greatly desired, a close commercial treaty with Great Britain. That was a matter which in the circumstances raised difficult issues for Great Britain, for the Americans wanted most of all to retain their old West Indian trade. Fox held that the political and commercial arrangements should be kept separate, since the former were subject to the approval of France and, moreover, the latter required full consideration. So no arrangement for a commercial treaty was included in the Peace. Yet there seemed every intention at first to complete the political with a commercial settlement. Shelburne contemplated it, and so did Pitt, and the American commissioners waited on in Europe for a separate negotiation. But they gradually perceived with great disappointment that the matter had hung fire. Franklin in bitterness wrote "England will get as little by the commercial war she has begun with us as she did by the military".

On the other hand the Peace had given the English, on a subject in which their honour and feelings were deeply engaged, a promise of no value. This concerned the Loyalist population. The Continental Congress could not compel the several colonies to relax the severity of their laws against the Loyalists, and though Vergennes sympathised in this matter as in some others with the English view, in the end the Peace contained only a promise that Congress would recommend to the States that persons who had not taken up arms should be allowed to return, and that those who had should not be prevented from recovering their property and leaving the country. These clauses of the Peace had been subject to severe criticism in Parliament, which thought that better terms might have been obtained, and Shelburne did not attempt to justify them. He argued simply that there was no alternative; we had either to accept them or continue the war; it had been necessary to sacrifice to some extent the interests of the Loyalists—"A part must be wounded, that the whole of the Empire may not perish".[1] As had been expected, the Loyalists gained little benefit from these ineffectual provisions. The Americans, impoverished and exasperated by the war, abated in nothing their persecution of those who had been on the losing side. The Loyalists who had fled did not return and many others followed them into exile. Great Britain, anxious to keep her hold over the fur trade of the interior, retaliated by not handing over the frontier posts as she had engaged to do in the Treaty, and, further, by ignoring the commercial proposals of the Americans. So matters stood in the early months of Pitt's administration, and the prospects of cordial relations with America were already clouded.

At the same time it was becoming clear how great an influence the issue of the war would exert on the future of Canada. The Peace deprived her of her historic connection with the Mississippi valley. Though French settlement was not extended beyond the lower reaches of the St Lawrence, French explorers and traders had penetrated south as well as west, and the natural direction of Canada's growth had appeared to be towards the heart of the Continent. Henceforward she must look for the opportunity of her expansion north of the Great Lakes and over the great western plains where the factors of the Hudson's Bay Company carried on their trade. Moreover, the British settlement, which had not come after the conquest, was now begun by a migration from the United States. Many of the Loyalists were coming in, and since the Peace, emigrants from England had turned to Canada. Canada was becoming a real British colony, and a colony of a new character, a land of two races and two religions. An unexpected destiny was appearing before her—to unite in one nation the two peoples for whose conflicts she had so long provided the arena. The Home Government which had hoped ten years before to settle for a long time the affairs of Canada, saw there, as in India, the whole question reopened and large issues of colonisation and colonial government presented for consideration.

In the West Indies Rodney's victory over de Grasse in 1782 had restored to some extent the fortunes of the war and saved us perhaps from sacrifices to France and Spain more considerable than those eventually forced upon us. The West Indies had passed the height of their prosperity, but they were still the treasured children of the Empire, and with the loss of the American colonies their relative importance was much increased. Their trade was large. In the decade 1770–80 its total value exceeded four million pounds a year. Here the Peace had arranged for a mutual restoration of conquests, and in addition we had surrendered to France Tobago, which we

[1] *Parl. Hist.* XXIII, 412.

had gained in 1763. For the supply of cotton this island was considered "of the utmost value to the manufactures of this country". But "cotton", said Shelburne, "...will always find its way to our door".[1] The West Indies had long done a thriving trade with the neighbouring colonies, whence many of the needs of the sugar plantations were most easily supplied, and their interests were bound up in the settlement of the commercial question with America. While this matter remained in abeyance, the trade was controlled by temporary regulations renewed from year to year which satisfied neither the Americans, deprived of their near and familiar market, nor the islands, which looked to America as their surest source of supply for food and timber. Scarcity constantly afflicted the British plantations, and the Governors had frequently to use their dispensing powers and open colonial ports to a freer trade than the regulations enjoined.

There were signs too that other issues would arise in which the islands were closely concerned. In June 1783 a petition of the Quakers against the slave trade was laid before Parliament. It was the beginning of that long struggle between Great Britain and her plantation colonies about the slave trade and slavery which in the end was to revolutionise their economic life. But at present the mother country did not trouble them with her new humanitarianism: she was more concerned for their security and progress. In their interest expeditions were sent to the Pacific with the object of importing the bread-fruit tree, which merchants and planters thought would provide cheap food for slaves. The tree was transplanted, but its fruit was not appreciated in the West Indies. Yet though Bligh never helped to feed the slaves, his first expedition (1787) had its imperial significance, for it resulted in a mutiny, a great feat of navigation, and a colony planted by the mutineers in Pitcairn Island.

Across the Caribbean Sea the Peace with Spain dealt with the long dispute about our logwood cutters. Spain recognised their right to carry on their operations on a part of the coast of the Bay of Honduras, subject to her sovereignty over the country, and we agreed that all British settlers on other parts of the Spanish Main or islands should withdraw to this area. The settlers complained of the boundaries fixed by the Treaty and of the lack of security for their operations. By the Convention of London, 1786, Spain extended a little the boundaries within which she was prepared to allow the cutting of logwood and made some other concessions, the British on their side evacuating the Mosquito Coast.[2] Our settlers, chiefly cotton planters, were removed and our old connection with the Indians on this coast came to an end. In the same year a superintendent, Colonel E. M. Despard, was sent to Belize. But relations

[1] *Parl. Hist.* XXIII, 415.
[2] Burdon, Sir J. A., *Archives of British Honduras*, I, 154–6.

with the Spaniards remained difficult, for the Spanish Government would not recognise the right of the settlers to organise government in territory under its sovereignty. The great object of Spain was to check illicit trade with her colonies, but neither Government could prevent what the subjects of both desired.

In the East Indies we had been obliged to restore to the French their settlements and rights of trade. But while we gave back with one hand we took with the other. Cessions were extracted from the Dutch which went far to compensate us for losses elsewhere. In the belated Treaty of 1784 they surrendered Negapatam and agreed not to interfere with British navigation in the Indian seas, an agreement which opened to us regions where they had claimed a commercial monopoly.[1] The war had cost them dear. Sir James Harris said it had ruined their Eastern possessions and commerce. The Dutch East India Company, at their last meeting at Middelburg, "expressed their apprehensions on the interpretation England might put on that article of the definitive treaty which allows a free trade in the East".[2] And our East India Company were not slow to take advantage of their new opportunities.

Our relations with European rivals were only a part of the many-sided problem of Indian politics. There remained the struggle for power in Southern India in which we were involved and which reached an indecisive conclusion at the Peace of Mangalore with Tipu in 1784. The great issue of government, too, which the conquests and mismanagement of the East India Company had created was engaging the principal attention of Parliament in the autumn of 1783.[3]

One other matter arising out of the American War, which must have seemed relatively trifling amongst great issues of trade and policy, but which for various reasons excited a good deal of attention, was the disposal of criminals sentenced to transportation. It had long been the practice to hand them over to contractors who disposed of them profitably to planters in America where their labour was in demand. This system was said to have answered every good purpose which could be expected from it. The American War brought it to an end, and it is strange how much inconvenience the cutting of this particular connection with our old colonies, the existence of which had hardly been noticed, now inflicted on a much embarrassed Government. As the judges continued to pass sentences of transportation the prisons were filled to overflowing, and as the efforts of John Howard had made prison reform a public question, the Government had to face constant enquiry and criticism. Long before the war ended the Government knew that a fresh place or places oversea

[1] Koch and Schöll, *Traités*, I, 462.
[2] F.O. 37/5 (in Harris's despatch of 28 Dec. 1784).
[3] See *C.H.B.E.* IV, ch. x.

must be found, and a committee of the House of Commons was making careful enquiries. No decision, however, had been reached when Pitt took office, nor was reached for several years after. But like the question of the Loyalists the matter was forcing to the front the idea of new colonies.

Such were the general consequences of the war in our dominions oversea. Though apart from the great cleavage with America the enormous power we had acquired in 1763 was not much diminished, the war was in many ways a turning-point in the history of the Empire. In 1763 the Empire was for the most part Anglo-Saxon in population, and primarily colonial in character, while its centre oversea was in America; in 1783 the balance of interest and power was shifted towards the East, in Bengal was the only great dependent population, and of Anglo-Saxon colonies we had only the West Indies, Nova Scotia and Newfoundland. Even in America the war cut the channels along which events moved. It caused the Loyalist migration, and so originated the British settlement of Canada, and raised the problem of the future form of government in new colonies. It placed the West Indies in a new situation, checking the ordinary course of their trade, and so raised for reconsideration the navigation and commercial policy of the Empire. It affected our views about colonisation and colonial government. It changed our military and naval problems on the North American continent. The frontier we had defended before 1763 we had now to attack, and the frontier we had attacked we had now to defend. We must look now for new markets and new sources of supply for our factories and shipyards. Masts, hemp and flax were needed for the navy, and we must try to encourage their production in our American possessions. Our expanding industries were increasing the demand for cotton, silk, sugar, wool and dyes, and the value of tropical and semi-tropical colonies was proportionately increased. Their trade was to assist us in the great struggle that was drawing near. Moreover, the war diminished our interest in the slave trade and made easier the way for the abolitionists: the emancipated colonies set us an example by fixing a date for its abolition. It created for us difficulties in dealing with our convicts, and drove us to a solution fraught with immense consequences.

With the imperial scale now tipped in favour of the East, our trade and political responsibilities in Asia became our greatest interests oversea. To guard the communications with India was now the principal naval problem, to protect and extend our Indian possessions the chief military task. The Mediterranean became important not only for its trade, but as a route to the East. Egypt suddenly assumed an unexpected significance. To that country, which Napoleon described as the most important in the world, we, unlike the French, had been strangely indifferent. Now, as if awakened by a blow, we grew conscious of its importance to our dominion in Asia. Our Government was urged to get Egypt, build up in Western Asia the trade we had lost in America and possess the two gardens of the world, Bengal and Egypt.[1] The Cape of Good Hope and Ceylon equally took a more prominent position in the eyes of the conquerors of India. Without loosening her grip on the West, where the West Indies, the new and struggling settlements in Canada, the Newfoundland fisheries, constantly engaged her attention, England turned towards the East where for thirty years through peace and war the growth of her power was to proceed without interruption. And, as it proceeded, her outlook in Europe shifted. France seemed a less formidable rival, and a new danger loomed up in Russia with her possibilities of overland communication into Central Asia. This coming change soon cast a faint shadow before it, for while France offered no help to Tipu in 1788 when the struggle in Southern India was renewed, in the crisis of 1791 in Eastern Europe, when Pitt intervened to check the triumphant progress of Catharine II, the Russian Government was considering a proposal to send a force from the Caspian Sea to attack the British in Bengal. And Pitt's own foresight of the transition appears in his unsuccessful attempt to check the Russian advance against the Ottoman Empire. He feared for our trade in the Black Sea and saw the remoter consequences of Russia's southward expansion. In the spring of 1791 we were on the verge of a Russian war. "This little Britain," writes Horace Walpole, "commonly called Great Britain, is to dictate to Petersburg and Bengal, and cover Constantinople under these wings that reach from the North Pole to the farthest East! I am right sorry for it, and hope we shall not prove a jackdaw that pretends to dress itself in the plumes of imperial eagles!"[2] But fear of Russia had not yet become a force in British politics; and public opinion, indifferent to Oczakoff, averse from war and preferring Russia to Turkey on religious, political and commercial grounds, compelled him to draw back.[3]

It is not our business here to describe the changes in the government of India which transferred the responsibility from a commercial company to Parliament and instituted the dual control which was to last till 1858, or the wars by which British power was extended and established in Southern India. That story is told elsewhere in this history.[4] But we have to remember that the affairs of India were continually before both Parliament and the public. Her hands forced by circumstances and men whom she had hitherto hardly tried to control, England in this decade definitely and deliberately

[1] Dalrymple, Sir J., *Queries* (1788), pp. 75–85.
[2] *Letters*, VI, 411–12. "I hope we shall avoid the folly of a Russian war," wrote Gibbon, "Pitt, in this instance, seems too like his father." To his stepmother, 18 May 1791. Prothero, *Gibbon*, II, 249.
[3] Herz, G. B., *British Imperialism in the Eighteenth Century* (The Russian Menace—a crisis of 1791). [4] See *C.H.B.E.* IV, chs. X and XIX–XXII.

accepted vast responsibilities in India. The British public had not welcomed the political activities of the East India Company, but they recognised in the work of Clive and Warren Hastings a great achievement and were not discouraged by their failure in America from undertaking a far harder task. So the march of empire had not ceased in the West before it was heard in the East, and the same House of Commons and Ministry which resigned a great part of America accepted expansion in India. The Indian question proved large enough to bring about the downfall of Fox and North, but Pitt carried through in the following year a Bill reconstructing the government of British India. The displacement of the Company seemed to some a breach of faith, and Gibbon, balancing "such an Empire", "not to be lost for trifles", against "the faith of Charters, the rights of property", hesitates and trembles.[1]

The awakened public conscience which delivered India from the misgovernment of the East India Company appeared also in the impeachment of Warren Hastings. Burke appealed "from British power to British justice", and for eight years the greatest man England has sent to India defied his accusers in Westminster Hall. The House of Commons in 1773 had declared that Clive had rendered "great and meritorious services to this country", and the House of Lords in April 1795 acquitted Hastings on all counts. The plain fact was that the country was becoming proud of the conquest of India, and while anxious to prevent and reform the evils which had followed it, would not allow the splendour of the result to be obscured in the condemnation of the means. "It is astonishing how little impression is made on the public by all the strong matter that has been brought forward during the course of the trial", wrote Lord Sheffield to Mr Eden, in July 1788. To the same correspondent two years before he had written what was no less illustrative of the other side of the matter: "It was not suited to the temper of the times to declare profit a justifiable and proper motive for going to war."[2] No man arraigned commercial companies as agents of Government in more sweeping terms than Adam Smith, but even he would not withhold his recognition of the high demeanour with which the Councils of Madras and Calcutta had faced and overcome their dangers.[3] With a new sense of responsibility had come a new interest in the East. In 1784 an Asiatic Society was founded, the product of Sir William Jones's "boundless curiosity concerning the people of the East", and he wrote proudly of it to Warren Hastings in 1791 "our Society still subsists, and the third volume of their Transactions is...advanced".[4]

[1] Prothero, *Gibbon*, II, 86.
[2] *Journal and Correspondence of Lord Auckland*, 10 May 1786, 29 July 1788.
[3] *Wealth of Nations* (ed. J. S. Nicholson), p. 265.
[4] Sir William Jones to Warren Hastings, 20 Oct. 1791. *Letters of Sir William Jones*, p. 159.

So, then, in this decade, when British settlement in Canada and Australia was just beginning, the affairs of India assumed a new place in our policy; her government was earnestly debated in Parliament, her wrongs engaged the sympathies of our greatest orators, her history and arts the interest of our foremost scholars; in her wars our future soldiers were being trained, and the development of her economic resources by British capital began. At the same time the East India Company pushed forward their activities in the Malay region, buying the island of Penang off the Malay peninsula from the Sultan of Kedah (1786). We were feeling our way into the Straits. It had for some time been a cause of concern to us that we had "no place of safety east of the Bay of Bengal for ships to take shelter in". Such a place was needed for the China trade which our Government was hoping at this time to extend by diplomatic means. Grenville described this object in 1789 as "of considerable importance". But Lord Macartney's mission to Peking in 1792 failed to achieve its purpose. The Dutch watched with anxiety our movements in a region which they regarded as their preserve. We wanted to be sure of a free navigation through the Malaccas; they feared lest we should establish ourselves in the archipelago among the Spice Islands and threaten their privileged position. After the recovery of our influence in Holland in 1787 we tried for some years to come to an arrangement with them on the basis of our restoring Negapatam and acquiring Trincomalee and a station for the purpose of our trade in the Eastern Seas. But the negotiations fell through in 1791, and Negapatam, for which the Dutch had hoped, was not restored. Our rivalry with them in the Malay region continued for thirty years before a lasting settlement was reached. To the west of India in the Persian Gulf towards the end of the eighteenth century England had attained a position to which none of her competitors could then lay claim.[1]

While trade was increasing in the East, it was not declining in the West. The course of events after 1783 went far to justify the arguments of Adam Smith against the colonial monopoly as well as to disappoint the ambitions of the French, for to acquire the American trade had been one of their objects in the late war. The Americans preferred English goods to French, and the French merchants could not give the long credits necessary in the trade.[2] Versailles had not crippled the commercial activities by which England lived. Trade was soon seen to obey other laws than those of politics and drifted back into the old channels. How little England was to be affected by the loss of the American monopoly was not indeed at first apparent, and meantime what answer was to be returned to the American desire for reciprocity? Ministers wished to save the

---

[1] Wilson, Sir A. T., *The Persian Gulf*, p. 179.
[2] Bemis, S. F., *Jay's Treaty*, p. 29.

American trade, as the Americans wished to save their West Indian trade. But the navigation and trade policy of the Empire formed an elaborate and stiff tradition, and the shaping of it to the new circumstances was no easy and obvious matter. Were the Americans to enjoy their old liberty of trade? Was it to the interest of the Empire, of the West Indies in particular, that they should? Or were they to be made to feel at once their new position as a foreign nation? Opinion was divided. Eden (the future Lord Auckland), who was an important authority and had accepted a post on the new Board of Trade, opposed "the modern plan of gratuitous and endless concessions". He did not wish to see "a total revolution in our commercial system", but thought we should remove the prohibitions on trade imposed during the war, and then proceed step by step.[1] Lord Sheffield's powerful defence of mercantilism in his *Observations on the Commerce of the American States* exerted great influence. In July 1785 John Adams, the first American minister to Great Britain, produced for consideration a draft treaty on a basis of most perfect equality and reciprocity, dealing not only with trade but with many vexed questions of international relations. When this was not accepted he modified his proposals, and in April 1786 put forward the commercial clauses alone. But Pitt's Cabinet, like Fox's, would not abandon the Navigation Act and hesitated to make permanent arrangements, though willing to do something by Order-in-Council.

Shortly afterwards (September 1786), the Government concluded a commercial treaty with France. How was it that we could make a treaty with France and not with the United States? The French Treaty did not touch the Navigation Act and colonial trade, while the Americans wanted an agreement that affected us on both these matters. The French, too, could retaliate by prohibitions on our trade, while the Americans during the critical period of their history could not do so effectively. However valuable American trade was to England, English trade was vital to America. To have lost it would have imperilled the new constitution. The two parties were not in an equal position.[2] In 1790 almost all the foreign shipping entering American ports was British, and of American exports nearly one-half went to British dominions.[3] Moreover, the Peace of Versailles had left no open wounds, while "the Treaty of Paris gave England and America plenty to quarrel about besides commerce, shipping and manners". The Loyalists, the frontier posts, American debts to British merchants were issues productive of mutual recrimination and ill-will and were fatal to the commercial negotiations.

So the matter dragged on, our reluctance to abandon our old policy being intensified by this friction, while in the course of the decade the Loyalist question was settled on other lines than those for

[1] *Parl. Hist.* XXIII, 602–7.
[2] Bemis, *Jay's Treaty*, pp. 33–6.　　　[3] Macpherson, *Annals of Commerce*, IV, 325–6.

which the British Government had vainly asked. At last the outbreak of war with France raised new and serious questions of neutral
rights and showed American sympathy strongly on the side of the
French. Faced with the danger of another American war, Pitt's
Cabinet was willing to come to terms, and Washington, no less eager
to avoid European entanglements and to find a peaceful way out
of Anglo-American difficulties, sent over Chief Justice Jay as envoy
extraordinary. Jay had been one of the American Commissioners
to negotiate peace in 1782 and Adams had written of him then:
"He don't like any Frenchman."[1] "He can bear any opposition to
what he advances", wrote Auckland to Grenville, "provided that
regard is shown to his abilities...almost every man has a weak and
assailable quarter, and Mr Jay's weak side is *Mr Jay*."[2] In 1794
the Treaty which goes by his name was negotiated. "Jay's Treaty
surpasses all that I feared", wrote Monroe the American minister
in France,[3] and it brought France and the United States to the verge
of war, for France held that the United States ought to maintain
her neutral rights and Jay had failed to insist on them. The concessions offered by Great Britain were not considerable—the frontier
posts were to be evacuated; the questions of American debts to
British merchants, the seizure of American ships during the war, and
the Maine-New Brunswick boundary were referred to mixed commissions; direct trade with British possessions in Europe and the East
Indies and in small vessels with the British West Indian islands was
opened to the Americans.[4] The Treaty removed the immediate
danger of war and some causes of friction, but it was a poor substitute
for that generous arrangement between the two nations for which
leading men on both sides were prepared at the time of the Peace.
Looking back it is hard not to regret that those who had given so
much could not have given the little more that was needed to lay a
basis of friendship between the divided branches of the Anglo-Saxon
race. The difficulties that caused the failure are apparent, but they
were not insuperable to a minister who had thought the object worth
the price. Meanwhile American trade had justified the hopes rather
than the fears of ministers, and "the loss of the Thirteen Colonies
had made singularly little difference to British prosperity",[5] an
experience which Castlereagh was able later to hold up for the
example of Spain.[6]

"Magnanimity in politics", said Burke, "is not seldom the truest
wisdom." This high virtue in these years neither country had

---

[1] Willson, Beckles, *American Ambassadors to France*, p. 14.   [2] *Dropmore Papers*, II, 578.
[3] Willson, Beckles, *American Ambassadors*, p. 70.
[4] See Bemis, *Jay's Treaty*, ch. XIII.
[5] *C.H.B.F.P.* I, 149. Talleyrand, who was in the United States 1793–6, analysed with
much acuteness the causes of the astonishing growth of Anglo-American trade so soon
after the separation. See *Mémoire sur les relations commerciales des Etats-Unis avec l'Angleterre.
Par le Citoyen Talleyrand.*   [6] Webster, C. K., *Castlereagh*, I, 71.

attained, and both were to find the truth of Burke's epigram. England with deplorable consequences missed her opportunity of American friendship; America sent her Loyalist sons to make Canada British. We must now turn to consider the policy of our Government towards these exiles and the manner in which their migration affected the future development of the Empire.[1] In the debate on the Peace Shelburne had accepted the principle of compensating the Loyalists if they suffered. As compared with continuing the war in the faint hope of exacting better terms for them the policy of compensation had both economy and good sense to recommend it. A war which was not worth continuing to preserve the unity of the Empire certainly could not be continued to exact a few million pounds. It fell therefore to Parliament to provide for the Loyalists, and in June 1783 commissioners were appointed to enquire into their losses and report on their indemnification. Amongst the Loyalists were soldiers, officials, clergy, professional men, the more conservative elements of society and some few persons of substantial wealth. Some from the southern colonies had gone to the West Indies to grow cotton and indigo, but the majority had gone to Nova Scotia whence many migrated into the province of Quebec along the St Lawrence above Montreal. Thus, after much moving about and a good deal of suffering inevitable in the circumstances, the Loyalists distributed themselves, the majority in Quebec, others in New Brunswick, Nova Scotia and the West Indies, the Home Government making generous grants to relieve their necessities. In June 1788 the question of compensation was debated in the House of Commons. Pitt thought that compensation could not be claimed as a matter of strict justice, but that the sufferers had a strong title to the generosity and compassion of the country. He divided them into four classes—residents in America who had lost property in America, residents in England who had lost property in America, residents in America who had lost incomes there, and claimants from West Florida which had been ceded to Spain. He proposed that small losses should be compensated in full and that the amount of compensation should diminish in proportion to the magnitude of the claim. He wished to make "a liberal and a handsome compensation".[2] The House cordially agreed. Over two million pounds was voted; and, including what had already been paid, the compensation amounted to over three millions. In these peculiar circumstances a section of the old empire was grafted into the new. Unfortunately the episode embittered for some years the relations of Great Britain and the United States, but its consequences were far-reaching. Nova Scotia was changed from a strategic post to a real colony, Anglo-Saxon colonisation began on the St Lawrence, and Canada was strengthened with a new population and a Loyalist tradition.

[1] See also *C.H.B.E.* VI, ch. VII.   [2] *Parl. Hist.* XXVII, 610–13.

The question of compensation was only a part of the problem created by the Loyalist migration. Far more important was the change in the conditions of our remaining colonies which their arrival produced. Carleton urged the liberal treatment of the Loyalist settlers and a generous attitude to our colonies. He thought it "indispensably necessary to establish the most close and cordial connection with the provinces which have preserved their allegiance...every source of jealousy or suspicion should be done away for ever".[1] For the benefit of the Loyalists who had settled north of the Bay of Fundy, Nova Scotia was in 1784 divided and the province of New Brunswick established, with an elected Assembly.[2] Cape Breton Island also was made a separate province under a Lieutenant-Governor. Prince Edward Island, separate since 1769, was placed under the Governor of Nova Scotia. The object of the seniority given to the Governor of Nova Scotia, as later to Carleton,[3] was to centralise the administration and avoid the delay of continual recourse to Great Britain and so to improve the government of the group.[4] The American War had naturally inspired the Government with fears for the "permanency of the connection" with our remaining colonies and a consideration of the means by which it might be secured. They were not indeed without apprehensions of the democratic temper of their old subjects. Trade too was a prime consideration. Could the remaining colonies grow up to take the place of the American colonies in the West Indian trade?

The reorganisation of the Atlantic group was barely completed before the government of Quebec demanded reconsideration. Clearly the Quebec Act was now no final settlement and the whole question must be reopened. The new-comers did not desire to live under French law or an autocratic system. A most complex situation confronted the Government, and petitions and counter-petitions from various sections of the population increased the difficulty of discerning the real wishes of the colony. Two races of different political traditions and capacities were juxtaposed in a vast country, the lines of whose future progress were as yet unknown. Justice to the new-comers was hard to reconcile with justice to the old inhabitants—the desire to grant free institutions with the prudence bitter experience dictated. Pitt instituted careful enquiries, and in 1786 Carleton, created Lord Dorchester, was sent out as Governor-General in North America, and the Government waited for his advice. Pitt was slow in coming to a decision and in 1790 excused his delay on the ground that it was their duty to render the plan "as perfect as the nature of the case would admit". The consideration of a new colonial con-

---

[1] Carleton to Townshend, 15 March 1783. See McNutt, W. S., "British Rule in Nova Scotia, 1713–1784" (an unpublished thesis in the Library of the University of London), p. 438.
[2] See *C.H.B.E.* vi, pp. 190–1.
[3] *Ibid.* p. 195.   [4] Sydney to Parr, 29 May 1784. See McNutt, *op. cit.* p. 451.

stitution at the time certainly raised far-reaching issues. It was a different problem from the establishment of New Brunswick, which naturally inherited the constitution of the province from which it was severed. What was to be our future colonial policy? What was to be learned from the experience of the past? Our relations with France were such that it was necessary to walk warily in French Canada. While Pitt deliberated, our old colonies established their new commonwealth and France let loose on the world the torrent of her revolutionary thought. At home opinion was dividing and tempers were inflammable. When at last the Canada Act came before Parliament in 1791, Burke claimed to consider the first principles of government. He would not copy the American system, nor "ship off to Canada a cargo of the rights of man". Such cautions were needless, for the Act showed rather a cautious reaction from than a bold acceptance of democratic ideas. It certainly did not offer to the French the liberty and equality which their mother country was now extending to her remaining colonies and which might, however unacceptable, have been theirs, had not the fortune of war placed them under another flag; nor to the Loyalists that control of their own life which they had exercised not so long before in another part of the continent. Nor did it attempt to realise the theory of Adam Smith, that colonies should be represented in the Parliament of the motherland and bear a proportionate share of imperial expenses. The idea of colonial representation in the British Parliament, so much agitated during the controversy with America, seems to have vanished from the political horizon after the American War as completely as if it had never appeared upon it. No one seems to have contemplated offering seats in Parliament to the *habitans* of Quebec any more than to the *Zemindars* of Bengal. What had not been found practical for the American colonies must have appeared purely visionary for any other.

The object of his policy, Pitt said, was "to put an end to the differences of opinion and growing competition that had for some years existed in Canada between the ancient inhabitants and the new settlers from England and from America on several important points, and bring the government of the province, as near as the nature and situation of it would admit, to the British constitution".[1] To achieve these ends he proposed to divide the province into two parts so as to give each nation "a great majority in their own particular part, although it could not be expected to draw a line of complete separation", and to establish in each province a Legislature consisting of a small elected Assembly and a Council composed of members for life or hereditary members, should the King confer hereditary titles. The French province would keep its own laws unless it preferred to change them. In both provinces the Protestant clergy

[1] *Parl. Hist.* xxviii ,1377.

would be maintained by a permanent appropriation of land. It is not necessary for our purpose here to say more in detail of the Act, as its provisions are described in a later volume of the History.[1] Here we are concerned only with the outlook of the Government and the objects it was pursuing.

In framing their policy the Government followed their own judgment and not that of the man on the spot. Carleton had not recommended the immediate grant of a representative Assembly, but the Government decided in favour of it, and following on that decision, determined on the division of the province. These two decisions, together with the attempt to put restraints on colonial democracy, formed the three cardinal points of their policy. Regarding the first, the view in official circles in England was that a constitution must be granted. The tradition of British policy, the neighbourhood of the American States and of the other British colonies made this essential. Canada could not be governed by force and the risk involved must be taken. And if to be done it were best done quickly. "It is a point of true policy", wrote Grenville, in his secret communication to Dorchester (20 October 1789), "to make these concessions at a time when they may be received as matter of favour, and when it is in our own power to regulate and direct the manner of applying them, rather than to wait till they shall be extorted from us by a necessity which shall neither leave us any discretion in the form, nor any merit in the substance of what we give."[2] This was real political wisdom and showed that some lessons from the recent past had been learned.

To grant an Assembly would meet the wishes of English merchants and Loyalist settlers, but what of the French? For their sake the province must be divided. Again Grenville is quite explicit on the main reason for this. "When the resolution was taken of establishing a provincial legislature...to be chosen in part by the people every consideration of policy seemed to render it desirable that the great preponderance possessed in the upper Districts by the king's ancient subjects and in the lower by the French Canadians should have their effect and operation in separate legislatures: rather than that these two bodies of people should be blended together in the first formation of the new constitution and before sufficient time has been allowed for the removal of ancient prejudices by the habit of obedience to the same government and by sense of a common interest."[3] The Government had taken pains to ascertain the feelings of the French Canadians towards a change of Government and the reasons for their objection to a House of Assembly, and their object was to remove any apprehensions the French might feel about the security of their religion, customs and nationality—to preserve to them in fact the advantages

---

[1] See *C.H.B.E.* VI, pp. 197–200.
[2] Shortt, A. and Doughty, A. G., *Constitutional Documents*, I, 969.   [3] *Ibid.* I, 986.

of the Quebec Act. It is interesting that the King emphasised the importance of this. In a note to Grenville, who was busy drafting the Act in the autumn of 1789, he writes that he trusts the plan has been drawn "with as much attention to the interest of the old inhabitants who, by the capitulation, have every degree of right to be first attended to, as its ever having been started in Parliament will permit". He would have preferred to leave the matter alone for some years.[1] Pitt, in the debate in April 1791, declared the division of the province "the most material and essential part" of the bill.[2] It is not necessary to accept Lord Durham's view that the object of the division of the colony was to weaken it and ensure more easily its subordination to Great Britain.[3] The division was an act of consistency, convenience and justice. On the other hand, it does not seem that Pitt believed the preservation of French nationality a good in itself. When Fox criticised the separation and urged that the most desirable thing was for the French and English inhabitants to unite "and coalesce as it were in one body", with English laws, Pitt agreed, but maintained that that end was most likely to be realised if no pressure were put upon the French,[4] and the concluding phrase in Grenville's letter to Dorchester, already quoted, showed that he presaged a future union.

If the risk of granting a constitution must be taken could it not by wise precautions be minimised? Might we not profit by experience and avoid those defects in the constitutions of our old colonies which had hastened their independence? Could we not strengthen our monarchical power, and sow the seeds of aristocracy beyond the Atlantic? We had let the old colonies take their own way and grow up as they could and we had lost them. Could we not correct the too great freedom of the old colonial policy by exercising more control over colonial institutions and the growth of colonial society? A paper forwarded to Dorchester with the first draft of the constitutional bill contained the suggestions on which the measure was founded and notes on the points in which the old colonial governments were now thought to have been defective.[5] It was argued that they never really had the British constitution. Full scope had been given to the principles of democracy, but "no care was taken to preserve a due mixture of the monarchical and aristocratical parts of the British constitution". We should labour therefore to establish a "respectable aristocracy" in the remaining colonies, and to constitute the Upper House of the Legislature in such a manner that it should have a real strength. So, in the provisions of the bill relating to the Legislative Council, to an hereditary aristocracy and also to

[1] *Dropmore Papers*, i, 530, George III to Grenville, 13 Oct. 1789.
[2] *Parl. Hist.* xxix, 113.   [3] *Durham Report* (ed. Lucas, Sir C. P.), ii, 65 *sqq.*
[4] *Parl. Hist.* xxix, 113.
[5] Shortt and Doughty, *Constitutional Documents*, i, 970-87.

an established Church, the attempt was made to introduce into colonial life some conservative elements which might restrain the democratic tendencies of the age. The object of these provisions, wrote Grenville, is "both to give to the upper branch of the Legislature a greater degree of weight and consequence than was possessed by the Councils in the old Colonial Governments, and to establish in the provinces a body of men having the motive of attachment to the existing form of government, which arises from the possession of personal and hereditary distinction".[1]

Thurlow thought an hereditary aristocracy would create an independent interest in the colony. He held that the want of dependence upon the mother country in their form of government was at the root of our failure with our old colonies. We had given too much political liberty, which "must necessarily include sovereignty and consequently independence". He wished "to preserve the greatest degree of habitual influence possible in the executive branch of the government".[2]

"With regard to taxation," Pitt said, "to avoid the occasion of a misunderstanding similar to that which had formerly taken place, no taxes were meant to be imposed by the Parliament respecting Canada, but such as might be necessary for the purposes of commercial regulation; and in that case, to avoid even the possibility of a cavil, the levying of such taxes, and their disposal, should be left entirely to the wisdom of their own Legislature."[3] In saying this he did no more than confirm a concession Parliament had already made.

On the vexed problem of imperial defence, Grenville, who seems to have been largely responsible for drafting the measure, was of opinion that colonies ought to bear their part of the cost of the government and defence of the Empire. This recalled the views of Adam Smith. But as "no general system of this sort has ever been adopted by us", he thought it impossible to introduce it into our relations with Canada.

On the question of uniting the St Lawrence colonies the wisdom of experience spoke in Chief Justice Smith's recommendation "to put what remains to Great Britain of her ancient dominions in North America under one general direction". In the past, he argued, all America had been "abandoned to democracy", and Great Britain should have found the cure, in the creation of a power upon the Continent itself to control all its own little republics and create a partner in the legislation of the Empire, capable of consulting their own safety and the common welfare.[4] Dorchester supported this and

[1] Shortt and Doughty, *Constitutional Documents*, I, 989.
[2] *Dropmore Papers*, I, 504.
[3] *Parl. Hist.* XXVIII, 1378.
[4] Chief Justice Smith to Dorchester, 5 Feb. 1790. Shortt and Doughty, *Constitutional Documents*, I, 1018–20.

advised "a General Government for His Majesty's Dominions upon this Continent, as well as a Governor-General", in the general interest of the provinces and of the unity of the Empire. Grenville replied that the matter had received consideration, "but, I think it liable to considerable objection. The principle of reuniting the executive government has already been acted upon".[1] Dorchester repeated the suggestion in 1793 to Dundas who had succeeded Grenville as Home Secretary. Dundas's refusal was emphatic: "it requires reasons more forcible than any which have yet occurred to me, to convince me that such a confederacy amongst the distant dependencies of the Empire, can either add to its own strength or to the real happiness of the different provinces."[2]

The measure of the concession that had been made to Canada depended on the manner in which the colonial Government was conducted. The suitability of its provisions to Canadian conditions time alone could show. That Canada never enjoyed real self-government under it may not have been Pitt's intention, but certainly Fox spoke with prophetic insight when he said that the bill held out to the Canadians "something like the shadow of the British constitution but denied them the substance", words destined to find an echo in Lord Durham's famous Report forty-seven years later. But, considered in relation to the time when it was passed, within a decade of the loss of the old colonies, and to the obscure and changing circumstances to which it was applied, the Act may be adjudged as an honest experiment. Unhappily the times proved unfavourable to an experiment on liberal lines, for within two years the cloud of war fell over the scene.

If Pitt was less successful in his Canadian policy than his care and sincerity in the matter deserved, if he laid up here a heritage of trouble for his successors, the expedition which he despatched to Australia was destined to achieve results far beyond what were intended or imagined. "Throughout history", says Emerson, "heaven seems to affect low and poor means", and there is surely no more signal illustration of this than that a great commonwealth traces its origin to a penal settlement. Amongst the problems which the loss of America imposed on an embarrassed Government was, as we have already seen, that of finding a new place to which criminals sentenced to transportation could be despatched.[3] For a satisfactory solution of the problem a distant place must be found, whence escape would be difficult, and also a place where the convicts could soon maintain themselves by their own labour, or the expense would be considerable; if possible, too, a place where their exertions would in the end

---

[1] Chief Justice Smith to Dorchester, 5 Feb. 1790. Shortt and Doughty, *Constitutiona Documents*, I, 1027.
[2] Shortt and Doughty, *Constitutional Documents*, II, 106–8.
[3] See also *C.H.B.E.* VII, ch. III.

contribute to the progress of British commerce and navigation. It was always before the mind of the Government that convict labour should be made useful to the State. To a committee of the House of Commons in 1779 Joseph Banks, President of the Royal Society, made the suggestion of Botany Bay—a seven months' voyage, as he explained, from England, where the natives would probably offer no opposition, and where the soil, though in large part barren, was sufficiently rich to support a considerable population. A large number of persons, he thought, should be sent, and the settlement would certainly require a full year's allowance of food and necessaries. In so vast a country he considered that a colony would in time grow up and become a market for England.[1] To the same committee, John Roberts, a former Governor of Cape Coast Castle, recommended a place high up the Gambia River, but the evidence of European mortality in Africa was disquieting. The committee reported in favour of the establishment of a colony or colonies of young convicts in some distant and healthy parts of the globe, which they thought "might prove in the result advantageous both to navigation and commerce".[2] Some years passed but no action was taken and the question grew more urgent. In 1783 Banks's suggestion of colonising New South Wales was repeated by James Maria Matra, a Corsican who had been with Cook in the *Endeavour*. He thought that we might thus "atone for the loss of our American colonies", and that the Loyalists could find an asylum there. We could also develop our Eastern trade and hold a position from which in time of war to threaten the Spanish or Dutch colonies. After conversing with Lord Sydney about the prospect, he added as a postscript the alternative proposal of sending convicts.[3] By an Act of 1784 the Government took power to transport convicts to any place appointed by Order-in-Council. In a debate (11 March 1784) Mr Hussey suggested New Zealand. Then rumour ran that the Government had in mind the coast of Africa. In March 1785 Burke in emphatic language denounced this: "The gates of hell were there open night and day to receive the victims of the law." The idea was disclaimed by Pitt, and when the matter was raised again in May, he declared that owing to "a very great hurry of public business" no decision had yet been reached. In July 1785 Lord Sydney told a committee of the House that no plan existed—that different ideas had been suggested but they were either made in conversation or were not worth attention. This committee favoured the idea of a settlement in Africa. Gambia and Guinea, they were clear, would not be suitable. But on the south-west coast between the Portuguese and the Dutch settlements, on the Bay of das Voltas, they thought an excellent site could be found. Here it would be possible for our Indiamen to find

[1] *Commons Journals*, xxxvii, 311.   [2] *Ibid.* p. 314.
[3] Barton, G. B., *History of N.S.W. from the Records*, pp. 423–9.

refreshment, and a base useful for the whale fisheries and for commerce or for hostilities in the South Sea might be established. Many American families might go there, and emigration, which was now flowing to the United States, might be diverted to our own dominions. Their outlook was wider than the convict problem. In fact they recommended the scheme only if it were on other grounds, commercial and political, desirable to establish a colony in South-West Africa.[1] So the Government investigated the African suggestions, which included also an establishment on the "Caffre Coast", an English Cape Colony.[2]

Meanwhile Admiral Sir George Young had submitted in the previous January a plan for the settlement of both Loyalists and convicts in New South Wales.[3] The settlement, he argued, might become a port of call for the China trade, then engaging serious attention at home, and New Zealand flax might be cultivated in the interests of the navy. Out of these schemes a plan at last emerged. Matra's postscript became the Government's policy. On 6 December 1786 an Order-in-Council fixed the eastern coast of New South Wales or some one or other of the adjacent islands as a place for the reception of convicts. The following January the King's speech announced without detail that a plan had been formed, and a Statute was passed establishing a Court of Criminal Jurisdiction on the east coast of New South Wales.[4]

Pitt had enquired anxiously in December 1786 about the probable expenses of the expedition.[5] He was in correspondence with Lord Camden about the proposed Statute,[6] but otherwise the scheme seems not to have engaged his personal attention. Once the decision was made the preparations were hurried forward. In May the fleet sailed, to be forgotten as soon as out of sight. The most pregnant event of these years was speedily obscured by Indian and domestic affairs. Thus inauspiciously began the colonisation of Australia.

Yet the Government deserve credit for the insight which chose the right man for the work. Captain Arthur Phillip was a choice as happy as Cook—a man capable of laying the foundation of a colony and animated by that vision. But for his capacity and courage the expedition might have been a disaster. The Government gave him too the powers of the Governor of a colony and not of a prison, and a sphere of action wide enough for the grandest results.[7] Phillip always thought of his work as the establishment of a colony, "a very essential service to my country". He would have no slaves and wished to introduce the family and the free settler as speedily as possible. "I would not wish convicts to lay the foundations of an

[1] C.J. XL, 1161–4.   [2] Rose, Pitt, 1, 435.
[3] Barton, History of N.S.W., pp. 429–32.   [4] 27 George III, c. 2.
[5] Barton, op. cit., p. 469.
[6] Rose, Pitt, 1, 439. Camden found in the Bill "a novelty in our constitution".
[7] For Phillip's Commissions see Historical Records of Australia, 1, 1, 2.

Empire", he wrote.[1] It cannot be said that the Government recipro-
cated his views or concerned themselves with more than the solution
of their urgent administrative problem. As for their choice of New
South Wales, they had in the end no alternative. Other colonies
were following the American example and convicts were repulsed
from the Mosquito shore[2] and from Newfoundland. Africa, which
the Government seemed to prefer, had proved impossible. There
remained only the Pacific. Thither the eyes of Europe were turning,
and the need to follow up the discoveries of Cook was no doubt
emphasised by news of the French expedition to the Pacific under
La Pérouse which sailed in 1785. So the Government took the risk,
despatched Phillip with a small military force, seven hundred and
fifty-six convicts and a commission that covered an enormous area
in the Pacific. Not supported by the hopes of a nation, but managed
with masterly prudence and care, the expedition succeeded, and Pitt
thus laid the foundations of a great state and added nearly half
Australia to the British Empire. But the story of the beginnings of
the colony belongs to a later volume of this History.[3]

That the Loyalists dropped out of the project is not surprising.
By 1787 the majority had settled down elsewhere. As for sending
free settlers, there was a fear of depopulation in England and opinion
did not favour emigration. The foundation of a free colony, whether
for Loyalists or other free settlers, might well prove a difficult and
expensive enterprise, but a penal settlement somewhere was a necessity, and to open the Pacific to trade was British policy.

Phillip arrived in Botany Bay on 18 January 1788, and going on
to Port Jackson founded there a few days later the settlement to
which he gave the name of Sydney in honour of the Secretary of
State. When, to their surprise, Phillip succeeded beyond expectation,
the Government persevered with their plan. Banks took a great
interest in the colony and was regularly consulted,[4] but neither the
method nor the place of colonisation escaped criticism. Wraxall
poured contempt on "a new colony of thieves and ruffians...under
the Southern pole". It was beyond reason or ridicule to transport
your citizens such a distance that but a few years before "Geography
itself had not extended its discoveries so far".[5] "Many", said
Mr Jekyll, in a debate in February 1791, "had their doubts as to
the wisdom of that system of colonisation", and Sir Charles Bunbury
did not think the place fit for the purpose.[6] Pitt admitted that Botany
Bay did not hold out "a prospect of luxury to exiles", but transportation was not intended to offer this. So far as the Government had

[1] Barton, p. 40.
[2] Burdon, Sir J. A., *Archives of British Honduras*, I, 146, 151.
[3] See *C.H.B.E.* VII, pp. 63–5.
[4] Barton, pp. lii, liii.
[5] *A Short Review of the Political State of Great Britain*, 1787.
[6] *Parl. Hist.* XXVIII, 1221–3.

yet heard, the condition of the felons was preferable to what befell them under the former mode of transportation. No cheaper mode of disposing of them had been found, and he did not know of any other place where they could be sent.[1] The early years of any settlement are full of difficulties which give ample occasion to the critic, and Sir Charles Bunbury returned to the attack again in 1793, alleging the expense of the colony and the ill effects of transportation on the criminal.[2] But the worst was now past, Australia awakened little interest in Parliament and penal colonisation appeared to have succeeded. Nothing illustrates better than the foundation of Australia how little Pitt's Government believed in new colonies, their principal care being the administrative problems connected with transportation; and the subsequent growth of Australia in spite of this indifference shows that the progress of colonies may depend less on the imagination and fostering of governments than on the exertions of ordinary people, adapting themselves to new circumstances and pursuing their own interests and opportunities in their own way.

The various suggestions for a settlement in Africa showed that that continent was now assuming a new importance in the eyes of Europe. The mortality of Europeans in tropical parts had given it a bad reputation, but the desire to know more of its resources and people was stimulated by the loss of America. Neither the merchant nor the philanthropist was satisfied to see this vast and populous land devoted solely to a desolating slave trade, and a movement began to take shape that was eventually to compass its abolition. Philanthropy and religion gained support from the quickened anxiety and interest in Africa, and the movement found its Parliamentary champion in William Wilberforce. Few of its supporters probably realised what "an obstinate hill" remained to climb. Vested interests were strong, humanitarianism cut across party lines and so was ineffective in politics. Yet real progress seemed to have been made when in 1792 the principle of gradual abolition was accepted by the House of Commons. And then upon this, as upon so much that was hopeful in the decade of peace, the shadow of war descended. Attempts to colonise in Africa, to explore the interior, to promote other forms of commerce than the slave trade, were also signs of the times, but of these developments and of the humanitarian movement which so largely inspired them an account will be given in a later chapter.

In our daring venture into the Southern Seas we began to reap the fruits of Cook's great voyages. But Cook had also drawn attention to opportunities of trade in the northern Pacific, and in 1785 the King George's Sound Company despatched Captain Nathaniel Portlock, who had served under Cook, with two vessels on an expedition to the north-west coast of North America. Portlock returned in 1788 having discovered that a lucrative fur trade might be opened with

---

[1] *Parl. Hist.* xxviii, 1223.   [2] *Ibid.* xxx, 955–61.

China.[1] Meantime, John Meares, from Calcutta, had embarked on the same enterprise and contemplated the establishment of a trading post in those parts.[2] The activities of our merchants soon attracted the jealous vigilance of Spain. Always suspicious of any coming of the English into the neighbourhood of her settlements, and in difficulties with her colonists who were agitating for direct trade with other nations, Spain seized the occasion to raise the question of her rights in the Pacific. At the time, we were getting a large part of Spain's home and colonial trade, and it was not to our interest to provoke controversy or engage in war. But the challenge was too signal and critical to be refused, and Pitt accepted it boldly with consequences of far-reaching importance.

Early in 1790 the British Government learned that in the preceding year some British merchants who, for the purpose of trade in furs and ginseng with China, had established a trading post at Nootka Sound on Vancouver Island—a region far beyond the limits of Spain's effective occupation in the northern continent—had been dispossessed by Spanish authorities, their ships seized and themselves maltreated.[3] In the dispute which followed Spain put forward the claim that the west coast of North America as far as latitude 60° N. was under her sovereignty, and desired that British subjects should no longer be allowed to trade, settle or fish in those parts. The British Government promptly demanded "immediate and adequate satisfaction" for the injury done. In Parliament Pitt described the Spanish claim as "the most absurd and exorbitant that could well be imagined", "indefinite in its extent" and originating "in no treaty, nor formal establishment of a colony", and Fox joined him in maintaining that occupancy and possession alone could give a title.[4] Both countries armed and appealed to their allies. Holland and Prussia expressed their willingness to support Great Britain, but France, though making warlike preparations, returned no certain answer to Spain. In France parties were divided; war would have suited the Royalists, but not their opponents. Russia and Austria likewise gave Spain no encouragement, and she was disappointed also of Britain's late opponents, the Americans, who were watching the crisis with natural interest. The United States were very anxious to get New Orleans from Spain and considered whether to encourage Great Britain to attack Louisiana in return for the cession to her of New Orleans or the Floridas. But they abstained, perhaps thinking that the fruit must drop some time into their hands and that they were better off without British neighbours on the Mississippi.[5] Gradually it became clear that French support could not be obtained by Spain

---

[1] Portlock, N., *A Voyage...to the North-West Coast of America, 1789*, p. 382.
[2] Meares, J., *Voyages from China to North-West America, 1788–9, 1790*.
[3] The senior captain, Meares, estimated the damage at 500,000 dollars apart from the loss of trade. Rose, *Pitt*, I, 563. [4] *Parl. Hist.* XXVIII, 770.
[5] Cox, I. J., *West Florida Controversy*, pp. 20–1.

on any terms on which it would be acceptable. Moreover, with her constitution in a state of flux and her navy in a state of mutiny, France was in no position for war. The Bourbon Family Compact which had been so formidable to Great Britain in the eighteenth century was dissolving in the politics of the Revolution. Isolated and faced with the menace of war, for Pitt now had ready ninety-three sail-of-the-line,[1] Spain abandoned her claims and came to terms with Great Britain. In July she promised reparation, and, by the Convention of October 1790, admitted the right of British subjects to navigate, trade and fish in the Pacific, provided they did not approach any part of the coast actually occupied by Spain, and to make settlements in places not already occupied. Great Britain on her side promised to prevent illicit trade with the Spanish colonies, and both Powers agreed not to make settlements south of the existing colonies of Spain. The actual compensation was referred to arbitration, and some years elapsed before the matter was finally closed.

Pitt's general conduct of this dispute came in for criticism at home. In the House of Lords, Lansdowne argued that it was a mistake to offend Spain, and that we had gained nothing by the controversy, for at any time we could assert our undoubted rights in the Pacific,[2] and Fox in a very able speech declared that we had put restraints on ourselves and made concessions rather than gains. Pitt admitted that we had not gained new rights, that we had possessed before the right to the southern whale fishery and the right to trade on the Pacific coast of North America, but he contended that we had gained advantages, for, whereas our rights had been previously disputed, they were now secured. Certainly, though theoretically we had the rights stated, actually we were disturbed in the exercise of them, as the incident showed, and the southern whale fishery was constantly harassed by the Spaniards. To get that matter settled was an advantage. It had, as was pointed out in the Lords' debate on the convention, "more than anything been a subject of jealousy to Spain".[3]

Why did Pitt take so strong a line on this occasion? The armament he prepared cost three millions, and war, had it come, must have cost immensely more. Great Britain had no desire to establish a settlement at Nootka; the place had no peculiar advantage for shipping or trade.[4] But the question of the open door in the unoccupied coasts of the Pacific was rightly seen by Pitt as a large issue, as well as a new phase of a perennial trouble. The far-reaching importance of his action on the future of Canada and on the relations of Great Britain with the United States could hardly be foreseen. The transcontinental expansion of the one might already be imagined, but

---

[1] *Journals...of Sir I. Byam Martin* (Navy Records Society), III, 382.
[2] *Parl. Hist.* XXVIII, 939–47.
[3] *Ibid.* 959–69.
[4] Grenville to St Helens, 1 Aug. 1793, quoted in *C.H.B.F.P.* I, 553.

hardly of the other. No doubt Pitt was thinking of trade rather than of colonisation, and would gladly have gone on to negotiate a commercial treaty with Spain had she been willing, but the possession of a "window on the Pacific" was to make all the difference to the future development of British North America. Taking then the occasion made by Spain and the opportunity offered by the "infinite embarrassments of France", he not only asserted a great principle and procured a settlement of a long-vexed question, but he also incidentally dissolved an ancient and formidable combination against our colonial power.

For the great steps that were taken in these years towards the rebuilding of the British Empire in new seas and continents the abatement of French rivalry and interference, so conspicuously illustrated in 1790, was a most favourable circumstance. After the Peace of Versailles the temper of France had been for a time highly pacific. The spirit of the philosophers rested upon the statesmen. Peace and commerce, the liberation of Europe from the shackles of monopoly, commercial treaties, were the objects of the age, and France entered willingly into these schemes. Financial difficulties contributed to exorcise the demon of war. Reforming ministers found full occupation at home. France seemed anxious to deal easily with England and not to pursue her advantage. Vergennes apparently wished England to continue her oversea activities and give her energies to commercial and colonial schemes rather than brood over her losses and cherish revenge. So the relations of the two countries were friendly. In the Peace of Versailles a step had been taken that might improve them further. A commercial treaty was contemplated. But Shelburne left office before it could be negotiated and Fox was opposed to it. He still thought of France under its absolute and military monarchy as "the natural foe of Great Britain", and in accordance with our traditional European policy wished to cultivate friendship elsewhere. But France pressed for the fulfilment of the undertaking, and Pitt, who believed that "a friendly connection seemed to be pointed out between them, instead of the state of unalterable enmity which was falsely said to be their true political feeling towards one another",[1] and who was ably supported by Eden, carried it through. It opened the prospect of better things. Our trade with France had been almost negligible. Soon it expanded and our merchants at least were to regret the subsequent war. The treaty had not been in force long before the domestic embarrassments of France became more serious, and gradually it was realised that the weight of France had been taken out of the balance of European politics.

Ever since his advent to power Pitt had been working to recover British influence in Holland. The opportunity came in the Dutch

[1] *Parl. Hist.* XXVI, 395.

crisis of 1786–7 when England and Prussia intervened to restore the stadholder and France was powerless to help her friends of the opposite party.[1] Pitt did not hesitate to use our rising strength and ran the risk of war had not France drawn back. So England recovered her traditional ally and was proportionately strengthened. Dutch friendship was of the utmost importance to our domestic security and our colonial power. If France prevailed in Holland, the outbreak of an Anglo-French war might expose our east coast to the Dutch navy, while the Cape, Ceylon and the Dutch East Indies might pass into French hands. It was not only the Thames but India that France threatened in Holland. This was no idle fear, for in 1786–7 the French were dreaming of the revival of their Eastern power by means of a Dutch alliance. They hoped to obtain Trincomalee from the Dutch and recover their position on the Coromandel Coast. Hence the importance of the struggle in these years for influence in Holland. The issue was to remain throughout the Revolutionary and Napoleonic wars of central importance between us and France, because on the independence of Holland rested both our security in Europe and the security of our power in the East.[2]

In April 1788 an Anglo-Dutch alliance was sealed and the two powers, in spite of French objections, arranged for the closest military and naval co-operation in the defence of their colonies in Africa and the East. The course of events in Holland brought England and Prussia together again, and by treaties between the three Powers in June and August 1788 the Triple Alliance was constituted which gave us again a voice on the Continent and a *point d'appui* of which we could make use in our exertions oversea.[3] "This great object", wrote Ewart to Pitt at a later date, ably summarising the result of our policy, "was accomplished at a very trifling expense to this country, though it gained more by it than by its most successful wars; as it thereby re-established its lost influence in Europe, secured its possessions in India, and unmasked the ruined state of France...."[4]

Meanwhile France was sinking into bankruptcy and unable to preserve her influence in Europe. In September 1788 Pitt said that the state of France promised us "a considerable respite from dangerous projects".[5] A great reversal of fortune had indeed been brought about. As Lord Loughborough wrote to Eden (13 October 1788) "France in the spring of 1787, ruling Holland, restoring her own provinces, re-establishing her fleets and armies, and building out the sea, has lost her influence in Holland and has neither money, credit, nor government".[6] While there was no intention in England deliberately to make profit of the difficulties of France it was im-

---

[1] See Rose, *Pitt*, I, chs. XV and XVI.   [2] *Vide infra*, chs. II, III.
[3] Koch and Schöll, *Traités*, I, 492–8.   [4] *Dropmore Papers*, II, 47.
[5] Quoted in Lecky, *A History of England during the Eighteenth Century*, v, 566.
[6] *Auckland Journal*, II, 239.

possible not to feel the advantage of her temporary incapacity. At a time so critical in the growth of our Indian power, when it still remained to be decided whether the Company would be the paramount power, or only one of the contending powers in India, France was paralysed. Though she gave Tipu's ambassadors "a splendid reception" at Versailles in 1788, she had to refuse him help. She could not aid the Indian princes as she had aided the American republicans, and break the British power in the East as she had broken it in the West. If so, she might have completed her revenge for the double catastrophe she herself had suffered in 1763. Her financial position would not allow it. Great Britain took her opportunity; Cornwallis who had failed in the West triumphed in the East, and before France was again in a position to act, the foundations of British power in India were broad-based across the sub-continent, in the hilly south as well as in the Gangetic plain; and beyond India the East India Company was feeling its way in Further India and China.

So too in the Pacific. French and English explorers had followed one another across its waters in the eighteenth century. The time was ripening for European penetration. But revolution and long wars preoccupied France, and England anticipated her in the annexation of its greatest area of vacant land. In 1788 we laid our claim to nearly the half of Australia—a claim which France was in no position or mood to dispute. Spain, paralysed by the weakness of her ally, was forced to yield, and the northern no less than the southern Pacific was laid open to British settlement. The weakening of the French Government amid the growing excitement and disorders of the Revolution was soon followed by signs of revolt in her dependencies, which exposed her Empire to the ambition of her enemies. About a retaliation on France of this kind Grenville wrote to Gower in August 1791: "The islands in the West Indies are not worth to us one year of that invaluable tranquillity which we are now enjoying."[1] The mood at home was still one of indifference to foreign affairs, to be grateful for and retain, if we could, our fortunate freedom from the confusions of Europe.

Such was the situation when the progress of events in France began to divide opinion in England. It was Burke who gave most forcible expression to sentiments hostile to the changes in France. In November 1790 he had published his *Reflections on the French Revolution*. In February 1791, in a *Letter to a Member of the National Assembly*, he, who had spoken for peace with Spain in 1790 when all voices were for war, declared in favour of foreign intervention against France. In April he broke with Fox in the debate on the Quebec Bill. But neutrality was still the policy of the Government. Pitt had no wish or intention to be involved in war with France so

---

[1] *Dropmore Papers*, I, 595; II, 181.

long as she threatened no vital interest of Great Britain. At the beginning of 1792 the Ministry was full of hope. England had recovered her prosperity. Her finances were in better order than ever before, her administration was improved, her influence in Europe, despite some checks, was as great as she could hope, she had friends and allies again, peace had established her power in India, part of Australia had been added to the Empire, new colonies were growing up in North America, she had drawn back from the Russian imbroglio, the Nootka negotiations, as our ambassador at Madrid reported, were *en bon train*. "Our good old island", wrote Auckland to Grenville, 3 July 1792, "now possesses an accumulation and completion of prosperity beyond any example in the history of the world."[1] Pitt spoke of that year as "the most productive of any in the history of this country". In the growth of population, the activity of trade, the progress of invention, the improvement of means of communication, signs of increasing strength revealed themselves. A new industrial era was dawning. Machinery was taking the place of hand labour, factories of home industry. Our cotton manufactures and exports were increasing at an enormous rate.[2] From the West Indies came in sugar, rum, cotton, coffee and other tropical products. The United States were the greatest single foreign market for our exports.[3] In the East Indian trade we were almost without a rival.[4] More and more we needed supplies of raw materials for our expanding industries, and new oversea markets for their products. Pitt was able both to add to the sinking fund and to remit taxation. England had recovered her economic position and was fast increasing her lead. She was more wealthy and prosperous than any other nation, while France was declining. It was hard to call a halt to such progress and tempt the uncertainties of war. But the state of France cast ever more gloomy and menacing shadows over this varied and pleasant prospect. Still, with the French navy mutinous, the French colonies rebellious, and the French Government weakened by successive crises and anxious to secure England's alliance or neutrality in case of continental war, perhaps nothing was to be feared. Certainly France seemed to have more troubles than ambitions oversea. So Pitt was determined to be hopeful, and in Europe to maintain what Gibbon called "our safe and prosperous neutrality". If he did not share the views of Fox, neither did he share those of Burke, and the slight reverberations of the Revolution in English opinion were not enough to deflect his policy in either direction. All turned on the conduct of France in Europe. She must not touch Holland. The Dutch alliance was an essential part of our European system and a pillar of our Eastern defences, and the recovery of it was Pitt's great achievement in

---

[1] *Dropmore Papers*, II, 286.   [2] Macpherson, IV, 132.
[3] Bemis, *Jay's Treaty*, p. 34.   [4] Macpherson, IV, 117.

foreign policy. The Emperor and the King of Prussia wished to draw Holland into their combination against France. Pitt exerted himself to prevent it. "This country and Holland", writes Lord Grenville to Lord Auckland, 6 November 1792, "ought to remain quiet as long as it is possible to do so."[1] In the same month England assured Holland of support if necessary.

The need soon came: the French declared the Scheldt open. Negotiations failed to settle this point. The Whigs divided and some joined Pitt, who now openly expressed his antipathy to the new system of the Revolution.[2] Chauvelin was dismissed and on 1 February 1793 France declared war. Much was said on the English side of subversive propaganda in England, but the essential matters were Holland with her colonies and Pitt's distrust of the actions and professions of France now in the full tide of aggressive war. Thus the decade of peace ended and England was embarked again on war, which Burke, with the uncanny prescience he had shown throughout, described as "the most dangerous war we were ever engaged in" and which he predicted would be long.[3] Peace with France had contributed much to British expansion during the ten years that had passed: war with France during the next twenty was to contribute even more.

[1] *Auckland Journal*, ii, 464.   [2] *Parl. Hist.* xxx, 271–4.
[3] *Ibid.* xxx, 386.

CHAPTER II

THE CONFLICT WITH REVOLUTIONARY FRANCE
1793–1802

THE French declaration of war on Great Britain and Holland on 1 February 1793 impressed even well-informed observers as a sudden outburst of revolutionary enthusiasm. But, in truth, the rupture came about largely as the sequel to a long series of disturbances centring in Anglo-French struggles for supremacy in the Dutch Netherlands, with all the resulting colonial implications. After the collapse of Britain's old Empire in 1783 efforts had thrice been made to abase her still further; and only the internal weakness and mutual distrust of France and other Powers availed to postpone a rupture to the year 1793. That calamity was due proximately to the revolutionary urge which incited the triumphant French Jacobins to overthrow the neighbouring monarchies and spread everywhere the principle of equality. But, as no people can ever cut itself loose from the past, so now the apostles of the new creed were destined little by little to drift back into the old courses, until, finally, a struggle, which began with a headlong rush of liberating zeal, swirled off into side eddies of commercial and colonial rivalry.

In all conflicts war methods tend to distort the original war aims; but in the present case the denaturalising process was both speedy and profound. For, as Great Britain and France could not effectively attack each other by direct means, both combatants resorted to indirect methods; and these led on to far-flung schemes which embroiled the world in a conflict reverting more and more to the traditional Anglo-French type. France sought to exclude the islanders from the Continent and they retaliated by mastering the oceans and lands oversea. During these efforts at would-be strangulation revolutionary principles were forgotten in the life and death struggle, which laid hold of all possible points of vantage and resorted to primitive naval and military methods never foreseen at the outset. From this war of the elements emerged the world of the nineteenth century— materialised, disillusioned and exhausted.

Early in this conflict there were signs that the war of democratic propaganda might degenerate into one of material aggression; for the French victories of the autumn of 1792 over the Austro-Prussian invaders exposed the Republic of the United Netherlands to the incursions of the Republicans, who saw the Dutch fleet, wealth and colonies almost at their mercy. Gallic enthusiasm mounted high; and by one of the series of aggressive decrees of November–December 1792 the French Convention annulled the rights of the Dutch to exclusive navigation of the River Scheldt below Antwerp, forthwith despatching war-vessels to assist in the reduction of that then Austrian stronghold. These actions and the threatening preparations of that ambitious schemer, General Dumouriez, on the Dutch frontier clearly presaged a renewal of the previous efforts of the French to achieve the subjection of the United Netherlands.[1] Already British statesmen had come to see that far more was at stake than the survival of the Barrier System, for which in time past their predecessors had often sacrificed great colonial gains. Above and beyond the safety of the Thames there was a wider issue—the preservation of the Dutch colonies. Near the mouths of the Scheldt, Meuse and Rhine was to be decided the question whether the Dutch or the French would rule at the Cape of Good Hope, in Ceylon, and in Guiana.

The naval issue alone would have raised the Scheldt problem to the first rank; for a century of experience had shown that, with the growth in size of ships, failure must attend all efforts to invade England from the cramped and shallow harbours of Northern France. Therefore French war efforts had almost always been directed against British commerce and colonies. But now, as mistress of the deep and capacious estuaries of Zealand and Holland, France might hope to deal the far more effective home-thrust against London.[2] Accordingly, as the Anglo-French dispute became acute at the end of 1792, Maret, head of the Department of Foreign Affairs at Paris, wrote to an English agent, "We are ready; our armies are there; liberty summons them; and it is in Holland that we shall strike the first blow against England."[3] Still more significant as a sign of the world-wide projects of the forward wing in the French Convention was the speech of a former naval officer, Kersaint. Speaking as mouthpiece of the Diplomatic Committee, and in view of the now imminent rupture with the islanders, he predicted the triumph of France, the champion of liberty and equality. The English, he said, were weakened by internal discontents and by the resolve of the Irish and Scots to achieve independence. Moreover, their governing classes depended largely on foreign trade, in which other peoples were largely their factors. Let France, then, by a vigorous naval offensive, attack the sources of this wealth, which would soon dry up.

The credit of England (he proceeded) rests on fictitious riches, which are widespread and essentially personal (*mobilières*). Her public wealth, restricted to the Kingdom, is almost entirely in her Bank, and all this fabric is sustained by the prodigious activity of her seaborne trade. Asia, Portugal and Spain are the best markets for the produce of her industry. We must close them by opening them to all. We must attack Lisbon and Brazil, and send an army to help Tippoo Sultan....If you know how to direct the naval war it will pay the costs of the land war, and perhaps France...will owe to her naval victories the strengthening of her liberty.[4]

[1] *Vide supra*, ch. 1; also *C.H.B.F.P.* 1, 223–30.
[2] *Spencer Papers* (Navy Records Society), 11, 251; *Dropmore Papers* (Hist. MSS. Comm.), 11, 365–7, 371, 379.   [3] *Correspondence of W. A. Miles on the French Revolution*, 11, 36.
[4] *Histoire parlementaire*, xxII, 375–7.

To dismiss this harangue as mere windy rhetoric would be to misread revolutionary psychology. The Jacobins, *exaltés* both by creed and by achievement, breathed a confidence which thrilled to its depths a people now in the heyday of an unparalleled rejuvenescence. In fact the new democracy, coalescing with the older nationalism, begat a political force which promised to overbear all monarchies. Brissot's Anglophobe oratory having on February 1 led the Convention unanimously to declare war on England and Holland,[1] the Jacobin leaders urged on the people either "to dictate peace on the ruins of the Tower of London" or to dry up the sources of England's corrupting wealth. Invasion or a war on colonies and commerce: such is the alternative which inspires French policy towards England in the Revolutionary and Napoleonic Wars. Of that policy Napoleon is the greatest executant; and the recurring failures of the direct thrust at London conduce to the spread of an ever widening conflict from which emerge the European and colonial systems of the nineteenth century. From first to last the significant events of the long struggle spring from that deep-rooted conception, the artificiality of the wide-flung British Empire when contrasted with the solid and self-contained might of France.

The French Jacobins might well be elated. Their victories over the Germanic Powers in 1792 had revealed the weakness of the old order, and their energy was winning the enthusiastic support of a nation soon to become a nation in arms. If, with their unlimited man-power, they controlled the Netherlands and the Rhineland, they could defy the neighbouring States, whose top-heavy structure, internal discontents and mutual jealousies ill fitted them for conflict with a compact organism standing four-square on four seas. On the other side Great Britain, like her prospective allies, was not sure of her own people; and there is force in the contention that the French should have left her alone, a prey to internal difficulties.[2] Her small army, recently reduced by Pitt to 18,000 men, was, in part, needed to keep order; recruiting also was difficult; a general enrolment of the militia involved grave risks, and not until later did the volunteer movement give some additional security against invasion. As to the defencelessness of the colonies the situation in Jamaica affords singular proof. Early in 1792 Lord Grenville warned the Governor that, from the general state of Europe and from the continuance of tranquillity which this country has just cause to depend upon, "Ministers had decided to reduce the garrison from 1868 British troops to 800—the level of the years of peace 1764–75; and any more must be supported by local funds".[3] The reduction took place, whereupon fear of a

[1] *Histoire parlementaire*, XXIV, 200–7; Perroud, C., *J. P. Brissot, Correspondance et Papiers*, p. 381.   [2] Chevalier, E., *Histoire de la Marine française, 1792–1815*, I, 47.
[3] C.O. 138/42, Grenville to Gen. Williamson, 7 Jan. 1792; C.O. 28/63, Dundas to Governor of Barbados, 3 Aug. 1792.

servile revolt soon induced the Governor to apply for two regiments from Halifax.

France might also not unreasonably hope to contest with England the supremacy of the seas and therefore of the world. The British navy was ill-prepared for war. In 1783 (so Admiral Byam Martin declared) "there was not a sound ship in the Fleet". The younger Pitt deserves immense credit for working hard to restore its efficiency, and for his "vigilance in watching over the colonial, maritime and commercial interests of the country". Well supported by the able Controller, Sir Charles Middleton (later Lord Barham), he constructed nine sail-of-the-line and repaired sixty, besides many frigates, so that by 1793 as many as ninety-three sail were seaworthy out of a possible total of 113.[1] The chief problem, however, was to man them. After the cessation of the sharp tension with Spain and Russia in 1790–1, Pitt too hopefully counted on the permanence of peace,[2] and in his persistent and revivifying efforts for economy[3] so far reduced the number of seamen that the Government now had to rely on the press gang to fill up the complements even of the Channel, Mediterranean and North Sea fleets. Consequently, not until 14 July 1793 was the Channel Fleet ready for sea. Meanwhile the North Sea Fleet was barely able to cover the transports conveying the brigade of Guards destined for the defence of the Hollandsdiep. Even in September, the Admiralty was anxiously awaiting the arrival of the East and West Indian convoys which would provide good hauls for the press gang.[4] Later, the First Lord, Lord Chatham, claimed that by immense efforts in the year 1793 he increased the crews of the Royal Navy by 56,337 men.[5] Very few people shared his satisfaction at the work of the navy, which at first was far from effective.

Indeed, the British Government was ill-prepared for a struggle with an enemy who marshalled vast masses of men ready to dare and die; for not until 26 November 1792 did it expect a rupture with France.[6] Then, too, its organisation for war was old-fashioned and slow. Worse still, the task of fanning to a generous glow the smouldering loyalty of the people transcended the power of George III and his Ministers, in none of whom was there a flicker of war genius. True, the King often displayed keen common sense; but at his right hand stood a peace Minister, whose economies in peace time contrasted strangely with his diffuse and sometimes wasteful efforts during the war. There is a spice of truth in the remark of a severe critic, William Windham, that, owing to an "inveterate prudence, an instinctive horror of indiscretion", Pitt would "never fairly lay himself out

---

[1] *Journals of Sir T. Byam Martin* (N.R.S.), III, 380–2; James, W., *Naval History of Great Britain* (edit. of 1902), I, 51–3, App. I.
[2] Rose, *Pitt*, II, 32.
[3] *Auckland Corresp.* II, 457.   [4] *Dropmore Papers*, II, 443.
[5] Chatham MSS. in P.R.O. (Mem. of Lord Chatham to George III).
[6] *Dropmore Papers*, II, 319, 332, 339, 341, 344, 351; *Auckland Corresp.* II, 419, 465.

ventre à terre so as to win the prize in the race of renown and glory".
Indeed, during most of the long war Pitt was a pale reflection of the
blazing sun of Chatham.

Nor did the colleagues of Pitt make good these deficiencies. At
the Foreign Office his cousin, William Wyndham, Lord Grenville,
won respect by hard work, consistency and tough patriotism; but
his cold and repellent personality was apt to freeze supporters and
hearten opponents. Far different was the jovial Henry Dundas.
Aggressive and pliable, bountiful and adroit, keen and acquisitive,
he figured by turns as the ministerial wire-puller, the manipulator
of Parliament, and the weaver of far-flung designs. Even as Secretary
of State for Home Affairs up to 1794, he influenced war policy far
more than that nonentity at the War Office, Sir George Yonge, or
than the second Lord Chatham, whose lethargic ways at the Admiralty won him the *soubriquet* of the *late* Lord Chatham. Yet Dundas,
for all his presumption (which has been severely castigated as the
cause of our many disasters),[1] had some redeeming gifts. He had a
vision of Empire, and he strove hard, first for its preservation, then
for its strengthening at vital strategic points. By long control of the
India Board and its vast patronage he virtually directed affairs in
the East Indies, and he directed them well; but he also had a keen
sense of the value of the West Indies as forming the keystone of our
commercial system. Moreover, though Pitt and he often attempted
far more than they could execute, their actions were prompted by
a pardonable belief in the superiority of our sailors and soldiers, and
the almost uncanny faculty of England to win through.

Meanwhile, the British Empire was in danger; for the French navy
far from being weak,[2] was formidable in *matériel*. Thanks to the
efforts of Louis XVI and his Ministers, its sail-of-the-line and frigates
were, class for class, superior to the English in tonnage, speed and
gun-power (in the last respect by one-sixth). Of French sail-of-the-
line seventy-six were rated as serviceable, but of these eight mounted
from 110 to 120 guns, our largest (of the *Victory* class) being nominally
of 100 guns. How many of the seventy-six were ready for sea by the
spring of 1793 is not known; but the Convention had ordered in all
fifty-four to be ready, and our historian James reckoned fifty as
ready built.[3] Thus, in view of its far lighter responsibilities, the
French navy almost warranted the boast of its Minister, Jean Bon
St André, that it was the most powerful in the world.[4] This estimate,
however, left out the factors of seamanship and discipline. The
Revolution had impaired the former and destroyed the latter. After
causing almost all the naval officers to emigrate, it had thrust into
their place merchant captains or others, who were now elected by

---

[1] Fortescue, Sir J., *History of the British Army*, vol. IV, *passim*.
[2] Sorel, A., *L'Europe et la Révolution française*, III, 245.
[3] James, *Naval History*, I, App. 6.   [4] Chevalier, *Histoire*, I, 50–6.

the crews on a system of indirect election. Discipline was thereby undermined at its source, and mutinies often happened when an admiral or a captain acted in a way displeasing to the crews. Consequently, though the Brest fleet straggled to sea five weeks before Lord Howe's force put out from Spithead, yet little harm was done to British commerce and much to the fleet itself by collisions. By good fortune it evaded contact with Howe, whose bad luck was phenomenal.

Such, then, was the situation in the spring of 1793. At first sight the auguries seemed favourable to Great Britain; for she joined a coalition already including Austria, Prussia, Sardinia and Naples, and soon to include Spain, the Empire, Portugal and, nominally, Russia. Appearances therefore favoured the assumption (still widely held) that she joined a great monarchical league for the purpose of stamping out French democracy. The known facts of the case are at variance with this assumption, which leaves out of count both the aggressive policy of the French extremists then in power, the inner weakness and mutual jealousies of all neighbouring States, and the resolve of the Pitt Administration, if possible, to keep the peace.[1] Never, indeed, has there been a league so imposing yet so hollow; and never a combatant so isolated, yet drawing such stores of strength and confidence from that defiant isolation. It is a truism to say that great States lose their strength in a coalition; and certainly Great Britain lost far more than she gained by joining this loose-jointed league. Acting alone, she would have known where she was; acting with exigent and often untrustworthy allies, she had to meet their demands for a fleet, a landing force and a subsidy, or for all three at once, with scanty and often diminishing help from them. Thus, she had immediately to despatch a brigade of Guards to defend the Hollandsdiep, in which she succeeded, only to be drawn into the Flemish campaign, which the Prussians thereupon failed to support.[2] Again, as her three Mediterranean allies bargained for the despatch of a strong British fleet to those waters, she sent off Admiral Lord Hood with, in all, nineteen sail and twenty-three smaller craft for objects which led on to the Toulon adventure and, after its failure, to the occupation of Corsica.

These extensions of the navy's responsibilities would by themselves have told against that simple and direct strategy which made for success in the Seven Years' War. But also our own and allied merchants demanded protection for their commerce in a way which often distracted naval policy. Yet, whatever the dogmas of strategists, such protection was necessary; for the navy had to shield the Empire and its commerce from Bengal to Canada and Jamaica. Across the Atlantic the problem was especially complex; for, the loss of the

[1] *C.H.B.F.P.* i, 224–39; Sorel, iii, 215–21.
[2] *Dropmore Papers*, ii, 388, 399, 425, 432.

thirteen American colonies having eviscerated the old Empire, the defence of the sundered halves presented grave difficulties in view of the marked unfriendliness of the United States,[1] and the determination of their shippers to defy our Navigation Laws in the West Indies. But the crisis which now arose in that valued group of colonies was so urgent as to call for more detailed notice.

As has before appeared,[2] the West Indian gambit was the favourite opening of France in the naval war; for in that wealthy archipelago, particularly in the smaller islands, a vigorous aggressor could generally sweep the board. Nowhere in the outer world did conditions so favour the assailant and damn the defender—a fact patent to many adventurous spirits from Drake to Napoleon. Moreover, as trade with the Caribbean increased in value, conquests in that inviting arena quickly depressed credit at London, Paris or Madrid, and broke the "will to war" of the stricken State. Thus, in 1760–2 the elder Pitt resolved by heavy blows in that quarter to clinch the recent successes in Canada and India, and compel both France and Spain to a peace. Similarly, two decades later, those Powers sought to deal us the *coup de grâce* at Jamaica; and, though England lay almost open to invasion and the Gibraltar garrison was half starving, the Admiralty despatched a great fleet under Rodney to save the sugar islands. He succeeded, and his success enabled England to speak with her enemies in the gate. If, even then, the knock-out blow was attempted in that quarter, was it not likely to be still more fatal after the loss of the American colonies left the British West Indies the richest asset in the economy of Empire? In September 1782 Sir Charles Middleton reckoned the value of property in St Christopher and ten of the lesser British islands to exceed £15,000,000, while they were also "an immense nursery of seamen", and "the most productive of our colonies".[3] Our capital invested in the West Indian trade was also estimated at £70,000,000 as against £18,000,000 in that of the East Indies; and shipping and import duties bore nearly the same proportion. Further, the sentimental connection was strong, witness these words of a West Indian planter—"England draws to it all that is good in the Plantations.... If we get a little money we remit it to England. They that are able breed up their children in England."[4]

But besides these motives there were others certain to lead to sharp collisions in the Caribbean. Both British and French squadrons were invitingly weak. The former consisted of the fifty-gun ship *Trusty* (Vice-Admiral Laforey) and a few small craft on the Leeward Islands station, and a similar force on the Jamaica station; while the small French squadron, based on Fort Royal in Martinique, was paralysed

[1] *Dropmore Papers*, III, 520–30; Bemis, *Jay's Treaty*, chs. I–V.
[2] *C.H.B.E.* I, 508, 510, 512, 518, 711–12, 741.
[3] *Barham Papers* (N.R.S.), II, 61, 70.
[4] Edwards, B., *History of the West Indies*, II, 460, 477.

by the political feuds in that island. Indeed, when the local Republicans finally worsted the Royalists, the latter fled to Trinidad in three small warships, leaving behind only one frigate fit for service. Thereupon the Republicans awaited powerful succours preparing at Brest.[1]

Even worse was the condition of the formerly rich and flourishing French colony in San Domingo. In the western part of that great island there had grown up a community which excelled in the cultivation of sugar, the yield per acre exceeding that of Jamaica by two-thirds, while its shipping formed a large part of the French total to and from the West Indies, estimated at 600 craft.[2] Yet that wealthy society, based on slave labour, had dissolved under the breath of egalitarian zeal; for when Paris set free all the slaves in the French colonies, the news aroused the blacks to wild hopes and the masters to stubborn resistance. Hence came servile risings which wrecked the settlements of San Domingo and sent hundreds of refugees flying for their lives to Jamaica. In response to their piteous appeals for help Governor Williamson, unable to spare any soldiers, sent arms and supplies, which only partially met the crisis. The French colonists meanwhile despatched to London Malouet and Charmilly with the official offer to place San Domingo under the protection of George III.[3] About three weeks before the rupture with France Dundas warned them

that unless this country is involved in actual hostilities with France, it is impossible for His Majesty, consistently with the line of conduct which he has invariably followed, to aid or in any degree to countenance any plan of operations affecting the internal concerns of France either in that country or in any of its dependencies. If hostilities do take place, which is highly probable, it will certainly be a part of the plan of operations pursued by this country to extend the protection of H.M.'s Government and of the King's arms to the French West India colonies, so as to preserve the whole group from utter subversion.[4]

A similar proposal brought by Royalist delegates from Martinique and Guadeloupe was also accepted on condition that those islands should either revert to the House of Bourbon if it regained the throne, or be exchanged for equivalent British colonies that might be lost in the war. Meanwhile the French inhabitants were to take the oath of allegiance, as in Canada, and enjoy the free use of their religion.[5]

On the surface, then, everything seemed to promise an easy transfer of the French West Indies to Great Britain and almost warranted Dundas's hopeful parenthesis—"if indeed serious resistance is appre-

[1] Adm. I/316, Laforey to Stephens, 19 Jan. 1793.
[2] Edwards, *West Indies*, II, 471; III, 146. Lokke, C. L., *France and the Colonial Question*, pp. 16, 28, 29.
[3] *C.H.B.F.P.* I, 560–1; *Dropmore Papers*, II, 388; Edwards, *History of...San Domingo*, passim.
[4] C.O. 137/91, Dundas to Williamson, 12 Jan. 1793.
[5] Adm. I/4157, Dundas to Major-Gen. Bruce, 27 Feb. 1793.

hended".[1] But he, Williamson and the French planters, all over-rated the numbers and efficiency of the French Royalist levies as much as they underrated the fighting powers of mulattoes and blacks, exasperated by oppression and now fired with fanatical zeal for equality. With the men of colour, too, were ranged those incalculable factors—the heats, the rains and the deadly miasma of woods and swamps. In a struggle between whites and blacks (for such it was at first) the former needed almost equal numbers and constant reinforcements to hold out against the heavy handicap of climate. Moreover, the French soon possessed a clear naval superiority in those waters—a sign that they intended to sweep us out of the West Indies. When Charmilly returned thither to concert with Williamson the occupation of San Domingo, the latter soon found that France had there one sail-of-the-line and four frigates, against which the small Jamaica squadron under Commodore Ford was helpless, while the French frigates also intercepted the necessary supplies of food. For naval reasons, then, the plan was reluctantly postponed. Williamson indeed asserted that "had the commodore only two line of battle ships, I have not the least doubt but possession might be taken of all the French colonies from Port au Prince round to Aux Cayes"; for our troops were fit for any service.[2] But soon, in view of the growing ferment among the negroes of Jamaica, he felt it risky to weaken too much the local garrison.

Equally dark was the outlook in the Leeward Islands; for in 1792 and 1793 France sent out thither large reinforcements, which over-powered the Royalists and sent those of Martinique and Guadeloupe flying to Trinidad or Dominica. About 4000 of them in Dominica soon became "very riotous and insolent", so that Admiral Laforey had to expel some and keep a frigate there to overawe the rest.[3] The position of Dominica between the two French islands was especially difficult; for propinquity to the French possessions always spread the levelling contagion. But all the British islands were in danger; and from none could the garrison be wholly withdrawn for offensive operations.

Thus the French Jacobins could count not only on the strategic advantage of possessing a first-class base in Martinique, but also on the far greater power of their levelling propaganda, which, while ranging the few whites with the Union Flag, massed the hordes of blacks and mulattoes under the tricolour. No wonder, then, that the French strained all the resources of their disorganised dockyards to despatch a formidable squadron to the West Indies. Having inherited from Louis XVI a powerful navy, they rightly decided to use it offensively in the quarter where they were the strongest, and

---

[1] C.O. 137/91, Dundas to Williamson, 4 June 1793.
[2] Ibid. Williamson to Dundas, 31 July 1793.
[3] Adm. 1/316, Laforey to Stephens, 19 Jan., 14 March 1793.

we were the weakest. Early in March, then, eight sail-of-the-line and two frigates got away from Brest. On the 9th they were sighted in the Bay of Biscay, and subsequent news pointed to their having joined a convoy off the north-west of Spain. Thereupon, on March 17, Pitt, Dundas and the Admiralty, surmising that their objective was the West Indies, issued orders that Rear-Admiral Alan Gardner, then about to convoy East Indiamen to Cape Verde, should receive reinforcements raising his squadron to seven or eight sail and proceed to the south-west for the purpose of intercepting the French expeditionary force. Thus, in the hurry caused by this alarming news, an East Indian convoy was to be left exposed in order to protect our almost unprotected West Indies,[1] a course of action harmonising with Pitt's statement to Grenville, that the West Indies must be protected even if our Mediterranean force was thereby delayed.[2] The evidence just set forth refutes the assertions that Pitt and Dundas went out of their way to attack the French West Indies.[3] On the contrary, it was the French who attacked us there; and British action was in reality defensive.

Arriving at Barbados on April 27,[4] Gardner heard that Laforey with the local force had lately recovered the small but rich island of Tobago, lost by the Peace of Versailles. In other respects the West Indian campaign of 1793 effected nothing. Major-General Bruce, military commander at Barbados, on receipt of assurances of effective help from the Royalists of Martinique if a suitable British force should land, decided to make the attempt. Setting sail on June 10, he, near Martinique, joined Commodore Murray's small blockading squadron, which, with the help of two French Royalist warships, had been cutting off supplies and had detained several American vessels. The French batteries foiled Bruce's first attempt to land, but on June 16 he succeeded at Fond Capot and planned an advance before dawn on the fortified town of St Pierre. His force consisted of some 1100 British and 800 French Royalists; but these last, while advancing in the darkness, became confused, fired on one another and retreated in haste. Bruce, finding them so untrustworthy, decided to re-embark all the troops. This tame withdrawal of course heartened the Republicans everywhere, and the affair showed how little reliance could be placed on Royalist auxiliaries. Gardner then proceeded northwards to St Christopher, and there on July 17 received the Admiralty orders of June 6 to return to England, after detaching two sail to Jamaica to guard the homeward convoy.[5] He did so on August 1 with five sail and four smaller craft, leaving behind six frigates and sloops to guard the Leeward Isles. Superficially con-

---

[1] Adm. 1/4157, Dundas to Adm. (Secret), March 1793.
[2] *Dropmore Papers*, II, 402, where the letter is wrongly dated.
[3] Fortescue, Sir J., *British Army*, IV (pt. 1), 78–80, 134, 135, 325, 350.
[4] Adm. 1/316, Gardner to Stephens, 22 April 1793.
[5] *Ibid*. Gardner to Stephens, 25 June, 24 July 1793.

sidered, his voyage seems a failure. But probably his arrival in those waters alarmed the French commander, Rear-Admiral Sercey, whose movements after reaching Martinique are mysteriously null. Williamson, on finding that he had disappeared, sent our squadron with the 13th regiment to occupy the town of Jérémie in the south-west of Domingo, which it easily effected on September 20, and soon afterwards relieved the hard-pressed Royalists of the fortress, Mole St Nicholas. Our men, however, soon found themselves beset by want of food and harassed by the coloured forces holding the hills that commanded the adjacent plain. Only 300 Royalists joined us.[1]

Meanwhile the British Government was preparing to despatch to the West Indies an expedition under Vice-Admiral Sir John Jervis and General Sir Charles Grey. The wisdom of sending thither four sail, fourteen smaller warships, and many transports with 6000 troops on board is questionable in view of the then severe strain on our man-power. In Flanders and the Rhineland the efforts of our Austrian and Prussian allies, now bent less on Paris than Warsaw, had been dilatory and weak. Also on September 8 the Duke of York's force besieging Dunkirk was driven back by a relieving French army. Accordingly, the "march on Paris", hoped for in the spring, was held up on the French frontier. Further, the fiery demands of Burke for help to the Royalist peasant bands of Brittany and Poitou led to some belated and therefore unsuccessful attempts at succour. Still greater was the strain after August 29, when the British and Spanish fleets were invited into Toulon by the hard-pressed Royalists of Provence. Admiral Hood, having only 1626 troops, and receiving insufficient help from allies, found himself committed to the unexpectedly difficult task of defending extensive positions around the city against the Republican levies which threatened his fleet in the inner harbour. Thus, in Flanders, the Rhineland, Brittany, Poitou, Provence, as well as in the West Indies, the titanic efforts of the Republican armies, acting on interior lines, threw back on the defensive the over-confident and ill-concerted allies, spread out over an immense circumference.

For Great Britain, with her puny forces, the problem of war strategy now became extremely difficult. Indeed, it could be solved only by clear thinking followed by resolute action. Obviously the future of the Empire and of the world depended largely on a due assessment of war aims and of our available resources. Yet very little, if any, evidence exists as to any careful examination of the problem with the help of experts. Dundas worked at it, and apparently without such help. In May 1793 he wrote to Grenville that, after careful examination of the "objects" (we should now say "objectives") of our naval forces, he, in full confidence, allocated them as follows:

[1] C.O. 137/91, Williamson to Dundas, Sept. 8, Oct. 8; Col. Dansey to Williamson, 25 Oct. 1793.

Channel Fleet, 25 sail; Mediterranean, 20; West Indies, 12; East Indies, 5. Postulating that the West Indies must be made perfectly secure, he urged that an expedition should set sail thither before September 20, it being highly desirable meanwhile to send 4000 or 5000 men to Gibraltar either for service in the Mediterranean, or for setting free that garrison to proceed to the West Indies.[1] At that time, long before the reverses in Martinique and near Dunkirk, this plan, though wide-flung, was not hopelessly diffuse. It postponed action in the East Indies, where we were comparatively at ease; and, by placing in the forefront the West Indies, it promised to end the Jacobin-negro alliance which threatened all the British islands as with a red-black plague.

But the events of September–October blasted all hopes of preparing steadily for a definite scheme of warfare. Instead, the whole degenerated into a scramble to send off fleets and troops wherever they seemed to be most needed. In the last resort the fault lay with the Prussian Government, which, instead of sending to Flanders the stipulated contingents amounting to 52,000 men,[2] marked time in the Palatinate. An undue strain therefore fell on us in Flanders. That campaign, together with efforts in Brittany, Toulon and the West Indies, depleted our scanty man-power, and that, too, despite the shrewd warning of George III: "The misfortune of our situation is that we have too many objects to attend to, and our force consequently must be too weak at each place." He therefore urged the retention in Flanders of seven battalions about to be withdrawn to the West Indies.[3] The critical state of the Flemish campaign fortunately hindered such a withdrawal; but in the Mediterranean the rival calls from Toulon and the West Indies led to a tragi-comedy. In October, when Hood still hoped to hold Toulon, Ministers ordered four sail and two regiments to be withdrawn from his command in order to join Jervis's West Indian expedition. By the time they reached Gibraltar Hood's outlook was so dark that they were ordered back to him, but arrived too late to help in thwarting Bonaparte's successful attack.[4] Meanwhile Lord Chatham had failed to inform Jervis that they were countermanded; and he and Grey long protested at the inadequacy of their force.

In justice to Ministers it should be remembered that trustworthy advices from Tobago warranted the hope of certain success in the West Indies. Still, cautious men like Lord Auckland pointed out to Grenville (November 7) that our first objective should be Paris, and that victory there would lead to the acquisition of the French West Indies, while diversions of force from the main effort might "risk

---

[1] *Dropmore Papers*, II, 407 (there wrongly assigned to July 1793).
[2] *Ibid.* II, 434, 441, 446–51.
[3] Rose, J. H., *Pitt and Napoleon; Essays and Letters*, p. 225; Fortescue, *British Army*, IV (pt. I), 141.
[4] Rose, J. H., *Lord Hood and the Defence of Toulon*, pp. 50–2.

the fate of the whole war". Grenville, however, deprecated the giving up of the West Indian expedition as likely to "give an impression of alarm".[1] Thus, for non-military reasons, the directing trio (Pitt, Grenville and Dundas) starved the efforts in Flanders which, if pushed on vigorously by the allies with united forces, should have ended the war. The radical cause of the British failure was the pursuit of secondary objectives on the circumference of the Empire before the main effort had been duly provided for. The lesson it taught, apparently, has never been thoroughly learned. Probably it is unattainable under a parliamentary system which demands the satisfaction of diverse mercantile interests.

Jervis's expedition, putting out from Spithead in mid-November, did not reach Barbados until 7–10 January 1794. The delay in his arrival was doubly unfortunate; for a virulent fever then raging laid low 1200 of his men; and in any case half of the best campaigning season was now over. Nevertheless, such was the energy of Jervis and Grey that the latter forced a landing in Martinique, in a bay near Fort Royal, while Major-General Thomas Dundas succeeded in taking St Pierre. The two forces then made their way through hilly and wooded country towards Fort Royal, the seamen dragging guns up almost incredible slopes in order to overpower the defence, which collapsed on March 21.[2] Equal success attended the attacks on St Lucia and Guadeloupe; so that by the end of April Jervis informed the Admiralty "that all the French islands in those seas were reduced". The Duke of Kent, who had played a creditable part in this campaign, thereupon returned to Canada where trouble was brewing with the United States.[3] Jervis and Grey now set up administrations based mainly on old French law, and left them largely in the hands of the chief inhabitants. The charge of corruption brought against the commanders is without foundation; but the culpable conduct of the British Governor of St Lucia may have accentuated the Republican reaction in that island, which led to its loss in 1795.[4]

Such a swing round, which nearly lost us Grenada and St Vincent, was in the nature of things; for the coloured people were fanatical for liberty, especially when they saw the British garrisons dwindle from disease and receive no reinforcements, while the French put forth great and successful efforts. Here again the issues at stake had not been duly measured as against man-power. The Home Government should have strained every nerve to send out betimes strong reinforcements and to cut off those of the French. Neither was done

---

[1] *Dropmore Papers*, II, 438, 454, 464.
[2] Tucker, J. S., *Memoirs of Earl St Vincent*, I, 119; Willyams, C., *Campaign in the West Indies*, pp. 15–81; *Admiral James's Journal* (N.R.S.), pp. 228–41.
[3] *Dropmore Papers*, III, 520–7. Friction was allayed by Jay's Treaty of Nov. 1794. See Bemis, *Jay's Treaty*, chs. VI seqq.; *Works of John Q. Adams*, I, 203–10.
[4] Willyams, *Campaign in the West Indies*, chs. VIII, XI.

effectively, the result being that two frigates, one corvette and four transports, with 1500 troops, got away from Rochefort in April 1794, and in June reached Guadeloupe. Their leader, Victor Hugues, excited the mulattoes and negroes to a general and successful effort against the British garrison, now enfeebled by disease and the death of General Dundas. Thereupon Grey's attempt at recovery by the depleted garrison of Martinique failed owing to the weakness of his force and a mistake in the line of attack; Guadeloupe was lost (July 1794), and Hugues boasted that two frigates and 800 Republicans had worsted six sail-of-the-line and 8000 chosen troops.[1] By systematic cruelty and cunning he now cowed the Royalists and doubled the energies of the negroes. Meanwhile, Jervis and Grey, both seriously ill and disgusted with Dundas, returned to England; and the crisis became increasingly serious in the Windward and Leeward groups.

Equally dark was the outlook in San Domingo. As has already appeared, the towns of Jérémie and Mole St Nicholas had been easily occupied. So too were St Mark and Tiburon late in 1793. Our efforts should have been limited to the ports commanding the approach to Jamaica; for with cruisers based on them the Jamaica trade would be moderately safe. But the difficulty of holding these isolated posts and leaving the interior to a fierce and active enemy was so obvious as to lead on to the attempt of mastering some of the hill country and most of the western coast. Then, under the strain of ceaseless vigilance in those fever-stricken woods and plains, fever exacted a deadly toll. In May 1794, when the survivors began to despair, hope revived with the arrival of three regiments from England under Brigadier-General Whyte. He led them, while still fresh from the voyage, against the capital, Port au Prince, which, with twenty-two richly laden merchantmen, proved an easy prey. The gain was illusory; for the heats of midsummer and the miasma of neighbouring marshes soon laid low forty officers and 600 men. Moreover, the Republicans, who recruited their bands from wandering hordes in the interior, both harassed us on land and sent forth from the smaller ports, Jacmel and Les Cayes, numerous privateers to prey on the Jamaica trade, which suffered the loss of some thirty vessels in a twelvemonth. Edwards, who knew the place well, judged that the right policy was to hold these and other posts of naval importance and destroy and evacuate Port au Prince.

Another adverse circumstance was the lack of help from our Spanish allies in the east of the island. Indeed, their conduct on several occasions, especially in leaving the French Royalists of Fort Dauphin to be massacred by the blacks, implied extreme jealousy at the allied successes, an attitude probably prompted from Madrid.[2]

---

[1] Fortescue, *British Army*, IV (pt. 1), ch. XIV; *Ann. Register* (1795), p. 186; *Adm. James's Journal*, pp. 243–5. [2] Edwards, B., *West Indies*, III, chs. X–XII; *C.H.B.F.P.* I, 257, 561–3.

The chief enemy, however, was yellow fever, against whose ravages neither the Home Government nor officers on the spot took adequate precautions. Despite all the lessons of experience the Government sent out the last reinforcements so late that they arrived after the beginning of the hot and rainy season, the result being that, at the end of December 1794, out of 1490 British troops in San Domingo 738 were sick, while, of the local troops in our service, out of 1925 only 407 were in hospital.[1] Early in 1795 the situation became very critical,[2] the struggle being clearly dependent on the survival of the fittest. It is therefore strange that Ministers did not adopt the suggestion of General Williamson to conciliate the mulattoes by granting privileges,[3] which would have ranged them on our side.

The losses sustained in the West Indies were so great that persistence in those enterprises, especially in San Domingo, seems indefensible. On strictly military grounds they were so at a time when not only Flanders but Corsica claimed all available troops. Yet the Caribbean policy of Ministers was doggedly maintained, and not without reason; for the struggle was in 1795 more and more shifting to the economic sphere, in which the West Indies were of transcendent importance. But even on naval and military grounds Ministers had good cause for hope. The first activities of Victor Hugues soon petered out; and in a few islands the negroes were contented and fought well for us.[4] Also, thanks to the successes of Admirals Howe and Bridport, the French navy suffered severely in 1794–5, its total losses amounting to eleven sail-of-the-line and fifty-six smaller craft, while those of the British navy were slight.[5] Accordingly, the occasional reverses of our troops in the West Indies furnished no cause for despairing of success in a sphere where the last word lay with the navy. As for the heavy losses of our troops by disease (often due to carelessness of the officers or lack of proper medical supervision)[6] no one in that age considered them a sufficient reason for abandoning our most valued group of colonies to France and her murderous black allies. Moreover, in 1795 the enemy seemed on the verge of financial collapse,[7] and no means of assuring it seemed so certain as that of cutting off his West Indian supplies. Finally, the fast-growing cotton industry of Lancashire and Lanark demanded all possible imports of raw cotton, which came largely from the West Indies, for the southern plantations of the United States were then ill developed, besides being, for political reasons, an uncertain source of supply. Economic motives thus prompted the continuance of our West Indian efforts, which have generally been viewed solely from a military standpoint.

[1] Edwards, *West Indies*, III, 184.
[2] C.O. 117/94, Williamson to Duke of Portland, 5 March 1795.
[3] C.O. 137/92, Williamson to Dundas, 19 Jan. 1794.
[4] *Diary of Sir J. Moore* (ed. Maurice, Sir F.), I, 240.
[5] Troude, O., *Batailles navales de la France*, II, 394, 459.
[6] Pinckard, G., *Notes on the Expedition to the West Indies* (espec. Letter 15); *Diary of Sir J. Moore*, I, 235, 239.   [7] *Dropmore Papers*, II, 452; Mallet du Pan, *Mémoires*, II, ch. 6.

In the latter part of 1795 an urgent crisis arose in Jamaica; for French agents retorted on our Royalist campaign in San Domingo by stirring up the dreaded Maroons who held the spurs and clefts of the Blue Mountains. These wild blacks, sprung from the slaves who escaped from their Spanish masters during the Cromwellian conquest,[1] were often reinforced by runaways and the human spindrift of the Caribbean, until, as the Abbé Raynal had foretold, they threatened to overrun the island. In July 1795, when the British garrison had been largely drafted to San Domingo, their chance came; and the black terror lurking in the impassable clefts known as the Cockpits threatened to deluge the plains below. At once the Governor, the Earl of Balcarres, proclaimed martial law, called out the militia and ordered back 800 newly arrived British troops, who, after putting in at the island, had sailed for San Domingo. Luckily, the Maroons of the eastern districts remained quiet, and few slaves joined the rebels. But those of Trelawny parish held firm in the fastnesses and often ambushed their white assailants with heavy loss. By degrees Balcarres and Colonel Walpole cut them off from the provision grounds of the slopes so that they were reduced to raiding the negroes' plots, thereby infuriating their natural allies. Accordingly, Balcarres raised mulatto and black companies against them, and, when the struggle lengthened out, procured 100 Cuban bloodhounds to hunt them from the Cockpits. This hateful device brought a manly rebuke from George III, who ordered him at once to send back the dogs.[2]

After some twenty fights the Trelawny Maroons surrendered (30 January 1796); but, as nearly all did so after the stipulated date, Balcarres and the Assembly (to the indignation of Colonel Walpole) ordered their expulsion, and 556 were shipped to Halifax, there to be supported by Jamaican funds till 1798. Meanwhile, the panic among the whites led the Assembly stubbornly to oppose Portland's proposal to raise in the island a black regiment for service in San Domingo, and it enrolled only a limited number of negroes. Nevertheless, bills were soon passed for improving the moral conditions of the negroes, raising the stipends of the clergy by £5000 and prohibiting the importation of all negroes above twenty-five years of age, as being irreclaimable.[3] After this terrible crisis the credit of Jamaica rose rapidly—a sign that Abbé Raynal's prophecy had been widely believed. The crisis none the less weakened British efforts against San Domingo and lessened the hope of success in that island.

[1] See *C.H.B.E.* I, ch. XIII.
[2] C.O. 138/34, Balcarres to Portland, July 19, 24, Aug. 14, 29, Sept. 27, Oct. 7, 27, 1795. C.O. 137/96, same to same, Oct. 18, 25, Nov. 16, 1795; Jan. 1, 30, Feb. 15, 1796; Portland to Balcarres, Jan. 8, Feb. 5, March 3, 1796.
[3] *Ibid.* Balcarres to Portland, March 26, May 12, 1796. C.O. 137/97, May 21, 23, 1796; and letters of W. D. Quarrell on H.M.S. *Dover* and at Halifax.

We now turn to the Mediterranean. The experience of the last four wars had shown that the issue of events on the outer fringe of the Empire depended largely on gaining control of that sea; for the traditional French opening was with the Toulon fleet. In order to counter any such move Admiral Hood had, early in 1794, occupied Corsica. Other reasons for this step were the central position of the island, its excellent harbours, its forests of hard timber,[1] and the prospect of gaining recruits from its brave and mainly monarchist population. French statesmen and admirals set great store by Corsica, which the Duc de Choiseul, the instigator of the French conquest of 1769, estimated as exceeding in value any West Indian island or even Canada.[2] In 1793 the island patriot, Paoli, raised his countrymen in an effort to expel the French, that "nation of atheists and regicides". Seeing his only hope to be in help from England, he sent assurances to Sir Gilbert Elliot, our civil commissioner at Toulon, that, with English help, the liberation of Corsica would be an easy task. Elliot, on a visit to the chief early in 1794, found him and his 2000 followers at the end of their resources, the sum of £4000 being necessary to ensure their continuance with him. In reply to Dundas's letter of 7 March 1794, asking on what terms the union of Corsica with Great Britain could be effected,[3] Paoli promised that, after the expulsion of the French, the islanders, assembled in the General Consulta, would elect George III as their King. On 31 March 1794, Dundas expressed to Elliot his assent to a plan of union—"as the future preservation of it [Corsica] does not appear likely to be attended with any expense or inconvenience which can be set in opposition to [the] advantage". He stipulated that the constitution of Corsica and the laws relating to religion, property, collection of taxes, should continue as at present, subject to such changes as might be made by the Corsican Legislature, and to the assent of His Majesty, as signified by the British Governor. The executive power was to be vested in this official, who, acting as Viceroy, would command the troops and have the right of veto on legislation.[4] A general agreement was arrived at on these questions.

The compact, though vague and certain to lead to misunderstandings, at first suited both parties; for the Corsicans urgently needed succour, and, after the loss of Toulon, and constant friction with the Spaniards, Hood had no sure base during the winter gales. No place of shelter was so advantageous as the Gulf of San Fiorenzo in the north-west of Corsica, whence his fleet and cruisers could effectively watch Toulon and harass the flank of the French army then striving to invade the Italian Riviera. As ships' guns at many points commanded the Corniche Road leading to the pass north of

[1] Nicolas, Sir N. H., *History of the Royal Navy*, i, 479; ii, 5.   [2] Choiseul, *Méms.* p. 245.
[3] Brit. Mus. Add. MS. 22,688, Dundas to Paoli, 7 March 1794.
[4] W.O 70/1 B; Lady Elliot, *Life and Letters of Sir G. Elliot*, ii, 213–17.

Savona (the military key of Italy), the defence of the Peninsula depended largely on Hood's force based on San Fiorenzo. Accordingly, he prepared to drive the French Republicans from the fortresses of San Fiorenzo, Bastia and Calvi, still easily held by them against the sporadic efforts of the Paolists; and, by a series of daring moves, landing parties from our fleet, led by Nelson and tardily supported by our troops, achieved that result (April–August 1794).[1] Meanwhile, at midsummer, a popular Consulta convened at Corte by Paoli acclaimed George III as King of Corsica and recognised Sir Gilbert Elliot (later first Earl of Minto) as Viceroy.

Thus began a highly interesting experiment. Corsica now figured in the line of succession of Mediterranean bases for which William III and Marlborough had striven. As such it was eminently desirable. Indeed, owing to the ruggedness of the island and the clannish aloofness of its inhabitants, the many attempts at its conquest have been prompted mainly by naval considerations. These certainly induced the action of the Pitt administration. Distracted by a dozen imperious claims, Ministers (now reinforced by the Portland Whigs) left the Viceroy, the admiral and the general to their devices. The new possession, in fact, was regarded as a second Gibraltar. Often Elliot complained that during three or four months he received no instructions from the new Secretary of State, the Duke of Portland.[2]

In this slipshod way began the effort at combining the claims of an enlarged naval base and a Crown colony. Experiments on the same line were soon to be tried at the Cape of Good Hope, Ceylon, Trinidad and Mauritius. These, for reasons which will appear later, have developed into great and flourishing colonies. The case of Corsica, however, was exceptionally difficult owing to the instinct of opposition to all government ingrained in the long-oppressed islanders. Jean Bon St André had summed them up as understanding only anarchy, and their leaders only despotism. In such a case to hit the happy mean is not often granted to mortals, particularly stolid northerners inapt to fathom southern versatility, the diverse intrigues of the Pope, the local Jacobins and the aggrieved Paolists. For Paoli now chafed at the promotion of some non-Paolists, and his rage mounted high when, after long delays at Westminster, a decoration was despatched to him and unaccountably disappeared *en route*.[3] The incident gave rise to many conjectures, that of Paoli and his clique being that either the British Ministers or Elliot had stolen it. More serious was the discontent caused by those infractions of liberty, the imposition of laws and the collection of taxes.[4] As for the administration of justice *à l'Anglaise*, it encountered many obstacles in an island where the murders had mounted to 1400 a year. Trial

[1] Nicolas, Sir N. H., *Dispatches of Nelson*, 1, 362–482; *Diary of Sir J. Moore*, 1, 48–116.
[2] Elliot, *Sir G. Elliot*, ii, 267–76, 326.
[3] W.O. 70/1, Portland to Elliot, Sept. 1795.   [4] Elliot, *Sir G. Elliot*, ii, 313–15.

by jury, introduced by Elliot, became proleptically Gilbertian; for, if, in that land of the vendetta, a jury ever dared to convict, straightway twelve blood feuds were started by the relatives of the murderer against his legal executioners. Yet, in the main, Elliot by good sense and firmness won his way; and no outbreak occurred when, for the sake of peace and quietness, he contrived that George III should invite Paoli to an involuntary and well-pensioned retirement in England. The Paolists themselves were relieved at his departure. "Supremely an actor" was Lady Elliot's verdict.[1] Colonel (Sir) John Moore, who was equally difficult, also went home. Portland approved both actions, commended Elliot's educational efforts, which included a university at Corte, and said he hoped Oxford and Cambridge would help.[2]

The British administration of Corsica could, however, succeed only during a long term of peace or a triumphant war; and hopes of success waned rapidly when Schérer and Masséna routed our allies at Loano and threw open the Riviera corridor into Italy (November 1795). But how came the British fleet, based on San Fiorenzo, to permit this incursion? The answer is to be found at Whitehall. Pitt had reluctantly decided to make a drastic change at the Admiralty in order to infuse method and punctuality into the despatch of business; and the official wheels clanked less slowly, and fleets sailed more promptly, when Lord Chatham was replaced by George, second Earl Spencer (December 1794).[3] The new First Lord, however, had the defects of his qualities; and when Admiral Hood, then on furlough, ventured to point out the inadequacy of the reinforcements destined for the Mediterranean fleet, he was promptly cashiered.[4] "Oh miserable Board of Admiralty", burst out Nelson, on receipt of the news. "They have forced the first officer in our Service away from his command. The late Board may have lost a few merchant-vessels by their neglect; this Board has risked a whole fleet of men-of-war."[5] Hood's successor, Admiral William Hotham, was beset by ill-health and by an accumulation of difficulties greater even than those which the veteran of seventy had triumphantly overcome. With undue caution Hotham failed to pursue an advantage gained over the Toulon fleet on 14 April 1795; and when Nelson boarded the flagship to urge a vigorous offensive, Hotham replied: "We must be contented, we have done very well." Nelson's comment should be written in letters of gold: "Now, had we taken 10 sail, and allowed the 11th to escape, when it had been possible to have got at her, I could never have called it well done." Also, when a similar opportunity was let slip on July 13, he wrote:

---

[1] Elliot, *Sir G. Elliot*, II, 327.
[2] Brit. Mus. Add. MS. 22,688. Letters of Duke of Portland to Elliot and Paoli; W.O. 70/1, Portland to Elliot, 5 Oct. 1795.
[3] Rose, J. H., *Pitt and Napoleon*, p. 235; *Spencer Papers*, I, 8–16, 31.
[4] *Naval Miscell.* (N.R.S.), I, 243–6.   [5] Nicolas, Sir N. H., *Dispatches of Nelson*, II, 42.

"Hotham has no head for enterprise"; also on August 19 (when commanding the light inshore squadron off Vado Bay): "Hotham hates this co-operation [with the allied army], and I cannot get him here;...but we expect Sir John Jervis, who, I understand, is a man of business." Unfortunately, before Jervis could retrieve the situation, the French, as we have seen, chased our allies to Savona and secured the chief portal of Italy. Thus, for reasons partly official, partly personal, the strategic advantages accruing from the possession of Corsica were lost; and, as Nelson had foreseen,[1] "the gold mine", Italy, was now open to the hitherto despairing financiers of Paris. From the blow dealt by the French conquest of that land the tottering Coalition never recovered. Austria, justly blaming the British navy for its half-hearted support, now inclined towards peace, while Pitt and Grenville wearied of helping an exacting and helpless ally. Nothing, indeed, in these critical years, 1795 and 1796, is more singular than the dearth of warlike talent on the monarchist side. Over against traditional Hapsburg mediocrity the French embattled speed, momentum and military genius of the highest order. Even at sea the battered fleets of Toulon and Brest now made head against the tame leadership of Hotham and Lord Bridport; for a gulf yawned between the age of Hood and Howe and that of Jervis, Duncan and Nelson. By signal ill-fortune our lean years were those when the exploits of Masséna, Bonaparte and their compeers carried the tricolour into the heart of Italy, Germany and Holland. In view of the deadlock in the Mediterranean, was it worth while to persevere in that quarter? On this question Ministers might well waver; for the startling changes in this Protean struggle now opened up both new dangers and new opportunities.

War is often a self-cancelling process; for blows aimed at the enemy often ricochet on to neutrals or allies. Such was now the case; and Pitt and Grenville may well have been bewildered when the struggle on which they entered in order to safeguard Dutch independence led to Dutch hostility. As has already appeared, the French, having the support of the powerful faction of the Dutch Patriots, attempted in March 1793 to overrun that land and control its fleet, its finance and its colonies. As that quaint fanatic, Anacharsis Clootz, said in the Convention—"C'est en Hollande que nous détruirons Carthage." Failing then, the Jacobins succeeded in the winter of 1794–5, when a severe frost held in its grip the waterways and yielded up the Dutch fleet an easy prize to the invaders. While the allied forces retired into North Germany, the Patriots set up the Batavian Republic. These events, followed soon by the retirement of Tuscany, Prussia and Spain from the Coalition, altered the whole outlook. The French, after attaining their natural frontiers, could now not only assume the offensive against Austria both in Germany and Italy, but also prepare

[1] Nicolas, Sir N. H., *Dispatches of Nelson*, ii, 26, 63, 70, 124.

to threaten England with invasion from the Dutch ports. On the other hand, the Dutch, and later also the Spanish, colonies were now exposed to Britain's naval action. Consequently, while her efforts slackened in Europe, they increased beyond the seas. Thus, the war now became world-wide; for clearly it was only by maritime and colonial action that the islanders could hope to wear down the increased military might of the French, and, as these retorted by great and victorious military efforts, their rôle, that of the Land Power, and Britain's, that of the Sea Power, became more and more sharply defined. The careers of a Napoleon and a Nelson lay enfolded in these tendencies of the year 1795, which foreshadow Austerlitz and Trafalgar, the Continental System and the Continental Blockade.

For the present the paramount issue was the Cape of Good Hope. It was clear that the French Republicans, now controlling Dutch policy and shipping, would attempt to seize that half-way house to India; for during the last war, the Cape, then in hostile hands, had proved an invaluable place of succour to hostile squadrons, enabling them to arrive in Indian waters in better condition than ours. "Whichever Power has the Cape may govern India"—such was the verdict of the East India Company at the end of that struggle.[1]

Naturally, then, Dundas, the watch-dog for the East Indies, took alarm at the first signs of a French conquest of Holland. So far back as 16 November 1794, he suggested to Grenville the despatch of an expedition, with authorisation from the existing Dutch Government, that of the Stadholder, to occupy Cape Town, thereafter protecting it "as a Dutch possession and for their behoof when peace is restored". In view of the Anglo-Dutch Treaty of 1788, which stipulated mutual assistance both in Europe and the colonies, the Cabinet decided, first, to assist the Dutch in making all possible efforts against the French invaders, but, in case of failure, at least to insist on retaining their complete independence of France.[2]

Primarily, the Cape concerned only the Dutch East India Company; but its maladministration and insolvency (to the extent of £10,000,000) exposed it to the risings of the burghers and the contempt of the Hollanders. In letters of January 1795 the now imminent danger of its acquisition by the French was pointed out to Dundas by Sir Francis Baring, Chairman of the British East India Company. Deprecating all notion of conquest, because "we have already too many drains on our population", he added that the Cape, in French hands, would be a serious danger; for "it commands the passage to India as effectually as Gibraltar doth the Mediterranean, and it serves as a granary for the Isles of France" (Mauritius, Bourbon, etc.). He further suggested the offer to its inhabitants of a large measure of self-government, the preservation of their laws

---

[1] Richmond, Sir H., *The Navy in India, 1763–1783*, App. VI.
[2] *Dropmore Papers*, II, 645, 646; Theal, G. M., *Records of Cape Colony*, I, 1–16.

and customs, and liberty to trade to our eastern possessions, though not to the Isles of France in war time. The Stadholder and the Princess of Orange fled from Holland and reached Harwich on 19 January 1795, proceeding thence to Kew Palace. On February 3, the Dutch East India Company warned its ships to leave British ports and made friendly overtures to the French Government.[1] A little earlier, our Ministers decided to make use of the Stadholder's authority to gain access to the Cape; and, as the French tightened their grip on Holland, the Stadholder ordered the commanders of all Dutch forts, plantations and colonies (notably of the Cape of Good Hope) to admit British ships and garrisons for protection against the French (1 and 7 February 1795).[2] Five weeks later, on the receipt of news foreshadowing hostile action by the Dutch, the British Government ordered its warships to detain their vessels, if necessary by force.[3]

Meanwhile Dundas collected forces in order to forestall those which France seemed likely to despatch to the Cape; and the urgency of the crisis explains the hurry and the risks which attended this singular expedition. Though the Brest fleet was neither blockaded nor even watched, the British forces straggled past it in three sections. On February 27 Commodore John Blankett sailed from Spithead with three sail and smaller craft conveying 515 troops under Major-General James Craig. On April 3, the Commander-in-Chief, Rear-Admiral George Keith Elphinstone, set out with three sail and three small craft but no troops. These, about 3000 in number under General Alured Clarke, could not start before May 15, under convoy of one sail. Clearly, Ministers were willing to take grave risks in order to be in time at the Cape. Fortune favoured them; for the French Government, resolving to throw its weight into Mediterranean affairs, had in December 1794 ordered six sail from Brest to join the Toulon fleet; and when these were sunk or battered by a tempest, it ordered out six others, which sailed on February 22, i.e. about ten days before Blankett entered the Bay of Biscay. At Brest, then, there remained only twelve sail and these mostly in bad condition.[4] Obviously, it was the new resolve at Paris to gain supremacy in the Mediterranean for the projected conquest of Italy, which depleted the Brest fleet at the very time when our three weak sections straggled across the Bay. In other words, French Mediterranean efforts facilitated our first really successful colonial effort in this war.

Clarke also had good luck; for, early in May, three French sail set out from Brest for convoy work in the Bay, i.e. about a fortnight before his almost unprotected transports crossed it.[5] In a military

[1] F.O. Holland, 37/57, Bentinck to Grenville, Jan.–Feb. 1795.
[2] Theal, *Records*, I, 27, 28.   [3] *Dropmore Papers*, III, 35.
[4] Chevalier, *Histoire*, II, 168, 201.   [5] *Ibid.* II, 202; James, *Naval History*, I, 262.

sense the Cape expedition was a desperate gamble; for, later, Dundas admitted that, even if it succeeded, "we have nothing else reserved to send there".[1] He also despatched it without field artillery or money, probably with the hope that the Cape Dutch would tamely obey the orders of their now exiled Stadholder.

But, even while Clarke's troops were beating out to sea, the French and Batavian (i.e. Dutch) Republics framed a treaty of close alliance (16 May 1795). France thereby acquired a money indemnity, all the Dutch lands south of the Rhine, and the right to make use of the port of Flushing, besides securing the present services of twelve sail-of-the-line and eighteen frigates, as well as half the Dutch land forces. In face of these provisions and of Article 4, exacting "an alliance offensive and defensive against Great Britain for ever",[2] the French guarantee of the "independence" of the new Republic was farcical. This alliance was unknown to Elphinstone, when, after joining Blankett near the Cape, he cast anchor off Simon's Town in False Bay (June 11). Forthwith he sent the Stadholder's letter overland to Governor Sluysken at Cape Town; but he and his Council, having no recent tidings from Europe, treated it with marked suspicion. Fearing the burghers, especially those of the country districts, some of whom were in active revolt against the Company, he first temporised and then rejected the British offer, as did the Council. In vain did Elphinstone and Craig renew the offer of British protection, with restitution to the old Dutch Government when restored. On June 25 Sluysken and the burgher councillors rejected it. The British officers then sent appeals to Governor Brooke at St Helena for troops, money and guns. They also detained Dutch East Indiamen in pursuance of the British Government's resolve of March 19.[3]

News of the Franco-Dutch alliance reaching Cape Town on June 28, Sluysken prepared to resist the British on the eastern spur of the Muizenberg, which commanded the road across the neck to Cape Town. Resolved not to be denied access to the capital, Elphinstone and Craig landed about 1500 men who, with the help of the ships' guns, rushed the post (August 7). Four weeks later Clarke's force arrived, bringing also money and field guns from St Helena. The latter included three brass pieces and trenching tools sent by Captain George Vancouver of H.M. sloop *Discovery*, who, on the return from his memorable voyage on the coast of what is now British Columbia, touched at St Helena at this interesting crisis and supplied some of the needs of the expedition. Clarke then prepared to move across the neck against Cape Town, while Blankett with four warships sailed round to threaten the place from the sea. The

[1] *Dropmore Papers*, III, 102.
[2] Martens, IV, 552; Koch and Schöll, *Traités*, I, 556; III, 149.
[3] Theal, *Records*, I, 40–99.

double menace sufficed; and after a short resistance the Governor surrendered (September 14). Thereupon the commanders declared the monopolies of the Company abolished, proclaimed internal free trade, and promised that no new taxes should be imposed. Nevertheless most of the burghers remained hostile; and when Clarke proceeded with his force to India, Craig had no easy task to hold the place. His position was indeed precarious until Elphinstone surprised and captured a Dutch relief expedition of two sail and seven small craft while sheltering in Saldanha Bay (17 August 1796). Thereupon nearly all the burghers, even those of Graaf Reinet, came in.[1]

Thus easily was secured a focal point in world strategy, which Blankett had well characterised as a feather in the hands of Holland but a sword in the hands of France.[2] That the latter made no serious effort to seize it is explicable only by her preoccupation in securing her natural frontiers and gaining supremacy in the Mediterranean. But after October 1795, when the Directory came to power at Paris, more attention was given to the navy and to the colonies; and in March 1796 Rear-Admiral Sercey sailed with three frigates and two corvettes, with troops on board, for Île de France. The corvettes were taken; but the frigates long harassed British commerce in the Indian Ocean.[3] The approach to the Bay of Bengal had, however, been safeguarded by an expedition from Madras which captured Trincomalee (August 1795).

Dundas deserves credit for the promptitude with which he struck at that strategic point commanding the Bay of Bengal. From the time of Clive every far-seeing man had discerned the need of securing a safe naval base as near as possible to the harbourless Coromandel coast. The landlocked harbour of Trincomalee was especially inviting. To its importance the great French commodore, Suffren, bore witness in letters written in 1782 during his desperate tussles with Admiral Hughes: "I think that the essential point is the capture of Trincomalee, as we can have no existence on the [Coromandel] coast without a port.... It would be the best prologue to our success in India." And again: "The importance of Ceylon is such that, if the English troops captured that island,...its recapture would be more important than all the other conquests wherewith one could begin a war in India."[4] How keenly the French coveted Trincomalee after its restoration to the Dutch appeared during the Anglo-French struggle of 1787 for supremacy in Holland. Secret orders were sent from Paris to Pondicherry for this seizure; but, on peaceful counsels

[1] Theal, *Records*, I, 103, 117–32, 208, 234, 431, 480, 502; *The Keith Papers* (N.R.S. ed. Perrin, W. G.), I, 303–28, 442–9. [2] *Keith Papers*, I, 214.
[3] Chevalier, *Histoire*, II, 240–2; Guyot, R., *Le Directoire et la Paix d'Europe*, p. 122; *Keith Papers*, I, 434; Clowes, W. L., *History of the British Navy*, IV, 282, 494.
[4] Troude, O., II, 228; Chevalier, *Histoire*, I, 389, 446, 460, 477. See, too, *C.H.B.E.* IV, pp. 324, 325, and Richmond, Sir H., *The Navy in India* (1763–83), Chapters VII–IX.

prevailing, the plan was countermanded.[1] On our side Dundas voiced the views of statesmen and merchants when, later, he wrote to Earl Spencer that "if the French are directly or indirectly in possession of the island of Ceylon, the French Minister of War would deserve to lose his head if we kept our Indian territories four years".[2] Accordingly, early in 1795, Dundas seems to have urged decisive action against Trincomalee; for advices to this effect reached Madras in July, whereupon the Governor, Lord Hobart, prepared an expeditionary force under Commodore Rainier and Colonel James Stuart, which, landing near that post, soon assured its surrender (26 August 1795).[3]

So prompt was British action as to forestall a singular intrigue set on foot by Hugh Cleghorn, formerly Professor of Civil and Natural History in the University of St Andrews. Lured away from that calm abode by the superior attraction of watching Jacobinical history in the making, he had plunged into the vortex of continental politics. While performing some work for our Government in Switzerland, he came into contact with an impecunious Comte de Meuron, who was colonel and proprietor of a Swiss regiment hired out by him to the Dutch East India Company and then serving in Ceylon. As that bankrupt Company rarely paid debts, de Meuron welcomed Cleghorn's hint that he should transfer his regiment to the British Government, a step likely to spare Ceylon a needless effusion of blood. Next, Cleghorn set forth to Henry Dundas the advantages of this patriotic-philanthropic scheme; and in February 1795 the Minister authorised the ex-professor to push on the affair, offering de Meuron a liberal *douceur*, which the Admiralty raised to £5000 so as to get the services of the regiment "for seven years certain". De Meuron was therefore able to satisfy his creditors and accompany Cleghorn to Ceylon, which, however, they did not reach until well after Stuart's success at Trincomalee. According to Cleghorn, the secret offer of a bribe brought five companies of the de Meuron regiment over to the British side. Certainly the Dutch defence of Colombo was weakened; and, when Stuart with some 5000 British and native troops landed near by, the capitulation soon followed (15 February 1796).[4] Cleghorn overrated his services, but he deserves credit for pointing out to Dundas the importance of Egypt and Ceylon, the position of the latter, at the tip of combustible India, being compared with that of "a long boat after a ship in flames".

The simile was not inapt; for British supremacy in the East was now imperilled by our retirement from the Mediterranean and its natural consequence, the attempt of France to seize the overland

---

[1] *Dropmore Papers*, I, 353, 606.
[2] *Spencer Papers*, II, 215.
[3] Turner, L. J. B., *Maritime Provinces of Ceylon* (1795–1805), p. 49.
[4] *The Cleghorn Papers*, pp. 276–82 (details corrected by Turner, pp. 71–83).

route to the East. The first link snapped in the chain of communications with the Levant was Corsica. Probably Pitt and his colleagues soon tired of holding that hornets' nest; for in his speech of 9 December 1795 he named Martinique, Cape Nicholas Mole and the Cape of Good Hope as the great acquisitions of the war, and made no mention of Corsica.[1] Indeed, the new Secretary at War, Windham, had informed Elliot that news from Corsica was like news from the moon; and he added: "The fault, I am persuaded, is not that anyone [of the Ministers] has thought or acted wrong, but that they have not thought at all."[2] The remark throws a flood of light on what is dignified by the name of colonial policy.

Moreover, as has been seen, the wonderful Corsican himself doomed to failure British rule in that island. Favoured by our weak action in the Mediterranean, he burst into Italy and soon shattered that venerable mosaic. Ever intent on driving the English from his island, he sent troops to occupy Leghorn and thence menace a landing. By way of retort Elliot ordered Nelson to occupy Elba (10 July 1796), the news of which event quieted the Corsican malcontents. But further tidings, that Spain was arming suspiciously and Naples was about to make peace with France, induced the Pitt Cabinet on August 31 to order the evacuation of Corsica. That decision was prompted by the signs of Spanish ill-will, which had its roots in the British occupations of Corsica, San Domingo and Demerara.[3] Further, on or about August 26, came the news that a French squadron, long sheltering and repairing in Cadiz, had been escorted far out to sea by the Spanish fleet[4]—a breach of neutrality which portended a joint attack either upon Corsica, San Domingo, Ireland, or on our ally, Portugal. In any case, naval concentration seemed necessary; and, our communications with Corsica being precarious, withdrawal thence and even from the Mediterranean had much to commend it. Curiously enough, on October 19, the very day on which Nelson brought off our last troops from Bastia, Ministers changed their minds. In the fond hope of encouraging further resistance from Naples they countermanded evacuation, and (with signal bad faith to the Corsicans) invited Catharine II of Russia to take over that island.[5] This last hope of clinging to the Mediterranean soon vanished, for the Tsarina died three weeks later. Meanwhile the Cabinet wavered. On October 28 Dundas, though ill and perplexed, sent a manly protest against the abandonment of the Mediterranean, as implying that whenever France and Spain joined hands we must scuttle from that sea and give up all hope of renewing our Italian alliances; whereas, thanks to Gibraltar, we could by firm action coop up the hostile fleets as in a cul-de-sac.[6] For the present,

[1] Parl. Hist. xxxii, 585.
[3] Parl. Hist. xxxii, 1287.
[5] Nicolas, ii, 291–3; Dropmore Papers, iii, 261.
[2] Elliot, Sir G. Elliot, ii, 331.
[4] C.H.B.F.P. i, 562, 563.
[6] Spencer Papers, i, 321, 324.

facts were too strong for him; but the future proved the soundness of his views.

As to the evacuation of the Mediterranean naval opinion was divided. Jervis, reviling the Corsicans for their "rascally baseness and ingratitude", regarded the abandonment of that island as the most fortunate event of his forty-eight years' service; but, deeming Elba in all respects desirable, he hoped we should hold it, as indeed the Government at first intended. Collingwood, agreeing with his chief's harsh judgment about the Corsicans, differed about Elba because Porto Ferrajo could easily be blocked. Nelson, finally a severe critic of the Corsicans, desired also to evacuate the Mediterranean, until confidence in Jervis and the defensive capacity of Elba led him decidedly to reverse his judgment. Apparently on this topic the Admiralty and War Office were at variance; for, early in November, the former decided finally to evacuate that sea; but, as the latter issued no order for the abandonment of Elba, its commander held on until April 1797, when he received a reprimand for not withdrawing earlier.[1] Meanwhile Spencer's plan of basing our Mediterranean fleet on Lisbon led to one fortunate result. Jervis, while making for the Tagus, met reinforcements, raising his fleet to fifteen sail, and early on February 14 off St Vincent sighted Cordova's Spanish fleet of twenty-seven sail in great confusion. In single line he drove between their sundered portions, and Commodore Nelson's glorious act of disobedience, in wearing H.M.S. *Captain* (74) out of the line and thus thwarting Cordova's move against the British rear, clinched the initial success. Not only were four large Spaniards taken but the rest were so demoralised that during three critical years that navy remained almost passive under blockade.[2]

The nullity of Spain was a godsend; for by this time the British fighting forces were greatly overworked owing to the diverse heavy drains upon them. Of these drains none was so exhausting as the efforts in the West Indies. It was of them mainly that Middleton wrote indignantly to Spencer (1 July 1795): "It is like a farmer wishing to occupy a large farm without money to manage it."[3] Certainly the farm (the British Empire) was large, but there was enough money for due management and defence if it had been judiciously used. We can now see that the mistake lay in not cutting our continental losses promptly after the utter collapse in the spring of 1795 and using our forces for the most profitable and least exhausting of the colonial enterprises. But fog hangs heavily over war (especially when waged by a Coalition), and much must be forgiven to those civilian leaders for not foreseeing the slackness or perfidy

[1] Tucker, *Memoirs*, I, 195, 235, 238; *Correspondence of Lord Collingwood* (3rd ed., 1828), p. 32; Nicolas, II, 172–4, 244, 289–305; Fortescue, *British Army*, IV (pt. I), 512; *Dropmore Papers*, III, 267.
[2] Nicolas, II, 331–49; *Spencer Papers*, I, 339–59.
[3] *Spencer Papers*, I, 19, 51.

of allies, the evanescence of French Royalist help, above all, the growing military strength of democratic France. There is force, however, in the criticism of Burke as to the futility of despatching costly expeditions to the West Indies to procure the wherewithal for the future peace bargainings. In October 1795, when another West Indian force was being scraped together, Pitt began to finger the olive branch; and Spencer, in balancing between San Domingo and Guadeloupe as the objective, named the former as desirable partly because of its "superior weight in the scale of negotiations...". Middleton preferred Guadeloupe because "it cannot possibly hold out, and, if taken, the other islands in the French possession cannot subsist of themselves".[1] The choice of the admiral for command also led to an unfortunate dispute. For administrative reasons Spencer insisted on advancing a junior, Rear-Admiral Sir Hugh Christian, over Admiral Sir John Laforey, who returned home in high dudgeon, while Middleton indignantly retired from the Admiralty Board.[2] This resignation (the third within six months due to Spencer's high-handed actions) left him with weak colleagues to confront naval problems of increasing complexity

In one respect this West Indian expedition marks a step in advance. Apparently it was the first on which medical experience was duly utilised. On September 28, Drs Johnson and Trotter of Haslar Hospital recommended that a physician should supervise the whole of the medical department, that a hospital ship should accompany the fleet, that the men's fare should include potatoes and pickled cabbage, with cocoa, etc., for supper, and that lemon juice, essence of malt and cream of tartar should be provided against scurvy, also calomel, bark, etc., against West Indian fever.[3] Delays, however, lengthened out owing to these and other preparations, for which the general in command, Sir Ralph Abercromby, was blamed by Dundas, who is now pilloried as the chief offender.[4] Whoever was to blame, the expedition started on November 16, two months too late for beginning operations in the healthy season. Another difficulty arose from the jealousy of Spain as to our intervention in San Domingo. In November 1795, Dundas secretly warned General Forbes of danger from the Spanish part of the island, and empowered him to use French Royalists to repel any encroachments.[5]

Ill luck was to beset the enterprise. Off Bridport Admiral Christian's stately array of eight sail and some 200 transports was struck by a hurricane, which strewed the Dorset coast with wrecks and drove the remainder up Channel, the battered survivors gradually creeping into Spithead. Putting forth again on December 9 he encountered

[1] *Spencer Papers*, I, 140, 150.   [2] *Ibid.* I, 165–90; *Barham Papers*, II, 418–24.
[3] *Spencer Papers*, I, 150–2.
[4] Fortescue, *British Army*, IV (pt. 1), 479.
[5] W.O. 6/6.

a succession of gales which buffeted his force to and fro during seven weeks. Only a few transports struggled to the ocean and made Barbados; nearly all dribbled back to Portsmouth to refit. These events gave the Government time to collect more troops, including foreign levies, for the reduction of San Domingo, which in January 1796 Pitt and Dundas placed first "with a view either to war or peace".[1] In February, however, Ministers preferred to begin at the tip of the Windward Isles, recapturing Grenada, St Vincent and St Lucia, then occupying the Dutch settlements on the Essequibo, and leaving San Domingo until later. Finally, St Lucia became the favourite objective, so notoriously so that a prominent officer in this expedition, Colonel [later Sir] John Moore, after touching at Barbados, noted in his diary: "It has been publicly known for some time past...that St Lucia was the object."[2]

The diary of that eager spirit flashes lurid lights on the course of events—the incredible confusion among troops and shipping at Portsmouth, the exhaustion of the foreign levies and discontent of our own soldiers, long tossed about the Channel, and now sailing for almost certain death. Nevertheless, the expedition straggled out from Spithead early in March 1796, and during the voyage or at Barbados the final allotment of officers to regiments, and of these to their spheres of action, took place. Abercromby, after calling at Barbados and Martinique, sailed for St Lucia. There the French and their fanatical black helpers were ready. Yet, as usual, a fleet moving a force quickly to the desired point baffled the defence, and Major-General Campbell, with Moore's active assistance, landed the 14th and 42nd regiments and secured a good position. Next, though the men were recruits, and the officers "young and without either zeal or experience", Moore led them on and gained rising ground connecting with the dominant position of Morne Fortunée. Through the month of May, despite heat and heavy rain, Moore and other officers pushed on, and on the 26th secured the surrender of that height and its stronghold with 2000 prisoners. Abercromby, confident in Moore's exceptional abilities, left him with some 4000 men to hold that important island, while the main body sailed for St Vincent and Grenada.

A serious crisis had arisen in St Vincent in March 1795, when the Caribs (now mainly negroid) broke loose from their reservation. Previously contented, they were roused by the levelling propaganda of Victor Hugues from Guadeloupe, and for a time threatened to master the whole island. In October, however, when three regiments arrived from England, the balance was restored, and the French and their native allies were driven back early in 1796. Late in that year it was decided to deport the insurgent Caribs to the island of Roatan

---

[1] *Dropmore Papers*, III, 166.
[2] *Diary of Sir John Moore*, I, 197.

off the Gulf of Honduras. St Lucia, St Vincent and Grenada were recovered at the cost of 800 casualties.[1]

In history the tragic side of man's life tends to overshadow his slow, prosaic work of upbuilding; and the annals of the West Indies, as often told, dwell chiefly on ravaged estates, fetid barracks, death-trap hospitals and crowded cemeteries. Yet in spite of internecine strifes, negro risings and yellow fever, this wondrous archipelago now became more than ever necessary to Europe, whose peoples struggled desperately for mastery even of half a dozen sugar islands. More-over, there was one area on the mainland which, when properly worked, proved to be a mine of wealth and real utility.

The Dutch settlements on the Guiana coast, Demerara and Esse-quibo, were now, after the Anglo-Dutch rupture of 1795, nominally hostile, though their estates and commerce were almost entirely in English hands. To quote from a later Memorandum drawn up in London concerning these settlements, they "have from the first been settled with British capital; as, long before they were captured in 1796, the greater part of the settled estates were British property, and, particularly in cotton, shipped, though not in a regular manner, to this country, producing an incredible profit to the growers, the soil being of a nature productive far exceeding that of our own [West India] islands".[2] It was natural, then, that these settlements should now apply to come under our protection; and they were peacefully occupied by our troops in April 1796. From a military standpoint this act has been censured as a scandalous diffusion of force "in order to secure the profits of a clique of merchants";[3] from the civilian's standpoint it was thoroughly justifiable in order to save from anarchy wealthy and semi-English settlements which already supplied Lancashire with great stores of cotton. The increase of prosperity in Demerara and Essequibo is shown in their exports to Great Britain during the first four years of our occupation:[4]

	Cotton (in bales)	Sugar (in hogsheads)	Coffee (in lb.)	Rum (in puncheons)
1797	2,425	1,483	1,937,230	720
1800	31,433	10,361	11,633,136	2,486

The increases continued up to the Peace of Amiens, when these Guiana settlements were retroceded to the Dutch, immensely enhanced in value.

Meanwhile, in the West Indian islands the outlook remained dark; for, as the Abbé Raynal had discerned, the weakness of their social structure everywhere invited overturn. To conquer was therefore

---

[1] Shephard, C., *History of St Vincent*, pp. 55–80 and App. 15; Fortescue, *British Army*, IV (pt. I), 441–9, 495.
[2] In C.O. 111/18.   [3] Fortescue, *British Army*, IV (pt. I), p. 432.
[4] Custom House Returns in C.O. 111/14; quoted in full in *C.H.J.* III (1929), 34–46.

always easier than to hold. This was now Moore's experience in St Lucia, so that he even pettishly accused Abercromby and Christian of running away from difficulties. These were increased by the Francophile fanaticism of the negroes and the heedlessness of British officers about the health of their men: "but", he added, "with a Roman instead of a modern exercise and discipline the troops in the West Indies might, I am convinced, be kept healthy." Owing, however, to carelessness and adherence to English customs and routine, the regiments melted away; so that he judged a reconquest easy by a small force sent from Guadeloupe. The fundamental difficulty was everywhere the same: "In the West Indies industry and cultivation do not contribute to the happiness of the inhabitants. All tends to the profit of the master, nothing to the comfort and convenience of the negroes."[1] Nevertheless, Moore, though sick and abnormally critical, deprecated evacuating St Lucia, because its occupation ensured tranquillity to the neighbouring islands.[2] Indeed, the abandonment of the West Indies to anarchy was unthinkable to men of that age, who generally agreed with Dundas that "the loss of Jamaica... would be complete ruin to our credit", and that the landing of 15,000 French from a superior fleet in Jamaica would be a greater disaster than in the British Isles.[3] Equally significant were the instructions of Portland and Dundas to Lieutenant-General John G. Simcoe (25 November 1796) on going out to command in San Domingo. He was urged to defend as large a space as possible so as to ensure an adequate revenue; but for this purpose to use French Royalists as much as possible, concentrating our men at the Mole, etc. Above all he must lessen expenses.[4]

The policy of holding on to the West Indies was partly justified by the increase in the value of the imports thence, from £4,183,000 in 1792 to £5,411,000 in 1798.[5] Thanks to colonial gains, which were chiefly in the West Indies, British shipping easily survived its exclusion from French, Dutch and Spanish ports. The total tonnage cleared from British harbours in 1792 was 1,563,000: in 1797–9 it averaged 1,250,000, but reached 1,445,000 in 1800. In these periods the proportion going to the West Indies rose from less than one-tenth to more than one-eighth of the whole.[6] Indeed, so generally prized were our gains in the two Indies as to prompt jealous taunts at Vienna that we protracted the war in order to complete those conquests.[7]

Seamen, in fact, hailed with joy the declaration of war by Spain in October 1796, as exposing her possessions to attack; and high were

[1] *Diary of Sir John Moore*, I, ch. IX.   [2] *Ibid.* I, 259.
[3] *Spencer Papers*, I, 138, Dundas to Spencer, 24 Aug. 1796.
[4] W.O. 6/6.   [5] Edwards, *West Indies*, v, App. 18.
[6] *Ibid.* v. App. 18; Tooke, T., *Thoughts on...Prices* (1824), App. II.
[7] [G. Morris] to Grenville, 5 Oct. 1796, in *Dropmore Papers*, III, 258.

the hopes at Martinique when Rear-Admiral Harvey with five sail and transports, conveying Abercromby and 3000 troops, weighed anchor for Trinidad. Arriving off Port of Spain near sunset, they sighted four sail and a frigate lying under the batteries; but in the night the Spaniards, caught unprepared with weak crews, fired the ships, and the next day surrendered the town without firing a shot (17 February 1797).[1] Never had there been so easy and profitable a capture.

The future of Trinidad also seemed full of promise. Under the stiff but energetic governorship of Colonel Thomas Picton, a mutiny among the coloured troops was suppressed and order established among the 3000 or more French mulattoes; roads were improved and illicit trade with the Spanish Main was encouraged. Knowing Spanish well, Picton early conciliated the Spanish proprietors and in general maintained their laws and customs, so that, on the approach of peace in 1801, they begged not to be handed back to Spain. Their Board of Cabildo stated that, thanks to the British occupation, they enjoyed a prosperity which contrasted with the scenes of licence and ruin in several islands; that they hoped for the grant of a stronger executive government than was common in British colonies, for Trinidad contained diverse peoples and was near to the mainland possessed by "our natural enemies". Referring to the fidelity of Canada after the Acts of 1774 and 1791, they now craved the like privileges, namely "the provisional continuation of our laws and religion", without any innovation until a representative Assembly could meet. Picton, in view of the doubtful French and Italian sections and the restive mulattoes, disapproved of instituting such an Assembly. His autocracy was resented by some English traders who raked up charges against him, which finally led to his recall but ultimate vindication. During his control of Trinidad, trade and prosperity increased. He warned the Home Government not to encourage immigration artificially from the other West Indies; for some of them were ruined by war or worked out by over-cropping; and Trinidad contained immense tracts of fertile land, unleased and untilled, suitable for the finest sugar canes. Settlers might therefore come from England, especially to the hilly and most healthy parts of the island. If the importation of negro slaves must be discouraged, as Parliament enjoined, could not natives from South America be imported for the cultivation of the staple produce, sugar? He foresaw also a great future for coffee, cotton and cacao, but declared labour essential for coffee picking, though less so for the two other products. He wished that the "pretended philanthropists" would examine the actual condition of the slaves, who were better clothed and fed and did less work than most European peasants.

Visitors to Trinidad also reported its fertility to be such that forty

---

[1] C.O. 296/1; Duro, F., *Armada española*, VIII, 133–7.

negroes working there would produce as much as a hundred in "the old islands". In August 1802 Lieutenant W. Layman, R.N., suggested a plan of importing Chinese coolies on our convict ships returning from Sydney; for the inhabitants of Trinidad, 17,718 in number, could not develop an area of 2400 square miles, most of which was even ungranted; and to exploit the untilled lands with Chinese would cost only £35,951,000 as against £67,578,000 by negroes; also new industries, such as that of palm oil for our soap manufactures, would soon flourish in Trinidad. Already the Government had seen the chance of settling there British immigrants in communities with their Anglican or Presbyterian pastors; and it is clear that the undeveloped natural resources of the island, including hard timber for the navy, soon induced the Government to insist on its retention.[1]

As an offset to the easy and profitable capture of Trinidad other West Indian enterprises proved to be failures. Abercromby's attempt on Porto Rico miscarried; and in 1798 circumstances led to the abandonment of San Domingo. This event resulted primarily from France having in 1795 acquired from Spain the eastern part of the island, and harrying us thence with the aid of fanatical hordes of negroes, who were immune to the fever so fatal to the British troops. General Simcoe had also been unable to keep down the expenditure to the total of £25,000 per month which Portland and Dundas had prescribed as the maximum; sickness had increased among our troops; and our Governors accused the French planters of diverting public money to "the worst ends of private peculation and inordinate cupidity".[2] The retention even of Mole St Nicholas with the tottering remnant of 1000 men being deemed impossible (though there Colonel Chalmers strongly dissented),[3] Colonel Maitland arranged with the capable negro chieftain, Toussaint l'Ouverture, for a peaceful withdrawal to Jamaica, the trade of which colony was not to be harassed (October 1798). On July 31 Maitland informed Balcarres that he made this compact "under the King's orders". Yet on September 11 Ministers ordered him to hold on and sent out General Knox to relieve him. The evacuation, however, preceded Knox's arrival.[4] Many French refugees fled to England, where they long received support from the Government.[5] As to the value of San Domingo, it may be measured by the efforts of Bonaparte in 1801–2 to recover it from anarchy. He despatched thither in all some 40,000 men, of whom very few returned to France. Even so, a Frenchman maintained that its reconquest was necessary to re-establish the commerce, manufactures and marine of France.[6]

---

[1] C.O. 295/1 & 2, Despatches of Colonel Picton, Duke of Portland and Lord Hobart.
[2] H.O. 30/1, Dundas to Simcoe, 9 June 1797.
[3] Chalmers, Col., *The War in San Domingo* (1803), pp. 70–80.
[4] C.O. 137/100 and 1/245; Fortescue, *British Army*, IV (pt. 1), 545–63.
[5] Pitt MSS. in P.R.O., no. 349.
[6] Lanion, A. P. M., *La dernière Expédition de San Domingue, ad fin.*

Our weakness in the West Indies in 1797–8 was accentuated by the mutinies in the British navy in the spring and early summer of 1797. Originating in the grievances of the seamen and the culpable neglect of the Admiralty even to notice them, these outbreaks spread from the Channel fleet to that of the Nore and infected many ships on distant stations. Never was England so near a collapse as when the Nore fleet blockaded the Thames, an event which in June sent down 3 per cent. Consols to 48, and palsied our efforts across the ocean.[1] Why the French, Dutch and Spaniards did not strike at us in our darkest days is a mystery which is not solved by the *recherché* explanation of the French Minister of Marine, that intervention then might have brought back the mutineers to their duty.[2]

Is it surprising that, even before the mutinies, Pitt should have decided to open negotiations for a general pacification? Indeed, what friend of peace would not seek to end this exasperating jumble, in which the would-be protector of Holland had become the captor of Dutch colonies; in which France, at first the emancipator of oppressed nations, was fast becoming their oppressor; in which the French army (once termed "Liberty on the march") was to prove itself the foe of parliamentary liberty at home, and England's navy dealt her an almost fatal blow? Above all, could an end be foreseen to these ever-increasing and ever-delusive aggrandisements, in which the military triumphs of the one side were constantly counterbalanced by the naval conquests of the other?

If the French Directory had sincerely shared the pacific desires of Pitt, the overtures which he set about in April 1797 might have led to a favourable issue. For, despite the disapproval of the King and the opposition of Grenville, he proposed to yield to France control of the left bank of the Rhine and to restore to her all the captured French colonies except Martinique. Thus, while gaining the "natural limits", she would regain St Lucia, the Saints, Tobago, her part of San Domingo, St Pierre and Miquelon, besides her posts in India. On the other hand, we demanded from her allies three valued strategic points—Trinidad from the Spaniards, the Cape and Ceylon from the Dutch Republic—retroceding, however, to the latter our captures—Demerara and its neighbouring settlements in the West Indies, and in the East Indies the Moluccas, the Bandas, Malacca, the Dutch posts in India, and perhaps Cochin. Our demands for Trinidad (valued more highly than St Lucia and Hayti), as also for the Cape and Ceylon sprang both from a true sense of their strategic value and from a just perception of the character of the Directors, eager for national gains and heedless about weak and dependent allies.

Nevertheless, under the double strain of the mutinies and of the miserable collapse of Austria, Pitt and his colleagues were soon fain

[1] Gill, C., *The Naval Mutinies of 1797*, p. 4 n.
[2] Desbrière, E., *Projets...de Débarquement aux Îles britanniques* 1, 258

to throw Martinique into the scales and to concede that the Cape and the posts in Ceylon should always be "free ports, open to all nations of the world". Even so the course of the negotiations at Lille, though ably conducted by Lord Malmesbury, rendered it doubtful whether these safeguards, along with Trinidad, would not be flung into the melting pot; for Spain not only abjured all thought of abandoning that island, but demanded that the Directors should secure for her Gibraltar and the Nootka Sound district; she even made a sporting bid for Jamaica. These lofty pretensions produced no lasting impression at Paris; but the Dutch demands for the Cape and Ceylon, urged with toughness and tact (perhaps also with bribes), won over the Directors, who saw themselves in fancy lords of the Dutch Republic, its fleet and colonies, and therefore masters of the golden East. Fears of some such consummation prompted Grenville and Dundas to make both the Cape and Ceylon a *sine quâ non* of peace. Pitt wavered about Ceylon; but perhaps on the issue of the Cape alone the peace effort would have failed. However that may be, the new Directory brought to power by the *coup d'état* of Fructidor (4 September 1797) cut short the discussions in an overbearing manner which ended all hopes of a compromise.[1]

Tools of the violent and militarist faction now dominant at Paris, the Directors soon rushed into aggressive schemes which served to array against them all Britons and the half of Europe. Both by land and overseas France and her henchmen snatched at universal supremacy—a colossal and bifurcating effort which Imperial Rome has alone achieved. Heedless of the warnings of history, the giddy *parvenus* of late whirled to the top at Paris, struck at Switzerland, Rome and the Rhineland, while they launched, first at the British Isles and then at the Levant, armadas which gave to the British navy its first great opportunities in the present struggle. By good fortune the crisis had already aroused to utmost vigour the faculties of Jervis and Duncan and now fanned to a flame the genius of Nelson. The repentant crews fought as never before; and behind the reunited navy stood a united British nation.[2]

For now was felt the welding effect of the blows aimed at us by the would-be conqueror of the East. The vanquisher of Austria set sail from Toulon on 19 May 1798 with an armada designed to ruin England by the conquest of Egypt and the destruction of British India—the last and greatest of the efforts which diverted the French Revolution into the paths of world conquest. Towards this oriental adventure the young Bonaparte was drawn by his romantic imagination, early stirred by the eastern *rêveries* of his friend Volney, and,

[1] Ballot, E., *Les négociations de Lille*, pp. 86–138, 188–276; Guyot, ch. xi; Malmesbury, *Diaries*, iii, 377–588; Rose, *Pitt*, ii, 321–27.
[2] See *Mémoires* of Mallet du Pan, ii, 363.

later, by the calculating conviction that only there could great
results be obtained.[1] Herein his ambition coincided with the colonising
bias of Talleyrand, who on 3 July 1797 had read to the Institute of
France a memorable essay on the advantages to be drawn from new
colonies. Premising that all the American colonies would soon be
independent, he urged the need of winning new lands, where hard
work and hope ("the veritable Lethe of Revolutions") would open
out a new future.[2] Accordingly the two, acting in general agreement,
gave an eastern trend to the negotiations for peace with Austria.
By sheer bullying, Bonaparte then secured for France from the spoils
of the Venetian Republic its fleet and the Ionian Isles—("more
interesting for us than the whole of Italy"). Next he arranged (in
Jove and Danaë fashion) a secret *liaison* with the French Knights
of the Order of St John at Malta. Then, after a survey of the preparations in the northern ports of France, he decided against any attempt
at invading England by the new flotilla, and on 23 February 1798
advised the French Directory, while keeping up the pretence of
invasion, to deal England the death blow by seizing Egypt and then
driving her from India.[3] Certainly the time seemed propitious. The
Mediterranean was a French lake. The ports of Spain and northern
Italy were under the control of France. Corfu was hers, and Malta,
too, by easy reversion after the demise of the corrupt and moribund
Knights of St John. Elsewhere all doors seemed closed, save to the
expectant Irish—an unpopular mission since Hoche's fiasco in the
December gales of 1796. Moreover, her henchmen, the Spaniards
and Dutch, were quiescent after the severe blows dealt by Jervis at
St Vincent and Duncan at Camperdown. Certainly the auguries
pointed away from the angry Ocean to the golden Orient. Thus,
Bonaparte finally persuaded the Directors secretly to push on the
eastern design as the easiest and speediest means of compelling
England to a peace.

But the French brain, ever the pointer in the colonial sphere, had
evolved another scheme, based on Île de France (Mauritius). The
French light squadron operating from that island, besides harrying
British commerce, had enabled the Governor, Malartic, to form a
connection with Tipu, the warlike ruler of Mysore. He, inheriting
the anti-British fury of his father, Hyder Ali, was now planning to
drive us from South India, and therefore appealed to Malartic to
send to the Malabar coast a mighty force of French, Malagasy and
Africans. Clumsily enough, the Governor published that appeal
(30 January 1798) which was known at Calcutta early in June.[4]

---

[1] Marmont, A. F. L. V. de, *Mémoires*, 1, 347.
[2] For the oriental trend in France see Lokke, C. L., *France and the Colonial Question*, pp. 93–100, 168–74, 182–96.
[3] La Jonquière, C. E. L., *L'Expédition d'Egypte*, 1, ch. v; Charles-Roux, F., *Les Origines de l'Expédition d'Egypte*, chs. v–vii; *Nap. Corresp.* Nos. 2103, 2419.
[4] *Wellesley's Despatches*, 1, 7, 17; *Ann. Register* (1798), p. 255; *C.H.B.E.* IV, 325 *seqq.*

There the new Governor-General, Lord Mornington (later the Marquis Wellesley) had already discerned the beginnings of an anti-British league; and he both reinforced our cruisers off the Malabar coast and sent warnings to London, which, about mid-June, convinced Dundas that the objective of the Toulon expedition was Egypt, *en route* for India. By that time it had occupied Malta.

The present generation cannot fully appreciate the perplexities of British officials in that age of torpid circulation of news. Now wireless telegraphy has almost equated the chances of the defender and the aggressor. Then, during long weeks, the aggressor had it all his own way before the defender knew where the blow had fallen. In fact, throughout the long struggle which now began between Bonaparte and the British Empire, our statesmen were heavily handicapped by slowness of news and their position on the outer fringe. In this sense London was (as Bonaparte phrased it) "a corner of the world, and Paris its centre"[1]; and in no campaign was the handicap so clogging as in that of the Levant, a fact which perhaps helped to attract thither that great calculator of combinations and chances. A sudden *coup* yielded Valetta to him in two days. Its recovery by British and native Maltese was to take two years.

Nevertheless, Pitt and his colleagues had already adopted a measure likely to lead ultimately to checkmate. The French threats to Naples and appeals for naval support which came thence and from Vienna, induced him to reverse the retrograde policy of October 1796 and to send back a fleet into the Mediterranean.[2] Though utterly in doubt whether the Toulon armada was intended for Naples, Lisbon or Ireland, Ministers yet saw (as Drake did in June 1588) that the one certain place of intercepting the enemy was off his own port. Thus, high politics and high strategy alike demanded the despatch of a fleet into that sea. Furthermore, Bonaparte's capture of Valetta soon demonstrated the unique importance of a Mediterranean base, hitherto unthought of by our officials, though Colonel Sir Mark Wood had already prophesied a French dash at Malta and Egypt for an eventual attack on India.[3] Certainly Malta had not yet figured in British naval policy. But now that island, long the eastern bulwark of Christendom, was to become a rock of offence and, later, the cause of a mighty war.

At once Dundas eagerly supported Pitt's forward policy in the Mediterranean, urging Spencer to send thither every ship that could be spared, even from the West Indies. Later, on August 27, he urged the need of preventing the French strengthening their army in Egypt, which would be "a deep wound to India". Spencer, however, deemed the French effort a "very Quixote-like expedition";

---

[1] *Nap. Corresp.* No. 10,662.
[2] *Dropmore Papers*, IV, 152, 167–72, 188; Rose, *Pitt*, I, 366, 367.
[3] *Letters of Colonel Sir Mark Wood*, 4 Nov. 1796 and 25 April 1798.

for he now hoped by means of Turkish and Russian help in the Mediterranean to cut them off in Egypt.[1] Both views were tenable. Spencer rightly believed that Bonaparte had overreached himself by exposing his communications with France to a crushing blow. Dundas maintained that French control of nearly all the Mediterranean ports would enable them to hamper our efforts in that sea and secure Egypt, which at the peace they would struggle hard to retain. The former view was based on strategic, the latter on diplomatic and general considerations. The course of events was destined to illustrate the importance of each.

At first, Bonaparte's flagrant sin against naval strategy brought condign punishment; for Nelson's crushing victory at the Nile (1 August 1798) imprisoned the French army in Egypt and ended for the time French supremacy in the Mediterranean. In September an Anglo-Portuguese squadron began the blockade of the French garrison in Malta, where the inhabitants, on hearing of Nelson's triumph, had risen against their recent captors; and in November Admiral Sir John Duckworth captured Minorca. Meanwhile, the Tsar Paul and the Sultan formed an alliance against France and sent their combined fleets to begin the blockade of the French in Corfu. In 1799, the evil results of Bonaparte's unsound move eastwards were still more manifest; for in Europe the Powers threatened by France framed the Second Coalition, whose armies nearly overwhelmed her; and in Asia the alarm spread by the Egyptian expedition and Malartic's foolish bluster led the Marquis Wellesley, well seconded by his brother Arthur, to strike promptly and successfully at Tipu's capital, Seringapatam (4 May 1799). By that triumph the Wellesleys carried forward those brilliant achievements which transformed a mercantile Company's domains into the Indian Empire.

The tale of the rebuffs dealt to France does not end here; for the British squadron despatched by Spencer to the Red Sea cut short French schemes for predominance in that quarter and prepared the way for the landing of a British force at Kosseir, while another, from Bombay, occupied the island of Perim. Further, Wellesley despatched a mission under Captain John Malcolm to Teheran and Baghdad which there counteracted French plans for an eventual march overland from Syria to India. Thus, on all sides the net of the Sea Power was flung wide around the French army in Egypt and began to close in.[2] The effort of Bruix's great fleet from Brest to break that Mediterranean blockade ended in the most singular fiasco in modern naval history (April–August 1799); and not until Bonaparte, by equally singular fortune, escaped from Egypt to France were sustained efforts made at Paris to save Malta and Egypt. As First Consul of

---

[1] *Spencer Papers*, II, 454–6.
[2] For details see Rose, J. H., "The Political Reactions of Bonaparte's Eastern Expedition", in *E.H.R.* Jan. 1929. Also Rose, J. H., *Life of Napoleon*, I, chs. 8, 9.

France he prepared small expeditions which sought to relieve General Vaubois and his brave garrison of 3000 troops then half-starving in Valetta. The Journal of that commander, kept regularly during the two years' siege, proves that he scorned the puny assaults of the few British troops and the ill-armed Maltese levies on those impregnable ramparts. "Provisions", he had written to the Directory, "and Malta will always belong to the Republic." His confidence was natural; for the task of maintaining a blockade of Valetta by sea, especially at night, taxed all the patience and skill of Keith and Nelson. The arrival of two swift blockade-runners with food in March and June 1800 enabled Vaubois to hold out until September 4, when he surrendered to the British general, Pigott. These, the outstanding facts of the long siege, demonstrate that the fate of Valetta depended essentially on sea-borne food, i.e. on the work of the British navy.[1]

Yet the dissolving effects of national and dynastic jealousies now began to depress the fortunes of Britain. The change set in over the Maltese question. There were now three claimants for the possession of that island; first, the moribund Knights of St John; second, their residuary legatee, the Czar Paul, who had lately been elected Grand Master by refugees of that Order, and now became their morbidly enthusiastic champion; third, the King of Naples, by virtue of ancient rights of suzerainty. Of these claimants the British Government at first strongly favoured the Tsar, hoping thereby (as in 1796 in the case of Corsica) to bring Russia into the Mediterranean to counteract France. In fact if the Russian fleet had arrived from Corfu in time to decide the siege, Malta must have been theirs, whereupon common opposition to France would have made the Anglo-Russian alliance Paul-proof. Far different was the reality. Paul became wildly Anglophobe, a mood stabilised by Bonaparte's skilful offer of Malta to him.[2]

Thus, in the autumn of 1800, was formed against us the League of the Armed Neutrals, a coalition, which, unlike that of 1780, was a stern reality, backed by the autocrats of the East and West for the crippling of the Sea Power. At once the islanders took up the challenge. Their war efforts, often diffuse and tardy, now ran straight and swift; for the navy was at stake.

At the end of every prolonged struggle the need for masts and large timber became urgent. English forests, worn down by the iron industry, could not repair the wastage of war; and the navy depended on those of New England, British North America and the Baltic lands. As the United States were unfriendly (a plan for the seizure of Canada being considered at Washington in May 1797[3]) and the lumber industry of New Brunswick, Nova Scotia and Canada was

[1] Hardman, W., History of Malta (1798–1815), ed. Rose, J. H., pp. 126, 142–4, 169–79, 301–3, 642.
[2] Ibid., pp. 218, 230; Paget Papers, I, 144, 255, 274; Dropmore Papers, VI, 250, 283–7, 384–9.
[3] Report of the American Historical Association (1903), II, 1025.

in its infancy, our dockyards depended on Baltic timber, the imports of which in 1799 exceeded five times over that supplied from British North America.[1] But every crisis in the Baltic stimulated lumbering in those colonies, with results favourable to their industry, wealth and population. Indirectly, the chief promoters of that trade were the Czar Paul and Bonaparte.

The dockyard crisis in 1800–1 being acute, England struck hard at the warder of the Baltic, and Nelson's victory at Copenhagen, following on the assassination of the half-mad Czar, virtually dissolved the hostile league. When fighting alone, with her back to the wall against half Europe, she found herself. Thus, by a singular fate, her new Prime Minister, Addington, the least warlike of men, now culled both in the Baltic and in the Mediterranean the laurels for which Pitt and Dundas had striven. For in the summer of 1801 the French were expelled from Egypt.

The wisdom of such an effort on our part was questionable when the northern horizon still loomed dark and Bonaparte's invasion flotillas crowded every harbour from the Texel to Brest. Why not leave the 30,000 marooned and homesick French to the workings of *ennui* and Egyptian insanitation, with some help from the Turks? Or if Abercromby's force, long gyrating off the coasts of Spain, must be employed somewhere, why send it without cavalry, siege equipment and money to Egypt, about which ministerial ignorance was dense?[2] Clearly, Dundas's Egyptian policy (for it was his) was a gamble, in which failure spelt disaster and success doubtful profit. But much could be said for it in view of bargainings at the ensuing peace; and a series of concentric moves against Egypt, now prepared for, promised success. Wellesley had ready at Bombay a force under General Baird destined for the Red Sea; and Sir Home Popham at the Cape was similarly inspired. The Bombay expedition was convoyed to Kosseir; but in the long desert march thence to Kenneh on the Nile the 3000 troops nearly perished of thirst; and both it and Popham's force from Suez were too late to share in the British capture of Cairo. There General Belliard with 13,000 French, largely sick and all half-mutinous, had surrendered to General Hely Hutchinson's force of 4000 effectives (27 June 1801). Menou's far more creditable defence of Alexandria ended with the capitulation of September 2; but again Baird's unlucky force was just too late to share in the honour of ending French rule in Egypt. In fact, Dundas had been guilty of far-flung and too ambitious designs. Science had not as yet rendered feasible a tripartite invasion of Egypt with any reasonable hope of a timely junction; and Belliard's central force at Cairo, if efficient and handled effectively, ought to have crushed our exhausted troops struggling from the Red Sea. Nevertheless, they reached

[1] Albion, R. G., *Forests and Sea Power*, pp. 292, 356; also, *vide infra*, chap. VI.
[2] Wilson, Sir R., *Expedition to Egypt*, ch. I.

Kenneh only eleven days after Hutchinson's capture of Cairo, and Alexandria only four days after its surrender.

But in the expeditions of Baird and Popham there is a higher significance beside which mere meticulous reckonings are dwarfed. Was it not worth running some risks to exercise the budding powers of the new British Empire for self-defence; to prove that it had passed the period of infancy when each child expected and received assistance from the motherland without yielding help in return, and that now, in the time of adolescence, even recent acquisitions could send forth succours completing a widespread concentration on a vital point? If Dundas erred in points of detail, he erred from excess of hope. He and his colleagues pointed out the way destined to be followed by Disraeli in 1878, by Australia and Canada in 1884 and 1899, and by all parts of the Empire in 1914.

Meanwhile Bonaparte's move India-wards led the British to strike their roots deeper in Ceylon. There they succeeded to a Government which had signally failed both to conciliate the natives and to develop the resources of an interesting and industrious community. The Dutch East India Company's rule of 140 years had, in 1796, easily collapsed; and after the British occupation of Colombo several of the Dutch officials and clergy were supported by the British authorities.[1] But thereafter the British East India Company failed in the admittedly difficult problem of governing Dutch, Eurasians and natives. For these and other reasons the Pitt Administration accorded extensive powers to the first Governor, the Honourable Frederick North, who landed at Colombo in October 1798.

He found the position somewhat improved,[2] but the Dutch were sullenly hostile, and the natives perplexed and angry at the many changes. In spite of cruel exactions by the Company's Malabar tax-gatherers, the treasury was nearly empty, and trade had declined, while relations with the Kingdom of Kandy were critical. Helped by the advice of Lord Hobart's Committee of Inquiry, North abolished the Company's oppressive fiscal methods and resolved "to restore to this justly discontented people the laws, usages, security and comforts of which they have been unjustly deprived". In the face of almost open opposition from our civil servants, several of whom he discharged, and tortuous intrigues from the Dutch servants whom he too trustfully retained, he succeeded in reforming the Revenue Departments and restoring discipline to the Civil Service and confidence to the trading community. Thereupon, with his usual excess of zeal, he sought to revive agriculture by reforms ill-adapted to that stationary society. He also imposed new taxes on legal papers and on the salt pans; but one on "joys and jewels" caused disturbances.

---

[1] Turner, L. J. B., p. 74.
[2] *Ibid.* p. 126. For details see the following sections; also *C.H.B.E.* IV, ch. XXIV; Mills, L. A., *Ceylon under British Rule*, ch. IV.

Nevertheless, he reported in August 1800 a revival in industry, and an increase in the efficiency of the new executive and judiciary. Both critical and impulsive, he pointed out the defects of Dutch administration and the immense possibilities of the island when the growth of coffee, cinnamon, tobacco and pepper was duly regulated, when also the destructive herds of wild elephants were lessened by capture, the trapping of 500 animals a year promising a steady profit of £30,000.[1]

With the Kingdom of Kandy the dealings of North were both unscrupulous and unsuccessful; but the story is told in another volume of this series.[2] Here we can notice only that his energetic administration led the Home Government to take the decisions embodied in the important but little noticed despatch of 13 March 1801. It announces that the Crown will assume direct control of Ceylon, the political activities of the Company ceasing at the end of 1801, though North will continue in office. Our aim is declared to be the just and fair treatment of the new subjects and the furtherance of their prosperity, so as "to ensure their attachment and promote the general interests and strength of the British Empire". The executive and legislative powers will rest with North, but he may consult certain leading inhabitants whom he may choose as a Council, though without putting questions to the vote. He will also administer justice, presiding over the Court of Appeal and the Criminal Court which he has instituted. The judges will be appointed by the Home Government, the Governor, however, nominating the local Justices of the Peace in accord with Indian precedents. To prevent immigration (undesirable in war time) no grants of land will be allowed, except in the town and district of Colombo; also recent purchases may be reversed. Regulations are then laid down for the cinnamon and pearl fishery monopolies. Strict economy is enjoined, the total garrison being limited to 3600 Europeans and two native or Malay regiments. For the security of the trade monopoly of the East India Company no unlicensed commerce will be allowed between Ceylon and any lands east of the Cape of Good Hope. As to the distracted native Kingdom of Kandy, it is hoped that the mission of General McDowell to that Court may lead to the establishment there of a British garrison which "will enable you really to direct the affairs of that State, keeping its forms but substituting a humane and stable policy for one of violence and usurpation so long proceeding". For the rest, North's proposals as to native schools are deferred until the time of peace, while another for the despatch of selected Cingalese youths for education at our universities, receives a polite but chilling dissent. He is urged to restore "the decayed agriculture" of Ceylon

---

[1] C.O. 54/2, North to E.I.Co., 12 Oct., 26 Nov. 1798; 26 Feb., 16 July 1799; C.O. 54/3; 13 and 30 Jan., 1 Feb., 4 April, 4 and 30 Aug. 1800; Turner, ch. vi.
[2] C.H.B.E. iv, 404–8.

by carrying out the wise proposals of Lord Glenbervie. Government will assist any gradual efforts; but "in the present state of the settlement the public mind must not be alarmed by great expenses. These improvements must therefore...keep pace with the increasing revenues and industry of the island". An able engineer will be sent out[1]—a sign that both the Pitt and Addington Administrations had resolved to retain Ceylon.

From the evidence now adduced as to the value of Ceylon and Trinidad it is easy to see why Pitt declared them "the two most valuable acquisitions we could select", and "the best calculated for confirming and securing our ancient territories".[2] As Ceylon was a bulwark to India so was Trinidad to our West Indies. Though Rodney and other naval men placed St Lucia above it in strategic importance, yet that of Trinidad was high. Further, Trinidad (six times as large as St Lucia) was almost free from the hurricanes that often devastated the latter; added to which most of its lands were unexhausted, and it contained forests of hard timber and a bituminous lake, both of high value for the navy. Besides, its people gave little trouble, while the mulattoes and blacks of St Lucia, as in all the French islands, were eager for equality and therefore turbulent, the estates also being heavily burdened by debt.[3] Finally, the contiguity of Trinidad to the Spanish Main promised a profitable trade and political influence. It was from Trinidad that Miranda and other "liberators" strove to overturn Spanish authority.

Such, then, was the general and colonial outlook in September 1801, when war-weariness induced the leading combatants to think of peace. The French were sated with continental conquests, now more and more distant and restive under their sway; and they and their allies had lost in all 81 sail-of-the-line, 187 frigates and 248 sloops,[4] losses which prevented any great naval effort. The British also could scarcely hope to attack France; or indeed any lands except Dutch and Spanish colonies. On the other hand the Union flag waved over all the French East and West Indies except Guadeloupe, Mauritius and its smaller neighbour. Of late the British navy had reduced the rich valley of the Surinam, besides Curaçao and other smaller Dutch possessions, and had swept from the seas French, Dutch and Spanish commerce, so that Bonaparte admitted to our plenipotentiary at Amiens, Lord Cornwallis, that France had "entirely lost its commerce and in a large degree exhausted its pecuniary resources".[5] On the contrary those of the British Isles steadily grew, even in the trying year 1801, when the revenue exceeded £33,000,000,

---

[1] C.O. 54/1.   [2] *Dropmore Papers*, VII, 49. Speech of 3 Nov. 1801.
[3] C.O. 253/2; Prevost to Portland, 24 Nov. 1798, 2 Feb., 1 June, 12 Nov. 1799, 8 March 1802.   [4] *Ann. Register*, 1801, App.
[5] F.O. 27/59, Cornwallis to Hawkesbury, 3 Dec. 1801.

as against £19,000,000 in 1795. Also the exports of British manufactures had risen in value to £25,699,000 in 1801 from £18,335,000 in 1793, and shipping proportionately.[1] Clearly, then, the Empire was flourishing, even amidst political isolation, and its gains of territory had mostly been over ductile tropical peoples as against those of France over Europeans who more and more resented her sway. Wellesley's prophecy, early in 1800, that Great Britain would soon be arbitress of the world, was not wildly improbable if her statesmen and allies stood firm.[2]

Certainly there was no reason for concluding a disadvantageous peace. For amidst the startling gyrations of this conflict there emerged two unchallengeable facts—the inner weakness of great sprawling Coalitions and the invincible strength of their protagonists. Hence the sudden breakdown of the monarchist coalition in 1795 and of the Armed Neutrality League in 1801. Their imposing exterior had but called forth the utmost efforts and the swift home thrusts dealt by France and Great Britain in those years of inspiriting isolation; and now, when almost stripped of adventitious aids, they stood forth, each unconquerable on its own element. France controlled the west and south of Europe, while Great Britain patrolled the seas and held in pledge the colonies of France, Spain and Holland.

Far-seeing assessors of the world forces now at work, already discernible in their main outlines, would have assigned the palm to the Sea Power. But all such assessment, except on a strictly trade basis, was beyond the ken of our statesmen, most of all of Addington, summoned, as he had suddenly been, from the Speaker's chair to the helm of state at an unexampled crisis. In a civilian called upon to confront Bonaparte, the natural impulse was promptly and thankfully to garner any gifts of fortune that had in reality been prepared for by his predecessors. With him, however, prudence spelt precipitation, which Bonaparte interpreted as fear. There were indeed some grounds for apprehension. Two bad harvests in succession had by the autumn of 1801 sent wheat up to 116 shillings the quarter; and fears of invasion beset pessimists like Cornwallis.[3] Affairs at Westminster were also all awry. George III clung to Addington as the warder of his Protestant conscience and scouted Pitt and Grenville as its would-be violators. The political world being thus in confusion, politicians at Westminster stood in slippery places. So hurried were their negotiations with France that, though good news was to be expected from Egypt, they signed the Preliminaries of Peace at London on October 1, the very day before news arrived of the surrender of Mcnou at Alexandria, an event already known at Paris.

Great Britain now agreed to restore to the French all her naval conquests, namely Martinique, St Lucia, Tobago and other sugar

[1] C.J. (1803–4). [2] Mems....of the Marquis Wellesley, I, 334.
[3] Cornwallis Corresp. III, 379.

islands, besides all their posts and factories in India and Goree in West Africa. To the Dutch she restored the Cape of Good Hope, Demerara, Essequibo and Surinam, besides Curaçao and several other small islands, retaining only the Dutch posts in Ceylon. Of her conquests from Spain she retained only Trinidad. She further consented to evacuate Egypt, Malta and Elba, the first reverting to Turkey, and Malta to the Knights of St John under certain safe-guards. The Ionian Isles became the Republic of the Seven Islands. On her side France agreed to evacuate the south of Italy, but she regained her West India Islands and other posts above named, also Miquelon and St Pierre off Newfoundland. These fisheries were to be placed on the former footing, subject to changes by mutual consent.

Such was this singular compact. The surrenders now made in this year of triumph surpassed those which Grenville contemplated as barely possible in the darkest days of the war. When England was burdened with defeated and demoralised allies, Grenville stated that His Majesty would restore as many oversea conquests "as may be judged reasonable in consideration of advantages to be procured to his allies and particularly to Austria"; and amidst her disasters of April 1797 he was ready to abandon all our West Indian conquests in order to save Vienna from Bonaparte. In that case England would retain only Ceylon and the Cape.[1] Even so, Austria preferred to make her own bargain with the conqueror, partitioning with him the Venetian Republic. Again in the war of the Second Coalition she finally made a separate peace with Bonaparte at Lunéville (February 1801), and we were therefore under no obligation to her or indeed to any Ally except "ever faithful" Portugal.

Why, then, did the Addington Cabinet now consent to sacrifices greater than those contemplated only for a time in the blackest month of 1797? If moderation in conquest is the first of virtues in empire-building, moderation in surrender is also a desirable quality. On the worst reckoning the war ended in a stalemate. But in that case, as in 1748, each side should have made equal sacrifices. Yet France now retained all her continental conquests; she continued to exercise control over the Batavian, Helvetic, Ligurian and Cisalpine Republics, and recovered every one of her former colonies, shifting to her Spanish and Dutch allies the burden of loss, namely Trinidad and Ceylon.

Naturally, then, Ministers were sharply censured in Parliament. In the Commons Thomas Grenville and Lord Leveson-Gower showed that our sacrifices were greater than those proposed in 1797, namely to the extent of the Cape, Surinam, Minorca, Elba and Malta. In reply Lord Hawkesbury deprecated such a comparison and pointed to the gain of Mysore as establishing our position in India; he also maintained that no cession in the West Indies was a real loss, nor was

---

[1] See *C.H.B.F.P.* i, 566, 573, for the relevant despatches.

that of Minorca or Malta; the former would always fall to a superior fleet, and, while regretting Malta, he declared it to be "no source of trade or opulence". Indeed our exports to the Levant amounted to only £112,000 out of total exports worth over £24,000,000. He further claimed that our acquisitions, Ceylon and Trinidad, were as valuable as those gains of 1760–3, Canada and Florida, which, with all their extent of territory, were not "real acquisitions". Our total trade with the West Indies now exceeded by one-third that of the pre-war years, so, too, that with the East Indies, while that with the Continent had nearly doubled. In this increase of commerce lay our security; for with it our navy would always increase, and that of France could never equal it. Pitt, as in private duty bound, supported the administration, but expressed great regret at the surrender of the Cape, which, however, he placed below Ceylon as a protection to India. Finally he affirmed that our gains in the two Indies were of such importance as to warrant the cession of Malta in order "not unnecessarily to mortify the feelings or pride of an enemy".[1]

In the Upper House Earl Spencer and Lord Grenville severely arraigned the peace as sacrificing our means of protection, especially in the Mediterranean, where we gave up everything and excluded ourselves. They fastened on Malta and the Cape as the most dangerous surrenders, "purchasing", added Grenville, "a short interval of repose by the sacrifice of those points on which our security in a new contest may principally depend". On the other hand St Vincent defended the terms of peace as satisfactory and honourable. Nelson also dilated on the immense expense of garrisoning Malta and the Cape, and affirmed that the latter port, now that East Indiamen were coppered, was the less necessary as a port of call. Indeed he dubbed it "merely a tavern on the passage, which served to call at and thence often to delay the voyage". The Lords, perplexed by this contest of authorities, supported the peace terms by 104 to 20.[2]

During the final negotiations at Amiens, our plenipotentiary, General Lord Cornwallis, sought to secure the retention of Tobago, an island inhabited and developed by Britons. In November 1800 these English colonists petitioned urgently against being sacrificed to France as in 1783; for their energy had cleared the island and made it prosperous so that it employed about fifty merchantmen manned by British seamen. If it continued with us, its commerce would soon bring £500,000 a year to the British exchequer, while its position to windward of Trinidad, also conferred great advantages.[3] Accordingly, Cornwallis sought to induce his opponent, Joseph Bonaparte, to concede to us Tobago if we cancelled a large sum due for the support of French prisoners. The First Consul, who insisted on

---

[1] *Parl. Hist.* XXXVI, 30–65; *Spencer Papers*, IV, 304, and *Naval Miscellany* (N.R.S.), III, 194–5.
[2] *Ibid.* pp. 157–90. *Bathurst Papers* (Hist. MSS Comm. 1923), p. 39; *Lord St Vincent's Letters*, I, 285.   [3] C.O. 285/7 *passim*.

recovering everything that France held in 1792, repelled this suggestion as dishonourable, but said he would give way on Tobago if we would give him "a few leagues around Pondicherry", which Cornwallis stiffly refused.[1] Finally, Joseph (with Talleyrand behind him) presented an even larger French account for the support of prisoners taken from the German and other forces subsidised by us. Cornwallis, thus cleverly outflanked, thereupon agreed to refer the debts to commissioners—a diplomatic way of surrendering Tobago. Subsequently he retired from trench to trench at Amiens, holding firm only against the Spaniards over Trinidad, to their infinite disgust with France. As to the Cape, he incautiously admitted the Dutch demand for full rights of sovereignty,[2] which (as was later pointed out) would enable them to cede it to France. The attempt to prop up the moribund Order of St John at Malta, with a Neapolitan garrison and a guarantee of its neutrality by the six Great Powers, caused wearisome discussions ending in an unsatisfactory compromise which Cornwallis deemed "as good a security for the Knights and for the island as under the present circumstances can reasonably be expected".[3]

Some time before the signature of the definitive treaty, the Addington Cabinet heard of the acquisition by France of the vast country of Louisiana from Spain—news which portended the adoption at Paris of a spirited colonial policy. Grave fears were therefore aroused as to our proposed surrenders of those strategic posts, Martinique and St Lucia. Yet Ministers and Cornwallis proceeded with the final negotiations at Amiens. In many quarters, however, the terms of that treaty (signed at Amiens on 27 March 1802) caused consternation. The Anglophile Russian ambassador, Vorontzoff, declared it the only compact since the time of Charles II at which Englishmen need blush.[4] Canning dilated on "the gross faults and omissions, the weakness and baseness and shuffling and stupidity" of the treaty.[5] Pitt nervously held his peace. Sheridan taunted him with wasting 200,000 lives and £300,000,000 and neither preventing French aggrandisement, nor gaining his much-vaunted "security", but only acquiring two islands, which should be called "Isle of Security" and "Isle of Indemnity".[6] With all seriousness Grenville and Windham censured Article X, which placed Malta in the hands of an Order whose total income could not possibly maintain a sufficient garrison, and that, too, a garrison of 2000 Neapolitans, whose realm was always at the mercy of the French. Nevertheless, Addington and his colleagues, by harping on the commercial benefits accruing from the peace, carried Parliament with them. They had now to learn that the mind of their rival was set, not on commerce, but on power.

[1] F.O. 27/59, Cornwallis to Hawkesbury, 3 Dec. 1801.
[2] Ibid. Cornwallis to Hawkesbury, 29 Jan., 5 Feb. 1802.
[3] Ibid. Feb. 9, 12, 16, 23; Cornwallis Corresp. III, 400–84; Rose, Life of Napoleon, I, ch. XIV.
[4] Dropmore Papers, VII, 93.   [5] Windham Papers, II, 184, 188.
[6] Sheridan, R. B., Speeches, V, 197.

CHAPTER III

THE STRUGGLE WITH NAPOLEON
1803–1815

By the end of the Revolutionary War the United Kingdom, in spite of serious blunders, had so far redressed its loss of influence in Europe by acquisitions overseas as to be able not only to endure but to profit by the strain of that desperate conflict; for, as has been seen, its exports and shipping increased in that period by more than one-third. In fact the British Empire was becoming a self-sufficing economic unit, knit together by the operations of the navy, and able to make head against French domination in the Netherlands, Germany and Italy. British gains were mostly in tropical lands which supplied vital needs; while those of France, though superficially far more impressive, were in neighbouring lands which could ill support exclusion from the tropics. Moreover, her acquisitions necessitated large armies of occupation, the expenses of which were, apparently, not always met by local requisitions. Certainly, in 1801 French finances were in great confusion, the Finance Minister, Gaudin, admitting a deficit of 100,000,000 francs. By rigid peace economies he reduced it to 11,500,000 francs in 1802; but, on the return of war in May 1803, he foresaw financial ruin ahead, and finally penned the verdict that it was "retarded solely by prodigies of valour and genius".[1]

Thus, it is probable that in 1801 the British Empire occupied a sounder financial position than France and her subject States.[2] But the advantages won by sea power were not obvious; for, indeed, its workings are, in general, obscure and cumulative. By degrees they affect the Stock Exchange and at length empty the larder; but they lack the sensational appeal of the advance of a conquering army. Indeed, throughout these wars the islanders remained unconscious of the vast reserves of strength inherent in sea power, while Napoleon trumpeted forth that the land was to conquer the sea.[3]

In the year 1801, then, Addington held the winning hand; but, diffident and tongue-tied, he faltered and threw up the game. Scarcely, however, were the Preliminaries of London signed than thoughtful men, if not bound by official reserve, declared their apprehensions. William Cobbett incisively dubbed the peace "a capitulation"; the Duke of Portland and Windham termed it "an armed armistice"; and though Pitt sought to save the face of his

---

[1] Méms....du Duc de Gaëte (1826), I, 188–92, 204. See, too, Mollien, Méms. I, 407 seqq.; Pasquier, Méms. I, 163.
[2] For French belief in the rottenness of England's financial state, vide supra, pp. 36, 37; also Lasalle, H., Les Finances de l'Angleterre (1803); Cunningham, Audrey, British Credit in the Napoleonic War, passim. [3] E.g. Napoleonic Corresp. No. 11,379.

friend Addington, the Pittites, especially Canning, declaimed bitterly against the needless surrenders to the French.[1] While the Foreign Secretary, Lord Hawkesbury, admitted in the House that the peace was a risky experiment, the confidential adviser of his colleague Castlereagh, privately foretold its imminent dangers; for, as it did not guarantee commercial relations with France, she would be free to exclude our trade, not only from all the European lands under her control but also from the colonies now about to be restored to her and her allies. From these colonial sources alone she would gain, and we should lose, trade worth at least £10,000,000 a year. She was also left free to build up a hostile commercial union with Spain, Holland and most of Italy, which might entail on us a further heavy loss. And what meant her great armament of forty-seven warships and 12,000 troops, despatched late in the year 1801 to San Domingo? If France and Spain were to maintain large forces in the Caribbean our expenses would increase, while our means of meeting them seriously decreased. Such a peace would be "our entire ruin".[2]

Though the foregoing estimate of an annual loss of trade of £10,000,000 may seem excessive, it ceases to be when the recent phenomenal progress of the conquered West Indies is duly weighed. The outstanding example was that of the colonies formerly Dutch— Demerara and Essequibo, which in the six years of the British occupation increased their exports of sugar to Great Britain twelvefold, those of raw cotton tenfold, and those of coffee sixfold.[3] Indeed, most of the conquered West Indian colonies prospered greatly under British rule, owing partly to the great influx of British capital, partly to the greater immunity of their exports from capture at sea. Therefore, the surprise and anger of the West Indian interest may be imagined, first, at the extensive retrocessions by the Peace of Amiens and, later, at the ensuing exclusion of British trade from all the colonies then retroceded to France and Holland. Our shipping also suffered by this one-sided peace, the vessels clearing outwards declining to the extent of 63,000 tons in 1802, a year of peace. Further, Bonaparte's recent acquisition of Louisiana from Spain seemed to prelude a vigorous New World policy, and its natural sequel, the driving of the Union flag from the Caribbean. Such an event would be disastrous; for the average exports of British manufactures to the West Indies had risen from £2,185,000 in 1790–2 to £3,561,000 in 1799–1801, and the corresponding imports thence from £3,877,000 to £5,101,000. Accordingly, there was a general demand that our sugar islands must be saved from Bonaparte's grasp; and the Addington Cabinet both protested against the despatch to San Domingo of that formidable French force and prepared to strengthen our West Indian squadrons and garrisons.

[1] *The Windham Papers*, II, 182, 185–7.   [2] *Castlereagh Corresp.* v, 25–28.
[3] Custom House returns in C.O. 111/4. For details see *C.H.J.*, October 1929.

Events proved that Bonaparte over-reached himself in the West. The prospect of French energy replacing Spanish torpor in the vast region west of the Mississippi aroused angry protests in the United States; and for a brief space common action by Great Britain and them seemed not unlikely. Fever, however, proved to be our best ally. In the great French expedition to San Domingo all the mistakes that had devastated the British forces were repeated. The crews and soldiers alike were too raw for the work; they arrived in February 1802 and soon were decimated by the rains of spring and the heats of summer. Nevertheless, in the winter of 1802–3 Bonaparte prepared to send two more expeditions, each of 15,000 men, to the same man-devouring island.[1] That service also absorbed nearly all his efficient warships, a fact which explains much in the subsequent negotiations.

In this affair, then, the initiative came from Paris, while Whitehall followed the new occidentation; and the same sequence was to happen in other regions; for Bonaparte had a colonial policy, while Addington and his colleagues had none, and gazed on doubtfully until some kind of action became necessary.

They began now to surmise that something was wrong in the Mediterranean. Despite the astounding assertion of the First Lord, the Earl of St Vincent, that the Peace of Amiens was "the very best this country ever made",[2] it was soon obvious that our forthcoming evacuation of Egypt, Malta and Minorca would leave the great Corsican free to make of the Mediterranean a French lake. His moves towards the establishment of a coastal control were clearly marked. Before the Treaty of Amiens was signed he had occupied Piedmont (postponing formal annexation until after the signature). Next, he sought to compel the King of Sardinia to exclude our ships entirely from that island. He also became President of the new Italian Republic with powers so extensive that rumour proclaimed him lord of the peninsula, forthcoming controller of the Mediterranean and the future conqueror of Egypt[3]—a forecast to which he himself lent strength by the annexation of Elba (August 1802).

Even before the pointer of the political barometer edged more and more clearly towards Malta, fears had arisen as to the fragility of the arrangements concluded at Amiens for the guarantee of the neutrality of that island. In view of Bonaparte's oriental designs its dominant strategic position and the strength of its capital marked it out as an object of envy. Yet the cumbrous provisions of Article X, relating to Malta, formed the outstanding example of Cornwallis's easy optimism; and if ever there had been any chance of the restored Knights of St John being able effectively to garrison the extensive ramparts of Valetta, it was destroyed by the subsequent subversive

[1] *Nap. Corresp.* Nos. 6456, 6570. [2] *Letters of Lord St Vincent* (N.R.S.), I, 285.
[3] *Paget Papers*, II, 42, Italinsky to Paget, 20 Feb. 1802.

action of France and Spain in confiscating their properties in those lands. Henceforth an Order, hated by the Maltese, and having an income of only £30,000 a year,[1] could not possibly defend the extensive walls of Valetta, and therefore needed outside support, which 2000 Neapolitan troops were to afford, whilst the guarantee of Maltese neutrality by the Great Powers would add an inviolable sanction.

But how (asked the critics, especially Grenville and Windham) could effective armed support come from the weak and decadent Kingdom of Naples, which had of late bought peace from France by excluding the shipping of all her enemies?[2] Would not the French, again masters of North and Central Italy, once more work their will on Naples? Was the support of Naples at Malta worth more than that of rotten timber to a bowing wall? Further, of what use was the collective guarantee of Great Powers who never agreed on anything? Apprehensions therefore centred in Malta, and little surprise was felt when Austria expressed dislike of Article X, and Russia and Prussia refused to act as guarantors.[3] As for the Sublime Porte, it warned us not to evacuate Malta. "The Porte", wrote Lord Elgin, British ambassador at Constantinople, "considers her interests and tranquillity secure while England possesses Malta, but not so after our abandoning it."[4]

Nevertheless, orders went forth from Downing Street for the evacuation of all the places now to be retroceded, including Egypt, Malta and the Cape. By degrees, however, British Ministers became alarmed at the extension of French control over neighbouring States. Along with news of the annexation of Elba came that of the assumption of the Consulate for Life by Napoleon, who now used his Christian name and adopted other monarchical customs. His will prevailed not only in France but in her dependent States, viz. the Italian, Ligurian, Helvetic and Batavian Republics. The independence of the last named was for us a vital issue; and apprehensions increased month by month at his persistent retention of French troops in Dutch fortresses and dominant influence over Dutch policy, which would enable him in due course to assume complete control at the Cape.

With the Dutch problem was closely linked the Maltese problem; for, in proportion as Napoleon's chances increased of dominating the sea-route to India through the submissive Dutch at the Cape, so much the more urgent for us became the need of safeguarding the overland route, the key to which was Malta. Thus, for cogent reasons, that island now became the crux of world policy. Its position in the gut of the central Mediterranean enabled a fleet based on Valetta

---

[1] Cobbett's *Annual Register*, II, 1206 (Debate of 3 May 1802).
[2] In Treaty of Florence (Feb. 1801), Koch and Schöll, *Traités*, II, 107; *Nap. Corresp.*, No. 5413.
[3] *Paget Papers*, II, 50-9; Hardman, W., *History of Malta* .pp. 445-65.
[4] F.O. 78/35; see too *Castlereagh Corresp.* V, 178.

to control the approaches to the Levant, the quarter on which, after the failure of his American designs, centred the fondest hopes of Napoleon.[1] It is therefore scarcely credible that Fox, usually a man of wide vision, should declare to the House of Commons that the forthcoming rupture with France occurred solely "for Malta, plain bare naked Malta, unconnected with any other interest".[2] By a singular but appropriate nemesis he lived on to attain to official responsibility and sobriety of statement, and in his last days rejected Napoleon's offer of peace in 1806 because it involved the sacrifice of a less important strategic centre, Sicily.

In the late summer of 1802 a statesman of remarkable insight had been probing the situation created by Napoleon's control of Louisiana, the four Republics named above and Elba. Castlereagh, the political heir of Pitt and the future protagonist of Europe against Napoleon, even now judged that we and other European States must withstand his encroachments, which threatened us alike on the Continent, in the Mediterranean, and in our colonial Empire. If (wrote Castlereagh) the First Consul attacked our immediate and vital interests, we had no choice but war, which, assuming that the national spirit held good, might be maintained even for ten years; but, the other Powers being cowed or apathetic, help from the rest of Europe was improbable; and we alone, even by a successful maritime war, could not rescue the Continent. Nevertheless, we should warn him that further encroachments, such as the acquisition of complete control over Holland, would not be tolerated.[3] No clearer forecast of the future ever appeared. Castlereagh saw the danger of looking on idly while Napoleon became master of all neighbouring States and therefore of the Dutch and Spanish navies and colonies. Still, if the Tsar Alexander held philanthropically aloof, while Austria skulked, and Prussia played the jackal to Napoleon, what was to be done? The problem was both colonial and continental. On its maritime side jealousy of England counted for much; on its continental side mutual jealousies clogged every step forward. Thus, as in a crystal globe, Castlereagh foresaw the prolonged isolation of England, the tardy and partial actions of our natural allies, the miserable breakdowns of alliances, in fine, the devastating tragedy of the next decade.

The actions of Napoleon for a time stiffened the attitude of the Powers; for in October 1802 he interfered so masterfully in Swiss affairs as to elicit protests not only from that people but also from Russia and Austria because he had lately guaranteed the independence of the Batavian, Helvetic, Cisalpine and Ligurian Republics.[4] Foreseeing the possibility of common action, the Addington Cabinet at once sent secret offers of help to Berne and countermanded the

---

[1] Browning, O., *England and Napoleon*, pp. 19, 29; *Paget Papers*, II, 72, 79.
[2] *Speeches of Fox*, VI, 526.   [3] *Castlereagh Corresp.* V, 29, 38.
[4] By the Treaty of Lunéville, Art. 11; Koch and Schöll, *Traités*, II, 103.

former orders for our evacuations of the Cape, Egypt and Malta. But, meeting with no effective response on the Continent, Ministers gave way, and on or about November 20 reissued orders for the evacuations to proceed.[1] This connection between our colonial and general policy is highly significant. The Cabinet had offered no protest when Napoleon annexed Elba; but on a matter of far less imperial concern, viz. Switzerland, they for a time stood firm, doubtless with the hope of framing a coalition of the Powers against France. Probably in the end, they acted on Pitt's advice as to merely "laying the foundation of a defensive system in Europe, rather than by involving ourselves *immediately* in a separate war only for the advantage of being able to carry it on with these possessions still in our hands". Even Pitt, however, ended by stating—"of course some new arrangement must, I suppose, be made about Malta".[2] This was inevitable; for the reason already noted. Similar advice came from Nelson. Though the great seaman had, earlier, belittled the importance of that island, yet now, in December 1802, he, naturally enough, revised his judgment. While declaring that England did not want Malta, he added that France must never have it; that the King of Naples was the rightful owner, but if he refused it, and Russia would not sign the guarantee, "we have no other choice but to keep Malta".[3]

Early in 1803 a sinister event added force to Nelson's last warning. On January 30 appeared in the columns of the official *Moniteur* the report of General Sébastiani sent by Napoleon as commercial commissioner to the Levant. Containing very little about commerce, it stressed the weakness of Turkey and the political chaos in the Ionian Isles and Egypt, affirming that 6000 French could reconquer that land. This official threat (for such it was) probably sprang from Napoleon's belief in intimidation by displays of overwhelming force. As Sorel has well pointed out, he never knew the English;[4] and his chief aim thenceforth was to terrify them into acquiescence with his hegemony in Europe and far-reaching plans in the Indies. Of course the Sébastiani Report only stiffened the British attitude. Hitherto it had been decidedly peaceful, as appeared in the reduction of the number of sail-of-the-line in commission from 104 early in 1802 to thirty-two early in 1803.[5] But now the horizon darkened. Cornwallis, who in November 1802 longed for peace, "unless we are ourselves assaulted" and some of the Great Powers would help us, now, in February 1803, deemed a rupture unavoidable. Such was the conviction of George III, who was reported as now being "extremely eager" for war, though it must lead to the loss of

[1] Browning, *England and Napoleon*, pp. 8–10, 152; Pellew, G., *Life of Lord Sidmouth*, II, 87; Driault, E., *La Politique Extérieure du Premier Consul*, pp. 280–92.
[2] Pellew, *Lord Sidmouth*, p. 87. See Pitt's views in *Diaries...of G. Rose*, I, 495.
[3] Nicolas, V, 36.
[4] Sorel, *Rév. franç.* VI, 261.
[5] James, W., *Naval History*, III, Apps. 10, 11.

Hanover.[1] Pitt believed that, in view of Sébastiani's Report, we must not give up Malta "without fresh and substantial security".[2] As for Nelson, he still hoped for peace but feared war would come. Meanwhile the British Government had resolved "not to enter into any discussions relative to the evacuation of Malta until we had first received satisfactory explanations on both these points", viz. Egypt and British interests as stipulated in the late Treaty.[3] Further, as considerable military preparations were going on in French and Dutch ports, the King on March 8 sent a message to the House of Commons announcing that precautionary measures would be taken here. Accordingly, the militia was called out and the press-gang set to work. The Government also instructed Lord Whitworth, its ambassador at Paris, to claim territorial compensation for the great extension of French territory since the peace, a principle whose justice Bonaparte and Talleyrand had conceded.[4]

Clearly such compensation must be found in Malta. A second warning, penned by Lord Elgin at Valetta on February 28,[5] as to the paramount importance of that island in safeguarding Egypt, probably clinched the resolve of Ministers, formed by April 13, to demand its retention during ten years and the absolute possession of the neighbouring islet, Lampedusa.[6] Bonaparte would not hear of this solution, and it was clear that he objected to our retaining anything more than Lampedusa or some other harbourless islet in the Mediterranean. He and Talleyrand fenced so as to gain time for their West and East India squadrons to reach places of safety;[7] but the British Government, discerning their naval reasons for this belated dalliance, declared war on May 18. Ostensibly the rupture occurred on our demand for a ten years' occupation of Malta, but in reality on the vital issue, that, after our evacuation of the Cape and Egypt, no other place than Malta offered any safeguard against the now avowed aims of Napoleon on Egypt and India. These facts refute the assertion that the responsibilities for the rupture were "much heavier on England's side".[8]

As to India some anxiety had already been caused, first by the report of one of our agents at Paris (10 November 1802), that Napoleon had great projects for India and hoped with the help of the Dutch eastern possessions, to "chase the English from Bengal"; for which purpose he was sending divisional generals to Mahé and Chandernagore, where only civilians were needed.[9] Further, on 6 March 1803, he had ordered a squadron with 1670 troops on board

---

[1] *Dropmore Papers*, VII, 151.   [2] *Ibid.* VII, 149.
[3] *Cornwallis Corresp.* III, 496–8; v, 49; Nicolas, v, 51.
[4] Browning, *England and Napoleon*, 7, 73, 121, 149, 162, 170.
[5] F.O. 78/38; printed in *E.H.R.* April 1921.
[6] Browning, *England and Napoleon*, p. 171.   [7] *Ibid.* pp. 181–90, 196–202, 213–38.
[8] Bainville, J., *Napoléon*, ch. XII.
[9] F.O. 27/70 (Advices and Intelligence).

to sail for Pondicherry *viâ* the Cape,[1] the rumour going forth that, by sending out small contingents, a considerable force might be gathered there without attracting notice. The secret instructions drawn up on 15 January 1803 to the commander, General Decaen, bade him carefully prepare for a war of several campaigns against the British, which not improbably might begin before 22 September 1804. In case of disaster he might fall back on some favourable *point d'appui*, whether Portuguese, Dutch or English, and there capitulate; but he was urged to hope for *la grande gloire*, which defies the lapse of centuries.[2] Decaen's careful survey of Cape Town during his stay there was in accord with his instruction to regard the Dutch as allies in case of war; and probably he regarded the Cape as a place to fall back on in case of misfortune.[3]

Considered as a test of the sincerity of Napoleon's desire for peace, the British demand for a ten years' occupation of Malta probed his designs not unskilfully. For, if he really desired a lasting peace, he could not, consistently with his recognition of the principle of compensation, refuse a claim for this limited occupation of an island, the plans for the neutralisation of which had utterly broken down. But, if he did not desire such a peace, it was far better for Britain to have the rupture at once, seeing that three French expeditions were at sea, that of Decaen and the last two expeditions to San Domingo. If, after giving these hostages to Fortune, Napoleon still refused the British claim, obviously he was bent on some object of transcendent importance, in the prosecution of which he was ready to incur grave risks to three expeditionary forces. The inference is therefore cogent that his ulterior aims were such as would lead to a fight to the death with the British Empire. He now made France ring with diatribes against *la perfide Albion*; but the well-informed knew that the rupture was due to his recent extensions of French power and his refusal of the British demands for a return to the *status quo ante pacem*.[4]

It is certain that Joseph Bonaparte, Talleyrand, Fouché, Masséna and the great majority of Frenchmen desired peace with England; but their efforts failed to bend the will of the First Consul, who, on receiving favourable news from Russia (probably as to a Franco-Russian entente in the East) thwarted their last efforts to avert a rupture.[5] As to the pacific aims of Addington and his colleagues, even after the publication of Sébastiani's Report, the despatches of General Andréossi, French Ambassador at London, bear decisive testimony. On 2 April 1803 he wrote to Napoleon: "The prayers, the needs and the wishes of this country are for peace." Again, on

[1] Prentout, H., *L'Île de France sous Decaen*, p. 29.
[2] *Nap. Corresp.* No. 6544; J. Tessier's article in *Revue historique*, 1881, xv, 349–81.
[3] See Rose, J. H., in *E.H.R.* (Jan. 1900) on Decaen at the Cape; also Prentout, *L'Île de France*, p. 32.
[4] Pelet de la Lozère, ch. 3; Chaptal, *Souvenirs*, p. 363.
[5] Browning, *England and Napoleon*, p. 265.

the 4th: "Everybody wants peace. By preserving the peace of Europe you will crush this country without appealing to the arbitrament of the mailed fist...and you are in a most favourable position to decide the world's destiny for all time."[1]

These warnings were true. By conceding a few points to Great Britain and concentrating on his navy, Napoleon would have had the world at his feet. But he lacked the qualities of prudence and moderation so necessary in empire-building. Having sold Louisiana to the United States (his only wise step at this crisis)[2] he resolved to carry through his oriental game, in which Malta must form the gambit. But his moves eastwards—his domination of Italy, annexation of Elba, Sébastiani's Report and Decaen's expedition—terrified the Addington Ministry into firmness, it being abundantly clear that open war was safer than a Napoleonic peace. With equal truth and wit Mme de Staël declared that, next to the fault of signing the Treaty of Amiens, that of not breaking it would have been the greatest.[3]

The prospects of Great Britain, after the surrender of the Cape, Martinique, and St Lucia, were far from bright. Her navy had been dangerously reduced during the peace; and not until 1806 did its sail-of-the-line muster the total of 104, reached in January 1802. In June 1804 our eighty-one sail were barely equal to the Franco-Dutch total of seventy sail, if joined (as was probable) by the Spaniards.[4] Fortunately, as we have seen, Napoleon's venture in San Domingo had locked up a considerable force there. Also, his ten sail-of-the-line in the West Indies being weakened or held fast by sickness, the squadron of Rear-Admiral Sir John Duckworth soon closed in on the chief garrisons, and finally reduced those of Mole St Nicholas and Cap François to surrender, the French preferring to capitulate to us rather than to the infuriated negroes under their ruthless chief, Dessalines.[5] In all, the French are reckoned to have lost 40,000 men in San Domingo,[6] besides many warships and transports, though one sail-of-the-line finally escaped to Cadiz and four made Ferrol,[7] where they were long observed by an English squadron. These casualties do not fully represent the harm done to Napoleon's plans. He could ill bear any diminution to his navy, for he now needed to be strong either in home waters or the East Indies; but, owing to the dispersion or loss outright of his West Indian squadron he was unable at any point to assume a vigorous offensive.

[1] Coquelle, P., *Napoleon and England*, pp. 53-7.
[2] See Rose, J. H., *Life of Napoleon*, I, 364–72.
[3] De Staël, *Considérations sur la Révolution française*, pt. IV, ch. V.
[4] *Barham Papers*, III, 42 ff.; James, *Naval History*, IV, App. 14.
[5] *Naval Chronicle*, XI, 61–3, Letters of Duckworth, etc.
[6] Dumas, *Vict. et Conquêtes*, XIV, 330; James, *Naval History*, III, 203–10.
[7] Chevalier, E., *La Marine française*, III, 83–5.

He therefore flung himself into the vast preparations on his northern coasts for the invasion of England, hoping, possibly, to deal her the home thrust, or, at least, to reduce her to the defensive and thus save from capture the French and Dutch colonies.

Whatever his aims, he failed. The British Admiralty, nerved by the traditions of Drake, Anson and Chatham, took adequate defensive measures at home but subjected the French fleets at Brest and Toulon (sometimes also at Rochefort) to distant but effective blockades, behind which it struck at the chief of the hostile colonies. In the East Indies, thanks to the foresight and firmness of the Marquis Wellesley,[1] Pondicherry and other French posts were never given up. Off Newfoundland, St Pierre and Miquelon were speedily occupied, thus depriving French cruisers of their bases for preying on the Newfoundland fishing fleet and the increasingly valuable trade in naval stores from Nova Scotia, New Brunswick and the St Lawrence. For by this time these colonies had replaced New England as sources of supply for timber, hemp and flax for the navy; and the rapid growth of this trade and that in grain enabled the British Islands to face the crisis resulting from the subsequent closing of the Baltic ports.[2] Further signs of our dependence on imported flax were the offer of prizes for its growth in and importation from British North America,[3] also the request of Simeon Lord and other traders of Sydney (April 1810) to found a settlement in New Zealand for growing flax for the benefit of New South Wales and the Royal Navy, with exclusive rights during fourteen years. The Board of Trade approved the proposal except the monopoly clause.[4]

As in 1793, so too in 1803, French designs in the West Indies compelled us to prompt action in that arena, where the recent retrocession to France of both Martinique and St Lucia endangered the whole of the British islands. Commodore Samuel Hood, commanding on that station, gained two notable successes. On 21 June 1803, with two sail-of-the-line and several smaller craft he struck suddenly at St Lucia, disembarking in Choc Bay troops which by mid-day rushed the outposts of Castries and by sundown carried the town itself. With vigour unabated they stormed at dawn the strong fortified position of Morne Fortunée. Thus, with the loss of twenty killed and 110 wounded, they recovered an island of great strategic importance as a look-out place on Martinique from to-windward. Next, a detachment proceeded to Tobago, which was regained with equal promptitude on July 1. Meanwhile, General Ernouf, Governor of Guadeloupe, threatened an attack in force on Antigua and its naval arsenal, which was practically defenceless and at the mercy even of

---

[1] Roberts, P. E., *India under Wellesley*, p. 149.
[2] Albion, R. G., *Forests and Sea Power*, pp. 352–5. Also *vide infra*, chap. VI.
[3] *Naval Chronicle*, XII (1804), 31–34.
[4] B.T. 1/1, 64. For New Zealand flax, see *C.H.B.E.* VII, Part II, ch. III.

privateers.[1] But the danger was ended by a dashing exploit. On September 5 Captain O'Brien in the *Emerald* (36) delivered a sudden and successful boat attack, which paralysed the French preparations.[2] We may note here that St Lucia soon recovered its former prosperity, Governor Brereton reporting in 1805 an increase in population (especially slaves); also in business firms, from eight in May 1803 to thirty-six. Castries alone exported 5,944,943 lb. of sugar in a year, besides large quantities of cotton, coffee, cocoa, rum and molasses.[3]

The British Government also sought to come to terms with Dessalines, the negro chief supreme in San Domingo, and instructed Duckworth to stipulate that any British subjects there should enjoy advantages equal to those of American traders, each nation importing only its own produce.[4] The speedy relapse of the island into anarchy invalidated all such efforts. But on the mainland of South America our seamen gained substantial successes, occupying with little or no resistance the Dutch settlements of Demerara, Essequibo and Berbice in September 1803, and Surinam in May 1804.[5] Thus early did the Dutch experience the hard lot of being forced to follow the lead of Napoleon. Losing their colonies and trade to our cruisers, they also suffered from his exactions on land; and, crushed between the upper and nether millstones, they have never recovered their former greatness as a colonising and commercial Power.

These colonial gains, along with others soon to be noted, served in part as a set-off to Britain's exclusion from European markets by which Napoleon sought to drain away her vitality. As one of our spies in Paris stated, he would need to make up for the inevitable loss of French colonies and commerce by overrunning neighbouring States in Europe; for only thus could he recoup those commercial losses and recover prestige among the impressionable French.[6] Here he achieved an easy success, occupying Hanover and South Italy without opposition; from the former he drew considerable sums, besides extending the coastal area whence British goods were excluded. The struggle therefore appeared more unmistakably than ever as one between the Sea Power and the Land Power, in which, from the nature of the case, neither side could win unless it utterly exhausted the resources of the other. In this trial of financial strength Napoleon sought to acquire an absolute control of the Continent, while the British retorted by mastering the resources of the tropics. In all essentials, then, the conflict became, on a greater scale, a resumption of that which was patched up in 1802.

---

[1] C.O. 152/85, Lavington to Hobart, 15, 30 July 1803.
[2] *Ibid.* O'Brien to Lavington, 6 Sept. 1803.
[3] C.O. 25/3, Brereton to Camden, 24 July 1805.
[4] C.O. 137/110, Hobart to Governor of Jamaica, 7 Oct. 1803.
[5] James, *Naval History*, III, 203-4, 296; *Naval Chronicle*, XII, 80. For the rapid progress in Demerara, see *C.H.J.* Oct. 1929.   [6] F.O. 27/70, Intelligence, 28 May 1803.

To this wearisome process of fiscal exhaustion the far more attractive plan of stabbing England to the heart offered an alluring alternative; and, as in 1798, before setting about his first effort at commercial strangulation from the East, Bonaparte had calculated the chances of a landing in Kent, so now he bent the energies of the French and Dutch to the task of "leaping the ditch". His colonial motive in making these colossal preparations, extending from Flanders to Brittany, has already been explained: but in this respect again his San Domingo venture had so far weakened the French navy that it could afford only a weak covering force to the Channel flotilla. On 31 May 1803 there were ready for sea at Brest only two sail-of-the-line, one frigate and two corvettes; many others needed extensive repairs, which would take long owing to the shortage of workmen and naval stores. At Toulon Nelson heard that seven sail were ready. At Rochefort there were four; and in addition to these were the four sail from San Domingo which had sought refuge at Ferrol.[1] Napoleon persistently treated that Spanish port as if it were subject to his control, and required extensive repairs to go on there. Even so, a French naval offensive was out of the question: it was useless for him to order twenty sail to be ready at Brest by December and similar increases at all naval stations from Genoa to the Elbe.[2]

On the British side Admiral William Cornwallis with ten sail (later kept up to an average of twenty) took station off Brest by 20 May 1803 and there began that long bull-dog watch which foiled Napoleon's plans of world empire. A little later Nelson began his equally memorable vigil off Toulon; and smaller squadrons often cruised off Rochefort and Ferrol. Thus Napoleon's invasion scheme was countered at the really crucial points, off his naval stations. He could therefore strike neither at Britain's colonies nor at her heart; for no seaman would consider seriously the invasion of England by a swarm of flat-bottomed craft, unprotected by sea-going ships. Further, there was little hope of his soon gaining the upper hand at sea; for our seamen were better trained, and our ships were better armed than his, namely, with carronades, which were deadly at close quarters.[3] The *personnel* also increased rapidly—a fact which refutes the allegations of slackness made against Lord St Vincent by the Grenville group and unfortunately adopted by Pitt.[4] He and other critics demanded many more gunboats to meet the invasion flotilla, which Napoleon feverishly increased; but fortunately St Vincent and the seamen resisted this move. They relied on our blockading fleets to hold up all the vast apparatus of invasion, and, like the elder Pitt in 1759, set about the work of wearing down the enemy's colonies and commerce.

[1] Leyland, J., *Blockade of Brest* (N.R.S.), I, pp. x–xii, 20–3, 34–45, 85–93, 128–45.
[2] *Nap. Corresp.* Nos. 6763, 6783, 7309.   [3] *Ibid.* 8428, 8830, 8887, 8938.
[4] *Letters of Lord St Vincent* (N.R.S.), II, 50–9, App. IX. But see *Barham Papers*, III, 15–24, for Middleton's criticisms.

Meanwhile, protected by the nation's guardians off Brest and Toulon, the vital sap of the British Empire flowed with force unabated. Despite sporadic losses to French and Dutch privateers, its shipping increased; 20,853 vessels cleared from the United Kingdom and the Plantations in the year ending 30 September 1803, as against 20,186 in the previous year of peace. In this increase British India had but a small share; for, despite the triumphs and annexations of the Marquis Wellesley's viceroyalty, her trade did not expand; and there was truth in the gibe of his enemy, Philip Francis, "Our Indian prosperity is always in the future tense."[1] But affairs were different in the West Indies. In the year 1804 as many as 170 ships sailed from England to the newly conquered West Indies, and 165 arrived thence, the total arrivals from all the West Indies being 637 and the sailings 677.[2] Clearly, the West India trade benefited by the ending of a one-sided peace. Also the Budget of April 1804 was so satisfactory that few new imposts were needed.[3] By contrast with the finances of France, which depended partly on contributions levied forcibly from alien peoples,[4] those of the United Kingdom promised ultimate triumph in this trial of strength.

We may pause here to note one important difference between the French Wars of 1793–1814 and that of 1778–82. In the earlier contest the British navy was too weak to keep the enemy fleets in their own ports. Consequently, they carried hostilities to the coasts of our colonies, and the chief battles were fought near them. But after 1793, and again after 1803, the great issues (except at the Nile) were decided off the enemy's coasts; and our colonies were immune from all but raiding squadrons, which were soon hunted down. Accordingly British commerce, which had dwindled in the American War, so far increased during the later conflicts as to enable Great Britain greatly to extend her Empire and effectively to subsidise her allies when the anti-Napoleonic reaction set in.

For the present, however, Napoleon's preparations for invasion caused much alarm in some quarters; and Pitt, at last yielding to the panic, helped to eject Addington. The new Pitt Administration, formed on 18 May 1804 (at the time of Napoleon's assumption of the imperial title), promised to organise national defence more effectively, though the substitution of Lord Melville (formerly Henry Dundas) for the Earl of St Vincent caused some apprehension. Lord Harrowby also brought little strength to the Foreign Office; Lord Camden took the Secretaryship for War and the Colonies, in which he was replaced in July 1805 by Lord Castlereagh. As Fox and the Grenville group disappointed Pitt's hope of forming a comprehensive

[1] Hansard, ii, 989.   [2] C.J. (1805), App. 39.
[3] Hansard, ii, 350.
[4] Napoleon reckoned these as amounting to two milliards of francs (Kerry, Earl of, *The First Napoleon*, p. 312).

and truly national Administration, the new Cabinet encountered stout opposition in Parliament.

At first, Melville acted cautiously at the Admiralty. Though we had a clear superiority in effective sail-of-the-line as against the French and Dutch, yet in view of the probable breach with Spain and the terrible strain on Cornwallis's blockaders off Brest, he deemed it advisable to allot to him double the number requisite for the blockade at any one time.[1] Thus, the traditions of Drake, Anson and Kempenfelt as to the vital importance of a strong western fleet were well maintained. But, naturally, the squadrons needed for colonial efforts remained weak until the great issue was fought out in home waters. Equally cautious was Camden. Until the new plans for raising troops and improving the Volunteers had taken effect, he refused to send troops out of the country, even on the urgent requests of Nelson for the rescue of Sicily and Sardinia from the grasp of the French. On August 29, however, he assured him that, when our defence measures were complete and the autumn gales rendered an invasion of England improbable, troops would be sent to the Mediterranean to prevent the loss of those islands.[2] The same resolve was now being formed by the Tsar Alexander, who took a keen interest in Italian and Mediterranean affairs. Therefore, in the winter of 1804–5, the two Powers drew together in order to preserve the balance of power in Europe, and both prepared to send to the Mediterranean expeditions for the eventual liberation of Italy.[3]

Meanwhile Napoleon had indulged high hopes of crushing England, witness the typical outburst of 2 July 1804. Premising that he had twenty-one (or twenty-three) sail ready at Brest, ten at Toulon, three at Rochefort, and four or five at Ferrol, also in his northern harbours 1800 armed small craft able to carry across 120,000 troops and 10,000 horses, he anticipated a speedy and victorious invasion. Confident also that his posts guilefully spread through South Italy would lure Nelson to Egypt, he planned a concentration of all the available French forces on the Channel, whereupon "let us be masters of the strait for six hours, and we shall be masters of the world".[4]

But close upon this brassy fantasia there sounded forth the first thin pipings of a change of *motif*. The reasons are not far to seek. He knew that from Ostend to le Havre he had no more than 900 gun-vessels actually ready, with 254 more equally held fast from Cherbourg to Rochefort.[5] Perhaps he had now taken to heart the warnings of experienced seamen as to the chances besetting a naval concentration and the acuter perils of successfully convoying 900

[1] *Barham Papers*, iii, 40–48.   [2] Nicolas, vi, 229 n.
[3] *Despatches relating to the Third Coalition*, ed. Rose, J. H., pp. 14–101; *C.H.B.F.P.* i, 335–9.
[4] *Nap. Corresp.* Nos. 7832, 7840, 7841.
[5] Desbrière, E., *Projets…de débarquement…aux Îles britanniques*, iii, 560–9.

units across the Channel from the narrow and shallow harbours of Picardy. Or it may be that his close study of English newspapers revealed the prosperity of the island realm, nourished from the two Indies and unaffected by the colossal preparations for invasion. Or, again, he may have wished to dangle before us a western lure in addition to that which actually did tempt Nelson eastwards for three weeks early in 1805. In any case it was necessary to do something; for the Parisians were beginning to scoff at *Don Quixote de la Manche*, and the favourite actor, Brunet, had delighted them by cracking nuts on the stage and adding the ironical comment "*Je fais des péniches*".[1]

Accordingly, Napoleon's thoughts swing away from the centre towards the circumference of this world war. If his *péniches* cannot reach Kent, may not his ships ravage the British Indies? He therefore proposes to send the four sail-of-the-line now ready at Ferrol to Martinique and Guadeloupe with 1600 troops on board;[2] but those ships being held fast, he stings Admiral Ganteaume with the taunt that some of the twenty-one ships now ready at Brest must slip out and effect something, part making for Ireland, others recovering Surinam.[3] Thus, while the flotilla counts for less in his thoughts, the two Indies rise in the scale; for on September 12 he plans to seize St Helena, evidently as a prelude to a blow at British India. On the 29th colonial plans definitely take the first place. He then orders Admiral Decrés, Minister of Marine, to prepare three expeditions; the first, carrying 3500 troops, will reinforce the garrisons of Martinique and Guadeloupe, and, to increase their security, will seize Dominica and St Lucia: the second, of 4000 men, will recapture Surinam and the other Dutch West Indian colonies, besides landing succours in San Domingo: the third, of some 1500 men, will capture Goree and other African posts, and then St Helena, where "the English are in blind security": and, cruising from that island as base, it will devastate their East Indian commerce. "Thus the English, attacked simultaneously in Asia, Africa and America, and being long accustomed not to feel the war, will have the proofs of their weakness brought home to them by these successive blows at the focal points of their commerce."[4]

Nelson's brain is working along parallel lines. On 6 September 1804 he writes to Sir Alexander Ball, Governor of Malta, foretelling a French blow at the West Indies for the capture of St Lucia, Grenada, St Vincent, Antigua and St Kitt's, "and in that case England would be so clamorous for peace that we should humble ourselves".[5] Thus both our great enemy and our great champion believe that war finance depends on the two Indies. Their convictions throw a flood of light on the higher strategy of the conflict.

---

[1] F.O. 27/70.   [2] *Nap. Corresp.* 7842.
[3] *Ibid.* 7994.   [4] *Ibid.* 8014, 8060, 8065.
[5] Nicolas, VI, 193; also the new Nelson letters in *Naval Miscellany* (N.R.S.), III, 179, 182.

The importance of the West Indies was increased by the Anglo-Spanish rupture in December 1804,[1] which ranged the Spanish colonial empire openly on the side of Napoleon and gave him the prospect of conquering by sheer mass. That event also opened out the vista of the partition of Portugal and her colonies between the French and Spaniards—a bait which Napoleon dangled before the Court of Madrid. The rupture, however, had been discounted both by Nelson and Lord Melville.[2] Besides, Napoleon expected the impossible from the Spaniards, two-thirds of whose crews had never been to sea.[3] Hence long delays and friction with him.

On the other side Pitt and his colleagues acted with a boldness far removed from the caution of 1796; they resolved to take the offensive in the quarter where Nelson deemed the Napoleonic system to be most vulnerable, the Mediterranean.[4] In short, both he and they decided to defend Great Britain and her Empire by attacking the enemy in a vital point. For a vigorous Mediterranean policy much could be urged. It was clear that in an offensive north of Naples a British fleet based on Malta would give efficient help, especially if a large Russian force from Corfu assisted. Acting together, the two Powers would attack Napoleon in a quarter where he was peculiarly susceptible; they would save Sardinia and Sicily from seizure, and thereby secure Malta as well as cover the Levant. Moreover, as the typical French opening was with the Toulon fleet, to corner it virtually covered both Great Britain and her East and West Indies. Accordingly, the Pitt Cabinet prepared (28 March 1805) to send to Malta an expedition of some 5000 men under Lieutenant-General Sir James Craig. His instructions warned him that the protection of Sicily from the French was his principal object.[5] During the long discussions as to the joint effort in South Italy, the Tsar repeatedly sought to induce us to give up Malta to him. Here he met with a rebuff; for Pitt (though consenting for a time to a temporary Russian occupation of Malta, if Britain could acquire Minorca) finally refused to win the Tsar's help by sacrificing to him the key of the Mediterranean.[6]

By a strange coincidence Craig's force nearly met Villeneuve's fleet off the south-west of Spain; for while England and Russia prepared a campaign in South Italy, Napoleon planned with the Toulon and Cadiz fleets to ravage the British West Indies and effect there a great concentration, which would tempt the British fleets thither, while his force, gaining in efficiency by the voyage, would

---

[1] See *C.H.B.F.P.* I, 334.
[2] Nicolas, VI, 248, 270, 314; *Barham Papers*, III, 42.
[3] Galiano, A., *Combate de Trafalgar*, I, 350; Fugier, A., *Nap. et l'Espagne*, I, ch. IV.
[4] Nicolas, VI, 105, 107.
[5] Bunbury, Sir H., *The Great War with France* (edit. 1854), pp. 181–6; Corbett, Sir J., *Campaign of Trafalgar*, ch. III.
[6] Rose, *Pitt*, II, 527, also *Third Coalition*, pp. 150–62, 173, 192.

secretly return to the Channel and convoy the flotilla to the coast of England.

Such, in brief, was his famous plan of 2 March 1805. It is often described in terms which imply that the West Indian move was merely a lure to tempt Nelson far away. But this is to misunderstand Napoleon's policy, in which the West Indies had by degrees attained a leading place. Thus, in December 1804, he ordered Admirals Villeneuve and Missiessy with the Toulon and Rochefort fleets to slip out and make for the West Indies, there to recapture Trinidad, St Lucia and the Dutch posts in Guiana, besides seizing Dominica and succouring a small French garrison still holding out in San Domingo. In this comprehensive programme Dominica held first place,[1] as menacing both Martinique and Guadeloupe. Villeneuve put out, only to be driven back for a time by a gale. Missiessy was more fortunate. After making Martinique he struck at Dominica, but with no lasting effect; for the British commander, General Prevost, withdrew his small force from the capital, Roseau, to Fort Rupert in the interior and held out successfully, so that Missiessy withdrew after exacting £7500 from Roseau. He repeated this device at St Christopher, Nevis and Montserrat, besides burning or capturing in all thirty-nine merchantmen (February–March 1805).[2] Hearing, however, of the mishap to Villeneuve's fleet, he made for Rochefort, which he reached without sighting a single British warship. Meanwhile, as has already appeared, Napoleon had decided to concentrate in the West Indies the fleets of Brest, Ferrol, Toulon and Cadiz, conveying some 4700 troops for action against the British colonies. Thereafter they were to return with a united force of more than forty sail to the English Channel for the great stroke on which hung the destinies of the world.[3]

On April 12 this already difficult scheme assumed a bewildering complexity. Hitherto he had ordered merely that his fleets long held in port should concentrate in the West Indies and speedily return thence to the English Channel; but on that day he read in the English newspapers of the alarm caused by Missiessy's raid. At once he resolved to make "those masters of the world on the cheap" rue their economies. His leading aim now was to capture the great convoy of sugar ships that usually left the Antigua rendezvous at the end of May. By this stroke he would ruin the West Indies, thus compelling England to send out troops and denude her own coasts. He therefore ordered the despatch of Rear-Admiral Magon with two sail to Villeneuve (then probably at Martinique), with new orders, that, as the Brest fleet had been delayed, he (Villeneuve)

---

[1] *Nap. Corresp.* 8206, 8231.
[2] C.O. 71/38, Prevost to Camden, 5 March 1805; Chevalier, *Histoire*, III, 131, 147; *Lloyd's Marine List* (1805); Fortescue, *British Army*, V, ch. VIII.
[3] *Nap. Corresp.* 8380–3.

must, in the time of waiting, do as much harm as possible to the British West Indies.[1]

Thus commerce destruction now stands first in the Emperor's thoughts. During the imperial progress from Lyons into Italy, his eager imagination pictures the West Indies at his mercy. Nelson having been lured off to Egypt, the 10,000 French troops now at or nearing Martinique may capture St Vincent, Antigua, Grenada— "And why should we not take Barbados?" Trinidad may be recovered, also Tobago, "for it is French". By the 29th he insists that the Brest fleet must set sail to reinforce Villeneuve and raise his conquering armada to fifty-six sail. As for the East Indies, 6000 French troops, setting out thither in September, will ruin the English Company.[2] In fact he pictures England as impaled on the horns of a dilemma. Either she will hold back her troops for defence against the Boulogne flotilla, in which case she will lose her colonies and be ruined; or, in alarm for her trade, she will send out large forces and be struck to the heart.

In point of fact, he was impaling Villeneuve and Gravina on a dilemma. These later commands, arriving in the unhealthy season, gave them work enough for a year, yet still bade them await Ganteaume's fleet at Martinique for the great issue in the English Channel. But now Nelson set them free. Early in June they heard the alarming news that that indefatigable pursuer had reached Barbados. It was true; for, as has been seen, he had already resolved to save the British West Indies if Villeneuve sailed thither. "I flew to the West Indies without any orders", he wrote, "but I think the Ministry cannot be displeased."[3] There he soon heard news portending the enemy's return to Europe. It was correct. Villeneuve and Gravina had judged rightly that this was their only alternative. In their three weeks' stay they had merely recaptured the Diamond Rock[4] and seized the valuable homeward convoy from Antigua.[5]

Nelson's dash to save the West Indies, far from displeasing the Admiralty, conformed to its policy of placing trade protection on a level with coast protection.[6] Very skilfully it contrived to effect both. For, on hearing news of the turn homewards of the combined fleet, Barham and Pitt (Pitt is known to have influenced this plan[7]) resolved to strengthen Cornwallis off Brest, so as to enable him, at need, to detach ships to Calder's force off Ferrol and there intercept Villeneuve and Gravina. Thus, on July 22, Calder was able to deal a sharp blow to the enemy, who three weeks later retreated to Cadiz,

---

[1] *Nap. Corresp.* 8574-82.
[2] *Ibid.* 8617-19, 8642, 8654, 8659, 8685 (23 April-4 May 1805).
[3] Nicolas, VI, 450.   [4] *Naval Chronicle*, XII, 201, 205.
[5] Desbrière, V, 681; Corbett, *Campaign of Trafalgar*, pp. 165-7.
[6] *Barham Papers*, III, 254. For Sir Home Popham's plan of using Gen. Miranda to revolutionise South America, see *Amer. Hist. Rev.*, April 1901.
[7] Rose, *Pitt*, II, 532.

thereby ruining whatever chances of invading England survived the Emperor's Protean strategy. Clearly, the bifurcating plan of campaign had hopelessly overburdened that heterogeneous, slow and now fever-stricken fleet (only two of the original Spanish units fought at Trafalgar[1]); and, as Napoleon was fully aware of its defects in *matériel*,[2] it is passing strange that this master of military home-thrusts should, in the more complex sphere of naval warfare, have mixed up a West Indian campaign with a great naval concentration for the domination of the English Channel. Only by superior skill could an ill-matched Franco-Spanish fleet leave Nelson and Cornwallis groping for them far away and thereby secure that domination "during some days".[3] But in truth, while the Emperor depreciated his admirals, he despised ours and their chief at Whitehall. "These much vaunted English...know nothing." "The English are in a regular muddle with orders and counter-orders." "Nothing more short-sighted than the English Government, occupied with internal cavilling and swayed by every rumour." Finally—"the Indies are ours when we want to take them".[4] Far different was the truth. The French attacks had harmed only Dominica and the Antigua convoy, while the valuable East Indian convoy reached port safely on September 5.[5]

After the Grand Army files away from Boulogne Rhinewards late in August, the story swings back to the struggle for the control of the two routes to India. Supremacy in the Mediterranean (*but principal de ma politique*) again becomes for Napoleon the dominant issue. At first he believes Craig's expedition to be for the Cape of Good Hope, and expresses satisfaction on hearing that it is in the Mediterranean; for England and Russia will never work together, least of all there.[6] His actions belie his words. For all his brilliant military successes at and near Ulm, his thoughts recur anxiously towards Sicily, and he issues imperative orders for the combined fleet to put out from Cadiz, join the Spanish ships at Carthagena and make for Naples, overwhelming the Anglo-Russian forces then reported to be there.[7]

This "powerful diversion" in the Mediterranean led to Trafalgar. Contrary to popular belief, Nelson's crowning victory was fought, not to save England from invasion, but to assure her position in the Mediterranean. Trafalgar saved Sicily from a French invasion; for when, after the disaster of Austerlitz, the new monarchical coalition collapsed and French troops began to march southwards on Naples, Craig prudently withdrew his troops from the mainland to Messina, "the place which had been originally our main object" (January

[1] Fugier, I, 390. [2] *Nap. Corresp.* 8309, 8469.
[3] *Ibid.* 8700. [4] *Ibid.* 8713, 8813, 8817, 8938.
[5] *Naval Chronicle*, xv, 337–9. [6] *Nap. Corresp.* 8794, 8807, 8813, 8817.
[7] *Ibid.* 9210. See Desbrière, *Trafalgar*, pp. 115–29, 227, for censures of this plan.

1806).[1] Thus, under cover of our fleet, began the British occupation of Sicily, destined to last for some eight years, and to form, with Malta, *une barrière infranchissable* against Napoleon's far-flung eastern designs. "Peace or war, you shall have Naples and Sicily", he writes in August 1806 to King Joseph, now King of Naples.[2] In truth, that resolve of his thwarted the attempt at a negotiation for peace in the summer of 1806, when Fox refused to sacrifice Sicily.

While Nelson's last and greatest triumph safeguarded the overland route to India, another smaller effort was about to secure the sea-route. As has been seen, Pitt deeply regretted the retrocession of the Cape of Good Hope to the Dutch; and their subsequent subjection to Napoleon intensified that feeling. Melville's opinion on the importance of the Cape has already appeared; and probably, even before his resignation of the Admiralty and the advent of Barham to office (April 1805), its recovery was discussed.[3] However, the defence of England and the West Indies thereupon occupied all thoughts until about 20 July 1805, when the question of the Cape again came up.[4]

The date is curious; for on or about the 9th the Admiralty heard that the Franco-Spanish fleet was on its way back from the West Indies to Europe; and there was the likelihood of the Cape expedition, cumbered with transports, meeting it. Nevertheless, late in July, owing to fears that the French were about to occupy the Cape, the Cabinet issued secret preparatory orders to Commodore Sir Home Popham and to Major-General Sir David Baird, commanding the troops then held in readiness at Cork. The fog of war still hung thick; for not until the end of July did news arrive of Calder's far from decisive success off Finisterre over the combined fleet, and for a few days its movements were utterly unknown. Therefore the fate of England still hung in the balance; and on August 3 Barham growled fiercely to Pitt as to his inability to keep up to due strength even Cornwallis's pivotal fleet off Brest, to watch the now active Dutch at the Texel, and to convoy our Russian allies then expected in the Mediterranean. "Circumstanced as we are", wrote the aged First Lord, "we must in the end meet with disgrace upon disgrace."[5] Nevertheless, as in April 1798, Pitt forced the hand of the Admiralty, and the Cape plan went forward.

Much could be said for his boldness. If the war was fast becoming one against colonies and commerce, Napoleon was certain to occupy the Cape, whereupon our East Indian trade must suffer severely from French and Dutch cruisers using it as a base of operations. Also

[1] Bunbury, *The Great War with France*, p. 212.
[2] *Nap. Corresp.* 10448, 10657; *C.H.B.F.P.* I, 348–55.   [3] Rose, *Pitt*, II, 532, n.
[4] *Castlereagh Corresp.* VI, 128–34; *Naval Miscellany* (N.R.S.), III, 197, 205.
[5] *Barham Papers*, III, 95; *Naval Miscellany*, III, 196–8, 205–16.

affairs in India portended the growth of a hostile confederacy,[1] which demanded precautionary measures. Further, on general grounds, it was well to recover our power of striking at hostile colonies of which Napoleon sought to deprive us by renewed threats aimed at London.

Indeed, as the West Indies had been saved by Nelson, the East now became the vital issue. And if, while guarding our own shores, we could secure the sea-route to the East by capturing the Cape, the scales of war would incline in our favour. Probably also Barham heard some reassuring news as to the naval situation; for on August 18 he wrote to Pitt: "I think this to be the proper time for the [Cape] expedition and India ships to sail from Cork. The sea is now open."[2] He therefore proposed to send a squadron of two-deckers to watch Ferrol, and behind that screen the Cape force would be in no great danger. In point of fact, the combined fleet was refitting in Cadiz when, on September 1, Baird with 4416 officers and men lately destined for the West Indies set sail from Cork for the East Indies, with instructions to take Cape Town on the way. Recent information showed that post to be held by 1500 troops of doubtful quality, while their warships could not move for lack of naval stores, and the inhabitants were well disposed to us.[3] Convoyed only by H.M.S. *Diadem* (64), Popham's scratch fleet rendezvoused at Madeira, where it met two more sail-of-the-line and three frigates. The crowd of fifty one ill-found, slow-sailing transports still had the good luck not to sight a single hostile ship, and, with the loss of only one unit, which foundered, the force hove in sight of Table Mountain (2 January 1806). From Cape Town no enemy craft disturbed their plans. Owing to the high surf on the open part of the coast, Popham finally decided to force a landing in Losperd's Bay, a little north of Table Bay. Even there the operation cost the lives of thirty-six men drowned, while only one was killed and four wounded. Advancing towards Cape Town in exhausting heat, Baird's men with little loss beat back General Janssens' force at Blauberg. Thereupon on January 10 Cape Town surrendered, and a week later Janssens' force and a burgher commando accepted Baird's terms.[4] They were more stringent than those of 1796, the right of imposing taxes being now retained, while all the French had to leave the Cape. But, as in the case of Nova Scotia in 1713 and Canada in 1759, private property was to be respected, liberty of public worship being also guaranteed.[5]

The oft-repeated statement that Trafalgar rendered possible the conquest of the Cape is incorrect; for Baird's force left Cork fifty days before that battle was fought. The links in the chain of causation were as follows. Napoleon's blow at the British West Indies, with a demonstration at the East Indies superadded, induced the Pitt

[1] *Castlereagh Corresp.* VI, 142–7.
[2] *Barham Papers*, III, 97.   [3] *Naval Miscellany*, III, 217–22.
[4] *Ibid.* III, 240–48; *Cape Records*, V, 222–60; *Naval Chronicle*, XV, 80.
[5] Theal, G. McC., *Records of the Cape Colony*, V, 261–5, 285.

Cabinet to prepare if possible to send from Cork a large force to the West Indies. Nelson's prompt pursuit of Villeneuve saved those colonies, and Calder's action of July 22 rendered it unlikely that the combined fleet would now invade the Channel. By August 18 Barham, trusting to its temporary inaction and his own precautionary measures, agreed that Baird's force might safely be diverted to the Cape; and it was half-way there before Nelson struck his last blow, which, when followed by that of Strachan at the relics of the enemy's fleet, precluded all likelihood of a great Franco-Spanish offensive. Trafalgar, then, for the present rendered impossible a naval counter-stroke against either the Cape of Good Hope or Sicily.

It is now clear that the conquest of the Cape of Good Hope and the securing of Sicily from Napoleon's grasp were due directly to the bold and far-seeing statesmanship of Pitt. As has been shown, he had consistently worked for the strengthening of the navy, and both in 1798 and 1805 was chiefly instrumental in inaugurating a vigorous Mediterranean policy.[1] He did not live on to see his reward. Just thirteen days before his death the Union flag was hoisted at Cape Town, and shortly afterwards the independence of Sicily was assured. The one event safeguarded the sea-route, the other the overland route to the East. In world history these incidents (almost unnoticed at the time) count for more even than Austerlitz and the collapse of the timorous old Europe which his example failed to energise and save. The tragedy of his career is that he passed away when total eclipse darkened all neighbouring lands, though, far away, the dawn of a new and stronger British Empire was clearly heralded. Could he have lived on for another two months he would have heard that both routes to the East Indies were secure and the West Indies placed beyond reach of molestation by Duckworth's crushing victory over a French raiding squadron off San Domingo.[2] That brilliant success (6 February 1806) brought the losses of the hostile navies within six months up to the total of thirty one sail-of-the-line, five frigates and five corvettes[3]—achievements never surpassed in the days of Chatham. Above all, the important posts in world strategy, muddled away at Amiens, had been recovered. And now they were to be held; for the great Peace Minister, at last a great War Minister, had, by his high-souled efforts, roused such a spirit in these islands that no compromise on these vital issues was thenceforth possible.

The sporadic and generally unsuccessful colonial efforts of Pitt's successors in the Grenville and Portland Administrations must be very briefly dismissed. The expedition against Buenos Aires originated in the desire of Commodore Popham to do something more profitable and spectacular than wait long at Cape Town. Disregarding the

[1] Rose, *Pitt*, I, 210–11, 377, 567; II, 124, 522, 527, 531–3.
[2] *Barham Papers*, III, 376–80; James, *Naval History*, IV, 98–103; Chevalier, *Histoire*, III, 250–5.   [3] *Barham Papers*, III, 274.

instructions which bade him proceed with his squadron to India,[1] he made a dash at Buenos Aires, which ended in a sharp reverse (July 1806). Before that finale was known in London Grenville wrote (22 September 1806) that Popham and his "agents" had aroused such hopes (obviously in mercantile circles) that the retrocession of Buenos Aires could not be thought of unless we gained "more for it in the way of security in Europe than I know how to shape or expect"; and, again seven days later, "rather than see all Spanish America fall into our hands, as it must now do in twelve months more of war, France would willingly give up Naples".[2] Wilder fancies never fogged the cautious brain of Grenville. He and Fox still clung to hopes of a peace which Napoleon had of late skilfully dangled before them; but Fox, when nearing his end, said that the Emperor was "playing a false game", and virtually closed the negotiations.[3] Nevertheless, Grenville and Windham, continuing the quest after security in Europe by a hunt after markets or bargaining assets in South America, despatched large reinforcements to La Plata, which enterprise, under that incompetent leader, General Whitelocke, ended in a disgraceful failure and our entire withdrawal.[4] Curiously enough, Napoleon's "Spanish blunder" of 1808 (soon to be noted) so enraged the Spaniards against him as to lead to an Anglo-Spanish alliance and, thereafter, to the voluntary opening of the very colonies into which we had tried clumsily to force a way. The new alliance (essentially between the two peoples) held good, even in that age of crumbling compacts, and it was proof against Napoleon's peace offers to us in 1810 on condition of throwing over the Spaniards.

It is time now to set forth and explain the vital issues in the Napoleonic War in its second and more definitely economic stage, 1806–12. At bottom the question was whether Britain's colonial conquests or Napoleon's continental conquests would weigh down the scale. Trafalgar and Austerlitz had decided the two rival supremacies; and, late in 1805, a British jurist could confidently assert that "not a single merchant ship under a flag inimical to Great Britain now crosses the Atlantic Ocean".[5] But on land all the signs favoured Napoleon. He controlled well-nigh all the coast from Hamburg to Leghorn; the sovereigns of Russia, Austria and Prussia bowed before him; the Spaniards, Dutch, West Germans and Italians were his vassals, Ferdinand, the nominal King of Naples, clinging on merely to Sicily. Was it, then, possible that the Sea Power, though supreme

[1] *Naval Miscellany*, III, 219–22, 238; *Naval Chronicle*, XIX, 30 ff.
[2] *Dropmore Papers*, VIII, 352. For our backing of Miranda's revolutionary efforts at Caracas, see Bagot, J., *George Canning and his Friends*, I, 266–8.
[3] Lord Holland, *Memoirs of the Whig Party*, II, 340; *C.H.B.F.P.* I, 352–55; Butterfield, H., *The Peace Tactics of Napoleon*, pp. 37–40.
[4] Fortescue, *British Army*, V, 12.
[5] Stephen, J., *Frauds of the Neutral Flags* (ed. Piggott, F. T., 1917), p. 59.

on the Oceans, the Mediterranean, in the two Indies, at the Cape and in West Africa, could hold out against these vast and compact resources? In the autumn of 1806, when Prussia fell before the conqueror, his power was overwhelming, and even the Titanic claim of his Berlin Decree (November 1806) that the British Isles were thenceforth in a state of blockade and isolation, seemed warranted by that all-victorious career. The retorts of the British Government in successive Orders-in-Council aroused more criticism than confidence,[1] and the political horizon was blackened by Napoleon's crowning triumph, the Treaty of Tilsit (July 1807), when Russia and Prussia joined his Continental System. They were soon to be followed by Denmark, in 1808 by Austria and in 1810 by Sweden.[2] As the only British acquisitions of the year 1807 were Curaçao, Heligoland and some of the Danish West Indies, the outlook overseas appeared of the gloomiest. Could the new and undeveloped lands acquired by the British navy make good the loss of direct access to the markets of Europe? Philippe le Bel, Philip II of Spain and Louis XIV in turn had vaguely planned the commercial isolation of England. After Tilsit Napoleon seemed about to accomplish it. He could then say to the Russian envoy: "Your master ought to command all on one side of the River Vistula, I all the other",[3] and he declared that British ships, "laden with useless riches...seek in vain a port from the Sound to the Hellespont".[4]

Yet in these years of his ever-increasing domination over Europe the Sea Power slowly but surely extended its sway. In 1808 Marie-galante and Désirade fell to the Union Jack; in 1809 Senegal, Martinique and Cayenne; in 1810 Guadeloupe, St Martin, Île de France [Mauritius], Île de Bourbon, the Seychelles, Amboyna and Banda.[5] Undoubtedly, the chief motive for this "mopping-up" process was to secure a monopoly of tropical products as a set-off to Napoleon's attempted exclusion of all British produce from the Continent. "If you will not allow it to go in, we will see to it that no other produce shall." Such in effect was the naval retort, increasingly cogent with every colonial conquest, and, incidentally, stirring up less odium than his domination of a dozen alien nations. For, while the Emperor sought to crown his System by the armed coercion of Russia, the islanders had already completed theirs by the occupation of Java (September 1811)—an event probably expedited by the despatch to the East of five French frigates which could be intended only for Batavia.[6]

The fundamental issue now was: Would the continental block, or

---

[1] Baring, A., *Inquiry into the Causes...of the Orders in Council.*
[2] For details, see *C.M.H.* vol. IX, ch. XIII; Heckscher, E. F., *The Continental System*, pt. II.
[3] Tatischeff, *Alexandre et Napoléon*, p. 140.
[4] *Exposé de la Situation de l'Empire* (24 Aug. 1807) in *Nap. Corresp.* 13063.
[5] For details of these captures, see James, *Naval History*, IV, 387; V, 69, 74, 190, 203–5.
[6] *Ibid.* V, 291–310.

the far-flung colonial chain, from Jamaica to Java, prove to be the more effective economic weapon? In sheer mass the former seemed overwhelming; but in reality it never was solid. Throughout northern Europe (except Denmark) merchants sought to keep up secret trade relations with England; and in 1808 when he strove to subject Spaniards and Portuguese entirely to his will, they defied him and espoused her cause, with the result that some of their ports and nearly all their colonies were thrown open to her trade.[1] Turkey also became neutral and opened back doors (notably Salonica) into Central Europe for British and colonial produce, the need for which became more and more acutely felt.[2] Indeed, there was an inextinguishable European demand for colonial produce, of which, by the year 1808, we had virtually complete control. Early in 1808, Castlereagh complained of the glut of that produce in our markets;[3] and, later, Liverpool merchants stated that their stocks of West Indian sugar were almost unsaleable.[4]

Accordingly, there ensued a long and intensely interesting struggle between Napoleon's resolve to exclude from the Continent the colonial produce with which our warehouses were bursting, and the resolve of the continental peoples to obtain it even at enhanced prices. True, some sub-tropical products could be grown in South France or Italy, but their transport by land to North Germany, Prussia and Russia was impracticable. Therefore these northern lands persisted in trading with British merchants, who alone could supply cheaply and in large quantities the tropical products on which all civilised peoples now depended, especially sugar and coffee, together with most of the silk, raw cotton (cotton-wool) and dyes needed for textile manufactures

This supremacy of British commerce was confirmed, first, by the extraordinary development of the textile industries in these islands,[5] secondly, by the Embargo and Non-Intercourse Acts of the United States (1808–9) which aimed at cutting off all intercourse with Europe. Though largely evaded, especially by enterprising New Englanders, these measures tended for a time to stimulate the British carrying trade to European lands, as well as the growth of cotton in the West and East Indies. Thus, in the very years when Napoleon sought to strangle British trade with Europe, it benefited by the comparative absence of competition at sea (which partly offset the war risks), and by the carriage of produce which continental peoples were eager to obtain; for they had little good machinery, few who could work it, scanty supplies of raw materials, and next to none of genuine coffee or cane-sugar. Tea the continentals could dispense

[1] For his plans for Spanish America, see *Nap. Corresp.* 13897, 13952, 13965, 13998; Melvin, F. E., *Napoleon's Navigation System*, pp. 54, 219, 269; Heckscher, pp. 176–8.
[2] For details, see Rose, J. H., *Man and the Sea*, App.
[3] C.O. 138/43, Castlereagh to Duke of Manchester (in Jamaica), 19 Jan. 1808.
[4] B.T. 3/11.   [5] *Vide infra*, ch. VI.

with, but they depended on British merchants for the most delightful of drinks: for coffee had become one of their necessary comforts; and when Napoleon's decrees banned the only means of obtaining it, frantic efforts were made to manufacture substitutes out of chicory, dried carrots, acorns and sunflower seeds. The Danes, who sought honestly to observe his decrees, finally had seventeen factories at work on this pathetic quest,[1] while they and the more restive and equally tobacco-loving Germans sought what solace was to be had from a certain odorous mixture of the leaves of gooseberries, chestnuts and cabbages.

But the success of Napoleon's vast fiscal gamble depended not only on coffee but on sugar, the consumption of which had increased greatly throughout Europe.[2] The imports into Great Britain had risen from 1,422,024 cwt. in 1791 to 2,331,398 cwt. in 1801–6, about half being normally re-exported to the Continent.[3] Indeed, the sugar habit had spread to such an extent that Napoleon now made special efforts to prop up his system at this its weakest point. Accordingly, he and his Minister Chaptal tried to galvanise both the infant beet-sugar industry of Achard and the still-born process of extracting sugar from grapes. As little sweetness came from the former, and only a viscous forbidding fluid from the latter, the demands for cane-sugar were clamant, though in 1812 it cost nine times as much in Paris as in London.[4]

Burdensome in all the Napoleonic States, the System pressed with special severity on the Dutch ports and those of northern Europe. In 1807–8 a citizen of Hamburg wrote of that city: "There is no longer any trade as it existed formerly", and "more than 300 vessels are laid up."[5] What wonder also that John Quincy Adams, who in 1809 went as American ambassador to Russia, found that people very hostile to Napoleon, while the Minister, Romanzoff, dubbed the French Emperor "a giddy-head in regard to commerce". In August–September 1810, Adams warned the French ambassador that the Continental System was "instead of impairing her [England's] commerce, securing to her that of the whole world, and was pouring into her lap the means of continuing the war". "You will lay the world under the most grievous contributions for her benefit and advantage." Such was the verdict of a bitter Anglophobe.[6]

In the year 1810, Napoleon completed his System by the annexation of Holland and the north-west coast of Germany. He also ordered the confiscation and burning of all British goods found in his Empire and dependent States; he sought to compel Russia to exclude British and suspect neutral shipping, and forced Sweden to

[1] Heckscher, p. 291.   [2] Edwards, *West Indies*, vol. v, App. 19.
[3] *Ibid*. Also *vide infra*, ch. XIII.
[4] Heckscher, pp. 292–4; Chaptal, *Souvenirs*, pp. 117–19.
[5] Perthes, F., *Memoirs*, I, 148, 162.
   Diary of John Quincy Adams, pp. 68, 72, 75.

declare war on the United Kingdom. The commercial struggle therefore entered on an acute phase which produced severe financial tension throughout the British Empire; and the fall in her exchange led Napoleon to believe that a few more turns of the fiscal screw would ensure a collapse. Yet, as has been seen, this time of strain witnessed the reduction of the remaining enemy possessions overseas, including Java in September 1811. Accordingly, the Sea Power kept pace with the Land Power in the race for supremacy; and the lists of British exports to the Continent show that, after declining from 1806 to 1809, they rallied in 1810, and were still very high even in the year 1811. It remains to account for this surprising phenomenon.

Britain's warfare (superficially unimpressive but lethally elusive) must have failed but for the great productivity of her West Indies. In truth, the part played by the East and the West Indies in this world drama is curiously unlike that pictured by the vivid imagination of Napoleon, and belied his contention that the chief source of power and wealth lay in the Orient. For, now that spices had been virtually replaced by West Indian sugar, the East Indies supplied but a small part of the products most desired by the continental peoples. The returns of the "official" values of the imports of our East India Company in this period are fragmentary; but the following are of interest:[1]

	1809 £ sterling	1810 £ sterling
Tea	3,567,812	2,164,396
Indigo	717,205	293,751
Cotton-wool	145,741	318,707
Raw silk	182,593	93,105
Spices	137,085	41,902
Sugar	81,252	25,289
Coffee	2,961	19,911

These figures are below the "declared" or real values; but though they are merely relative, yet they show the priority of tea, indigo and raw cotton, and the small imports of spices, East Indian sugar and coffee.[2] As continental peoples took little tea, the East Indies count for little in the commercial war with Napoleon. The reasons for their comparative backwardness are probably as follows. The regulations of the British East India Company cramped the natural developments of commerce; and in the dependency outside its administration, namely Ceylon, war with the Kandyans checked the hoped-for progress. Even in the more settled parts cultivation of all kinds was hindered by the irksome quasi-feudal restraints exercised by the "modeliars": "There is the strongest reason", wrote the Governor,

[1] *C.J.* (1810–11), App. A2.
[2] For the opposition of our West Indian interest to importation of East Indian sugar, see Ragatz, L. J., *The Fall of the Planter Class in the British Caribbean*, pp. 210 *seqq.*

"to believe that the present uncivilised state of this island...is much owing to the continuance of their authority, subversive of every amelioration and improvement, and acting in the strongest sense of that term distinctly as an *imperium in imperio*. I am sorry to say it appears that, since we got possession of this island, that power has been daily increasing." He added that his predecessor, North, had extended their authority over all the Cingalese parts of the island; and he advised its curtailment by all possible means, as the Dutch had wisely sought to effect.[1]

Friction also arose in Mauritius soon after its conquest owing to the enforcement of the new British law abolishing the slave trade. On this vital issue the people of St Louis offered armed opposition to the British authorities (November 1811); and in February 1812 Lieutenant-Governor R. T. Farquhar reported their strenuous opposition to his veto on the importation of slaves from Madagascar and Africa, on the ground that this new order of things "strikes at the root of their most valuable individual interests".[2] His reports show that the constant friction and ill-will diminished the productivity both of Mauritius and Île de Bourbon. True, these islands had now ceased to be the bases of French cruisers, which in 1807–9 had captured fourteen East Indiamen with cargoes of great value,[3] but, even after the capture of the two islands, our imports of East Indian sugar fell from 26,200 cwt. in 1810 to 20,405 cwt. in 1812, a decline which is inexplicable, especially when compared with the import of 125,155 cwt. in 1805, a year of greater war risks.

On the other hand all available statistics show the paramount importance of the West Indies during the Napoleonic War. Though our imports and re-exports of their sugar varied with the fluctuations of that mighty struggle, yet the continental demand for their produce was never seriously lessened even by the severest of Napoleon's exclusive measures. How could it be when French and German buyers were ready to pay from 5s. to 6s. a pound for cane-sugar, which sold for 4d. in Trinidad; also 7s. or more for coffee or raw cotton, which fetched 6d. or 16d. the pound respectively in the West Indies?[4] In such cases man's attempt to hinder the inflow from lands of superabundant plenty to lands of haggard scarcity is as vain as to check the winds; and, for all the efforts of the great Emperor, his coastal defences always leaked. What could his 20,000 *douaniers* avail against the persistent ingenuity of millions of would-be consumers and swarms of abetting smugglers?[5] It is therefore not surprising to find immense imports of sugar into Great Britain even in

[1] C.O. 59/27 Ceylon; Miscellaneous. Report of Lieut.-Governor General T. Maitland, 31 Jan. 1807. See, too, Turner, L. J. B., *Maritime Provinces of Ceylon*, pp. 202–9.
[2] C.O. 167/9.
[3] *C.J.* (1810), p. 713; cf. Prentout, H., pp. 496–509.
[4] Tooke, T., I, 308–11; C.O. 295/26—prices of Jan. 1811 in Trinidad, in *C.J.* (1811).
[5] Mollien, F. N. comte, *Mémoires*, III, 290.

the bad years 1812 and 1813. In each of these years respectively the following totals in cwt. arrived from the several places of origin:[1]

	1812	1813		1812	1813
East Indies	72,607	48,725	Barbados	156,196	81,586
Jamaica	1,455,954	1,340,825	St Christopher	150,705	125,262
St Croix	353,285	282,675	Tobago	122,778	97,451
Demerara	244,817	244,234	Martinique	80,302	134,585
Grenada	210,516	186,539	St Lucia	55,102	90,451
St Vincent	195,233	195,458	Guadeloupe	20,002	75,148
Antigua	187,961	153,106	Other countries	17,888	68,477
Trinidad	118,411	165,876			

These statistics challenge attention on several counts. First, they show that out of the total imports of sugar for 1812 (which are not the grand total; for those of Dominica and a few other islands do not figure in it) only one part in 192 came from non-British lands. Brazil, Cuba and other areas now very important then counted for next to nothing in our market; and, as we often compelled neutrals to unload in our ports, neutral competition for the time scarcely existed. Secondly, these great imports of sugar and other tropical produce were largely for re-export[2] through channels which will be noticed presently. Thirdly, the superior productivity of our older West Indian islands is very remarkable. In spite of all the talk about the exhaustion of their soil, Jamaica and the older Leeward possessions far surpassed the recent acquisitions, excepting Demerara whose fertility was remarkable.[3] Though Jamaican planters bitterly declared that the stoppage of the import of slaves since 1807 threatened them with ruin, yet, on the other hand, the cessation of all danger from the Maroons, as also from the Caribs in St Vincent, and from invasion in all the islands, begat a sense of security long unknown; and the high war prices seem everywhere to have stimulated production, the exports from St Croix being phenomenal in 1812. Further, anarchic Hayti was no longer a competitor; and British cruisers had so long cut off the French islands, especially Martinique and Guadeloupe, from trade with France that probably their plantations had suffered—a fact which may explain their low productivity in 1812 and partial recovery in 1813.[4] Similar remarks apply to St Lucia, while local storms probably account for the decline in Barbados and Tobago in 1813, and the ruin of Dominica in both years.

There remains the problem of Trinidad. As appeared in the previous chapter, the first Governor, General Sir Thomas Picton, foretold its speedy and well-sustained prosperity. But the island

---

[1] *C.J.* (1813–14), App. 10.
[2] See for details Edwards, *West Indies*, v, App. 20, 22.
[3] See the returns in C.O. 111/18; also Ragatz, p. 214.
[4] Webster, C. K., *British Diplomacy* (1813–15), p. 184.

seems to have suffered severely from the Embargo Act of the United States (1808), the local revenue declining seriously in 1809.[1] The production of sugar was also disappointing, being in 1812 only one-twelfth that of Jamaica. Petitions from the sufferers throw some light on the local difficulties. The London merchants trading with Trinidad declared (13 February 1812) that the trade and credit of that island had been constantly declining, owing to the operation of foreign laws, the inefficient and often unintelligible judicial system which favoured fraudulent debtors, and heavy import duties which exasperated honest traders and were the joy of smugglers. By way of cure the petitioners urged the introduction of legislative powers, fair taxes, English laws and legal procedure. In July 1812 John Sanderson of Trinidad presented a petition of its merchants as to "the forlorn situation of that long-suffering colony". Indeed, all the evidence available shows that something was radically wrong; and it would appear that the fundamental cause was a pedantic and pro-tracted clinging to Spanish laws and customs. English alone was used in its law courts in and after 1813, when exports largely in-creased.[2]

The effect of British cottons in undermining Napoleon's Conti-nental System was more important than that of sugar. But, as less raw cotton came from our colonies than from the United States[3] (whence by various devices it filtered through even in 1812–14), its influence need not be discussed here. The total imports, however, were larger than ever in 1810–11, and the value of our cottons then exported exceeded by about £3,500,000 a year those of 1806, the first year of Napoleon's ban on British goods. Far from his ruining Lancashire and Lanarkshire, those counties (thanks to increasing supplies from the New World) helped materially to defeat him.[4]

Unquestionably the West Indies were an important factor in England's commercial triumph. While British North America was still valued chiefly for furs, fish and timber, and sent only inter-mittent supplies of grain (none during the American War[5]); while West Africa ceased to supply slaves and furnished only Senegal gum, palm oil, ivory and a few objects of lesser value; while the Cape was merely a port of call; while Ceylon and Mauritius disappointed all hopes of rapid progress, and Governor Farquhar could seriously advise the abandonment of New South Wales in favour of Mada-gascar[6]—the West Indies steadily sent large quantities of the produce which baffled Napoleon's efforts at exclusion.

For all the bannings and burnings of British produce in his States late in 1810, our exports continued to be large, even in the trying

[1] C.O. 295/21.   [2] C.O. 295/32.
[3] *Vide infra*, ch. VI.   [4] See details in Rose, J. H., *Man and the Sea*, App. 4.
[5] *C.J.* (1814–15), App. 11.
[6] Mem. of R. T. Farquhar to Earl of Liverpool, 28 July 1812 in C.O. 167/10.

year 1811, as the following table of "official" values of British exports shows[1]:

	1809 £	1810 £	1811 £
Coffee	1,847,920	5,845,160	1,454,172
Sugar	783,963	1,713,130	1,470,994
Indian piece goods	822,345	1,179,728	1,082,115
Tea	714,939	703,724	569,360
Indigo	323,107	636,807	491,298
Cotton-wool	60,283	156,215	343,550
Dyeing woods	48,840	139,752	320,115

The phenomenal increase of these exports, except that of tea, in 1810 must have been mainly in response to continental demands. Our exports of refined sugar, together with those of cottons and woollens,[2] also increased so largely that they cannot be accounted for solely by the access lately gained to the Spanish and Portuguese colonies, whose demands were not large.[3] On the whole, it is safe to say that the United Kingdom could not have survived the financial strain of the years 1810–12 if it had not had almost sole control of the tropical products which the continental peoples insisted on obtaining. In short the British Isles were saved by the British Empire.

That rarely visible but ever-vitalising connector, the navy, not only assured to our merchants and manufacturers constant supplies of tropical produce but also occupied or utilised several posts whence deadly punctures could be administered to Napoleon's unwieldy and tightly inflated Continental System. These were Anholt, Heligoland, the Channel Islands, Gibraltar, Sicily, Malta and (finally) the Ionian Islands and Lissa. It will be well to glance at the services rendered by these outposts of Empire.

Anholt, an islet in the Cattegat, was seized from the Danes in May 1809; and in March 1811 their attempt with some 2000 men to recapture it was stoutly beaten off by the crew[4] (for administratively Anholt figured as a man-of-war). The islet also served as a look-out post, a rendezvous for furnishing news, collecting the Baltic convoys and aiding British or friendly blockade-runners. As the neighbouring lands needed our colonial or manufactured products and we needed their corn or naval stores,[5] the Baltic trade was of prime importance. To the Napoleonic veto on it, as arranged at Tilsit, Great Britain had speedily retorted by the seizure of the Danish fleet, and now by the far more effective device of granting secret trading licences to British, Russian and Prussian merchants for friendly intercourse which annulled or evaded the provisions of Tilsit and the Orders in Council. This illicit trade soon reached large proportions and seems

---

[1] C.J. (1810–11), App. 8B.   [2] Ibid. App. 8.
[3] British exports to Buenos Aires in 1813 were valued at £404,220, about one-ninth of those to the W. Indies (C.J. 1814–15, App. 11).
[4] James, Naval History, IV, 431; V, 222–6; Saumarez, Mems. II, 224.
[5] Vide infra, ch. VI.

to have revivified commerce, witness the declaration in 1809 of the Judge in the Court of Admiralty: "It is a notorious fact that the whole trade of the world is carried on under licences."[1] As this trade under licences to hostile ports was nowhere so important as in the Baltic, Sir James Saumarez, our admiral in that sea, had special instructions to favour it and not needlessly to harass the Russians. Consequently, in October 1809 one of his captains, Byam Martin, reported that that trade was fast increasing.[2] In June 1810 a convoy of some 600 vessels under neutral flags, but carrying British and colonial products, sailed to the Baltic; but then Napoleon intervened, compelling the Tsar, Alexander I, and other Baltic rulers to exclude or seize these cargoes and conform to his rigorous decrees.[3] From these blows our Baltic trade suffered severely. The commerce of Russia also practically ceased, and in the spring of 1811 her merchants petitioned Alexander to resume the licence system.[4] British credit also underwent a severe strain; and the importance of Anholt declined, until in May–June 1812 at the first rumours of a change of policy in Russia, two convoys of 170 and 200 British or friendly ships sailed for Gothenburg, where Byam Martin wrote that our trade was as active as ever, "an incredible quantity" of sugar coming in. He also rejoiced that exports of Baltic timber would now replace "the rotten stuff from America".[5] Again Anholt proved to be useful, besides serving as a rendezvous for our Baltic squadron which harassed the flank and communications of Napoleon's army in the Moscow campaign.[6]

In the North Sea Heligoland served as an important base for our secret trade to the Elbe and Weser areas. After its capture from the Danes in 1808 the British Government spent £500,000 in making a harbour and erecting warehouses, mainly for the import of British and colonial wares into Germany, though in that year and 1810 much German corn reached England through Heligoland.[7] Some 200 British merchants and agents settled in the island, which during four years hummed with activity, its chief settlement being dubbed "Little London". A scarcely credible estimate valued its imports at £8,000,000 a year, all being designed for Germany or Denmark.[8] Here, as at so many points, the Argus eyes and eager mind of Napoleon supply missing links in our information. Twice in the year 1810 he ordered Franco-Dutch squadrons to capture Heligoland, or at least to threaten attacks; for "the mere rumour that that entrepôt

---

[1] Quoted by Judge J. Phillimore, *Reflections on...the Licence Trade* (1811), p. 25.
[2] *Journals of Sir T. Byam Martin*, II, 18, 68, 70, 118, 141, 159.
[3] *E.H.R.* Jan 1903; Heckscher, p. 234; *Nap. Corresp.* 16881, 17041, 17071.
[4] F.O. 65/77, Letters from Petersburg, Feb.–April 1811.
[5] *Journals of Sir T. Byam Martin*, II, 176–80, 217.
[6] *Ibid.* II, 181–5, 287–92.
[7] Galpin, W. F., *Grain Supply of England in the Napoleonic War*, p. 179.
[8] Heckscher, pp. 168, 178–82.

was exposed has caused a very great sensation in London". Also, after his annexation of the north-west of Germany in December 1810, the official justification for that step stated that "the immense stores of Heligoland would always threaten to flow into the Continent, if a single point on the shores of the North Sea remained open to English commerce".[1] Certainly our agents in Heligoland were very enterprising, the firm of Mellish begging our Government to have the guard-vessels driven away even from Dutch ports so as to facilitate the running in of sugar, etc., from that island.[2] Great ingenuity was used in getting our colonial produce into the Elbe. The Hamburgers arranged for bogus funerals to a riverside suburb until inquisitive *douaniers* discovered the hearses on the return to be packed with coffee and sugar. Children, dogs and women were then pressed into the smuggling service; and so in one way or another the produce of the Indies filtered into Europe.[3]

Napoleon's rigorous control of North-West Germany had the effect of diverting British trade into more southerly channels. Thereafter it often reached Central Europe by way of Salonica or the Dalmatian coast and the Danube.[4] This change increased the importance of our Mediterranean trade, and added to the value of Gibraltar and Malta as entrepôts for British commerce. The ports of Sicily were of little service; for the whims and intrigues of Queen Maria Carolina, the boorish incapacity of Ferdinand I and "the oppressive and unjust ways of levying all duties", rendered trade very risky.[5] There is little direct evidence as to trading activities in Malta, which necessarily were secret; but after the Berlin Decree some thirty or forty British firms established branches in Malta to develop the clandestine commerce with Italy, which, under the protection of the navy, developed rapidly.[6] On 3 April 1812 a committee of London merchants petitioned the Board of Trade against allowing neutrals any privileges whatever for participating in this trade into the enemy's Mediterranean lands, which were now being supplied largely by us with British and colonial produce through Gibraltar and Malta, "the wants of the Continent being urgent, and the encouragement for speculation consequently great".[7] The services rendered by those ports appear in the few surviving statistics, which show the values of the imports of British cottons into them and the mainland adjoining, during and after the breakdown of the Continental System[8]:

	Gibraltar	Spain	Malta	Italy
1813	£1,983,294	£498,440	£2,413,360	£215,084
1815	£1,024,704	£994,294	£380,754	£1,241,130

[1] *Nap. Corresp.* 16384, 16991, 17197.   [2] B.T. 3/11.   [3] Heckscher, ch. III.
[4] *Ibid.* pp. 231–3, 244; Tooke, T., *History of Prices*, I, 311.
[5] Petition of British merchants in Sicily 17 Sept. 1811, in B.T. 3/11; also in B.T. 5/21 (petition of 16 Jan. 1812). For the British occupation of Sicily, see Bunbury, pp. 264–342, 357–405; *C.H.B.F.P.* I, 379, 380, 455–9, 490.
[6] Hardman, *History of Malta* (1798–1815), pp. 526, 537.   [7] B.T. 1/64.
[8] *C.J.* (1815), App. 11 (the returns for 1811, 1812, 1814 were destroyed by fire).

Clearly, then, Gibraltar and Malta were of great service for deflating the Continental System from the south; and, later, a traveller described the activities brought by the British into Malta, which he named an intermediary between East and West.[1]

Far more critical was the question of the Ionian Isles. As has been seen, Napoleon early in 1803 expected an easy reconquest; and many subsequent signs prove his keen interest in them and in the Morea which they covered. The British Government and Nelson were equally resolved to oppose his designs; and Spiridion Foresti, our Minister at Corfu, the capital of the Republic of the Seven Islands, sought to enhance British influence. The Russian occupation was very unpopular; and Foresti and others urged us at least to occupy some good port in the Adriatic.[2] A complete collapse occurred after Tilsit, when the Tsar Alexander's surrender to Napoleon involved the ultimate sacrifice of Russia's control over the Seven Islands as well as the Bocche di Cattaro. The victor began at once great preparations for occupying this fine harbour as well as Corfu in order to secure supremacy in the Adriatic and pave the way for a partition of the Turkish Empire.[3] In vain did Foresti warn us to forestall the enemy at Corfu and secure the allegiance of 200,000 devoted Greeks, most of them good seamen. Also Ali Pacha, practically the ruler of Albania and Epirus, promised effective help in opposing the French schemes.[4] We were too late; for, while our fleet action in the Mediterranean was tardy and therefore ineffective, that of France was prompt. Early in 1808 the Rochefort and Toulon squadrons, united under Admiral Ganteaume, eluded Admiral Collingwood's fleet in the Mediterranean and threw large garrisons into Corfu and neighbouring islands.[5]

This event affords one among many proofs that Napoleon's continued efforts to seize Sicily and his high-handed intervention in Spain aimed at the renewal of his grandiose schemes in the Orient,[6] for which Italy, the Ionian Isles and Sicily were to serve as bases. His "Spanish blunder", however, tore an irreparable rent in these designs and enabled us to retrieve our earlier mistakes.[7] Thus, in 1809, in answer to appeals from the provisional governments of most of the Seven Islands, British forces occupied Zante, Cephalonia, Cerigo and neighbouring islets, whereupon the Septinsular Republic was re-established under British protection.[8] Sta. Maura was recaptured from the French in March 1810. Ali Pacha, who feared

---

[1] Von Raumer, F., *Italy and the Italians*, II, 164.
[2] F.O., 42/9. Foresti to Mulgrave Feb. 14, March 1 (enclosing *Mémoire sur la Dalmatie* by Chev. de Tinseau). [3] *Nap. Corresp.* 12850, 12851, 13001.
[4] F.O. Ionian Islands, 9. Report on Corfu, etc., dated Kew, Nov. 1807.
[5] Clowes, v, 231, 240–5.
[6] *Nap. Corresp.* 13792, 13877–13936, 13997, 14005, etc.   [7] *Ibid.* 14161.
[8] F.O. 42/10, contains Memorials from Ithaca and Cerigo (October), and Zante (December) 1809, to Canning for protection.

French designs on Albania, aided us with men and supplies, also with timber for the dockyard at Malta; but the close blockade of Corfu proved very difficult in face of Napoleon's persistent efforts at succour from Italy and the Dalmatian coast. General Donzelot, its brave defender, held out to the end of the war. The other islands, despite proneness to faction and disorder, welcomed British rule, and benefited by the presence of firm but conciliatory administrators like General Oswald and Colonel Hudson Lowe, "to watch over the due administration of the laws"; and Foresti held that self-government, at least in turbulent Zante, would be fatal.[1]

From these islands as bases British warships pushed into the Adriatic and secured the central island of Lissa as a commercial depôt. Apparently, it proved serviceable to our clandestine trade with Italy; for Napoleon ordered that all cottons landed at Ancona and Venice be seized as British in origin; while Levantine cottons destined for France must come direct to French ports.[2] Further, in March 1811, a Franco-Venetian squadron, which set out from Ancona for the recapture of Lissa, was brilliantly defeated by Capt. Hoste's light squadron off that island, a victory which assured both our hold on that post and our supremacy in the Adriatic.[3] British commerce benefited greatly thereby; and probably to the following months may be referred the well-authenticated incident, that a firm of merchants employed 500 horses in transporting British produce from the Slavonic (Dalmatian) coast "overland to France, at a cost of about £28 per cwt."[4] Whatever Napoleon might think or say to the contrary, it was the continental consumers who paid for these extra charges.

An observer, who surveyed the colossal System piled up year after year by a seemingly invincible power, might deem this sparse string of islets, from Anholt to Lissa, a contemptible offset. He would err. For, thanks largely to these insignificant points, Napoleon's gigantic land-mass, now distended almost to bursting-point, was never sea-proof. At scores of points it leaked from the thrusts of the trident, impelled by sea power but rendered trebly effective by the imperious needs of a half-starving Continent. In the last resort Napoleon was beaten by cotton and dyes, by sugar and coffee.

The hopelessness of the effort, *Napoleon contra mundum*, appears in the comments of his Ministers, Mollien and Chaptal;[5] also in his own order of 5 July 1811 to Marshal Davout, the Napoleonic satrap at Hamburg: "Colonial merchandise and produce, whether coming from Sweden, Prussia or any place whatsoever, must be seized and confiscated, because they come originally from England."[6] Equally

---

[1] F.O. 42/12, Foresti to Wellesley, 20 Feb. 1811.   [2] *Nap. Corresp.* 16885.
[3] Clowes, v, 478–80; James, *Naval History*, v, 233–45; Chevalier, *Histoire*, III, 387–9.
[4] Porter, E. R., *Progress of the Nation*, p. 389.
[5] Mollien, *Méms.* III, 290–9; Chaptal, *Souvenirs*, pp. 274–8.
[6] Lecestre, *Lettres nouvelles de Napoléon I*, II, 142

discouraging was the fact that in 1812, when he sought to proscribe the use of all but Levantine cottons, British exports of the finer cotton-stuffs from the Indies were valued officially at £16,517,000.[1] In fact, the utter failure of his gigantic effort at strangling British commerce may be measured by the fact that the total revenue of the United Kingdom increased steadily from £103,000,000 in 1805 to £120,000,000 in 1808, £131,000,000 in 1811, and £162,000,000 in 1814, the revenue in each year but the last exceeding the total expenditure.[2]

The collapse of Napoleon's colossal boycott[3] was due in no small measure to the stubborn recalcitrance of Sweden. After he deprived her of Swedish Pomerania she was almost unassailable by his armies; and an open trade policy was inaugurated by Bernadotte, ex-Marshal of France and now Prince Royal and heir to the Swedish throne. Though he appeared in 1810 to accept Napoleon's *fiat* of war against England, yet both British and Swedish fleets skilfully marked time and often screened the operations of their merchantmen. The value of Sweden's imports from Great Britain rose as follows from 1805 to 1812: Groceries (including sugar) £33,812 to £483,600; dyes £14,796 to £104,651; linens and cottons £4850 to £235,600. In every item the increase in Sweden's imports from Great Britain was greater than in those of her total imports—a fact even more marked in 1813.[4]

In this gigantic strife of the elements a series of deepening pressures brought the cyclonic system to a climax in the year 1812. By that time the Sea Power held the tropics and the Oceans; the Land Power held or controlled all Europe except its islands and parts of its outlying peninsulas. The navy of the one and the armies of the other seemed alike unconquerable; for only in Spain could the combatants come to grips. Elsewhere the strife was Protean but none the less exhausting, as appeared in severe and prolonged financial crises foreshadowing a not distant collapse. And while their whole fabrics heaved and strained, the exterior parts cracked outright; for in the very month when the great Empire of the East shook off the new law of the land, the great Republic of the West defied the new law of the sea.

To trace here in detail the growth of the maritime feud between the United States and the United Kingdom is impossible.[5] Since the year 1807 war had with difficulty been averted owing to the acute friction which led to the passing of their Embargo and Non-Intercourse Acts. Though Napoleon's policy gave equal umbrage to

[1] Baines, E., *History of the Cotton Manufacture*, p. 243.
[2] Silberling, N. J., in *Quarterly Journal of Economics*, vol. XXVIII.
[3] Mollien, *Méms.* III, 318.
[4] See *C.H.J.* (1929) for fuller details, furnished by Dr E. F. Heckscher of Stockholm.
[5] See *C.H.B.E.* VI, ch. IX; *C.M.H.* VII, chs. IX, X; *C.H.B.F.P.* I, 356–8, 366, 367, 377–9, 522 ff.

that Republic, yet as Britain's maritime supremacy became more marked, resentment fell mainly on her; and many Americans advocated armed resistance to her. For, besides the grievances of the Eastern States against the British Navy, were those of the Western States against British agents, who were alleged (with scanty proofs) to be egging on Indian tribes to unite for offensive action against the outlying settlements. In February 1810 that typical frontiersman, Henry Clay of Kentucky, urged the Senate to choose, not war with Napoleon, but war with Great Britain:

because I believe her prior in aggression, and her injuries and insults to us more atrocious in character.... The conquest of Canada is in your power.... I verily believe that the militia of Kentucky are alone competent to place Montreal and Upper Canada at your feet.... Is it nothing to us to extinguish the torch that lights up savage warfare? Is it nothing to acquire the entire fur trade connected with that country and to destroy the temptation and opportunity of violating your revenue and other laws? [1]

Later, he declared also in favour of seizing East Florida from the Spaniards; and other "war-hawk expansionists" advocated a rupture with Great Britain because her alliance with Spain would naturally lead on to that step. After President Madison's advocacy of war preparations (November 1811), P. B. Porter of New York, Chairman of the Committee on Foreign Relations, pointed out the injury which could be inflicted on British commerce by American privateers, while the conquest of Canada and the cutting-off of naval stores and foodstuffs would soon humble the mistress of the seas, already deprived of those necessaries coming from the Baltic lands. [2]

Clearly, then, a large party at Washington believed in the easy conquest of Canada and overthrow of British power. Despite conciliatory overtures from London, the war party gained the ascendancy, and on 18 June 1812 carried the vote for the declaration of war against Great Britain by 19 to 13 votes in the Senate and 79 to 49 in the House of Representatives. [3] The declaration of war passed at sea a despatch from London rescinding the Orders in Council which were the ostensible cause of the war vote at Washington. On both sides the conflict was accepted with many regrets. These were widespread in New England, where languid recruiting atrophied the attacks on Canada; and after the first failures to invade Upper Canada from Detroit or Niagara, the American efforts on land became almost sectional. Ultimately their flotillas won the command of the Great Lakes; and their fine frigates and nimble privateers wrought much damage, even in our home waters and among the transports carrying supplies to Wellington in Northern Spain. But these strokes in and from the West did not vitally affect the great

---

[1] Annals of Congress (11th Congress), I, 579, 580, cit. Pratt, J. W., Expansionists of 1812, p. 40.
[2] Ibid. p. 50.
[3] Ibid. pp. 140, 163.

issues in Europe; for by various devices we got through American cargoes, especially cotton. Sea power also decided the Peninsular War, as Wellington generously confessed: "If anyone wishes to know the history of this war, I will tell them (*sic*) that it is our maritime superiority gives me the power of maintaining my army while the enemy are unable to do so."[1]

Far heavier were the blows which Napoleon drew on himself from the East. Russia, even more than Sweden, which had one great oceanic port, felt the pressure of his fiscal system. The secret reports from our agent at Petersburg revealed the general drift towards Bernadotte's secret proposal of a Russo-Swedish league and war with France.[2] The Tsar Alexander, however, long refused to abandon the Continental System until, late in 1811, sheer economic necessity led him to relax its severity and tax *articles de luxe* coming into Russia. The anger of Napoleon at this divergence from the policy of Tilsit thenceforth deepened. Indeed, he had all along shown a strange inability to understand the imperious needs of Russia. Thus, in February 1810, while allowing licences for the export thither of French and Italian wines and corn ("which is useful to my States") he refused to allow any for colonial wares, which she needed far more. In September he ordered the Prussian Government to impose a duty on such wares passing through its lands into Russia. He also insisted on the confiscation of the 600 ships then bound for Russia with colonial produce; for "under whatever pretext they hide, and whatever they do, they are English; . . . the blow to England will be terrible". By November 4 the 600 fraudulent neutral ships grew to 1200; and he charged the Tsar's Government with breaking the Treaty of Tilsit and spreading colonial produce through Germany "par 700 chariots venant de Russie". She must join France in compelling Sweden to confiscate the great stores of colonial merchandise sent by the English to Gothenborg.[3]

In the spring and summer of 1811 the growing bitterness of his complaints led Alexander to advance troops westwards; whereupon Napoleon saw in this step and in the rumoured arrival in Russian ports of 150 vessels disguised under the American flag, a resolve to break with France and renew trade with the British.[4] Disputes concerning the Eastern and Polish questions complicated the controversy; but in essence it was economic. On 1 May 1812 (O.S.) our agent at Petersburg reported that public opinion called for the freeing of Russian commerce from its Napoleonic shackles, and that, while Alexander hesitated, the Council of State declared that "there was but one way, that of opening completely the ports", provided

[1] *Journals . . . of Sir T. Byam Martin* (N.R.S.), II, 409.

[2] F.O. 65/77, Advices of 24 May 1811; Webster, C. K., *British Diplomacy (1813–15)*, pp. 92, 93.

[3] *Nap. Corresp.* 16224, 17040, 17071, 17099.   [4] *Ibid.* 18062.

that incoming vessels took back Russian produce exceeding by one-third the value of their imported cargoes. The outcry against Napoleon's fiscal decrees increased daily; and on May 28 (O.S.) Russia renewed a treaty of commerce with Portugal. Napoleon's Grand Army began to cross the River Niemen at midsummer, and soon afterwards appeared a ukase opening all Russian ports to British commerce on the old relations.[1]

Such are the relevant facts about the Franco-Russian rupture of June 1812. Their purport is clear. If Napoleon, instead of surrendering to the fatalistic idea that a rupture with Russia must come in spite of the desires of both Emperors, had calmly surveyed the vital necessities of Russia, he would have seen that her people, least of all, could do without colonial produce, and he would have humoured her in essentials. As for the notion that she was the chief distributor of such produce throughout Central Europe, it was wildly wrong; for what little she could get she needed for home consumption, besides which her powers of wide distribution inland were patriarchal at all times and null in winter. Sweden (as has appeared above) was the real culprit; and for once, as we have seen, Napoleon showed his discernment of that fact.[2] True policy, therefore, bade him humour Alexander in order to gain his support in coercing Sweden. Far from doing so, he turned more and more against him, and in the spring of 1812 angled for the friendly neutrality of Sweden, during his ensuing trial of strength with Russia.[3] It would seem, then, that this formerly clear thinker allowed his vision to be blurred by considerations arising out of the Eastern and Polish questions, or even by a gallinaceous sense of personal rivalry; whereas the dominant issue, namely the commercial strangulation of Great Britain, called for overwhelming pressure, not on Russia, but on Sweden. By attacking Russia Napoleon aroused the enmity of a great nation, previously half-dormant, and threw away half a million of men. By his own admission that whole venture was based on design. "I leave one place, I go to another"; so he said to Roederer, "I leave St Cloud, I go to Moscow, not for a whim or for my friends, but by mere dry calculation."[4] And it is now clear that he went there on a demonstrably false calculation.

To sum up; if British statesmen erred by insisting too long and too strictly on their maritime code, the error of Napoleon in clinging even longer and more strictly to his Continental System must be pronounced far more fatal. Let the policies of the two Powers be judged by their results. While, in June 1812, the sporadic severities of the Sea Power brought about the equally sporadic hostilities of a

---

[1] F.O. 65/77.　　　　　　　　　　　[2] *Nap. Corresp.* 17099.
[3] *C.H.B.F.P.* i, 385, 595–7; *Nap. Corresp.* 18702.
[4] *Journal du Comte Roederer*, p. 323. For his restlessness see Romanzoff's report of his words: "I must always be *going*. After the Peace of Tilsit where could I go but to Spain?" (*Diary of J. Q. Adams*, p. 90.)

young and ill-armed Republic, the grinding and protracted pressure of the Land Power aroused the determined hatred of a great and warlike nation entrenched in unconquerable solitudes. By the former event the British Empire was for a time harassed at sea and menaced in Canada; but the crisis served to elicit a new and exuberant feeling of Canadian loyalty, even among the French-speaking Canadians, for whom France now angled in vain. On the Moscow campaign Talleyrand passed the far-seeing verdict: "*C'est le commencement de la fin.*"

Such it proved to be in spheres other than military. The opening of Russia's ports not long after June 1812 afforded a welcome relief to our overcharged industrial system; but it also set free her stores of grain for export to half-starving England from which American privateers cut off Canadian corn-ships.[1] Thus, Napoleon's invasion of Russia produced mercantile and economic reactions which baffled the confident prophecies of a British collapse indulged in by Clay, Porter and other "war-hawks". Nor was this all. Russia's potentially immense man-power, pressing on the rear of Napoleon's shattered army, and her new commercial freedom, contrasting with the commercial bondage of Central Europe, galvanised that torpid mass into activity. Early in 1813 Prussia and North Germany rose against him; later, Austria and South and West Germany followed suit in what now became "a contest of nations". The Continental System forthwith collapsed;[2] and at the close of the year, the allies, aided by the Dutch, drove him beyond the Rhine. Even then their hostilities, reinforced by those of Wellington and the Peninsular armies, gave him no rest; and on 11 April 1814 he abdicated, dragging France down in his fall to her pre-revolutionary level.

This cataclysm was not only European, but world-wide; for the fall of Napoleon entailed the collapse of possible schemes like that of Terre Napoléon in mid-Australia and of a great Latin-American Empire; while, on the other hand, the conquests of the British navy could have assured absolute supremacy in every quarter of the globe. The world problem was solved in neither of these ways. The all-British solution was contrary both to the traditions of Westminster and to the promptings of the genius of Pitt, which now guided his pupil, Castlereagh, through the mazes of continental diplomacy. For the outlines of the peace of 1814–15 had been sketched in 1805 by the son of Chatham, who then gave form and substance to the visionary schemes of Alexander I.[3]

Further, the co-operation with Russia and other Powers, finally including the Dutch, imposed the duty of moderation even in the

---

[1] Galpin, pp. 247, 250; *Journals of Byam Martin*, II, 211–22.
[2] See *C.H.J.* (1929) for the huge exports from Heligoland to N. Germany in April 1813.
[3] Rose, J. H., *Pitt*, II, 523–5; *Napoleonic Studies* (Essay 2), and *Third Coalition*, 108–40; Webster, C. K., *Brit. Diplomacy*, App. 1; also his *For. Policy of Castlereagh (1812–15)*, I, ch. 1, § 5.

hour of victory. Also in the doubtful months of 1813 we had encouraged our allies by promising that the general peace would be
facilitated by the retrocession of several of the conquered colonies
(a fixed practice in British policy, as was shown in our previous
chapter[1]); but our maritime code must not be called in question.
At the end of the year, when the allies swept back the French to
the Rhine and Meuse, the British Government demurred to offering
extensive sacrifices overseas unless equivalent securities were to be
forthcoming in the continental peace especially on the side of Holland
and the Low Countries.[2] For the purpose of raising an effective
barrier against France on that side, our plenipotentiary, Castlereagh,
was empowered to offer that, if the French abandoned Antwerp
and other naval posts on the Scheldt, and if Holland, under the
House of Orange, were strengthened by gaining Antwerp, Juliers
and Maestricht with adjoining districts, we were prepared to restore
the Dutch colonies conquered in the war, except the Cape of Good
Hope, for which £2,000,000 would be paid. Also, with the view of
restoring equilibrium, especially as regards Spain and Portugal,
Great Britain would consider her other colonial conquests as objects
of negotiation; but she must retain Malta, Mauritius, Île de Bourbon,
the Saints and Guadeloupe, the last being a debt of honour to
Sweden.[3] Our colonial conquests from Denmark (except Heligoland)
would be available as bargaining assets in the Anglo-Danish-Swedish
negotiations then pending.[4]

After the signature of the peace with Denmark (14 January 1814),
by which she lost Norway to Sweden but regained her oversea possessions except Heligoland, the British Government further defined
its policy in an undated Memorandum on the Maritime Peace. Great
Britain had offered to sacrifice many of her colonial conquests "for
the welfare of the Continent"; for "her object is to see a maritime
as well as a military balance of power", which would be assured by
the independence of Spain and Holland. Also our cessions of conquered colonies would be greatest if France were reduced within her
ancient limits.[5] During the military reverses of February 1814 in
Champagne, Castlereagh wavered as to our retention of Tobago and
the Ionian Isles;[6] and for a time Napoleon might have signed a
favourable peace with the discouraged and disunited allies; but his
resolve to cling to Holland and Antwerp and his hope of an eleventh-
hour triumph lost him his last chance. Blücher's bravery and
Castlereagh's firmness revivified the Coalition, which, early in March,

---

[1] See also *C.H.B.F.P.* I, 268, 274 ff., 305–7, 425–32; and Butterfield, H., pp. 91, 101–3,
132, 145, 210, 282, 300.
[2] Webster, C. K., pp. 10, 11, 14, 45, 60, 89, 110, 117–19.
[3] See *C.H.B.F.P.* I, 594.
[4] Webster, pp. 123–6. For Anglo-Dutch relations, see Renier, G. J., *Great Britain and
he Netherlands (1813–15)*, 87–106.
Webster, pp. 126–8.   [6] *Ibid.* p. 146.

solidified in the Treaty of Chaumont, the harbinger of speedy triumph.[1]

Apart, then, from Napoleon's fundamental defect, untimely and steel-like obstinacy, the chief cause of his fall was his resolve to dominate the Netherlands. On several occasions has the fate of Europe been closely linked with that of those weak but wealthy lands. And now more than ever; for the Dutch colonies, added to those of France, would enable her to rival the British Empire; while the Dutch and Flemish harbours threatened its heart. Not without cause, then, had Napoleon written, "Holland is French and will be so for ever".[2] And, with equal reason on strategic grounds, he resolved in March 1814 at all costs to keep Antwerp,[3] "the pistol held at the head of England". Thus, that great port, a leading cause of the Anglo-French rupture in 1793, made of the Napoleonic struggle a war to the knife.

The paramount importance of the Barrier question over merely colonial considerations was at this time well expressed by Pitt's old friend, the Earl of Harrowby, to Earl Bathurst:

Antwerp and Flushing out of the hands of France are worth twenty Martiniques in our own hands; and though there will undoubtedly be a strong feeling [in England] against this concession, perhaps even against any concession, yet, if a peace can be concluded with all the Great Powers of Europe in union with us and with each other, I think that...there never was a period in history in which the prospect of so long and so secure a peace was offered to the world.[4]

The restoration of the Bourbon dynasty in the person of the gouty and unwarlike Louis XVIII afforded some guarantee to this effect; and during the negotiations Talleyrand scored several successes by enthroning the principle of legitimacy, which implied the adoption of the *status quo ante bellum*. True, this principle involved the loss of the revolutionary and Napoleonic conquests, with 15,360,000 subjects; but this sacrifice merely registered the fact that the armies of Europe now held down France and were determined to recover all, and more than all, they had lost. Many statesmen and publicists thought that by the Treaty of Paris (30 May 1814) France escaped too lightly, especially as she regained nearly all her old colonies. But in the House of Commons Castlereagh defended the treaty on the ground that "it is not the interest of this country to make France a military and conquering, instead of a commercial and pacific, nation".[5]

Nevertheless, the British Government, though ready to relinquish very much for the common good, decided, in view of the immense costs of the war and the extensive aggrandisements of Russia, Prussia

---

[1] Webster, pp. 160–8; Rose, J. H., *Napoleon*, II, 402–13.

[2] Lecestre, *Lettres nouvelles de Napoléon*, II, 293.

[3] Campbell, N., *Napoleon...at Elba*, p. 315. For our naval views and actions about Antwerp, see *Journals of Sir T. Byam Martin*, III, 16, 19, 28 ff.

[4] *Bathurst Papers*, p. 260.   [5] Hansard, XXVIII, 458.

and Austria, to retain another of her oversea conquests, namely Demerara; and Castlereagh no longer wavered about Tobago. Naval men also welcomed the French offer that, instead of the Saints, we should retain St Lucia, valuable for its look-out on Martinique. The urgent desire of France to recover the once wealthy island of Guadeloupe (now ceded by us to Sweden) was satisfied by a series of complex but friendly bargains, ending with our payment of £1,000,000 to Sweden by way of compensation.[1] The French also recovered their *comptoirs* in the East Indies, on condition of not fortifying them. Castlereagh explained to the House that we must retain Mauritius because "in time of war it was a great nuisance, highly detrimental to our commerce", the losses of which from Mauritius cruisers and privateers had been "incalculable".[2] For the like reasons we kept the Seychelles and Rodriguez; but Bourbon, as a less formidable base, reverted to France. She was also to resume her former treaty rights in the Newfoundland fisheries (a matter of grave umbrage to our colonists).[3]

The approaches to India by the overland route were also assured. So strenuous and persistent had been Napoleon's bid for the Levantine stepping-stones to India that the importance of England's retaining Malta was clear as noonday; and Addington's portentous blunder of relinquishing that "most important outwork of India" (as Nelson finally called it[4]) was now repaired. The island was acquired "in full right and sovereignty"—a sign that the musty suzerain claims of the former Kingdom of the Two Sicilies were repudiated as obsolete. Castlereagh's temporary wavering about the Ionian Isles was finally over-ruled and Great Britain acquired a Protectorate over them.[5] The lessons as to their importance, inculcated by the events of 1798, were not disregarded twice.

To the modern mind, accustomed to the sight of a dominating New World and of colonies equalling, or in some cases dwarfing, their motherlands, the anxiety of European statesmen to round off their home domains, and their slight appreciation of lands oversea appear incredible. A curious instance of this near-sightedness appeared during the negotiations for the establishment of the Kingdom of the United Netherlands. In order to strengthen that Barrier against some hypothetical Napoleon, British statesmen offered to restore, with two exceptions, the once wealthy Dutch colonies. But it soon transpired that some well-informed Dutch statesmen were far from eager to recover them. Lord Clancarty, British ambassador at the Hague, found van Nagel "willing even to forego their reacquisition upon an adequate indemnity" (probably in money); and

[1] Koch and Schöll, *Traités*, III, 267, 357, 371; Garden, *Traités*, XV, 349.
[2] Hansard, XXVIII, 463.
[3] *Ibid.* 458, 462. [4] Nicolas, V, 107.
[5] Webster, pp. 304, 319; *C.H.B.F.P.* I, 493; *Bathurst Papers*, p. 277; *Castlereagh Corresp.* X, 449.

he himself was sceptical as to their value except in the case of Demerara.[1] Very significant, too, were the secret comments of another Dutch Statesman, Falck (18 June 1814):

> To limit our West India possessions to those on the mainland, and those in the East to insular settlements, such is the result of our recent researches into our colonial system. The affair (*procès*) of the Cape is also irretrievably settled, and all that is granted us by way of purchase whether for it, Curaçoa, St Martin, St Eustatius and Saba, or for our *comptoirs* in Bengal or in the peninsula on this side of the Ganges, ought to be considered as unhoped-for profit. Of course our own interest ought to have brought us to abandon properties that are always onerous and already compromised by the least chance of war. What good fortune to find people complaisant enough to pay us for abandoning them![2]

This secret confession shows the Dutch colonial system as being then in the main a bankrupt concern, for the realisation of which any purchase money was a lucky windfall. In point of fact the Dutch Foreign Minister, van Nagel, did very good business in disposing of colonies which at that time the Dutch did not much want, and for which, with two exceptions, Great Britain was not eager. True, the young Prince of Orange went to London partly with the hope of facilitating the acquisition of the above-named colonies in order to "reconcile them [the Dutch] to their incorporation with the already defined part of the former Austrian Netherlands".[3] But if he hoped to secure the Cape and Demerara as a dowry for his desired union with Princess Charlotte, he failed, and in all respects.[4] Pitt's resolve to keep the Cape governed the situation.

Further, an influential petition of British West Indian merchants had, apparently, induced the Government not to give up Demerara, Essequibo and Berbice, as was the case in 1802. Therein they declared that, both before and after 1802, the inflow of British settlers and capital had practically Anglicised those settlements, more than £15,000,000 having been invested there in sugar, coffee and cotton estates, which had proved highly productive. They also pointed out that at present Holland "from its misfortunes is totally unequal to afford them the necessary support and protection". "It could not be considered a very great sacrifice on the part of Holland to divide with this country her possessions on that Continent [South America], which would be effected by restoring her most favoured colony of Surinam, in which very little British capital has been invested and a very small proportion of the population are British subjects." Finally, they declared that the ruined finances of Holland would be strained even in developing the great and fertile area of the Surinam basin.[5] Probably this influential petition prompted the subsequent

---

[1] *Castlereagh Corresp.* x, 55, Clancarty to Castlereagh, 17 June 1814. See too Renier pp. 84, 318 *seqq.*
[2] Colenbrander, *Gedenkstukken der algemeene geschiednis van Nederland* (1813–15), p. 606.
[3] F.O. 37/70, Clancarty to Castlereagh (Private), 8 June 1814.
[4] Colenbrander, pp. 614–16, 619–32, 641–44.
[5] C.O. 111/18. Forwarded by Hon. Geo. Rose on 19 Dec. 1813.

partition of Guiana, about two-thirds remaining British, the third part (Surinam) being retroceded to Holland. Later, the Earl of Liverpool defended our retention of most of Guiana because it was British in population and furnished a large part of the raw cotton needed by our manufacturers.[1] Naturally, as the fall of Napoleon heartened all his enemies, the Dutch became more exigent for the recovery of all their colonies—a claim which the British Government could not admit.[2]

Finally, by the Convention of London (13 August 1814) Great Britain restored to the Netherlands their former colonies of Java, Amboyna, Banda, Ternate in the East Indies; Curaçao, St Eustatius and some smaller islands in the West Indies; and agreed to pay for those which she retained (viz. the Cape, Demerara, Essequibo, and Berbice) the sum of £5,000,000, besides the £1,000,000 in respect of Guadeloupe. The sum of £2,000,000 was to be applied towards the satisfaction of outstanding claims on the Dutch Government and the strengthening of the new frontier of the Netherlands.[3] In one sense the aggrandisement of the Dutch State in Europe was in itself adequate reparation for the loss of the Cape and the Demerara settlements. Indeed a permanent union with the Belgic provinces, based on good and tactful government, would have provided complete compensation for the loss of these colonies.

Napoleon's bold bid for power in 1815 did not upset these colonial settlements, for, after Waterloo and his second abdication, both Castlereagh and Wellington again successfully urged the need of moderation towards the restored Government of Louis XVIII. "We ought", so wrote the Duke in August 1815, "to continue to keep our great object, the general peace and tranquillity of the world, in view, and shape our arrangement so as to provide for it."[4] The Germanic schemes for a partition of Eastern France were accordingly rejected, and only small frontier districts were ceded to the Netherlands and Prussia. In pursuance of this policy of not collecting trophies but of bringing back the world to peaceful habits, Great Britain exacted no additional colonial gains, and did not seize the opportunity for modifying the unfavourable arrangements for the Newfoundland fisheries. The war indemnity of 200,000,000 francs payable by France to her was to be spent chiefly in fortifying the new Dutch-Belgian frontier.[5] At last, after a decade of struggle, Pitt's dream of security seemed realised.

Meanwhile the Liverpool Ministry had selected St Helena as the place of Napoleon's detention, because it was inaccessible and

---

[1] *Castlereagh Corresp.* x, 132.   [2] Renier, p. 327.
[3] For details, see Webster, C. K., *Foreign Policy of Castlereagh*, i, 303–5, 540; Martens, C., *Traités*, iii, 30–33; Koch and Schöll, *Traités*, iii, 371, 410; Garden, *Traités*, xv, 349; also *C.H.B.E.* viii, pp. 211–13.
[4] Wellington, *Despatches*, xii, 599; so, too, Castlereagh in *C.H.B.F.P.* i, 508–11.
[5] *Castlereagh Corresp.* xi, 484–502.

"particularly healthy".[1] Yet fears of a rescue that might cost the world another war haunted Ministers and contributed to the last of the many annexations due to the Napoleonic nightmare, namely the Islands of Ascension and Tristan da Cunha,[2] which raised the total of British colonies from 26 in 1792 to 43 in 1816.[3] Thus, from first to last, his restless genius spurred on the British Government and nation to efforts otherwise unthinkable. From the Ionian Isles and Malta in 1797–8 to these last odd expedients in the wastes of the South Atlantic he acted unwittingly as *Mehrer des Reichs*; and the suspicion of many Germans, that we connived at his escape from Elba, is at least intelligible. "Great Britain is under weightier obligation to no mortal man than to this villain." So wrote Gneisenau soon after Waterloo.[4] With better sense and more insight did Chateaubriand declare that the British nation was an obsession to Napoleon and the cause of nearly all his mistakes.[5] But the frankest and most illuminating commentary on his career came from the Emperor himself. At Elba he said to a British visitor: "I made a mistake about England, in trying to conquer it. The English are a brave nation. I have always said that there are only two nations, the English and the French; and I made the French."[6] With equal justice might he have claimed that he made the second British Empire—hailed by a diplomat and thinker as both immense and indestructible.[7]

If Napoleon had realised his earlier scheme of world dominion, he would have ruled over all western and southern Europe, also the Spanish, Portuguese and Dutch Colonies, as well as Egypt, Syria, Mesopotamia, India and Central Australia (*Terre Napoléon*). Was this scheme, or the British plan of restoring, in the main, the conditions of 1791, more conducive to the welfare of mankind?

---

[1] *Castlereagh Corresp.* x, 434, 444.
[2] See despatches to and from Admiral Sir Pulteney Malcolm in *United Empire* (Oct. 1929).
[3] *State of the Nation* (1822), § 2.
[4] Müffling, F. K. F., *Passages from my Life*, II, 274.
[5] Chateaubriand, *Méms. d'outre Tombe*, Bk. 2 (p. 232, Nelson edit.).
[6] Broughton, Lord, *Recollections*, I, 180.
[7] De Pradt, D. D., *L'Europe après le Congrès*, p. 220.

CHAPTER IV

THE NEW IMPERIAL SYSTEM, 1783–1815

THE founders of the Second British Empire, remembering the disgrace of British misrule and extortion in India and the abdication to "democracy" in North America, were determined to govern with justice, to foster the welfare of subject races, and to be obeyed. These are the characteristics of the system of "Colonial Office Government", the origins of which the present chapter will attempt to trace. But while the new system was being worked out in the East, the old type of expansion by colonisation persisted in surviving in the West, and with it the constitutional dilemma which had previously defied solution. The American Loyalists who migrated to Canada and Nova Scotia and the people of Ireland desired to retain association with Great Britain, if it could be made compatible with local liberty. The Pitt Administration was deeply concerned to satisfy that desire with generosity, while being determined, as in the East, to exercise unquestioned authority. The two systems of imperialism, "domestic" and "tropical", now existed side by side within the same Empire. In the former, a solution was ultimately discovered which enabled a framework to be built up with autonomous associated nations at the apex and Crown Colonies at the base. Under the "tropical" system a parallel process in relation to coloured races was evolved. When order and justice had been achieved by centralisation of control, the further conception of native self-reliance was borrowed from the "domestic" system, producing in Africa "indirect rule" and in India expanding forms of self-government. In short, the two systems, springing from divergent conceptions of empire, reacted upon each other, constituting in each case a flexible political structure of ascending gradations. The experiments which were attempted during the period from 1783 to 1815 indicate the origins of this inter-reacting process and illustrate the underlying aims and ideas which gave rise to it.

Unexpectedly, perhaps, the greatest of these experiments is to be found in the record of Anglo-Irish relations. Although the history of Ireland, like the domestic history of Great Britain itself, does not fall within the compass of this work, Anglo-Irish relations during the years 1782–1800 assumed a unique character and importance in imperial policy. It is symptomatic of the attitude of Englishmen to Ireland that, because the Irish were represented in their Parliament for rather more than a century, they have persisted until recent years in regarding its history as primarily part of their own rather than conceiving of Ireland as the most important unit, politically and strategically, of an overseas empire. The constitutional experiment of association between equals, which was rejected by the Americans, was demanded and applied in the case of Ireland. A study of the manner in which the new device was operated and of how it came to be abandoned provides the key to much of the constitutional policy of Great Britain in relation to the Empire at large.

In February 1782 the Irish Revolution under the dynamic leadership of Grattan reached its climax at the Convention of Dungannon, when the delegates of a disciplined Volunteer Army, numbering some 40,000, passed resolutions denying the claim of the British Parliament to legislate for Ireland or to control Irish legislation through the British Privy Council, and demanding an independent judicature. After a vain attempt to induce Grattan to modify his demands, the Rockingham Administration, anxious to satisfy Ireland at almost any cost, surrendered. On 17 May 1782 two resolutions were passed through the Commons without a division offering a settlement on lines essentially similar to that offered, though too late, to the Americans in 1778.[1] The first resolution conceded the Irish demands in full by providing for the repeal of the Act of 6 George I, which affirmed the legislative supremacy of the British Parliament and the appellant jurisdiction of the British House of Lords in Irish causes. The second motion declared the indispensability of establishing the connection between the two countries "by mutual consent upon a solid and permanent footing". What the Ministry meant by these words was precisely explained in the House by Fox at the time and again three years later.[2] The two resolutions were intended as complementary parts of a constructive whole. The supremacy of the local Parliament in its own field was frankly conceded on the understanding that the two parties would then confer and negotiate a treaty to be solemnly ratified by both legislatures which would recognise and define the "superintending power" of Great Britain in what Fox described as matters of external or imperial concern.[3] As already mentioned, the proposals sent to America in 1778 had adumbrated a similar division of function as between local and external affairs. The suggestion was made for the third time by Lord Durham in 1839, when it became the basis of a new system. The form in which the proposed settlement was cast by Shelburne and Fox was far-sighted and statesmanlike. The recognition of Irish independence was to be followed by a voluntary acceptance of British authority in matters not specifically Irish. Most unfortunately on each occasion when an effort was made to secure recognition for the "superintending power" of the metropolitan Parliament, Irish susceptibilities were so wounded that refusal was inevitable; and with each refusal the alarm of British

[1] See Morison, S. E., *The American Revolution, 1764–1788. Sources and Documents*, pp. 186–203.
[2] *Parl. Hist.* xxiii, 16–48, 90–5; xxv, 966, 969.
[3] *Ibid.* xxiii, 26–7.

Ministers deepened until at last they abandoned the entire experiment by the Act of Union, so bequeathing a legacy of vexation and misery both to Ireland herself and to their own political descendants.

The initial effort in this direction was made by the Duke of Portland, as Lord-Lieutenant, in 1782, and took the form of trying to persuade the Irish Parliament to receive a bill which would have bound them to accept British supremacy "in all matters of state and general commerce". It would also have committed them beforehand to share the expense of any defensive or offensive war undertaken by Great Britain.[1] The attempt not only failed but turned the enthusiasm of the Irish for the Act of Repeal (22 George III, cap. 53) into cold suspicion of British sincerity. The damage was not repaired until the passage of the Act of Renunciation of April 1783, which formally and explicitly abolished appeals from Irish Courts and declared that the claim of the Irish people to be bound only by laws by the King in the Parliament of Ireland was "established and ascertained for ever".[2] One "safeguard" was obtained in the Irish statute of 21 and 22 George III, cap. 47, which superseded the procedure under Poynings' Law by which all bills had to be certified by the King in the Privy Council of Great Britain before discussion in Ireland. The new bill required that enactments of the Irish Parliament, before receiving the royal assent from the Lord-Lieutenant, must be submitted to the King, and unless returned without alteration under the Great Seal of Great Britain were void. Since the Great Seal could not be affixed except on the advice of a minister responsible to the British Parliament, this device was in theory a protection against legislation injurious to British or to general imperial interests. But it was a safeguard on paper only. An attempt to veto an enactment of the sovereign Parliament of Ireland on the advice of a British Minister would have been contested as a violation of the Act of Renunciation and have provoked a major crisis.

The real check upon which the British Cabinet relied to safeguard imperial interests was the employment of political "influence" in its most vicious form. The Viceroy, in effect, was Prime Minister, with his Chief Secretary as Leader of the House, backed by a solid majority of "King's Friends" who were bought with places, pensions, and titles. The system operated more deleteriously here than elsewhere. In the first place, the protection of British interests was surrendered to a *caucus* of territorial magnates whose support, expensive though it was, could not be relied on. A British Ministry could only count on their loyalty so long as their own tenure of office was unthreatened and so long as Government measures in the Irish Parliament did not clash with Irish national sentiment. So powerful and articulate was this latter force by means of the Volunteer organisation, that when

[1] See Portland to Shelburne, 6 June 1782. Printed in Grattan's *Life*, II, 291.
[2] 23 Geo. III, cap. 28, *Statutes at Large*, XIV, 320–1.

9-2

it was aroused even placemen ran for shelter to the ranks of the Opposition. In the second place, the identification of the imperial connection with a bought parliamentary majority inhibited the British from broadening the franchise, a reform which would have made government by corruption impossibly expensive. The situation, therefore, was that British statesmen were confronted with a sovereign legislature, which, not having acknowledged British supremacy in foreign affairs, defence, and external trade, as Shelburne and Fox had intended, was free at any time to pass resolutions for treaty relations on its own account with a Foreign Power; and their only protection against such perils was a weapon which bent in their hands whenever the position became critical.

The only satisfactory solution was to break through the oligarchic control and come to terms with the nation itself. Such a policy was urged upon Pitt and his colleagues about the year 1792 by Richard Wellesley, Earl of Mornington (afterwards the Marquis Wellesley) in an unknown State Paper of exceptional interest and importance. In this masterly document the writer presents a comprehensive survey of Irish discontent, analysing the past mistakes of British policy, and indicating the remedy along lines that are startling in their originality. The fatal flaw in Ireland, he maintained, was the absence of responsible government. Parliamentary self-government without ministerial responsibility was a fantastic anomaly and a parody of the parent constitution.

The responsibility of the servants of the State is the acknowledged principle of the British Government, nor can it be expected that the Irish, who are repeatedly told that, in point of constitutional liberty and security, they are now upon the same footing as the people of England, will be deprived of so important a right as that of calling Ministers to account, when they have betrayed their public duties. To convince them that every member of the domestic administration of their country is as truly, and legally responsible, as persons in similar situations in England, is an object of such material consequence, that it should always be kept in sight. The personal responsibility of Ministers is one of the great securities of the monarchy in England; and the personal responsibility of Ministers in Ireland is the only ground upon which British supremacy can be firmly built. The idea that the responsibility of the Government is in the Lord Lieutenant is false and unconstitutional. He represents the executive magistracy of England, the sovereign of Ireland, between whom and the people no difference can be properly supposed to arise.

The principles of Lord Durham and the Colonial Reformers were thus enunciated half a century before their day. Again like Durham, Wellesley was insistent that external affairs must be centred in Westminster. Ireland, as a member of the Empire, was too important to be controlled by any man or body of men save the Cabinet of England, "which, taking into its views all interests and relations of every part of the King's dominions, may direct and confine the force and resources of the whole to one common end".[1] There, admirably

---

[1] *Dropmore Papers*, III, 541–61 (Hist. MSS. Comm. 13th Report, App. Pt III). The document at Dropmore, which is evidently a copy, is unsigned, but internal evidence seems to point conclusively to Wellesley as the author.

expressed, is the central motive of imperial policy during the period succeeding the American Revolution.

Wellesley's proposition, in fact, amounted to this, that Ireland could be induced to leave imperial concerns in the hands of Great Britain by converting Irish autonomy into a working reality. But to Pitt and Grenville the price was evidently too high, the risk too great. Pitt lacked the originality of the great Chatham, while inheriting his essentially conservative temperament. His liberal but cautious mind sincerely desired to reform abuses, if it could be done without incurring the odium of innovation. He was acutely aware that the acceptance of Irish independence in 1782 without securing the intended reservations had left the situation perilously in the air. He accordingly strove to regain control in the external, that is to say, in the imperial sphere, but only by offering concessions which would have left the British domination of Irish domestic affairs intact.

The circumstances of Pitt's effort to reach a settlement in 1784–5 are of cardinal importance in understanding the principles of imperial policy applied by him and his colleagues and have been curiously misinterpreted by historians. In the negotiations which then took place Pitt approached the Irish question as an imperial problem and offered a compromise which turned upon the vital issue of imperial defence. In response to a request from the Irish Commons in May 1784, negotiations took place in London, resulting in the drafting of resolutions which would have established free trade between the two countries by reciprocal duties and have admitted Irish goods to free competition in the British and colonial markets.[1] In return the Parliament of Ireland was to bind itself by statute to a permanent appropriation of any future surplus in the Hereditary Revenue to the service of the Navy for the general defence of the empire. This revenue, consisting for the most part of customs and excise receipts, was expected to grow with the increasing wealth produced by an emancipated commerce, thus furnishing an assured and rising contribution towards imperial expenses. It was to be a bargain. Unless and until Ireland provided the quota, Great Britain would not grant the commercial benefits.[2] Moreover it was not sufficient for Ireland to provide for her own defence in her own way; she must contribute to the cost of a naval defence controlled from London. "There can be", wrote Pitt to Rutland, the Lord-Lieutenant, "but *one navy* for the Empire at large, it must be administered by the executive power in this country. . . . Nothing else can also prevent the supreme executive power. . . being distracted into different channels."[3]

Private consultation with their supporters convinced Rutland and his Chief Secretary, Thomas Orde, that the condition attached to the

---

[1] The original (eight) Resolutions are in H.O. 100/16, ff. 16–21.
[2] See Cabinet Minute of 5 Jan. 1785, Royal Archives, Windsor Castle; and Lord Sydney to the Duke of Rutland, 6 Jan. 1785, H.O. 100/16, ff. 11–14.
[3] Pitt to Rutland, 6 Jan. 1785 ("Secret"), *Pitt-Rutland Correspondence*, pp. 55–75.

British offer would make it unacceptable. When it became clear that the Ministry was determined to insist on a defence quota as a point of principle and also because it dare not face the British Parliament without an assured *quid pro quo*, the Lord-Lieutenant suggested that the Irish Parliament might be induced to spend the money *in Ireland* on the equipment and supply of a squadron stationed in Irish waters.[1] But the Cabinet rejected the proposal of an Irish Navy as "utterly inadmissible". Ireland must pay her share in maintaining a unitary force, "employed under the Executive Power of the Empire", for the protection of common commercial interests.[2] Pitt now found himself caught between two fires. On the one side he felt himself obliged to placate the formidable opposition in England by whittling down the terms of the original offer, and on the other to press the Irish for explicit guarantees of payment which aroused passionate anger. He had hoped to secure a prior enactment from the Irish Parliament providing a permanent and irresumable defence appropriation before approaching his own legislature. When that effort failed, he withdrew the eleven resolutions as passed by the Irish Parliament from the British Commons and allowed them to be re-cast. They reappeared as the twenty resolutions[3] in which the Irish appropriation was converted into an unalterable subvention; numerous commercial restrictions were introduced; and all British laws of trade, past and future, were to be accepted automatically by the Irish legislature. Starting from the position of offering a generous commercial settlement, Pitt ended by demanding a surrender of Irish autonomy in external affairs in its most extreme and unpalatable form.[4] The reception accorded to the amended resolutions in the Irish Commons on 12 August 1785 was such that the project was dropped and never revived.

Pitt and his colleagues conceived of the Empire as closely knit together by a mutual interest in privileges and burdens, its policy co-ordinated by the acceptance of British supremacy. The conception is clearly revealed in the foregoing episode and is characteristic of imperial policy during this period. The failure to apply it with success in Ireland postponed the evolution of colonial self-government for a generation. In 1785 Great Britain came within measurable distance of putting her relations with her Irish sister on a sound footing. Had she succeeded, the experience thereby gained and the precedents established would have been invaluable in her subsequent dealings with daughter states. In other words, Ireland came near to being the first Dominion, leading the way to a British Commonwealth of

[1] Rutland to Pitt, 14 Nov. 1784, Pitt Papers, G.D. 8/330; Same to Same, 13 Jan. 1785, H.O. 100/16; Orde to Pitt, 9 Jan. 1785, G.D. 8/329; Orde to Nepean, 24 Jan. 1785, H.O. 100/16.
[2] Sydney to Rutland, 1 Feb. 1785, H.O. 100/16.
[3] Printed in *Parl. Hist.* xxv, 934–42.
[4] See his speech on 25 July 1785, *Parl. Hist.* xxv, 978–9.

Nations. As it was, she disappeared from the imperial scene in 1800 and did not emerge again until the twentieth century.

The failure to reach a settlement in 1785 exerted an important influence on imperial policy, for it deepened the conviction in the minds of British statesmen that the existence within the Empire of a sovereign legislature, independent of Westminster, was a standing menace. The sole safeguard in which they trusted, the obedience of a "Government" majority in the Irish Commons, had failed them. The desertion of the placemen on that issue had proved that in the last resort the Irish nation, and not the British Cabinet, was the master of the oligarchic Parliament. The dangerous nature of the situation was emphasised in the Regency Crisis of 1788. When George III suddenly became insane in that year, Pitt proposed to hold the fort for himself and his royal master against Fox and the Prince of Wales by establishing the latter as Regent with strictly curtailed prerogatives. It was obviously essential that Ireland should follow the same course; and Pitt again relied on the placemen to follow the British lead by enacting an identical Regency Bill. But a constitutional difficulty at once emerged. The independent Irish Legislature was being asked to exchange the King of Ireland for a new executive authority manufactured in England by British statute.[1] Furthermore, they were being asked to obey a British Administration which the Prince of Wales would do his utmost to oust from power; and in any case he would be free to recall Buckingham, Pitt's nominee, and appoint a Lord-Lieutenant of his own who could employ Irish patronage to build up a Prince's party to rule Ireland. They were expected, in fact, to insult the man who would soon be in a position to put them out of business. They refused to do so, and the Viceroy-Prime Minister found himself in a minority of 74 to 128. Led by Grattan, they then passed a motion of their own, inviting the Prince to assume the regency of Ireland without restrictions. In short, the Crowns of Great Britain and Ireland were on the point of being two distinct and disparate entities. The danger was only averted by the providential recovery of the King.

The foregoing events had proved that the establishment of an independent parliamentary oligarchy was no answer to the constitutional dilemma which had defied solution in the case of the Thirteen Colonies. From the British point of view it was an unreliable servant, apt to be driven into revolt by the pressure of public opinion or by its own selfish interests. In the eyes of seven-eighths of the Irish people it stood for tyranny. When the movement towards national self-determination, stimulated by the example of America, was reinforced from revolutionary France, and Wolfe Tone in 1791 began his campaign for a national Parliament, it became clear that the ruling clique in Dublin was in peril. And by the same token the imperial bond, which was identified with it, was similarly endangered.

[1] Cf. Lecky, W. H., *History of Ireland in the Eighteenth Century*, II, 469 *seqq*.

Coming to the problem after drafting the Canada Act of 1791, Pitt, Dundas, and Grenville decided to apply the same policy of curbing republicanism by reliance on aristocracy regardless of creed. Their effort represents the last attempt to adjust the Irish constitution of 1782 to satisfy the opposing claims of imperial superintendence and local nationalism.

On 26 December 1791 Dundas conveyed to Westmorland, the Lord-Lieutenant, the conviction of the Cabinet that "a moderate and qualified participation" of Roman Catholics in political affairs must be conceded by the Protestant minority if they wished to avoid destruction.[1] Westmorland's reply was emphatic: the enfranchised Protestants were determined to defend their monopoly to the last ditch, and if he dared to introduce such a measure his administration would certainly be defeated.[2] Once again Pitt hesitated and then abandoned his project. When Westmorland suggested a legislative union with Great Britain as a possible means of escape from the danger, Pitt replied that the idea had long been in his mind. War and rebellion after 1793 settled the issue. The Act of Union in 1800 was frankly acknowledged by Pitt as the abandonment of an experiment which he had always regarded as dangerous.[3] He had approached the problem of an independent but discontented Ireland with a determination to secure unity of command and with zeal for her welfare. Had he possessed the imagination and decisiveness of great statesmanship it seems very probable that he could have achieved a working partnership with Irish nationalism and so gained a voluntary acceptance of British guidance in external affairs. But in 1785 and again in 1792 he faltered and the opportunity was lost. He failed in the great task of transforming a corrupt oligarchy, possessing ill-defined powers, into a genuine national Parliament with its functions adjusted to fit into the framework of the Empire because (apart from the opposition of the King and other obstacles) he did not really believe that it could be done. Instinctively he turned to unification. The concentration of executive and legislative power in the metropolis promised to remove the nightmare of Ireland in the hands of French republicanism and also to make possible the redress of her grievances by action in a united Parliament. This determination to rule, but to rule beneficently, is the keynote of the new imperial policy. The same principle of vigorous paternalism was being applied in India; and when strategical points such as the Cape, Ceylon, Mauritius, Malta and the Ionian Islands were acquired and held under the stress of war conditions, the same policy of centralised authority, over-riding local liberty, but fostering native welfare, was applied.

The year 1791 which saw the Pitt Administration attempt to

[1] Dundas to Westmorland, 26 Dec. 1791, H.O. 100/33.
[2] Westmorland to Pitt ("Private and Secret"), 1 Jan. 1792, Pitt Papers, G.D. 8/331.
[3] Same to Same, 13 Nov. 1792, *ibid.*

reform the constitution of Ireland also witnessed the passage of the
Canada Constitutional Act. In both cases the guiding principle was
the same. While Grenville was hammering out the Canadian constitution, his brother Buckingham was urging upon Pitt the necessity
of resisting republicanism in Ireland by reliance on the propertied
class, Catholic as well as Protestant;[1] and Burke, when advocating
the same course to Sir Hercules Langrishe, reminded him that the
same principle had just been applied to Canada.[2] The mind of
Grenville on the Canadian question is fully expounded in a confidential memorandum which he circulated among his Cabinet colleagues for criticism, and which became the foundation of the Act
itself.[3] It explains the reasoning and the purpose behind each provision of the proposed constitution. In his cogitations Grenville reveals
the lesson which the American Revolution had burned into the minds
of himself and his contemporaries. The despotic *régime* of the Quebec
Act of 1774 must be replaced by parliamentary institutions. A form
of representative government must be conceded, and conceded
graciously, for there was no option; but assemblies in the new Empire
must not be the masters of an impotent executive. That was the evil
thing "democracy", which had brought disaster in North America
and was now spreading anarchy in France. The boon to be offered
was the genuine British constitution, which preserved a perfect
equipoise between Crown, Lords and Commons, each of which was
powerful and capable of resisting encroachment upon its own allotted
sphere. It followed, then, that in a colonial constitution there must
be a strong executive, effectively exercising the power of veto and
other royal prerogatives, and a similarly potent Upper Chamber in
the legislature, checking and balancing the Governor on the one
hand and the elected House on the other. "To the want", wrote
Grenville, "of an intermediate Power, to operate as a check, both on
the misconduct of Governors, and on the democratical Spirit, which
prevailed in the Assemblies, the defection of the American Provinces,
may perhaps, be most justly ascribed, than to any other general cause
which can be assigned." Precisely the same device was suggested for
Ireland in the Wellesley memorandum: "I think the House of Lords
might be made use of to advantage...it consists of the principal
landed men in Ireland....And, if they were brought a little more
forward to public notice, they might be made a most powerful engine

[1] See Westmorland to Pitt, 1 Jan. 1792, Pitt Papers, G.D. 8/331.
[2] Burke to Langrishe, Jan. 1792, quoted by Lecky, *op. cit.* III, 32.
[3] General Cruickshank's surmise (*Papers and Records*, Ontario Historical Society, XVIII,
231, 233) that the memorandum was written for the use of the Cabinet by Grenville
himself is confirmed by Grenville's references to it (Grenville to Thurlow, 12 Sept. 1789,
Dropmore Papers, I, 506–10) and by his letter to George III, 12 Oct. 1789 (Royal Archives,
Windsor). It was forwarded by Grenville to Dorchester in Canada on 20 Oct. 1789
(Shortt and Doughty, *Constitutional Documents*, I, 969–70). For accounts of the Act see
C.H.B.E. VI, chap. IV; and Burt, A. L., *The Old Province of Quebec*, chap. XIX.

of Government; and if...a faction should prevail for a time in the House of Commons, might be interposed, with safety and effect, as a barrier against their attempts."[1] How were these two components of the machine, the Governor and the Council, which had suffered political atrophy in the old colonial system to be reinvigorated? Grenville tabulates the measures by which he hoped to gain that object. The underpinning of the executive had already been largely accomplished; but Grenville proposed a further and more startling accession of strength to that arm of government. In Great Britain and Ireland the King possessed a large hereditary revenue (although now exchanged for a Civil List) and it was very regrettable that the same resource had not been provided in the colonies. "Perhaps it is not too late, even now, for the adoption of such a system." If reservations were made of land adjacent to all future grants, the Crown would benefit by an assured and growing revenue.[2] In this conception of the Sovereign "living of his own", financially independent of Parliament, Grenville was imitating the British constitution not of his own time but of a bygone age. This proposal was the only one advanced by him which was not embodied in the Act, although the idea survived in a different form in the system of Clergy Reserves.

The parallel process of balancing the elected chamber by a powerful aristocracy was to be done by remodelling the Council. Hitherto, it had exercised executive as well as legislative functions like the Privy Council of the Tudors. There was now to be a Legislative Council constitutionally distinct from the Executive Council. This division would enable the members of the upper legislative body to be appointed for life instead of "during pleasure" as formerly; and their position should be further reinforced by conferring on them "some personal and hereditary distinction of honour and nobility". Thus, in each province a colonial House of Lords was to be established as the trusty and powerful ally of the imperial executive. In conclusion Grenville claimed that he had outlined "a form of government well adapted to promote the prosperity of that province, and free from the errors which have prevail'd in the constitution of the antient colonies".[3] When forwarding his memorandum to Lord Dorchester, he remarked that the international situation was very favourable "for the adoption of such measures as may tend to consolidate our strength, and increase our resources".[4] Once again the dual motive of the new imperial policy emerges—the fostering of prosperity and the consolidation of authority.

The problem of independent "democratic" assemblies in Ireland and North America was thought to be solved by assimilation to the

---

[1] Dropmore Papers, III, 557.

[2] Grenville repeated this suggestion in his letter to Lord Dorchester of 20 Oct. 1789 (Shortt and Doughty, op. cit. p. 970).

[3] The memorandum is printed in full by Shortt and Doughty, op. cit. pp. 969–87.

[4] Grenville to Dorchester, 20 Oct. 1789, ut supra.

British constitution of the eighteenth century. In the case of Ireland, as we have seen, an effort had been made to approximate thereto by calling into political existence a broad-based aristocracy, and when the attempt failed, assimilation was achieved by the expedient of absorption into the prototype itself. In outward form the new Canadian instrument more closely resembled the original than its American predecessors; but Canadians quickly discovered that what they had received was in practice more akin to the English constitution under the Tudors. The dilemma which had wrecked the First Empire was still unsolved. But curiously enough the new conception of uniformity carried within it the germ of a genuine solution. When the parent organism emerged from its static phase and began to grow again, the political structures assimilated to it began perforce to move also. The Reform Bill of 1832 made the Durham Report of 1839 possible.

The principle of relying on a strong local executive directly controlled from the metropolis was likewise applied to India. The *de facto* independence which had been gained by the British in India was from the imperial point of view even more menacing than that achieved by the thirteen colonies or by Ireland, for it threatened both to destroy the source of wealth and power to which Englishmen were looking as compensation for failure in the West and to imprint an indelible stain on the nation's honour. Unexpectedly a trading company had acquired a vast empire at a time when the State itself was engaged in a gigantic struggle with its European rivals. The interval between the Seven Years' War and the beginning of the American troubles proved too short to teach statesmen at home the nature of their novel responsibilities. When France and Spain joined with insurgent America, and Great Britain was fighting with her back to the wall, the Company's employees became indispensable and therefore masters of the situation. As soon as there was peace the realisation that the British name was held in general execration in India compelled a thorough reconstruction on material as well as humanitarian grounds. Instinctively British politicians of every party turned to centralised control as the remedy. For our present purpose it will be instructive to watch the mental processes of Fox and Pitt in their respective efforts to apply it.

Under the provisions of Fox's India Bill the management of the territories, revenues, and commerce of the East India Company was vested in seven members of Parliament headed by Earl Fitzwilliam, who were to supersede the Court of Directors and the Court of Proprietors. Subject to their instructions, nine proprietors, each of them holding a minimum of £2000 stock in the Company, were nominated as Assistant Commissioners "for the sole purpose of ordering and managing the commerce of the said united Company". Vacancies among the Commissioners were to be filled by His Majesty and among the Assistant Commissioners by a majority vote of the Company proprietors. A quorum of five Commissioners was authorised to remove an Assistant Commissioner found guilty of neglect or misdemeanour; and no person could hold office who supplied shipping to the Company, who was concerned in buying or selling its imports or exports, or against whom a charge of peculation or oppression in India appeared in the Company's records within two years before his nomination. Commissioners and Assistants were to be incapable of holding any appointment with the Company or exercising any other place of profit under the Crown. All charges of corruption, extortion, or disobedience, transmitted by the Governments in India, were to be examined within twenty days of their receipt and if no action was taken against the accused, the Commissioners must put their reasons on record. Finally, the King was empowered to remove any of them upon an address of either House of Parliament.[1]

A candid comparison of this bill with that worked out by Pitt and Dundas and placed on the statute book in the following year leads to the conclusion that Fox's measure was on the whole the more workable of the two. The bill illustrates two constitutional trends of great importance in the development of imperial administration. The exclusion of the Crown from Indian patronage and the proposal to establish a new executive authority for India, separate and distinct from the Cabinet, were gross blunders; but they exemplified a movement to assert the sovereignty of Parliament over colonial dependencies (as opposed to the claims of royal prerogative) which had been spasmodically in progress since the Revolution settlement. The extinction of the Board of Trade in 1782 had been similarly aimed at the Crown in its relation to the Empire. In the Whig tradition Fox was feeling his way towards a system of government for the Empire in which an omnipotent Parliament would itself control executive action overseas. When challenged on the constitutional orthodoxy of his India Board, he retorted that the argument " deprives you, at one stroke, of all the manifold advantages which result from every possible modification of colonization. What system of government can be applied to any foreign settlement or territory whatever, which is not proscribed by the same reasoning?"[2] Fortunately the ascendancy which Pitt afterwards acquired over the mind of George III made the acts of the Crown, in fact as well as in theory, the acts of ministers responsible to Parliament, and so removed the rivalry between the two in the government of dependencies.

The second important feature of Fox's measure is the determination evinced in its provisions to secure good government in India by the

---

[1] The text of the bill and of the companion measure "for the better Government of the Territorial Possessions and Dependencies in India" is printed in *Parl. Hist.* xxiv, 62–89.
[2] *Parl. Hist.* xxiv, 214.

direct subordination of the Company's servants to Parliament. Throughout the debates there is manifest the fear and detestation of a Governor-General who indulged in extortion and wars of aggression with impunity and of the peculators who battened on the misery of the people, secure from the reprobation of the Directors through the influence of their friends in the Court of Proprietors. All intermediate delegacies, for whom the Herculean task of reform must prove too strong, should be swept away: Parliament itself must rule. Furthermore, it must contrive a method by which Indian affairs could be removed to a large degree from the arena of party politics. A dependency, Fox maintained, could not be well governed without continuity of policy. One of the flaws in the government of Ireland was the rapid succession of short-lived Viceroys due to the alternation of parties at Westminster. India must be preserved from it if a just and durable system was to be evolved.[1] The central thought in Fox's mind was expressed in his offer on 16 January 1784 to allow his India bill to be re-cast from top to bottom, "reserving only, that it was made a permanent system, and that the seat of Government was established at home not in India".[2] And again, on moving for leave to bring in a new India bill a week later, he stated that he had only two fundamental principles from which he refused to recede: "that the system for the government of India should be permanent, rendered so by the authority of Parliament; and secondly, that the government should be at home....They were the essential grounds on which he had gone in all his propositions for India."[3]

The same principle dominated the mind of Pitt. When introducing his first India bill he claimed that it secured "a permanent, regular, systematic, and supreme control over all the political affairs of that vast country". As regards unification of control he went further than Fox in one respect and not so far in another. Instead of an independent India Board, executive authority at home must be rendered indivisible by linking Board with Cabinet and making the former analogous to a third Secretaryship of State put in commission. "It was necessary that one executive power should have the superintendence over the whole empire." On the other hand he held that the effectiveness of the central machine would be reinforced and not weakened by powerful administration on the spot: "I, for my part," he declared, "can never expect any duration, any consistency, any degree of permanency in the government either of India or any other of our dependencies, without a strong and permanent government is established in this distracted country."[4] A similar idea, it will be remembered, lay behind the careful buttressing of the position of the Governor in Upper and Lower Canada. For this reason the measure known as Pitt's India Act was less drastic in its disciplinary regulation of officials

[1] *Parl. Hist.* xxiv, 336.   [2] *Ibid.* 378.
[3] *Ibid.* 420.   [4] *Ibid.* 407–10.

in India than Fox's bill had been, and promotion in the civil and military services was left in the hands of the Governments of Bengal, Calcutta and Madras, though under the safeguard that it should be exercised according to seniority of appointment. The local executive, having been purified, was to be fortified and thereafter trusted. It was safer, said Pitt and Dundas, that power and influence in Indian administration should reside abroad, and a strong government in India was the only effective means of securing order and justice.[1] The Governor-General was accordingly made supreme not only over his own Council but also in relation to Bombay and Madras. The unification of power was carried further by the Amending Act of 1788 which enabled the Governor-General in emergency to act without the concurrence of his Council; and when Burke poured out the vials of his wrath against such arbitrary government, Dundas remarked that the Governor-General "was indeed invested with more power, but he had therefore the greater responsibility".[2] The process was carried further still in 1800 when the Marquis Wellesley received a supplementary commission as Captain-General and Commander-in-Chief of the land forces in India, which, wrote Dundas, would "have the complete effect of subjecting all the troops in India to the direction of the Governor-General, acting under the orders of the persons entrusted by His Majesty with the confidential conduct of Indian affairs".[3]

Concentrated power in India was to be guided through a similar concentration in Whitehall. The *desideratum* in the words of Lord Stormont was "a strong government in India, subject to the check and control of a still stronger government at home".[4] But here Pitt faltered. With his eye on political exigencies and impressed with a lively sense of the growing importance for Great Britain of oriental commerce, he took care to secure the prior assent of the Directors of the Company to his bill and paid a heavy price for their acquiescence. Instead of the homogeneous body proposed by Fox, consisting of a Board which controlled everything, while delegating commercial matters to nine Assistant Commissioners, elected by the Company Proprietors, Pitt divided Indian affairs into two mutually exclusive spheres, the one comprising political and revenue administration, and the other commerce. A Board of Control consisting of six unpaid Privy Councillors, including one of the Secretaries of State and the Chancellor of the Exchequer, was to take charge of the former, while the Court of Directors retained its original authority in commerce.[5] Two independent authorities, whose functions frequently overlapped, were bound together in a single administrative system. All despatches to India had to be submitted to the Board, which had no power to

---

[1] *Parl. Hist.* XXIV, 1094 (Pitt) and 1140 (Dundas).   [2] *Parl. Hist.* XXV, 1285.
[3] Dundas to Wellesley, 24 July 1800, C.O. 77/58.
[4] *Parl. Hist.* XXIV, 1297.
[5] *Statutes at Large*, XIV, 477–91 (24 Geo. III, 2nd Session, cap. XXV).

interfere in commercial policy, but which could alter or entirely
re-cast political despatches which the Directors had to sign and send
out whether they concurred or not.[1] A perusal of the correspondence
between the Board and the Directors reveals, as might be expected,
endless friction and accusations of encroachment.[2] During the war
period of 1793–1815, when commerce and politics became interlocked
as never before, Ministers frequently found themselves hindered and
embarrassed by opposing views in Leadenhall Street.[3] But although
Pitt's scheme of unification fell short in this respect, it achieved the
important result—and only just in time—of setting the government
of India directly under the hand of the Cabinet. When the Amending
Act of 1793 formally recognised the primacy of Dundas in Indian
Administration by creating a regular President of the Board, a
Secretary of State for India had to all intents been established.

The national effort to put its Indian house in order reveals formative
influences in imperial policy at large. The crusade of Burke to make
an example of Hastings for all time, and the determination of Fox
and Pitt in their several ways to stamp out aggression and misrule by
the centralisation of authority, indicate an awakened sense of moral
responsibility and a growing conviction that a vigilant and unitary
superintendence was the only reliable weapon. The speeches of Pitt
and many others during the Indian debates express the further
realisation that the humane treatment of subject races was not only
required by Christian ethics but was also a necessary condition of
profitable business. British imperialism in the nineteenth century
never entirely departed from that dual principle to which it owed
much of its success and most of its unpopularity with European rivals,
who tended to mistake enlightened self-interest for hypocrisy. The
principle itself and the administrative machinery through which it
was operated became the model for the government of all non-Anglo-
Saxon dependencies. In the period under review it may be termed
"Colonial Office Government". Subsequently, it was elaborated
into the Crown Colony system.

Before observing the application of the system in the acquired and
conquered colonies, it will be well to pay some attention to the central
organisation. When the American Secretaryship and the Board of
Trade were abolished under Burke's Act in 1782, the duties of the
former were taken over by the Home Office and those of the latter
were distributed, some being undertaken by committees of the Privy
Council. From 1782 to 1786 the colonial business of the Home Office

---

[1] Cf. Sir Wm. Foster, "The India Board, 1784–1858". *Trans. Roy. Hist. Soc.* 3rd Series,
xi, 61–85.
[2] One of many examples of collision between the two took place in Feb. 1788. See
Minutes of the Board of Control (India Office), i, 211–18, and Correspondence of the
Board with the Court of Directors, i, 230–3.
[3] See, for example, Dundas's heated protest to the Chairman against the Company's
interference in foreign affairs, 13 July 1798, C.O. 77/57.

was handled in the first instance by a small staff of clerks, known as the "Plantations Bureau" under Mr Grey Elliott as Under-Secretary; but in 1786 its work was merged into the general routine of the Office. On 5 March 1784 a new standing committee of Council was established, consisting of eighteen members, and described as the Committee "for the consideration of all matters relating to trade and the plantations". In colonial affairs this Committee for Trade (as provided by Burke's Act) was excluded from patronage and did not receive despatches and petitions from the colonies unless forwarded for some special reference by the Secretary of State. It concerned itself with every aspect of commercial policy, shipping, land grants, and settlement, and with the review of colonial legislation on reference from the Privy Council.[1] The incessant industry and expert knowledge of its only President, Charles Jenkinson (subsequently Lord Hawkesbury and first Earl of Liverpool) quickly endowed it with an authority analogous to that of the old Board of Trade. Such important matters as the policy to be adopted towards American ships and merchandise in the British West Indies, measures to prevent the Newfoundland Fishery from becoming a "colony", the terms of the proposed treaty with Ireland in 1785, the new Navigation Law (popularly known as Hawkesbury's Act), and the suggested abolition or restriction of the Slave Trade, were investigated and reports submitted, which in every case determined the policy of the Ministry. The minutes of the Committee with their *verbatim* reports of witnesses' evidence and the enormous file of deposited memorials and statistical returns constitute a detailed documentary history of British colonial and foreign trade between 1784 and 1801.[2] In August 1786 it was reconstituted as "the Committee of the Privy Council for Trade and Foreign Plantations" with an enlarged clerical staff. Its terms of reference were the same, but in addition to the original members the following were appointed *ex officio*: the First Lord of the Treasury, the First Lord of the Admiralty, the two Secretaries of State, the Chancellor and Under-Treasurer of the Exchequer, the Speaker of the House of Commons, and (provided that they were Privy Councillors) the Paymaster of the Forces, the Chancellor of the Duchy of Lancaster, the Treasurer of the Navy and the Master of the Mint. The Speaker of the Irish House of Commons and any British Privy Councillor holding office in Ireland were also included. Jenkinson, now Lord Hawkesbury, was nominated President, with Grenville as his deputy.[3] From now on the most assiduous members of the Committee, apart from the President, were Pitt and Grenville. These two

---

[1] Cf. Manning, H. T., *British Colonial Government after the American Revolution*, Yale Historical Publications, Miscellaneous, xxvi (1933), chap. iii, and Lingelbach, A. L., article in *Amer. Hist. Rev.* xxx, 701-27.

[2] The Minutes comprise the series B.T. 5 and the documents ("Board of Trade Miscellaneous") the series B.T. 6 in the P.R.O.

[3] See B.T. 5/4, pp. 1-3.

were also frequently present at the India Board. When it is remembered that Pitt was controlling expenditure at the Treasury Board, and that Dundas, and afterwards Grenville, was in charge of colonial correspondence at the Home Office, it will be realised that every branch of imperial administration was within the direct cognisance of the "triumvirate".

Reduced in volume as colonial business was after 1783, its attachment to the Office of the Secretary for Home Affairs overworked that Department. The Secretary was responsible for domestic affairs, which involved a regular correspondence with each Government Department,[1] for Ireland, and for the Empire, exclusive of India. When an Irish crisis was in progress and despatches were being exchanged with the Lord-Lieutenant every twenty-four hours (which before 1800 happened not infrequently), other business tended to be neglected. But on the whole the enquiries of colonial Governors in their despatches were answered with reasonable punctuality and at the direction of the Secretary himself. There appears to have been no definite allocation of clerks to any of the three fields for which the Office was responsible, and the Secretary with his Under-Secretary dealt with incoming correspondence, whether domestic, Irish, or colonial, as it arrived. An able Under-Secretary, such as Sir Evan Nepean, was in the habit of conducting a correspondence of his own with departmental secretaries at home, with the Chief Secretary in Ireland, and with colonial Governors. These last in particular found it very convenient to be able to express their needs and grievances informally, leaving it to the discretion of the recipient to pass on the information to the Secretary of State. By this means also much useful information and advice was transmitted to the colonies which would have been difficult to incorporate in formal despatches.

The similarity, already noted, between British policy in Ireland and in Canada in this period was clearly not unconnected with the circumstance that Irish and Canadian despatches were delivered to the same building and were dealt with by the same persons. And when colonial administration was transferred in 1801 from the Home Office to the War Office, the policy of direct rule was not likely to be weakened by a Minister immersed in the conduct of a world war in which colonial dependencies as sources of supply and strategic points were vital factors. Thus the machinery of imperial control at home consisted as regards India of the Board of Control, managed by Dundas; for commercial policy and the review of colonial legislation, of the Committee of Council for Trade and Plantations, conducted by Jenkinson; and for Ireland and the Colonies, of the Home Office and subsequently the War Office. While other Committees of Council

---

[1] There is much useful information about the Colonies in the correspondence of the Home Office with other Departments, notably in the three series: H.O. 28, H.O. 32 and H.O. 35.

formally reviewed Irish legislation and acted as a Supreme Court of Appeal in colonial causes, the Council itself functioned as a kind of clearing house. Ministers submitted debatable points of law and policy which the Council referred to the appropriate Board or Committee and gave effect to the resulting recommendation by Orders-in-Council. Linking these various parts and co-ordinating the whole, were the two Secretaries of State. Operating at the will of the machine and responsible to it were Governors-General and Governors endowed with wide powers. In outward form this structure did not differ substantially from that in existence before 1783; but the growing ascendancy which Pitt acquired over his ministerial colleagues on the one side and the monarch on the other laid the foundations of the modern Cabinet system and so *inter alia* effected a cohesion in imperial administration previously unknown.

The territories within the Empire in the period under consideration, exclusive of Ireland, India, and Canada, may be divided into two categories: the surviving remnants of the Old Empire on the North American seaboard (reinforced by the Loyalists) and in the West Indies, and foreign colonies acquired by conquest during the wars with Revolutionary France and Napoleon. In the former the normal type of colonial constitution, consisting of Governor, nominated Council and elected Assembly, was adhered to. The only exception was Cape Breton, which because of its meagre population was ruled by a Governor and a small Council of officials until its reunion with Nova Scotia in 1820. A detailed consideration of constitutional policy in the established British Colonies is unnecessary, for the evolution of the new imperial system is not to be found there. But certain trends in this field merit attention, since they help to explain the course of action adopted in the new areas peopled by non-British Europeans and native races. The maritime colonies of Nova Scotia, New Brunswick, and Prince Edward Island were as yet too weak seriously to take up the challenge presented by an immovable executive confronting a potentially irresistible legislature; and in the West Indies the loss of political leaders by the growth of absentee landlordism relegated those colonies to a political backwater.[1] The attitude of Secretaries of State towards colonies already enjoying representative institutions (or in the case of the migrating Loyalists claiming them as a right) may be summarised as a scrupulous regard for local constitutional privileges previously recognised and a desire to prevent encroachment or innovation. Further retreat would entail a surrender in North America to the republicanism of the United States and would open the door in the West Indies to French Jacobinism. The equipoise between executive and legislature, regarded as the essential characteristic of the British constitution, was to be reproduced as far as possible in the colonies. The quality of the British con-

[1] Ragatz, L. J., *Absentee Landlordism in the British Caribbean*, 1750–1833, *passim*.

stitution was twice blessed, for its insistence on a strong colonial executive in imitation of the monarchy was a bulwark against subversive movements from outside and at the same time the safest guarantee of the imperial connection. In respect to the surviving parts of the Old Empire Ministers were dealing with units which were either in their infancy or in a state of political decline. In particular the economic and strategic dependence of the West Indian islands upon Great Britain was such that political submission was in the long run inevitable. Had that not been so, the emancipation of slaves in 1833 would have produced a second "American" Revolution. Moreover, the fact that the Imperial Government was paying the salaries of the Governor, the judges, and other civil administrators as well as bearing a large proportion of the cost of the military establishments restrained the local legislatures from exerting that day-to-day pressure which had characterised the policy of their American predecessors. Ministers were well aware of the value of this asset. When Drury Ottley was appointed Chief Justice of St Vincent in 1787 it happened that no salary was allotted to him. Repeated petitions to Lord Sydney, the Secretary of State (1782–89), failed to elicit an answer. At length, "despairing of any redress from Government", Ottley caused the circumstances of his case to be explained to the island Assembly, which unanimously agreed to allow him a stipend out of local revenue. Such a solution was not however acceptable to Lord Sydney, who informed Ottley's agent, "that it was by no means proper for the Judges in the Colonies to be dependent upon the Colonial Assemblies for their support". It was therefore Sydney's wish that an official refusal should not be urged, "as it was the intention of Ministry, so soon as they might have leisure to consider of the subject, to make proper provision for the Law Officers in the colonies".[1] The Assembly's offer was accordingly withdrawn.

The responsibility of executive officers to the imperial authority was insisted upon, not only as a check upon local ambition, but as a protection against arbitrary conduct. An illustration of this comes from Cape Breton. As so often happens among officials in small isolated communities, the Lieutenant-Governor, William Macarmick, was at loggerheads with Abraham Cuyler, the Secretary, Registrar, and Clerk to the Council. Cuyler was charged before the Council with various misdemeanours, Macarmick acting as prosecutor, cross-examining the defendant, and also giving evidence, as did two of the Council. They thus gave judgment upon their own testimony. Dismissed from all his offices, Cuyler appealed to the Privy Council. On hearing the case the Committee for Colonial Appeals sternly reprobated these proceedings as "unwarrantable" and highly necessary to be discountenanced. Moreover, in their view the case presented

---

[1] Ottley to Dundas, 29 Aug. 1791, Pitt Papers (West Indies Miscellaneous), G.D. 8/350.

further and more serious implications. The Governor had used his Council, not merely to remove a Councillor, but to dismiss an imperial officer. In all such cases "the Governor is to exercise his own judgment and he alone is personally responsible, whether he does it of his own head or by the advice of his Council". "If", added the Committee, "under the pretence of giving advice to the Governor, the Council were to exercise an authority of this dangerous nature, no public officer, nor indeed any other person, would be safe from such enquiries." Cuyler had already been sufficiently punished for his insolence: the graver charges had been refuted: he must be reinstated in his offices forthwith.[1] In short, it was deemed essential that the imperial power should control its own servants and not allow any self-constituted local authority to intervene.

At the same time the lesson of the American revolt made the Government careful to avoid offending colonial susceptibilities whenever possible. The treatment of Barbados, where a strong tradition of local privilege had existed since the days of the Protectorate, is a case in point. On the recall of Governor Cunningham, who had aroused the fury of the Barbadian Legislature, in June 1782, a special effort was made to conciliate the islanders. The new Governor, David Parry, was furnished with Instructions which differed in material points from those of his predecessors.[2] With respect to the vexed question of appropriation of supply, the usual clause forbidding the Governor to allow any public money to be issued except by warrant under his own hand by and with the consent of the Council was qualified with the following addition: "Provided however...that if any money bill shall be presented to you for your assent, the provisions of which...although not conformable to this our Instruction, shall nevertheless be agreeable to the usual and established custom and practice in bills of a similar nature in our said island, You may give your assent thereunto, anything herein contained to the contrary notwithstanding." In justifying "the ground of this essential alteration" to the Lord President of the Council the Secretary of State explained that it had been a long-established custom of the Barbados Assembly and frequently permitted by the Crown to insert a clause in money bills providing that the disposal of the money so raised should be lodged in commissioners named in the Act.[3] Governor Cunningham had raised a storm by standing to his Instructions and refusing assent to any money bill which vested the expenditure in hands other than his own. In this significant instance imperial theory had been adjusted to suit colonial practice.

A further important concession granted in these Instructions related to the imposition of fees in the island. Exorbitant fees had long been

[1] Privy Council Register, P.C. 2/135, pp. 139–44 (15 June 1790).
[2] Parry's Instructions, dated 6 Sept. 1782, occupy a volume of their own, C.O. 29/20.
[3] Draft letter to the Lord President, 27 Aug. 1782, C.O. 28/59, ff. 354–7.

a grievance in the West Indies, and the Barbados Assembly in particular had denied the legality of fees established by order of the Governor-in-Council. Governor Parry was accordingly instructed to propose that the Assembly themselves should draft a bill establishing a permanent table of fees payable to public officers, which should be "as little burdensome as possible".[1] "It seems very proper", runs the official comment, "to prevent any exertion of authority under His Majesty's Instructions which may create dissention between the Governors and the governed." A further "Office" memorandum in noting the new Instruction about money bills provides an excellent summary of the position adopted by the Government towards the old colonies. The altered Instruction permitted the Governor "to assent to such Acts as are consistent with the usual and established custom of the island, but does not authorise him to consent to any new or improper innovation or incroachment on the part of the Assembly".[2] But a policy of maintaining the constitutional *status quo* could only be successful if Ministers at home devoted a vigilant attention to administrative detail, and this they were not prepared to do. In company with most of his West Indian colleagues, Governor Parry repeatedly insisted that he could not maintain the prerogatives of his office unless his suggestions were supported by Government. How could he expect to exert an "influence" in the Assembly analogous to the manipulation of the British House of Commons by Administration unless local patronage was dispensed in accordance with his recommendations? But Secretaries of State usually turned a deaf ear to such proposals: colonial patronage played too useful a part in the political game at home.[3]

Notwithstanding the concessions granted to Barbados in 1782, Parry five years later admitted that he was fighting a losing battle. "The inconsistencies and irregularities practised in this Government", he wrote, "and the encroachments made upon the Royal Prerogative are beyond conception great." Many amendments were necessary to save the Governor and Council from being undermined "by the vast weight of pecuniary influence that already has been, and in future will be thrown into the democratic scale".[4] By 1806 the situation had not improved. In that year Lord Seaforth, then Governor of Barbados, cited the various inroads into executive authority made by the Assembly and went on to propose the intervention of Parliament as the only remedy. A Commission should be sent out to investigate the divergent privileges claimed by colonial legislatures, and its recommendations should form the basis of an Act "to reduce them all to the analogies of the Mother Country, and establish all their rights, privileges and modes of proceeding upon

[1] *Ibid.*; cf. Privy Council Register, P.C. 2/131, p. 286 (5 May 1786).
[2] "Remarks on the Barbados Instructions", C.O. 29/59, ff. 452–4.
[3] See, for example, Parry to Nepean, 21 Oct. 1787, C.O. 28/61, ff. 91–4.
[4] Same to Same, 18 Dec. 1787, *ibid.* ff. 116–19.

identically the same footing".[1] A consummation devoutly to be wished; but Ministers of the time held a rooted objection to airing colonial problems in Parliament and so providing grist for the Opposition mill.[2] The previous occasion of parliamentary intervention after 1765 had not been noteworthy for the happiness of its results. Moreover, they themselves regarded constitutional problems in the Atlantic and Caribbean colonies with a mixture of aversion and indifference; aversion because the problems bristled with difficulties, and indifference because they were absorbed elsewhere in the task of creating a new imperial system on a different basis. It was symptomatic that this passivity did not extend to commerce. Their efforts before the outbreak of war in 1793 to substitute the British North American colonies for the United States as the source of supply for timber and provisions in the West Indies and to replace American by British shipping in those waters were vigorous and unremitting. The old island colonies, as well as those acquired by conquest, received close attention as the producers of sugar and (even more important during this period) of cotton for Lancashire mills; and under the "free port" system many of them were exploited as avenues through which British manufactures were insinuated into the Spanish empire. The rapid rise of England to industrial pre-eminence and the economic repercussions of a world war were shifting the emphasis of her imperialism.

The "Ceded Islands" in the West Indies, that is to say, the French islands of Grenada, Dominica and St Vincent, which after being ceded to Great Britain in 1763 were recaptured by France during the American War and returned by the Treaty of 1783, constitutionally occupy an intermediate position between the old British settlements and the foreign islands captured after 1793. They are of interest for our present purpose, since they represent a link in the history of the incorporation of foreign administrative systems into the British Empire, thus connecting French Canada with Dutch Guiana and Cape Colony. The declared intention of establishing an Assembly in Canada which was reversed by the Quebec Act was fulfilled in the case of the French Islands, while the Canadian precedent of according political recognition to Roman Catholicism was followed. They are the sole examples (apart from Lower Canada) of the normal British colonial constitution being applied to a foreign population.[3] The experience gained from the experiment was hardly calculated to encourage a repetition of it elsewhere. Although weak in numbers the Anglo-French communities were far from being docile. When Governor Orde of Dominica in 1786 informed the Council that His Majesty had sent an engineer to fortify the island and recommended

---

[1] Seaforth to Cooke, 3 March 1806, C.O. 28/74. Quoted by Manning, *op. cit.* pp. 67–8.
[2] Cf. *ibid.* pp. 68–70.
[3] There were many British planters in each of the three Islands, but the French appear to have been in a majority.

that a sufficient quantity of negro labourers should be furnished to work on the fortifications, both Council and Assembly agreed. But when the former attempted to amend the proposed joint Address to the Governor by providing that the required slaves would be supplied "when called for by His Excellency", the Assembly unanimously rejected the proposed insertion. A violent quarrel ensued, in which the latter refused to give way. The bill as eventually passed provided that the slaves would be furnished by a committee of the Assembly on requisition from the engineer in charge. Equally heated was a controversy in the same year which arose from the refusal of the Assembly to continue to pay for the upkeep of an armed force, which had been raised to suppress a slave revolt. Orde maintained that the task of dealing with the revolt had been delegated to him and the Council, and that the Assembly could not suddenly revoke that authority and refuse further payment to the men whom he had engaged to fight for them. To his charge that they were directly breaking their word solemnly pledged the Assembly retorted that apparently the Governor still denied their clear right to decide when and how public money was to be expended, and Orde was obliged to submit.[1] The upshot of these and other quarrels was an appeal from the Assembly to the Privy Council for Orde's dismissal. The proceedings which followed dragged on from June 1790 until April 1793 owing to the dilatoriness of the Assembly in forwarding documentary evidence; and, incidentally, they illustrate the patience of the Privy Council in dealing with colonial complaints. The charges were eventually dismissed as altogether frivolous.[2] This comparative new-comer to the Empire had proved as haughty and as quarrelsome as the original members.

The situation existing in the island of Grenada and the manner in which it was handled exerted an important influence upon constitutional policy with respect to acquired dependencies. In obedience to his Instructions, which followed the standard form, General Melville in 1763 called an Assembly and required each member to subscribe to the declaration against the doctrine of transubstantiation, thereby excluding the French from the Legislature. Although an Ordinance three years later granted them the franchise, the position was thereby exacerbated; for the British minority resented the control over elections which the French acquired, while the latter refused to accept a legislature from which they, the majority of the electorate, were excluded. French candidates were elected to the Assembly, but were refused admission. The island was in a tumult. In alarm the Grenada

---

[1] Copies of the Minutes of the Dominica Council, 13 April–24 July 1786 and of the Assembly, 13 April–13 July 1786. Privy Council—Unbound Papers, P.C. 1/61, bundle 15.
[2] Privy Council Register, P.C. 2/135, pp. 106–11 (5 June 1790); pp. 134–9 (15 June); p. 275 (1 Oct.); pp. 436–7 (1 Feb. 1791); pp. 478–82 (19 Feb.); pp. 487–8 (24 Feb.); P.C. 2/136, pp. 115–30 (21 May); pp. 185–92 (25 June); pp. 185–296 (25 June, 30 June, 6 July, 3 and 4 Aug.); p. 387 (3 Dec.); P.C. 2/137, pp. 331–2 (21 Jan. 1792); pp. 76 and 267 (14 June and 19 Dec.); P.C. 2/138, pp. 147–59 (8 April 1793).

Proprietors in London approached Lord Hillsborough (in 1768) and prevailed upon him to secure the approval of the Privy Council to an Order permitting the participation of the French in the Legislature and in public office. Stormy scenes followed; but eventually French members were admitted to both Council and Assembly. Unfortunately the behaviour of the French population after the capture of the island by France in 1779 so embittered the British subjects, that when they came into their own again in 1784, they passed repressive legislation against the French and announced their determination "to shut them out of the Council and Assembly for ever".

A petition on behalf of the aggrieved colonists and a counter-petition from the Grenada Agent were considered by the Privy Council in May and June 1787; but their Lordships in some perplexity postponed a decision. Further petitions in 1789 obliged the Privy Council to face the issue. The argument of the British settlers was that, although His Majesty had the right to establish what form of constitution he thought fit in a conquered or ceded country, he could not by his prerogative make any alteration in the fundamentals of the constitution originally granted: "that having once established a protestant Government by excluding the Roman Catholics from the Legislature, his prerogative did not warrant him to introduce a Popish Mixture into the Government without the consent of the people, whose right to assent or dissent...attached from the time the Commission was carried into execution by calling an Assembly."[1] The argument thus advanced was referred in a written "Case" to the Law Officers of the Crown,[2] who decided that the contention of the British inhabitants was correct: that when the Crown had established a constitution in 1763 it thereafter possessed no prerogative power of amendment.[3] The Order-in-Council of 1768 was thereafter invalid, nor could the cession of Grenada to the British Crown in 1783 be regarded as a new acquisition and so revive the prerogative power. Thus the wise recognition of French Catholic privileges in Canada accorded under the Quebec Act and confirmed by the Act of 1791 was reversed in the case of Grenada. A short bill passed through Parliament would have removed the difficulty raised by the Law Officers' ruling. But, as already noted, recourse to Parliament in colonial matters was not favoured by Ministers. It is also possible that the alarming prospect of a pro-French majority in the Assembly of a vulnerable island was not without its effect. At any rate, this particular model of the British

[1] The above account is drawn from (i) Governor Lucas to Sydney, 9 April 1786 (C.O. 102/15; a copy in Pitt Papers, G.D. 8/348); (ii) Governor Mathew to Grenville, 30 May 1789 (C.O. 102/16, also in G.D. 8/348); (iii) Petition to the Privy Council by the Marquis de Casaux and J. L. André, Agents for the French inhabitants of Grenada (G.D. 8/348).

[2] Privy Council Register, P.C. 2/134, pp. 509–20 (18 Feb. 1790); also Unbound Papers, P.C. 1/62, under same date.

[3] Law Officers' Reports, H.O. 48/1, ff. 376–81 (10 June 1790).

constitution was in future to be worked by subjects who were British-born. As will be subsequently noted, the same policy was adopted though by a different method in Guiana. As a constitutional precedent the decision had far-reaching implications. Since it had been held that the Crown could not alter a constitution of its own creation once it was in being, it followed that in all conquered territories the initial form in which local sovereignty happened to be established became at once rigid and definitive, unless and until the authority of Parliament was invoked. This circumstance provides a further reason for the chariness of the Colonial Office in formulating constitutions for conquered dependencies and the careful investigations which usually preceded any such formulation.

Thus the policy of Government in relation to the old established colonies in the West Indies reproduced features similar to that pursued in Canada; on the one hand, a rehabilitation of the executive, and on the other, a careful regard for the privileges of the local legislature—so repeating the balance of the parent constitution. The ideal equipoise was never achieved, because in these colonies the executive officer on the spot was insufficiently supported by the executive at home. The Ceded Islands for their part represented the conquests of a previous generation and had been provided as a matter of course with constitutions of the normal colonial type. But the experiment of working representative institutions with a mixed population of British and foreign stock had been unhappy. To the impatience engendered by the turbulence of the British islands was added the fear of an Assembly being controlled by the supporters of a foreign power. And, lastly, it had been learned that if the Crown once established local representation, the terms of the concession could be neither recalled nor modified. Is it surprising that experience of this kind taught the statesmen of the post-1783 era that, when they themselves acquired colonies by conquest, the better way was to break with an unprofitable tradition and imitate the centralised method applied in India by continuing the autocratic machinery conveniently inherited from their Spanish and Dutch predecessors?

We have now to consider the policy of the British Government with regard to dependencies conquered after 1793, and in this connexion it is important to bear in mind the character of the legal basis on which it subsisted. The indeterminate position of the Crown in respect to conquered territories was defined in Lord Mansfield's famous judgment of 1774 in the case of *Campbell* v. *Hall*. It was then determined that Hall, the Collector of Customs in Grenada, had acted illegally in levying an export duty of $4\frac{1}{2}$ per cent. on sugar exported from the island by Campbell. The Collector had done so on the authority of Letters Patent of 20 July 1764, which imposed this duty in Grenada as in the case of Barbados and the Leeward Islands. But Lord Mansfield ruled that since an Assembly had been officially and publicly promised and a Governor commissioned to convoke such a body, the King had thereby divested himself of the power of taxation in the island. No tax could therefore be levied except by representatives of the people themselves or by the British Parliament.[1] The subsequent ruling which for the same reason denied the power of the Crown to alter the Grenada constitution in favour of the French was thus an amplification of Lord Mansfield's decision. In delivering judgment, the latter laid down six fundamental propositions, which may be summarised as follows: (i) A conquered country becomes a dominion of the Crown and therefore subject to the legislative power of Parliament. (ii) The conquered inhabitants become subjects and cease to be aliens. (iii) Articles of capitulation and peace treaties under which the country is surrendered or ceded are inviolate. (iv) The local law and legislation of every dominion is the true rule for all questions arising there, and Englishmen while in residence enjoy no privileges distinct from the natives. (v) The laws of a conquered country continue in force until they are altered by the conqueror. (vi) The Crown by virtue of its prerogative has power to alter old laws and make new ones for a conquered country, but subject to two *provisos*—that this power is subordinate to that of the King in Parliament, and secondly is incapable of functioning contrary to fundamental principles. The Crown, for example, could not exempt an inhabitant from the imperial laws of trade or from the authority of Paliament.[2] A further point stressed by Lord Mansfield was the fact that the Commission issued to the Governor of Grenada had reserved no right of legislation by the King or by the Governor-in-Council pending the summoning of an Assembly. By implication, therefore, the Crown possessed the right to reserve to itself legislative authority and to exercise its own discretion as to time and form in transferring that authority to a representative body. This right was duly exercised in subsequent years.[3]

The constitutional experience gained in a variety of fields up to the outbreak of war in 1793 was accordingly cumulative in its influence. The need for stricter control in Ireland, in Canada, and in the old West Indian colonies, the necessity of direct rule in India, the unhappy effects of applying representative government in the Ceded Islands, and the significant implications of the legal judgments of 1774 and 1790 in the case of Grenada, were factors which all converged in the same direction of authoritative rule when new areas were conquered and added to the Empire. When therefore Sir Charles Grey, the Commander-in-Chief in the West Indies, in 1794 requested

---

[1] The power of Parliament to impose taxes in the Colonies was renounced four years later under the Act 18 Geo. III, cap. 13.

[2] Lord Mansfield's judgment is printed in full in Shortt and Doughty, *op. cit.* i, 522–31.

[3] Cf. Keith, A. B., *Constitutional History of the First British Empire*, pp. 16–17.

that Governors be appointed and civil constitutions be established without delay in the recently conquered colonies of Martinique and San Domingo, Commissions and Instructions were drawn up which represented a clear break with traditional form. From the Commissions all references to a Council and Assembly and local powers of legislation disappeared, while the Governor's Instructions were new instruments. The government of these French colonies was to revert to the *ancien régime* in operation there before 1789, subject to modifications which might subsequently appear to be necessary. All executive powers, civil and military, were vested solely in the Governor. A small consultative Council was to be selected by him, but, as with Governors in India, he was free to act contrary to their advice, provided that the reasons of the dissenting Councillors were put on record and transmitted to the Secretary of State. Councillors might be Roman Catholics and in that case would take the oath prescribed by the Quebec Act. The Roman Catholic faith was to be maintained, although all Protestant forms of worship were to be tolerated. French law and French courts were retained, and the old fiscal system was to be continued without the addition of new taxes and under the direct superintendence of the British Treasury.[1] In fact, the principles of government which had been established in French Canada by the Quebec Act, and which changing circumstances had thwarted in that region, were now revived in the case of the French West Indies. Moreover, as might be expected, these Instructions became the "Office" model for Governors appointed to colonies subsequently conquered, not only in the Caribbean but also in eastern waters. It is not inapt, therefore, to describe the policy embodied in the Quebec Act of 1774 as the basis of British Crown Colony government.

The manner in which the British Government dealt with the island of Trinidad after its capture from the Spaniards in 1796 is particularly significant in this respect. Trinidad was large and fertile, only requiring enterprise and capital to become a source of great wealth. It contained some 910,000 acres of cultivable land of which the Spaniards had developed only one twenty-fifth part; and it was estimated that about 420,000 acres of this undeveloped land was suitable for the cultivation of sugar. Moreover, it was situated close to the front door of the Spanish empire, and if incorporated into the British "Free Port" system would immensely accelerate the process of smuggling British manufactures into Spanish America. The potentialities of the Island in this respect were already known to British merchants, who for some years had been taking advantage of the free port facilities offered by the Spanish Government itself.[2] Under what

---

[1] Manning, *op. cit.* pp. 341–4.
[2] Cf. "Reasons for continuing the collection of the 3½ per Cent Duties at Trinidade", enclosed in Cochrane's letter of 19 Sept. 1800, Melville MSS. II, f. 94 (Rhodes House Library, Oxford).

form of administration was the new acquisition to be governed and developed? The terms of the Commission and Instructions issued to the first Governor, Colonel Thomas Picton, in 1801 closely followed those adopted for Martinique and San Domingo. The island was to be ruled according to its ancient institutions under a Governor enjoying autocratic powers. But in the case of Trinidad this apparently simple solution presented peculiar difficulties. In the first place the Spanish constitution (which conformed to the standard type in South America) vested in the Governor executive and judicial powers exceeding those possessed by any British Viceroy, but at the same time imposed the usual substantial checks through the superintendence of the provincial *Audiencia* and the power of the *Cabildo* or municipal authority in the chief town. These checks were, of course, unknown to the British constitution. Furthermore, the population was not predominantly Spanish but consisted of a majority of free negroes, many settlers from the French Islands, and a number of British planters. If the island was to be organised as a great emporium for Spanish-American trade, English commercial law and courts competent to administer it were important *desiderata*, and British merchants opened a sustained campaign to acquire these advantages together with a constitution of the normal British type. The cry of Adam Lymburner and the merchants of Montreal and Quebec was being repeated.

On the other hand under the influence of the Humanitarians in England the case of Trinidad was used to exert pressure in an unexpected direction. After calling for information with regard to the island, Canning on 27 May 1802 submitted a motion in the House of Commons that His Majesty be petitioned to refrain from granting any allotments of new land in the island until regulations had been approved by Parliament to prevent the extension of cultivation from causing an increase in the slave trade. In an eloquent speech he urged the House to take this opportunity of making a complete break with the traditional plantation system in the West Indies. To clear the ground and to convert Trinidad into a vast sugar-producing factory would, he computed, cost the lives of one million negro slaves. And to what end? The price of sugar, already a glut on the London market due to war conditions, would be ruinously lowered; the island would be weakened in the face of external foes by the standing menace of a slave revolt; and England would have proved that when put to the test she could not resist riches even at the price of human misery. Here was a golden opportunity to break away from the vicious plantation system and inaugurate a new system of colonisation in the Caribbean. "Do not", he cried, "make large grants or sales to great capitalists. Look for your settlers among classes of men who will be induced to become residents in the island." And he submitted a number of suggestions for securing such a population. Colonisation along these lines, he frankly admitted, would not produce as large a quantity of sugar to swell the Custom House entries for the first few years. "But are you to raise a sum of money, or to found a colony? Would you lay the foundation for the returns of a twelve-month, or for the greatness of an age? I hope, the latter."[1] Although the motion was not adopted, Addington promised that no land grants in Trinidad would be made until the report of the newly appointed Commissioners had been received and carefully considered. Canning's motion had been a plea for the intervention of Parliament. As such, it failed. The knowledge that if Parliament were allowed to meddle with colonial questions, the Government would inevitably become involved in the struggle between Humanitarians and planters, sharpened the determination of Ministers to rule the new empire themselves. But although the unlimited powers of the Imperial Government in ordering the new colonies was to be wielded by the Cabinet instead of Parliament, the demand that they should be exercised to further nobler ends in colonisation was not without effect. Subsequent efforts to persuade the old West Indian Colonies to ameliorate slave conditions were a failure, but the same policy was *imposed* on Trinidad by the famous Ordinance; and when the Albany Settlement was established in South Africa, slavery of any kind was forbidden within its borders. Just as Burke and Fox in flaming words had insisted that unlimited centralised authority was the only effective means for the cleansing of Indian administration, so the enemies of slavery, in revolt against plantation conditions but thwarted by planter oligarchies, saw the unrestricted prerogative power in conquered colonies as a weapon with which to enforce humanitarian principles.

These circumstances convinced Lord Hobart, the Secretary of State, that Trinidad should if possible be developed by free labour and that the establishment of representative institutions was to be avoided until the case in its favour had been conclusively proved.[2] The Commission of Enquiry promised by Addington and consisting of Governor Picton, Colonel Fullarton and Captain Hood, was instructed to make a thorough investigation of the conditions obtaining in the island. They were to recommend a form of government adapted to an exceptionally heterogeneous population, to examine the code of laws and advise on any changes which they might deem desirable, and to offer suggestions for the colonisation of the island, bearing in mind that the climate did not preclude settlement by Europeans.[3] Unfortunately Fullarton's fiery temper and the despotic methods of Picton quickly occasioned such vituperative quarrels between them that government fell into complete confusion and the

[1] *Parl. Hist.* xxxvi, 854–82.
[2] See Hobart to Picton, 18 Feb. and 26 June, 1802, C.O. 285/2.
[3] Hobart to the Commissioners, 16 Oct. 1802, C.O. 295/3.

planters followed their rulers into two bitterly hostile factions.[1] The administrative problem had to wait until the recall of the Commissioners and their replacement by Governor Hislop in 1804. To him Hobart at once propounded his views. The Canadian and West Indian colonies offered three types of constitution from which to choose: the standard model of Governor with Council and Assembly; secondly, Governor and Council only; and thirdly, the type obtaining in conquered territories in which the Governor was the sole delegate of the sovereign authority of the Crown. Hobart made it clear that he himself favoured the Governor-and-Council model of the Quebec Act, because in his view the objective was "the gradual advancement of the colony to such a state as will enable His Majesty in due time to extend to it the further benefits of the constitution of the other British colonies". The power of the Governor and Council to enact ordinances would make possible the gradual introduction of British law.[2] Hobart thus conceived of the constitutional structure of the Empire as a coherent organism, within which the subordinate units gradually approximated in form to the parent prototype. Under such a system each new-comer to the Empire would at once enter a probationary stage, from which it was possible to rise by steady gradations to the full status of representative government.

Hislop responded to these suggestions by sending his Attorney-General, Gloster, to England with a draft constitution, which the latter had prepared in the form of a parliamentary bill, together with an explanatory memorandum. After giving his reasons for rejecting an elective Assembly as well as a gubernatorial autocracy, Gloster advocated the formation of a Council of life members, which in addition to the legislative functions of the Quebec Council should have power to impose taxation. When Gloster arrived in England, however, the Addington Ministry had fallen and the Napoleonic menace relegated the affairs of Trinidad to the background until the year 1810. By that time the renewed pressure of London merchants interested in Trinidad compelled a decision. After considering the representations of the merchants who urged the introduction of English commercial law, and of the colonists who wanted an Assembly which should include French, Spaniards and British but not the free people of colour, Lord Liverpool finally decided to leave things exactly as they were. His reasons for the decision are revealing. The Gloster plan for a nominated legislature commended itself but was rejected from a fear that Parliament would not give its consent to a constitution which (with the solitary exception of Cape Breton) had no counterpart in the Old Empire. The alternative then was either

---

[1] See Fullarton's defence of his conduct to Earl Camden, 10 July 1803, Melville MSS. ii, ff. 106–9.

[2] Hobart to Hislop, 22 Feb. 1804, C.O. 295/8. This important despatch is described in full by Manning, op. cit. pp. 354–6.

to establish a system of government analogous to that of the other
West Indian islands or to retain the rights of Crown and Parliament
in a new colony entire and unimpaired. On general grounds Liverpool informed Hislop that he had decided to stand by the latter
course, but more particularly so in the case of Trinidad because the
creation of an elective chamber there would vest power in the hands
of a non-British majority. Moreover, the duty of enforcing the recent
Act abolishing the Slave Trade made it especially important that the
imperial power should retain its legislative authority in any new
colony which owned slaves. Trinidad was, therefore, to have no local
legislature of any kind which might thwart the supreme will of
imperial authority expressed through the Governor.[1] In laying down
the principle that the normal type of British colonial constitution was
inapplicable in a non-British community, and that in any case the
central government must retain power in its own hands in order to
mould new colonies to its purpose, Liverpool was applying a policy
in Trinidad which was already in operation at the Cape and elsewhere, and was also giving to it a general formulation for the future.
The external pressure of a world war which called for direct control
over the economic and strategic resources of conquered colonies, the
fact that the new subjects were non-British, potentially hostile, but
without claim to British liberties, and the determination in England
to enforce a detested humanitarianism, were varied factors which
strangely conjoined to create "Colonial Office Government". Under
these converging influences Liverpool arrived at a conception which
(unlike that of Hobart) set the conquered Empire as a thing apart
enclosed in a rigid mould of its own.

On passing from colonies captured from the French and Spaniards
to those conquered from the Dutch, the same principles, varied in
their application by local conditions, are found in operation. The
colonies of Dutch Guiana—Demerara, Essequibo and Berbice—
were occupied by a British force in 1796, were surrendered under the
Treaty of Amiens and reoccupied (permanently) in 1803. The terms
of the Capitulation governing the second occupation of Demerara
and Essequibo were exceptionally favourable to the colonists and
guaranteed to them their ancient institutions even more explicitly
than in the case of other conquered colonies.[2] Under the first article
the conquerors promised that "The laws and usages of the colony
shall remain in force and be respected, the mode of taxation now in
use shall be adhered to, and the inhabitants shall enjoy the public
exercise of their religion in the same manner as before the capitulation". No new establishments were to be introduced without the
consent of the local legislature; and (under article 14) "Should any

[1] Liverpool to Hislop, 27 Nov. 1810, C.O. 296/4.
[2] The terms of the Berbice Capitulation did not provide such explicit guarantees, and
local institutions were accordingly modified by the Central Government without difficulty.

difficulties arise in consequence of any dubious expressions occurring in the present Capitulation, the same shall be explained and construed in the sense most favourable to the Colony ".[1] Indeed, these guarantees of the *status quo* were more comprehensive than the Secretary of State desired. His despatch of 4 August 1803, which among other things ordered the levying of the 4½ per cent. duty in *all* conquered colonies, reached Lieutenant-General Grinfield some hours after the signing of the Capitulation. The Demerara Court of Policy promptly protested against the impost as a violation of the settlement just signed. In reporting his failure to give effect to Hobart's orders, Grinfield aptly remarked that since "Military Men cannot be considered as acquainted with Financial and Legislative matters, it might be proper for a general outline to be given to the Officers Commanding on Expeditions for Conquest for their guide in the granting Terms of Capitulation ".[2]

It so happened that the Dutch constitution, inherited and perpetuated in Demerara and Essequibo, was not dissimilar in spirit from that proposed for Trinidad in 1804. While providing a local "aristocracy" to assist in internal administration, it left supreme legislative and executive control in the hands of the imperial power. The chief component of the constitution was the Court of Policy, which was entrusted with the maintenance of order, the issuing of local ordinances in conformity with directions from the parent state and with the duty of advising the Governor in all political and financial matters. The Court consisted of four *ex-officio* members, including the Governor and four elective members, two from Demerara and two from Essequibo. As the Governor had a casting vote, the official element could usually control the Court. The previous consent of the Governor was necessary for the introduction of any measure, although he possessed no subsequent power of veto. Less in accord with British traditions were the two Courts of Justice, one for each settlement, both consisting of an *ex-officio* President and six elected members. The third branch of the constitution was known as the Combined Court, which exercised the power of taxation and of examining accounts. It consisted of the members of the Court of Policy and six colonists elected separately to act as financial representatives. With the exception of these last, who (after 1796) were chosen by the freeholders, the election of all non-official members was indirect through a College of Electors or "Kiezers", who were themselves chosen for life by the planters. The power of the Combined Court in financial matters with its large elective majority might have become formidable but for the fact that the revenue resources were

[1] A copy of the Capitulation, dated 18 Sept. 1803, is in C.O. 111/5. The document is printed in *Parl. Pap.* 1848, xxxix.
[2] Grinfield to Hobart, 2 Oct. 1803, C.O. 111/4. Cf. Memorandum of the Court of Policy against the 4½ per cent. duty, 1 Oct. 1803, *ibid.*

divided into two funds, known as the "Government" and the "Colony" Chest respectively. While the latter was supplied by taxes levied by the Combined Court, the former (comparable to the Royal Revenue in Ireland) was derived from a capitation tax and other fixed imposts and was entirely under official control. The Government Chest except in abnormal times provided the salaries of the Governor and other officials and defrayed the cost of maintaining the fortifications and other military charges.[1]

The Duke of Portland was quick to appreciate the value of a standing revenue outside the control of the colonial legislature. All expenditure under that head was to be accounted for by the Governor and its necessity proved.[2] In 1801 Governor Beaujon was instructed to transmit the outstanding balance of the Government Chest amounting to £6293 to England;[3] and when acknowledging its receipt, Portland explained that the sum had been consigned to the Treasury, "to remain at His Majesty's disposal, subject provisionally to the discharge of any expences which may be necessarily incurred on account of the Public Service of the colony; and any further sums which may be received on the same account will be disposed of in a similar manner".[4]

Despite these very convenient devices in the Dutch system for the maintenance of central control, the situation which arose in the Guiana colonies revealed serious defects in the new British policy of ruling foreign settlements through their ancient institutions. Any form of centralised administration requires unremitting attention and a detailed acquaintance with the local conditions of each unit. But the retention of inherited institutions (adopted to satisfy the inhabitants and to perpetuate an autocratic tradition) entailed in addition an expert knowledge of the political and legal structure of the French, Spanish and Dutch empires. How was a hard-worked War Office, burdened with colonial administration while absorbed in the conduct of a world war, to cope with such technicalities? The Secretary of State and his staff did well under such conditions to deal with trade problems and the distracting task of enforcing ameliorative measures for slaves without touching the complexities of internal government. The remaining alternative was an expert Governor and Law Officers with specialised knowledge on the spot. But they were hard to find. The first two Governors of Demerara and Essequibo, Beaujon and Bentinck, were Dutchmen: but their successors were British military men. The administrative history of the colony from the recall of Bentinck

[1] The functions of the two Chests are fully described in a memorandum, "Remarks on the Sovereign and Colonial Chests of Demerary", enclosed in Sir Wm. Myers's letter to Earl Camden, No. 19 of 30 Sept. 1804, C.O. 111/5. Cf. Governor Bentinck's account to Lord Liverpool, 12 April 1810, C.O. 111/10.
[2] Portland to Beaujon, 31 March 1800, C.O. 111/4.
[3] Beaujon to Portland, 10 Feb. 1801, ibid.
[4] Portland to Beaujon, May 1801, ibid.

in 1812 until the settlement of 1831–4 represents a series of efforts to adapt old and half-understood customs to meet changing needs. The results were unsatisfactory and created discontent and dissension. "The real difficulty", it has been well remarked, "lay in the antithesis between Dutch forms and English ideas."[1]

The reforms of Bentinck's successor, Major-General Carmichael, and their outcome illustrate the inherent difficulties. Bentinck himself had been authorised to carry out certain changes, such as the substitution of English for Dutch as the official language, the amalgamation of the Demerara and the Essequibo Courts of Justice for the sake of economy, and the definition of the powers of the College of Electors and of the Financial Representatives in the Combined Courts; and this he was preparing to do when he was suddenly recalled. Carmichael, who was put in temporary charge until a successor should be appointed, was directed to reform immediate abuses but to refrain from any material alteration in the general system of government. Characteristically, he decided that, having once begun, he must go much further and make a clean sweep. His revolutionary reforms aimed at the establishment of two principles: the political ascendancy of the British element in the colony and the maximum degree of assimilation of the Guiana constitution to that of Great Britain. The electoral franchise was extended to include the professional and commercial classes (who were English), and the reconstituted College of Electors, chosen by the new electorate, was to hold office for two years instead of for life as formerly. Its members were also to supersede the Financial Representatives in the Combined Court. In the case of the latter body he not only confirmed their taxative powers but granted them the right, hitherto disputed, of appropriating supplies.[2] The constitution so established overthrew the Dutch system without reproducing the essential features of the British.

Carmichael's faith that the British Parliament was "the most perfect of all models of legislation",[3] and that "the ancient system of colonial government, however pure and consistent at the period of its formation...may require temporary changes to assimilate it to the mother country",[4] characterised the ideas of statesmen twenty years earlier, when the perfect balance of the British constitution was upheld as the sovereign antidote for American democracy and French Jacobinism. But the perils of war and the dread of revolution at home had hardened men's minds. The British constitution was all very

---

[1] See Penson, L. M., "The making of a Crown Colony" (*Trans. Roy. Hist. Soc.* 4th series, IX, 107–34).

[2] Carmichael's actions and intentions are fully described by him in his despatches and their numerous enclosures to the Secretary of State dated respectively 28 April, 3, 4, 15 and 28 May, 5 June (C.O. 111/12); 8 Sept. (Nos. 9 and 10), 11 and 12 Oct. 1812 (C.O. 111/13).

[3] Address to the new College of Kiezers, 10 Oct., enclosed in despatch of 11 Oct. 1812.

[4] Address to the Court of Policy, enclosed in despatch of 3 May 1812.

well for those who understood its aristocratic principles; but foreign communities, like the working classes in Great Britain itself, were most safely managed by direct methods. Carmichael (who was a dying man) was peremptorily ordered to refrain from further change. Yet so over-mastering were the pre-occupations of the central government in the midst of a great war that the promised directions for constitutional reform never materialised. An acting Governor had exceeded his instructions and remodelled a constitution after a pattern which careful examination at home would doubtless have rejected. Yet having been introduced, Carmichael's defective arrangements persisted for twenty years until the general reform of the Crown Colony system in 1831. Although the constitution of a unified British Guiana which was then established was allowed to reproduce many old features, Crown Colony governments thereafter ceased to be anglicised forms of old French, Spanish or Dutch models, and were approximated to a uniform standard.[1]

Passing from the Atlantic colonies to those of the Mediterranean and the Indian Ocean may be compared to entering a new wing of a factory, where new inventions, recently patented, are being tested amidst the noise of eager voices and newly made machinery. The vast wealth and power which accrued to Great Britain in India not only accelerated the transfer of imperial interest from the West to the East but gave rise to a new conception of imperialism. Other factors contributed to this change. The British people had come to believe that American independence, which removed a rival from within the ring-fence, was not so much a loss as an economic gain. Secondly, the new Canada was a disappointment: it had not become the granary for the West Indies, as had been hoped, and political friction in Lower Canada was unpleasantly reminiscent of the Thirteen Colonies. Against the West Indian planters there was a rising tide of disgust: commercially the old sugar colonies were becoming an expensive luxury and on moral grounds a source of discomfort. These circumstances tended to drive the lesson home that colonisation was the least profitable and the most troublesome method of doing business overseas. The rapid rise of Great Britain to supremacy in industry led her in this period to conserve and not to dissipate the technical skill of her artisans and her producers of food and to look for vaster markets than her own people could ever create by settlement. She planned a great commercial "empire" in the Mississippi basin and another in Spanish America, where British manufactures could be exchanged for raw material without incurring the burden and friction of political responsibilities. The former plan proved to be a dream only, and the latter was delayed. But in India and in the Far East generally the need was satisfied. Honour and self-interest

[1] Penson, *op. cit.* pp. 131–4.

alike compelled the nation to provide efficient government in India; and, as we have seen, they did so by means of a concentration of autocratic power. Moreover, Cornwallis's complete anglicisation of the Indian Services illustrates a further point of policy in the new system. "In every colony where the British flag flies", declared Carmichael in Demerara, "the ascendancy should be with it, and... the executive government must become English."[1] Experience in India had proved that the government of Asiatics must be strong and even-handed, while the traditions of the Quebec Act, continued in the conquered colonies of the Caribbean, implied that British ascendancy should be combined with due respect for French or Dutch institutions and privileges. When, therefore, strategic points guarding the sea-routes to India, such as Cape Colony and Ceylon, fell into the hands of Great Britain and she was confronted with the task of ruling non-British Europeans and a non-European population, she devised modes of government which were based upon that dual experience. Moreover, the appreciation of British statesmen that they were building an Asiatic empire on lines new to the British system, and were building for posterity, inspired a vigorous initiative in their administration which was lacking in the case of the colonies in the West.

For these reasons then the Commission and Instructions issued to Lord Macartney, the first Governor of Cape Colony after its occupation in 1795, conformed in general to the West Indian models already noted, particularly as regards the vesting of executive power solely in the Governor and the preservation "as nearly as circumstances will permit" of the ancient laws and institutions. But they were also *ad hoc* documents carefully designed to meet peculiar circumstances. The presiding genius of the new empire, Henry Dundas, was determined to convert the Cape into an impregnable fortress for the defence of British territories in India. Special efforts were therefore made both to guarantee British supremacy and to conciliate the Dutch. On his side the Governor was endowed with unique powers, being given authority to enact ordinances having the force of law and a wide latitude to carry out administrative reforms. On the other hand, a series of fiscal and commercial improvements were indicated in order to render the British *régime* as palatable as possible to the new subjects, while the Dutch personnel of the Services and their judicial, ecclesiastical, and local organisations were retained. Such extensive powers in the hands of an incompetent Governor such as Sir George Yonge could be dangerous; but until the advent of British settlers in 1820, bringing with them ideas of political liberty, and of the missionaries who imported new notions about Kaffirs and Hottentots, the system of paternal despotism achieved a large measure of success.[2]

[1] Address to the new College of Kiezers, 10 Oct. 1812, C.O. 111/13.
[2] For the history of the British administration at the Cape between 1795 and 1822, see *C.H.B.E.* viii, chaps. vii and viii.

Cape Colony was not only an island of European settlement in the African continent but a fortress—the Gibraltar of the Indian Ocean. The character of British rule was accordingly dictated by strategical considerations and its scope limited to the control of the Dutch community through its own institutions. The vast problem raised by the presence of Hottentots within and Kaffirs without was as far as possible ignored.

The conquest from the Dutch in 1796 of that other Indian fortress, Ceylon, presented the British with a situation exactly the reverse. In this case the Dutch element was relatively unimportant, consisting almost entirely of administrative officials; while the population to be reckoned with (Sinhalese and Tamil) was an organized Asiatic society, representing though in primitive form a medley of ancient cultures and religions. The principles and methods that were adopted are of unique interest in the history of the Second British Empire, and the experience gained left a permanent mark on imperial policy.

The first lesson to be learned was that the art of ruling native races is a thing of infinite variety not amenable to standardisation. The natural impulse after the conquest was to treat Ceylon as part of the British territories in India for the protection of which it had been acquired. In any case the claims of the East India Company, whose troops from Madras had conquered it at a cost of £12,000, would have been difficult to resist. Ceylon was therefore granted to the Company in 1796, and the Madras Presidency (which had begun to establish its officials there in 1795 before the completion of the conquest) became responsible for its administration. A military Governor was appointed with certain vague civil powers; but for all practical purposes the civil government was put into the hands of a Madras Civil Servant, Robert Andrews, as the Resident and Superintendent of Revenue. Under him were a group of Madras Civilians in charge of Districts. The details of the system are uncertain, but it seems that Andrews and his subordinates, while chiefly concerned in the collection of revenue and the management of the pearl and cinnamon monopolies, also exercised administrative and judicial functions. Apparently each District was subdivided into a number of smaller units, managed under the supervision of the British Assistant by *aumildars*, who were natives of the Madras Presidency, and who brought with them a swarm of petty office-holders. The substitution of these *aumildars* for the Sinhalese officials, known as *mudaliyars*, obliterated the most important feature of the Dutch system. The Dutch had ruled the limited coastal areas under their control by the easy expedient of selecting *mudaliyars* from among the chief Sinhalese families and leaving in their hands extremely wide powers over the ryats. Such a system abandoned the latter to continual oppression and injustice but avoided trouble. The importation of a corps of rapacious foreigners from India, who were entirely ignorant of local usage and tradition, went to the extreme of interference while providing a more vicious form of government than that of their predecessors. It aggravated the lot of the ryats, alienated the dispossessed Sinhalese nobles, and provided an excellent opportunity for the Dutch burghers, who had held aloof and refused to take the oath of allegiance, to make mischief.[1] To complete the picture, the Madras officials abolished the native system of land tenure, by which from time immemorial land had been held in return for services, and introduced the Madras revenue system. They also connived at, and many actively participated in, extensive peculation and extortion carried on by their Indian subordinates, an abuse which was rendered fatally easy by the Madras practice of combining the functions of tax farmer and magistrate in the same person. The upshot was a formidable revolt which broke out in June 1798, and which was not finally suppressed until about February of the following year.

Even before the actual outbreak of rebellion, Lord Hobart, who was then Governor of Madras, had received disquieting reports from Ceylon. He accordingly decided to appoint a Committee of Investigation, consisting of Colonel de Meuron as President, Colonel Agnew, the Adjutant-General in Ceylon, and the delinquent Andrews. Undeterred by the presence of this third member, de Meuron and Agnew carried out a searching enquiry and submitted a report, the recommendations of which were approved by the Madras Government in May 1798. The Madras revenue system was abolished and the ancient Sinhalese system restored. Service land tenure was re-established; the Madras native officials and tax farmers were to be sent back to India; and the *mudaliyars* were to be reinstated with restricted magisterial powers, and (most important) they were to be directly under the chief executive officer and independent of the Revenue Department. The sagacity of de Meuron and Agnew brought peace. When the Honble. Frederick North, the first Governor under a new system, arrived in September 1798, he gladly accepted the far-sighted proposals which they had put forward.[2]

The years 1798–1802 were for Ceylon a period of attentive trial-and-error on the part of the Imperial Government. The experiments which were tried and failed indicate the lines of thought which Dundas and his colleagues were pursuing and explain why the system of administration which was ultimately adopted was unlike any form previously attempted. The decision to put Ceylon under the direct authority of the Crown was made before news of the Sinhalese rebellion could have reached England and was possibly due to the failure of the peace negotiations at Lille, where the return of Ceylon to Holland

---

[1] In 1797 most of the pure-bred Dutch departed to Java, but those of mixed Dutch and Sinhalese blood stayed on and subsequently became invaluable to the British as minor administrative officials.

[2] See Mills, L. A., *Ceylon under British Rule, 1795–1932*, chap. III.

had been contemplated. But Ministers had overlooked the vested interests of the East India Company, which strenuously protested against a measure which might tend to weaken "an united authority in India". Dundas as Secretary of State and President of the Board of Control was supreme in such matters and planned to incorporate Ceylon into the Indian system but with a status of its own similar to that of Madras and Bombay. The Governor and the members of the Civil Service were to be appointed by the Crown, but they were to be under the direction of the Governor-General in India and the Court of Directors, who were themselves controlled in all non-commercial matters by Dundas at the Board. Revenue, including the cinnamon monopoly, was the concern of the Company. The Governor was to exercise all legislative and executive authority without even the check of an Advisory Council as in the Indian Presidencies. The personnel of the Civil Service, who were placed directly under his orders, were to be drawn from the Services in India. This last provision was decided upon after Governor North had left England. He had understood that a group of young men whom he was taking with him after selection by Dundas and himself would be allowed to form the nucleus of a separate Ceylon Civil Service under the immediate supervision of the Secretary of State; but his wish was not gratified.

The mind of Dundas is clearly shown in these arrangements. For him India was the focal point in all his plans, administrative, military, and commercial. Ceylon was important, not yet on its own account, but as an outlying province of India. The Asiatic Empire in all its parts was to be moulded to a standard form and directed by centralised authority. Arising from the same attitude of mind, he had even contemplated the inclusion of the Cape in the Indian administrative structure. Greater knowledge, however, soon taught his fertile mind that Ceylon possessed intrinsic potentialities and peculiar needs.

The character of Frederick North, with all its failings, was not unsuited to the situation in which he found himself. Versatile and volatile, he was a man of intense but passing enthusiasms, who was for ever discarding incompleted schemes of reform for others of greater promise. Although he could make a clean sweep of rapacious officials, he did not know how to prevent the recurrence of their misdeeds. But the integrity and generosity of his mind established the welfare of the natives as the prime duty of government. On arrival he found that the administration of justice was virtually at a standstill. According to his instructions he was to re-establish the Dutch system of courts and jurisprudence, making such reforms as should prove requisite. As a necessary preliminary he employed Mr (later Sir) Edmund Carrington, a Calcutta barrister, to compile a legal code in accordance with the principles of Roman-Dutch Law. The system of criminal and civil courts which he then established was with some modifications embodied in the Charter of Justice of 1801. As regards revenue he divided the colony into thirteen Provinces, administered by Agents of Revenue under the direction of a new Board of Revenue and Commerce. But his chief contribution to the future of Ceylon was his exposure of the evils caused by the employment of officials from Madras. Their dislike of the appointment of an outsider as Governor grew into angry hostility when North's investigations began to reveal the corruption and extortion of which many were guilty. To the Court of Directors he described the "obstinate spirit of opposition to my authority, and intrigue against my person, which have rendered the first nine months of my government so ineffective in the establishment of your interests and the protection of the people".[1] The dismissal of some of the worst offenders had a salutary effect upon the remainder, but the problem was not thereby solved. The Directors compelled him to fill the vacancies from the Madras Service and in effect to accept its dregs, for no man of ability was prepared to sacrifice the higher salaries and better prospects of promotion in India; and even when the men secured were honest, they were entirely ignorant of the languages and customs of Ceylon. Fortunately the revelations of North and his insistent advice that good government could only be established through a specialised Ceylon Service totally separate from India convinced Dundas that a mistake had been made. For some time the latter had been absorbing information about Ceylon—from books and despatches and from men with first-hand knowledge—with the same remarkable assiduity that he had shown on first assuming responsibility for India. On 30 December 1800 he informed the Directors that he had resolved to convert Ceylon into a Royal Government on the same footing as the Cape of Good Hope.[2]

The administrative arrangements of 1796, of 1798 and of 1801 represent three stages in the evolution of a new policy. Underlying all three was the principle that imperial interests demanded that the Government of Ceylon should be "blended" with that of India. At the same time the changes indicate the gradual recognition of another principle, that imperialism is stultified unless like the quality of mercy itself it becomes mutually beneficial, the governing country receiving the advantages of political and economic profit and in return fostering the welfare of subject races by the employment of methods adapted to their specific needs. The reforms of 1798 had for imperial purposes retained Ceylon as an integral part of the Indian *régime*. The form of government established in 1801 abandoned compromise: the political connection with India was abolished and Ceylon was equipped with a political, financial and judicial system of its own. In the process of designing it, Dundas had considered the two existing types of imperial government, the traditional "indirect" method

---

[1] North to the Court of Directors, 30 Jan. 1800, C.O. 54/2.
[2] Dundas to the Court of Directors, 30 Dec. 1800, C.O. 55/61.

through local legislatures, and the new form of direct rule as worked out in India and applied through the medium of "ancient institutions" in the conquered colonies of the Caribbean. As the basis of the Ceylon model Dundas unhesitatingly chose the Indian form. On the present resumption of authority by the Crown "it was far from being proposed", he explained to North, "to assimilate that island or its government to our colonies in the West Indies. But on the contrary whatever experience has shown to be politically wise in the Government of the British Territory on the Continent of India, and appears...applicable to the situation of Ceylon, it is the inclination of His Majesty's Government to preserve or to adopt." Some of "the principal motives" in the new scheme had suggested themselves on a consideration of North's correspondence:

> The complete legislative power must remain, as it now is, vested in the Governor alone, subject to revision and confirmation or rejection at home....It may however be advisable for the sake of more solemnity and as affording the means perhaps of giving more satisfaction in the country...that you should form to yourself a Council with which you would consult on all great and important occasions.... At the same time it is not to be understood that the Members of this Council, or any majority of them, are to have any share of the Legislative or Executive Authority, which, as I have already stated, is vested in you alone; or that they are to be responsible for any Opinions and advice they may give in that Capacity.

In such a Council "it would be inexpedient to allow any question to be put to the vote", but any Member differing from the Governor should be at liberty (as in India) to enter a Minute on the Proceedings stating the grounds of his dissent. It should consist of not more than five persons, three of whom should be the Chief Justice, the Commander of the Forces, and the Principal Secretary: a fourth member might well be the Head of the Revenue Department. "But on this point, and with respect to the fifth, you will exercise your own discretion and judgment upon the spot, as also in suspending or ceasing to require altogether the attendance of any of the Members."[1]

Converted by North to the necessity for a separate Civil Service, Dundas drew up a scheme with his usual care, which characteristically allowed considerable latitude to the Governor on the spot. Promotion was normally to be by seniority, unless the Governor thought fit to exercise his discretion in favour of exceptional ability; and there was to be no outside interference, since "nothing can be more unjust and heartbreaking to young men...than to labour under the apprehension of having their services superseded by favour and interest at home". All vacancies were thus to be filled by the Governor from within the Service: the appointment of Army officers and other Europeans resident in Ceylon was expressly forbidden. Recruits were drawn from youths at home of about fifteen years of age, who were selected

---

[1] Dundas to North, 13 March 1801, C.O. 54/5 (another copy in C.O. 55/61). This despatch, which runs to 127 paragraphs, accompanied the new Commission and Instructions sent out to North.

by the Secretary of State and sent out as "writers". The scale of salaries ranged from £300 for a writer to £3000 for the Principal Secretary. Two years later a pensions scheme, which North had worked out on instructions from Dundas, was approved. Government and servant each contributed 10 per cent. of the salary to a trustee fund, from which pensions became payable to senior officials after eight years' service and to the junior grades after twelve.[1] Following a practice which was being adopted in the case of all Crown colonies, Dundas also provided for the appointment of a Crown Agent in London to be selected by the Secretary of State but paid for by the colony. His duties were those of a general business agent for the colonial government. Crown Agencies frequently went to members of the Colonial Office staff, and Ceylon was fortunate in getting the services of William Huskisson.[2]

Equally important perhaps were the judicial arrangements which were treated separately in a royal "Charter of Justice". In his comments on the Charter Dundas stated that the principles followed by North in reconstituting the Courts had met with his strong approval and were the basis of the new system. The declared aim was accordingly "to preserve inviolate to the natives of the Island their local habits, their ancient tenures, distinctions and religious observances...and to secure to all classes of the people the protection of the laws by an effective administration of justice". The Judiciary consisted of two branches, one for Europeans and the other for the Sinhalese. For the former a Supreme Court of Judicature was established, consisting of a Chief Justice and one Puisne Judge appointed by the Crown, which exercised a comprehensive jurisdiction in all cases in which resident Europeans were involved. The constitution of courts for native cases was a more difficult matter. A framework was provided by the creation of a new High Court of Appeal (comprising two Supreme Court Judges and the Governor) and by instructions for the establishment of Justices of the Peace in the Districts for the trial of minor criminal and civil cases. With respect to the intermediate provincial courts North was left to continue his previous experiments, always having regard to native usage. For a time he revived the old Dutch courts, known as *Landraats*; but his disgust at their inefficiency caused him to replace them in November 1802 with five Provincial Courts presided over by civil servants. These courts exercised an extensive civil but limited criminal jurisdiction. A new Charter of Justice in 1810 provided for a number of alterations, notably the introduction of trial by jury, but the main outlines survived. The obliteration of Sinhalese law by the Dutch caused the

---

[1] Dundas to North (a separate despatch, also dated 13 March, on Civil Service arrangements), C.O. 54/5. Cf. Mills, *op. cit.* pp. 42–4.

[2] Cf. Penson, L. M., "The Origin of the Crown Agency Office". *E.H.R.* xl (April 1925), 196–206.

emergence of a system of jurisprudence which seems to have been predominantly Roman-Dutch in principle, modified by British procedure and unwritten native custom.

Equally significant was the economic side of the scheme. Ceylon, like India itself, was to be a commercial preserve. Its external trade remained solely in the hands of the East India Company; its internal resources—the cinnamon plantations and the pearl fisheries—were to be a Government monopoly; and in order to protect the interests of both Government and people, European colonisation was prohibited. No land could be held by foreign Europeans, and except in the District of Colombo British subjects themselves could hold land for seven years only, grants in perpetuity being forbidden.[1] In all other respects Dundas had learned that his previous adherence to the Indian model had been a mistake; but his strong reaction against the West Indian "plantation" system had led him to place Ceylon in an economic isolation which threatened to be suffocating. On assuming control of colonial affairs in 1810, Castlereagh immediately raised the ban against European settlement.[2]

The years 1805 to 1810, during which Ceylon was ruled by General (later Sir) Thomas Maitland, saw the paper scheme of 1801 transformed into an administrative machine functioning with smooth precision. The idealism of Frederick North had unfortunately been coupled with extravagance and with inability to control unprincipled subordinates. Maitland on the other hand was a born administrator. He was a martinet and supremely confident in the correctness of his own judgments. "I must differ extremely", he once wrote to Castlereagh, "with any man however high that can conceive...that I am bound to conceal any opinion I entertain because...it differs in some degree from that entertained in other quarters."[3] Corruption was rooted out and a strict control over expenditure established; and while drastic economies were effected by abolishing unnecessary posts, inadequate salaries were increased. By 1808 Maitland had reorganised the Civil Service along lines which remained substantially unaltered until 1834. The sole object of Government, he declared, was to further the productivity of the island by "generally increasing the prosperity and happiness of the natives". Perhaps the most difficult problem in this connection was that of restraining the *mudaliyars* and their underlings from oppressing the ryats. For this purpose the Collectors of Revenue were reorganised, and three sitting Magistrates were appointed in the Districts with instructions to try minor cases on the spot and to refer all important native cases direct to the High Court.[4] When ill-health compelled Maitland to retire to

---

[1] Dundas's despatch of 13 March 1801 (*ut supra*), paras. 36, 37 and 40.
[2] Castlereagh to Governor Maitland, 5 June 1810, C.O. 54/38.
[3] Maitland to Castlereagh, 21 Feb. 1810, C.O. 54/38.
[4] Maitland to Windham, 28 Feb. 1807, C.O. 54/25.

England in March, 1811, a new type had been added to the system of Colonial Office government. The form of administration applied to foreign European communities in the "plantation" group of dependencies was adapted in the case of Ceylon to fit the circumstances of an oriental people. In both branches of the new system the underlying principles were the same.

We have now examined the methods employed in the government of oligarchies consisting of French and Dutch planters, and secondly of communities which were entirely Asiatic. It remains to give some account of British policy in governing illiterate European peasants who were accustomed to the traditions of feudal aristocracy but strongly imbued with local patriotism. The territories in which this third experiment in direct rule was carried out, namely, Malta and the Ionian Islands, were, as regards geography, culture, commerce and strategy, predominantly European. In a general European war they were therefore directly and intimately involved. Occupying key positions off the southern coasts of the battle-area, they were coveted by the belligerent Powers who feared their acquisition by the enemy. When Napoleon taught the British to regard the retention of Malta as a national necessity, the policy adopted in the ruling of it inevitably subordinated every other consideration to that of preserving British authority.

As Lord Liverpool afterwards remarked, "the circumstances under which the British authority has been established in Malta, present a case bearing no analogy to any other instance in the modern history of this Kingdom".[1] The established rulers, the Knights of Malta, had been expelled by the French in 1798. The French invaders had themselves been driven out in 1800 by a British force in co-operation with the islanders, who in a representative "Congress" enthusiastically acclaimed the sovereign of Great Britain as their ruler. Yet before the surrender of Valetta the Commander of the British Forces had proclaimed the intention of his Government to restore the Knights after Maltese grievances had been redressed.[2] But whether or not Malta was to pass to other hands at a future peace settlement, the British Government decided in the meantime to retain possession. Absolute control of the fortress was to be secured while leaving the Maltese and their institutions as much alone as possible. In May 1801 the Secretary of State, Lord Hobart, terminated the temporary military *régime* by establishing a form of dual dictatorship in the persons of the Military Commander and a new officer, termed the Civil Commissioner, who was to have charge of the revenue and the civil administration. In his Instructions to the newly appointed Commissioner, Mr (later Sir) Charles Cameron, Hobart laid down

[1] Liverpool to the Commissioners, 1 May 1812, C.O. 159/4.
[2] See Lord Hawkesbury's speech in the Commons, 13 May 1802, *Parl. Hist.* xxxvi, 764.

certain broad principles. For the present the government of Malta was to be conducted without altering the laws and regulations under which the revenue and civil affairs of the island had been managed heretofore, unless any such alteration "shall appear to the officer commanding His Majesty's Forces, to be required for the safety and defence of the Island, or to be so evidently beneficial and desirable as to leave no doubt of its expediency or of its being generally acceptable to the wishes, the feelings, and even the prejudices of the inhabitants". The administration of justice and police was accordingly to continue as under the Knights of St John, subject only to directions from England and to such deviations as the Commander-in-Chief might on a sudden emergency deem requisite. Malta was in fact a fortress, and at every point the civil arm (itself autocratically con- trolled) was to be amenable to the over-riding discretion of the military authority. The same considerations caused Hobart to retain the old government monopoly of purchasing and retailing foreign corn upon which the Maltese depended. The system produced a considerable revenue. "As a constant and useful check over the people in the hands of government, I am convinced that it ought to be adhered to as an arrangement no less politic on our part than provident towards the Maltese themselves." Commercial prosperity was to be fostered by attracting to Malta the trade of the Eastern Mediterranean through the development of her unique quarantine facilities and by granting to Valetta the advantages of a "free port". Finally, with regard to the inhabitants, the Commissioner was "to use every endeavour consistent with your public duty, to meet their wishes, to show yourself indulgent even to their prejudices and to omit no fair opportunity of conciliating their affection and ensuring their fidelity to the Government under which they are now placed".[1] It will readily be seen that in these Instructions Hobart made no attempt to give precise definition to the powers of the Commissioner except as regards his ultimate subordination to the Commanding Officer. For the rest he was free to interpret the general principle of conciliation and non-interference by his personal management of every department of civil administration, subject only to the super- vision of the Secretary of State at home.

The principle of preserving local privileges (now firmly established as a necessary feature of the new imperial system) was strikingly exemplified in the case of Malta under the Treaty of Amiens. Article X stipulated the conditions under which the Order of St John of Jerusalem was to be re-established. "The arrangement therein provided for", wrote Hobart to Cameron, "has been made with so

---

[1] General Instructions of Hobart to Cameron, 14 May; Supplementary Instruction of 20 May; Hobart to the Commander-in-Chief at Malta, enclosing "Substance of a Pro- clamation" announcing Cameron's appointment, 21 May 1801; Hobart to Cameron, 15 Sept. C.O. 159/3.

much consideration by His Majesty's Ministers, and has been contended for by them with so much perseverance in the negotiations
at Amiens, that I allow myself to hope it will be considered by the
Maltese as forming for them a Charter of the most essential political
rights." The grievances which the inhabitants had endured during
the previous *régime* of the Knights were to be obviated for the future
by the admission of Maltese members to the Order. It was further
provided that at least one-half of the municipal officers and one-half
of the military establishment were to be composed of native Maltese.
On the commercial side the British "free port" policy was to be
continued, "which cannot fail", Hobart prophesied, "in a short time
to render the island of Malta the greatest depôt of the Levant".[1]

The British purpose in enforcing the acceptance of these terms at
Amiens had been to ensure the future independence of the island by
substituting Maltese for French influence among the Knights and by
establishing a cordial co-operation between the reconstituted Order
and the native population which would unite them in its defence.[2]
The arrangement would have had the effect of placing the preponderance in the government of Malta in the hands of the Maltese
themselves. When therefore the bellicosity of Napoleon and British
stubbornness prevented the evacuation of the island in accordance
with the Treaty and caused a renewal of the war in May 1803, the
Addington Ministry was confronted with a delicate situation. Maltese
independence had been publicly proclaimed in an international
treaty, and the Maltese deputation in London had taken their leave
"with every testimony of gratitude and satisfaction".[3] Hopes had
been raised that could not now be gratified, for the resumption of the
struggle with Napoleon rendered the continued control of Malta as
a naval and commercial base of the highest importance. Indeed the
rival claims of imperial and local interests have proved more difficult
to reconcile in the case of Malta than in almost any other territory
within the Empire. For the present the British Government was
content to pursue its former policy of ensuring its authority through
the autocracy of the Civil Commissioner and of winning the allegiance
of the population by preserving their institutions. Sir Alexander Ball,
Cameron's successor as Civil Commissioner, was well qualified by his
character and knowledge of the island for this dual task. As Captain
Ball he had been the first British Commander-in-Chief in Malta after
the reduction of Valetta: as Commissioner his understanding of the
native Maltese and his unremitting attention to their welfare made
his name long remembered and revered among them.

In pursuing this policy of satisfying the Maltese population the
British Government was however disregarding the claims of the local

---

[1] Hobart to Cameron, 31 March 1802, C.O. 159/3.
[2] See Lord Hawkesbury's speech, May 1802, *Parl. Hist.* xxxvi, 764-5.
[3] Hobart to Cameron, 30 April 1802, C.O. 159/3.

aristocracy. In 1802 the noble families of Malta had been on the point of becoming masters of a neutralised independent island. The unexpected turn of events by which they continued to be subject to the autocratic rule of a single Englishman was naturally unpalatable. Led by the Marchese Testaferrata, they began a campaign for Maltese "Home Rule". They asserted, and cited grants from the Kings of Aragon to show that from 1282 onwards they had enjoyed effective self-government under an executive officer (the *Capitano di Verga*), controlled by an elective Assembly known as the *Consiglio Popolare*. It was insisted that the subsequent efforts of the Order of St John of Jerusalem to curtail these privileges had been uniformly resisted until 1782, when the Grand Master, Rohan, had forced a despotic system upon them. The proclamation of Captain Ball after the surrender of Valetta to the effect that the privileges of the Maltese would be respected and their ancient laws continued in force was accordingly interpreted as a promise to revive and continue representative government in the form of the *Consiglio Popolare*; and the acceptance of British sovereignty by a "Congress" consisting of deputies from each *casale* (which Ball had summoned for the purpose) was treated as a solemn act of the Maltese Legislature and not as that of an *ad hoc* convention.[1]

The success of the Testaferrata party in London during the peace negotiations made their subsequent disappointment correspondingly acute. But since the British Government had recognised the claims of Maltese self-government at Amiens, they hoped that the British *régime* would now be modified to admit them to a share in political power. An agitation was accordingly begun to secure support for the party in the island and at the same time to bring pressure to bear upon the Ministry in London.[2] While the Whig Ministry of "All the Talents" was in power there was some chance of success, for William Windham, the Secretary of State, seems to have been sympathetic.[3] But with the return of the Tories under Portland in 1807 the hopes of Testaferrata and his supporters began to fade. Thereupon Testaferrata himself repaired to London and submitted to Bathurst a statement of his party's demands, which included the re-establishment of the *Consiglio Popolare* and the institution of trial by jury with a right of appeal in all cases to the *Consiglio*.[4] In April 1812, Testaferrata was informed that the Government did not consider that the papers presented by him were in fact authorised declarations of the wishes of the Maltese people. It was, however, intimated that Commissioners were about to be sent to Malta to examine fully into its laws and

[1] See Maltese petition to the King, 10 July 1811, and the Marchese Testaferrata to Earl Bathurst, Jan. 1812. Printed by Hardman, W., *History of Malta...1798–1815*, ed. J. H. Rose, pp. 509–11, 512–15. Cf. Eton, W., *Authentic materials for a history of...Malta*, pp. 80 *seqq.*

[2] Eton, *op. cit.* Cf. Bunbury to Oakes, 18 Sept. 1811 ("Private"), C.O. 159/4, §§ 56–8.

[3] Cf. Eton to Windham, 16 June 1807, B.M. Addit. MSS. 37,887 (Windham Papers, vol. XLVI).

[4] Testaferrata to Bathurst, Jan. 1812 (*ut supra*).

administration.[1] The Government had in fact made up its mind to establish a permanent system of civil administration in Malta. It had also decided that the new constitution should not concede the principle of local representation. In arriving at this decision the British Ministers had some justification. The claim for self-government on historical grounds was unconvincing. Moreover they cannot have contemplated with any enthusiasm a possible repetition of the Corsican experiment. When that island became "united" with Great Britain in 1794 and its inhabitants elected George III as their king, the British Viceroy, Sir Gilbert Elliot, had found the Corsican Legislature a thorny problem. To establish Testaferrata as the Paoli of Malta was clearly undesirable.[2] Furthermore, the complete failure of the "English Constitution" which Bentinck established in Sicily at this very time (March 1812) was in large measure to vindicate the Ministers' judgment with regard to Malta.

The three Commissioners who were appointed in April 1812 under the Great Seal were General Oakes (who was both Civil Commissioner and Commander of the forces in the island), William à Court, formerly *Chargé d'Affaires* at Palermo, and John Burrows, late Chief Justice in Dominica. The instructions which Lord Liverpool drafted for their guidance are a precise statement of imperial policy. The existing form of government, he explained, was a temporary makeshift, which had left existing institutions untouched. But the Maltese themselves were demanding a revision of the legal code, a regular system of civil government, and formal annexation to the British Crown. Moreover the influx of British merchants and foreign traders from all parts of the Mediterranean, attracted by British protection and the "free port" arrangements at Valetta, had enabled the island to make the fullest use of the commercial opportunities offered by the war.[3] Accordingly the complaints of British residents that commerce was obstructed by obsolete laws and defective courts of justice must be carefully examined.

Turning to the administrative side, Liverpool clearly indicated the lines which the Commissioners' report was expected to follow. It must be a basic principle that the military authority should be free from all restraint in superseding the civil power whenever the security of the island appeared to demand it. It was therefore desirable that "as often as practicable" the supreme power, both civil and military, should be vested in the same person. From such premises the conclusion followed inevitably that the claims advanced by Testaferrata and his supporters in their petition were "inconsistent with the local circumstances, and incompatible with the safety and tranquillity of the island". "The leading principles", added Liverpool, "by which the views of the Prince Regent's Government are

---

[1] See Testaferrata to Bathurst, 21 April 1812, Hardman, *op. cit.* pp. 516-17.
[2] *V. supra*, pp. 52-4.   [3] Cf. chap. III, *supra*.

guided, are, to give to the Maltese and all residents in Malta, as large a share of civil liberty as is consistent with the military circumstances of the island: to ensure to them a just and impartial administration of justice: to maintain an official system of internal police: and to establish such Regulations as may protect commerce and encourage domestic industry."[1]

The Report of His Majesty's Commissioners on the affairs of Malta (1812), which comprises 259 folio pages with substantial appendices, is not only a political and commercial history of the island during the British occupation, but a document of exceptional interest in illustrating contemporary views on imperial administration.[2]

On investigation the Commissioners came down heavily against the theory of an ancient Maltese Legislature. Prior to 1428 when the Knights of St John arrived, the *Consiglio Popolare* had indeed existed but as an electoral college choosing the members of the *Consiglio dell' Università*, which was merely a municipal body entrusted with the superintendence of markets, the purchase of corn, and the upkeep of roads and public buildings. This body had possessed the right of preferring complaints to the Crown respecting the affairs within its immediate jurisdiction, but never upon any occasion had it arrogated to itself the right of legislation nor in any way presumed "to interfere with the uncontrolled exercise of the executive power". Under the Knights even this measure of local self-government had fallen into disuse. "The result of our enquiries", they wrote, "has been the most firm conviction that these claims so loudly urged by turbulent and interested individuals, are totally without foundation, and that at no period of their history did the Maltese ever possess the slightest pretension or right to a deliberative and legislative Assembly." To introduce the principle of elective representation now would have disastrous results. The populace was violent in temperament, illiterate, and grossly superstitious: its deputies would be at the mercy of a few unscrupulous politicians who would turn the credulity of their associates to their own profit. When "a few disappointed and factious persons" clamoured for institutions which they were perfectly aware were "totally unfitted to the character and genius of the nation", it was not difficult to discern the presence of self-seeking intrigue beneath the cloak of patriotism. The establishment of a popular Assembly "would indeed be a rallying point" for all such elements and enable them "to loosen the reins of government" and so attain their various ends.

[1] Liverpool's Instructions to the Commissioners, 1 May 1812, C.O. 159/4.
[2] The Report is in C.O. 158/19 and the commercial Appendices in C.O. 158/20. A few extracts were printed by Hardman (*op. cit.* pp. 517–23), who remarks: "This Report has never been made public in its entirety, but extracts have occasionally appeared, notably one in a return asked for by the House of Commons and ordered to be printed on the 17th June, 1846." Until recent years the official Malta files in the Public Record Office were not open to the public.

Furthermore, the people themselves were completely satisfied with a government which had brought them an amazing degree of prosperity. Not only had the Port of Valetta attracted to itself a large share of Levantine trade, but when Napoleon had imposed the Continental System, immense quantities of colonial produce and British manufactures had been smuggled into Europe from Malta by way of Marseilles, Leghorn, Naples, Ancona, Trieste and Salonica. Another powerful stimulus had been provided by the American Embargo Act of 1808, the operation of which had greatly raised the demand for Levantine produce in London. Between 1810 and 1812 the export of manufactured goods from Malta had reached an annual average of £800,000. The number of English ships arriving at Valetta had risen from 291 in the year 1801 to 460 in 1811, while the number of Maltese arrivals had increased from 1349 to 2510 during the same period. The only important section of the community, said the Commissioners, who had not greatly benefited were the Maltese aristocracy. "The higher orders, whose stationary revenues have not kept pace with the general increase of wealth, we found less sanguine in their views and expectations. They look with somewhat of a jealous eye on the prosperity which surrounds them; and it is from this class that a small leaven of discontent has arisen...[which] must from this period be watched by the vigilant eye of Government." On every ground therefore they earnestly recommended the refusal of a popular Assembly "as a measure fraught with the greatest danger, and involving the most ruinous consequences". The generality of the people wanted nothing better than "a more intimate and indissoluble union with Great Britain". In that phrase, frequently repeated by Ministers and colonial administrators, is expressed the keynote of imperial policy in the years of the world war.

Representative government then was to be rejected. "To graduate our ideas", wrote the Commissioners, "of the perfection of a government by the approximation it bears towards our own, is a mode of reasoning as unjust, as it is erroneous." The reverse opinion had been strongly held before the struggle with Jacobinism and Napoleon. The alternative for Malta was a form of the Crown Colony government which had been worked out in the conquered dependencies. The Commissioners freely admitted that the existing personal rule of the Civil Commissioner could not go on. "There is nothing to interpose between his pleasure and its exercise, nor to guide him, but his own discretion." Because his powers were virtually unlimited, being undefined, he hesitated to make use of them. The Public Secretary and Treasurer were of great assistance in administrative routine, but they shared none of his responsibility. Similarly in his capacity as supreme court of appeal he was assisted by the *Signatura*, consisting of four Maltese lawyers as "Auditors", who were removable at pleasure. But this body was Counsel, not a Council. It could not operate in any way as a check upon the unlimited authority of the Commissioner. The Council which they proposed would consist of four English and four Maltese subjects, the English to consist of the Commissioner, the Secretary, the Treasurer, and one other, and the Maltese members of the two present Auditors, a member of the nobility and another "of citizen class". The Civil Commissioner was to have a double vote, "which will give that preponderance to the side of the English so absolutely necessary to be maintained". This Council should perform the judicial duties of the *Signatura* (which should be abolished) and also advise on all other matters relating to the civil administration. The Maltese members should be nominated by the Commissioner but should hold office for life unless removed by order of the Secretary of State. Certain specific limitations of the Civil Commissioner's power were proposed. Lord Liverpool's hint that the Civil Commissionership and the military command in Malta might be concentrated in one person was adopted.

The aims of the Commissioners in devising this constitution, as stated in their report, are worthy of attention in that they reflect the views of the Ministry at home and are of general application to the system of Crown Colony government:

In framing the materials for this new Council...it has been our object to take away from him [i.e. the Civil Commissioner] every privilege which might hereafter be exerted to injure or oppress, but to leave him in the undisturbed possession of those, which may be necessary to give force to his Government and to ensure the welfare of the State....All pretence for the clamour, which has been raised for the institution of a deliberative Assembly will be at once annihilated. A regular channel of complaint [to the Crown] will be open to every class of the inhabitants, and with so powerful a representation in the Council, it will be impossible that they should petition in vain.

On the legal and judicial side the Commissioners gave it as their opinion that the grave miscarriages of justice which took place were due not so much to the laws themselves, which were framed on equitable principles, as to the manner of their execution. Their description of the procedure in the Grand Civil and Criminal Courts was devastating. In future judges should receive a fixed salary and be forbidden to receive fees: their practice of selecting cases for hearing, hastening some and deferring others, should be terminated, as also their habit of interviewing litigants out of court. All process should be conducted in open court throughout and verdict should be delivered within ten days of the hearing in writing, and in Italian instead of Latin. The multiplicity of criminal appeals which caused the detention of accused persons for prolonged periods should be obviated by abolishing appeals except in capital cases. Their heaviest condemnation fell upon the commercial court, known as the *Consolato del Mare*. "The arts and evasions, the frauds and chicane, the influence and delay" which characterised that Court were such that the law was becoming a dead letter. No security or protection was

12-2

expected by the British merchant, who preferred to put up with a certain loss rather than waste time and money in fruitless litigation. Whenever possible they resorted to private arbitration. The abolition of the *Consolato del Mare* was accordingly recommended, and in its place was proposed a mixed court of British and Maltese merchants with right of appeal to a judge assisted by one British and one Maltese assessor whose decision should be final. Since the commercial section of the ancient Maltese code was quite unsuited to the existing conditions, it was suggested that power should be given to a Board consisting of equal numbers of British and Maltese lawyers, assisted by some of the leading merchants, to draft amendments as required. The demand for trial by jury was rejected as being totally inapplicable in the case of the Maltese.

As regards revenue administration it was proposed that the Board of Administrators should be abolished. This board of Maltese officials had been established by the British on their first arrival because of their own ignorance of local procedure. The Treasurer was now fully acquainted with the processes, and it was clearly desirable that the administration of all branches of finance should be placed "under the immediate direction of an Englishman". To the proposal of an English official that direct taxation might be introduced the Commissioners returned an emphatic negative. Taxes except for occasional and specific purposes had not been imposed under the rule of the Knights, and Great Britain had repeatedly promised to conserve ancient privileges. "The adoption of such measures would render the people dissatisfied, and mistrustful, and would give some countenance to the cry for the establishment of a representative Assembly, through which contributions could be levied and taxes imposed."

On 15 July 1813 the redoubtable Sir Thomas Maitland, whom we have already seen at work in Ceylon, was appointed the first British "Governor" of Malta.[1] A fortnight later Earl Bathurst sent him a copy of the "very able" Report of the Commissioners and in a covering despatch stated that the Government had resolved to act upon their proposals with certain modifications. The general desire of the Maltese to be "acknowledged publicly as subjects of the British Crown" was to be gratified by a formal proclamation in that sense as soon as Maitland reached the island and by the establishment of the civil authority upon a permanent footing. The system of government decided upon by Bathurst left the power of the Governor even more unfettered than the Commissioners' Report had done. "The authority of the Governor is limited only by the orders of the King. He is responsible to His Majesty and to his country for his conduct; but his discretion is not to be shackled by any person or by any body of persons resident in Malta." Whether there was to be a Council at all was to depend entirely upon the

[1] The Office copy of his Commission and Instructions is in C.O. 159/4, pp. 175–216.

Governor's discretion. If he so decided, the number of members must not exceed six excluding himself. The Bishop of Malta, the President of the High Court of Appeal, the Public Secretary, and the Treasurer would be members *ex officio*, the remainder to be appointed (and removed) as the Governor desired. The Governor alone was to have the right of introducing business for discussion. The members were not to vote but merely to deliver their opinions. They were however to have the right of sending to the Governor a written expression of dissent within twenty-four hours of a meeting, and if they thought fit, to require its transmission to the Secretary of State. As previously recommended the Governor was also to be the senior military officer in the island.

As regards the laws and courts of judicature Bathurst substantially adopted the Commissioners' recommendations. Defective and inadequate though the laws were, a sudden or radical alteration of the Code was inadvisable. But the Governor was given full power to effect a gradual revision at his own discretion. As a preparation for such reform, glaring abuses in the practice of the courts must be rectified along the lines suggested in the Report. A commercial court adapted to the merchants' needs was to be established in place of the *Consolato del Mare*. Its organisation and the drafting of a new commercial code were to be undertaken by an English barrister, who would be sent out as the permanent legal adviser to the Governor with the title of King's Assessor. The judges of the civil and criminal courts were to be natives of Malta; the judges of the Commercial Court and the President of the Court of Appeal might be either Maltese or British. The use of torture was to be abolished. A new appellant system was devised to supersede the old *Audienza* and *Signatura*. For civil cases there was to be a High Court of Appeal, consisting of a President (appointed by the Secretary of State), one of the civil judges who had not tried the cause in the first instance, and one criminal judge. The judges were to sit by rotation. Appeal from this Court was subject to the discretion of the President. If granted, the case went before a Supreme Court of Justice, which was to be composed of the Governor, the President of the Court of Appeal, the Public Secretary, and two judges selected by the Governor. In criminal cases there was to be no appeal, except that a convicted person might petition the Governor who was to exercise an absolute discretion.

The central purpose of British policy is summed up in the concluding passage of Bathurst's despatch. The "affections and interests" of the native population were to be identified with the British connection by the fostering of commercial prosperity on the one side, and, on the other, by a "gradual advancement in the condition and information of the people". To that end Maitland was recommended to devote his constant attention to the diffusion of the English language in place of the Arabic *patois* of the populace and the Italian of the upper classes. All proclamations should be issued in English as well as Italian and the proceedings of the High Court should be conducted in English. The establishment of public schools where the reading and writing of English might be taught would be of very beneficial effect; "and I am to request you will promote such Establishments, and give them the support of Government".[1]

The rule of Maitland in Malta from 1813 to 1824 does not fall within the chronological limits of this chapter, nor is an examination of it necessary for our present purpose. It was marked by the same strongly defined characteristics as was his administration in Ceylon: a tireless devotion to the welfare of the inhabitants, a ruthless demand for efficiency alike from himself and his subordinates, a contempt for native magnates, and an expressed conviction (usually justified) that the Home Authorities were wrong and he himself right. It only remains to indicate parallel lines of policy on the part of the British Government in designing a form of government for that other Mediterranean acquisition, the Septinsular "Republic" of the Ionian Islands.

The French occupation of the Ionian Islands in 1807 after the secret Treaty of Tilsit was a direct threat to the Turks whose Empire Napoleon was planning to partition and to Great Britain in the eastern Mediterranean. If the islands, on the other hand, came under British control, another important commercial base would be acquired for the "puncturing" of the Continental System after the manner so profitably adopted in Malta and elsewhere.[2] In 1809 Cephalonia and Zante petitioned Great Britain to restore "their national independence", and an expedition under Vice-Admiral Collingwood and General Oswald was sent to occupy the islands. Little resistance was encountered from the French, except at Corfu, where the garrison held out until 1814, when it was ordered to capitulate by Louis XVIII. On 2 October 1809 General Oswald at Zante issued a proclamation promising the Ionians that the British would "establish a free independent government, with the uncontrolled exercise of their religious, civil and commercial rights".[3] In so doing Oswald pledged his Government to an administrative task of the utmost difficulty. To find a middle course between the claims of local liberty and of imperial interest was proving a sufficiently formidable task in the case of Malta where local patriotism was not so sharply defined as in the Greek Islands. Moreover, the previous attempts of the Ionians to govern themselves as an independent republic (between 1800 and 1806) had collapsed in complete confusion, and order had not been

---

[1] Bathurst to Maitland, 28 July 1813, C.O. 158/19. Another copy in the Entry-book, C.O. 159/4, pp. 219–60. Short extracts are printed by Hardman, *op. cit.* pp. 256–530.
[2] Cf. *C.H.B.F.P.* i, 387.
[3] *British and Foreign State Papers*, 1815–16, p. 251.

restored until the establishment of a Russian dictatorship. How then was the dilemma to be resolved between the demands of an imperial power requiring control for strategical reasons and the aspirations of a people whose desire for freedom was only rivalled by their political incapacity?

The British reacted to the problem by imitating their own procedure in Malta. Pending a peace settlement the Islands were held on behalf of the Allies, and each was administered by a British military officer with plenary powers, "aided by the advice and assistance of the most worthy inhabitants" and in the name of the Septinsular Republic.[1] In April 1812 it was decided that the Ionians should be permitted to bear the British Flag and be thereby entitled to as full protection of their commerce as if they were British subjects.[2] Six months later a more regular form of government was established. In reply to Ionian requests that they should become "permanently united with Great Britain", Castlereagh indicated that while the war continued it was impossible to make permanent arrangements for their government, but that since the frequent changes among military commandants had proved inconvenient, the Government had decided to appoint a Civil Commissioner, "who shall be entrusted with the civil and military authority, in the same manner as has been practised at Malta".[3] The instructions issued to the Commissioner (Lieutenant-Colonel James Campbell) on his appointment in February 1813 closely followed the Maltese precedent.[4]

At the Congress of Vienna the British Ministers at first evinced no desire to retain the islands as British possessions. But by February 1815 opinion was veering round, and after the Hundred Days their cession to Great Britain was all but agreed to by the Allied Powers. At the last moment, however, Russia raised difficulties on the ground that she had previously guaranteed Ionian independence which had been violated by France after the Treaty of Tilsit. On 5 November 1815 a Treaty was signed at Paris which defined the future status of the Islands. Under article I they were to form "a single, free and independent state, under the denomination of the United States of the Ionian Islands". The second article laid down that the state so constituted should be placed "under the immediate and exclusive protection of His Majesty the King of Great Britain", the other contracting Powers renouncing every right and particular pretension. According to the third article the Islands were to regulate their internal organisation with the approbation of the Protecting Power; and the latter was to "employ a particular solicitude with regard to legislation and the general administration of those States". His

---

[1] See Oswald to Castlereagh, 8 Oct. 1809, Addit. MSS. 20,184, f. 3.
[2] Liverpool to Bentinck, 13 April 1812, W.O. 6/57.
[3] Castlereagh to Toscardi, 21 Oct. 1812, W.O. 1/760.
[4] Bathurst to Campbell, 27 Feb. 1813, C.O. 136/300.

Britannic Majesty would appoint a resident Lord High Commissioner, "invested with all the necessary power and authorities for this purpose". Subsequent articles provided that the Commissioner should convoke and direct the proceedings of a Legislative Convention for the drafting of a new constitutional charter.[1]

The international status created by this Instrument bears some analogy to that obtaining in the cases of Iraq and Egypt in modern times. The Ionian "Mandate" was a peculiarly difficult if not impossible one to administer. How was article I, which proclaimed the political independence of the Ionian State, to be reconciled with the third article which enjoined the Protecting Power to appoint a resident Commissioner armed with all the necessary authority to give effect to British "solicitude" in matters of legislation and general administration? The delicate art of training an undisciplined people to stand politically on their own feet, of striking a mean during the probationary process between undue interference and an over-hasty surrender of the levers of control calls for consummate statesmanship. Great Britain required another century of experience in adjusting her outlook and methods to the claims of nationhood in the English-speaking Dominions and in India before she was equipped to fulfil the obligations of trusteeship in its most exacting form, that is to say, the type of trusteeship which consciously aims at its own elimination by becoming unnecessary.

During the autumn of 1815 when the cession of the islands to Great Britain had been expected, Bathurst and Maitland had agreed that the Ionians must be trained under a form of Crown Colony administration. Representative government might be considered at a later stage after they had been prepared for it. Their ideas did not change when the cession of a dependency was altered to the creation of a protectorate over an "independent" State. In conveying this news to Maitland, Bathurst warned him not to convoke the Legislative Convention for the drafting of the constitutional charter until he had had time to become thoroughly acquainted with the Ionians and their social and political alignments. Above all things he must see to it "that they entertain no wild speculative notions respecting government and that they do not imagine that they can make a constitution as they would make a pudding according to a British or French receipt....I do not imagine that a system of popular representation and public discussion is what they will be ripe for, tho' it should not be so stated to them for many years to come."[2] The upright and masterful "King Tom", as Maitland was aptly nicknamed in Malta, needed no such bidding.[3]

---

[1] An official (printed) copy of the Treaty is in C.O. 136/7. It is printed by Xenos, S., *East and West* (London, 1865), pp. 226–8, and by Hertslet, Sir E., *The Map of Europe by Treaty*, I, 337–41.
[2] Bathurst to Maitland ("Private"), 2 Dec. 1815, C.O. 136/300.
[3] See his address to the Primary Council, 3 Feb. 1817, C.O. 136/7.

The "Constitutional Chart" which the Ionian delegates conveyed to London in May 1817 for the approval of the Protecting Power established a piece of political machinery which would have intrigued the Abbé Sieyès. In effect it created a British Commissionership as powerful as that in Malta behind an elaborate façade of self-government. A copy of the Chart has been preserved which contains Maitland's own marginal comments written for the edification of the Secretary of State.[1] They explain his purpose in the shaping of each device. The Senate consisted of a President and five other members in whom were vested the functions of an Executive and Legislative Council. The Senators were elected by the Legislative Assembly from among its own members on nomination by the President. After a stiff struggle the Ionian deputies gave way to Maitland's determination that the President himself should be appointed by the Crown. As regards the ordinary Senators it was sufficient, remarked Maitland, that the power of the veto should ensure the choice of well-disposed persons. The power of initiation lay with the President alone but subject to the check that each Senator might once only in each session of Parliament bring forward a proposition if the Commissioner approved of it. The Senate was divided into three Departments, General, Political and Financial; but no departmental act was to be held as ultimately valid until the Senate had approved in its collective capacity. One office, that of Secretary to the General Department, was reserved as a Commissioner's appointment. The holder of the post, explained Maitland, would be an Englishman, so that "nothing can be done from day to day without its being instantly reported to the Lord High Commissioner". The Senate appointed (subject to the Commissioner's veto) to all posts under the General Government including the Regents and Judges in the respective islands. It could also initiate legislation and while Parliament was in recess possessed the right of making regulations subject to the Commissioner's approval which had *pro tempore* the force of law.

The Assembly was composed of twenty-nine elected and eleven "integral" or *ex-officio* members. The latter comprised the six Senators, the Regents of the four great islands, and one of the Regents from the three smaller islands (Ithaca, Cerigo and Paxo) sitting in rotation. The election of the President of the Assembly was controlled with the same double veto of the Commissioner as was the election of Senators. The Assembly possessed the right of initiating legislation concurrently with the Senate and with the Commissioner himself acting through the Senate. In practice, however, the Legislature did little more than register the Commissioner's decrees. "I introduced all the bills",

---

[1] "Copy of the proposed Constitutional Chart for the United States of the Ionian Islands, as approved of unanimously by the Legislative Assembly", C.O. 136/7. I am indebted to Mr C. Willis Dixon, who has made a special study of Maitland's career, for drawing my attention to this copy of the Chart and to several other related documents. The Constitutional Chart is printed in *British and Foreign State Papers*, 1816–17, pp. 647 *seqq.*

wrote Maitland to Bathurst in 1818, "which have hitherto been
passed. I think there is no prospect of this not being the common
course of things."[1] A bill passed by the Assembly could be vetoed
by the Senate, which in that case must send down its reasons to the
Lower House within three days. Such a bill could not be reintroduced
in the same session. Normally the approval or dissent of the Commissioner to a bill was final, but power was reserved to the Protecting
Sovereign to intervene and cancel any law by Order-in-Council
within one year of its enactment. The obedience of the Assembly
(particularly important in the matter of voting supplies) was secured
by using the "integral" members as a Finance Committee and by a
curious and very effective device for manipulating the elections. In
the event of a dissolution of Parliament either at the end of its normal
term of five years or at the will of His Britannic Majesty the Commissioner chose five members from the retiring Assembly, who with
the Senators constituted a "Primary Council". This body drew up
a list of 58 candidates, two for each of the 29 constituencies. The
electorate, formed on a narrow franchise, chose one of the two
nominees in each case. This provision, Maitland explained, was "the
very keystone upon which the whole fabric rests". "The Primary
Council is the great engine upon which (by their double lists) the
elections are secured in favour of the Government. And it will be
perceived that if the Government, in addition to the five members
named on this emergency, gets only one of the six Senators to go
with it, the elections are secure—an immense power vested in the
Government, but one absolutely necessary under the circumstances
of the country." The details of the local government of the islands
need not detain us, for, as Maitland remarked, they were "more for
show than substance". Real power was vested in the British Resident,
whom Maitland chose solely for his capacity and to whom he delegated
wide responsibility.

The basic aim of the system was to secure the happiness of the
people and to safeguard imperial interests by the imposition of direct
authority. Local aristocracies were as far as possible ignored, because
they were suspect as potential oppressors on the one side and as
mischief-makers in respect of imperial authority on the other. The
flat refusal returned to the demands of the Testaferrata party in Malta
has already been noted. In the case of the Ionian Islands the terms
of the Anglo-Russian agreement under the Treaty of Paris necessitated
the employment of more indirect methods, but the underlying policy
was the same. The power of the British Administrator of those islands,
wrote Maitland in 1816, should be devoted to "standing forth as a
real protector of the people against the vices of their own rule".[2]
Four years later he wrote: "The old nobles of the head families look

[1] 6 May 1818, C.O. 136/7.
[2] Maitland to Bathurst, 27 Feb. 1816, C.O. 136/5.

with disgust at anything like protecting the people from their tyrannical and arbitrary control." "The only real and true method of administering government here for the benefit of the people, is in fact to maintain all the powers in the hands of His Majesty's Lord High Commissioner."[1]

The temper of the age which remembered the American Revolution, which had witnessed the rise of Jacobinism and the consequent menace of Napoleon, preferred to guarantee freedom from disorder rather than trust the individual with a liberty which, if misused, might bring down the entire edifice, but which alone could train him to be a reliable co-operator. Crown Colony government broke through the tradition of trying to govern by representative institutions colonies which could never stand alone. The system of centralisation was not in itself a solution, although it tided over a period of external peril and provided an effective instrument for the exercise of trusteeship. When Lord Durham devised a means by which colonial freedom could be conceded without entailing disruption, the necessary flexibility was achieved. Crown Colony government then found its proper place in the imperial mechanism: a form of tutelage in which static units were retained under efficient and benevolent control, and out of which progressive units, of whatever nationality, could be led by ascending gradations to an ultimate self-determination.

[1] Maitland to Bathurst, 10 Jan. and 15 Feb. 1820, C.O. 136/4.

CHAPTER V

THE ABOLITION OF THE SLAVE TRADE

IN the middle of the eighteenth century the problems arising from the contact between the peoples of the different continents—problems which loom so large at the present day—had scarcely been envisaged, still less discussed or dealt with. If the relations between Englishmen at home and Englishmen in the American colonies under the old Commercial System were conceived as mainly an economic question, the relations between Englishmen and the coloured races seemed to be still more simply and exclusively a matter of business. Trade and nothing else was their concern in Asia. The conduct of Englishmen in India was regarded as the private affair of the East India Company, and public opinion in England was chiefly interested in the maintenance of the Company's property. In North America and the West Indies, similarly, the contact and the conflict between British settlers and the native races roused no feeling of moral responsibility in the mother-country. If the Imperial Government bestirred itself to check the American colonists' inevitable westward advance and their no less inevitable occupation of the Redskins' lands, the motive was not humanitarian; it was partly to prevent the Indians from being dangerously embittered against the British and becoming the instruments of French aggression, and partly—especially after the annexation of Canada in 1763—to safeguard the peaceful operation of the Indian fur-trade. In the West Indies, again, the early dealings of the British immigrants with the aboriginal population of the islands had excited no attention at home. The question was apparently never discussed in Parliament until 1773, when an enquiry was held into the ill-treatment of the Caribs at St Vincent.[1] Englishmen at home, in fact, only cared about their Indian silk or American tobacco or West Indian sugar; they did not care, and hardly knew, at what human cost it was obtained. And this indifference to any other than the commercial aspect of the old imperialism, this lack of interest or imagination as to the dealings of their white kinsmen with the brown man of India or the red man of America, is the chief explanation of their attitude to the relations between white and black, to the connection of Britain with the third continent, Africa. It is in this last field that the dominance of the old commercialism is revealed in its most naked and repulsive form. For Englishmen went to Africa, not merely, as they went to Asia, to trade, but to trade chiefly in Africans.

[1] Lecky, W. H., *History of England in the 18th Century* (1917 ed.), vii, 357.

The growth and character of the slave trade have been described in a previous volume.[1] How was it that the whole slave-system, of which the Trade was an essential part, was tolerated so long by the Christian sentiment of England or Europe? It was partly due, no doubt, to ignorance, indifference, and lack of imagination on the part of the stay-at-home public as to the realities of the system. But it was also due to practical considerations, to the strength of the case that could be made for the continuance of the system.

The key to it lay in the West Indies; for the economic welfare of their West Indian colonies was regarded throughout the eighteenth century as vital to the prosperity of their European possessors. It is not strange that British statesmen at the close of the Seven Years' War questioned whether Canada or Guadeloupe was the more valuable acquisition to the Empire or that in the War with Revolutionary France Pitt and Dundas sacrificed so many British lives in trying to occupy more "sugar-islands", since no less an authority than Pitt himself could declare, in proposing his income-tax in 1798, that of the incomes derived from overseas (including Ireland) and enjoyed in Britain, four-fifths were derived from the West Indies.[2] And if the prosperity of the West Indies was regarded as essential to that of Britain, the maintenance of slavery and of the trade which fed it were regarded as essential to the prosperity of the West Indies. "The impossibility of doing without slaves in the West Indies", wrote an apologist for the Trade in 1764, "will always prevent this traffic being stopped. The necessity, the absolute necessity then, of carrying it on must, since there is no other, be its excuse." It was thought, moreover—and not without reason—that any attempt by British opinion to interfere with slavery or the Trade would be regarded by the West Indian colonists as an intolerable interference by the mother-country in their domestic concerns. Finally, there was the carrying trade to be considered, of which the trade in slaves formed so great a part; and not its profits only, but its contribution to British naval power. It seemed foolish for Britain to withdraw from the Trade unless all her maritime rivals, and particularly France, agreed to do so at the same time; and it seemed certain that no such universal international agreement was obtainable. Altogether it was a strong case, and it was backed by the combined "vested interests" of the planters and the traders and their associates, whose representatives in Society and in Parliament constituted a "West Indian party" similar to that of the East Indian "nabobs".

But if, for these reasons, the idea of interference with the slave system was so long neglected by British statesmen, and ruled out of practical politics, the consciences of individual Englishmen could not

---

[1] *C.H.B.E.* i, chap. xv.
[2] Speech of 3 October 1798; Pitt's *Speeches* (1806 ed.), iii, 317; cited by Trevelyan, G. M., *British History in the Nineteenth Century*, p. 88.

be silenced. Protests were audible in early days, and presently they multiplied. It was in religious circles, naturally, that the first voices were raised, and George Fox may perhaps be regarded as the originator of the Humanitarian Movement, since in 1671 he recommended the Quakers in Barbados to be kind to their slaves and after a term of years to set them free.[1] In 1675 the great nonconformist, Richard Baxter, repudiated the "heinous sin" of slave piracy in his *Christian Directory*,[2] and in 1680 Morgan Godwyn, an Oxford clergyman, composed a pamphlet denouncing the brutalities of slavery which he had witnessed in Barbados.[3] In 1688 the Society of Friends, true to their founder, began their long campaign of protest at a meeting of German Quakers at Germantown, Pennsylvania; in 1696 the Yearly Meeting of the Pennsylvanian Quakers as a whole advised Friends "not to encourage the bringing in of any more Negroes"; and in 1727 the British Quakers passed a resolution declaring that "the importing of negroes from their native country and relations by Friends is not a commendable or allowed practice and is therefore censured by this meeting".[4] In 1758 the last-named body definitely warned, and in 1761 disowned, all Friends who continued to participate in the Trade,[5] and similar decrees of expulsion were passed by their fellows in America in 1774 and 1776.[6] The Quakers were the only religious community to act as a community, but leading members of other religious bodies were not slow to echo individually the protests they had raised. In 1755 Bishop Hayter,[7] and in 1766 Bishop Warburton,[8] condemned the Trade from the pulpit; and whereas Whitefield[9] during his residence in the American colonies had accepted and defended slavery as a necessity, to be ameliorated rather than abolished, John Wesley[10] in 1774 attacked the whole system and the trade that fed it.

Meantime the general current of thought was moving in the same humanitarian direction as the special teaching of religious communities and leaders. The slave system was clearly incompatible with the ideas of the eighteenth-century Renaissance in England and in France. Locke denounced it with curt logic and Montesquieu with elaborate sarcasm. And when the theorists proceeded from the rights of individuality to the natural goodness of man and discovered a dubious proof of the latter doctrine in "the noble savage", the anomaly of slavery became still more obvious. A new interest, moreover, in the

---

[1] Clarkson, T., *History of the Abolition of the Slave Trade* (London, 1808), I, 111.
[2] Baxter, R., *Christian Directory*, Part II, chap. XIV.
[3] Godwyn, M., *The Negro's and Indian's Advocate* (London, 1680).
[4] Clarkson, I, 113.
[5] *Ibid.* I, 113–16.   [6] Turner, E. R., *The Negro in Pennsylvania*, pp. 72–7.
[7] Clarkson, I, 58.
[8] *Ibid.* I, 61.
[9] Tyerman, L., *Life of Whitefield*, II, 169–70, 205–6, cited by Klingberg, F. J., *The Anti-Slavery Movement in England*, pp. 48–9.
[10] Wesley, J., *Thoughts upon Slavery* (London, 1774).

primitive peoples of the world was excited and a new sympathy aroused on their behalf by a new phase of overseas exploration. The narratives of Dampier, Tasman, Anson, Captain Cook and others were widely read. Specimens of Red Indians, Esquimaux and South Sea Islanders were to be seen in England. And since the sense of colour prejudice, at least among Englishmen at home, was apparently still as dormant as in the days when Shakespeare wrote *Othello*, the idealised black man soon appeared in English literature. Mrs Aphra Behn, whose youth had been spent in Surinam, took a negro for the hero of her most famous novel, *Oroonoko or the Royal Slave*, which was published in 1696 and dramatised by Southerne. Defoe condemned the slave trade in his *Poor Man's Plea...on the Reformation of Manners* (1698), advocated kindness to negroes in his *Life of Colonel Jacques* (1722), and drew an immortal picture of a truly "noble savage" in *Robinson Crusoe* (1719). And if the portrait of the negro girl in Sterne's *Tristram Shandy* (1759) is scarcely on the great scale of "Man Friday", it is drawn with no less sympathy. Nor were the poets behind the prose-writers. Pope in the *Essay on Man* (1733), Thomson in the *Seasons* (1726–30), Savage and Shenstone all alluded to the tragedy and pathos of the kidnapped and subjected negro. Thomas Day, better known as the author of *Sandford and Merton*, wrote a poem on *The Dying Negro* (1773). It is significant, finally, that the high priest of the literary cult in London hated slavery and the Trade with a hatred that was vehement even for him. So strong indeed was Samuel Johnson's prejudice on that account against the West Indian system that he once startled a company of "very grave men" at Oxford by calling a toast to "the next insurrection of the Negroes in the West Indies".[1]

The evils of the slave system were thus becoming steadily better known and more discussed as the eighteenth century drew on; but any definite or effective attack on it might still have been long delayed if the slave-owners themselves had not precipitated the conflict by introducing slavery into England. It was doubtless natural that planters coming home on holiday or to settle down on retirement should prefer their old black servants to new white ones; but they failed to realise how the presence of an increasing number of slaves—there were at least 10,000 in England by 1770—would affect opinion in the Old Country. Slaves ran away sometimes in England just as in the colonies; and, if they knew what was supposed to be the law, they appealed to kindly Englishmen to get them baptised and give them godfatherly protection from their pursuing masters. This method of escape became indeed so popular that as early as 1729 the West Indian community appealed to the Law Officers of the Crown,

---

[1] Boswell, *Life of Johnson* (1904 ed.), II, 153–6. Boswell did not share his hero's views on this subject. An exhaustive list of writers against Slavery and the Trade is given in Clarkson, *op. cit.* vol. I.

Yorke and Talbot, who declared that neither residence in England nor baptism affected the master's "right and property" in the slave and that "the master may legally compel him to return to the Plantations".[1] Still more decisive was the judgment of Lord Chancellor Hardwicke in 1749 that a runaway slave could be legally recovered.[2] So slavery continued, no longer far away beyond the range of Englishmen's imagination, but under their very eyes. Advertisements of slave auctions appeared in the newspapers. Rewards were offered for the capture of runaways and their safe disposal on shipboard, and the earning of such rewards became one of the disreputable professions of riverside London. This forcing of the hard facts of the slave-system on the attention of Englishmen had a more practical effect than the appeals of divines, the arguments of political theorists, or the humane sentiments of novelists and poets. It was hard facts that inspired in one Englishman such a fierce and persevering hatred of slavery and its concomitants that he was able presently to achieve the first definite step in the abolition of the whole system.

It happened that in 1767 Granville Sharp (1735–1813), a clerk in the Ordnance Department and a student of philology, was brought into contact with the peculiarly brutal case of a slave in London who had been ill-treated by his master, set adrift as useless, and, when restored to health, kidnapped again into slavery. From that time Sharp set himself to contest the law which tolerated such inhumanity. Undeterred by the view of Blackstone himself, who told him that the Yorke-Talbot ruling must stand, he worked hard at the law and produced a book on *The Injustice and dangerous Tendency of tolerating Slavery...in England* in which he resuscitated the earlier opinion of Chief Justice Holt that every slave entering England became free.[3] Shortly after its publication he rescued a slave from a ship about to sail for the West Indies by means of a writ of *habeas corpus*. The law, it seemed, could cut both ways; and in 1772, Sharp brought the issue to a head by prosecuting the master of a fugitive slave called Somerset for detaining him on shipboard. Chief Justice Mansfield was one of the judges; and, though he was personally anxious that the case should be settled out of court, he could not evade a decision which at a stroke set over 14,000 slaves at liberty and destroyed property worth more than half a million pounds. On June 22 the court held that the state of slavery was "so odious that nothing can be suffered to support it but positive law". "Whatever inconveniences, therefore, may follow from this decision, I cannot say this case is allowed or approved by the law of England; and therefore the black must be discharged." Six years later, the Scottish judges delivered a similar decision in the case

---

[1] Howell, *State Trials*, xx, 80, 81, 82.
[2] *Ibid.* xx, 1, 82.
[3] *Report of cases determined by Sir John Holt*, p. 495.

of Joseph Knight. Since the Somerset judgment covered Ireland as well as England, the state of slavery thus ceased to exist after 1778 on the soil of the British Isles.[1]

The fact that it continued to exist on British soil overseas was overshadowed for the moment by the War of the American Revolution; but after 1783 all the circumstances were propitious for a further attack on it. The American colonies were out of the arena; and it was a far less formidable task for humanitarians in the mother-country to assail the domestic institutions of the West Indian planters now that the more numerous and independent slave-owners in the mainland colonies were no longer at their side. With the coming of peace, moreover, British politics entered on a new phase. Sobered by their humiliating defeat, Englishmen, with the younger Pitt as a new kind of leader, began to set their house in order; and, if retrenchment came first, reform was also in the air—free trade, the conciliation of Ireland, Parliamentary Reform, a new *régime* for British India. Alongside such liberal causes the abolition of slavery could find a natural place, and alongside the last of them particularly. In the years between the suicide of Clive in 1774 and the impeachment of Warren Hastings in 1788 public opinion on the question of British rule in India was transformed. The idea that the British connection with India could be regarded as a mere matter of commerce, which, except for the requisite minimum of regulation, lay outside the purview or control of Parliament, was abandoned; and in its place, by the combined influence of Burke's passion, Fox's humanity, and Pitt's sense of justice, a new system of ideas was established—that the commercial connection involved for the stronger of the two parties a moral obligation to ensure, as far as might be, that the weaker party did not suffer from that connection; that this, in turn, involved the exercise of direct control by Parliament over the East India Company's Indian administration; and that all such exercise of political power was, in Burke's words, "in the strictest sense a trust". In other words the modern doctrine of "trusteeship" with regard to weak or backward races had taken its place in British politics. And obviously it could not be limited to India. If the British people had awakened to a new sense of duty towards Asiatics they were bound very soon to feel the same sense of duty towards the weaker, more backward and far more brutally treated Africans. Nor, lastly, must it be forgotten that the Evangelical movement was now at the climax of its power over English minds, strengthening the new humanitarian impulses, demanding the application of Christian principles to all human relations, seeking everywhere for a salutary sense of sin. That sense was awakened, in some degree, by the scandals in Bengal. But these at their worst were transient and had already been suppressed. A far

---

[1] Prince Hoare, *Memoirs of Granville Sharp* (London, 1820); Howell, *op. cit.* xx, 1–82; Yorke, P. C., *Life of Hardwicke*, ii, 472–3.

more glaring case for a conviction of national guilt was awaiting recognition in English actions on the Slave Coast of Africa.

It happened, moreover, that in the period of the American War several eminent and influential names had been added to the roll of those who, for a century past, had individually and disconnectedly assaulted slavery and the trade. Adam Smith, who in his *Theory of Moral Sentiments* (1759) had drawn a somewhat extravagant contrast between heroic negroes and their sordid masters, argued more coldly in the *Wealth of Nations* (1776) that slave labour was uneconomical. Though he admitted that the profits of sugar and tobacco plantations enabled their owners to afford the expense of slave cultivation, "the experience of all ages and nations, I believe", he wrote, "demonstrates that the work done by slaves, though it appears to cost only their maintenance, is in the end the dearest of any".[1] Thomas Paine's essay on slavery in Philadelphia (1775) was little known in England;[2] but Robertson's *History of America* (1777) and *Charles V* (1769) and Paley's *Moral and Political Philosophy* (1785) were widely read by their countrymen and in all three books slavery was denounced as contrary to Christianity. The war, too, had created many new readers, and there appeared several new editions of Burke's *European Governments in America* (first published in 1761) which boldly asserted that the sufferings of the negro slaves "in our colonies" were worse than those of any other subject people in any other place or age.[3] And, meantime, a vigorous attack on slavery had been opened by two great men in France. The Abbé Raynal's voluminous treatise on the East and West Indies (1750), which included a detailed account of African slavery, soon reached its seventh edition in France, and several English translations of it (1777–85) provided the humanitarians in England with "a vast storehouse of information".[4] Condorcet's *Réflexions sur l'esclavage des nègres* (1781) was also read on this side of the Channel: and English enemies of the slave trade began to hope that French public opinion might move side by side with British and so eliminate one of the strongest arguments against abolition.

It was in a promising atmosphere, then, that the Quakers, once more to the fore, took the first step towards an organised abolition movement. In 1783 they opened their campaign with a petition to Parliament against the Trade;[5] and in the same year the "Meeting for Sufferings", a sort of standing committee of the Society, was directed to give special attention to the cause, and a small committee of six was formed for the special purpose of considering "what steps they should take for the relief and liberation of the negro slaves in the West Indies and for the discouragement of the slave trade on the

[1] *Wealth of Nations*, book I, chap. VIII; book III, chap. II.
[2] *Writings of Thomas Paine*, I, 4 *sqq.*, cited by Klingberg, *op. cit.* p. 53.
[3] 1770 ed., II, 124.   [4] Swinney, S. H., in *Western Races and the World*, p. 130.
[5] *Parl. Hist.* XXIII, 1026.

coast of Africa".[1] The efforts of these two bodies resulted in some effective propaganda. Before long they secured a place in some of the London and provincial newspapers for any articles they chose to supply. In 1784 they composed a pamphlet on *The Case of our Fellow-creatures, the oppressed Africans*, 12,000 copies of which were distributed among ministers, members of Parliament, judges and so forth. In 1785 they promoted the circulation in England, specially in the public schools, of *A Caution to Great Britain and her Colonies in a Short Representation of the calamitous state of the enslaved negroes in the British Dominions* by the French-American Quaker Anthony Bezonet (1713–84).[2] Meanwhile, the Quakers were finding allies no less earnest than themselves. The most eminent was Granville Sharp, who had continued ever since the Somerset case to work privately for abolition. In 1784, Dr Porteous, then bishop of Chester, preached a sermon on the negroes' wrongs, which was published by the Quaker Committee.[3] In the same year the Rev. James Ramsay, who after nineteen years in St Christopher had returned to a Kentish parsonage with a firm determination to alleviate the evils he had witnessed, entered the field with the first of a series of outspoken pamphlets on slavery and the Trade.[4] Soon afterwards a recruit came forward who was destined to do more than any other man, with one exception, to bring about the triumph of the cause. Thomas Clarkson, son of the headmaster of Wisbech Grammar School and a student at St John's College, Cambridge, had been led to examine the slave trade for the purpose of the senior Latin Essay competition of 1785. The theme prescribed by the liberal-minded Vice-Chancellor, Dr Peckard, who had devoted a recent sermon to the iniquities of the slave trade, was *Anne liceat invitos in servitutem dare?* Clarkson won the first prize and his essay was published in an English translation. But, in the meantime, he had become obsessed with the horrors of the Trade; and having made the acquaintance of Dillwyn, a member of the Quaker Committee, and of Sharp and Ramsay, he decided in 1787 to abandon the clerical career he had begun and to devote his life to the cause of abolition.[5]

The propaganda in which this little group of philanthropists had so far been engaged had been aimed at the whole slave system—at slavery as well as the slave trade. As time was to prove, the two evils were inseparable; the Trade could not be completely killed as long as slavery survived. But in the course of their discussions the Abolitionists determined to attack the Trade first. It was the easier part of their gigantic task. Public opinion might be convinced that slavery was a necessity in the West Indies and yet be persuaded that it could continue to exist by means of natural reproduction without the importation of more negroes from Africa. The abolition of slavery, again, meant the destruction of private property worth several million

---

[1] Clarkson, i, 120.   [2] *Ibid.* i, 121–2.   [3] *Ibid.* i, 98.   [4] *Ibid.* i, 101.
[5] *Ibid.* i, 117–26, 230.

pounds; the abolition of the Trade would only destroy one means of adding to that property and divert a certain amount of capital to other commercial fields. A better defence, too, could be made for slavery; there were many humane slave-owners and many happy slaves. But the operations of the Trade—the seizure or purchase of free men and women and the brutalities of the "Middle Passage"— were morally indefensible. Nor would concentration against the Trade leave slavery unharmed: the attack on the one stronghold would go far to undermine the other. But even if the objective were thus limited, its attainment remained immensely difficult. The act of abolition could only be an Act of Parliament, and the propaganda might be wasted if it were not brought to bear inside as well as outside Parliament. Its members, so far, had shown no eagerness to right the negroes' wrongs. Thrice in the last five years the issue had been raised in the House of Commons. In 1776 David Hartley, the member for Hull, had moved that "the Slave Trade is contrary to the laws of God and the rights of men", and Sir George Saville had supported him.[1] In 1783 the Quakers had presented their petition.[2] In 1785 another petition for "the extinction of that sanguinary traffic" was presented by Poulet and Hood, members for Bridgwater, on behalf of the inhabitants of that borough; and they reported to their constituents that it had been ordered "to lie on the table" and that "there did not appear the least disposition to pay any further attention to it".[3]

The House, in fact, had accepted the doctrine laid down by Lord North, with all his usual urbanity, in response to the Quakers' petition. "It did credit to the feelings of the most mild and humane set of Christians in the world. But still he was afraid that it would be found impossible to abolish the Slave Trade...for it was a trade which had in some measure become necessary to almost every nation in Europe; and, as it would be next to an impossibility to induce them all to give it up and renounce it for ever, so he was apprehensive that the wishes of the humane petitioners could not be accomplished."[4] It might well seem a hopeless task, indeed, to win over a majority of the apathetic Commons, not to mention the Lords, to the cause of abolition unless one of the great political leaders took it up. And of this there was no prospect. Abolition could not be made a party cry. If there were men in both parties who would not prove irresponsive to a humanitarian appeal, there were men also in both who were either directly connected with the West Indian interest or drawn by temperament or conviction to the defence of the Trade. A leader, therefore, who committed himself to abolition, might well split and smash his party. For that reason, and also because he judged the strength of the opposing forces to be insuperable, Burke, who in 1780 had drafted a code of regulations for the reform and ultimate sup-

[1] Clarkson, i, 84.   [2] Parl. Hist. XXIII, 1026.
[3] Clarkson, i, 107.   [4] Parl. Hist. XXIII, 1026.

pression of the Trade, had gone no farther,[1] and Fox, as he hinted presently, had also shrunk from espousing a cause which appealed so strongly to his warm humanity. Pitt, though at this time his sympathies were quite as deeply engaged, was unlikely to rush in where Burke and Fox feared to tread at the risk of alienating the majority of his followers, destroying his personal ascendancy, and thus being forced to leave unfinished his primary political task—the restoration of British strength and spirit after the losses of the American War. If nothing, then, could be expected of the party leaders, the only hope left was that some powerful free-lance might be inspired to raise the unpopular flag, possessed of enough ability, prestige and persistence to rally supporters from both parties and in due course to create an abolition party of his own.

By what might well have seemed a stroke of providence, such a free-lance was available. William Wilberforce, the son of a Yorkshire merchant and the contemporary and intimate friend of Pitt, had made a highly successful entry into public life. Having served a brief political apprenticeship as member for his native town of Hull, he had come to the front by securing one of the important seats for Yorkshire at the critical election of 1784. His natural eloquence and beautiful voice had captivated the Commons, who dubbed him "the nightingale of the House". His personal charm, his infectious high spirits, his love of talk and song and laughter had captivated Society. If he had not yet acquired the weight and steadiness needed for a Cabinet post, it was obvious that this gifted, well-to-do and popular young man had a great career ahead of him. But in 1785 his pursuits and ambitions, his whole attitude to life, were suddenly and completely transformed by an Evangelical "conversion". For a time he shunned society and repudiated politics; and when presently, influenced partly perhaps by Pitt's affectionate tact, he resumed his place in Parliament, he could no longer take his old, vivacious share in the party game. Something higher than allegiance to his party or even to Pitt now claimed his voice and vote; and some higher call, too, was needed than current political issues if his sense of Christian dedication were to find a satisfying outlet in a parliamentary career.

At this appropriate moment several influences converged to interest him in the cause of the negroes. The Rev. John Newton, whose spiritual aid he had sought at this crisis of his "conversion", had himself captained a slave-ship in those unregenerate days which he now depicted in such lurid hues from the pulpit of St Mary Woolnoth. Then in 1786 Wilberforce was reintroduced by Sir Charles Middleton (afterwards Lord Barham) and his public-spirited wife to Ramsay, whom he had met three years before. In 1787 Clarkson called on him, presented him with a copy of his prize essay, and was invited to call

---

[1] Morley, J., *Burke*, p. 187; Wilberforce, R. and S., *Life of William Wilberforce*, I, 152 (henceforth cited as *Life of Wilberforce*).

frequently again. Regular meetings for the discussion of the subject were presently arranged at Wilberforce's house in London at which Granville Sharp, Clarkson, Ramsay and other sympathisers attended; and Wilberforce began to make enquiries among the London merchants connected with the Trade. Finally, in the course of the same year, Pitt himself, who had seen, no doubt, which way his friend's mind was moving, suggested that he should "give notice of a motion on the subject of the Slave Trade". But Wilberforce now scarcely needed prompting. The call of abolition was precisely the kind of call for which he had been waiting—a call above all party bias, an irresistible call to a Christian conscience—which, he soon believed, came straight to him from God. So, before the end of the year, the decision was definitely taken, and Clarkson obtained leave to publish it to the world. To the Abolitionist Committee it was the best of news. "His position as member for the largest county," wrote Granville Sharp of the new leader, "the great influence of his personal connections, added to an amiable and unblemished character, secure every advantage to the cause."[1]

No time was now lost. Wilberforce's resolution was to be brought forward early in 1788 and the Abolitionists spent the intervening winter in busily preparing their case. Clarkson set out on the first of those many journeys of enquiry, in the course of which he was to travel (so he afterwards computed) no less than 35,000 miles,[2] and the fruits of which were to do more than anything else to equip the Abolition Movement with its requisite armament of facts. On this occasion he visited Bristol, Liverpool and Lancaster, seeking out and interviewing anybody associated with the Trade, listening to gruesome stories of barbarity, measuring the quarters assigned to slaves in slave-ships, collecting specimens of leg-shackles, handcuffs, thumbscrews and mouth-openers, checking muster rolls to prove the high mortality among the seamen, and so forth. Wilberforce, meanwhile, was no less busily engaged in London, studying fresh evidence as it came in, canvassing the cause among members of Parliament, and consulting frequently with Pitt. And Pitt, for his part, was warmly sympathetic.[3] With a divided Cabinet, in which the enemies of abolition included Thurlow, Dundas and Sydney, he could not make it a Government measure. And Wilberforce quite agreed. "It was", he said, "in no sense a party question."[4] But Pitt was prepared to give his whole-hearted individual support to Wilberforce's resolution, and he greatly assisted the collection and publication of evidence by instructing the Trade Committee of the Privy Council to enquire into and report on the condition of British trade with Africa.[5] He at-

[1] *Life of Wilberforce*, I, chaps. IV–VI; Clarkson, *op. cit.* I, chaps. IX, X; Harford, J. S., *Recollections of W. Wilberforce*, p. 139.
[2] Clarkson, II, 470.   [3] *Life of Wilberforce*, I, 158–63.
[4] *Ibid.* I, 165.   [5] *Ibid.* I, 166.

tempted, in the meantime, to undermine one of the strongest arguments of the opposition—the continued participation of other nations in the Trade. On 7 December 1787 he wrote, in support of a letter from Wilberforce, to Sir William Eden, British Ambassador at Paris, directing him to sound the French Government with a view to an Anglo-French agreement "to discontinue the villainous traffic". "The more I reflect on it," he wrote again, "the more anxious and impatient I am that the business should be brought as speedily as possible to a point": and since Eden was shortly to be transferred to Madrid, he added: "If you see any chance of success in France, I hope you will lay your ground with a view to Spain also. I am considering what to do in Holland."[1] The outcome was disappointing. The French ministry were evasive. They meant, it seemed, to wait and see what positive results were obtained by the humanitarians in England before committing themselves.[2] And, if France held back, it was useless to press the question on Spain and Holland. Abolition, it was becoming evident, could not be carried with a rush. "Called at Pitt's at night," noted Wilberforce in his diary early in 1788; "he firm about the African trade, though we begin to perceive more difficulties in the way than we had hoped there would be."[3]

On 8 May 1788 the campaign was opened, but not by Wilberforce. In March, his health, always delicate, had completely broken down. His recovery, indeed, was almost despaired of; and, while the Abolition Committee discussed the question of finding another parliamentary leader, Wilberforce sent for Pitt and obtained from him a promise not only to move the resolution but to do anything else which Wilberforce himself might have done.[4] Pitt kept his word. He at once took over the personal superintendence of the Privy Council enquiry.[5] He invited Granville Sharp to Downing Street and discussed with him the Committee's policy.[6] And in due course, in a studiously moderate speech, he moved the resolution committing the House to consider the Slave Trade in the next session. Not till then, he pointed out, when the Privy Council report would be available, could any of the issues be decided, as for instance the question of regulation *versus* abolition. Fox was less cautious. "I have no scruple to declare at the onset", he said, "…that the Slave Trade ought not to be regulated but destroyed." Burke likewise committed himself to abolition. Very little was said in opposition. The West Indians were reserving their defence, and only one of their party broke silence with an impatient assertion that abolition was "unnecessary, visionary, and impracticable". The resolution was carried *nem. con.*[7] But before the session ended, both attack and defence became, as it happened,

---

[1] For the letter in full, see Rose, J. H., *Life of Pitt*, i, 459.
[2] *Journal and Correspondence of Lord Auckland*, i, 266–7, 269, 277, 304–8.
[3] *Life of Wilberforce*, i, 161.   [4] *Ibid.* i, 169.
[5] *Ibid.* i, 170.   [6] *Ibid.* i, 171.   [7] *Parl. Hist.* xxvii, 495–506.

more definite. Sir William Dolben, member for Oxford University, having visited a slave-ship then lying in the Thames, was so horrified at the arrangements for packing the slaves between decks that he promptly gave notice of a bill for limiting the number of slaves carried in proportion to the tonnage of the ship. In the debate on the second reading the champions of the Trade abandoned their reserve and denounced any attempt to regulate the Trade as tantamount to its destruction. It was a false move, for it forced Pitt at least halfway into the open. If Parliament were not allowed at any rate to regulate it, he would vote, he declared, "for the utter abolition of a trade which is shocking to humanity...and reflects the greatest dishonour on the British senate and the British nation". This decisive lead ensured the passage of the bill on the third reading by 56 to 5; and when it was resisted in the Lords, by Thurlow, who derided it as the product of a "five days fit of philanthropy", by Rodney, who expressed a sailor's anxiety as to losing commerce to the French and weakening our strategic hold on the West Indies, and other peers, Pitt bluntly let Grenville know that if the Bill were thrown out, he would not remain in the same Cabinet with its opponents. On June 30, the Bill was carried by the narrow margin of 14 votes to 12.[1]

Wilberforce, meanwhile, had made a surprising recovery. In the autumn he was back in London; and again the winter was spent in diligent preparation. Ramsay and Clarkson—"Wilberforce's white negroes", Pitt called them—were often working eight or nine hours a day with their leader; and at this period the cause obtained another vigorous recruit in James Stephen, who had lived for the past eleven years in St Christopher and watched the slave system at close quarters. Nor was the other side idle. At public meetings all over the country, in petitions to Parliament, in the press and in a shower of pamphlets, abolition was denounced as involving the commercial ruin of the nation and slavery defended as a means of bringing the savages of Africa into contact with a higher civilisation. In April 1789 the Privy Council Committee presented its report. It stated no case for or against the Trade, but confined itself to the evidence given before the Committee and information otherwise obtained. Both sides could find material in it; but it was bound to tell on the whole against the Trade, if only because it was the first authoritative statement of the atrocities the Trade involved.[2] There was now no reason for further delay, and on May 12 Wilberforce moved a series of resolutions condemning the Trade in a speech of more than three hours' duration.[3] It was a masterly presentation of the case for abolition and was warmly praised by Burke, but it had little immediate effect. Though

[1] *Parl. Hist.* xxvii, 576–99, 638–52; Rose, J. H., *William Pitt and National Revival*, pp. 461–2.
[2] *Report of the Lords of the Committee of Council etc.* (1789).
[3] *Parl. Hist.* xxviii, 41–67.

Pitt and Fox and Burke unequivocally supported Wilberforce, the Opposition succeeded in postponing further discussion till the next session on the plea that the House of Commons ought itself to hear the evidence and not take it at second hand from the Privy Council Committee. On the other hand, a bill to amend and continue Sir William Dolben's temporary Act of the previous year was smoothly passed.[1]

Early in 1790 the hearing of evidence was begun before a Select Committee. The evidence of the Trade was taken first, and at its conclusion the Trade party daringly attempted to obtain a vote against abolition without hearing the other side. But Pitt's firmness and the Commons' sense of fair play prevailed; and the evidence against the Trade was duly heard. There was no time for further action before the session ended in June. A General Election followed which increased Pitt's majority. The ensuing six months were spent by Wilberforce and his collaborators in laborious study of the new evidence—there were nearly 1400 folio pages of it—and on 18 April 1791 he moved to bring in a bill to abolish the Trade. It was again a powerful speech, and again the great trio supported him. "How can we hesitate a moment", asked Pitt, "to abolish this commerce in human flesh which has so long disgraced our country and which our example will contribute to abolish in every corner of the globe?" But though the conscience of the House was beginning to be roused by the repeated recital of the evils of the Trade, the majority were not ready for a measure so radical and confiscatory as abolition. "The leaders, it is true", said a back-bench member, "are for abolition. But the minor orators, the dwarfs, the pygmies will, I trust, this day carry the question against them. The property of the West Indians is at stake; and though men may be generous with their own property, they should not be so with the property of others." The motion was defeated by 163 votes to 88.[2]

The Abolitionists might well have been discouraged. Indeed, the aged Wesley, in a letter written in the previous February, a week before his death, had told Wilberforce that he saw no hope of his success unless he had been divinely selected "to be an *Athanasius contra mundum*". The movement, moreover, was gravely affected by the reaction on British opinion of events abroad. It had seemed at its outset as if the French Revolution could do nothing but good to the negroes' cause. The ideas of freedom and equality, set before the world in the Declaration of the Rights of Man, were clearly applicable to black men as well as white; and when Clarkson had visited Paris in 1789, to establish contact between the Abolition Committee and *Les Amis des Noirs*, a society which had been founded on the model of the Committee in the previous year, with Condorcet as its president, he had found far more apparent enthusiasm for his cause than in London.

[1] *Parl. Hist.* xxviii, 68–101.
[2] *Ibid.* xxviii, 311–15; 711–14; xxix, 250–359.

But as in England so in France, the merchants and the planters rallied in the Trade's defence; suspicions were awakened of English good faith; Clarkson was violently attacked in the newspapers; and nothing was done.[1]

Meanwhile the French authorities were being confronted with another aspect of the "colour problem". The mulattos in the fertile and populous colony of San Domingo demanded equal rights with the white settlers, and in 1790 there was a small rising, quickly suppressed. In May 1791, the National Assembly rashly decreed equality for mulattos born of free parents; and at once the great majority of them, whose mothers had been slaves, were up in arms. Treated like slaves themselves, they called on the slaves to revolt. Some 100,000 responded. Two thousand whites were massacred; and the colony was plunged into a long and brutal "servile war". The contagion spread, moreover, to the other French islands and finally to the British island of Dominica, where a small slave rising, easily suppressed, broke out in the course of 1791. Already distrustful of the new French ideas, conservative-minded Englishmen interpreted these events in the West Indies as proof of the unwisdom of hastily applying theory and sentiment to practical politics. The opposition in Parliament stiffened against abolition. Yet, at the same moment, the movement in its favour in the country at large was growing daily stronger. Spurred on by their defeat in the session of 1791, the Abolitionists had organised a regular campaign of agitation—the first of its kind in British history and the precedent and model for the many similar campaigns which presently became a familiar feature of British public life.[2] The Abolition Committee planned and controlled it. Clarkson was its chief agent in England, Dr Dickson in Scotland. The result of their work was the creation of Corresponding Committees, linked to the parent body in London, in every important urban centre in Britain, and the organisation of petitions. Subsidiary efforts were a call, which was widely answered, to abstain from the use of West Indian sugar, and the wholesale distribution of copies of *The Negro's Complaint* by Cowper (who had already attacked the Trade in *The Task*) and of a cameo, made by Wedgwood, an ardent Abolitionist, which depicted a negro piteously entreating aid. The campaign was vigorously pressed throughout the winter; and when Wilberforce early in 1792 again gave notice of an abolition motion, the House of Commons was assailed by what was in those days a quite unprecedented volume of petitions—312 from England and 187 from Scotland. Only five petitions were presented in support of the Trade, two of them from individuals and a third in favour of regulation. Even Liverpool, despite all the prophecies of her ruin, made no move.[3]

---

[1] Clarkson, I, 446–93. [2] Trevelyan, *op. cit.* p. 51.
[3] *Life of Wilberforce*, I, 333–69; Clarkson, II, 188–92, 346–55.

This remarkable manifestation of public opinion could not fail to make some impression on the House of Commons; and if French ideology and the fall of San Domingo could be effectively paraded in the Trade's defence, its opponents had also a new argument from abroad in the fact that, on March 16, the Danish Government had given a lead to Europe by decreeing that the Danish slave trade should cease in 1802. Thus the debate of 2 April 1792 brought the cause of abolition far nearer to victory than it had yet been or was again to be for several years to come. Wilberforce's opening speech excited more sympathy, and, in its account of one particularly atrocious action on the part of certain slave-traders, more indignation, than any of his previous efforts. The temper of the House was such, indeed, that the Trade party was obliged, for the first time, to compromise. Their chief spokesman on this occasion was Dundas; and his reputation for common sense, his standing in the Government and his intimacy with Pitt gave weight to his suggestion that, if abolition must come, it should be gradual. Dundas was supported by Addington (the Speaker) and by Jenkinson. And when, at the end of the long debate, Pitt made perhaps the finest speech of his life—"one of the most commanding displays of eloquence they had ever heard", said Fox, Grey and Windham afterwards—a speech which closed, as the early sunlight streamed through the windows of the House, with the famous prophecy of dawn in Africa—he was unable to efface the impression Dundas had made or to overcome the attractions of a compromise. Dundas's amendment, which made the motion read "That the Slave Trade ought to be *gradually* abolished", was carried by 193 votes to 125.[1] Three weeks later Dundas outlined his "gradual" policy in a series of resolutions, the most vital of which fixed the date for abolition at 1 January 1800. Wilberforce, Pitt and Fox again pleaded for immediate abolition; and, though the majority naturally refused to rescind its previous decision, the date was put forward to 1796 by 151 votes to 132.[2] This was no mean success. It was, indeed, a substantial proof of the great advance which the cause had made in the country and in the House within the last twelve months. "This is more than I expected", wrote Wilberforce, "...we are to contend for the number of slaves to be imported, and then for the *House of Lords*."[3] The italics were justified, for the Upper House was less susceptible to public opinion, it could ignore those numerous petitions, and it was at least as open to "West Indian" influence as the House of Commons. The King, moreover, who had once chaffed Wilberforce about his "black clients",[4] was now known to be strongly against abolition. The Abolitionists, on the other hand, could count on Grenville—whom Pitt had appointed in 1790 to succeed Sydney as

[1] *Parl. Hist.* xxix, 1055-1158; *Life of Wilberforce*, i, 345-6.
[2] *Ibid.* xxix, 1204-93.   [3] *Life of Wilberforce*, i, 349.
[4] *Ibid.* i, 344.

the minister in charge of colonial questions and had raised to the peerage as a counter-weight to Thurlow's party—and on Dr Porteous and other bishops. But the balance was uneven: and on May 3 the majority of the Lords, led by Thurlow, showed themselves opposed to abolition in any form or at any time and, bent on obstruction, decided to hear the evidence on the Trade all over again in committee of the whole House. Only seven witnesses had been heard, at intervals, when on June 15, the session closed.[1]

The delay was disastrous. The negroes' cause, which had come so swiftly to the front of British politics in the summer of 1792, was thrust as swiftly into the background in the autumn by events in Europe. Before the year was ended the character of the French Revolution had completely changed, and on 1 February 1793 its new leaders declared war on Britain. The Abolition movement, like other liberal movements, was bound to suffer in general from the reaction against Jacobinism in France and in particular against its effects in the French West Indies. Clarkson, moreover, had impulsively declared his sympathy with the Revolution at a London meeting—"a mischievous thing for the cause you have taken in hand", Dundas was quick to point out to Wilberforce.[2] And Wilberforce himself did not escape the suspicion of a Jacobin taint. A pacifist on principle, he was uneasy from the first as to the rightness of the war, and, in the course of 1794 and 1795, he even broke for a time with Pitt and agreed with the Foxites in demanding peace. It was easy, therefore, in that strained atmosphere for the champions of the Trade to link abolition and Jacobinism together. The existence of the movement, declared Lord Abingdon, proves that "we too have in this country our Condorcets, our Brissots, our Abbé Grégoires, and our Robespierres".[3] "Your friend Mr Wilberforce", remarked Windham to Lady Spencer, "will be very happy any morning to hand your Ladyship to the guillotine."[4] Even so close a humanitarian ally as Burke was temporarily alienated by Wilberforce's pacificism.[5]

If the cause was thus injured by the Revolution, it was still more injured by the war. There was a natural inclination to concentrate only on war measures and to defer all others, and especially one so drastic and controversial as abolition, till peace returned. And the old arguments against weakening the mercantile marine and producing trouble in the West Indies were obviously strengthened by the war. Most damaging of all, perhaps, was the effect of the war on Pitt's attitude to abolition. More and more as the attainment of a sound peace eluded him and as the burden of his office grew heavier, Pitt felt disinclined to spend his energies, create division, and weaken his authority by continuing his first and vehement support of a cause which had nothing to do with victory. Englishmen, in general, felt

[1] *Parl. Hist.* xxix, 1349–55.　　[2] *Life of Wilberforce*, i, 343–4.
[3] *Parl. Hist.* xxx, 655.　　*Life of Wilberforce*, ii, 72.　　[5] *Ibid.*

much the same. In 1793 the sentiment of the country towards abolition cooled as fast as it had warmed in 1792. "I do not imagine", wrote a Yorkshire correspondent to Wilberforce, "that we could meet with twenty persons in Hull at present who would sign a petition that are not republicans." And similar reports came in from other counties.[1] In these circumstances the progress of the cause in Parliament inevitably ceased. In the Commons in 1793 a bill introduced by Wilberforce, to obtain a measure of abolition by prohibiting the Trade with foreign countries was defeated in a tiny House by 31 to 29. In the Lords, after an acrimonious debate on the main position, the formality of hearing evidence was continued. Seven more witnesses were heard that session.[2]

Thus the Abolition Committee of which Wilberforce, who had at first remained outside it on the ground that his influence would be strengthened by independence, was now a regular member, found there was little it could do. It rarely met in 1794, only twice in each of the next three years, and after 1797, not at all till 1804. Meanwhile, the invaluable Clarkson had fallen out of the ranks. Another exhausting, and this time a disappointing, journey in the winter of 1793 had broken down his health and he withdrew into retirement, where he composed his detailed *History of the Abolition of the Slave Trade*, published on the morrow of its attainment, in 1808. Abolition, in fact, would have disappeared altogether from politics during those hard years if Wilberforce, believing, as he did, that his crusade was divinely appointed, and, as he said, that war time was the very time for a nation to rid itself of guilt, had not persisted, session after session, in forcing his cause on the memory and conscience of Parliament. In 1794 the coalition of the Portland Whigs with Pitt weighed the scales still further against him; for most of them, including Portland, supported the Trade and obtained assurances from Pitt that abolition would not be made a Government measure. Dundas, moreover, frankly confessed to Wilberforce that he had used all his influence with Pitt and other Ministers "to prevent any question on the subject being agitated, at least during the war".[3]

None the less, Wilberforce reintroduced his Foreign Slave Trade Bill in 1794 and actually carried it. But the attendances were small and the interest slight, since everyone knew that the House of Lords would throw it out—as it did by 45 votes to 4. Two more witnesses were heard in the Lords that session, and thereafter the enquiry was dropped altogether. Wilberforce, nevertheless, returned to the charge. In 1795 he reminded the Commons that 1796 was the date fixed by their own resolution for abolition, and moved for a consideration of the question. But he was voted down by 78 to 61, and Dundas carried by the same majority a counter-resolution postponing "gradual

[1] *Life of Wilberforce*, II, 18. [2] *Parl. Hist.* xxx, 513–20, 652–60, 948–9.
[3] *Life of Wilberforce*, II, 49.

abolition" till after the war. In 1796 the tide seemed for a moment to be turning. Wilberforce succeeded in carrying a bill for abolition in a year's time so far as the third reading, but then he lost it by the narrow margin of 74 to 70. On the other hand in 1797, a year of severe financial strain, he was refused leave even to introduce his bill and in each of the next two years his fate was the same. Equally fruitless were the attempts made in 1798 and 1799 by a Slave Trade Limitation Bill to protect from the ravages of slave-traders that part of the African coast in which the new colony of Sierra Leone had been planted.[1]

This persistent ventilation of the question was not so useless as it may well have seemed. It is noteworthy that the champions of the Trade no longer attempted to palliate its evils; no one now defended it except as an economic and political necessity. Moreover the direct appeal to humanitarian sentiment was steadily widening its range. As the Abolitionists had foreseen, the slave trade and slavery hung together. As early as 1791 Pitt himself had raised the "rather delicate point" of emancipation if and when the slaves could be raised from their degraded state to a capacity for civilised life. And though emancipation still lay far beyond the horizon, there were now moderate men among the "West Indians" who were anxious to improve the conditions of slavery, and even thought it possible that better health and greater fertility among the slaves might some day render further importation unnecessary. On the proposal of C. R. Ellis, a member of an old West Indian family and one of the leaders of those "moderates", an address was carried in 1797, directing that the colonial legislatures should be requested to take measures to improve the welfare of the slaves, though Wilberforce and Pitt and Fox opposed it as virtually sanctioning the Trade and indefinitely postponing its abolition. In 1799, again, two ameliorating Acts were passed—one repealing an Act of George II permitting slaves to be sold for the repayment of their masters' creditors, the other enforcing more space between the decks of slave-ships and authorising bounties to captains and surgeons for a low death-rate on the "Middle Passage".[2] Thus, while the planters in the West Indies were as truculent as ever—the Jamaica Assembly, in answer to the Address of 1797, denied the right of the Imperial Parliament to enact abolition against its will—the West Indian party in England no longer felt bound to oppose every attempt to interfere with slavery or to regulate the Trade.

The fortunes of war, moreover, had raised a new economic issue. On the one hand, the removal of enemy shipping from the high seas had greatly increased the British share of the whole Trade; it was estimated that British ships were carrying double the number of slaves by 1807 that they had carried in 1793. On the other hand the

<hr />

[1] *Parl. Hist.* xxx, 1439–49; xxxi, 467–70, 1321–45; xxxii, 737–63, 862–902; xxxiii, 251–94, 569–76; xxxiv, 1118–38.   [2] 28 Geo. III, c. 54.

occupation of the French and Dutch colonies in the Caribbean enabled the sugar grown therein to compete on equal terms with British West Indian sugar in the British market, provided that enough slaves were imported to grow it. And to some at least of the Trade's defenders it seemed unwise to permit these islands to be stocked with slaves if there was any chance of their being restored to their previous owners at the end of the war. Hence some "moderates" of the West Indian party had supported Wilberforce's attempts to carry a Foreign Slave Trade Bill; and hence also, when the Abolitionists pressed on principle for an Order-in-Council to prohibit slave imports into the conquered colonies, the "moderates" were again on their side. In 1800, though the majority of their party, less far-sighted or less apprehensive of foreign competition, repudiated such a compromise, they even went so far as to suggest a suspension of the Trade for five years.[1]

Nor, finally, was the attitude of Parliament quite hopeless. The House of Lords to all appearance was as obdurate as ever; but in the Commons, though the Trade could muster sufficient stalwarts to defeat nearly all Wilberforce's direct attacks, the great majority or members were at least not hostile enough to abolition to attend the debates and help in voting them down. In personnel, again, if the cause had lost a good friend in Windham, who would once have "rather let Liverpool and the Islands be swallowed up in the sea than this monstrous system of iniquity be carried on",[2] but consistently opposed abolition after 1798, it had gained a better friend in Canning. Despite his close friendship with the Ellis family, Canning declared himself for abolition in 1797 and contributed a notable speech to the debate of 1799, asserting, *inter alia*, that the colonial legislatures, if left to themselves, would never make any effective reforms—an interesting prophecy in the light of his experiences some twenty years later.[3] But of all the personalities involved Pitt's was dominant; and it became more and more evident during these years that, as long as Pitt remained in power, there was no real hope for abolition till the war was over. It is not easy for latter-day historians to doubt that Pitt was sincere in his hatred of the Trade since, up to the end, neither Wilberforce nor Clarkson doubted it. But, for reasons already stated, Pitt refused to break with his anti-Abolitionist supporters in the Cabinet or the Commons in the middle of the war. He still loyally supported Wilberforce with logical, unequivocal and sometimes eloquent speeches in almost every debate on the question and sometimes even after he had tried to dissuade his friend from raising it. But he could do no more. He could not make abolition a Government measure. And, whatever might have happened if Wilberforce's

---

[1] *Parl. Hist.* XXXIII, 1376–1415; XXXIV, 518–66, 1092–1140; *Life of Wilberforce*, II, 257–78, 329–38. [2] Clarkson, *op. cit.* I.
[3] See Canning's letter to Pitt (1799) printed in Rose, J. H., *Pitt and Napoleon*, pp. 321–4.

resolution had been carried unamended in 1791, only as a Government measure could abolition be carried after 1793.

While the progress towards its primary goal of abolition was thus at this time almost imperceptibly slow, the Humanitarian Movement was quietly strengthening its inner forces behind the scenes and finding less obstructed outlets for its energies. It gained greatly in force and cohesion by the concentration of its leadership in one community, which, since its most prominent members lived in the same suburban village, became known as "the Clapham Sect". Its patriarch was Granville Sharp (1735–1813), whom James Stephen's son described in after years as "the abiding guest and bosom friend" of the younger brethren. The next in seniority was Charles Grant (1746–1823) and the rest of the group—John Shore (1751–1834), William Smith (1756–1835), James Stephen (1758–1832), Edward Eliot (1759–97), John Venn (1759–1813), William Wilberforce (1759–1833), Henry Thornton (1760–1815) and Zachary Macaulay (1768–1838) were more or less contemporaries. Among other intimates and constant guests, who did not live at Clapham, were Clarkson, Isaac Milner, Charles Simeon, Thomas Gisborne, Thomas Babington and young John Bowdler. And growing up into the "Sect" were the members' children, of whom the younger Charles Grant and James Stephen were presently to play great parts in humanitarian politics, the one as Colonial Secretary and the other as permanent head of the Colonial Office. In this remarkable community Wilberforce was the dominant figure, and next to him Henry Thornton, a wealthy bachelor, the son of one of John Newton's most devoted disciples. Thornton's house was the regular meeting-place of the "Sect", and Wilberforce lived with him there from 1792 till, on his marriage in 1797, he made a home for himself next door. Neighbours and intimate friends, some of them linked by intermarriage, they were an extraordinarily homogeneous fraternity, living in comfort but not in luxury, and giving largely to charity. They were mostly Evangelicals, every Sunday they listened to John Venn's sermon in the parish church; and their private life was inspired and regulated by the same strict but unpretentious piety. They were all more or less directly engaged in politics or public service. The elder Grant, after a successful career as an official of the East India Company joined the Court of Directors, of which he was chairman in 1805; Sir John Shore (afterwards Lord Teignmouth) was Governor-General of Bengal (1793–8), Zachary Macaulay was Governor of Sierra Leone (1794–99), Wilberforce, Henry and John Thornton, Stephen, Smith and Eliot (whose premature death in 1797 was as heavy a blow to Pitt as to Wilberforce) were all in the House of Commons for various terms. Nominally Smith was a Whig, the others Tories; but they were all, like Wilberforce, really "independants", speaking and voting with a sense of responsibility higher than that of party allegiance. And this independence, together with their notorious integrity, gave them a peculiar authority in Parliament and outside it. "The Saints", they were called, and the nickname was only half a joke. Governments and parties and public opinion in general were bound to respect, and not seldom to defer to, this little group of upright and disinterested men when, as on any humanitarian theme, they spoke from the heart and with one voice.[1]

It was the energy and idealism of the "Saints" that created the first British colony in Africa. The Somerset judgment of 1772 had produced a difficult social problem. Some fourteen thousand slaves had been suddenly set free in England, and many of them had quickly fallen into beggary. These unfortunates at once engaged the sympathy and the purse of Granville Sharp, and in 1786 a "committee for relieving the black poor" was organised with Samuel Hoare and the Thornton brothers among its members. The result of its discussions was the adoption of a proposal made by Dr Smeathman, a naturalist who had lived for four years at Sierra Leone, where since the days of Queen Elizabeth Englishmen had traded mainly for slaves but also for gold, ivory, hides and other products. Smeathman's suggestion that the destitute negroes should be transported *en bloc* to this fertile district of their native Africa was attractive to the Abolitionists for more than the particular reason which had inspired it. From the first they had regarded the destruction of the slave trade as only the negative half of their work. They had always urged the necessity—and none more forcibly than Pitt—of doing something positive towards the civilisation of Africa, if only by way of amends for the wrongs inflicted on the Africans by the Trade. A colony of repatriated negroes under British control might serve as at least a starting-point for that great task; and it might also serve to prove the constant assertion of the Abolitionists that a profitable "legitimate" trade could be developed with Africa to replace the trade in slaves. The Government welcomed this solution of a tiresome problem and provided the cost of transport; and in the spring of 1787 some 400 negroes and 60 whites were landed at Sierra Leone and proceeded to erect a township on a block of fertile coastland, about 20 miles square, by St George's Bay, which had been purchased from King Naimbanna and in 1780 was ceded to the Crown by him as a liege of the King of England.

It was soon clear that colonisation, particularly on the west coast of Africa, was not as easy as it seemed. Many of the colonists, both white and black, were dissolute, undisciplined, and lazy. The managers of the adjacent British and French slave depots at Bunce Island and Gambia Island were naturally hostile to the enterprise and did all they could to make trouble. The season, moreover, for

---

[1] *D.N.B.*, *sub nom.*; Sir J. Stephen, "The Clapham Sect", in *Studies in Ecclesiastical Biography*, pp. 521–82.

starting the colony was ill-chosen. The fever-bringing rains set in before the new-comers were acclimatised; and at the end of the first year half of them were dead. The ranks of the survivors were still further thinned by desertion; but they struggled on, raising enough food to meet their immediate needs, until in 1789 the final blow fell. One of the many petty conflicts arising from the slave trade had resulted in the destruction of a neighbouring chief's village by a British party. In indiscriminate revenge, the chief gave the colonists three days' grace to abandon their little town and then burned it.[1]

But the "Saints", as has been evident, could not be easily discouraged. In 1790 they made a new start. They formed "The St George's Bay Association" for "opening and establishing a trade in the natural productions of Africa". Again the Government was sympathetic, and in 1791 the Association was invested with a charter and incorporated by Act of Parliament[2] as "The Sierra Leone Company", with Sharp as president, Thornton as chairman, and Grant and Wilberforce among its directors. Although in this new venture, unlike the African Chartered Companies which had preceded it, commercial profit was regarded as a secondary end of admittedly uncertain attainment, a considerable capital was raised from philanthropic subscribers, Thornton himself investing over £2000. And public interest was increased by the Government's decision to aid the re-birth of the colony by transporting thither over twelve hundred negroes who had fought on the British side in the American War and had been settled after demobilisation in 1783 in the uncongenial climate of Nova Scotia. Meantime some sixty of the previous colonists had been collected and the building of a new town, called Freetown, begun. The Company's capital was raised to nearly £240,000, and stores and equipment were plentifully provided. A church, a hospital, and warehouses were erected. Schools were established and well attended. In 1791 the Company sent out Mr Falconbridge, who was acquainted with the coast and had aided Clarkson in obtaining evidence against the slave trade, as its agent in charge; but in 1792 he was dismissed as incompetent and a brother of Clarkson, a lieutenant in the navy, was appointed as first Governor of the Colony, with a Council of eight, reduced shortly afterwards to two. In 1793 Clarkson was succeeded by his senior Member of Council, William Dawes. But neither money nor men could save the second settlement from the same kind of difficulties as had assailed the first. Malaria was soon rife again. Among other visitations of a tropical nature, the colonists suffered from "incredible swarms of ants". Once a ship, laden with over four thousand pounds' worth of African produce for England, was completely destroyed by fire. And again the enfranchised negroes, especially those from Nova Scotia,

[1] Martin, E. C., *The British West African Settlements, 1750–1821*, pp. 103–9, and authorities there cited.   [2] 31 Geo. III, c. 55.

proved unsatisfactory. They clung to the town and refused to work on the land. They demanded a more democratic constitution, sent delegates to plead their cause in England, and, when these returned unsatisfied, broke out in a feeble and short-lived rebellion. Clearly the colony was again drifting to disaster, when in March 1794 Zachary Macaulay took over the government from Dawes.[1]

Macaulay was born in 1768, the son of the minister at Inverary. After an unsatisfactory start in business in Glasgow, he obtained, by the patronage of a relative, Sir Archibald Campbell, ex-Governor of Jamaica, a post as under-manager on a sugar plantation in that island. There he spent four lonely and unhappy years; but on his return to England in 1789 he was befriended by Babington who had married his sister, converted by him to the Evangelical way of life, and introduced into the "Clapham Sect". He went out to Sierra Leone as a volunteer in 1791 and was taken into the administration as Second Member of Council in 1793. A man of great determination and fired with a desire to right the negroes' wrongs, he now set himself obstinately to his difficult task; and the colony had begun slowly to right itself, when in September 1794 a French squadron, piloted by an American slave-captain, appeared. No resistance was offered, and Macaulay appealed to the French Commodore to recognise that the colony was of no military value and was the product of French principles of freedom and equality. But the colony was bitterly denounced by the American and British slave-traders; and the Commodore asserted his inability to restrain his men. So Freetown was thoroughly pillaged by the Jacobin sailors and most of its chief buildings burnt. "Every house," noted Macaulay in his diary, "was full of Frenchmen who were hacking and destroying and tearing up everything which they could not convert to their own use. The destruction of live stock... was immense."[2] Soon after, Macaulay's health broke down; but in 1795, after a short rest in England, he was back at his post. And now, at last, the tide definitely turned. The disaffected negroes, alarmed perhaps by the French attack, were readier to submit to discipline; the damage to the town was made good; agriculture increased; in 1798 there were 300 houses and 1200 inhabitants in Freetown, and a profitable trade had been opened up with the interior. So, when Macaulay retired in 1799, he could claim that the colony was no longer only an experiment; and in the next year the Government recognised this fact by raising the status of the Company. A "Charter of Justice" was conferred on it, which constituted the settlement "one independent and separate colony by the name of the colony of Sierra Leone". The Company was endowed with full territorial rights over the ceded area subject to a nominal rent to

[1] Martin, *op. cit.* pp. 109–25.
[2] Martin, *op. cit.* pp. 125–6; Viscountess Knutsford, *Life and Letters of Z. Macaulay*, pp. 58–82.

the Crown, empowered to purchase other adjacent land and authorised to appoint a Governor and Council with full executive authority within the colony and to legislate for it either directly or through the Council. Provision was made for municipal government in Freetown and for the administration of civil and criminal justice. Towards the cost of civil government and defence annual grants-in-aid were voted by Parliament. Soon after this rise in status the Company was again troubled (October 1800) by disaffection on the part of the Nova Scotian negroes, who claimed that their lands had been promised to them free of taxes and refused to pay a newly imposed quit-rent. But the subsequent revolt was again easily suppressed, this time with the help of some 500 Jamaica Maroons, who, having themselves rebelled in 1795, had been transported to Nova Scotia and had recently been transferred to swell the mixed population of Sierra Leone.[1] So the colony struggled on, beset by the old difficulties of inducing the settlers to work at agriculture and of protecting the inland trade from interference by the slavers, until, in 1807, the directors of the Company petitioned for the transfer to the Government of responsibilities they were not financially strong enough to bear. On 1 January 1808, Sierra Leone, the child of the Humanitarian Movement, took its place by Act of Parliament as a Crown colony in the imperial system.[2]

Another creation of the Movement, in which the "Clapham Sect" was closely interested, was the African Association, founded in 1788 "for the discovery of the interior parts of Africa". It was this Association that commissioned Mungo Park in 1795 to make his first African journey, which resulted in the first European discovery of the upper waters of the Niger. Its success led to a second expedition in 1805, under Government auspices, when Park lost his life in following the course of the Niger seawards. Thus, from the outset, exploration and philanthropy went hand in hand in Africa. To the geographers the penetration of the Dark Continent was a gain for European science; to the humanitarians it was a letting-in of light, a first step towards the civilisation of the Africans.

At this period, finally, the great missionary Renaissance began. The campaign against the slave system, the foundation of Sierra Leone, the promotion of discovery were all the products of the new sense of responsibility for the welfare of the native races with whom the British people had been brought in contact; and in the eyes of religious-minded Englishmen, especially those who had been influenced by the Evangelical revival, the most obvious means of promoting the natives' welfare was to convert them to Christianity. It is no accident, therefore, that the most famous British enterprises in the modern mission field were inaugurated just at this time. And

[1] V. supra, p. 51.
[2] 47 Geo. III, sec. 2, c. 44; Martin, op. cit. pp. 126–41.

again the "Saints" were to the fore. In 1786 David Brown, a friend of Charles Simeon, began his chaplaincy at Calcutta and discussed with Grant the idea of a great mission in India. In 1792 the Baptist Missionary Society was founded and William Carey landed in Bengal. In 1798 the undenominational "Missionary Society", afterwards called the London Missionary Society, was founded. Meantime, in 1790, Grant had returned to England and communicated his schemes for an Indian mission to Wilberforce. One result was the latter's vigorous but unsuccessful attempt to secure the inclusion of some provision for the moral and religious improvement of the natives of India in the Charter Act of 1793. From 1797 onwards plans were discussed by Simeon, Grant, Wilberforce, Venn and Henry Thornton for the creation of a new organisation which should embrace Africa as well as India; and in 1799, a small meeting in London, with Venn in the chair, established The Society for Missions to Africa and the East, better known as the Church Missionary Society. Wilberforce and Grant were among its first vice-presidents, Henry Thornton was treasurer. The foundation, lastly, of the British and Foreign Bible Society in 1803 was mainly Wilberforce's work. Its first president was Lord Teignmouth.

But throughout these years the main object of the Humanitarians, however distant the prospect of its attainment might seem at times to be, was still the destruction of the slave trade, and to that end all their efforts were concentrated when, soon after the birth of the new century, the chances and changes of politics began at last to combine in their favour. Pitt's resignation in 1801 and the Peace of Amiens in 1802 encouraged hopes of a new era. But when Wilberforce, in 1803, after two years' silence was preparing to move once more his customary resolution, he was forced to abandon it by the news of an impending resumption of hostilities. "You can conceive", he wrote to Babington, "what would be said by Lord Hawkesbury and Co. if I were to propose abolition now."[1] But this, as it happened, was the dark moment before dawn. Early in 1804 the Abolition Committee resumed its suspended activities, strengthened now by the inclusion of Stephen, Macaulay and Henry Brougham, who had revealed his interest in imperial questions and his hostility to the slave system in his book on colonial policy published in the previous year.[2] And their hopes were raised by the reappearance of division in the West Indian party. The "moderates", alarmed at reports of the great fertility of the annexed Dutch colonies, and afraid, as Wilberforce put it, "lest they should be in the situation of the owners of an old and deep mine who are ruined by the discovery of some other where the ore can be obtained almost on the surface", once more put forward a proposal for suspension, only to be beaten again by their own extremists who argued that,

[1] *Life of Wilberforce*, III, 88.
[2] *An Inquiry into the Colonial Policy of the European Powers*, Bk. IV, sec. II.

once suspended, the Trade would never be revived.[1] But the split
had gone deep; and in the debate of 30 May 1804 Charles Middleton
(later Lord Barham), a leading "moderate", who had hitherto played
a consistent part in the Trade's defence in Parliament, confessed himself a convert to downright abolition. It was in that debate that the
final triumph of the cause began. The subject of it was only too
familiar—Wilberforce's perennial resolution; but the attendance was
much larger than in previous years, and it was swelled by some 33 or
34 new Irish members, created by the Act of Union and all, at least
for that occasion, convinced Abolitionists. Pitt and Fox briefly expressed
their unchanged sentiments and the debate as a whole was short. But
its result was surprising. One hundred and twenty four members
voted for the motion and only 49 against it![2]

Late on the same night, the inner circle of the "Sect" settled the
main lines of the Abolition Bill; and on June 7 Wilberforce moved the
second reading. It was carried, despite strong opposition from
Windham and Castlereagh, by 102 to 44.[3] On June 12 the Bill passed
its committee stage. The majorities were falling owing to the efforts of
the West Indians and the defection of the Irish group; but Pitt, back
in office since May, despite rumours that his faith in abolition was
dead, supported the bill in every debate and swept aside a last attempt at obstruction. On June 27 the third reading was carried by
69 to 33.[4] But the final victory was still delayed. On the ground that
there was not time enough left that session to fight the bill through the
Lords, the Cabinet, still of course divided on the issue, decided to hang
it up till the next year; and the consequent debates in the Lords,
though no divisions were taken, revealed the strength of the opposition. Eldon (the Lord Chancellor), Hawkesbury (a Secretary of
State), and Westmoreland (Lord Privy Seal), all spoke against the bill.
So did the Duke of Clarence, with the other members of the royal
family beside him prepared to vote as he did.[5] "One session" commented Wilberforce "in such a case as this is not much",[6] but the
session of 1805 provided the most exasperating of all his disappoint-
ments. Strained almost to breaking-point by the burden of the war
and seeking to strengthen his weak Government by an alliance with
the Addington group, Pitt begged Wilberforce to postpone his controversial bill for yet another year. Wilberforce refused. The bill was
again introduced. The first debates were favourable; but, while Fox
was not as confident as usual, Pitt, for the first time, abstained from
direct support; and the second reading was lost by 77 to 70.[7] No less
disappointing were Wilberforce's efforts to secure executive action
prohibiting the import of slaves into the conquered Dutch colonies,
especially Guiana. Pitt definitely promised to issue a proclamation;

[1] *Life of Wilberforce*, III, 163–6.   [2] Hansard, II, 440–75.   [3] *Ibid.* II, 543–58.
[4] *Ibid.* II, 863–75.   [5] *Ibid.* II, 926–33.
[6] *Life of Wilberforce*, III, 181.   [7] Hansard, III, 521–2, 641–74.

but, preoccupied by the rise of Napoleon's power in Europe and the formation of the third Coalition, he procrastinated. The requisite Order-in-Council was not issued till September.[1] And then the war once more filled the political stage. In quick succession came Ulm, Trafalgar, Austerlitz. In January 1806 Pitt died.

It has been said that abolition was unattainable as long as Pitt was alive; but this is only true on the assumption that circumstances would never have forced George III to permit Pitt to form the coalition he desired with Fox and so to create a national Government in which the supporters of the Trade, if any, could have been safely overridden. As it was, Pitt's death provided precisely those compelling circumstances. The King could not evade the Coalition of "All the Talents", with Grenville as its chief and Fox as Foreign Secretary. And a first instalment of abolition, a comprehensive Foreign Slave Trade Bill, applying to annexed as well as foreign colonies, was brought forward as a Government measure and quickly passed through both Houses. It was followed by a resolution for total and immediate abolition. It was moved in the Commons by Fox, who, unlike Pitt, regarded the cause of abolition as at least as important as the conflict with Napoleon and declared on this occasion that, if abolition were the only achievement of his public life, he would be content. It was carried by 114 to 15; the Lords likewise accepted it by 41 to 30. In the last few weeks of the session, a bill was rushed through to prevent the Trade from employing new shipping and so attempting a last great *coup* before the clearly impending end.[2] Thus, with the "West Indians" divided, the old anti-Jacobin outcry long dead, French rivalry in the Trade at least temporarily suppressed by the war, opinion in the country, as Clarkson, who had emerged from retirement and made another of his journeys in the winter of 1805–6, reported, again warm for abolition, especially among the younger generation, all the circumstances were now once more as favourable as in 1792.

None the less, the vigour and rapidity of the achievements of 1806 were mainly due to Fox; and when he died in the autumn of that year, it was fitting that his last hours should be cheered by the knowledge that the triumph of his favourite cause was certain. On 2 January 1807 the final Abolition Bill was read a first time in the House of Lords. In its ultimate form, the first clause stated that "all means of dealing and trading" in the purchase of slaves in Africa or in their transport to the West Indies or anywhere else was thereby "utterly abolished, prohibited, and declared to be unlawful", and that any British subject acting to the contrary should be fined £100 for every slave so purchased, sold, or transported. Clause II declared that British ships engaged in the Trade would be forfeited to the Crown.

[1] *Life of Wilberforce*, III, 183–5, 216–17, 230–4.
[2] Hansard, VI, 597–9, 805, 917–19, 1021–5; XII, 31–4, 227–36, 580–603, 801–9, 1143–5.

Further clauses provided for the penalisation of insurance contracts for safeguarding the Trade; for the payment of bounties to officers and seamen for all slaves captured from British ships or from enemy ships in war time; and for the placing of such captured slaves at the disposal of the Crown either for service in the army or navy or for a limited regulated apprenticeship to private persons. The Opposition still put up a fight. Papers were demanded, petitions presented, counsel heard; but the old obstructive plea for evidence was refused. On February 5 the second reading was carried by 100 to 36, and the third reading, without a division, on February 10. On the same day the bill was read a first time in the Commons, and on February 23 after a one-sided debate—the only outstanding speech coming from Solicitor-General Romilly, whose tribute to Wilberforce provoked an overwhelming ovation—it passed the second reading by 283 to 16. An amendment in committee to postpone the operation of the bill for five years was defeated by 175 to 17, Canning opposing it. Windham, who had hitherto voted silently against the bill, scornfully questioned whether the Trade would actually be diminished by the abolition of the British share in it; and Castlereagh asserted that the only positive results of the bill would be to undermine the loyalty of the West Indian colonies and to create a great smuggling trade. But it was useless now to divide the House; the bill was read a third time on March 16; and a week later it returned to the Lords for the confirmation of a few small amendments. The imminent fall of the Coalition Government seemed to threaten a disaster at the eleventh hour; but the Tory leaders, including not only the sympathetic Perceval but the hostile Eldon, Hawkesbury and Castlereagh, declared that they had accepted Parliament's decision. And, as it happened, the old Government was still in office when, on March 25, the King's assent was given and the bill became law.[1]

Thus closed in victory the first period of the Humanitarian Movement. It had made an effective entry into the vast field covered by the relations between the white and coloured peoples of the British Empire. And, if much remained to be done in the coming century, if even on the one issue of the slave trade the pessimism of Windham and Castlereagh was to be fully justified, if the shadow of the Arab slave trade loomed beyond the European, at least the "Saints", by single-minded devotion to one cause through the dark days of war, anti-Jacobinism, unpopularity and personal abuse, had achieved the first and hardest step towards the destruction of an evil seemingly indestructible, had wakened the conscience of the British people and planted a humanitarian tradition in the heart of British politics.

[1] 46 Geo. III, c. 36; Hansard, VIII, 257–9, 431–2, 468–9, 601, 613–18, 657–72, 677–83, 691–3, 701–3, 717–22, 829–38, 940–95, 1040–53; IX, 59–66, 114–40, 146; *Life of Wilberforce*, III, 272–305.

CHAPTER VI

THE INDUSTRIAL REVOLUTION AND THE COLONIES, 1783–1822

THE publication of Smith's *Wealth of Nations* coincided exactly with the American Declaration of Independence. In the *Wealth of Nations* "fire engines" are mentioned but not steam engines. A year earlier James Watt had entered into partnership with Matthew Boulton at the Soho Works, Birmingham. He adopted the "sun and planet" on his engines to produce rotary motion in the year that Cornwallis surrendered Yorktown; he utilised the expansive power of steam to obtain the double stroke for his pistons in the year that Rodney beat De Grasse and saved the West Indian sugar colonies. While the Shelburne cabinet was turning the preliminaries of peace into the Treaty of Versailles (Jan.–Sept. 1783) Richard Arkwright's first patent was running out and Henry Cort of Gosport was working at the specifications of his not altogether original patent for making wrought iron quickly and cheaply by the puddling process. A handful of inventions, even of the greatest, are not an industrial revolution; but their occurrence just at that time was a signal, to those who could read it, that if what King George in the distress of defeat would call "this once respectable empire" should regain respectability, be remodelled or rebuilt, the requirements of the homeland from her colonies and her whole economic relation to them might differ greatly from what Clarendon, Walpole or Chatham had known.

Those requirements, as conceived in Clarendon's day, had been scheduled—on the side of demand—in clause eighteen of the great Navigation Act (12 Car. II, c. 18), Sir George Downing's "enumeration" clause. The plantations were to send to England all their sugar, tobacco, cotton, indigo, ginger, fustic and other dye-woods—their subtropical and warm temperate zone produce, in short. In the rest of their produce England had been less interested. She had no intention of submitting to plantation competition in the supply of goods which she believed herself capable of producing. She fed herself, generally speaking, and intended to go on feeding herself. The raw material of her one really great manufacture, wool, she possessed in abundance. Though, as time went on, in Walpole's day and Chatham's, she increased her imports of certain grades of wool, these were not grades which any of the colonies of the Old Empire could provide; and throughout the first three quarters of the eighteenth century she took more trouble to prevent British and Irish surplus wool from being smuggled abroad contrary to the law than in opening up fresh sources of supply. The superfine wool that she required from overseas had never yet been produced in a young country. To the last the northern temperate colonies of the Old Empire had not enough to give her of the things of which she stood in great need. So late as 1766 they were described—by an English writer[1] it is true—as "greatly distressed" for "returns", "in order to pay the balance of their trade with England".

There were industrial raw materials which England had long been glad to draw from them, but had never drawn in sufficient quantity, in spite of "enumeration", tariff preferences and bounties. These were primarily the "naval stores" for which she had been dependent time out of mind upon the Baltic lands—great masts and spars; flax and hemp; tar, turpentine, pitch and the best iron. To encourage colonial production, bounties on the import from America of masting-timber; hemp; tar, pitch and turpentine, had been offered under Queen Anne (3 and 4 Anne, c. 10). Nearly £46,000 was paid out in bounties on American naval stores in 1775;[2] and the policy of marking the best American timber trees with the "broad arrow" for the King's navy had helped to alienate America from the King. One of the bounties, that on masting-timber, only expired in 1781. The hemp bounty, which had expired in 1741, was revived and associated with a bounty on undressed flax "much about the time that we were beginning sometimes to court and sometimes to quarrel with our American colonies",[3] that is in 1764 (4 Geo. III, c. 26). They were voted for twenty-one years, and so were still current after the Treaty of Versailles. The British Isles raised so little hemp and used so much flax that these bounties had met with no regular opposition from any domestic interest. In spite of them the colonial "distress for returns" persisted in the 'sixties of the eighteenth century; and the man who so described it, Malachy Postlethwayt in the 1766 edition of his *Dictionary of Commerce*, was writing at length about a great scheme for developing all the "naval store" trades of the colonies and employing "not less than 100,000 men...in the woods", in order to relieve the United Kingdom of its dependence on Baltic supplies and terminate a most one-sided and to all mercantilists undesirable trade, a trade carried on "in Norway ships, navigated by Danes", as a result of which "crowns and half-crowns...have circulated far more plentifully in Norway than in England for many years past".[4]

By that time the timber problem was no longer a problem in "naval stores" only, and had assumed a character which was to be accentuated as the industrial revolution swung forward. The drain of specie to the Baltic to pay for timber, which Postlethwayt alleged to be greater than the drain to the East, had grown, he said, "especially

[1] Malachy Postlethwayt; see below, p. 218.
[2] Albion, R. G., *Forests and Sea Power*, App. B, p. 418.
[3] *The Wealth of Nations* (ed. Cannan), II, 144.
[4] Preface to the 1766 ed. of the *Dictionary*, p. 5.

of late years, since the spirit of house-building has been so prevalent in this kingdom". That spirit became much more prevalent as the new towns bulged out between 1780 and 1820 and London continued to grow as it had long been growing. Whilst Postlethwayt was writing, Parliament was dealing with the timber question. The bounties on the importation of American timber which it voted for nine years in 1765 (5 Geo. III, c. 45) were not on masting-timber, which already had its bounty, but on "good deals" and "other squared timber", for ship and house building; but they produced very little of either.

When the Old Empire had fallen, when many of its commercial arrangements had become obsolete, and most of the bounties connected with its trade had run out, the timber position remained unaltered. Newfoundland and British North America were richer in forests than the lost dominion, though not so rich in men. By 1782 New Brunswick was sending the masts which New England would no longer send. Great Britain was poorer in woodlands than she had ever been, and required more timber every year as she became more populous, more industrial and more urban. Scandinavia and the Baltic remained her most convenient sources of supply as they had been thirty years earlier when the London timber merchant was "furnished with Deal from Norway, either in Logs or Plank; with Oak and Wainscot from Sweden; and some from the Counties in England";[1] and so on. Colonial timber was admitted tax-free down to 1798; very lightly taxed—never at more than 2s. a load—thereafter, at times or for special purposes being again admitted duty-free. European fir-timber paid 4s. 1d. a load from 1783 to 1787; 6s. 8d. from 1787 to 1797; 10s. from 1797 to 1802. (The untaxed value of the load varied during these years from about £1. 10s. 0d. to £3. 0s. 0d. in time of peace and from about £3. 0s. 0d. to £6. 0s. 0d. in time of war.)[2] These preferences were not enough to countervail the natural and acquired advantages of the European supplies. Between 1788 and 1802 Great Britain imported nearly 3,000,000 loads (say tons) of squared fir timber from Europe; from all her American colonies only 19,429 loads—an average of some three or four small ship's cargoes a year. To these must, however, be added the masts and spars—true "naval stores"—and various kinds of small timber which were not all returned in loads. But in 1802 British America sent only some 7500 loads of masts, oak timber and plank, and fir-timber against 247,000 loads of all these kinds from Europe.[3]

With the resumption of war in 1803 the prices of Baltic timber rushed up. That year more than 10,000 loads came from the colonies in natural response to the stimulus of price. Timber from British America could now bear the long Atlantic freight. Thereafter the colonial imports grew fast, the Home Government encouraging

[1] Campbell, J., *The London Tradesman*, ed. of 1757, p. 167.
[2] Tooke, T., *History of Prices*, II, 417.   [3] Figures in Albion, *op. cit.* pp. 420 *sqq.*

them by raising repeatedly the duties on European timber. The Russian alliance with Napoleon, followed by Sweden's acceptance of the Continental System and of war with England, made an absolute famine of Baltic timber not impossible; though Canning crushed the Danes to keep the Sound open and Admiral Saumarez held the Baltic from 1808 to 1813, doing what he could for the trade in naval stores. Memel fir was the standard continental timber quotation on the London market. Tilsit is not many miles upstream from Memel. In 1808, the year after the meeting at Tilsit, when the timber-shipping season opened, the price of Memel fir ran quickly up to £17 a load. This prohibitive level was not maintained—nor was Alexander's alliance with Napoleon—but for the next four years the price was not often below £10. In 1808 the duty on this continental timber was 27s. 4d.: in 1811 it was doubled: in 1812 it was fixed at 64s. 11d. In the next year peace in the Baltic broke the prices and, after Waterloo, the Memel quotation fluctuated between £3. 15s. 0d. and £2. 5s. 0d.; but the duty remained. It was fixed at a round 65s. in 1819. The exaggerated war-time preference had been imposed to meet a real danger and to induce shipowners to open up the North American trade: Government in 1810 had guaranteed such a preference as would secure them freights. Maintained for years after the peace, it had changed the whole course of trade, so that in 1821 the use of Baltic timber was confined to "the more valuable description of buildings".[1]

That year only 99,000 loads of squared foreign firwood were imported against 318,000 loads of colonial. Over 1500 ships and nearly 18,000 British seamen were now engaged in this North Atlantic timber trade. Commercial critics of the system complained that, at a cost to the consumer calculated some few years later at £1,000,000 a year, the mother country was subsidising the "superfluous shipping"[2] of British America, a great deal of which—so they argued—was hardly worth maintenance. Lumbering had been stimulated extraordinarily in the colonies, over-stimulated there can be little doubt. Timber was said to constitute half the exports of the province of Canada. It was argued that if the merchants of New Brunswick were prevented, by any change in British policy, from drawing against timber shipments "all importation of British goods must cease".[3] The argument was probably good, for a historian from New Brunswick has said that "the preference to colonial lumber...practically created the colony".[4]

The industrial revolution, with its accompaniments and its consequences, had more than doubled the British demand for imported timber within twenty years (1802–21). In twenty years more the

---

[1] *First Report on Foreign Trade, Parl. Pap.* 1821, VI, p. 9.   [2] *Ibid.* p. 6.
[3] Joseph Marryat in Hansard, IV, 542.
[4] Davidson, J., *Commercial Federation and Colonial Trade Policy*, p. 9.

demand would double again. The needs of war; the response to those needs from colonies where tree-felling, in reason, was locally desirable and, even when unreasonable, had been declared imperially expedient and made artificially profitable; the absence for six years after the peace of any discernible British timber policy, except the policy of dealing gently with a shipping interest which had lost the transport employment of war time and was over-supplied with tonnage now that ships had no longer to wait for convoy—these things had created a great economic problem which would occupy public men and influence imperial politics for a generation.

The attempts of eighteenth-century legislators to make the Old Empire more nearly self-sufficing in flax and hemp had been even less successful than their attempt to make it self-sufficing in timber. These attempts were not revived after 1783. Raw flax came in free down to 1798. Hemp was not heavily taxed. The standard quotations for both commodities were Baltic quotations—Petersburg and Riga. (It was not until Courtrai ceased to be French, after the fall of Napoleon, that the fine Flemish flax could once more be quoted regularly.) During the wars the duties on both were raised, but only for revenue purposes. Though the quotations for both ran up dangerously in 1808–12, it was never possible to launch a policy like that adopted for timber. The lost American colonies had been in the habit of sending supplies, not of flax but of flax seed to Ireland. Canada began to do the same in the new century; but the Canadian supply was not nearly enough to save Ireland from a flax crisis when both Russian and United States seed supplies were interrupted by policy and war between 1808 and 1814.[1] So the beginnings of industrial revolution in the linen manufacture early in the nineteenth century had very little colonial significance at that time, although they aroused interest in the possibilities of flax growing in New Zealand, and Norfolk Island.[2]

Iron, a manufactured raw material itself subject to industrial revolution, was in a very different position from these vegetable raw materials from the temperate zone. The old American colonies had exported it. Just when they were being lost, the Darbys and their imitators, with Henry Cort, his predecessors and followers, were rendering the eighteenth-century imperial iron policy obsolete. That policy had only taken its final shape since 1750. There is no doubt, though the figures are uncertain, that during the first half of the eighteenth century, Britain had regularly imported more bar iron— mostly Swedish and Russian—than she had produced. Some patriotic pamphleteers had joined with the biased industrialists who wanted cheap bar in protesting against the omission of iron from the list of colonial "naval stores" eligible for bounty under the Act of 1703,

[1] Gill, W. C., *The Rise of the Irish Linen Industry*, p. 224.
[2] *C.H.B.E.* VII, Part I, p. 327; Part II, pp. 33, 147.

since England's dependence on Sweden and Russia had its strategic risks. Diplomatic trouble with Sweden in 1717–18 and again in 1737–8 had advertised the danger; but partly owing to official apathy and partly to the conflict of interests at home—iron producer *versus* iron user—no steps had been taken to stimulate colonial production until the notorious Act of 1750 (23 Geo. II, c. 29) which forbade the colonists to erect mills for working iron and also exempted colonial pig iron and bar iron shipped to London from the payment of import duties.[1] In 1764 (4 Geo. III, c. 15) colonial iron was "enumerated", except when exported to other parts of America or to Asia or Africa. The Seven Years' War had again underlined the risks of too much dependence on Sweden and Russia, neither of which powers had been on England's side. At that time (1761–5) the colonies were sending yearly an average of 3100 tons of iron, mostly pig, against a foreign import of 40,900 tons, all wrought bar. Ten years later (1771–5) the colonial average was 4800 tons, the foreign 44,300 tons. The American iron was still mainly pig, but the colonies had at least begun to make their contribution to an imperial need.[2]

The need was still great, assuming the desirability of imperial self-sufficiency, because the whole British make of pig iron, at the time of the American Declaration of Independence, was probably not much greater than the import of the much more valuable foreign bar iron. Twelve years later (1788) the British output of pig is supposed not to have been more than about 68,000 tons, though there had been marked progress during the later 'seventies and the 'eighties, especially in the supersession of charcoal smelting by coke smelting. In 1788 something like one-fifth of the whole "make" of pig was supplied by the twenty-six surviving charcoal furnaces, scattered over twelve or fourteen English, Welsh and Scottish counties. Then came a more general use of steam-power for the furnace blast and of coke as fuel; the war demand after 1793; a sharp rise in the price of imported bar in 1796; increased import duties; and very rapid improvements in the puddling and rolling processes, especially at the iron-works of Merthyr Tydfil. By 1812 a single South Welsh iron-master, Richard Crawshay of Cyfarthfa, was turning out 10,000 tons of bar in the year. Eleven years later (1823), when the industry had recovered from the severe post-war depression, the aggregate British make of pig was some 442,000 tons, of which not much less than a half came from Wales.

The course of important international trades had been reversed—by invention, aided, it is true, as in the diversion of the timber trade, by climbing war-time duties, but by invention primarily. Down to 1800 the annual import of foreign bar had been still something like

40,000 tons. (In 1790 the duty was 56s. 2d. and in 1800 75s. a ton; prices in bond fluctuating between £14 and £21.) During the difficult war years of 1808–13 the average amount of foreign bar secured and retained was 12,700 tons a year.[1] For the five years 1818–22 the average annual export of British bar was over 32,000 tons, together with some 10,000 tons of pig-iron and castings. Foreign iron could not be dispensed with entirely, because the best cutlery steel was still made from the very best Swedish charcoal-smelted bar; but only 10,000 tons, paying duty at the rate of 130s. a ton, were taken in 1822. Except for fine steel making the foreign iron was no longer wanted. Nor was foreign steel, of which England had been an importer from the middle ages down to the decade 1770–80. Steel was in fact being exported, not only in every kind of tool and implement but also in considerable quantities unmanufactured.

Britain after Waterloo clanged with iron like a smithy. A visiting foreigner noticed that even in quiet English gardens "huge cylinders of iron" were dragged along the walks and across the lawns. There was no longer any need to stimulate colonial production and export; nor did either the old or the new colonies yet contain any but the most local and insignificant iron industries. If, however, any British possession had been capable of export, its pig iron would have been admitted at 1s. 3d. and its bar iron at 3d. against the foreigners' 130s. a ton. Neither came. The duties were mere fossils of a policy, which in the eighteenth century had been alive, or, if the description be preferred, permits to enter an inaccessible market issued to those who had none of the licensed goods to sell.

Two years after the great Navigation Act had ordered the Plantations to send their cotton only to England, the total import from them all in a year was 7500 bags: six years later, in 1668–9, it was 1000 bags fewer.[2] Cotton was grown more or less in most of the British West Indies—including Barbados, Jamaica, and several of the Leeward Islands; but, as the figures show, the quantity sent by any single island was never considerable. In the 8 years 1671–9 Jamaica sent only 876 bags. But as the English consumption at that time was very small, the result was regarded as not unsatisfactory, and it was argued in the 'seventies that Plantation supplies had materially lowered the prices, hitherto regulated, from the markets of the Levant. Throughout the first three-quarters of the eighteenth century, in spite of the great growth of the West Indian sugar industry and the fact that most of the cotton used in England still came from Smyrna, West Indian cotton kept a place in the English market; but for many years little came from the old English islands. In 1762 a

---

[1] The figures for 1812 do not exist. No doubt the imports in the later years of the war were mainly for cutlery—and weapons.
[2] From the Board of Trade Papers, quoted in Beer, G. L., *The Old Colonial System*, I, 40 n.

pamphleteer, arguing in favour of the retention of Guadeloupe rather than Canada, based his argument on the assertion that Guadeloupe had sent to England over £100,000 worth of cotton in 1761 and that none of the old Plantations had sent any appreciable quantity.[1]

Although her total import of cotton was still small, averaging about 4,750,000 lb. a year from 1771 to 1775, England had already become something of a depot for Western Europe: in 1775 Turgot is found reversing a mercantilist policy three-quarters of a century old by authorising French manufacturers to buy in England as a corrective to high prices in France.[2] During the American War of Independence the English consumption was just beginning to grow rapidly: by 1782 it had reached nearly 12,000,000 lb.: in 1792 it was over 33,000,000: in 1802 nearly 57,000,000: in 1822, 143,000,000 lb. Down to 1783 what little cotton had come from the thirteen colonies—only a few bales, so far as is known—had been nearly all West Indian transshipped. When, in 1784, an American vessel landed eight bags at Liverpool they were held up in the customs until it was proved that they really were United States produce: the fact at that time seemed *a priori* improbable.[3] Ten years later an important United States cotton export still seemed improbable; for John Jay agreed with Lord Grenville in November 1794 that—in return for certain privileges granted to American shipping in the West Indian trade—no sugar, coffee or cotton should be exported in United States bottoms, except to United States ports, "either from His Majesty's Islands or from the United States", until two years after the termination of the war between France and England.[4] The British negotiator's object was to retain all the island sugar, coffee and cotton freights for British ships. The American negotiator supposed that he was not making an important sacrifice when he accepted the words "from the United States", because the United States had no important export trade in any of the three commodities. It seems he was not fully informed: cotton export, as a regular trade, had begun: some thousands of bales had been shipped even in 1791: but his mistake was natural. The Senate may have been better informed when it declined to ratify this particular clause of his treaty in 1795—a year made a great difference in the cotton trade at that time—but neither country could yet have realised that in losing the thirteen colonies Britain had lost the fields which would feed her new staple industry.

A sharp rise in cotton prices during the War of Independence had stimulated cotton growing all over the West Indies. The swift

[1] *An Examination of the Commercial Principles of the Late Negotiation*, pp. 36–40 [? By Wm. Burke]. See Beer, G. L., *British Colonial Policy, 1754–65*, pp. 147–9.
[2] Circular to the Farmers General of 13 June, 1775. Turgot, *Œuvres* (ed. Scholle), v, 92.
[3] Bolles, A. S., *Industrial History of the United States*, p. 55.
[4] The text (App. VI) and a very full discussion in Bemis, S. F., *Jay's Treaty, a study in Commerce and Diplomacy*.

expansion of the British industry during the next decade maintained the stimulus. The Levant could not increase its shipments and Lancashire began to look for new sources of supply.[1] It turned first to South America and India. Consignments of Brazilian cotton are known to have arrived in 1781: probably they were not the first. From 1788 there is a continuous series of market quotations of "Pernambuco". In that year the East India Company was approached. Shipments were arranged but the cotton was not what the spinners wanted; so in 1792 the shipments were discontinued for a time. Brazil was not yet sending very much or very good cotton. The ten years from the Treaty of Versailles to the outbreak of the war with France might be called the West Indian age of the British raw cotton trade. West Indian cotton was the best on the market; it was also by far the most abundant. It has been calculated[2] that during the five years 1786–90 the West Indies supplied nearly 71 per cent. of the manufacturers' consumption; the Mediterranean over 20 per cent.; Brazil nearly 8 per cent.; the East Indies and the United States the tiny balance. Ten years later (1796–1800) the proportions of a greatly increased consumption were—West Indies $35\frac{1}{4}$ per cent.; the Mediterranean $18\frac{1}{2}$ per cent.; Brazil $11\frac{1}{2}$ per cent.; the East Indies, where trade had revived in connection with a sharp price rise in 1797–8, 9 per cent.; a few miscellaneous sources $1\frac{3}{4}$ per cent.; and the United States 24 per cent. The figures for the West Indies include all the islands and also Guiana. As cotton was admitted duty free at this time, the customs officials had no need to enquire too closely into the place of its growth. Figures given in a pamphlet of 1788[3] suggest that perhaps not more than half of the West Indian cotton was at that time British grown.

In the interval (in 1792–3) Eli Whitney had invented the saw-gin for separating the cotton-wool from the seed, a process which was particularly difficult and expensive when the cotton was short in the fibre, as most of the Georgian and Carolinian cotton then was, the growth of the long-fibred "sea-island" variety having not yet been taken in hand. Regular quotations of American cotton on the English markets begin in 1793.[4] The war price rise of the late 'nineties encouraged cotton growing in the United States still further: in 1800 they sent about 40,000 bales, that is some 16,000,000 lb., or considerably more than the whole British consumption of 1783. American speed and the limitless American territory alarmed the cramped and conservative West Indian interest. "The quantity produced in Georgia and Carolina", a trade circular stated in 1801, "and on the banks of the Mississippi, in favourable seasons, will, in point of weight,

[1] Ellison, T., *The Cotton Trade of Great Britain*, pp. 81 *sqq.*
[2] By Ellison, *op. cit.* p. 86.
[3] *Important Crisis in the Calico and Muslin Manufactory.* See Chapman, G. J., *The Lancashire Cotton Industry*, p. 143.
[4] The quotations are for "bowed Georgia".

exceed all the West Indian Islands put together, and will have a serious tendency to depress the value of our own [i.e. British] West India cotton. The consumption of New Orleans and inferior Georgia is become very general, and already precludes the sale of middling and inferior West India at the proportionate price we have formerly been accustomed to."[1] Competition was beginning at the bottom, as it usually does, and working upward.

The West Indies were still leading both in quality and bulk at the beginning of the nineteenth century. The British imports of 1803, for example, are reckoned to have been—West Indies, 57,000 bales; the United States, 45,000; Brazil, 28,000; the East Indies, 10,000. But within the next few years America rushed ahead and the West Indies declined not only relatively but absolutely.[2] The American embargo of 1808–9 and the war of 1812–14 barely checked the flood of American cotton. Even in 1813 Britain secured 38,000 bales smuggled out of the Southern States or shipped openly to neutral ports and so to England. The main effect of these partial interruptions was to encourage, not West but East Indian exports, unhappily for the East India Company and the private importers; for the East Indian trade was slow, the bulk of the Indian cotton was bad, and quantities of it were left on the importers' hands in 1810–11, when American stocks accumulated during the embargo were released. In 1812–14 the Company was able to get rid of its dead stocks and was tempted by high prices to import again on a large scale. This it continued to do for some years after both the American and the French wars were over, with the result that for a time Indian cotton formed a larger proportion of the total import into Great Britain than at any earlier or later date, except during the American Civil War. But it was not a profitable trade. In the early 'twenties the East India Company was struggling to get rid of its stocks, even exporting 10,000 bales of Bengal cotton from England to China. The East Indian imports of the late 'twenties were barely half what they had been for the years 1816–20.

The position in those post-war years was that the United States now sent $47\frac{1}{4}$ per cent. of the British imports; the East Indies $26\frac{1}{2}$ per cent.; Brazil nearly 16 per cent. and the West Indies less than 7. Ten years later (1826–30) America would be sending $74\frac{1}{2}$ per cent., the West Indies $2\frac{1}{4}$ per cent., the East Indies $9\frac{1}{2}$ per cent.; and the transition from the West Indian age of a generation earlier to a United States age would be completed. Prophetic, but not at the time important, was the arrival of a little Egyptian cotton on the English market in 1822.

West Indian cotton growers had not merely failed for lack of space to meet the now enormous demands of the British spinners. Their

[1] Quoted in Ellison, *op. cit.* p. 85.
[2] *Vide supra*, ch. III for the importance assigned to Demerara cotton in 1814.

aggregate production had been declining steadily since the opening years of the century. During the quinquennium 1816–20 it was not half what it had been in 1803. In the succeeding decade it was to be halved again, falling to some 13,000 bales a year in the late 'twenties, less than had been sent just before 1783. The United States, having first cut into the market for "middling and inferior West India", took to growing the fine, long-fibred, "sea-island" cotton on the isles at the mouth of the Savannah and along the coast of South Carolina, so competing with the best that the West Indies could produce. There were also fiscal causes at work. No preferential treatment worth mentioning had ever been given to empire cotton before 1819. All cotton came in free down to 1798, and from 1798 to 1801 West Indian, the more valuable article, actually paid more than its then most important competitor, Georgian. In 1803 the duties on all cotton were assimilated, at 2d. a lb., except that on Brazilian cotton, which was not brought into line until 1809; and they remained uniform, with a reduction to about 1d. a lb. after the wars, until the British West Indian cotton was given a preference, of about $\frac{1}{4}d$. a lb., in 1819, and something more in 1822. No amount of preference could have drawn out of the West Indies the quantity, or out of the East Indies the quality, of cotton which Lancashire and Lanarkshire required in the nineteenth century. In this handling of cotton duties, it may be noted, the legislators of the war period showed much more economic insight than is sometimes credited to them. Duties on an exotic raw material are no doubt vicious in principle under any system of political economy; but income was needed; the manufacturing industry could bear it; and the post-war duty of about 1d. a lb. only worked out at so much as 10 per cent. *ad valorem* when cotton was very cheap. In 1821 it was replaced by a 6 per cent. *ad valorem* duty for foreign cotton.

All through the years during which the headquarters of cotton supply were being transferred from the West Indies to the United States, West Indian sugar, the old staple of the islands' trade and the real source of their wealth, was taxed more lightly than East Indian, and so much more lightly than foreign sugar that the latter only came to England at all to be bonded for re-export. The duty on West Indian raw sugar, as stabilised after Waterloo, was more than 1d. a lb. less than that on East Indian, and about 4d. a lb. less than the prohibitive duty on foreign sugar.[1] But this did the West Indies little good between 1818 and 1822. The occupation of Dutch Guiana, Tobago, Trinidad and Santa Lucia during the wars had greatly increased the area of British controlled West Indian sugar territory. Moreover, Guiana in particular was more fertile than some of the old sugar colonies such as

[1] The sugar duties were so complex that exact statements would have to be exceedingly long, and so are not attempted.

Antigua. All this new territory, except the eastern half of Guiana, was retained at the peace. So too, half way to the other side of the world, was the highly developed sugar colony of Mauritius; but its sugar did not get easily into the British market until it was given the same tariff treatment as the West Indian in 1825. In the early 'twenties the West Indian interest was fighting to retain its privileged position—for there was a sugar surplus on the home market as it was. Raw "muscovados"—the West Indies sent nearly all their sugar raw—which had generally fetched a good deal more than 40s. a cwt. during the wars, had run up towards 100s. in 1814 and had kept above 40s. till 1818, averaged 32s. 3½d. in 1821 and 31s. 9½d. in 1822. It was alleged in 1825 that, as a result of falling prices, most of the land of the West Indies had changed hands of late years. "The planter who continues in possession of estates finds himself in the last extremity", one West Indian advocate wrote.[1] Another tried to excite public sympathy and retain the preference by a story of a planter who, after a few years in Antigua, went home and drew £5000–7000 a year from his estate. He sent his eldest son to a public school and as a Fellow Commoner to Christ Church. He charged £30,000 on the estate for his wife and children, and now the eldest son, brought up with great expectations, was getting nothing and the portions were unpaid.[2] Critics suggested that such high living was as typical of the planters as their undoubted misfortunes.[3]

At home, the maintenance of war taxation and the agrarian and industrial distresses of the years after the wars had kept the consumption of sugar until 1821 almost at the point reached twenty years earlier, in spite of the growth of population. If anything, it was rather less in 1821 than in 1801, so far as can be ascertained. The consumption per head had fallen in the interval by perhaps one third. West Indian rum and molasses had lost their old-time outlet on the American mainland. West Indian sugar which could not be absorbed by the English market found a difficult vent on the Continent; firstly because the continental markets did not want muscovado, but "clayed"—that is partially refined—and refined sugar; secondly, because whatever they wanted could be supplied more cheaply from the fertile lands of Cuba and Brazil which had not, like the British colonies since 1807, lost the right to import slaves from Africa. Here the argument for preference blended with attacks on the policy which had "at length virtually suffered...the Saints to legislate for the colonies".[4]

Coffee, which enjoyed with sugar a preference that amounted to a

---

[1] Masson, J. P., *A Letter to Ministers suggesting Improvements in the Trade of the West Indies*, etc., 1825, p. 37.

[2] Turner, S., *A Letter to C. R. Ellis, Esq.*, 1825, p. 13.

[3] E.g. *The West Indies as they are* and *England enslaved by her own Slave Colonies*; both anti-slavery pamphlets of 1825.

[4] *A letter to C. R. Ellis, Esq.*, p. 9.

monopoly of the home market, was perhaps more profitable, but it was a much smaller and more difficult crop. Ostensibly, consumption in the United Kingdom increased about sevenfold between 1790–2 (when it was only 1,000,000 lb. a year) and 1810–12; but no doubt much of the coffee described as "retained for home consumption" was in fact re-exported. However these figures for 1810–12 were arrived at, there was no improvement in them during the next decade. Britain had ceased to be a smuggling depot for Napoleonic Europe, and her home demand had not proved expansive enough to satisfy the planters. There was at least the consolation that the British price in the early 'twenties—unlike that of sugar—was better than it had been since 1807. But coffee was not grown at all on many islands and was only a secondary crop in Jamaica and Dominica and in Guiana, the chief homes of what were called "coffee mountains". Other crops, of which the cocoa of Trinidad and Grenada was perhaps the most valuable, were of even less importance. In imperial economy the West Indies were what they had always been, the sugar colonies. The industrial revolution had affected them but little, either directly or indirectly, except by raising hopes of profit from cotton which they were not in a position to secure. Down to 1822 it had not even succeeded in building up a new mass of demand for their staple "luxury" export and its two great by-products; though the fault lay not with the revolution but with government. The retention of the income tax and a halving of the sugar duties, after Waterloo, might have done much for the sugar colonies.

Postlethwayt's *Commercial Dictionary* had referred in 1774 to the "incomparable wool" of Spain, "which all their neighbours, and nobody more than our clothworkers, can testify to exceed any in Europe". It was the only foreign wool then much used in England and it was used only—at that time and for many years later—by the fine cloth manufacturers of the West. East Anglia relied on the long English "combing" wool; and for the rougher industry of Yorkshire the ordinary British "clothing" and "combing" wools were good enough. In the 'eighties the imported wool, nearly all coming from Spain, Portugal, Madeira or the Canaries, was never worth less than 3s. 9d. a lb., when the average value of all British wool was about 8d. The quantity of the import in 1789 was some 1200 tons. What the weight of the British clip was at that time is not known; but it is not likely to have been less than 30,000 tons. Improvements in manufacturing processes during the later years of the eighteenth century, and the need for meeting the competition of fine French cloth after the commercial treaty of 1786—your well dressed Englishman, in the years just before the Revolution, was prepared to pay his tailor a stiff price for a coat of warranted French cloth—led to a rapid increase in the import. In 1800 it approached 4000 tons, still nearly all

from Spain and Portugal, and it was worth 4s. 10d. a lb. All this
time wool, like cotton, was admitted free. Throughout the wars, and
down to 1820, the duty was never so much as 1d. a lb., though the
price from 1803 to 1819 was never below 6s. Once, in the year of
Moore's retreat to Corunna, it reached 19s. 10d.[1] From 1820 to
1825 the duty stood at 6d.: then the 1d. duty was restored. So there
was no long-period obstacle to the entry of foreign wools other than
the obstacles of war.

New and important foreign sources of supply had developed since
the wars. A change of commercial policy in Spain during the later
eighteenth century had led to the export of Spanish sheep to many
European countries, including Great Britain, where they came into
the hands of King George. From King George's flock at Kew some
were eventually taken by Captain John Macarthur to New South
Wales.[2] They also went to Holland and thence to the Cape of Good
Hope. But the countries which were first successful in breeding
important fine-woolled flocks from them were France, Saxony and
Silesia. France had too well-developed a manufacturing industry to
become a large exporter, though once, in 1818, she sent to England
nearly 1000 tons of wool; but the agrarian states of Eastern Germany
began to export very freely so soon as conditions permitted. A little
wool had come from Germany since just before 1800, but the effective
trade begins with the relatively huge import of between 1500 and
2000 tons in 1814.

In 1818 the total import of wool of all kinds ran up to the surprising
total of 11,000 tons, exactly twice the average of the four preceding
years. It was this which alarmed the landed interest and produced
the 6d. duty; for the whole British clip probably did not exceed
45,000 tons and, pound for pound, the imported wool was three
times as valuable as the British. In spite of the duty the imports had
worked back nearly to the 1818 level by 1824. The English demand
for fine wool had become fierce. German supplies could now meet
it. Spanish no longer could. In 1818 Spain and Germany were about
level. When the market was opened wide again, in 1825, Germany
sent over 12,000 tons; Spain not a third of that.

At this moment of manufacturers' need empire-grown wool was
coming on the market, not yet, it is true, in very large quantities, but
in a way which indicated clearly enough the commercial and industrial future. This is not the place to tell the purely Australian story of
how the first fleet sailing for Port Jackson had taken in sheep at the
Cape, or of the struggles and successes of Captain John Macarthur.[3]
According to the English official records some wool—245 lbs.—came
for the first time from "New Holland" in 1806; but several years
earlier Macarthur had in fact taken home samples of wool bred from

---

[1] Prices from Tooke's *History, passim.*   [2] *C.H.B.E.* VII, Part I, p. 101.
[3] See *C.H.B.E.* VII, ch. VII etc.

merino sheep bought for him at the Cape in 1797. Experts had seen it in 1803 and declared it to be "of very superior quality, equal to most which comes from Spain".[1] Ten years later imports on a commercial scale began. In 1826, five hundred tons of wool were for the first time imported from "New Holland" in a single year. Finally, in 1828, an expert witness told a House of Lords Committee that the Australian wools though "of varied qualities" all possessed "an extraordinary softness which the manufacturers here so much admire that they are sought for more than any other description of wools". He stated that, owing to the shortage of return freights from Australia, he could "bring wools from Sydney, or Hobart Town, at a less expense per pound than from Vienna or Leipsic"; and he foretold with confidence that "fifteen or twenty years hence we shall have as much wool from those colonies as we shall want in this country of the finer kind".[2] His forecast was not seriously incorrect.

Although Australia got her first sheep from the Cape, and Cape wool arrived in fair quantities on the London market while Australian shipments were still experimental and small, exports from Cape Town grew slowly. A certain amount of merino wool was shipped; but it was not, at this time, either good enough or abundant enough to make its mark among British dealers. The largest quantity of Cape wool imported in any one year down to 1828 was rather more than 20 tons in 1822, a figure which "New Holland" had exceeded in 1815. How much of this was of good quality is not known; but it is known that the ordinary wools of the Cape early in the nineteenth century, especially the "natives' wool", were rough, of the class known later to the wool trade as carpet wools. That the Cape merino wool, which was to take an important place on the international wool market later in the century, was not yet much considered is shown by its omission from the very complete enquiry into the wool trade carried out by the Lords' Committee of 1828. Even twenty years later, when G. R. Porter was preparing the third edition of his *Progress of the Nation*, the wool trade of the Cape was not reckoned important enough to deserve more than a bare mention.[3]

The import trade from the East Indies had never been a "plantation" trade by legal definition. "Enumeration" had not applied to it: the Company was free, for example, to ship Indian cotton to China. So little was the trade of a plantation character in the later seventeenth century, that it gave rise to the famous controversies over the importation of Indian printed calicoes and chintzes, and so to the "Calico Acts" of 1700 (11 and 12 Wm. III, c. 10) and 1721

[1] Macarthur Onslow, *Some Early Records of the Macarthurs of Camden*, p. 65.
[2] *House of Lords Committee on the Wool Trade*, 1828, p. 40.
[3] Porter's *Progress*, ed. of 1851, p. 774. Porter gives some statistics of the exports of Cape wine etc., but merely refers to wool.

(7 Geo. I, c. 7), with their complex reactions on British fashions, British smuggling, and the rising cotton manufacture. The Acts by no means ended the import of Indian textiles by the Company. Some were brought to be printed here or for re-export;[1] many could be classed as muslins which were outside the Acts. And although the invention of Crompton's "muslin wheel" led to the curtailment of these imports after the decade 1770–80, they were still of importance in 1822. They were accompanied by regular and irregular imports of Eastern curios and "China-ware"; yet most of the goods brought from the East towards the end of the eighteenth century had something of what might be called a plantation or colonial character of the old sort. Such were the drugs, spices and dye-stuffs, especially indigo, the raw silk—both from India and China—and the raw cotton with which, as has been seen, experiments were made from 1788 onwards. But all these came from "old" countries; the European "planter" had as yet no hand in their production. The tea from Canton, which had become a more important item of the Company's trade decade by decade throughout the eighteenth century, was never seen growing by an Englishman. The wild tea of Assam, which suggested the possibility of tea-growing in India, was only discovered in, or about, 1826. The cotton experiment—the cotton was all native grown—was a praiseworthy attempt of the Company to meet by purchase and shipment the new industrial demands of the home market. Now and again, between 1810 and 1814, the Company also shipped very small consignments of East Indian wool; but shipments did not become regular until "free traders" were admitted to share in Indian export business, in the latter year. The shipments were never important, for there was no fine wool in India and plenty of rough wool at home.

After the loss of its Indian monopoly in 1813 the Company steadily curtailed its export business from India, concentrating on the China trade, of which it still had the monopoly, and drawing most of its dividends from tea, of which it sold from £3,000,000 to £4,000,000 worth yearly. Down to 1822 it shipped some "nankeens" from Canton, and down to 1824 some silk; thenceforward, until it lost its Canton monopoly also in 1833, tea only. From India, in the 'twenties, it was sending little but raw silk, indigo, and some muslin with other fine cotton fabrics. The bulk of the indigo trade, which was growing very fast indeed to meet the needs of the British cotton and wool dyers, had now fallen into the hands of the private exporting houses in Calcutta. They had also taken over a trade of some national importance, though of no great size, which had been developed earlier by the Company—the munitions trade in saltpetre. For seventy years at least the greater part of the saltpetre used in English

---

[1] The first Act prohibited the import of printed calicoes; the second Act their use. Neither Act forbade their production.

powder factories had come from India. When the Company ceased to ship Indian cotton, after its unhappy experience of that trade in the years about 1820,[1] it was the private traders who kept the reduced and unprofitable business alive, until from an unsuccessful trade for consumption it became a modestly successful trade mainly for re-export during the 'thirties. The private traders also had a hand in the export of Indian silk; and they did most, if not all, of the growing export of shellac and rice. They were mainly responsible for the at first unsuccessful attempt to secure equal treatment for East and West Indian sugar, using or causing to be used the argument that the Indian grower was a freeman, the home consumer a freeman taxed to help slave-owners; and they were making a start with the export of hemp and hides.

The United Kingdom, as has been seen, had never been able to apply, nor had her statesmen always wished to apply, the full underlying assumptions of the older mercantilism—that she should supply herself from her own resources with those essential foods and raw materials which her geographical position enabled her to raise; that she should draw from colonies and the East Indian trade the tropical and sub-tropical produce which her industries and her luxurious consumption required; and that she should find outlets for her growing surplus of manufactures in the colonies, in Eastern markets, and in European countries which would send her in exchange it might be treasure or it might be wine or raw silk or olive oil—at any rate something which would not compete sharply with any of her own or with any of her colonies' produce. With some reluctance she was prepared to take from temperate lands goods which were supplementary to her own, rather than directly competitive with them. Hence the rather unpopular Baltic trades and the essential suspensions of the eighteenth-century Corn Laws in times of shortage. *A fortiori*, supplementary supplies from the temperate colonies were received and encouraged, above all the naval stores.

That ordinary foodstuffs could be desirable as a regular supplementary import had not seemed likely during the first three quarters of the eighteenth century. But it happened that Britain, more industrial and more populous than formerly, became, on the balance, a corn-importing rather than a corn-exporting country, in the very years in which she lost the American colonies. So the fact stands in retrospect. But the reversal was at the time hardly perceptible and there was then no fatal necessity of permanence about it. British agriculture was making most satisfactory progress. Plenty of land remained to be cleared and drained. Ireland, in the language of the day, was still almost completely "unimproved"; and there were the temperate colonies, especially British North America, and above all

[1] *V. supra*, p. 226.

Upper Canada where United Empire Loyalists in flight from the United States were clearing potential corn-fields. Their right to share on privileged terms in the supply of the mother country was recognised by the Corn Law of the late eighteenth century, Pitt's law of 1791 (31 Geo. III, c. 30). Although they were not able to make any important contribution to the great need of England during the next ten years, she adhered to her policy. The law of 1804 (44 Geo. III, c. 109) fixed the price level at which wheat might be imported on payment of a small rather than an almost prohibitive duty—2s. 6d. instead of 24s. 3d.—at 63s. a quarter for foreign wheat but at 53s. for colonial. Finally the great Corn Law of 1815 (55 Geo. III, c. 26), into which was introduced the new principle of absolute prohibition of import for consumption until the standard price level had been reached, placed that level at 80s. for the foreigner but only at 67s. for the British subject. From May 1816, until October 1819, the official English monthly average price was always above 67s. and the market in consequence always open to colonial corn. It was only in October 1820 that a spell of continuous low prices set in. Then, until the end of 1824, the official average kept well below 67s. as the result of a succession of good harvests both in Britain and Ireland. For five years imports were negligible and in two of the five there was no import at all.[1] The colonial preference did not work. When, in 1825, a rise in prices made Government anxious and it was decided to tax Canadian wheat for two years at only 5s. a quarter irrespective of any price limits, Huskisson was estimating that Canada's maximum capacity of supply was not more than 50,000 quarters.[2] Although he expected so little from her, he argued that corn was the staple product of the colony; that with it she paid for her takings of British goods; and that it was unjust to leave the Canadian consigner in standing uncertainty as to whether or not the working of the corn-price averages in England would allow him to sell his corn there.[3] Probably Huskisson made too much both of Canada's dependence on this branch of her trade and of England's obligation in connection with it. Canada had a timber trade as well as a corn trade; and the British consumer was making a real sacrifice in order to maintain the former trade in that state of prosperity into which war policy had called it. But it is at least interesting, and at most much more than merely interesting, to see Canada's potentialities as a contributor to the food needs of the United Kingdom recognised just when men of various schools were being forced to consider the chance that, in spite of agricultural progress and a recent spell of cheap food, the years of self-sufficiency for the increasingly industrial and ever more densely peopled islands might be drawing to an end.

[1] Strictly, none in 1822 and 2 quarters in 1821, according to the official figures.
[2] In 1818 the import had been no less than 1,593,518 quarters.
[3] Hansard, XII, 1097.

Not much interest was shown in the notion of a self-sufficient empire during the forty years that followed the Treaty of Versailles. In more than half of those years writers and statesmen were preoccupied with war. *The Wealth of Nations* had discredited many of the economic arguments by which the notion, in itself military rather than economic, had been buttressed. Hopes of a long, even of an age-long, peace after Waterloo drove military arguments into the background. True, Patrick Colquhoun, writing in the flush of victory between Leipzig and Waterloo, of the *Wealth, Power and Resources of the British Empire,* had spoken of his task as a developing of "the general system of national economy...applicable to the wide extended British Empire"; but he had not in fact developed any national-imperial system. The growing manufacturing interest wanted markets, any markets. Merchants wanted perfect freedom to buy and sell. The rising school of the political economists taught that their wish was in harmony with the best nature of things. Adam Smith had cared passionately for empire, if not for self-sufficiency. In an index to Ricardo's *Principles* (1817) the word "empire" is not found. More important perhaps than all, in their influence on conduct rather than on ideas, were the coarse facts of British trade with the lost dominions, which remained a magnificent market. In the great prosperity of the years between 1783 and 1793 it had begun to seem that Britain had gained by throwing away an empire. It might have been argued plausibly, during the crisis of the French Wars, that she was saved by her trade with the United States. She was certainly saved by her trade with the American continent and islands.

Had commerce with the United States been in any way one-sided, its practical influence might have been less. An increasing dependence for cotton on the Southern States of the Union might have seemed dangerous, had not both Southern and Northern states been such excellent customers. Independent, they fulfilled their old function as buyers of British goods more satisfactorily than they ever had when dependent. If the declared values of British exports are to be trusted—and although there are risks in using them, they are at least a reasonable index to the relative importance of different branches of trade—during the three years 1805–7 the United States took very nearly one-third of all the "produce and manufactures" exported. In 1808–9, when owing to political differences the United States halved their purchases, "America exclusive of the United States" took nearly half the exports—the countries are not further differentiated in the official statistics of the years 1805–11; and they include British possessions. No doubt some of these exports went into the United States through back doors. In 1810, when United States buying was again active, the American continent and islands took very considerably more than half the exports—£26,600,000 out of £45,800,000. In 1815–18, when the Anglo-American war was over, the United States alone took a full quarter. That war would have been much more destructive to British commerce had not Europe been opened again, just when it began, by the military events of 1812–13 in Spain and Russia.

After the peace came a shrinkage in the nominal value of exports, owing to the general fall in prices, and a settling down of trade into channels in which it flowed more regularly and at more constant levels. In the 'twenties the United States took, on the average, as nearly as possible one-sixth of the total British exports; or in round figures £6,000,000 worth. They were the largest single customer of the British manufacturers. It is perhaps more remarkable that the British West Indies, before they were hit so hard by the low sugar prices of 1822–3, were taking from £4,000,000 to £5,000,000 worth of British exports yearly. In the late 'twenties they were not such good customers, but even then they rarely fell below £3,000,000, that is, roughly, one-twelfth of the total exports.

West Indian controversialists made great use of these remarkable figures and of the perfect conformity of the West Indian trade to the old notions of imperial intercourse. The West Indies, one of them wrote in 1823, had "no one rival art or vocation to compete with the British manufactures": "not a brick or a hat, scarcely even any sugar . . .in a refined state"[1] was made there. They also based claims to the consideration of the British Parliament on another feature of their trade which had been inherited from the old colonial system, and on its consequences—the obligation to buy all the manufactures which they required in England. They could get more cheaply than from England, one who was perhaps their ablest advocate argued in the same year, "iron, glass, cordage, sail-cloth, Osnaburgs, cotton and coffee bagging, checks, linens of every description, silks. . .paper hangings, cheese, wines, brandy, geneva and soap".[2] Some of these things, it is obvious, could be had more cheaply from Europe; but probably the iron, cordage, sail-cloth and cotton and coffee baggings could have been got most easily from New England.

The West Indians pointed out further that, in the years 1818–23, their demand for United Kingdom produce very greatly exceeded that of the East Indies, even if to the true Indian demand were added that of China. They might even have strengthened their case by arguing that they took more than the whole of Asia and Africa put together, as in several years of that quinquennium they actually did—according to the returns of the custom house. British North America was far behind them as a buyer: even ten years later it had not become a serious rival. Altogether the export trade of the mother country to

---

[1] *A Statement of the Claims of the West India Colonies to a protecting duty against East India sugar,* 1823, p. 45.
[2] Marryat, Joseph, *A reply to. . .various Publications recommending an Equalisation of the Duties,* etc., p. 81.

all parts of the New Empire, including the China trade of the East India Company, for the years 1820–22, came to rather less than one-third of her total export trade, or in round figures £10,000,000 out of £36,000,000. It was decidedly greater than her trade with the United States, but was comparable with it. It was almost exactly equal in value to her trade with all those parts of America which were not British territory.

Industrial change since 1783, besides greatly increasing the gross amount of British exports—both intra- and extra-imperial—had made one major change, and one very important minor change in their character; but as yet no more. The major change was, of course, the almost unbelievable expansion of the export of cotton goods—from an average of only some hundreds of thousands of pounds in the years 1780–3 to over £16,000,000 in 1820–3.[1] The important minor change was the appearance of a considerable export of iron and steel side by side with the much older export of hardware and cutlery. But the average value of the iron and steel was only about £900,000 a year; that of the hardware and cutlery not much more. Exports of woollen fabrics had increased; but so much more slowly than those of cotton that their value now stood a poor second, at a little over £6,000,000, whereas for hundreds of years before 1780 they had headed the exports. These three groups of commodities—cottons; woollens; iron and steel, manufactured and unmanufactured, between them amounted to full two-thirds of the declared exports in 1820–3. Of the remaining exports the most important were linen, which was largely Irish; refined sugar, an export which further emphasises the importance of the West Indian trade; and brass and copper wares, in that order. The rest of the long list was highly miscellaneous.

The demand of the West Indies for the miscellaneous wares, under compulsion of the imperial trade system, has already been illustrated. They were excellent markets also for the staple goods, especially for the coarse cotton and low woollen "slave cloths". Of raw iron and steel they took very little, but plenty of hardware and tools. Yet at every point they were being outdistanced by the United States, with their huge slave-demand and white man's luxury demand in the South, and their demand for everything that a mixed agricultural and industrial white population can require in the North. For the woollens, both fine and coarse, the United States were decidedly the best of all markets. Although they grew so much of the cotton, and had a cotton industry of their own, they imported great quantities in all its various manufactured forms. For iron and steel and iron and steel goods they were again the best single market. The refined

---

[1] The values of 1780–3 are not stated more precisely because of the "notoriously unreliable character" of eighteenth-century customs accounts. See Wadsworth, A. P. and Mann, J. de L., *The Cotton Trade and Industrial Lancashire, 1600–1780*, p. 145.

sugar they did not want: Cuba was too near; but they were great buyers of miscellaneous manufactures, brass and copper wares, furniture, instruments, and all sorts of articles for personal use.

British North America had a demand almost identical in character with that of the northern States of the Union—useful, expanding, but definitely secondary in size, not as yet very much greater than that of the foreign West Indies. South Africa and Australia, as markets, were still in their infancy.[1] The lesser and scattered British possessions claim no separate treatment; but something should be said of the very important transition stage at which trade with the East had arrived in the new century. Formerly India had sent luxuries, or at least rarities, and fine cotton manufactures. Now she was sending raw cotton in bulk through the Company; and private merchants were beginning to ship cheaper and rougher raw materials such as hides and hemp. England in the past had sent treasure and some oɪ her finer manufactures. When the rough raw materials began to come west, plain Manchester cotton goods were working east to pay for them.

It was hardly to be expected that the conservative administration of the Company, for so long an importer of cotton fabrics, would take an active part in reversing the trade. A little was done; but it was not until the private merchants took the business in hand, after 1814, that the foundations of the British export of cotton manufactures to India were really laid. During the next eight years the export became considerable; but it was still quite a subordinate part of the huge shipping business in cotton goods in 1820–2, to be reckoned not in millions but in hundreds of thousands of pounds. China, where the Company's monopoly survived, was penetrated still more slowly. A trial shipment of Manchester cottons was made so early as 1790; but they were thought by the Chinese "much too costly, and not held in such estimation as many of their own manufactures".[2] More than thirty years later, the Company sold off a total consignment of only £5000 worth of calicoes and velveteens at a loss of sixty per cent. The Manchester men were to argue, when giving evidence against the maintenance of the China monopoly, that a freer trade would have been more successful.[3] Perhaps they were right. They were able to show that the whole export trade to India—not only that in cottons—had grown and become more varied since the ending of the monopoly there; but it is not certain that the cotton trade, however free and competitive, could have forced its way into China before 1822. It

[1] The declared value of exports to the Cape of Good Hope in the three years 1820–2 averaged only £235,000 a year; those to "New Holland" £156,000. The Cape trade grew slowly in the following years, the Australian rather more rapidly. In 1830 the Australian trade stood at £315,000 and it had been higher in 1827. For comparison it may be noted that Barbados alone in 1830 took £272,000 worth of British exports.

[2] Morse, H. B., *The East India Company Trading to China*, ii, 180.

[3] *Reports on the Affairs of the East India Company, Parl. Pap.* 1830, v, Q. 5016 and *passim*.

only did so slowly after the termination of the Canton monopoly of the Company in 1833, as costs of producing and transporting the Manchester goods fell.

Down to 1824–5 the Company still sent general merchandise, including some cotton goods, to India; from that time forward it sent only stores for its army and civil government. To China it shipped religiously to the last those woollens to find a "vent" for which it had worked so hard for generations. Its shipments in 1821 were valued at £702,000 free on board and in 1829 still at £600,000. An East India official explained to a parliamentary committee in 1832 that the woollens were sent, even when the "vent" was not good, as a matter of tradition and duty, an equivalent for the monopoly as it were: "it was considered a moral obligation", he said.[1]

Trade by monopoly and "moral obligation" was very near its end in the early 'twenties. Freedom and competition, freedom good and bad, competition creative and destructive, were the marks of the dominating industry of the day. It would get its cotton where cotton was long and cheap: let the West Indies grow cotton like that. Industries revolutionised later, or not yet revolutionised at all, were imitating it. The colonies were markets like any others, and hardly of the best. Only a few wool dealers and users were looking forward with confidence and satisfaction to the development of colonial raw material supplies, complementary to those of the mother country, which would relieve a great industry from dependence on the foreigner. Timber dealers not directly interested in the North American colonies, together with most timber users, were ready to welcome a reduced dependence on colonial supplies, provided they got lower prices, while arguing at the same time—and not incorrectly—that North America had, and might expect to retain, a natural monopoly at both ends of the scale, the cheapest lumber and the finest masts and spars. Iron masters asked for no help from anyone and would give none: they had their raw material: their goods would batter their way into all markets. It was no longer necessary to worry about colonial nail making and "slit-mills". The monopolistic colonial sugar-trade, surviving intact from the old commercial system, was threatened both by "the Saints" and by a hungry people who would tire of paying 8d. a pound for the cheapest sugar in order that the West Indian proprietors, the "mass" of whom "either returned to England after the acquirement of their fortunes or had always resided"[2] there, might retain their vested interests and be saved from the mortgagee. Colonial bulk-trades in foodstuffs and in raw materials other than timber were only just beginning to be outlined, in short uncertain strokes, on futurist canvases. There was but a tiny population of true colonists in the whole Empire. There was not a steamboat

---

[1] *Committee on East India Company's Affairs, Parl. Pap.* 1831–2, x, Q.887.
[2] *A Statement of the Claims, etc.,* p. 51.

afloat that could get to any colony by steam alone. The export of machinery had barely begun: its export to foreign countries was fenced about with prohibitions. Before the industrial revolution could impart a decided twist to imperial economic relations or to colonial life, the colonies must grow—they were growing—the revolution proceed—it was proceeding—and some surviving restrictions must be abandoned. Statesmen were just beginning to consider their abandonment.

CHAPTER VII

ANGLO-FRENCH COLONIAL RIVALRY, 1815–1848

THE settlement of 1815 flouted Richelieu and Colbert no less than Napoleon, their successor. Walled in by united Europe, France found herself also restricted in the wider world. Though she was once more in possession of nearly all her old colonies,[1] her situation could only remind her of her former wide dominion and unbounded aspiration overseas. And in every continent her prosperous and triumphant rival, it might seem, was Britain. In Europe, the countrymen of Nelson and Wellington, of Pitt and Canning, now gained islands which controlled the Elbe, the Adriatic and the Aegean, while in more distant regions their empire was reckoned by Frenchmen to embrace some 117,000,000 souls.[2] A nation thrice as numerous as the British, looking back upon two centuries blazing with great French names and resplendent French triumphs in Europe, could not remain contented with the poor 2,000,000 of their own restored colonial empire.

If indeed the question of colonies and commerce had ever stood alone, the course before French statesmen would have been clear. History and the fierce pride of their people must have driven them to reconstruct and reinvigorate their navy and their commercial fleet. Unassailable by land so long as she remained unaggressive, France must apply her superiority in numbers, organisation, diplomatic skill and military power to gain victory over Britain in the regions where such superiority would be decisive. Twenty-three years after Waterloo Britain, in a French view, was a vast manufactory, a great laboratory, a universal counting-house; France, a rich farm, turning itself into a factory.[3] A few years later, the expenditure upon the French navy had been doubled, and Commodore Napier could declare that it was in better condition and equipment than our own,[4] which after 1815 was reduced to little more than the total in 1792.[5] Such progress, made while European and internal politics absorbed the chief energies of French rulers, only hints at what true statesmen might have achieved.

France, however, remained France; a "phosphoric nation"[6] forgetful of her naval defeats, always tempted towards continental aggrandisement and distracted by continental memories, always proud of her

---

[1] For details see Chapter III, *ad fin.*
[2] Dupin, Baron C., *Essais sur l'organisation progressive de la marine et des colonies*, p. 10.
[3] Cf. Raikes, T., *Journal*, 21 May 1838.
[4] F.O. France, Cowley to Aberdeen, 23 June 1845, no. 265.
[5] *C.H.B.F.P.* II, 18.
[6] Raikes, T., *Journal*, 27 May 1835.

willingness to sacrifice profit to prestige. Incarnate in Thiers, her ablest son, she exhibited the peculiar restlessness which a Scottish diplomat laboured to define as "a craving after something imaginary or unpossessed...that political marasmus...undermining the prosperity of France".[1] Such restlessness was remote indeed from the quiet sacrifice and steady preparation which colonial and commercial ascendancy required. France was, moreover, handicapped not only by the *malaise* and exhaustion inevitable after a quarter of a century of upheaval but also by the inheritance of a problem which might well demand a century for its solution. She had accepted under *force majeure* a constitution largely prescribed by the Tsar Alexander and upheld by Britain and her other foes. It was true that the social system left by the Revolution and the laws and institutions created by Napoleon were to be preserved and administered by the hereditary kings of France. But could a monarchy which proscribed the tricolour and the *Marseillaise* be really national? Could it preserve its independence of the ultramontane clergy? Above all, could it, if constitutional, retain its power to govern, or would Parliament, as in Britain, absorb the real power? In Louis XVIII France possessed one of the wisest of her Bourbon sovereigns, but it may be doubted whether her problem could have been solved by any king. It was almost certain that much of her reviving energy would be wasted in internal friction, and that no king or minister would be able to devise or to carry out a policy of real progress. Commerce and colonies, therefore, must rank below home politics as well as foreign, until internal harmony had been achieved.

In Britain, victorious at a great financial price, the danger was real though less severe. Here the aristocracy, which had defied the Revolution and Napoleon, survived unbroken and national policy remained unchanged. In Europe, the treaties of 1814–15; throughout the world, peace and commerce—such formed the sacred "interests" of Britain. But the British Government, like the French, and indeed like almost every Government in Europe, could not trust the mob, and dreaded the contagion of revolution. The years since 1789, with their growth of population and industry, and with the automatic protection of the agricultural interest vital to the prosecution of war, had created a domestic situation which the sudden transition to peace must render dangerous, while at the same time they had checked Britain's almost instinctive adaptation of her constitution to new needs. In 1815 the rotten boroughs of pre-Revolutionary days retained their ancient rights and silently commended to masses in Leeds and Manchester the doctrine of the Rights of Man. Faced at once with social misery and with the spiritual ancestor of Bolshevism, the rulers of Britain feared that "the whole thing might break up", and Castlereagh arranged for the sale of his wife's jewels when the

---

[1] F.O. France, Hamilton to Palmerston, 25 May 1832, no. 62.

expected storm should come.[1] As after the European convulsions of a century earlier and a century later, common fear of revolution gave the Governments of France and Britain a strong impulse towards mutual support. After Waterloo, this tended to be chiefly the support of the Bourbons by the ministers of the Georges. It took shape in the avoidance of demands likely to make the restored government unpopular with the French, and by diplomatic help in French dealings with the Allies. The best return which France had it in her power to make lay in the avoidance of encroachments on her neighbours or of an undue intimacy with Russia.

The antagonism between Britain and France which pervaded the eighteenth century was being gradually replaced in the nineteenth by antagonism between Britain and Russia. British and Muscovites, indeed, lived far apart, remained strangers to each other's language, and derived neither intimacy nor enmity from their respective churches. They had lately been allies against the French and they were destined in a later age to renew their alliance against other foes. It was possible to dream of a noble co-operation between them, the old power and the new, the manufacturing and the agricultural, the maritime and the continental, each contributing to enlarge the realm of order and of civilisation. But Russia's enormous army and her dubious past, her menace to British markets[2] and British lines of transport, the presence throughout Europe of intriguers in Russian pay, her patent aspirations after naval power, above all her threat to India—all these forced British statesmen into opposition to the dark and unbounded projects of the Tsar.[3] In Louis XVIII Alexander saw a prince whom he had protected during years of exile and had finally established on the throne. The Bourbon also embodied that divinely sanctioned monarchy by ancient title which was represented and championed by the Romanov, while he also inherited the traditional French antagonism to the rival Caesar at Vienna. To dispose of the power of France, where the duc de Richelieu, a former governor of Odessa, soon became premier, as he already disposed of some lesser European states, was naturally a flattering prospect to an autocrat whose place within the European circle was barely a century old. France, moreover, could supply Russia with the money and goods of which she stood in need, and could secure and powerfully advance her entry into the Mediterranean. Many motives therefore impelled the Tsar, himself not unmenaced by revolution, to court the king whom he had made the gaoler of the Revolution in its birthplace.

After Waterloo, then, France had reasons of convenience for seeking an understanding with Britain, and Britain had even more

---

[1] Webster, C. K., *The Foreign Policy of Castlereagh, 1815–22*, p. 498.
[2] Pokrovsky, M. N., *Russkaya istoriya*, IV, 19–20 *et passim*; Crawley, C. W., *The Question of Greek Independence*, pp. 4–7.
[3] *C.H.B.F.P.* II, 8–13.

urgent motives for seeking an understanding with France. Modern history, indeed, is a record of successful alliances between the two powers when their common civilisation is imperilled, whether by the Habsburgs in the sixteenth and seventeenth centuries, or by Russia in the nineteenth, or by Germany in 1914. But for an enduring and cordial understanding between them it is necessary to bridge a cleavage which was never broader than at the Bourbon Restoration. The hatred then so widely felt for France among Germans and Spaniards was shared, if to a lesser degree, in England. To Englishmen the French were "the enemy", as forgetful veterans still called them in the Crimea. Men verging on middle age had spent almost all their adult years cooped up within an island whose whole future was menaced by France. Older men recalled the slaughter of Fontenoy, the disasters and triumphs of the Seven Years' War, and the loss of America through France. And this enemy nation seemed to them in part godless, in part idolatrous, a tyranny and an anarchy by turns, but always intent upon closing markets to British goods and upon stealing away British trade. It can hardly be wondered that Nelson wished the whole nation exterminated, that the first Lord Malmesbury, for all his tried diplomacy, declared that no Prince of Wales should visit Paris save as a conqueror, or that Raikes described as "highly satisfactory" the news that our allies had lost near 3000 men at Antwerp.

Despite their hatred and contempt, the British flocked to France for pleasure, but few French save ex-prisoners knew Britain at firsthand. To Frenchmen, with rare exceptions, the British were a nation of callous egotists, whose staggering success was due partly to their indecent energy and partly to undeserved good fortune. The days of French reverence for British philosophy and British liberty had gone by, and Normanby complained that the critic who ventured to praise Shakespeare in France must take care to express a caveat in favour of Racine.[1] To French reactionaries and revolutionaries alike British religion and British politics were abhorrent. The suspicion that the million Protestants of France were in danger roused Protestants in Britain, but Reformés and Anglicans were not identical or even intimate. To French Catholics both the Church of England and the English sects seemed cold and hypocritical, while the emancipated deemed them narrow and superstitious. A French Royalist likewise must find the British insubordinate, while the French Left could not but contrast the haphazard chartered liberties of Britain with the radiant universal liberty which the Revolution had proclaimed. Even if within a few years of the peace Boulogne seemed to be a British town and 40,000 British lived in Paris, even if for appreciable periods a political entente could be maintained, there must remain for many years a deep

[1] Normanby, Marquis of, The English in France, i, 169; cf. Hall, J. R., The Bourbon Restoration, p. 192.

mutual distrust between the nations and much latent ill-will. Individual Englishmen and Frenchmen could be friends and the more enlightened members of both nations found matter for mutual respect, but such contacts were relatively rare. The wife of a British ambassador in Paris declared herself convinced that any amalgamation in Society was impossible.[1] The British public was ready to believe the worst of France and to resent it, while French statesmen had Paris, the French press and the Deputies against them when they worked for the *entente*, and with them whenever they defied Britain. Again and again after the French Restoration the politic friendliness of the sovereigns and their ministers failed to overcome the discord between their subordinates, diplomatic, administrative and naval, a failure which inevitably cast suspicion upon the good faith of the governments themselves.

Mutual ill-will between France and Britain therefore conditioned their relations during the generation (1815–48) which divided the fall of the first Napoleon from the advent of his nephew to power. For more than one-fifth of that interval, between the Second Peace of Paris (20 November 1815) and the fatal twelfth of August 1822, when Castlereagh took his life, their domestic progress moved within the framework created by his sane and skilful policy. It was of vast importance for both countries that during these critical years their relations should be shaped by a statesman who, like Wellington and Aberdeen, was by training not insular but European. Harmony with Metternich and Austria, a discreet manipulation of Alexander's ambition to control three continents, a sympathetic regard for the moods and trials of France—all these were secured by placing British policy in the hands of one whom his fellow-Europeans respected for unfeigned devotion to the common cause.

Few governments have ever faced a harder task than that of Louis XVIII when he succeeded Napoleon in a humiliated and diminished France. French society itself was a new creation. The Revolution had transformed it into something which seemed to resemble the open champaigns of its native landscape, in contrast with those manifold enclosures which characterised both land and life in England and society in historic France. In this post-Revolutionary society, where the middle classes had acquired a firm predominance and the lower novel freedom, there was no organ of government which unquestionably represented the nation. Louis XVIII at best symbolised deliverance from invasion and from a *régime* which many of his subjects had detested. But to the masses he could promise little. The main work of the Revolution and of Napoleon could not be undone, and the restored monarchy must seem to embody the triumph of rejected principles and of alien armies over France. Thus the King was forced to be the leader or the tool of

[1] Willson, B., *The Paris Embassy, 1814–1920*, p. 79.

a royalist party rather than the rallying-point of the whole people. The ministers indeed were of his choosing, but the Chambers could make their continuance in office difficult if not impossible. The French Parliament, however, for all its newness, was hardly more representative of the people than was the contemporary Parliament in Britain. A franchise embracing some 100,000 electors, with great possibilities of governmental pressure on both electors and elected, forbade the Crown to regard a victory in the Chamber of Deputies as a definitive success. Embarrassed alike by the constitution and by the spirit of revolution, the restored monarchy found in the church and in the royal family allies of doubtful value. While keen observers held for twenty years after Waterloo that religion in France was dead or dying, the Catholic church was attempting a reactionary programme in politics which formed a constant danger to the Crown. At the same time the indiscreet language and behaviour of the royal princes jeopardised the future of the dynasty, and the Bourbons were at bitter feud with their cousins and possible heirs. Futile in politics, the Royalists talked of setting aside the renunciation for which a century earlier half Europe had shed its blood, and of restoring to the succession their Spanish cousins, perhaps the worst rulers in the world.

Louis XVIII and his advisers none the less could not fail to see that the first requisite of the monarchy was a firm throne, that this postulated a loyal army and an acquiescent nation, and that without showing some spirit in foreign policy they could secure neither. A spirited foreign policy demanded first the full restoration of France to her place among the Powers, and, second, the relaxation of the fetters imposed on her by the treaties of Vienna. Most galling were those debarring her from expansion towards Belgium, the Rhine and Italy, thus closing her frontiers to French-speaking populations which, as she had some reason to believe, desired to come within them. Chafed by the treaties, apostles of monarchy like Chateaubriand were ready to wage war for mere prestige, while revolutionaries might still hope to conquer by propaganda. Cooler heads, however, could perceive that while it was dangerous if not suicidal to challenge Europe by attempting aggrandisement, much might be done by diplomacy, notably in Spain, while Italy, where Bourbon princes also still survived, offered possibilities of future intervention. But two facts appeared beyond all doubt—that immediate prestige could not be gained by colonisation and that for the time being no friendship could equal in value that of Britain. For France to attempt aggrandisement overseas was to strike with her weaker arm, to drain her treasury for distant and doubtful profit, to flatter her people less if successful, and, if unsuccessful, to offend them more than by attempting aggrandisement in Europe. Above all, though the Prince Regent was the protector of France, Wellington a fair umpire and

Castlereagh a European statesman, it remained true that to send a French ship anywhere was to make Britain suspicious, and that to attempt colonial expansion was to ensure her jealousy and opposition. These considerations, which held good for many years, were strongest when, as after Waterloo, a new French government was struggling to hold its ground.

For three years, until the Aix-la-Chapelle Congress had withdrawn the army of occupation as from the end of November 1818, consolidation and emancipation threw foreign and colonial politics into the shade. Guided by the honourable and modest duc de Richelieu, whose natural regard for Russia Britain wisely did not resent, France survived a royalist frenzy like that of the English Restoration. With an electoral law which gave only one in three hundred of the people votes, and an army ballot which called up less than two and a half times as many, France, stable for three years, could be received again into the full comity of nations. During these years of domestic and European effort, none the less, some notes had been struck which long re-echoed through that colonial disharmony which had not, as men supposed, been extinguished by the surrender of France to Britain. Most penetrating among these was the discord of the slave trade. The accustomed apathy of the British people with regard to foreign politics gave place to keen excitement when morals and religion were at stake,[1] and the cause of the negroes had become the cause of conscience. "I am unable", wrote Wellington from London to his brother, "to describe to you the degree of frenzy existing here about the slave trade."[2]

Napoleon, hoping to propitiate Britain, had decreed that slavery itself was illegal in French possessions, and Britain hoped that Louis might confirm the decree.[3] It soon became evident, however, that France, intent upon developing her restored colonies, and suspicious of British motives, was not sincere even in abjuring the carriage of slaves from Africa. Early in 1817, Britain protested that the trade was carried on under the eye of the French authorities in Martinique and Guadeloupe, and next year the Governor of Goree was found to be appropriating a hundred francs for every slave exported.[4] Thus began an interminable and wearisome series of efforts by Britain to manœuvre France into line, an agitation which inevitably discounted the attraction of the *entente* as against a French connection with the less humanitarian absolutist powers. At the same time Britain noted with close attention the renewed exclusion of foreigners from trade with the French colonies, and the suspicious activities of Catholic missionaries, who were sent especially to the Île de France and to

---

[1] *Correspondence and Conversations of A. de Tocqueville with N.W. Senior*, i, 22.
[2] Willson, *op. cit.* p. 30.
[3] F.O. France, Stuart to Castlereagh, 26 May 1815, no. 80.
[4] *Ibid.* 20 January 1817, no. 23 and 19 February 1818, no. 66.

Canada, even when it was hard to fill vacant cures in the mother country.[1] France, for her part, learning that Britain intended exploration in Africa, begged her to take note that a Moroccan instructed by Cuvier and others was to join in Egypt the caravan from Mecca, to work up the Niger towards its source and thence to make his way to Senegal.[2] A proposed development in that region was indeed partly checked by the Chamber, but the French proceeded to revive their pre-Revolutionary plans for gaining a footing in Madagascar. Even while weakest, France showed herself resolved to develop her meagre empire overseas and to increase it.

During the four years (October 1818 to August 1822) in which an emancipated France had to deal with Castlereagh, the same tendencies continued. Although a prey to party strife, which prompted Liberal plots and Royalist schemes of reaction, the nation steadily regained prosperity and international prestige. While Britain drew further from Alexander's European concert, the would-be Areopagus of the Powers, France approached its doors. Lured by Russian offers of profit from the revolt in Greece, and by hopes of regaining her old influence in the Levant, she toyed with the idea of a Mediterranean squadron equal to the British.[3] The common constitutionalism of the two Western nations seemed likely to form a less potent bond than that which linked continental governments against revolution. France, moreover, grew year by year more likely to become a manufacturing competitor of Britain. Schemes for the mutual relaxation of tariffs faded: British rolled iron was threatened with exclusion from France: our ambassador reported that information was being systematically drawn from England, and that a hundred steam-engines were forging iron where six years earlier there had been none.[4] The French, moreover, were attending closely to the possibilities of navigation with the aid of steam, a development which might destroy British preponderance by sea.[5] Meanwhile, in defiance of treaties, the British were excluded from Senegal, and posts on the Gambia were established by the French. French slave-traders, with a cynical disregard of natural history, fitted out a ship at Havre to convey "mules" from the coast of Africa. One expedition was prepared for Madagascar, another, "merely for scientific purposes",[6] was sent to round Cape Horn. The premium granted to cotton grown in French Guiana was extended to Senegal, and an *entrepôt* for colonial produce established at Goree.

These activities, the legitimate and the questionable alike, caused Britain less concern, however, than French policy towards the revolted

---

[1] F.O. France, 13 August 1818, no. 322 and 14 September 1818, no. 364.
[2] *Ibid*. 8 December 1817, no. 490.
[3] Crawley, *op. cit.* p. 22.
[4] F.O. France, Stuart to Castlereagh, 10 December 1821, no. 337.
[5] Cf. *Ordonnance* of 8 August 1821.
[6] Register of despatches, Paris, July 1821, no. 213 (F.O.).

Spanish-American colonies. The colonists had never recognised the rôle of Joseph Bonaparte, but the restoration of Ferdinand VII in 1813 had not been followed by a restoration of their allegiance to Spain. In the years which followed Ferdinand had clearly failed to regain his sovereignty either by conciliation or by force, but the Spanish nation would not tolerate any abandonment of the claims of their rulers. In these circumstances great prospects opened before France, either of recovering her hold on Spain by sympathetic activity in one direction, or of making the revolted colonies substantially her own by the reverse. For some years the belief that recognition by a Great Power would be tantamount to annexation was plausible.[1] Legitimacy pointed towards aiding Spain; Liberalism, towards recognising the new nations. Honour, the British might well opine, forbade separate or at least secret French action in either sense, since in the common interest Britain had scrupulously refrained from taking many profitable opportunities of intervention, although commercially she was in close touch with the colonists. The limited trading rights grudgingly accorded to her at the Peace of Utrecht had in practice been consistently exceeded and in spite of Spanish resentment the intercourse which benefited both the colonist and the English merchant had continued throughout the eighteenth century. Faced by the Continental System and, on account of her growing industrialisation, more than ever in need of markets, England had seized on the chances offered by the colonies after their revolt. They, hard pressed for revenue, were eager to admit duty-paying goods, and trade had continued accordingly. It was clear therefore that Britain must watch with the closest interest any move which might affect their future. In 1818, however, the French were tempted into an intrigue for the establishment of Bourbon monarchies across the Atlantic, which, if successful, might have proved a great commercial and colonial *coup d'état*. The discovery could not fail to prejudice Franco-British friendship, nor to impel Castlereagh in his last days towards a liberal policy in Latin America.

The untimely death of Castlereagh (12 August 1822) placed power in the hands of Canning, a statesman less Continental in outlook, less conciliatory in temper and more ready both to rouse and to obey the people. Meanwhile leadership in France had passed (December 1821) into the able hands of Villèle, and an ultra-Royalist majority in the Chamber rejoiced in the prospects of reaction. Official relations with Britain, however, remained excellent, despite the perplexing problems resulting from the Greek revolt. By relaxing the Navigation Laws, Britain qualified her ships to carry the produce of her colonies to France. Common jealousy of the United States helped to harmonise the West Indian policy of the two nations, and the dangers from pirates in the Spanish islands produced a satisfactory local

[1] Cf. Adams, C. F., *Memoirs of J. Q. Adams*, IV, 26 November 1823 and *passim*.

entente. When attacks upon Louis XVIII by popular societies in Madrid resulted in acute tension with Spain, which since 1820 had been dominated by a military revolution, Britain hastened to offer mediation. Villèle, though not unjustifiably militant when informed that Spain was offering Britain a commercial treaty, stood firmly on the side of peace.

Spain, where legitimate monarchy was now enslaved, had indeed become the question of Europe. Britain strove for non-intervention. Russia was resolved to intervene. France, pleading danger from disease but in reality dreading revolution, had already placed an army on the frontier. At this crisis she was spurred to action by Chateaubriand, a superb and moving rhetorician whose convictions were never more than the formulae of his rancours and desires.[1] Having sent Villèle, as he proudly confessed, an untrue account of the wishes of the European Congress at Verona,[2] he became Minister of Foreign Affairs at the close of 1822. In the following spring, the duc d'Angoulême led 95,000 men across the Pyrenees, and the white flag of the Bourbons seemed to have triumphed over the tricolour, the symbol of revolution. This French stroke, by no means widely popular in France, menaced and embarrassed Britain. It might result, indeed, as was predicted at the secret session of the Chamber on 8 February, in rendering France the protectress of Spain, with Cuba as a new Jamaica, and an enfranchised South America as her grateful client.[3] To captivate both Spain and the rebels, and at the same time to defy France, absolutist Europe and the United States, must however overtax even Canning's genius. Far more probable was friction with France from questions of privateers, contraband, blockade, right of search, unneutral service—all the usual concomitants of neutrality by sea, and it would be well if Britain did not find herself confronted by a new Bourbon league whose efforts to regain Spanish America would be supported by the absolutist Powers.

Angoulême's swift success inspired the French Government to address ours in a tone to which we had been unaccustomed since the Restoration.[4] In June, Chateaubriand received assurances of the support of the Allies in case Britain should assist Spain.[5] A few weeks later (after the French fleet's successful bombardment of Cadiz which thereupon surrendered to the Spanish Royalists) our ambassador described the French Government as aiming, both in Spain and the colonies, at direct ascendancy, "which they think cannot under any contingency be counteracted by the influence of Great Britain".[6] The Tsar, it was known, had been making enquiries about the Spanish

---

[1] Palaeologue, M., *The Romantic Diplomatist*, p. 143.
[2] Chateaubriand, *Congrès de Vérone*, I, 173.
[3] F.O. France, Stuart to Canning, 10 February 1823, no. 42.
[4] *Ibid*. 5 May 1823, no. 182.
[5] *Ibid*. 12 June 1823, no. 256.
[6] *Ibid*. 7 July 1823, no. 307. See also Chévalier, *Hist. de la Marine française*, p. 14.

settlements in America and about the possibility of consolidating his own possessions. He might be tempted to take California, Peru and Chile while France established a Bourbon prince in Mexico.[1]

The natural consequence of such gestures was to draw together the threatened powers, Britain and the United States. While American agents were reported as active in Mexico and Cuba, Mr Gallatin at Paris was expressing his conviction that his Government viewed with satisfaction every attempt at colonisation by Great Britain in the north-west.[2] France soon discovered that her triumph in Spain implied a costly occupation of the country for an indefinite length of time, and that at sea she was not powerful enough to challenge both Britain and the United States. Hence she showed eagerness for the co-operation of Britain in the Peninsula, and for a Congress to establish Bourbon monarchies overseas. She viewed with the utmost nervousness every British movement towards the New World, especially such as suggested the imminence of commercial, if not political, recognition of the independence of the Spanish colonies. But the new friendliness of the United States aided Canning[3] to avert the Congress by demanding that they should be invited. Rather than admit "a government...whose political principles are directly at variance with those of every other Power" Villèle would forego the Congress. "For the sake of a simple local advantage", he maintained, "the United States would always be disposed to overset the arrangement upon which their plenipotentiary may agree."[4] The new year found Paris deeply impressed by the Monroe message of 2 December 1823, which proved that no Congress could hope to restore the colonies to Spain. Chateaubriand, indeed, professed himself satisfied that Monroe had not been prompted by Canning, and that his (Monroe's) veto on colonisation was directed only against the claims of Russia to make the northern Pacific a closed sea.[5] France could not deny that Polignac had in October 1823 abjured intervention in Spanish America, while in Spain itself the cruel and obstinate Ferdinand VII seemed by his conduct to mock her policy in restoring such a monster to power. Early in June Chateaubriand was abruptly dismissed.

France, it was clear, had gained little by her attempt to revive the glories of Henri IV. As a constitutional power, her intervention had been out of keeping, while as a colonial and sea power she was not yet strong enough to challenge Britain. Before 1823 was at an end, Villèle had declared that ministers fully understood their interests to be the same with those of Britain upon many points, especially colonial.[6] Such an attitude did not forbid the choice of a path leading

[1] Adams, *op. cit.* 26 November 1823.
[2] F.O. France, Stuart to Canning, 26 May 1823, no. 219.
[3] Temperley, H. W. V., *The Foreign Policy of Canning*, p. 118.
[4] F.O. France, Stuart to Canning, 4 November 1823, no. 568.
[5] *Ibid.* 13 January 1824, no. 30.
[6] *Ibid.* 28 November 1823, no. 619.

to rivalry in the future. Reinforced by his brother-in-law, Bassaynes, who had governed the Île de Bourbon and visited many British possessions, he planned a Government department of Colonies, strengthened the naval forces in the West Indies and off Brazil, and utilised the occupation of Spain to threaten the pirate ruler of Algiers. Regiments of the line were to replace colonial battalions, and 4000 men therefore assembled at Brest. Above all, in accordance with British precedent, the new field in Spanish America was carefully surveyed. "Not a month passes", wrote our ambassador in July 1824 from Paris, "without the arrival or departure of obscure agents to promote the interest of France in the South American states."[1] In August the agents were avowed, a measure which necessarily terminated French protests against the despatch of their British rivals. In Portugal, however, and indeed almost all over the world, "frequent demonstrations of imprudent zeal" on the part of their subordinates called for repression by the French ministers in the interests of the *entente*.[2] Until English sea-power could be safely challenged, France might intrigue and the Tsar entertain grandiose designs, but there the matter must end. Until that day Latin America, unlike Europe, might feel free to develop unhampered by the intervention of crowned reactionaries.

Such was the situation, official friendship veiling a colonial rivalry which must grow with time, when the long-expected death of Louis XVIII took place (September 1824). Although the accession of his bigot brother threatened a James II in the place of a Charles II, Villèle, it might be hoped, would really rule. At first indeed Charles X won hearts by unexpected generosity and moderation. His overture to Orleans, with the reminder that only an infant stood between the duke and the French crown, constituted the first admission by any king since Louis XIV that the renunciation by the Spanish line was valid.[3] Although French merchants in Brazil complained that preferential duties were accorded to their British rivals, France showed all possible official sympathy with the mission of Sir Charles Stuart, lately our ambassador at Paris, to compose the differences between Brazil and the mother country. The perplexing question of St Domingo, moreover, was handled with restraint and wisdom. In 1795 the French had acquired the whole of an island formerly divided between France and Spain. To rule it proved, however, a task beyond their powers, for the vexed question of slavery defied settlement and kept the islanders in constant revolt. A force sent out by Bonaparte was compelled to withdraw (1803) and in 1804 the country declared its independence. At the Restoration in 1814 the French asserted their title but allegiance was refused. Until,

---

[1] F.O. France, 5 July 1824, no. 340.
[2] *Ibid.* 31 May 1824, no. 272.
[3] *Ibid.* 23 September 1824, no. 492.

therefore, the question of sovereignty could be settled, the position of countries engaged in trade with the islanders was delicate in the extreme. French pride and the principle of legitimacy supported Villèle's earlier argument that "the recognition of a black empire founded upon insurrection and upon the massacre of the white population would have a most pernicious moral effect". Negro risings in both French and British West Indies and upon the mainland were indeed not seldom apprehended. Britain however doubted "whether a *de facto* government of negroes, established for twenty years, whose subjects had commercial intercourse with all nations, was not more dangerous in a state of proscription than when admitted into the society of the nations of the world", and in June 1825 France named the price of recognition. The negro rebels were granted a fortnight in which to agree to pay an indemnity of 150 million francs with a preference of 50 per cent. to France over the next most favoured nation. Failing acceptance, their ports would be blockaded.[1]

French success in St Domingo, however, fell far short of that achieved by Britain through Canning's triumphant recognition of the Latin American republics and his admirable settlement of Brazil.[2] France, fettered by her duty to legitimacy, was compelled to look on while Britain and the United States divided the commerce of these nascent states. When her warships convoyed Spanish transports to Cuba she was unequivocally informed that no plea whatever would justify in the eyes of the British Government the introduction of any French force into the Spanish islands.[3] Remembering the Family Compact, however, and secure that neither Britain nor the United States would allow the other to appropriate Cuba, she refused to sign any self-denying agreement with regard to this or any other of the Spanish West Indies,[4] and, early in 1826, she sent for the first time a large naval force to the Havannah. But it was Jesuits and Greeks rather than South Americans who during that year taxed her energies, and once again something like a general *entente* with Britain became possible. French equanimity, none the less, was tested by an Order-in-Council regulating the trade of their ships with the British West Indies and colonies upon the mainland. This Order, retorting as it did upon the French their own illiberal principles, evoked the sorrowful protest that it made their nation an exception and imposed upon them duties of which the superior British industry had no need.[5]

The chequered year 1827 prolonged the apparent pause in the colonial rivalry between France and Britain. Domestic politics and the fortunes of the Greeks more than ever absorbed the attention of both nations. In France, Villèle's reactionary measures ended in his

[1] F.O. France, Granville to Canning, 13 January and 14 June 1825, nos. 13 and 126.
[2] Temperley, *op. cit.*
[3] F.O. France, Granville to Canning, 6 June (secret and confidential) and July 1825, no. 148.
[4] *Ibid.* 25 and 29 August 1825, nos. 175 and 179.   [5] *Ibid.* 25 August 1826, no. 260.

fall (December 5). In Britain, the Catholic Emancipation question issued in the brief premiership of Canning. "Canning," wrote Greville on April 13, "disliked by the King, opposed by the aristocracy and the nation, and unsupported by the Parliament, is appointed Prime Minister." The reception of this news by the French Court, ministry and hierarchy was gloomy in the extreme, though the Liberals saw in it the glimmering of a brighter day for France and Europe.[1] A hundred days, and Canning was no more, but his rule had procured the treaty of London (July 7), signed with France and Russia for the settlement of the affairs of Greece. Of this the fruit was Navarino (October 20) and soon the French and British were exchanging compliments and decorations. In the delight at "the spirited and successful resistance...to the naval operations of the Turks", our ambassador wrote from Paris, "the hostile feelings which used to exist between the nations seem to have subsided here".[2]

Although the French were frankly warned that neither the British Parliament nor public shared their new-born enthusiasm for the Greeks, while in May Wellington is said to have threatened war,[3] the *entente* gained ground during the following year. In Martignac, Charles X found a moderate and at first a popular minister, while the advent of Aberdeen at the Foreign Office in June portended a policy of mildness and conciliation. The King, mindful of kindness received during his exile, was doubtless sincere in his expressions of delight that public opinion remained favourable to intimacy with Britain. Together the two states watched the growth of the formidable *Zollverein* and the Russian invasion of Turkey. They were at one with regard to the despatch of a French expedition to the Morea and the recognition of Donna Maria in Portugal. The police needed no British solicitation to suppress the Irish agitators in France, while friendly verbal communications sufficed to end a fishery dispute on the Newfoundland coast. One gentle warning, indeed, was uttered when the French were credited with plans for a convict station in Australia, "the extension of the British establishments in that country", our ambassador declared, "having already embraced every part of the coast".[4]

The complete victory of the Russians in the Turkish campaign of 1829 helped to strengthen the *entente*. As the French shrewdly reasoned, the right of protection over the Christians of Turkey and Persia to which Russia aspired might prove worse than limited cessions of territory.[5] To the disgust of the Russians, allied squadrons appeared off Constantinople, and a peace was signed at Adrianople which secured Greek independence without destroying the balance

[1] F.O. France, Hamilton to Canning, 16 April 1827, no. 32.
[2] *Ibid*. Granville to Dudley, 2 and 9 November 1827, nos. 160 and 169.
[3] Crawley, *op. cit.* p. 107.
[4] F.O. France, Stuart (then Lord Stuart de Rothesay) to Aberdeen, 18 August 1828, no. 62.   [5] *Ibid*. 5 October 1829, no. 388.

of power. In the days of the Polignac ministry (August 1829 to July 1830), however, while the apprehensions of the French were being more than fulfilled by the swifter *tempo* of reaction, rivalry with the British was more prominent than co-operation. French activity in West Africa seemed to warrant the charge of systematic encroachment in order to monopolise the trade of the rivers down to the Gambia. Whether or no their rights on the coast of Madagascar had been ceded with Mauritius, the French were preparing to assert them by force. In the Levant they were striving to oust British traders, and there were plans for French steamship companies in the Mediterranean and in the Baltic.

All this however paled before the invasion of Algiers. In striking at Algiers, France seemed to the British to be grasping at the control of the whole southern shore of the Mediterranean. The American minister at Paris deplored the threat to "the only plausible motive which can be alleged in Congress for incurring the expense of maintaining a naval establishment in time of peace".[1] For Algiers stood for the Barbary Powers, hitherto an incorrigible nest of pirates, openly defiant of their nominal overlord the Sultan, and defiant even after such measures as Lord Exmouth's bombardment in 1816 or the visit of a Franco-British squadron three years later. The occasion of Polignac's stroke was the insult to a flag of truce incidental to an ineffectual French blockade. Britain, refusing the invitation to co-operate, suspected from the first the development of the scheme and its dangerous implications. Mehemet Ali, the Viceroy of Egypt, even offered to attack the Barbary Powers by land. Such independent action by one vassal of the Porte against others imperilled the theory of Turkish unity, and opened vistas of the seduction of France by Russia to do all that Britain most abhorred. To the end of January 1830, indeed, Polignac persisted in denying that any French expedition was preparing. "H.E.'s persausion [*sic*] of d—d falsehood of this assertion", runs the gleeful entry of the attaché who indexed our ambassador's report to Aberdeen. The French, it seemed, counted too much on advantage in the impending elections to forego the expected victory, and, lying at Constantinople also,[2] evaded mediation. However Stuart might rage, Polignac would say no word that hinted at an intention, still less a pledge, to abandon the occupation.[3] The French press commented bitterly on the parallel armaments of Britain at Gibraltar, Malta and Corfu; Stuart even intrigued with the supporters of Villèle; but Algiers fell on July 5, and this event was thought to presage a new partition of the Ottoman Empire.

Next month, Charles X was on his way to England and his minister to the dubious shelter of a gaol. The immediate and inevitable effect

[1] *Ibid.* 16 July 1830, no. 341.
[2] *Ibid.* 29 March 1830, no. 131.
[3] *Ibid.* Granville to Palmerston, 18 March 1833, no. 94.

of the July Revolution was to increase the importance of Britain in French eyes. Both the fugitive King and his destined successor turned for advice to Stuart, and all parties sought British goodwill. As Louis Philippe, Orleans was accepted by Britain as by France—"faute de mieux, crainte de pis".[1] While he paraded the tricolour and was ready to erase the lilies from his shield, he promptly disclaimed the system of revolutionary proselytism conspicuous in 1792 and the territorial aggrandisement which was the dream of the younger classes. He discouraged the approaches of the Republicans of Paris to those of London, sent Talleyrand, the *entente* incarnate, to St James's, and sought in Britain the counterweight to Russia, where the Tsar showed an invincible detestation for a prince who had stolen his cousin's crown. France, as his minister was soon to declare, must ally herself with Britain, and favour every measure which might increase the strength and population of Prussia. With such associates and with her own power to arm on the revolutionary scale, she might forbid Russia to cross the Vistula.[2]

The King, who at fifty-seven thus set himself to please old and young, royalist and republican, France and Britain, was wont to conceal his "secret, crooked, boxed-up character"[3] behind an unfailing torrent of fair words. A man of considerable ability and great experience, physically courageous, unbiased by patriotism, religion, vice or pride, his dominant aim was to preserve his seat upon the throne, so that he might promote the interest of his numerous family and enlarge his ample fortune. Although he professed that he would make the Charter a reality and even that he looked for guidance to the Chambers, he believed himself the most persuasive and the wisest of men and was always an absolutist at heart. With such a disposition, he naturally sought for Foreign Secretaries who would defer to his opinions and for ambassadors with whom he could maintain an independent correspondence; and French interests naturally suffered. The *entente* seemed at first the indispensable prop of his throne, but with principles rather German than British, he might well prefer an alliance with the absolutist Powers, whose armies alone could distract those of France from their proper function of guarding the dynasty against insurrection. While he would be eager to develop commerce and such colonies as promised profit, he was the least likely of kings to risk a costly and dangerous struggle for the sake of national prestige. Tory eyes soon perceived that he might have made a thriving tradesman but could never be a glorious king.[4]

While France was still shaken by a revolution which had cost some thousands of lives and caused 28,000 Government servants to lose

---

[1] Raikes, T., *Journal*, 22 February 1833.
[2] F.O. France, Stuart to Foreign Office, 26 November 1830, no. 654.
[3] Heine, H., trans. Leland, C. G., *Works*, VIII, 34.
[4] Raikes, T., *Journal*, 31 July 1835.

their places,[1] the nation was profoundly thrilled by risings in Belgium and in Poland like her own . The Belgian revolt meant that the system of strong monarchies arrayed as the gaolers of France was breaking down, that rich territories coveted by France for centuries might be hers, and that her King, already sensitive to the moral quarantine in which he was placed by legitimist Europe, might have a second monarch among his sons. The Polish revolt meant that the Tsar, whose menaces to France had reconciled even Brittany to the conscription,[2] would be occupied with his own affairs. More deeply than the Spanish and the Belgian movements, which were characterised by "religious feelings in which the French do not participate", it touched the heart of France.[3] The Government could therefore take a high tone with Spain, declaring that, since Spanish armaments could threaten only France, the French would cross the Pyrenees unless they were abated.[4] But, apart from legitimacy and the rights of the King of Holland, a movement that might render Belgium French touched the most sacrosanct of British interests. This Louis Philippe realised, but as yet neither his throne nor any other institution was solidly established. At a time when Paris might struggle for a republic and the provinces for a federation, a French King who truckled to Britain could only expect to be overthrown.

It was therefore of vast importance that at this crisis the management of foreign affairs in Britain passed into new and skilful hands.[5] Palmerston, who with other Canningites had enabled Grey and the Whigs to replace the Tories under Wellington, was the living refutation of Castlereagh's lament, "after me no one understands the affairs of Europe". In temper he remained what he had been at Harrow, "the pluckiest and strongest boy in the whole school"; in principles he derived through Canning and Pitt from Chatham; he was perfect in French, in organisation, in Parliamentary talent, in clearness of judgment and of expression; he possessed unflagging powers of work and unfailing patience. Thanks to Palmerston above all other men, the terribly complex Belgian problem was solved within a year, on lines which a century has only deepened. The achievement ranks the higher that the temper of the French was further tried by the interference of Austria in Italy, by the triumph of Russia over the Poles, and by the refusal of the Powers to raze certain Belgian fortresses which in a country now neutralised seemed only to threaten France. The weakness of the monarchy, moreover,

---

[1] According to Guizot, F.O. France, Stuart to Aberdeen, 13 September 1830, no. 495.
[2] *Ibid.* Stuart to Palmerston, 10 December 1830, no. 681.
[3] *Ibid.* 17 December 1830, no. 700.
[4] *Ibid.* 17 December 1830, no. 704.
[5] For sharply conflicting estimates of Palmerston, cp. Beust, *Memoirs*, 1, 242, "the very ideal of a Foreign Minister", with Vitzthum, *Denkwürdigkeiten*, p. 113, "an adroit juggler but a second-rate politician". A. Cecil depreciates his powers and his Belgian triumph, *British Foreign Secretaries*, pp. 147, etc.

appeared by many signs besides its subservience to Britain. In 1831 the students of Paris and the workmen of Lyons were conspicuous for disturbances, the Government was forced to replace Napoleon's statue in the Place Vendôme, the capital was more than once disturbed by sympathisers with the Poles, and it was significant that the well-to-do National Guard was shirking duty. French morale seemed low at a time when the morale of many nations was tested to the utmost by the cholera, a disease which swept off seven hundred persons in Paris within eight days, and in Casimir-Périer robbed France of an invaluable statesman. While the west remained the home of legitimacy and the south was conspicuous for Bonapartist, Republican and economic discontent, Paris in June 1832 had to be placed in a state of siege—a step which happily revealed the unsuspected popularity of the King.[1]

With the passing of the Reform Bill (June 1832), a measure warmly welcomed by the French Government, and with the achievement of a solid *entente* with regard to Belgium and Italy, Franco-British relations entered upon a phase which lasted until July 1840. With one short interruption, power remained in Whig hands, while Palmerston made the Foreign Office his own preserve. The common enemy to be watched was Russia; the greatest danger, disunion regarding distracted Spain. The Government of Louis Philippe, doomed to be illegitimate and uninspiring, could never safely dispense with British friendship, while, in its struggle to make the French rich and therefore well-affected, British co-operation was invaluable. France, however, though swift to welcome British capital and enterprise for her new railways, remained slow to free her slaves or reduce her tariffs. Colonial questions still lay in the background, with rivalry always latent and sometimes obvious. In general, however, the history of Franco-British relations during the first decade of Louis Philippe is that of a mutually profitable *entente*.

In March 1832, indeed, the British showed some perturbation at the report of a French expedition to New Zealand. *La Favorite*, it appeared, had set out for the islands before the July Revolution but with no authority to make a settlement. In spite of the ferocity and cannibalism of the Maori race, the country had long attracted the attention of the French, while the British Government showed itself loath to undertake fresh adventures. The year 1830, however, saw the rise of a British ministry which favoured colonisation and of a French *régime* under which the projects of its predecessors were abandoned.[2] But the interests of France in the whaling industry, in spreading Catholicism and in developing French power and prestige, were not extinguished by the Revolution of July, and her connection with New Zealand could not be finally severed by the mere behest of Britain.

[1] F.O. France, Hamilton to Palmerston, 11 June 1832, no. 84.
[2] Harrop, A. J., *England and New Zealand*, ch. v.

In sharp contrast to the new attitude of France, Britain reasserted her dormant title to the Falkland Islands, over-riding the claims of Buenos Aires. Commercially the islands had little value save as a centre for vessels engaged in whaling and sealing, but as a strategic point in the South Atlantic and on the Horn route to Australia and to the Pacific Coast of America, it was important that they should be prevented from falling into the hands of France or of the United States. It was an "Admiralty" rather than a Colonial Office move, but the French might feel that here again they were being thwarted by a power which already owned more than her fair share of the globe. For the time being, none the less, suspicions of her designs in the Pacific were obscured by graver questions as to the stability and the policy of her Government at home. The French obviously needed an *entente* against Russia in the Near East, since the Turkish empire was about to crumble under the attacks of the Viceroy of Egypt. They desired also concert by sea, holding that a demonstration by the joint squadrons would allay fears of a maritime war. At this time, moreover, a French army, with the hesitating approval of the British, was moving upon Antwerp to coerce the Dutch. Louis Philippe, always at a loss for ministers, had won with difficulty the acquiescence of Britain in his choice of Soult, declaring that the *cliché* of the marshal was "I am the apostle of peace", and that Guizot and Thiers would answer questions in the Chamber and give the Cabinet a due civilian complexion.[1] The King's reputation for courage was now enhanced, but the value of his alliance further discounted, by the first of many attacks upon his life. Pistols and muskets, bombs, airguns and infernal machines—all were discharged at "the tyrant", until it came to be noted as a curiosity that five whole months had passed without an attempt at his extermination.[2] As he grew older and still remained in peril, Britain must feel less and less confidence in a policy which depended upon his survival. This was particularly the case with the design of liberalising commercial relations, in which Louis Philippe often professed to be foiled by his ministers, and they, if apparently converted, by the Chamber. This situation was illuminated by the events of 1833. The King then promised to sanction the export of raw silk, but a law in fulfilment of French promises regarding customs found no active supporter among the ministers and was rejected by the Chamber. British cotton twist and tin must therefore wait for admission, and Broglie, although faced with threats of retaliatory duties by Britain and conceding the evils of protection, held out no hope that coal and iron entering France by sea would be taxed as low as those brought in by land.[3] Such failures in economic comradeship inevitably affected the attitude of a commercial nation towards

[1] F.O. France, Granville to Palmerston, 28 September 1832 (separate), most secret and confidential. [2] Raikes, T., *Diary*, 20 December 1836. [3] F.O. France, Granville to Palmerston, 21 June and 27 December 1833, nos. 137 and 320.

17-2

French colonial enterprise. For the moment attention centred on Algiers. The successors of Charles X warned Britain frankly that, while the French people valued her alliance, war even with her would be popular if withdrawal from Algiers were the alternative.[1] At the same time they gave indications that France might in time abandon of her own accord this costly burden. The hatred of the inhabitants, due in part to the oppression and rapacity of French Governors, was indeed notorious, and years later it was said that anyone who ventured half a league beyond the outposts would lose his life.[2] The interior remained, in fact, largely unconquered. Difficulties of geography and climate reinforced the hostility of the inhabitants, and the magnitude of the task may be judged by the steady increase in the French forces before the task could be completed. Less than 18,000 in 1831, in 1839 they numbered 54,000, and in 1847, 107,000. Such a drain on her resources could not but weaken France in other matters.

With the important exception of the Peninsula, however, the *entente* appeared to flourish in every field until November 1834, when Thiers, Guizot and their friends resigned, and William IV suddenly drove the Whigs from office. The abolition of slavery by Britain, at a cost in French reckoning of five hundred millions, gave the lie to the many who had attributed to hypocrisy our constant agitation for the negroes, but although in 1831 Louis Philippe's Government had agreed to a Convention with us for mutual rights of search of all suspect slavers, it was not renewed in 1841. The need for the *entente* was illustrated by the prostration of the Sultan before the Tsar in the treaty of Unkiar Skelessi (6 July 1833) and by the growing intimacy of the absolutist Powers. Its value received demonstration when the two fleets dominated the Mediterranean, and when Turkey and Egypt were persuaded to remain at peace and to turn their thoughts towards reform. France even reduced some of her tariffs and tonnage dues as a compliment to Britain.

The *entente*, however, was weakest where it was expressed in a formal treaty of alliance—on the side of Portugal and Spain. Palmerston's Quadruple Alliance of 1834 belonged to that class of covenants of which the late Triple Alliance is the most famous, in which states whose dissonance is incurable become partners to guard against mutual surprise. France could not sincerely desire British predominance in the Peninsula and remained Carlist at heart. While a foreign female regent, against her own convictions, was forced into making a show of Liberalism, Spain fell into a savage anarchy which the Western Powers could at least unite to oppose. The future of the young queen, Isabella, however, promised to divide France and Britain without uniting Spain.

The brief interval (December 1834–April 1835) during which Peel

---

[1] F.O. France, June 1833, no. 140.
[2] Raikes, T., *Diary*, 20 July 1839.

and Wellington replaced Melbourne and Palmerston in office witnessed little change in the *entente*. A serious dispute between France and the United States with regard to American claims for repayment evoked the good offices of Britain.

Wellington deprived our ambassador at Constantinople of the power lately conferred upon him of making war by summoning the fleet, while the French refused to co-operate in an endeavour to convince Don Carlos that the game was up. When the Whigs returned, the Spanish struggle continued to fill the foreground of *entente* politics, although in November Paris was roused by the Tsar's speech at Warsaw foreshadowing the extinction of Poland, while a considerable French force sailed to the West Indies to frustrate American reprisals. To the persistent friction generated by the French occupation of Algiers was added that due to an interminable controversy about the claims of British merchants for the interruption of their trade with Portendik, north of the river Senegal.

From 1835, Palmerston declared later, French policy began to change to systematic endeavour to undermine our interest in every quarter of the globe. The next important landmark in the history of Franco-British relations, however, was the advent as Foreign Minister of Thiers (February 1836). This tiny myopic journalist from the south, whom Heine described as "all brain", was perhaps the most forceful French statesman between Napoleon and Gambetta, and like them of mingled race. Though careless of opposition and an avowed protectionist, he began by lauding the *entente*, which his master described as the basis of the repose of the world. To Austria he bluntly declared, "You do what you like with Cracow and Poland, and we, in concert with England, must and will do what we like in the Peninsula".[1] On many sides this concert was maintained, though Thiers insisted on his right to send a squadron to Tangier to deter Morocco from aiding the Algerines. But a "warm altercation" with Granville, when the French navy was thought to be protecting the Carlists against the British, revealed his real mind, and the outburst was the more significant because he doubtless spoke for France. British agents, he declared, were everywhere anti-French, Dawkins in Greece, Ponsonby at Constantinople, our consul at Barcelona, our auxiliary legion at San Sebastian.[2] His attempts at a more active policy in Spain, however, cost him his office (August 1836). He was succeeded by Guizot, who had written on the history of England and respected her, while the suave but suspicious Molé, whom the King regarded as his own mouthpiece, took the portfolio of Foreign Affairs.

In the next fifteen months the *entente* wore very thin, but with the capture of Constantine (October 1837) the French gained a great

[1] F.O. France, Granville to Palmerston, 3 June 1836, no. 214.
[2] *Ibid.* 13 June 1836, no. 234.

colonial triumph and virtually secured supremacy in Algeria. The friction among the *entente* forces off the coast of Spain continued to be acute, and relations were further embittered by the discovery of an attempt by Villiers to negotiate an Anglo-Spanish commercial treaty. When, in February 1837, Paris learned that King William's speech to Parliament paid no tribute to his ally, much excitement prevailed, and Louis Philippe declared himself deeply wounded. The shock to his ministry at least was greater since Louis Bonaparte's attempt at Strassburg had shown that no jury in the east of France would convict a Bonapartist, while in the great manufacturing towns much distress prevailed. In October, the British prepared a deliberate indictment against the French agents in Spain, Portugal and Greece.[1] With Russia threatening Greece, however, the *entente* was still too serviceable to be discarded, and at the end of a year in which his life had been threatened thrice, Louis Philippe claimed that France had never been more prosperous and contented.[2]

Signs quickly followed that if France were prosperous and her government secure, colonial rivalry with Britain would become unveiled. Early in 1838, the *Journal des Débats*, which was known to be subsidised by the Government, advocated assistance to those Canadian rebels whom "American self-styled patriots"[3] were already helping. A Frenchman landed in New Zealand as its bishop appointed by the Pope, a French corvette followed, and the arrivals of French whalers increased sixfold.[4] At the same time French designs on Tunis were persistently suspected by the British. But the most prominent feature of the year was the establishment by France of blockades of Mexico and Buenos Ayres, while the French in Guiana (Cayenne) were charged with encroaching on Brazil. Their disloyal conduct in Spain, moreover, seemed to reach a climax when sufficient French horses reached the Carlists to render Madrid unsafe.[5] Friction with Russia, however, the greatest safeguard of the *entente*, continued undiminished. While the French dreaded lest aggression by Mehemet Ali and his Africans should give the Tsar a chance to defend the Sultan, they summarised their reply to the Tsar's diplomatic discourtesies by evicting the Russian ambassador from his hotel and installing the Turkish in his place.[6]

Although divergence regarding Syria made the *entente* more hollow than before, in form it was assiduously maintained, and in August 1839 the French Government warmly welcomed the mention of their friendship in the Queen's Speech.[7] Incidents such as their prohibition

[1] F.O. France, 13 October 1837, no. 314.
[2] *Ibid.* 18 December 1837 (confidential).
[3] Letter from a Michigan citizen enclosed by Granville, 19 March 1838, no. 86.
[4] See *C.H.B.E.* vii, pt. ii, p. 71 and Harrop, *op. cit.* pp. 102, 103, 107. The bishop was wrongly suspected of political designs.
[5] F.O. France, Granville to Palmerston, 26 October 1828, no. 303.
[6] *Ibid.* 5 October 1838, no. 280.
[7] *Ibid.* Bulwer to Palmerston, 31 August 1839, no. 25.

of corn export regardless of existing contracts, or their system of marching pauper foreigners and refugees to the coast and embarking them for England, or press charges against Britain for exciting rebellion in Algiers, merely indicated afresh that the co-operation between the two States was based on temporary convenience rather than on abiding interest or goodwill. What was prominent and indeed vital was the new phase into which the Eastern question passed with the death of Sultan Mahmoud in July. The helplessness of the Turks as against Mehemet Ali on the one hand and Nicholas on the other was swiftly placed beyond dispute. How was the integrity of Turkey to be preserved?

The strongest force in shaping British policy was at this time Palmerston, while in France the King could at least veto any action which was not demanded by an overwhelming outcry of the people. Such an outcry, resting upon no calculation, began to be threatened for the cause of Mehemet Ali as the natural ally of France in the east. The King, fearing Russia, Mehemet and his own people, demanded that the Sultan should be urged to grant at once his minimum demands. Palmerston, on the other hand, thought Russia "a great humbug" and Mehemet a greater, while, with every wish to be friendly towards France, he had no intention of sacrificing British interests to a cautious and self-seeking king. Grant Mehemet an independent Egypt, he demonstrated with good-humoured frankness to the French, "and the whole coast...from Morocco to the gulf of Alexandretta would then be in your power....This would never suit us".[1] His policy was to group the Powers, Russia included, in support of that indubitable principle of public law and prime British interest—the integrity of the Turkish empire. If Russia could be induced to champion this principle, he had little fear either of Mehemet or of France, so long as Louis Philippe was on the throne. France, he held, had been changed by a generation of prosperity, and her king would not risk his crown to gratify the hot-heads of Paris. Britain, therefore, did not shrink from receiving in the autumn the special mission of the Russian Brunnow, who argued that Mehemet should be limited to his pashalik of Egypt. France, on the other hand, maintained that it would be suicidal to attempt to dispossess him of Syria, Arabia and Candia, which he had conquered. No dependence, argued Soult, could be placed upon Russian observance of a treaty, nor was it likely that Nicholas would sacrifice his gains at Unkiar Skelessi by making Turkey a component part of the European system.[2] Palmerston proved the better judge.

Apart from the Eastern question, the *entente* seemed during the first half of 1840 to have taken a new lease of life. France, it is true,

[1] Guizot, F., *An Embassy to the Court of St James's in 1840*, p. 40.
[2] F.O. France, Bulwer and Granville to Palmerston, especially 27 September and 21 October 1839, nos. 76 and 326.

warned Britain that in the interests of Algiers she could allow no attack upon Tunis, and Britain renewed her enquiries about French designs upon New Zealand. In the preceding year, indeed, which Louis Bonaparte's *Des idées napoléoniennes* made memorable, "L.B." had published four striking articles on New Zealand in the *Journal des Débats*. While Britain was colonising the islands, L.B. declared, France found her colonial empire reduced to Algiers, "three decrepit islands, a stretch of burning sand at Senegal and the murderous marshes of Guiana". In reality, although the numbers of the British colonists in New Zealand were steadily increasing, the Government at home had long shown the utmost reluctance to a proclamation of sovereignty over the islands. The missions, which had flourished there since the arrival of Marsden in 1814, were anxious to preserve the natives from the disastrous effects of settlement, whether by convicts or others, and their opposition reinforced the desire of the Colonial Office to avoid a step which, it judged, would necessitate the maintenance of costly armed forces on the other side of the globe. Despite the enthusiastic advocacy of Edward Gibbon Wakefield, a move might have been still longer delayed had it not been for the suspicion aroused by the action of the French Government in supporting the formation of a colonising company. Wakefield's arguments had been powerfully aided by every rumour of French designs. In each country the advocates of colonisation were pressing their governments to take action, and in each it was by playing on sentiments of jealousy and distrust that results could most easily be obtained. The formation of the French company may be said to have decided the issue. Captain Hobson was sent to treat with the Maoris for the recognition of British sovereignty and when, shortly afterwards, a French expedition arrived, it was to find that it had been forestalled.[1] Besides the incessant soothing explanations of the King, France offered and received many proofs of friendship. Commissioners were drafting new arrangements for promoting mutual commerce. Soult frankly condemned the French missionaries for trespassing on the Protestant preserves in Tahiti.[2] Britain arbitrated between the French and Mexico. When England, as the French ambassador in London remarked, had "two wars on hand, one in China for pills [opium] and another at Naples for matches",[3] France laboured successfully to compose the latter, a sordid dispute arising out of the grant of a sulphur monopoly, to the great detriment of English trade in that commodity. The British return, which in Thiers' view would abolish fifty years of antagonism,[4] was to surrender with gracious promptness the bones of Napoleon. But in July Thiers, who in March had begun

---

[1] *C.H.B.E.* vii, pt. ii, ch. v and Harrop, *op. cit.* ch. v.
[2] F.O. France, Granville to Palmerston, 17 February 1840, no. 62.
[3] Guizot, *op. cit.* p. 85.
[4] *Ibid.* p. 101.

his ministry by breaking with ceremony to tell Granville of his wish to cement the alliance, declared to Granville's lieutenant that the alliance was at an end. "You think", added the King, "that France may be bullied into anything."[1]

This rupture of the *entente* in 1840, the results of which rather than the history concern us here, was due to the signature in London of the treaty of July 15 by the four Powers, excluding France. Mehemet, they agreed without her knowledge, should be compelled to quit Syria. On July 11, Guizot had written to Thiers that the direct overture of Mehemet to the Sultan which France was inspiring seemed to the remaining Powers to ruin the concert and to be "the complete and personal triumph of France at Alexandria and Constantinople".[2] The French were only the more infuriated by the knowledge that Palmerston had assiduously sought their co-operation and had given them warning after warning that if they stood aloof the integrity of Turkey would be upheld without them. How would Thiers revenge himself for having been proved wrong? And could Mehemet really be coerced?

For some months a general war threatened. France vastly increased her forces, and Thiers declared that she would soon have 900,000 men under arms. A sober calculation, however, suggested that only one-third of this number could be marched to the frontier,[3] while the French threats had roused a new and formidable spirit on the German side. Thiers gave place to the cooler and milder Guizot; Mehemet collapsed; and the year closed with characteristic explanations by the King. The French army, he maintained, was only big enough to guard against revolution at home and to hold Algiers, both necessary services to Europe, since Algiers had been converted from a nest of pirates into a land where all nations might colonise and grow rice and cotton.[4] Louis Philippe thus spoke in his accustomed character "as a shrewd *préfet de police* to keep the peace of the world".[5] He had indeed profited by the crisis, for Paris was now to be fortified. French critics jeered at a costly plan which would cripple their trade in order to plant two thousand guns in a rampart against a chimerical coalition of Europe.[6] But the guns commanded a capital in which revolt was no chimera, and a throne sustained by the tremors of the bourgeoisie might be safer within their range.

The new year (1841) soon showed that under Louis Philippe and Guizot the cold fit had succeeded to the hot. Even though Austria and Prussia had demanded French disarmament, the King dared to

---

[1] F.O. France, Bulwer to Palmerston, 20 and 27 July 1840, nos. 22 and 36.
[2] Guizot, *op. cit.* p. 200.
[3] F.O. France, Bulwer and Granville to Palmerston, 18 September (private and confidential) and 6 November 1840, no. 316.
[4] *Ibid.* Granville to Palmerston, 25 December 1840 (most confidential).
[5] Raikes, T., *Journal*, 27 January 1841.
[6] *Ibid.* quoting Molé, 25 March 1841.

decree a reduction from 433,000 to 344,000 men. In the spring Bulwer reported that the nation, when called on to pay the bill, had entirely recovered from its military paroxysm. The Convention of London (13 July), regulating the status of the Straits, once more ranged France beside the other Powers. There were signs, indeed, that a nearer connection with Austria and Prussia, Powers formidable to France and akin in spirit to her King, might perhaps replace or supplement the *entente*.

While shunning war, however, the French Government showed high spirit and wide vision in contemplating aggrandisement overseas. When Louis Philippe disclaimed projects for acquiring Barcelona or a Balearic island, Tunis or Morocco, he as usual overstated his case. The Pyrenees, he declared, would be impenetrable if he had his wish, for France had no need to seek further acquisitions in Europe or elsewhere.[1] But the French were pressing on with the construction of steamers; they sent a mission to Tunis; they chose men of note and ability to explore Greece, Germany and the Balkans; they sought prestige and profit on the African coast of the Red Sea, in Madagascar and in Chile; and they were already deeply interested in plans for the marriage of the queen of Spain. Although the influence of Prince Albert made for vigilance, it was certain that the substitution of Aberdeen for Palmerston at the Foreign Office (August 1841) meant that mild judgments of the French initiative would replace brisk and clear-sighted guardianship of the world-wide interests of Britain.

Nearly three years later, Palmerston denounced the Tory Government for "almost licking the dust before their French ally", with the result of making her every day more encroaching and more hostile. Neither the insult nor the hostility, however, originated with the French King or minister. Guizot could point out that the cry of the rioters of Marseilles was not more, "À bas les Anglais!" than, "À bas Guizot!"[2] and the Chambers were always ready to attack him for subservience to Britain. From the opening days of 1842 until 2 August 1844, when old Lord Cowley told him that the Pritchard affair was really serious, the inevitable clash between two unfriendly rivals had been preparing in an official atmosphere of mutual courtesy and conciliation. In 1842, for example, it was the Chamber that carried a naval increase against the Government, while the outcry of French manufacturers compelled ministers to strike at British linen and linen yarns. If France signed a treaty against the slave trade only to refuse ratification, French popular clamour against conceding any longer the right of search was genuinely to blame. The Portendik claims were sent to arbitration: new postal and fishery regulations seemed on the verge of establishment: concert in many

[1] F.O. France, Bulwer to Foreign Office, 19 November 1841 (secret and confidential).
[2] *Ibid.* Cowley to Aberdeen, 22 March 1844, no. 156.

parts of the world was maintained, and a treaty of commerce planned. A stern remonstrance by Britain against the King's scheme for a customs union with Belgium did not fail of its effect. If, in December 1842, France announced her annexation of the Marquesas Islands, her legal and moral right to do so could not be denied.

A French forward movement in the Pacific, none the less, roused the liveliest suspicions in Britain. It presented itself at a time when our commerce seemed to be declining, in conjunction with a great and successful effort to increase the commerce of France. Guizot's "grow rich" and the King's appetite for property were classic; commercial negotiations with the German States, Sardinia and Belgium were on foot; the idea of a Franco-Belgian *Zollverein* had not been abandoned; Algiers was being fiercely hammered into shape; the manifold advance in Africa continued; the Government proposed to favour colonial canes by destroying the beetroot sugar industry at a cost of forty millions; the French were clearly setting stepping-stones for an immediate advance on China. Something of this might be attributed to the need for distracting Frenchmen from the hollowness of a rule which had lost its *raison d'être*, something to the fears for the future of a dynasty now tragically robbed of its heir. But the consequent British distrust and the French dislike of Britain found vent in mutual indictments on the ground of religion. Only a few months after the tricolour had been hoisted in the Marquesas, the dominion over other groups—the Friendly Islands, Tahiti, the Sandwich Islands, the Society Islands—was in question, and in some of these regions Protestant missionaries had done much for civilisation. The French, among whom a widespread religious revival was proceeding, regarded them as heretics or as British propagandists, while the British were never more keenly anti-papal. Guizot, himself a Protestant, uttered in March 1843 a declaration of policy the apparent straightforwardness of which Palmerston could hardly have surpassed. "We have nothing to conceal", he declared, "with respect to our proceedings in the Pacific. We should gladly avail ourselves of any means of strengthening or improving our possessions of the Marquesas, but beyond this we have no views of conquest or appropriation of any kind."[1] Within three months, however, he was defending a project for further establishments in the Pacific, and expatiating to the Chamber on their advantages for whaling, commerce and the spread of the Catholic faith.[2] Tahiti was taken under French protection. Twenty-nine British residents expressed their thanks, while twelve Protestant missionaries declared their loyalty to the new *régime*, but the change produced immediate friction between the French and British consuls. At the same time it was not clear how far French ambitions went with regard to New Zealand. It was

---

[1] *Ibid.* Cowley to Aberdeen, 20 March 1843, no. 110.
[2] *Ibid.* 12 June 1843, no. 131.

certain that they envisaged strict parity with the British in China, where Britain had secured the opening of the so-called treaty ports.[1] Nearer home, French policy towards Spain, Tunis and Morocco embarrassed Aberdeen, while unofficial French sympathy with Ireland took offensive forms. Ledru Rollin, the bastard of a famous mounte-bank,[2] celebrated the fall of the Bastille by opening a subscription for O'Connell's "Repeal", and declared that a new War of Inde-pendence would find France as active as did the old.[3]

In the new year, 1844, the French Opposition journals raged against Britain, and in reply to Thiers Guizot hinted that the *entente* fell short of an intimate alliance and amounted only to an under-standing with regard to Greece and Spain.[4] To these the spring months added Texas, which both Powers were anxious to save from the United States. The energy of Stratford Canning at Constantinople, moreover, procured for both nations concessions with regard to worship. The surprise visit of Nicholas I to England, though peculiarly offensive to Louis Philippe, and believed by all his subjects to be aimed at France, produced a momentous illusion as to Aberdeen's attitude towards Turkey, but failed to change British policy or to rupture the *entente*. In August, however, the arrest of Pritchard at Tahiti[5] suddenly brought the two nations to the very verge of war. The British held that their consul had been vilified and flung into a dungeon in the tropics by a usurping tyrant, although a British warship was lying close at hand. In the French view, a scoundrel who had renounced his consulate, falsified papers and stirred up insurrection, had been lawfully and necessarily confined. The states-men on both sides must jeopardise their political future to save the nations from the consequences of their Parliaments' demands. A stage combat was suggested, mutual goodwill was shown, and finally France censured the delinquent without recalling him and voted a restricted compensation by a majority of only eight.

A visit of Louis Philippe and Guizot to London removed all traces of official disharmony and proved to Russia that the country which the Tsar had honoured with his presence would welcome the pariah king. In the eyes of many of his subjects, however, the visit seemed obsequious, and they continued to clamour for the denunciation of the agreements which gave France and Britain the right to search each other's ships for slaves. Parliament, on the other hand, felt just as strongly that no concession should be made. The limited *entente* therefore continued to bear this constant handicap. While in France British enterprise, British capital and British labour were making

---

[1] F.O. France, 3 May 1843, no. 170.
[2] *Ibid.* Normanby to Palmerston, 14 May 1848, no. 325.
[3] *Ibid.* Cowley to Aberdeen, 17 July 1843, no. 298.
[4] *Ibid.* 5 January 1844, no. 13.
[5] *C.H.B.F.P.* II, 184.

railroads, a new protectorate, that of the Gambier Islands, was enlarging the French dominion in the Pacific.

During the year 1845, the colonial rivalry of the two nations continued on the lines already clearly indicated. Joint action in matters indifferent, courtesy and conciliation between the Governments, but jealous egotism between the nations—such relations hardly promised future peace. Texas proved a common disappointment; Switzerland, where the Jesuits were active, a common anxiety. Africa, North, East and West, produced the accustomed crop of suspicions; Polynesia, the accustomed disputes about obscure islands. "It is the constant habit of French agents abroad", our ambassador at Paris complained, "to impute their failings to our intrigues", and they found credence in the highest quarters.[1] A novel field for misunderstanding appeared in Muscat, where activity, which the French declared to be purely commercial, was construed as part of a plan for establishing at Zanzibar and elsewhere public and private depots of merchandise and munitions.[2] On the other hand, a grandiose plan for establishing French commercial intercourse with China failed on a nearer view of the essential facts. Neither nation, it appeared, drank the staple export of the other, while to import Chinese silks would endanger home production, and to send French silks to China would be absurd.[3] What was painfully obvious to the British was that the French were becoming ever more able to embark on distant schemes. Since 1837 the expenditure on their navy had doubled, and had reached 120 million francs. At the same time French commerce had gradually increased to almost twice its volume in 1831. As Minister of Foreign Affairs, Guizot had already declared (30 March 1843) that his country desired a network of strong places on the strategic and trade routes of the world so that French trade and influence might be furthered, and it was in pursuance of this plan that, when Britain obtained Hong-Kong (1842), efforts were made to find for France a station which could afford her similar advantage. Moreover, as the girl-queen of Spain grew older, the question of her future husband became increasingly grave. All these dangers, however, left Aberdeen's composure undisturbed. While he filled the diplomatic corps with nonentities and revived the old sophism that colonial questions should not involve the mother-countries,[4] he produced no better policy than the dogma that the Spanish marriage was the affair of Spain, provided only that the bridegroom were not French.

The year 1846, momentous both for the Orleans dynasty and for the *entente*, found the King dreaming of control over the Spanish

[1] F.O. France, Cowley to Aberdeen, 6 June 1845, no. 237.
[2] *Ibid*. 3 March 1845, no. 103.
[3] *Ibid*. 7 November 1845, no. 441.
[4] *Ibid*. 13 and 20 October 1845, nos. 401, 413.

empire, and his minister of spreading French civilisation over the whole of Africa.[1] In February, all France seemed to receive with indescribable anxiety and interest the new commercial plans of Peel, the admiration of her Conservatives being tempered with fear lest the return of the Whigs in Britain should bring about the fall of Guizot.[2] In novel accents, the *Journal des Débats* praised "the most pure, disinterested and patriotic" motives of Britain. Both countries were soon at issue with the United States, France on account of President Polk's attack on Mexico, where she still hoped for a Bourbon monarchy, and Britain on account of his dictatorial impolicy in the Oregon dispute. For the head of a great State to accept the verdict of a party convention on a complex and long-disputed question of international law was an affront to civilisation, and "Fifty-four forty or fight" challenged the whole *entente*. Happily for the peace of the world, the Tory ministry lasted long enough to effect a settlement by negotiation. Few statesmen shared the regal calm with which Aberdeen could ignore the insults of an inferior or the Christian meekness for which foreign politics in general afford but little scope. In July, however, the dreaded Palmerston returned to office. Guizot would have been more than mortal if a return in kind for the surprise of 1840 had not proved attractive, while both King and minister could not but endeavour to stem the tide of their unpopularity by a national success. When Palmerston's policy of alliance with the Spanish Liberals to oppose French aggrandisement in and through their country was substituted for the *laissez-faire* of Aberdeen a bold stroke seemed to be invited. "Our line", Guizot could claim, "has never varied, a Bourbon on both thrones, but not the same."[3] The outcome was an inhuman deception which drove Queen Victoria, Palmerston and the British public into fury. On August 24, Normanby, who had brought new vigour into the embassy at Paris, was received with the utmost distinction by Louis Philippe, who at once established him on the intimate footing of an *ambassadeur de famille*. On August 28, he recorded long conversations with both King and minister on the marriage of the queen of Spain. On September 3, he was already hurrying back to London to discuss the *coup d'état* by which the queen herself was to marry a Bourbon reputed impotent, while her sister and heir-apparent espoused the French King's son.

Both at the moment and in the long run, the foul stroke failed to bring the expected advantage. To the French public, the Spanish marriages might well seem a Bourbon job rather than a national triumph, and though they had nicknamed Louis Philippe "the Englishman", they showed him no special gratitude for thus shaking off the bonds of Britain. Queen Victoria, with Prince Albert's aid,

[1] F.O. France, 6 March 1846, no. 116.
[2] *Ibid*. 6 February 1846 (private and confidential).
[3] Cf. *Ibid*. Normanby to Palmerston, 1 September 1846, no. 14.

sent "a tickler" to the King, while the strength of the British protest
to Spain astonished the absolutist Powers.[1] When these, at Cracow,
abolished the last vestige of independent Poland, France could
extract no more than a futile British protest, while her policy of
recognising the Bey of Tunis as independent was foiled by Britain,
who thus won the gratitude of the Turk at her expense.[2]

The history of 1847, none the less, upheld the truth of Palmerston's
belief that the common interests of France and Britain would dissipate
all ordinary clouds. Both were preoccupied with distress at home, and
Britain with an acute commercial crisis, while in the spring Paris
had to assist no less than 350,000 persons.[3] In Spain, French policy
seemed to provide "a series of surprises founded on deception", but
in Portugal the two Powers worked in concert. Although British
representatives opposed French at Madrid, at Athens, in South
America and even in Paris, much quiet co-operation was compelled
by the logic of facts. French and British admirals on the African
station uniting to put down human sacrifices formed a fitting counterpart to French and British statesmen uniting to keep Switzerland at
peace. Both there, where the federal forces proved strong enough
to suppress the separatist Sonderbund and to drive out the Jesuits,
as well as in Italy, where the new nationalism challenged the old
régime, Palmerston and his Liberalism represented the real mind of
France.

For in 1847 it had become abundantly clear that France had another
mind than that of Guizot. To Normanby, the annual celebration of
the three glorious days of July seemed to be a popular fête without
any popular feeling, a routine rejoicing at the source of perpetual
disappointment.[4] While railways and free trade had already dispelled
much anti-British prejudice, the unfulfilled promises of local railroads
by official candidates at the French elections had paved the way for
"a revolution of contempt". In the autumn, when it seemed impossible
to conceive any Government more unpopular,[5] apathy gave place
to a general and spontaneous ebullition. Banquets were held in
honour of Reform, the purification of the Chambers from corrupt
functionaries being deemed more urgent than the extension of the
franchise. At the close of the year, moreover, the King's speech from
the throne made it impossible for the Opposition to ascribe the guilt
of reaction to his ministers and not to him.

When 1848 dawned, Louis Philippe still ruled by fear—fear of
the Communards, which had caused vast withdrawals from the
Savings-Bank in Paris, and such fear of the Crown as a numerous
and well-placed army might inspire. At the end of January, the

[1] F.O. France, 2 October 1846, no. 36.
[2] Ibid. 27 November 1846, no. 86.
[3] Ibid. 9 April 1847, no. 113.
[4] Ibid. 2 August 1847 (private and confidential).
[5] Ibid. 19 November 1847, no. 325.

Sicilians were known to be demanding the constitution of 1812, while the French Government was determined to prevent the banquets and to refuse all prospective engagements as to Reform. It had never been intended, said the Minister of Justice, to confer the right of political discussion upon Frenchmen.[1] The Opposition, defeated in the Chamber by a majority which fell from 110 to 33, summoned the people to a peaceful demonstration, but significantly and illegally directed the National Guards to fall in according to their legions.

Such was the situation which in the last fortnight of February brought about an exception to the rule that French revolutions do not happen in the winter.[2] Although many English residents had quitted a capital to which discontented reformers had been streaming from the provinces, and which contained an ever-dangerous mob, the constitutionalism of both Government and Opposition encouraged expectations of a peaceful issue. When Guizot resigned, the funds rose, the barricades were torn down, Paris was illuminated, and crowds cheered Thiers and his associates in the streets. But a single shot provoked a volley from the troops, and in the resulting storm the Orleans monarchy collapsed.[3] On February 24, a provisional government, mainly Republican, had generated itself, but the anarchy in Paris was complete. The mob found arms in abundance at Fort Vincennes, and the Communards burned the King's residence at Neuilly.

Happily for France and for the world, the Provisional Government included Lamartine, who rose to the very height of the occasion. For sixty hours he defied an infuriated rabble which was half drunk and which had 12,000 muskets in its hands. At a moment when the Communards, though few in number, might by their union and desperation have shattered the framework of society, and when a revolutionary government might have gambled upon foreign war, Lamartine avoided alike the methods of 1792 and of 1918. While marauders were shot by dozens, the death penalty for political offences was abolished. The tricolour was upheld against the red flag; religion was respected; the interest on government stock was promptly paid; the Orleans fortunes remained inviolate. While he hoped that the hours of work might be reduced from eleven to ten by mutual agreement, Lamartine denounced the *organisation de travail* as nonsense. Slavery was abolished, and a National Assembly convoked in which Algiers was to be represented. Desiring above all things the British alliance, he repudiated connection with the Chartists or with the disloyal Irish. "I can never hear of Irish nationality", he declared, "except as identical with English."[4] Towards Italy, now in the

---

[1] F.O. France, 10 February 1848, no. 70 *et passim*.
[2] Cf. Heine, *op. cit.* VIII, 276.
[3] F.O. France, Normanby to Palmerston, 24 February 1848, no. 92.
[4] *Ibid.* 15 March 1848, no. 162.

throes of war and revolution, he shaped his policy to conform to that of Britain.

It could not indeed be supposed that Lamartine's energy and ascendancy would endure for long; or that France would for long abandon her colonial and commercial rivalry with Britain. In May the Minister of Agriculture and Commerce, known as a former proprietor of hells and brothels,[1] declared to the National Assembly that the events of February had broken the English alliance for ever. As the Government weakened and the social situation grew swiftly worse, the danger of some rash stroke increased. Paris trembled before the hordes who flocked to the National Workshops, including, it was said, 20,000 liberated convicts. The Minister of Agriculture proposed agricultural colleges and settlements as a panacea.[2] When the provinces rose against taxation, and Paris was placed in a state of siege, rumours of foreign instigation became rife, and men talked of an alliance between Britain and Russia to paralyse France by civil war. In the autumn, the Prefect of Police wished to close the clubs and prohibit banquets. To influence the elections, the Government once kept back the morning posts for six hours, fearing lest press attacks on themselves should arrive before their refutations in the evening papers.[3] Under manhood suffrage, the constituency of the Seine gave Lamartine no more than 4000 votes. In her despair and hatred of the Republic, France turned to Louis Bonaparte. "History affords no parallel", wrote Normanby, "to this spectacle of all the eminent men of all former political parties uniting in support of a man whom no one of them would personally have selected."[4] The new President, however, represented all parties in desiring the good-will of Britain.

The effect of the French convulsions of 1848 therefore had been to re-establish an *entente* which brought her much valuable guidance before the close of that tormented year. Italy, Germany, Denmark, the Danubian principalities—all invited foreign intervention, but towards all the cautious policy of Palmerston gave a lead to France. A sympathetic watching of the attempts of other populations to be free, timely remembrance that among the Italians "there was no feeling so dominant as the desire to owe their independence to themselves alone",[5] joint mediation if and when their failure seemed inevitable—such were the methods by which Britain helped France to recover. The colonial and commercial rivalries were lulled, though in France free trade principles were losing ground. It was recognised that her merchant ships were too costly to compete with the British on equal terms. The new President, a prisoner in France from 1840

---

[1] *Ibid.* 14 May 1848, no. 325.
[2] *Ibid.* 18 June 1848, no. 399.
[3] *Ibid.* 10 December 1848, no. 777.
[4] *Ibid.* 12 December 1848, no. 778.
[5] *Ibid.* 3 May 1848, no. 292.

to 1846, came from his refuge in London full of determination to make his country great and prosperous by developing the concert with Britain. Would he succeed in establishing his power? And could his power prevent the latent hostility between the rivals from breaking forth anew? The years 1848 to 1870 were destined to supply the answer.

CHAPTER VIII

COLONIAL PROBLEMS AND COLONIAL POLICY, 1815-1837

To the Britain of 1815 peace was all important and consequently international affairs hold the centre of the stage after the close of the great wars. Fortunately some of her ablest statesmen held the seals of the Foreign Office from 1815 to 1837 and did their work so well that the country enjoyed peace for nearly forty years. This long period of external tranquillity enabled Britain to deal with arrears in the field of political reform and to make progress towards the settlement of important social and economic questions. While foreign and domestic problems thus occupied British statesmen, those pertaining to the overseas empire tended to fall into the background. Not until the year Queen Victoria ascended the throne did the two rebellions in the Canadas compel serious attention to the question of colonial relations.

But this lack of public interest does not mean that nothing of importance happened in the colonies and in the relations between them and Britain. On the contrary, the years 1815-37 were for the Empire eventful and formative years. They witnessed a steady growth of the settlement colonies, the adoption of a new emigration policy, the undermining of the economic bases of the old imperial system, the impact of English humanitarianism upon the colonies and colonial frontier policy, the gradual relinquishment by Downing Street of detailed supervision of local affairs in the more important dependencies, the adoption of improvements in their administrative machinery, and the formulation of new theories concerning colonial government. In examining these changes, their causes will be asked; and for answer we must turn to the history of the United Kingdom at this time, for without a knowledge of this, British imperial history cannot be understood.

The Tory government of 1815 had a large majority, facing an Opposition that was weak and divided. But by 1830 the Tories lost public confidence and were succeeded by the Whigs, who in 1832 passed the great Reform Bill. Changes and reforms had, however, been inaugurated by the Tories. The liberal wing of that party, Canning, Huskisson and Peel, came into control in 1822 and there followed Peel's administrative reforms—an improved criminal code and an effective police system, Huskisson's modifications of customs and trade regulations and Canning's liberal foreign policy. Moreover, in 1828 and 1829 the privileged position of the Established Church was impaired by the repeal of the Test and Corporation Acts and the admission of Roman Catholics to the House of Commons. Hence, while the Tories were yet in power, the nation shook off fear and complacency and began to attack the citadels of privilege. The Reform Bill sapped the most towering of these—the position of the landed aristocracy.

The first reformed Parliament, elected in 1832, contained a small but potent leaven of reformers. They launched strong and successful attacks on the system of sinecures, the high cost of the imperial government, the trading monopoly of the East India Company, and the Elizabethan Poor Law. The great Act which abolished slavery in the British Empire was in the main the result of the effective pressure exerted by the non-partisan Anti-Slavery Society; and party lines were broken in the fight over the important Factory Act of 1833. The Act which created a supreme court for the British Empire, the Judicial Committee of the Privy Council, passed without debate.[1] The impulse towards reform was national rather than party.

The shift in the balance of political power effected by the Reform Bill and the results of several other reform measures greatly influenced the Empire and imperial policy; but other factors must be appreciated before the latter can be understood, particularly the general social and economic condition of Britain and the influence of the industrial and commercial classes and of the humanitarians. The year 1815 brought peace abroad, but not at home. The demobilisation of the army and the navy, the collapse of the war industries, and the effects of the technological changes, later labelled the Industrial Revolution, resulted in the largest unemployment problem that England had yet faced. Wages and prices of manufactured articles went down, while the price of corn was kept high by a protective tariff. There were riots and demonstrations which the Government met by calling out the military and by repressive legislation. After 1820 economic conditions improved, but not much. In 1825, a Select Committee sent a questionnaire to every parish in England containing the query whether it was customary for married labourers with children to receive aid from the poor rates. The overwhelming majority replied in the affirmative.[2] Wages and conditions of labour were bad in England, worse in Scotland and worse still in Ireland, partly owing to the great increase in population which had taken place since 1750. Population had become "redundant". The gloomy prophecy of Malthus, that the growth of the population would outrun that of the food supply, seemed verified. The poor rates were high; and the Government began to look upon the increased population as a menace instead of as a source of strength. The poor

---

[1] 3 and 4 Wm. IV, cap. 41. An Act for the better Administration of Justice in His Majesty's Privy Council.
[2] *Parl. Pap.* 1825, IV (334).

and the unemployed of Britain were then willing to migrate despite the length and the dangers of the voyages to the colonies; and the Government encouraged them to go.[1] It was a great change of national policy, for since 1660 emigration had been officially discouraged and the eighteenth-century colonies had been peopled from non-English sources.

The Industrial Revolution created on the one hand unemployment and an industrial proletariat and on the other increased wealth in the hands of a few. There arose a class of enterprising, hard-headed promoters, who had scant reverence for the old as such—men whose aim was more business. Their economic and political influence grew apace. They regarded the Empire from a profit and loss point of view; and they found in the United States an important source for cotton and an excellent market for manufactured goods. Developed, populous, and civilised communities were the best markets; the resources of Africa and of the Pacific Islands were little known. Hence the new capitalists favoured relaxing the old Acts of Trade and Navigation, and they looked coolly upon colonial ventures which might increase the burden borne by British taxpayers.

Strangely mixed with business sentiment in early nineteenth-century Britain was the humanitarian. Some humanitarians were business men and Christians, like the Buxtons and the Whitbreads; others were business men and not Christians, like Robert Owen; still others were Christians and not business men, like William Wilberforce and Lord Ashley. Some humanitarians were conservative, others were radical in politics. Their inspiration came from many sources, but the most important was the Bible. The majority of them were deeply moved by the Christian emphasis on the fatherhood of God and the brotherhood of man and by the admonition to go forth and preach the gospel to all nations. Humanitarianism was then a tremendous force in British social and political life; and by its championship of slaves and aborigines it profoundly affected the course of British imperial history.

Moreover, the relative inefficiency of the governmental machinery and the often disorganised state of the national finances contributed to accelerate the outflow of emigrants. The picture drawn by Sir Robert Peel in 1841, while in opposition, of the Chancellor of the Exchequer sitting by a pool of "bottomless deficiency fishing for a budget", fits several of those who held that position in the years 1815-37. For eleven of those years the national budget showed a deficit.[2]

Like the Empire to-day, the Empire in 1815 was scattered and

[1] Buer, M. C., *Health, Wealth, and Population in the Early Days of the Industrial Revolution*; Carruthers, W. A., *Emigration from the British Isles*, pp. 32–56; Cowan, Helen, *British Emigration to British North America*, pp. 43–64.
[2] Knowles, L. C. A., *The Economic Development of the British Overseas Empire*, 2nd ed. i, 96.

diversified, but it was small in comparison. None of the colonies possessed a large European population or much economic strength. The Empire was based on sea power and existed for the benefit of trade. These two considerations decided which of the occupied territories should be kept after the Napoleonic wars. Of the conquests made since 1793, Heligoland, Malta, the Ionian Islands, the Cape, Mauritius, the Seychelles, Ceylon, three provinces of Dutch Guiana, St Lucia, Tobago and Trinidad were retained. Two of these, the Cape and Guiana, had hinterlands, but the former was then valued only as a half-way station to India and the latter neither then nor later has been important for European colonisation.

The seven colonies of British North America had a total population of about 600,000. More than half of these were found in Lower Canada, then as now mainly French in population, language and custom. Upper Canada had about 80,000 white settlers, the majority of whom were of British origin, with the Loyalist refugees who had come from the United States after the Revolution and their descendants dominant in the political and social life of the province. Their devotion to the British Crown had been twice tested, in the war of American Independence and in that of 1812–14, but since Upper Canada then attracted other Americans, fear was entertained that the new arrivals might draw the province into the orbit of the United States.[1] North and west of the Great Lakes lay a vast region where roamed large herds of buffalo, some Indians, and a few trappers and fur traders. Here Britain had claims to an immense area, but its boundaries were still undefined and its economic significance as yet slight.

The West Indian colonies had increased in number and diversity during the Revolutionary and Napoleonic wars. All were plantation colonies whose population of about one million was overwhelmingly slave. The whites formed approximately one-tenth of the total— among these the British dominated, though Dutch, French and Spanish planters and traders remained in the colonies recently acquired, and Bermuda and the Bahamas had a strong American Loyalist element. The West Indies had been, and in 1815 still were, very important in the economy of the Empire, but their prosperity and importance were on the wane.

On the African side of the South Atlantic, the island of St Helena, which for a century and a half had been a port of call for the ships of the East India Company, had importance thrust upon it in 1815 by becoming the prison for Napoleon. Sierra Leone, founded as a place of refuge for liberated negroes, competed in wretchedness with the older British trading stations on the shores of the Gulf of Guinea. With the cessation of the slave trade in 1808 their importance had practically vanished. All had an unsavoury reputation as the "white

<hr>

[1] *C.H.B.E.* vi, 225, 254.

man's grave". At the Cape, the white population of 35,000 were mainly of Dutch origin with an important admixture of French Huguenot blood, and the majority of the whites found in Mauritius and the Seychelles were French. On the other hand, the Australian settlements were exclusively British, and all of them, New South Wales, Van Diemen's Land (later Tasmania), and Norfolk Island, were prison camps; although in New South Wales an increasing number of free immigrants arrived yearly. Ceylon, captured from the Dutch, and the small stations, Penang, the Province Wellesley, and Bencoolen, which the Company held east of the Bay of Bengal, had few European inhabitants. In India the British controlled the north-east and some inland territories in the southern section of the peninsula, and their conquest of the whole had become a matter of "manifest destiny". Nearer home Britain held Heligoland, Gibraltar, Malta and the Ionian Islands. These were all useful for the maintenance of her naval supremacy, but unimportant for trade or settlement.

At the peace negotiations with France, Lord Castlereagh and his colleagues had shown great moderation. They appreciated the folly of compelling the foe to accept crushing terms. So trading stations in India, islands in the West Indies, and the fishery rights off Newfoundland were restored to France. Criticised in the House of Commons for the lenient peace terms, Castlereagh replied loftily that the object of a peace treaty was peace and that France deprived of colonies and natural resources would certainly plot revenge. She should be left with a balanced empire.[1] The sound common sense of this none will deny. On the other hand, it is also clear that Castlereagh secured for Britain all that he and the British Government thought Britain needed. The new possessions safeguarded her naval power in the North Sea and in the Mediterranean and the sea route to India. Moreover, they assured her a plentiful supply of sugar. Here again Castlereagh thought in terms of a balanced empire—based on trade, not on colonisation. This view he shared with both contemporaries and successors. To Grey, Peel and Wellington, Britain's colonies constituted an honourable obligation and were an asset only in so far as they aided trade. Consequently those statesmen showed no desire to extend the imperial boundaries. Sir Stamford Raffles' bold step in acquiring Singapore, which he persuaded the East India Company to purchase from the Sultan of Johore, 1819, was disapproved, but not re-traced;[2] the Anglo-Dutch treaty of 1824 gave Malacca to Britain in exchange for Bencoolen, and the Dutch predominance was recognised in the other occupied islands of the East Indian

---

[1] Speech in the House of Commons, 29 June 1814: Hansard, xxviii, 460–4. See also speech by Lord Liverpool in the House of Lords, 28 June 1814: *Ibid.* xxviii, 371.
[2] Coupland, R., *Raffles*, pp. 97–9; Egerton, H. E., *Sir Stamford Raffles*, pp. 190–5. See chapter xvi.

Archipelago.[1] But opportunities to gain control over Tahiti and other islands in the Pacific were neglected;[2] and in the 'twenties Britain considered giving up her posts in Western Africa.[3]

What Britain has Britain holds might be an appropriate description of her frontier policy. She would not surrender to the state of Maine land in dispute with New Brunswick, the resistance was prompt and effective;[4] and fear that France might seize Western Australia caused her in 1829 to make sure of her title to the entire island continent.[5] Threats to the security of existing frontiers led to some small annexations in South Africa and to larger ones in India and Burma.[6] But apart from these, the new acquisitions were limited to the island groups of Ascension and Tristan da Cunha so as to insure against possible efforts to rescue Napoleon, Bathurst and McCarthy's island in Western Africa, and the Falkland Islands.[7] The last named were apparently seized because of their importance for whaling—the oil from the whale was superior to that from the palm as lubricant for the machines of Manchester.

The reasons for the non-expansionist policy of the British Government at a time when opportunities, judged by the elastic moral code of imperialism, were easy and attractive, may be briefly summarised as the absence of foreign rivals; a lack of interest on the part of merchants and industrialists in territorial expansion; and the championing of the rights of natives by the humanitarians. The two latter reasons may be further elaborated.

When Britain in 1816 temporarily destroyed the naval power of the Barbary States, the Mediterranean was made safer for commerce, and among the beneficiaries the British traders were, of course, not the least. The republics in Latin America at this time provided new fields for trade and new markets for British goods. Trade with the United States expanded greatly in the period. Cotton from the southern states of the American Union drove West and East Indian cotton out of the English market; and at the same time the United States proved an excellent customer for British iron and steel products. Huskisson's trade and tariff policies stimulated trade with the continent of Europe. In two regions, however, West Africa and the Far East, the trading interests urged advances or opposed withdrawals. In the former, the anti-slavery interests supported the traders in asking Government aid

---

[1] Treaty signed in London, 17 March 1824: *British and Foreign State Papers*, 1823–24, XI, 200–1.

[2] Scholefield, G. H., *The Pacific, Its Past and Future*, pp. 9–10, 35.

[3] Lucas, C. P., *A Historical Geography of the British Colonies: West Africa*, pp. 119–20. See Chapter XIX.

[4] Moore, John Bassett, *History and Digest of the International Arbitrations to which the United States has been a Party*, I, chap. IV.

[5] *C.H.B.E.* VII, pt. I, 129–31.

[6] Lucas, C. P., *Historical Geography: South and East Africa*, pp. 107–62; Roberts, P. E., *A Historical Geography of the British Dependencies: India*, Part I, pp. 276–99.

[7] Goebel, Julius, *The Struggle for the Falkland Islands*, chap. IX. See Chapter XIV.

for exploring the interior. The "Saints" helped the merchants on the ground that if Africa could be opened to legitimate trade, the illicit trade in slaves would come to an end. And when the British Government in 1827 decided to withdraw from the Gold Coast, the step was opposed by the traders who agreed to administer the posts with an annual subsidy from the Government.[1] In the Far East the abolition of the trading monopoly of the East India Company in China meant that henceforth the British Government must protect British trade in that country. Friction soon developed, and before long the stage was set for the first Anglo-Chinese war.[2]

From the time of their beginnings in the eighteenth century, the British missionary societies had chosen fields of work outside the Empire. They were especially active in the South Pacific; and John Williams, who was perhaps the greatest among the British missionaries in that field, asked in 1837 for support on the ground that the missionaries found "new havens...for our fleet; new channels are opened for our commerce; and the friends of our country are everywhere multiplied".[3] That British influence was spread by missionaries cannot be gainsaid, but as true ministers of the Gospel they soon arrayed themselves in opposition to the traders who debauched and the colonists who wished to despoil the Pacific islanders. The conflict between the missions and the trading and colonising interests came to a head in New Zealand. The missionaries wished that a British protectorate should be established over the islands without opening them to colonisation.[4] Thereby they earned the hatred of Wakefield and his associates. The missionaries lost, but the provisions in the Treaty of Waitangi which aimed at safeguarding the rights of the Maori to the land were due to their influence.[5]

Similarly at the Cape they championed the cause of the natives and checked political expansion. They aided the Griquas to organise something resembling states beyond the frontiers of Cape Colony, and they opposed colonial encroachment upon native territory. An important temporary success, scored by them in 1835, when Sir Benjamin D'Urban, Governor at the Cape, received orders from home to abandon the Queen Adelaide territory seized in a Kaffir war,[6] indicates perhaps the high-water mark of missionary influence at the

[1] Buxton, Charles, *Memoirs of Sir Thomas Fowell Buxton*, 5th ed. pp. 369–71; Ellis, A. B., *A History of the Gold Coast of West Africa*, pp. 192–3. See chapter XIX.

[2] *C.H.B.F.P.* II, 215–19.

[3] Williams, John, *A Narrative of Missionary Enterprises in the South Sea Islands*, pp. 587–8.

[4] Marsden, Samuel, *The Letters and Journals of*, ed. by John Rawson Elder, pp. 497–508; Ramsden, Eric, *Marsden and the Missions*, pp. 66–74. See also evidence of J. Beecham of the Wesleyan Missionary Society, and of Dandeson Coates of the Church Missionary Society before Select Committee on State of New Zealand, 14 and 15 May 1838: *Parl. Pap.* 1837–38, XXI, No. 680, pp. 243, 294.

[5] *C.H.B.E.* VII, pt. II, 55.

[6] *C.H.B.E.* VIII, 313–14. For extracts from the famous despatch, Glenelg to D'Urban, 26 December 1835, see Bell, K. N. and Morrell, W. P., *Select Documents on British Colonial Policy, 1830–1860*, pp. 463–77.

Colonial Office. The then Colonial Secretary, Lord Glenelg, a vice-president of the Church Missionary Society, and several of his subordinates, notably James Stephen and Henry Taylor, were closely identified with missionary and humanitarian movements. Thomas, later Sir Thomas, Fowell Buxton, the abolitionist, led the friends of the aborigines in the House of Commons; he presided over the Select Committee which in 1835–37 studied the native question within and on the borders of the Empire, and was also a founder of the Aborigines Protection Society which from time to time has been a thorn in the flesh of enthusiastic empire builders. The missionary ideal of a British trusteeship for the natives may have been visionary, yet it was a noble one.

From the standpoint of geographical expansion, the imperial policy of these years may be described as one of lost opportunities, but within the ring fence of existing boundaries settlements were pushed forward, the wilderness subdued, and population grew rapidly. In British North America population increased from about 600,000 to more than 1,500,000 in the twenty-two years under discussion. Prince Edward Island showed the smallest rate of increase and Upper Canada the largest—nearly fourfold. At the Cape the white population approximately doubled; in Australia the number of colonies grew from two to four and the population from about 15,000 to about 150,000.[1] In Lower Canada and at the Cape a goodly share of the increase was due to natural causes, but elsewhere immigration from the British Isles helps to explain the rapid growth. Exclusive of transported convicts, nearly 400,000 men, women and children left the British Isles in these years to seek new homes in British colonies. When the period opened emigration was discouraged; at its close the Government was aiding and subsidising emigrants on a large scale.[2] The primary reasons for this change of policy were unemployment and distress at home; among the secondary may be mentioned the availability of land in the colonies as a means for rewarding naval, military, or political services, and the efforts of promoters of emigration, among whom Wakefield holds the first place.

Emigration had been prohibited during the war on the ground that a large population meant more man power. After the war, the Government first cautiously made land grants to discharged officers and privates and to Highlanders in distress, then repealed the anti-emigration laws, and in 1819 Parliament voted £50,000 for sending about 5000 British settlers to the eastern districts of the Cape Colony as a means of strengthening this frontier against the Kaffirs.[3] Two years earlier a Select Committee on the Poor Law had recommended

[1] These figures are based on estimates.
[2] Carruthers, pp. 60–112, 305. The statistics for emigration are incomplete. Carruthers gives those based on customs returns, but they do not include the South African settlers of 1820, nor any for Australia until 1825.
[3] See Edwards, I. E., *The 1820 Settlers in South Africa. A Study in British Colonial Policy.*

"that all obstacles to seeking employment wherever it can be found, even out of the realm, should be removed; and every facility that is reasonable afforded to those who may wish to resort to some of our colonies".[1] And in the same year that Parliament first appropriated money for sending settlers to the Cape, the Poor Law Committee repeated the earlier recommendation and referred pointedly to the unoccupied land in the colonies where "the labour of man, assisted by a genial and healthy climate, would produce an early and abundant return".[2] But the Tory government of that day was slow to adopt the suggestion, the Cape experiment proved more costly than had been anticipated, and the Colonial Secretary, Lord Bathurst, was anxious to keep colonial expenditure down.[3] However, as we have seen, in 1822, new men began to give new directions to various policies, and Robert, later Sir Robert, Wilmot Horton became Parliamentary Under-Secretary of State for the Colonies.[4] He was an enthusiastic champion of emigration as a remedy for poverty, low wages, and unemployment. Looking upon the colonies as an integral part of the mother country, with identical interests, he judged that the removal of the redundant population of the latter to the waste lands of the former would help to adjust the available capital and labour to wages, and cement and make perpetual the union between Britain and her colonies.[5] So persuasive was he that Parliament subsidised the emigration of paupers from Ireland and England by grants of £15,000 in 1823, £30,000 in 1825, and £20,480 in 1827. The majority of these emigrants were sent to Upper Canada.[6] The grants were large, if one considers the state of the budget, but they had no perceptible effect upon the problems of poverty and unemployment which remained as pressing as ever. Resort was then had to the use of colonial lands for the purpose of financing a transfer of people. In 1826 more liberal regulations were adopted for the granting of land to individual settlers;[7] and the Canada Land Company, chartered in that year, obtained nearly 2,500,000 acres in Upper Canada at a low price on condition that roads should be built, other improvements made, and settlers brought out. Similar companies were later organised to operate in Lower Canada and in Australia, and Thomas Peel and his associates obtained 1,000,000 acres for their colony of Western Australia.[8]

[1] Quoted by Madgwick, R. B., *Immigration into Eastern Australia*, p. 72.   [2] *Ibid.* p. 73.
[3] A report of the Navy Transport Department of 30 January 1821 shows that down to that time £86,760 had been spent on transporting and victualling the settlers at the Cape: *Parl. Pap.* 1821, xiv, No. 45.
[4] At first Robert John Wilmot; the name Horton, from his wife's father, was added in 1823. After that he was usually spoken of as Wilmot Horton. He was knighted in 1831.
[5] Horton, Robert Wilmot, *An Inquiry into the Causes and Remedies of Pauperism*. First Series, pp. 18, 25, 51–3, 65–6.   [6] Cowan, chaps. v and vii.
[7] For regulations of 1826 see C.O. 325/26; *Documents Relating to the Constitutional History of Canada*, ed. by A. G. Doughty and Norah Story, pp. 348–50; Madgwick, 54–5.
[8] *Lord Durham's Report*, ed. by C. P. Lucas, iii, 45, 59; Roberts, S. H., *History of Australian Land Settlement*, pp. 45–70.

But to Edward Gibbon Wakefield falls the honour of persuading the Government to inaugurate a constructive land and emigration policy which combined and improved upon the principles of Horton and of the land companies. Wakefield originated a plan of systematic colonisation which included using the proceeds from the sale of land in the colonies as a fund to aid emigration. In 1829 he published *A Letter from Sydney*, in which the evils resulting from the haphazard methods of granting land and promoting colonisation are clearly shown. With the organisation in 1830 of the Colonisation Society a "pressure group" was formed to spread the new doctrine. Wakefield's scheme of colonisation differed from that of Horton in its emphasis upon selecting the prospective colonists with the view of establishing a well-balanced colonial society—a new England at the very outset. He was more interested in creating nuclei for states than in integrating the Empire. This plan for an emigration policy was approved by the Whig government of Earl Grey, in which Lords Goderich and Howick held respectively the posts of Colonial Secretary and Parliamentary Under-Secretary. The new regulations dealing with the disposal of colonial lands, framed in 1831, embodied the Wakefield principles of sale at a fixed upset price, the utilisation of the funds thus obtained to aid emigrants, and the careful selection of emigrants.[1] The "shovelling out" of paupers was to be discontinued. But old habits die hard, and among the women sent to Australia as assisted emigrants, 1832 –35, were many who were morally undesirable.[2] And parts of the report of the Select Committee on the Disposal of Lands in the Colonies, 1836, read as if they had been lifted from a pamphlet by Horton.[3]

Early in the 'thirties Wakefield organised a company for the purpose of founding a colony in South Australia. His plan met with opposition at the Colonial Office because the legal adviser at that office, James Stephen, regarded it as unsound and unworkable. Wakefield then modified his plan and secured approval for it by an Act of Parliament, which constituted a departure from the old method of founding colonies by royal charter. His colony of South Australia dates from 1836.[4]

Changes had taken place in the relations between Britain and her dependencies since the successful revolt of the thirteen American

[1] C.O. 325/26. The Wakefield theory is discussed by Roberts, pp. 73–93. Madgwick, pp. 75–83, presents a good analysis and comparison between the theory o f Wakefield and the theories of his predecessors.

[2] Madgwick, pp. 96–111.

[3] The report emphasised that in all matters connected with emigration the interests of Britain and of the colonies were identical and that the transfer of superabundant labour from Britain to the colonies would open new channels of industry and commerce and increase the prosperity of the United Empire: *Parl. Pap.* 1836, xi (512), p. v.

[4] The story of this controversy is told by Mills, R. C., *The Colonization of Australia, 1829–1842*, pp. 218–58; and by Price, A. G., *The Foundation and Settlement of South Australia*. The views of Stephen are summarised by Hall, Henry L., *The Colonial Office: A History*, pp. 159–64.

colonies; but the two basic principles of the old colonial system remained unaltered—the political power of the Imperial Government was supreme and the economic interests of the colonies were subordinated to those of the mother country. Parliament recognised only a few self-imposed limits on its right to legislate for the entire Empire; the Crown refused to admit that the colonists might control or supervise executive action; and the old regulations concerning trade and navigation were technically still in force. In theory this system of dependence and centralised control remained in operation until after Queen Victoria had ascended the throne, but actually it had been greatly modified long before, and an attempt may now be made to trace the course of change.

Even in 1815 the British Empire served as an excellent illustration of "unity in diversity". The supremacy of the Imperial Parliament was considered absolute. In the colonies founded by English immigrants the Common Law of England prevailed, while ceded and conquered colonies usually retained their old laws and institutions. These colonies were under the immediate control of the Crown which might legislate without specific Parliamentary sanction until a colonial legislature had been established.[1] From the standpoint of the constitutional lawyer this arrangement might seem logical and even simple, but in actual practice it presented many and puzzling variations. For instance, in New South Wales, which had become a settlement colony, the Governor promulgated ordinances without Parliamentary sanction until the passage of the Judicature Act of 1823. The legislative power of the Crown was supposedly non-existent in colonies with legislatures of their own, but the Crown continued to control legislation through the appointed legislative council, the Governor, and the reviewing and veto power over colonial laws. In several of the colonies with legislatures of their own, the legislative and executive councils were identical.[2] The Governor could therefore initiate legislation and veto laws not to his liking or reserve them for the signification of His Majesty's pleasure. A Colonial Act, even though approved by the Governor, might be disallowed if it were contrary to the law of England or violated the principles of the regulations governing trade and navigation. The colonies occasionally nullified the reviewing power by passing annual laws or by not sending the Acts home. These methods of circumventing imperial regulations worked, however, for only short periods. Ordinarily all colonial laws were carefully

---

[1] These principles had been clearly stated by Lord Mansfield, 1775, in Chapman *vs.* Hall. See Clementi, Sir Cecil, *A Constitutional History of British Guiana*, Appendix S. For a convenient summary of the constitutional law of the British colonies at this time see Clarke, Charles, *A Summary of Colonial Law*, pp. 3–25. See also speech by Brougham in House of Commons, 23 March 1819: *Hansard*, xxxix, 1138; and Speech by Sir James Mackintosh, House of Commons, 18 July 1822: Hansard, New Series, vii, 1701–5.

[2] Not until 1832 were the two councils separated in New Brunswick, and in Nova Scotia in 1837. See Martin, Chester, *Empire and Commonwealth*, pp. 163, 173 and Lucas, *Lord Durham's Report*, i, 83–84.

scrutinised and occasionally some were disallowed.[1] The whole system was unpopular in the colonies and often resulted in hardship. Even with the best will and intention on the part of the Colonial Office, the slow means of communication and the lack of co-operation between the departments which had to be consulted on colonial laws meant delayed decisions and confused judgments.

Some of the West Indian colonies had elective Assemblies dating from the first half of the seventeenth century. Those of the Canadas originated with the Constitutional Act of 1791. That these differed in point of view and in legislative practice was only natural. But the variations in institutions found among the colonies with representative government were slight in comparison with those of the Crown colonies. Except the Australian, which as a Government venture were Crown colonies, these colonies had been acquired at different times and from various countries, and the terms of capitulation or cession had varied. Consequently, Lower Canada and St Lucia had the old French law antedating the Revolution and the Code Napoléon; Mauritius had the old French criminal law and in other fields the Code Napoléon; British Guiana, the Cape and Ceylon kept the Roman Dutch Law, changed to some extent by the Batavian Republic; Trinidad retained the law of Spain; Malta preserved a Maltese Code; Heligoland had Danish law; and British India had no unified legal system. In most of the colonies, except Malta and Heligoland, the laws of the old home lands had been altered in order to fit local conditions before they passed under British rule; after that they might be changed by the King in Council unless specific laws or rights had been guaranteed by treaty.[2]

How the division of the legislative power in the colonies between Parliament and Crown worked may be seen by comparing the introduction of constitutional government in New South Wales with its introduction at the Cape. When it was realised that the former was a settlement colony, Parliament in 1823 passed an Act which created a supreme court and a Council, while the Cape, a conquered and ceded colony, received these institutions from the Crown by executive instrument. Ordinarily Parliament did not interfere in colonial matters, but when aroused it freely asserted its absolute supremacy. Thus the ancient prerogative of the Crown to found colonies by charter was overridden when Parliament in 1834 passed an Act for the founding of South Australia; and the precedent established when the Canadas, in 1791, received their constitution from Parliament was adhered to when Newfoundland in 1832 was

[1] See Reports of the Law Officers, C.O. 323. James Stephen, who became legal adviser to the Colonial Office in 1813, examined the laws carefully; he was loth to recommend disallowance even though the colonial laws might be carelessly drawn and not conform in every particular to the corresponding English law. The charge that he delayed decisions has no foundation.
[2] Clark, op. cit.

granted a constitution. Spurred by the strong anti-slavery sentiment in England, Parliament on several occasions affirmed its power to interfere with slavery in the West Indies despite the vigorous assertions by the colonies concerned that the question was a local one which fell within the province of the local legislatures.[1] And when the West Indian colonies remained deaf to warnings and admonitions, the Imperial Parliament used its supremacy by passing in 1833 the Act which abolished slavery. But this was practically the sole instance in our period of Parliament disregarding and running counter to the prevailing political opinion in the colonies. The general tendency was to heed colonial requests for greater freedom. In Australia, South Africa, and British North America, the Imperial Government in response to local demands gradually divested itself of responsibility for purely local affairs.

Except in matters pertaining to slavery, and trade and navigation, the power of Parliament was seldom invoked in colonial matters. Now and then a champion of economy might start a debate on the uselessness of the Colonial Office or on the cost of colonial defence, but these debates were rare. The dependencies were left in charge of the administrative departments, which were rarely asked to render an account. Consequently, the records of these departments are better sources for a study of colonial policy than are the pages of *Hansard* and the *Statutes*. The latter, however, are needed to complete the picture of a crumbling colonial system.

Since it was based on trade, it is proper and fitting to begin our examination of the decay of the old system with an analysis of the early modifications of the Trade and Navigation Acts. This decay started with the successful revolt of the thirteen American colonies; it was hastened by the Industrial Revolution. In the eighteenth century, the West Indian colonies had been encouraged to grow tropical produce, receiving timber, food stuffs and other necessities from the colonies on the mainland. When the most important of these became independent the principles of the Trade and Navigation Acts applied to their commercial intercourse with the British West Indies. But the needs of the West Indies could not be supplied by the remaining English colonies in America or by England. The West Indies were threatened with economic ruin, and since they were important in the economic life of the Empire and had influential spokesmen at Westminster, their interests could not be sacrificed on the altar of consistency. Hence Britain in 1794 agreed to permit direct trade between her West Indian colonies and the United States. This trade was interrupted by the war of 1812-14, and the barriers against it were not removed completely until 1830, when a lively trade followed. Other modifications of the commercial system of the Empire were effected by the establishment of free ports in the West Indies and

---

[1] Schuyler, Robert Livingston, *Parliament and the British Empire*, chap. v.

in British North America, and by the right granted to the Dutch planters in the newly acquired portions of Guiana to continue their trade with the Netherlands. Under the pressure of the new conditions due to the Industrial Revolution, Huskisson in 1825 secured the passage of an Act allowing the merchants of Prussia to trade with British colonies.[1] Moreover, British consumers began to complain that the preferences and restrictions on shipping imposed by the Navigation Acts amounted in reality to taxing them for the benefit of colonists and shipowners. The objections to the timber preferences in particular were voiced very strongly, though as yet without effect.[2]

The conflict between the old and the new in imperial economic policy and government which waxed so strong in the 'forties can be noticed also in the 'twenties. Both sides scored gains and losses. The Australian wool growers in 1825 lost the small preference which their produce had till then enjoyed in the British market, yet in the same year the preference on Canadian wheat was increased. The preference on West Indian cotton was lost, while that on sugar was retained. Indeed, the sugar preferences gave rise to a prolonged and complicated struggle, not so much of the old commercial policy against freer or free trade as of old and favoured sugar producers against the new ones. In this case, the opponents of the existing order could invoke the slogan of a unified and integrated imperial policy. The West Indian sugar colonies of Britain had long had a virtual monopoly of the English market, shared, of course, by the newly won West Indian colonies, Trinidad, Tobago, St Lucia, Demerara, Berebice and Essequibo, but withheld from Mauritius, also a sugar island. Mauritian planters and traders began to demand an equalisation of the sugar preferences, and they were soon joined by merchants trading with the East Indies. Manchester wished to increase its export of cotton goods to India, but freight rates were high since return cargoes were difficult to obtain after American raw cotton had driven Indian cotton out of the English market. Indian sugar offered a possibility if the preferences could be equalised. Thus East was pitted against West. The latter had the stronger lobby at Westminster. Mauritius gained in 1825 the equalisation desired, but India had to wait another ten years.[3] Monopolies were unpopular in the England of the early nineteenth century and hence the East India Company fought a losing battle in defence of its commercial rights. The monopoly of the trade with India, except in tea, was lost in 1813, that in the tea and

---

[1] See chapters VI and XI. See also Clapham, J. H., "The Last Years of the Navigation Acts", in *E.H.R.* XXV, 480–501, 687–707; and speech by F. J. Robinson, later Viscount Goderich and Earl of Ripon, in the House of Commons, 1 April 1822: Hansard, New Series, VI, 1414–25.

[2] See statement by Alexander Baring, afterwards Lord Ashburton, in the House of Commons, 24 March 1835: Hansard, Third Series, XXVII, 214. The timber preference amounted to 45s. per load, and it was claimed that shipowners found it profitable to take timber from the Baltic to North America and re-ship it to England as colonial produce.

[3] See chapter XI.

China trade went in 1833. But the principles of an integrated Empire apparently did not apply to the Indian trade. Cotton goods manufactured in India were subject to a 30 per cent. tariff in England, while only 2½ per cent. was levied on English goods in India.[1] Thus Lancashire strangled the cotton industry of the East. Self-interest formed the basis for the policy of preferences, and ultimately self-interest caused it to be abandoned. Doubtless the preferential tariff arrangement for a time benefited both Britain and the colonies. The latter, however, felt the need for using the tariff as a means of increasing revenue. This seems the most plausible explanation of the practice adopted by some West Indian colonies to impose heavy duties on each other's produce. It was winked at so long as the duties were not levied on British goods.[2]

Acting on the theory of a unified and integrated Empire the Government sought to maintain a single monetary standard and to anglicise law and customs in conquered colonies. Particularly in Australia, the lack of a proper medium of exchange caused much hardship in the early days. The Spanish dollar was then widely used all over the Far East, and in part to replace this the Treasury in 1825 made an arrangement whereby British silver coins could be distributed throughout the Empire.[3] Reforms of governmental institutions at the Cape and in Trinidad aimed at introducing English laws and institutions to replace those of Holland and Spain. Similarly, the abortive plan for the union of the Canadas, in 1822, contained proposals for discouraging the use of the French language and for bringing the Roman Catholic Church in the colony under the Act of Supremacy. Sometimes, however, it appears that British officials in a colony were more zealous in promoting anglicisation than were those at home. A case in point is the Cape ordinance of 1827 which required of jurymen a knowledge of English. The population was overwhelmingly of Dutch stock and except in Cape Town few of the Afrikanders knew English. The ordinance, therefore, placed service on juries within the reach of comparatively few persons. It was sharply criticised by James Stephen because "it establishes an invidious distinction, which must be galling to the feeling of the Dutch inhabitants. It tends also to discourage the extension of the English language. If Dutch-men might sit in the Jury Box, the strongest possible motive would arise for studying the language used in the Court of which they were members."[4]

---

[1] Redford, Arthur, *Manchester Merchants and Foreign Trade, 1794–1858*, pp. 112–13.

[2] James Stephen, reporting on certain Acts from Barbados, 8 July 1814, noted that it had been established by usage although perhaps contrary to imperial regulations, that the colonies could regulate the trade between themselves even to the extent of imposing prohibitive duties. He objected, however, to Dominica Act, No. 217, of 1818, which imposed a duty of 2½ per cent. on all export and import, and to St Lucia ordinance, No. 18, of 1822, which imposed a similar levy on goods not sold by residents of the island, on the ground that these levies might fall on British goods: C.O. 323/40, 42.

[3] Chalmers, Robert, *A History of Currency in the British Colonies*, pp. 23–4, 417–25.

[4] Report of 20 December 1828: C.O. 323/45.

On this point, the sentiments of Stephen had they been known at the Cape would have won him praise from the Afrikanders. Not so those which he held on the issue of equality of all races. The famous 50th ordinance, which decreed legal equality irrespective of race and colour,[1] Stephen described as "an Act of great value introducing many most important amendments of the former law, and highly deserving not merely of sanction but of the approbation of His Majesty".[2] That this does not represent simply the passing personal opinion of the legal adviser is clear from the instruction sent to Sir Benjamin D'Urban, Governor of British Guiana, 5 March 1831: "And we do...enjoin and command you", this despatch declares in solemn language, "not to propose or assent to any Ordinance whatever by which persons of African or Indian birth or descent might be subjected or made liable to any disabilities or restrictions to which persons of European birth or descent would not be also subjected and made liable."[3] Thus both at the Cape and in the provinces of British Guiana, the Colonial Office aimed at maintaining equality before the law for all free persons. The spirit of English humanitarianism was then strong in the men who administered the British Empire.

The same spirit is seen in the attitude of the Colonial Office toward slavery. With the abolition of the slave trade in 1808, the question of preventing evasions of the law by smugglers became of considerable importance. The enemies of slavery proposed a system of slave registration. It was accepted by the Government and in 1812 a slave registry was set up in Trinidad by Order-in-Council. This was later extended to other Crown colonies; but when Wilberforce in 1815 introduced a bill in the House of Commons for compulsory registration of slaves in all slave colonies, the West India interest offered strong opposition and the bill was withdrawn. The Colonial Secretary, Lord Bathurst, however, suggested to the colonies in question the advisability of such a registry, and the suggestion was followed by all except Bermuda. In 1823 Thomas Foxwell Buxton, who had succeeded Wilberforce as leader of the anti-slavery forces in the House of Commons, introduced a motion for the gradual extinction of slavery in Demerara, a Crown colony. Canning, speaking for the Government, opposed the motion and offered a substitute which affirmed the need for improving the lot of the slaves. This was carried and was conveyed to the slave colonies by Lord Bathurst in a circular despatch of 28 May 1823. In the ten years that followed, the so-called policy of "melioration" was tried; but it foundered on the rock of West Indian intransigence. Led by that of Jamaica, the legislatures stoutly maintained that slavery as a local institution came under their jurisdiction. They defied both the abolitionists and the Imperial

---

[1] *C.H.B.E.* VIII, 290.
[2] Report of 9 January 1829: C.O. 323/46.
[3] Clementi, p. 444.

Government; and model slave codes prepared in England were disregarded, except in the Crown colonies.[1] However, the appointment of special officials to watch over the treatment of the slaves, known as the slave protectors, was a great step forward. The *Anti-Slavery Reporter* could now cite Blue Books in support of its contentions. As Sir Henry Taylor has put it: "the howlings and wailings of the 'saints' were seen to be supported by unquestionable facts, officially authenticated."[2]

The historic fight for the abolition of slavery in the British Empire had many aspects besides the constitutional and the humanitarian. There were cross currents. Some sprang from sentimental sources, others from those of self-interest. The West Indies were the old valued colonies; the institution of slavery had been set up with the knowledge and sanction of the Home Government; it represented property, and England was tender towards vested interests. The Church of England could not be severe with its offshoot in Jamaica, where respectable rectors had slaves and sometimes ill-treated them.[3] English West Indian traders, planters living in England, holders of plantation mortgages with friends and relations formed a resourceful and energetic group. They organised the West India Association, and they maintained a powerful lobby in the House of Commons, where Charles Ellis and Joseph Marryatt, champions of the West Indian interest, led a compact body of fifty to sixty members. Against them were the "Saints", the anti-slavery, humanitarian forces, which after 1823 followed the banner of Thomas Fowell Buxton, a rich brewer and philanthropist. He lacked the great personal charm of Wilberforce and was not an effective speaker; but he was sincere and earnest and commanded respectful attention. Allied with him was Henry Brougham, next to Canning perhaps the best speaker in the House of Commons. When inspired, the oratory of Brougham reached a high level; and outside the House his popularity was great. Behind them were the Anti-Slavery Society, founded in 1823, and the Nonconformist missionary organisations. From the outset, the West Indian planters had looked upon Baptist and Wesleyan missionaries as sworn enemies. In 1824 a missionary, John Smith, was sentenced to death in connection with the Demerara revolt and died in gaol. His martyrdom provided Brougham with a text for an impassioned attack on slavery.[4] Still, the Dissenters, though fairly numerous and certainly vociferous outside, mustered few votes inside the House, until after the passage of the Reform Bill. But the "Saints" obtained support from the worshippers of Mammon. As already explained, the

---

[1] Burn, W. L., *Emancipation and Apprenticeship in the British West Indies*, pp. 55–100; Klingberg, Frank J., *The Anti-Slavery Movement in England*, chaps. VIII and IX; Mathieson, W. L., *British Slavery and its Abolition*, chaps. II and III.
[2] Taylor, Sir Henry, *Autobiography of*, Am. ed., I, 102–3.
[3] Burn, pp. 63–4.
[4] *Ibid.* p. 82. See chapter IX.

Mauritian and East Indian interests fought the West Indian on the issue of sugar preferences. And the advocates of freer or free trade were little impressed with the plea that slavery was necessary for the economic life of the West Indies: Manchester was not restrained by brotherly love for Jamaica. But even combined, these forces failed to make real headway against the West Indian interest in the un-reformed Parliament.

It was otherwise at the Colonial Office. Here the legal adviser, James Stephen, son of one of the ablest and the most uncompromising of the Abolitionists, scrutinised West Indian legislation, blocked efforts of West Indian assemblies to hamper the work of Noncon-formist missionaries, and riddled the arguments presented in favour of denying slaves elementary human rights. The slave was, he con-tended, a British subject; and as such he was entitled to the protection of British law.[1] That the Colonial Office was hostile to slavery is evident from the rules drawn up to govern the granting of land to the emigrants sent to South Africa in 1820. The land so granted should not be worked by slaves. Twelve years later the regulations for the alienation of land held by the Government in British Guiana stipulated "that such lands or any part thereof shall not be cultivated by the labour of Slaves".[2] The Colonial Office watched the effects of the Government's "melioration" policy, and in a memorandum of 1 December 1832 it pointed out that the policy had failed and that the evils of slavery could be cured only by abolition. By then the anti-slavery campaign was nearing its climax. A slave uprising in Jamaica, December 1831, had been put down with great savagery, thus supplying anti-slavery orators with excellent ammunition. The Abolitionists found in Daniel O'Connell, the leader of the Irish, a most valuable ally; and a new propaganda organisation known as the "Agency Committee", guided and inspired by George Stephen, fourth son of the old Abolitionist leader, mobilised public opinion so effectively that the first reformed Parliament passed the great Act which outlawed slavery in the British Empire.[3]

The experiment of apprenticeship, instituted by the Emancipation Act, proved a failure. The distinction between emancipation and freedom was too subtle to be understood by the majority of the negroes. They believed that the planters had cheated them, and the planters on their side often strove to exploit the apprentices in whom they no longer had a proprietary interest. The special and stipendiary magistrates appointed to supervise the enforcement of the Emancipa-tion Act met with opposition and ill-will from planters and planter-controlled legislatures and juries. At the Colonial Office, James

[1] Burn, p. 59; C.O. 323/40–50 *passim*.
[2] Instructions to Sir Benjamin D'Urban, 5 March 1831. Quoted Clementi, pp. 447–8.
[3] Stephen, George, *Anti-Slavery Recollections*, pp. 129–36, 253–8.

Stephen and Henry Taylor complained of the want of good faith in the West Indies. And when the former, in 1836, was appointed to the important post of Permanent Under-Secretary of State for the Colonies the negro had a powerful friend at court, the more so since the then Colonial Secretary, Lord Glenelg, shared Stephen's point of view on natives and former slaves. The permanent staff at the Colonial Office finally arrived at the conclusion that the apprenticeship system was unworkable and that representative government in the West Indies must come to an end.[1] Parliament agreed concerning the apprentices and terminated the experiment, 1 August 1838; but the proposal to suspend the constitution of Jamaica met with so much opposition that it had to be dropped.

The question of the position of the Church of England in the colonies cropped up repeatedly in the discussions over negro slavery in the West Indies and is of sufficient importance to merit separate treatment. Not until the end of the old Empire did the church establishment become an issue in discussions between the mother country and her colonies. True, the agency for the Church of England overseas, the Society for the Propagation of the Gospel in Foreign Parts, received some aid from the Government, and it was assumed rather vaguely that the overseas possessions were included in the jurisdiction of the Bishop of London. But problems connected with Church and religion in the colonies received scant attention from either Church or lay authorities until after the American Revolution. In 1787 and 1795 respectively the bishoprics of Nova Scotia and Quebec were established; the next to be created was that of Calcutta, 1814, and five more were added between that date and 1837. At this time the representatives of the Church of England assumed as by right that it held a privileged position in the Empire. And until the 'thirties the Government generally supported these pretensions. The Parliamentary grant to the Society for the Propagation of the Gospel increased from £1800 in 1814 to £22,664 in 1825, and then dropped to £15,532 annually until 1832, when it was reduced to £13,750. The grant for 1833 was £8250, for 1834 £4000.[2] The bishoprics of Jamaica and Barbados, created in 1824, were well endowed by the Imperial Government. In 1825 the Governor of New South Wales was ordered to set aside one-seventh of the public land for a corporation which should support the Church of England in Australia and establish schools for the education of children in accordance with the tenets and principles of that Church. Similarly, the Governor of British Guiana was commanded in 1831 to provide schools with

---

[1] Burn, chaps. IV–VIII; Findlay, G. G. and Holdsworth, W. W., *A History of the Wesleyan Methodist Missionary Society*, II, 311–17. This account of the working of the apprenticeship system is based mainly upon the journal of Henry B. Britton, at that time missionary on the island of Nevis.

[2] *Classified Records of the Society for the Propagation of the Gospel*, pp. 758, 825–6.

instruction in religion "according to the Doctrine of the United Church of England and Ireland".[1]

By this time, however, the opposition to the special privileges accorded to the Established Church was gaining strength both in England and the colonies. In England the opposition was signalised by the repeal of the Test and Corporation Acts, 1828, and in the colonies it was revealed by a growing insistence upon complete religious equality. This was recognised, although somewhat reluctantly, by the Colonial Office. For instance, Stephen recommended for disallowance a Nova Scotian Act of 1819 which authorised the Governor to license dissenting ministers to perform marriages "without adhering to the form prescribed by the Book of Common Prayer". He gave as grounds for this advice that the Church of England was established by law in Nova Scotia; that the new Act provided for equality in the exercise of an important function of the clerical office; that the dissenting minister might not be properly trained for clerical duties; that the income of the regular clergy would be reduced; and that the innovation facilitated marriages without sufficient publicity. In 1826 he likewise objected to an Act from Lower Canada which granted ecclesiastical power to church bodies other than the Churches of England and Scotland and the Roman Catholic Church.[2] A change of heart is noticed in the report of 27 August 1829, on an Act from Lower Canada instituting a Protestant registry. He now observed: "the state of the world is very unfavourable to the maintenance of exclusive ecclesiastical pretensions, and it is evident that the exclusive privileges of the English Church in Canada, cannot be supported—except at the expense of great unpopularity."[3] His superiors shared this belief. Lord Glenelg in 1835 admitted the futility of choosing "any one Church as the exclusive object of Public Endowment" in Australia; and the Colonial Office disapproved of Colborne's endowment of Anglican rectories in Upper Canada.[4]

For a time it appeared that the Government might support all colonial churches without granting special favour to any one. Canada had three distinct church establishments, the Church of England, the Church of Scotland, and the Roman Catholic Church. The Church of England claimed a position of pre-eminence and throughout our

[1] For instructions concerning land to be set aside for Church and schools in New South Wales see Bathurst to Brisbane, 1 January 1825: H.R.A. Third Series, XI, 438–9. For British Guiana see Clementi, p. 450.

[2] Reports on Nova Scotian Act, No. 953, of 1819, 18 August 1819 and on Lower Canadian Act, No. 550, of 1826, 2 September 1826. C.O. 323/41 and 43.

[3] Report on Act No. 606, of 1828. A year earlier he had written with reference to an Act, No. 1260, from Nova Scotia, which dealt with religious organisations and societies: "It is, I presume, vain to attempt to secure to the Church of England on the North American Continent, that species of monopoly of secular privileges which it enjoys in this Country, nor does it seem probable that the real interest of that Church would be promoted by maintaining any such exclusive principle." Report dated 29 November 1828: C.O. 323/45 and 46.

[4] Dunham, Aileen, Political Unrest in Upper Canada, 1815–1836, pp. 99–100.

period its spokesmen asserted that it had exclusive rights to the Clergy Reserves, amounting to the equivalent of one-seventh of the land alienated by the Crown—which the Constitutional Act of 1791 had set aside for the support of the Protestant clergy. But English legal and official opinion supported the contention, put forward by the Church of Scotland, that Canada was a British colony, consequently the two established Protestant churches of Great Britain should share the Clergy Reserves. The scheme of 1822 for a union of the Canadas included, as we have seen, a provision for bringing the Roman Catholic Church in Canada under the Act of Supremacy. The union plan failed; and it is doubtful if the proposal concerning the Roman Church could have functioned. Nevertheless, the Government gave support to the Roman Catholic clergy,[1] and even the Dissenters occasionally received aid. In South Africa the Dutch Reformed Church was by far the strongest, and this was recognised, although perhaps not in exact proportion, in the Government's grants for 1832 to the churches at the Cape. The funds were divided as follows: Dutch Reformed, £4200; Church of England, £1850; Roman Catholics, £200; and Presbyterians, £200.[2] The Church of England was considered established in the older West Indian colonies, and the Moravians, Baptists and Wesleyans met with resistance when they began missionary work among the negroes. But the Government finally decided that the Dissenters should not only be tolerated but aided. Parliament in 1835 granted the Society for the Propagation of the Gospel £7500 for 1835 and £7160 for 1836 and at the same time voted £5000 to the Wesleyans for each of these two years; the funds were to be used for the education of negroes in the West Indies.[3] After 1831 direct Government support to the colonial churches was decreased, both for reasons of economy and because the practice of aiding individual churches involved the Home Government in colonial religious controversies.

Beginning in the early 'twenties the Imperial Government gradually divested itself of responsibility for purely local affairs in colonies with a considerable white population. The West Indies formed an exception to this; but the apparent inconsistency was due to the special conditions found in the sugar colonies. Here a small and decreasing white population exploited a large black and coloured. The situation was further complicated when the non-Europeans became free, acquired property, paid taxes, and still were denied political rights and even full legal protection. To check the exploitation of the many by the few seemed desirable, but it was not feasible without reducing

[1] Despatch, Goderich to Dalhousie, 5 August 1827, ordered that out of Crown revenues payments should be made to the Protestant clergy £5150, to the Catholic Bishop £1000: Doughty and Story, pp. 405–6.

[2] *Records of the S.P.G.* p. 272. In Van Diemen's Land Governor Arthur supported all churches: Forsyth, W. D., *Governor Arthur's Convict System*, p. 39.

[3] *Records of the S.P.G.* p. 195; Findlay and Holdsworth, II, 322.

the power of assemblies elected on the basis of a narrow franchise. This was the point of view not only of humanitarians inside the Colonial Office, but of such an ardent colonial reformer as Charles Buller.[1] When complaints against the existing governmental autocracies at the Cape and in New South Wales became insistent, the Colonial Secretary, Lord Bathurst, showed an earnest desire to have them studied on the spot. For this purpose he devised the expedient of sending commissioners from England to study and report to the Colonial Office on the local conditions and problems. New South Wales was in the unusual position of being a settlement colony governed under a system used ordinarily in only conquered or ceded colonies. The explanation of the anomaly is, of course, that the earliest Australian colonies, New South Wales and Van Diemen's Land, were prison farms, governed under prison discipline. With the arrival of free immigrants a need for change arose, and when the freed and free population of New South Wales outnumbered the convicts, the colony had to be given a governmental system suited to freemen. This became imperative after the Imperial Government in 1831 had adopted a land and emigration policy peculiarly adapted to the needs of Australia. But the stigma of transportation had to be removed before the lands of Australia could be considered attractive to the labouring population of England. Transportation and free popular institutions could not exist side by side. The question was further complicated by the fact that some employers of labour in New South Wales looked upon transportation as needful in order to insure a supply of labour. Hence in the 'thirties the issue between an autocratic Home Government and a strongly held colonial desire for more freedom was not a clear-cut one. The Home Government slowly relaxed its control over local affairs in New South Wales. By 1830 a free press, trial by jury and a legislative council had been conceded. The advocates of more complete self-government organised in 1835 the Australian Patriotic Association which maintained a Parliamentary agent at Westminster. The first so appointed was Sir Henry Lytton Bulwer; he was succeeded by Charles Buller, who bluntly informed the Australians that transportation was incompatible with free institutions. Given the choice they preferred the latter, and a Select Committee with Sir William Molesworth as chairman recommended, 1838, that transportation should cease; this was put into effect in 1840 and representative institutions were granted to New South Wales two years later.[2]

Similarly at the Cape, many issues complicated that of colonial self-government. The inhabitants of Dutch stock had little experience of self-government save in purely local affairs, and its relations with

[1] Schuyler, p. 192.
[2] *C.H.B.E.* vii, pt. i, 146–74; Melbourne, A. C. V., *Early Constitutional Development in Australia. New South Wales, 1788–1856*; Sweetman, Edward, *Australian Constitutional Development.*

the West Indian assemblies might well cause the Imperial Government to hesitate before it established deliberative bodies in a colony where slavery existed. Furthermore, the large native population inside the colony and on its borders caused the missionaries and their friends in England to emphasise the needs for a check upon the colonists. Commissioner J. T. Bigge, who had investigated the situation in New South Wales, was sent to the Cape, and in conformity with the wishes of his conservative chief, the Colonial Secretary, Lord Bathurst, he cautiously advised some changes in the local institutions. The first instalment came in 1825 when the Governor was given an advisory council with little power. Two years later the Supreme Court of the colony was made independent of the Governor, two non-officials were added to his Council, and magistrates took the place of the old unsalaried *heemraden*—a change far from pleasing to the Boers. The reformers at the Cape were not satisfied, but they split on the issue of slavery. A similar cleavage was noticed in the House of Commons over the question of more self-government for the Cape. The champion of the West Indian interests, Joseph Marryatt, favoured it, while Dr Lushington, the Abolitionist, spoke in opposition. And since the anti-slavery forces were in the ascendancy they blocked an immediate grant of local autonomy. In 1833 two councils, an executive and a legislative, replaced the advisory one. The legislative council of ten to twelve members included five officials and five to seven burghers chosen by the Governor. This small beginning of representative government was carried a step farther in 1836 with the establishment of elective boards in the towns and villages at the Cape.[1]

Even in British North America racial and religious issues complicated that of local self-government. Newfoundland had no resident Governor until 1817. The population, slightly more than 50,000, was poor and under the economic dominance of merchants of the western fishing ports who equipped the fishing fleet that went out every spring and returned in the autumn. Ever since the Restoration Irish Roman Catholics had formed the majority of the settlers, and after 1815 a large number of Irish poor went to or were dumped on the colony. This created an Irish Roman Catholic problem which was used as an argument against granting representative government. After 1830 the anti-Papal cry lost some of its political effectiveness and in 1832 Newfoundland received an elective assembly which did not, however, exercise real power until the end of the decade.[2]

In the Maritime Provinces and in the Canadas, factional strife as well as racial and religious animosities delayed the extension of local autonomy. Prince Edward Island was dominated by absentee landowners even more completely than was Newfoundland by the West

[1] *C.H.B.E.* VIII, 359–66.
[2] *Ibid.* VI, 429–31.

Country merchants. Consequently, when Lord Goderich in 1832 suggested the separation of the executive from the legislative council in the Maritimes, the concession was accepted by New Brunswick but rejected by Prince Edward Island. Nova Scotia had the oldest legislative assembly in British North America, dating from 1758. To this colony had come a large number of Loyalist refugees, an immigration which caused New Brunswick to be organised as a separate colony in 1784. But, as in Upper Canada, the majority of the Loyalists gave strength to the Tory element in the population, and not until our period draws towards its close did the reformers secure a competent and effective leader in Joseph Howe.[1] Nova Scotia and Upper Canada each had a political coterie labelled the "Family Compact" which claimed a monopoly of devotion to British institutions. In Lower Canada the racial issue was sharply drawn between the French Roman Catholics who controlled the Assembly and the Protestant English minority entrenched in the executive and legislative councils. Since the Canadas were the colonies with the largest European population and also possessed extensive power of local self-government, their struggle for more autonomy was regarded as the touchstone of colonial policy.

So long as the Tories were in power at home, it was perhaps natural that imperial support should be given to the existing order. But even in colonial policy a distinction must be drawn between the old and the new Tories. Huskisson held the seals of the Colonial Office for an altogether too short span of time in 1827–28. He wished to conciliate the Canadians, and when the Governor, Lord Dalhousie, in 1827 disallowed the election of the radical leader, Louis Joseph Papineau, as Speaker of the Assembly, Huskisson administered a reprimand.[2] The royal prerogative should not have been invoked in the speaker-ship fight. In a similar manner the action of the Tories of Upper Canada, 1831, in expelling the agitator William Lyon Mackenzie from the Assembly, was disapproved by the Colonial Secretary, Lord Goderich, who advised the Canadian Tories to ignore the libels published by Mackenzie.[3] In harmony with this attitude he surrendered the control over Crown revenues in Lower Canada. Goderich was much under the influence of James Stephen. The latter's opinion concerning Canadian affairs, as recorded in a report of 1 May 1831, is, therefore, of special significance. Stephen wrote that observation and experience

have convinced me that the rejection of Bills passed by the Canadian Assemblies can scarcely be productive of advantage in any case excepting such as directly affect the Trade and Navigation of this Kingdom. The attempt to regulate the internal

[1] *C.H.B.E.* vi, 270–86.
[2] Doughty and Story, p. 419.
[3] Dunham, pp. 135–7. When Mackenzie visited England in 1832 he had several interviews with Lord Goderich, who "was sincerely anxious to gain information and to redress what grievances he could": *ibid.* p. 131.

Government of the Province [i.e. Lower Canada] in opposition to the wishes of the local Legislature, cannot but terminate in defeat and strengthen the popular at the expense of the monarchical interest. The Crown has neither influence nor authority to oppose to the power of the Assembly, and ineffectual resistance to their demands I conceive more pregnant with mischief than the most decided system of non-interference could be.[1]

Nor were these liberal opinions on colonial policy confined to the Colonial Office. Sir James Mackintosh, a prominent member of the Whig party, echoed the sentiments of Burke when on 28 February 1816 he urged the House of Commons to look to the love of the people of Canada for England as the only durable bond of union. Twelve years later he spoke of that union as an alliance, and said that Britain should assure the Canadians of "a full and efficient protection from all foreign influence; full permission to conduct the whole of their own internal affairs; compelling them to pay all reasonable expenses of their own government, and giving them, at the same time, a perfect control over the expenditure of the money; and imposing no restrictions of any kind upon the industry or traffic of the people."[2] The Committee of the House of Commons appointed in 1828 to study the Canadian problems reported in favour of allowing the colonies complete control of local finance.[3] And Lord Howick, Parliamentary Under-Secretary for the Colonies, speaking in the House of Commons, 18 February 1831, advised the Imperial Government to avoid vexatious interference with the local affairs of the colonies. Britain should protect them against foreign attacks, promote their prosperity, and teach them to combine with the mother country for the common welfare in peace and common defence in war. If so treated and so taught, Howick felt convinced that the colonies would remain loyal to Britain. They would, he averred, be more useful as willing allies than as dissatisfied subjects.[4]

But these sound and statesmanlike ideas were not so easy to put into practical operation in the early 'thirties. As in the day of Burke, they ran counter to the accepted view of empire and of the position of colonies. Moreover, the Canadians presented difficult demands. Those from Lower Canada included complete control over all revenues raised in the province and an elective legislative council. The Imperial Government conceded the former in 1831, but insisted that in return the colony should guarantee adequate salaries for judges and other civil officials. This request was refused.[5] An elective legislative council meant that both houses of the legislature would be in the hands of the French Canadian majority. To give them power over the English minority and control of the gateway to the interior of British North America seemed risky, especially since they

[1] C.O. 323/45.
[2] Speech in the House of Commons, 2 May 1828: Hansard, New Series, XIX, 320.
[3] For report of Committee see Doughty and Story, pp. 466–77.
[4] Hansard, Third Series, II, 690.
[5] C.H.B.E. VI, 245.

might wish to turn to their old home land, France. Nor was the situation in Upper Canada much simpler. American influence in the province seemed on the increase; the Loyalist element deserved support both from the standpoint of past services and because they were staunch defenders of imperial unity; furthermore, the programme of the radicals—responsible government—was a novelty. Lord John Russell, one of the most liberal among the English statesmen of that day, declared in the House of Commons, 6 March 1837, that if the Canadians

persist in maintaining that it is absolutely necessary that there should be an elective Legislative Council and an Executive Council subservient to the Representative Assembly, then it must very shortly come to this, that they should also have a governor of their own nomination, for none other would do their bidding. If this be the proposition of the Assembly of Lower Canada, it is in another form nothing else than demanding the total independence of the colonies from the mother country.[1]

Independence Britain would not concede, and Lord John Russell's views were endorsed by an overwhelming majority in the House of Commons.

There was no lack of good will on the part of the Colonial Office. Its patronage in Canada was given up; Lord Glenelg in 1835 expressed himself in favour of a large measure of colonial self-government; and a commission was sent to Canada to study the situation; but no solution was or perhaps could have been found at this time. The uprisings that followed in December 1837 were small and speedily put down, but they administered a mortal blow to the old colonial system of the British Empire.[2]

In the disputes with the Canadas, as well as in those over the founding of South Australia, the frontier policy in South Africa, and the annexation of New Zealand, critics of the Government made the Colonial Office their target and these attacks have been continued by latter-day historians. Something must therefore be said of its personnel and methods. In 1801 the third secretaryship, that for War and the Colonies, came into existence. Colonial affairs were apparently handled by a separate office almost from the beginning, although the Colonial Office did not really function until 1812, when Henry Goulburn was appointed Parliamentary Under-Secretary of State for the Colonies.[3] Its separate machinery was completed when the office secured a Permanent Under-Secretary in 1825. Lord Bathurst was Secretary of State for War and the Colonies in the Liverpool Government, 1812–27. Then followed a period of brief tenures: William

---

[1] Hansard, Third Series, xxxvi, 1303. On 14 April 1837 Russell stated that an elective Legislative Council and an Executive Council responsible to the Assembly would be "inconsistent with the relations between a colony and the mother country": *ibid.* xxxvii, 1277.

[2] Egerton, H. E., *A Short History of British Colonial Policy*, 9th ed. p. 262; Lucas, *Lord Durham's Report*, i, 90–105.

[3] Manning, Helen T., *British Colonial Government after the American Revolution, 1782–1820*, p. 483. For a good sketch of the Colonial Office in this period see Burn, chap. iii.

Huskisson, Lord Goderich, Sir George Murray, Lord Stanley, T. Spring-Rice, Lord Aberdeen, until 1835, when Lord Glenelg entered the office held by him for four unhappy years. Lord Bathurst does not occupy a front rank among British statesmen and his conduct of colonial affairs has been severely criticised. Some allowance must be made, however, on account of the times and especially the difficult situation at home. The records show him to have been industrious and well-meaning. The appointment of special commissions to study the conditions in New South Wales and at the Cape and the issue of "Blue Books" on colonial affairs inaugurated by him show laudable intentions and convey the impression that he has not received his meed of praise.[1] Among the six men who occupied the office, 1827–35, Huskisson doubtless stands first as administrator. Sir James Stephen, a competent critic, spoke of Huskisson as a man with "a dominant understanding". He ranks with Peel as an administrator; he combined a wide knowledge and a clear understanding of the economic problems of the Empire with a genuine sympathy for the colonial point of view. Had he been given six years instead of six months as head of the Colonial Office his term might have become as epoch-making in imperial history as was that of Joseph Chamberlain seventy years later. Three of the others, Goderich, Stanley and Aberdeen, reached the position of prime minister, so that talent was not lacking.[2] Storms have raged over Lord Glenelg and his term as Colonial Secretary. He had the misfortune of incurring the enmity of Wakefield and Charles Buller, both bitter controversialists, and of failing in his efforts to pacify the Canadas. He retired under a cloud in 1839 and has suffered much at the hands of historians. At the time of his resignation Stephen wrote: "He is the tenth Secretary of State under whom I have served, and from the most certain knowledge I can declare that of the whole list he is the most laborious, the most conscientious, and the most enlightened Minister of the public."[3] And Sir Thomas Fowell Buxton said of him: "I ought to know

[1] Wilmot Horton, in defending his former chief, Lord Bathurst, asserted that "for daily sedulous discharge of the peculiarities of his office as Colonial Secretary, no public man who has ever filled that situation has been more remarkable." Horton, R. W., *Exposition and Defence of Earl Bathurst's Administration of the Affairs of Canada*, p. 40. The issuing of a "Blue Book" for each colony began in 1822 and by 1835 the returns were complete from all Crown colonies, but those with representative government often withheld important information. See evidence by Peter Smith, senior clerk in the Colonial Office, 1 June 1837, before Select Committee on Colonial Receipt and Expenditure: *Parl. Pap.* 1837, VII (516), pp. 40–1. For a discussion of the early use of Royal commissions see Manning, p. 539.

[2] Some doubt might be entertained concerning the talent of Lord Goderich, but the evidence cited above, p. 298, note 3, shows him as sincerely desirous of understanding the problems of Canada. For an estimate of Lord Stanley, Colonial Secretary 1833–34, 1841–45, see Morrell, W. P., *British Colonial Policy in the Age of Peel and Russell*, pp. 32–5. Gladstone, who served under Lord Aberdeen at the Colonial Office, noted his "serious and earnest benevolence, and practical competency for affairs", 8 April 1835, Black Leather Book of Secret Memoranda, p. 25: Gladstone Papers at the British Museum.

[3] Stephen, Caroline, *The First Sir James Stephen*, p. 56: Letter to Mrs Austin, 12 February 1839. Stephen was very critical of his friends; and the fact that Glenelg was his "intimate personal friend" hardly detracts from the value of the estimate.

something of Colonial Secretaries for I have worried each of them in succession for twenty years.... There is not one of them who, in my estimation, has acted more conscientiously, or of whose anxiety to do justice to Negroes, Caffres, Hottentots and Indians I feel more assurance than Lord Glenelg."[1] The last sentence furnishes a clue to the reasons for his failure; another was supplied by Stephen when he said concerning Glenelg that "in all my intercourse with mankind I have never known a man so amiable, guileless and true". No profound knowledge of political history or public life is required to appreciate Stephen's further remark about the incompatibility of Glenelg's "temper and principles with the tempers and with the rules of action to which we erect shrines in Downing Street".[2] Unfortunately, the friend of the oppressed, the "guileless and true", seldom wins in the race for political success and glory.

Among the Parliamentary Under-Secretaries, Wilmot Horton, 1821–27, deserves special mention because of his championship of assisted emigration and his views on inter-imperial relations. He was not a man of first rate ability, but his energy and perseverance enabled him to achieve a modicum of success. Lord Howick, 1830–33, at a later date left his mark on colonial policy; W. E. Gladstone served too short a period, January–April 1835, to make an impression. The first Permanent Under-Secretary, R. W. Hay, 1825–36, has been described as a kindly sensible man with many social and other extra-official interests. He carried on a large private correspondence with colonial officials, but apparently learned little and understood less of the practical problems connected with colonial administration and policy. The man who left the deepest impression on colonial affairs was Hay's successor as Permanent Under-Secretary, James Stephen.

This powerful and enlightened public official became legal counsellor to the Colonial Office in 1813 and to the Board of Trade in 1825. He was made Assistant Under-Secretary in 1834, promoted to the Permanent Secretaryship two years later upon the retirement of Hay, and served in this capacity until 1847. Thus the greater portion of his time of service in a high position falls outside the limit set for this chapter; but long before his final promotion he wielded much influence in the affairs of the colonies. Indeed, Lord Stanley told Gladstone in 1839 that six years earlier when he assumed the duties of the Colonial Office "he found Stephen in the habit of reporting on Colonial Laws in such a form as that his reports might at once go to the Colonies, with the alteration of a few words, at the commencement and close, in character of despatches".[3] The organisation of the Colonial Office was almost wholly the work of Stephen, who devised a system of taking care of incoming and outgoing despatches, collecting

---

[1] Quoted in Stock, Eugene, *History of the Church Missionary Society*, 1, 452–3.
[2] Stephen, pp. 56–7. For eulogy of Glenelg by Joseph Howe, see his *Speeches and Letters*, ed. by J. A. Chisholm, 1, 612.
[3] Entry in Gladstone's Black Leather Book dated 19 April 1839.

reports and memoranda, and handling the heavy inter-departmental correspondence. Strictly honest, sincere and deeply religious, he introduced and maintained a high standard of efficiency and integrity in the public service. By birth and early association he belonged to the Clapham Sect and the Abolitionist group. Hence his admission in 1829 that he had been "devoted not exclusively but mainly to promoting, as far as was compatible with the duties of my office, the extinction of slavery".[1] Allusions have already been made to his work in that field. Both before and after the passage of the Emancipation Act, which, incidentally, was drafted by Stephen, he worked hard to protect the negroes of the West Indies as well as the natives in and outside the British Empire against oppression at the hands of the whites.

In his official capacity, Stephen scrutinised the often not too sound schemes for colonisation presented by Wakefield and his friends. Thereby he aroused their hatred; and the malicious slander published by Charles Buller about Stephen as one who neglected the welfare of the colonies has been too long accepted as true. Careful examination of the available records shows that both as counsellor and when he combined this position with that of Permanent Under-Secretary, Stephen was enlightened in his humanitarianism and remarkably free from the vice of legal pedantry. He had, of course, to call attention to the discrepancies whenever they occurred between colonial laws and the laws of England, had to help to enforce the legislation against unsound money, and keep a watch over the interests of the mother country. But he fully appreciated that since the conditions in the colonies differed from those of England, the details and forms of English law could not always be followed. He grew more liberal in his views as his experience increased; and it is somewhat surprising to find that Stephen in 1828 upheld the colonial against the English opinion on the subject of pauper emigration. Reporting on a Nova Scotian Act aimed at the exclusion of pauper immigrants, 29 November 1828, Stephen wrote:

It appears to me that no sound principle can be referred to in justification of the practice which has so long and extensively prevailed, of imposing upon the Colonists the charge of maintaining British and Irish paupers. If such persons were sent into an English Parish, they would be liable to be sent back to their homes. When introduced into a transatlantic Colony, this is impossible. The only course that remains is to take security that for a limited time they shall not be burthensome.[2]

Even more startling was the opinion recorded by him when reporting, 21 November 1832, on a Jamaican Act imposing "restraint on the liberty of publication", an opinion which it might not have been prudent to record a few years earlier. "No improvement", he wrote, "was ever yet effected except through the medium of discontent with

[1] Stephen, p. 16, extract from a letter written to a cousin in 1829.
[2] C.O. 323/45.

some existing Law or usage, and a people who must always remain satisfied must ever remain stationary."[1]

By the middle of the 'thirties two other men remarkable for their culture and breadth of view held subordinate positions in the Colonial Office. Of these, James Spedding soon left the Civil Service to devote all his attention to literature; but Sir Henry Taylor remained until his retirement in 1872. Taylor was the author of a remarkable treatise, *The Statesman*, which supposedly portrays James Stephen. Spedding and he shared the humanitarian views of Glenelg and Stephen. No wonder that the Colonial Office was obnoxious to the empire builders. By 1837 that Office had achieved a fair degree of efficiency with definite assignment of men to its various divisions. Henceforth, the delays in transacting the business it was supposed to handle were due not to the Colonial Office but to the fact that so many other departments and boards had to be consulted on colonial matters, and several of these were often extremely negligent.[2]

Among the accusations then levied against British colonial administration was that unfit men were appointed to high office, that these were given too much power and too high salaries, and that many of them were absentees. All these charges had some foundation. After the Napoleonic wars a number of generals had to be given appointments and the colonies offered convenient berths. Stephen at one time referred to the period as one "replete with abuse", and even as late as 1837 Sir G. Cornewall Lewis asserted that the scum of England was poured into the colonies.[3] This was an exaggeration, but in a period when great nobles commanded many votes in the House of Commons, Governors closely related to them, as Lord Charles Somerset to the Duke of Beaufort, could not be recalled whenever they had shown incapacity. This was remedied in part with the reform of 1829, which limited appointment of Governors to six years.[4] The high salaries complained of, especially by the Canadians, who made inconvenient comparisons with the cost of government in the United States, were a legacy of the eighteenth century. It had then been customary to fix the salary of a Governor upon the basis of social rank. A duke however incompetent must perforce be given a good position and a high salary. Reductions were, however, effected by taking men of less exalted rank and this became easier after the passage of the Reform Bill. At a time when it took on the average nearly four months to reach the Cape and six months to reach New South Wales, the men on the spot had to be upheld, though this did not mean that they were never reprimanded. The general principle concerning the treatment of Governors as stated by Lord Stanley was

[1] C.O. 323/48. The most recent estimates of the character and work of Sir James Stephen are by Burn, chap. III, and Hall, *passim*.

[2] Hall, pp. 30–1.

[3] Lewis, George Cornewall, *Letters of*, ed. by G. F. Lewis, p. 90.

[4] *Parl. Pap.* 1836, XXXIX (537).

"before the public, you must always support them...reserving the privilege of writing private admonitions".[1] In the matter of sinecures substantial improvements were made. A Select Committee on Sinecure Offices in the Colonies reported in 1835 that, in 1812, seventy-one offices in the colonies were either sinecures or the duties were executed by deputies, but that in the year of the report only four were held by officers not resident in the colonies.[2]

As our period closes the Colonial Reform movement had begun. This movement was in the main due to the work of Edward Gibbon Wakefield and to the demands for changes which came from the North American colonies. It should be kept in mind, however, that Sir James Mackintosh and others had long argued in favour of a liberal colonial policy. Wakefield's name is linked with the land and emigration policy which the Government adopted in 1831, with the founding of South Australia, and with the annexation and colonisation of New Zealand. His positive and enduring achievements are those connected with colonisation. He aroused interest and created faith in colonies at a time when, as we have seen, there was little economic or political demand for them. Herein lies his title to fame as an empire builder. In the field of government his contributions were less significant. His attacks upon the Colonial Office were unfair and vindictive. He helped to weaken confidence in the existing political system, but he did not possess knowledge and appreciation of the problems connected with colonial and imperial government. He was throughout a company promoter, a speculator in land. Still, he apparently interested Charles Buller, Lord Durham and Sir William Molesworth in the problems of empire. They had the knowledge and the experience of government which he lacked. But not until Buller and Durham had studied colonial problems on the spot in Canada were they able fully to appreciate the true meaning of the political concessions demanded by the Canadians. Durham's great contribution to the cause of imperial reconstruction was made in his masterful and justly famous report on Canada, 1839, and Buller's essay on *Responsible Government*, 1840, has become a classic.[3] Molesworth was less spectacular, he had not the genius of the other two. His contributions to the cause were made in solid speeches in the House of Commons and in financial aid. Among the others who supported the colonies in the House of Commons, J. A. Roebuck, the agent for Lower Canada, had little political insight; and Joseph Hume, the radical, and George Grote, the historian of Greece, who both appear to have been separatists, were too theoretical to be effective. The colonial leaders, Robert Baldwin of Upper Canada and Joseph Howe of

---

[1] Gladstone, Black Leather Book, p. 84. See also Burn, p. 322; Hall, p. 111; and Melbourne, p. 111.
[2] *Parl. Pap.* 1835, xviii (507), pp. 3–12.
[3] For the text of Buller's essay see Wrong, E. M., *Charles Buller and Responsible Government*, pp. 87–170.

Nova Scotia, saw perhaps more clearly on the issue of colonial self-government than did any of the English reformers. And well they might, for their experience was first hand.

Looking back from the year of the accession of Queen Victoria to that of Waterloo, changes are noticeable in colonial policy and administration, especially in temper and outlook. The colonies moved within an imperial orbit with England at the centre. They were not yet in a position "to set the tune"; that was done in England. Hence the importance of the political and economic changes and of the changes of thought in England on the development of the Empire. The Industrial Revolution, the financial embarrassments that beset England after the war, the struggle for and the passage of the Great Reform Bill, the improved standards in administration, the growth of a spirit of liberalism and the great humanitarian movement, all in various ways are reflected in the English attitude toward the colonies and their problems. The expansion of the Empire and the progress of colonial self-government were slow in the years 1815–37. The Government of England was, however, susceptible to the pressure of groups whether they advocated political reform, abolition of slavery, or reform of the tariff. The technique of such groups was improving. Francis Place had been skilful in his advocacy of repeal of the Combination Acts and the passage of the Reform Bill; the tactics of George Stephen were a great improvement upon those used by Wilberforce and Buxton in their struggles for freeing the negroes— they were fully as skilful as those of Place. These lessons were apparently not lost upon a born promoter and agitator like Wakefield. By clever appeals to lofty idealism, imperial sentiments, and ordinary human cupidity, he could and did achieve results. In the later 'thirties the stage was set for new and rapid changes. At home James Stephen, the guiding spirit of the Colonial Office, favoured reform in colonial administration and policy, an attitude not based upon abstract theories but upon practical experience. Public opinion had become accustomed to reform; the most aggressive elements in the population, the commercial and industrial, advocated changes in the economic policy of the Empire which would and did have far-reaching effects upon imperial relations; these elements saw nothing to be gained from continual squabbles with the colonies, nor were they afraid of concessions that might lead to complete colonial autonomy. They were willing to let the colonists have what they wanted. This attitude of mixed liberalism and indifference offered opportunities for advocates of colonial reform—Wakefield, Buller, Durham and Molesworth. And then a crisis in the Canadas called for constructive measures. The reformers at home had suggestions, and those of North America, like Baldwin and Howe, had plans for meeting the existing emergency. The year 1837 is also the year of Buxton's Aborigines Committee and of Molesworth's Committee on Transportation. Both were omens of great significance. Boers of South Africa were on trek seeking new homes where they would not be disturbed by English ideas in government, religion and social relations—another portent of great moment for the British Empire. Meanwhile the steamship had passed the experimental stage. By 1837 steamships began to appear east of the Straits of Singapore. An agency for imperial expansion which also served as a link between the far-flung portions of the British Empire had come into existence. A new era was dawning.

CHAPTER IX

THE EMANCIPATION OF THE SLAVES, 1807–1838

THE Evangelical revival in the Church of England, which had inspired the philanthropic activities of "the Clapham sect", made rapid progress in the first quarter of the nineteenth century. As late indeed as 1808, the year after the abolition of the slave trade, the *Christian Observer* estimated that not more than a tenth of the clergy, perhaps only a twentieth, were Evangelicals; but in 1828 Keble regretfully noted "the amazing rate at which Puritanism seems to be getting on all over the kingdom".[1] Being mainly a middle-class movement and closely allied with Dissent, it could not but expand with the new alignment of social forces which foreshadowed the Reform Bill; and its influence can be discerned in the growth of missionary and humanitarian enterprise.

It would have been strange at such a time if the work done, but not completed, in 1807 had escaped attention; for the abolition of the slave trade as conceived by its promoters was a beginning rather than an end. Nothing could have been further from their intention than to follow up their success by demanding emancipation, for which they thought the negroes quite unfit; but they none the less believed that they had set in motion a chain of consequences which must issue in freedom. As the planter would no longer be able to replace the wastage of labour by importation, he would be constrained in his own interest to husband his stock. The negroes would be better fed, better housed, and more leniently worked. Marriage and the care of children would be encouraged; moral would follow physical improvement; and James Stephen, the most extreme of the Abolitionists, spoke for them all when he said that "they looked to an emancipation of which not the slaves but the masters themselves would be the willing authors".[2] It was necessary, however, for the fulfilment of their hopes that British participation in the slave trade should be actually as well as legally cut off; and they were impelled by their interest in the negro race to work for its general suppression.

These were, or rather became, the two main objects of the African Institution which was formed under high political patronage on 15 July 1807. Its original design, as set forth at great length in its first report, was to act as a sort of general staff for the army of pioneers, merchants and missionaries which was to take advantage of the op-

---

[1] Coleridge, Sir J. F., *Memoir of Rev. John Keble*, p. 176.
[2] Wilberforce, R. I. and S., *Life of William Wilberforce*, IV, 242.

portunity now offered for the civilising of Africa, and so "to repair the ruin and degradation which we have contributed to bring upon her".

The slave trade of the United States was to become illegal—eight months after ours; that of France, Spain and Holland had been arrested by the war; and, the Portuguese having but one small settlement north of the Equator, it was estimated that over 2000 miles of coast would be thrown open to legitimate commerce. The Spanish slave trade was, however, almost immediately revived under British protection owing to the outbreak of the Peninsular War; the Americans, and even the British, developed a contraband traffic; and the African Institution exhausted itself in combating these evils till it expired from lack of funds in 1826. What might have been accomplished under more favourable conditions may be conjectured when we find it supplying information to Captain Tuckey for his unfortunate attempt to ascend the Congo; sending out seeds and plants which had been obtained from India and the model of a mill for cleaning rice from the husk; trying to introduce palm-leaves as a substitute for hemp in the making of ropes; and establishing a school at Sierra Leone.

Meanwhile the Abolitionists were beginning to suspect a flaw in their automatic device for the amelioration of slavery. The planters did not seem to be adapting themselves to the new conditions, and the colonial Assemblies were certainly not enforcing this process by changes in the law. Wilberforce wished above all to legalise and promote marriage amongst the slaves, and thought that the planters must agree with him if only in order to arrest the depopulation which could no longer be counteracted by the slave trade. He was therefore anxious to secure facilities for religious instruction; and one of his earliest interventions was to assist the Methodists to procure the recall of a proclamation in which the Governor of Demerara had prohibited meetings for worship on the estates after sunset. In this and other instances he was not unwilling to humour Ministers in "doing things by private communications";[1] but these secret conclaves were abhorrent to Wilberforce's brother-in-law, Stephen, who had no idea of cleansing the Augean stable of the West Indies "with a government muck-fork", and insisted as early as 1811 that nothing effectual would be done "to check colonial crimes till we blazon them to the English public and arm ourselves with popular indignation".[2]

Stephen's disposition was naturally inflammable, and eleven years' experience of slavery when he was practising at the West Indian bar had made him the most vehement of all its adversaries—"full ten degrees above me", was the estimate of Wilberforce.[3] He considered the persistence of abuses as proof that the planters were still counting

---

[1] Wilberforce, R. I. and S., *op. cit.* IV, 242.
[2] *Ibid.* pp. 239, 241.
[3] *Ibid.* p. 241.

on importation, and, fantastic as this opinion was, it had a sub-stratum of truth. The Act of 1807, enforced by a vigilant navy, had largely achieved its purpose; but something more than pecuniary penalties was needed to extinguish so lucrative a traffic; and in 1811, at the instance of the African Institution, slave-trading was made a transportable offence.[1] This, however, did not satisfy Stephen. What he wanted was so ready a means of testing the right of property in slaves that nobody could have anything to gain by importing them, and his plan was to supersede the present defective registers by one which should be thoroughly reliable. Perceval, his friend and patron, who was then Prime Minister, consented to give effect to this idea in the Crown colony of Trinidad, and did so, shortly before his assassination, in 1812.[2] He agreed with its advocates that Parliament should be called upon to enact a uniform registration law, but advised them to wait for a year "to see how the engine should work in Trinidad";[3] and nothing further was done till 1815. Early in that year appeared *Reasons for establishing a Registry of Slaves*—a bulky pamphlet, professing to be a report of a committee of the African Institution, but known and acknowledged to be the work of Stephen. Here he admitted that the number of negroes imported into most of the colonies had been very small; but, by making no allowance for the accuracy of the new register in Trinidad as compared with previous returns, he arrived at a conclusion which could only mean that negroes had been smuggled into this island at the rate of several thousands a year; and he maintained that the bare possibility of importation elsewhere would be enough to deter the planters from improving their system, which he denounced as "the most extreme and abject form of slavery that ever degraded and cursed mankind". Lord Liverpool, when he was approached in March, said that, as there was no proof of smuggling, he could not ask Parliament to impose registration on the chartered colonies.[4] Stephen, who sat for a Treasury borough, resigned his seat; and Wilberforce warned the Premier in a confidential letter that he might soon have to start a popular agitation on behalf of the slaves.[5] On June 13 the long deferred bill was brought in by Wilberforce, who had to content himself with its being read once as a hint to the colonies to set up registers on this model for themselves. On this occasion he admitted that the prohibition of the slave trade had probably not been violated in Jamaica; but a year later, in moving for certain returns of population, he endorsed the latest and wildest aberration of Stephen—that the Jamaica planters had forestalled the Transportation Act by importing no fewer than 14,000 slaves.[6]

Meanwhile news had been received of an alarming outbreak in

[1] 51 Geo. III, c. 23. [2] Wilberforce, R. I. and S., *op. cit.* IV, 132.
[3] *Ibid.* p. 20. [4] *Ibid.* p. 244. [5] *Ibid.* p. 250.
[6] Hansard, XXXI, 772; XXXIV, 1182; Stephen, J., *Second Letter to Wilberforce in defence of Registry Bill* (1816), p. 158.

Barbados, where on Easter Sunday 1816 the slaves rose and wrecked or damaged sixty estates. Only one white person was killed, but several hundreds of the blacks were slain or executed. They are said to have believed that freedom was being illegally withheld from them by their masters; and they may well have thought so, for Stephen's pamphlet had provoked violent replies, and he and his associates were charged in the colonial press with having declared for emancipation. In 1819, when all the colonies had established registers, an Act was passed requiring duplicates to be lodged with a registrar in London and invalidating the sale or mortgage in this country of any slave who had not been entered in his books. The periodical registration of slaves, descriptive and not merely numerical, was no doubt a check on their ill-treatment; but the controversy as to whether the system should be adopted by the colonies or imposed upon them by Parliament was certainly not worth the contention it provoked—especially in view of Clarkson's subsequent admission that illicit imports, at all events after 1811, existed only in Stephen's imagination.[1]

The Abolitionists had now involved themselves in a renewal of hostilities with the planters; but ostensibly they were fighting merely to secure what they had gained in 1807; and Wilberforce, though the oppression of his "poor black clients" cost him sleepless nights, could not bring himself to open his campaign for the amelioration of slavery. He was unwilling to embarrass the Government in its efforts to procure a general suppression of the slave trade; and he was also deterred, first by political disturbances at home, and then by an economic crisis in the West Indies. Even Stephen, somewhat cowed by the storm he had raised, was on the side of caution; and not till 1823 did an appropriate opportunity appear.

The planters were in a position which exposed them to other enemies than the philanthropists. Quite a number of peers and members of Parliament—not to mention their relatives—were proprietors in the West Indies; and this connected them with the City, since their working capital was supplied by the houses to which they consigned their sugar, and moreover the merchant was often also a proprietor. The West India Association in London consisted of non-resident proprietors and merchants, and was said to be dominated by the latter. Shipowners and manufacturers had their place in this combination; and it was said in 1825 that "there were no less than fifty-six members of the House of Commons deeply and personally interested in the continuance of colonial slavery", who all voted "in a compact body".[2] The East India Company had of course its group of merchants and ex-officials in Parliament, but these in number and cohesion were much inferior to the West Indians.

[1] Clarkson, T., *History of Abolition of Slave Trade* (ed. 1838), Preface. Gardner shows that there had been no importation into Jamaica, *History of Jamaica* (1873), p. 253.
[2] Lushington in *Anti-Slavery Reporter*, No. I.

It so happened that these two interests had just come into conflict. The East India Company had recently been turning its attention to sugar; and in 1813, when the Company obtained a renewal of its charter but had to give up its monopoly of commerce, the West Indians had succeeded in imposing a differential duty of 10s. on the importation of sugar from Bengal. Five years earlier, the law which required them to send all their sugar to this country—which could import no other—had been modified, and in 1822 it was repealed.[1] The East Indians now demanded that in return for this indulgence the 10s. duty should be taken off; and on the rejection of their claim they and the Abolitionists joined forces, both professing to believe that, if the planters were exposed to competition from India, they would be compelled to reform, if not to abolish, slavery. Natural as this alliance was, it could not but quicken in its opponents the sense of injustice which had been excited by the register dispute. The East Indians posed as apostles of free trade, though all they wanted was to be allowed to participate in the West Indian monopoly; and the Abolitionists rather overdid the part imposed upon them by their allies. Not only did they make speeches and publish pamphlets against the 10s. duty, but in their collective capacity they went so far as to suggest that fiscal reform might solve the West Indian problem more effectively than the direct interference of Parliament.[2]

They were now at last to take the field, but not under their veteran commander-in-chief. Wilberforce, always fragile and now in his sixty-fourth year, felt himself too infirm to continue in this post, and his choice of a successor fell on Thomas Fowell Buxton, who had recently become prominent as a speaker on prison and criminal law reform; but one learns with some astonishment from his diary that he had thought of selecting Thomas Whitmore, the East Indian leader in Parliament.[3]

In January 1823 a society was formed in London for the mitigation and gradual abolition of slavery, which called itself, for shortness, the Anti-Slavery Society, and became the parent of many similar societies in other towns. The Duke of Gloucester, cousin of George IV, was the president. Amongst the vice-presidents, including five peers and fourteen members of Parliament, were Wilberforce, Clarkson, Stephen, William Smith, Buxton, Stephen Lushington, Lord Suffield, Sir James Mackintosh, Brougham and Whitmore; and on the committee were Zachary and Thomas Babington, Macaulay. Such imposing patronage is in signal contrast to the small and obscure beginning of the society formed in 1787; but it must be remembered that, whilst Granville Sharp and his friends had aimed at nothing short of the abolition of the slave trade, the men of 1823 were thinking primarily of the amelioration of slavery and of abolition only as its natural but

[1] 3 Geo. IV, c 45.
[2] *Second Report (1825) of Anti-Slavery Society.*   [3] *Life of Wilberforce,* v, 129.

distant result. Even in 1832, when amelioration might well have seemed hopeless, some of Buxton's "special friends and faithful supporters" had not yet despaired of "gradual extinction through the agency and cordial concurrence of the planters".[1]

The personal continuity of the two movements was impaired when Wilberforce retired from Parliament in 1825 and Clarkson soon afterwards was incapacitated by illness; but the three other veterans continued to work with all their former energy. Smith, who had represented Norwich since 1807, was invaluable as head of the Dissenting interest in Parliament. Zachary Macaulay had edited for many years the *Christian Observer*; and the *Anti-Slavery Reporter* was started under his direction in 1825. All important documents and speeches relating to the controversy were summarised in this monthly journal, which served also to link up the various local societies; and the articles and comments, almost all by the editor, were carefully authenticated. Stephen as a pamphleteer was equally indefatigable. "You and Stephen", wrote Wilberforce to Macaulay, "are the authors-general for our cause."[2] Buxton had been predisposed to accept the succession to Wilberforce by his relations with the Quakers, to whom belonged his wife, Hannah Gurney, and her sister, Elizabeth Fry. He brought into the movement the eminent civilian Lushington, Lord Suffield, and Mackintosh, who had co-operated with him in prison reform; and the first of these, who had entered Parliament just in time to speak in favour of the Slave Trade Abolition Bill, became his most trusted lieutenant.

It had been decided that Wilberforce should write the manifesto of the movement, and in March appeared his *Appeal on behalf of the Negro Slaves*. There were systems of slavery reputed to be harsher in practice than the British, but on the legal and social side it merited most of the strictures passed upon it in this pamphlet. The degradation of the slaves was extreme, for they had no legal status, such as was secured to them in the Spanish, and nominally at least in the French, colonies. The murder of a slave was indeed a capital crime; but this gave them no real protection, because their evidence was not admitted against a free person, whether white or coloured. Slaves could not be legally married, and their domestic relations were imperilled by the law which rendered them liable to be sold, individually or collectively, in payment of their owner's debts. In 1797 a British statute[3] which sanctioned this abuse was repealed,[4] and the Assemblies were exhorted both by their friends in Parliament and by the Colonial Office to prohibit the sale of slaves apart from the estate; but Tobago was the only chartered colony in which this reform had been, or was to be, effected. The Spanish usage which empowered the slave to pur-

---

[1] Buxton, C., *Memoirs of Sir Thomas Fowell Buxton*, p. 279.
[2] Knutsford, Viscountess, *Life and Letters of Zachary Macaulay*, p. 385.
[3] Geo. II, c. 7.   [4] 37 Geo. III, c. 119.

chase his freedom at an adjudicated price was unknown in our colonies, and even voluntary manumission was discouraged. Two-thirds of the slaves were employed in the production of sugar, the most uncertain and speculative of tropical industries, and also the most laborious, especially in the crop season when the mills were kept running all night; and it is significant that the indictment of slavery, in so far as it took account of industrial conditions, was based wholly on sugar. In other occupations, such as coffee-growing, where the slaves could not be worked in gangs under a driver,[1] they had a much easier lot; and the mildest form of servitude was to be found in British Honduras and Bermuda, where it was applied mainly in wood-cutting, boat-building and fishing. About 70 per cent. of the proprietors were non-resident. This was a misfortune for the slaves; but most of the resident proprietors were too poor to avoid over-working their gangs, and the large estates, despite the absence of their owners, were admittedly the best managed. Anything that had been accomplished for the elevation of the negroes was due to the missionaries, Methodist, Moravian and Baptist, who in some of the smaller islands worked under the patronage of the planters, but met with great opposition in Jamaica and Barbados.

Slavery had no compensations, but it had its alleviations. Though the slaves could not legally hold property, they were never disturbed in the possession of their dwellings and gardens, and could even dispose of them at death. They had usually allotments which sufficed not only for their own subsistence, but to supply the town population with fruit and vegetables. By this means they were enabled to purchase the gay holiday attire which so surprised visitors, and in some cases to practise thrift; but, as Sunday was their market day, it was by no means a day of rest.

The decrease of population was referred to in Wilberforce's pamphlet, and is worthy of attention as the evidence most relied on for ill-treatment. It is difficult to estimate the annual waste of life on the plantations before the abolition of the slave trade, as importation was required for new as well as old estates, but the most competent authorities reckoned it at about $2\frac{1}{4}$ per cent. As two-thirds of the negroes imported were always males and all of them were adults, depopulation could not but continue for some time after 1807; but for the six years 1818–24 the average annual decrease had fallen to $\frac{5}{8}$ per cent.[2]—a result much less unfavourable to the planters than the Abolitionists were willing to admit. That the population actually maintained itself had been their plea in former days, when they

---

[1] It was the irresponsibility of the negro driver, and not the amount of labour he could enforce under the lash, which constituted the cruelty of this system, as was proved after emancipation, when what had been a day's work under slavery became the standard for task-work, and the task could easily be done in five or six hours.

[2] *Anti-Slavery Reporter* (1827), II, 12.

wished to prove that the colonies could dispense with the slave trade.[1]

Wilberforce's survey was confined to the West Indies; but there were two other slave colonies, and in one of these the process of reform had already begun. The Cape of Good Hope had been ceded to Great Britain in 1814. Dutch slavery in the form it assumed at the Cape was supposed to be an exception to its general harshness; but even there neither indulgence nor protection was secured to the slaves by law.[2] A proclamation[3] intended to supply this defect was issued by the Governor, Lord Charles Somerset, in March 1823. Its main objects were to promote the diffusion of Christianity by offering certain advantages to baptised slaves and their owners, and to limit punishment and the hours of labour; but, as Burke said of the West Indian slave codes, it "lacked an executory principle", and perhaps the only clause that could not easily be evaded was that which made baptised slaves eligible as witnesses. The proclamation was confined to the negroes, and had nothing to do with an anti-slavery motion in regard to the Hottentots which had occupied the House of Commons in the previous summer. Unlike the West Indies, Cape Colony was a field for emigration; and the Abolitionists were anxious that the influx of British settlers, which began on a considerable scale in 1820, should not be a means of enslaving the natives. A clause to prevent this was already inserted in all grants of land; but Wilberforce feared that settlers remote from Cape Town might violate the condition, or even start slave-trading with neighbouring tribes; and on 25 July 1822 he moved an Address recommending the Hottentots to the King's "benevolent care". This was agreed to after a long debate, but without a division, the Government having announced that a royal commission, which was to visit the Cape and other colonies, would be instructed to enquire into the points mentioned by Wilberforce.[4] We shall see later that the condition of the Hottentots was much worse than might have been supposed from the debate, though Wilberforce was in communication with a missionary who had just returned from South Africa.[5]

Mauritius, the remaining slave colony, was also a recent acquisition, having been conquered from France in 1810 and retained at the Peace of 1814. Here alone the British slave trade survived after it had been made felony in 1811; and, if Stephen's attention had been drawn to this quarter, he could easily have established his case. The matter was taken up in Parliament in 1826, and from an enquiry which was soon

---

[1] *Parl. Hist.* (1791), XXIX, 267, 338; *Edinburgh Review* (1804), V, 233; *Westminster Review* (1824), I, 366.
[2] *Anti-Slavery Reporter* (1827), I, 289. For slavery at the Cape see *C.H.B.E.* VIII, chap. X.
[3] Printed in 18th *Report* (1824) *of the African Institution*, p. 183.
[4] Hansard (1822), VII, 1796.
[5] See *C.H.B.E.* VIII, 247.

afterwards held in the island it appeared that the slave trade had been carried on to a considerable extent down to 1818 and may have continued in some measure "at a much later period". Fraud and evasion made a complete fiasco of the register which was established in 1816—so much so that, ten years later, it was found necessary to "commence again the whole process of registration".[1]

The anti-slavery campaign in Parliament was opened on 15 May 1823, when T. F. Buxton moved that "the state of slavery is repugnant to the principles of the British constitution and of the Christian religion", and ought to be gradually abolished "with as much expedition as may be found consistent with a due regard to the well-being of the parties concerned". This idea he proposed to carry out by declaring free all children born after a certain date, and by establishing for the existing slaves certain reforms which he had communicated to Earl Bathurst, the Secretary for War and the Colonies. They were to be inseparable from the estate, to be admitted as witnesses, to have the right of purchasing their freedom by instalments and the benefit of religious instruction, marriage and the observance of Sunday. Measures—"but what I cannot say"—were to be taken to restrain the master's power of punishment, and a substitute was to be found for the driving system. Canning, who replied for the Government, thought it too late in the day to raise either the religious or the constitutional objection to slavery, and did not at all approve of emancipating infants whilst their parents were kept in bondage; but he acknowledged the necessity of securing Sunday to the slaves as a day of rest and of attaching them to the soil; and on the question of the whip he gave the Abolitionists more than they had asked or even thought prudent, declaring that it must be wholly abolished in the field and no longer inflicted as a punishment on women. He moved as an amendment that effectual and decisive measures should be taken to ameliorate the condition of the slaves; that "through a determined and persevering, but at the same time judicious and temperate, enforcement of such measures", the House looked forward to such an improvement in the character of the slaves as should prepare them for freedom, and was anxious for the accomplishment of this object at the earliest period "compatible with the well-being of the slaves themselves and with a fair and equitable consideration of the interests of private property". He made it clear, however, that the Government would adhere to the policy they had adopted on the register question, enforcing the reforms in the Crown colonies but merely recommending them to the chartered colonies, though he added that, if the latter should prove contumacious, Ministers "would not hesitate to come down to Parliament for counsel".[2]

---

[1] *Parl. Pap.* 1829 (292) xxv.
[2] Hansard (1823), IX, 258–87.

The Abolitionists had no faith in the colonial Assemblies. Reluctantly and not without protest, they concurred in this decision; but they were somewhat reassured by the professed readiness of the West Indian leaders to accept the resolutions. A week later, they supported Whitmore's motion for a select committee on the sugar duties; but on this question the "mighty and inveterate and obstinate combination"[1] —so it seemed to its opponents—could muster no more than thirty-four votes.

This defeat and the failure of his proposal to emancipate the children of the slaves seem to have greatly discouraged Buxton and to have convinced him that the attainment of his object was even more distant than he had thought. In a letter of the following November to Mackintosh, who had not yet supported the cause in Parliament, he said that he was "alarmed at the prodigious strength of the West Indian party", but that, if Mackintosh as well as Brougham could be relied on for assistance, "I doubt not that the sons of the present slaves will be raised to a state of villeinage and their grandsons will be freemen".[2]

Reforms for the gradual amelioration of the slave system were to be introduced first into Demerara, a Crown colony in which slavery still retained some of its Dutch harshness; and Bathurst lost no time in setting to work. In his despatch of 28 May 1823,[3] accompanying the resolutions of the Commons and a report of Canning's speech, he said that he could not then deal with all the proposed reforms, but would confine himself to two which he was sure the Court of Policy would deem it an honour to adopt—that the flogging of women should be absolutely interdicted, and that drivers should be forbidden to use or even to carry the whip. The Abolitionists were much better informed in this matter than Bathurst. They knew that the women slaves were always said to be far more difficult to manage than the men, and they were aware of the sentimental as well as practical importance that was attached to the whip; and Wilberforce, when he heard of the despatch, called it "positive madness".[4] The Governor, General Murray, himself a planter, received the despatch early in July; but delays in giving effect to the instructions precipitated a crisis such as had convulsed Barbados some years before during the Register dispute. The slaves understood that some "good thing", which the more ignorant believed to be their freedom, was being withheld from them. In the district between the Rivers Demerara and Mahaica, where missions had made most progress and aroused a religious fervour among the slaves, feeling was still more embittered by restraints on attendance at chapel which had recently been imposed. Here on 18 August there was an outbreak in which some 13,000 slaves were soon involved. They showed great self-restraint, neither looting nor

[1] M'Queen, J., *The West India Colonies*, p. 331.
[2] Buxton, C., *op. cit.* p. 135.
[3] *Parl. Pap.* 1824 (427) XXIV.
[4] *Life of Wilberforce*, V, 201.

burning, but two whites, who resisted the search for arms, were killed. The revolt was cruelly suppressed, and the Governor believed it to have been "plotted at the Bethel chapel on Mr Post's estate".

Copies of the Demerara despatch and its enclosures had been sent to the chartered colonies; and in a despatch of 9 July they were furnished with a summary of the other reforms which they were expected to adopt. Sunday markets were to be abolished as soon as provision could be made for religious instruction, and savings banks were to be established. Slaves who could produce a certificate from their religious teachers that they understood the nature of an oath were to be admitted as witnesses, except where the interest of the master or the life of a white person was concerned. Marriage was to be recognised, and husbands and wives and children under fourteen years of age were not to be sold separately. Slaves were not to be flogged till the day after the offence, and then only if a free person or a certificated witness was present in addition to the owner or overseer; and a record was to be kept of all floggings which exceeded three lashes.[1]

Bathurst's despatch of May 28 had been quite enough to excite a storm of indignation in Jamaica. Meetings were held in every parish at which the most violent resolutions were passed; and the same spirit prevailed in the Assembly, where it was even suggested that the King should be petitioned to dismiss the Colonial Secretary. Denunciation of the despatch in Jamaica was at least as likely to excite the slaves as its suppression in Demerara; and at the end of the year a plot for a rising was said to have been discovered. Eleven negroes were hanged and as many transported; but the evidence was little better than gossip, and became still more suspicious when two negroes, on whose testimony most of the prisoners had been convicted, were banished from the island as "persons of a most dangerous character". Plots even more nebulous were reported from Trinidad and St Lucia; and at Bridgetown in Barbados "a party of respectable gentlemen" demolished the Wesleyan chapel.

The news from Demerara and the West Indies was accepted as confirming the fears of those who had predicted that nothing but mischief could result from a popular agitation in favour of the slaves; and Buxton encountered a feeling which he described as not "opposition but virulence". At the opening of Parliament in February 1824 the Abolitionists were perturbed by a passage in the King's Speech in which the West Indian problem was referred to as "beset with difficulties" and soluble only by means "in which caution shall temper zeal"; but they were more disappointed than surprised—for they had been told what to expect[2]—when the despatches were laid before both Houses on March 16. It then appeared that the "petty refractoriness" of the chartered colonies was to be treated with nothing more

---

[1] For this despatch see *Parl. Pap.* 1824 (427) XXIV.
[2] Buxton, C., *op. cit.* (1848), pp. 143, 144.

drastic than a further course of "temperate but authoritative admonition", but that the programme of reform, which insurrection had frustrated for the moment in Demerara, was to be carried out at once in Trinidad. Further, something was to be done for religion and morals. Canning admitted that the Church of England in the West Indies had hitherto concerned itself only with the whites. "It was no more calculated for the negro than for the brute animal that shares his toils." This reproach was to be removed by the erection of two bishoprics in Barbados and Jamaica, the occupants of which would be expected to provide for the religious education of the slaves. The policy thus announced met with no opposition in the Lords, but Buxton and Wilberforce strongly protested.

That the anti-slavery movement was making headway in the country is shown by the fact that the number of petitions to Parliament had risen from 225 in the last session to nearly 600; and the exultation of its adversaries in Parliament was now to be checked. General Murray had followed up his suspicions as to "the Bethel chapel on Mr Post's estate" by having its pastor tried by court-martial; and John Smith, the missionary in question, had been sentenced to death, but recommended to mercy. The Governor remitted this recommendation to the Colonial Office, but, before a reply could be received, Smith, who was consumptive, died in prison, 6 February 1824. Brougham, on June 1, moved an address to the Crown in which the whole proceedings were unsparingly condemned, and this occasioned a long and animated debate.[1] There were several charges against Smith, but the only one which was found to have been fully established was that he knew of the intended rising and did not give information. Smith had over-estimated his power to control the negroes. Their designs, in so far as they amounted to an actual struggle for freedom, were certainly unknown to him; but he was fully aware that they were talking of forcing the planters to concur with them in an application to the Governor for Bathurst's "new law"; and, if there was any distinction between the rioting and the rebellion of slaves, it was not likely to be intelligible to their masters. The prosecution may have been inevitable, but little can be said for the manner in which it was conducted.

There were two reports of the trial, one official, the other drawn up by Smith's legal adviser, and from a comparison of these it appeared that hearsay evidence had been freely admitted against but not in favour of the accused. Whether it was due entirely to Smith's religious teaching that the rebels had refrained from bloodshed may be doubted in view of the previous revolt in Barbados; but the colonists themselves were of opinion that what discredited them most in the eyes of the British public was a letter of Mr Austin, the only Anglican clergyman in Demerara, in which he said that "nothing but those

---

[1] Hansard (1824), xi, 962–1076, 1206–1315.

principles of the gospel of peace", which Smith had been inculcating, "could have prevented a dreadful effusion of blood here and saved the lives of those very persons who are now, I shudder to write it, seeking his life". Canning, thinking it impossible to come to a satisfactory decision, was content to move the previous question, and even that was carried in a good House by a majority of no more than forty-seven.[1]

An Order-in-Council for the amelioration of slavery in Trinidad had been laid before Parliament on March 16,[2] and it deserves attention because the chartered colonies were expected to take it as their model. This ordinance did not by any means restore to the slaves of Trinidad the full enjoyment of the privileges they had had before the British occupation; but it revived or confirmed two articles of the Spanish code which were important additions to Bathurst's scheme—the institution of a protector of slaves and the recognition of the slave's right to purchase freedom from his master at a price which, if not settled by mutual consent, was to be determined in the last resort by an umpire. As the Order had been framed in Trinidad, it was proclaimed there, in spite of considerable opposition, as soon as the revised draft was returned from London; but great difficulty was experienced in extending it to the other Crown colonies, where it had to be adapted to Dutch or French law. The most obnoxious article was that relating to compulsory manumission, and in Demerara and Berbice[3] the non-resident proprietors succeeded in holding up this reform for three years by appealing against it to the Privy Council. Members of Parliament connected with the West Indies had promised to support Canning's policy in 1823; but in 1826 not only did they associate themselves with the appeal to the Privy Council, but a pamphlet, written by Alexander M'Donnell, the secretary of the West India Committee, and professing to express its views, then appeared under the significant title, *The West India Legislatures Vindicated from the charge of having resisted the call of the mother country for the amelioration of slavery.*

Obstructed in the Crown colonies, the policy of the Government was not likely to find favour where it was merely recommended for adoption. Bathurst's despatch enclosing the Trinidad Order reached Jamaica in September 1824. The agitation of the previous summer was at once renewed, and in a more confident spirit, for the planters were elated at the rebuff of their adversaries in Parliament, and looked forward hopefully to the coming of their bishop as likely to curb the activities of nonconformist missionaries. There had recently been a disturbance amongst the slaves in which some horses and

[1] *Parl. Pap.* 1824, XXIII (373, 465, 565); *Report of the Case,* 1824, Preface and pp. 182, 189, 197; *Substance of the Debate* (with "some new facts" in Preface), 1824; Hansard (1824), XI, 961–1076, 1206, 1213; *Edinburgh Review* (1824), XL.
[2] Printed in Hansard (1824), X, 1064.
[3] United to Demerara in 1831 to form British Guiana.

mules were killed. The Assembly could thus refer to "the present season of alarm", and maintained that, as reform had been postponed in Demerara, so it ought to have been deferred in Jamaica in circumstances "infinitely more critical". A bill to admit slave evidence under certain restrictions did not even find a seconder. Next year, when introduced in a still more limited form, it was thrown out by a majority of nearly two to one; and the Governor, the Duke of Manchester, in proroguing the Assembly expressed his regret that they had not recognised "the necessity of doing something, if not to disarm your enemies, still to satisfy friends, and, more than all, to convince Parliament that the urgent representations of His Majesty's Government have not been entirely disregarded".

In Barbados popular feeling seems to have run even higher than in Jamaica, and here we meet for the first time with the plan of evasion which was to be generally adopted. Instead of frankly accepting or rejecting the articles of the Trinidad programme, the local Legislature consolidated and amended its own slave laws, and professed in doing so to give effect as far as possible to the suggestions of the Home Government. As the alleged reform consisted rather in modifying old laws than in enacting new ones, it was almost impossible to judge how much or how little had been done; and good and bad elements were so closely interwoven that, as was afterwards said in Parliament, the Crown could not reject the relics of barbarism, which were purposely retained, without sacrificing the "salutary new provisions".[1] In August 1824 the Assembly of Barbados was engaged in this work, and, though the Trinidad Order had only just arrived, as many of its provisions were said to be included as could safely be adopted; but the Council was so far from sharing this opinion that it rejected the bill as rather worse than the existing law. Next year the bill passed, and the Assembly, in an address to the Governor, declared: "If it is determined that we shall be the victims of fanaticism, prejudice and injustice, we must submit; but neither threats nor persuasion will ever induce us to put the finishing hand to our own political, perhaps natural, existence."[2]

A disposition not quite so intractable was shown in some of the smaller islands, and notably in Tobago; but these exceptions to the rule were far from allaying the agitation which had now cast its network of societies over the whole country. In the third report of the London Anti-Slavery Society, adopted in December 1825, full credit was given to the Government for its ability and zeal, but it was asserted that the papers laid before Parliament showed the hopelessness of trying to extinguish or even to mitigate slavery "without the direct and authoritative interference of the Imperial Legislature".

[1] Hansard (1826), xv, 1319.
[2] Parl. Pap. 1825, xxvi (205); Second Report of Anti-Slavery Society; Reporter, i, 81; Hansard (1826), xiv, 1018; xv, 1293, 1300; Mathieson, W. L., British Slavery and Its Abolition, pp. 159–63.

The same opinion was expressed by Buxton in presenting a petition from the people of London in March 1826; but Canning maintained that "so hasty and precipitate a course" would be inconsistent with the cautious and gradual abolition which was all that had been contemplated in 1823; and he announced that another attempt would be made to bring the colonies to reason. An Act comprising the whole Trinidad Order was to be drawn up under the direction of Ministers and submitted to each of the colonial Legislatures; and, in order to strengthen the resolutions of 1823, they were to be submitted for approval to the Lords. On the same evening the question of the recent trials of slaves in Jamaica was brought before the House by Denman who declared that in these proceedings judicial oppression had "reached the highest pinnacle of its power". All the unscrupulous devices employed by the prosecution, including what Lushington called "hearsay evidence with a vengeance", were exposed in the debate; and one of the members connected with the West Indies wrote thus to a friend in the colonies: "On the question of the trials there was only one feeling in the House that such a state of law was utterly indefensible. You can scarcely form a conception of the strong impression which these trials have made on the public mind."[1] There was no difficulty in inducing the House of Lords to confirm the resolutions; and the West Indian peers hardly needed the warning of Lord Dudley and Ward, himself a Jamaica slave-owner, that "they could not afford to disregard the cry of indignation which had come from every corner of the kingdom".[2]

Brougham was of opinion that to make a fresh appeal to the humanity and good sense of the colonists would be a mere waste of time, and on May 19 he moved that the House early in the next session should consider measures to effect its purpose. Canning met this proposal by moving the previous question; but in reply to Ellis, the West Indian leader, he vindicated compulsory manumission as the most essential feature of the Government scheme. "*This* clause is the way out of that system, the opening by which slavery itself may *escape* gradually, and as it were imperceptibly, without the shock of a convulsion."

Meanwhile the new method of dealing with the colonies was being applied in a manner somewhat less drastic than that which Canning had proposed. In his despatches of May 11 and 21 Bathurst sent out eight drafts of legislation, embodying the several items of the Trinidad Order, and required the law officers of each colony to digest them into bills. The result of this final effort fully justified the prediction of Brougham. The small colony of Nevis was the only one which accepted the bills. Everywhere else they were either thrown out or not even allowed to be brought in; and the only pretence of compliance consisted in a professed readiness to amend the slave codes.

[1] *Anti-Slavery Reporter*, I, 207. [2] Hansard (1826), XIV, 1160.

The earliest replies from the colonies arrived at the end of the year; but the papers were not laid before Parliament till the summer of 1827. By that time Lord Liverpool was ill, and a Ministry dependent on the Whigs had been formed by Canning. Under these liberal auspices something would probably have been done to enforce the resolutions had Canning lived; but he died on August 8, and his Ministry survived him under Lord Goderich for only five months. The rigid Toryism of the Wellington Government (January 1828 to November 1830) would hardly have allowed them to coerce the planters, nor had they much inducement to do so, for the anti-slavery movement had been suspended for a year and a half before they came into power, and did not revive, at least in Parliament, till their term of office was nearly at an end. From July 1826 to January 1828 only some half-dozen petitions were presented to the House of Commons, this being the period of expectancy as to the West Indies and of Ministerial changes at home. In 1828 the trickle of petitions again became a flood; but Buxton was dangerously ill; Brougham, who had undertaken to bring forward the question, also fell ill; Lushington, having been appointed Judge of the London Consistory Court, was too much occupied to take his place; and Denman was temporarily out of Parliament. In 1829 the agitation again died down, extinguished temporarily both in Parliament and in the country by the controversy as to Catholic Emancipation. It is somewhat remarkable that the same Ministry which removed the civil disabilities of Nonconformists and Catholics at home should also have enfranchised the free coloured population in the Crown colonies; but a measure of more importance was one for the protection of the natives of South Africa.

Wilberforce had been anxious, as we have seen, to prevent British settlers in Cape Colony from making actual slaves of the Hottentots; but a great deal more than this was needed to secure their freedom. That they had not been actually exterminated is the best that can be said for their treatment during the century and a half of Dutch rule; and, if their condition became even worse after the permanent British conquest in 1806, this was due mainly to the fact that the demand for labour, owing to the abolition of the slave trade, had greatly increased. In 1809 a proclamation was issued which shows both the humane intentions of the Governor, Lord Caledon, and the extent to which he had been imposed upon by those whose interest it was that the Hottentots "should find an encouragement for preferring entering the service of the inhabitants to leading an indolent life".[1] Under a subsequent proclamation, issued by Sir John Cradock, afterwards Lord Howden, in 1812, masters were empowered to apprentice the children of Hottentots, born during the service of their parents, from the age of eight to that of eighteen.

[1] See *C.H.B.E.* VIII, 280 *seqq.*

Some degree of independence was still possible for the Hottentots if they attached themselves to one of the mission settlements which had been formed by the Moravians, and later by the London Missionary Society; but even here, whilst occupying a fraction of the soil which had once been their own, they were liable to demands for labour from the neighbouring farmers. In South Africa as in the West Indies the Moravians had always maintained good relations with the local Government. Less successful in this respect, the London missionaries were also hampered by the inferior quality and situation of their land; and their settlements, being supposed to encourage idleness, were harassed by the local authorities, who obstructed their admission of Hottentots and discriminated heavily against them in the exaction of public services and taxes. In 1819 the London Missionary Society sent out two representatives to report on the state of its missions. One of these, Dr Philip, came home in 1822 in time to advise Wilberforce on the subject of his motion; but it seems to have been agreed that to expose the condition of the Hottentots at a time when no reform was to be expected would serve only to excite hostility against the missions.[1] On his return to South Africa, Philip was examined by the commissioners whose attention had been directed to the natives in consequence of Wilberforce's motion; and the information he furnished was used to some extent in one of their general reports, but mainly in a special report which was called for later and not printed till 1830.

Philip now warned the Cape Government that, if the Hottentots were not rescued from their degradation, he would appeal on their behalf to the British Parliament and people. With this object he returned to England in 1826; and two years later, after trying without success to obtain satisfaction from the Colonial Office, he put his case before the public in two substantial volumes. That the Government realised the effect of this exposure was shown when Buxton proposed to raise the question in Parliament, and was told that his motion would be accepted if he brought it forward without making a speech. Accordingly on 15 July 1828 he moved an address to the Crown that such instructions should be sent to the Cape "as shall most effectually secure to all the natives of South Africa the same freedom and protection as are enjoyed by other free people of that colony, whether English or Dutch". But the Governor, influenced by a report which was dated as early as April 3, had already resolved to emancipate the Hottentots; and all the grievances of the latter were swept away by an ordinance of July 17, which was subsequently ratified as an Order-in-Council.[2]

---

[1] Philip, J., *Researches in South Africa illustrating the condition of the Native Tribes* (1828), II, 450.

[2] Philip, *op. cit.* Preface, pp. xxi–xxiv, II, 373, 380, 450; *Parl. Pap.* 1829 (50), XXV; 1830 (584), XXI; *Commons Journals*, LXXXIII, 536.

On the question of slavery the Wellington Ministry took care to make known in a circular despatch of 1828 that it had no intention of departing from the policy of Canning; but this announcement was not likely to cause much alarm in the West Indies; for the compliance of the colonies, which Brougham described as "so slow as to be imperceptible to all human eyes save their own", was accepted by the Prime Minister as sufficient to avert "any strong censure".[1] This complacent optimism had become intolerable to the Abolitionists, when in 1830 they renewed the struggle which had been practically suspended for four years. At an enthusiastic meeting in May the London Anti-Slavery Society resolved to petition Parliament that slavery should as soon as possible be abolished, and that all British subjects born after a certain date should be declared free; and the petition was entrusted to Brougham on the ground, as stated by Lushington, "that scarcely a decent hearing could be obtained in that House by any other member on this subject".[2] Parliament, soon after Brougham had discharged his task, was dissolved; the "July Revolution" at Paris, which occurred whilst the general election was in progress, gave a powerful impetus to the cause of parliamentary reform; and, though the Tories had still a majority in the new House of Commons, Wellington resigned on November 2 and was succeeded as Prime Minister by Earl Grey. It was not only "the battle of English liberty" that had been fought and won at Paris,[3] but also the battle of negro emancipation; for the party which had given to the anti-slavery movement both its political and its religious strength was now in office, and Brougham was Lord Chancellor. Of 2600 anti-slavery petitions presented in the autumn of 1830, no fewer than 2200 were said to have come from Nonconformists.

Not even a Whig Government could be expected to abolish slavery till it had disposed of the far more urgent question of parliamentary reform; and meanwhile the Abolitionists had to content themselves with a new device for giving effect to the discredited policy of amelioration. The late Ministry, in February 1830, had issued an Order in Council applying to all the Crown colonies, which admitted slaves without restriction as legal witnesses; but it was acknowledged to be deficient in other respects, and enquiries had been instituted with a view to its completion. The Abolitionists had no better friend in the Ministry than Viscount Howick, son of the Prime Minister and Under-Secretary for the Colonies. In April 1831 he announced that this ordinance was to be revised,[4] and that a reduction of sugar duties would be offered to the chartered colonies on condition that they

---

[1] Hansard (1828), XVIII, 978; XIX, 1466.
[2] *Anti-Slavery Reporter*, III, 264.
[3] *Edinburgh Review* (1830), LII, 1.
[4] For the extraordinary proceedings in Mauritius, when the revised Order-in-Council was received there in March 1832, see Mathieson, *British Slave Emancipation, 1838–1849*, pp. 218 *seqq.*

adopted it "word for word". Canning had foreshadowed fiscal *penalties*, not benefits, if the colonies proved obdurate; but the Tories were too exasperated by the Reform Bill, which had recently been introduced, to hear reason. Peel attacked the proposal as an outrage on the self-respect of the colonies; and it was no sooner known in Jamaica than the planters indulged in an orgy of denunciation. Meetings were held all over the island at which they presented themselves as the victims of "uncompensated emancipation", declared that the consequences would be a servile war too horrible to contemplate, and even talked of putting their slave property under the protection of the United States. In Jamaica, as formerly in Barbados and Demerara, the belief soon spread amongst the slaves that their "free paper" had arrived and was being suppressed. The planters confirmed them in this delusion by their wild talk of hoisting the American flag; and the climax of indiscretion was reached when the *Jamaica Courant* published a rumour that the troops had received "secret orders to remain neuter or to act against us in the event of disturbance". On December 27 an insurrection broke out among the slaves. It was confined to the north-west corner of the island and only two whites were wantonly killed; but houses and sugar-works were systematically fired.

The time had gone by when an act of violence such as this could stem the current of anti-slavery feeling in Britain. The general election of 1831 had given a large majority to the Whigs, hitherto holding office without power; and soon afterwards a rift disclosed itself in the Anti-Slavery Society. The younger and more zealous members had been urging that nothing effectual would be done in Parliament till means had been taken to increase the "pressure from without"; and under the leadership of George, fourth son of James Stephen, and Joseph Sturge, a Quaker merchant of Birmingham, they set up the Agency Committee—so called because it employed agents to lecture and organise. The Committee was independent of the parent society, though its circulars were issued from the same address. The object of the new body was political as well as philanthropic, and indeed the two movements could not be dissociated. The West Indian proprietors and merchants knew that slavery would not long survive the establishment of a middle class franchise. They were anxious on more general grounds to preserve the nomination boroughs, through which the sugar colonies were indirectly represented in Parliament; and the tacit alliance of borough-owners and slave-owners was disclosed by Lord Wynford: "God forbid that there should be anything like a forcing of the master to abandon his property in the slave. Once adopt that principle and there was an end of all property."[1]

Not one of the chartered colonies had closed with the Government offer, or rather, they had all rejected it; but they were suffering from

[1] Hansard (1832), XII, 630.

acute commercial depression; a hurricane, which proved twice as destructive as the Jamaica rising, had added to their distress; and the Government in April 1832 agreed that the state of their interests should be referred to a committee of the Lords. Buxton, regarding this as "a pretext for delay", resolved to counter it in the Commons, and moved that a committee should be appointed to consider measures for the extinction of slavery. The Government offered to accept his motion if he brought it into line with the resolutions of 1823, and, as the Reform Bill had not yet passed, great efforts were made to induce him to give way; but he stood firm and was supported by no fewer than eighty-nine members. Much information was collected by the two Select Committees, but both confined themselves to reporting the evidence, without giving any conclusions adduced from it.

The Reform Bill became law on June 7, but, though Parliament did not sit after August 16, it was not dissolved till December 3; and the Agency Committee displayed great energy at the general election, exacting pledges, publishing lists of candidates who favoured its policy and placarding the towns and villages with its favourite poster, "Am I not a man and a brother?"[1] When the first reformed Parliament met, however, in February 1833, Buxton was "affronted and vexed" to find no mention of slavery in the King's speech. He at once gave notice that he would move for abolition, and the Government then announced that they would take up the question and introduce "a safe and satisfactory measure"; but it was not till Buxton rose to propose his motion that they named a date, April 23.

The truth was that Ministers were not finding it easy to draw up a scheme which should be both "safe and satisfactory". They all wished to free the negro, but could not agree as to how his labour was to be secured to the planter. Lord Goderich, the Colonial Secretary, was dominated by Howick and two members of the permanent staff, James Stephen and Henry Taylor. Taylor proposed that the slave should be assisted to purchase his freedom by instalments; but Howick had a scheme of his own worked out for him by Stephen. The slaves were to be unconditionally set free, and a loan of £15,000,000 was to be given as compensation to their owners. Labour of specified duration and for fixed wages was to be enforced "with the aid of the proposed police"; and land used for growing food was to be taxed in order to make it difficult for the negroes to obtain a subsistence without working on the estates. The Cabinet, mainly under the influence of Brougham, rejected this scheme, as also did the West India Committee;[2] and another plan, very like that ultimately adopted, appears to have been under consideration, when Goderich for political reasons was replaced by Stanley.

[1] Stephen, Sir G., *Anti-Slavery Recollections* (1854), pp. 166, 167.
[2] Taylor, Sir H., *Autobiography* (1885), I, 124, 125, 127-9.

The loss of Goderich, who became Lord Privy Seal and Earl of Ripon, was regretted by the Abolitionists, especially as it was followed by the resignation of Howick; and there had been a fresh outburst of agitation when Stanley addressed the House, not on April 23, but on May 14. On this occasion he applied himself rather to showing the necessity of his measure than to explaining its purport; and the details will be found in the newspaper reports of a statement which he had made four days earlier to supporters of the Government. Slavery was to be abolished. In other words, the slave codes, which ten years of pressure had failed to ameliorate, would cease to exist; but, whilst slaves under six years of age were to be emancipated, the rest were to be apprenticed, at the most for twelve years, to the planters. For three-quarters of the day or week they were to work as before, except that they could be punished only by magistrates responsible to the Home Government. For the remaining quarter they were to work, if so disposed, as free labourers, and the masters were to see that a certain proportion of their earnings was set aside as a compensation fund. If it be asked how the masters could recover the value of their slaves through the accumulation of wages which they themselves had paid, the answer is that they were to have a loan of £15,000,000, which, if Parliament desired to relieve the slaves, might be made a gift. Stanley concluded by moving the adoption of his scheme in five resolutions; and, Howick having argued at great length that there could be "no intermediate state between slavery and freedom", the debate was adjourned. When it was resumed (May 30), the Government announced that they had decided to relieve both the slave-owners and the slaves by making a present of the £15,000,000; but this did not satisfy the West Indians, who resolved to ask for a gift of £20,000,000 and a loan of £10,000,000, which might or might not be repaid according as the experiment of free labour succeeded or failed. They were promised the additional £5,000,000, but not the loan. The concession was made on the principle of what Stanley called buying the goodwill of a business; but it was doubtful whether this valuable asset had after all been obtained; for, just before the resolutions were adopted, it was proposed on behalf of the West Indians that, to induce them "to co-operate cheerfully", they should have a one-half reduction of sugar-duties and a guarantee of £15,000,000 against loss[1]— demands which were, of course, refused.

The Abolition Bill was introduced on July 5, and had undergone only one important alteration when it became law—to come into effect eleven months later—on August 28.[2] In the previous autumn, when the Abolitionists were conferring with the Government, they had put forward a scheme not unlike that of Stanley, except that it

---

[1] *C.J.* LXXXVIII, 482.
[2] An extension of four months was allowed to Cape Colony and of six months to Mauritius.

provided for the remuneration of labour and was to last for only one or at most two years.[1] Nevertheless, when the resolutions were being discussed, Buxton had moved to dispense with the apprenticeship, and then to accept it if wages were paid. Both these motions were withdrawn; but a motion that the duration of the apprenticeship should be cut down to the shortest period necessary to accustom the negroes to wage-earning was lost by only seven votes. The Government then decided to reduce the term for predial or field apprentices from twelve to six years, and for non-predial apprentices from seven to four years. The apprentice could at any time be released by his master, and could compel his discharge by purchasing it at a valuation. The great majority of the petitions had been for immediate and uncompensated emancipation; but the Agency Committee which prompted this demand had greatly overrated its power, and all the anti-slavery societies were dissolved.

The Commissioners of Compensation did not enter on their duties till September 1835;[2] and much ill-feeling was aroused as soon as it became known that the rate would vary with the demand for labour, and consequently would be much higher in the new colonies than in the old. It has often been remarked that slave property was valued for compensation at about half its market price; but the planters were to be deprived of their negroes only in so far as the latter might not be available as free labourers; and we have seen that both the scheme of Goderich and the original scheme of Stanley contemplated merely a loan, the idea being that any loss occasioned by the change of system would be but temporary. The sum voted by Parliament was not to exceed £20,000,000; and the amount actually disbursed in satisfaction of claims was £18,669,401.

When the abolition of slavery had been secured, if not accomplished, Buxton again turned his attention to South Africa; and the aborigines within Cape Colony having been rescued from their miserable condition, his object now was to protect the tribes on its frontier. This was a more delicate, if not a more difficult, task; for, whilst the colonists were clearly responsible for their treatment of the "tame Hottentots", it could not be assumed that they were wholly to blame for the state of chronic hostility in which they lived with their savage neighbours. This, however, was the assumption made by Buxton when in July 1834 he moved an Address to the Crown for the protection and amelioration of native races and devoted most of his speech to the "commando system". As a method of reprisal against the Kaffirs, this system dated only from 1817 and recently had been much restricted; but Buxton identified it with the murderous forays of the Boers in former days against the Bushmen, saying that "the system con-

[1] *Correspondence of William Wilberforce* (1840), II, 524.
[2] See Wastell, R. E. P., History of Slave Compensation, 1833–45, an unpublished thesis in the library of the University of London.

tinued with its usual ferocity"; and he did not mention the perpetual thefts of cattle which were its motive, if not its justification. Spring Rice, an "old friend and coadjutor" of Buxton, was at this period Colonial Secretary. He seconded the motion of the latter and even suggested that in the next session he should move for a Select Committee, but took him severely to task for his unfair treatment of the colonists.[1] Buxton, however, was confirmed in his opinion by the outbreak a few months later of the sixth Kaffir War. Lord Glenelg, the new Colonial Secretary, agreed with him and in December 1835 intimated that the territory which had been conquered from the Kaffirs must be restored to them on the ground that they had been "urged to revenge and exasperation by the systematic injustice of which they have been the victims".[2]

A Select Committee to consider the state of the aborigines in British Settlements was appointed, with Buxton as chairman, in July 1835, and was reappointed in the two following sessions. The evidence disclosed a striking contrast between the Bushmen of New South Wales, who had been found incapable of assimilating either Christianity or civilisation, and the natives of the Society Islands and New Zealand, who in both respects had proved amenable. One of the South Sea witnesses was John Williams,[3] who has been described as "the most successful missionary of modern times". His successes were not confined to the religious sphere; for he told the Committee how he had extracted lime from coral, had constructed eight or ten sugar mills, and with his own hands had built a ship which was so successfully imitated by his converts that they had now many vessels of twenty to fifty tons burden. But perhaps the most interesting fact elicited was the success in mediation to which the missionaries ascribed their influence over the Maoris.[4] Five of them had pitched their tent for three days between two large forces equally well armed, and had succeeded at last in winning over "a very dreadful savage" to whom had been confided the question of peace or war.

South Africa, which accounted for two-thirds of the witnesses, was, however, the main field investigated by the Committee, and was equally conspicuous in the Report, drawn up by Buxton with the assistance of Dr Philip and signed on 26 June, 1837.[5] The Report was an indictment of European colonisation for the many calamities it had brought on native races (except in so far as it had been accompanied by missionary exertions), and was naturally more successful in developing this theme than in suggesting remedies. New territories were not to be acquired without the sanction of Parliament, and representatives of

[1] *Mirror of Parliament*, 1 July 1834.
[2] See *C.H.B.E.* vol. VIII, ch. XII.
[3] See *ibid.* vol. VII, pt. I, p. 333.
[4] *Ibid.* pt. II, ch. IV.
[5] For the Report see *Parl. Pap.* 1836, VII and 1837, VII.

the colonists, whether nominated or elected, were not to be consulted in the protection of the aborigines; but on the question of the attitude to be adopted towards independent tribes the writers of the Report do not seem to have known their own minds. As a general rule, treaties were to be avoided, because the contracting parties could not negotiate on equal terms; but some arrangement should be made with border chiefs for the punishment of aggressions; missionaries should be encouraged to form "schemes for advancing the social and political improvement of the tribes"; and not only were the parts of Glenelg's despatch of 26 December 1835 which prescribed an elaborate system of treaties embodied in the Report, but the propriety was urged "of a strict adherence to these regulations".[1]

The apprenticeship was established in all the slave colonies except Antigua and Bermuda, which had declared for immediate emancipation. There was little evidence amongst the planters of the goodwill for which Stanley had recommended the additional £5,000,000; but the peaceable and orderly behaviour of the negroes must have astonished the Duke of Wellington, who had said that we might be reduced to "the necessity of destroying the black population";[2] and, but for the exceptional difficulties which were encountered in Jamaica, the period prescribed for the experiment would in all probability have been allowed to run out. The Jamaica Abolition Act was accepted as qualifying for compensation in the confidence that its imperfections would be removed. The Assembly did pass an amending Act, but its operation was limited to the end of 1835, when it was allowed to expire, and was not renewed till provision for this purpose had been made in Parliament. Most of the Jamaican planters had so arranged their hours of forced labour that the free time of the negroes included Friday afternoon as well as Saturday; but the persistence of a minority in claiming the whole of Friday was a constant cause of trouble. In many cases indulgences which custom had secured to the slaves were denied to the apprentices; the court for regulating the purchase of freedom was so unfairly constituted that they had usually to pay an exorbitant price; and, though no female apprentice could be judicially flogged, women as well as men were flogged by way of maintaining discipline in prison. This abuse, though it had no necessary connection with the apprenticeship, could not fail to be identified with that system, and was soon aggravated by the institution of treadmills. Most of these were so badly constructed as to be mere instruments of torture; and prisoners of both sexes were flogged—as well as battered by the wheel—if they could not catch the step. Jamaica had two excellent Governors during this period and contrived to get rid of both. The Marquis of Sligo, who inaugurated the apprenticeship,

---

[1] The Aborigines Protection Society, now amalgamated with the Anti-Slavery Society, was founded in 1837 as an outcome of this Committee.
[2] Hansard (1833), xx, 518.

came into conflict with the Assembly and was recalled; and the same fate awaited his successor, Sir Lionel Smith, who had been transferred from Barbados, because he had there succeeded in conciliating the planters.

As early as October 1835 a meeting was held at Birmingham to petition for "entire emancipation". Joseph Sturge was the leader of the movement; and the next year, when a Select Committee of the Commons had reported that there was "much reason to look forward with confident hope to the result of this great experiment", he and three others sailed for the West Indies on a mission of investigation. What they saw there was of course mainly what they had come to see; and on their return two publications were issued. One was a short pamphlet in which an apprentice who had been grossly ill-used narrated his experiences,[1] the other was a book written mainly by Sturge;[2] and the object of both was to prove that the negroes were being worse treated under the restraints and safeguards of the apprenticeship than they had been as slaves. This view, though adopted in our general histories, was as mistaken as it was inherently improbable, and could never have gained credence had it not also been asserted that the Special Magistrates appointed for the protection of the apprentices were, with few exceptions, the tools of the masters. Some of them were so; but it would be easy to show that the great majority of these over-worked and under-paid officials acquitted themselves with admirable fidelity and zeal, and well deserved the high encomium bestowed upon them by an ex-Governor of Jamaica.[3] The most distinguished of their number was John Daughtrey, who in July 1837 considered "the gradual improvement of the people under the present system" as so indubitable that he knew no well-informed person "who makes it even a question".

Sturge's book, which was published early in 1838, made a great impression. Brougham, then out of office, was the first leading statesman to identify himself with the agitation, which he described as the most general and determined he had ever known; Buxton and Lushington, who at first held aloof, soon joined it; and it was claimed that at the end of May over 3000 petitions had been presented to the House of Commons. Various abuses in the working of the apprenticeship had been pointed out by the Select Committee; but the Jamaica Assembly was as deaf to all appeals for the reform of that system as it had been to similar appeals for the amelioration of slavery. In April an Abolition Amendment Act was passed which empowered the Colonial Governors to legislate for this purpose by proclamation. As the apprenticeship was part of the compensation secured to the slave-owners, Ministers opposed three motions for its abolition, one of

[1] *The Narrative of James Williams* (1837).
[2] Sturge, J. and Harvey, T., *The West Indies in 1837*.
[3] *Jamaica under the Apprenticeship*. By a Proprietor [Lord Sligo] (1838), pp. 32–7.

which was carried by three votes in a snatch division; but they were anxious that the Assemblies should themselves give it up; and a stage had now been reached at which their representations might be expected to prevail.

The non-predial apprentices whose labour was unrestricted were entitled to be released on August 1 of this year; and their number had hitherto been estimated at no more than a sixth of the whole. In the rules drawn up for the guidance of the Commissioners of Compensation, estate artisans, such as coopers, masons, carpenters and smiths, had been classed as predials, presumably on the ground that their labour, like that of the field-workers, was limited to forty-five hours a week. The Abolitionists had always complained of this classification; and in a despatch dated as late as March 30, the colonies were informed that, in the opinion of the Crown lawyers, the apprentices in question were non-predials. The planters had now to reckon with the loss of their artisans; they had also either to give up the apprenticeship or to continue it as amended by Parliament; and it is not surprising that the Legislatures of all the chartered colonies decided, one after another, that the partial emancipation due on 1 August 1838 should be made general.

There may have been no alternative to this cutting short of the apprenticeship after Sturge's agitation had excited the negroes, but it was certainly a very bad introduction to the new régime. The Select Committee of 1836 had expressed its anxiety that the "solemn engagement" should be preserved "inviolate"; and, though Ministers had contrived to maintain the good faith of Parliament, they had done so only by pressing, if not forcing, renunciation on the colonial Legislatures. The whole trouble had arisen from the intransigence of the Jamaica Assembly; but the penalty was not confined, like the provocation, to Jamaica; and Barbados was probably not singular in thinking that it had suffered for the sins of another colony. Nor was it the planters alone who complained of injustice; for it was only, as a rule, by saving their earnings for extra labour during the apprenticeship that the negroes could buy themselves out, and the many who had recently purchased their freedom now found that their savings had been wasted. Sir Lionel Smith found it difficult to answer their complaints.

Two things were essential to the introduction of wage-labour in the slave colonies—laws to regulate its operation and money to meet its expenses; but no provision had been made for the first of these purposes, and little, if any, for the second. The Orders-in-Council which defined the policy of the Home Government in regard to such matters as contracts for labour, vagrancy and squatting were not issued in London till September and October 1838; and, as the Assemblies had had to legislate without waiting for guidance, their enactments were almost all disallowed.[1] Nothing was so likely to discourage the

---

[1] See *Parl. Pap.* 1847-8, XLV (419).

negroes from working on the plantations as irregularity in the payment of wages, and this in many cases was inevitable. It had been made known that very few planters in Jamaica were "prepared with money payment"; and silver was so scarce in the island during the first few weeks of emancipation that cheques were used for such small sums as a dollar or even a shilling. The Crown colonies, having had to wait for the decision of the chartered colonies, were necessarily the least prepared; and Trinidad is said to have had only four days' notice.

These were temporary defects; but the fundamental difficulty remained that the abolition of slavery had been accomplished, not as the outcome of the long course of preparation recommended by its supporters, but as the only step possible after that policy had been successfully opposed.[1] It may be said that, though the civilising process had been frustrated before emancipation, it might at least have been tried later; but this task, if we can imagine it being undertaken by the West Indian legislatures, must have been based on compulsion, and any attempt to coerce the ex-slaves for their good would certainly have been denounced in this country as a violation of their freedom. In fact, for some years after 1838 almost the sole object of the Colonial Office was to see that the Abolition Act was not surreptitiously infringed; and Joseph Gurney was not the only person who thought that the emancipated classes needed nothing more for their development than to be left to themselves. "Only let freedom alone and all will be well."[2] Earl Grey, the former Viscount Howick, when he became Colonial Secretary in 1846, was more than ever convinced that the regulated emancipation he had suggested would have been the better plan. Realising that it was now too late to tax the grounds of the negroes, he proposed to make them pay for schools and hospitals; but this also proved to be impracticable, and it is significant that, in spite of his anxiety to stimulate and elevate a people "so unfortunately addicted to idleness", the one really successful measure of his administration was the scheme for importing Indian coolies which more than restored the prosperity of Mauritius and Trinidad and did almost as much for British Guiana.

[1] On this point see Livingstone, W. P., *Black Jamaica*, p. 32.
[2] *A Winter in the West Indies* (1840), p. 114.

CHAPTER X

COLONIAL SELF-GOVERNMENT
1838–1852

I

OF all the governments which ruled England in the nineteenth century hardly one can have seemed less fitted to strike out a bold line in imperial policy than the second Melbourne administration. The Whigs had carried a series of great statutes remodelling the institutions of government, and now they were stale. Reforming energy was on the wane both in the party and in the country, and although the favour of the girl who became Queen in June 1837 had raised their drooping prestige they returned from the polls with a majority in the Commons of only twenty or thirty. The defection of O'Connell and the Radicals might turn the balance, and Lord John Russell's declaration against any further extension of the franchise strained Radical allegiance.[1] In the Lords ministers had against them not only the usual Tory majority but their late colleague, the eccentric and formidable Brougham; Durham, the other potential Radical leader, had also been excluded from Melbourne's Cabinet. The ministry was weak both in counsel and in debate, and nowhere weaker than in its Colonial Secretary. Charles Grant, Lord Glenelg, was conscientious and hard-working, and his conciliatory temper did not always lack appreciation in the colonies; but he was woefully deficient in judgment and decision, and his conduct of affairs found stern critics not only on the Radical benches but in the Cabinet itself. Nevertheless, he enjoyed the affection and respect of the great civil servant whom he had recently raised to be permanent head of his department.

In James Stephen's case the convention which ignores the personality of English public officials was persistently broken.[2] In accusing him of indifference to colonial interests and a desire to interfere out of season, critics like Roebuck, Buller and Wakefield were ludicrously wrong. They were less wrong in magnifying his influence. But a qualification is necessary. On ordinary routine matters, particularly while Glenelg was Secretary of State, it is true that Stephen's influence, though not obtruded, was immense; it was the natural result of his industry, knowledge, ability and public spirit. But when a colonial

---

[1] See *The Greville Memoirs*, Nov. 1837.
[2] See Hansard, 3rd series, XXXVI, 1337 (6 March 1837), XL, 385 (23 Jan. 1838).

issue reached the stage of real political and parliamentary importance it passed out of Stephen's hands for decision by the Cabinet.[1] Such for some time had been the case with regard to the Canadas.

On 22 December 1837 the British public was startled by the news of insurrection in Lower Canada. To most Englishmen it was a bolt from the blue, but North American affairs had long perturbed the Colonial Office and the Cabinet.

In 1828 and 1834 Committees of the Commons had considered the grievances of Lower Canada, in 1831 revenues had been surrendered by Parliament to the Canadian legislatures, and in 1835 the Whigs had sent out the conciliatory Gosford as Governor and a commission of inquiry. But all in vain. The Quebec Assembly persistently refused to vote supplies, and in March 1837 the Home Government reluctantly appealed to Parliament. Both Houses passed by large majorities Lord John Russell's ten resolutions, which refused the Lower Canadian demands for constitutional change and authorised the payment of Canadian salaries in arrear out of the proceeds of colonial taxation. Baulked of their hopes, but encouraged by the speeches of the English Radicals, the bolder French-Canadian leaders rose in arms in November; an even feebler outbreak followed in the Upper Province. Both risings were easily suppressed, but their importance was exaggerated in England. They served to force Canadian, and colonial, affairs to the front and enabled, indeed compelled, the Government to take more drastic measures than would otherwise have been possible. Ministers could count on Conservative support, and even O'Connell disapproved Papineau's action.[2]

After acute dissension the Cabinet decided against the repeal of the Revenue Act of 1831 and in favour of the temporary suspension of the Constitution Act of 1791, so far as concerned the Lower Canadian legislature; the Governor was for the time being to exercise a limited legislative authority in conjunction with a special council, and was to summon thirteen persons from each of the two provinces to meet for the purpose of submitting a permanent scheme to Parliament. A bill introduced in January on these lines passed with little opposition, but Peel's criticism secured the omission from the preamble of all reference to the proposals for shaping a new constitution. To the Radicals the bill seemed oppressive and despotic to the last degree; only one thing mollified them, the selection for Governor-General and High Commissioner of one of their own chiefs, Lord Durham.[3] An early advocate of reform of Parliament and chairman of the

---

[1] *The Greville Memoirs*, 12 March 1839.

[2] The Act surrendering revenues (often called the Ripon Act) is 1 and 2 Will. IV, c. 23. For encouragement of the Canadian Opposition by English Radicals see the Commons debates of 6 and 8 March and 14 April 1837, Hansard, vols. XXXVI, XXXVII. For O'Connell see Mulgrave to Russell, 6 Jan. 1838, Russell Papers, P.R.O.

[3] See Memoranda by Russell and Howick in Russell Papers, P.R.O. The bill is in *Parl. Pap.* 1837–8, 1, 253 sqq.; it became law as 1 and 2 Vict. c. 9.

committee which drafted the famous bill, "Radical Jack" had retired in 1833 from the Cabinet of his father-in-law, Lord Grey; next year he had come out openly as the unofficial leader of those Reformers whom the late Act failed to satisfy. His advanced views and fiery temper made him a difficult colleague, and he was distasteful to Melbourne on both personal and public grounds. In June 1837 he had returned from the St Petersburg Embassy, and though he owned allegiance to the Government, he was a dangerous man unmuzzled. He had ability, courage amounting to rashness, and a considerable popular following; so it was politic of Melbourne in July to offer him the Governor-Generalship of Canada. Durham had then refused the thankless task; now, when the offer was repeated in a greater emergency, he accepted with misgivings. His several commissions appointed him Governor of the two Canadas, Nova Scotia, New Brunswick and Prince Edward Island, High Commissioner for the two Canadas, and Governor-General of the whole of British North America, including Newfoundland—a mandate of unprecedented scope. The instructions supplied him by Glenelg explained that his main duty was to prepare the way for a return to a system of free government, and included the suggestions, dropped from the bill, for the convocation of delegates from the two Canadas in an advisory capacity.

Having invoked the "cordial and energetic support" of the Cabinet in his task of "awful responsibility", and the "generous forbearance" of the Tory peers, Durham chose his staff with the greatest care; its two most distinguished members, Edward Gibbon Wakefield and Charles Buller, were both already prominent in colonial affairs, Wakefield as the promoter of the systematic colonisation of South Australia and New Zealand, Buller as Agent for the Australian Patriotic Association of New South Wales and member of the House of Commons Committee on Transportation.[1] The new Governor landed at Quebec on 29 May 1838. It was the first time that a statesman of both Cabinet and ambassadorial rank, already distinguished in national and European politics, had been sent out to govern a British colony; the first time also that enthusiasts for the imperial connection had been placed by Government in a position to apply their theories. Durham promptly dismissed all but one of his predecessor's Executive Councillors—a striking break with tradition—and opened up friendly relations with the President and people of the United States. But the story of the auspicious beginning and stormy close of his five months' reign belongs rather to the history of Canada and to the biography of English parties and personalities than to the development of colonial policy, except in so far as the controversy illustrates the possibilities of misunderstanding in days

[1] Hansard, XL, 240–3 (18 Jan. 1838).

before the telegraph and the frivolous manner in which colonial interests could be subordinated to personal caprice.[1] It will be more useful for our purpose to observe how opinion stood at home in the months preceding the presentation of Durham's Report.

The debates on the Ten Resolutions of March 1837, on the Lower Canada Government bill, and on Molesworth's motion of 6 March 1838 censuring Glenelg's administration—a motion which was enlarged by the Tories to include the ministry collectively—provide unusual opportunities of learning the views of the politicians on the colonial situation.[2] These views may be summarised in two propositions: the colonies are bound to leave us some day; but we must not, and will not, let them go now. It is clear that the great majority of members in all parties, whether regretting the prospect or not, believed that the colonies would separate from the mother country eventually. The disruption of the old empire two generations before was an ever present memory, and it seemed that history was repeating itself. Colonial assemblies were as unreasonable as ever, their democratic views pointed to republicanism, and the last sixty years had produced no talisman of concord. But on this occasion the mother country would not have the heart to fight against a clearly expressed colonial opinion, whether from expectation of defeat, dislike of force, or a belief, flowing from economic theory, that the colonies were not worth fighting for. Only Charles Buller and a handful of other Liberals had faith that wise treatment might preserve the connection.

On the other hand, the feeling was almost as universal that the time for separation was not yet come, and that its likelihood in the remote future ought not to affect present policy directly. Colonies, said Russell, the Leader of the House, increased England's strength and prestige. Moreover, the Canadians of British origin showed no desire to separate, and to abandon them would be base. Peel was ready to face war with the United States on this issue; Melbourne, while thinking it possible that eventual separation would mean no "material detriment" to the mother country, was clear that it would be a serious blow to her honour, and deprecated its discussion; the Radical Molesworth claimed to yield to none "in a desire to preserve and extend the colonial empire of England"; and Roebuck himself was not prepared to see Canada become part of the United States. Those who, like Brougham, declared that the colonies were worth nothing to Great Britain and that their loss would be a positive advantage to British trade were a tiny minority.[3] It was generally agreed that in present circumstances England must hold on to her

---

[1] See *C.H.B.E.* vol. VI, ch. XI.

[2] See Hansard, vols. XXXVI, XXXVII, XL, XLI.

[3] For Peel's views see Parker, C. S., *Sir Robert Peel*, II, 355; Hansard, XXXVII, 1279, XL, 72; for Melbourne's, Reid, S. J., *J. G. Lambton, Earl of Durham*, II, 137, Hansard, XL, 882; for Molesworth's Hansard, XLI, 483; for Roebuck's, Hansard, XXXVII, 1210, 1228, XL, 735 ff.; for Brougham's, Hansard, XL, 213.

colonies, do her best for them, and make the most of them. The connection should be maintained as long as possible: the colonies should be allowed free institutions and given conciliatory treatment; then, if part we finally must, we should part as friends.

But what did free institutions and conciliation mean? To grant demands incompatible with a colonial relationship would lead only to premature separation. Free institutions meant, in effect, institutions as like those of the mother country as possible, and it must be remembered that in 1838 the British constitution was regarded as essentially "a mixed form of government", duly combining the monarchical, aristocratic and democratic elements. The loss of the thirteen colonies proved to the Whig-Tory mind the danger of an excess of democracy, and the provisions for Legislative Councils and an endowed church in the Canadian constitutions of 1791 were intended by Pitt and Grenville to counterbalance it. Granted that colonial soil was not congenial to aristocracy, it seemed in 1838 all the more important not to weaken the monarchical element by conceding the demand for elected senates, smacking as it did of American republicanism. There was equal opposition to the proposal that the Executive Councils should be made responsible to the Assemblies. All agreed that these Councils were unsatisfactory in composition as in function, but it was generally held that, were their status assimilated to that of an English Cabinet, colonial subordination would be at an end.[1] As regards legislation, Parliament followed Burke and Canning in wishing to interfere as little as possible. Glenelg declared it "unconstitutional" to intervene in the internal concerns of a colony enjoying representative government unless for grave cause and when other means had been exhausted.[2] In the matter of taxation the principle of the Act of 1778, whereby Parliament declared that it would not henceforward tax the American colonies for revenue, was regarded as sacred; but the Assemblies did not control all the revenues of the provinces, and the refusal of the Lower Canadian Chamber to vote a fixed Civil List in return for the sources of income surrendered by Parliament in 1831 made it certain that no further concession would be sanctioned except as part of a bargain.[3] On the negative side, the right of disallowance was certainly exercised in many cases that now seem surprising, but it was the professed policy of the Colonial Office to use it only when the interests or the honour of the mother country was involved. Glenelg wrote even of the reservation of bills as an "extreme right".[4]

Such being the general temper, there was little cry for vengeance

[1] See the second and third reports of the Gosford Commission, *Parl. Pap.* 1837, xxiv, 50.
[2] Glenelg to Head, 5 Dec. 1835, *Parl. Pap.* 1836, xxxix (113), p. 60; reprinted in Kennedy, *Statutes, Treaties and Documents of the Canadian Constitution*, 2nd ed. p. 319.
[3] The Act of 1778 is 18 Geo. iii, c. 12. In New Brunswick the Crown lands and revenues were surrendered in return for a Civil List in 1837; see *C.H.B.E.* vi, 279.
[4] Glenelg to Gosford, 17 July 1835, *Parl. Pap.* 1836, xxxix (113), p. 50.

on the French-Canadians: they were regarded as a backward people, deluded by agitators, and, though several speakers urged the union of the two Canadas, Glenelg disclaimed any intention of effecting it without the consent of both provinces.[1]

Lord Durham disembarked at Plymouth on November 30, in disgrace with ministers and bitterly resentful at their treatment of him. Though tempted both by his own feelings and by Radical exhortations to lead an attack on the Government in circumstances which seemed promising, with unusual self-restraint he resolved to set first the interests of Canada, where a second futile outbreak had just occurred, and for the next two months he slaved at his Report. Wakefield was already in England, Buller arrived on December 21, and there were informal means of ascertaining the views of prominent ministers. On January 31 Glenelg received the document in proof; on February 8 a large part of it appeared mysteriously in *The Times*, and it was soon afterwards laid before Parliament. Clear, incisive and readable, before many months passed it had been studied and discussed throughout the Empire.[2]

Before leaving England Durham had satisfied himself that the claims of French-Canadian nationalism were inadmissible, and that Canada must be made thoroughly British. In his secret despatch of August 9 he argued that the conflict of races in the Lower Province was far more acute and fundamental than was understood in England and that the constitutional deadlock was only one example of its effects.[3] He developed this theme in the Report: "Never again will the present generation of French Canadians yield a loyal submission to a British Government; never again will the English population tolerate the authority of a House of Assembly, in which the French shall possess or even approximate to a majority."[4] Convinced that the preservation of French-Canadian nationality was neither possible nor desirable, and rejecting absolutism as alike inefficient, unlikely to last, and bound to create friction with the United States, he concluded that only a popular government, in which an English majority should permanently predominate, could ensure tranquillity to Lower Canada.[5] This pointed to a fusion of its government with that of one or more of the surrounding provinces, and he explained how his early predilection for a federal system including the Maritime Provinces, which might be expected to lead in time to a complete legislative union, had yielded to the arguments for a legislative union of the two Canadas, creating a single province in which 550,000 English would outweigh

---

[1] Hansard, XL, 885 (8 Feb. 1838).
[2] See generally New, Chester, *Lord Durham*, chap. XXI and, for a discussion of the authorship of the Report, his Appendix; also *C.H.B.E.* vol. VI, ch. XI. For J. S. Mill's intervention see his *Autobiography*, pp. 215–17, and *Westminster Review*, Dec. 1838.
[3] Reprinted in Lucas, Sir C., *Lord Durham's Report*, vol. III.
[4] Lucas, I, 53.
[5] *Ibid.* p. 303.

450,000 French. Only the pressure of circumstances prevented him from advocating the immediate legislative union of the whole of British North America. In one of the most eloquent passages of the Report he urged the material and moral advantages of such a policy. The greater the scale of the union, the more might be hoped from the growth of a "national feeling", which, so far from fostering a desire for separation, would be likely to lessen it, since the colonists so united, freed from undue interference by Downing Street and from fear of the overwhelming preponderance of the United States, would attain a loftier self-respect, both individual and collective, and find satisfaction in their new nationhood. But public opinion in the Maritime Provinces was not ripe for the merger, whereas Lower Canada could not wait. Durham therefore advised the prompt introduction of a bill repealing the Act of 1791 and uniting the Canadas as a single province; there should be provision for the eventual admission of the other colonies by agreement, and a single supreme executive and a single Court of Appeal for British North America should be established at once.[1]

But Durham did not believe that swamping the French population in an English mass would of itself bring peace. A radical change in the method of government was necessary.

It is impossible [he wrote] to observe the great similarity of the constitutions established in all our North American Provinces, and the striking tendency of all to terminate in pretty nearly the same result, without entertaining a belief that some defect in the form of government, and some erroneous principle of administration, have been common to all.... It may fairly be said, that the natural state of government in all these Colonies is that of collision between the executive and the representative body. In all of them the administration of public affairs is habitually confided to those who do not co-operate harmoniously with the popular branch of the legislature; and the Government is constantly proposing measures which the majority of the Assembly reject, and refusing its assent to bills which that body has passed.

Such disharmony seemed to "indicate a deviation from sound constitutional principles or practice". Representative government had been made to work in England, after the conflicts of the seventeenth century, through the recognition that the King could not hope to rule by ministers not possessing the confidence of the Commons. It was idle to suppose that a representative body with any experience would be content to act as a mere law-making and tax-raising instrument confiding the direction of policy to an irresponsible clique of officials.[2] There were various ways of making a government "responsible". In the United States responsibility was secured through a popularly elected executive, and there were some who desired an elected Executive Council in Canada. But this, in Durham's view, was inconsistent with monarchy, and he himself

[1] Lucas, I, 304–25.
[2] *Ibid.* pp. 72–81.

favoured the solution henceforward known as "responsible government" *par excellence*.

Every purpose of popular control might be combined with every advantage of
vesting the immediate choice of advisers in the Crown, were the Colonial Governor
to be instructed to secure the co-operation of the Assembly in his policy, by
entrusting its administration to such men as could command a majority; and if
he were given to understand that he need count on no aid from home in any
difference with the Assembly, that should not directly involve the relations between
the mother country and the Colony.

These issues might be defined as constitutional amendment, foreign
relations and external trade, and the disposal of public lands. The
change would involve government "by means of competent heads
of departments" instead of "the present rude machinery of an
executive council", and it could probably be effected by instructions
contained in a single despatch.[1] But, in order to start the colony fair,
Parliament should set up elective municipal bodies, revise the constitution of the Legislative Council, surrender all revenues (except
from public lands) in return for an adequate Civil List, secure a
permanent tenure and income to the judges, prevent money grants
from being proposed in the legislature except on the initiative of the
Crown, and repeal the existing law on the subject of Clergy Reserves.

Should these reforms be promptly adopted, Durham looked forward
to an indefinite maintenance of the imperial tie. He had found in
Canada an affection for the mother country which only a continuance
of misgovernment could destroy. "The British people of the North
American Colonies", he wrote, "are a people on whom we may
safely rely, and to whom we must not grudge power." He based his
estimate of their future conduct not on a pessimistic retrospect of
events to the south sixty years before, but on personal acquaintance
and democratic sympathy. "The experiment of keeping colonies and
governing them well, ought at least to have a trial, ere we abandon
for ever the vast dominion which might supply the wants of our
surplus population, and raise up millions of fresh consumers of our
manufactures, and producers of a supply for our wants." And, after
all, the colonists did not exist for the sake of the mother country.
England's first duty was to secure the well-being of her colonial
children, and honour demanded that, if eventually separation should
come about, the British colonies "should not be the only countries on
the American continent in which the Anglo-Saxon race shall be found
unfit to govern itself".[2]

The principal features of this Report as an imperial document of
permanent importance are, in the first place, its confidence and
courage, in contrast with the defeatism of many; secondly, the
outspoken determination that the language and institutions of the
country must be British; thirdly, the readiness to allow the colonists

[1] Lucas, I, 279–82.
[2] *Ibid.* pp. 285, 331, 310.

a constitution similar to the English constitution not of the seventeenth, but of the early nineteenth century; and, lastly, the refusal to be perturbed by the possibility that the colonists might not always acquiesce in the restrictions laid on their autonomy.

The Government had intended to introduce a Canada bill before Easter.[1] But it was the curse of colonial administration that important decisions were delayed because ministers or Parliament were occupied with other business. This is particularly true of these last years of the Whigs, which have been described as "one long political crisis". Even in 1839 Canada had to yield precedence to the troubles of another colony. Moreover, Cabinet dissensions over Jamaican affairs brought to a head the distrust of Glenelg's capacity long felt by Russell and Howick. His colleagues agreed to drop him, much to James Stephen's indignation, and at the beginning of February he was replaced by the Marquis of Normanby, formerly Earl Mulgrave, a popular Irish viceroy and a former Governor of Jamaica, but a man of no great parts.

Discussing the Canadian problem with Russell in December Melbourne had been inclined to continue the suspension of the constitution of the Lower Province and to leave the others alone. A permanent general settlement must be based on a popular franchise; but it was agreed that the French-Canadians, who formed the vast majority in Lower Canada, must not regain their predominance, and Melbourne was reluctant to juggle with the representative principle. He preferred therefore to temporise.[2] But by the beginning of April, fortified by Durham's advice, the Cabinet resolved on a legislative union of Upper and Lower Canada, and Russell announced this decision to the Commons on May 3.[3] That very night began the Jamaica debate which resulted in the ministry's resignation, and but for the young Queen's refusal to dismiss her Whig ladies it would have fallen to Peel and Stanley to give Canada a constitution and a Governor. Back in office, but badly shaken, on May 13, the Whigs decided not to attempt to pass their Union measure during 1839, but they submitted to Parliament resolutions on the subject and later the text of a bill. Russell explained, in moving the resolutions on June 3, that it would be difficult, in view of democratic opinion across the United States border, to prolong despotic rule, and that a confederation of all five provinces was judged impossible for geographical and other practical reasons. The new colony composed of the two Canadas should be made thoroughly British and should receive municipal institutions. But it would be wise to postpone for a while the first meeting of the united Assembly, and indeed all discussion of the

[1] Hansard, XLV, 206, 919 (11, 27 Feb. 1839).
[2] Melbourne to Russell, 23 Dec. 1838, *The Melbourne Papers*, ed. Sanders, p. 444.
[3] *Ibid.* (2 April 1839); Broughton, Lord, *Recollections of a Long Life*, v, 183; Hansard, XLVII, 756, 765; for Russell's views see a memorandum in his hand of 28 March 1839 in the Russell Papers.

details of the new constitution, and for the present merely to define and extend until 1842 the powers of the Governor and Special Council of Lower Canada.[1] The Government's delays and changes of plan were derided by their critics, but in view of Upper Canadian strictures on Durham's Report the decision to postpone permanent legislation was not seriously challenged, even by Durham himself. Urgent as he had been for prompt action, he recognised the need of obtaining for the new settlement a broad basis of consent, and he deserves all credit for subordinating personal feelings to the good of the Empire.[2]

But though the session of 1839 left Lower Canada still without a constitution, steps of profound importance had been taken before its close. Not only had the Government decided to unite the provinces, but the seals of the Colonial Office had been entrusted to no less a personage than Russell himself. Melbourne had learned at length that "the firm and effective management of the colonies is vital to the interests of the Empire".[3] Russell knew little about the colonies and he lacked Durham's greatness of conception, but he had energy, confidence and goodwill, and never shirked responsibility. Hardly less important was the choice of Charles Poulett Thomson, the President of the Board of Trade and a member of the Cabinet, to be Governor of the Canadas.[4] Thomson possessed wide commercial, parliamentary and departmental experience, his self-confidence equalled Russell's own, and he was on intimate terms with both Russell and Durham. These three friends between them inaugurated a new system of colonial government.

Russell explained to Thomson in his confidential instructions that his first duty was to discover the wishes and secure the co-operation of the Canadians in the matter of the Government's Union policy. A brief allusion to the topic of "the nature and extent of the control which the popular branch of the united legislature will be admitted to exercise over the conduct of the executive government, and the continuance in the public service of its principal officers" was expanded in two despatches which have become classics in imperial history.[5] Ever since the publication of Durham's Report this topic had been engrossing attention in Upper Canada and Nova Scotia, and it is necessary to know what was meant.

From earliest times the Royal colonies had possessed Governors and Executive Councils modelled on the Stuart system of domestic

---

[1] Hansard, XLVII, 1254 seqq. The bill introduced for this purpose did not in its final form (2 and 3 Vict. c. 53) extend the period; the limit of 1 Nov. 1840 remained unaltered.

[2] The Government's changes of plan may be traced in Hansard, XLVII, 1273 (3 June), XLVIII, 96 (10 June), 207 (13 June), 1007 (28 June). They themselves attributed them to Canadian, their opponents to domestic considerations.

[3] Melbourne to Lansdowne, 19 August 1839. Torrens, W. M., Memoirs of Lord Melbourne, II, 311.

[4] The administration had been conducted since Durham's departure by Sir John Colborne, afterwards Lord Seaton.

[5] Russell to Thomson, 7 Sept., 14, 16 Oct. 1839, Parl. Pap. 1840, XXXI [211] reprinted in Kennedy, pp. 416–24.

government. The Councils, like the Privy Council at home, had varied functions, judicial for instance, and appointments were normally for life. Unlike the Privy Council they acted also as legislative Second Chambers, and they did not necessarily include the heads of the colonial departments. Neither Councillors nor heads of departments were normally members of the elected Assemblies; on the other hand, in the colonies possessing separate Legislative Councils Executive Councillors commonly sat in these bodies.[1] It is misleading, therefore, to think of Executive Councillors or of the heads of colonial departments as corresponding to English ministers. The colonial form of government was, in fact, not parliamentary: it bore a closer resemblance to the constitution of the United States as originally devised than to the British system in the nineteenth century. It was only possible for John Simcoe, the first Lieutenant-Governor of Upper Canada, to speak of the provincial constitution as "the very image and transcript" of that of Great Britain because in the eighteenth century the essence of the British constitution was held to lie in the blend of the monarchical, aristocratic and popular elements and in the separation of powers. The importance of the Cabinet system was not yet recognised: there is no mention of it, for instance, in Russell's *Essay on the English Government* published in 1821, and it may be that not before Walter Bagehot wrote did it become a commonplace of theory.[2] Lord Durham was the first British statesman to insist that if the colonies were to enjoy British political institutions these must include an executive responsible to the popular assembly.

Not everyone, however, was beguiled by Simcoe's phrase. As early as 1808 the Governor of Lower Canada told Lord Castlereagh that "the Canadian party" claimed "that there exists a Ministry here, and that in imitation of the Constitution of Britain that Ministry is responsible to them for the conduct of Government".[3] But it was not, apparently, till twenty years later, when the clash between established interests and reformers had produced something like opposing parties in Upper Canada, that the demand for an executive responsible in the English sense to the legislature was first clearly stated by Dr William Baldwin, a wealthy Irish settler in Toronto. It was accepted by a group of Baldwin's political friends, and formally adopted by the Lower Canadian House of Assembly in February 1836 as well as, more vaguely, by the Nova Scotian Assembly in April 1837; but in no province had there been much clear thinking on the subject, and it was left to William Baldwin's son Robert to give the doctrine full expression in the letter which he wrote to

[1] Separate Legislative Councils were established in the Canadas in 1791, in New Brunswick in 1832, in Nova Scotia and Prince Edward Island in 1838. See *Parl. Pap.* 1839, xxxiv, 579.
[2] See Dunham, A., *Political Unrest in Upper Canada*, pp. 161-4.
[3] Craig to Castlereagh, 5 Aug. 1808, Kennedy, p. 224.

Glenelg on 13 July 1836 and two years later submitted to Durham.[1] The plan consisted in

nothing more than having the provincial Government, as far as regards the internal affairs of the Province, conducted by the Lieutenant Governor (as Representative of the paramount Authority of the Mother Country) with the advice and assistance of the Executive Council, acting as a Provincial Cabinet, and composed of men possessed of the public confidence, whose opinions and policy would be in harmony with the opinions and policy of the Representatives of the People.

The Executive Councillors "would generally if not uniformly be in one or other House of Parliament, and would there form a centre of Union, and in fact act as a sort of balance Wheel to the constitution". He believed that the adoption of this "English Principle" would strengthen the attachment of the people to the mother country and "place the Provincial Government at the head of public opinion".[2] He did not propose or intend that even in purely colonial affairs the Lieutenant-Governor should exercise no personal control of policy: the function of his ministers would be merely to advise; the decision in the last resort would be his.

We have seen that Parliament in 1837 declined to grant this concession, but that Durham none the less recommended it. In adopting Baldwin's plan he changed the emphasis somewhat and struck a bolder note. His English experience made him think of the heads of departments (whom Baldwin had not mentioned), rather than the Executive Council, as the instruments of popular government, and he had the courage to advise that the Governor should receive "no aid from home in any difference with the Assembly, that should not directly involve the relations between the mother country and the Colony"; further, he enumerated the classes of subjects which did so concern the mother country.[3] Some of his successors found his exposition ambiguous. It is true that he uses the word "responsible" in differing senses and that the picture of a Governor carrying out "his" policy "by means of competent heads of departments", the word Cabinet being nowhere used, might suggest a William III rather than a Victoria, or even than a William IV. But there is no real obscurity if we assume that Durham allowed for a gradual development. It is clear from the Report that the existing British system was his ideal, but he explained in his last speech in Parliament that he did not propose to take all steps at once.[4]

[1] See generally Dunham, chap. x; New, pp. 335–42, 411–15; for Lower Canada see Kennedy, p. 331, and the 2nd and 3rd Reports of the Gosford Commission (*Parl. Pap.* 1837, xxiv, 50) including especially the evidence of J. Neilson and R. E. Caron (pp. 130, 132); for Upper Canada see Head to Glenelg, 21 April 1836, and enclosures (*Parl. Pap.* 1836, xxxix, 391); for Nova Scotia see Chisholm, J. A., *Speeches of Joseph Howe*, i, 104, 114, 154; R. Baldwin's letter to Glenelg is in C.O. 42/434, and is printed, along with his covering letter of 23 Aug. 1838 to Durham, in Kennedy, pp. 335, 367.
[2] Kennedy, pp. 338, 339.   [3] Lucas, ii, 280, 282.
[4] See Thomson to Russell, 15 Dec. 1839, C.O. 42/298, p. 209; Metcalfe to Stanley, 24 April, 4 Aug. 1843, Kaye, Sir J. W., *Life and Correspondence of Lord Metcalfe*, ii, 477; *Selections from the Papers of Lord Metcalfe*, ed. Kaye, pp. 411 *seqq.*; Lucas, ii, 278, 327; Hansard, xlix, 880 (26 July 1839); *C.H.B.E.* vi, 306.

The Cabinet were not converted by Durham's arguments. Russell instructed Thomson to say nothing which might countenance the theory of "what is absurdly called responsible government".[1] He would not admit its soundness even as regards the internal affairs of a colony, since even here the Home Government could not divest itself of responsibility for "the honour of the Crown or the faith of Parliament or the safety of the state". But in practice he was prepared to act on the lines traced by Durham. "Her Majesty has no desire to maintain any system of policy among her North American subjects which opinion condemns"; it is her intention "to look to the affectionate attachment of her people in North America as the best security for permanent dominion", and the new Governor will earn her approval "by maintaining the harmony of the executive with the legislative authorities". The execution of such a policy must be based not on positive enactment but on practical experiment in mutual forbearance.[2] At the same time Russell did much by another despatch to free the hands of Governors for action on the line indicated: heads of colonial departments and Executive Councillors were to know that henceforward their offices must not be regarded as held during good behaviour, as had virtually become the case. Public policy, or even a change of Governor, would now be taken as sufficient cause for their removal.[3] The former of these despatches was not published till March 1840, but the latter was made known in the colonies at once and created considerable stir both there and at home, where it increased the Duke of Wellington's dislike of the Government's Canadian policy.[4]

Neither despatch was in fact altogether novel in principle. Recent Secretaries of State had urged Governors to include a popular element in their Executive Councils, and Glenelg had accepted the recommendation of the Gosford Commission that Councillors should be made removable at the Governor's discretion.[5] What was new was the confidence and vigour behind the phrases, and the selection for their translation into action not of some Peninsula veteran but of a young man "with House of Commons and Ministerial habits", of

[1] See speeches of Russell on 3 June 1839, Normanby on 26 July 1839, Hansard, XLVII, 1268, XLIX, 844; Russell to Thomson 4 Oct. 1839, *Letters from Lord Sydenham to Lord John Russell*, ed. Knaplund, p. 32.

[2] Russell to Thomson 14 Oct. 1839, *Parl. Pap.* 1840, XXXI [211], p. 13. Russell wrote in 1870 that in 1836 he had been satisfied by Robert Baldwin's assurance of Canadian loyalty; "and when I held the seals I practically acted upon it, though I did not concur in the theory". *Speeches of Earl Russell*, I, 154. It is noteworthy that Thomson conferred with Durham before sailing for Canada. New, p. 526.

[3] Russell to Thomson, 16 Oct. 1839, *Parl. Pap.* 1840, XXXI [211], p. 15.

[4] Hansard, LV, 241, 507 (30 June, 7 July 1840). For Melbourne's replies see *ibid.* 270, 516. The despatch was originally drafted at the beginning of September and had then no connection with the Responsible Government issue or with Canada; Butler, J. R. M., *Camb. Hist. Journ.*, II, iii, 248 *seqq.*

[5] See Correspondence in *Parl. Pap.* 1839, XXXIV (579) and Glenelg's minute in *Canadian Archives, Report for 1923*, p. 247.

first-rate ability, untiring energy, and high political courage.[1] A situation had been reached where only experiment could determine how far, if at all, Durham's views and Russell's might be reconciled in practice. No one in England knew what "responsible government" would mean in North America, and because parliamentary processes were unfamiliar there no one could know in North America either. It was enough for the reformers that the system in force was irresponsible and was hateful. Everything therefore depended on the man chosen to conduct the experiment; and the Whigs served the Empire well in that after sending Durham to prospect and report they sent Thomson to see what could be done and do it.

The new Governor brilliantly executed the first part of his commission by winning the consent of both Canadian legislatures to the scheme of union and so averting Tory opposition in England. Peel had to calm the angry misgivings of the Duke of Wellington, and Russell felt constrained to drop the clauses establishing municipal institutions by which both Durham and Thomson had set such store; but otherwise the Union bill of 1840, as redrafted by Thomson with the expert help of Chief Justice Stuart, passed without difficulty through a Parliament weary of colonial controversy. Besides constituting a single province of Canada with a single legislature, the Act provided for a fixed Civil List in return for the surrender of the Crown's hereditary revenues and reserved to the Crown the initiative in votes appropriating public money.[2]

Lord Sydenham fully deserved the peerage and "red riband" awarded him as the tokens of "complete success". Besides carrying the union he induced both Houses at Toronto to pass a Clergy Reserves bill which, he said, was worth ten unions; he secured by provincial enactment the municipal institutions which the Union Act denied him; and before his death he had, with the help of a loan guaranteed by the Imperial Government, set Canadian finances on their feet and initiated indispensable public works.[3] But the importance of his career in the story of the development of colonial self-government lies in the fact that he devised a new rôle for the Queen's representative and so prepared the way for a new type of colonial policy, built on British, not American, lines. He laid his finger on the worst defect of the Canadian system: there was no organic connection between executive and legislature. The Government did not initiate or control legislation, it had no effective spokesman in the Assembly, its officers were not even united in supporting a common policy. The remedy which he applied was to form, under his own leadership, a team of men whom a majority of

[1] The phrase quoted is Thomson's own, Scrope, G. P., *Memoir of the Life of Charles, Lord Sydenham*, p. 245.

[2] The equal representation of Upper and Lower Canada, adopted in the Act, had been suggested by Colborne; to Normanby, 19 Aug. 1839, *Parl. Pap.* 1840, xxxi [211].

[3] Knaplund, P. (ed.), *Letters from Lord Sydenham etc.*, pp. 44, 155.

the Assembly would support, and with their help to drive useful measures through. They were in fact a ministry, the first Canada had seen; for all the members of his first Executive Council for the united province held official posts, and all his heads of departments had seats in the Assembly, except one who was a Legislative Councillor. By the success of his methods he educated the Canadians, and educated Russell, with whom he carried on an intimate private correspondence, in the application of parliamentary methods to a colony; he carried the process so far and so fast that by the end of the first session of the united legislature he had assented to a declaration that, while the representative of the Sovereign must be responsible to the imperial authority alone, his chief advisers "constituting a provincial administration under him, ought to be men possessed of the confidence of the representatives of the people".[1] His fatal accident has deprived us of the letter to Russell in which he would have justified his acquiescence in something so very like "what is absurdly called responsible government". But Charles Buller was right in saying: "It does not matter very much what the Government repudiates or what it recognises, for certain it is that in the Parliament of United Canada it has created a power from which no Government in this country will be able to withhold that voice in the selection of its rulers, which Lord Durham showed to be a necessary consequence of representative institutions."[2]

The success of Sydenham's *tour de force* was due partly to his own adroitness and vigour, partly to the admitted need of the great measures which he secured for the province, and partly to the weakness of party ties in the new Assembly. His death forestalled the embarrassments bound to occur when the pendulum swung away from him, all the more surely since he had failed to win the confidence of the French-Canadians. He seems never to have faced the question of what would happen should he no longer find subordinates willing and able to carry his policy through the Assembly. Lord Falkland in Nova Scotia, who by Russell's instructions was trying, with smaller strides, to follow in the same path, said frankly that the Governor must resign.[3] Sydenham's scheme of being his own Prime Minister was admirably suited to a period of transition, while a colony was learning what parliamentary government meant. But he was wrong in believing that his system would run itself; serious difficulties were certain to confront the new Governor whom Russell's successor would appoint.

Events in the Maritime Provinces, in accordance with their loyal and constitutional traditions, were less dramatic than in the Canadas,

---

[1] Resolutions of Legislative Assembly 3 Sept. 1841, printed in Kennedy, p. 458.
[2] Lucas, III, 376. Durham died on 28 July 1840, Sydenham on 19 Sept. 1841.
[3] Russell to Falkland, 18 Aug. 1840, C.O. 218/32; Falkland to Russell (Private), 29 Nov. 1840, Russell Papers, P.R.O.

but here, too, the period 1837–41 was one of even drastic change. New Brunswick was content to have secured the surrender of Crown lands and revenues in return for a Civil List, and Sir John Harvey, appointed Lieutenant-Governor in 1837, made things work smoothly[1]. But in Nova Scotia, where the franchise was very low and where the reforming party had recently found an energetic leader in Joseph Howe, a young journalist of great courage and resource, the Assembly came to an open breach with the Council in April 1837. On appeal being made to London, Glenelg, while rejecting the Assembly's inchoate demand that public officers should be rendered responsible to it, agreed to the creation of a Legislative Council distinct from the Executive Council and was prepared to transfer the Crown revenues on the same lines as in New Brunswick.[2] But the conservative sympathies of the Lieutenant-Governor, Sir Colin Campbell, neutralised the conciliatory spirit of Downing Street, and friction continued even after July 1839, when rival delegations from the two Houses of the Legislature pleaded their causes before Normanby. Joseph Howe, who had remained at Halifax, was greatly disappointed by Russell's speech of 3 June renouncing Durham's theories, and addressed to him in reply the four celebrated Letters in which the case for limited colonial autonomy was argued more fully than before.[3]

Russell's despatch on the tenure of offices[4] was published in both New Brunswick and Nova Scotia, and in both led to misunderstanding. At Fredericton Harvey let his heads of departments and Executive Councillors understand that henceforward opposition to the policy of the Government would involve loss of office, as the result of this "very important change".[5] In Nova Scotia the Assembly claimed that the despatch conceded the principle of responsible government, ingeniously insisting that it must be interpreted in the light of Sydenham's pronouncement of 14 January 1840 in which he assured the Assembly of Upper Canada that he had received instructions to govern "in accordance with the well understood wishes and interests of the people, and to pay to their feelings, as expressed through their representatives, the deference that is justly due to them".[6] Russell did not think it worth while to correct Harvey's "mistake". In Nova Scotia, where the Assembly, not content with passing a formal vote of no confidence in the Executive Council, had proceeded to demand the Lieutenant-Governor's recall, he judged matters more serious, and while approving Campbell's refusal to agree to the collective removal of the Council instructed Poulett Thomson to visit Halifax

[1] See *C.H.B.E.* VI, 277–80. Cf. Glenelg's minute in *Canadian Archives, Report for 1923*, pp. 229–30, and Harvey to Durham, 16 Aug. 1838, summarised *ibid.* p. 110. Of Harvey's five Executive Councillors three were members of the Assembly.
[2] See correspondence in *Parl. Pap.* 1839, XXXIV, 579.
[3] Kennedy, pp. 384 sqq.
[4] Above, p. 347.
[5] Harvey to Russell, 24 Dec. 1839, C.O. 188/66.
[6] Kennedy, p. 432.

and report on the situation.[1] Thomson diagnosed the same fault as in Canada, a complete absence of parliamentary methods of government, and Russell appointed a Whig peer, Lord Falkland, in Campbell's place to put Thomson's suggestions into practice.[2]

The Colonial Department was mainly concerned in these years with the colonies already possessing representative government. But in echelon behind them, at different stages of political development, were other colonies which desired it. In March 1841 Lord John Russell stated as a general principle that "whenever you had a settlement of British subjects well established in a place, you should give them free and popular institutions".[3] In spite of the party feeling which had led to deadlocks in Newfoundland, he would rather amend its constitution than withdraw representative government. In granting the island an elected Assembly for the first time in 1832, Goderich had approved the same principle, with a reservation for "those colonies in which the people are separated from each other by distinctions analogous to those of caste".[4]

The existence of exactly such distinctions in the penal establishments of Australia checked their development long after a population of free immigrants had settled there alongside the convicts and "emancipists", as former convicts were called.[5] Until about 1840 the hostility between the party of the emancipists and the more aristocratic or "exclusive" free settlers and officials was the chief feature of the social and political life of New South Wales. Since 1828 the legislative authority had been the Governor and a nominated Council of fourteen, of whom seven were officials and nearly all were taken from the "exclusive" section.[6] The Act of 1828 was due to expire in 1836, and in this year both parties expressed their views to the Home Government by petition. The "exclusives", important in substance rather than numbers, asked only for an increase in the unofficial element in the Council. The "emancipists", who on the advice of Henry Lytton Bulwer, their English patron, had recently organised themselves into the Australian Patriotic Association, demanded as alternatives either two Legislative Chambers, of which

[1] Harvey to Russell, 24 Dec. 1839, with minutes by Vernon Smith and Russell, C.O. 188/66; Russell to Thomson, 30 April 1840, with enclosures; Russell to Campbell, 30 April 1840, Can. Archives, G. 47; Melbourne in the House of Lords, 30 June 1840, Hansard, LV, 270 (see above, p. 347, n. 4); Martin, C., *Empire and Commonwealth*, pp. 186–93.

[2] Thomson to Russell, 27 July 1840, Can. Archives, G. 391 and *Letters from Lord Sydenham to Lord John Russell*, ed. Knaplund, p. 81; Martin, C., pp. 194–8.

[3] Hansard, LVII, 716.

[4] Goderich to Cochrane, 27 July 1832, *Parl. Pap.* 1839, XXXIV, 579. For Newfoundland see *C.H.B.E.* VI, 428–30.

[5] The population of New South Wales numbered just over 77,000 in 1836, of whom nearly 28,000 were convicts; of Van Diemen's Land, over 40,000 in 1835, of whom nearly 17,000 were convicts. Martin, R. M., *History of the Colonies of the British Empire*, 1843.

[6] See Melbourne, A. C. V., *Early Constitutional Development in Australia (New South Wales)*, pt. II, ch. VI, pt. III, ch. II, and *C.H.B.E.* vol. VII, pt. I, ch. VI.

one should be elective, or a single "blended" Chamber, a portion of whose members should be nominated and the remainder elected.[1]

Australia was in those days some four months distant from London, and the need for thorough consideration was made a reason in the session of 1836 for merely renewing the Act of 1828 for a year. The same procedure was in fact adopted until 1842, partly owing to the pressure of affairs in England, partly because conditions were changing fast in the colony. In 1837 there was every excuse for delay: Chief Justice Forbes and James Macarthur, the leader of the "exclusives", were both in England, three new books on the affairs of New South Wales required to be digested, and in April the House of Commons appointed a Select Committee, with Molesworth as its chairman, to investigate the subject of transportation. This last step was of crucial importance, since it stood to reason that so long as New South Wales and Van Diemen's Land could be described as convict stations Parliament would not give them "free institutions". There was good ground to suppose that the Committee would recommend the abolition of transportation and that the Government would carry out the recommendation; in one respect Russell and Glenelg anticipated its findings by agreeing to discontinue the practice of "assigning" convicts in the colonies to work for private employers.[2] The issue was one where the moralist, the humanitarian, the rationalist and the systematic coloniser could work side by side.

Meanwhile Stephen, with the help of Forbes and Macarthur and later of Charles Buller, Bulwer's successor as Agent of the Australian Patriotic Association, was at work on a reformed constitution which should make some concession to the representative principle without either entrusting power to ex-convicts or distinguishing invidiously between them and free settlers. Belief in the virtue of an elective municipal system was much in vogue, in connection with England, Ireland and the Canadas, and an attempt was made to solve the Australian problem by introducing one in New South Wales, whereby local bodies should exercise a suspensory veto on the measures of a nominated council at Sydney. After much discussion and shortly before his departure for Canada, Buller with Macarthur's approval submitted a plan providing for a single Chamber, partly nominated, partly indirectly elected through municipal councils. Glenelg circulated the plan in bill form to the Cabinet; but it met with objection, and the fact that the Transportation Committee was still sitting gave an excuse for postponing decision.[3]

---

[1] Bourke to Glenelg, 13 April 1836, *Parl. Pap.* 1846, XXIX (400). Some such scheme had been recommended by Governors for some years; see Sweetman, E., *Australian Constitutional Development.* See also Melbourne, A. C. V., pt. III, chs. VI, VII.

[2] See interdepartmental letters of 15 and 29 April 1837 in *Parl. Pap.* 1837–8, XXII (669), p. 260.

[3] C.O. 201/257; Buller to Glenelg, 15 April 1838 (copy) in Russell Papers: Hansard, XLII, 479 (9 April 1838); Sweetman, chs. XI, XII; Melbourne, pt. III, ch. X.

At length in August 1838 Molesworth's Committee reported in favour of discontinuing transportation to New South Wales and Van Diemen's Land as soon as possible.[1] From that moment the grant of self-government to all the Australian colonies in due course was assured. Sir George Gipps, the new Governor of New South Wales, repeated his predecessor's criticisms of the existing Legislative Council and advised, as suitable for the present transitional period, a single "blended" Chamber, of whose members one-half to one-third should be directly elected; ex-convicts, if qualified, should be allowed the franchise but should not be eligible.[2] Gipps had already opened the sessions of the Council to the public, and though a new constitution was again deferred, the renewing Act of 1839 gave the Council power to remodel the judicial system in a "liberal" direction. Next year Russell introduced a bill giving the colony, for ten years, a Legislative Council of thirty-six members, of whom twenty-four would be elected. But the bill was dropped after the first reading, and the measure eventually passed did little more than renew the Act of 1828; proposals for the subdivision of the colony which aroused fierce opposition when known in Australia were modified in deference to Peel's objections.[3] When the Whigs left office, New South Wales was still without representative government. Things were moving, however, in the colony as well as at home: immigrant wage-earners formed a new democratic element, and the two hostile parties were being brought together in defence of their economic interests against the policy of the mother country. Insistence on Crown control of revenue from land sales, the transference to the colonial treasury of charges for gaols and police, the cessation of assignment and transportation, the adoption of Wakefield's views on the sale of land, and finally Russell's intention of partitioning the colony, all these tended to unite free settlers and "emancipists" until, in 1841, James Macarthur himself declared that the distinction should cease to count politically and pronounced for representative government.[4]

In Western and South Australia no such divisions had ever existed. These colonies had no penal taint, but had both been recently founded as communities of free settlers by Act of Parliament.[5] The obstacles to self-government were those of infancy, their small population and financial embarrassments, though such considerations had

---

[1] *Parl. Pap.* 1837–8, XXII (669). By Order-in-Council of 22 May 1840 New South Wales was withdrawn as from 1 Aug. 1840 from the list of settlements to which convicts might be sent.

[2] Gipps to Glenelg, 1 Jan. 1839, C.O. 201/284.

[3] Hansard, LV, 360 (30 June 1840); Melbourne, pt. III, ch. xi. The Act of 1840 is 3 and 4 Vict. c. 62.

[4] See Melbourne, pp. 213, 230 and pt. III, chap. XII; Sweetman, chap. XIII; *C.H.B.E.* vol. VII, pt. I, pp. 160–3.

[5] 10 Geo. IV, c. 22; 4 and 5 Will. IV, c. 95. See *C.H.B.E.* vol. VII, pt. I, ch. VIII. According to Martin, R. M., *History of the Colonies of the British Empire*, pp. 461, 471, the population of Western Australia was about 2000, that of South Australia about 3000, in the later 'thirties.

not prevented the grant of assemblies in the seventeenth century. Now, however, the Home Government felt a greater responsibility.[1] Western Australia possessed an Executive and a Legislative Council, the latter enlarged in 1838 to contain two unofficial nominated members.[2] South Australia, which Wakefield and his friends had wished to found as a proprietary colony, exposed to the least possible interference from Downing Street, suffered at the outset from a curious division of authority between a Governor and Council responsible to the Secretary of State and a Resident Commissioner subject to a board of South Australian Commissioners meeting in London. The founding Act declared that "a constitution of local government" might be established by Order-in-Council when the population reached 50,000, but as late as 1840 the figure was barely 10,000. Almost immediately steps were taken to secure some unity of control, and in 1840 the functions of the South Australian Commissioners were transferred to Russell's new Commissioners for Land and Emigration.[3]

The formation of New Zealand into a British colony offers a more dramatic example of the clash of ideals and methods between the Wakefield group and the Colonial Office. But here matters were complicated by the presence of a native population. It was an age of committees and reports, and, just as Canadian and Australian destinies were moulded by the opinions of Lord Durham and the Committee on Transportation, so the Report of the Aborigines Committee of 1837 bulks large in the history of New Zealand and South Africa. After a gloomy survey of the results of contact between Europeans and uncivilised races when not "attended by missionary exertions", and of the dangers likely to arise from British expansion, the Report expressed the view that natives could not safely be entrusted to the protection of white settlers and must therefore be kept, so far as possible, under the control of the executive government, "whatever may be the legislative system of any colony". The acquisition of native lands by British subjects should be declared illegal and void, and new territories should not be annexed without the sanction of Parliament. The Committee believed that the late war in South Africa[4] was due to "systematic forgetfulness of the principles of justice" in dealings with natives, and approved Glenelg's recent instructions to Sir Benjamin D'Urban renouncing his annexation of Kaffir territory on the eastern frontier of the Cape of Good Hope. Regarding the recent emigration of Dutch Boers from the colony

---

[1] See Stephen's memorandum of 14 July 1832, C.O. 13/1 (extract in Bell and Morrell, *Select Documents on British Colonial Policy*, pp. 199 *seqq*.).

[2] See correspondence in *Parl. Pap.* 1846, XXIX (400); Sweetman, pp. 337 *seqq*.

[3] *Parl. Pap.* 1840, XXXIII, 35. See for South Australia generally C.O. 13/1, and *Parl. Pap.* 1841, XVII (129), 1846, XXIX (400).

[4] The Kaffir War of 1834–5.

as an act of pure aggression against the natives, the Committee hoped they would be apprised "that while retiring beyond the protection of the British Government, they have not ceased to be responsible to its authority". Similarly, the new settlement at Port Natal must be carefully watched. Turning to the South Sea Islands, the Committee rejoiced that no attempt had hitherto been made to subject the islanders to the dominion of any European race, and expressed suspicion of plans to colonise New Zealand.[1]

This report exactly expressed the attitude of the Colonial Office under its Evangelical chiefs, painfully conscious of one aspect of the dual mandate but fearful of any extension of imperial responsibilities.[2] The policy of Glenelg and Normanby and Stephen was to treat with savage tribes almost as if they were civilised nations and to discourage European adventurers from meddling; they should leave the land to the natives and the natives to the missionaries.[3] This policy did not appeal to the Dutch farmers of the Cape, with their more intimate experience of Kaffir ways. To many of them it seemed that the Government, in some matters so meddlesome, was in this failing to perform its most elementary duties, and when at length, in quest of broader acres and a larger liberty, they pushed beyond its frontiers, north of the Orange River and east of the Drakensberg, into lands which it declined to annex, they bitterly resented its refusal to recognise their independence; it would neither protect its subjects nor allow them to protect themselves.[4]

In New Zealand the hands of the Government were forced. By the end of 1838 they were coming to realise that it was too late to keep the Maoris from contact with any Europeans except missionaries, and that if the contact were unregulated the Maoris had no chance at all. Political authority of some sort must be assumed in New Zealand; so, after deciding to supersede the existing Resident by a Consul, they proceeded to invest the Consul designate, Captain William Hobson, R.N., with the additional character of Agent, in order to negotiate a treaty with the chiefs, whose independence and sovereignty the Queen recognised, for the cession of certain ports and districts.[5] But it was not till June 1839 that the Treasury were informed by the Colonial Office of the proposal to annex certain parts of New Zealand to New South Wales.[6]

[1] *Parl. Pap.* 1837, VII (425).

[2] Glenelg, Sir G. Grey and Stephen were all prominent members of the Church Missionary Society.

[3] See the Report of the House of Lords Select Committee on the Present State of the Islands of New Zealand, *Parl. Pap.* 1837–8, XXI (680).

[4] For the Great Trek see *C.H.B.E.* vol. VIII, ch. XIV. An imperial Act of 1836, the Cape Punishment Act (6 and 7 Will. IV, c. 57), empowered the Cape authorities to punish offences committed by British subjects in territories adjacent to the colony up to the twenty-fifth latitude.

[5] Glenelg to Gipps, 1 Dec. 1838, C.O. 202/37; Stephen to Backhouse (at the F.O.), 12 Dec. 1838, *Parl. Pap.* 1840, XXXIII [238], drafts in C.O. 209/4. The existing Resident, James Busby, was appointed in 1832. See generally *C.H.B.E.* vol. VII, pt. II, ch. V.

[6] Stephen to Spearman, 13 June 1839, Normanby to Hobson, 14 Aug. 1839, *Parl. Pap.* 1840, XXXIII [238]. Various drafts of Hobson's instructions are in C.O. 209/4.

Meanwhile Edward Gibbon Wakefield and his friends had decided to act. A joint-stock company was formed, capital and colonists were procured, and on 5 May a party of pioneers sailed from the Thames. With their arrival in New Zealand in August the systematic colonisation of the islands began.[1]

Hobson appeared in New Zealand waters in due course at the end of January 1840, and in a few days he had negotiated the required agreement, the famous Treaty of Waitangi, with the native chiefs.[2] The North Island thus became British territory and part of New South Wales. British sovereignty over the southern islands was proclaimed in May, as by right of discovery, in time to forestall a French expedition bound on a similar quest.[3] In November, under an Act passed in August, New Zealand was detached from New South Wales to become a Crown Colony under a Governor and a small nominated Legislative Council.[4] In the same month Russell, cutting loose from Stephen's views, came to an agreement with the Directors of the Company in England, and the grant of a charter in February 1841 seemed to regularise its position.[5] But the harmony did not last. In the colony Hobson and the emigrants failed from the first to work together, and at home, even before Russell left office, further misunderstandings and disputes arose between Downing Street and the Company. There were faults on all sides. The Company acted rashly and at times illegally; Gibbon Wakefield was regarded as an unscrupulous intriguer, and neither at home nor in the colony did his friends treat the authorities with tact or respect. On the other hand, the Government might fairly be blamed for vacillation and pedantry and for taking a mean view of their commitments as regards both money and men. Quite apart from the later dispute as to their financial engagements to the Company, both the Governor they sent out and the staff and equipment allowed him were totally inadequate for the occasion. Compelled, said Stephen, to choose between a considerable increase of the Army and Navy, at a time when troops were urgently needed at home as well as in India and in North America, and "a very defective protection of the vast transmarine empire" which was being extended "in every quarter of the Globe", the Government had decided for economy.[6]

The Canadian and Jamaican emergencies and the ubiquitous activities of the Wakefield group brought the colonies in these years into exceptional prominence, and the new interest was reflected in

[1] See Durham to Normanby 22 May 1839 and other correspondence in *Parl. Pap.* 1840, XXXIII [238].
[2] See *Parl. Pap.* 1840, XXXIII (560).
[3] *Parl. Pap.* 1841, XVII (311). For French activities see *C.H.B.E.* vol. VII, pt. II, pp. 70–6.
[4] See 3 and 4 Vict. c. 62; *Parl. Pap.* 1841, XVII (311), pp. 24 *seqq.*
[5] The Charter was dated 12 Feb. 1841.
[6] Minute of 21 Sept. 1839, C.O. 209/4.

three treatises written at this time by three Englishmen who all afterwards filled important public positions.

In April 1840, while Lord Durham was still alive, Charles Buller republished anonymously three articles on "Responsible Government for Colonies", expanding the doctrines of the Durham report and describing in terms entertaining, but most unfair to Stephen, the baneful influence of "Mr Mothercountry" in colonial internal affairs.[1] As to matters of imperial concern, which he believed with Durham to be easily definable, he shared the view expressed in the previous year in Joseph Howe's *Letters to Lord John Russell*, that colonial opinion would gladly acquiesce in control from Downing Street.

George Cornewall Lewis, who lived to hold high cabinet office, in his classic essay *On the government of dependencies*, which appeared in 1841, treated his subject with a wealth of historical knowledge and sound practical judgment.[2] Distinguishing between colonies and dependencies and regarding a self-governing dependency ("supposing the dependency not to be virtually independent") as a contradiction in terms, he held that a wise "dominant" country "would voluntarily recognise the legal independence of such of its own dependencies as were fit for independence; it would, by its political arrangements, study to prepare for independence those which were still unable to stand alone; and it would seek to promote colonisation for the purpose of extending its trade rather than its empire, and without attempting to maintain the dependence of its colonies beyond the time when they need its protection". Preoccupied as he was with the dilemma of dependent or not dependent, he failed to appreciate the possibilities of such a "virtual independence" as might result from a system of popular self-government should the dominant power voluntarily abstain from interference.[3]

Professor Herman Merivale, Stephen's successor at the Colonial Office, showed a keener vision in his Oxford "Lectures on Colonisation and Colonies".[4] He drew a contrast between the principles of recent and former colonial policy: our ancestors "cared for the most part little or nothing about the internal government of their colonies, and kept them in subjection in order to derive certain supposed commercial advantages from them. We give *them* commercial advantages, and tax ourselves for their benefit, in order to give them an interest in remaining under our supremacy, that we may have the pleasure of governing them".[5] He declared that in the American colonies the mother country had of late exercised closer control than formerly,

---

[1] First published in the *Colonial Gazette*, Dec. 1839, Jan., Feb. 1840; reprinted in Wrong, E. M., *Charles Buller and Responsible Government.*
[2] See Sir Charles Lucas's edition of 1891.
[3] Lewis, Sir G. C., pp. 289, 324.
[4] Delivered 1839–41; reprinted in 1861 and, ed. K. Bell, in 1928.
[5] Merivale, H., reprint of 1928, p. 78.

notably in the case of church establishments and waste lands, and that the denial of representative institutions to the Australasian colonies was "a remarkable novelty in British policy". He questioned whether it was wise to enforce a period of probation before an infant colony acquired self-government: it had not been so in New England, and it was doubtful if size had anything to do with capacity for self-rule.[1] Like Lewis, Merivale saw only two ways of treating a colony, absolute government and absolute freedom; but he thought both alternatives compatible with a political connection with the mother country.

> The mere political link of sovereignty may remain, by amicable consent, long after the colony has acquired sufficient strength to stand alone. Existing relations may be preserved, by very slight sacrifices, on terms of mutual good-will. But this can only be by the gradual relaxation of the ties of dependence. The union must more and more lose the protective, and approximate to the federative character. And the Crown may remain, at last, in solitary supremacy, the only common authority recognized by many different legislatures, by many nations politically and socially distinct.[2]

II

The accession of Peel's historic ministry to power in September 1841 meant for the colonies a change of persons rather than of principles. The new Secretary of State, Lord Stanley, had presided over the department already as a Whig, and neither he nor his successor, Gladstone, wished colonial policy to become a party issue; they differed little on broad grounds of principle from Russell and approved the tenor of his despatch on responsible government.[3] Both they and Peel felt strongly that at any rate in the case of the adolescent colonies the continuance of the connection, which though advantageous to Great Britain was far more so to them, must depend on their own goodwill and co-operation.[4]

The Tory chief realised how fateful for the interests of the Empire were the decisions now to be taken. Peel believed "that the relation in which England stood at present to the Canadas involved considerations far more important than those which affected its relations with any state of Europe", and he now offered Stanley the seals of the Colonial rather than the Home Office "from the honest belief that it was the more interesting and more important of the two". But such interest was not shared by public opinion, in Parliament or outside. When, in July 1844, Stanley was at his own wish called up to the Lords, he declared that he was wasted in the Commons, where "Colonial affairs seldom come on, and when they do, they are to be discussed before an audience who know nothing about them,

---

[1] Merivale, H., pp. 105–7, 631.
[2] *Ibid.* p. 633. Cf. the fine peroration on p. 634.
[3] Stanley to Russell, 12 July 1841, Russell Papers, P.R.O.
[4] See Peel's speech of 13 April 1840, Gladstone's of 29 May 1840, Stanley's of 2 Feb. 1843, Hansard, LIII, 1063 *seqq.*, LIV, 724 *seqq.*, LXVI, 123.

and take no interest in them".[1] In October 1842 T. C. W. Murdoch, who had gone out to Canada with Thomson as Civil Secretary and continued under his successor, returning to the Colonial Office, reported on the ignorance as to Canadian affairs not only of English society and English newspapers but even of the Secretary of State.[2] For in spite of Stanley's vigour and prestige he was not a happy choice. He was too pugnacious and rhetorical, too aristocratic and too authoritarian, to understand or sympathise with the proud, suspicious colonial democrats who claimed to be treated as full Englishmen. Stanley regarded the colonies as integral portions of the British Empire, no doubt, but as essentially subordinate, owing loyalty to the policy of the Queen's ministers as well as to the Queen's person; the Whigs held the same view, but they were less emphatic in asserting it.[3]

The North American colonies were still the post of difficulty and, until Ashburton smoothed out the frontier controversy with the United States, of danger also. Peel and Stanley spared no trouble in selecting Sydenham's successor. If they did not find a House of Commons man, as Sydenham had hoped, they avoided a soldier and chose a diplomat of purest water, a wit of Canning's school and circle, that Charles Bagot who had once gained golden opinions at Washington and had negotiated the limitation of armaments on the Great Lakes. They chose him partly for his American record, partly as "a perfect gentleman in manner and feelings".[4]

The Tory leaders had accepted the Union, not without misgivings, as the only means of maintaining a British parliamentary majority in the Canadas. They expected the Canadians likewise to accept the Act whole-heartedly, in the matter of the Civil List, for instance, and to co-operate in working the "great experiment".[5] On that understanding they were prepared to admit the French-Canadians to favour and to allow the government to be conducted on the lines indicated by Russell to Sydenham. Stanley instructed Bagot to invite the aid of all classes, without respect to race or creed, granted only "Loyalty to the Queen, attachment to British connection, and an efficient and faithful discharge of Public Duty". He was to consult, as far as consistent with his duty to the Home Government, "the wishes of the mass of the Community", to withdraw them from the discussion of theoretical topics to the calm consideration of practical improvements and to make use of the ablest men "without reference to distinction of local party, which, upon every occasion,

[1] Hansard, LIV, 1121 (12 June 1840); Peel to Stanley, 30 July 1844, Stanley to Peel, 27 July 1844, Parker, III, 158, 155.
[2] Murdoch to Bagot, 18 Oct. 1842, Can. Archives, Bagot Papers.
[3] See Stanley to Bagot, 8 Oct. 1841, Glazebrook, G. P. de T., Sir Charles Bagot in Canada, p. 129.
[4] See Knaplund, "The Buller-Peel Correspondence regarding Canada, 1841," Can. Hist. Rev. vol. VIII.
[5] Stanley to Bagot, 17 May, 3 June 1842, Can. Archives, Bagot Papers.

you will do your utmost to discourage".[1] But the application of these
generous principles involved acute controversy in the course of the
next four years.[2] Both in Canada and in Nova Scotia the demand
for party government was resolutely pressed, and in Canada the
issue was complicated by the resurgence of the French-Canadian
party allied with the Reformers from the Upper Province.

In the early phase of Cabinet government in England the sovereign
ruled through his ministers; later his ministers ruled through the
sovereign. The change was effected through the consolidation of
ministries by party connection. It was the intention of Howe and
Huntington in Nova Scotia, of Baldwin and La Fontaine in Canada,
to carry through a similar change by similar means.[3] But such was
not Stanley's intention. While accepting the general principle that
government should be carried on in the colonies in accordance with
the views of the majority of the population, he could not agree that
the Governor was to be a mere machine; nor did he believe that
when Durham wrote in his Report of a "system of administration
by means of competent heads of departments" he had envisaged any
such development. The resolutions accepted by Sydenham in September 1841 clearly implied mutual forbearance and good sense.[4]
Party government in the colonies was open, in English eyes, to the
further objection that colonial parties had not the cohesion, permanence, or sense of responsibility of parties at home. Peel did not
think that, "in a small community", party could "govern with any
advantage", and the letters of Bagot and Elgin are eloquent with
scorn for the low standards of colonial public life.[5]

In Canada suspicion of party was embittered by suspicion of
disloyalty. Durham's policy of anglicising the French was never tried
in fact; it was too ruthless to be carried through by Englishmen. The
hope that at least British predominance would be secured was
frustrated, as Tories at home had prophesied, by the alliance, planned
as early as April 1839, between the French-Canadians and the
followers of Robert Baldwin.[6] By July 1842 it was clear that no
administration could stand against them, and when the Legislature
met in September, Bagot's Council, whom for the most part he had
inherited from Sydenham, advised him to invite the French-Canadians,
as a party, to join in a coalition government.[7] Stanley had already
shown restiveness at Bagot's approach to one French-Canadian
suspected of adherence to the rebels of 1837, and he and Peel had

---

[1] Stanley to Bagot, 8 Oct. 1841, Glazebrook, p. 126.
[2] See *C.H.B.E.* VI, 315–23.
[3] For Huntington see Martin, C., *op. cit.*, p. 176. L. H. La Fontaine, a cool-headed and
vigorous realist, became leader of the French-Canadians after Papineau's withdrawal.
[4] *v. supra*, p. 349. For Stanley's views see Hansard, LXVI, 247 (7 Feb. 1843), LXXV, 39 *seqq.*
(30 May 1844).
[5] Hansard, LXXV, 75 (30 May 1844).   [6] Martin, C., pp. 244, 256 *seqq.*
[7] Harrison to Bagot, 11 July, Draper to Bagot, 16 July, Bagot to Stanley, 28 July 1842,
Kennedy, pp. 464–72; Bagot to Stanley, 13 Sept. 1842, Can. Archives, Bagot Papers.

urged the Governor to resist the tainted party as long as possible. Stanley saw something "unnatural" and

not very creditable in discarding the faithful adherents of British connection and administering the Province by placing in high office such men as La Fontaine and Viger, the former of whom was among the most violent of the old French party and the latter in prison for sedition *at least.* I am not prepared to carry the notion of colonial responsible government to such a length, and I cannot but recollect that we, as Ministers *here*, are a responsible body, responsible to a public opinion, which in my judgment such a course would universally revolt.[1]

But such protests arrived too late. Choosing, as a diplomatist, to negotiate while there were still cards in his hand, Bagot had already reconstructed his Cabinet; henceforward it contained five of the Baldwin-La Fontaine group along with six old members, and it commanded a triumphant majority in the Assembly.[2] As the reconstruction had not followed on a vote of the House, an open surrender to the principle of responsible government was avoided, but Bagot admitted that it was in practical operation, and such was the general opinion in the province.[3]

The Cabinet at home were disgusted by what they considered Bagot's mismanagement, but they realised the difficulty of his position and supported him in Parliament when the incident was discussed. The Tories had been "indignant", Greville tells us, having "no taste for the independence and supremacy of a Canadian parliament"; but there was not sufficient interest in colonial affairs to make more than a temporary stir.[4] The incident was in fact a turning-point in the transfer of ultimate authority from the Governor to the Assembly, and Bagot's subsequent illness furthered the process. But if this was loss from the official standpoint, it was all gain that the French-Canadians no longer brooded apart in sullen resentment but had begun to co-operate in the building of a new nation under the British flag.

Though Peel and Stanley had not disavowed Bagot, they hoped that for his successor they had found a stronger man. Sir Charles Metcalfe, a Liberal personally unknown to them, had won fame as a firm but conciliatory administrator in India and Jamaica, and his appointment was generally applauded. But neither in India nor in Jamaica had his initiative been subject to such checks as Bagot's Council, consolidated by Bagot's illness, now sought to impose on him. He was prepared to accept the position as it had been under Sydenham, but not to be a mere tool in the hands of his "Cabinet", nor to allow them the full use of the Governor's patronage for the

[1] Stanley to Peel, 27 Aug. 1842, Can. Archives, Bagot Papers.
[2] See Bagot's despatches of 26 Sept. 1842 to Stanley, printed in Glazebrook, pp. 129-50.
[3] Bagot to Stanley, 28 Oct. 1842, Can. Archives, Bagot Papers; Roebuck's speech of 7 Feb. 1843, Hansard, LXVI, 244; Metcalfe to Stanley, 24 April 1843, Kaye, J. W., *Life and Correspondence of Lord Metcalfe*, II, 478.
[4] Parker, III, 379-86; *The Greville Memoirs*, 29 Oct. 1842; see debate of 7 Feb. 1843, Hansard, vol. LXVI.

benefit of their party. Until the publication of Russell's circular on the tenure of colonial offices, all Crown appointments had been virtually for life and were made within the official circle; there was no distinction between "political" and "permanent" posts. Russell's circular for the first time discriminated between the two, but not with any precision, and it was not surprising that an Executive Council of the new type should claim to control patronage as the Governor's advisers had done in the past. Metcalfe, on the other hand, wished "to make the patronage of the government conducive to the conciliation of all parties", and he was loth to hand over the keys of the citadel to men whom he believed to be essentially disloyal.[1] "The British party" was in fact the only section with which he could sympathise, and it is clear that Stanley shared his feelings. While disclaiming any desire to re-establish the old bureaucracy of Upper Canada, Stanley had told Bagot that such stalwarts were the men to fall back on in difficulty; he now instructed Metcalfe to stand firm on the issue of patronage.[2]

Baldwin and La Fontaine however regarded this issue as inseparably connected with the greater one of responsible government. Matters came to a head in November 1843, and all the Executive Councillors but one resigned. Metcalfe, undaunted, continued to carry on the government in the teeth of a hostile Assembly, and in doing so received the approval not only of his Conservative chiefs but of an almost unanimous public opinion at home, including Russell and Buller. When at the end of 1844 a dissolution gave him a small majority, his firmness seemed triumphantly justified. But his rule became identified with that of a party, and both Peel and Stanley wrote as if the connection with Great Britain depended on the continuance in power of his supporters.[3]

In Nova Scotia, despite the absence of any taint or suspicion of disaffection, things had run a very similar course. The coalition contrived by Sydenham broke down in 1843 largely owing to personal differences in the Council, and the same issue of party government came to the fore. Falkland believed, like Metcalfe, that the success of the Reformers would reduce the Governor to a cipher and tend towards separation; like Metcalfe he dissolved and won his election; like him he reluctantly became himself identified with a party. Hope, Stanley's parliamentary Under-Secretary, recognised that party government was in fact in being and was prepared to accept it, so

[1] See Dawson, R. M., *The Civil Service of Canada*; Russell to Thomson, 16 Oct. 1839, Kennedy, p. 423; Kaye, *Life and Correspondence of Lord Metcalfe*, II, 477 *seqq.* and *Selections from the Papers of Lord Metcalfe*, pp. 404 *seqq. passim.*

[2] Stanley to Bagot, 17 May 1842, Can. Archives, Bagot Papers; Stanley to Metcalfe, 1 Nov. 1843, Morrell, W. P., *British Colonial Policy in the Age of Peel and Russell*, p. 60.

[3] For opinion in England see the debate of 30 May 1844, Hansard, vol. LXXV; Peel to the Queen, 30 Jan. 1844, Stanley to Metcalfe, 18 June 1845, Kaye, *Life and Correspondence of Lord Metcalfe*, II, 583, 596.

long as it did not "encroach on the prerogative of the Crown".
But Stanley would not agree; he set his hopes on Falkland's success.[1]

The apparent success of the Governor in both Canada and Nova
Scotia deluded the Home Government into the belief that the settled
opinion of the colony was behind him. In New Brunswick no clear
demand for responsible government was heard until 1845, when
friction had been caused by a foolish appointment and other injudicious
action on the part of the Lieutenant-Governor. Consequently
Metcalfe's successor, Lord Cathcart, a soldier appointed in view of
the threat of trouble with the United States over the Oregon boundary,
was instructed by Gladstone, the new Peelite Secretary of State, that
he could not do better than follow in Metcalfe's footsteps. Like his
predecessors he should avoid "abstract declarations on the subject
of what has been called responsible government", and, while respecting the Assembly as the main organ of the deliberate sense of
the Canadian community, which "must determine the form of
Canadian laws and institutions", and regarding popular favour as
a "presumptive" title to his own, he must retain in the last resort
his own responsibility in making appointments, preferring when
possible men of proved loyalty to the throne and unconnected with
"narrower or more questionable" political ties.[2]

The representatives of the Crown on both sides of the Atlantic
were still obsessed with a conception of loyalty and patriotism which
was not only restricted and unimaginative but positively dangerous,
because incompatible with the growth alike of national and of
democratic feeling in the colonies. They should have taken warning
from Metcalfe's complaint that "the whole colony must at times be
regarded as a party opposed to Her Majesty's Government. If any
question arises, such as that, for instance, of the Civil List, in which
the interests of the mother country and those of the colony may appear
to be different, the great mass of the people of the colony will be
enlisted against the former." This spirit was "not confined to any
particular party", and could not therefore be attributed to dislike
of the British connection.[3] It was disappointing to Stanley to find
this feeling unchanged by the preference on Canadian wheat granted
by the mother country in 1843 as a gesture of goodwill, and to see no
response to his hopes that Canada would take an effective share in
its own defence.[4] To Stephen it appeared that Canada had "become,
in everything but the name, a distinct State", enjoying complete
self-government in internal affairs; he himself thought this development inevitable, and pointed out the "very pregnant fact" that there
were almost as many Europeans in Canada in 1846 as there had been

[1] Falkland to Stanley, 2 March 1844, with Minutes by Hope and Stanley, C.O. 217/186.
[2] Gladstone to Cathcart, 3 Feb. 1846, Can. Archives, G. 123.
[3] Metcalfe to Stanley, 13 May 1845, Kaye, *Selections etc.*, p. 459.
[4] Canada Corn Act, 6 and 7 Vict. c. 29; Stanley to Metcalfe, 18 July 1843, 16 Sept.
1845, Can. Archives, G. 117/122.

in the thirteen colonies seventy years before. About this time he remarked in his diary that it was not unlikely that the next Governor-General of Canada would be the last.[1]

In Australia the first session of the 1841 Parliament bore fruit in three important Acts passed practically without opposition. By the Waste Lands Act of 1842 the Wakefield principle that the unsettled tracts of the colonies should be kept at the disposal of the Crown and never alienated except by sale was applied to all the Australian colonies and to New Zealand.[2] By a later Act New South Wales received the instalment of representative government which had been under consideration since 1836. The cessation of transportation, the increased number of free immigrants, and the reconciliation of the two local parties had made the concession much easier. Stanley's measure was based on Russell's bill of 1840; it gave the colony a Legislative Council of thirty-six members, of whom twenty-four were to be elected by voters possessing an estate of £200 or occupying a dwelling worth £20 a year. There was no discrimination against ex-convicts. Canadian experience was drawn upon in the provision for municipal institutions and in the reservation to the Crown of a revenue of over £80,000 beyond the control of the local Legislature.[3] Stanley explained that the continuance of transportation to Van Diemen's Land had prevented the Government from proposing a similar measure for that colony.[4]

Action as regards South Australia was indicated by the Report of the Select Committee of 1841, on which Stanley and Gladstone had served, along with Howick, Sir George Grey, and Molesworth. After considering the deplorable state of the finances of the colony, the Committee had recommended that its anomalous constitution should be remodelled on more orthodox lines, the Queen in Council being empowered to infuse an elected element into the legislature in due course.[5] A bill to this effect was accordingly passed in 1842 and a Legislative Council of seven nominated members was set up. Stanley announced that he was not prepared to add elected members until satisfied that the colony was self-supporting and a permanent Civil List obtainable.[6]

In New South Wales the restricted measure of self-government

[1] Minute of 12 Jan. 1846, C.O. 42/531 (extract in Bell and Morrell, p. 87); Stephen, L., *Life of J. F. Stephen*, p. 49.
[2] 5 and 6 Vict. c. 36; see Hansard, LXIII, 880 (26 May 1842) and Stanley to Gipps, 5 Sept. 1842, C.O. 202/45.
[3] 5 and 6 Vict. c. 76. Stanley had consulted both James Macarthur's brother, Edward, and Charles Buller, and had adopted some of Buller's suggestions. See Buller to Stanley, Nov. 1841, C.O. 206/62. The population was now over 130,000, of whom over 52,000 were free immigrants. See *C.H.B.E.* vol. VII, pt. I, ch. VI.
[4] Stanley to Franklin, 5 Sept. 1842, *Parl. Pap.* 1846, XXIX (400), p. 30.
[5] *Parl. Pap.* 1841, IV (119), XVII (129). The Sir George Grey who sat on the Committee is to be distinguished from George Grey, the colonial Governor.
[6] 5 and 6 Vict. c. 61. See Hansard, LXIV, 990 *seqq.* (5 July 1842) and Stanley to Grey, 6 Sept. 1842, 2 July 1843, 8 Feb. 1845, *Parl. Pap.* 1846, XXIX (400).

conferred by the new Act provoked from the outset the controversies between elected representatives and independent executive from which such polities are rarely free. Economic depression made discontent sharper, and friction increased during the remainder of Gipps's term of office: there was no Upper Chamber, as in Canada before 1838, to share the Governor's unpopularity, but he was less at the mercy of the Legislature for revenue.

The retention of an independent statutory income in the hands of the Crown was one of the main grievances of the squatters and other propertied interests represented on the Legislative Council; the other was the management of the waste lands and of the revenue from them which had likewise been placed out of their control. In 1844 the Council, adopting the Reports of two Select Committees, made energetic protests on these points and also petitioned the Queen that the Government might be "henceforth conducted on the same principle of responsibility, as to legislative control, which has been conceded in the Canadas". The Durham Report had been published and studied in the colony as early as 1839, and Wentworth, the prime mover of the protest, was obviously influenced by it; but it is not clear how far the implications of parliamentary government had been thought out.[1] Gipps, on the other hand, who had visited Canada in 1836 as a member of the Gosford Commission, believed that, if the independent revenue were surrendered, it would be impossible to maintain the necessary supremacy of the mother country, and suggested that the suspension of the new constitution for ten years might prove the only solution.[2] Stanley had no intention of making the required concessions. He declined to discuss the "abstract" and "vague" topic of responsible government,[3] and he would not admit that either justice or expediency demanded that the first occupants of Australian soil should be allowed to dispose of its vast vacant spaces. Already in 1841 and 1843 he and Stephen had rejected this principle in resisting local desires for the importation of coloured labour at the public expense.

There is not on the globe [wrote Stephen] a social interest more momentous—if we look forward for four or five generations—than that of reserving the continent of New Holland as a place where the English race shall be spread from sea to sea unmixed with any lower caste. As we now regret the folly of our ancestors in colonising North America from Africa, so would our posterity have to censure us if we should colonise Australia from India.... To introduce [coolies] at the public expense would be to countenance and affirm the favourite theory of all colonists that the first settlers in a new country become the proprietors of it all; and that the affairs of it are to be conducted for their benefit rather than for the benefit of the metropolitan state.[4]

[1] Report of Committee on General Grievances, C.O. 201/350, extracts in Bell and Morrell, p. 83. See Sweetman, pp. 191 *seqq.*; Smith, W., "Canada and constitutional development in New South Wales", *Can. Hist. Rev.* June 1926; Melbourne, pt IV, chaps. V, VII, and p. 384.
[2] Gipps to Stanley, 1 Jan. 1844, 13 Feb. 1845; Morrell, *British Colonial Policy*, pp. 97, 98.
[3] Stanley to Gipps, 20 Aug. 1845; Sweetman, pp. 193, 364; Melbourne, p. 320.
[4] Minutes of 17 July 1841, 12 Sept. 1843, C.O. 201/310, 333; Morrell, p. 90.

However the blame be distributed, relations between the Government and the elected Councillors were severely strained when Gipps went home in July 1846.

In New Zealand and South Africa the issue of self-government was complicated by the divergent interests of natives and Europeans. Stanley inherited in either case embarrassing commitments to native chiefs and at least the makings of a feud with the settlers. His relations with the New Zealand Company, which during four years grew steadily worse, were exposed to the public eye by a Select Committee of the Commons and by a three nights' debate.[1] The primary dispute over the Company's land claims involved fundamental differences of opinion as to the relationship possible and proper between a European Government and Maori chiefs. The action of the Melbourne Cabinet in treating them as a sovereign independent Power was now very widely disapproved, but among those who agreed in regretting the treaty of Waitangi there were differences as to its interpretation. The Committee of 1844, under Howick's chairmanship, condemned alike the policy of Glenelg and Normanby leading to the treaty, the illegal precipitancy of the Company, and Stanley's general tendency in the controversy to magnify the rights of the natives and belittle those of the colonists. Peel of course supported Stanley in public, but he could not approve his handling of affairs.[2] By the time the battle royal opened in the session of 1845, Captain Robert Fitzroy, appointed Governor in 1843, had plunged the colony in confusion, and war had broken out with the Maoris. A demand put forward in the Commons for self-government for the settlers found Sir James Graham and Peel friendly, but they preferred to make a beginning with municipal institutions.[3] Before leaving office Stanley replaced Fitzroy by George Grey, fresh from the struggle against financial chaos in South Australia, and showed a more conciliatory temper towards the Company and the colonists. He would not concede an elected central legislature, but he agreed that the dispersion of the white settlements pointed to municipal self-government with wide powers, equality between the two races being always observed, and he was prepared to allow delegates from the municipal councils to sit on the Legislative Council.[4] Gladstone went further and invited Grey to make suggestions for the extension of the representative principle, since the Government wished the colonists to undertake the management of their own affairs as soon as possible,

---

[1] *Parl. Pap.* 1844, XIII (556); Hansard, LXXXI (17, 18, 19 June 1845). See also Hansard, LXXVIII, 658 sqq., 1094 sqq. (11, 18 March 1845).

[2] Peel to Ingestre, 9 July 1845, *Parl. Pap.* 1845, XXXIII (517 I); Morley, J., *Life of Gladstone*, I, 298.

[3] Hansard, LXXXI, 926, 950 *seqq.* (19 June 1845).

[4] See correspondence in *Parl. Pap.* 1845, XXXIII (517 I), 661; Hansard, LXXXII, 807 *seqq.* (21 July 1845); *Parl. Pap.* 1846, XXIX (400).

subject to the rule that "the Crown should stand in all matters between the colonists and the natives".[1] A bill on these lines was prepared for the 1846 session, but the fall of Peel's Government left action to the Whigs.[2]

In South Africa Stanley had no New Zealand Company to plague him, and, of the Governors, Napier at least was a wiser man than Hobson or Fitzroy. But there were tough Boer farmers determined on self-government and Kaffir and Zulu tribesmen far more aggressive, as they were far more powerful, than the Maoris. Glenelg's policy had been to prevent the Boers from tyrannising over the natives, but not to increase the area under direct British rule. The two aims were in fact incompatible. It was at Port Natal that troubles first came to a head, compelling the Government to recognise facts.[3] A small British settlement there, in Zulu territory, had received a wave of trekking Boers in 1837. British troops sent to preserve peace had been withdrawn in December 1839, and the Boers had declared a republic. But their high-handed dealings with the natives made a renewal of British intervention inevitable. Russell eventually ordered the re-occupation of the place, and when negotiations with the Boers had failed a force was sent for this purpose in April 1842. The consequent fighting induced the Governor, Sir George Napier, to disregard a despatch from Stanley reverting to the Glenelg policy of withdrawal, a policy which had Stephen's approval but was based on ignorance of local conditions. Stanley then acquiesced in the necessity for annexing Natal, but gave directions for consulting the Boers as to their future form of government.[4] When, however, the new territory received a constitution in 1844, it was placed under the legislative authority of the Cape, with only a Lieutenant-Governor and an Executive Council of its own.[5] Meanwhile, north of the Orange and on the eastern frontier of the Cape, the policy of treaties with the native chiefs was adhered to or resumed, and no further annexation was sanctioned until the outbreak of the Kaffir war in 1846.

Stanley could hardly be expected to grant self-government to the Trekkers in Natal before it had been won by their parent colony. The Cape had enjoyed a nominated Legislative Council since 1834, and municipal elective institutions since 1836; but in April 1842 Stanley replied unfavourably to a petition from Cape Town for an elected Assembly, though Napier supported it. Stanley's main

[1] Gladstone to Grey, 31 Jan. 1846, *Parl. Pap.* 1846, XXIX (400), pp. 79, 80.
[2] Hansard, LXXXVII, 809 (22 June 1846), LXXXVIII, 349 ff. (6 Aug. 1846). See generally *C.H.B.E.* vol. VII, pt. II, ch. V.
[3] See *C.H.B.E.* vol. VIII, chs. XIV and XV.
[4] Napier to Stanley, 25 July 1842 (extract in Bell and Morrell, p. 490); Stanley to Napier, 12 Oct., 13 Dec. 1842, C.O. 49/36; as in New Zealand, there was some fear of foreign intervention.
[5] See Napier's proclamation of 12 May 1843, Bell and Morrell, p. 495; Stanley to Maitland, 25 May 1844, *Parl. Pap.* 1847-8, XLII [980].

objection was the diversity of the population, which must make the due apportionment of electoral power an insoluble problem.[1] Later on, in laying down principles for the administration of Natal, he insisted that the law should recognise no distinction of race or colour.[2] The argument that representative institutions were unsuitable where they must result in the suppression of one race by another was used also by Radicals; by Brougham, for instance, on the subject of the Cape Town petition, and by Buller in the Jamaica debates of 1839.[3] The difficulty was certain to arise with the abolition of slavery in the colonies and the growth of democratic feeling at home.[4]

III

The replacement of Stanley in December 1845 by the more conciliatory Gladstone was only an incident in a change in imperial policy profoundly affecting relations with the colonies. The basis of the old empire had been essentially economic, and though many holes had been knocked in the mercantilist code since 1822, the regulation of colonial trade for the general advantage was still regarded as one of the natural functions of the imperial legislature. Merivale, we have seen, had argued that economic privilege was now accorded at the expense, rather than for the benefit, of the mother country, and the Parliament elected in 1841 had heard sharp criticism of the working of colonial preference; nevertheless, as late as 1843 a substantial new preference had been given to Canadian wheat and flour.[5] The repeal of the Corn laws showed that henceforward the reduction of the cost of living at home would be the prime object of statesmen in Great Britain, and foreshadowed the repeal of the preference on colonial sugar and timber. In equity this policy implied the renunciation by the imperial Parliament of the right to restrict colonial commerce by tariffs and shipping regulations. Accordingly the new Russell administration passed a British Possessions Act in 1846,[6] allowing the legislatures of the American colonies to repeal duties laid by Parliament on their imports, and three years later repealed the Navigation Acts. The effect of these changes was naturally to make men revise their traditional views on the meaning and value of a colonial empire.

The third Earl Grey, Russell's Colonial Secretary, was not like his three immediate predecessors destined for the premiership. But he was a man of unusual ability and prestige with peculiar qualifications for presiding over the change of policy. As Viscount Howick

---

[1] Stanley to Napier, 15 April 1842, *Parl. Pap.* 1846, XXIX (400).
[2] Stanley to Napier, 13 Dec. 1842, C.O. 49/36.
[3] Hansard, LXIV, 276, XLVII, 833 ff.; see Taylor, Sir H., *Autobiography*, I, 250 *seqq.*
[4] For constitutional development in South Africa see *C.H.B.E.* vol. VIII. ch. xv.
[5] Canada Corn Act, 6 and 7 Vict. c. 29; *v. supra*, p. 363.
[6] 9 and 10 Vict. c. 94.

he had professed the Free Trade creed for twenty years with almost religious devotion, and no Member of Parliament had shown a keener or more sustained interest in colonial affairs. As Under-Secretary in his father's Reform administration Grey had been concerned with the surrender of certain revenues to the Canadian legislatures, and more intimately with the introduction of Wakefield's principles in Australia. Later he had stood in the Cabinet for a conciliatory treatment of Lower Canada and had given general approval to Durham's Report. Never an easy colleague, he had resigned office in September 1839, and after Durham's death, though not sharing all the enthusiasms of the Colonial Reformers, he had served as a connecting link between them and the official Whigs. He regarded the Empire as a solemn trust as well as a source of power and glory, and to him the victory of Free Trade meant no slackening of interest in the colonies. His parliamentary Under-Secretary, moreover, was the Durhamite, Benjamin Hawes, and it was arranged further that he should have assistance from Charles Buller.[1]

In October 1847 James Stephen retired from the Colonial Office. He had never worked happily with the Colonial Reformers; he was too distrustful of Wakefield's adventurous schemes and lack of principle. But there was no denying his ability and devotion, and he made repeated attempts to reduce the delays in colonial business caused by the methods of other departments. In his place Grey appointed Herman Merivale. The post had been previously offered to James Spedding and then to Henry Taylor, who returned the compliment later by describing Grey as "the most laborious, able, public-spirited, and honest-minded" of the eleven Secretaries of State under whom he served.[2]

To Lord Grey's active and critical mind it seemed that long arrears of self-government were owing to several of the colonies, and he set himself without delay to provide New Zealand, Australia, and the Cape with representative institutions. Yet there was another matter still more urgent. "You are fortunate", wrote Buller to Joseph Howe, "in now having a Colonial Secretary who has sound views of Colonial Policy: but the good results of Lord Grey's administration cannot be achieved all at once. We must wait some time ere we can find Governors to carry his views into effect."[3] Fate was kind: within a few weeks of taking office Grey secured, to succeed Cathcart in Canada, one who was to become the most eminent of all British

[1] For Grey's attitude on the treatment of Lower Canada in 1837, see the Russell Papers in the P.R.O.; Melbourne to the Queen, 27 Dec. 1837, *Letters of Queen Victoria*, I, 98; Howick to Melbourne, 29 Dec. 1837, *The Melbourne Papers*, ed. Sanders, p. 423; Esher, *Girlhood of Queen Victoria*, I, 251 *seqq.*; for his reception of Durham's Report see *Canadian Archives, Report for 1923*, p. 338. For Buller see reference to Howick papers in Morrell, p. 203.

[2] Taylor, I, 235; II, 30, 92.

[3] Buller to Howe, 10 Sept. 1846, *Can. Hist. Rev.*, Dec. 1925, p. 316. Buller said that "almost the sole business of the Colonial Office should be to breed up a supply of Good Colonial Governors".

colonial governors. James, eighth Earl of Elgin, a fine scholar and speaker, had just returned at the age of thirty-five from a successful administration of Jamaica. He was a Peelite Tory, but Grey acted as Stanley had done in Metcalfe's case and appointed the best man available, though a political opponent and personally unknown to him.[1] Before Elgin sailed for Canada, however, he had married Grey's niece, Lord Durham's daughter, and he had learnt Grey's views as to how British North America must be governed. Grey had acclaimed the principles of Durham's Report at the time, particularly as regards "allowing to the colonists the most complete self-government upon matters of mere internal regulation and local interest"; but he had explained in Parliament later that he could not approve of the executive government being "directly responsible to the Colonial Assembly". He had apparently believed, much as Russell had, that Durham's general scheme could be put into practice without the acceptance of the theory associated with his name. But he had thought Metcalfe's policy wrong.[2] Now, in the autumn of 1846, he was called upon to give instructions in a concrete case, in answer to an appeal from Sir John Harvey, the new Lieutenant-Governor of Nova Scotia.[3]

Lord Falkland's feud with the reforming party had made matters very difficult for his successor. Consequently, when Harvey, who did not believe in "responsible or party government", tried to induce members of the Opposition to re-enter the Executive Council on a coalition basis, he met with no response. He proceeded to lay the situation before the Secretary of State. Lord Grey's reply, stating "the general principle upon which the constitutions granted to the North American colonies render it necessary that their government should be conducted", is rightly regarded as the charter of colonial freedom in the Second Empire.[4] Harvey, he wrote, must avoid identifying himself with any party, and should support his existing Executive Council as long as they could carry on the government satisfactorily. He must make it clear that any transference of political power from one party to another was due not to his own wishes but to those of the people. Conversely, in supporting his Councillors for the time

[1] Both Stanley and Gladstone, as well as the Queen, had wished Elgin to be Governor of Canada; Morison, J. L., *The Eighth Earl of Elgin*, p. 76; Knaplund, P., *Gladstone and Britain's Imperial Policy*, p. 42; *Letters of Queen Victoria*, II, 47.

[2] Grey, *Colonial Policy of Lord John Russell's Administration*, I, 208; Howick to Durham, 7 Feb. 1839, *Canadian Archives, Report for 1923*, p. 338; Hansard, LIV, 746 (29 May 1840). Cf. the views expressed in his speech of 26 Jan. 1838, Hansard, XL, 577. For his judgment on Metcalfe, see Grey to Elgin, 2 June 1847, 5 April 1849, Can. Archives, Elgin-Grey Correspondence.

[3] Harvey had been transferred from New Brunswick to Newfoundland in 1841, and from Newfoundland to Nova Scotia in Aug. 1846.

[4] Harvey to Grey, 15 Sept. 1846, with enclosures, C.O. 217/193; Grey to Harvey, 3 Nov. 1846, *Parl. Pap.* 1847-8, XLII (621), p. 7, reprinted in Kennedy, p. 494. Cf. Grey's memorandum dated 3 Oct. 1846, C.O. 217/193. Livingston points out in *Responsible Government in Nova Scotia* (p. 207) that Grey to a considerable extent adopted Howe's arguments.

being, he must avoid any suggestion of objecting personally to their opponents, and he must refuse to exert the authority of the Crown improperly, on their advice, for party objects. But this refusal must be exercised with the greatest discretion, and with the knowledge that it would be a legitimate ground for the Councillors' resignation; a course they would doubtless adopt if they believed that public opinion would support them.

> Should it prove to be so, concession to their views must, sooner or later, become inevitable, since it cannot be too distinctly acknowledged that it is neither possible nor desirable to carry on the government of any of the British provinces in North America in opposition to the opinion of the inhabitants.[1] Clearly understanding, therefore, that refusing to accede to the advice of your Council for the time being upon a point on which they consider it their duty to insist, must lead to the question at issue being brought ultimately under the decision of public opinion, you will carefully avoid allowing any matter not of very grave concern, or upon which you cannot reasonably calculate upon being in the end supported by that opinion, to be made the subject of such a difference.... The adoption of this principle of action by no means involves the necessity of a blind obedience to the wishes and opinions of the members of your Council; on the contrary, I have no doubt that if they see clearly that your conduct is guided, not by personal favour to any particular men or party, but by a sincere desire to promote the public good, your objections to any measures proposed will have great weight with the Council, or should they prove unreasonable, with the Assembly, or, in last resort, with the public.[2]

The outstanding features of this despatch were, first, the recognition that the final decision in colonial affairs, involving ultimately the issue of separation, must rest with the people of the colony; and secondly, the faith that the people might be presumed to be reasonable and well disposed to the mother country. It was the failure to see these two points in their true connection which had for ten years created in the minds of most British statesmen an intractable dilemma. The dilemma had never troubled Durham, and Durham's son-in-law, now arriving in Canada with Grey's despatch in his pocket, could tell his bride that he had "adopted frankly and unequivocally Lord Durham's view of government".[3]

As Russell had followed up his despatch on responsible government with a second on the tenure of offices, so another historic pronouncement was demanded from Grey by circumstances in Nova Scotia. The colony was small, the able supporters of the old system pointed out to him; there was hardly material for two alternative administrations; moreover, the Executive Councillors remained distinct from the heads of departments, and it seemed hard on the latter, in the absence of a pension fund, to introduce the American spoils system

---

[1] This sentence was substituted by Grey for a sentence in his memorandum stating that "the recognition of what is called responsible government" was, whether wise or the reverse, "at all events irrevocable".

[2] Cf. Grey to Elgin, 22 Feb. 1848. Can. Archives, Elgin-Grey Correspondence, quoted below, p. 373.

[3] To Lady Elgin, 31 Jan. 1847, Walrond, T., *Letters and Journals of James, Eighth Earl of Elgin*, p. 35. See an interesting letter in the Canadian Archives, written by Elgin to Grey, 8 Oct. 1852, on receiving the manuscript of Grey's *Colonial Policy*.

at their expense. The Sydenham method of parliamentary government had not, in fact, been introduced at Halifax, and the implications of Russell's tenure of offices despatch had not been understood.[1] Grey was therefore constrained to explain the British practice, by which only the highest offices are affected by party victories, whereas the great majority of public servants, dissociated from party politics, hold virtually "during good behaviour". He believed that this distinction might well be introduced in the North American colonies and that the peculiar circumstances of Nova Scotia presented "no insuperable obstacle to the immediate adoption of that system of parliamentary government which has long prevailed in the mother country, and which seems to be a necessary part of representative institutions in a certain stage of their progress".[2] Grey's two despatches were not published at once; but in January 1848, when a newly elected House of Assembly passed a vote of no confidence in the existing Council, the Council promptly resigned, and Harvey thereupon called on J. B. Uniacke, once a Tory but now leader of the Liberals, to form a new administration. In explaining to the House of Commons what had happened, Henry Labouchère said it might be seen "that the principle of responsible government was in active operation in Nova Scotia".[3]

But if it was in Nova Scotia that the principle was first officially recognised, it was on the larger stage of Canada, with its racial divisions and memories of bloodshed and with the challenge of democracy across the border, that its working was put to the supreme test and the importance of the Governor's part demonstrated. Elgin at first maintained in office the ministers he inherited from Metcalfe, making, with their approval, a vain attempt to obtain French-Canadian assistance. When after a General Election the new Assembly pronounced against them, he sent for the Opposition leaders, with whom Metcalfe had quarrelled, and gave them his full confidence and backing.[4] Grey supported Elgin unreservedly in this "great experiment", though not without anxiety, since he suspected there was "a difference in the capability of the Anglo-Saxon race for self-government from that of the other European races".[5] But so little did he share Stanley's views that he was prepared to see Papineau himself in office should the majority in the Assembly demand it.

If we overrule the local legislature [he wrote to Elgin], we must be prepared to support our authority by force, and in the present state of the world and of Canada,

---

[1] See Livingston, W.R., *Can. Hist. Rev.* June 1926, pp. 125–9.
[2] Grey to Harvey, 31 March 1847, *Parl. Pap.* 1847–8, XLII (621), p. 29; Kennedy, p. 496.
[3] Hansard, XCVI, 803 (17 Feb. 1848). Labouchère had been Under-Secretary of State for the Colonies in 1839; he became President of the Board of Trade in 1847. See also the debate in the Lords on 26 March 1849 on Fairbanks's resignation, Hansard, CIII, 1257 *seqq.*
[4] The vote of the Assembly was on 3 March 1848; the ministry resigned on March 4; Elgin sent for La Fontaine and Baldwin on 7 March.
[5] Grey to Elgin, 22 March 1848, Can. Archives, Elgin-Grey Correspondence.

he must in my opinion be an insane politician who would think of doing so. It does not however follow that you are by any means powerless; if your advisers insist upon an improper course of proceeding, the line to take is freely to place before them the objections to it, but to yield if they insist up to the point when they have put themselves so clearly in the wrong that public opinion will support you in resistance.... I cannot help believing that the advantages of the present connection are so entirely on the side of Canada that by following this course you will be supported in resisting everything to which you cannot consent with honour and consistently with the real interests of this country. If not, I do not see how separation can be prevented.... Your influence with the members of your Ministry, which will be founded on the conviction (I trust generally entertained) that you are no partizan of their opponents, and have no other object but to promote the true interests of the Province, will, I trust, enable you to restrain them from any really objectionable measures.[1]

Lord Grey's two despatches to Harvey had now been published; becoming known in Canada in February 1848, they showed such a new mind in Downing Street that even Papineau was reported to have been "staggered" and to have "for a moment admitted that perhaps *Perfide Albion* might be sincere".[2] Later in the year the repeal by Parliament of the section in the Union Act making English the only official language of the province sealed the abandonment of Durham's anglicising policy.[3] It was Elgin's opinion that the Opposition leaders had been admitted to power in the nick of time to save Canada from French or Irish disturbances inspired by the events of 1848 in Europe. It remained for him to face the anger of the old party of ascendancy, embittered by economic grievances, of which the most obvious was the withdrawal of the preference so recently given to Canadian wheat and flour.[4]

The real test of Elgin's courage and of the sincerity of the Imperial Government and Parliament came with the Rebellion Losses Act of 1849. The new Canadian ministry, following the precedent of a previous Act concerning Upper Canada, proposed to compensate such Lower Canadians as had not actually been convicted of treason for any unjust damage they might have suffered in the suppression of the risings of 1837 and 1838. Though vehemently opposed by the local Tories, the bill passed the Assembly with a majority of both French and English votes, passed the Legislative Council, and received the Royal Assent from the Governor-General, who deliberately chose to take any resulting odium on his own head rather than transfer it to the Queen's advisers. Riot and insult followed in Canada, and at home speakers in both Houses of Parliament hotly demanded that the Act should be disallowed unless so amended as to make it clear that no rebel would receive compensation. Gladstone and Herries led the attack in the Commons, Brougham, Lyndhurst, and Stanley in the Lords. But Russell and Grey stood firm, and once

[1] Grey to Elgin, 22 Feb. 1848, Can. Archives, Elgin-Grey Correspondence.
[2] Elgin to Grey, 17 Feb. 1848, *ibid.*
[3] 11 and 12 Vict. c. 56; Elgin to Grey, 4 March 1848, *ibid.*
[4] *V. supra*, p. 363.

again Peel gave them his powerful help; they had a majority of 141 in the Commons, of 3 only in the Lords.[1] It was a momentous occasion; the Commons had decided by an overwhelming vote that Parliament would not interfere in a matter of primarily Canadian concern, though it might wish that the Canadian legislature had acted otherwise. Undoubtedly the decision helped to secure the failure of the movement for annexation to the United States which was engineered by some despondent Montreal merchants later in the year.

In all these troubles Elgin could rely on Grey's steady support. Week by week the two friends, like Russell and Thomson before them, opened their hearts to one another in the incomparable letters now preserved at Ottawa. The aspirations of the one were often negatived by the other as impracticable, but in matters involving the principle of self-government, such as the need for repealing the Clergy Reserves Act of 1840, they saw eye to eye, and they collaborated with harmony and success in the great constructive work of creating a new rôle for the Governor and so, as Elgin put it, bringing "the theory of constitu-tional government in a colony from the region of chimeras into that of facts".[2]

In the apologia which Lord Grey published soon after his retirement from office he explained what conditions must be fulfilled, in his opinion, to make possible the successful working of responsible government, or, as he preferred to call it, parliamentary, or party government. The community must not be a very small one; the population must be in an advanced stage of civilisation, and must have "had the advantage of some training by the working of a free constitution of a simpler kind", including, he was inclined to add, some devolution of authority to municipal bodies.[3] In the other North American colonies these conditions were only partially fulfilled. In New Brunswick the material for a proper party Cabinet was lacking, and, though in principle responsible government was conceded in 1848, it was not in full operation until 1854.[4] Prince Edward Island was even more backward. After consulting Elgin in 1847, Grey believed that the immediate introduction of responsible government was inadvisable, but in view of the wishes of the local Assembly he sanctioned it in 1851.[5] In Newfoundland, where a "blended" Chamber had been introduced in 1842, the former bicameral system was restored in 1847, with an undivided Executive and Legislative

---

[1] Hansard, cvi, 189 seqq., 305 seqq. (June 14, 15), 450 seqq. (June 19, 1849). See also ciii, 1125, civ, 1102, cv, 467, 561.

[2] Elgin to Grey, 26 July 1851. See also Elgin to Grey, 5 July 1850, Grey to Elgin, 17 July, 21 Aug., 1 Nov. 1850, 31 Jan. 1851, all in the Elgin-Grey Correspondence.

[3] Colonial Policy of Lord John Russell's Administration, i, 33–5.

[4] See Head to Grey, 6 Nov. 1850, printed in Bell and Morrell, p. 133.

[5] Elgin thought it had the worst of all forms of colonial government—an oligarchy of irresponsible officials; to Grey, 14 Sept. 1847, Can. Archives, Elgin-Grey Correspondence; Grey to Bannerman, 31 Jan. 1851, printed in Bell and Morrell, p. 136. See Parl. Pap. 1847, xxxviii (566).

Council. The demand of the tiny Assembly for responsible government was refused by Grey and his successor, but was eventually conceded in 1854.[1]

The pioneer position of the North American colonies lends their early constitutional development an importance to which that of Australasia and of South Africa cannot pretend. After each principle had been conceded in America, its adoption elsewhere was only a matter of time. The achievement of the Russell administration was to give representative government on the New South Wales model to three more Australian colonies, and to prepare the way for its prompt concession in New Zealand. Lord Grey attempted, indeed, to deal with New Zealand first; his antecedents gave him much more sympathy than Stanley with the colonists and less exalted views of the Maoris' rights to the land. He carried a bill through Parliament in 1846 empowering the Queen to establish in New Zealand a complicated structure of municipal councils and provincial legislatures, with a General Assembly at the top; this constitution was to apply only to the districts settled by Europeans, but within these areas natives literate in English were eligible for the franchise.[2] But the Governor, who had now practically quelled the Maori rising, protested forcibly that the scheme would in fact exclude from the franchise the great mass of the natives who formed the majority of the population of the North Island, and might provoke a fresh outbreak; he urged therefore that it should apply to the South Island only.[3] Lord Grey bowed to these objections and obtained from Parliament the suspension of the Act, save for certain clauses, in both islands for five years. In the interval it was hoped that the "amalgamation" of the two races might proceed harmoniously, and the Governor was encouraged to make a start with municipal and provincial institutions.[4] In land policy, too, Lord Grey was content to yield to the Governor's advice;[5] in New Zealand, as in Canada, he showed that he could recognise and trust a man of real quality. Relations with the New Zealand Company at home were set on a basis acceptable to both the Directors and the Government by an experimental concordat negotiated by Charles Buller in 1847;[6] the experiment did not in fact succeed, and the company surrendered

[1] 5 and 6 Vict. c. 120, 10 and 11 Vict. c. 44; see *C.H.B.E.* VI, 428–32.
[2] 9 and 10 Vict. c. 103. See Earl Grey to G. Grey, 23 Dec. 1846, enclosing copies of the new Act, Charter, and Royal Instructions, *Parl. Pap.* 1847, XXXVIII [763], p. 64. For Stephen's influence in the drafting of the Charter see Melbourne, p. 342, n. 4.
[3] G. Grey to Earl Grey, 3 and 13 May 1847, *Parl. Pap.* 1847–8, XLIII [892], pp. 42 *seqq.*
[4] 10 and 11 Vict. c. 5; see Earl Grey to G. Grey, 20 and 30 Nov. 1847, *ibid.* pp. 46 *seqq.*; also speeches of Labouchère, 13 Dec. 1847, and Grey, 29 Feb. 1848, Hansard, XCV, 1003, XCVII, 3.
[5] See Marais, J. S., *The Colonization of New Zealand*, pp. 253–84, Morrell, pp. 321, 328–31.
[6] See Stephen to Trevelyan, 6 May, Earl Grey to G. Grey, 19 June 1847, *Parl. Pap.* 1847, XXXVIII [837]; Hansard, XCIV, 190 (12 July 1847); *C.H.B.E.* vol. VII, pt. II, p. 85.

its charter in 1850, but not before it had arranged for the planting in the South Island of two new vigorous communities by the Otago and Canterbury settlers.[1]

Lord Grey's first thoughts were little happier in the case of Australia. Local circumstances seemed to him to demand the separation of the Port Phillip district (now Victoria) from New South Wales, and by the bill effecting the partition he proposed also to revise the constitution given to that colony in 1842. He would replace the single "blended" Chamber by two Houses, of which the more popular should be elected indirectly, as in the abortive New Zealand constitution of 1846, by reformed municipal bodies. He intended further to grant representative government at once to South Australia and Van Diemen's Land as well as to the new colony of Victoria, and in certain circumstances to Western Australia, and he outlined a federal scheme to include the Australian colonies.[2] When the despatch in which Grey explained his views was published in New South Wales, opinion showed itself chiefly in condemnation of the proposal for indirect election; he was obtuse not to have foreseen how unacceptable this would appear to colonists already possessing the direct franchise, who had, moreover, flatly refused to recognise the District Councils prescribed for them from England. So evident was the unpopularity of his scheme that Grey did not present the intended bill in the session of 1848.[3] He explained that he had no wish to impose on a colony a form of government to which it objected or was even indifferent; he was willing to drop indirect election and a Second Chamber, and he would gladly see the colonial Legislatures co-operating in the framing of their own constitutions.[4] Further, to ensure the best possible consideration for his amended proposals, he referred them to a special committee of the Privy Council. Its Report, drafted by Sir James Stephen, adopted and amplified Grey's own opinions. Calling attention to the change in policy by which representative institutions had been granted to none, except New South Wales, of the sixteen colonies acquired since 1800, it stated an abstract preference for the old system of Governor, Council and Assembly, but in the present case recommended that the New South Wales model should be followed; it proposed however that, subject to imperial veto, the colonial Legislatures should have power to vary the scheme and to alter the enacted Civil Lists.[5] The Report was circulated to the Australian Governors and formed the basis of the bill introduced in June 1849.

[1] See *Parl. Pap.* 1851, xxxv [1398], [1402].
[2] Grey to Sir Charles Fitzroy, 31 July 1847, *Parl. Pap.* 1847–8, xlii (715); Bell and Morrell, p. 93.
[3] Hansard, cv, 1125 (4 June 1849) and cvi, 1120 (2 July 1849).
[4] Grey to Fitzroy, 31 July 1848, *Parl. Pap.* 1847–8, xlii (715); Bell and Morrell, p. 104.
[5] *Parl. Pap.* 1849, xxxv [1074]. The members of the Committee, besides Grey and Stephen, were H. Labouchère, Lord Campbell and Sir E. Ryan. It was technically "the Board of Trade", or rather the "Committee of H.M. Privy Council for Trade and Plantations". Grey had by now become converted to the "Blended House"; Grey, *Colonial Policy*, ii, 97.

Reintroduced in February 1850, when there had been opportunities of learning local opinion, the Australian Colonies Government Bill was debated more thoroughly than any colonial measure since the Canada Union Bill, and shared the honours of the session with Don Pacifico and Papal Aggression. On the whole it was favourably received and its second reading was challenged in neither House. The provisions for a fixed uniform tariff, for federal control of waste lands, and for a federal legislature were eventually dropped; but amendments setting up bicameral legislatures, giving the several colonies control of their own waste lands, and restricting the imperial power of disallowance to defined subjects, were all defeated.[1] Parliament was not prepared to surrender imperial control in the last resort, but expressed a widespread desire to treat the colonists like Englishmen and give them the institutions they wanted; no doubt undue importance was attached to the form prescribed for these in what was admittedly no final measure. The topic of responsible government was hardly touched on, perhaps because the certainty of its eventual concession was generally recognised.[2]

Acceptable as the new Act might be to the three colonies deriving from it their first instalment of self-government, it gave little cause for rejoicing in New South Wales. There the franchise had indeed been extended, but the colony had been partitioned, and the retention of the waste lands, the land revenue, and a Civil List under the control of Downing Street denied its insistent demands. The land, taxation and transportation aroused far keener local interest than political institutions, and Grey's disregard of the view of the majority in these respects outweighed his various concessions.[3] The Legislative Council launched a protest as its expiring act, a protest which the new Council reaffirmed. Grey's reply to the first was conciliatory in tone but not repentant.[4] It fell to his successor to answer the second, but by then circumstances had been altered by the grant of a liberal measure of self-government to New Zealand.

In May 1850 the Government had been satisfied that the time was ripe to grant the desire of the New Zealand colonists for representative

[1] For the importance attached to the last point in New South Wales see *C.H.B.E.* vol. VII, pt. I, pp. 280, 281.
[2] The bill became 13 and 14 Vict. c. 59; see *Parl. Pap.* 1850, xxxvii [1160], [1182], 1851, xxxv [1303], esp. Grey to Fitzroy, 30 Aug. 1850. Grey gave the populations of the four colonies as: N.S.W. 171,000, Vic. 51,000, S.A. 49,000, V.D.L. 70,000, Hansard, cxi, 1223.
[3] E.g. as regards the Casual Revenues and Customs patronage: for the former see Melbourne, pt IV, chap. v; for the latter see Grey to Fitzroy, 8 Aug. 1850 (circular despatch), *Parl. Pap.* 1851, xxxv [1303], p. 42. Grey, following Gladstone, had intended to reintroduce convicts in New South Wales in 1849; see Melbourne, pt IV, chap. x and *C.H.B.E.* vol. VII, pt. I, p. 176; Bell and Morrell, pp. 308-11.
[4] Fitzroy to Grey, 18 June 1851, 15 Jan. 1852, Grey to Fitzroy, 23 Jan. 1852, *Parl. Pap.* 1852, xxxiv [1534], pp. 10, 20, 25; Bell and Morrell, pp. 137-41; Hansard, cxxii, 914 *seqq.* (18 June 1852).

government, and a bill had been planned for the following session.[1] Pressure of business, however, compelled its postponement for a year. For the session of 1852 the Whigs had prepared a measure on lines suggested by Sir George Grey, the Governor, and they announced it in the Queen's Speech, but it fell to the Tory Pakington to introduce and carry it.[2] The geography and history of the New Zealand settlements made a centralised government impossible at present; the Act therefore established six provinces, each with an elected Council and elected Superintendent, but the constitution was not strictly federal, since the General Assembly for the whole colony had concurrent and superior legislative powers and the Governor could disallow provincial bills. The central legislature was to consist of two Chambers, the one elected on the same franchise as the Provincial Councils, the other nominated for life by the Crown. A Civil List of £16,000, including £7000 for native purposes, was assured, and "the Crown reserved power to maintain the laws, customs and usages of the Maoris within proclaimed districts"; but the Assembly was given control of waste lands and empowered to some extent to amend the constitution.[3] As in the debates on the Australian bill, Parliament showed its willingness to give the settlers the institutions they desired, and Conservatives, Peelites and Whigs co-operated to pass the bill before the 1847 parliament was dissolved in June. It was henceforward certain that the demand of the Australian colonists for the management of their waste lands could not long be denied.[4]

In South Africa the issue of self-government was still overshadowed by frontier policy, which meant native policy; it was over native policy that troubles with the Boers had begun and continued. The problem was far more difficult than in New Zealand, owing to the vastly greater numbers and territory involved. Lord Grey's plans for New Zealand showed that he was not at one with Exeter Hall in his attitude to natives; on the other hand, he was desirous to protect them from Boer aggression, even outside British territory, to Christianise and to civilise them.[5] This desire was limited, however, by an unwillingness to pay the price. He was reluctant to extend the frontier and still more reluctant to incur expenses which would need

---

[1] Hansard, cx, 1408, 1427 (13 May 1850). See G. Grey to Earl Grey, 30 Nov. 1849, *Parl. Pap.* 1850, xxxvii [1280], p. 104; Earl Grey to G. Grey, 19 Feb. 1851, *Parl. Pap.* 1851, xxxv [1420], p. 193.

[2] Hansard, cxix, 323 (10 Feb. 1852); Earl Grey to G. Grey, 23 Feb. 1852. *Parl. Pap.* 1852, xxxv [1483], pp. 5 *seqq.*

[3] 15 and 16 Vict. c. 72. See Pakington's speech of 3 May and Grey's of 22 June 1852 (Hansard, cxxi, 102 *seqq.*, cxxii, 1155 *seqq.*). For the claims of Wakefield and Adderley see Marais, p. 293. See also *C.H.B.E.* vol. vii, pt. ii, pp. 97–9.

[4] See Pakington to Fitzroy, 15 Dec. 1852, *Parl. Pap.* 1852–3, lxiii [1611] (extracts in Bell and Morrell, p. 265).

[5] See extracts from the Howick Papers, Bell and Morrell, p. 522. Grey was satisfied that the Kaffirs' attack on their neighbours in 1846 was "entirely unprovoked"; Grey, *Colonial Policy*, ii, 198.

parliamentary sanction; this reluctance was prudent, since British public opinion cared much more for economy than for South Africa.[1] The event showed that here at least there was no place for philanthropic imperialism on the cheap.

Grey's term of office began with one Kaffir war and ended with another. The outbreak of the first, in 1846, sealed the doom of the treaty policy maintained with modifications since 1836. Grey was inclined to make a protectorate of the district between the Fish and Keiskamma rivers, with the Kaffir tribes organised under British officers.[2] But Sir Harry Smith, the forceful optimist whom he sent out as Governor at the end of 1847, in rapid succession extended the area under British sovereignty to the Kei on the east, and to the upper Orange and then to the Vaal on the north.[3] Grey sanctioned these large annexations with progressive reluctance, insisting that the colonists must be warned not to expect the imperial Treasury to pay for any more Kaffir wars and that the mother country could bear no financial responsibility for the administration of the new Orange River Sovereignty.[4] The Privy Council Committee, to whom the general question of the South African possessions outside the Cape was referred in 1849, reported that the disavowal of this annexation would mean worse evils, particularly to the natives, than its maintenance.[5] But, highly as the Committee valued the social and religious improvement of the natives, they would not assert "that it could be either wisely or justly prosecuted at the expense of the public revenue either of this kingdom or of the colony of the Cape of Good Hope".[6] It was the view which Grey had taken in the case of Natal, where he wished to rule as far as possible through the chiefs, gradually civilising the natives and inducing them to work.[7] In each of the two new territories a small Legislative Council was established, and the administrator was warned not to look outside for financial help.[8] But though Grey endorsed the Committee's recommendation that further annexations without parliamentary authority should be formally forbidden, he continued to feel, like his predecessors, a responsibility for the behaviour outside British territory of those whom he still considered British subjects. As late as November 1850 he was prepared to authorise a punitive expedition against the Boers north

[1] *Ibid.* II, 248.
[2] Grey to Pottinger, 2 Nov. 1846, *Parl. Pap.* 1847-8, XLIII [912] (extract in Bell and Morrell, pp. 502 *seqq.*).
[3] Smith to Grey, 18, 23 Dec. 1847, 3 Feb. 1848, *Parl. Pap.* 1847-8, XLIII [969].
[4] Grey to Smith, 31 March, 21 June 1848, *ibid.*
[5] The decision was due to Russell; Morrell, p. 299.
[6] See enclosure in Grey to Smith, 26 July 1850, *Parl. Pap.* 1851, XXXVII [1360], pp. 85 *seqq.*
[7] Grey to Pottinger, 4 Dec. 1846, to Smith 10 Dec. 1847, 19 June 1848, *Parl. Pap.* 1847-8, XLII [980], pp. 93 *seqq.*, 137 *seqq.*, 221 *seqq.*
[8] For Natal, see copy of Letters Patent dated 2 March 1847 in Grey to Smith, 16 March 1848, *ibid.*; for Orange River Sovereignty see copy of Regulations in Smith to Grey, 26 March 1849, and copy of the abortive Letters Patent in Grey to Smith, 25 March 1851, both in *Parl. Pap.* 1851, XXXVII [1360].

of the Vaal and to introduce a bill extending the jurisdiction of British magistrates to the Equator.[1] The events of 1851 caused a complete change of policy.

Meanwhile steps had been taken towards the grant of representative government to the Cape.[2] Grey desired Sir Henry Pottinger, the new Governor, in November 1846 to prepare a considered reply to Stanley's as yet unanswered despatch of 1842; Grey informed him that the Government entertained "the strongest prepossessions in favour of [the representative] system of colonial polity", and declared that some difficulties might be wisely encountered,

and some apparent risks well incurred, in reliance on the resources which every civilised society, especially every society of British birth or origin, will always discover within themselves for obviating the dangers incident to measures resting on any broad and solid principle of truth and justice. On such a basis, as I am convinced, rests the policy of intrusting the remote dependencies of a metropolitan state with the largest powers of self-government, in whatever relates to their internal and local affairs.[3]

An answer came in due course from Sir Harry Smith enclosing official opinions from his Councillors: Stanley's objections based on geographical dispersion and racial divisions were not considered decisive, and it was agreed to recommend one legislature for the whole colony, formed of two Houses, one elected and one nominated. A draft Order-in-Council establishing a constitution modelled on those of Canada and New Zealand was included.[4]

Lord Grey replied in February 1849 that the Government had decided in principle to grant representative institutions to the Cape, and as in the Australian case the question was referred to the Board of Trade Committee of the Privy Council. Their Report was sent to Cape Town in January 1850. A few days later Russell announced in Parliament that it was intended to give the Cape an elected Second Chamber.[5] The Committee, in other words Grey, had decided that nominee Councils carried little weight, and that the ultra-democratic "republican" device which the French-Canadians had once demanded in vain was really more conservative. Seeing that "what has been termed 'responsible', but what would more correctly be described as 'parliamentary' or 'party' government" was not suited to the Cape, it was undesirable that officials should be eligible to sit in the Assembly and so risk entanglement in party contests; but they might attend and speak, without voting, in either House. There should be provision for a Civil List as in the Australian bill, and appropriations

[1] Grey to Smith, 26 July, 12 and 29 Nov. 1850, ibid. The bill was to amend the Act 6 and 7 Will. IV, c. 57, v. supra, p. 355.
[2] See C.H.B.E. vol. VIII, ch. xv.
[3] V. supra, pp. 367, 368. Grey to Pottinger, 2 Nov. 1846, Parl. Pap. 1847–8, XLIII [912] (extract in Bell and Morrell, p. 91).
[4] Smith to Grey, 29 July 1848. Parl. Pap. 1850, XXXVIII [1137]; a very important part was played by William Porter, the Cape Attorney-General.
[5] Grey to Smith, 12 Feb. 1849, ibid.; Hansard, CVIII, 553 (8 Feb. 1850).

for native purposes should be unalterable save with the consent of the Secretary of State.[1]

So far all had gone well for Grey's plans in the colony and at home. Now Nemesis struck. Alike in New South Wales and in South Africa he was punished for his well-intentioned wilfulness in attempting to impose convicts on a colony without due regard for local opinion. At the Cape the atmosphere was poisoned for several years by the indignation aroused by the Neptune incident, and its repercussions prevented the constitution from coming into force during Grey's tenure of office[2].

So satisfactory had been the tenor of Sir Harry Smith's reports that the outbreak of another Kaffir war at the end of 1850, and Smith's failure to suppress it, were stunning blows to Grey. His whole South African policy came up for discussion in the Cabinet and for attack in the Commons, where the main interest of the Colonial Reformers was now diverted from Australia to the Cape. Then in September 1851 came news of trouble with the natives in the Orange River Sovereignty and of the Boers' refusal to support the Queen's authority in the field. If it was true, as the Resident unwisely asserted, that two-thirds of the Boers in the Sovereignty were rebels at heart, then to remain there for the benefit of the natives was mere "quixotic philanthropy". Russell became convinced that withdrawal was the right course and Grey so informed the Governor.[3] Smith vehemently disagreed, but in January 1852 the Assistant Commissioners sent out from home felt constrained, as a diplomatic measure, to break with previous British policy and recognise the independence of the Boers north of the Vaal; in the same month the Cabinet recalled Smith.[4] In issuing instructions to the new Governor, George Cathcart, Grey spoke of "the absolute necessity of a revision of the system of policy hitherto pursued on the Cape frontier".[5] It was the old story; in 1852 as in 1846, a new policy needed. But whereas then he had looked to more active measures, he now thought of a restriction of obligations. It was a sad end to his schemes, and to his career; for within three weeks he was out of office, never to enter a ministry again though he lived to be ninety-two.

During Lord Grey's term of office a keen but transient breeze of

---

[1] Enclosure in Grey to Smith, 31 Jan. 1850, *Parl. Pap.* 1850, XXXVIII [1137]. For the difference of opinion between Russell and Grey in Dec. 1849 as to the proposed Second Chamber see Morrell, p. 280; for the views of Stephen, who was not a member of this Committee, see a most interesting memorandum in Bell and Morrell, p. 116 (from C.O. 48/289).

[2] See *C.H.B.E.* vol. VIII, ch. xv.

[3] Grey to Smith, 15 Sept. and 21 Oct. 1851, *Parl. Pap.* 1852, XXXIII [1428]; see references to Howick Papers in Morrell, p. 302. The withdrawal was actually effected by the Convention of Bloemfontein, 25 Feb. 1854, Eybers, p. 282.

[4] Grey to Smith, 14 Jan. 1852, *Parl. Pap.* 1852, XXXIII [1428], p. 253; for the Sand River Convention (17 Jan. 1852) see *Parl. Pap.* 1852-3, LXVI [1646], pp. 29 *seqq.*; Eybers, p. 358.

[5] Grey to Cathcart, 2 Feb. 1852, *Parl. Pap.* 1852, XXXIII [1428], p. 256 (extract in Bell and Morrell, p. 528). For the course of events generally see *C.H.B.E.* vol. VIII, ch. XIV.

interest in colonial affairs ruffled the surface of English public life before the gloom of the bad times yielded to the prosperity of the fifties. Famine in Ireland and trade depression brought emigration into prominence.[1] Nor could politicians fail to reflect on how the new commercial policy and the relaxation of control implied in responsible government at Montreal were likely to affect England's position as an imperial power. Both these developments were of course highly objectionable to the party led by Stanley and Disraeli. It was clear, moreover, that free trade and other grievances were causing widespread discontent in the colonies themselves. There was trouble in Jamaica, Guiana and Ceylon in 1848; the Montreal riots and annexationist agitation in Canada in 1849 were followed by the controversies with Australia and the Cape over transportation. Colonial malcontents visiting England, like Lowe and Fairbairn, aided and instructed the administration's domestic critics. "The forty colonies, it appears, are all pretty like rebelling just now", wrote Carlyle in 1850; "and are to be pacified with constitutions."[2]

Wakefield and his party seized the occasion to demonstrate in force with pen and tongue. Their chief, recovered from his two years' disablement and relieved by Buller's death at the end of 1848 from any need of sparing the Government, published next year the fullest exposition of his views on colonisation and colonial government, savagely venting on Lord Grey and the department his accumulated wrath at the hampering of his schemes for New Zealand.[3] The book contained the sketch of a model constitution, under which the settled colonies might enjoy general powers of self-government, certain fields, such as military affairs, foreign relations and waste lands, being reserved by charter for imperial control; colonial Governors should hold office during good behaviour, possibly for life, but the charter should provide, first, that none of their acts should be valid unless performed on the advice of an Executive Council, and secondly, that the Executive Council should be *ipso facto* removed by an address of no confidence from the Assembly; it was important that the franchise should be comparatively high.[4] At the same time Wakefield inspired the formation on a broad basis of a new Colonial Reform Association; it included both eager colonial enthusiasts, like J. R. Godley and C. B. Adderley, and leading champions of economy, like Cobden and Milner-Gibson, whose main interest in the colonies was to make them self-supporting. There was a "fever for economy", and when long bills were presented for obscure Kaffir wars economists were furious.

[1] Grey called it "a reigning fancy of the day". To Elgin, 16 Nov. 1848, Can. Archives, Elgin-Grey Correspondence.
[2] "*Downing Street*", p. 2, in *Latter-Day Pamphlets*. Cf. the letter of 13 Aug. 1852 from Lord Robert Cecil to the Rev. H. Palmer in Cecil, Lady Gwendolen, *Life of Robert Marquis of Salisbury*, 1, 34.
[3] Wakefield, E. G., *A View of the Art of Colonization*, 1849.
[4] *Ibid.* (ed. Collier, 1914), pp. 297–321.

"Under the pressure of great distress and financial embarrassment," wrote Grey in May 1848, "there is a growing disposition in the House of Commons and amongst the public to grumble at the heavy cost of our colonies."[1] By making colonial self-government and the cessation of all normal expenditure on the self-governing colonies its two main objects, the promoters of the society spread their net wide. Gladstone, though not a member, supported them, and Disraeli toyed with the idea of at least joining forces with them for an attack on the Government.[2]

Besides the frequent discussions on the affairs of particular colonies, several debates were initiated in these years on colonial policy as a whole. Francis Scott, the advocate of the New South Wales Legislature, pleaded in a thin House in April 1849 for a select committee on colonial relations. J. A. Roebuck in the same year, inspired by American expansion west of the Alleghanies, produced a scheme, both in book and in bill form, for a fundamental statute to regulate the stages of colonial political development from first settlement to federal union.[3] But the most persistent and learned parliamentary champion of the Colonial Reformers was Sir William Molesworth, who in July 1848, June 1849, and April 1851 opened discussions with long spoken essays, carefully memorised, statistics and all, demanding investigations into the whole field of colonial government and insisting that inefficiency, extravagance and discontent were the necessary result of the excessive centralisation of power in Downing Street. Molesworth believed that the Cape was worthless to Great Britain and that no harm would be done if the North American colonies became independent or joined the United States—a junction which Roebuck wished above all things to avert—but he did not propose to abandon Canada.[4] Whether Cobden actually wished for separation is not clear; in any case he cared little for the political, compared with the "commercial and moral", connection.[5]

Disraeli was convinced that the policy of "what are called Colonial Reformers" meant the dissolution of the Empire, and suggested to his chief a vague scheme for colonial representation at Westminster, which might help to counterbalance the democratic influence of the English towns.[6] Grey expressed his own misgivings as to the trend of opinion in a well-known passage in a letter to Elgin.

There begins to prevail in the House of Commons, and I am sorry to say in the highest quarters, an opinion (which I believe to be utterly erroneous) that we have no interest in preserving our colonies and ought therefore to make no sacrifice for

[1] To Elgin, 4 May 1848, Can. Archives, Elgin-Grey Correspondence. See e.g. the Commons debates of 25 Feb. 1848 and 13 June 1851, Hansard, XCVI, 1353 seqq., CXVII, 737 seqq. III, 233–7.
[2] Disraeli to Stanley, 17 Dec. 1849; Monypenny, W. F. and Buckle, G. E., Life of Disraeli, III, 233–7.
[3] Hansard, CIV, 313 seqq., CV, 928 seqq.; Roebuck, The Colonies of England.
[4] Hansard, C, 816 seqq., CVI, 937 seqq., CXV, 1364 seqq.   [5] See Morrell, p. 488.
[6] Disraeli to Stanley, 28 Dec. 1849, to Derby, 9 Sept. 1851; Monypenny and Buckle, III, 237, 333–6.

that purpose. Peel, Graham and Gladstone, if they do not avow this opinion as openly as Cobden and his friends, yet betray very clearly that they entertain it, nor do I find some members of the Cabinet free from it.[1]

This feeling was not universal. Carlyle, whose views probably more truly represented the common man, was astonished at the willingness of the governing class to let the colonies go, and protested with superb eloquence in the name of the ordinary instinct of Englishmen.[2] But the faint hearts were no doubt supported by the belief, not really surprising in minds familiar with the recent history of the early English and Spanish colonies in America but not with the existing colonial conditions, that responsible government, whether one wished it or not, must eventually lead to separation. Grey knew how damaging was the effect in Canada of defeatist views publicly expressed in England, when accentuated by unpopular acts of imperial power, like the repeal of the Corn Laws, and by the attraction of prosperity across the border. He would have liked to gratify the Canadians by economic favours, such as help with the Halifax-Quebec railway; but in the existing temper of the House of Commons that was impossible. It was a vicious circle. Imperial policy and indifference caused despondency and disaffection in the colonies, and these, reported home, made Englishmen still less willing to sacrifice aught for such unfriendly kinsmen. In 1848–9 even Elgin and Grey doubted whether Canada could be kept for the Empire.

The official pronouncement of the Government's attitude was made by the Prime Minister in February 1850. Addressing himself chiefly to the Colonial Reformers, Russell argued that both honour and interest forbade the abandonment of the colonies. They immensely increased our prestige and therefore our strength; if cast off by us, they would assuredly turn for protection to some other Power; nor could we escape our responsibility for protecting natives and minorities. To refuse to contribute to their defence would amount to abandonment. But in return for defending them we had the right to demand that their commercial policy should conform to that of the Empire. He claimed that his administration was in fact promoting self-government in the colonies and reducing the United Kingdom's commitments as fast as practicable; the work could only be done gradually.[3] The speech made a good impression, but it contained at the end a passage in which Russell anticipated the possible eventual decision of some colonies to sever the imperial tie. To the House of Commons this peroration no doubt seemed perfectly natural, but in Canada it aroused the indignation of Robert Baldwin, the man whom Sydenham

[1] Grey to Elgin, 18 May 1849, Can. Archives, Elgin-Grey Correspondence. Graham said "that we ought to limit instead of extending our colonial empire, that Canada must soon be independent...", *The Greville Memoirs*, 13 Feb. 1848.

[2] "New Downing Street" (13 April 1850), pp. 27–37, in *Latter-Day Pamphlets*.

[3] For what had actually been done in the way of reducing garrisons, see Morrell, pp. 475–7, 490, 497–9.

and Metcalfe had distrusted and denounced; and Elgin, reporting the incident, exhorted the Secretary of State: "You must renounce the habit of telling the Colonies that the colonial is a provisional existence. You must allow them to believe that without severing the bonds which unite them to Great Britain they may attain the degree of perfection and of social and political developement to which organised communities of freemen have a right to aspire." Grey in reply agreed in deprecating "all reference that can possibly be avoided to eventual separation", but urged that Russell had only spoken the truth in saying that the time *might* come, that if it did we ought to allow the separation to take place amicably, and that in the meantime we ought to prepare the colonies for self-government; he repeated, too, his fears that the attitude of the Commons—and he again mentioned the Peelite leaders—was "calculated to render their retention extremely difficult".[1]

Perhaps the most interesting of the proposals of the Colonial Reformers was one, clearly borrowed from the United States constitution, for a statutory delimitation of matters of imperial and local concern, whereby the Crown's right of interference would be restricted.[2] This revolutionary project, supported by Gladstone, was stoutly opposed by Russell and Grey and thrown out by the House of Commons. The powers of the Crown, the exercise of which thus remained in the discretion of ministers, consisted mainly of the right of instructing Governors and the right of disallowing colonial Acts. The formal Royal Instructions issued during this period show no fundamental innovations, except such as naturally followed on changes of constitution.[3] Much more important were the informal instructions conveyed to Governors in despatches, sometimes when they entered on their duties, and thereafter as occasion arose.[4] It was by such means that Thomson and Harvey and Elgin were directed to transform the system of colonial government; and no more need be said than to point out that the amount left to the Governor's discretion varied greatly with the colony and with the Governor. Stephen held in 1846 that in the case of Canada a wise Secretary of State must leave almost everything to the Governor, and that Stanley had in fact so acted.[5]

In the matter of colonial legislation, Benjamin Hawes told the House of Commons in April 1849 that in the three North American colonies most advanced in self-government the use of disallowance and of the Governor's veto had become rare; in other colonies it was

[1] Elgin to Grey, 23 March, Grey to Elgin, 19 April 1850; see Morison, J. L., *British Supremacy*, pp. 262–66; the rise in Elgin's confidence since 1849 is remarkable.
[2] See Wakefield, pp. 298 *seqq.*; Molesworth, Hansard, cvi, 965 (26 June 1849).
[3] Poulett Thomson had been invited to redraft his own; R. V. Smith to Murdoch, 3 Dec. 1840, Can. Archives, G. 183.
[4] Durham, Thomson, Bagot and Cathcart received initial "instructions"; Metcalfe and Elgin did not.
[5] Minute of 12 Jan. 1846, C.O. 42/531.

less so, but in the eighteen months ending June 1848 objection had been taken to only 55 out of 912 colonial laws sent home. He pointed out that in the major differences between imperial and colonial opinion, namely on emancipation, fiscal policy, waste lands and transportation, it was Parliament, not the department, which was the deciding authority.[1] Grey expounded his own policy with regard to disallowance in the book which he published soon after his resignation as a defence of his official career. Here again, much depended on the degree of stability and responsibility attained by the individual colony. Like Stephen, he was for reducing interference to the minimum and, at least in a self-governing colony, he was not disposed to disallow a law simply because he thought it unwise. But in some matters, which could not be specified beforehand, interference was justified, inasmuch as they concerned the honour of the Crown or the interest of the Empire as a whole. Convinced as he was of "the absolute necessity of the commercial policy of the whole Empire being uniform and consistent", he instructed Head in New Brunswick not to assent to any bill granting bounties, and in Canada he was prepared to disallow measures of retaliation against the trade of the United States.[2]

Of all Grey's predecessors in the Colonial Office few had been such able men as he, and none had studied colonial affairs so long and so earnestly. It was a cruel irony that such a man shaping policy at a time when public opinion showed for once some interest in the colonies should have been written down a failure. This was largely because so much was expected of him, and because his discomfitures were more spectacular than his successes and, coming after them, eclipsed them in the popular eye. South Africa, above all, was the grave of his reputation; yet here, it is claimed, he was the first statesman to evolve a real native policy and understand the responsibilities of empire.[3] He may be blamed for not standing by Smith to the end; but Smith's optimism had deceived him in the past, and the drive for retrenchment in England made a long-sighted policy very difficult. Among his characteristic defects disloyalty to subordinates did not rank, as his treatment of Sir George Grey and of Elgin witnesses. It is indeed one of his great services to the Empire to have selected and supported Elgin, as Russell selected and supported Thomson seven years before. When we compare the system of colonial government in 1852 with the system in 1838, there is no sharper contrast than in the calibre of the men filling the great proconsulships. In sending out statesmen like Durham and Thomson the Whigs set a

[1] Hansard, c, 875, civ, 343 seqq. (25 July 1848, 16 April 1849).
[2] Colonial Policy of Lord John Russell's Administration, i, 19 seqq.; Hansard, ciii, 1272 seqq. (26 March 1849); Grey to Elgin, 13 June 1851, Can. Archives, Elgin-Grey Correspondence. For Grey's views on fiscal uniformity see Grey to Elgin, 25 Oct. 1850, 15 Feb., 9 May 1851, ibid.
[3] See Morrell, British Colonial Policy, chaps. xix, xx, on Grey's attitude and achievement.

standard which the Tories did their best to maintain; Elgin, as it happened, was the choice of Stanley and Gladstone as well as of Grey. Both parties also share the credit during this period of having, after 1839, sent no second-rate man to Downing Street. But the Whigs may claim one further merit: that both in 1839 and in 1846 they saw a change of system to be necessary in the government of the North American colonies, and that by effecting the change they opened a way by which the Second Empire might be preserved.

CHAPTER XI

THE MOVEMENT TOWARDS FREE TRADE,
1820–1853

IT was Adam Smith who gave currency to the term "Mercantile System"; and he meant it for reproach. The mercantilists assumed that one nation's profit was another's loss. They believed in regulation and restraint, and set an inordinate value on the treasure accruing to a nation from a favourable balance of trade. Modern historians use the term in an extended sense. They define it, for example, as the economic expression of militant nationalism. They contrast it with the parochialism of the pre-nation state and with the supposed cosmopolitanism of the nineteenth century. But if we designate the period 1820–53 as "the fall of mercantilism", the wider interpretation is misleading. For it suggests that England then fell away from nationalism, when in fact the tendency was the other way. In 1820 the imperial spirit was still strong, but in 1853 it was faint. The country had become absorbed in its social problems, and its policy of trade discouraged the imperial tie. It is better to speak of the movement towards free trade, and to avoid thus a term which is used neither by the statesmen of the period, Huskisson, Peel and Gladstone, nor by the contemporary historians, Tooke and Newmarch. Huskisson, to whom above any other the introduction of free trade is due, regarded the policy which he pioneered as a breach with "the old and hopeless system of prohibitory protection"[1] which had ruled hitherto. He says "protection," not "mercantilism." When he revised the tariff, it was with a view to removing "useless and inconvenient restrictions".[2] He contrasted the inert monopoly of Spain with the prospering freedom of England. But he was not a free trader at the expense of empire, and in this he followed his intellectual master Adam Smith. "An open trade," said Huskisson in 1825, "especially to a rich and thriving country, is infinitely more valuable than any monopoly, however exclusive, which the public power of the State may be able, either to enforce against its own Colonial dominions, or to establish in its intercourse with other parts of the world."[3]

Adam Smith published the *Wealth of Nations* in 1776; the free trade movement as a conscious effort began in 1820. The interval of forty-four years embraced the industrial revolution in its most crucial phase and the long war with France; and both of these momentous hap-

---

[1] Huskisson, W., *Speeches*, II, 344. [2] *Ibid*. II, 506.
[3] *Ibid*. II, 321.

penings prepared the way for a new policy of trade. The industrial revolution broke down the old routine, and the French war, as is the fashion of wars, speeded the progress of industrialism. Therefore the fiscal changes which followed after 1820 were in accord with social and technical changes which preceded and accompanied them. Moreover, the war put a premium on a form of trade which was not unlike "free" trade in its original connotation of interloping. For during the war, with the sanction of government, privateering and blockade-running were exalted into national virtues. To them Napoleon opposed his Continental System, but the free traders prevailed against him. They used the supremacy of their navy at sea to penetrate the Continent on two flanks, from the Baltic Sea and German Ocean in the north and from the Mediterranean in the south. In 1813 a further large instalment of free trade was secured, when the monopoly of the East India Company was taken away in all but the China trade.

For the five years from 1815 to 1820 England was absorbed in the task of returning to peace, but two events in these years greatly aided the passage to a new trade policy. The first was the suppression of the Barbary pirates in 1816, which made the high seas for the first time reasonably safe. It helped the weaker powers even more than it helped England, but it was done by England in pursuit of a purpose to which she was consistently faithful from 1807 onwards, the suppression of the slave trade and of slavery. The second event was the resumption of cash payments, decreed in 1819 and accomplished in 1821. This restored the free market in gold. The free traders, Huskisson and Peel, were prominent in securing the resumption and in holding fast to it. Free gold and free goods went hand in hand, and were themselves part of a wider programme of freedom in other relations of life, social, religious and civil.

It has often been remarked that Great Britain owes free trade to the Tories; and this in the main is true. The reforms of Huskisson were the final economic effort of the long-established Tory Government in the unreformed House of Commons. He himself did not come to the Board of Trade till 1823, and already something had been done. In 1820 the merchants of London, inspired by Thomas Tooke, launched their petition in favour of full free trade, and in the same year the Government instituted an enquiry into the foreign trade of the country, which resulted in the legislation of 1821 and 1822. In 1821 the prohibitive duties on Baltic timber were lowered: in 1822 the Navigation Laws were subjected to their first revision. For this work the credit belongs to Thomas Wallace, Vice-president of the Board of Trade since 1818. The Government, meanwhile, was preparing the way for a more liberal trade policy by granting recognition to the new republics of Central and South America. Then came Huskisson to expand the work and give it comprehensive form. In three years,

1823, 1824 and 1825, he instituted a policy of commercial reciprocity with foreign powers, removed the long-standing prohibition on the import of foreign silks, revised and reduced the whole tariff and carried the revision of the Navigation Laws a stage further forward. It has not infrequently happened that measures of liberalism have been thwarted by the first succeeding depression. Huskisson's testing time came with the commercial crisis at the end of 1825, and he had to defend his policy against those who attributed the distress to the new fiscal system. In this he was triumphantly successful in what are perhaps his three greatest speeches: 24 February 1826, "The effects of the free trade system on the silk manufacture"; 12 May 1826, "The state of the navigation of the United Kingdom"; 7 May 1827, "The state of the British commercial shipping interest". He used the occasions to show the enormous superiority which England enjoyed as the result of supremacy in naval power and the new machinery. Perhaps his most novel appeal was to the value of foreign competition as a stimulus to enterprise.

The hall mark of true statesmanship is the power to prefer the substance to the shadow when the shadow is enshrined in tradition and sectional interest. Huskisson realised that the independence of America and the decline in the power of Holland had created a new situation, which made the old Navigation Laws and the system of discriminating duties which had come to be attached to them at once useless and obstructive. "Our Navigation Laws", he said, "have a twofold object. First, to create and maintain in this country a great commercial Marine; and secondly, to prevent any one other nation from engrossing too large a portion of the navigation of the rest of the world."[1] That nation had formerly been Holland, and now it was the United States. America (he proceeded to argue) had been strong enough to secure trade with England on equal terms as well as entry into her colonial trade: the true policy of England was to extend to others what America had extorted for herself by the Treaty of 1815. The new countries of Central and South America, therefore, were promoted to equality with the United States in the Navigation Law of 1822; and similarly the countries of Europe in 1825 were allowed a share in the colonial trade on condition of reciprocity.

Huskisson's policy, however, was the reverse of passive, and he never forgot the interests of the colonies. When the United States took exception to the policy of imperial preference, demanding empire rates for themselves, he met retaliation with retaliation. "This", he said in 1825, "is a pretension unheard of in the commercial relations of independent states. It is just as unreasonable as it would be, on our part, to require that sugar or rum, from our West-India Islands, should be admitted at New York upon the same terms and duties as the like articles, the growth and production of Louisiana."[2] When

[1] Huskisson, *Speeches*, III, 2. [2] *Ibid.* II, 315.

Holland would not open her colonial preserves, he imposed on her the extra rates immortalised in Canning's rhyming despatch:

> In matters of commerce the fault of the Dutch
> Is offering too little and asking too much.
> The French are with equal advantage content,
> So we clap on Dutch bottoms just twenty per cent.

The tariff was then so high that it was possible both to give preference to the colonies and to reduce the foreign rates. But in the matter of the Baltic timber duties, he refused further reduction on the ground that it would injure the Canadian timber trade—"Canadian timber, considering that it grew in one of our own colonies, and was transported in our own ships, was a most valuable trade to Great Britain."[1] And although neither he nor Canning was able to liberalise the Corn Laws, yet he secured for Canada in 1825 a concession which opened English ports to Canadian wheat at all times. Moreover, even when he had finished his revision of the Navigation Laws, he retained all that then was, or for long enough had been, important in that system, the reservation to British shipping of sea transport within the Empire and of the long haul from distant parts to England. When he resigned in 1828, the trade of the colonies was virtually as free as the trade of Scotland or the Channel Islands. They could export and import freely in their own ships, or in ships of the other country. A preference determined by the mother country was given to British goods, but the colonies retained the proceeds of the differential rate, and on their side enjoyed corresponding preferences in the English market. With characteristic thoroughness Huskisson made a survey of the Empire and assigned to the staple product of each part a worth-while preference. He did not, however, grant fiscal autonomy. That came of itself later.

The French war, while it gave an impetus to trade and industry, piled up burdens of taxation; and these left England after 1815 with a tariff and a system of indirect taxation which were painfully overloaded and highly obstructive to trade. The commercial interests got their way in 1816 when they secured the abolition of the income tax; and this meant that far too much revenue had to be raised by the taxation of commodities. Fortunately, however, Huskisson was able to prove that, in spite of British naval power, he could not repress smuggling where duties were excessive. Therefore, when revising the tariff 1823–5, he took as his guide the level which, if exceeded, would be evaded by the smuggler. This he fixed at 30 per cent.; and he urged that it was not the state alone which would benefit. "Let the state have the tax, which is now the reward of the smuggler, and let the consumer have the better and cheaper article, without the painful consciousness that he is consulting his own convenience at the expense of daily violating the laws of his country."[2] The case was strongest

---

[1] *Ibid.* ii, 362. [2] *Ibid.* ii, 342.

where the article was prohibited. In defending his silk policy he said (Feb. 1826) in one of his liveliest sallies: "Nay, Sir, if strangers were, at this moment, ordered to withdraw from the gallery; and every member were called upon (of course in secret committee) to produce his handkerchief with the understanding, that those who had not prohibited handkerchiefs in their pockets were obliged to inform against those who had—I am inclined to believe, that the informers would be in a small majority. Upon every information allowed under this prohibitory law, the chances are that the informer and the constable have Bandanas round their necks, and that the magistrate, who hears the charge, has one in his pocket."[1]

By 1830 merchants and manufacturers, on the whole, were converted to the new policy, but they had come round very nervously, and they were by no means ready to part with the moderate protection which they still enjoyed. They were, as Huskisson said in 1825, all great advocates for free trade except in their own calling; and in one particular he failed altogether to move them. The prohibition on the export of machinery was continued, and it was not removed till 1843. Huskisson, in accordance with his policy of removing restrictions on exports, tried to remove this restriction also, but the manufacturers of Lancashire evinced the liveliest alarm. J. Deacon Hume, his right-hand man in the codification of the tariff and for many years after that the Permanent Secretary to the Board of Trade, told a House of Commons Committee in 1841 how upon one occasion Mr Huskisson held up a small article of machinery to a deputation saying: "So, gentlemen, then the prosperity of the trade of this country depends upon our preventing this thing from being carried out of it."[2] Indeed, it was only when painful experience showed that by prohibiting the export of the whole article an encouragement was given to the illicit export of tools and machine parts, that the ban on export was removed.

It has sometimes been said that Huskisson was not a whole-hearted advocate of free trade, and it is true that he did not make a fetish of it. He conceived of it as part of a constructive policy. He removed encouragements that had become obstructions and replaced them by realities. Moreover, in approaching free trade by degrees, he adopted the only course which was possible for a statesman. And in one great respect he was the convinced disciple of Walpole. He desired to make England the entrepôt of world trade; therefore he abolished the harsh penalties on foreign shipping which made the use of English harbours a ruinous expense, and he enlarged the warehousing system both in London and the provincial ports. He saw that England could not retain for ever the pre-eminence which she enjoyed in 1815, and he sought further prosperity in a course which combined concern for

[1] Huskisson, *Speeches*, ii, 512.
[2] Committee (H. of C.) on the laws affecting the exportation of machinery, *Parl. Pap.* 1841, vii (201), Q. 23.

England and the Empire with concern for the progress of world trade and world peace. "*Noblesse oblige*", he says in effect, time and again, to his wavering supporters.

Huskisson's policy was in accord with fundamental tendencies. He met squarely the new situation in America without truckling to that sensitive democracy. He saw that each was in sufficient need of the other to impose conditions. For whatever might be the estrangement between their governments, economic forces bound the two countries together in the first half of the nineteenth century as never before or since. This was the age of the Cotton South, the producer of the raw material which fed England's premier industry. Meanwhile the American North was importing heavily from England for capital development. English houses exporting on commission had their agents in New York, and import was similarly organised. To handle cotton a special class of cotton broker arose in Liverpool, linking up the importer with the manufacturer. The credit that was needed for import and export came in the first instance from England. Although, until the Civil War, America had an important mercantile marine, yet her foreign trade was to an increasing degree orientated on England. She traded with China, but bought the dollars needed for that trade by sending cotton to Liverpool. The pattern of Atlantic trade was very different from what it had been in the mercantile age. Then it was a jealously guarded triangular monopoly—North America, the West Indies, England. Now for passengers and emigrants the Atlantic was becoming a ferry of sail and steam, in which American and Canadian enterprise were prominent. American owners ran fast sailing packets between New York or Boston and Liverpool: after 1833, when the China trade was thrown open, American clippers brought tea to London in record time. Great Britain replied with steamships. In 1840 Samuel Cunard of Halifax, Nova Scotia, founded in England the Cunard Steamship Line. The shipowners of Liverpool and Glasgow, using at first sail and then steam, divided their time between the St Lawrence and the Gulf of Mexico, fetching timber from the former in the summer season and cotton from the latter in the winter. Thus was evolved a great trade in staples of export from the countries of the New World, in exchange for the capital and people and quality merchandise of the Old.

By the end of the 'forties England was carrying out to America hundreds of thousands of distressed Irish as well as some of her own people and emigrants from the Continent of Europe. Thus the underlying forces worked against a policy of empire even in the liberal form conceived by Huskisson. Between 1815 and 1850 England greatly increased her Empire, and this should have made her imperially minded, but she enjoyed at the same time an even greater increase of trade and influence in the United States themselves, in Latin America, and in the Far East. Her own colonies and even the populous East were unable to absorb the wealth of manufactured goods which she poured out from her wealth of imported raw material. For this the markets of Europe were essential; and to Western Europe 1820–53 was the period of English invasion, when the machine-made produce of England ousted their own hand-made goods, and when English and Scottish engineers, and sometimes Irish navvies as well, equipped them with their first railways. They, too, shared in the free trade movement, but it meant to them something very different. To Prussia, engaged in the formation of a German *Zollverein*, it meant a new free trade between the formerly separate parts of the German nation. To France it was a venture in political liberalism rather than a change of fiscal faith. To Belgium it was a way of becoming again a source of supply to the great nations which surrounded her. To all it was a means of catching up with the commercial advantage of England.

Huskisson's eye was usually on North America—on British North America and the United States. Although he included India in his scheme of empire, his imperialism was a colonial imperialism. As member for Liverpool, he had a particular affection for shipping and the Canadian trade of timber and wheat. And he assisted further the industrial north when he facilitated by appropriate tariff action the importation of another great raw material of manufacture, Australian wool. He turned instinctively from the insular confinements of the West Indies to the new continents within the Empire. Canada was one such, Australia another. In 1822 Captain John Macarthur won medals for his new Australian wool, which rivalled the best merino of Saxony, and by 1840 Australia was a serious rival of Germany.[1] By 1850 she was easily first, and thus in thirty years a new despised area of settlement relieved England from her age-long dread of a shortage of wool. Cotton in the American South and wool in Australia were produced under conditions of increasing returns. British shipping carried them to the ports of Liverpool and London. The mills of Lancashire and Yorkshire manufactured them under conditions of equally increasing returns. It was at this period that the doctrine of increasing returns found its way into the body of economic doctrine, as expounded, for example, by Nassau Senior.

And, to the south-east of Australia, was yet another vacant land, New Zealand. Traders came down from Sydney to supply the whaling boats there, and introduced, as always, drink and disorder among the sailors and natives. Then came the exploitation of timber. "The timber", we are told in 1840, "was deemed an object of importance to the British Navy; and ships chartered by Her Majesty's Government have for many years visited New Zealand to supply the royal dockyard with spars."[2] Finally, New Zealand, following

---

[1] For the growth of the Australian wool trade, see *C.H.B.E.* vol. VII, pt. I, pp. 184 *seqq.*
[2] Report of Committee on New Zealand, *Parl. Pap.* 1840, VII (582). Appendix—Statement by Church Missionary Society of February 1840.

Australia, added to the supply of wool.[1] The whalers, incidentally, helped the textile industries of England, for the spermaceti oil which they won was ideal for cotton-spinning machinery. It raised the revolutions of machinery by "500 out of 4000".[2] Railway engines employed the less valuable palm oil. Thus we see the circumference of empire furnishing raw materials in bulk to the mother country in the centre; and the episode was repeated from every quarter of the world. England was still in the main feeding herself, and her intensive agriculture was a part of the new industrialism. Huskisson, in his speech of May 1827, alluded to the 40,000 tons of shipping, mainly foreign, which brought in bones for the purpose of manure. They came from the coast between the Scheldt and the Eider.[3] Twenty years later British shipping went farther afield for a similar purpose. This time it was the guano of Peru, in which Nova Scotian as well as English shipping played a prominent part. By 1850 it was a very great trade. "The sales of Peruvian Guano", Tooke tells us, "by Messrs Gibbs for the last three years have been 1852, 118,000 tons; 1853, 135,000 tons; 1854, 177,000 tons; in all 430,000 tons; which at £12 per ton, represents an expenditure by farmers of £5,160,000."[4] And after the Crimean War Sir John Bennet Lawes, the founder of Rothamsted, shocked public sentiment by sifting the Crimean battlefields for yet more bones. But these things do not make imperial policy. They are just the silent items of imperial growth.

In 1830 the Whigs came into power. They effected an important financial reform when they overhauled the excise. By abolishing the beer duty in 1830 they gave the country free beer, and in 1840 through Sir Rowland Hill they gave it the greater boon of the penny post. But, lacking the courage or the will to impose an income tax, they were unable to continue the reduction of the tariff, which had reached a level where further reductions would involve a temporary loss of revenue. Free trade, however, as we have insisted, was more than a reduction of import duties, and the reformed House of Commons in its first year of legislation passed two great acts of liberation, which enhanced the freedom of trade. In 1833 it abolished the institution of slavery in the colonial empire, which mainly affected the West Indies and South Africa, and in the same year it abolished the monopoly of the East India Company in the China trade. East and West were now free, and their increasing produce flowed freely into the crowded mouth of the Thames.

Until 1802 London had no docks. In 1802 the West India Dock was completed, in 1808 the East India Dock. The dock companies were given a monopoly of their trade for twenty years, but in 1823,

---

[1] See also *C.H.B.E.* vol. VII, pt. II, pp. 32, 147.
[2] *Parl. Pap.* 1840, VII (582). Q. 1047.
[3] Huskisson, *Speeches*, III, 102.
[4] Tooke, T., *History of Prices*, V, 194.

since the tide was setting in against monopoly, it was not renewed. Rival dock companies were encouraged; and for mutual protection in 1838 the East and the West India Dock Companies amalgamated. By this time the West India trade had passed its zenith, and the East India Docks were too small for the liberated eastern trade. The amalgamation, therefore, was an economy as well. The commodities *par excellence* of the West Indian and East Indian trade were sugar and tea. It is the habit of people in the British Empire to take sugar in their tea and to drink tea more frequently than any other people in the world, except, perhaps, the Dutch. The habit is a reflex of imperial history. To William Cobbett it was a shameful betrayal of the national beverage, beer. "I view the tea-drinking as a destroyer of health, an enfeebler of the frame, an engenderer of effeminacy and laziness, a debaucher of youth, and a maker of misery for old age." And the luxury was becoming a necessity: which caused a certain Chinese governor to remark to his emperor, "By tea-reins your Majesty can control the English".[1]

The emancipation of 1833 dealt the West Indian sugar planters a heavy blow. And very soon a chorus of lamentation arose from the West Indian interest, which in the eighteenth century had been the most powerfully organised voice in British trade. In 1842 there was a great rehearsal of woe before the House of Commons. "The labour", said one planter, "seems to melt away in freedom." "The negro", said another, "looks upon the wages system which compels men to turn out continually at the ringing of a bell, at a certain hour, to be the same as slavery, and he detests it, and escapes from it wherever he can."[2] Not only did the adults work less, but they used freedom to withdraw their children altogether. Formerly children had done the cleaning and the weeding, but now it was necessary to employ a gang of adults. This great upheaval left its trace on English economic thought. Rather unfairly, economists have used it as the classical case of sluggish labour, content with the customary standard, which when paid more will work less.

Two remedies were possible. One was fiscal, a retention of the preferential rate which from the beginning West Indian sugar had enjoyed. At first the West Indies enjoyed a preference not only over foreign countries, but over other parts of the Empire as well. But in 1825 Mauritius, which had been acquired from France in 1810, and retained at the peace of 1814, was given the West Indian rate, and in 1835 the East Indian rate was equalised with this. Further competition was threatened in the 1840's when the policy of the free breakfast table was in the ascendant; and Peel's successor, Lord John Russell, provided for a reduction of the foreign rate over a period of

[1] Report of Committee on the affairs of the East India Company, China Trade, *Parl. Pap.* 1830, v (644), Q. 3712.
[2] Report of Committee on West Indian Colonies, *Parl. Pap.* 1842, XIII (479), QQ. 3054.

5 years, after which time (July 1851) there would be a uniform rate of 14s. per cwt. for West Indian, East Indian and foreign sugar alike. The West Indian planters offered a bitter resistance, and their supporters in Parliament, led by Lord George Bentinck, compelled the Government in 1848 to prolong the differential duty. "We have saved the colonies." "It is the knell of Free Trade"—he cried. But it was only the postponement. Gladstone equalised the rates in 1854.

The West India interest, though still powerful in the 1840's, could not have enjoyed so long a respite, if they had not been supported by the anti-slavery forces. For slavery prevailed in Brazil, a rival source of sugar supply; and the treaty of 1825 with Brazil having expired in November 1843, Peel in 1844 was at liberty to impose duties which discriminated between the free labour and slave labour sugar of foreign countries. The proposal gave rise to angry controversy. It was denounced by the opposition as hypocritical and quixotic, but Peel persisted and with difficulty carried the clause which imposed on foreign countries, "the sugar of which Her Majesty has declared to be admissible, as not being the produce of slave labour", a rate less than half that imposed on other foreign sugar. The distinction remained until Russell replaced it by his five years scheme, and though it lasted barely three years (1844–7), it is of importance as showing the material sacrifice which the country was still prepared to make in the interest of human freedom. For, slavery apart, England had every reason, political and commercial, for avoiding a breach with a traditionally friendly Brazil.[1]

The second remedy for West Indian distress was that eventually adopted, a new supply of labour; and this saved the West Indies, though it did not save West Indian sugar in the end. European labour was impossible. A batch of Welsh emigrants who came out in 1841 died off or returned in penury almost at once. Some persons suggested that they might adopt the Wakefield system of withholding land, so that the negroes would have to work for wages: others that they might be imported as free labour from West Africa, but letters from Sierra Leone discouraged this. "Love of country", they were told, "is a remarkable characteristic of African negroes...this feeling at times and under compulsory absence runs into a passion, producing disease by its very excess and not infrequently death."[2] There remained the East, and the East was not unwilling. The importation of coolie labour from India was legalised for Jamaica, British Guiana and Trinidad in 1844. It was the organised and farthest-flung wave of the great migration that had been in process in Indian and China waters since the British fleet had helped in suppressing piracy there. The Chinese led the way, moving south to Cochin China, Singapore,

[1] See Cady, J. F., *Foreign Intervention in the Rio de la Plata*, 1838–50.
[2] Report of Committee on West Indian Colonies, *Parl. Pap.* 1842, XIII (479). Appendix, Letter from Sierra Leone.

Java and Borneo. Natives of India joined in the flow, which reached Mauritius about 1850, and East Africa somewhat later. The West Indian flow was composed of natives from India and was carefully controlled by the British Government in India. It gave satisfaction both to the coolies and the planters. It was a great effort of imperial policy. Sugar and tea met in England in the tea-cup. West and East met again on the sugar plantation itself.

The trouble in the West Indies, however, was much deeper than lack of labour. They, the little tropical islands, had passed their prime. If the world's geography had been different, they might have been the territorial entrance to the great continents adjacent to them. In the old days they were a centre for the supply of slaves to the mainland. From Jamaica illicit trading had been conducted with the colonies of Spain and Portugal. But the independence of these countries and the opening of a legal trade between England and South America sapped the commercial advantages which they had hitherto enjoyed. Henceforth England's contact with South America was direct. The commercial treaties which England signed with the countries of South America were exceptionally favourable to herself. Thus, by the treaty of 1825 with the Argentine, British merchants were put on an equal footing with the citizens of that republic in the matter of trading privileges and port and tonnage dues, while at the same time, as British citizens, they were exempted from forced loans and compulsory military service.

Figures of British exports for 1830 show the relative importance of different areas at that time. The United States took 6·1 millions sterling: South America, with Mexico, 5·2: the British West Indies 2·8 and the foreign West Indies 0·9. In home waters the countries of Europe took 14. South America had hardly reached the period of continental penetration. The contacts there in the main were coastal. The course had been charted by that strange free-lance, Admiral Cochrane, when in the 1820's he won unbelievable victories over the fleets of old Spain and old Portugal. But continental development was obstructed by fierce war in or between the new republics. It was England's way to make trade for herself by backing the winning side. Her interest in South America was entirely commercial, in opposition to the dynastic ambitions of France and Spain.

A great impetus was given to British trade along the west coast of South America by the establishment of the Pacific Steam Navigation Company in 1840 on the initiative of the American Consul in Ecuador, William Wheelwright. This coast was very well suited to development by steamship; for the calms and currents of the Pacific made sailing tedious, and the serrated coastline forbade land travel by coastal route or railway. South America, indeed, had no coal, but this promoted a new British export, the delivery of coal to coaling stations; and the Pacific Steam Navigation Company led the way in the introduction of the fuel-saving compound engine. When the gold rush to California set in, the British Government extended its mail contract with the Company to Panama. Already in 1846 the Company had made Liverpool its headquarters, and in that city Valparaiso, Antofagasta, Callao and Guayaquil became household words. Until the opening of the Panama Canal in 1914 the route to the Pacific coast of North America was round Cape Horn. The gold seekers moved on from California to British Columbia, and this brought new trade to British shipping. California itself developed as an agricultural region, and became, when the gold rush died down, a considerable exporter of wheat to Liverpool. This kind of foreign trade was very different from the old regulated trade within the limits of empire. The shipping crept along the continents and traded with all and sundry, now in the regions of formal empire, now in those of informal empire, now with an island whose crops or deposits could be easily lifted, and now with mainland ports which showed the way to the continental interior. The intensive penetration of the hinterland was the task of a later generation. In the Argentine alone, and mainly since 1880, Great Britain has invested over £300,000,000 in railways and allied activities.

The other liberating Act of 1833 (3 and 4 William IV, c. 93) formed the concluding stage in the opening of eastern trade to British merchants and merchant shipping. The first stage came in 1813, when the monopoly of shipping between India and England was taken from the East India Company. Monopoly lost, the Company abandoned its Indian trade altogether; and for the next twenty years (1813–33) devoted itself to two branches of enterprise, to the operation of ships between Suez and Bombay (which involved marine survey work in the Indian Ocean) and to the China tea trade, which was its main commercial occupation. Its monopoly in the latter was qualified, being complete only in respect of the importation of tea from China to the United Kingdom, and of the exportation of manufactures from the United Kingdom to China. The monopoly of import extended to South Africa, at which certain of its regular ships touched, and to Canada, to which special ships were sent. S. Cunard and Company were the Canadian agents of the East India Company and when the first direct shipment, 6517 chests in the *Countess of Harcourt*, reached Halifax, Nova Scotia, on 29 May 1825, the local rejoicing was great. But in eastern waters the Company was only the leader among other English traders there; for it gave tea licences to "country" ships, trading from China to the different ports of Asia, in which was included for this purpose New South Wales. Furthermore, other nations traded with China, the Portuguese to a slight extent, the Netherlanders, and in particular the Americans. After 1815 the United States were very active in the Pacific. The ships of John Jacob Astor took the silver dollars of South America, the furs of

North America and the sandal-wood of Hawaii to Canton and sailed back with tea and silks round Cape Horn. The British, on the other hand, approached China through India. It was for them an extension of the Indian trade, just as was the early trade with Australia and New Zealand.

A witness before an East Indian Committee of 1840,[1] in presenting an estimate of the total of India and China trade, stressed this point. "The whole trade (he said) is one connected trade." And he framed the balance sheet accordingly:

Exports from India and China to England ... 9·6 millions

of which the two largest items were indigo from India and tea from China. On the other side he gives the "mode by which per contra is paid for", in millions sterling as follows:

Manufactures to India	...	...	...	...		2·5
,, China	...	...	...	...		0·6
Remittance of private fortunes	...	...	...		0·5
East India Co.'s home charges	...	...	...		3·0
Opium sent to China	...	...	...	...	3·4	
Cotton ,,	...	...	...	...	1·0	
					4·4	
Less return of bullion from China to Calcutta and Bombay	...	...	...	...	1·4	3·0
						9·6 millions

The import of opium into China was illegal; nevertheless it was the main means by which Chinese exports were paid for. Silver dollars and Indian raw cotton made up the difference. The opium came either from Smyrna in Turkey or from India, which was the chief source of supply. The East India Company had the monopoly of its growth there, though they did not themselves load it on their own ships. The country traders took it to Chinese waters, and native smugglers took it ashore. The Chinese authorities professed a profound contempt for the foreign trader. They welcomed birds' nests and sea-slugs, but for the ways and wares of Europe they had no use. In 1821 a Chinese governor said of the Christian merchants: "They are a mercenary, gain-seeking set of adventurers, whom reason cannot rule; the dread of not making money is that which alone influences them."[2] That was the official view, but as an English trader remarked, "practice and profession are much at variance in China". For the smuggling was conducted in the open light of day. The Chinese Government boats would manœuvre around and report periodically to the authorities at Canton that they had swept the seas of smuggling ships, but the smuggling went on just the same. The opium was unloaded from one side of the ship, while the Mandarin watch-boats lay along the other. The smugglers and the Mandarin

[1] Report of Committee on the Petition of the East India Company for relief, *Parl. Pap.* 1840, VIII (527): G. G. de Larpent, Chairman of the East India and China Association formed in 1836.
[2] *Parl. Pap.* 1830, V (644), Q. 3712.

boats were believed to have an understanding; and the smuggling of opium was merely the prime illegality. The country ships traded north of Canton with forbidden ports. Saltpetre was "an article that by law is always obliged to be sold to the Government, but it is principally sold to the outside dealers who give higher prices for it".[1] It was used by the Chinese for gunpowder and fireworks. While the Company's monopoly lasted, the Company kept some sort of order in the trade. When this was removed, the smuggling was intensified and an open breach with China ensued. Palmerston wrote to the British Agent in China in 1839 that Her Majesty's Government could not interfere for the purpose of enabling British subjects to violate the laws of the country with which they traded.[2] None the less Great Britain was a party to the so-called "opium war" of 1839–42, which resulted in the extortion of trading concessions from the reluctant Chinese and in the cession to Great Britain of Hongkong.

When the merchants of England were pleading for the opening of the Indian trade in 1813, they were thinking mainly of a share in the import trade from India. It hardly seemed possible then that England should supply India, the home of the cotton manufacture, with English cottons. None the less by 1840 this change had come, and it was visible, not only in India, but in that great theatre of trade which Sir Stamford Raffles had won for Great Britain in 1819, namely Singapore and the regions farther east, to which the possession of Singapore gave access. Witnesses of 1840 speak of the change in the East as a "recent" revolution. Says one: British manufactures are not confined to the English in India, "they are spreading all over the country, particularly the Manchester goods and the Glasgow goods: in fact it is a question of cheapness. Cheapness has forced our manufactures into India, and as long as we can, by the power of machinery, make them cheaper, though they may not be so durable as their own, yet that is nothing compared with the cheapness which to a poor people is the first object they have in view."[3] Says another: "Almost all the natives, high and low, in the neighbourhood of Calcutta are clothed with English cottons."[4] England, thanks to her fleet and the enterprise of Raffles, held Java for a few years, before she established herself finally in Singapore. According to a trader of 1830, "When I first went to Java in 1811, they were almost exclusively clothed in Chinese manufactures, and I witnessed a revolution there which almost clothed them in European manufactures during the time I was there."[5] The Chinese in the Straits Settlements were keen and progressive traders. They assisted English merchants in obtaining the patterns and shapes which would suit the Chinese and Malays. More-

[1] *Parl. Pap.* 1830, v (644), Q. 4595.
[2] *Parl. Pap.* 1840, VII (359), Q. 479.
[3] *Parl. Pap.* 1840, VIII (527), Q. 201.
[4] *Ibid.* Q. 660.
[5] *Parl. Pap.* 1830, v (644), Q. 3497.

over, many of the Chinese went back to China after a time and took back with them a preference for English goods, so that the result was a second India. At first the Chinese obtained from India the raw cotton which they made into their own durable clothing. Then came the machine-made product of England, which, being cheaper, was invincible. By the aid of cheapness and an illegal drug, "free-trade" England conquered the East commercially.

Peel dominates the 1840's; and though assuredly it was not his wish, he was dominated himself by the struggle for Corn Law Repeal, which was launched from Manchester in 1839. Huskisson bequeathed to him a tariff of moderate dimensions, marked by a lively and sympathetic imperialism. For empire Peel did little except in one notable instance, the Canada Corn Act of 1843. In return for a duty imposed by Canada on American wheat, Canadian wheat and flour were admitted into England at a nominal rate of 1s. per quarter of wheat. But that it was no part of an active imperialism is shown by his refusal to extend the privilege to the new colonies of Australia, despite the impassioned appeal of William Hutt, the member for Gateshead, in a noble speech of 1845.[1] For the Tory squires, whom Peel was anxious to conciliate, feared a breach, however imperial, in the sacred fabric of the Corn Laws.

In his budgets of 1842–6 Peel carried the tariff to within sight of complete free trade. The protective element was the rate on manufactured goods. Huskisson left it at 30 per cent. Peel took it first to 20 per cent. and then to 10 per cent., silk exceptionally being granted 15 per cent. Furthermore, he abolished the duties on nearly all raw materials, together with the tax on imported coal, which he had himself imposed in 1842 to finance the tariff reductions of that year. He was able to do this only because he had the courage to reimpose an income tax; for the duties on raw materials, like those of the excise, yielded substantial revenue.

Although from 1791 onwards there was an imperial side to the Corn Laws, it was strictly subordinate to their national aspect. The law of 1815 created a situation which made the Corn Laws the central point of controversy in the national life during the next thirty years. Huskisson tried to modify it and failed. Peel modified it along Huskisson's lines in 1842, but it brought him no relief because Manchester was bent on total repeal. To the industrial mind the Corn Laws were the last great restriction on freedom of export. They introduced, said the Anti-Corn Law League, a fundamental disharmony into the economic scheme. They made trade irregular, they obstructed the export of Lancashire cottons to pay for Polish corn; and when further it was made to appear that they were a landlords' monopoly which starved the poor, the populace was mobilised in support of repeal. Other nations owing to their area and situation have not

<hr />

[1] Hansard, Third Series, LXXX, 301.

experienced a similar crisis. Holland depended on foreign foodstuffs long before she passed into modern industrialism. America continued to be a great exporter of foodstuffs and raw materials long after the appearance of large-scale industrialism in her northern and eastern States. But the size of Great Britain was such that she became on the balance an importer of foodstuffs in the opening years of the Industrial Revolution. Thanks to the ceaseless improvement in animal and arable husbandry, she was able to feed her own people until 1846, despite their rapid growth in numbers, mainly from her own soil. The Corn Laws were repealed at the time when their continuation would have involved for the first time serious social hardship. The agriculturists resented being called monopolists, and indeed Adam Smith would have agreed with them. They were not prepared to surrender the heritage of a permanent and almost model agriculture. Above all, they were not prepared for the social humiliation which the triumph of the Corn Law repealers would signify. They stood for the old England, the repealers for the new. In 1846 the phrase "fall of mercantilism" becomes peculiarly inappropriate, for 1846 saw the fall of landlordism, the triumph of the merchant and manufacturer over the landlord and farmer.

Three years later, in 1849, that other great limb of economic policy over the centuries was cut away. The Navigation Laws, which Huskisson had left full of real strength, were repealed with the exception of the clause reserving coastal shipping, and this went in 1853. The repeal produced murmurs among the shipowners and protectionist die-hards. But there was no need of an Anti-Navigation Law League. They went because they had become inappropriate. English trade had broadened into a world trade, which ran in and out between the countries of formal and informal empire. The laws irritated other countries without helping England and were likely to invite tariff retaliation by the growing power of Prussia. Huskisson's fear of the pre-eminence of America was now losing significance. The sailing ship was still very important, but each decade the steamship (thanks in part to the screw-propeller) was gaining—the steamship made of iron and using coal, the two materials in which England possessed a great comparative advantage of production. The old appeal to the nursery of seamen was in part met by the reforms which Sir James Graham had instituted in the Admiralty in the 1830's; and a long-service personnel was secured by the Act of 1853. But to the colonies Corn Law repeal appeared an act of imperial ill-faith. Canada in the early 'forties had built up a prosperous corn trade largely on the strength of the preference in the British market; and when this went she was seriously damaged.[1] Having lost the corn preference which she valued, she was not loath to see the repeal of the Navigation Laws, which limited the shipping in the St Lawrence.

[1] See *C.H.B.E.* VI, 250, 380–2, 386.

She and other colonies now passing over to self-government took the tariff policy of the mother country as an invitation to go each their own way; and this way, because their areas were continental, took them to protection.

The anxiety of England in the 1840's to get rid of imperial preference, either by the colonies to herself or by herself to the colonies, seems an excess of fiscal purity. Certainly it was not due to pressure from the colonies. The key to it, perhaps, is to be found in India and the East. A parliamentary report of 1840 examining into East Indian affairs contains this notable sentence:

Colonial possessions scattered over the four quarters of the globe and legislatively dependent on the acts of a distant government, can only be maintained in peaceful and willing obedience by making strict justice and impartiality the sole guides of every legislative proceeding by which they may be affected.[1]

This was at a time when cotton goods from India into England paid 10 per cent., while English cottons into India paid $3\frac{1}{2}$ per cent.: when Indian silk goods into England paid 20 per cent., while English silk goods into India paid $3\frac{1}{2}$ per cent.: and when Indian cottons entering Ceylon paid twice the rate of those coming from England or from Europe! And if empire rates were claimed, what was the British Empire? Was Mysore included, which was a portion of the British dominions in everything but in name? Was the territory of the Nizam? Was Central India as a whole? "Internally they are independent but externally their relations are managed by us", it was said of the last.[2] Perhaps, then, it was to avoid these problems of differential treatment that Great Britain moved towards the simpler uniform rate, which was most simple when it was no rate at all, in other words when there was free trade. In 1850 free trade was not disruptive of an empire such as England had. For that empire, in addition to being scattered, was of very dissimilar composition; and in both hemispheres formal empire was the near neighbour of informal empire. The West Indies fringed South America. British India surrounded native India and was the avenue to Singapore and Hong-Kong, both of them British outposts in regions of foreign dominion.

When Lord Durham went to Canada, he found there (in the language of his Report) two nations warring in the bosom of a single state—the English and the French. Disraeli found the same in England, two nations—a nation of the rich and of the poor. While free trade was being fulfilled, England was awakening to the evils arising from the conditions of work in factory and mine, from the prevalence of truck and intemperance, and from the lack of housing and sanitation. These were problems which required constructive

---

[1] *Parl. Pap.* 1840, VIII (527), Report XIX.
[2] *Ibid.* Report VIII.

legislation; and it was forthcoming in the great Acts of 1842, 1847 and 1848, for mines, factories and public health respectively. Tory philanthropy forced them upon a Liberalism whose enthusiasm lay elsewhere. For statesmen of liberal outlook conceived that they were making a decisive contribution to the welfare of the workers and the poor, when they consulted the interest of consumers, who in the mass were the working poor. In providing the people with cheap bread, cheap sugar, cheap tea and the like, Peel and Gladstone did their social best. They were individualists, their belief in free enterprise and self-help was unshaken. But they believed also that a country which enjoyed a good and economical government and plenty of food and clothing was a happier country for the mass of the people, and that it was within the province of government to make these things possible. The fiscal policy of free trade was for them the means by which their social goal could be most surely attained, and this made them cold to a policy of empire which appeared to put power before plenty.

The career of James Silk Buckingham (1786–1855) reflects the change from imperialism and foreign adventure to pacifism and domestic preoccupation.[1] He began life as a Cornish lad in the mercantile marine. His first command took him to Nassau in the Bahamas, to engage in the smuggling trade with South America. Then he went to Smyrna and Egypt, where he offered his services to Mehemet Ali. From Egypt through Mesopotamia he reached India. Refusing to command a slave galley to Zanzibar, he was offered by John Palmer, the Indian banker, the editorship of the *Calcutta Journal*. But like Cobbett he was an imperial Radical. For championing the cause of a free press he was in 1823 "transmitted" to England and his paper suppressed. In England he entered Radical politics and interested Lord Durham in self-government for the colonies. He founded the *Oriental Herald* and *Colonial Review* in 1824 and the *Athenaeum* in 1828, and during 1829 he spoke in the cities of the north of England against the East India Company's monopoly in China. They called him "Lord Hum" for the noise he made, and he was returned to the reformed parliament as member for Sheffield. His imperial days had ended. He turned to the campaign for marine reform, protesting again impressment and the exploitation of sailors. In 1834 he wrote the report of the Committee on Intoxication, in which he exposed the victimisation of seamen on land, and in 1838–40 he travelled through America, lecturing on temperance and peace. His career spans the generation which divides the imperialism of the Napoleonic War from the social and pacific inclinations of 1850.

Laissez-faire England was consistently liberal. Free trade in goods and gold was matched by the free export of capital and persons. In the eighteenth century the emigration of artisans was forbidden by

---

[1] Turner, Ralph E, *James Silk Buckingham, a social biography*.

law; and Huskisson removed this check on freedom in 1824. The Liberals took it ill when, having abolished slavery in the Empire, they were invited to look inside their factories and abolish slavery at home. But they saw more readily that the protection which was necessary for women and children in factories was also necessary for families of emigrants. The Factory Act of 1802 is the beginning of a series which culminates in 1847. Similarly the Passenger Act of 1803 (43 Geo. III c. 56) is the beginning of a series which culminated in the Act of 1855, "the Magna Carta of the emigrants", as it has been called. Just as the early Factory Acts were evaded, so in deference to mercantile protest the early Passenger Acts were relaxed with the result that disease and accident increased. But in the 1840's, when the immigrant flood swamped the machinery of reception and carried disease inland, Canada in self-defence imposed her own controls. The colonies, following the practice of the United States, became in time self-governing in the admission of people as well as of goods. The problem of emigration became a problem of immigration, and England turned her attention from emigration ships to the protection of seamen under the Merchant Shipping Acts.

Between 1815 and 1850 the migration of people was very active in three parts of the Empire—Canada, the Straits Settlements, Australia and New Zealand. The flow into Canada was part of the greater flow from Europe to North America, and Canada's problem was to obtain a respectable share of this spontaneous movement. She resented the instinct of the mother country to unload paupers on her. The problem of reaching Canada was comparatively simple. The difficulty was to keep the settlers when they arrived. Geography was the deciding factor here. The settlers moved on to the United States, and the turn of Canada did not come until the free land of America was exhausted and the Canadian West could be reached by rail. In the Straits Settlements the flow was an Asiatic one. Because of its unique strategic situation Singapore grew with the rapidity for which new continents, less happily placed, have sighed in vain. It was a base for an attack on the agricultural and mineral resources of Malay, of the tin-bearing islands of Banka and Billiton, of Java and of Borneo. When England exchanged Bencoolen in Sumatra for Singapore, she made the most fruitful deal in her imperial history. There were two avenues into China waters. That by the Sunda Straits between Sumatra and Java was under Dutch control. The second was by the Straits of Malacca, at the tip of which is Singapore. So long as traffic came round the Cape, one afforded as good an entry to the China Sea as the other, but when in 1869 the Suez Canal was opened, Great Britain found herself in control of the ideal steamship route to China, Gibraltar-Suez-Aden-Singapore. Thus Singapore became the key point of Eastern commerce. From its foundation in 1819 Singapore was a resounding advertisement for Free Trade.

Sir Stamford Raffles foresaw that a town where commerce was untaxed and harbour-regulations were almost non-existent would prove an irresistible attraction. His policy was soon justified, merchants flocked to Singapore from every part of the Archipelago and the Far East, and every effort of the Dutch to prevent them proved unavailing.... The merchants of Singapore, Chinese as well as European, always regarded free trade as the palladium of their city, and firmly, and on the whole successfully, resisted the periodical attempts of the [East India] Company to tamper with it. To its continuance, and to their spirit of daring enterprise, they owed their continued prosperity.[1]

South of the East Indies lay the Antipodes, the recipients of the third stream of migration; and here, especially on the northern and western side of the Australian continent, population was as hard to establish as it was easy in Malay. The story of this settlement is told elsewhere.[2] The process was slow for many reasons—distance from England, the desire of the Home Government to isolate convict settlement, the effort of the missionary societies to save the natives from exploitation by the white man. But wool and gold hastened free settlement and provided occupations on which Australasia could grow without dependence on Asiatic labour. In fine, the horizon of new settlement within the Empire was as wide now as it had been in the days of the Pilgrim Fathers.

Easier circumstances at home went hand in hand with greater opportunities overseas. By 1850 the aftermath of the Napoleonic war had been removed, and social England was in better state than at any time since 1815. Chartism had burnt itself out. The hand-workers had moved out of their long agony into machinery. The Corn Laws were dead. The revolutionary upheaval of 1848 did not stagger England for a moment. After 1848 Western Europe ventured on the path of liberalism which England had been treading for some years, though in some countries they retraced it speedily; and the atmosphere was favourable for the International Exhibition of 1851, at which Manchester celebrated the gospel of Manchester. Overseas there was a new magnet. Gold, that great fertiliser of settlement, was found in California in 1848, and soon after in the British Empire: first in Australia, and then in succession down to our own time, in New Zealand, British Columbia, South Africa, the Yukon, West Africa and Northern Ontario. Instead of pouring out under the drag of distress, as the Irish poured out after 1845, the youth of high spirit rushed off to the gold fields with enthusiasm. The bad days of convict settlement and pauper-shovelling, the disheartening days of planned colonisation of the Wakefield type, which produced so few settlers in the end, disappeared. Emigration became spontaneous and the freshly mined gold moved across the oceans to raise prices and set in

[1] Mills, L. A. "British Malaya 1824–67". *Journal of Malayan Branch of Royal Asiatic Society*, Nov. 1925, p. 189.
[2] See the history of the new settlements in Australia and New Zealand, *C.H.B.E.* vol. VII, pt. I, chs. VI and VIII, pt. II, ch. V.

motion new trade, alike in the East and West. The origin was often enough within the British Empire, yet gold was not conceived of as a commodity of empire. The goldfields were a gathering place of the nations, and the gold, when mined, moved on its exalted course, as that one commodity which might enter every nation without let or hindrance.

An empire so scattered and disparate as the British could hardly reveal an organic unity, especially under conditions of free trade. It was, however, at all times possible for her statesmen to display a greater or less skill in reconciling imperial expansion with the commitments of foreign policy. In Huskisson's time economic policy and diplomacy were in full and open accord. He made the Presidency of the Board of Trade an office of liaison between foreign policy and British trade. It was possible because of the perfect friendship between Canning and himself. In March 1825, when thanking the Levant Company and its Chairman, Lord Grenville, for the gracious surrender of their charter, he informed the House that the duties formerly performed by the Company would now belong to the Crown with a saving to merchants in consular charges of something like 2 per cent. of the value of the trade. This was a measure of freer trade and Gladstone would have exulted in the economy, but Huskisson made it subordinate to considerations of diplomacy.

> In the present state of a great part of the countries in which these consuls reside, and looking, moreover, to our relations with Turkey, as well as with other powers, to the delicate and important questions of international law, which must constantly arise out of the intercourse of commerce with a country in a state of civil war,— questions involving discussions, not only with the contending parties in that country, but with other trading and neutral powers,—it is impossible not to feel that, upon political considerations alone, it is highly expedient that the public servants of this country, in Turkey, should hold their appointments from the Crown.[1]

After his time imperial policy lost its drive. Free-trade England was in the safe keeping of Peel and Gladstone, but the free-trade Empire of their generation owed less to them than to Palmerston, the mettlesome Whig, who presided at the Foreign Office from 1830 to 1841 and again from 1846 to 1851, and to his strong servant Stratford Canning, ambassador *par excellence*, who had begun in 1808 his contact of fifty years with the Near East. Although Peel was not Chancellor of the Exchequer, he was in charge of the great budgets of his ministry, and in the last of these, 1845, when he was reducing tariffs right and left, he nevertheless asked for an increase in naval expenditure, which was scarcely in harmony with the pacific outlook of orthodox free trade. But how could he avoid it: with the China War but recently concluded, with Afghanistan the graveyard of a recent British disaster, with France on the alert in the Mediterranean, West

---

[1] Huskisson, *Speeches*, ii, 358.

Africa and the Pacific, with the Dutch and English settlers at blows in Natal, with the Argentine rent by civil turmoil to the great prejudice of British commerce, and with the steamship presenting a new demand for naval outlay—for those steamboats which were so important in running down pirates and slavers? Hence his Chancellor, Goulburn, had to plead that "an increase of about £1,000,000 in the naval estimates was required to provide for the protection of an extended colonial empire and growing commerce, for the new naval stations which had been established on the coast of Africa, in the Pacific and in the China seas, and to maintain 'a respectable steam navy suitable to a peace establishment'."[1] The spirit of Palmerston, indeed, never died, and he, rather than Peel, was the successor of Huskisson in imperial achievement.

Gladstone brought to the Exchequer in 1853 the pent-up zeal of financial genius and the spirit of the International Exhibition of 1851. He completed the great work of his predecessors and added as his peculiar contribution a system of taxation which rested for the first time in the world's history on free trade. The colonial preferences which survived were to him as great a nuisance as the outworn complications of the Navigation Laws on which Huskisson in his day had poured scorn; but he was polite even towards colonies. He said in his budget speech of 1853:

> We propose in many instances where there are at present differential duties in favour of British possessions, to merge these differential duties altogether by lowering the foreign article to the level of the colonial, but where we are not able to lower the foreign article to the level of the colonial, we have not thought it would be considerate in any case to raise the duty on the colonial article.

What magnanimity! Huskisson could never have delivered himself of this if he had lived to be a hundred. However, in the following year, England declared war on Russia; and, in analysis, the Crimean War was nothing but a war in the Near East for the assurance of access to that Far East in which a trading company had grown into an imperial dominion. To follow the history of the tariff beyond 1853 is to deal in anti-climax. For only the remnants of protection remained, and these Gladstone swept away in his completing budget of 1860. Peel, as he fell, had given to the nation untaxed bread, Gladstone in 1853 halved the duties on a long list of fruits and dairy products and in 1860 abolished them. Peel had dispensed with the duty on cotton wool, Gladstone freed cotton yarn in 1853 and manufactured cottons in 1860, the year in which all duties on imported manufactures ended. In the matter of the imperial preferences, or "differential" duties,[2] as they were now regarded, Gladstone was

---

[1] Page, W., *Commerce and Industry*, p. 156.

[2] The 'differentials' by the colonies in favour of the mother country had disappeared as the result of the passage of 5 and 6 Vict. c. 49 (1842), the last of the British Possessions Acts, followed by 9 and 10 Vict. c. 94 (1846), an Enabling Act, inviting the colonies to abolish the small differentials which remained after the Act of 1842.

faithful to the principle which he laid down in 1853. The colonial was reduced to the foreign rate and held at that until both could be reduced or abolished. In 1854 the duties on colonial and foreign sugar were equalised: in 1860 those on wine and spirits: in 1863 those on tobacco. The preferences on manufactured silk and on timber went in 1860. Silk, the privileged child of English tariff history, was henceforth not only without preference, but without protection. The timber duties brought in money and therefore remained till 1866, when the national purse was strong enough to remit this surviving tax on an important raw material, which Gladstone dubbed "the very essence and quintessence of political folly."[1] The significant tariff episode of these years occurred overseas. In 1859 Canada used the fiscal freedom conferred, nay forced, upon her by the mother country to introduce a tariff which protected her manufactures against those of other countries including England. Once again in British economic history two kinds of freedom were in conflict.

1833 has yielded two landmarks of policy—the abolition of slavery in the West Indies and the opening of the China trade; and there is a third. For in 1833, at the request of Turkey, Russia sent ships and troops to Constantinople to rescue that "drowning man", the Sultan. The Turkish Empire, which in 1820 had sprawled across the eastern Mediterranean from Bosnia to Alexandria, was in disintegration. Mehemet Ali, the Albanian conqueror of Egypt, whose career coincides in time with that of Stratford Canning, occupied the avenue to the East. France by her occupation of Algiers in 1830 had begun her African empire, introducing there a policy of peace and gallicization, which was her version of the colonial policy of Lord Durham and his school. England feared that with Russia pressing down from the north and France edging eastwards in the south, the gateway to the East would be closed. Already de Lesseps and the French engineers, among whom were some ardent disciples of St Simon, were proposing canals and barrages to Mehemet. The spirit of Napoleon lived again in Egypt. What should serve for an Aboukir Bay? England's reply was the extension of a protective arm over Turkey and the development of steam communications with India.

Before and while English engineers were busy with the projection, and construction (1851–8), of the Alexandria-Suez Railway, the East India Company through its splendid Bombay Marine, which from 1838 onwards was converted to steam, did work of imperial importance by its surveys of the coastline from Bombay to Aden and from Aden up the Red Sea to Suez. For the first time all this region was intensively mapped. Purely for naval reasons, on account of its excellent harbour and its convenient position as a coaling depôt, Aden was occupied in 1837–9. Here, as later in Socotra and at many

---

[1] See Buxton, S., *Mr Gladstone—A Study*, p. 61.

points of Africa, the naval captains forced the pace. We have spoken already of the connected whole of the India and China trade. These events in the Arabian Sea were part of it. France was developing her empire on inner lines, running fast steam-packets from Marseilles to Algiers and Alexandria. America, while gaining ground on the Atlantic, was losing some of her old strength in the round-about trade with China. Her boats would set off for nothing less than a world cruise, taking goods from place to place, Smyrna, New York, Hawaii, Canton. They carried floating super-cargoes; that is to say, each boat conducted its own trade. England, with her trunk route of East Indiamen from England to India and China and with permanent residents in her trading factory at Canton, was working towards a new and modern conception of long-distance steamship service. When the East India Company withdrew from trade, steamship lines arose to take over its work, and when in 1869 the Suez Canal was opened the evolution was completed. Steamships plied from England to the East by water, touching British stations the whole way. Thus the Suez Canal was the culminating point of more than half a century of effort towards rapid and unbroken contact with the East.

In the history of the steamship, as we ordinarily tell it, there is obviously a gap. We place the steamboat on the river and cross-channel services of Great Britain about 1816. In 1819 an American steamship, the *Savannah*, is heard of in the Atlantic. At last in 1833 the Atlantic was genuinely crossed under steam by a Canadian vessel, the *Royal William*, but it was not until 1838 that it was conquered from the British side. What were the English and Scottish builders doing? Their eyes were on the Mediterranean and Arabian Seas, which in technical opportunity came midway between channel and ocean service. In 1823, the year when Huskisson began his reforms, India suddenly became steam-conscious and in 1825 the steamship *Enterprise* struggled out from Falmouth to Calcutta under steam most of the way. But the decisive voyage was that of the *Hugh Lindsay*, Bombay-built, which reached Suez from Bombay in a month, thus enabling the mails which she carried to reach England in half the usual time. The urge to development came from the English community in India desirous of quicker passenger transport and quicker postal communications. Their efforts were supported by enthusiasts like Thomas Waghorn, who made for themselves a new business career as mail and package carriers. After the success of 1830 the East India Company ran a regular service from Bombay to Suez. The Mediterranean end was supplied by a combination of private and government effort. The Peninsular and Oriental Company (P. and O.) launched its first steamship in 1829 for service between Falmouth and Gibraltar. Admiralty steam packets in 1832 were in service between Gibraltar and Malta, the weak link in the chain being the Admiralty sailing packet which continued the service from

Malta to Alexandria. In 1839, a year before the Penny Post, England and France concluded a postal convention for the conveyance of mails to India *via* London-Marseilles-Malta.

Between 1840 and 1853 the Peninsular and Oriental expanded up to the point at which it was able to render an integrated service. It received its first mail contract in 1837 and its charter in 1840, and took over the conveyance of mails the whole way to Alexandria. In 1842 it made its appearance in Eastern waters. The despatch of the *Hindustan* from Southampton for Calcutta on 24 September 1842 was an object of national celebration. As long as the East India Company operated its marine, the Peninsular and Oriental omitted the Bombay-Suez route and concentrated on the Calcutta-Madras-Ceylon-Suez service. In 1845 the mail contract was extended to cover service to Singapore and China. Thus at this time there were two services a month each way, Suez-Bombay by the East India Company, Suez-Ceylon and points beyond by the Peninsular and Oriental. Australia was not long in demanding steamship service, which came, like some of her early banking, by way of extension from India. And South Africa was in the stream of the same progress. The *Enterprise* had called at Cape Town in 1825, and ten years later, the *Hope*, the first South African coasting steamer, arrived there. But it was not till the first mail steamer, the *Bosphorus*, reached Cape Town in January 1851 that "Table Bay changed its rôle of half-way house to the East and became, instead, the terminus of steamship communication between the Mother Country and her southern colony".[1]

The steamship was only for that class of traffic which could afford it—well-to-do passengers, mails and parcels. The bulk of produce as well as the bulk of passengers, to wit, the emigrants, were still conveyed in sailing vessels. This was true in all waters. Nassau Senior noted how in 1850 "many British vessels carry emigrants to New York and after landing them proceed to the southern ports for cotton, or to Canada for timber".[2] And London owners were heavily engaged in the emigrant trade to the East. The great White Star Line was itself the reorganisation of an earlier line composed of American-built clippers sailing to Australia. It was not until the middle 'fifties that the Inman Line built specially designed screw steamers for service from Liverpool to Philadelphia and thereby captured a large slice of the emigration traffic on the Atlantic. To India the great significance of the steamship was the saving of time for persons and news. In 1820, when the East Indiamen were at the height of their prowess, it took from five to eight months to send messages from London to Calcutta, and perhaps two years to get an answer. At this time a journey to Constantinople might take two months. In 1850

---

[1] Marischal Murray, *Ships and South Africa*, p. 7.
[2] Senior, N. W., *Industrial Efficiency and Social Economy*, i, 344.

by the Overland route (Alexandria-Suez) it took only one month from London to Calcutta. And the steamships prepared the way for the cables which they laid and which followed their course. This was the achievement of the 1860's. For Great Britain the Indian Mutiny of 1857 was the last great example of delayed news which was of vital import. By 1870 communication was a question of hours, while now it is one of minutes. The regulation of shipping and the en-couragement of particular trades, which was natural enough when commerce was small and risky, had no place in a world order in which trade flowed out in every direction in search of a regular profit. The revolution in transportation was complementary to the change from interrupted handicraft to the continuous output of the machine; and it forged solid financial ties with distant countries. The development of communications with the East stimulated, and was stimulated by, the establishment of Exchange Banks in India and China. The produce itself came round the Cape: while the bills of lading were posted overland and discounted on arrival in London. When the produce itself arrived, the bill had matured.

In 1853, the concluding year of our period, we are still in the pre-railway age of the British Empire. There the ocean steamship preceded by a short while the continental railway. The early railways of England, 1825–50, had as their complement overseas the early steamships which plied in sheltered waters in the Mediterranean, up African rivers, along the straits and gulfs of Asia. America by 1850 was more advanced. The railway was half-way across that continent, and the Mississippi carried a great steamship tonnage. But the continents of the British Empire as yet were barely touched. In 1853 there were only 200 miles of railway in Canada and virtually none in Australia. The building of railways there and elsewhere—South Africa, the Argentine, India and the Far East—and the erection of harbours at the points where railways and steamships met, was the special task of the half century and more from 1853 to 1914. It was then that Great Britain became a really great exporter of capital.

But the story of expansion has its sinister side. An age notable for its economy in money was lavish of natural resources and human life. At home there was the exploitation of women and children: abroad the expropriation of native peoples and the waste of natural resources. The failing was not peculiar to the British Empire. The Americans, for example, as they settled the Middle-West, virtually exterminated the Red Indians. The English in India, though they brought order and good government, penalised ruthlessly the native cotton manu-facture. The English were embroiled in New Zealand with the Maoris in long and exasperating wars. There was waste of natural resources as well. One example may be quoted from the India volume of this history. We remember Congo and Putumayo easily, these being the sins of others. We should do well to remember also the early history of the coastal strip of Burma, stretching south from India towards Penang.

The timber traders—discharged warrant officers and ship's mates—never visited the forests but sent out Burmans who made the jungle folk, timid Karens, extract timber for little or nothing; the Karens burned several forests to discourage such visitations. In 1842 better firms appeared but as these had the ear of government the result was to accelerate exploitation—Durand's removal placated Calcutta firms whose leases he had cancelled. By 1850 the forests were ruined.[1]

We have surveyed the history of England for thirty-three critical years. Its policy begins imperially and ends nationally, but the facts behind the policy are imperial throughout. It was an age of free trade and imperial increase. Perhaps the greatest fact behind the detail of policy and incident is the steady progress of the mother country to metropolitan stature in an economic sense. Increasing areas of the world became furnishers of staple raw materials and of valued articles of personal consumption in such mass that in some cases these entered the list of common wants. As foreign trade grew, so shipping grew and opened up new fields for the talent of the marine engineer and the use of British coal. As shipping grew, so docks and harbours grew, the outward and visible sign in England of the revolution in transport on the high seas. Now that we are feeding once more at the ample bosom of Mother Protection, we find it hard to recall the zest of free trade. We conjure for it in retrospect an artificial title "The Fall of Mercantilism". To the merchants and manufacturers of that age it was the rise of a new system, in which commerce was sovereign over agriculture, and not only over agriculture, but over empire itself. We think of free trade as planless and passive. They, by the aid of free trade, took empire in their stride. By free trade they secured political empire, and something more, which we may call economic empire. Although imperialism was at a discount, empire itself was at a premium. When these men turned their back on the old way of empire, it was with no thought of surrendering the wealth of empire. The age of Gladstone was as far as that of Adam Smith from desiring an England which by the surrender of empire should have accommodated herself to the real mediocrity of insular circumstance. Every reflecting man from the Tories of the right to the Radicals of the left realised, in 1853 as in 1828, the ineluctable truth of Huskisson's memorable words, "England cannot afford to be little. She must be what she is, or nothing".[2] England never had any intention of parting either with her colonial trade or with the governance of India. Is it surprising, then, that others thought Englishmen hypocrites, and mistrusted them where they were wholly sincere, as in their zeal for the suppression of slavery?

[1] *C.H.B.E.* IV, 567.
[2] Speech on the Civil Government of Canada, 2 May, 1828 (*Speeches*, III, 287).

CHAPTER XII

PROBLEMS OF SETTLEMENT

(I) TRANSPORTATION

THE idea of transportation as an auxiliary of colonisation was advocated before England became possessed of any overseas territory and, as we have already seen,[1] during the history of the old Empire the practice of transportation provided a supply of labour to the southern colonies of North America and to the West Indies that was not generally unwelcome. An important section of the Habeas Corpus Amendment Act, 1679 (sec. XIV), enabled any person convicted of any felony to pray in open court to be transported beyond the seas, whereupon the court might give permission for transportation in lieu of the execution of the sentence imposed. The statute passed by Parliament in 1717 (4 Geo. I, cap. 11) was designed to make the system more efficient. The preamble explains the reason. It had been found that punishments inflicted had not been effectual because "many persons to whom the royal mercy hath been extended upon condition of transporting themselves to the West Indies" had returned "to their former wickedness and been at last for new crimes brought to a shameful and ignominious death". Moreover, in many of the colonies and plantations in America "there is great want of servants who by their labour and industry might be the means of improving and making the said colonies more useful to the nation". It was therefore provided that any person convicted of petty larceny should be, as conveniently as might be, sent to one of the colonies for seven years; receivers of stolen goods were to be transported for fourteen years. The courts which convicted them were to hand them over to persons who should contract to convey them to America; and if any transported person returned before the expiration of the term of the sentence he should be punishable with death. Contractors who undertook to ship convicts to America were paid a bounty of £5 a head, in addition to the profit from the sale of their human cargo.

A statute of 1719 (6 Geo. I, cap. 28) enabled justices of the peace to contract with persons for the transportation of convicted persons, and additions were made, by Acts passed in later years, to the number of offences for which transportation was prescribed. A further Act of 1768 (8 Geo. III, cap. 15) enabled judges to order persons convicted of capital crimes to be transported for any period which might be deemed appropriate. The preamble of this Act explained that under

---

[1] See *C.H.B.E.* I, Index, Transportation.

the former system there had been delay in securing the King's pardon, which, in capital cases, had been granted to offenders on condition of their being transported. Consequently prisoners lay for several months in gaol, "whereby they are rendered less capable of being useful to the public of America to which they are sent". The Act was also important inasmuch as it defined the legal position of such persons after they were handed over to the contractors who conveyed them to the colonies. The contractors were to have "a property and interest in the services of the said offender" for the term of the sentence imposed; and this property and interest in the services was transferred to the plantation owners to whom the contractors sold their rights. The distinction between property and interest in services, and slavery, was one which had to be insisted upon as legally valid several times in the later history of transportation.

Thus, by the time of the rupture of the connection between the North American Colonies and Great Britain, transportation was a well-established part of the penal system. The cessation of it would have involved a total revision of British criminal jurisprudence, and an increase in the number and size of gaols in the United Kingdom. None of the judges recommended any alternative method of punishment and no responsible politician condemned transportation as undesirable either from the British or the colonial point of view. The outbreak of the War of Independence, stopping transportation to America, afforded an opportunity of overhauling the system. The stoppage was attended by great inconvenience and suffering and confronted the Government with a difficult problem. Hulks were moored in ports, in the Thames and in other rivers, and were filled with condemned persons, whose detention thereon was considered as equivalent to transportation. The gaols were terribly overcrowded. Burke stated in 1785 that there were then not less than 100,000 convicts undergoing an ordeal "infinitely more severe than could be inflicted in the utmost rigour and severity of the laws". But even Burke, though he considered that transportation made "no distinction between trivial crimes and those of greater enormity; all indiscriminately suffered the same miserable fate, however unequal their transgressions or different their circumstances", made no move to change the system. He did on another occasion voice the opinion that "the whole system of the penal laws was radically defective", but he suggested no definite alterations. The opposition to the Pitt Government in the House of Commons when the Bill was introduced in 1787 "to enable His Majesty to establish a criminal judicature on the eastern coast of New South Wales and the parts adjacent", was vigorous and watchful. But Fox, Sheridan and the Whig stalwarts, Wilberforce and the humanitarians, Burke and the philosophers, the jurists and the parliamentary rank and file, raised no objection and the bill was passed unanimously. Everybody seemed to be glad that a country had been found in the far-off south seas where there would be no interference with transportation, where there was plenty of room, and the very remoteness of which was an additional advantage.

For some years the Home Government had been trying to solve their problem. Attempts were made to land convicts from Great Britain in the former colonies, as well as in Newfoundland and Honduras. In 1789 Pitt's foreign minister, W. W. Grenville, felt called upon to point out that "the landing convicts in the territories of the United States, even if the masters of the ships perform their contracts for so doing, is an act highly offensive to a country now foreign and independent; and as such, very improper for the Government to authorise. And it is, besides, an act of extreme cruelty to the convicts, who, being turned on shore without any of the necessaries of life, are either left to starve, or, as has sometimes been the case, are massacred by the inhabitants." The attempt to land convicts in Honduras was opposed by the settlers[1] and a contingent of eighty Irish convicts sent to Newfoundland was rejected by the Governor (1789) on the ground that Newfoundland was "neither a Colony nor a Plantation". "We have no law", wrote Grenville, "to compel the colonies or Newfoundland to receive them."[2] Investigations for a suitable place on the African coast for a penal settlement yielded no satisfactory result.[3] At last the solution of the problem seemed to be found in the establishment of the new settlement in New South Wales.[4]

One striking difference distinguished transportation to New South Wales from the earlier system. In the American colonies, the convicts were employed in labour upon estates controlled by colonists; in New South Wales, there were in the beginning no colonists to employ them. The whole work of building an organised community had to be undertaken *ab initio* by convict labour. It might have been expected therefore that care would be taken in the selection of the convicts for this purpose. But no attempt was made to choose from the mass of prisoners under sentence in Great Britain such as would be most useful as colonists. No regard was paid to moral or physical fitness or even to the length of sentence. Prisoners were huddled into the transports with undiscriminating recklessness. Those whose moral delinquency was not deep were mingled with depraved persons such as Governor Phillip described: "most notorious offenders, every one of whom is as great a villain as ever graced a gibbet".[5] The tendency was to lower all to a level of

[1] See Burdon, Sir J. A., *Archives of British Honduras*, I, 146, 151, 153, 169.
[2] Historical MSS. Commission; *Dropmore Papers*, I, 541–9, 552.
[3] See Rose, J. H., *William Pitt and National Revival*, pt. I, pp. 432–7.
[4] *Vide supra*, pp. 24–8 and vol. VII, pt. I, ch. 3.   [5] *H.R.A.*, I, 235.

degradation; though even in this society there were "convicts of both sexes who were never known to associate with the common herd".[1] Prisoners who had not more than eighteen months or two years of their sentences to run were sent. Later, in consequence of the protests of Governors, it became usual to select, first, those condemned to transportation for life; secondly, those under sentence for fourteen years, and thirdly, those sentenced to seven years who were judged to be bad characters. It also became customary not to send men over fifty years of age.[2]

The transports for conveying prisoners to New South Wales were engaged by tender, at "so much per ton for the run". The cost of transportation varied from about £17 to £37 per convict.[3] Until 1816 the Government did not provide medical supervision for the ships, which were frequently overcrowded, and in some cases the conditions were no better than those in which African slaves were shipped to the West Indies.[4] A meagre scale of rations was provided, but the convicts did not always get their due, and were "worn out by want and long confinement" before they reached their destination. Punishments were extremely cruel. There are instances of convicts being kept in irons throughout the long voyage from England to Australia, and of men being chained together for eight months. "I believe", wrote Phillip, "that while the masters of the transports think their own safety depends on admitting few convicts on deck at a time, and most of them with irons on, which prevent any kind of exercise, numbers must always perish on so long a voyage, and many of those now received are in such a situation from old complaints, and so emaciated from what they have suffered on the voyage, that they will never be capable of any labour."[5]

Governor Macquarie pointed out in 1814 that the many scandals which occurred upon the transports were chiefly due to defective medical supervision. After the Peace of 1815 the Government had more ships and more naval doctors to spare and improvement was possible. It was a remarkable fact that in not one instance had there been an outbreak of contagious disease upon a ship employed exclusively in bringing out women convicts. "From the women there was nothing to apprehend with regard to the safety of the ship and they had therefore unrestrained access to the deck." But ships which brought out male convicts exclusively were dens of fever.

Convicts in New South Wales, and later in Van Diemen's Land, were either employed at work for the Government or were assigned

---

[1] Collins, *Account of the English Colony in New South Wales* (ed. of 1910), p. 40.
[2] See the evidence taken before the Committee on Transportation, 1812, *Parl. Pap.* 1812, II, p. 77.
[3] The Journal of P. G. King (*H.R., N.S.W.*, II, 514) gives a detailed account of the way in which transports were fitted up and guarded.
[4] See the description written by the Rev. R. Johnson of the transport *Surprize* in 1790. *H.R., N.S.W.*, I, pt. 2, p. 387; and that of Captain Hill, *ibid.* p. 367.
[5] *H.R.A.* I, 188.

to settlers. The assignment system was devised for enabling the free settlers to procure their services, but there were no free settlers during the first five years, and no considerable number till after 1825. A person to whom convicts were assigned possessed a legal property in their services. He had to feed and clothe them according to a regulation scale, and if they committed offences, or their conduct was unsatisfactory, they might be brought before a magistrate. Governor King (1801) stated that it had been a custom for those to whom the labour of convicts had been assigned to "chastise them by horse-whipping and beating them for real or supposed offences and neglect of work". He issued peremptory orders against this practice.

The punishments inflicted by magistrates were frequently very severe. It was not uncommon for them to order from twenty-five to one hundred lashes for idleness or negligence. Wages were paid; and as a rule employers who had both convicts and free labour made no distinction between the wages paid to the two classes. Indeed, the punishment most dreaded by the convicts was to "bring them down to the Government regulations", which meant depriving them of rations to which they were not entitled under the prescribed scale. There were periods when assignment absorbed so much of the convict labour that there was insufficient to enable the Government to proceed with necessary public works. Scandals also arose through the excessive assignment of servants to persons living in Sydney, and Governor Darling (1827) directed that convicts should as far as possible be assigned to persons living in the country, "in order that they may be out of the reach of enjoyments which are open to those who reside in the town". There were instances of convicts being followed to New South Wales by their wives, who thereupon obtained their own husbands as their assigned servants. There were also cases in which there was reason to believe that the wives of convicts had committed offences in England in order that they might be transported, "as a means of joining their husbands".[1]

Lord John Russell once stated in the House of Commons that the assignment system was a form of slavery; and there is, indeed, little to distinguish the two methods of compulsory labour, except the technical distinction between property in the person, as in slavery, and property in the services, as in assignment. But as a means of opening up a new country, wherein at the beginning no kind of industry could be expected to be remunerative unless it were provided with the cheapest kind of labour, it could be defended, if not justified.

The tendency to dwell upon the grim aspects of transportation has obscured the fact that for many who endured this punishment it opened the path to affluence. As early as 1798 it was realised by one of them that "the convicts here lead a happier life than the

---

[1] *H.R.A.* xiv, 114.

labouring poor of Europe", and another in a letter to England observed that fortunes were to be made in the colony. When the interior was opened up, exceptional opportunities were presented to enterprising men to occupy land and produce wool for export. Large areas were taken by "squatters" who, as the word was originally employed in Australia, were very often ex-convicts. Men of this class became possessed of property worth as much as £40,000: and incomes mounting to two and three thousand pounds per annum were not rare. When tales of the wealth accumulated by some convicts reached England, the Secretary of State reminded the Governor that the colony had been founded to be a place of "real terror" for malefactors.[1] It seemed to him to have defeated its own ends. But it was not within the power of any Government to prevent such results. The economic opportunities presented by a vast country with expanding commerce, increasing population, and cheap land and labour, were open to those who were shrewd enough to use them. It was through the irony of circumstance that the gate of torment opened for them upon the way to prosperity.

No provision was made for taking back to Great Britain convicts who had served their sentences. In this respect the system made no distinction between a man sentenced to transportation for seven years for a comparatively trivial offence, and one who had received a heavy sentence for a serious crime. "No obstacles were thrown in the way",[2] but the convict had to make his own arrangements. He might have saved enough money, or might secure employment on a ship, but he could expect no help from the Government. Expirees or emancipists, as they were variously called, were encouraged to become settlers, and when they took advantage of the terms offered to them were likely to prosper. But there were very many idle and worthless people who, as Phillip said, "dreaded punishment less than they dreaded labour", and who were so inured to crime that nothing would divert them from it. Hunter commented on "the vast number of bad characters who are let loose in this way, and who have no means or opportunity of getting out of the country, becoming a dangerous and most troublesome pest".

But it was not about the status of people as depraved as these that the acute emancipist question arose which so greatly troubled a succession of Governors. In strict terminology there was a distinction between expirees and emancipists, the former being persons who had become free through the expiration of their sentences, the latter

---

[1] Earl Bathurst to Macquarie 30 January 1819 (*H.R.A.* x, p. 7): "Bear in mind that transportation to New South Wales is intended as a severe punishment applied to various crimes, and as such must be rendered an object of real terror to all classes of the community." At a later date (*H.R.A.* xii, p. 584, 24 September 1826) Lord Bathurst expressed concern that "the dread of transportation amongst the lower classes in this country is much diminished".

[2] Collins, *English Colony in N.S.W.* p. 121.

persons who had been pardoned by the Governor in the exercise of the power committed to him. But both classes were concerned in the issue which so greatly disturbed the administration and retarded the grant of free institutions to the colony.

The political aspects of the dispute are discussed in volume VII of this work, and need not be further considered here. An emancipist question inevitably arose when there were some thousands of ex-convicts, many of them men of good standing in the community and not morally inferior to the "free" immigrants and the official class who refused to associate with them. Not only did Governors Macquarie and Brisbane show marked sympathy for them, but independent visitors to New South Wales formed favourable impressions of emancipists as a class. The impassioned feeling against them died hard, and did not totally disappear till the convict system itself was abolished and the institution of representative government formed lines of cleavage on worthier issues.

The political prisoners form a class apart. Batches of Irish "exiles" were transported for participation in the insurrection of 1798.[1] But not all the Irish prisoners were transported for political offences. There were many before 1798 who had been convicted for ordinary crimes. Governor Hunter found them particularly troublesome, and complained that "if so large a proportion of these lawless and turbulent people, the Irish convicts, are sent to this country, it will scarcely be possible to maintain that order which is so essential to our well-being". The political offenders began to arrive in considerable numbers after 1800, and Governor King did not think ill of them, though he had been alarmed lest they should prove dangerous. The Irish transportations were conducted so loosely that no papers were sent out to show for what periods prisoners had been sentenced; indeed, there were hundreds of cases in which no record had been kept in Ireland. They were tried by court martial, sentenced, put on board the transports, and conveyed oversea without the formality of an entry of their names and convictions. Officers of the French expedition commanded by Baudin which visited Australia in 1802 met some of these embittered men, and were convinced that if an attack were made upon Port Jackson the Irish convicts would rise in rebellion. François Péron reported that as soon as the news circulated that the French flag had been seen in the harbour, "the Irish commenced to flock together".[2] There was a revolt in 1804, but it was easily suppressed, as the population generally gave no support to the Irish.[3] Two of the leaders of the 1798 rebellion were Protestants, Joseph Holt, a Wexford farmer, whose *Memoirs* give a lively picture of life in New South Wales and Norfolk Island, and Henry Fulton, a

[1] See vol. VII, pt. I, pp. 75-6.
[2] See Péron's report in Scott, E., *Life of Matthew Flinders*, 455.
[3] See vol. VII, pt. I, p. 99.

clergyman, who became senior chaplain of the colony, a magistrate, and Church of England minister at Penrith, where he died in 1840.[1]

The beginning of trade unionism in England brought a small group of prisoners to Van Diemen's Land. The Dorchester labourers were victims of the determination of the Whig Government then in power to suppress this movement. George Loveless and his associates in 1833 formed a union to maintain wages in the Dorsetshire village of Tolpuddle. They took an oath to be loyal to one another in the event of an employer reducing wages below the common rate, and pledged themselves not to work with any member who divulged the secrets of the society or violated its obligations. The taking of this oath enabled the authorities to put the men on trial under an Act passed at the instance of the Pitt ministry for dealing with the Naval Mutiny at the Nore (37 Geo. III, cap. 128). Loveless and five others were convicted and sentenced to seven years' transportation.

The case evoked intense sympathy for the men, not merely on personal grounds but also because it was admitted that the Government had taken action against them with the object of suppressing the trade union movement. Lord Howick, speaking on the case in the House of Commons, said: "These were the first persons who were detected, and ministers were in hopes that the punishment of them would be a check to the similar dangerous proceedings of others."[2] The Lord Chancellor, Brougham, in his *Memoirs*, stated that he had favoured the proceedings against the Dorchester labourers, "agreeing as I did that these trade unions were in the nature of conspiracies of the worst kind".[3] In 1836 as the result of persistent appeals to the Government the six Tolpuddle convicts were pardoned and returned to England. George Loveless published a naive and pathetic little book, *Victims of Whiggery*, wherein he gave an account of his life in Van Diemen's Land.[4]

The Canadian rebellions in 1837–8 brought a large contingent of prisoners to New South Wales and Van Diemen's Land. The Sydney *Monitor* of 28 February, 1840, announced the arrival of the ship *Buffalo*, bringing fifty-eight persons "convicted of being concerned in the recent disturbances in the Canadas". The colonial authorities were instructed to "keep these prisoners distinct in every respect from others".

These Canadian cases raised novel considerations. The prisoners were tried by courts martial consisting of fifteen military officers.[5]

[1] Holt's *Memoirs* were published from his manuscript after his death; see also Lecky, *History of Ireland*, IV, 291.

[2] Hansard, XXII, 938. [3] Brougham, *Memoirs*, III, 323.

[4] *The Book of the Martyrs of Tolpuddle*, published by the Trades Union Congress Union Council, and Firth, M. and Hopkinson, A., *The Tolpuddle Martyrs*, were issued in connection with the centenary of the convictions, 1934. On the legal aspects of the case see Hurst, Sir Gerald, "The Dorchester Labourers", *E.H.R.*, January 1925.

[5] See *Report of the State Trials before a general court martial held at Montreal in 1838–9*, 2 vols., Montreal, 1839.

After a large number had been condemned to death and several had been hanged, the Governor-General, Lord Durham, being anxious, for humanitarian and political reasons, that the death penalty should not be further inflicted, summoned a special council, which passed an ordinance providing that prisoners convicted of treason were to be transported to Bermuda.[1] When, however, eight prisoners reached that colony, the Governor, Sir S. R. Chapman, objected that he could not receive them as convicts. Both his law officers and the Chief Justice (T. Butterfield) held that "he had no power to impose restrictions upon them with a view to their detention in Bermuda".[2] Bermuda was a colony to which convicts were sent from Great Britain, chiefly for military offences,[3] but it was denied that the Government of another British possession could deposit prisoners upon "the pleasant isle". In Great Britain the law officers of the Crown (J. Campbell and R. M. Rolfe) advised the Secretary of State that so much of Durham's ordinance as directed the prisoners to be transported to Bermuda and kept under restraint there was "void". The power of the Government of Lower Canada was confined to its "general sovereign legislative power within the province".[4] Durham still maintained that the power of the Canadian provincial government to punish by transportation was indisputable, and that he as Governor-General "had power to appoint the place to which any person should be transported". But the Secretary to the Government of Bermuda, in a letter to the eight prisoners, whom he addressed as "Gentlemen", officially informed them that they were to consider themselves as exempted from restraint.

The eight prisoners, with four others, were then removed to England, where they were placed in Liverpool gaol with a view to transporting them to Van Diemen's Land. But a strong agitation on their behalf had been aroused, headed by J. A. Roebuck, who, with remarkable energy and eloquence, maintained that they were illegally imprisoned. Application was made to the Court of Queen's Bench for a writ of habeas corpus, which was granted by Mr Justice Littledale. The twelve prisoners were brought to London, and the case was argued for several days, Roebuck, who appeared as one of their counsel, contending that "if men were to be detained it must be by the law of England; no authority in Canada had power to deport".[5]

Ultimately, Lord Abinger, in delivering judgment, said that the Court did not think it necessary to pronounce upon the point that the Legislature of Canada had no authority to make any law other than one binding within the province. The Court could not, however,

---

[1] Minute Book of Executive Council, 3 July 1838; Canadian Archives, Ottawa. Bermuda was chosen because it would not "affix a character of moral infamy on the exiles". See also *C.H.B.E.* VI, 294–7.
[2] P.R.O., Bermuda, C.O. 37/99; 29 July 1838.
[3] See Whittingham, F., *Bermuda, a Colony, a Fortress and a Prison*, pp. 186–226.
[4] Lord Glenelg to Lord Durham, 18 August 1838.   [5] *The Times*, 16 January 1839.

order the gaoler to release the prisoners, inasmuch as they had confessed treason. "But", Lord Abinger added, "if the prisoner (John Grant, whose case was taken to test the legality of the twelve) cannot be lawfully transported under his present circumstances, it is presumed that the Government, upon being so certified, will take proper measures for prosecuting him for the crime of treason in England. For these reasons we are of opinion that the prisoners must be remanded."[1] This being a clear intimation that the Court was doubtful about the legality of the proceedings, and it being impracticable to bring witnesses from Canada and retry the prisoners in England, Lord John Russell advised the Queen to "grant them a pardon on condition of their entering into their own recognisance not to return to Canada nor to appear within fifty miles of the Canadian frontier".[2]

There still remained in Canada a large number of men who had been convicted and sentenced to death for treason. Sir George Arthur, who was appointed Lieutenant-Governor of Upper Canada during the rebellion, had previously been Lieutenant-Governor of Van Diemen's Land, and was a strong believer in transportation as a reformatory discipline.[3] He persuaded his executive council to recommend that free pardons be granted to the younger prisoners and that the remainder be transported. The Secretary of State approved, and measures were at once taken to transport 141 prisoners, 83 from Upper Canada (Kingston) and 58 from Lower Canada (Montreal), to Australia and Van Diemen's Land. Of those transported from Upper Canada, 78 were United States citizens. They had been sentenced to death, the offence they had committed being described on the Return of Convicts as "piratical invasion of Upper Canada". The sentences were commuted to "transportation for life".[4] The prisoners were conveyed in H.M.S. *Buffalo* direct from the St Lawrence to Australia, those from Upper Canada being landed at Hobart, whilst those from Lower Canada, all of whom were French, were sent to Sydney. Sir John Franklin, the famous Arctic explorer, then Lieutenant-Governor of Van Diemen's Land, reported that he had "not allowed these men to pass through the usual ordeal of the convict barracks, not wishing them to be thrown amongst the usual class of thieves and rogues who are kept in such places of punishment",[5] and similar consideration was shown to the French-Canadian prisoners in New South Wales.

In 1844–5, when danger of further disturbance had died down in

[1] *The Times*, 6 May 1839.
[2] Russell (Home Secretary) to the Marquis of Normanby (Secretary of State for the Colonies), 13 July 1839; *Reports relating to Canada*, 1840, document 23.
[3] See Arthur's *Defence of Transportation*, 1835; also Forsyth, W. D., *Governor Arthur's Convict System*.
[4] Sir George Arthur's despatch to Marquis of Normanby, 19 July 1839. Canadian Archives, Ottawa.
[5] Franklin to Lord John Russell, 16 February 1840.

Canada, free pardons were granted to the remaining prisoners;[1] a few had died, and two made their escape in American ships. One of the latter was James Wait, who, on his return to the United States, published a narrative of his experiences. Five other American prisoners, and two French-Canadians, also published books. Of these, the most valuable is Francis Xavier Prieur's *Notes d'un condamné politique de 1838*, a pathetic and sincere work, which gives an intimate account of the ticket-of-leave system as he endured it. The American books are full of bitterness and angry disillusionment; and three of them —those by Miller, Wright and Marsh— are venomously untruthful.

The violent phases of the English Chartist movement occasioned the transportation of John Frost and two of his associates for their participation in the riots at Newport, Wales, in 1839. Frost had been sentenced to death for high treason, but there was an appeal on a technical point, which was argued before a court of fifteen judges, the majority of whom decided that the conviction was good in law. But as there was difference of opinion among the judges the Government commuted the sentence to one of transportation for life. Frost served for nearly fifteen years in Van Diemen's Land. He worked in the chain gangs on the roads for a while, and was afterwards employed as a police clerk and in other clerical capacities. In 1854 he received a conditional pardon, which stipulated that he should not return to England. He went to the United States, but after receiving a free pardon he returned to England, where he lectured on "the horrors of convict life". In 1857 he published a *Letter to the people of Great Britain on Transportation, showing the effects of irresponsible power on the physical and moral condition of convicts.* A few other Chartists were transported, but the great majority were imprisoned at home.[2]

The last two batches of political prisoners were connected with the Young Ireland movement of 1848 and the Fenian conspiracy of 1867. The best known among the men of '48 was John Mitchel, whose *Jail Journal*, published in the United States after his escape from Van Diemen's Land in an American ship in 1853, gives an account of convict life. The Fenian convicts, about sixty in number, were sent to Western Australia, which was the only penal colony remaining in Australia when they were transported. The most eminent of these was the poet John Boyle O'Reilly, who escaped in an American whaler, and attained distinction as a man of letters in the United States, where he resided for the remainder of his life.

There was no notable change in opinion upon the policy of transportation until the second quarter of the nineteenth century. The House of Commons Committee which enquired into the system in

[1] See *Hobart Gazette* and *Sydney Gazette* at various dates during December–January 1844–5.
[2] Gammage, R. G., *History of the Chartist Movement*, pp. 133, 180–3, 348.

1812, under the chairmanship of the Hon. George Eden, concluded that the colony of New South Wales was "in a train entirely to answer the ends proposed by its establishment".[1] The Committee which enquired into the state of the gaols of the United Kingdom in 1819, under the chairmanship of the Rt. Hon. Charles Bathurst, made some observations upon "that singular and extensive establishment", New South Wales, but took it for granted that the system was permanent. John Macarthur, who gave evidence, informed the committee that the motives which impelled free settlers to go to the colony were "the excellence of the climate, their obtaining grants of land from Government instead of being obliged to purchase them, and also their being enabled to employ convicts as labourers, which renders labour decidedly cheaper"; and the committee appeared to accept this as satisfactory.[2] J. T. Bigge, who was sent out as Commissioner to investigate in 1819, and reported in 1822–3, made suggestions for improving the system and extending it by new settlements, but he did not allege that it failed as an efficient and desirable mode of dealing with criminals.[3] The Select Committee on Criminal Commitments and Convictions, 1828, strongly defended the system. Nor was there, so far, any colonial demand for the discontinuance of transportation. The economy of New South Wales depended upon cheap convict labour. One of the inducements offered to settlers was that landowners would be able to get such labour. There were only two classes in New South Wales, labourers and employers; the latter did not desire the cessation of a system by which they profited, whilst the former had no voice in the matter. It is a striking fact that when questions relating to New South Wales were debated in the House of Commons, there was no demand, even from the advocates of free institutions, for the ending of transportation. The colony had been started for that purpose and must be maintained for it; transportation was part of the accepted order of things.

The change of opinion came from both ends at about the same time. In Great Britain Jeremy Bentham's influence upon political thought swayed the philosophical radicals; and Bentham provided a plan of prison reform which aimed at making transportation unnecessary by the building of reformatory penitentiaries at home. Romilly and Mackintosh in the House of Commons attacked the whole criminal procedure, and Peel took up the question in his measures for consolidating the criminal law. Public men began to doubt whether the system was not a great mistake. The group of colonial reformers, prominent among whom were Sir William Molesworth and Charles Buller, assailed it because it was detrimental to wholesome colonisation. Wakefield, who knew the inside of Newgate, was a resolute foe of the convict system. The Act

---

[1] *Parl. Pap.* 1812, II (341).
[2] *Ibid.* 1819, VII (579).　　　　[3] *Ibid.* 1822, XX (448) and 1823, X (33), (136).

permitting the colonisation of South Australia prohibited the sending of convicts there and none were transported to New Zealand.[1] No Governor had tried harder than Sir George Arthur in Van Diemen's Land to make a penal colony a success, and his failure to do so contributed to convince ministers that transportation as a means of colonisation must be abandoned. Assaults were launched against the system on moral and humanitarian grounds by writers who followed the lead of Archbishop Whately and Sydney Smith. Its reformative efficacy was impugned; the horrors by which it was attended were stressed; it was denounced as the most costly and least defensible method of punishment.

Richard Whately, Archbishop of Dublin, published his *Thoughts on Secondary Punishments* in 1832 and his *Remarks on Transportation* in 1834. The books contained eloquent and powerful attacks upon transportation. They directed attention to the main purpose of penal legislation, which was, he maintained, the prevention of crime, not "reclaiming hardened villains and Australian forests". He argued that in fact transportation had in many instances meant not punishment but reward; that in most cases it brutalised and degraded; that it was a form of slavery; and that there was a strong case for an enquiry as to whether the system ought to be continued. Sydney Smith, in essays marked by his characteristic mixture of wit and sound sense, insisted that transportation had failed both to reform and to punish. He instanced "a wicked little tailor" who wrote home that he was "as comfortable as a finger in a thimble, that, though a fraction only of humanity, he had several wives, and was filled every day with rum and kangaroo". While the Secretary of State, Lord Bathurst, was "full of jokes and joy", public morals were sapped to their foundation, an extreme profligacy of manners was the chief product of the system, and the colony which had cost the British taxpayer some millions of pounds had increased rather than diminished crime.

The consequence of these attacks was the appointment by the House of Commons in 1837 of a select committee, over which Sir William Molesworth presided, to enquire into the efficacy of transportation as a punishment, its influence on the moral state of society in the penal colonies, and how far it was susceptible of improvement. The report of this committee, with its evidence and appendices, forms by far the most valuable collection of first-hand information on the subject.[2] Three members, Lord John Russell, Lord Howick (afterwards Earl Grey) and Sir George Grey, became Colonial Secretaries; Sir Robert Peel had already evinced interest in the subject by his criminal law reforms; whilst Charles Buller and the chairman were experts on colonial politics. Nearly all the twenty-

[1] South Australia Act 1834, Sect. 22; for New Zealand see vol. VII, pt. II, pp. 72–3, 77.
[2] See *Parl. Pap.* 1837, XIX (518) and 1837–8, XXII (669).

three witnesses had had personal experience of the system. The report contained a searching examination of the law and principles upon which transportation was founded, and of the manner in which it had been conducted. The conclusions were: (1) that transportation to New South Wales and Van Diemen's Land should be discontinued as soon as practicable; (2) that crimes when punishable by transportation should in future be punished by confinement with hard labour, at home or abroad, for periods varying from two to fifteen years; and (3) that to prevent a recurrence of those social evils which had been found to result from transportation as hitherto conducted, penitentiaries established abroad should be confined to places where there were no free settlers and wherein effectual security could be taken against such settlers coming.

It should be observed that these recommendations did not include the total abolition of transportation. The committee still contemplated the establishment of penitentiaries abroad and it may be inferred that in this respect the report was the result of a compromise. Some members of the committee, including Molesworth and Buller, were certainly in favour of ending the system; others were not. But its continuation on the plan proposed was clearly impossible. If New South Wales and Van Diemen's Land were no longer to be used for the purpose, where else could the advocates of transportation hope to find a place to which convicts might be sent? And where was there any prospect of excluding free settlers if the territory were suitable for them? It seems probable that Molesworth and Buller, unable to carry the majority with them, induced the committee to make recommendations which would inevitably lead to abolition; and that, in fact, happened.

Indeed, the report condemned transportation so emphatically that its continuation in any form for any considerable time was hardly conceivable. The two main characteristics of the system as a means of punishment, it was averred, were "inefficiency in deterring from crime, and remarkable efficiency, not in reforming, but in still further corrupting those who undergo the punishment". These qualities of inefficiency for good and efficiency for evil were inherent in the system, "which therefore is not susceptible of any satisfactory improvement". Condemnation in such unqualified terms, taken together with the recommendation of continuance in some other place in a modified form, seems evidence of a clash of opinion which found expression in an inconsistency. Statistics collected by the committee showed that from 1788 to 1836, 75,200 convicts had been transported to New South Wales; and 27,759 had been sent to Van Diemen's Land since 1817. The total convict population of New South Wales in 1836 consisted of 25,254 men and 2577 women; whilst in Van Diemen's Land there were 14,914 men and 2054 women. In Norfolk Island, the number in 1837 was above 1200, most of them having been re-transported for offences committed in New South Wales. In addition there were at that date about 900 convicts in Bermuda.

The immediate effect of the publication of the report was that the Government determined to stop transportation to New South Wales; and an Order in Council of 22 May, 1840, proclaimed that after 1 August of that year no more convicts should be sent to that colony, though Norfolk Island and Van Diemen's Land might still be used for the purpose. But the Government was not prepared to end the system completely and it was even proposed by the Secretary of State that King Island in Bass Strait should be used for a convict establishment. Governor Gipps raised a strong objection to that course because of the facilities which would be afforded for escape, all the islands in Bass Strait being close to the track of ships. The difficulties in the way of giving effect to the compromise suggested by the committee were patent.

The first reactions to the report in Australia were unfavourable to abolition. The document, as Gipps reported to the Secretary of State, produced "a considerable sensation" in Sydney; but the sensation was one of fear of the consequences of abolition. Especially was there consternation as to "the prejudicial effects which the evidence was likely to produce on the colony". A petition signed by a large number of the inhabitants protested that much of the evidence presented a false and over-coloured picture of the social condition of the colony. The Legislative Council carried twelve resolutions for presentation to the Imperial Government;[1] and these stressed the point that the character of the colony had been traduced and misrepresented. The sudden discontinuance of transportation, the Council insisted, would deprive the colonists of convict labour, would thus curtail their means of purchasing Crown lands, and would consequently diminish the funds available for promoting immigration. The Legislative Council at this date was, it must be remembered, a nominee body, consisting of officials and landowners, and the latter, especially, did not view the discontinuance of transportation with favour because of its effect on the supply of labour. It might have been expected that there would be support for abolition from other quarters, but there was no marked movement in Australia to abolish transportation until the Rev. John West (a Congregational Minister sent out by the London Missionary Society in 1839) formed the Anti-Transportation League. As the report of the transportation committee, published a few weeks before he left England, contained much information about his new field of work, he naturally read it; and soon after he arrived in Launceston, Van Diemen's Land, he formed the league which was thereafter to exert much influence on Australian opinion, and to bring into existence an abolitionist party.

[1] See Bell and Morrell, *Select Documents*, pp. 286–7.

Meanwhile the British Government became unpopular in New South Wales because it had deprived the landowners of the regular flow of labour which enabled them to work their estates. "Many of the acts of the Home Government affecting this colony during the last ten or twelve years have been received by the colonists with more or less disfavour", reported Sir George Gipps in 1843; and he instanced "the abolition of transportation and assignment, which deprived the colony of cheap labour", as an additional provocation.[1] There was also the grievance of throwing on the colony the whole expense of maintaining its police and gaols.

A reaction in favour of transportation ensued in Great Britain. There was not yet a sufficiency of gaols, and the policy of crowding convicts upon hulks had been resumed. After a debate in 1841, initiated by Viscount Mahon, the House of Commons carried a motion that it was highly inexpedient to increase the number of convicts permanently confined on the hulks in Great Britain.[2] He quoted from the New South Wales petition in proof of the contention that so far from the inhabitants of that colony being opposed to transportation, the change introduced had excited the strongest feelings of opposition and disapprobation. He advocated the formation of a new penal colony in the north of Australia, and urged that transportation should be conducted so as to secure that "while we cast abroad the seeds of future empire, we should at the same time attain the two great objects of all penal legislation, to deter and to reform". Both Lord John Russell and Lord Howick, speaking for the Government, denied that there was any intention to abolish transportation entirely; they had simply determined to diminish it.

The new policy, therefore, raised fresh perplexities. The Government could not ignore the opinion expressed in the House of Commons, nor could they disregard the view pressed upon them by the petitioners from New South Wales and by the Governor. Moreover, the pouring of an increased number of convicts into Van Diemen's Land created an acute situation there. A petition to the House of Commons from that island in 1846 represented that free settlers were being driven out through the crowding in of convicts. The petitioners spoke of "the frightful result of the present convict system", and prayed that transportation might cease till the number of convicts in the country was reduced.

At the same time there was a demand for labour in the newly-settled province of Port Phillip (later named Victoria). Public and private representations were made to the Colonial Office that Port Phillip could easily absorb a certain amount of convict labour. Immigration societies favoured this policy. In Australia, therefore, the situation was that one colony complained of the cessation of transportation, a second complained because too much of it was proving

---

[1] *H.R.A.* XXIII, 199.   [2] Hansard, 1841, LVII, 522.

ruinous, whilst a third, which had only lately come into being, was urgently in need of labour.

At this time, also, the English prison commissioners were anxious to try an experiment with a new system. A model prison had been erected at Millbank upon Jeremy Bentham's "panopticon" plan, six large wings radiating from a common centre. The new penal system involved the detention in Millbank, for disciplinary preparation, of persons sentenced to transportation. After a period of servitude there, they were drafted to another model prison at Pentonville, which was opened in 1842. Here the prisoners were set to useful labour; if they were illiterate they were taught; they were brought under moralising influences; and, though they were placed in solitary confinement for breaches of discipline, they were at the same time able to earn by good conduct a mitigation of sentence. But transportation was an essential part of the Pentonville system, which, as officially explained, was based on the assumption that there would be a demand for labour in the colonies. It was intended that, as a rule, prisoners should be kept under observation in Pentonville for at least eighteen months, and at the end of that period the prison commissioners were empowered to select such as appeared to have profited from the treatment and send them abroad. When they landed in the colony to which they were consigned, they were to be given "conditional pardons". The holder of a conditional pardon was free to go where he pleased, provided he did not return to Great Britain during the currency of the sentence originally inflicted upon him. It meant, therefore, that those who were transported under the conditional pardon system would not be assigned servants in the old New South Wales sense, but would be unrestrained subject to the condition mentioned.

In November, 1844, the ship *Royal George* arrived at Melbourne with a company of conditional pardon men on board. It became at once apparent that, notwithstanding that landowners in the Port Phillip province had asked for convict labour, the attitude of the towns-people was quite different. When it was known that persons on the *Royal George* had been sentenced to seven years' penal servitude, two years of which they had already served in Millbank and Pentonville, bitter indignation was expressed. A meeting under the presidency of the Mayor of Melbourne protested against the introduction to Port Phillip of "expatriated villains from the gaols of England, either under the fanciful name of exiles or of any other appellation". The landowners just as stoutly maintained that they must have labour from this source if they could not get it otherwise. "I do not choose to be ruined for virtue's sake", said one of their spokesmen; and another declared that "labour we must have, and if we do not get it from Pentonville we shall have it from Van Diemen's Land". "Pentonvillains", as they were called, were never welcomed in Port Phillip during the five years when they were sent to the young colony, though the superintendent, Latrobe, reported that there never was the slightest difficulty in getting immediate employment for them.

The resistance to transportation in Australia was not strong enough to command attention till Melbourne and Sydney each contained a sufficient number of free immigrants to form a public opinion in opposition to the system; and this urban opinion was influenced by different interests and motives from those which moved the landowners of the country districts. Since 1835 funds derived from the sale of lands had been devoted to paying bounties to encourage free immigration. During the following decade thousands of people were brought to Australia by this method, and as their families grew up in the land of their adoption, the evils attendant upon convictism became repellent to them. Bushranging made life and property insecure for farmer and squatter, and the towns were beset by thieves. A desire to clear the country from a system which poured pollution into it took root and developed into a political question.

In March, 1849, the Governor of New South Wales, Sir Charles Fitzroy, visited the Port Phillip District. Shortly before that time there had been public meetings in Melbourne at which resolutions were passed demanding that no more convicts should be sent. The agitation was stimulated by an announcement by the Secretary of State for the Colonies, Lord Grey, that in future prisoners should be sent out with tickets-of-leave, as well as with conditional pardons. This meant that the small amount of prison discipline, which had modified the worst of the old system in some degree, was to be partially abandoned. Fitzroy, impressed by the strength of the opposition, declared that it would be obviously unjust to land more convicts in Port Phillip, that he had already remonstrated with the Home Government against doing so, and that he had given authority to stop any more from being landed. On his return to Sydney he was perplexed by a like remonstrance from the townspeople there, who insisted that New South Wales also ought to be freed from receiving more convicts. Fitzroy then stated that he had no power "to prevent the importation of prisoners or their distribution in the country", and that Port Phillip must take a share of them. The Melbourne people realised that they would have to take prompt measures on their own account.

The critical moment arrived when the ship *Randolph* reached Port Phillip on 8 August. The Mayor convened a meeting, at which speeches were delivered inciting the people to "resist the landing of such cargoes" even by force if necessary. The executive officer of the Government at Melbourne at that date was styled the Superintendent; he was responsible to the Governor at Sydney. In this crisis the Superintendent, Latrobe, took upon himself the responsibility of avoiding a breach of the peace by ordering the *Randolph* to sail to Sydney. When she arrived there, public feeling was also inflamed to such an extent that Fitzroy did not venture to permit the convicts to land, but sent them on to Moreton Bay, where a new penal offshoot from New South Wales had been founded in 1824. When the ship *Hashemy* arrived in May 1850, the same course was adopted. It was thus the determination of the free immigrants which finally broke up the transportation system.

The policy of the Imperial Government, however, was not to abandon transportation. Lord Stanley, Secretary of State in 1844, affirmed that the Government "hold it indispensable that within the Australian colonies receptacles should be found for all the convicts and exiles who may be sent from this country in execution of judicial sentences. This is so momentous an object of national policy that we can acknowledge no conflicting motive as of sufficient importance to supersede it." Lord Grey, too, the Whig Secretary of State, was at one with his Tory contemporary in this regard. "The country", he said, "is perfectly justified in continuing the practice of transportation to Australia, the colonies being only entitled to ask that, in arrangements for conducting it, their interests and welfare should be consulted as far as possible." He dwelt upon the bad effects that would be produced in England if she were compelled to retain her own criminal population. "What will be the consequence when some two or three thousand men, who under the existing system would be permanently removed from the United Kingdom, are to be annually turned loose on society?"[1] The official head of the Colonial Office failed to realise that there was a society of reputable persons in the colonies which had an equally strong objection to criminals being "turned loose" upon them.

At the time when this movement of resistance was being developed in the country which had had the largest experience of transportation, the Government determined to extend it to South Africa.[2] The idea was first mooted in 1842, when it was at once made clear that neither the British nor the Dutch inhabitants of the Cape would welcome such an experiment. But the Government disregarded these warnings. In September 1848 an Order-in-Council was passed declaring the Cape of Good Hope a place to which convicts might be sent. The ship *Neptune* was already on the way with the first cargo of "conditional pardon" prisoners when the inhabitants of Cape Town became aware of the decision of the Imperial Government. An anti-convict association was formed whose members were pledged to resist the landing of the "exiles". The force of public opinion induced Sir Harry Smith to disregard his instructions, and he undertook not to permit the convicts to land pending the receipt of further directions from Great Britain and confirmed this decision by a proclamation of 17 July 1849. The *Neptune* arrived in September, but not a man was landed. The situation was relieved by the receipt of a despatch from Lord Grey

[1] Grey, Earl, *Colonial Policy*, II, 310.   [2] See *C.H.B.E.* VIII, 369–72.

ordering the ship to take her freight to Van Diemen's Land, and the Order-in-Council was shortly afterwards revoked.[1]

In 1849 the Order-in-Council enabling ticket-of-leave prisoners to be sent to New South Wales and the Port Phillip district was also revoked, and in Van Diemen's Land the activities of the anti-transportation league were successful in securing the abandonment of the system in that island in 1852. Between 1841 and 1852 the large number of 35,378 prisoners of the Crown had been deposited there. Transportation to Norfolk Island was abandoned in 1855.

Australia now had good reason to hope that the last had been seen of a system which, though it had conferred economic advantages upon the country in the early years of colonisation, had become repugnant to the people. The new era of responsible government had dawned. Van Diemen's Land, the scene of the convict system at its worst, had turned its back on the past by changing its name to Tasmania (1853). It was, therefore, disappointing to the southern and eastern colonies when in 1849 Western Australia requested that convict labour might be introduced, and when in 1850 the first convict ship landed its company of exiles at Perth.[2] This departure from the policy to which the remainder of Australia was by this time deeply pledged was due to economic causes. The Colonial Office, influenced by Wakefield's ideas, which enjoined the sale of land at a fixed minimum price, had compelled the administration to sell land in Western Australia at a minimum of £1 per acre. The same price prevailed in New South Wales, where the prospects were at the moment more advantageous. It was not likely that an intending settler would pay £1 per acre for land in Western Australia when he could get it for that price in the Port Phillip District or in the settled areas beyond Sydney. The uniform price prevented the Western Australian administration from offering more favourable terms to settlers than were offered elsewhere. A committee of the Legislative Council in 1844 pointed out that "the alteration in the land regulations, fixing the minimum price of Crown lands at 20s. per acre, has had a powerful and baneful influence upon the conditions of the colony, and consequently on the revenue, by putting a stop to the sale of Crown lands—no money sales, with the exception of a few town allotments having been made since 1 December 1842—and to the introduction of capital". Trade was paralysed, the Treasury was embarrassed, the credit of the colony declined.

There was an outcry when it was suggested that the British Government should be asked to relieve the situation by the inauguration of transportation. In July, 1844, the Legislative Council resolved that "no dearth of labour can be so extreme as to call for or to warrant our having recourse to such a hazardous experiment for a supply".

[1] See the Cape Town resolutions in Bell and Morrell, *Select Documents on British Colonial Policy*, p. 312. Morrell, W. P., *The Colonial Policy of Peel and Russell*, pp. 403–6, gives an account of the resistance movement in Cape Town.
[2] See vol. VII, pt. 1, pp. 228–30.

But during 1845–6 public opinion began to swing round to the opposite view, notwithstanding that the Governor, John Hutt, pointed to the manner in which the other Australian colonies had freed themselves "from this system as from a pestilence". A new Governor, Fitzgerald, took office in 1848. Before he left England the Government, aware of the trend of opinion in Western Australia, directed him to enquire whether the colony would be prepared to receive convicts from Pentonville. His enquiries brought the question to a head. The Governor reported his opinion that if it were desired by the British Government to establish another penal colony in Australia, the majority of the inhabitants of Western Australia would be glad to learn that that site had been chosen for the purpose. There is no reason to doubt that the Governor correctly gauged the state of public opinion. An Order-in-Council was accordingly passed in May, 1849, enabling convicts to be sent to Western Australia, and from 1850 to 1868 they were sent. During that period 9720 male prisoners were received; no women were included. One result was to prevent Western Australia from enjoying responsible government till 1870, when the system of government which had been inaugurated in the other Australian colonies fifteen years earlier was commenced under the governorship of Sir Frederick Weld.

In 1856 the House of Lords appointed a select committee to enquire into transportation.[1] It reported that the system appeared to have been conducted with advantage to Western Australia, with satisfaction to the colonists, and with benefit to the convicts themselves. But whilst there had been careful selection of the convicts transported at the beginning, the committee found that since 1853 "the worst and most flagitious class of offenders, some of them, indeed, utterly unfitted for transportation under any system", had been sent. There is no doubt as to the economic advantage that the revived system conferred upon Western Australia, but by 1868 the opinion prevailed that for the advantage of this colony, and of Australia as a whole, it ought to cease. The Colonial Office too was opposed to its continuance. The improved prison and penal system of Great Britain had also removed the problem of the convict from the number of acute difficulties, and after 1868 no more British prisoners were transported.

That transportation was an important element in modern colonisation is apparent not only from British experience in the North American colonies and Australia, but also from French methods in Canada and Louisiana, and in a lesser degree from those of the Portuguese in Brazil. The foundation of colonies in distant lands and the establishment of industries in them involve large investments of capital and a plentiful supply of labour. Failing an unusual impulse to emigration, such as peopled the Puritan and Quaker settlements

[1] See Report in *Parl. Pap.* 1856, XXIV (124).

of America, colonies in the seventeenth and eighteenth centuries had small prospect of success. The American colonies which received convict labour benefited from it economically, and as far as can be ascertained were not much prejudiced by it. The Declaration of Independence, which catalogued all imaginable grievances, did not include this among them. In Australia, the rough work of preparing an untamed territory for settlement was performed by using the only source of labour supply available at the time. It was not, on the whole, good economic labour, but the value and greatness of the work done by it cannot be doubted. As Charles Darwin observed in 1836, by "converting vagabonds most useless in one country into active citizens of another, and thus giving birth to a new and splendid country, it succeeded to a degree perhaps unparallelled in history"; and again, "It is a magnificent testimony to the power of the British nation. Here, in a less promising country, scores of years have effected many times more than the same number of centuries have done in South America."[1]

In all colonies where convict labour was used, there came a time when, settlement having grown to adequate proportions, local opinion turned against it. That was so in the American colonies before the Revolution, and in southern and eastern Australia when free immigration outnumbered the bond element, shortly before the great gold discoveries. Even in Bermuda, where the convict class was small and the system mild in its characteristics, a proposal to introduce juvenile delinquents from Great Britain provoked the House of Assembly (11 September 1838) to protest against it "as a measure fraught with the most pernicious consequences".[2]

Undoubtedly convictism had its vicious features. It was attended often by hideous cruelties. It produced the plague of bushranging in Van Diemen's Land and New South Wales. But the reformatory purpose was fulfilled in many thousands of instances, and in innumerable others it opened prospects of happy and prosperous life to persons who otherwise would have languished in poverty and crime. Romancers and manufacturers of "faked" reminiscences have created a false impression by lurid sensational writing and presenting individual instances as typical. The Legislative Council of New South Wales was well within the mark when, in one of its resolutions of 17 July 1838, it insisted that "many men who previous to their conviction had been brought up in habits of idleness and vice, have acquired, by means of assignment, not only habits of industry and labour, but the knowledge of a remunerative employment which, on [their] becoming free, forms a strong inducement to continue in an honest course of life".[3]

[1] Darwin, C., *Journal...of the various countries visited by H.M.S. Beagle*, 1839 edition, p. 532.
[2] P.R.O., Bermuda, C.O. /37/99.
[3] N.S.W. *Parl. Pap.* 1839, xxxiv.

On the other hand, transportation delayed that radical reform of the penal system of Great Britain which was long overdue when Jeremy Bentham advocated a new prison discipline, and philanthropists, following the lead of John Howard, exposed the horrors of insanitary gaols. As long as criminals could be shipped to the Antipodes, the motive for prison reform did not impel any Government to make humane provision at home. Only when it became apparent that the colonies would not much longer tolerate the system, were effective steps taken towards reform.

Transportation subsided exactly at the period when a fresh impulse to British colonisation was given by the work of the Colonial reformers and the theories of Edward Gibbon Wakefield. Fallacious as those theories were in some respects, they exercised enormous influence. The new spirit, which viewed the expansion of the Empire in the South Seas as a glorious British achievement, broke with a tainted past and inspired a nobler future.

PROBLEMS OF SETTLEMENT

(II) EMIGRATION AND LAND POLICY, 1815–1873

IN the mass movement which, after 1815, transferred seven million inhabitants of the United Kingdom to the colonies and the United States within sixty years, the dominating facts are the condition of wretchedness which forced most of them to seek an escape from Great Britain, and the struggle for existence, not always successful, through which the transference and new settlement were accomplished. The history of the movement includes few leaders of dominating importance; but from the general mass there stand out, especially in the earlier years, certain groups of common folk, largely from the Scottish Highlands and Islands, whose adventures revealed more powers of organisation and co-operation than the rest; and some dreamers, or gallant gentlemen, mainly English, who, venturing to conceive of a colonial empire strangely unlike that which existed, proceeded by their efforts to make their dreams come true.

Emigration on an extended scale was not a new thing in 1815. It has been calculated[1] that, in the years before the Declaration of Independence, 20,000 Northern Irish and Highland Scots emigrated annually; and certainly from 1784, when the first reinforcement of Highlanders left to join their fellow-countrymen in the Canadian Glengarry, down to the Sutherland evictions, band after band from the Highlands passed over to Canada. But the years immediately following 1815 mark a new dispensation in emigration. The causes which operated were many, and varied widely in their operation from district to district. The actual reduction in armed forces meant something; as late as 1826 and 1827 the ex-service man, English, Scottish and Irish, officer and private, bulks largely in emigration petitions.[2] But the new movement was not caused chiefly by demobilisation. In manufacturing districts like Belfast, the Clyde and Forth isthmus, and Lancashire, the unsettlement of trade after the war, and still more, the transition from manual to mechanical means of production created desperate distress, and drove the labouring classes in these regions in thousands to combine in emigration societies, clamouring in petitions for parliamentary aid, and when hope there failed, to struggle somehow out of the death-in-life conditions in Britain. Weavers, like those who appeared before the Select Committee of 1827, had no illusions about the future of their handicraft: They knew perfectly well, they said, that machinery must go on, that it will go on, and that it is impossible to stop it.[3] Sometimes

---

[1] Johnson, S. C., *Emigration from the United Kingdom to North America*, p. 2.
[2] *Third Report from the Select Committee on Emigration*, 1827, Appendix No. 1. *Parl. Pap.* 1827, v.
[3] *Third Report*, p. 48.

they miscalculated the probable duration of wage depression, although their most cherished memories or brightest hopes of adequate payment seem to have reached no higher than twenty shillings a week. But a Paisley weaver may be allowed to put the point not only for Scotland but for all distressed regions in 1827: "It has been utterly impossible for us to pay this year any rent to our landlords, consequently the little property we now possess becomes theirs; and we cannot expect that they will let us houses for another term. We have no other prospect but that we shall be turned to the street, without a blanket to cover either ourselves or children, or implements to work at our trades."[1]

In southern agricultural regions where public unwisdom could only attempt to grapple with an impossible situation by poor law administration which simply intensified the evil, there was less intelligence, perhaps less conscious suffering, little initiative, and almost no co-operation among the dulled minds of farm labourers. But there an idea originated of using, and also saving, poor relief by emigration through mortgaging the poor rates. Proprietors thinking, sometimes unselfishly, for those too wretched to think for themselves, attempted to evade a more resolute method of meeting agricultural problems by despatching their "redundant population" overseas. When the Select Committee asked a former overseer of the Parish of Great Horwood in Buckinghamshire, "You are of opinion that if the poor in that part of the country where you live were made sensible of the independence which, under circumstances of industry, they might obtain as emigrants, there would be no continued disposition on their part to refuse to become emigrants", his answer reflects a kind of dumb despair, the fruit of servitude driven into extremity by social mismanagement, "I should think not, but such a case has never been proposed to them, and I cannot answer for it."[2] The same witness acknowledged in language which sounds more ruthless than was intended that "there are many of them now going to the United States from several parts of our country.... I have this morning seen a friend of mine who says a gentleman in Kent is sending them off by wagon loads now." Their fate seems to have been less dreadful than the method of riddance deserved, for some of them were sending later for "their relatives and friends".[3]

Evils beyond remedy, and regions beyond despair, meet the student of early nineteenth-century Irish emigration. A landed class, usually absentees without a sense of responsibility or shame, and a peasantry with no education, foresight, or economic intelligence, had produced, out of the natural advantages of Ireland, an agricultural system incredibly mismanaged and disastrous. They had, by 1820,

---

[1] Adam Millar to Archibald Campbell, Esq. M.P., *Third Report*, p. 59.
[2] *Select Committee, Second Report*, 1827, *Parl. Pap.* 1827, v, p. 106.
[3] *Ibid.* p. 107.

at any rate, peopled this confusion with at least a million too many inhabitants; no poor law had been provided, and so thoughtlessness and recklessness, Irish and British, had produced a condition beyond parallel in civilised communities at that time.[1] The spectre which haunted and continued to haunt every English ministry, until famine, disease, and panic flight did for England and Ireland what they had insufficient intelligence to do for themselves, was the Irish population question. That was the dominating cause of mass emigration in the earlier nineteenth century, and the reason why governments and colonisers failed to affect the chief currents of emigration.

The Highlands of Scotland presented another variety of motive. It was true, as Lord Selkirk had pointed out in 1806, that the clan system, by its break-down after 1746, threatened to reproduce in the Highlands a situation somewhat similar to that in Ireland. But the population was always far less in numbers; the nature of the soil forbade any sentimental hunger for land; and not only were the clansmen far higher in the possibilities of civilisation than the poor Irish, but their chiefs were usually neither aliens nor absentees. Economic forces, that is the sum total of common selfish tendencies, had displaced clan settlements first by cattle and then by sheep. Not even with kelp and fisheries, and certainly not with ambitious schemes for reclamation of waste lands, could the increasing population be retained in Scotland. Many of the clansmen passed to the Lowlands, now and then, as in David Livingstone's case, to reveal their Norse inclinations to wander at some generations' remove. For the rest, a series of reasonably well-managed transplantations continued to keep the Highland problem well within the limits of rational solution. Individuals like the Rev. Alexander Macdonald and Lord Selkirk, in many other cases the proprietors or chiefs, arranged schemes of co-operative emigration.[2] The existing settlements of those who had arrived in Canada after a first residence in the older American colonies, and a growing number of Gaelic speaking communities scattered over British North America, drew with a fairly constant attraction. Among the petitions summarised for the Select Committee of 1827 is a characteristic document from the proprietor of the island of Coll, illustrative of Highland motives: "Applies on behalf of several thousand souls in the Hebrides for aid towards emigration. He himself last year sent out 300 souls from one of his islands, and he can now spare 1500 from his estates, and would be willing to pay, for a limited number of years, the interest of money expended in their emigration; the emigrants themselves afterwards paying it in an annuity."[3]

[1] *Passim* in the *Reports* from the Select Committees of 1826 and 1827. *Parl. Pap.* 1826, IV, and 1827, V.
[2] *Canada and Its Provinces*, vol. XVII, chapter on "Pioneer Settlements".
[3] Appendix No. 1 to *Third Report*, p. 504.

Men's needs being always stronger than the intelligence of their rulers, it is hardly surprising that the British Government, in the earlier years of the new emigration, was quite unequal to the demands made on it. With unquestionable goodwill the many Colonial Secretaries from Bathurst to Normanby solved some specific problems, made more than the average number of administrative blunders, and, in the long run, were, with their Under-Secretaries, spectators of, rather than actors in, the process. Taken together with the permanent officials, their natural gifts were those of regulation rather than of creation, and allowing to the most competent of them, James Stephen, full credit for his conscientiousness, and to the most earnest of the parliamentary Under-Secretaries, Wilmot Horton and Howick, praise for good intentions and much zeal, they differed from Mrs Partington mainly in that they swept to assist, not to retard the tide. Parliament, which in this matter meant the House of Commons, rather than the Lords, exhibited all the characteristics natural to a democratic institution faced with need for immediate action. They inquired and discussed, did little, and let the rush of emigration carry them along. The majority of them, like their constituents, were indifferent to questions which seemed to affect little their own immediate interests. Colonial debates, whatever the subject, were unpopular. Within the meagre circle of those who cared there were some, like the Chancellor of the Exchequer in 1815, who thought of the direction of emigration mainly as a means of preventing British subjects from passing into the United States.[1] There were passionate opponents like Michael Thomas Sadler who thought "that the best colonies we could plant, with respect to the interests of the agriculture and manufactures of England, were those which might be established in the uncultivated deserts of our European empire";[2] stiff legal opponents like Sir James Graham who held that "the system of emigration was contrary to the spirit of our laws, and opposed to many of our most ancient regulations";[3] and merely confused thinkers, like Joseph Hume, who alternated between suggestions that "it might even be advisable to transport them [unemployed workmen] without their consent", and equally wild and foolish words in condemnation of emigration. Apart from the colonial or emigration enthusiasts, the constructive and intelligent opinions of Parliament on the subject were best expressed by men like Huskisson and Peel, who saw the need for, and usefulness of, emigration, but who also saw, as the enthusiasts did not, the extremely limited scope within which the emigration as a remedy for redundancy would operate.[4] Peel defined his own as "rather a medium view of the question"; holding that a rational system of emigration would lead

[1] Hansard, xxx, 52.
[2] Ibid., Second Series, xxi, 1729.   [3] Ibid. xvi, 299.
[4] Ibid. xvi, debate of 15 February 1827, and xxi, debate on redundant population, 4 June 1829.

to effects the most beneficial to the country by affording facilities to
its impoverished inhabitants of bettering their condition, but that the
relief would be neither immediate nor general.[1] Peel's ultimate conclusions usually coincided with the line of action which Englishmen
actually followed; but although it is difficult to prove him wrong, his
activities were characterised by a kind of leisurely fatalism. He and
his followers were carried onwards helplessly by events, and the
people had generally solved or partially solved their problem before
Government intervened. Besides all this the British Parliament, alike
in its approval and its disapproval of emigration, thought only of the
strictly British point of view, and legislated with the vaguest idea of
what the colonial communities themselves really wanted.

Apart from the sheer pressure of misery on the labouring population, which was the primary motive in emigration, the most important
factor was the stimulus given by a series of individuals. The work of
the more important of these will be dealt with later, but it is impossible to ignore the pioneer and ill-fated efforts just before 1815
of the Earl of Selkirk; the unbalanced but penetrating wisdom of
Robert Gourlay, who not merely turned his later life into a kind of
colonising crusade, but in the introduction to his *Statistical Report of
Upper Canada* foreshadowed all the more vital of Gibbon Wakefield's
conclusions;[2] and the quick imagination of John Galt, whose handling of the Canada Land Company must count as an important
episode in the history of early nineteenth-century colonisation.

The trouble with most of the earlier enthusiasts was that they were
obsessed with single ideas or sets of ideas; that they failed to relate
their own wisdom to that of others; and that lack of balance, and
exaggeration, offended the nice sense of proportion which, if it keeps
the average Englishman from doing anything, at least keeps him
from doing anything actively ridiculous. What could one do but
smile when men like Gourlay argued that "by simple means, and
within 20 years, the Poor Laws of England may become a dead letter
and all need for such in Ireland be done away".[3] The average
politician rejected in such men not wisdom but wisdom without discretion, presented by enthusiasts whose preoccupation with isolated
truths made them bores and simpletons.

It may seem capricious to omit mention of the economists or merely
academic thinkers who made the early nineteenth century a classic
age in economic thought. But, after all, their sphere and their experience were naturally domestic, and they found abundance of
material to work on at home. Besides this they lived in surroundings
sharply separated from the voiceless human misery at home, which
produced emigration, and the bitter fight for life overseas which

[1] Hansard, Second Series, XVI, 505–9.
[2] Mills, R. C., *Colonisation of Australia* (1829–42), pp. 137 *seqq.*
[3] Hansard, Second Series, XVI, 142: Petition from Robert Gourlay.

follow it. At best they were political analysts living in cities and libraries, wise after the event and even less prophetic than the common man. Malthus, whose views on redundant population attracted the attention of all who were grappling with the problems of colonisation, and Macculloch, the contemporary "respectable" economist, lose something of their impressiveness when dragged into the rough country of colonial adventure. They might advise or give evidence before Select Committees, but the resistless current of the great folk-wandering brushed them and their principles aside without apology.

To secure a proper sense of proportion in appreciating the earlier experiments in emigration, the statistics of British and Irish population between 1800 and 1840 must be borne in mind. In 1801 the population of Great Britain had been 10,942,646, and the estimated population of Ireland "nearer five than four millions". By 1821 these figures had increased, in Britain to 14,391,631, and in Ireland to 6,801,827. By 1831 the population of the United Kingdom was over twenty-four millions, to which Ireland contributed nearly a third. In the quarter century from 1815 approximately a million souls had emigrated, of whom, down to 1840, 499,899 went to British North America; 417,765 to the United States; 58,449 to Australasia, and under 10,000 to South Africa. Of the Australian emigrants by far the greater number did not emigrate until after 1836.[1] The vast majority of these emigrants drew no advantage from Government, beyond the information furnished publicly, and the rather inadequate control exerted over the owners and masters of emigrant ships.[2] In 1823, before the rush became uncontrollable, the Government experiments for the year affected a bare thousand, men, women and children, while the mass emigration amounted to 16,387. Even the larger numbers sent out in 1825 were only one-seventh of the emigration of that year. In 1831, when Wilmot Horton's methods were beginning to give place to the ideas of Wakefield, the annual numbers rose to 83,046. In 1847, with every official agency hard at work, and in the midst of a period of colonising propaganda, systematic colonisation sent some 5000 settlers to Australia and New Zealand, while a quarter of a million, mainly Irish, escaped to America as best they could, without the covenanted mercies of the State.[3]

Two witnesses of the highest respectability and importance have left records based on first-hand experience of the hard facts of the earlier emigration as it was conducted, not in blue books and debates, but in real life. In 1838, after eight years of a reforming government in Britain, Lord Durham, in introducing evidence of the entire inadequacy of all attempts to guide the process, expressed his surprise

[1] Johnson, S. C., *op. cit.* Appendix 1, Statistical Tables relating to Emigrants.
[2] See Walpole, K. A. in *Trans. R. Hist. Soc.*, 1931, pp. 197–224.
[3] Johnson, p. 344.

"that emigration of the poorer classes to the Canadas did not entirely cease some years ago" and explained its continuance by the sheer ignorance of what had happened to earlier settlers.[1] In 1847 Lord Elgin, writing as Governor-General to the Secretary of State for the Colonies, drew appalling pictures of the complete failure in control of the Irish emigration of that year. "The immigration which is now taking place", he wrote to Earl Grey, "is a frightful scourge to the province. Thousands upon thousands of poor wretches are coming here, incapable of work, and scattering the seeds of disease and death. Already five or six hundred orphans are accumulated at Montreal, for whose sustenance until they can be put out to service, provision must be made."[2] Nor was it only the ports which felt the scourge of governmental incapacity. In October, when Elgin was riding through what is now Ontario, he spoke of the consequences of this uncontrolled rush affecting the "remote hamlets to which the poor wretches had penetrated carrying with them their disease and pauperism".[3]

The meaning of these facts is obvious. The history of earlier nineteenth-century emigration cannot be written from the ordinary State records of Great Britain, although these give the numbers emigrating. A new movement from the British Isles had begun, which recalls the "great emigration" of the seventeenth century. In great part it evades research; and we are dealing only with the fringe of the subject, while the substantial part lies buried with the errors, sufferings and impotence of some hundreds of thousands, many of whom earned not even the official immortality conveyed by the registration of death.

To this fringe, however, it becomes necessary to turn.

From 1815 to the Irish famine of 1845 three periods may be distinguished in the development of emigration.

The first of these is a time of specially conducted or directed settlements. Something of the story has been told in another volume,[4] since the province of Upper Canada, after 1815, was the favoured region for colonising experiments. It will suffice, so far as British North America is concerned, to say that parties of assisted emigrants from England, Scotland and Ireland were personally conducted to, and assisted in, such settlements as the Talbot colonies, Perth, Lanark and Peterborough. In these years too, after the founding of the Canada Land Company, John Galt made his most interesting and useful experiment in the Huron country. He anticipated Wakefield in the idea of devoting the proceeds of Crown lands to make a fund in aid of emigration, and on the basis of his work in Upper Canada was founded much of the future prosperity of the western part of the pro-

[1] Lord Durham's *Report* (ed. Lucas, C.), II, 243.
[2] *The Elgin-Grey Papers, 1846–56*, vol. I, 58, 59.
[3] *Ibid.* vol. I. Letters with references of this kind between August and October, 1847.
[4] *C.H.B.E.* vol. VI, ch. X (B).

vince. His claims to be regarded as one of the true leaders in emigration may be stated in his own words: "The Canada Company had originated in my suggestions, it was established by my endeavours, organised, in disregard of many obstacles, by my perseverance, and, though extensive and complicated in its scheme, a system was formed by me upon which it could be with ease conducted."[1]

Elsewhere the impact of immigration was much less conspicuous. The movement to Australia was very slight, if the transportation of convicts, some 2447 a year, be ignored. In 1821 there were only 320 immigrants, and not even the founding of Western Australia raised the numbers very high. Until 1823 there was a gentle flow, carefully guided by government, to Cape Colony. Benjamin Moodie, assisted by the imperial authorities, took out some 200 Scottish mechanics in 1817—one of the rare cases in which apparently the settlers kept their bargain made in Britain; after 1819, at Somerset's recommendation, nearly 5000 individuals, at one time or another down to 1822, settled on very favourable terms and apparently with success, although not without promise of trouble from their Kaffir neighbours; and in 1823 John Ingram, conducting, at the Cape, an experiment parallel to that of Peter Robinson in Canada, introduced 452 Irish men, women and children, who according to credible report "soon raised themselves above the rank of servants".[2]

But already the second period had commenced, the years when Wilmot Horton did his best to guide British emigration. Horton's best monument lies in the massive volumes of Emigration Reports published in 1826 and 1827. For the rest, he took his Under-Secretaryship of State for the Colonies very seriously, wrote a multitude of letters and pamphlets, and directed, at second hand, two quite useful experiments in emigration, but the recording angel's judgment was anticipated by the Imperial Parliament, which failed to take him quite seriously, and, having given him some freedom in the Select Committees on Emigrants, refused to pass any of his more elaborate measures.

Obsessed, and not unnaturally so, with the Malthusian idea of a redundant population, Wilmot Horton had convinced himself that emigration offered itself as the most natural solution to his difficulties. England and Scotland demanded, and Ireland clamoured for, some remedy for chronic unemployment. In Ireland there was no poor law; in Scotland the mere rudiments of a system, and in England pauper legislation offered not assistance so much as additional difficulties. It was his conviction that the removal of a mere section of the distressed population would assist the fortunes of the entire agri-

---

[1] Galt, J., *Autobiography*, II, 157.
[2] Theal, G. M., *History of South Africa since 1795*, III, 219–24; 226–39, 421–2. It will be apparent from this chapter that South African facts enter far less into a study of the emigration and land policy of the time than do those of British North America and Australasia. Other issues there proved more exciting, if not more important.

cultural and industrial population. Sometimes he calculated on an emigration initiated by a Government loan but ultimately financed through repayment in the form of annuities by the emigrants assisted. Sometimes he thought that the parishes might accomplish his desires through mortgaging their rates, incidentally thereby diminishing their expenses; in effect he relied on both methods.[1] He thought little of the communities to which he meant to consign his emigrants, but he did understand that his responsibility extended beyond the mere emigration of redundant paupers to their actual settlement, and, in a vague way, by means of his system of repayments, he anticipated Wakefield's balance of capital and labour in the colonies. One of the conclusions of the *Third Report*, in 1827, was that "a principle of supply may be adjusted, at an early period, under which the Colonists of the Cape and of New South Wales and Van Diemen's Land may receive precisely that proportion of labour which is suited to their wants, while at the same time the independence which an indefinite supply of fertile land provides for the labourer, after a few years of exertion, will tend progressively to transmute all such labourers into colonists, and to create fresh demands for labour from the population of the mother country".[2] Apart from more grandiose plans, his most ambitious practical scheme was based on a loan of £1,140,000, by which in three years 19,000 families, i.e. a population of 95,000, would be transferred to the colonies, there to repay Great Britain from the surplus wealth created by their efforts.[3]

Horton's two efforts at legislation failed, and some were of opinion that he helped to kill the very anaemic interest which existed in the subject. He must receive credit for two legitimate and scientifically calculated experiments in pauper emigration, in 1823 and 1825; and Lord Howick, in an unsuccessful measure in 1831 which borrowed most of its ideas from his predecessor in office and interests, paid a reasonable tribute to the man whose example had inspired him.[4] If slightness were not in politics the sin against the spirit, one might hold that Wilmot Horton never received, nor will receive, his due. But the limitations of all that he did are self-apparent. At a time when emigration demanded first-rate powers of exposition in its advocate, he impressed his contemporaries as a bore. He thought mainly of pauper emigration, nor did he distinguish, among the paupers, between the fit and the unfit; and he failed to see the unsuitability of most of those whom he meant to benefit for the kind of redemption which he was providing. He was ridiculously optimistic as to the possibilities of financing his measures through repayments by settlers and from poor rates. He never envisaged to himself the extent of the evil for which his remedies were so ludicrously inadequate, and he had the Home official's natural incapacity for thinking of the colonies as anything more than dumping grounds for

[1] Mills, *op. cit.* pp. 27–52.   [2] *Third Report, on Emigration*, June 1827, p. 37.
[3] *Ibid.* pp. 18–22.   [4] Hansard, Third Series, II, 880.

the failures of English civilisation. Charles Buller was unfair in labelling his work as "shovelling out paupers";[1] but his real inadequacy is revealed when placed in juxtaposition with the opposition of Michael Thomas Sadler, who erred even more flagrantly on the other side of the emigration question, but whose passionate realisation of what the poor were and what they felt, turns Wilmot Horton's best plans into something more futile than moonshine. Howick, then, when he pronounced his eulogy of Horton in 1831, was really composing the obituary notice of the man, his plans and his failures, though Horton afterwards did some very good work as Governor of Ceylon, 1831–7.

A third period, that of the systematic colonisers, had already begun. Much that the group accomplished lies outside the province of emigration and land settlement, but since Edward Gibbon Wakefield's main thesis concerned both of these subjects, an estimate of his work finds here its natural place. It will have been noted that in co-operative emigration and land settlement the main bodies of intelligent settlers were of Scottish origin, as, later, it will be obvious that Ireland provided the passive suffering crowd whose numbers constituted the most impressive feature in the emigration of the century. In this third period, which witnessed the creation of new fields of colonisation, in addition to settlements in established colonies —which indeed was one of pioneering in the proper sense of the word—the dominant spirits were mainly English. One might venture on the generalisation that English pioneers of the governing classes were as supreme in this field of creative colonisation as Highland and Lowland Scots were in the effective communal organisation of territory already marked out for settlement, but not yet settled.

The starting point is somewhere about 1829, when Wakefield's gaol reflections began to take definite shape in the "Letters from Sydney" which he published in the *Morning Chronicle*.[2] That year, as Wakefield's ill-natured and inaccurate criticisms help his readers to remember, also saw Thomas Peel make an effort at settling Western Australia, which places him, in spite of his failure, in this new class of "creative emigrants".[3] It was the first feeble effort of the nineteenth century to give England new colonies, to people these with a community neither pauper nor convict, but representative of the English community and to create, as a first essential to success, a labouring class, changing perhaps in the individuals, but always present to make capital and land living factors in the colony. It was all astonishingly English. As Canada still retains a certain Scottish or even Highland flavour, Australasia, which was created by Englishmen, still (except in Otago) remains distinctly English in tradition. Begun by Phillip, explored by Grey, Sturt and Eyre, advertised by Wakefield, taken hold of by English gentlemen, Australia and New Zealand carry on the

---

[1] Hansard, Third Series, LXVIII, 522.
[2] In book form, *A Letter from Sydney*, 1829. [3] Mills, ch. III.

story begun under Elizabeth and developed by the English Puritans.

Colonial historians have been more anxious to explain Wakefield's published opinions than to estimate what he actually accomplished. The opinions are obvious enough; for Wakefield, whose ideas were fruitful rather than varied, proclaimed them with unblushing repetition in circular, letter, pamphlet and book, from the Sydney letters down to the *Art of Colonisation*. The demand of a price for land sufficiently high to restrain speculative buying and premature acquisition of land by labourers, and sufficiently moderate to hinder no legitimate purchaser; the employment of the proceeds mainly as an emigration fund for the maintenance of a steady supply of labour to the colonies; the careful selection of men, and especially of women, of the right ages and classes as emigrants; the concentration of thought, not on the community relieved of its redundant population, but on the community about to be created—that, Wakefield thought, was the true evangel of colonisation.[1]

Consideration of his views on land sales may for the moment be postponed. But what were his distinctive contributions to the emigration problems of his day?

Whatever he may have intended, it is plain that in practice he troubled little about the "redundancy" question. The additions to the free population of Australia between 1836, when South Australia began, down to 1846, amount in eleven years only to 103,348. Or, to put the matter more graphically, in the chief year of stress, 1847, when the redundant population took matters into its own hands by passing, 250,000 strong, across the Atlantic, the southern colonies received not quite 5000 settlers.[2] Clearly Wakefield's practice had little to do with Wilmot Horton's dreams or Malthusian fears.

He was really bent on "colonisation for its own sake". With as little practical gift for pioneering as Sir Walter Raleigh himself, he aspired like Raleigh to found new kingdoms overseas; and whatever other conjectural parents South Australia and New Zealand may claim, they exist very largely because Wakefield planned that they should exist.

He held, too, that the emigrants to such new communities should possess, in simplified and modifiable form, something like the social strata of the Mother Country. In Canada, Highland communities revealed the democratic possibilities of the clan system with the chief removed. In Australia and New Zealand, Gibbon Wakefield hoped to see capital and labour persist, only in rational and humane form, and with labour easily able to transform itself into capital. It was this social conventionality of Wakefield which for the first time made emigration respectable. His *New British Province of South Australia*[3] held out inducements not only to ambitious labourers, but also to the

---

[1] *Passim* in all his colonial writings.   [2] Exactly 4949. Johnson, *op. cit.* Appendix 1.
[3] E.g. *The New British Province of South Australia* (1834), ch. IV.

struggling and aspiring middle class, to "young men of good fortune and what is called mean birth", and even, although with hesitation, to children and grandchildren of the highest families in the land.[1] It was as sound an idea as any colonial projector ever conceived; it was bound to succeed. South Australia not only started with a Masonic Lodge, a newspaper and a social tone; it had churches with pews to let, and if one may believe an early chronicle,[2] in the English Church at least, every sitting was taken in one day. This was the beginning of the period in which Dr Arnold of Rugby had dreams of his later years spent in an Australian bishopric; when Charles Kingsley and Thomas Hughes made these colonies natural resorts for heroes and heroines; and Thomas Carlyle, who used relentlessly his Scottish prerogative of preaching to exclusively English audiences ideas conceived in Scotland, pictured the leaders of the people finding a new vocation in organising some kind of "Emigration Service".[3]

Wakefield achieved this result because he was an advertiser of genius. As has been said, he was not specially prolific of ideas, but no man ever succeeded more perfectly in forcing on the public what ideas he had. Without any foolish self-consciousness, he spoke with that kind of certainty which always convinces the British public. Reading them coldly, a hundred years after they were written, one sees flaws in the little trade circulars which he published to make men emigrate to South Australia and New Zealand; but in 1834 and 1837 the glamour of Wakefield's eloquence concealed their weaknesses. He was able to delude men into doing the right thing, because he had first deluded himself. Like another incredible coloniser of the period, Wilkins Micawber, "one might have supposed him a child of the wilderness, long accustomed to live out of the confines of civilisation, and about to return to his native wilds".

Besides this he proved himself, within strict limits, a unique centre of political influence. The colonies were founded, emigrants of the right sort, and in the correct numbers, were despatched, communities of the most wholesome nature sprang up, partly because this remarkable man gathered round him an informal and sometimes refractory staff of influential public men. Some of them followed him; others co-operated; and still more borrowed ideas from him while rejecting his system as a whole. There were systematic colonisers like Howick whose constructive policy was largely Wakefieldian; others assisted his projects by the opposition which they offered to them. But all had felt the stimulus of Wakefield's enthusiasm, and that stimulus converted them from officials and amateurs into statesmen.

With the Wakefield period came the creation of the Board of Colonial Land and Emigration Commissioners. From 1840 until, in

---

[1] *Ibid.* pp. 126, 127–9.
[2] Stephens, John, *The History of South Australia*, 2nd edition (1839), p. 222.
[3] Carlyle, T., *Past and Present*, Bk. IV, ch. III.

1873, the Board of Trade took over from the commissioners the relics of their duties, this body played an important official part as delegates of the Colonial Office in emigration affairs; and their annual reports provide the drab epic of the great years of the nineteenth-century exodus. A temporary commission had come into existence in 1831, with T. F. Elliot of the Colonial Office as Secretary, and had furnished information, provided loans, and substantially reduced the fares to Australia.[1] To it the South Australian Commission had succeeded, men whom Wakefield might petulantly call "ignorant and careless amateurs", but who nevertheless owed their existence to Wakefield's projects; and, in 1837, T. F. Elliot was appointed Agent-General for Emigration under the Colonial Office. The *Report* of the Earl of Durham, and, more definitely, Wakefield's appendix on Land and Emigration, forced the Whig ministry to undertake specific measures for the control of the whole field of emigration. So it happened that, in January 1840, Elliot, Torrens and Edward Villiers took over all duties previously exercised by other bodies and became the Board of Colonial Land and Emigration Commissioners. It was their business to provide easily accessible information about the colonies, to control the sale of waste lands, to direct the emigration for which land sales provided money, and to superintend the application of the Passengers' Acts which protected the emigrants on their voyage. From the nature of their office the commissioners were bound to find that, as self-government became real in the colonies, their authority and activities must diminish, but this diminution in no way reflected on the usefulness or energy of the Board. It was rather a measure of the success of directed emigration. The annual reports contain a full account of their activities as well as the record of their lingering decease. From the outset Canada lay outside the sphere of their activities, although information from British North America was furnished with more or less fullness. By 1855 the provinces of New Zealand had their own emigration agents at work, and a year later Victoria gave notice that the Board must be prepared to surrender its functions to a colonial agency. So the process of decentralisation went on, until in 1865 the report for the year confessed that "the only Australian emigrants of whom the selection is now in our hands are female domestic servants for Victoria, and a limited number of mechanics, agriculturists and female servants for Queensland, and the emigrants sent to Western Australia out of the Parliamentary vote".

Now and then came a flicker of fresh energy, as when in 1859 the commissioners undertook the conveyance to India of the women and children of soldiers serving there, and the Cape Parliament requested them to manage the entire business of emigration for them—although

---

[1] *Report from the Commissioners of Emigration*, August, 1832. *Parl. Pap.* 1831–2, XXXII.

in the latter case the reason given was that the affair was too limited for the employment of a separate agency. But by 1860 they were beginning to outlive their usefulness. So, when the administration of the Passengers' Acts was transferred to the Board of Trade, the commissioners' reports came to an end in 1873, and they themselves, quietly and after a decent lapse of time, disappeared in 1878. During the forty-three years of their effective existence they were directly responsible for all systematic efforts made in the control of emigration, and in a dry and arithmetical way they wrote the history of the great uncontrolled movement of these years.[1]

In many ways the founding of the colony of New Zealand was the most characteristic episode in this stage of controlled and systematic emigration, for it provides the nearest approach attained to successfully accomplished intention in colonisation. No doubt even in the years before the Irish famine uncontrolled emigration, especially to North America, was always greater in amount, and sometimes immensely greater, than the movement led by the systematic colonisers. Besides this, it is plain that neither in South Australia nor in New Zealand were the plans and principles of Wakefield and his friends carried out as they desired, nor were the results of their efforts always those on which they had calculated. But an entirely new class of emigrants answered their appeal in considerable numbers. The division and sale of lands proceeded according to a fairly regular scheme, and, in spite of expenses greater than had been expected, and disputes between the New Zealand Land Company and the Imperial Government, a colony was established after an interval of time amazingly short and at a cost ridiculously small.

The most notable achievement of the founders of New Zealand was that they induced a non-emigrating class to emigrate. Wakefield was under no illusions as to the difficulties here. "The whole emigration to Upper Canada and New Zealand", he wrote in 1849, "furnishes no instance of the ultimate settlement of a gentleman's family with satisfaction to themselves and their friends at home."[2] Yet although there existed great reluctance in England, disappointment in New Zealand, and, even where success was reached, an impatience to return to the mother country, many of what may be called the governing, middle, and professional classes emigrated; many remained overseas, and, of those who returned, some had done real work before they left. Edward Jerningham Wakefield's companions in his pioneering days in New Zealand included men of wealth and authority—at an early day in New Zealand society there was an aristocracy as well as a democracy, with its "Wakefield Club" and social functions.[3] When Thomas Arnold, son of the great Rugby

[1] *Reports of the Colonial Land and Emigration Commissioners*, in *Parl. Pap.* 1842–73.
[2] Wakefield, E. G., *Art of Colonisation* (1914 ed.), p. 220.
[3] Wakefield, E. J., *Adventure in New Zealand from 1839 to 1844*, vol. i.

headmaster, began his wandering career with an attempt to cultivate his father's holdings in New Zealand, he sailed thither in company with Captain Cargill, formerly of the Connaught Rangers, and a most respectable contingent of Scottish Presbyterians, and his colonial friends included Alfred Domett, some army officers, and sons of English landowners.[1] In the first group of 512 which sailed to colonise Canterbury in the South Island, there were 363 cabin passengers;[2] and among the settlers of the next decade was Samuel Butler, who not only played Bach's fugues on the piano which he had carted to his hut in "Mesopotamia", but who returned to Britain in 1864 with his original £4400 increased to £8000 and invested in New Zealand at 10 per cent.[3] It is perhaps the most interesting fact, here, that in the days when Lord Dalhousie's hand was sore on Sir Henry Lawrence he too thought of New Zealand as a refuge for his later years. Numerically this "gentleman" class might be negligible, but in at least two new colonies they assisted to success the efforts of Wakefield and his friends in controlled and systematic emigration.

Meanwhile a fresh chapter in the transfer of population had begun, the Irish exodus after the Potato Famine of 1846. It would be worse than useless to attempt an exact description of the conditions in Ireland which led to the most revolutionary change in nineteenth-century imperial history. But it is worthy of note that Daniel O'Connell, when he opposed the Whig Poor Law proposals for Ireland, urged Melbourne to spend something like the twenty millions, which had recently been spent on freeing slaves, in a heroic measure of Irish emigration before conditions in Ireland should end in absolute disaster. It was Lecky's grave judgment "that the true source of the savage hatred of England that animates great bodies of Irishmen on either side of the Atlantic" was not so much the penal laws, the Rebellion, or the Union, as "the great clearances and the vast un-aided emigrations that followed the famine".[4] Thomas Carlyle's savage and indignant description of Westport Poorhouse in 1849 gives first-hand evidence of what English legislation produced in place of systematic settlement overseas. "Human swinery has here reached its acme, happily; 30,000 paupers in this union, population supposed to be about 60,000.... Abomination of desolation; what can you make of it! Outdoor quasi-*work*: three or four hundred big hulks of fellows tumbling about with shares, picks, and barrows, 'levelling' the end of their workhouse hill;...five or six hundred boys and lads pretending to break stones. Can it be a *charity* to keep men alive on these terms!"[5]

It was one of those occasions when, Government having really

---

[1] Arnold, T., *Passages in a Wandering Life*, chs. III–IV.
[2] *Colonial Land and Emigration Commissioners. Report for 1851.*
[3] Jones, H. Festing, *Samuel Butler*, vol. I, chs. VI–VII.
[4] Lecky, W. E. H., *Leaders of Public Opinion in Ireland*, II, 184.
[5] Carlyle, T., *Reminiscences of My Irish Journey in 1849*, pp. 201–2.

demitted office, the people blindly and with fearful sacrifices stumbled towards the only possible solution to their troubles.[1] They departed *en masse* for North America. For once, the official arithmetic becomes melodramatic. From 129,851 in 1846, the emigration numbers shot up to 258,270 in 1847. In the eight years from 1847 over two million and a half emigrants left the British Islands, the *annus mirabilis* being 1852 with 368,264.[2] Doubtless many Englishmen and Scotsmen, some of them in misery, were included in these numbers, but the overwhelming mass was Irish. In March 1851 the census showed a fall in the population of Ireland of 1,659,330, and the fall was to continue.[3]

Faced with so great a tragedy, even the most competent and the most benevolent could do little. Landlords like Lord Lansdowne arranged their own system of assisted emigration.[4] The Board of Emigration Commissioners tinkered with the Passengers' Act, administered an increased vote to assist indigent emigrants to Canada, added new officials in Ireland and at Liverpool, and assisted the passengers of vessels which put back in distress. But the outward movement in panic brushed them and their efforts aside. In the rush of 1847 more than 6000 died on the passage across, and quarantine stations, hospitals and the roads to settlements in Canada were encumbered with the sick and dying of the great mass movement.[5]

After the first wild rush was over, the expatriated Irish began to work their own system of assisted emigration. Few events in the chequered history of Ireland do more credit to that incalculable people than the assistance which the exiles sent back to bring their relatives to America. "It is not unfair to assume", said the Commissioners' *Report* of 1849, "that three-quarters of the whole expense of the emigration from Ireland last year was defrayed by those who emigrated in previous years." By 1862 the sum thus transmitted from America to Ireland had amounted to twelve million pounds. These events changed the course of British history in the nineteenth century; and, since it is clear that, from 1846 onwards, the Irish emigration was even at lowest comparable in numbers to that from England, the imperial and international implications of the movement both for the British Empire and the United States must form an inspiring theme for the social historians of the twentieth century.

It seems relevant to ask what became of these armies of the Irish poor, more especially in the region which chiefly attracted them, the United States. John Mitchel, whose *Jail Journal* records his impressions in 1853–4, was surprised at the way in which the masses faded into the general population of the United States. "They get

---

[1] Written strictly with reference to the Irish emigration, and more especially with reference to the main flow across the Atlantic.

[2] The actual distribution of these numbers was, U.S.A., 244,261, B.N.A., 32,876, Australia, 87,881. The effects of the discoveries of gold in California and in Australia must be allowed for, but the numbers for Ireland unaffected by gold rushes were great. See *Colonial Land and Emigration Commissioners' Reports*, especially that of 1853.   [3] *Ibid.* 1848–55.

[4] Trench, W. S., *Realities of Irish Life*, ch. VIII.   [5] *C. L. and E. C. Report*, 1848.

railroad cars", he said, "on the very evening of their arrival, and are whirled away to where loving friends are awaiting them on the banks of the Wabash, or hard by some bright lake on Michigan; or else they get immediate occupation in the city itself where there is always a fine demand for broad shoulders and willing hands."[1] The general evidence is less rose-coloured. Canadian experience proved that there they provided unskilled labour for the new public works and railway construction of that period. American official evidence is clear that "three-fourths of the Irish stay in New England and the Middle states (principally in Massachusetts, New York and Pennsylvania) where the commercial and manufacturing interests are seated; and they are found in the South and West only where there are great public works in construction".[2] They began, at once and naturally enough, to prove a source of anxiety to the Canadian and British Governments, and they provided the Fenians with willing members. When the American Civil War broke out they joined freely on both sides, and in the judgment of a competent authority, "the Irish regiments were in no whit less trustworthy than those purely American".[3]

Alike in dramatic quality and far-reaching political consequences the Irish exodus occupies the central place in the history of nineteenth-century emigration. It is well to remember that not until 1869 did the numbers of the Irish emigration fall below those from England.[4]

The remaining years of the period contain nothing so significant as the efforts of the Wakefield school, or the mass movement from Ireland. The history of emigration to 1873 is not unlike a register recording the alternation in Great Britain and Ireland between prosperity and distress. In spite of the comfort and security of Victorian days among the possessing classes, there were always three-quarters of the population so insecurely established that any decline in national prosperity sent a far from negligible margin overseas to find there some means of keeping alive. Happily for the social peace of the country there was still a great demand for labour, especially in the United States, and only an incipient movement to protect overseas settlements from the ill effects of unrestricted immigration.

The discovery of gold in Australia for some years varied the normal course of events. The first stream of adventurers in New South Wales and Victoria came naturally from the surrounding colonies, 8000 leaving Van Diemen's Land in 1851 for the diggings.[5] But the total emigration to Australia in 1852, 87,881 in number, reflected the new movement, and the figures of such a year as 1857, in which 36,000 unassisted emigrants stand beside 24,000 assisted,[6] prove that the

---

[1] Mitchel, J., *Jail Journal*, 372.
[2] *Report of Superintendent of Census* (U.S.A.) for 1 December 1852.
[3] Henderson, G. F. R., *Life of Stonewall Jackson*, II, 340.
[4] *C. L. and E. C. Report*, 1870.   [5] *Ibid.*, 1852.
[6] *Ibid.*, 1858.

character as well as the numbers of Australian emigration had for the moment changed. A similar discovery of gold in New Zealand resulted in a very marked increase of the inflow of population there after 1861.

For the rest, the history of emigration reflects more or less the social history of the United Kingdom. In the 'fifties a rise in prosperity kept labourers so well off that they were little inclined to seek a doubtful future overseas; while at the end of the period, about 1869, distress in England raised the emigration from England once more above that from Ireland. The greater events in Europe and America had their natural effects on emigration. The Crimean War and the Indian Mutiny, affecting the emigrating class through increased recruiting, lowered the numbers for these years, although in 1857 a number of volunteers from the German legion were sent out to South Africa and settled on the Eastern frontier.[1] In addition to recruiting, commercial crises in Canada and the United States, distress in Australia, and prosperity in the United Kingdom lowered the numbers; and, about this time, the emigration commissioners began to notice the return of men "who having acquired prosperity have come back to enjoy it in the mother country".[2]

A little later the official reports record a new feature in the passenger lists from British ports—a marked increase of foreigners travelling through Britain for destinations mainly in the United States and Canada. These came chiefly from Teutonic and Scandinavian countries, as many as 13,000 Norwegians, Swedes and Danes out of a total Canadian list of 30,000 passing to British North America in 1867. By 1869 the numbers had mounted to over 65,000, and in 1872 to 79,000. Those interested in Bismarckian statesmanship will note with interest that for 1870 there was a decrease in the foreign outflow of over 17,000, and that the decrease "took place not in the six months during which the Franco-Prussian war was in progress, but in the six months which preceded".[3]

As the Irish flood subsided, and the new colonies more and more assumed responsibility alike for land revenues and immigration policy, the reports of the commissioners on which this account is mainly based declined in size and importance. But just before the end, when leisure from serious duties provided the commissioners with intervals for reflection, they summarised the events which they had witnessed and, in a small measure, controlled. Their summaries reveal to what extent the Victorian era deserves to be called the great age of colonisation. Out of rather more than four millions who passed from Britain to North America between 1847 and 1869, practically all had gone unassisted by Government, and of the three and a half millions who travelled steerage, the passage money

---

[1] *C. L. and E. C. Report*, 1857.   [2] *Ibid.*, 1859.
[3] *Ibid.*, 1871.

amounted to £15,000,000. In other words the people of Great Britain and Ireland, aided by their friends in North America, had furnished a subvention for emigration amounting to £650,000 a year. In addition to this the Board had provided 1088 ships carrying 339,338 emigrants, colonial funds providing well over £4,000,000 for their fares. The Government of Great Britain could at least congratulate itself on the fact that it had witnessed a revolution without needless expense to itself. Whether the boasts of strict Manchester men, in these days with Bright and Gladstone at their head, will stand the scrutiny of a less orthodox economic age may be doubted. The advocates of financial economy have usually ignored those occasions on which it is more profitable to spend money in relieving clamant national needs than to allow it to collect in the pockets of private individuals. To a proposal to relieve acute distress in London in 1869 by expenditure on emigration the official answer was: "The proposal was resisted on the ground that such a grant would put an end to the contributions from private sources by which emigration is now carried on; that it would impose on the class who pay taxes an unnecessary burden; and that the better class of labourers would not emigrate, while a pauper emigration would be refused by the colonies and the United States."[1] The answer cannot easily be refuted. Between 1815 and 1872 there passed from the United Kingdom 7,561,285 souls, about a million and a half to Canada, four millions to the United States, one million to Australasia, and not quite two hundred thousand elsewhere—an astonishing achievement for the common people, who paid the cost in money, labours, sorrows, sickness and death. Doubtless, on the hard terms which nature exacts, the conditions which prevailed during the folk-wandering were the only possible conditions, human wisdom and goodness being, as they are, limited. But it seems strange for any government or academic school of thought to exalt their and our impotence into a moral principle, and to impute to themselves virtue for having adhered strictly to a *laissez-faire* policy. It seems rather occasion for the melancholy confession that government goes only a little way, and that, after our inconsiderable energies have exhausted themselves, men like the rest of animate creation are at the mercy of incalculable powers which indeed provide answers to the problems raised by human heedlessness, but at a price which only Calvinistic theologians or unflinching pessimists can contemplate without dismay.

There were, however, two regions in which a government concerned with emigration could not follow a policy of *laissez-faire*: the transport, by sea, of emigrants, since the conditions of life on board ship made crowded and ill-regulated voyages occasions of disease and death; and the granting and sale of land where the Imperial Govern-

[1] *C. L. and E. C. Report*, 1870.

ment, being by far the greatest landowner in the world, had perforce to conduct the whole business of land transfers, registering its decisions in Statutes of the Realm and Orders-in-Council.

Legislation in the form of Passengers' Acts began with a statute in 1803,[1] in part inspired by the Highland Society. That Act was called for because of the hardships suffered by passengers on emigrant ships, and because it had become necessary to regulate the numbers, and safeguard the barest necessities of life to the emigrants. As the importance of emigration traffic grew, defects in the Act revealed themselves, and there was great activity and some controversy in the years between 1820 and 1842. Experimental legislation in 1823 and 1825 was cancelled by an Act in 1827 which marked the temporary victory of extreme *laissez-faire* views on the transportation of emigrants. But the results of unrestrained selfishness revealed themselves so instantaneously that 1828 saw a new and simpler statute passed, in which the really effective change was that the Colonial Office took over the responsibility of administration from the Customs officials; and a comprehensive Act of 1842 summarised the lessons of 20 years' experience, and gave the new Board of Land and Emigration Commissioners authority for vigorous enforcement of its conditions.[2]

The substance of the statutes was dictated by the natural features of life on board ship. The number of passengers per vessel must be restricted; the ships tested and proved seaworthy; the supplies of food and water guaranteed; the owners and captains bound down to fulfil their duties. When the regulations were evaded by emigrant vessels which sailed from ports free from inspection, it became necessary to name certain recognised ports of departure. Lists of passengers must be delivered to the chief officer of customs; and surgeons provided for all vessels carrying over one hundred people. Like all novel legislation, the earlier Passengers' Acts were honoured at least as much in the breach as in the observance. For no system of laws is any stronger than the machinery provided for its enforcement, and passenger legislation, like factory legislation, depended for its efficiency on competent inspection. Here as in most other colonial matters, Lord Durham's *Report* was a decisive event. Although the comprehensive Act of 1835 seemed to have safeguarded emigrants, and although official reports congratulated their compilers on the fact that "every effort had been made for the ease and safety of their transit", Durham, Wakefield and their informants revealed conditions of the most hopeless confusion and waste of life. In almost every department regulations had been violated. Filthy ships, ill-ventilated and without decent sanitation, had bred diseases which did not cease with the voyage. Numbers were in excess of the legal limits, lists of passengers

[1] 43 Geo. III, c. 56.
[2] Walpole, K. A., *Emigration to British North America under the early Passenger Acts*. An unpublished thesis in the Library of the University of London, summarised in *Trans. R. Hist. Soc.* 1931, pp. 197–224.

were carelessly or intentionally falsified; so-called doctors exhibited an ignorance which was only equalled by their presumption; and provisions and water often ran short, or were supplied by captains at famine prices. One sentence, quoted from the most responsible authority at Quebec, stamped itself on the minds of all the readers of the *Report*: "I am almost at a loss for words to describe the state in which the emigrants frequently arrive," wrote Dr Morris, the inspecting physician of the port of Quebec. "With a few exceptions the state of the ships was quite abominable, so much so that the harbour-master's boatmen had no difficulty at the distance of gunshot, either when the wind was favourable or in a dead calm, in distinguishing by the odour alone a crowded emigrant ship."[1]

As direct consequences of the *Report* followed the creation of the Board of Land and Emigration Commissioners, whose duties, down to 1873, included the administration of passengers' legislation, and a new and stricter Passengers' Act in 1842. Judging from the facts of Atlantic traffic the results seem to have been quickly beneficial. The death rate per hundred of those embarked fell from 1·019 in 1840 to 0·38 in 1843.[2] Successful actions were taken against captains or owners exceeding the limit of passengers, against the purveyors of unwholesome provisions, and against the fraudulent agents who tried to fleece the ignorant before sailing. The new efficiency of control may be best illustrated from a typical case of assistance rendered to unfortunates in 1843. In July the *Catherine* sailed from Tobermory in Mull for Cape Breton and Quebec with about 220 adult passengers on board. After five weeks at sea she put into port at Belfast in a very leaky condition. Officials under the Board provided a store for the reception of the distressed Highlanders, and strictly examined the methods by which the master of the vessel had distributed supplies. In less than a fortnight the *John and Robert*, a good vessel well supplied, cleared out of port apparently with most of the original passengers and landed them at a harbour in the maritime provinces and at Quebec in good health. Since the emigrants in Quebec were all destitute, the emigration authorities there forwarded them at the expense of the department to Toronto and Glengarry.[3]

Discrimination must be made between the more strictly controlled and assisted traffic to Australia and New Zealand, and the busier but less official traffic across the North Atlantic. It may be assumed that on the vessels, about 1100 in number, which carried the assisted emigration to Australia, New Zealand and the Cape between 1847 and 1869, conditions were strictly in accordance with regulations.[4] Certainly on such model voyages as those in which Edward Jerningham Wakefield, Thomas Arnold and Samuel Butler took part, something more than mere legal comfort was provided. "I have had the

[1] Lord Durham's *Report* (ed. Lucas), II, 243.
[2] *C. L. and E. C. Report*, 1844.
[3] *Ibid.*, 1844.
[4] *Ibid.*, 1870.

getting up and management of our choir", wrote the author of *The Way of All Flesh*, at the end of his journey. "We practise three or four times a week; we chant the *Venite*, *Glorias*, and *Te Deums*, and sing our hymns. I have two basses, two tenors, one alto and lots of girls, and the singing certainly is better than you would hear in nine country places out of ten."

A certain notoriety attached to the experiment made by Mr Vere Foster in 1850 of sailing in the emigrant ship *Washington* to obtain "an insight into the condition and prospects of Irish emigrants from the time of their leaving this country".[1] His general charges were that the passengers were treated with needless harshness by the officers; that provisions were issued capriciously and negligently; that the medical inspection had consisted of the questions: "What's your name? Are you well? Hold out your tongue. All right." He thought the sanitary conveniences filthy and attributed the death of twelve children through dysentery to "the want of proper nourishing food". But the captain of the vessel denied the accuracy of the indictment, and the commissioners did not feel confident enough to take action. At the end of the period, after a Royal Commission in 1851, and legislation in 1852, 1853 and 1855, conditions had changed completely from the wretched confusion which Lord Durham had reported. An unofficial body, calling itself "the sanitary commission of *The Lancet*", published in 1873 the results of an inspection of vessels based on the Liverpool trade, which proved that in that region at least there was little cause for complaint.[2] They thought that the separation of the sexes might be more strictly regulated; that the hospitals and sanitation and ventilation could be improved; and that the duties and powers of the emigration medical officers ought to be increased. "But", they added, "we are bound and indeed very glad to record our strong sense of the active and intelligent way in which the present system is worked both by government officials and by the shipowners."

Meanwhile, on the routes both to Australia and to America, new mechanical developments were creating improvements more naturally and quickly than statutes or inspectors could. By 1840 Samuel Cunard had begun his great steamship company, and his Atlantic "liners" were quickly followed by those of other companies. The length of the voyage was reduced by three-quarters, and better and larger vessels carried greater numbers with but a tithe of the old discomforts. The transference from sail to steam on the American route took place with startling speed. By 1863, 44 per cent. of the emigrants crossed in steamships; in 1867, 93 per cent.; and recognised points of departure like the Clyde and Liverpool ceased altogether to send their pas-

[1] Copy of a letter addressed to the Land and Emigration Commissioners by Lord Hobart, *A. and P.* 1851, *Parl. Pap.* 1851, XL (198).
[2] *A Report on emigrant ships* (London, 1873).

sengers to America by sailing ships. Here at any rate, one must conclude, the results of carefully planned legislation seconded by strict administration, and, towards the end, supported by advances in mechanical science, had done much to minimise the sufferings of emigration.

Equal in importance with the emigration from Britain of the "redundant population" was the settlement of the population on the waste lands of the colonies. But here the British Government occupied a position of unusual complexity and difficulty. Although the average Cabinet and Parliament consisted largely of landowners, the experience at their disposal was English and undemocratic; the agents through whom their measures became operative were far removed from their control; and the needs and novel circumstances of the pioneering population were unusually difficult to appreciate and remedy. Many of the factors which had already aggravated the Irish land question were present in this new situation, and threatened to create an equally grave land question in all the greater colonies. It was indeed a fortunate circumstance that successive concessions of self-government ultimately removed the responsibility of land settlement from British hands, and left the colonies to make their own mistakes. The period during which colonial land policy affected the ministries of the United Kingdom ended with the grants of Home Rule to the great colonies: in the North American provinces between 1840 and 1852; in Australia (without Western Australia) after 1855; in New Zealand after 1852; in the Cape (without Natal) in 1872.[1]

Before the years of the great Emigration Committees and *Reports* it would be misleading to speak of anything like an informed and consistent land policy, although certain general ideas had already been appreciated in Great Britain. From first to last the influence of men on the spot like Dorchester, Sir George Gipps, and "Governor" Grey, who knew their own minds, the connection with political questions such as French nationalism in Canada, the reflex effects of schemes directed like transportation or poor-relief emigration towards relief of home problems, these and such as these were the irregular forces contributing to the formation of a British policy. Only after 1831 was any systematic effort made to deal with land problems strictly from the point of view of land, and not a few of the innovators after 1831 suffered from inadequate practical experience. In an account of land policy, therefore, it is difficult to avoid the appearance of dispersion and inconsecutiveness, the truth being that on the point the ideas of English statesmen were really confused and inconsecutive.

The growth into a policy must be traced from an earlier point than 1815, for the new empire with its land problems came into existence with the cession of Canada, and the formation of a penal settlement in Australia. The centre lay at first in Canada. In the instructions to,

---

[1] Keith, A. B., *Responsible Government in the Dominions*, ii, 1047–53.

and advice received from, the Governors, more particularly Guy Carleton, Lord Dorchester, the earliest beginnings may be traced. We are not here concerned with the fluctuations between English and French principles of land tenure which occupied the years between 1763 and 1791.[1] Suffice to say that, if the Irish question had ever been studied with the fidelity and imagination which Dorchester gave to his Canadian task, the history of Irish land would have been very different.

At the outset, in 1763, the Government recognised one of the chief dangers which in the future, as in the past, was to beset the paths of land legislators: "the monopoly of lands in the hands of land jobbers from the extravagant grants made, in the old colonies, by some of Your Majesty's Governors".[2] Governors were therefore duly instructed to make strict conditions with regard to settlement and cultivation, and Dorchester at least recognised the evils which absentees could inflict on a colony. Exact statements of the amount of land to be granted to individuals were drawn up, "100 acres of land to every person being master or mistress of a family for himself or herself, and 50 acres for every white or black man, woman, or child of which such person's family shall consist", with the possibility of an additional 1000, provided "they are in a condition and intention to cultivate the same".[3] As time passed, and especially after 1791, the idea was accepted that portions should be reserved for the Crown and the clergy, with the curious result that Church and State soon found themselves practising, with all the usual evil results, all the worst habits of the speculating monopolist, and inflicting irreparable injuries on the young community. Another recurring feature, frequent enough to be called an item of policy, was the habit of rewarding soldiers or men of the embodied militia with grants of land after the wars with which the century started. These grants, being as useless as they were easy to make, either complicated the problems of non-cultivation, or fell into the hands of jobbers, without assisting those for whom the benefit was intended. As late as 1837 applications from men who had served in 1812 were still straggling in, and over 500,000 acres in military grants were without claimants. These individual military concessions must of course be distinguished from planned and directed settlements such as that of Perth, in upper Canada. For a time, however, in British North America, in spite of serious errors, the British Government showed some recognition of the evils to be checked and of the methods by which this could be done. Thanks to the genius of an able soldier, Dorchester, the new elements of policy were introduced with enlightened sympathy towards the colonists.

---

[1] See *C.H.B.E.* vol. VI, chs. VI and VII.
[2] Shortt, A. and Doughty, A. G., *Documents relating to the Constitutional History of Canada*, I, 137.
[3] *Ibid.* Instructions to Murray and Dorchester, I, 196, 315.

Meanwhile, at the other side of the world, Admiral Phillip was administering a land policy suited to the needs of a convict settlement. In accordance with his instructions he issued grants to freed convicts ("emancipists") of 30 acres per single man, and 50 acres per married man, with rations for twelve months.[1] At the same time he held that "the sending out settlers who will be interested in the labour of the convicts, and in the cultivation of the country" was absolutely necessary, and it became the practice in New South Wales to allow the free settler not more than 100 acres above the amount granted to an emancipist.[2] Dorchester and Phillip were however in a fortunate position. They were men of strong character, possessed of a very clear view of their responsibilities; and they were further assisted by the limited emigration of the period in which they ruled.

When the flood-gates opened after 1815, there followed the period, *par excellence*, of land grants, marked by passivity at home, and confusion overseas. The characteristics of this shameful interregnum in imperial land administration have been drawn by a master hand in Appendix B of Lord Durham's *Report*. The British North American provinces furnished the most appropriate examples of incoherence because there the local influence of the Executive and Legislative Councils co-operated with the imbecility of some of the Governors to produce reckless profusion and real jobbery. It is important to emphasise local influences. Imperial policy doubtless failed, especially in ignoring the lessons of contemporary American practice, and in allowing the land administration to be carried on "by colonial authorities for purely colonial purposes".[3] Still the outstanding fact was the failure of the colonial Councils and their friends in intelligence and honesty. The story is a monotonous one; *bona fide* settlers hampered in their strenuous efforts by ineffective surveys, complicated fees and costly delays; schemes, planned for the settlement of townships under leaders, turned into gambling projects by respectable land-jobbers; private grants shared in by Governors, councillors and even bishops—so that the North American colonies became wildernesses of plundered land, lying waste until such time as the clearing work of hard-working small-holders should add the requisite value to the reserved estates. It was merely by good fortune and not by wise judgment that the greatest grant to a single monopolist, the Canada Land Company, really helped on the development of Upper Canada. When that corporation took over nearly 2,500,000 acres of excellent land, and with it many of the powers usually exercised by government alone, the enterprise and public spirit of the agent, John Galt, stood in glaring contrast to the unenterprising greed of less ambitious land-grabbers.[4] In Australia a process similar, although planned on a far

[1] Becke, L. and Jeffery, W., *Admiral Phillip*, p. 228, and see vol. VII, pt. I, pp. 69–70.
[2] Phillips, M., *A Colonial Autocracy*, p. 12.
[3] Lord Durham's *Report* (ed. Lucas), III, 37.
[4] *Canada and its Provinces*, III, 334–5.

less magnificent scale, was going on. Yet, with a simplicity reflecting more credit on his heart than his head, Goulburn could write with all seriousness that "huge grants of land to individuals have been the bane of all our colonies, and it has been the main object of Lord Bathurst's administration to prevent the extension of this evil by every means in his power".[1]

If the rise of emigration was the direct cause of much of this degeneration, by way of compensation the new interest in emigration was a chief factor in the evolution of a policy. Beginning with some such proposition as that of Colonel Torrens, that "emigration was merely the application of the redundant capital and population of the United Kingdom to the redundant land of the colonies",[2] the pioneers of modern colonisation slowly worked out a rational system for the distribution of waste lands. Robert Gourlay, in the introduction to his *Statistical Account*, pleaded for the sale, and opposed the grant, of waste lands and urged the expenditure of the proceeds from land on assisted emigration. John Galt, too, in the days before the systematic colonisers, challenged Wilmot Horton's method of emigration through parochial assistance, holding it "constitutionally better than his measures that a price should be put upon the Crown Lands in the Colonies, and that from the sales of them a fund available for purposes of emigration should be formed".[3]

But all the other advocates of a systematic land policy faded into obscurity after Edward Gibbon Wakefield began his propaganda. Before dealing with this side of Wakefield's work, however, something must be said about one obvious source of inspiration which affected Wakefield and his school. The history of the expansion of the United States westward has never received the attention it deserves as a means of elucidating parallel problems in British imperial advance. In the case of land the neglect is culpable. By 1830 a huge stretch of new country, west of the old states, had been peopled by four and a half millions of American colonists, and in 1820 two Acts of Congress reshaped the land policy of the Union.[4] The chief features of that policy may be fitly given in the words of a British land reformer: "There is one uniform price fixed of $1\frac{1}{4}$ dollars per acre",[5] said H. G. Ward in his speech on the Waste Lands of the Colonies in 1839.

No credit is given. There is a perfect liberty of choice and appropriation at this price. Immense surveys are carried on, to an extent which strangers have no conception of. One hundred and forty millions of acres have been mapped and planned at a cost of 2,164,000 dollars. There is a General Land Office at Washington with forty subordinate district offices, each having a Registrar and Receiver.... Maps, plans, information of every kind are accessible to the humblest persons.

[1] Phillips, *op. cit.* p. 111.
[2] Hansard, Second Series, XVI, 493. [3] Galt, J., *Autobiography*, I, 349.
[4] Turner, F. J., *Rise of the New West*, pp. 71–141.
[5] Hansard, Third Series, XLVIII, 852.

There is also the best check on the proceedings of these offices by the means of annual reports to Congress, while at the same time every facility is given to individual enterprise. A man, if he pleases, may invest a million dollars in land. If he miscalculate it is his own fault; the public is, under every circumstance, the gainer.

Here then at a critical point in imperial development had arisen a huge parallel experiment in sale of land by the State. When the British Government had conferred grants of land on half a hundred different principles, mostly wrong, and had operated through the edicts of a Secretary of State, the United States was binding itself by Acts of Congress, and parting with land on a strict and uniform system. Imperial surveys were conspicuously inefficient; the surveys and registration of the United States were prepared for all emergencies. Great Britain, fearing the speculator, encouraged him by its complicated blunders; in the United States men were left free to do as they pleased within the limits of the Acts, the corrective power entering with the passage west of great throngs of rude but competent pioneers, whose schemes of local government, once they had set up their little settlements, restrained monopolists by local rates. One great advantage the Republic possessed. Its expansion was hampered by no dividing seas. Its border population, trained in the best and hardest school of land settlement, pushed on, driven by pressure of population from the east. If colonisation and land settlement are the same thing, then the most efficient colonisers in the world in 1830 were the rude communities of which Abraham Lincoln was a characteristic product. American land administration was succeeding because it prescribed the simplest possible conditions, defined and maintained by authority of Congress, and persisted in them without hesitation or change.

At this point Wakefield entered the field. Hostile alike to the prevailing system of land grants, the uneconomic and anti-social concession of great solitary estates, the absence of any connecting link between land grants and the provision of labour, and the irresponsible authority of local autocrats and Colonial Office officials, Wakefield brought together from all available sources the system connected with his name. His chief handicap was that, never having visited a colony,[1] he could not check his imaginative logic with concrete experience. He held that land should be sold, and at such a price as would prevent labour prematurely turning to uneconomic landowning—but he must be allowed to state his own doctrine of the "sufficient price".

In founding a colony [he wrote in his latest work] the price might be so low as to render the quantity of land appropriated by settlers practically unlimited; it might be high enough to occasion a proportion between land and people similar to that of old countries, in which case, if this very high price did not prevent emigration, the cheapest land in the colony might be as dear, and the superabundance

---

[1] I.e. during the period in which his views developed.

of labourers as deplorable, as in England; or it might be a just medium between the two, occasioning neither superabundance of people, nor superabundance of land, but so limiting the quantity of land as to give the cheapest land a market value that would have the effect of compelling labourers to work some considerable time for wages, before they could become landowners. A price that did less than this would be insufficient; one that did more would be excessive; the price that would do this, and no more, is the proper price. I am used to call it the sufficient price.[1]

For obvious reasons he refused to name any definite sum, but he always thought of the price as high; in the Canterbury settlement £2 per acre, with an additional £1 for church and education, was counted appropriate to act as a regulating price. It was to be, as in the United States, unvarying, and no limits were to be put to the amount which might be purchased. He and his group all held that it should be named and enforced under the authority, not of a minister, but of an Act of Parliament.

The creation of an emigration fund from land sales was not at first necessarily connected with the idea of the sufficient price. "So completely is production of revenue a mere incident of the price of land", he said, "that the price ought to be imposed, if it ought to be imposed under any circumstance, even though the purchase money were thrown away."[2] In actual fact the two ideas became indissolubly connected, and from the connection flowed other conclusions. In his most theoretic mood Wakefield imagined that some kind of mathematical proportion could be established between the amount of land sold, the sum of money provided by the land fund, and the number of labourers required for the land, and brought out by means of the fund. Needless to say, no such proportion could exist, except in the most general way. Arguing in the same theoretic fashion, Wakefield came more and more to distrust auction as a means of determining the price. His latest position was that "selling by auction may serve other purposes than that of determining the sufficient price by means of competition, but when employed for this purpose, which it cannot serve, it is a self-delusion and a cheat".[3]

It is impossible here to follow Wakefield into the metaphysics of his system or to elaborate any analytic criticism of it. But the surest and soundest criticism which it received came from attempts made by responsible statesmen to put it into practice, and the modifications which colonial common sense imposed on the original Utopian plan. In the colonies, it is well to remember, "the exploded fallacies of the Wakefield theory" met with little favour.[4] The earliest victory was registered in 1831 when Goderich decided that "no land shall be disposed of otherwise than by sale, a minimum price (say five shillings an acre) being fixed, but this price not to be accepted until upon

---

[1] Wakefield, E. G., Art of Colonisation, ch. XLVII.
[2] Ibid. p. 376.   [3] Ibid. p. 355.
[4] Declaration and Remonstrance of the Legislative Council of N.S.W. 1 May 1851.

proper notice it shall appear that no one is prepared to offer more"[1]
—a double violation of the principle, since the price was too low,
and the method of raising it public auction. Then came the South
Australian Act of 1834, where in section 6 the commissioners were
instructed "to make such orders and regulations for the surveying and
sale of such public lands at such price as the said commissioners may
from time to time deem expedient...provided that no part of the
said public lands shall be sold except in public for ready money, and
either by auction or otherwise as may seem best to the Commissioners, but in no case and at no time for a lower price than the sum
of twelve shillings".[2] All the sales money was to form an emigration
fund. In 1836 Wakefield was the most influential witness before the
Select Committee on the disposal of lands in the British colonies. The
Whigs, advancing towards his position, raised the fixed price of
colonial land from five to twelve shillings, and in 1840 determined on
twenty shillings as a fixed price not to be modified by auction sales,
a council of perfection which roused the anger of New South Wales
and speedily produced its own abrogation. From first to last, whether
directly and positively, or by a kind of negative stimulus or irritation,
Wakefield gave the land policy of New Zealand its characteristic
turn, and as late as the 'seventies the Canterbury settlement remained faithful to the strictest doctrine of the sufficient price. As for
the growing reputation of the man, nothing is more amazing in the
late 'thirties and early 'forties than the respect with which his
authority in land policy came to be accepted, even although his
eulogists had an uncomfortable habit of interrupting the perfect logic
of his theory. When H. G. Ward introduced his colonial land resolutions in June 1839, he, Molesworth, Labouchere and Howick all not
merely paid tribute to the prophet but openly accepted his doctrine;
and when the House of Commons sat in Committee on the South
Australian Acts in 1841, Lord John Russell,[3] speaking still as Colonial
Secretary, referred to "an exceedingly sound and useful principle—
that uncultivated public lands in a colony, instead of being, as in
former times, granted in very large proportions to individuals without
the means of cultivating them, should be sold at a certain price, and
the produce thus obtained should be employed in sending labourers
to the colony".

But the Durham mission and *Report* furnish a unique example of
Wakefield's influence in colonial land policy, as they also illustrate
its limitations. Once only, in Canada and in 1838, did members of
the Wakefield group occupy a position of commanding authority, and
issue their recommendations with all the weight of official proposals.
The land policy of the *Report* and its Appendices furnished a searching

[1] Goderich to Darling, 9 January 1831; in Bell, K and Morrell, W. P., *British Colonial
Policy*, p. 197.
[2] 4 and 5 William iv, c. 95; Bell and Morrell, pp. 205–7.
[3] Hansard, Third Series, LVII, 247.

test of the practical value of Wakefield's programme in detail. The general importance of what Durham, Buller and Wakefield did was very great. Their description of the evils of the old land system was so full of unforgettable details, and so completely justified as an exposure of shameful mismanagement, that it operated with all the power of destructive legislation. At the same time the resolute sincerity of their demand for intelligent and scientific reforms made continued inaction impossible.

But their control of the situation ceased at that point. Wakefield and his more faithful disciples were useful as advisers only for an early, simple and very transient period in the growth of a young colony. When that stage had passed, their enthusiasm remained fruitful but their practical programme could no longer be applied without extensive modifications. That programme they now proposed as a policy for British North America. As a remedy for the evils created by earlier unrestricted land grants, Wakefield's main suggestion was a tax of twopence an acre on wild lands, with the alternative that the tax might be paid in land.[1] To land still ungranted he proposed to apply with occasional variations the Wakefield system over its whole extent. The new Canadian policy was to be simple, uniform and equal: a fixed, and not an upset price, with sale by auction banned; no credit, or payment in instalments; no restriction on the amount of land which might be bought; a "sufficient price" to facilitate settlement without leading to excessive and premature acquisition of land by settlers; a simple method of issuing titles and registration; and surveying really adequate. Since circumstances forbade a scientifically sufficient price, Wakefield proposed ten shillings per acre as a second best. The whole amount of the purchase money was to be spent, partly on public works, partly in providing for an increased emigration.[2]

The *triumvirate* spoke with less certain voice on the authority to which the administration of the new land and emigration laws was to be entrusted. It cannot be denied that their final proposal named an imperial authority, and in the Appendix Wakefield asked that the agent through which the Government worked should be a British Commission, with colonial assistants, regulating the disposal of public lands, the imposition of tax on wild lands, the selection and transport of emigrants, and the spending of the loan by which the whole process was to be expedited.[3] But even Buller and Wakefield declared that if the Parliament of Great Britain should consider the reforms inexpedient, it was their duty "to relinquish formally their control over this matter to the Colonial Legislature";[4] and Durham, whose acceptance of Wakefield's views was always modified by his own lofty liberal imperialism, seems to have permitted his conception of a

---

[1] Lord Durham's *Report* (ed. Lucas), III, 81–9. [2] *Ibid.* III, 95, 113.
[3] *Ibid.* III, 128–9. [4] *Ibid.* III, 40, 130.

United British North America to include in its details the surrender to such a Union of the disposal of public lands and the territorial revenue.[1]

Canadian facts were, however, stronger than Wakefield's doctrines. The Union Act handed over all territorial as well as other revenues to the United Provinces, in exchange for a permanent civil list; and with the revenues naturally went control of land. Whatever may have been the wisdom of the surrender, it was inevitable. The earliest reports of the Land and Emigration Commissioners—Russell had accepted Durham's advice on that point—confessed that Canadian legislation retained all money from land sales as part of the general revenue of the colony, and that, in Canadian emigration, the main object of the Commissioners had already been limited to "ascertaining, by regular returns, the manner in which it is conducted, and guarding against or punishing any infraction of the law, by which only it is in any degree regulated".[2] Perhaps the cruelest blow was dealt by Sydenham, whose realism had little patience with Wakefield's ideas. He quickly made up his mind that "Wakefield's plan of bringing out labourers by the sale of lands was utterly impracticable; that the emigrants were, in great majority, more suitably employed on public works than in qualifying through agricultural labour for land-owning; and that, in the rush of voluntary emigrants to America, all that his government could do in directing emigration was to forward men to districts where work was waiting for them".[3] The systematic colonisers, then, found themselves in the position ultimately reached by all projectors of New Jerusalems. The angel with the golden measuring rod, the walls and gates and jewels and streets of gold were fading like an unsubstantial pageant, but thousands of struggling men and women were now finding it easier to earn their daily bread.

An idea really simple, the abolition of land grants and a fair minimum price for colonial land, had now been accepted; with the further proposition that all, or a substantial proportion of, the revenue thus raised should form an emigration fund. Party arguments, the conscientious reflections of some responsible ministers, and the shrewd business instincts of colonial buyers and owners of land, had lopped off some of the extravagances and the excrescences of the system as Wakefield himself had laid it down. It mattered little that in the opinion of its creator his theory "had never had anything like a fair trial anywhere" and that "the professed trials of it had been something not only different from it, but utterly at variance with it in reality".[4] Prophets are seldom willing to admit that the half is greater than the whole.

So it happened that when the logical issue of the long process came

---

[1] Lord Durham's *Report*, II, 314, with note by Sir Charles Lucas.
[2] *C. L. and E. C. Report*, 1842.   [3] Bell and Morrell, pp. 219–21.
[4] Wakefield, E. G., *Art of Colonisation*, p. 25.

in Stanley's Australian Land Sales Act of 1842,[1] the result was not something which Wakefield could accept as an expression of his doctrines. At the same time it was certainly not in accordance with colonial opinion. Nevertheless, it marked an improvement on the earlier policy so great as to amount to a revolution. The details of the Act belong properly to Australian history; but the principles on which it was constructed form the revised land policy of the British Empire stated authoritatively in a statute. In brief, these were the fundamental points:

1. In introducing the measure Stanley announced that it was not right that any Secretary of State should possess the power of making changes without authority. His policy took the form of an Act of Parliament.[2]

2. In place of systems differing in the various colonies, the same system was to apply to all the colonies—that of "one regulated upset price, below which no land should be sold, and at which there should be a permanent sale".[3]

3. To meet some of the objections raised by the opponents of sale by auction, although no town or suburban[4] lots might be sold otherwise than by public auction, land in the country sections, which had been put up but not sold, might be sold by private contract at the upset price.

4. Sales were to be for what was really ready money, one-tenth at the time of sale, and the remainder a month later.

5. While charges incurred in the survey and management of the land might be met out of the proceeds of the sales, at least one half of the total amount was to be spent on emigration.[5]

While the Act pleased neither the Legislative Council of New South Wales, to whom it seemed to set a prohibitory price on the soil, nor yet the sheep farmers, to whom it granted merely annual licences, it was a reasonable attempt to blend Wakefield's doctrines, American practice, and the shrewd criticisms of colonial Governors. It was the most elaborate and the last comprehensive attempt made by the Imperial Parliament to solve the problems of colonial land.

Meanwhile another aspect of the land question was being thrust by natural development on the Imperial Government. From an early date it had become apparent that pasturing, and especially sheep farming, were at least as important a source of wealth in New South Wales and the other settlements as agriculture. But the conditions under which land might be occupied, and the price paid, by sheep farmers, or, as the Australians termed them, squatters, had obviously little relation to those which applied to agricultural land. It was difficult for legislators or theorists in Great Britain to define the proper relation between the two forms of utilising the land. Wakefield, for example, was on such a point ludicrously inadequate. His most enlightened critic[6] is too lenient when he says, "While he did not overlook the importance of pastoral industry, he considered that its interests should be subordinate to those of agriculture". As late as

---

[1] 5 and 6 Vict. c. 36.   [2] Hansard, Third Series, LX, 82.   [3] *Ibid.*
[4] Technical terms describing land within the limits of an existing or contemplated town, and land within the distance of 5 miles from the nearest point of an existing or contemplated town.
[5] 5 and 6 Vict. c. 36.   [6] Mills, R. C. in *The Colonisation of Australia*, p. 112.

1849, when his *Art of Colonisation* appeared, he showed none of that definite and practical comprehension of the "squatting" problem which alone would have made his views worthy of attention. As for the Government, the impulse towards defining a policy came in equal proportions from the doctrines they had already accepted with regard to arable land, from the arguments of interested classes in Australia, and from the forcible criticisms of able governors like Sir George Gipps. British ministers were, after all, rather inexperienced arbitrators handicapped by their lack of first-hand knowledge of the subject. Under such circumstances it was inevitable that the parties in possession, in this case the great squatting lessees, should win the day.

At first leases had been allowed within the older settled districts. Then, when a series of great discoveries down to 1836 opened up vast tracts of land peculiarly fitted for sheep farming, the squatters overflowed into the new wilderness. The determination of policy lay in the hands of autocrats on the spot like Bourke and Gipps; they created a system of licences which brought little into the exchequer but at least kept some control over the actual situation. But the three parties mainly concerned remained uneasy. The squatters desired greater security, the Government looked for a more substantial income, and in the colony a party strongly opposed to squatters' privileges was coming into existence.[1]

The terms of the Act of 1842 forced on a decision. The section[2] which allowed "licences for the occupation, for any time not exceeding 12 calendar months..., of any Waste Lands of the Crown" confirmed the sheep farmers in their sense of insecurity; and the Bill which Lord Stanley submitted in 1845 for colonial comment provoked an elaborate and able statement of squatting claims from stock-holders in New South Wales.[3] The definitive stage in British policy came with the Waste Lands Occupation Act of 1846, and the "Squatting" Order-in-Council of 1847. Land was then divided into settled, unsettled and intermediate. In the unsettled regions leases were granted for terms not exceeding fourteen years in duration; the rent was to be proportioned to the number of sheep or cattle which the run was capable of carrying, and the definition of the run was in terms which eliminated smaller holdings; the runs were not to be open to sale, except to the lessees, during the continuance of the lease; and at the expiration of leases the holders had the option of buying the land at a price not less than £1 per acre.[4] "At one stroke the flock owners of the wide interior were to be turned into leaseholders. In a moment a vested interest was created to protect which powerful influences have ever since struggled, quite naturally, but to the infinite harm of progress."[5] The process by which the Imperial Parliament arrived at a policy

[1] See vol. VII, pt. I, ch. 7.   [2] Section 17.   [3] Bell and Morrell, pp. 236-40.
[4] Earl Grey, *Colonial Policy*, I, 314-18; Bell and Morrell, pp. 241-9; Roberts, S. H., *History of Australian Land Settlement*, pp. 186-7.
Reeves, W. P., *State Experiments in Australia and New Zealand*, I, 227.

with regard to pasture lands, and the terms in which it defined that policy, have a significance more far-reaching than the subject with which they dealt. An economic issue of primary importance to the colonial community, and one in which local interests were dia-metrically opposed to each other, had been settled by a Home Government not merely aloof from colonial opinion on the subject, but really without that special knowledge of the situation which was the first essential for successful legislation. It was not difficult for Earl Grey to write, with the complacency which must ever haunt Whitehall, that by his Orders-in-Council "all the encouragement they could fairly require has been given to the sheep and cattle farmers...while at the same time the Crown lands have not been improvidently alienated before they have acquired the value they must ultimately derive from being wanted for an increasing population".[1] But in New South Wales, John (later Sir John) Robertson, whose experience embraced both agricultural and pastoral farming, gave a much less flattering report.

While the agriculturist has been absolutely excluded from leasing any portion of the public land [he wrote in 1855] and thwarted, harassed, and dispirited at every turn in his efforts to obtain the submittal of such lands to sale, and subjected to public competition at auction before suffered [sic] even then to purchase, the grazier has been allowed to use them under a system of leases, affording him the greatest possible facility of possession, and at the lowest imaginable rental...and absolutely without competition.[2]

When overseas interests have developed their own definite and irreconcilable parties, and when the imperial arbitrator does not possess sufficient practical knowledge to be fair to either side or to himself, the case for imperial control automatically disappears. The final stage in colonial land policy had now been reached. With the publication of Lord Durham's *Report* the era of colonial self-govern-ment officially began, and with self-government the idea that the colonies should control their own land policy and land revenues. The connection between the two developments has already been traced in the case of Canada; and the Canadian example was followed in all the other colonies as they became autonomous. When New Zealand received its constitution, the General Assembly, although not the Provincial Councils, received the power "to make Laws for regulating the Sale, Letting, Disposal, and Occu-pation of the Waste Lands of the Crown in New Zealand".[3] About the same time the gold rush in Australia raised the whole consti-tutional question in a very acute form, and brought the problems of Australian land into marked prominence. It mattered little when Earl Grey protested, from the Colonial Office, that although property in waste lands was a question of expediency and not right, he did not think that the time had come for change; and the plea in his *Colonial*

[1] Grey, Earl, *Colonial Policy*, I, 315–16.
[2] Parkes, Sir H., *Fifty Years of Australian History*, I, 81–2.   [3] 15 and 16 Vict. c. 72.

Policy, if eloquent, was already obsolete, that the Crown should still act as Trustee for the benefit of all its subjects.[1] Events were too strong for Downing Street and its opinions, and within the same year in which Grey urged his views, it fell to the short-lived first Derby Ministry to assure the colonists in New South Wales through their Governor that "under the new and rapidly changing circumstances of New South Wales the time is come at which it is their (the Cabinet's) duty to advise Her Majesty that the administration of these lands should be transferred to the Colonial Legislature, after those changes in its constitution have been effected which are adverted to in the petition".[2] So New South Wales and Victoria followed Canada and New Zealand, to be themselves followed by every other colony as it attained its majority.

An attempt has here been made to trace the well-intentioned, but not always equally well-informed, efforts of the Imperial Government to administer the waste lands of the Empire. Since many of the worst scandals which that Government found it hard to remedy came from colonial greed and dishonesty as much as from British supineness, it was hardly to be expected that an agrarian golden age would quickly follow the termination of imperial control in the colonies. After all, Home Rule is best defined as the right of a people to misgovern themselves. An eminent colonial authority, without any intention of praising imperial wisdom by contrast, confesses that "the problem of settlement under the perfect tenure is far from being solved", and that "in no branch of state work, perhaps, has success been so chequered with failure as in the management of the estate which England fifty years ago handed over—a princely endowment to the young colonies then about to try their hands at self-government".[3] In some such mood of modesty, the colonial critics of Great Britain will perhaps admit that from first to last her statesmen, even in land, meant desperately well; that a few imperial statesmen like Dorchester attained more nearly to an understanding of their section of the subject than anyone not born and bred in Great Britain, and that if the average British Ministry erred often and grievously through ignorance or mere passivity, the rogues and monopolists who profited so willingly from official blunders were usually characteristic products of early nineteenth-century colonial training.

[1] Earl Grey to Sir C. Fitzroy, 23 January 1852; in Bell and Morrell, pp. 262–5; Grey, *Colonial Policy*, I, 318–19.
[2] Sir J. Pakington to Sir C. Fitzroy, 15 December 1852. The petition had asked for financial control in exchange for a satisfactory civil list.
[3] Reeves, *op. cit.* I, 194–5.

CHAPTER XIII

THE CROWN COLONIES, 1815–1845

(i) THE SUGAR COLONIES

THE close of the Napoleonic Wars brought peace in the military sense, but, as we have already seen,[1] ushered in a prolonged period of conflict between the planting interests, both in the colonies and at home, and the newly awakened humanitarianism in England.

Although the slave trade had been formally abolished by the Act of 1807, it did not immediately disappear in all parts of the British Empire. In the recently conquered island of Mauritius great difficulty was experienced in its suppression. Under a weak Governor, Sir Robert Farquhar, the trade continued illicitly on a large scale; though it must be remembered that he was hampered by the difficulty of reconciling an exclusively French population to British rule. In the West Indies, also, there was the suspicion, much exaggerated by rumour, that the trade was still being carried on. To provide a check against this the Government established by Orders-in-Council a system of slave registration in Trinidad in 1812 and in St Lucia in 1814. In 1815 Wilberforce introduced a bill to enforce slave registration in all the colonies, but objections were raised both in England and in the colonies that such action by the Imperial Parliament would be unconstitutional, since it would override the local legislatures, and that (registration involving some expense) it would amount to taxation without representation. The bill did not pass, but on this occasion the threat was sufficient and all the colonies adopted measures for setting up a register of the slaves, though nowhere on such efficient lines as in Trinidad. Unfortunately, in Barbados, the question of registration became confused in the minds of the negroes with emancipation and resulted in 1816 in an insurrection of the slaves. Neither side was slow to draw the moral—the planters, that ill-judged interference at home with their affairs could only lead to further upheavals and ultimate disaster; and the reformers, that such outbreaks merely reflected the intolerable burden of slavery and emphasised the need for a lightening of that burden.[2]

For some years after 1815 the Abolitionists waited to see whether their hopes would be justified: namely, that the economic interests of the planters would lead to a great improvement in their treatment of the slaves, now that the supplies of new negroes from without had

---

[1] See chapter IX.
[2] Edwards, Bryan, *History of the West Indies to 1820*, II, 102–7.

been cut off. But it gradually became clear from the despatches of the Governors and the reports of the missionaries that little improvement was to be expected from this cause. In January 1823 the Society for the Mitigation and Gradual Abolition of Slavery throughout the British Dominions was founded. In May of the same year Canning proposed and the House of Commons unanimously adopted a series of declarations supporting "effectual and decisive measures for ameliorating the condition of the slave population in His Majesty's colonies", and looking forward to their ultimate emancipation. The attempt that was made in the ensuing ten years to secure the reform of the colonial slave codes has been described in an earlier chapter,[1] but attention must here be drawn to its political effects in the colonies.

In 1815 the British possessions in the West Indies consisted partly of colonies which had long been under British rule and possessed representative institutions, and partly of colonies conquered in the recent war, namely Tobago, British Guiana (Demerara and Berbice), Trinidad and St Lucia. Of these, Tobago, which had been given an elective Assembly in 1768, but was subsequently ceded to France, was the only new colony to be allowed the old representative system. In the other three colonies and in Mauritius, with their large foreign populations (Dutch, French or Spanish) outnumbering the English, it was thought undesirable to establish elective assemblies, and the legislatures were subordinated to the executive; completely in Trinidad, St Lucia and Mauritius, and partially in British Guiana.

The Colonial Office first dealt with the simpler problem afforded by this small group of colonies. The Governor of Trinidad, Sir R. Woodford, was asked to draft a reformed slave code on general lines suggested by Earl Bathurst, and this code was imposed by Order-in-Council on Trinidad in 1825; a similar code was adopted, after some opposition, by the nominated Council of St Lucia in 1826. In Mauritius also there was very strong local feeling against the code, which was not finally enforced until 1830. Peculiar difficulties arose in British Guiana (Demerara and Berbice) owing to the existence of semi-representative institutions which had been inherited from the period of Dutch rule. In Demerara there was a Court of Policy consisting of ten members, five being officials appointed by the Governor and five colonists appointed by the College of Kiezers—a body composed of seven members elected by the colonists for life. The Governor had a casting vote. In addition to the Court of Policy there were also six elective Financial Representatives holding office for two years. The Financial Representatives and the Court of Policy sitting together constituted the Combined Court which had the right to vote taxation to meet the estimates drawn up by the Governor. The precise powers of these two bodies, the existence of which had

---

[1] See chapter IX.

been expressly recognised in the capitulation of 1803, were not clearly defined, and this difficulty caused continual friction.

The Colonial Office, anxious not to raise the constitutional question unnecessarily, began by transmitting a copy of the Trinidad slave code to Demerara with the request that the Court of Policy should enact a similar code. At the same time (in 1824) it sent out a distinguished soldier, Sir Benjamin D'Urban, to be Governor of the colony. D'Urban had been Governor of Antigua and was sympathetic to the colonists, but despite his friendly persuasion the Court of Policy insisted on inserting amendments which were unacceptable to the Government. After a long period of fruitless negotiation the Colonial Office in 1830 enforced the acceptance of its own provisions by a Consolidated Order-in-Council applicable to all the Crown Colonies.

In Berbice the Governor was assisted by a Council of six members, chosen by him from a panel of twelve elected by the colonists. This Council of planters proved completely recalcitrant over certain important items in the slave code submitted to them—notably the abolition of the driving whip and the flogging of women. Its opposition was maintained until 1826, when Sir H. Bentinck, the Governor, was instructed to supersede it by a Council nominated by himself. The new Council, which passed the code in the same year, did not function for long, however, for in 1831 Sir Benjamin D'Urban succeeded in securing a sufficient measure of agreement for the Colonial Office to unite Demerara and Berbice as the colony of British Guiana, with one Court of Policy, one College of Electors and six Financial Representatives for the whole area.

In the meantime the imposition of the slave code on Demerara had given rise to a violent controversy. The colonists contended that the Court of Policy was their legislature and that the action of the Crown had been unconstitutional and had infringed the terms of the capitulation of 1803. It is worthy of note that when the union of Demerara and Berbice had been decided on, the instrument by which this was effected took the form, not of an Order-in-Council, but of a new Commission and Instructions to Sir Benjamin D'Urban. Finally, in 1832, the Colonial Office defined its attitude towards the claims of the Court of Policy in a declaration by Lord Goderich, the Colonial Secretary, in which he formally asserted the right of the Crown to legislate by Orders-in-Council in all the captured colonies.[1]

The position regarding the older colonies with representative institutions was much more complicated. In 1833 Bathurst had sent a circular despatch to the Governors of all these colonies in which he outlined the measures of reform that were desirable and urged their immediate adoption. This step was greeted by a storm of protest

[1] Penson, L. M., "The Making of a Crown Colony: British Guiana, 1803–33", *Transactions of the Royal Historical Society*, 1925, pp. 124–8. Clementi, Sir Cecil, *Const. History of British Guiana.*

throughout the West Indies. The Canning resolutions and the proposals of the Government were denounced as illegal interference in the colonies' internal affairs—a battle cry which rallied all the planters in defence of their ancient liberties. Nor were constitutional rights the only ground on which the colonists opposed a thoroughgoing reform of the slave codes. They had been suffering from economic depression since 1815 and therefore resisted any changes which would weaken their hold over their dwindling supplies of slaves. To the influence of these factors must be added the general temper of a white ruling class living in the tropics and long accustomed to absolute domination over a slave population—a ruling class, moreover, which had not experienced the workings of the Evangelical Revival and was completely out of touch with the feeling at home on such matters as Sunday markets or the marriage of slaves.

For ten years, from 1823 to 1833, the struggle continued.[1] The Government applied as much pressure by way of exhortation and warning as was consistent with its general policy of avoiding direct intervention. The island legislatures responded by rejecting the model codes and substituting their own measures, which fell far short of what the Colonial Office wished and public opinion in England demanded. By 1830 the sands were running out. In May of that year the Anti-Slavery Society openly advocated the immediate liberation of the slaves; and when in 1831 there was a serious, if easily suppressed, slave revolt in Jamaica it was felt that the time had come to cease dallying with the policy of amelioration. Changes of Government delayed matters for a while, and allowed the colonists a little more grace, which they continued to abuse as in the past. Finally, in 1833, the Reformed Parliament passed the Act for the Abolition of Slavery throughout the British Colonies.[2] The Act brought slavery to an end and, as part compensation to the slave owners, provided for a period of apprenticeship for the former slaves which was to come into force in August 1834. This period was to last four years in the case of nonpredial slaves and six years in the case of predial slaves. The former category consisted of domestic slaves and all others not usually employed in agriculture or in the manufacture of colonial produce; the predial slaves were those engaged in field work and employed on the estates. The hours of labour of the predial apprentices were limited to forty-five per week, during which they were required to work for their existing masters without pay, but receiving free food, clothing, housing and medical attendance. In the spare time remaining to them the apprentices were free to work if they wished on the plantations in return for wages. They were allowed to anticipate the end of the apprenticeship period by purchasing their complete freedom from the proprietor. If they were idle or refused to obey orders they were

---

[1] Mathieson, W. L., *British Slavery and its Abolition, 1823–1838*, chap. III.
[2] See chapter IX.

liable to be flogged, but the infliction of punishments arising out of the apprenticeship system was placed in the hands of special stipendiary magistrates appointed from England.

Finally, the planters were to receive (as a maximum) the sum of £20,000,000 in further compensation for the loss of their slave property, but only subject to the condition that the local legislatures of the Chartered Colonies passed laws for carrying into effect the Abolition Act, and that those laws were approved by the King in Council.

The political developments in the sugar colonies, which we have briefly sketched, can only be understood in relation to their economic and social background. The economic position of the colonies after the Napoleonic wars was influenced by a number of general causes, which in a large measure lay outside their control, but by which they were all in varying degrees affected.

The abolition in 1807 of the slave trade, so far as the British colonies were concerned, destroyed what had been the foundation of their economic structure and development. Without a continual inflow of fresh slaves it was impossible in the long run for cultivation by slave labour to be conducted on a paying basis, especially having regard to the tendency for the slave populations of the islands (excepting Barbados) to decline in the absence of recruitment from outside. While the slave trade was still in existence, the price of additional slaves constituted an adjustable factor in the cost of production, and it was possible to counteract to some extent the effects of a fall in the price of sugar by a fall in the import price of slaves.[1] It was also profitable to drive the slaves harder so long as the problem of replacement did not present much difficulty. As a consequence of the abolition of the trade the British West Indies suffered, from 1815 onwards, from the severe competition of sugar produced in the very fertile Spanish colonies of Cuba and Porto Rico and in the Portuguese colony of Brazil, which, despite all the diplomatic efforts of the British Government and the liability of foreign slave-trading vessels to capture by British cruisers, were able to secure large numbers of slaves from Africa. It is true that the heavy duties on foreign sugar prevented its importation into Great Britain for home consumption, but the effect on the West India growers was none the less real, for the foreign sugar was exported to the Continent of Europe, and thus diminished the re-export of colonial sugar from England and lowered its price there. The same humanitarian movement in England, which led to the abolition of the slave trade, also caused the introduction of many measures tending to increase costs of production for British planters as compared with foreign producers, for example, the limita-

[1] Cf. the statement of a Cuban planter in 1830 in *Statements relating to the State of the British West Indies, Parl. Pap.* 1830-31, IX, p. 533.

tion of the hours of slave labour and the enforced maintenance of the aged and infirm.

The necessities of war finance and the costs of the convoy system had led to the raising of the British sugar duties to a very high level. In 1789 the duty on West Indian sugar was 12s. 4d. per cwt., but it was gradually increased until it reached its highest point in 1813 of £1. 10s. per cwt. In 1819 it was fixed at £1. 7s., at which figure it was maintained till 1830, the duty then falling to £1. 4s. On sugar from Mauritius and India an additional duty of 10s. per cwt. was levied until 1825, when the duties on Mauritian and West Indian sugar were equalised in the face of great opposition from the West Indian interests. It was not until 1836 that the differential duty on sugar from British India was removed. This high specific duty checked consumption and kept up the price of sugar in the English market for the benefit, not of the planters, but of the British Exchequer. The average consumption per head of the population of the United Kingdom for the inflation years 1801 to 1814 was 18 lb. 7 oz., while in the following thirty years of peace it was only 17 lb. 3 oz.[1] Further, it was a long-standing grievance of the colonists that the Home Government, in order to stimulate the demand for corn, refused to allow the use of sugar and molasses in the manufacture of spirits in the United Kingdom, and also maintained much higher duties on rum than on British and Irish (especially Scotch and Irish) spirits. In the case of British plantation coffee, the duty in 1819 was 1s. per lb., while foreign coffee paid 2s. 6d. per lb., but these duties were halved, with a great resulting increase in consumption, by the Act 6 George IV, c. 111, which came into force in January 1826.

With the end of the war the price of sugar in bond in London, which had reached its highest level of £3. 9s. 9d. per cwt. in 1814, fell rapidly to £1. 16s. 2d. in 1820 and to £1. 4s. 11d. in 1830. At the latter date the duty of £1. 7s. caused an addition of 108 per cent. to the net price of the sugar. The fall in price was due, partly to the deflation of the English currency and the consequent fall in the general price level; partly to the fall in freights and insurance at the end of the war; and partly to increased supplies of sugar to the British market from British Guiana, Mauritius and India, and of foreign sugar to the Continent. The first two of these causes also gave a certain amount of assistance to the West Indian planters, because they lowered the prices of foodstuffs and stores imported from England. It was stated in evidence in 1832 that the average cost of production of sugar in the British West Indies had fallen from £1. 0s. 10d. per cwt. in 1807 to 15s. 10d. in 1830.[2] But it is clear from the figures given above that the decline in the cost of production was by no means

---

[1] *Appendix to Report of Select Committee on Sugar Duties, Parl. Pap*, 1862, XIII, p. 319.
[2] Minutes of Evidence before the Select Committee on the State of the West India Colonies, *Parl. Pap.*, 1831–32, XX, Q. 410.

commensurate with the decrease in the market price of sugar in England.

The restrictions imposed on their trade by what still remained of the old colonial system increased costs of production in the British West Indian colonies. The fact that, until the amending Acts of 1822 and 1825, these colonies were constrained, for example, to buy all the manufactured articles they required from Great Britain, was, it is true, no longer very burdensome to them, for none of the other countries could rival England's manufactures in cheapness after 1815. Nor were the prohibitive duties on the imports of refined sugar into England of much importance, for after the abolition of the slave trade the colonies lacked both the labour and capital necessary to operate refineries with success. Again, the shipping restrictions of the Navigation Acts had not seriously affected the interests of the West Indian planters so far as trade with Europe was concerned. Their real grievance was bound up with the checks that were imposed on their very important trade with the United States.

From 1794 to 1806 a very considerable volume of trade, at times of an illicit character, was carried on between the United States and the West Indies. In 1815, after seven years of interrupted commerce and war, a commercial convention was signed between Great Britain and the United States by which what was in effect most favoured nation treatment was mutually accorded and discriminating duties in each country on the ships of the other were abolished. But the West Indies were expressly excluded from benefiting by the main provisions of this convention, and from 1815 to 1830 direct trade between the West Indian colonies and the United States was precarious and costly—once laid under complete embargo (1827 to 1829)—and always subject to heavy discriminating duties on both sides. During the periods when direct commercial relations were entirely prohibited, a good deal of trade continued to be carried on in a roundabout way by the transport of American goods to Canadian or Newfoundland ports or to French and Danish islands in the West Indies, whence they were transhipped to the British West Indies, the whole operation naturally causing considerable extra expense. Even after 1830, when minor concessions on both sides enabled the resumption of shipping and normal commerce between the United States and the West Indies, protective duties were almost as effective in hindering trade as had been the former policy of monopoly and exclusion.

The burden on the colonies between 1815 and 1830 which resulted from these restrictions and diversions of the normal course of trade was appreciable. Amongst the most important of the external requirements of the planters were provisions (especially herrings and other salt fish, but also flour and meat) for feeding their slaves;[1]

[1] See Rose, J. H., "West India Commerce as a factor in the Napoleonic Wars", *Cambridge Hist. Jour.*, 1929.

timber for construction purposes, and staves and shingles for making rum casks and the hogsheads and barrels in which sugar was packed. The most natural and much the cheapest source of supply of most of this produce was the United States. But it was precisely on these articles that the heaviest duties were levied if they came from other than British possessions and the import of foreign fish was entirely prohibited.

The Navigation Acts also tended to raise freights against the colonists, for their exports (mainly sugar and rum) were bulky articles which were carried almost entirely to Great Britain; on the other hand, the manufactures they chiefly imported thence naturally required less shipping, and voyages out to the colonies were not infrequently in ballast. The bulky provisions and timber imported from the United States were carried to a considerable extent in American ships which went back in ballast, because there was only a small market in the United States for West Indian sugar and rum, and American ships were not allowed to carry plantation sugar to England. Thus single voyage freights had to be paid on a great deal of both incoming and outgoing cargoes.[1] The importance, however, of this disability, which lasted until the abolition of the Navigation Acts in 1849, is lessened by the fact that the American ships trading with the West Indies were mostly of small size and would not have been well adapted for carrying cargoes of sugar across the Atlantic to England.

It should be noted that the restrictions of the "colony system" did not apply to Mauritius or British India, and this was one of the reasons why the West Indian planting interests so bitterly opposed the equalisation of the duties on sugar from the East Indies. They felt themselves very hardly used when in 1825 this extra duty was removed so far as Mauritius was concerned (6 George IV, c. 76), and the extension of the navigation laws to Mauritius by the same Act did little to allay their grievance.

There was a heavy external drain on the resources of the colonies. This was caused by a combination of absentee landlordism, the mortgaging of plantations to British capitalists, and the existence of many patent places, pensions and other claims for which the colonies were liable. The Leeward Islands, for example, from 1663 to 1838 paid the Crown a tax of $4\frac{1}{2}$ per cent. on the gross value of all exported produce. Thus there was always a very large excess of exports from, over imports to, the sugar colonies.

The expansion of British colonisation in North America and Australia during the first half of the nineteenth century diverted in other directions the main stream of emigration of men and capital. There is good reason to believe that the Englishmen who migrated to the West Indies at this period were not for the most part men of very high quality. The growing sentiment against slave ownership

---

[1] Clapham, J. H., "Last years of the Navigation Acts", in *E.H.R.* Oct. 1910, p. 701.

was no doubt partly responsible for this, but, whatever the causes, the effects on the fortunes of these colonies were serious and far-reaching.

Finally, for nearly the whole of the first half of the nineteenth century British colonial sugar and coffee enjoyed a complete monopoly of the British market. If the revenue duties on colonial produce were high, foreign tropical produce was loaded with duties so heavy as to be prohibitive. This was the essential counterpart of the restrictions of the colonial system and explains why the West India interests were comparatively docile under grievances the existence of which was undeniable. The attitude of the colonies can be seen from the following extract from a memorandum submitted on their behalf to the Board of Trade in 1830:[1] "The inhabitants of Jamaica conceive that they are entitled to advantages in return for this code of prohibition, restraint and taxation. The privilege of exclusively supplying the mother country with our staple commodities is the equivalent, which has had the sanction of long time and mutual recognition, and a ratification which has been designated as more solemn than any which an Act of Parliament could confer."

The economic history of the West Indian colonies, of British Guiana and of Mauritius is largely the story of the sugar industry there. Just as the prosperity of Egypt to-day is almost wholly dependent on cotton, so the well-being of these possessions was bound up with the prices and conditions of production of a single crop—sugar, with its by-products, rum and molasses. Adam Smith quoted as a common saying in his time "that a sugar planter expects that the rum and the molasses should defray the whole expense of his cultivation, and that his sugar should be all clear profit".[2] While this was far from being true after 1815, whatever may have been the case in 1775, it is certain that rum was a valuable source of revenue to the planter and one that he almost always neglected to bring into account when making a statement of his position before official committees of enquiry. There were or had been other products which at different times had had a measure of importance in the West Indies, in particular, cotton, coffee, cocoa, ginger and pimento. Already in the early years of the nineteenth century West Indian cotton could no longer hold its own in the face of the competition of the United States and the shortage of labour. British Guiana, alone of our American possessions, was still able to export in 1830 a quantity of cotton worth mentioning.

Jamaica had developed the cultivation of coffee on a considerable scale during the Napoleonic Wars,[3] especially after the insurrection of the slaves in San Domingo in 1791. But, with the coming of peace and the expansion of coffee growing in Cuba and Brazil, the supplies

---

[1] *Statements relating to the...British West India Colonies, Parl. Pap.* 1830–31, IX, p. 491.
[2] *Wealth of Nations*, ed. Thorold Rogers, I, 166.
[3] *Vide supra*, chapter III.

to the European markets were greatly increased and prices fell. Between 1830 and 1835, when the domestic consumption of the United Kingdom had largely increased as a result of the lowering of the import duty from 1s. to 6d. per lb. in 1825, it was still not more than 50 per cent. of the total importation, the balance having to be exported to the Continent in the face of protective duties and the competition of coffee from colonies which still benefited from the slave trade. However, despite low prices, coffee continued to be a secondary crop of considerable importance in Jamaica, and also in British Guiana and Dominica, until after the emancipation of the slaves.

The remaining products of the West Indies ranked much below those already mentioned, partly owing to the high duties levied on them. Cocoa had once been cultivated to some extent in Jamaica, but had almost disappeared there by the beginning of the nineteenth century; its chief West Indian source was then the island of Trinidad. Ginger was still exported in appreciable quantities only from Jamaica and Barbados, and pimento, or allspice, from Jamaica alone. It may be noted, however, in the case of coffee, cocoa, ginger and pimento, that the domestic consumption of those articles in the different islands was considerable in the nineteenth century, and that their local importance, especially in Jamaica, was therefore greater than would appear from the quantities exported.

During the Napoleonic Wars the fortunes of the British West Indies fluctuated according to the changing level of prices of their chief products, sugar, rum and coffee, in England. In 1807, when these colonies were in a state of acute distress, the first of the parliamentary enquiries into their condition was held. Their misfortunes were found at that time to be due mainly to the great fall in prices caused by the transport of sugar and coffee from the French islands to Europe in neutral American vessels.[1] A drastic change occurred in the British attitude towards neutral trade with enemy possessions, which led to the interruption of this trade and, finally, contributed to cause the war of 1812 with the United States. Prices rose again after 1807 and the plantations were prosperous in spite of high freights, war insurance and losses from privateering.[2] Although prices fell sharply in 1816 and continued with slight fluctuations to move downwards, conditions were not unprofitable on the better managed estates until the severe slump of 1830–31. The slump was largely occasioned by the expansion of production in the newly acquired colonies of British Guiana (Demerara and Berbice) and Mauritius. The former contained a large area of exceedingly fertile soil which had been thinly settled by the Dutch, and was rapidly colonised by the British, who

[1] *Report of the Committee on the Commercial State of the West India Colonies, Parl. Pap.* 1807, III, p. 5.
[2] *Vide supra,* chapter III.

converted the land near the coast into large sugar, coffee and cotton plantations. Steam engines were imported and the plant was up-to-date and efficient. Mauritius was hampered until 1825 by the differential duties which kept her sugars out of the British market. But owing to imperfect administration the slave trade had been allowed to continue there on a considerable scale until 1818, when it was effectively checked, though it did not entirely disappear for several years after that date.[1] The equalising of the duties in 1825, combined with an abundant supply of slave labour and of virgin soil suitable for sugar cultivation, enabled production to expand very rapidly, imports of sugar into the United Kingdom from Mauritius rising from 93,723 cwt. in 1825 to 485,326 cwt. in 1830. This expansion contributed to a severe fall in the price of sugar in England, which reached £1. 4s. 11d. per cwt. in 1830 and £1. 3s. 8d. in 1831.

A further circumstance affecting the sugar colonies was the anti-slavery agitation, both in England and the colonies, and the dire forecasts uttered by the friends of the planters of their irremediable ruin if slavery were to be abolished, which damaged their credit in England, rendered their estates unsaleable, and led to the foreclosing of many mortgages. Some of the effects of this lack of capital can be seen in the great reduction in the annual export of brass and copper manufactures, machinery and mill work to the West Indies, which fell from an average of £121,033 for the years 1828-30 to £38,866 for the years 1831-34. Accordingly a new Select Committee was appointed in 1830 to enquire into and devise remedies for the plight of the sugar colonies, which was aggravated by the hurricane that devastated Barbados and the Leeward Islands in 1831 and by the slave-rising in Jamaica at the end of the same year. Mauritius did not come within the scope of the terms of reference of the committee, except so far as her output was a contributory cause to the fall in sugar prices; she enjoyed at this period subsidiary markets for both sugar and rum, especially in Australia, the Cape of Good Hope and Madagascar, and for this and other reasons was less affected by the cheapness of sugar in England than were the West Indies and British Guiana.[2]

The evidence given before the committee, besides stressing the general causes affecting the economic conditions of the sugar colonies which have been mentioned above, threw a good deal of light upon certain features of their economic system which were of great importance. These were the prevalence of absentee ownership; the indebtedness of the planters to mortgage holders in England; and the financial relations between the planters and the West India merchants.

It is difficult to say precisely at what stage in the development of

[1] Cf. *Report of Commissioners of Inquiry upon the Slave Trade at Mauritius*, Parl. Pap. 1829, xxv, p. 76.
[2] Cf. Pridham, C., *England's Colonial Empire*, vol. I, *The Mauritius*, pp. 155-9.

the West Indies the typical form of ownership became that of the absentee. During the course of the eighteenth century there was a gradual but continuous tendency for wealthy and successful proprietors in Jamaica and other islands to retire to England to enjoy their wealth. Their estates were managed by bailiffs to whom they gave a power of attorney, and who were universally known in the sugar colonies as attorneys, the term having no legal connotation. This tendency to forsake the tropical climate and restricted society of the West Indies for the amenities of English life was reinforced by two further factors. The wealth and display of these West India nabobs led to a great eagerness amongst many who had capital in England to purchase properties in the West Indies, and such people, often entirely ignorant of the conduct of sugar or coffee estates, naturally left the management in the hands of the island attorneys. Moreover, where estates had been mortgaged to London merchants and the latter had foreclosed, the merchants often preferred to retain the estates, operating them through an attorney, in preference to selling them on the open market. As a result, by the early part of the nineteenth century, the proportion of resident proprietors had fallen, until, in most islands, they were in a small minority. This prevalence of absentee ownership in the sugar colonies is an outstanding feature of their history and it is important to see the effects of the system.

The duty of the attorney was to exercise a general superintendence over the management of the estate, to order all necessary supplies for the estate from England or elsewhere, drawing bills on the proprietor (or more usually on the merchant to whom the sugar or coffee was consigned on behalf of the proprietor) to cover the expenses defrayed during the course of the year. The attorney was paid as a rule a commission amounting to 6 per cent. on the gross value of the produce shipped.[1] He was responsible for appointing an overseer to conduct the actual work of cultivation and to manage the estate; and he also appointed two or three book-keepers to keep a check on the field work and in general on the overseer. The attorney, therefore, had a position of enormous importance, while the distant proprietor was practically powerless to control his actions. An attorney commonly had a number of estates under his superintendence, and if dishonest, he could put into his own pockets the greater part, if not the whole, of the net proceeds of an estate, while, if, as often happened, he was merely negligent in visiting the property,[2] the overseer had a free hand and could enhance greatly the small nominal salary which he enjoyed. Where the attorney was able and conscientious, the estate was well administered, but, even so, a payment of 6 per cent. on the gross value of the produce shipped was a very heavy burden

[1] Edwards, Bryan, *The History, Civil and Commercial, of the British Colonies in the West Indies* (ed. of 1807), ii, 300.
[2] "I venture to say that not half of the estates are visited by their attorneys once a year", Bigelow, J., *Jamaica in 1850*, p. 88.

on the estate. "The absentee proprietor is compelled to draw everything from the estate and return nothing. He turns all its produce into money and ships it home as fast as possible. None of it is invested in labour-saving machinery, in manuring or in any other way for the benefit of the estate, but all goes to keep down a foreign interest account, to pay off mortgages or to be expended upon his support elsewhere."[1]

An inexperienced or inexpert proprietor was most likely to make his estates pay if he left them in the hands of an able attorney, but it was seldom that an English owner visited his West Indian property without discovering the existence of long-standing abuses and serious waste which his presence enabled him to rectify.[2]

Even worse than the evils of absenteeism were those associated with the existence of heavy mortgages upon the great majority of the estates in the sugar colonies. There were three main causes of this condition. The first and least important type of mortgage arose out of the custom, prevalent in the latter part of the eighteenth century, whereby the owner of an estate imposed upon it charges for marriage portions, annuities, interest on legacies, etc., which had to be met before he could draw upon the produce for his own use.

Secondly, there was much speculative purchase and sale of estates, which changed hands very frequently. The purchaser of an estate valued at £20,000 would put up perhaps £5000 of his own money and would raise the balance on mortgage, hoping either to be successful with his own operation, or that a favourable turn of the market would enable him to re-sell at a profit. The third type of mortgage was a result of the financial relations between the owners of estates and the West Indian merchants.

The normal method of finance was for the proprietor to find the fixed capital, i.e. the land, machinery, slaves, etc., and for the circulating capital to be provided by merchants, most of whom resided in London or Liverpool, though some were domiciled in the colonies. Some of the largest English merchants had branches or agencies in the colonies. The planters secured advances from the merchants against the produce before it was shipped. If the crop was a poor one, or prices fell in the home markets, the planter found himself in debt to the merchant. If the debt could not be paid off quickly or accumulated until it became of considerable amount, the merchant would take out a mortgage on the planter's property. Whenever the planter had to have recourse to the merchant for financial advances, but, above all, when his estate was "encumbered" with a mortgage, he found himself completely tied to his merchant.[3] All his produce

---

[1] Bigelow, J., *Jamaica in 1850*, p. 82.
[2] Much evidence both for and against absenteeism was taken by the Select Committee on Sugar and Coffee Planting, *Parl. Pap.* 1847–8, XXIII, Parts 1–4.
[3] Minutes of Evidence before Select Committee on the State of the West India Colonies, 381, *Parl. Pap.* 1831–32, XX, Q. 667.

had to be shipped through the merchant, either in the merchant's own vessels or in vessels chartered by him.[1] The boat went to the English port assigned by the merchant, the produce was sold by him, and all stores not purchased in the colony had to be bought and shipped back to the estate through him. The merchant, having the whole of the produce under his control, drew his interest of, say, 6 per cent. on the money lent on mortgage; he sold the sugar to the wholesale grocer in England, advancing the money for the duty but charging a commission of $2\frac{1}{2}$ per cent. on the gross selling price (i.e. *cum* duty).[2] By the custom of the trade the sugar was sold at from two to four months' credit, but if the buyer defaulted and could not pay, the loss was borne, not by the merchant but by the planter. Finally, the merchant obtained a commission on all stores bought through him for the plantation, and, if he paid cash, a very considerable discount on the credit price charged to the planter. By a curious custom the planter was allowed to import free of freight a volume of coal or other stores corresponding to that of the sugar or coffee exported to England.[3] It is not surprising to find merchants admitting frankly that their chief incentive in advancing money to the planters lay in the merchanting profits to be derived from the transport and sale of the produce rather than in the nominal interest received on the loans.[4] The merchant's main concern was that as much produce as possible should be extracted from the soil and exported, irrespective of its cost of production or its profitableness to the planter. Edwards describes a class of merchants who lent money to a new proprietor at the beginning of his operations, with the aid of which he carried out the arduous work of clearing and planting the land and erecting the buildings. When the time came for buying negroes and stock, the lender demanded immediate repayment, with the result that a forced sale was hurried on; no bidders appeared but the creditor himself, who had the estate knocked down to him at his own price. He says that this practice was especially common in Jamaica. On the other hand, he goes on to say that there were other cases where the merchants had no desire to become planters but had found themselves forced to take over an unprofitable estate or lose their money altogether.[5]

It would be unfair to lay upon the West India merchants as a class the stigma of oppressive and extortionate conduct towards the planter. They performed valuable and essential services for the planter: they financed his current requirements; they advanced the duty and marketed his crop; and they provided regular lines of specially constructed vessels at the times required.[6] The age-long

---

[1] Minutes of Evidence before Select Committee on the State of the West India Colonies, *Parl. Pap.* 1831–32, xx (381), Q. 2677.
[2] *Ibid.* QQ. 669–73 and Q. 1431.   [3] *Ibid.* QQ. 2379, 2535, 2761.
[4] *Ibid.* QQ. 1075–81.
[5] Edwards, B., *op. cit.* II, 302–5.
[6] *Parl. Pap.* 1831–32, xx (381), QQ. 2662, 2698.

conflict between the liner and the tramp—or "seeking vessel", as it was then termed—and the complaint of the shipper against being tied to the former with its higher rates, are to be found clearly set out in the evidence before the committee of 1831–32. This committee, in their Report, exonerated the merchants from the general charge of sharp practice and dishonesty, and held that the planters who were financially dependent on the merchants merely suffered the inconvenience and loss resulting from their lack of ready money and powerlessness to finance themselves. There seems little doubt, however, that the general scale of charges was high, having been fixed in the period when the slave trade was still in operation and when high prices and large profits were the rule rather than the exception. The burden, both of the interest and the merchanting charges, was endurable so long as the price of sugar continued at a level satisfactory to the producer. But with low and falling prices the fixed interest on the mortgage often absorbed all and more than all the net income of the estate. The arrears accumulated at compound interest until the creditor foreclosed and the estate was sold up.

Thus estates changed hands with great frequency and new capital was continually being brought into the plantations only to be lost in a few years. The whole business of plantation ownership was, and always had been, highly speculative: it appealed to the gambling instinct of men rather than to any sober calculation of risks and probable profits. Edwards remarked at the beginning of the nineteenth century: "Though perhaps not more than one man in fifty comes away fortunate, every sanguine adventurer takes for granted that he shall be that one."[1] The readiness with which, from 1815 onwards, capital was invested in the West Indies whenever there was the slightest improvement in conditions is a proof that the tradition of the sudden rise to fortune of so many sugar nabobs in the past exercised enduring influence and that sugar cultivation was rarely unprofitable in the long run in spite of occasional years of very low prices. It is significant that a witness, who had been managing estates in Trinidad since 1829, could not remember the depression of 1830–31, when giving evidence in 1842.[2]

The sugar colonies derived little benefit from the Report of the Select Committee of 1830. The committee was unable to approve the adoption of any of the more drastic proposals put forward by the colonists, and contented itself with recommending that an examination should be made into the financial possibilities of a reduction of the British duties on colonial sugar, that facilities should be given to the indebted colonists to borrow money at a low rate of interest with a sinking fund spread over a long period of years, and that a number

---

[1] Edwards, B., *op. cit.* II, 306.
[2] Evidence before Select Committee on West India Colonies, *Parl. Pap.* 1842, XIII (479), Q. 4066.

of minor changes be made in the system of regulations and restrictions on colonial trade.

The Government ignored even the modest recommendations of the committee; the sugar duties were not lowered, and in other respects the burdens against which the colonists complained were left unaltered. Thus the long-standing grievance of the $4\frac{1}{2}$ per cent. duty[1] on all gross produce exported from the Leeward Islands remained and was not abolished till 1838; while, when the vacuum pan method of producing sugar of a much finer quality than the ordinary muscovado was introduced into British Guiana early in the 'thirties, it was decided by a Treasury ruling of June 1833 that such sugar was liable to the prohibitory duty of £8. 8s. per cwt. on imported refined sugar.[2] In one respect, however, the evidence of the very real distress prevailing in the West Indies influenced Parliament, for in 1832 an Act (3 William IV, c. 125) was passed empowering the issue of Exchequer Bills up to a maximum of £1,000,000, the proceeds to be used to relieve the losses sustained by the planters in Jamaica owing to the insurrection of 1831, and in Barbados, St Vincent and St Lucia, owing to the hurricane of the same year. Of this sum £500,000 was allotted to Jamaica.

The Report of the committee on the commercial state of the West Indies was published in 1832 when the agitation for the emancipation of the slaves was at its height. In 1833 the Abolition Act was passed by the Imperial Parliament, and from 1 August 1834 (in Mauritius 1 February 1835) slavery was replaced by a period of apprenticeship designed to be a transitional measure pending complete emancipation in from four to six years' time.

Two colonies—Bermuda and Antigua—instead of accepting the period of apprenticeship, voted for immediate abolition. In both cases the relations between the planters and the slaves appear to have been exceptionally good. Of Antigua it was said that the slaves there had reached a higher level of religious and social development than in many of the other colonies.[3]

Antigua was a small and densely populated island, with some 30,000 slaves and no undeveloped land; all provisions were imported and the negro had no alternative but to work. The planters had the foresight to realise that the apprenticeship system would be difficult to operate, and their wisdom was justified in the event. One planter, looking back on the great leap-in-the-dark of 1834, declared: "I would rather have given up my compensation money, as it was called, than have been kept in hot water for six years by the appren-

---

[1] See *C.H.B.E.* vol. I, p. 292.
[2] Minutes of Evidence before the Select Committee on Sugar Duties, *Parl. Pap.* 1862, XIII (390), Q. 29.
[3] *Papers relative to the Abolition of Slavery in the British Colonies, Parl. Pap.* 1835 (1), p. 535.
[4] Minutes of Evidence before the Select Committee of the House of Commons on Sugar and Coffee Planting, Part I, *Parl. Pap.* 1847–8, XXIII (123), Q. 9160.

ticeship system."[4] The good will of the negroes was gained from the outset, and though this was severely strained by the low rates of wages paid at first for free labour, the sudden transformation from slavery to freedom was accompanied by no upheavals or any serious decline in production. The planters did their utmost to raise the standard of comfort of the enfranchised negroes by establishing stores in different parts of the island for the sale of silks, wines, perfumery and other articles of luxury. In consequence imports increased and the desire of the negroes to earn money was stimulated. Within two or three years of emancipation the value of land had risen appreciably, and, while this cannot be dissociated from the rising prices of sugar in the English market, it was a vindication of the belief that the cultivation of sugar by free labour could be carried on at a profit.

The Abolition Act was drafted in outline and many highly important matters of detail were left to the colonies. As in 1823, so again in 1833, the Crown Colonies were legislated for by an Order-in-Council, of which a copy was sent to the self-governing colonies to serve as a model. With the bait of compensation spread before them the majority passed laws for the enforcement of the Act which were largely, if not wholly, acceptable to the Colonial Office. Some measure of co-ordination, so far as the executive side of government was concerned, had been secured by a loose federation of the Leeward Islands—Antigua, Dominica, Montserrat, Barbuda, St Kitts, Nevis— and the Virgin Islands in 1832, the Governor-in-Chief having his seat in Antigua. A similar Federation was formed for the Windward Islands in 1833, when Barbados, Grenada, St Vincent and Tobago were united under one Governor in Barbados. In both cases the lesser islands were administered by Lieutenant-Governors who reported to the Colonial Office through the Governor. All the colonies retained their own laws, systems of justice and elected Assemblies. The centralisation thus obtained related only to the relation between the colonial representatives of the Crown and the Home Government. Indeed, when the Governor of Antigua in 1837 very sensibly convened a General Council and Assembly of all the legislatures of the Leeward Islands to meet at Antigua in order to discuss the problems arising out of the abolition of slavery, his action was disavowed by the Colonial Office and the meeting had to be cancelled.

Jamaica, with 312,000 apprentices out of a total of 670,000, received about £6,150,000 out of the aggregate sum of £16,589,000 actually paid in compensation for the freeing of the slaves. She regarded herself, with some justice, as having been badly treated in the allocation of the compensation money, for the basis adopted favoured the newer colonies with unexhausted soils such as Trinidad and British Guiana. Hence, although she had, surprisingly, been the first colony to pass an Abolition Act, it was not long before serious disagreement arose between the colonists and the Home Government. The Colonial Office had approved the Jamaican Act on condition that an Amending Act was passed. This was done but was allowed to lapse at the end of a few months. The Governor, the Earl of Sligo, himself a large proprietor, did his utmost to bring the Assembly to reason but became involved in a dispute with it over a question of breach of privilege and was recalled in 1836. Before he left the island, however, the Home Government on his advice had taken the unusual step of passing a bill through the House of Commons providing that the Amending Act should be prolonged to 1840 unless this had already been done in the Jamaican legislature. The Act was in fact renewed in July 1836. The Earl of Sligo was succeeded by Sir Lionel Smith, who as Governor of Barbados had shown firmness in his dealings with the apprentices and was regarded with favour by the planters.

It was not long before the new Governor found himself at loggerheads with the colonists. His predecessor, mainly through ignorance, had tolerated abuses of the apprenticeship system in such matters as the number of working hours, the valuation of apprentices for immediate freedom, the withholding of allowances in kind, and the treatment of prisoners. All Sir Lionel Smith's representations on these matters were ignored by the Assembly, but most of the abuses were remedied by an Amending Act which was passed, largely with Jamaica in view, by the Imperial Parliament in April 1838. Only a few months had elapsed before there came the sudden unexpected ending of the apprenticeship system throughout the sugar colonies.

As has been stated above, the term of apprenticeship fixed in the Abolition Act of 1833 had been six years for the predial and four years for the non-predial slaves. The latter would therefore be completely free on 1 August 1838. But the Act had not specified to which category the important class of estate artisans belonged, and it was not until May 1838 that the Colonial Office notified the colonies that these artisans were to be reckoned among the non-predials. The planters therefore found themselves in the difficulty that if apprenticeship continued after August 1838 they would no longer be able to compel the services of the estate artisans, while they would remain subject to the restrictions imposed by the Amending Act of 1838. The apprenticeship system had proved difficult to work and was not popular with the planters themselves, and in addition there was a widespread fear of revolt among those who were not released from bondage. These considerations, which were urged on the colonies by the Colonial Office, proved decisive, and with varying degrees of reluctance on the part of the local legislatures, they all passed Acts terminating apprenticeship completely on 1 August 1838.

The feeling of reluctance was greatest in Jamaica, where it was only partially mitigated by the belief in the colony that the objectionable Amending Act of May 1838 would lapse with the end of apprenticeship. What they had most resented in this Act was the power given to the Governors of colonies (including those with legislative assemblies) to legislate by proclamation in regard to certain matters, especially the conduct of prisons. The Home Government, however, was not prepared to tolerate a return to the old *régime* under which women were flogged in prison and the treadmill was extensively used.[1] Accordingly a bill was hastily passed through Parliament in July 1838, entitled "An Act for the better Government of prisons in the West Indies", by virtue of which the Governors obtained the power to take over the regulation and management of prisons. The Jamaican Assembly at once resisted; it met in September 1838 and, after declaring in violent language that its constitutional rights had been grossly invaded, refused to carry out its functions so long as the Prisons Act remained in force. Consequently a number of expiring laws, including even that providing for a police force, were not renewed, nor were any measures devised to deal with the needs of a free society. The Governor dissolved the Assembly but found the new body equally recalcitrant. It seemed clear that the only way out of the deadlock lay in recourse to the ultimate sovereignty of the Imperial Parliament, and in April 1839 Lord Melbourne's Government introduced a bill in the House of Commons to suspend the constitution of Jamaica for five years. The bill was hotly contested and Lord Melbourne resigned. He returned to office in the following month and a much milder measure was then brought forward which was further weakened by amendments in the House of Lords. In its final form the Act merely empowered the Governor-in-Council to revive the expiring laws if the Assembly failed to do so.

Through no fault of his own the planters had become so antagonistic to Sir Lionel Smith that there was no prospect of his being able to restore friendly relations between the Crown and the Assembly. He was therefore recalled and Sir Charles Metcalfe, who had distinguished himself as an administrator in India, was sent out to replace him in September 1839. The choice was a good one, for Metcalfe proved himself to be a Governor of exceptional capacity. His instructions were to conciliate the colonists and to secure their cooperation. By the exercise of much tact and skill, and with a real understanding of their difficulties, he succeeded in persuading the Assembly to comply with the wishes of the Colonial Office. The appropriate legislation was enacted, and the emergency powers of the Governor remained in abeyance. Metcalfe's policy was continued by his successor Lord Elgin, also a man of great ability, and proved for the time being eminently successful. So this tempestuous colony enjoyed a brief period of comparative quiet until a fresh and equally violent conflict arose out of the equalisation of the sugar duties in 1846.

[1] Mathieson, W. L., *op. cit.* p. 311.

In one other colony, British Guiana, a serious constitutional struggle developed during the early stages of emancipation. Here the precise powers of the Combined Court in regard to finance were even more in dispute than those of the Court of Policy in regard to other legislation. The colonists claimed that they possessed, and that the terms of the capitulation had guaranteed to them, the full measure of financial autonomy enjoyed by colonies with elective Assemblies, including the right to modify the Civil List, i.e. the salaries of the Governor and other members of the Administration. This claim the Colonial Office denied, contending that the powers of the Court related only to supply, or the voting of taxes, and not to appropriation, or the decision as to the allocation of expenditure. During prolonged negotiations lasting from 1834 to 1836 the British Government compromised to the extent of admitting the right of the Combined Court to discuss the other estimates provided that a satisfactory Civil List was voted for seven years. In 1840 the large increase in administrative expenditure consequent on the abolition of slavery, and the higher working costs to the planters under a system of free labour, led to an agitation for the reduction of the estimates. The introduction that year of new estimates, which provided for an expenditure nearly twice as great as in the preceding period, brought matters to a head. The Combined Court refused to vote the supplies for the Civil List unless some of their demands were granted, and, in particular, unless a satisfactory immigration ordinance was guaranteed. For some months neither side would move and no taxes were collected in the colony, but eventually a compromise was again reached. The Colonial Office gave way over the immigration ordinance, while the Combined Court agreed to vote the Civil List.[1] It was further decided, by an Order-in-Council of 1842, that the Court was entitled to strike out or reduce any item of the estimates except those in the Civil List or those secured by law. This was but one of many instances during the nineteenth century of concessions extracted by the colonists by means of their control over finance—a control which was recognised up to a point by the Colonial Office but which was never sufficiently clearly defined. The resulting friction and obstruction proved a serious handicap to the progress of the colony.[2]

Although in 1834 slavery had disappeared as a legal and social institution, many of its economic characteristics were retained under the system of indentured labour which prevailed during the brief period of apprenticeship. The negro could neither leave his master's plantation nor could he cease from working during the forty-five hours per week which he was legally compelled to give to his master in exchange for food, clothing and houseroom. If the negroes under slavery had supported themselves by the cultivation of provision

[1] Rodway, J., History of British Guiana, III, 57–60.
[2] Report of the British Guiana Commission; Parl. Pap. 1927, VII [Cmd. 2841], pp. 50–51.

grounds, as was very generally the case, they were allowed 4½ hours off a week for this purpose, thus reducing their compulsory working week to 40½ hours. This provision opened the way to endless friction. Subject to the limitation of the total number of hours, it was left to the employers to distribute them as they thought fit. The arrangement which was most popular with the negroes as a rule was 9 hours a day for four days and 4½ hours on the fifth day, leaving Friday afternoon free. But in many cases, especially in Jamaica, the 8-hour day was adopted, often as a punishment, to the great dissatisfaction of the negro, who thereby lost his Friday.

The intention of the Abolition Act had been that the customary allowances to the slaves, such as salt fish and meal, should be continued, but the planters not infrequently abolished these allowances altogether, partly as a measure of economy and partly in order to bring an added pressure to bear on the negroes to hire themselves out for wages. Alternatively, the allowances were valued at a certain sum and set off against extra labour performed by the negroes.[1] In parts of Jamaica and British Guiana the lot of the apprentice was a harder one than had been the lot of the slave. The planters, realising that their period of domination was drawing to a close, and fiercely resentful of the agitation of the Anti-Slavery Society and of the interference of the Imperial Parliament, were resolved to extract the uttermost from the negroes while they still had the mastery over them, though this was not true of all the islands or of conditions universally in any island.[2]

The new system would have brought with it far greater abuses had it not been for the special stipendiary magistrates, of whom in the first instance one hundred were appointed and paid by the British Government to administer justice under the Abolition Act as between the planters and the apprentices. The power of ordering punishment was taken from the planters and from the island justices, who were almost invariably themselves representatives of the planting interests, and was given to the special magistrates sent out from England. After apprenticeship had been in operation for some time, it was found that additional special magistrates were needed and considerable numbers of the local inhabitants were nominated by the Governors of the colonies to act in this capacity. Many of these, contrary to the intentions of the Imperial Act, were either planters or connected with the planting interests. An immense amount of criticism and obloquy from both sides was directed against the special magistrates, who were both over-worked and under-paid, but the evidence shows that with relatively few exceptions they did their work well and fairly under exceedingly difficult circumstances.

Considerable advantage was taken of the right given by the

---

[1] Sturge, J. and Harvey, T. *The West Indies in 1837*, 2nd ed. (1838), p. 459.
[2] See Hansard, XLII, 47–59.

Abolition Act to the apprentices to purchase their freedom outright. In the first twenty-two months in Jamaica alone 998 apprentices purchased their freedom by valuation and paid £33,998 currency (equivalent to £20,387 sterling) or approximately £34 currency per head.[1] The valuations were carried out by a tribunal of three, composed of two special magistrates and one local justice of the peace. In case of disagreement the special magistrates could refuse to approve the valuation, in which case the transaction could not be completed, but, as a rule, an average was struck at which the valuation was fixed. The appraisements were widely criticised, and with a good deal of justice, on the ground that they were frequently much too high, being well above the rates at which slaves had been sold before the apprenticeship.

The repercussions of the apprenticeship system upon the economic interests of the planters were much less serious than they had feared. There was undoubtedly more difficulty than formerly in getting sufficient workers during the crop season, and for the manufacturing processes where continuous labour for long stretches was essential. Slaves had worked in the mills from fourteen to sixteen hours daily, but apprentices not more than twelve, and then only if high over time rates were paid. Much time also was lost owing to the necessity for referring disputes over the performance of work, questions of discipline, etc., to the stipendiary magistrates.[2] On the other hand, the decrease in the supply of labour consequent upon the diminution in the number of hours of compulsory labour was partly compensated for by the extra work done more or less voluntarily for wages, and by the introduction on a considerable scale of machinery and of the system of piece wages. Moreover, the planters benefited to an important extent from the compensation money paid by the British Government to the owners of slaves. The share of Jamaica alone was £6,149,934 and many individual proprietors had very large sums allotted to them. These sums were only partially available for investment in improvements such as steam engines, new machinery, etc., which were urgently needed in order to economise labour, for a considerable proportion of the compensation money passed to the mortgagees who held liens on West India property. Many of these had lost all hope of recovering their loans, and they were quick to seize the opportunity to put in their claims and to secure a ruling giving them priority over the proprietor himself when the money came to be distributed. Nevertheless, the gain even to the encumbered proprietor was appreciable; he could free his estate from debt, or at least lighten the burden materially and so save the interest that he

---

[1] Minutes of evidence before the Select Committee on Negro Apprenticeship in the Colonies, *Parl. Pap.* 1836, xv (560), Q. 5863.

[2] Evidence before Select Committee on West India Colonies, *Parl. Pap.* 1842, xiii (477), Q. 1407.

had been paying for many years past. With the lessening of indebtedness and the waning of the agitation of the anti-slavery party the selling value of properties rose, and for a brief time the credit of the planters stood higher than for several years past.

Fortunately, also, for the planters, the reduction of the duty on plantation sugar from 27s. to 24s. per cwt. in 1830 and the low prices ruling at that time had stimulated consumption in England, and, with an improvement in trade, prices had been rising since 1831. The widely advertised fears of the colonists that emancipation would destroy the sugar industry had led after 1834 to considerable speculation in sugar, the price of which in bond in London rose to £2. 0s. 10d. per cwt. in 1836—the highest average level since 1819. Against these favourable factors must be set the fact that costs tended to be higher, as the planters were losing at least 16 per cent. of the former compulsory working hours and were compelled to pay wages for any extra work performed over and above the stipulated forty-five hours.

In order to show the effects of apprenticeship upon output it is necessary, in the absence of comparable figures of production or export, to take the quantities imported into the United Kingdom. Domestic consumption at this period was small in all the colonies, and, with the exception of Mauritius, practically the whole of the exports of sugar and coffee were sent to the mother country. Even in the case of Mauritius, the volume of sugar exported to other countries was normally only a small proportion of the whole. Taking five years of slavery, 1829–33, and four years of apprenticeship, 1835–38, the average annual import of sugar to the United Kingdom from the British West Indies (including British Guiana) in 1829–33 was 3,917,912 cwt., and in 1835–38, 3,487,801 cwt.; the corresponding figures for Mauritius were 470,155 cwt. in the earlier period and 549,872 cwt. in the latter period. In the case of coffee the decline was more serious—from 23,645,639 lb. to 16,731,360 lb. for the whole of the West Indies. Thus, while the output of sugar in Mauritius increased appreciably (a fact which was partly accounted for by the introduction of about 12,000 Indians between 1834 and 1837 to work in the plantations) the output of West Indian sugar decreased by nearly 11 per cent. and of coffee by as much as 29 per cent., by far the greatest part of the falling off in production being attributable to one colony only—Jamaica, where the apprentices were most harshly treated. Elsewhere the changes in either direction were not very large, though there was an appreciable expansion of output in both Barbados and British Guiana. But neither in these colonies, nor in Mauritius, could it be said that apprenticeship was a success. From whichever angle it is regarded, whether as a term of probation to prepare the negroes for ultimate emancipation, or as an integral part of the compensation to be paid to the planters, it failed to achieve its objects, and there was universal dissatisfaction with the system.

The final emancipation of all classes of workers in 1838 was due to several causes—the colonists' realisation of the shortcomings of the apprenticeship system; the fear of revolts and uprisings on the part of the predial negroes if their period of servitude were prolonged beyond that date; the desire to forestall the possibility of an over-riding Act of the Imperial Parliament; and the decision of the Colonial Office that estate artisans must be considered non-predials and must therefore be emancipated in 1838. Thus, as we have already seen, the legislatures of the different colonies introduced and passed bills abolishing apprenticeship on 1 August 1838. In Mauritius, owing to the later date at which the apprenticeship system came into force, complete freedom was deferred until 1 April 1839.

The new state of society involved very comprehensive changes in the legal and social institutions of the colonies. Many laws in force under slavery had to be repealed or modified, while new laws needed to be introduced. The most important of the latter dealt with the respective rights of masters and servants; the prevention and punishment of vagrancy; the prevention of "squatting", i.e. the unauthorised occupation of land; the organisation of police forces; the regulation of the militia; and the maintenance of the poor. The passing of these laws gave rise to much friction between the British Government and the colonial legislatures. The Colonial Office, dominated by the doctrines of the Manchester School and harassed by Exeter Hall and a widespread agitation,[1] opposed a rigid veto to any measures put forward by the colonists involving compulsion or coercion. If a free labour market worked well in England, it should also succeed in the West Indies, and no restraint must be imposed on the operation of the laws of supply and demand. Colonies in which there was much free land were not allowed to pass drastic measures against squatting, and not even the plea that colonial vagrancy laws merely reproduced the provisions of English statutes sufficed to secure their approval.[2] The situation was further complicated by the fact that some of the chartered colonies had passed legislation in the years 1834–38 which had been allowed on the ground that new measures were so urgently needed that it would be undesirable to hold them up unless for very strong reasons. Moreover, the apprenticeship period being a legal continuation of a semi-slavery, restrictions could be permitted which would not be compatible with a state of complete freedom.[3]

Difficult and knotty problems arose at once out of the contract of

[1] Hansard, XLIII, 409 seqq.
[2] Cf. Lord Glenelg to Sir E. J. M. Macgregor, 31 August 1838, Parl. Pap. 1839, XXXVI (323).
[3] Cf. Lord J. Russell to Sir C. T. Metcalfe, 26 April 1841, Parl. Pap. 1841, Sess. 2, III [341], p. 568.

service between master and servants. When Antigua abolished slavery completely in 1834 she passed an Act based on the system of hiring prevalent at that time in English rural districts.[1] Under this Act the receipt of a week's wages was *prima facie* evidence of a "general hiring" for a period of twelve months, subject to the right of either party to withdraw on giving one month's notice. The Act also imposed a fine of £10 on anyone employing a person under a general hiring on another estate. But when other colonies sought in 1838 to enact similar legislation their measures were, without exception, disallowed at home. A considerable time necessarily elapsed before laws could be passed which the Colonial Office would approve, and in the meantime the negroes became accustomed to the absence of any legal restraint on their disposal of their labour. In any case the insistence by the Colonial Office on a written contract for any period exceeding one month was sufficient to render any such provision nugatory, for the negroes had an overwhelming prejudice against putting their name to any legal document, fearing that they were being induced to sign away their newly acquired freedom. They were also supported in their unwillingness to enter into contracts by the advice of the missionaries, the stipendiary magistrates and the colonial authorities. Except in Antigua, where the system of annual hirings was allowed to continue with satisfactory results for the time being, the normal form of contract of employment was the informal daily or weekly hiring. It is probable that in the larger colonies no contract system would, in the long run, have been effective or enforceable in practice, but elsewhere the planters would have benefited considerably if the Antiguan system could have been put into operation in 1838. Here, as in other respects, the colonists suffered from the failure of the Home Government to understand their problems and difficulties. They were also the victims of the premature termination of apprenticeship which took the Colonial Office as much by surprise as it did the colonists themselves. No preparations had been made in anticipation of the change, none of the most necessary adjustments had been thought out, and a bewildered and resentful community moved straight from the vexatious complexities of apprenticeship into a state of freedom.

The reform of the system of justice in the colonies was long overdue. It was notorious that both civil and criminal justice were very indifferently administered in most of the colonies. In some colonies the laws had never been printed, and existed only in manuscript; in others, e.g. Trinidad and St Lucia, the laws and methods of legal procedure were based on those in force when the colonies were captured from their former holders. In general, too, much power in both civil and criminal matters was in the hands of local justices of

---

[1] The first Act (1834) was unacceptable in some particulars to the Colonial Office, but, as passed in an amended form on 6 August 1835, it was approved.

the peace who were almost always themselves planters or associated with the planting interest. Most of the judges in important civil courts were men devoid of legal training. Litigation was slow, uncertain and exceedingly costly.

In most of the colonies the chief method of reform consisted in the continuation of the jurisdiction of the stipendiary magistrates in matters affecting the relations of master and servant. In Jamaica alone, the feeling against the special magistrates, who, in their view, had been forced on the islands by an Act of the Imperial Parliament and who had superseded the local justices, was so intense that, though a reduced number of stipendiary magistrates continued to function after the termination of apprenticeship, they were only allowed to act in conjunction with the local justices, by whom their recommendations were frequently over-ruled.[1]

Further, except in Jamaica, a bench of two or three stipendiary magistrates was constituted a Court of Appeal from the decisions of the local justices and other courts of primary jurisdiction. Finally, though the details differed widely in different colonies, obsolete and archaic courts were abolished and judges with legal experience and training were appointed to the higher court. The criminal law was at the same time revised so as to bring it into closer harmony with English practice. These reforms were not accomplished at once and many years passed before they were completed and made general throughout the colonies.

The most immediately urgent question in August 1838 was the rate of wages to be paid for labour. The planters, especially in Jamaica, very quickly paid the penalty for one of the many injustices that had been perpetrated during apprenticeship. The value at which the apprentices could then buy their immediate freedom had been based on an estimated monetary value per day which was multiplied by the number of working days still to run till the end of apprenticeship. It was to the planter's interest therefore to fix the value as high as possible, and it was notorious that the negroes were assessed proportionately much higher than their market value under slavery. Furthermore, the planters were prepared during the same period to pay from 2s. 6d. to 3s. 6d. (currency), and even more during crop time, for extra labour on Friday and Saturday. This was appreciably more than they were willing to pay or than many of them could pay normally under the new system. The negroes expected to receive at least as much as they had been getting during apprenticeship and were bitterly disappointed when they found that the current wage which most planters were prepared to offer in Jamaica was 1s. 8d. per day for first grade field labourers. On some estates the planters refused to pay more than 1s. 0½d. with the result that their negroes refused to work at all at that rate; on others the negroes

---

[1] Pringle, Hall, *The Fall of the Sugar Planters of Jamaica*, p. 53.

demanded 3s. 6d. to 4s 6d. a day, which was much more than the planters could afford. Both the missionaries and the stipendiary magistrates incurred the odium of the planters by advising the negroes not to accept abnormally low rates of wages, but on the other hand, they discouraged the negroes from putting forward unreasonable and extortionate demands. The rate of wages varied widely in different colonies, being highest in British Guiana and in Trinidad, where the soil was the most fertile and the population the smallest in relation to the area under cultivation or available for settlement, and lowest in Barbados with its dense population and in some of the older and most impoverished of the smaller islands. In Mauritius wages were kept down by the immigration of coolies from India. Comparison is rendered difficult by the fact that from 1840 onwards it became increasingly common to charge rent for the labourers' houses and provision grounds as a partial set off against wages, which, however, then tended to be higher than on those estates where rent was not demanded. Also, in some of the colonies, allowances of food, rum, etc., which were part of the regular maintenance of the negroes under slavery, were continued after emancipation. In most cases where these allowances had been made they were withdrawn after 1841 when the fall in the price of sugar led to strenuous attempts to lower wages and thereby reduce the cost of production.[1] In British Guiana and Trinidad the shortage of labour was such that it was very difficult to secure uniformity of action among the planters, and the individual planter who tried to reduce wages found himself faced as a rule by the loss of most of his workers.[2]

In general, the rate of wages had a complex reaction upon the supply of labour. On the one hand, if wages fell below a certain level it paid the negro better to withdraw altogether from estate labour, cultivate a small plot of land and sell his surplus produce on the market; while, on the other hand, high wages resulted in his being able to cover his modest requirements with the proceeds of only three or four days' work a week. The money rate of wages varied in 1840 from 9d. (sterling) a day in the smaller islands to from 1s. 8d. to 2s. 6d. per day in Trinidad and British Guiana. In most of the colonies piecework was extensively resorted to for certain classes of work, such as weeding, cutting cane-holes, etc., and proved as a rule more satisfactory than payment by the day. The size of the task was governed by schedules drawn up under slavery or during the emancipation period and represented what was considered a fair day's work for a slave of average strength, but it was found under freedom that a good labourer could easily do a task in from 4½ to 5 hours.[3] In Barbados,

[1] Evidence before Select Committee on West India Produce, Parl. Pap. 1842, XIII (479), QQ. 3915.
[2] Ibid. Q. 2573. Cf. also Premium, Barton, Eight Years in British Guiana, p. 143.
[3] Papers relating to the Affairs of British Guiana, Parl. Pap. 1841, XVI [321], p. 152.

where labour was plentiful, the piecework system was little employed owing to the feeling that it led to work being scamped and rendered the negroes more independent of their masters.[1]

Under a slave economy the planters' chief requirements for running their estates were purchased abroad and almost the whole of the produce was sold out of the colony. A system of free labour involved a very large demand for additional currency, especially of small denominations suitable for paying wages and for the retail purchases of the negroes. As one planter complained: "In a state of slavery the planter may go on from day to day and from year to year upon credit, working the estate by the labour of the slaves; but in the present state of society he cannot move an inch unless his pockets are full of money."[2] Except in Jamaica and British Guiana there was no paper money in circulation prior to the abolition of slavery. Every colony had an extraordinary miscellany of coins; in most of the West Indian Islands gold doubloons, Portuguese Johannes, escudos, eagles, etc., were current or were used as money of account. The commonest silver coin was the Spanish dollar, but there were also large quantities of American dollars in circulation and some British silver coins. In British Guiana the currency consisted of Dutch guilders and Spanish dollars. The trade figures and public accounts were kept as a rule in terms of £ currency, and the rate of exchange in terms of sterling varied from year to year and from colony to colony. Some of the difficulties associated with the establishment of a wage system were undoubtedly due to the shortage of fractional currency.

Complaints were most frequent on this score in Jamaica, in spite of the fact that the legislature had devoted £200,000, out of the £500,000 loan made to the colony in 1836 by the Imperial Parliament, to the acquisition and import of half-crowns, shillings and sixpences in British silver. Subsequently the Assembly remitted funds to England and brought out £10,000 in 3d. and 1½d. silver coins.[3] In British Guiana the colony of Demerara had a considerable paper currency based on securities invested in England. In 1834 the Court of Policy resolved that the interest on these securities, amounting to £5000 per annum, should henceforward be remitted in silver coin.[4] Large sums of money in the same form were also sent out to the colonies by the West India merchants, but great difficulty was found in keeping it in circulation. In some cases the merchants in the colonies bought up the silver and sent it home as a cheaper method of remittance than by buying sterling drafts.[5] Another important

[1] Evidence before Select Committee on West India Produce, *Parl. Pap.* 1842, XIII (479), Q. 1490.
[2] Evidence before Select Committee on Sugar and Coffee Planting, *Parl. Pap.* 1847–48, XXIII, Part II (184), Q. 9075.
[3] Minutes of Evidence before Select Committee of the House of Commons on Negro Apprenticeship in the Colonies, *Parl. Pap.* 1836, xv (560), Q. 5518.
[4] Halliday, Sir A., *The West Indies*, p. 195.
[5] Minutes of Evidence before Select Committee of the House of Commons on Colonial Accounts, *Parl. Pap.* 1837, VII (516), Q. 1104.

source of loss arose out of the trade between the West Indies and the United States; the merchants of the latter refused to accept produce and demanded payment either in sterling bills on London or else in cash.

The fundamental obstacle in the way of the circulation of English silver money in the West Indies had been that, under an Order-in-Council of 23 March 1825, the shilling had been undervalued in terms of the Spanish dollar, with the result that, while the latter together with the gold doubloon continued to circulate, the former was largely driven out.[1] In 1838 this error was rectified and the dollar and the doubloon were correctly rated at 4s. 2d. and 64s. sterling respectively. By degrees, in all the West India Islands and British Guiana, sterling became the unit of account, though it was not until the effects of the gold discoveries of 1849 and 1851 were fully felt that the dollar was finally driven out of circulation.

Before the apprenticeship period banking, other than that carried on by the large commercial houses, was virtually unknown in the sugar colonies, but the new demand for a medium of exchange led to the establishment of banks on a considerable scale; in some of the colonies part of the compensation money for the freeing of the slaves was employed in this way.[2] In 1836 the Colonial Bank for the West Indies was incorporated with a capital of £2,000,000, the bulk of which was subscribed in England. Its headquarters were in London, but its chief offices were in Jamaica, with branches in all the more important islands and in British Guiana. The notes of the bank were convertible into silver. Its general policy was based on Scottish banking methods (especially the cash credit system) which were regarded as the most suitable for the area in which it was operating.[3]

By virtue of the slave codes the slave was entitled to a certain standard of food and houseroom. The usual way in which the bulk of the food requirements of the slaves, apart from salt fish, was met, was by the allocation of a certain quantity of land which the slave could cultivate in his own time and on which he could grow his own food. These provision grounds in colonies with a great deal of land, such as Jamaica, British Guiana and Trinidad, were fairly extensive, and the negro could often meet his own needs and have a surplus over to take to market. On the abolition of apprenticeship there was no general uniformity in the method of treatment of these grounds.

At first the planters were restrained by the provision of the Emancipation Act empowering the negroes to remain for three months in undisturbed possession of the houses and grounds which they occupied and cultivated on the estates where they had been working, and in the case of the sick and infirm this was extended to 1 June 1839. But

---

[1] Chalmers, R., *Colonial Currency*, p. 24.
[2] E.g. the Mauritius Commercial Bank, founded in 1839. Cf. Baster, A. S. J., *The Imperial Banks*, p. 77.
[3] Martin, R. M., *Statistics of the British Colonies*, p. 20.

when this period came to an end, the planters had uncontrolled rights over the whole of their property, and in many cases, above all in Jamaica, they pursued a policy which was both oppressive and unwise. Rents were fixed at an exorbitant figure, sometimes in the form of a poll tax on every member of the family over ten years of age. Where the wages paid were 1s. 8d. per day, the rents varied from 3s. 4d. to 5s., and even more per week. If the negro could not pay, he was ruthlessly evicted. Sometimes when the rent was a few shillings in arrears, the planter, instead of seeking to recover the debt in a court of summary jurisdiction, brought the case before the Court of Common Pleas, where the costs amounted to several pounds.[1] One of the stipendiary magistrates in Jamaica observed: "I fear that most of the managers are endeavouring under the colour of law, both in the rent and ejectment cases, to establish a system of compulsory labour, and the plan of entirely depriving the people of their grounds now appears the mode most universally adopted."[2]

In Barbados the usual practice at first was to demand no rent if the negro worked a full week on the estate, but for every day's absence from work a rent charge was made. In many other islands labourers with houses and provision grounds were given lower wages than those who came from outside to work on the estate. In British Guiana, where the shortage of labour was especially great, the planters did their utmost to keep the negroes on the estates by making no charge for rent and by improving the labourers' cottages.

As time progressed, conditions gradually became stabilised in Jamaica as well as in the other colonies, rents were fixed at reasonable levels, and there was a growing tendency in colonies where the practice at first had been to make no charge for rent, for the owners to realise the advantage to be derived from rent payments. But in most cases the negroes remained tenants at will, which acted as a deterrent to their making any improvements and provided a strong incentive to them to settle on freehold land away from the estates. The rent payment also continued in large measure to be mixed up with the payment of wages, in the sense that higher rents were commonly demanded from labourers who did not give their labour to the estate, and that the proprietors deducted the rent from the weekly wage. This gave rise to frequent disputes and dissatisfaction on the part of the negroes and was generally regarded by contemporary observers as the most important hindrance to good relations between the negroes and the proprietors.[3]

The effects of the abolition of slavery upon the supply of labour on the estates depended upon two main factors: the personal relations

---

[1] *Extracts from Parliamentary Papers relating to the West Indies*, 1839 (London, 1840), p. 150.
[2] *Ibid.* p. 147.
[3] Sir C. T. Metcalfe to Lord J. Russell, 30 March 1839, *Parl. Pap.* 1841, Sess. 2, III [341], p. 336; Evidence before Select Committee on West India Produce, *Parl. Pap.* 1842, XIII (479), QQ. 1473, 5529, 6692; Sewell, *The Ordeal of Free Labour in the West Indies*, p. 158.

existing between planters and their labourers, and the ratio in each colony of population to land fit for cultivation. While the latter was the more fundamental consideration, the former was decisive in individual cases. Many of the Jamaican planters in the early days after emancipation could not adapt themselves to the new conditions. It was altogether alien to their traditions and their temperament to reason and appeal where once they had ruled by the lash. The independence of the negroes was galling to them, and they sought by every means in their power to retain their authority, some even going to the lengths of destroying the provision grounds of the negroes, ejecting them from their houses and killing or maiming their stock. These men later paid the penalty of their actions, for their workers migrated to other estates or to native villages established on unoccupied land. Even the best treatment on the part of the proprietor or his attorney did not always receive an appropriate response, and in some cases the only apparent explanation of the unsatisfactory labour conditions on a particular estate was that the negroes had been drawn from a specially unruly African tribe.[1] In addition to rent difficulties, a fruitful cause of trouble lay in the frequent irregularities in the payment of wages. Sometimes these were due to the arbitrary action of the planter, but more often to genuine inability to find the money at the time required, either because of the shortage of money of small denominations or because the funds were not available.

While these considerations played a certain part, the principal factor was undoubtedly the ratio of population to land. In Barbados, Antigua, Dominica, St Kitts and St Vincent, population was relatively dense and there was very little free land not taken up. There was no alternative left to the negroes but to work on the estates. Here the complaint was not so much of a shortage of labour as a whole, as of the irregularity of the supply of labour owing to the unwillingness of the negroes to enter into more than daily contracts and to the fact that they rarely worked continuously throughout the week. To some extent this was fostered by the discontinuous nature of sugar cultivation itself—"at some seasons 160 may be required in the field, at others there may not be work for 50 or even 20".[2] During the actual cutting of the crop and the manufacture of the sugar continuous labour of from twelve to sixteen hours a day was necessary, and this labour it was very difficult to get under conditions of freedom, while where it was not available a portion of the cane crop or of the sugar was often spoiled. Even in the colonies with dense population there was an appreciable reduction in the numbers of labourers on the estates. Almost all the children and the greater number of the women were withdrawn after the termination of apprenticeship. To

[1] Cf. Sir C. T. Metcalfe to Lord J. Russell, March 30, 1840, *Parl. Pap.* 1841, III, p. 420.
[2] *Extracts from Parliamentary Papers relating to the West Indies*, 1839 (London, 1840) p. 89.

these must be added the considerable number of negroes who became porters or dock workers, or who went into retail commerce to supply the new demands which had sprung up in a state of freedom. Against this reduction in the supply of labour must however be set certain increases. Firstly, large numbers of free black and coloured people who during slavery and apprenticeship would not touch field work were attracted to the estates in the early days of freedom by the prospect of earning wages. Secondly, there was a numerous class of domestic slaves, a proportion of whom also took up field work. Moreover, the decline in the number of labourers was less in reality than in appearance, for under slavery, after the abolition of the slave trade, the proportion of non-effective workers on any estate was high. Estimates vary, but as a rule only from one-third to one-half of the total number of slaves on a plantation were active labourers at any one time. Further, wherever task work prevailed, more was accomplished in a given time than under slavery or apprenticeship. Even under time-wages the free labourer did not have the inducement to malinger and "go sick" which was so common a practice during slavery. On balance, however, there can be no doubt that the supply, and, what was even more important, the continuity of labour were diminished, above all during the crucial crop season, which lasted five months out of the year and covered not only the cutting of the canes and manufacture of sugar but also the work of manuring and planting the new season's canes.

The other group of colonies comprised British Guiana, Trinidad, Mauritius, St Lucia and parts of Jamaica. Here there was an abundance of land available for settlement by the negroes, the population was relatively sparse, and further development depended primarily upon an increase in the supply of labour. It is necessary to make a sub-division within this group. Jamaica and St Lucia were both old colonies, much of the land in which had become exhausted for both sugar and coffee planting. It is true that in Jamaica there was a great deal of territory entirely uncultivated, but the larger part of this was mountainous, or far distant from the centres of population and lacking in means of communication, or poor and infertile soil. In contrast to most of the other colonies, the output of sugar in Jamaica had been declining ever since the years immediately after the Napoleonic Wars; coffee also had shown a large decrease since 1824. Even so the inertia of the old slave system and the ever-present hope of a favourable movement of prices had kept in cultivation many estates which were either unfavourably situated or else at a disadvantage owing to poor soil.

The abolition of slavery caused some of these estates to go out of cultivation, and a number of the negroes on them became available for the remaining properties. But unfortunately the relations between planters and negroes were nowhere so unsatisfactory as in Jamaica.

The constant friction on many estates over questions of wages, rent and the hire of provision grounds, aggravated as it was by the uncompromising temper of the planters, led to the permanent withdrawal of much labour from the estates. At the same time it must be remembered that their difficulties were exceptionally great and that they were harder hit financially by emancipation than the planters in any other colony. On every side they met with opposition—from the British Government, the colonial authorities, the stipendiary magistrates, and, in particular, from the missionaries. The last named had gained the confidence of the negroes in a number of ways: they preached a highly emotional type of religion well adapted to the temperament of the negroes; they were insistent in proclaiming the doctrine of equality; they agitated, in season and out of season, for what they judged to be the political and economic interests of the negroes; and they were far more active in both religious and educational work than the representatives of the Established Church to which the planters belonged. Most of the missionaries were Dissenters and they carried some of the bitterness of religious differences at home into their work in the colonies. Though their feud with the planters was mainly based on humanitarian grounds, it bore also something of the nature of a class struggle. Where the missionary element was strong, as in Jamaica and to a lesser extent in British Guiana, the relations between the planters and their labourers were certainly less harmonious than elsewhere, and for this the missionaries, with their honest but one-sided zeal, were not always wholly free from blame.[1] An additional factor in the situation was that the British public gained most of its impressions of life in the sugar colonies from missionary reports, which were apt to be highly coloured and not representative of conditions as a whole.[2]

The cumulative effect upon the Jamaican planters of this atmosphere of mistrust and suspicion was to enhance their feeling of exasperation with a state of society which had been forced upon them, and to render them frequently blind even to the most obvious dictates of prudence and self-interest.[3]

British Guiana, Trinidad and Mauritius were all colonies in which the cultivation of sugar on a large scale was a comparatively recent development and there was a very great deal of fertile land, easily accessible, which had not been granted to the colonists by the Crown. Here the position of the labourers was the strongest, for the demand for their services was so great that wages were forced up to a high figure, and at the same time it was easy for the negro either to buy

[1] Cf. Merivale, H., *Lectures on Colonisation and Colonies* (1861), p. 323; Dalton, H. G., *History of British Guiana*, I, 288–9, II, 148–9. See also below pp. 512, 513.

[2] Rodway, J., *op. cit.* III, 32.

[3] For the state of mind of the Jamaican colonists in 1840 see *Autobiography of Sir Henry Taylor*, vol. I, ch. xv. Also Despatch of Sir C. T. Metcalfe to Lord J. Russell in *Parl. Pap.* 1841, Sess. 2, III [314], p. 441.

land cheaply or to "squat," i.e. to take possession of ungranted Crown lands. Although Acts were passed against squatting, they did not prove very effective, while attempts to pass really drastic Vagrancy Acts were discouraged by the Colonial Office. In these colonies the problem was partly one of high wages and labour costs, and partly of shortage and irregularity of labour supply. The effect of these factors in restricting output was greatest in British Guiana, which was least able to supplement its labour supply by effective immigration. The greatest withdrawal of negro labour from the plantations took place in Mauritius, owing chiefly to the very strong prejudice felt there by the negro against a type of labour so closely associated in his mind with slavery. A special magistrate of Mauritius estimated in 1840 that out of a labour force of 30,000 apprentices employed on the cultivation of sugar not more than five thousand males could be induced to engage as field labourers for one year after the end of apprenticeship. He added: "The late apprentice population considers the cultivation of the soil to be the most degrading occupation in which the human race can be employed. Field labour is in my opinion ended for ever among the emancipated negroes of Mauritius."[1] It is noteworthy that the colonies in which this sentiment was the strongest—Jamaica, British Guiana and Mauritius—were those in which the slave trade had been most active during the period just prior to its abolition. In Barbados, Antigua and certain other of the smaller colonies the bulk of the population consisted of Creoles who had worked for generations on the land and had developed a very different attitude towards the cultivation of the soil, more akin to that of a race of peasantry.

An important consequence of the scarcity of labour which resulted from the abolition of slavery was the introduction of labour-saving devices. The most important of these was the plough, which sometimes was used directly for cane planting, but more commonly to break up the soil preparatory to the digging of cane holes by hand. During slavery there had been very little incentive to use any kind of implements other than the primitive hoe and cutlass; most weights were carried on the head and the grinding mills and other plant for the manufacture of sugar were operated either by wind or by cattle. A very considerable saving of labour could be achieved by the employment of the plough, the wheelbarrow, in a few cases trucks on wooden or iron rails, the cane and megass elevator, and the steam engine. But such new methods were introduced very slowly, largely owing to the conservatism and prejudices of both planters and negroes. Even where there was willingness to adopt labour-saving devices,

---

[1] *Correspondence relative to Indian Labourers in Mauritius*, 1840, XXXVII (331), p. 737. It may be noted that the Mauritian negroes from the East Coast of Africa were distinct in race and type from the West African negroes who had been brought to the West Indies and British Guiana.

circumstances often rendered this impossible. Much of the land was hilly and not suited to the plough; while in British Guiana the extent to which the plantations were intersected with open drains and canals was equally unfavourable to its use; again, the ignorance of the natives and their lack of care caused a heavy wastage among the horses and consequent expense to the planters. In British Guiana, where the steam engine had for long been employed in the sugar mills on most of the estates, conditions were peculiar, for the average scale of cultivation was very much larger than in any of the other sugar colonies. Its colonisation by the British (a large proportion of the settlers was Scottish[1] or Barbadian[2]) was quite recent; there was no long tradition of small proprietorship, and, from the outset, the scale of operations and the capitalisation of the estates had been large.

In other colonies the steam engine was still rarely to be found by 1845. In some islands the regularity of the prevailing winds favoured the windmill;[3] in Antigua the frequency of drought and consequent shortage of water was a barrier to the steam engine; moreover, it was necessary to import the fuel from England; and it was difficult to find skilled mechanics to repair engines which had broken down. Finally, lack of capital was in many cases a decisive impediment.

As soon as the Emancipation Act was passed, and the colonies were faced with the fact that they could rely in future only on the labour which the negroes were willing to perform, the question of immigration was taken up with great enthusiasm as a panacea for all the ills caused by the new *régime*. At the outset the movement was largely confined to three sources of labour—migration within the islands, importation of Europeans, and immigration of Portuguese from Madeira. In addition to these there was a small number of freed negroes released from captured slave-ships belonging to other nations and of negroes coming in from the United States.

The great scarcity of labour in British Guiana and Trinidad had caused wages there to be much higher than in the neighbouring islands, and there was in consequence a natural tendency for labour to move to the more highly paid districts. This was stimulated by the action of the planters in sending agents to recruit for them with specious promises of little work and enormous pay, but it was also retarded by the strong sentimental attachment of the negroes to their own soil. The principal loser was Barbados, which boasted of having the densest population in the world—about 800 to the square mile—from whence considerable numbers were drawn to British Guiana, Trinidad and St Lucia.

[1] Halliday, Sir A., *The West Indies*, p. 117.
[2] Bronkhurst, H. V. P., *British Guiana and its Labouring Population*, p. 67.
[3] Even in the present century the majority of the sugar mills in Barbados are still moved by wind power.

The extent of the movement was influenced both by economic and geographical considerations, such as contiguity. A witness in 1847 explained that Tobago had kept its labourers because, the island being to windward of Trinidad, the negroes had not been able to get across[1]—a testimony to the small development of steam navigation in the West Indies at that time.

Grenada suffered considerably from the migration of its negroes to Trinidad, the prevailing religion in both islands being Roman Catholic—a circumstance which impeded a similar movement from Protestant St Vincent.[2] There seems to have been no tendency for Barbadians to go to Jamaica. The exodus of negroes from the low-wage colonies was viewed with scant favour by the planters, and pressure was brought to bear on the legislatures to restrict this movement as much as possible. Acts were passed in Barbados, St Kitts, St Vincent and other islands, requiring intending emigrants to obtain a certificate from the justices of the peace, which could be withheld on various grounds, such as indebtedness or the fact that they would be leaving behind them persons who had been dependent on them for support. Such measures, however, were discouraged as far as possible by the Home Government as being an arbitrary interference with the freedom of movement of the individual. But in 1842 the Colonial Office yielded to the representations of the older colonies to the extent of forbidding those colonies which had immigration schemes financed out of public revenues from offering bounties for the introduction of Creoles from the West India islands.

Even apart from the effect of the restrictions imposed upon the inter-island migration of negroes, the results for the negroes themselves who migrated seem to have been rarely satisfactory. Under different climatic conditions their mortality was great, and the tales of hardship spread by the returned negroes deterred many of their fellows from seeking to better their lot in this way.

None of the other classes of immigrants referred to above was of so much importance as the West Indians. European labourers, in particular, were conspicuously unsuccessful in the West Indies. Jamaica during apprenticeship introduced some hundreds of Germans and some thousands of Irish and Scotch, but they were unable to withstand the combined effects of the climate and of an often excessive consumption of alcohol, and they succumbed in such great numbers that the experiment was given up as a failure.[3] A few Portuguese came from Madeira to British Guiana in 1835 and considerably larger numbers were introduced in the years 1840 to 1842, but they

[1] Evidence before Select Committee on Slave Trade, *Parl. Pap.* 1847–8, XXII (536), Q.6324.
[2] Evidence before Select Committee on West India Produce, *Parl. Pap.* 1842, XIII (479), Q.2691.
[3] Evidence before Select Committee on East India Produce, *Parl. Pap.* 1842, XIII (536), QQ.853, 1590, 7317.

suffered so severely from sickness that in 1842 further immigration from this source was for a time prohibited.

A very material check to the immigration movement came when the British Government by an Order-in-Council of 30 July 1839 prohibited any contracts from being made in the Crown Colonies with labourers except in the colony in which the labour was to be performed. The whole course of immigration was changed by this measure. Previously the individual planter had sent out agents at his own expense to hire workers for his estate—as a rule with a contract of from one to three years. The disallowing of such contracts forced the colonists to have recourse to a system of general bounties on immigration, financed out of the revenues of the colony. This was a severe blow to the colonists and caused great resentment among them, but was in harmony with the British Government's policy of refusing to sanction any attempts to reintroduce servile conditions under the cloak of voluntary contracts. Originally the Order applied to Europeans as well as to all other classes of immigrants, but it was found impossible to attract skilled artisans, who were needed in growing numbers with the increasing use of steam engines, ploughs, etc., without a fixed contract of employment, and the Order was rescinded in respect of immigrants from Europe in 1841 and from North America in 1843.

Once the flow of negroes within the islands had dwindled to small proportions, the colonists cast their eyes on two great possible sources of supply—the West Coast of Africa and India. In regard to the former, many ambitious schemes were mooted for buying up slaves and transporting them to the free life of the West Indies. But to all such proposals the Colonial Office turned a deaf ear, for it was held that any such demand for African negroes must inevitably stimulate the slave trade within the continent of Africa. The most that the Government would sanction up to 1845 was that liberated Africans landed at Sierra Leone and St Helena should be allotted in certain proportions amongst the different colonies, under a scheme controlled entirely by the Home Government.

It may be observed that the colonists were more embittered by the generally negative attitude of the Colonial Office towards immigration than by almost any other part of its policy after the abolition of slavery. Exeter Hall and the missionary element as a whole in England and many of the colonies were opposed to immigration for a number of reasons. They feared that the conditions of work of the immigrants, especially under indenture schemes, would in fact amount to a revival of slavery; that serious abuses would arise from the recruitment of labour in other countries; and that the planters would use their immigrant workers to force down the wages and standards of living of the newly enfranchised negroes. They, therefore, put pressure with some success on the Colonial Office to impose restrictions on immigration, which not only greatly increased its cost to the colonists, but also rendered it difficult for them to introduce fresh workers on a large scale or to derive full benefit from those who were brought in.

The remaining chief source of supply was British India with its enormous population accustomed to hard work and low wages. Mauritius, as was natural from its geographical position, was the first colony to introduce Indian coolies, and as many as 24,000 were brought in between 1834 and 1838, 50 per cent. of whom came over in the single year 1838. In this same year 406 were brought to British Guiana. In both colonies the Indians were induced to sign indentures for five years. Considerable abuses, however, arose, and in 1839 the Government of India prohibited all further emigration from India. This prohibition continued in force until 1842, when it was abrogated so far as Mauritius was concerned. It was then laid down that the Mauritian Government should appoint and pay a Protector of Immigrants in Mauritius and emigration officers at the three Indian ports from which emigration was permitted—Calcutta, Madras and Bombay. The indenture system was abolished, but the colony undertook to repatriate at its own expense all Indians who had resided five years in the colony.[1] In the three years, 1843–45, as many as 57,145 Indians entered Mauritius, of whom 34,525 came in the single year 1843.

The relative importance of immigration during the early years after emancipation in the colonies chiefly concerned can be seen from the following figures:[2] Jamaica, with a registered slave population in 1832 of 310,707, had a total immigration of 7346 between 1834 and 1845. For British Guiana the corresponding figures were 82,824 slaves and 22,333 immigrants; for Trinidad, 22,359 slaves and 14,853 immigrants; for Mauritius, 63,146 slaves and 81,990 immigrants, down to and including 1845. In all the colonies the effective number of immigrants was considerably diminished by heavy mortality, especially in the early stages, by repatriation, and by the transfer of many immigrants from agriculture to commerce or other occupations. On the other hand the total numbers given for slaves included domestic slaves and children as well as many who were not employed in the cultivation of sugar, for which purpose the immigrants were almost exclusively required. It will be seen that the volume of immigration between 1834 and 1845 was insignificant in the case of Jamaica, of appreciable magnitude in British Guiana and Trinidad, and of overwhelming importance for Mauritius.

[1] On this whole subject see *Correspondence relative to Indian Labourers in Mauritius, Parl. Pap.* 1840, xxxvi (331), pp. 289 *seqq.* and further correspondence in *Parl. Pap.* 1841, Sess. 2, iii (66), pp. 287 *seqq.*; *Parl. Pap.* 1842, xxx (26), pp. 189 *seqq.*; *Parl. Pap.* 1843, xxxv (148), pp. 127 *seqq.* and *Parl. Pap.* 1844, xxxv (356), pp. 275 *seqq.*
[2] Cf. *Tenth Report of Colonial Land and Emigration Commissioners, Parl. Pap.* 1850, xxiii [1204], pp. 132–3.

It remains to translate the sum of the foregoing considerations into terms of output. Adopting the classification of Merivale,[1] the sugar colonies may be divided into three main classes, to which Mauritius may be added as a separate class by itself. First, there were the colonies enjoying a relatively dense population with little or no unoccupied land; of these Barbados and Antigua may be selected as the outstanding examples. Secondly, there were colonies which had long been settled and where the most fertile land had all been taken up and exploited but where there was much inferior land either undeveloped or under cultivation which could not be cultivated in the absence of high prices and cheap labour—Jamaica, St Vincent, Grenada. The third class, consisting of British Guiana and Trinidad, was characterised by the existence of much fertile land not yet cultivated, together with a sparse and scanty population. Mauritius must be placed alone, because its proximity to India enabled it to draw, to an almost indefinite extent, upon the human resources of that country. The following table shows the average annual export of sugar to the United Kingdom from the above colonies:

Imports of sugar into the United Kingdom in cwts.

	Average of five years 1829–33	Average of four years 1835–38	Average of four years 1842–45
Whole of the British West Indies and British Guiana:			
	3,917,912	3,487,801	2,582,291
Colonies of the first class:			
Barbados	333,311	409,356	335,451
Antigua	159,704	143,878	188,994
Colonies of the second class:			
Jamaica	1,384,111	1,040,070	677,896
St Vincent	224,638	194,228	132,106
Grenada	201,941	161,328	79,903
Colonies of the third class:			
Trinidad	305,034	295,787	312,026
British Guiana	893,615	935,599	537,132
Mauritius	470,155	549,872	605,763

The falling off in output for the whole of the West Indies and British Guiana, which was appreciable during the apprenticeship period, was very much greater during the years 1842–45, when some of the worst difficulties of the period immediately succeeding emancipation had been overcome, but when the price of sugar in the British market was steadily falling and the planters were facing the possibility of the removal of the preferential duties which they had enjoyed so long. The colonies of the first class referred to above show a general consistency in all the periods, but those of the second class show a continuous decrease in output, specially marked in the years 1842–45.

---

[1] Merivale, H., *op. cit.* pp. 339–45.

In Jamaica, hitherto much the largest individual producer of sugar, production in the latter period was less than half that in the years just before the apprenticeship system came into force. In the third class, Trinidad, thanks to a steady inflow of labour, chiefly from the other West Indian islands, was able to maintain her output with little change, but British Guiana, with her much larger area, suffered very severely from the shortage of labour which she experienced as soon as emancipation was completed. Finally, Mauritius was enabled to expand materially the cultivation of the sugar cane with the aid of a big influx of coolies from India, and although in area only one-sixth of Jamaica, she produced in 1842–45 nearly as much sugar as the latter colony.

Upon the negroes themselves the *immediate* effects of complete emancipation were largely favourable. There was at first a general consensus of opinion that, whatever might be the difficulties and hardships of the planting community, the negroes had benefited enormously from the change. In the larger islands where they had access to provision grounds, where land could be bought and wages were relatively high, their economic position was eminently satisfactory. Their provision grounds gave them a large degree of independence, they were free to work when they would, and, as the planter found to his cost, they could easily maintain themselves on three or four days' work in the week. Fortunately for him the needs of the negroes were not limited to a bare subsistence, otherwise the inducement to work for wages would have been virtually non-existent. They proved to be very fond of luxurious and ostentatious expenditure, e.g. smart clothes, good furniture, wines, and on these and similar expensive articles they willingly spent large sums of money. Further, they had a passionate desire for the religious education of their children; in Jamaica they maintained by their contributions the missionaries who ministered to them, and would subscribe to the limit of their capacity towards the building of churches and schoolrooms. Throughout the later years of slavery and in the difficult period of change and adaptation to the new state of freedom the missionaries were devoted and self-sacrificing friends of the negroes. While the clergy of the Established Church had in too many cases been lazy and indifferent to their welfare, prone rather to share the prejudices of the planters than to risk their displeasure by defending the cause of the negroes, the missionaries lent them their whole-hearted support. Even though they were not always entirely wise in their advocacy, their influence, especially during the period of apprenticeship and later of freedom, was a restraining and a helpful one. It was largely due to their efforts that the disturbances, which many had feared would be the result of the new order of society, did not take place. The greater part of the religious and educational activities in the sugar colonies were carried out by the missionaries, and to them more than to any one else such moral progress as the negroes made was due.

The Governor of Jamaica, after a tour of inspection through the island in 1840, reported that he had "found the peasant remarkably comfortable, with money in plenty, and independent, and their own masters in a greater degree, I believe, than any peasantry in the world".[1] Some indication of the greater prosperity of the negroes can be gained from the large increase in imports of foodstuffs, clothing, etc., which characterised the early period of emancipation, while the qualities of the goods imported also improved.

(ii) THE BAHAMAS, BERMUDA, BRITISH HONDURAS

The Bahamas. After a brief period of prosperity during the Revolutionary wars at the end of the eighteenth century, when they were a centre of trade with the enemy colonies of France and Spain, the Bahamas relapsed into a condition of poverty and stagnation. The American Revolution led to a considerable influx of Loyalists who brought with them the cultivation of cotton, but by 1815 this occupation had been practically destroyed by the cheap cotton of the Southern States and had ceased to have any importance. From then onwards the trade of the Bahamas was on a very small scale, consisting mainly of the export of salt, sponges and other local produce to the United States, while an important source of income to the islanders consisted in the salvage of wrecked vessels.

Prior to the abolition of slavery there was much friction between the Assembly and the Crown as represented by the Governor. The Assembly obstructed the anti-slavery movement as much as possible, and on one occasion—from 1830 to 1832—refused all financial supplies when the Governor endeavoured to introduce measures to mitigate the lot of the slaves.[2] After the completion of emancipation the relations between the Assembly and the Crown were free from acute struggle.

The only constitutional change of importance was made by Letters Patent of 12 January 1841, which abolished the old Council and created two separate bodies, a Legislative Council and an Executive Council, each consisting of not more than nine members, nominated by the Crown.[3]

For this change, the earliest example in the West Indies of the division of the Governor's Council, the motive was the desire of

---

[1] Metcalfe to Russell, *Parl. Pap.* 1841, Sess. 2, III [341], p. 422. It must, however, be remembered that Metcalfe was judging the condition of the Jamaican negro largely by Indian standards. Cf. Thompson, E., *The Life of Lord Metcalfe*, p. 346.
[2] Martin, R. M., *The British Colonies*, vol. III, *West India Islands*, p. 160.
[3] Malcolm, H., *Historical Documents relating to the Bahama Islands*, p. xviii.

the Governor to benefit by the advice of two prominent members of the House of Assembly whom he wished to nominate to vacancies in the Advisory Council. As this body also fulfilled the functions of a Privy (Executive) Council, their nomination would have involved the resignation of their membership of the Assembly. Hence he suggested to the Colonial Office the separation of the Council into two bodies, one with advisory and the other with executive functions.[1]

Bermuda. The prosperity of Bermuda was largely influenced by the volume of trade and the conditions governing commercial relations between the West Indies and the United States. For some years after 1815 Bermuda was the centre of a very active trade as a result of the exclusion of American vessels from the West Indies and the use of Bermuda an an entrepôt port for both American and West Indian produce. But she lost the advantages of this position by the Anglo-American agreement of 1822, and although for many years she benefited to some extent through the facilities afforded by the ware-housing system, these also finally disappeared when the system was abolished in 1843, and her carrying trade, which had long been declining, dwindled into insignificance.

The main revenue of Bermuda was derived from the money brought to the colony by the British naval dockyard, the construction of which was begun in 1810, by the naval hospital, and by the convict establishment on Ireland Island.[2] The latter was peculiar in that the convicts were employed solely on government work and were not allowed to be employed for private benefit or to be discharged in the colony.[3] Bermuda shared with Antigua the distinction of being the only British colonies to emancipate their slaves outright in 1834, without adopting the transitional system of apprenticeship.

With a population in 1845 of about 10,000 the Government of the colony was of the full representative type, with a Governor, a nominated Council and an elected Legislative Assembly of thirty-six members. As the members of both the Council and the Assembly were paid $2 for each day on which they sat, the panoply of government was a matter of considerable expense to the colonists.

The franchise was more narrowly restricted than in any of the West Indian colonies, being entirely dependent on a property qualification in the form of land. This was originally the ownership of a freehold of a total value of £24, but was raised in 1834 to £60 in order to lessen the danger of a transfer of power to the newly enfranchised negroes.

[1] Shattuck, G. B., *The Bahama Islands*, p. 535.
[2] Williams, W. F., *An Historical and Statistical Account of the Bermudas*, p. 49.
[3] *Bermuda: A Colony, a Fortress and a Prison*, by a Field Officer, p. 176.

British Honduras. The settlement of British Honduras, with an area of 6000 square miles and a total estimated population in 1805 of 3635, was dependent for its economic existence upon the export of mahogany and logwood. It also acted to some extent as an entrepôt for European manufactures intended for other Central American countries and as an export point for certain of their products, such as cochineal, indigo and sarsaparilla. Logwood for dyeing, of which there was a substantial re-export to the continent of Europe, had been the principal export during the early history of the colony, and at one time the price reached the high level of £100 per ton. The largest export appears to have been 18,000 tons in 1756, but by 1783 it had fallen to 7000 tons and during the first half of the nineteenth century it was much lower; between 1829 and 1836 the annual export averaged only 1828 tons. Towards the end of the eighteenth century the price was from £8 to £10 a ton, but in 1835 it was stated that the demand had fallen off greatly owing to the introduction of substitutes and that the price was only £5. 10s. a ton.[1] Mahogany was a much more important export than logwood in the nineteenth century, and in spite of high import duties into England, which were not abolished till 1846, the industry of cutting and shipping mahogany to Europe was one which yielded appreciable profits, the chief limiting factor being the supply of labour. Prior to 1834 the bulk of the work was carried out by slaves, but in 1834 the apprenticeship system was introduced and, as in other British colonies in the West, slavery was completely abolished in 1838. The change was accompanied by no such dislocation in the labour market as occurred in most of the other colonies where the plantation system existed.

The place of slavery was taken by a somewhat rigid Masters and Servants Act, hirings being made at Christmas, as a rule for the ensuing year, and being completely binding on both parties for the period agreed upon.[2] The dependence of the labourers on their employers was enhanced by the custom under which part of the wages —often from four to six months—was commonly advanced by the employer.[3] Custom and the peculiar conditions of the industry rendered this system acceptable to both parties and it was not interfered with by the Colonial Office.

The political constitution of British Honduras was gradually evolving during this period from its original anomalous simplicity towards a modified form of Crown Colony government. The position in 1815 was that the head of the Government was the Superintendent, who was responsible to the Crown but held his commission under the Governor of Jamaica. There was a representative assembly called

[1] Burdon, Sir J. A., *Archives of British Honduras*, II, 37.
[2] Chief Justice Temple, in *Journal of the Society of Arts*, v (1856–7), 121.
[3] Fowler, H., *A Narrative of a Journey across...British Honduras*, p. 120.

the Public Meeting, which comprised all the free inhabitants of the settlement, though there was a property qualification for voting and an executive body of seven Magistrates annually elected by the residents with voting rights. The Public Meeting passed laws and voted taxes, while the Magistrates were entrusted with the appropriation and expenditure of the public revenue in accordance with the votes of the Public Meeting.[1] The Magistrates were also the sole Court of Justice until 1819, when a Criminal Court for serious offences was established by Act of Parliament. From time to time friction arose between the Public Meeting or the Magistrates and the Superintendent, whose position was rendered the more difficult because of the continued state of uncertainty as to the legal status of the settlement. The original constitution established by Burnaby's Code in 1765 had made no provision for a Superintendent, and the settlers constantly appealed to the shadowy claim of Spain to uphold their contention that the settlement was not a proper British colony. The Superintendent in 1822 complained that "The great delicacy with which the British Government has acted towards the Court of Madrid has retarded the introduction of a more regular form of Government and the unavoidable difficulties which naturally result from the present anomalous system must be considered to have been endured, rather than excite any misunderstanding with Spain".[2] He went on to say: "The Settlers have always submitted to the exercise of this authority [that of the Superintendent] with great distrust and reluctance, but seeing, if used with justice and discretion, it is so very reasonable in its nature, they have seldom of late years made any decided stand against it, altho' they have ever looked upon it as an unjust usurpation, and are always willing enough to set it aside."[3]

By degrees, however, successive Superintendents enlarged the scope of their executive authority and contrived, despite the opposition of the settlers and the rather lukewarm support of the Colonial Office, to restrict the rights of the Public Meeting. In 1832 the Superintendent assumed the function of appointing the seven magistrates who exercised control over the finances of the colony, and who had been elected hitherto by the Public Meeting. The Superintendent also reserved to himself the right to legislate by proclamation whenever he considered it necessary, and to refuse to allow the Public Meeting to debate any motion until he had approved of it.[4]

In 1840 the Superintendent appointed an Executive Council to assist him in the administration of affairs, and in the same year a proclamation was issued stating that "the law of England is and shall

---

[1] Memorandum of the Superintendent, 24 November 1834. In Burdon, Sir J. A., *op. cit.* II, 360.
[2] Superintendent Colonel Arthur to Major-General Pye, 3 April 1822, in Burdon, Sir J. A., *op. cit.* II, 256. Colonel Arthur became in 1824 Lieutenant-Governor of Van Diemen's Land. [3] *Ibid.* p. 257.
[4] Gibbs, A. R., *British Honduras*, pp. 104–5.

be the law of this settlement or colony of British Honduras":[1] thus abrogating in principle if not always in practice the ancient legal usages and customs which had been in force hitherto.[2] An important dispute arose over the control of finance, the Public Meeting seeking to impose certain conditions and restrictions upon the administration by the Magistrates of the funds voted by the Meeting, while the Magistrates and Superintendent, supported by the Colonial Office, contended that the executive authority was alone responsible for the control of expenditure. On an appeal being made by the Public Meeting to the Secretary of State for the Colonies against the encroachments on their rights and privileges, the reply was received in 1842 that the Public Meeting was "authorised to continue to exercise its legislative powers, harmoniously if it can with the Executive, each taking usage as the rule by which their respective powers are to be defined".[3] On the other hand, when the Superintendent in 1842 urged that the Public Meeting had fallen into disrepute and that there was a general desire for its abolition, the Colonial Office replied that, as there was no present prospect of cession of sovereignty by Spain, local usage must continue and the Executive Council be dissolved if it could not avoid collision with the Public Meeting.[4] In the following year the Secretary of State ruled that the Public Meeting had no legislative powers and was merely a creature of usage, its powers being defined as the making of rules for the conduct of the settlement subject to the consent of the Superintendent, "and that it is for the advantage of all parties that the Superintendent and the Public Meeting should severally keep within the limits which custom and public convenience have assigned to their respective functions".[5] In 1844 a change was made in order to curb the independent authority of the Magistrates, by making them ex officio members of the Executive Council and requiring all supplies in future to be granted by the Superintendent-in-Council.

(iii) CEYLON

Under the Portuguese, and also under the Dutch, colonisation in Ceylon had been confined to coastal districts, and both these powers had encountered great difficulties from the independent kingdom of Kandy which controlled the centre of the island. With the coming of the English it was certain that the existence of this dual authority could not long be maintained. A sufficient reason for intervention was afforded in 1815 by the gross maltreatment of some native traders who were British subjects. War was declared, and, helped by the defection from the King of many important chiefs, who had been alienated by his misgovernment, the British troops speedily defeated

---

[1] Burdon, Sir J. A., *op. cit.* II, 411. [2] *Ibid.* III, 174.
[3] *The Handbook of British Honduras* (London, 1889), p. 34.
Burdon, Sir J. A., *op. cit.* III, 56. [5] *Ibid.* III, 65.

the Kandyans.[1] By the terms of peace the kingdom of Kandy was formally annexed to the British Crown, thereby bringing to an end a native rule and independence which had lasted for upwards of 2300 years. The sudden replacement of the native monarchy by British rule inevitably involved the nobles and priests in some loss of prestige and status, even though they were confirmed in most of their former powers. The people also, who had fought for centuries against Portuguese and Dutch in the maritime provinces, were ill at ease under a foreign yoke. Discontent increased rapidly and flared up in a serious rebellion in 1817. A pretender to the throne, whose cause was strengthened by the theft of the sacred tooth of Buddha from its shrine in Kandy, started a revolt which soon became general throughout the former kingdom. The British troops, hampered by the nature of the country and suffering severely from disease, had great difficulty in putting down the rebellion, and additional troops had to be brought from India. The rising was finally quelled in October 1818. Steps were at once taken to reorganise the administration of the interior; the influence of the nobles was further curtailed by increasing the number of Agents of Government and giving them more extensive functions. The native chiefs and officials were completely subordinated to the Agents of Government (the equivalent in Kandy of the Collectors in the maritime provinces), who now exercised almost all the powers previously belonging to the chiefs, including the right to exact *rajakaria*, or forced unpaid service. The central administration of Kandy remained in the hands of a Board of Commissioners responsible to the Governor.

The absence of means of communication had been one of the chief causes of the difficulty experienced in putting down the rebellion of 1817–18. Hence, on the restoration of peace, military roads were driven into the interior, in particular the great road from Colombo to Kandy, which was begun in 1821 and completed ten years later. There were unsuccessful attempts at rebellion in 1820, 1823 and 1824, and the fear of further insurrections led to the maintenance of a considerable military establishment in Ceylon, with the result that for many years there was a large annual excess of expenditure over revenue. It was in fact chiefly for reasons of economy, but partly on account of the disturbed condition of the interior, that the unusual step was taken of appointing military officers to most of the chief posts of Agents of Government in Kandy.[2]

The civil service of Ceylon had been organised after the British conquest in 1796 largely on Indian lines, as was only natural in view of the fact that between 1796 and 1802 it was administered, at first as a dependency of the Madras Presidency, and then under the joint control of the Crown and the East India Company.[3] The service was

[1] See vol. IV, p. 408. [2] Mills, L. A., *Ceylon under British Rule, 1795–1932*, p. 64.
[3] See vol. IV, ch. XXIV.

reorganised under Governor Sir Thomas Maitland (1805–11) and was brought to a high state of efficiency,[1] in which it remained until the desire of the Colonial Office to balance revenue and expenditure in view of the continual deficits led to important changes. Many of these changes, which were carried out on the recommendation (the Colebrooke Report)[2] of a Commission of Enquiry appointed by Parliament, were unwise, and were strongly opposed by the able Governor, Sir Robert Wilmot Horton (1831–37), who had reluctantly to enforce them. Not merely were drastic reductions made in the salaries of civil servants, but pensions were abolished and the rate of promotion slowed down. The effect of these measures on the efficiency of the civil service was quickly apparent. The service became unattractive to men of ability and the whole standard was lowered. Thus an important regulation of 1822, under which promotion of the junior officials was conditional on a satisfactory knowledge of the native languages, was allowed to fall into disuse. Moreover, civil servants, while not permitted to engage in trade, were allowed to own coffee estates and to sell the produce. The decline in salaries discouraged them from attending to their official duties and led them to devote a large part of their time to the cultivation of their estates. The administration of the colony deteriorated so seriously that the Colonial Office became alarmed. Minor reforms were made in 1837 and 1839 and finally in 1845 Lord Stanley revoked most of the changes of 1833. Salaries were raised, pensions restored, the regulations requiring a knowledge of native languages were strictly enforced, and civil servants were not merely forbidden to acquire lands in future but were required in many cases to dispose of their existing estates within a brief period.[3] Promotion according to merit was re-established. However, it was not possible quickly to restore efficiency to a demoralised civil service, and the Kandyan revolt of 1848 was partly due to the defects which had been allowed to creep into the system and which could not at once be eradicated.[4]

From 1803 to 1833 Ceylon had been governed as a Crown Colony, but the Governor had been supreme, subject to the Colonial Office, with only an Advisory Council of official members. In 1833 this Council was renamed the Executive Council and there was added a Legislative Council composed of nine official and six unofficial members nominated by the Governor from among the chief merchants and estate owners in the colony. In this way the autocratic powers of the Governor were lessened and the administration was brought into somewhat closer touch with the people, although the very mixed

---

[1] de Silva, C. R., "Ceylon under the British Occupation: its Political and Economic Development," 1795–1833, I, 287. (An unpublished dissertation in the Library of the University of London.)

[2] An interesting and on the whole sympathetic account of the Colebrooke proposals is to be found in de Silva, C. R., op. cit. pp. 640–73.

[3] Ibid. p. 76.   [4] Mills, L. A., op. cit. p. 77.

composition of the population made representation necessarily incomplete. In addition to the British there were the Sinhalese, forming the main bulk of the inhabitants; the burghers, descendants of the Portuguese and Dutch; Tamils; Moors; Malayans and others. It had originally been intended that half the unofficial nominated members of the Legislative Council should be European and half natives. The Governor's instructions forbade the nomination of any unofficial member holding an office under the Crown, and it proved impossible at first to find suitable persons with a knowledge of the English language who were not in the employ of the Government. The latter difficulty was overcome in 1836 when sanction was obtained "to allot salaries to the natives who might be selected members of the Legislative Council, equivalent to the emoluments of the offices relinquished by them at the time of their appointment".[1] Even so, it was not easy to fill the places reserved for natives, for in 1849 we find the six unofficial members of the Council composed of four Europeans and two burghers, but not a single representative of the Sinhalese.[2] A further reform of importance, advocated by Colebrooke, was carried out in 1834 when the Kandyan and maritime provinces were united and a uniform administration was organised for the whole island.

In the past Ceylon had known slavery and a form of quasi-feudal land tenure (service tenures) involving the right of the King or of subordinate chiefs to exact unpaid service, or *rajakaria*. Both *rajakaria* and slavery persisted for a time under British rule. In 1801 Governor Frederick North (later Lord Guilford) had attempted to abolish service tenures, but the laws he then passed were not enforced by his successors. When the Kandyan administration was revised in 1818 the power to exact *rajakaria* for official purposes, such as roadmaking, was taken from the nobles and given to the Agents of Government. The actual task of calling out the ryats, or occupiers of service lands, remained however with the native officials, and this afforded opportunities for discrimination and extortion. In 1832 *rajakaria* on Government account was abolished, although, as was pointed out by Governor Horton, this action was highly inconvenient at a moment when it was difficult to hire labour in the colony and when many of the Kandyan roads begun by Governor Barnes had not been completed. There remained only the right of the Kandyan nobles and the Buddhist temples to exact *rajakaria* from their own tenants, a right which they enjoyed until 1870, when it was replaced by fixed annual money rents.

Slavery in Ceylon, having been mainly domestic in character, was mild and comparatively free from abuses. Largely from reasons of

[1] *Addresses delivered to the Legislative Council of Ceylon by Governors of the Colony*, pp. 17–18.
[2] Minutes of Evidence before the Select Committee on Ceylon, *Parl. Pap.* 1850, XII (66), Q. 5930.

policy connected with the abolition of *rajakaria*, the Government moved slowly and with caution in dealing with this question. Regulations were adopted in 1806 and again in 1818 for the compulsory registration of slaves in the maritime provinces, and provision was also made for the manumission of slaves at a valuation fixed by arbitrators. As a result slavery gradually became extinct in those parts of the country in which the regulation was enforced, but continued on an appreciable scale in the Kandyan districts, until it was finally abolished there also in 1845.[1]

In the early years of British rule Ceylon was famed principally for cinnamon and pearls. The former had been made a Government monopoly by the Dutch, and this monopoly was continued for a while by the British; but its enforcement entailed the maintenance of many oppressive restrictions and it was finally abandoned in 1833, the cultivation of and trade in cinnamon being thrown open to all, and its exportation permitted subject to an export duty of 3s. per lb. The consequence was a very serious decline in revenue, which fell from £147,550 in 1832 to £60,117 in 1840 and to £26,890 in 1845. The export duty proved to be much too heavy in view of the competition of cinnamon from Java and of an inferior but much cheaper substitute, *cassia ligula*, grown in China and on the Malabar coast of India. Although the duty was lowered by stages until in 1843 it was 1s. per lb., the price declined so much in the European markets that much of the land under cinnamon trees was allowed to go out of cultivation or was converted to other uses, especially the growing of coco-nut palms.[2] The pearl fishery likewise was a monopoly, though of a peculiar type. The Government controlled the oyster beds and sold to speculators the right to fish the beds, which it declared to be open. Prior to 1837 the revenue thus received was often considerable, but for twenty years after that date the principal pearl fishery in the island was closed and receipts in most years were smaller than expenditure. In addition to these sources of revenue the Government also retained fiscal monopolies in salt and the sale of arrack.[3]

In the period from 1815 to 1830 economic development was slow. Ceylon was regarded chiefly as an important military station; even the roads which were constructed were built mainly to secure the pacification of the country. This was consistent with the policy, based on political and military considerations, which had led the British Government at the peace of 1815 to retain Ceylon while restoring Java to the Dutch. Hence it was long before attention was devoted to exploiting the economic resources of the colony.

By far the most important export of Ceylon during the latter part

[1] Tennent, Sir J. E., *Ceylon*, 1, 435.
[2] Cf. Caffer, J., "The Cinnamon Trade of Ceylon", in *Journal of the Royal Asiatic Society*, 1846, pp. 368–80.
[3] *Report of Sir J. E. Tennent on Finance and Commerce of Ceylon in 1847–8, Parl. Pap.* XLII, [933], pp. 158–64.

of the period under review was coffee. During the twenty years 1815 to 1835, although the export of coffee steadily increased, it still consisted almost entirely of the native-grown, badly prepared berry, which fetched very low prices in the English market. The early experiments at cultivation by the Dutch and British had been unsuccessful owing to the choice of ground in the lowlands. But when plantations were formed in the uplands, following the example of one of the early British Governors, Sir Edward Barnes, who laid out a plantation on his estate at Gampola in 1825, it was found that coffee of the highest quality could be grown in Ceylon. The creation of the coffee industry, which transformed Ceylon "from a sluggish military cantonment into an enterprising British colony"[1], was brought about by two main causes—the virtual disappearance of coffee production in the West Indies following the emancipation of the slaves, and the equalisation in 1836 of the duty on East Indian and West Indian coffee imported into the United Kingdom. For ten years prior to 1836 East Indian coffee paid a duty of 9d. per lb. and West Indian of 6d., but in 1836 they were equalised at 6d. per lb. The decrease of supplies from the West Indies raised coffee prices in England and, by 1840, both the technical and the commercial success of coffee cultivation in Ceylon were well established, with the result that from 1840 to 1845 there developed a veritable coffee mania. A rush took place to the hitherto unexploited jungles in the hill country that has been likened to that to the Australian gold diggings. Capital poured into the country, and it was estimated that by the end of 1847 about £3,000,000 had been invested in coffee planting, chiefly by Europeans.[2] Between 1840 and 1845, 268,000 acres of Crown lands were sold for coffee plantations, much of which was bought by speculators, but a great deal also by civil servants. By 1845, "the previous Governor and the Council, the military, the judges, the clergy and one half the civil servants had penetrated the hills, and become purchasers of Crown lands".[3] The lands were sold at first at a uniform price of 5s. per acre and the profits of re-sale were often large.

As in other colonies, the expansion of cultivation brought with it a large additional demand for labour. The coffee plantations were in the interior and the Kandyan population of the uplands, who had been accustomed for centuries to the primitive agriculture necessary to grow their food, had neither the aptitude nor the inclination to work for the European planters on their estates. The competition for labour soon forced wages up to a high level, which proved very attractive to the low-paid coolies of Southern India. A big flow of immigration set in from the Malabar coast, the numbers entering Ceylon

[1] Tennent, Sir J. E., *Ceylon* (London, 1860), II, 229.
[2] Minutes of Evidence before Select Committee on Sugar and Coffee Planting, *Parl. Pap.* 1847–8, XXIII, Part II (184), Q. 14,311.
[3] Tennent, Sir J. E., *op. cit.* vol. II, 231.

rising from an annual average of 6600 for the three years 1841 to 1843 to an average of 73,700 for the two years 1844 and 1845, though many of these immigrants did not remain long in the island, but returned to their own country with their savings.[1] The combined effect of the inflow of capital and of the increased supply of labour can be seen in the exports of coffee, which rose from 41,863 cwt. in 1839 to 178,603 cwt. in 1845. The output for the first of these years consisted almost entirely of native-grown coffee, but in the later year about one-half the total amount exported came from the newly established plantations. The native coffee was inferior in quality and fetched relatively low prices in the English market.

Besides cinnamon and coffee, there were three other products of Ceylon which were of considerable commercial importance—betel nuts, tobacco and the products of the coco-nut palm. The market for betel nuts and tobacco was found chiefly in India, but also in other parts of the East, while coco-nut oil and coir were shipped to Europe.

Ceylon during this period affords an important contrast to all the other tropical colonies which have been discussed in this chapter, owing to the comparatively small extent to which her economic life was dominated by British capitalists. By 1845 the plantation system was only just becoming predominant in coffee cultivation and beginning to assume some importance in the coco-nut industry; in cinnamon planting the European purchasers of the former Government gardens had a hard struggle to compete with the product of the natives; while of all other commodities the native, owning and cultivating his own land, was the sole producer. Ceylon had thus been spared the evils of the slave trade and of slave plantation labour.

When the British took over the island from the Dutch they acquired a colony confined to a narrow strip along the coast. The interior was a wild and savage country, and even in Colombo the Dutch "owing to the precarious nature of their relations with the people of Kandy were careful not to erect their dwellings beyond the guns of the fortress".[2] The Dutch had regarded Ceylon as a trading station rather than a colony, and their possessions were restricted to a number of coastal fortresses such as Colombo, Galle and Jaffna. Under British rule the whole island was occupied and opened up for political and economic development. Before the conquest of Kandy the British garrisons and civil servants were concentrated in the maritime districts, but after 1815 they were dispersed over the interior of the island. "This measure," says Pridham, "though divesting the places referred to of their great charms, in a social point of view, was politically necessary; and whatever improvements have since been effected in the interior are, in great measure, to be ascribed to the

[1] Rigg, J., "On Coffee Planting in Ceylon", in *Journal of the Indian Archipelago*, VI, (1852), 126.
[2] Tennent, Sir J. E., *Ceylon*, II, 153.

new field thus opened to the activity of men, who, in addition to their ordinary civil duties, found it expedient to devote the remainder of their time to agricultural pursuits."[1] The greatest change in the social and economic conditions of the colony came, however, from the immigration of capital, European settlers and Indian labour which followed the rise of coffee planting in the interior. To the garrison and the administrative officers were now added large numbers of British planters, men for the most part who hoped to get rich quickly, and to return to England with a fortune—an attitude which influenced the type of settlement during this period. "You cannot convince an English settler that he will be abroad for an indefinite number of years; the idea would be equivalent to transportation: he consoles himself with the hope that something will turn up to alter the apparent certainty of his exile; and in this hope with his mind ever fixed upon his return he will do nothing for posterity in the colony. He rarely even plants a fruit tree, hoping that his stay will not allow him to gather from it. This accounts for the poverty of the gardens and enclosures round the houses of the English inhabitants."[2]

The expansion of commerce led to the rise of a number of ports, notably Colombo, Trincomalee, said to have been described by Nelson as "the finest harbour in the world",[3] and Galle.

From all this economic development the Sinhalese themselves, especially the Kandyans, kept aloof. While they profited indirectly from the increase in the wealth of the island, they were reluctant to work on the plantations, and left the rapidly growing retail trade mainly in the hands of the Moors and Muhammadan inhabitants.

The Dutch had established a considerable number of Government schools in the maritime provinces, but these were neglected for many years. During the Governorship of Horton, however, when the throwing open of Government service to the natives emphasised the importance of education, more attention was devoted to this matter. But in 1836 the total sum allotted to education was only £3600, though by 1841 this had increased to £12,600. The greater part of the teaching was in fact in the hands of the various religious denominations. Public health was cared for by the establishment of hospitals and by measures to prevent the spread of infectious diseases, especially smallpox and cholera. In general, however, apart from the great benefits conferred by the maintenance of order and an impartial system of justice, and the relinquishment of *rajakaria*, the administration was slow in taking steps to improve the conditions of the majority of the population.

[1] Pridham, C., *Ceylon and its Dependencies*, i, 206.
[2] Baker, S. W., *Eight Years Wanderings in Ceylon*, pp. 98–9.
[3] Martin, R. M., *Statistics of the British Colonies*, p. 371.

CHAPTER XIV

INTERNATIONAL COLONIAL RIVALRY

(I) The New World, 1815–1870

DURING the thirty years between the Treaty of Versailles (1783) and the Treaty of Ghent (1814) questions of international politics were almost entirely confined to the Old World, and American affairs lost the commanding position they had held during the preceding three-quarters of a century. But with the return of peace it became clear that a radical and permanent revolution had come about in world politics. In the seventeenth and eighteenth centuries the rivalries of the European Powers had been extended to the New World, and the struggles of England against France and Spain for opportunities of colonial trade and development in America had contributed materially to the decisions reached in Europe. But during the Revolutionary and Napoleonic wars not a single major engagement had been fought beyond the Atlantic; British sea-power had barred the ocean routes to all hostile fleets, and the effective struggles were confined to the land and waters of the Old World. Behind that shield the infant nation of the United States had overcome its first growing-pains without foreign interference or even a dread of it, and the peoples of Latin America had planned their schemes for independence with impunity. Even in the Caribbean, a cock-pit of strife for two centuries, France had been helpless before the British forces and disastrously failed in her attempt to recover her colony of San Domingo from its revolted slaves. Napoleon's grandiose schemes to restore a French empire in Louisiana had never got beyond the paper on which they were written. By the secret convention of San Ildefonso (Oct. 1800) Spain had agreed to retrocede the old French colony in exchange for Tuscany, but as soon as news of the scheme became public passionate resentment was aroused in the United States, and President Jefferson sent a special envoy to Paris to effect a compromise or even buy outright the French claims (1803). By that time his failure in the West Indies and new prospects in the East had led Napoleon to change his policy. He was ready to renounce Louisiana in order to concentrate his full strength on the capture of the East Indies, and by accepting the American offer of purchase he expected to win the firm friendship of the United States and their help against England.[1] By the resulting treaty the whole of the immense valley of the Mississippi and its tributaries, with all the vast

---

[1] For a detailed account of Napoleon's changes of policy at this time see Rose, J. H., *Life of Napoleon*, I, 365–72.

possibilities of future development across the prairies to the slopes of the Rocky Mountains, passed peacefully into the hands of the new rising Power, and in the interior of North America only the United States and Great Britain were left to colonize the richest unoccupied territories in the world.

In the later negotiations concerning the Louisiana purchase the United States contended that it included the territory of West Florida which had been a British colony between 1763 and 1783 but was returned to Spain by the Treaty of Versailles. The Spaniards refused to accept this contention and the dispute dragged on for several years, but at last by the treaty of 1819 both East and West Florida passed into the possession of the United States, and thus both sides of the very important Florida Channel, the main gateway from the Caribbean, fell into the hands of the English-speaking Powers, the United States holding the western shore and the British their colony of the Bahamas on the east. Nominal Spanish sovereignty on the northern coast of the Caribbean was confined to the undeveloped territory of Texas which was to play a part in Anglo-American relations in later years when the new independent Republic of Mexico had succeeded to the Spanish claims.

The effective separation of the politics of the New World from those of the Old was practically complete long before the Peace of 1815, and Britain could hand back a few remnants of their former American possessions to France and Holland at Vienna with the comfortable certainty that they afforded no hopes of expansion or even of effective commercial competition. Henceforward she had only one rival in America and that the Power with whom in international politics, inspired as both were by similar ideas derived from a common history, she was more often in unison than in conflict. Against the intrusion of European Powers into the affairs of the western hemisphere Great Britain and the United States were certain to unite, and, after the short and uneventful war that kept them apart from 1812 to 1814, this soon became manifest. International rivalry in the New World lay, as a rule, quite apart from other questions of world politics.

Most of the outstanding questions which had been left over at Versailles in 1783 were settled by the Jay Treaty of 1794. The frontier forts on the Canadian border were handed over to the United States, and it was agreed to refer the question of the disputed north-eastern frontier between Maine and New Brunswick for settlement by a joint Commission, but the questions of maritime rights and the fisheries were left undecided, and it was the former of these that caused the outbreak of war between the two Powers in 1812. That war played an important part in the history of Canada,[1] but it was at the time of little importance to the Empire as a whole except to emphasise

---

[1] See *C.H.B.E.* vi, ch. ix, especially p. 233.

the need of more wheat and timber from British North America. Its main influence was on the direction of the future development in North America. The flow of American emigration across the Great Lakes into the fertile lands of Upper Canada was arrested, and their settlement was henceforward under the undisputed lead of the United Empire Loyalists, who had victoriously opposed an American invasion, and the many Scottish immigrants, who flocked in as soon as the war was over. Both elements contributed to the growth of a common patriotism among English-speaking Canadians, which was certainly not American but was the nucleus round which a new nation began to shape itself. The war also had a beneficent influence by bringing together with common memories the English and French-speaking Canadians. Together they had repulsed the invasion from the south and had learned respect for one another's valour and loyalty. As a consequence the rapidly growing movement from the United States into the western lands was to be paralleled by a similar movement directed not from the distant United Kingdom but by Canadians both of British and French stock from the communities on the St Lawrence and the northern shores of the Lakes. The westward expansion was henceforward to be dual and to flow in two separate streams, one on either side of the mid-continental watershed which was vaguely recognised as a dividing-line though not yet accurately delimited. That delimitation was to be the principal question of Anglo-American diplomacy for many years, and it was a unifying influence in imperial development that Canadian opposition to the claims of the aggressive American frontiersmen had to be voiced by British diplomatists. Just as the French rivalry along the western frontier in the eighteenth century had held the thirteen colonies to their British allegiance, so American rivalry played its part in the consolidation of the new Empire.

The negotiations for the Treaty of Ghent were marked by a mutual reluctance to drive matters to extremes, and in the result the settlement was merely a return to the *status quo ante*.[1] The British maritime claims, which had led to the outbreak of war, were left unsettled, but they lost their danger. They were not exercised during the long succeeding period of peace and a new era had dawned by the middle of the century. No settlement of the frontier questions was reached, and they were left to be solved piecemeal by the traditional American device of joint boundary commissions.[2] The Lake of the Woods marked the westward end of the boundary to be thus delimited.[3]. The British plenipotentiaries strove to revive the old eighteenth-century idea of a buffer Indian state in the western lands, but the Americans rejected it, and the British did not persist. The question of American

[1] *Brit. and For. St. Pap.* II, 357–64.
[2] See chapter XXIII.
    Brit. and For. St. Pap. II, 357–364. Arts. VI and VII.

trade with the British West Indies was left over for separate negotiation, as were the disputes about the fisheries which were of great import- ance to the settlers in Newfoundland. A temporary Commerical Convention arranged in 1815 was succeeded in 1818 by a General Convention for ten years,[1] which was later extended indefinitely and cleared up many of the outstanding difficulties. Great Britain re- linquished her claims to control the open-sea fisheries on the New- foundland Banks, while the Americans abandoned their contention that they had a right to special privileges on the coast of the colony. This did something to emancipate the Newfoundlanders from the restrictions upon British sovereignty in the colony, although until 1904 they were still bound by the old provisions of the treaty of Utrecht upon the French shore, which had remained practically unaltered by the treaties of 1783, 1814 and 1815.

The most dangerous question left over by the Treaty of Ghent was cleared up without attracting any particular public attention on either side of the Atlantic, although subsequent events have shown its outstanding importance both to Canada and the United States. In the negotiations of 1814 the British put forward a proposal for the limitation of armaments upon the Great Lakes and along the frontier, but this was rejected by the Americans, and after the peace both sides began to build up naval forces upon the Lakes. In 1817, however, John Quincy Adams, then the American Minister in London, brought forward a new proposition for mutual disarmament, and though Castlereagh somewhat hesitated owing to the defenceless situation of Canada in face of the much stronger power of the United States, he finally consented to proceed. A short agreement was con- cluded by the exchange of Notes in Washington between Richard Rush, the American Secretary of State, and Charles Bagot, then British Minister in the United States. By this Rush-Bagot Agreement,[2] which was ratified by the Senate in 1818, mutual disarmament upon the Lakes was agreed upon, and the forces on either side were reduced to those sufficient for police purposes. Although the agreement only related to the naval forces of the two Powers upon the inland waters between them, the precedent thus adopted has extended to the whole frontier, and neither side has deemed it necessary to erect fortifications or to maintain military forces for defence against the other. By the Convention of 1818 it was generally accepted that the forty-ninth parallel (coinciding roughly with the watershed) was to be the frontier between the Lake of the Woods and the slopes of the Rocky Mountains, and so the longest land frontier of the Empire has made no demands upon its military forces. The delimitation of the frontier between the islands in the Bay of Fundy and in the St Lawrence

[1] *Commercial Treaties*, ii, 387.
[2] *Brit. and For. St. Pap.* v, 1200–1. *U.S. Treaties and Conventions*, pp. 415–18, and see chapter xxiv.

River and the Great Lakes was agreed upon by joint commissions established under the Convention of 1818, but it was impossible to reach agreement upon the Maine boundary. Attempts were already being made by both sides to open up the Oregon country between the Rocky Mountains and the Pacific Ocean, but neither was ready as yet to particularise its claims in that largely unexplored region, and it was mutually agreed that for ten years the Oregon country should be freely open to the citizens of both powers without prejudice to the claims of either.

The treaty of 1819 by which Spain ceded the whole of Florida to the United States[1] had also an important bearing upon the Pacific slope of the continent. Down to that date the western boundary between Louisiana and Spanish territory had never been defined, for the country was unoccupied and almost unexplored. Now by the third article of the treaty Spain withdrew her territorial claims as far south as the forty-second parallel and so relinquished any interest in the Oregon country. The viceroyalty of Mexico was in successful rebellion against the rule of Old Spain and the interest of Madrid in the Pacific coast was therefore very slight, but it was of importance that the new Mexican Republic as the legatee of Spanish claims should be restricted to the south, for it left Great Britain and the United States alone concerned with the valuable northern region.

Their joint interests soon demanded defence, for another claimant appeared from the north. During the latter part of the eighteenth century Russian enterprise had been extended right across the land mass of Asia to the coast of Kamschatka and Bering Strait. In pursuit of the furs of the sea-otter and the seal Russian adventurers passed across the strait to the American coast and established trading ports to the southward where they trafficked with the aboriginal tribes of Indians.[2] In the late eighteenth century Spanish expeditions had come into contact with the Russians and established territorial claims up to the southern limit of their enterprises, but in the Nootka Sound dispute of 1789–90[3] Great Britain had successfully interposed her claims and it was left to Captain George Vancouver in 1793–4 to carry out detailed exploration of the coast and thus to establish British rights to prior discovery. By the end of the eighteenth century all the Russian enterprises on the American coast had been brought into the hands of a semi-official corporation called the Russian-American Company in which the Czar Alexander I had a direct personal interest. In 1821 he issued a ukase by which he claimed the whole Bering Sea as a Russian preserve and warned off all foreign ships from visiting the Northern Pacific coast as far south as the fifty-first parallel. This decree ran directly counter to the traditional

[1] *U.S. Treaties and Conventions*, p. 1017.
[2] For exploration on this coast see *C.H.B.E.* vi, 407–8.
[3] See above pp. 28–31.

American claims to free navigation of the open sea and carried Russia's claims far to the south of her effective occupation. The United States at once protested and proposed to Great Britain a joint remonstrance in St Petersburg. In July 1823 John Quincy Adams as Secretary of State to President James Monroe emphatically declared to the Russian Minister in Washington that the United States would oppose the establishment of any new Russian settlements in America to the south of those already occupied according to the principle that "the American continents, by the free and independent condition which they have assumed and maintain, are henceforth not to be considered as subjects for future colonisation by any European Powers".[1]

Canning, the British Foreign Secretary, would not enter into joint action to curb the Czar's exaggerated pretensions, but preferred to maintain British rights on the Pacific by independent representations to Russia. His reluctance was due in part to the fact that the question was involved in the more important controversy about French intervention against the revolted Spanish colonists in South and Central America. Russia's theoretical pretensions, combined with France's practical schemes for carrying into the New World her victorious armies, which had just re-established despotism in Spain, were a very real danger, but Canning believed that Alexander would not persist, and he was right.

In April 1824 Russia withdrew her claims and consented to a treaty with the United States whereby the southernmost limit of her enterprises was fixed at 54° 40′;[2] this was followed by a similar Convention with Great Britain in February 1825,[3] and thus the whole of the Pacific coast between 42° and 54° 40′ was left to the English-speaking Powers without any possibility of foreign intervention. This was of the highest importance to both, for it meant that sooner or later their ambitions of two centuries to extend their sway from the Atlantic right across to the Pacific Ocean could be achieved.

While the immediate practical result of the crucial negotiations of these years was the exclusion of Russia from Oregon, the question of French intervention in the affairs of the revolted Spanish colonies demanded a far larger share of the attention both of Great Britain and the United States. The three important principles that embody what has since been called the Monroe Doctrine were proclaimed by President Monroe in his Message to Congress of 2 December 1823. They are quoted here in his actual words:

(1) That the American continents, by the free and independent condition which they have assumed and maintain, are henceforth not to be considered as future subjects for colonisation by any European Powers.

(2) With the existing colonies or dependencies of any European Power we [i.e. the United States] have not interfered, and shall not interfere.

[1] Adams to Twyll, 17 July 1823. See Ford, W. C., "John Quincy Adams and the Monroe Doctrine", *Amer. Hist. Rev.* (1902), VII, 676–96; VIII, 28–52.
[2] *U.S. Treaties and Conventions*, pp. 931–3.   [3] *Brit. and For. St. Pap.* XII, 38–43.

(3) But with the Governments, who have declared their independence and maintained it, and whose independence we have, on great consideration and on just principles acknowledged, we could not view any interposition for the purpose of oppressing them, or controlling in any other manner their destiny, by any European Power, in any other light than as the manifestation of an unfriendly disposition towards the United States.[1]

The very definite declarations of the Message did not cover a territory like Oregon where rights were not yet delimited. Together Great Britain and the United States could warn off other Powers, but that warning was only effective because of the strength of the British fleet, and Canning was not willing to accept any restriction of British expansion or interests in America. He told Richard Rush, then American Minister in London: "If we were to be repelled from the shores of America, it would not matter to us whether that repulsion was effected by the ukase of Russia excluding us from the sea, or by the new Doctrine of the President excluding us from the land. But we cannot yield obedience to either."[2] To the British Commissioners dealing with the Oregon disputes he was equally emphatic. If the American Commissioners raised the Monroe Doctrine as limiting British rights, they were to say that "His Majesty's Government reject it in the most unequivocal manner. Whatever right of colonising the unappropriated portions of America has been hitherto enjoyed by Great Britain, may still be exercised in perfect freedom."[3] To this uncompromising pronouncement the United States made no reply, and when the Oregon question came up for definite decision twenty years later, the British negotiators went into the discussion with free hands.

At the end of 1824 the official preliminaries for the recognition by Great Britain of the new republics of Latin-America as independent Powers were completed, and a radical change was wrought in the political situation in the Western Hemisphere which left Great Britain and the United States as the only rivals for influence with them. Thus the question of our policy in the Caribbean came into the forefront again from the comparative neglect in which it had lain since the Peace of Paris in 1763. Then it had been our aim to curb the rivalry of France in the West Indies; now it was the policy of the United States with which we were concerned, and for the twenty-five years from 1825 to 1850 the most difficult passages of Anglo-American diplomacy related to Caribbean problems.

While the colonies on the mainland were successfully vindicating their independence of Spain, the island colonies of Cuba and Porto Rico were still retained under the Royal power. In 1825 it appeared that France was planning to send troops to occupy Cuba. Her

---

[1] For details concerning the antecedents of the Message see *C.H.B.F.P.* II, 68–76. For the Message see Richardson, J. D., *Messages and Papers of the Presidents*, 1789–1897, and see below, chapter XXIII.
[2] Quoted by Temperley, *C.H.B.F.P.* II, 73.   [3] *Ibid.* II, 73, n. 1.

nominal pretext would be to support the royal government, but as it was common knowledge that she was trying to restore her control over Haiti, formerly her colony of San Domingo, there was strong ground for supposing that she had ulterior designs on Havana, the fortress that commanded the exit from the Caribbean through the Florida Channel. To check such designs Canning proposed to France and the United States a joint declaration by which all three Powers would promise never to annex either Cuba or Porto Rico. France hesitated, but Adams flatly refused and instead informed the French Government that the United States would never consent to the occupation of the islands.[1]

Other actions of Adams confirmed Canning in the idea that under the cover of the Monroe Doctrine he was cherishing ambitious designs to make the United States dominant in the Caribbean. To such designs Great Britain must necessarily be opposed, not only because of her ancient and still valuable West Indian colonies, but because of the policy to which Canning attached so much importance, that of cultivating our influence in the new republics in Mexico and Central America. Parallel with this were the long drawn out disputes over American commerce in the British West Indies, to which reference is made in another chapter. In July 1826 all trade and intercourse were prohibited between the British West Indies and the United States in other than British vessels, and Adams, now President of the United States, countered by refusing to allow British vessels from the West Indies to enter American ports.

The President's Messages to Congress about the Pan-American Congress at Panama and many injudicious speeches delivered in the course of the debates in Washington added to the dangers of the situation and seemed to indicate that the United States might claim a right to prescribe to Great Britain her course of action in her West Indian colonies, a claim the British Cabinet was naturally determined to withstand. Britain's unremitting efforts to put down the slave trade and to persuade other Powers to join her in those efforts roused the fears and hostility of the slave-owning interests in the southern United States, and it was upon their opposition to Adams's Pan-American ideas and his suspected friendliness to Bolivar's ideals of slave emancipation that his Caribbean designs foundered. But they left behind much distrust on both sides of the Atlantic, and when in 1833 emancipation was proclaimed throughout all the British Colonies, the southern slave-owners became the leaders of anti-British feeling in the United States with direct influence upon Caribbean policy.

In 1829 Andrew Jackson succeeded Adams in the Presidency and it was feared that his aggressive anti-British sentiments would make relations in the Caribbean even more difficult, but both he and his

---

[1] Quoted by Temperley, *C.H.B.F.P.* II, 232.

successor, Martin Van Buren (1837–41) were too much occupied elsewhere to take up Adams's West Indian ambitions. During their Presidencies the danger-point in Anglo-American relations turned again to the Canadian boundary. In 1827 a Convention had been negotiated referring the dispute about the frontier between Maine and New Brunswick to the arbitration of the King of the Netherlands. He gave his award in 1831 dividing the territory between the contestants, but the Senate refused to accept the award and so the matter remained undecided.[1]

Feeling between the Canadians and their neighbours, the frontier farmers in the States, especially of New York and Maine, ran very high during the 'thirties. When William Lyon Mackenzie raised the standard of revolt in Upper Canada in 1837 he found many sympathisers across the Lakes, who, despite the obligations of neutrality, did all they could to supply the rebels with arms and munitions. On the collapse of the rebellion, Mackenzie fled to the American side of the border and there endeavoured to arouse his sympathisers to armed intervention by raids into Canada. The resulting affair of the *Caroline* is described elsewhere;[2] it aroused considerable heat, to the detriment of Anglo-American relations, but it was only one of many similar scuffles on the border, and the cooler heads in London and Washington would not allow such minor frontier troubles to cut across the broad lines of policy. The Maine boundary caused more difficulty, and in 1839 seemed to threaten real danger. In the so-called "Restook[3] War" riotous assemblies of lumber-men on either side were arming for battle and the local legislatures were ready to support them, but the Cabinets in London and Washington wisely checked the frontier hot-heads. By 1840 each side had stationed regular troops in the disputed region and things had quieted down. The Governments both of Maine and New Brunswick agreed under pressure to leave the dispute to the central authorities, and their armed militia were withdrawn.

Besides the Oregon boundary, which could wait, there were three parts of the frontier which were in dispute: (1) between Maine and New Brunswick, (2) at the head of Lake Champlain near the United States' fort at Rouse's Point, where faulty surveying had traced the forty-fifth parallel too far to the south, and (3) between Lake Huron and the Lake of the Woods. In each region the expansion of enterprise and especially the forward march of American settlers were making the difficulties acute. Daniel Webster, one of the leading statesmen in the United States, became Secretary of State in March 1841,[4] and he was convinced that in face of the internal dissensions then threatening the Union it was necessary to clear up external difficulties

---

[1] See chapter XXIII.
[2] See *C.H.B.E.* VI, 269 and below, chapter XXIII.
[3] Or Aroostook: see *C.H.B.E.* VI, 280–1.
[4] First under President Harrison, and on his death a month later under Tyler.

amongst which those with Great Britain loomed largest. Lord Palm-erston, Foreign Secretary in the Melbourne Cabinet, had brusquely repulsed earlier American proposals for compromise, but on the formation of Sir Robert Peel's ministry, when he was succeeded by the more conciliatory Earl of Aberdeen, the way lay open for the accommodation of disputes that both countries clearly needed. In October 1841 Webster began new overtures to settle the boundary question by direct negotiations, and Peel and Aberdeen were both convinced that those overtures ought to be accepted, especially in view of the menacing situation in Canada.[1] In December therefore Aberdeen informed the American Minister in London that the Government had determined to send a special envoy to negotiate direct with Secretary Webster in Washington and with full power to make a final settlement.

This was a step of the highest importance for the future of amicable relations between the two great English-speaking Powers in the New World, and in their choice of the envoy the British Government showed that they were determined to do all that was possible to achieve success. Alexander Baring, Lord Ashburton, knew the United States by long personal experience, and with a charming American wife he was *persona grata* in the society of Washington. Into the details of the negotiations which were carried on by personal and largely informal conference between Ashburton and Webster we need not enter.[2] The boundary questions were expected by the British Govern-ment to present the greatest difficulty, but the two negotiators saw that the only thing to do was to wipe the slate clean of the disputes of nearly sixty years and to split the difference. The boundary through the Great Lakes and the St Lawrence was settled by mutual conces-sions and the grant of reciprocal rights of navigation; at the head of Lake Champlain the *status quo* was recognised and the well-developed American settlements there remained in the United States, but the north-eastern boundary was more difficult. Webster, however, with considerable courage defied the obstinate States of Maine and Massachusetts and accepted Ashburton's claims, leaving the States to be bought off by a grant from Federal funds. The agreements reached were embodied in a treaty in 1842, and in the face of much bitter censure Webster succeeded in securing its ratification by the Senate. Ashburton, too, was bitterly attacked in England for what Palmerston called his "surrender", but after some months of acri-monious discussion it was generally recognised that he had rendered great service to the Empire by getting rid of uncertainties likely to prove increasingly dangerous as settlement proceeded. An ironical fact appeared in the course of the discussions after the treaty. Each Government had had in its possession maps bearing upon the dis-

---

[1] See *C.H.B.E.* vi, ch. xii, especially p. 317.
[2] For a summary account and references see *C.H.B.F.P.* ii, 247–53.

putes, but neither had produced them because on each side they supported contentions of the other.[1]

It was expected that the conclusion of the Webster-Ashburton Treaty would usher in better relations between the two Powers, but in this it failed, because the Democratic party then in the ascendant in the United States found its greatest support in the Southern slave-owning States where anti-British feeling ran high owing to distrust of our policy in the Caribbean. No party in Great Britain wished to increase our colonial responsibilities, and especially no one desired to add to our troubled West Indies, but the Americans persistently suspected British designs for the annexation of Cuba. No British statesman ever cherished such designs, though both Palmerston and Aberdeen were opposed to an extension of American power in the Caribbean. Their main interest lay in Texas, which was being rapidly overrun by American adventurers and wrenched from its nominal dependence on Mexico. The intricate moves and counter-moves that the Texas question led to between 1827 and 1845 need not concern us here,[2] but it should be remembered that they were closely bound up with British policy in the Caribbean and Central America and so reacted upon our territorial claims in the western hemisphere.

In 1840, during the last days of the Melbourne ministry, Palmerston decided to recognise the independence of the new Republic of Texas, but it was left to his successor, Aberdeen, to carry out his intention. In concert with Guizot, the French Foreign Minister, Aberdeen sought the adhesion of the United States to a tripartite convention to put pressure on Mexico to acquiesce in Texan independence. His main idea was to preserve the balance of power in the Caribbean and to use Texas as a buffer-state against the rapidly growing power of the United States, but the Americans refused, for the Democrats wished to annex the territory and thus to add a new slave-owning State to the Union. The question was little understood by the British public, but in the American press and in Congress it caused a lively agitation. Aberdeen's proposals were taken as evidence of British duplicity and they did much to fan the flame of American aggressiveness along the western frontier.

In the Presidential campaign of 1844 the Democratic party appealed to this anti-British sentiment for support of their candidate, James K. Polk, and in Congress they strove to resist British influence in Texas by a counter-move elsewhere. The Oregon question had slumbered under the arrangement of 1827 for joint occupation, but in the campaign the Democrats loudly voiced American claims to the whole territory right up to the Russian border. Their slogan "Fifty-four Forty or Fight" swept the country and undoubtedly

[1] *Brit. and For. St. Pap.* xxx, 360–7.
[2] See *C.H.B.F.P.* ii, 254 *seqq.*

helped to win the election for Polk in November 1844. In the last days of Tyler's administration the British Government suggested the reference of the question to arbitration, but the retiring President would do nothing to tie his successor's hands. Polk, in his Inaugural Address in March 1845, was most uncompromisingly direct. He coupled Texas and Oregon together as regions where the interests of the United States called for a stout resistance to British ambition.

The news of the rising anti-British agitation across the Atlantic was already causing much uneasiness in England, for responsible public men had been under the impression that the Webster-Ashburton Treaty of two years before had cleared the obstacles that impeded Anglo-American friendship.

The President's Message, however, contained so gratuitous an official rejection of British claims repeatedly acknowledged in previous negotiations that the British Government prepared to defend its position, and for a moment there seemed danger that the dispute would end in war; but in reality the danger was nearly past, for Polk was deeply involved in plans for war with Mexico and both sides were ready for a reasonable compromise.

Into the question of Polk's extraordinary extension of Monroe's Doctrine against European colonisation in the western hemisphere it is unnecessary here to enter, for it had no practical effect and was never generally accepted. But the President's actions in Texas had an important bearing upon British policy in the Caribbean and must be mentioned. In the December session of 1845 Congress sanctioned the annexation of the Republic of Texas as a new State of the Union, and all Aberdeen's plans for supporting it as a buffer against the extension of American influence on the shores of the Gulf of Mexico were brought to naught. He tacitly acquiesced in the annexation and the way was open for the settlement of the Oregon dispute.[1] The treaty provided for the extension of the boundary along the forty-ninth parallel from the Rocky Mountains to the Pacific Ocean. The whole of Vancouver Island was assigned to Great Britain and her sovereignty was recognised over the valley of the Fraser River where her settlers and the agents of the Hudson's Bay Company had mostly congregated, while the basin of the Columbia River was left to the Americans. This was fitting, because the colonists who had come over the mountains from the United States had begun to develop that region and it was there that Jacob Astor had his fur-trading establishments. The ratification of the Oregon treaty by the Senate in June 1846 practically ended the controversies about the British North American frontier. From the Atlantic to the waters of the Strait of Juan de Fuca everything was settled and only a minor question of the islands in the strait remained.

[1] Moore, J. B., *International Arbitrations*, I, 154–7.

At the very moment when the Oregon negotiations were successfully terminated, Frémont was encouraging the American settlers in California to rise against their Mexican governors by stories of British designs to annex the territory, which were entirely apocryphal. The device was successful, however, and in July 1846 the American flag was officially raised at Monterey, then capital of the province, and California was formally proclaimed as annexed to the United States. It was not until two years later, after a disastrous war, that Mexico recognised accomplished facts by the Treaty of Guadalupe Hidalgo (1848), and the two English-speaking Powers were left side by side without a competitor in temperate North America. At San Francisco and the mouth of the Fraser they looked out on the Pacific from new angles, and the affairs of that vast ocean took on a fresh importance in world politics.

While the Anglo-American disputes in the north were settling down with almost equal satisfaction to the claims of both sides, the principal centre of dispute was again shifting to the Caribbean and a troubled period of five years followed that ended in 1850 with the retirement of Great Britain from a field of policy in which since Cromwell's conquest of Jamaica in 1655 she had played a leading part. Down to the middle of the nineteenth century Caribbean policy had always demanded a share, and sometimes a very important share, of the attention directed by British statesmen to extra-European affairs. After that date, although Great Britain relinquished none of her West Indian colonies, her interest in them had no bearing upon her attitude to world politics; it was solely domestic and economic. The last steps by which this important change was brought about must therefore claim some attention as the closing phase of a long epoch in our colonial history.

We have already mentioned the unobtrusive withdrawal of Aberdeen from his Texan policy when Texas became a State of the Union, but we have said nothing as to what was happening farther south. From the days of Charles II onwards it had been England's ambition to secure a preponderant share in the trade of the Spanish colonies, and although her various efforts to secure a footing there were an almost unbroken series of failures, some traces of her early claims upon the Central American coast survived into the nineteenth century. Jamaica was intended to be the emporium of the trade and it was especially in connection with that colony that the vestiges of early aspirations remained. Those aspirations had failed before the unfaltering determination of the Spanish Crown to exclude all foreigners from the trade of the Indies. When the colonies became new independent republics and opened their ports to foreigners in the 'twenties Great Britain secured a large share of their oversea trade, but was faced by the acute competition of the merchants of the United States. This competition for influence in the republics brought about in Polk's Presidency and that of his successor Taylor a direct challenge to Britain's surviving claims.

When buccaneering and piracy were suppressed, the filibusters took to logwood cutting along the remote rivers and creeks on either shore of the peninsula of Yucatan. Their primitive camps were at first established in the closing years of the seventeenth century round the Laguna de Terminos at the bottom of the Gulf of Mexico, but the Spaniards drove them thence and they congregated in the creeks (round what later became known generally as Belize) which behind their sheltering cays and shallow waters were more remote from Spanish attack.[1] There were constant disputes during the eighteenth century about the legality of their settlements there, but Britain would never accept the contention of Spain that her sovereignty extended over that region, where admittedly she had never established effective occupation. After the Peace of 1783 Spain reluctantly recognised the legality of the British occupation of Belize,[2] but she would not accept the vague semi-protectorate that Britain claimed to exercise over the Moskito Indians who inhabited the swampy region to the south of Cape Gracias à Dios through which the San Juan River drained Nicaragua into the Caribbean.

The principal Central American communities, Nicaragua, Guatemala, Honduras and Costa Rica, had finally won their independence from Spain early in the 'twenties and the whole region became a loose federal republic called "the United States of Central America", but they were the scene of unending guerilla wars in which adventurous filibusters from North America played prominent parts. Great Britain strove through the ministers she appointed to the various republics to exert a calming influence on this perennial anarchy in order to foster her Central American trade and protect the interests of her bondholders, but her efforts to interfere aroused the jealousy of the Americans, and during the 'forties Central American affairs played a distinct part in exacerbating Anglo-American relations. The trouble centred in two questions, the status of the British colony at Belize and the revived proposals for a trans-Isthmian canal between the Caribbean and the Pacific.[3]

By the Convention of London of 1786 Great Britain agreed with Spain that all British settlers should be evacuated from the Moskito Coast and the adjacent islands, and in return Spain recognised the district round Belize as open to the enterprises of the logwood cutters, though without any explicit acceptance of British sovereignty in that region.[4] Neither side carried out this arrangement, for Spaniards from Honduras and Guatemala never left the settlers at

[1] See Burdon, Sir J. A., *Archives of British Honduras*, 1, xii–xv, Introduction by A. P. Newton.

[2] By the Convention of London, 1786. Burdon, J. A., *ibid.* 1, 154–6.

[3] Williams, M. W., *Anglo-American Isthmian Diplomacy, passim.*

[4] Burdon, Sir J. A., *Archives of British Honduras*, 1, 154–6.

Belize in peace until after their disastrous repulse at the "battle" of St George's Cay in 1798. On the other hand British colonists remained on the Moskito Coast and in the islands in the Bay of Honduras, especially Ruatan. A serious effort was made to establish a satisfactory organisation of the Government at Belize in 1814 when an able and energetic soldier, Major (later Sir) George Arthur, was appointed as Superintendent in supreme military and civil command in place of the inexperienced local men who had previously been appointed to the post by the Governor of Jamaica.[1] He remained in the Settlements until 1822 and organised the government on a much firmer and more orderly footing. About that time British subjects were becoming more numerous in the territory of the Moskitos, and they gathered especially at the mouth of the San Juan River where they developed a primitive port called Blewfields (or Greytown) which was known to the Spaniards of Nicaragua as San Juan del Norte. In 1839 the government of Belize was fully organised, though it was still known only as a Settlement until 1862. With the reorganisation increased attention was paid by its Superintendent to the boundary disputes and to what was going on at Blewfields and in the Bay Islands.[2]

The cause of this increased interest was the revival of projects dating back as far as the sixteenth century for the cutting of a canal to link the waters of the Caribbean to the Pacific, and the rival attempts of British and American concession hunters to persuade the new Central American Republic to grant them valuable privileges for its construction. Two routes in particular were especially considered, the first across the Isthmus of Panama through the territory of the Republic of New Granada and the second by way of Lake Nicaragua and down the San Juan River with its exit into the Caribbean at Blewfields. In 1830 a Dutch company secured a concession from the Republic of Nicaragua to exploit the latter route, and although nothing came of it, the Nicaraguans realised the obstacle to their interests that arose from the British claims to the Moskito Territory, and, prompted by American projectors, they tried to secure the help of the United States in contesting those claims.[3]

In the debates in Congress which followed President Polk's re-enunciation of the Monroe Doctrine in the more exaggerated form to which we have already referred, British designs in Central America were pointedly mentioned as evidence of aggression, and when the United States had occupied California the projects for an isthmian canal came into the forefront as a means of avoiding the difficult land route across the plains or the long sea voyage round Cape Horn to the new State of the Union. In 1846 the United States secured

[1] *Ibid.* II, 169–77; cf. above, chapter XIII.
[2] The disputes concerning the boundaries of the Settlement at this period are set out at length in a series of notes by W. E. Gladstone, *Archives of British Honduras*, II, 367–74.
[3] Fish, C. R., *American Diplomacy*, pp. 291–2.

a treaty from New Granada conveying the sole right of communication across the Isthmus of Panama[1] and this left the Nicaragua route as the only one open to British concessionaires. Their agents, with the approval of the colonial government at Belize, were determined to urge the claims of the Moskito Indians to the full, and in 1847 the Nicaraguans were expelled from Blewfields and the British consul there in his official capacity of Protector of the Moskitos hauled down the Nicaraguan flag. This led to an attack by the armed forces of Nicaragua and the arrest of certain British officials. In consequence British warships were sent to Blewfields, drove out the Nicaraguans once more and in March 1848 extorted a treaty from the republic which recognised the sovereignty of the Moskitos under a British protectorate.[2]

Matters had gone so far that Palmerston, now once more Foreign Secretary, was compelled to direct his serious attention to this question, especially so because anger was rising in the United States and the whole subject of our policy and interests in the Caribbean was at stake. Affairs were still critical when President Polk was succeeded in March 1849 by the more conciliatory Taylor with John M. Clayton as Secretary of State. Neither side wished to drive matters to extremes, for more important things than Central America demanded friendly relations between them. Many responsible Americans believed that Britain was planning to establish a protectorate over Costa Rica and the Republic of Honduras, and the somewhat tactless proceedings of some of the British diplomatic representatives in the region seemed to lend colour to their suspicions. In reality, however, it was then the settled general policy of the Cabinet to accept no further colonial responsibilities and especially not to extend our difficulties in the West Indies where our depressed island colonies imposed such constant burdens on the Colonial Office. Palmerston showed an unusually conciliatory tone in his communications to the American Minister in London. He disclaimed any intention of forming any new British colonies in Central America and accepted a proposal from the United States for a joint guarantee of the neutrality of any isthmian canal.[3]

The negotiations for a formal treaty were entrusted to Sir Henry Bulwer, British Minister in Washington, and in 1850 he agreed with Secretary Clayton upon a draft convention by which both powers bound themselves not to colonise or assume or exercise any dominion over any part of Central America. Palmerston accepted the draft and Clayton, after much difficulty, succeeded in getting the treaty ratified by the Senate. The Clayton-Bulwer Treaty, as it is known, was of course specially concerned with the isthmian canal projects,

[1] *U.S. Treaties and Conventions*, pp. 195–205.
[2] *Parl. Pap.* (1847–8), lxv, 152–3.
[3] Williams, M. W., *op. cit.* and below, chapter xxiii.

but it has a wider importance in our imperial history, for it must be taken as the formal expression of the policy which had long been shaping in the minds of British statesmen of all parties. This was the definite limitation of our interests in the Caribbean to the maintenance of the *status quo* and the avoidance of any extension of political responsibilities in the West Indies and the neighbouring lands.

That this meant no abandonment of rights that Great Britain already possessed was formally recognised in a statement by Clayton to Bulwer that the United States did not construe the renunciation of territorial interests by Great Britain as extending to her settlement in Belize and its dependencies. What these dependencies were still led to difficulties, and in 1850 the Bay Islands came into question. Certain American adventurers were endeavouring to occupy the islands which had been loosely attached to Belize since the eighteenth century. Palmerston sent orders to the Governor of British Honduras to prevent American encroachments, but he was ready to come to a settlement of the outstanding difficulties both in the Bay Islands and in Moskito Territory. Before matters could be arranged, however, the dispute was carried into the maelstrom of American domestic politics. Anti-British slogans again played an important part in the Presidential campaign of 1852, as they had done eight years before. The Republic of Nicaragua had appealed to the United States for active support against British pretensions upon the Moskito Coast, and this appeal was made just when public opinion was excited over Cuban affairs. Spain was trying to secure a tripartite guarantee of Cuba from Great Britain, France and the United States, and this was supposed to mask a British design to purchase the island to recompense her bondholders for their loans. Such suspicions were baseless, but they cannot be neglected, for they made Anglo-American relations more difficult and so affected policy.

The Senate set up an inquiry into British proceedings in Belize and the Bay Islands, and the establishment by letters patent in March 1852 of a separate colonial administration in the islands[1] was one of the causes of a scathing report, which denounced the letters patent as a flagrant violation of the Clayton-Bulwer Treaty by the seizure of territory rightly belonging to the Republic of Honduras, and went on to claim that Belize itself was part of Guatemala's territory and that the British settlers were intruders. This report was the product of the fire-eating Democratic expansionists from the South who wanted to secure the hegemony of the Caribbean in order to add fresh slave-owning territory to the Union.[2] In order to bring pressure to bear on Great Britain and so compel her to withdraw from the Caribbean, the Southern Democrats wished to accentuate the attitude of the United States on Canadian questions, but the Northerners in

---

[1] Burdon, Sir J. A., *Archives of British Honduras*, III, 156–7.
[2] Williams, M. W., *Anglo-American Isthmian Diplomacy*.

the President's Cabinet would not agree, and so the negotiations concerning the fisheries of Newfoundland, reciprocity with Canada and the West Indies were kept separate and proceeded on independent lines.

The fishery negotiations and the trade questions with Canada are treated elsewhere in this work[1] and need not concern us further here. But it must not be forgotten that they were going on concurrently and certainly affected the senators who had to ratify any agreement that might be reached. The diplomatists might keep matters in water-tight compartments, but laymen would not do so. There were long debates on the Monroe Doctrine in Congress in 1853,[2] and repeated references were made to British encroachments in Nicaragua and the Bay Islands as being counter to the doctrine and demanding strong measures for their repulse. Lord Clarendon, in his long correspondence with James Buchanan, Secretary of State to President Fillmore, firmly resisted the aggressive extension of the doctrine that Polk had voiced and which the Democrats in the Senate wished to implement even at the cost of war. The whole dispute was intimately mixed up with the intricate diplomatic manœuvres concerning Cuba which were then in train.[3] But Buchanan's mistakes in his Cuban policy, which seriously diminished the prestige of the Democratic party, made him unwilling to drive matters to extremes in the face of Clarendon's firm yet conciliatory attitude on Caribbean affairs, and on the other side Britain's preoccupation with the Crimean War made it possible for those who, like Cobden and Roebuck, wished to promote an Anglo-American *rapprochement* to prevent any over-insistence on British claims. Disraeli took the lead in furthering a movement for compromise in the important debates on Anglo-American relations in the House of Commons in 1856, and Clarendon attempted to find a way out of the difficulty in 1857 by sending a special envoy to the United States and Nicaragua to negotiate a settlement, as Ashburton had done with Webster in 1846. But Sir William Gore Ouseley, to whom the task was entrusted, effected nothing, the state of affairs in Central America was going from bad to worse owing to the intrigues of French and American adventurers, and in 1858 the annexationist party in the United States boastfully proclaimed their intention of tearing up the Clayton-Bulwer Treaty and seizing the land through which any trans-isthmian canal must pass.

A solution came owing to the change in the domestic situation in the United States. Civil war was fast approaching and President Buchanan could spare little attention from the critical state of affairs at home for foreign adventures. The Central American republics, aware that they could expect no effective support from the north, were

[1] *C.H.B.E.* vi, 386–9.   [2] *C.H.B.F.P.* ii, 273.
[3] *Ibid.* ii, 274.

ready to listen to the conciliatory proposals which the British Envoy, Charles Wyke, made them in 1859. A series of treaties was concluded; with Honduras in November 1859, by which Great Britain consented to withdraw from the Bay Islands in return for certain frontier concessions and the recognition of British Honduras;[1] with Nicaragua in January 1860, by which the British protectorate over the Moskitos was limited in scope;[2] and with Guatemala in April 1859, by which the inland frontier was regulated and the colony of British Honduras recognised.[3]

By these treaties the political situation in the Caribbean was stabilised, and until the outbreak of the Spanish-American War in 1898 no further change was made. The West Indies were removed from the rôle of a constant irritant in Anglo-American relations, and their interest to Great Britain henceforward lay wholly in the economic field.

The main causes of international dispute in the western hemisphere in which Great Britain was concerned affected the United States, but in the far South there was a long-standing controversy where our opponent was the new Latin-American Republic of Argentina and where the United States generally supported the British case. This related to the Falkland Islands, the sovereignty of which was disputed between Great Britain and Spain in the period after the Seven Years' War.

The islands were called by the French the Iles Malouines (corrupted by the Spaniards to Las Malvinas), since they were at first used by the sailors of St Malo as a base for their illicit trade with the Spanish colonies in the South Seas. Spain claimed the islands as a part of her Indies and so closed to foreigners, but she had never colonised them. A small colony of Acadians was established by Bougainville in East Falkland in 1764,[4] and in the following year Commodore John Byron, acting under the orders of the Admiralty, established a post on the fine harbour of Port Egmont in Saunders Island;[5] for its strategic importance, as commanding the entrance to the Straits of Magellan and the route round Cape Horn, had been pointed out by Anson after his celebrated voyage of 1740-4.[6] Spain protested against the occupation of the French colony and secured its removal in 1767 when she established definite occupation there, but the British remained at Port Egmont. In 1770 that post was attacked by a Spanish expedition from Buenos Aires and the British were expelled. The English Government, however, by diplomatic and naval pressure compelled its restitution, and from 1771 to 1774 there was an acute dispute as to the sovereignty over the group.

[1] *Brit. and For. St. Pap.* XLIX, 13–19.
[2] *Ibid.* L, 96–106.   [3] *Ibid.* XLIX, 7–13.
[4] Koebel, J., *The Struggle for the Falkland Islands*, p. 226.
[5] *Ibid.* pp. 231 *seqq.*   [6] *Ibid.* p. 195.

Finally, however, Britain decided to evacuate Port Egmont but without any formal relinquishment of the rights she claimed.[1] From 1775 onwards the Spaniards had a Governor in the islands, but their colonising efforts were unsuccessful. By the third Article of the Nootka Sound Convention of 1790 Great Britain agreed with Spain that on the east and west of South America her subjects should not form "any establishments on the part of the coast situated to the south of the parts of the same coast and of the islands adjacent already occupied by Spain",[2] but this did not preclude the rights of her fishermen to land on the coast and erect temporary huts for the purpose of their fishing. The Spaniards maintained that this article recognised fully their sovereignty over the Falklands, where they undoubtedly had a colony.

In 1806 the Governor of the islands, hearing of Beresford's capture of Buenos Aires, abandoned his post, but although the British soon left Buenos Aires and the royal government was restored, no new Governor was sent to the Falklands and the colonists were left to themselves. In 1811 the few who remained were removed by order of the governing revolutionary *junta* at Monte Video, and the islands were left derelict without permanent inhabitants.[3] They were constantly visited by increasing numbers of British and American whalers and sealing ships who were working in the South Atlantic, and their economic importance was obviously growing. In 1820 the Government of the United Provinces of La Plata despatched an ill-equipped frigate to take formal possession of the group, and her commander found as many as fifty vessels of different nationalities in the island harbours. A note was dispatched to foreign governments informing them of the resumption of ancient Spanish rights, but it remained unheeded. In 1823, after the recognition of the new republic by the United States, an Argentine Governor was appointed to develop a new colony in the Falklands, but little was done until 1828, when Louis Vernet, a Hamburg merchant who had been naturalised in La Plata, was granted the whole of the islands with exclusive fishing rights and made political and military Governor for the Republic of the whole territory of Las Malvinas and Staatenland.[4] Woodbine Parrish, the British Minister in Buenos Aires, protested and claimed the islands as British territory, a claim in which he was supported by the Home Government. The protest, however, was disregarded by the Argentine authorities, and matters dragged on through 1829 and 1830 until they were brought into prominence by Vernet's attempt to exercise his exclusive fishing rights.

In July 1831 three American sealing ships were seized by Vernet as infringing his orders. One escaped, and another was allowed to

[1] Koebel, J., *op. cit.* chapters XVII–XVIII.   [2] Martens, F., *Recueil de Traités*, IV, 497.
[3] Boyson, V. F., *The Falkland Islands*, pp. 81–2. Koebel, J., *op. cit.* p. 433.
[4] *Brit. and For. St. Pap.* XX, 420.

go after giving security, but he compelled the third to sail with him to Buenos Aires for adjudication by a properly constituted court. The American Minister, George Slocum, violently protested when Vernet and his capture arrived, and with the support of Silas Duncan, commander of an American naval vessel then in the Rio de la Plata, he demanded that Vernet should be handed over to him to be tried as a pirate.[1] What was really at stake, of course, was Vernet's exclusive fishing privilege which neither the American nor the British sealers would acknowledge. Failing compliance with his demands, Duncan sailed for the Falklands, destroyed all the Argentine munitions there and carried off several prisoners to Monte Video. A few months later the Argentine Government sent out a new Governor with a detachment of exiled soldiers to re-establish the colony, but they revolted and murdered him and the islands became the scene of much disorder.

Meanwhile the British Government, having received no reply to Woodbine Parrish's protest of 1829 and learning from the United States of what was going on, determined to assert its claims. A naval sloop on the South American station was ordered to proceed to the Falklands and restore order. In December, 1832, the British flag was raised again at Port Egmont and in January, 1833, Captain Onslow proceeded to Berkely Sound where he found the Argentine commander, informed him that Great Britain was determined to exercise the rights of sovereignty over the whole of the Falkland Islands and demanded his withdrawal. In the face of superior force the Argentinians could do nothing but submit, and Onslow was left in undisputed possession. A few days later he sailed away, leaving the islands with no more government than before but with a few British survivors of the derelict colony at the mercy of the remains of the half-breed convicts who had formed the garrison.[2]

Interest shifted to London where the Argentine Minister was instructed to protest to Palmerston against the forcible expulsion of the Buenos Airean garrison and ask for redress. The representation was treated very cavalierly, for it remained unanswered for six months and then Palmerston pointed to the restitution by Spain of the post at Port Egmont in 1771 as an evidence of her acknowledgment of British sovereignty. The Government of the United Provinces, he continued, could not reasonably have anticipated that the British Government would permit any other state to exercise a right derived from Spain which Great Britain had denied to Spain herself. Weak and divided as the Argentine Provinces were at that date, they could do nothing more, and they could get no help from the United States which refused to invoke the Monroe Doctrine against claims which to President Jackson seemed to antedate the Revolution. Further

[1] Koebel, J., *op. cit.* pp. 439 *seqq.* Boyson, V. F., *op. cit.* pp. 91 *seqq.*
[2] Boyson, *op. cit.* p. 99.

protests in London carried the matter no further and it was closed as far as Great Britain was concerned in 1842, when Lord Aberdeen informed the Argentine Minister that as we were preparing for the establishment of a full colonial government in the Falklands, Great Britain would permit of no infraction of her inalienable rights.[1] His statement referred to the Act of Parliament which had been passed in 1841 to permit the establishment of a new penal station for the transportation of convicts.[2] The passing of the Act meant the beginning of the modern colony whose uneventful further history need not concern us.

With the outbreak of the Civil War in the United States Anglo-American relations passed into a different phase which will be dealt with in a later part of this work; but we may note that the new President of the United States, Abraham Lincoln, soon after his inauguration expressed his willingness to enter into a new treaty with Great Britain for the suppression of slave trading.[3] The treaty was concluded in April 1862[4] and orders were issued to the United States vessels in African waters to co-operate with the British squadrons. By 1865 their joint action against the slavers was effectual and the West African slave trade was exterminated.

Of boundary questions only one remained, that concerning the islands in the Strait of Juan de Fuca between Vancouver Island and the State of Washington. The two nations had practically agreed to refer the matter to the arbitration of the King of Prussia in 1860, but, before further steps could be taken, the Civil War had broken out and the matter rested until 1872 when after arbitration by the German Emperor a compromise line was accepted,[5] and thus the long Canadian boundary was delimited from end to end.

When the Union forces were unmistakably getting the upper hand and it became certain that the United States would come out of the war with unimpaired vigour, the minds of some leading American statesmen turned to ideas of territorial expansion of the most ambitious sort. Charles Sumner, for example, a leading senator, suggested the cession of Canada to the United States as compensation for the indirect damages caused to the Union by the *Alabama* and other commerce raiders during the Civil War. Sumner was in touch with many leading Englishmen who held what were called "little England" ideas, and he believed that Britain was anxious to get rid of her colonial burden. That Canada was ripe for annexation he was

---

[1] *Brit. and For. St. Pap.* XXI, 1005.
[2] The Act 6 and 7 Vict. c. 13 provided for the establishment of settled government in the islands.
[3] For the negotiations see *Brit. and For. St. Pap.* LIII, 1424–38.
[4] *U.S. Treaties and Conventions*, pp. 454–66, and see below, chapter XXIII.
[5] *C.H.B.E.* VI, 549–50.

certain, but, like most other leading Americans, he had little conception of the rising tide of Canadian nationality.

Of more practical importance was the less grandiose policy of William H. Seward, Secretary of State to Lincoln and afterwards to President Johnson. In 1859, before the war, responsible Californians were suggesting that, in order to safeguard the growing interests of the United States in the Pacific, Russia should be approached with offers to purchase the territory of Russian America which, as we have seen, came down as far as 54° 40' where it touched British Columbia. The Russians were not unready to consider the idea, but nothing could be done during the war. In 1867 the Czar made the first advances, and after some bargaining the terms of the purchase were agreed upon. The treaty, in which this Alaska Purchase was arranged, was drawn up by Seward and Sumner, who was then Chairman of the Foreign Relations Committee in the Senate and was responsible for securing its ratification. The success which crowned it, whereby the United States so vastly increased its hold on the Pacific Coast, confirmed Sumner in his idea that by firm but peaceful pressure he could secure a like pliability in Great Britain. So the last European flag would disappear from the American coast and the Stars and Stripes would wave everywhere from Bering Strait to the Mexican border. The sequel falls beyond the end of the period here dealt with and will be traced in our next volume.

(II). Great Britain and France, 1848–1870

Between 1848 and 1870, every Great Power suffered something like a transformation. During these years the economic changes natural to the railway age were in many cases less revolutionary than the changes in the framework of the state. Britain, with the Second Reform Bill (1867), moved at the gentlest pace, and the great Liberal cabinet of 1868 proved remarkably aristocratic in its membership. Yet in Britain the premiership of a Wellington had become as unthinkable by 1870 as the premiership of a Gladstone was in 1848.

The United States entered the period an unstable confederation of less than 23,000,000 people, with slavery and secession among their political rights. They passed out of it more than 38,500,000 strong, a free and united nation. France began and ended as an unconvincing and insecure republic, but it was the rise, the splendour and the virtual abdication of an autocracy that filled the period and changed the outlook of the people. Italy in 1848 was hardly conceived of: 1870 added Rome to a monarchy ruling the entire peninsula. The Russia of Nicholas I seemed to Europe a despotism based on slavery, despising the West but upholding western autocrats by force. Before 1870, the Russia of Alexander II was accounted a nation of freemen, thankfully importing from the West her choicest judicial, municipal and educational institutions. The atlas of 1848 presented Austria, Prussia and Germany as powers distinct though territorially intermingled. In 1870 the dual monarchy of Austria-Hungary had arisen, while a new Germany was being based upon expanded Prussia. Europe thus transformed had assumed collective responsibility for the Turkish Empire, which was now recognised as a European power.

Britain, less taxed than any rival by internal struggles, had most energy to spare for development overseas. As yet, however, the time when governmental effort should be made to fulfil an imperial destiny, or to create allied daughter-nations, or to export redundant workers had hardly come. Whatever party was in power, Britain continued to take anxious care for India, making the Turkish Empire sacrosanct because its collapse might place the routes to India in hostile hands. She never failed to protect her possessions overseas, nor did she obstruct their natural development. But the lesson taught by American secession joined with the strict balance-sheet methods of leading Victorian minds to check dreams of dominion over regions not easily accessible to British ships. "No news would here be received with greater pleasure", wrote the Foreign Secretary from London at the end of 1865, "than that Canada had declared herself independent or had annexed herself to the United States."[1] The Queen, stipulating for an independent monarchy under a British prince, welcomed the notion of Canadian separation.[2]

From Britain's point of view, international rivalry in the colonial sphere, where it existed, offered very simple problems. Her own principles were fixed, and there were but three Powers, France, Russia and the United States, whom she could seriously regard as rivals. The government of the United States, with which she had been twice at war, was regarded in some quarters as our natural enemy. Founded on repudiation of British control and British ideas of government, susceptible to the promptings of Irish emigrants and rebels, often insulting in public pronouncements and in diplomacy, it was credited with the design of appropriating our American markets and possessions on the first convenient occasion. Fear of the United States contributed not a little to our careful abstention from many of the international disputes in Europe.

From Russia under Nicholas I came a nearer and a wider peril. That gigantic land-power, which a sea-power, and indeed hardly any power, could hope to check, menaced both our markets and our empire. How far India was ever really endangered, preceding chapters will have shown. A Cossack force had once been sent to conquer it. Russians in their more exalted moments might declare that their frontiers marched with themselves and that only the waves of the ocean could give them pause. The Russian government was able to

[1] Clarendon to Cowley, 4 December 1865, Wellesley, F. A., *The Paris Embassy*, p. 291.
[2] Cf. Lord Newton, *Lord Lyons*, i, 292, for similar views of cabinet ministers.

send us news that the Indian Mutiny was imminent. Before the Suez Canal was opened in 1869, the British route to India compared more unfavourably than thenceforward with that of Russia. And Russian statesmen were naturally alert to sharpen the sword of Damocles that they held, or seemed to hold, over Britain's head. But the theory which prevailed in Britain for half a century, that the expansion of the Russian empire in Asia arose from a deep plan to conquer India, ranks with the later theory that continental manufactures were evidence of a conspiracy against British trade.

The Russian hegemony over Europe, however, was such that in 1849 only the western Powers were really independent. From the North Cape to the Bosporus, all nations seemed to obey the Tsar's behest, "Tremble before us and obey." More serious for Britain was the Russian assault upon her trade. As the growth of other sources of supply rendered her less dependent upon Russian grain, the tendency of Russia to manufacture for herself and to protect her own manufactures was naturally increased. Her tariffs were extended to Poland, Moldavia and Wallachia. Circassia and even Turkey herself seemed likely to go the way of Bessarabia, and trade routes like those to the Caspian to be cut by the Tsar's decrees.[1] Russian activities against us were felt in China, and Egypt could not be regarded as entirely safe. Such facts go far to explain why the dominant aim of British diplomacy must be to prevent Russia from successfully approaching France. But France herself might confront us with a danger weightier by far than could arise from any other source. A great military power which might be also a great naval power, our traditional enemy and close neighbour, confined since 1815 within unnatural frontiers by treaties drafted and upheld by us, compelled daily to observe us occupying great possessions of which we had deprived her, could France be trusted or even expected not to seize an opportunity for revenge?

At the same time, France and Britain marched together at the head of civilisation and were in many ways each other's daily aid and comfort, as nature seemed to have designed. Closely connected by trade, they formed also the twin stronghold of free institutions in a mainly despotic Europe. United, they could do much to preserve peace in the world and to enrich their subjects. Divided, they deprived Europe, Asia and perhaps America of the strongest check on Russia and the autocracy that she sustained. Sensible of all this, British statesmen comported themselves towards France in a manner which might well seem unintelligible between friendly neighbours. They showed their sincere desire that her government should be strong and her people prosperous. Preferably, but by no means indispensably, she should practise, as we did, constitutionalism and free trade. With whatever government she might choose we desired

[1] Pokrovsky, M. N., *Russkaya istoriya s drevneishi'h vremen*, IV, 38 seqq. (1924).

a cordial understanding, the two powers maintaining constant correspondence and, wherever possible, treating questions all over the world by joint or parallel action. But at the same time we frankly set ourselves against the natural consequence of strong government and national prosperity—expansion. Whether France desired to secure economic influence over Belgium, or a return to the frontiers of 1814, or a protectorate over the head of her national religion, or a great position in Africa or farther afield, Britain was always grudging, impeding and opposing to the utmost of her power.

To carry out this policy, Britain invariably sent to Paris the ablest diplomat at her command, gave him a splendid embassy with almost Cabinet rank, and more and more tended to deal with the French Government through him rather than through the French ambassador in London. He was supported in France by accredited military and naval observers, and the official correspondence of British diplomats in the Peninsula and in Italy passed through his hands. While on the one hand his constant preoccupation must be to watch for any sign of inconvenient enterprise by France, on the other he must carry out his employers' free translation of what neighbourliness implies. With whatever perplexity we were confronted, from enabling railway guards to communicate with drivers to the best way to plan kitchens for lunatic asylums, our unvarying practice was to enquire of France. A war scare between the two countries interrupted our requests for specimens of French percussion arms, but the Foreign Office saw no incongruity in inviting French artists to design a monument to the Duke of Wellington.

Happily for both countries, the Revolution of 1848 found Russell and Palmerston in power. Russell spent a large part of his long life in extolling the Revolution of 1688, while Palmerston could see that if France called herself a republic and elected a Bonaparte chief she was really tending towards order and the *entente*. Even the French restoration of the Pope in 1849 meant that yet another part of Europe returned within the old framework, and that Austrian action was anticipated and thereby Austrian influence restricted.

While the indispensability of the Prince President was gradually becoming clear to France, many of the characteristics of his rule were impressing themselves upon Britain and upon Europe. The year 1849 began with a declaration by his ministers that extreme moderation backed by firmness would be shown to the rest of the world, and to England *la plus parfaite franchise*.[1] Before January was out, France had offered proportionate disarmament, and in the autumn she declared that 60,000 men would be disbanded as a demonstration on behalf of peace.[2] Eagerness to join Britain against Russia in the

---

[1] Normanby to Palmerston, 2 Jan. 1849. Citations dated but not otherwise attributed come from the Foreign Office archives, France, vol. 168 *seqq*.
[2] *Ibid.* 19 September 1849.

Near East, hints of the President's lack of prejudice against free trade, even a suggestion that passports between London and Paris were superfluous, all promised well for the *entente*. In Prince Louis and his government Britain could not fail to see a valuable ally against their common foe, the Reds. Towards the designs of Austria to create a Great Germany including all her empire, France and Britain were unanimously opposed. In Palmerston's phrase such a power would be "a public nuisance", while France declared that its formation would offer her the choice between disgraceful acquiescence and a disastrous war.[1] Both powers, moreover, viewed with like concern "the increasing pretensions of the United States to exclude any power not American from any concern in the affairs of that part of the globe".[2] Their *entente*, prompted immediately by Cuba, soon embraced all colonial questions and in particular promised success to the British plan for constructing a railway in Egypt.

Why, then, were these years marked also by mutual distrust and friction? The answer must in part be simply hereditary habit, particularly the tradition of rivalry prevailing among French and British agents in distant lands. The violence with which Palmerston treated Greece in the affair of Don Pacifico (1850) brought about the recall of the French ambassador from London. The protection given in England to international assassins and the invective or the wounding patronage of the English press formed a constant menace to good relations. Worse than all else perhaps was the ineradicable suspicion attached in Britain to the very words "France" and "Bonaparte", and nurtured by Louis Napoleon's policy with regard to Italy. Before he had been President a year, he had driven Garibaldi from Rome and reinstated the Pope. Then was inaugurated that French protectorate which prompted Palmerston to define the difference between "occupation" and "business"—"the French are in occupation of Rome but they have no business there". A French protectorate, indeed, was preferable to that of Austria, a less Liberal power, and its exercise was costly and burdensome to France. The British, none the less, regarded it from the first as proving its author ambitious and insincere. If it gave Louis Napoleon a hold upon the Italians, it always militated against his *entente* with Britain.

On the second of December 1851, choosing an untroubled moment and thereby gaining the advantage of surprise, Louis Napoleon freed the nation from its legal shackles by armed force. Outside the capital, France responded with an almost unanimous vote of confidence, and empowered the liberator to draw up a new constitution. Upon Britain, the effects of the *coup d'état* were swift and far-reaching. The fall of Palmerston, the fall of the Whig administration, the establishment of the coalition under Aberdeen and the precipitation of a war

---

[1] Normanby to Palmerston, 3 February 1851.   [2] *Ibid.* 22 July 1850.

with Russia—all these were perhaps surpassed in ultimate importance by the increase in British distrust of Napoleon.

The year 1852, which opened thus inauspiciously for the *entente*, saw the Empire in fact proclaimed, but the relations between the governments of France and Britain were actually drawn closer. Repeated *plébiscites* proved that the masses supported the new Napoleon, and the successors of William of Orange could hardly contest his title. The reports of the rapture shown at his presence in rural France counted for more than even the figures of the ballot. There was much indeed in Napoleon's proceedings to shock a British mind. We lamented the virulence with which his government persecuted the press, and shook our heads over the reckless expenditure and jobbery which defaced the creation of the new network of French railways.[1] When Napoleon at Marseilles spoke of the Mediterranean as a French lake, the power which ruled Malta and the Ionian Islands promptly demanded explanations. But the assurances of non-aggression that had been given regarding Belgium and Tunis were unequivocally repeated, despite the crowned orator's "poetical image" of a sea covered with the merchantmen of France.[2] At Bordeaux Napoleon declared that the coming Empire stood for Peace, a peace which meant war on ignorance, want and irreligion, to be waged by roads and railways, by steamships and the assimilation of Algeria. His policy, in a word, would be peace under the treaties of 1815.[3] Thus relieved from the menace of French arms, Britain could not refuse to face the menace of French arts. Napoleon, moreover, declared that, when she was fit for it, he intended to give constitutional liberty to France.[4]

The treaties of 1815 were in fact broken by the accession of a Bonaparte to the French throne. That Britain, their architect and upholder, was the first to condone the breach, may be ascribed to her favourable experience of Napoleon's four years in office, and not least to his attitude towards Russia. It was something, indeed, that Cowley, her new ambassador in Paris, could discuss with Drouyn de Lhuys at the Foreign Office "the general disregard shown by the United States government for international law",[5] a topic which as of old evoked a perfect understanding. But Britain valued far more highly the proofs that the new autocrat in France now stood far apart from the Tsar, who had welcomed his triumph over revolution. In 1852 Napoleon's zeal to please his Catholic subjects by claiming rights over the Holy Places in Jerusalem had led to a struggle at Constantinople against Russia and the Eastern Catholic claims. While

---

[1] Cowley to Granville, 5 July 1852.
[2] Cowley to Malmesbury, 29 September 1852.
[3] Simpson, F. A., *Louis Napoleon and the Recovery of France*, p. 195; Cowley to Clarendon, Wellesley, *op. cit.* p. 32.
[4] Cowley to Granville, 22 January 1852.
[5] Cowley to Granville, 27 September 1852 (concerning the Lobos Islands).

he agreed with Cowley that French policy had been to blame, Drouyn declared that his master would rather be pounded in a mortar than yield to the dictation of Russia.[1] No declaration could be more pleasing to British ears.

How, during the summer and autumn of 1853, a war which no Great Power desired became inevitable, forms an amazing history which may not be recounted here. The significance to Britain of the French alliance against Russia was illustrated when the Russians, bursting into the "Independent Tartary" of contemporary maps, triumphantly arrived at Khiva. Soon Afghanistan alone would stand between India and themselves, and, if French secret sources of information were to be trusted, they calculated on making short work of Afghanistan. France, acting on later German lines, could have made many profitable bargains for herself from our necessities, but she gave us full sympathy, and, when necessary, material assistance, towards the defence of our Indian Empire. In China and in the Pacific the *entente* likewise flourished. The French occupation of New Caledonia as a convict station perturbed Britain less than the smallest forward movement overseas in normal times. In Paris, indeed, everything was done in a hurry and without reflection, and none save Napoleon could bind the government.[2] But though momentary execution wavered, the main principles remained unchanged and chief of all was loyalty to Britain. Napoleon's proposal that against Russia Britain should provide the fleet and France the army ought to have driven away all our doubts.

Throughout the two Crimean campaigns (1854–5), and the parallel battles of secret diplomacy, French loyalty remained untarnished. Napoleon had strength enough to carry the war to a victorious end, but with him, as with the allied nations, reaction inevitably followed. Early in 1856, his doctors were talking of an exhausted nervous system and diseased organs,[3] while statesmen pointed out that to manage everything himself and at the same time indulge in dissipation must overtax his strength. The British, who had wished to fight on, though not, as he suggested, in order to free the Poles, were disappointed both by the war and by the peace. Although Russia had been thrown back in both northern and southern Europe and shackled in the Black Sea, she remained untrammelled in the Caucasus, and, worst of all, became widely popular in France. Walewski, Napoleon's kinsman and Drouyn's successor, was reputed entirely Russian. Napoleon himself, whom the war had brought to the pinnacle of fame and power, had no longer any grievance against the Tsar, and naturally claimed a new independence in foreign policy. Britain, for reasons which he could not consider sound, had been insistent that he should

[1] Cowley to Clarendon, 19 March 1853.
[2] Cowley to Clarendon, Wellesley, *op. cit.* p. 30.
[3] Clarendon to Cowley, Wellesley, *op. cit.* p. 96.

disapprove the proposed canal at Suez, and the union of Moldavia and Wallachia which their inhabitants desired. She now vigorously opposed his intervention in the cause of order in Spain, but sought it in the affairs of Naples. When he suggested that France should give Britain a free hand in Asia Minor and America, in return for liberty to extend Christian domination in Morocco, Britain replied that it was impossible to bind future administrations, or to further the power of France, whose future sovereigns were likely to be hostile to herself.[1] All this was accompanied by press attacks, which Napoleon felt deeply, while Britain was traditionally the protector of the far more scurrilous Belgians, and of the men who conspired in London against his life.

Napoleon's sense of honour and of duty to France and to his new-born heir none the less preserved his loyalty to the *entente*. Early in 1856 he had declared that the days when France coveted Madagascar and other islands had gone by, and he acted accordingly.[2] He himself and his ministers continually repressed the rage of French agents abroad against their British colleagues. When the United States insulted Britain by expelling her minister, the French showed that they regarded the quarrel as their own. In 1857, to the disappointment and disgust of Russia, France gave us invaluable help in concluding peace with Persia. Above all, when the Indian Mutiny broke out, and Britain, in Clarendon's phrase, existed as a nation by the grace of Louis Napoleon, we received every sympathy and courtesy from the French, who even permitted us to hurry reinforcements across their soil.[3]

The magnanimous loyalty of Napoleon to the *entente* when at the summit of his fortunes emphasises the ugliness of the relations between France and Britain which swiftly followed. The danger to the Emperor from Mazzini and other refugees had long rendered France uneasy.[4] Remonstrances against sheltering such men had been addressed to Belgium, Switzerland and Sardinia, but most of all to Britain. Britain answered that her law courts could not act on mere suspicion, and that France was continually sending refugees to Dover, thus making her a sort of penal settlement for undesirables.[5] Early in 1858, the most ghastly of all attempts at assassination was perpetrated by Orsini. Although his associates were men against whose arrival from France Britain had protested, and although Orsini himself had been denounced to the French by our police, the public on both sides of the Channel soon seemed eager for war. A French Crimean regiment begged to be allowed to seize the Emperor's enemies in England,[6] while the Commons overthrew Palmerston's government for proposing to alter

---

[1] Correspondence between Cowley and Clarendon, 28 December 1856 etc.
[2] Cowley to Clarendon, 8 January 1856.
[3] Wellesley, *op. cit.* p. 136.   [4] Cowley to Clarendon, 8 July 1857.
[5] Cowley to Clarendon, 26 December 1857.   [6] Wellesley, *op. cit.* p. 153 n.

our defective law against aliens. The governments preserved the peace, the British aided by the knowledge of our unique impotence while India absorbed our forces, the French by the instinct for a splendid gesture which prompted Napoleon to send Pélissier as his ambassador to London. That irresistible Crimean hero accepted the unwonted rôle, stipulating only that he should not be called upon to speak English or to tell a lie.[1] Napoleon, moreover, showed in regard to everything save press offences a unique appreciation of what our government could and could not do. It could, and did, help to remove the suspected refugees to the United States, but it could not interfere with the verdict of a British jury. The acquittal of Orsini's colleague, Bernard, which filled the Empress with indescribable stupefaction, since the defence charged her husband with moral responsibility for Orsini's crime,[2] evoked in the Emperor himself only sad doubts as to whether Franco-British friendship could possibly continue. The two nations and their governments, in his view, resembled mutually sustaining pyramids. Draw the bases apart, and the summits would tremble, until at last they fell in common ruin.[3] Had not this moment come?

In these successive crises of the *entente* and "scares" in Britain, however, it is notable that France never took the steps which must precede a direct threat to our shores or to our empire overseas. To give her friendship to Russia or to the United States might threaten us indirectly. Even to consider the possibility of an economic union with Belgium must arouse our resentful suspicion. But no more direct threat came from the Second Empire than the completion of a great harbour at Cherbourg and the equipment of a moderate fleet. In June 1858 a careful precautionary survey of France by British agents proved that, as usual, rumours of hostile preparations led only to a mare's-nest. Colonel Claremont, our military attaché, found the people "totally indifferent to anything but their own interests, always inclined to boast and cry out against England, but very much alarmed when they fancy matters are really becoming serious".[4] Much of our policy for many years was based upon the belief that this was true. Nearly twenty years before, Palmerston had defied France in the belief that a quarter of a century of peace must have changed her temper. "What Frenchman nowadays", asked Cowley, "thinks of anything but putting money into his pocket?"[5] The country, none the less, had some 150,000 men always available for an aggressive movement, and, as she had shown in China, the spirit of adventure lived on.[6]

The next year, 1859, brought the first occasion on which the keen-sighted British ambassador, who had studied Napoleon almost from

[1] Wellesley, *op. cit.* p. 162.
[2] Cowley to Clarendon, 8 March 1858; Wellesley, *op. cit.* p. 263.
[3] Cowley to Malmesbury, 30 April 1858.   [4] Cowley to Malmesbury, 2 June 1858.
[5] Wellesley, *op. cit.* p. 165.   [6] Cowley to Malmesbury, 23 August 1858.

the *coup d'état*, was forced to doubt his sincerity.[1] Clarendon at the same time thought him on the road to ruin—"the fate of every sovereign of France who deserts us to run after other gods".[2] The occasion for the breach was, of course, the French threat of war with Austria, and, in a less degree, the French policy of subservience to the interests of Russia. Many, indeed, like the reigning Tsar, could not understand why a man who had won the highest position in the world should thus adventure it,[3] for the issue of the war was uncertain, and the indignation of England was as nothing compared with the indignation which inflamed the German people. Napoleon, however, had an honest and dominant desire to free the Italians, and he believed that until Italy was settled his own dynasty would never be secure. To give Sardinia the Adriatic for her frontier, moreover, would entitle France to receive her own natural frontier of the Alps, by the transfer of Savoy and Nice. Hence, while Britain looked on with undisguised disapproval, events moved swiftly from Napoleon's "inexcusable language"[4] to the Austrian ambassador on New Year's day until July 11, when the two Emperors met to arrange for peace. To propitiate Britain, with Palmerston and Russell now in control, France made great offers overseas. Assurances regarding Egypt and Morocco, and plans for the substitution in French colonies of coolies from India for negroes from Africa followed in quick succession. France reiterated her resolution not to interfere in Madagascar, and her willingness to co-operate in China. She established good relations with Belgium, and held out hopes of settling the perennial disputes with Britain about fishing rights off Newfoundland. It was none the less noted as ominous both that Napoleon told his finance minister that France must be self-sufficing,[5] and that the peace was not allowed to dispense her from maintaining efficient armaments by land and sea.

Among the Italians, no agreement between France and Austria could stem the tide of nationality, and our leading statesmen believed that they were justified in seeking Italian unity and freedom. The year 1860, therefore, opened with the curious paradox that while the British volunteers were arming to resist Napoleon, the British Foreign Secretary was meditating an alliance with Napoleon to defend Italy and Sardinia.[6] But when our European policy succeeded, and what Thiers called a "new Prussia beyond the Alps" was established on the flank of France, no considerations of friendship or diplomacy restricted Russell's protests against the cession of Savoy and Nice. In vain the French claimed that the Alps were a decree of the Almighty, that the Second Partition Treaty had contemplated the union now arranged, that in 1792 these provinces had cheerfully accepted conquest and

[1] Cowley to Malmesbury, 5 April 1859.   [2] Wellesley, *op. cit.* p. 179.
[3] Cowley to Malmesbury, 1 April 1859.
[4] Cowley to Malmesbury, 3 January 1859.
[5] Cowley to Russell, 16 December 1859.
[6] Walpole, S., *Life of Lord John Russell*, II, 322 *seqq.*

that their inhabitants were eager to join France. In a strange scene Napoleon asked the Russian ambassador what England would have done if he had questioned her annexation of Perim in 1857.[1] In August, French and British forces landed near Taku and marched victoriously to dictate peace terms at Peking. But although every other Great Power remained unmoved, Russell continued to declare that Switzerland was in danger, that the balance of power was overthrown, that the Emperor had broken his promise to respect the treaties of 1815, and that the French would be led on to further acts of aggression. The price of Savoy and Nice was the firm belief of Britain that the Second Empire in France was dishonest.

The situation seemed the more extraordinary and the strain on the *entente* was rendered still greater when in January 1860 Napoleon forced his people into the famous free trade treaty negotiated by Cobden, and when, in October, Russell, who had denied the right of the Savoyards to join France, proclaimed that the Romans and Neapolitans had the right to join Sardinia. The upshot was that Britain substituted a vigilant association with France for the intimate confidential alliance of four years before.[2] The Prince Consort shared the German view that Venice was an outwork of Germany, and that, there or on the Rhine, the Germans would be the Emperor's next victims, after which England's turn would come.[3] To many, as to the Queen, France was once more "the universal disturber of the world".[4]

Despite the harmonious character of Franco-British co-operation in China, new suspicions of French naval power arose. Before the Italian war, Claremont had described Napoleon's expectation of a revolution in warfare by sea and his own of a future French attack on Britain.[5] Now popular works of reference could record impressive figures. The French navy in 1860 was said to number 461 vessels carrying 12,520 guns. In ten years it would be increased by 150 ships of war and 72 steam-transports.[6] A first-class steam frigate was to be named the *Ville de Nice*. The personnel of the navy and marine included 90,298 men, or nearly double the usual annual average of the British navy. Was it safe to trust with such a force a military autocrat who had already surprised two empires?

In other fields, moreover, and notably in Syria "the Emperor of Europe" showed a desire to assert his power. France urged that excesses committed by the natives of the Lebanon against the Christian Maronites necessitated Christian intervention. Russia countered by proposing the same remedy for Turkish massacres in Bosnia, Herzegovina and Bulgaria. Failing a collective intervention, the French

---

[1] Cowley to Russell, 7 March 1863, *Letters of Queen Victoria*, 1837–61, III, 391.
[2] Wellesley, *op. cit.* p. 207.   [3] Cowley to Russell, 10 August 1860.
[4] *Letters of Queen Victoria*, III, 399.
[5] Cowley to Malmesbury, 23 August 1858.
[6] Beeton, *Dictionary of Universal Information*, p. 511.

entered Syria alone, and it became the task of Britain to prevent an eastern counterpart to their occupation of Rome.

The events of 1861, however, did much to show the two countries how closely their interests were intertwined. "The alliance of England", a rare French voice asserted, "is so dear to us because she adds to our power to accomplish good things, and because united with her there is no barbarism possible in Europe."[1] It was at least evident that the sympathy of France with the Poles was likely to make her distasteful to Russia, that Napoleon had gone far towards the English doctrine of free trade, that he was proposing to open French colonial ports to foreign shipping, and that some constitutional concessions were seriously in his mind. The rumour of a project for annexing the island of Sardinia was denied. The continuance of 20,000 French troops in Rome, however, taxed the ingenuity of British no less than of Italian statesmen, and there were rumours that the idea of a pan-Scandinavian kingdom had found an entry into the Emperor's brain. Outside Europe, on the other hand, the *entente* seemed real and pervasive. A convention for the importation of coolies into French colonies was signed. British co-operation with France and Spain for procuring redress from Mexico was requested. Napoleon declared himself hostile to the desire of his Marine and Colonial Ministers to annex Saigon, assuring our delighted ambassador that, while we needed naval stations all over the globe, the scanty French colonies were not worth their annual cost.[2] Weightiest of all, France took a firm stand by our side in face of the perils arising from the civil war in North America.[3] While some at least among our statesmen were surmising that Napoleon might settle separately with the Americans or avenge himself by making us eat dirt, he in fact held firmly to his first profession "that the insolence and presumption (*outrecuidance*) of the North merited a severe lesson, and that he hoped it might be given them".[4] The loyal support given by France to Britain was only strengthened when the *Trent* outrage brought us to the very verge of war, and history can hardly endorse the contemporary explanation that this was due to the hopes of the French that we should force open the Southern ports and give them cotton,[5] for at the same time Napoleon's unchanging ideals were receiving abundant and fateful illustration in the affair of Mexico.

The Mexican adventure, "the grand idea of the reign", which played a great part in the downfall of the Empire and the consequent reconstruction of the world, had already for several years been taking shape. In the first months of the Crimean war, a Mexican refugee had sought to enlist both France and Britain for a restoration of the

[1] *Revue contemporaine*, cit. *The Times*, 18 April 1861.
[2] Cowley to Russell, 2 July 1861.
[3] Clarendon to Cowley, Wellesley, *op. cit.* p. 224.
[4] Cowley to Russell, 2 July 1861.
[5] Cowley to Bulwer, Wellesley, *op. cit.* p. 226.

monarchy. Clarendon, with his wonted urbane realism, spoke strongly
of the danger of rousing the resentment of the neighbouring republics,
and of provoking war with the United States. Drouyn, more com-
bative and notoriously mendacious, declared the project "not unacceptable to the French government", and represented it to Britain
as designed to place a Spaniard, not an Austrian, upon the throne.[1]
But at that time, even to secure a diversion if the United States should
side with Russia, France could not advise the Mexicans to run the
risk, and the project languished. Seven years of unrelieved ruin in
Mexico, however, only strengthened its hold upon Napoleon's imagination. From his first accession to power, he had been filled with
what a British confidant characteristically styled "comprehensive
projects of a beneficent character".[2] Comprehensive and beneficent
beyond parallel was a scheme promoting at once nationality,
monarchy, Catholicism, reconciliation between the dynasties, the
commerce and influence of Europe, payment of debts to Frenchmen
and glory to the Emperor of the French. But for the Monroe Doctrine,
dreamed Napoleon, France might lead a European coalition to easy
victory, and a new Austrian empire would reconcile the old to the
endowment of Italy with Venice.

In 1861 the United States seemed irremediably divided. Napoleon
leapt at the opportunity which the consequent suspension or extinction
of the Monroe Doctrine must afford. Magnifying into certainties his
hopes of Mexican support and of Austrian acquiescence, and rejoicing
to champion the well-being of mankind, he repudiated the British
proposal to renounce interference by force, and pressed on a tripartite
intervention. Spain and Britain were at least willing to share in
sending ships to demand the payment of debts due to their subjects.
For several years Mexico occupied the Emperor's mind and steadily
drained away his power.

The natural consequence of adding a new preoccupation to the
standing difficulties arising from the question of Venice and from the
French occupation of Rome was to make Napoleon less than ever
likely to seek new quarrels elsewhere. At the close of 1861 France
was reducing her army, taking anxious care for her finances, and
propitiating Britain by decrying the Suez Canal.[3] This, her Foreign
Minister declared, could never become a paying concern, as the
works at each end would be enormous, and he showed his pleasure
at being rid of the idea. Early in 1862 the close concert with Britain
in dealing with the United States was emphasised anew, and friendly
overtures were made to Prussia and to Russia.[4] At fifty-four, moreover,
Napoleon was beginning to find his strength inadequate to the paternal
government of France. Everything pointed to the avoidance of fresh

[1] Cowley to Clarendon, 5 June 1854.   [2] Normanby to Palmerston, 4 June 1851.
[3] Cowley to Russell, 15 November, 5 and 19 December 1861.
[4] Cowley to Russell, 15 August 1862.

complications, yet the British Premier firmly believed that the Emperor was about to launch a general war for Venice and the frontier of the Rhine. Cowley, in a masterly memorandum, destroyed the idea, declaring that, despite the nation's jealousy of England, Napoleon would never voluntarily bring her into the field against him.[1] In October Drouyn, resuming office, declared that England would be his greatest difficulty, since with her he could find no common point of view of the Italian question. On all other questions, however, and especially those connected with the East, she commanded his concurrence.[2] This was the more important because the question of the Greek succession once again threatened the *entente*.

During the 'sixties, indeed, every year seemed to add to the distraction of France by European politics from expansion in the wider world. She had done well, it is true, in Cochin China, and was dreaming of vast trading developments southward from Algeria, when suddenly all her attention was absorbed by the sufferings of the Russian Poles. Soon every class among his subjects was crying out for Napoleon's intervention.

Questions enough existed to imperil peace. Poles against Russia, Germans against Denmark, Italians against Austria, the Pope and his protector, anarchy upon the Danube, excessive armaments in every great Continental power—in face of all these Europe folded her hands lest France should claim that any reform entitled her to a revision of the treaties of 1815. With the opposition parties visibly gaining ground in France and the dynastic future insecure, with a British Premier incurably distrustful, a Foreign Secretary of inimitable rudeness and a bitter press, it is hardly surprising that Napoleon showed himself morose as never before, that he and his minister were not unfriendly to the thought of a war that would vindicate their congress scheme,[3] or even that France became apathetic towards the homeland of the new Princess of Wales. The year 1864, therefore, opened with unpromising efforts on the part of Britain to patch up the *entente* and to save Denmark from mutilation.[4]

The war of Austria and Prussia against unaided Denmark (February–October 1864), which dismembered the Danish monarchy and placed many Danes under German rule, at least proved to France and Britain their impotence when disunited. By midsummer Drouyn was declaring that the only alliance worth anything was that between these two powers, a union which could govern the world.[5] But the conduct of Britain with regard to Denmark confirmed his inference from her conduct with regard to Poland—that when war was in the offing she could not be relied on. Although, earlier in the year, said

[1] Cowley to Russell, 10 January 1862; Wellesley, *op. cit.* pp. 234-40.
[2] Cowley to Russell, 17 October 1862.
[3] Cowley to Russell, 25 December 1863.
[4] Cowley to Russell, 7 January 1864; Wellesley, *op. cit.* pp. 258-9.
[5] Cowley to Russell, 20 June 1864; Wellesley, *op. cit.* p. 268.

Drouyn, the United States had given assurances that they did not intend to interfere with the proceedings of the French in Mexico,[1] where the Archduke Maximilian had at last accepted the crown, the failure of French policy in the New World was hardly less evident than in the Old. When, on the eve of Grant's successes, the American House of Representatives denounced "a monarchical government erected on the ruins of any republican government in America under the auspices of any European power",[2] it was not difficult to guess their meaning or to forecast the consequences. Before the end of the year Napoleon must choose between the danger of Maximilian's collapse if the French withdrew, and the wrath of his own people and of the Americans if they did not.

Meanwhile a quiet year in Europe had given scope for the display of greater energy overseas. The Suez Canal had reached a stage at which its works could be proudly exhibited to all nations. Algeria received the honour of an imperial visit. After more than thirty years' occupation, Napoleon complained, a yearly expenditure of some sixty million francs and the presence of some 80,000 soldiers could not protect a few French colonists.[3] The Mohammedans, who outnumbered the European settlers by nearly 150 to 1, detested European institutions, and the time had come to substitute a system of protection of native rights. At the same time the gradual evacuation of Mexico was planned, and Drouyn refrained from resenting "what he would call American language: it was difficult to know whether it was *intended* to be offensive or not".[4] Common action with Britain was taken in many quarters of the globe, notably in the endeavour to keep peace between Spain and Chile. Although Britain felt obliged to decline Napoleon's invitation to a defensive alliance against the United States, she was able to assure Napoleon of her whole-hearted friendship, such confidence had he inspired by his pacific conduct and assurances of late years.[5] Since 1860, indeed, Britain had had leisure to repent of her outcry about Savoy and Nice. She had seen crisis after crisis, Polish, Danish, American, pass, without any attempt by Napoleon to put his supposed revolutionary ambitions into practice. Delane of *The Times* could only wish that the French were as devoted to their Emperor as were the English. Even Palmerston, just before his death (October 1865), declared that "all old sentiments of rivalship and antagonism as between Englishmen and Frenchmen are on our part extinguished".[6]

In the year which followed (1866), all else was dimmed by the Prussian triumph at Sadowa on July 3. A few hours' fighting showed

---

[1] Cowley to Russell, 12 February 1864.
[2] Grey to Russell, 30 April 1864.
[3] Cowley to Russell, 28 April 1865.
[4] Cowley to Russell, 5 August 1865.
[5] Cowley to Clarendon, 4 January 1866.
[6] Palmerston to Cowley, 3 September 1865; Wellesley, *op. cit.* p. 287.

that the balance of European power had been overturned. Thenceforward France found herself compelled to struggle by diplomacy, and finally by force of arms, against a Germany militant and conquering as in the days of Charles V. From Sadowa to Sedan, rivalry with Britain overseas remained impossible for France.

In August, 1867, the Austrian and French Emperors and their ministers met at Salzburg. A general though guarded *entente*, distasteful from the first to Russia as well as to Prussia, was developed and discussed between them during the succeeding years. It failed to secure from Prussia the fulfilment of her treaty obligations towards her ex-Danish subjects. But it proved to all the world that the Austrian Emperor condoned Napoleon's share in the Mexican tragedy of May, 1867, when his brother had been shot by the triumphant Juarez after the French had departed.

The year 1868, which witnessed few great events, was passed in almost intolerable tension. The Prince of Wales summed up the general view of the situation—"things don't look too friendly or comfortable". It was something that the French gained time to accustom themselves to the new greatness of Prussia, and that outbreaks of war fever proved to be Parisian and transient. The new Italian monarchy and the new Austro-Hungarian constitution, moreover, had everything to gain by lapse of time. Such overseas questions as arose were mainly familiar, though Prussia claimed a share in the settlement in Tunis on the ground that a firm in conquered Frankfort had interests there.[1] With the spectacle of Prussian progress alarming France, neither friction between French and British agents in China nor the complaints of the London Missionary Society about French intolerance in the Loyalty Islands were likely to disturb the old *entente*. No better agent than Lyons could have been found for averting the troubles that come from over-sensitiveness or interference. It was natural to him to refer complainants from the Society Islands to their local consul and his consummate dissuasion of Sultana Fatima, who arrived from the Comoro Islands to secure the Queen's support against France, must have strengthened his influence in Paris.[2]

France began the new year (1869) in a pacific mood which was unbroken for eighteen months. The Emperor, whose speech was notably conciliatory and pacific, was still served by La Valette, a minister who tried to soothe Beust when the Prussian press maligned him,[3] and who styled war between England and the United States a crime of *lèse-civilisation*.[4] Though firm that Prussia must not cross the Main, and bold enough to say that if she provoked France the French guns would go off of themselves, he described his policy as not to make a noise in a sick man's room,[5] and acted up to his pro-

[1] Lyons to Stanley, 14 May 1868.
[2] Lyons to Stanley, 29 June etc. etc. until 25 September 1868.
[3] Lyons to Clarendon, 1, 7 and 8 January 1869.
[4] Lyons to Clarendon, 3 June 1869.   [5] Lyons to Clarendon, 2 April 1869.

fessions. No man could be more firm for the *entente*, and the *entente* meant intimacy with the power whose first interest was always peace in Europe.

The pacific spirit of the French government was conspicuous in a dispute with Belgium which held the attention of Europe during the spring of 1869. From its first beginning, the Empire had set out to make the nation rich. This was the railway age, and France had constructed or acquired many railways beyond her frontiers. Her natural reply to the *Zollverein* lay in the economic sphere, and her minister protested against those who impugned her motives. "He did not suppose", he declared, "that it would be considered criminal of France to endeavour to form more intimate commercial relations with her neighbours."[1]

During the first half of the year, moreover, France had co-operated with Britain in declining to guarantee the neutrality of a Panama Canal, or the sovereignty of Colombia. She had shaped her policy in Tunis as Britain desired, and she looked forward to the neutralisation of the new canal at Suez. The two powers had acted in concert to compose the differences between the Sultan and the Viceroy of Egypt. When La Valette resigned, his successor was the Prince de la Tour d'Auvergne, the eminent representative of France in London.

Thus the *entente* with Britain pursued its quiet course. Plans for a new French harbour to connect with Dover came from a British firm; large ferry-boats were contemplated: the two powers combined to check friction in Siam, to remonstrate with Russia regarding Montenegro and the lower Danube and to arrange for territorial exchanges in West Africa. No offence, it was agreed, would be given if Protestant Britain did not concur in denouncing the decree of Papal Infallibility of which France stood in dread.[2]

For many months, however, Bismarck had been secretly preparing to challenge France in Spain. Always at heart a rebel,[3] he resented the French claim to interfere in Germany, as he had resented the Austrian hegemony of 1850–66, between the landmarks of Olmütz and Sadowa. The throne of Spain stood vacant, and it proved hard to find a king. The succession question gave Bismarck his opportunity.

The war, which men believed for many years to have arisen from French jealousy of German unity and from Napoleon's ambition for the Rhine, swiftly brought about the hegemony of a new German Empire over Europe and with it the mutilation and eclipse of France. Hemmed in as never before upon their own continent, the French at last sought compensation and prestige beyond the seas. Their great career in Africa and Asia developed with the unfeigned encouragement of Bismarck, for it promised to divert the energies of France

[1] Lyons to Stanley, 31 July 1868.
[2] Lyons to Clarendon, 14, 17, 22, 23 (629–31) June and 3 July 1870.
[3] Ludwig, E., *Journal of Royal Institute of International Affairs*, VI, v, 286.

from her revenge and to embroil her with Italy and Britain. When, however, Germany herself came to desire colonies and to need open markets overseas, the question assumed another colour. The twentieth century was to witness new colonial rivalries between Germans, French and British which did much to heighten the international anarchy of its pre-war years. In the colonial as in many other spheres, 1870 sowed the seeds of 1914.

CHAPTER XV

THE ROUTES TO THE EAST, 1815–70

THERE are two roads to the East to be considered: the ancient route from the Mediterranean basin overland to the Red Sea or the Persian Gulf, and the much more recent but longer ocean route round the Cape of Good Hope. The political history of these two routes between the years 1815 and 1870 turns primarily upon the efforts of Great Britain, France and Russia to control one or both of them.

Russia, as a Black Sea and would-be Mediterranean Power, was directly interested only in the route through the Levant. Between 1799 and 1807 she had shown a lively interest in the fate of Piedmont and Malta, and of the Ionian Islands, which she feared Napoleon might use as a base from which to seize Egypt; but throughout the long French wars she had also continued Catherine the Great's policy of pressing southward upon the decaying Ottoman Empire in the direction of the Bosporus and Asia Minor, and down through the Caucasus by way of Tiflis and Baku upon the decrepit monarchy of Persia.

France, as an Atlantic and a Mediterranean Power, was interested in both routes; but of the two she was more keenly interested in that through the Levant. She had always engrossed a larger share of the trade of those parts than her British rival and, on the morrow of the disastrous Seven Years' War, Choiseul and his followers had dreamed of a French Egypt and Arabia, a canal linking the Nile with the Red Sea as in the days of the Pharaohs, diplomatic supremacy in Syria, Mesopotamia and Persia, and an open road for an attack on the British in India. Perhaps also French influence, radiating from the Île de France (Mauritius), might dominate the Moslem east coast of Africa and make connection with the main line of the French advance eastward at Suez at the head of the Red Sea and at Muscat (Oman) at the mouth of the Persian Gulf. Dreams such as these had found partial fulfilment in Napoleon's Egypto-Syrian campaign and in his later schemes for an advance upon India by France and Russia in alliance with Persia, whose Shah still claimed to be overlord of the Afghan Amirs and of the Mogul himself.

Great Britain, like France an Atlantic and a Mediterranean Power, valued the Cape route more highly than the Levantine. Its value increased in her eyes after the close of the Seven Years' War, when the centre of gravity of her commercial empire began to swing away from the Atlantic to the Indian Ocean. Thrice, between 1781 and 1806, she had raced France for the control of the Dutch Cape Peninsula, the key position on that route, the point of Africa at which ships sailing to and from India most conveniently made landfall. Her interest in the Mediterranean was less simple. She maintained her naval power in the inland sea as a vital factor in the European balance of power; but though British business men or their Greek and Jewish agents had long been active in its ports, the trade was of only secondary importance to her, and she did not share France's dreams of political supremacy in the Middle East. On the other hand, as far back as 1775, British officials and important despatches had passed to or from India by the Levant.[1] It was as a means of communication, as a passage for mails and passengers to whom time was a serious consideration, that this overland route became of increasing importance to her after the Vienna settlement. Thenceforward British policy was vitally concerned with both routes to the East, linking up with British fortunes those of the many states and peoples that lay along the line from Lisbon to Peking, and presently to Sydney and Wellington also, whether by way of Suez, Basra, or Cape Town.

By the year 1824, when the Eastern Question had emerged in its modern form, the world was able to estimate how vastly the British hold upon the two routes had been strengthened during the past thirty years. At the outbreak of the Revolutionary Wars in 1793, the English East India Company had controlled directly or indirectly perhaps one-tenth of India. In 1824 it was paymaster and guardian, Vakil-i-Mutlaq, to the Mogul, and controlled nearly the whole of the sub-continent up to the frontiers of Ranjit Singh's Punjab and the territories of the Amirs of Sind in the lower Indus valley. It had indeed lost the monopoly of the India trade in 1813, but it still jealously reserved to itself the profitable though somewhat ignominious traffic with the haughty Chinese, the chief remaining source of its dividends.[2] Meanwhile, during the past thirty years, the volume of British imports from the East had increased threefold and of its exports thither more than fourfold.[3]

The transit of this great and growing trade was much more securely guarded than it had been in 1793. Then there had been singularly few British posts in all the 11,000 miles from the English Channel to the Bay of Bengal; after St Helena, an outpost of the East India Company in mid-ocean, there had been no British possession until Madras, while the approaches to India had been ringed round by French and Dutch stations. Now all that was changed. On the western side of Africa, the French had regained their stations: Goree, Albreda and the rest, near the British Gambia, and the Dutch

---

[1] Hoskins, H. L., *British Routes to India*, p. 10.
[2] Clapham, J. H., *An Economic History of Modern Britain*, i, 252.
[3] Hoskins, *op. cit.*, p. 87.

and Danes still held their trading posts near Great Britain's on the
Gold Coast; but the British had added Ascension and inaccessible
Tristan da Cunha to St Helena, and were finding Sierra Leone, once
a mere refuge for freed negroes, an invaluable base for the "sentimental
squadron" which had already begun its long campaign against the
slavers of the West Coast. At the far eastern end of this maritime
empire, Van Diemen's Land and Norfolk Island had been occupied,
and New South Wales, originally a "receptacle" for convicts and
dispossessed peasants, was growing fast now that it was regarded
also as a suitable outlet for men of means and their dependants,[1] and
had begun to send its wool regularly to London. In between, the
ring of hostile foreign stations had been shattered beyond repair.
To Penang in the Malay Peninsula the East India Company had
added Singapore (1819), and Malacca, close by, in exchange for
Bencoolen, its one foothold in Dutch Sumatra (1824). The annexation
of Burmese Aracan and Tenasserim gave the Company control of
most of the eastern shores of the Bay of Bengal (1824–25), while the
Crown had taken Dutch Ceylon, whose fine harbour of Trincomalee
commanded the entrance to that bay. In terms of the Vienna settlement the French had indeed recovered Bourbon, which lacked a good
anchorage, and their interests in Madagascar; but the British had
deprived them of Mauritius, Rodriguez and the Seychelles, bases
which had proved dangerous to trade in time of war. Finally, to
make the ocean route more secure, the British had taken the Cape
Colony from the Dutch and planted British settlers on its dangerous
eastern or "Kaffir" frontier behind the secondary harbour of Port
Elizabeth; while in an attempt to direct the commerce of that route,
it had made Cape Town and Mauritius free ports (1819–20).[2]

Similarly, Great Britain's hold upon the Mediterranean route was
much firmer than before. Since the final loss of Minorca ten years
previously, the one strong place that she held in 1793 on all the long
line from Land's End to Bombay had been Gibraltar. Now, in 1824,
Gibraltar was still hers, backed by the old alliance with faithful
Portugal which gave British squadrons the shelter of the Tagus
estuary in case of need. The less reputable working arrangement,
whereby in times past the Barbary pirates had supplied Gibraltar
with fresh meat and, as a rule, left British shipping alone for a consideration, was falling into desuetude.[3] Britain had less need of such
a desperate shift now; the United States had taken strong measures
against the pirates under her very eyes, and she herself had sent Lord
Exmouth to bombard Algiers (1816). On the other hand, to Gibraltar
Great Britain had added Malta, "the strongest place in Europe",[4]

[1] Fitzpatrick, B., *British Imperialism and Australia, 1783–1833*, pp. 14, 226 ff.
[2] *C.H.B.E.* VIII, 232–3.
[3] Parkinson, C. N., *Edward Pellew, Viscount Exmouth*, pp. 419 ff.
[4] *C.M.H.* IX, 751.

and the Ionian Islands centring round the naval base of Corfu. British influence was predominant at Constantinople, all the more since the Crown had taken over the diplomatic functions of the expiring Levant Company (1821–25), while farther east the British had gained prestige by their recent victories over the French and their Asiatic allies. The one part of the Middle East in which British influence stood lower than that of another European Power was Egypt. The East India Company had improved its prospects of trade in the Red Sea by a commercial treaty with Aden (1802), but in Egypt itself the Albanian, Mehemet Ali, aspired to build up an empire and, realising that he must have Western help to that end, had turned to France as the more sympathetic and weaker of the two European Powers that lay nearest to him.

For nearly a decade after 1815 Great Britain was preoccupied with the problems of post-war recovery and the maintenance of the Vienna peace settlement. A threat to the Mediterranean side of that settlement was most likely to come from France or Russia, either in the Iberian, Italian or Balkan Peninsula. It was Britain's interest to uphold the *status quo* in all three areas, to discourage the union of either of the first two under a single strong government and, above all, to prevent the domination of any one of the three by an external Power.

During the early post-war years, Russia promised to be the disturbing element. It was disconcerting that the Czar Alexander, in spite of his constant talk of peace, should maintain a huge army on a war footing and station a large part of it on the Pruth; but the Ottoman Empire still stood apparently unshaken and buttressed by the British naval power at Corfu. Great Britain did not look for serious disturbance in that quarter; rather did she expect trouble in the central and western Mediterranean. The years 1816–17 were full of rumours that the Czar meant to acquire one of the Balearic Islands as a base against the Algerine pirates, and it was known that Russian agents were busy in Italy.[1] In 1820 revolts flared out in Spain and Naples. Britain stood back while Austria dealt with the Neapolitan rebels; but neither she nor Austria would hear of Russian intervention in Spain. It was Bourbon France which forcibly restored absolutism at Madrid. The French in Spain were hardly more to Britain's taste than the Russians, for France was recovering fast and Toulon was a formidable rival to Malta. In 1827, while the French were still on Spanish soil, the British risked landing an expedition at Lisbon to uphold the rights of the child queen against the claims of her absolutist uncle, Dom Miguel; but, a year later, the French and British troops were gone and Iberian problems ceased for a time to threaten the Mediterranean equilibrium (1828).

---

[1] *C.H.B.F.P.* II, 7, 13, 35.

Meanwhile, a dangerous and prolonged crisis had arisen in the Levant. The Powers, especially Great Britain and Austria, had long been alarmed lest the Greek rising of 1823 should tempt the Czar to take action single-handed against the Ottoman Empire. This Alexander did not do; but in 1824 the conflict plainly ceased to be a matter of purely Turkish concern. Sultan Mahmud, realising that the Greeks had gained the upper hand at sea, reluctantly called to his aid his over-mighty vassal, Mehemet Ali, Pasha of Egypt.

For twenty years past, and mainly under French guidance, Mehemet Ali had been building up a great Egyptian empire. He had first established his power at Cairo by massacring the Mamelukes, and had then adopted as much of Western military, naval and commercial methods as would serve his turn. Master of the new Egypt, he had occupied the Holy Places in Arabia and reduced the desert Wahabi to temporary quiescence, conquered the Sudan and founded Khartum (1823), and extorted Crete from his unwilling Turkish sovereign (1822). His fleet now crushed the Greeks in island after island. In the following year, in return for the promise of Syria, Damascus and the Morea, he sent his son Ibrahim to stamp out rebellion in mainland Greece (1825).

Ibrahim's drastic measures called forth European intervention. When he prepared to sweep the Greeks out of the Morea to make room for Arabs or Egyptians, Canning threatened to interpose the British fleet between him and his base at Alexandria. Then the new Czar Nicholas I threatened Britain's overland route to the East by attacking Persia, and obliging Sultan Mahmud to sign the Convention of Akkerman which gave Russia considerable powers of control over Moldavia and Wallachia and also over the Bosporus and the Dardanelles (Oct. 1826). To prevent Russia, and perhaps France also, from going too far on their own account, Canning called upon them to take common action with Britain. By the Treaty of London (July 1827) the three Powers agreed that there should be an autonomous Greece paying tribute to the Sultan as overlord. Then, to stop the bloodshed, they sent a joint fleet to the Morea. There, a few weeks after Canning's death, the allied fleet destroyed the Turco-Egyptian flotilla in Navarino Bay (Oct. 1827).

The Wellington Ministry, dismayed at this "untoward event", which revealed the weakness of the Ottoman Empire, Britain's ancient ally, allowed the control of events to pass into the hands of France and Russia. French troops swept the Turkish garrisons out of the Morea, and since the Sultan had, in fury at the news of Navarino, denounced the Convention of Akkerman, the Russians crossed the Pruth. Their hands were free, for they had just ended their Persian war by the Treaty of Turcomanchai, which increased their dominions south of the Caucasus (1828), and the Sultan, who had followed Mehemet's example by slaughtering his unruly Janissaries, had had no time to train a modern army. Being in no state to resist the Russians, Mahmud was forced to accept the Treaty of Adrianople (Sept. 1829), which gave the Czar the Danube delta and promised to Greece autonomy in terms of the Treaty of London.

While the centre of the Ottoman Empire was thus falling under Russian domination, the French Bourbons invaded Algeria (1830). The fall of the Bourbon Monarchy and the outbreak of revolutions in various parts of Europe made it impossible for Great Britain to take vigorous action; for she and Orleanist France soon found themselves entangled in the problem of Belgium, while Louis-Philippe declared that if he were to be held to his predecessor's promise to evacuate Algeria as soon as the national honour had been satisfied, his shaky throne would fall. At last, however, Great Britain, France and Russia settled the Greek question, and in January, 1833, young Prince Otho of Bavaria landed from a British frigate at the Piraeus as king of an independent Greece of modest dimensions. Forthwith the French, who had conquered much of the Algerian coast belt, announced that they were masters there and that Algeria was to be to them what India was to the British (March 1833).

Meanwhile the Czar and Mehemet Ali had not been idle. Sultan Mahmud had refused to pay Mehemet the promised price of the aid which had brought him so little good. Mehemet determined to take it. With the exultant support of a strong body of French opinion, he sent his son to conquer Syria. Ibrahim overran that province and then, crossing the Taurus mountains like another Antiochus, shattered the main Turkish army at Konieh (Dec. 1832). The road to Constantinople lay open, and Mahmud, having first appealed in vain to preoccupied Britain and semi-hostile France, turned in desperation to Russia. In the end Mehemet Ali, already master of the Suez route to the East, kept Syria, Damascus, and Aleppo, the gateway to the Euphrates valley and the Persian Gulf, while Russia bound the Sultan by the Treaty of Unkiar Skelessi to close the Straits to states at war with Russia but to leave them open to Russia (June 1833). For the eight years of its term, that treaty promised to make of the Ottoman Empire a Russian protectorate.

Meanwhile improving means of communication were fast giving to the Levant route an unprecedented importance in the eyes of Great Britain as the line along which governmental and business control could be best exerted in Asia, which was already taking, in goods and bullion, close upon one-eighth of Britain's total exports.[1]

The year 1825 that saw the opening of the Stockton and Darlington railway, the first public railway in the world, saw also the first steamships on both the routes to India. The British Government attached small armed steam-packets to the Mediterranean squadron, and a

---

[1] Clapham, *Economic History*, I, 250.

private company sent the *Enterprise*, under steam and sail, round the Cape to Calcutta in 113 days. The experience of the *Enterprise*, weak and wasteful of fuel on a long ocean run where coal was only to be had at Cape Town, threw doubt on the suitability of the Cape route for steamships. That doubt was soon reinforced by the proved superiority of the Mediterranean-Red Sea route with its more frequent ports of call. In 1828 the Bombay Marine had taken to steam to the disgust of its officers and men. Two years later it deservedly assumed the name of the Indian Navy and despatched the *Hugh Lindsay*, built of Indian teak with British engines, from Bombay to Suez.[1] The mail reached London in fifty-nine days instead of the customary seventy or eighty. Thereafter progress was rapid in spite of the dangers of the Red Sea navigation. In the middle 'thirties mails went from England by government packet to Malta and were there transhipped for Alexandria, while passengers either accompanied the mails or went overland to Marseilles to sail direct to Alexandria by a new sub-sidised French line (1835), or to Trieste and thence by the Austrian Lloyd ships to Alexandria by way of Constantinople. A private transport company conveyed them to Suez, and from that point they went on to Bombay in the steamers of the reluctant Indian Navy. The Cape was not given a regular steam mail service for another twenty years.

In times past the Turkish Sultans had objected to Christian navigation in the Red Sea, so close to the Holy Places of Islam. Mehemet Ali, the new guardian of those shrines, had no such scruples, but did everything he could to encourage the use of the Suez route, if only for the sake of the tolls. At the cost of the lives of 20,000 fellaheen he improved the Mahmoudieh canal, which linked up Alexandria with the main stream of the Nile, and eagerly debated the rival merits of a canal from the Nile to the Red Sea and a railway from Alexandria to Suez. He decided in favour of the railway and was so confident of British approval that he ordered the material.[2] That approval was not forthcoming, and the railway gear was left to rust upon the quay (1835).

Conceivably, had Mehemet waited for a year or two until after the first British railway boom of 1836–37 had finally established the superiority of the locomotive engine over both the stationary engine and cable and the road steam-carriage,[3] his fortune might have been better. As it was, the British Government feared that it might be called upon to guarantee traffic to a railway whose success would increase the importance of a pro-French Pasha, and made up its mind to try the alternative route through northern Syria and down the Euphrates, which was much less firmly controlled by Mehemet than the

[1] Hoskins, *British Routes to India*, pp. 95 ff., 108 ff.
[2] *Ibid.* p. 231.
[3] Clapham, *Economic History*, I, 381 ff.

road through Suez. An experiment with two steamers in 1836, however, was not a success, and this route as a whole proved to be as unhealthy as was its rival. The spasmodic use of the Euphrates route was gradually abandoned, and meanwhile the facilities on the Suez route were multiplied. The semaphore signal was installed between Cairo and Suez; a Franco-British convention for the carriage of the mails furnished the model for those conventions which were soon to cover the world with an international network of postal services (1839), and in December 1840 the Peninsular and Oriental Company began to run regular steamship services between England and India on both sides of the Isthmus of Suez.[1]

During the early years the P. and O. mailboats traversed stormy political waters. The storm had been beating up for some time past. It is true that the Eastern Question, which involved nothing less than the fate of the Ottoman Empire, was more or less quiescent from the middle of 1833 until the middle of 1839, especially as the Czar had soon intimated that the Treaty of Unkiar Skelessi was merely a "historical relic";[2] but during those years there had been grave and prolonged trouble in the Iberian Peninsula at the western end of the Mediterranean route, and increasing unrest all along its eastern extension from the Persian Gulf to the frontiers of India.

In 1833 civil war broke out in Portugal and Spain. Great Britain did not intervene officially in either country, but, to make sure that Louis-Philippe did not intervene in Spain, Palmerston included France in a Quadruple Alliance with Great Britain and the lawful governments of the two Iberian states (1834). The Portuguese Civil War was soon ended; but in spite of the assistance of French and British Foreign Legions, the Spanish Government could not quell the Carlists until August 1839. The French Legion, meanwhile, had been transferred to Algeria, where it beat down the resistance of Abd-el-Kader so effectively that Great Britain presently recognised the French occupation (1843); but when the French followed up their success by invading Morocco and bombarding Mogador and Tangier from the sea, the British Government warned them bluntly that annexation in that quarter, almost opposite Gibraltar, would constitute a *casus belli*.[3] The French prudently drew back (1844).

The Treaty of Unkiar Skelessi had set the stage for much that followed in the Middle East. The French ceased to support the Turkish Sultan and smiled once more upon Mehemet Ali. Soon their agents were busy in Syria, Mesopotamia, and Persia, even in India itself, on whose north-western frontier European officers, the ablest of them Frenchmen, had made Ranjit Singh's Sikhs a most formidable fighting force.[4] But it was Russia rather than France that

[1] Hoskins, *British Routes to India*, pp. 247 ff. [2] *C.M.H.* x, 557.
[3] Phillips, A., *Modern Europe, 1815–1899*, p. 236.
[4] Grey, C., *European Adventurers of Northern India, 1785–1849*.

caused Great Britain anxiety in the near approaches to India. Secure upon the Black Sea and the Straits, Russia seemed to threaten British India either by the shorter but almost impossible road through the Khanates of Khiva and Bokhara, or by the longer but more practicable road through Persia and the three Afghan principalities of Kabul, Kandahar and Herat. Were the Russians to predominate there, only the Punjab and Sind would lie between them and the East India Company's frontier along the Sutlej river.

Towards the end of his term of office as Governor-General, Lord Bentinck had given an indication of what was coming by concluding commercial treaties with the Punjab and Sind, and by allowing the Afghan, Shah Shujah, an exile in British India, to assert his claims in arms to the throne of Kabul against Dost Mohammed (1834). Shah Shujah's attempt failed, and during the next year or two Russian and British agents competed for control over Persia and Afghanistan. At last the Persians besieged Afghan Herat (Nov. 1837). Lord Auckland, Bentinck's successor, promptly despatched an expedition to the Persian Gulf, and followed that up by treaties with Ranjit Singh and Shah Shujah, the claimant to Kabul (1838).

The expedition against Persia was attended by swift success. A Persian attempt to storm Herat failed; the siege was raised and peace made on terms which left British influence predominant at Teheran. To confirm this British ascendancy on the Gulf, a commercial treaty was presently concluded with the Imam of Muscat (1839). Meanwhile Auckland had established Shah Shujah on the throne of Kabul and of Kandahar also; a Russian demonstration against Khiva broke down, and the British Government was reassured to learn from the Czar himself that his troops were in no way intended for an attack upon India (1839).

Nor was that all. The British reinforced their diplomatic hold on the Levant route to the East by annexations. In February, 1839, they obliged the local Sind Amir to cede Karachi,[1] which gave them the control of the mouths of the Indus and closed the principal Indian market for African slaves. In the same month, having found that Socotra was useless as a coaling station, they occupied Aden partly by persuasion and partly by force, and, a little later, confirmed their hold on the southern outlet of the Red Sea by binding the Somali chiefs on the African shore immediately opposite never to make treaties with another Power without informing the British authorities (1840).[2]

The Ottoman Sultan had recommended the British, a year or two back, to make sure of Aden before Mehemet Ali forestalled them.[3] After his acquisition of Syria, the Pasha of Egypt had begun to call

[1] C.H.B.E. IV, 527.
[2] Coupland, R., *East Africa and its Invaders*, pp. 465 ff.
[3] C.H.B.F.P. II, 182.

himself Viceroy and to enlarge his borders. By the close of 1838 he had confirmed his authority in Kordofan, Sennar and Kassala, and sent his troops as far up the White Nile as Fashoda, while to the east his soldiers held down nearly all Arabia and he himself made no secret of the fact that he intended to take Muscat and, if all went well, Bagdad also. He then declared himself independent and thereby challenged the right of his Turkish sovereign to the Khalifate, the guardianship of the Holy Places which were already in Egyptian hands.

This rapid growth of the power of Mehemet, with the help of French experts and the undisguised approval of political opinion in France, which was fast extending its hold upon Algeria, alarmed the British Government and public. They agreed with Palmerston that Napoleon's dreams must not be suffered thus to come true, that "the mistress of India cannot permit France to be mistress directly or indirectly of the road to her Indian dominions",[1] especially now that Mehemet's monopolies were damaging British trade in defiance of the commercial treaty which H.M. Government had recently concluded with the Sultan for the whole of the Ottoman Empire. In 1839 the crisis came to a head quickly. The Egyptian army effected a junction with its fleet on the Arabian shore of the Persian Gulf, and occupied Bahrein Island. Both fell back when the British Government warned them that an attempt to establish Egyptian authority on the Gulf would not be "viewed with indifference",[2] and to enforce the point the British temporarily occupied Bahrein Island themselves. Thereupon the eager Sultan, confident in the powers of his new Prussian-trained army, declared war upon Mehemet Ali (June 1839).

It was a rash venture. The Turkish army was sent flying at Nisib; Sultan Mahmud died of shock at the news, and the Turkish fleet went over bodily to the Egyptians. Mehemet, however, made no further move, and the Powers had time to debate how best to shore up the tottering Turkish Empire. The point of danger was that the French were determined to keep Mehemet Ali in Syria and Palmerston was resolved to turn him out. Palmerston induced the other Powers to go forward without France. They offered to secure for Mehemet the hereditary pashalik of Egypt and, since he was now nearly seventy years old, the administration of southern Syria for life (July 1840).[3] Then, while France in fury put her army and navy on a war footing, a joint British, Austrian and Turkish squadron anchored off Beirut. It was the signal for which many Syrians, groaning under the weight of Egyptian taxation, monopolies and conscription, had long

---

[1] Hoskins, *British Routes to India*, p. 268.
[2] Temperley, H. [W. V.], and Penson, L. M., *Foundations of British Policy from Pitt* (1792) *to Salisbury* (1902), p. 127.
[3] *C.M.H.* x, 569.

been waiting. Some of them rose, and when the allied squadron bombarded Beirut, many others joined them. Beirut and Acre fell, and, as the Egyptian troops retreated hurriedly southward, the allied fleet moved on to Alexandria. There Mehemet accepted terms at the hands of Sir Charles Napier, the British admiral. He was to lose Crete, Syria and Arabia, but to keep Egypt and its Sudanese dependencies (Nov. 1840).

At this stage Louis-Philippe eased a dangerous strain by dismissing the warlike Thiers and calling in Guizot, who proposed that both the Suez and Euphrates routes to the East should be neutralised since they were "a great interest to all of Europe".[1] Palmerston would not have it so; he was determined to clip the wings of France in spite of the difficulties that were accumulating on British shoulders farther east. The Afghan adventure had led to unexpected and dangerous complications; the Sind Amirs were restive; Ranjit Singh was dead and the Punjab was fast sinking into chaos, while a war with China, begun at the close of 1839, was not yet ended. Palmerston had his way. The Sultan and the Pasha formally accepted the terms proposed at Alexandria, and Egypt and the Sudan became hereditary possessions of the house of Mehemet Ali; but it was only after the four Powers concerned had ratified the agreement that they admitted France to their councils. They indeed rejected Guizot's proposal that the whole of the Ottoman Empire should be placed under the guarantee of the five Powers, but together with France they signed the Convention of the Straits, reaffirming "the ancient rule of the Ottoman Empire" that, when itself at peace, the Sublime Porte should close the Bosporus and Dardanelles to the warships of all other states (July 1841).[2]

Thus, at the risk of war, Palmerston had ended French hopes of dominating the Levant, and re-established British prestige at Constantinople and even at Cairo. Persia also came over definitely to the British side as against the Russians, and Lord Ellenborough, having cut British losses in Afghanistan, by recognising Dost Mohammed, safeguarded the Indian frontier by annexing Sind (1843). Finally, the Treaty of Nanking gave the British Hong-Kong, opened Shanghai and several other Chinese ports in addition to Canton, and secured for British subjects in China something of the capitulary privileges which they had long enjoyed in the Ottoman Empire, and for their official representatives liberty to speak on equal terms with the servants of the Son of Heaven (Aug. 1842).

British relations with Orleanist France had been strained during the long Syrian crisis, and were to be further strained for some years thereafter by French activities in many parts of the outer world and not least on or near the Cape route to the East. Very few Englishmen

[1] Hoskins, *British Routes to India*, p. 284.
[2] *C.M.H.* x, 572; *C.H.B.F.P.* II, 180.

and no British Government of that time desired more territory overseas, certainly not in Africa. Apart from the northern littoral which
flanked the Mediterranean route to the East, and perhaps the
Cape Colony, they took little interest in that vast continent. Africa
was for them simply something to be circumnavigated on the way
to India or a lurking place for slavers. For the purpose of hunting
down slavers and safeguarding the trade route, Great Britian had all
she needed in Sierra Leone, St Helena, which had been transferred
from the East India Company to the Crown in 1834 to bring it within
the scope of the Emancipation Act, the Cape Peninsula and Mauritius.
As for the islands of the Pacific, they were as dust in the British balance.

Great Britain was none the less watchful lest France, in pursuance
of Guizot's avowed policy of spreading a network of French stations
round the world,[1] should threaten her trade routes. French activities
in the western Indian Ocean, through whose waters the traffic on the
overland and ocean routes to the East must pass, aroused her
suspicions. British trade with the long stretch of African coast
eastward of Cape Town, and with the adjacent islands, was negligible;
the one occasional port of call close to the African mainland was
Johanna, one of the Comoro Islands at the northern end of the
Mozambique Channel.[2] For the rest H.M. Government was
concerned only to put down the Arab and European slave trade on
the East Coast, and desired annexations so little that it remained
unmoved even by the plea that a mainland station would facilitate
its suppression. It shelved the treaty, ceding the southern shore of
Delagoa Bay, which Captain Owen had signed with local chiefs in 1823
and gave no recognition to the protectorate which he and his successor
managed to exercise over Mombasa (1824–26).[3] It was content that
Radama, the Hova ruler of most of Madagascar, should have signed
a treaty forbidding his subjects to indulge in "the Trade" (1817),
and that the Imam of Muscat, who was also ruler of Zanzibar and
nominal lord of Mombasa and the other Moslem towns upon the
coast between Cape Guardafui and the northern limits of Portuguese
Mozambique, should have forbidden it to foreigners in his dominions
utterly, and to his own subjects with any part of British India (1822).[4]

A little later, again, H.M. Government had rejected requests from
Cape Colony that it should forestall the Americans by annexing Delagoa
Bay or Port Natal (Durban), where a handful of British and Colonial
traders had been established by leave of the neighbouring Zulu king
since 1824[5], and heard with equanimity that the United States, first
of all Western Powers, had made a commercial treaty with Muscat-

[1] *C.H.B.F.P.* II, 263.
[2] Coupland, *East Africa*, p. 160.
[3] *Ibid.* pp. 217 ff.; *C.H.B.E.* VIII, 453.
[4] Coupland, *East Africa*, pp. 199, 215.
[5] *C.H.B.E.* VIII, 324.

Zanzibar (1833). It had displayed hardly more interest when the French bombarded Tamatave in revenge for the expulsion of their own and most of the British traders from Madagascar, and Charles X talked of conquering the whole of the island. The July Revolution had ended that dream and Ranavalona, widow of Radama, brusquely declining the offer of an Orleanist protectorate (1831), had shown herself hostile to all things European. Thereafter there had been no cause for anxiety until the time of the final Mehemet Ali crisis. Then the French became active all along the line from Muscat to Tamatave.

In 1840 French and British consuls appeared at Muscat and when, in the following year, the Imam removed the seat of his government to Zanzibar, both followed him, for Zanzibar was the centre of a coastal empire with which the French of Mauritius and Bourbon had long had trading connections and in which many traders from British India were already domiciled. Meanwhile the French had tried to induce the Imam's eldest son to allow them to build forts at Barawa and Mogadishu far to the north of Zanzibar, and failing there had hurried southward and forced a protectorate upon the ruler of Nossi-bé, off the northern end of Madagascar. Palmerston, believing that the island belonged to Muscat, protested; but when he discovered his mistake, he yielded, with what grace he might, only to learn that the French had extended their protectorate over one or two neighbouring islands including Mayotta, "a little Gibraltar" (1842–43).[1] The British redressed the balance in a measure by concluding an anti-slave trade treaty with the Sultan of Johanna, and by annexing the Boer republic of Natal on the African mainland not far from the southern outlet of the Mozambique Channel (1843). The reluctant decision to hold this unwanted territory with its sand-blocked harbour was taken mainly on grounds of internal South African policy; but the decision was perhaps reinforced by the hope, a hope destined to be disappointed for many years, that Natal coal would be useful to steamers on the Cape route to the East, and certainly reinforced by the suspicion that French intrigue had encouraged the Boer resistance to the Queen's troops.[2] Great Britain would take no risks, so she kept Natal; but she took no steps to occupy the almost useless harbour of St Lucia Bay close by, which the Zulu king had ceded to her, and, in Madagascar, helped the French to bombard Tamatave, whence Ranavalona had once more ejected the European traders (1845).

Meanwhile, far to the north, the French were dominant once more in Mehemet Ali's Greater Egypt; their missionaries were busy in Abyssinia, whence the King of Kings was driving out the Protestant missionaries, and Frenchmen were trying to buy land in the Imam's African dominions. At Zanzibar, the French consul joined forces

---

[1] Coupland, *East Africa*, p. 449.
[2] *C.H.B.E.* VIII, 330–1; Uys, C. J., *In the Era of Shepstone*, pp. 8, 19.

with leading Arabs who resented the increasing restrictions that were being imposed upon their slave trade. The British had induced the Imam to narrow the slave-trading "corridor" between Africa and Asia so as to exclude newly-annexed Karachi (1839), as a prelude to abolishing slavery in British India (1843). Backed by an imposing array of warships, the consul obtained a most advantageous commercial treaty for his country; but, on the other hand, he and his Arab supporters gained such a dangerous hold upon the Imam's eldest son that the Imam dispossessed his heir and arranged that on his own death his African territories should go to the second son and his Asiatic to the third (1844).[1]

The British followed up their advantage by persuading the harassed Imam to forbid the export of slaves from his African dominions and the import of African slaves into his Asiatic possessions (1845). It was a great step forward, and all the more effective in that the Ottoman Sultan and the Persian Shah presently promised that no African slaves should be landed at their Gulf ports (1847–48); but there was one traffic on the East African coast which the British could not stop, and which further strained their relations with the French. France had long ago forbidden the slave trade, but the status of slavery still existed in her tropical islands in both hemispheres. Finding it increasingly hard to keep up their labour supply by smuggled slaves, the colonists of the French African islands moved their Government to ask for leave to recruit indentured coolies in British India. That leave had been given reluctantly to Mauritius and some of the British Caribbean colonies soon after the Emancipation Act of 1833, but it was now refused to the French. Hence, for nearly twenty years (1843–61), in spite of British protests, the French imported from the Moslem East Coast "free immigrants" who differed from slaves only in the temporary nature of their servitude and their somewhat better treatment on the plantations.[2]

For fully ten years after the closing of the Mehemet Ali crisis in 1841 the Eastern Question lay dormant, and Great Britain, drifting ever farther away from France, drew so near to Russia that the Czar Nicholas could discuss with the undecided Aberdeen what should be done when the expected collapse of the Ottoman Empire took place (1844).[3] Nevertheless, British anxiety for the stability of the Mediterranean balance was awakened more than once; by the twofold Spanish royal marriages which threatened to set an Orleanist some day upon the throne of Spain, and still more urgently by the storm of revolutions that swept over Europe in 1848. During 1848–49 Great Britain stood aside as far as possible from the troubled Continent, though Palmerston, who hoped to see a reformed Kingdom of the Two Sicilies firmly established in the immediate neighbourhood of

---

[1] Coupland, *East Africa*, p. 454.
[2] *Ibid.* pp. 427 ff. [3] *C.H.B.F.P.* II, 343.

Malta, went very far in giving help to the Sicilian rebels.[1] He even called in Louis Napoleon, President of newly-republican France, to help him in the thankless task and, long after Napoleon had turned aside to restore the Temporal Power at Rome, joined with him in warning off Russia from the Danubian Principalities; for, though Napoleon might not be so convinced as was Palmerston of the necessity for a strong Austria as a counterpoise to Russia, he fully agreed with him that the Turkish Empire must be maintained against a Russian advance towards the Straits or the Levant.

The popular movement in neighbouring Italy stirred the Ionian islanders who already envied their Greek brethren the democratic institutions which they had recently forced upon King Otho (1843).[2] The British protectorate had never been popular, partly because most of the islanders felt that their government, with its aristocratic Senate and Chamber in which the old Venetian families predominated, did too little for them and too much for the mixed Greek, Italian and Jewish population of Corfu, and partly because it stood in the way of their union with the Greek kingdom. Hence there were risings, political and agrarian, in Cephalonia and elsewhere in 1848–9. Once these had been suppressed, the British Government, which had just set up a partly elective council in the island fortress of Malta in keeping with the colonial reforms of the day, gave the Ionian Islands a more democratic constitution (1849). It thereby increased the influence of the annexationists, who waxed vociferous a few months later when a British squadron blockaded the Piraeus to enforce the claims of Don Pacifico, a Gibraltar Jew, and other British subjects against the Greek Government. A settlement of this dispute was presently effected through the good offices of France (April 1850), but Palmerston, fresh from his famous "civis Romanus" speech, would not hear of the transfer of the Ionian Islands to Greece lest the French or the Russians should establish themselves at Corfu.

It was indeed no time for Britain to loosen her hold on the eastern Mediterranean. British trade might be falling behind that of Austria and France in the Levant and even in parts of Italy, the Austrian Lloyd fleet might dominate the shipping of those parts; but for all that, Britain was sending considerable quantities of coal to Italy and taking in return the Italian oak which was so acceptable to the Admiralty; British cottons were going in ever-increasing volume to the Ottoman Empire whose mohair was esteemed highly by the Yorkshire weavers, and, now that the Corn Laws had been repealed, the wheat of Odessa was finding a ready market in the United Kingdom. Moreover, British banking still predominated in the Mediterranean countries, and British prestige stood higher than ever at Constantinople, and at Cairo also where the young anglophile

[1] C.H.B.F.P. II, 315.
[2] On the Ionian Islands and Greece vide C.H.B.F.P. II, ch. XIV.

Abbas had succeeded Mehemet Ali (1849–53). But, as ever, Britain was more interested in what lay beyond the Levant. Her consumption of jute, tea, coffee and other Asiatic commodities was rising fast; India was for her a source of cotton supply second only to the United States, and to India, Ceylon, and China she was sending a vast bulk of cotton goods.[1] Further, the East India Company had made itself master of all India up to the mountains of the north-west by conquering the Sikhs (1845–49), and of all the shores of the Bay of Bengal and the mouth of the Irrawady river by defeating the Burmese (1852–53).[2]

France, Napoleonic once more, seemed to be the most likely disturber of this British peace. Her annexation of New Caledonia had raised an uproar in half Australia (1853); but that was far away. More disquieting was the restoration of military rule in Algeria almost immediately after the shortlived Second Republic had incorporated it as part of France; while repeated talk of a Suez canal and rumours of renewed French activity in Madagascar and Zanzibar, where French trade was fast outstripping that of all other nations, portended trouble on both the British routes to the East. Behind it all the French traffic in "free immigrants" went on faster than ever since the Republic had abolished the status of slavery in the overseas empire (1848), and in 1854 it was even extended to Portuguese East Africa. Britain strengthened her position in the Mozambique Channel by concluding a commercial treaty with Johanna (1850), and it was partly at least because French subjects had asked for the concession that she persuaded the Imam of Muscat-Zanzibar to cede the tiny Kuria-Muria group off the south-eastern shores of Arabia so that a Liverpool company might monopolise the guano deposits and thus supplement existing supplies from Peru and the Guano Islands off the south-west coast of Africa (1854).[3]

Jealous and suspicious of one another though they were, France and Great Britain presently found themselves involved as allies in the long Crimean war. By the Treaty of Paris, in March, 1856, the Powers guaranteed the integrity and independence of the Ottoman Empire and recognised the Sultan as a member of the Concert of Europe; Russia gave up a strip of Bessarabia which cut her off from the Danube; the Straits Convention of 1841 was reaffirmed, the Black Sea was neutralised, and Russia and Turkey engaged not to have fortified bases upon its shores.[4]

As long as the alliance between France and Great Britain held good, Russia would be denied all hope of access in arms to the Mediterranean and, in face of the general guarantee to the Turkish Empire by the Powers, would find it dangerous to press down upon the Levant route to the East at any point on the western side of the

[1] Clapham, *Economic History*, i, 481 ff. [2] *C.H.B.E.* iv, 548 ff., 562.
[3] Coupland, *Eas tAfrica*, pp. 524 ff. [4] *C.H.B.F.P.* ii, 387 ff.

Persian frontiers. It was in Persia and still more in India itself that grave peril now threatened the British. Bahadur Shah the Mogul, believing with justice that John Company intended to make an end of his shadowy office, had turned for help to the Persian Shah, the ancient overlord of the house of Baber (1855). At the outbreak of the Crimean War, the Shah, anxious to pay off old scores against Russia, had offered to co-operate with the Allies. Rebuffed, he swung over to a benevolent neutrality towards the Russians, and presently promised the Mogul the combined support of the Persian and Russian Empires and proclaimed a holy war against the Company.[1] The Indian Government struck swiftly. Having secured the friendship of the buffer state of Afghanistan by a treaty with Dost Mohammed (1855), it sent an expedition to the Persian Gulf. Bushire was occupied, and, though the Shah took Herat with the aid of a French engineer officer, the British occupation of Muhammarah forced him to relinquish his prize and to acknowledge the independence of Afghanistan (1857). The Gulf expedition thereupon returned to India just in time to take part in crushing the Mutiny. When peace was restored to India eighteen months later, the last of the Moguls, his sons dead, had departed to end his days at Rangoon, and the Company, his overwhelming vassal, had also passed away, bequeathing its powers and responsibilities to the British Crown (1858).[2]

News of the Indian Mutiny had reached London in forty days; but whereas, during the Crimean War, troops had been sent from India to the Black Sea by the Suez route with the ready consent of all concerned, the first reinforcements were now sent to India round the Cape and none were sent overland for three desperate months. A Select Committee afterwards revealed that this choice of routes had been dictated by "political and other considerations", a formula which undoubtedly covered the fear of incurring the hostility of Napoleon III.[3]

Napoleon used Britain's necessity as a means of breaking down her opposition to the cutting of a canal through the Isthmus of Suez.[4] Cherished as an ambition since 1834 by Ferdinand de Lesseps, the then French consul at Cairo, the project of an isthmian canal did not come within the realm of practical politics until 1847, when the aged Mehemet Ali appointed an international commission of inquiry. The French, who strongly desired the canal, were encouraged by the cautious optimism of the French and Austrian commissioners, while the British, at that time in what Ruskin called their "ferruginous temper", stood out for a railway from Alexandria to Suez similar to

---

[1] *C.H.B.F.P.* II, 415.; *C.H.B.E.* IV, 606.
[2] *C.H.B.E.* V, 208, 607.
[3] Hoskins, *British Routes to India*, pp. 399 ff.
[4] For the history of the Suez canal see Fitzgerald, P. H., *The Great Canal at Suez, its political, engineering and financial history*; Hoskins, *British Routes to India*; and Wilson, Sir Arnold Talbot, *The Suez Canal, its past, present and future*.

those with which they were so industriously covering their own islands, and which Lord Dalhousie was planning for India on a grand scale. They took comfort from the blunt opinion of the British commissioner that a non-tidal canal would simply be "a stinking ditch". Thus began the twenty years' war of the Suez canal, a struggle which had a profound effect upon the mutual relations of Great Britain and the Second Empire. The British could not deny that a navigable canal would offer an unbroken voyage from England to Indian ports less by anything from two-fifths to one-third than that by way of the Cape, less by about one-fourth to the South China ports, and appreciably less even to Australasia;[1] but they knew that while a railway would probably be a British undertaking, a canal would certainly be French. Meanwhile, they honestly believed that a navigable canal was impracticable, and the Foreign Office warned the Sultan, whose firman was legally necessary for such a work, that the French would stop as soon as they had constructed a deep fortified entrenchment severing Egypt from the rest of the Ottoman Empire.[2] To the last, multitudes of Englishmen were convinced that the canal scheme was "a blind for the occupation of Egypt by France".[3]

At one moment, in the early days, a House of Commons committee debated the advisability of encouraging steam communications with India, the Far East and Australasia by the "all-red" route round the Cape (1851). Australia was sending to the United Kingdom half its supplies of wool, the Cape Colony was adding its quota, and the tide of emigration was rushing in spate to the new goldfields at Bendigo and Ballarat. Steamships, too, were improving in range and power; steam gunboats were harrying the slavers on the West Coast[4] and, in the very year of the Commons committee, the General Screw Steam Navigation Company essayed to give the Cape Colony its first steam mail service. But H.M. Government decided to concentrate upon the Suez route and, as if to confirm it in its decision, the Screw Navigation Company failed presently to fulfil its contract.[5] For some years yet the Cape Colony must be content to receive its mails by sailing ship.

The British Government's decision to concentrate on the Suez route was a natural one, for they had won the first round in the canal war. Abbas Pasha had called in British experts to build him a railway and by the close of 1853 the track was in working order between Alexandria and Cairo. Then came a swift reversal of fortune. Abbas died on the eve of the Crimean War, and his successor, Said, declared in favour of France and a canal. In November 1854, while the battle

[1] Knowles, L. C. A., *The Economic Development of the British Overseas Empire*, I, 16.
[2] Hoskins, *British Routes to India*, pp. 309, 349; Ashley, E., *The Life of Henry John Temple, Viscount Palmerston*, II, 325.
[3] Dilke, Sir C., *Greater Britain*, p. 568.
[4] Rose, J. H., *Man and the Sea*, p. 257.
[5] Theal, G. M., *History of South Africa since 1795*, III, 137, 150.

smoke hung heavy over Inkerman, Said gave de Lesseps a concession, which, subject to the Sultan's approval, promised him lavish grants of land and ample supplies of cheap labour for the cutting of an isthmian canal. The canal was to be international, on the principles recently laid down for the projected Nicaraguan canal by the British and United States Governments (1850);[1] but, international or not, the Emperor of the French at once enrolled Said in the Legion of Honour and promised the canal project his unswerving support.

The French and British Governments agreed to shelve the canal question for the duration of the war lest it should break their united front against the Russians, while Said tried to meet British objections by issuing a revised concession which provided, *inter alia*, that the canal should remain under Egyptian sovereignty and should be "a neutral passage" open at all times to the merchant vessels of all nations on equal terms (Jan. 1856).[2] It was in vain. Once the Treaty of Paris had been signed (March 1856), the struggle was resumed more fiercely than ever. Alarmed at confident talk in Paris of coming French domination on the East Coast of Africa and in Madagascar, "an Australia all our own",[3] the British forestalled the French by annexing Perim Island between Aden and the African mainland, and, while thus strengthening their hold on the southern outlet of the Red Sea, looked with favour upon a British company which proposed to build a railway and electric telegraph from a point on the Syrian coast down the Euphrates valley to Basra on the Persian Gulf. Such a railway would establish British predominance in Syria and Mesopotamia, cut across all possible lines of Russian advance southward, and, it was hoped, quash the Suez canal scheme. In spite of the offer of a French group to build the railway without the moderate financial guarantee demanded by their British rivals, the Sultan gave his firman. The British group declined to internationalise the project by joining hands with the French, and though de Lesseps' appeal to the business men of Britain over the heads of their rulers met with some success, it was well understood that the British Government would support the Euphrates railway. But the Indian Mutiny had broken out and British reinforcements were going out round the Cape for "political and other reasons". Palmerston, fresh from an interview with Napoleon at Osborne, unexpectedly threw over the Euphrates project. Fearing a combination of France and Russia against it, he could do no other; but it was significant that British troops soon began to go to India by the Suez route, and that the Emperor presently suggested that, to save more time, they should travel through France to take ship at Marseilles.[4]

Enough of the *bonne entente* on which the Mediterranean balance depended had thus been saved to enable British and French troops to

[1] *C.H.B.F.P.* II, 268.
[2] Hoskins, *British Routes to India*, p. 317.
[3] Coupland, *East Africa*, p. 457.
[4] Hoskins, *op. cit.*, pp. 330 ff., 402 ff.

co-operate in two campaigns in China (1857–60). With the diplomatic support of the United States and Russia, their Governments bound the Chinese Emperor by the Treaty of Tientsin to receive the ambassadors of foreign Powers and to open the interior of his vast empire to Western missionaries and traders.[1] Meanwhile the Sultan doggedly refused to ratify Said's concession to de Lesseps. Perhaps he held that a canal was unnecessary now that Said had after all carried on Abbas's railway from Cairo to Suez (1858). De Lesseps' reply was to open his subscription lists. Within the month rather more than half the shares had been taken up, the vast majority by Frenchmen, often in small blocks. On 25 April 1859 the first sod was cut.[2] A week later Napoleon III and Victor Emmanuel of Sardinia precipitated a Mediterranean crisis of the first magnitude by declaring war on Austria.

Great Britain viewed Napoleon's new adventure with suspicion and alarm. Since the close of the Crimean War, she had learned to regard her French ally as much more actively dangerous than her late Russian enemy. Not content with an army that far outnumbered the British, Napoleon seemed set upon challenging Britain's maritime supremacy, and now, whatever its result, his Italian war was bound to alter the balance of power in the Mediterranean. The worst that could happen from the British point of view was the general conflagration that must ensue if Russia were drawn in. Even if the struggle was localised, an Austrian victory would throw Italy into the melting-pot; while the expected Austrian defeat would weaken Britain's traditional ally against France and, since 1856, against Russia also, and might lead to the planting of a Bonaparte or a Murat upon the throne of Naples, an ill neighbour to Malta, or even to the creation of the united Italy which Victor Emmanuel and Cavour desired.

The Austrians were soon swept out of Lombardy, and though Napoleon unexpectedly came to terms with them, leaving Venetia under Hapsburg rule, he took from his ally Savoy and the port of Nice as the price of his aid, while province after province declared for union with Sardinia. Haunted by the fear that Cavour might offer Genoa or even the island of Sardinia to Napoleon in return for helping him to take Venetia by force,[3] the British Government turned away for a moment to deal with a sudden threat to the *status quo* in the western Mediterranean opposite Gibraltar. The Spanish Government, hoping to unite the factions that plagued it by a foreign adventure, sent a punitive expedition into Morocco. Great Britain, who had not hesitated to warn Orleanist France off this dangerous ground, intimated that no annexations would be permitted.[4] Then, as the Spaniards, honour satisfied, withdrew, Sicily revolted against its Bourbon king. By the

[1] *C.M.H.* xi, 807, 817.
[2] *C.M.H.* xii, 430 ff; Wilson, *Suez Canal*, p. 22.
[3] *C.H.B.F.P.* ii, 446.
[4] *C.M.H.* xi, 564.

end of July 1860 the island was in the hands of Garibaldi's Redshirts, who were cheering for "Italy and Victor Emmanuel".

While the Garibaldians were overrunning Naples, and the Sardinians were forcing their way through the Papal States to head them off Rome and its French garrison, another Mediterranean crisis flared up, this time in the Levant. In May 1860 the unorthodox Moslem Druses of the Lebanon, who made no objection to the presence of British and other Protestant missionaries, massacred their Catholic Maronite neighbours, who had been nominally part of the French nation ever since the days of St Louis. The consuls-general of the Powers at Beirut, backed by a Franco-British squadron, had just managed to quell the uproar, when the Moslems of Damascus sacked the Christian quarter with the willing help of the Turkish garrison (July 1860). Napoleon suggested that Egyptian troops should be called in to restore the Sultan's authority; but Great Britain, remembering Mehemet Ali, would not have it so. But since the mutual massacres were threatening to spread to the coastlands full of Greeks and Jews, who would undoubtedly call upon Russia for aid, Great Britain reluctantly agreed that French troops should support a joint pacificatory commission of the Powers. So, "partant pour la Syrie", the French landed at Beirut and speedily restored order (Aug. 1860).[1]

During the year of diplomatic bickering that followed this French occupation of Syria, the last shreds of the *bonne entente* were dissipated. The British were alarmed at the recent strengthening of the French garrison at Rome, and at the intervention of a French squadron to prevent a Sardinian bombardment of Gaeta, refuge of the Neapolitan Bourbons; they were nervous lest the French landing in Syria should form a precedent for similar action in the Balkan peninsula; they were angry that they themselves should be fighting a losing battle over the Suez canal at the very moment when British engineers were laying a Mediterranean-Red Sea cable to Karachi by way of the Kuria-Muria Islands, their guano deposits now sadly depleted. In response to a personal appeal from de Lesseps backed by the French subscription lists, Napoleon had thrown the whole diplomatic weight of his empire behind the canal project. On making peace with Austria he had bound her to second his efforts and had presently secured Russia's aid also.[2] Thus supported, Said had become defiant. He had recently taken up the unallotted canal shares,[3] close upon half of the total, and now declared that, firman or no firman, nothing but force should stop the canal. In face of that Britain strained every nerve to get the French out of Syria; but it was only in June 1861, after the jealous Powers had at last agreed that the Lebanon should be administered by a Catholic Armenian, that Napoleon's troops marched down to their ships.[4]

C.H.B.F.P. II, 451 ff.
C.M.H. XII, 431.

[2] Hoskins, *Routes to India*, pp. 358–9.
[4] C.H.B.F.P. II, 451.

The years that immediately followed the French intervention in Syria were marked by renewed rivalry between the French and British in the outer world, and by a notable concentration of British force in the Mediterranean. Anglo-French competition was not serious on the West Coast of Africa. The British annexation of Lagos (1861) was in no way a reply to the extension of French authority on the Senegal and Gaboon-Ogowe rivers, but the only means of suppressing the principal slave market upon a coast on which British influence had been enhanced by the purchase of the Danish stations (1850); nor was it from fear of the French that Great Britain annexed the Guano Islands (1861–6), but rather to advance the interests of the Cape Colony which took over these dependencies a few years later (1873).[1]

The need for British watchfulness was greater on the East Coast of Africa, for that coast was in a sense a prolongation of the Suez canal and had been brought by the steamship much closer than before to Britain's overland route to the East. In Madagascar, at the southern end of this long coast, the French Government upheld the lavish concessions which the feeble successor of Queen Ranavalona had given to a French adventurer,[2] and subsidised the Jesuits who had ventured back together with the Protestant missionaries. Napoleon, moreover, at last broke down British opposition to French labour policy in that region. For some years past French warships had escorted the vessels which carried "free immigrants" from the Moslem and Portuguese mainland to Réunion (Bourbon) and the Comoros, and when the Lisbon authorities, under British pressure, had tried to stop the traffic, two French battleships overcame their scruples by anchoring in the Tagus (1858).[3] A little later, however, the sugar planters of Natal obtained leave from the British Government, successor now of the Company, to recruit coolies in British India (1860). Next year, a like permission was given to the French, and so the trade in "free immigrants" died away; but to check unwelcome French interest in South-eastern Africa, Great Britain disinterred Owen's treaty of 1823 and claimed the southern shore of Delagoa Bay on behalf of Natal (1861). She thus entered upon a controversy with Portugal which was only ended fourteen years later by the arbitration of the President of the French Republic (1875).[4]

Farther north, the separation of Zanzibar from Muscat that had been arranged in 1844 was effected, not without the intervention of the Government of India to compose differences between the two heirs of the Imam (1856–61). French trade with Zanzibar and its dependencies was now losing ground to that of the Americans, Germans and British Indians; but it still overshadowed British trade and, to be on the safe side, Great Britain induced France to recognise

[1] Theal, *History of South Africa*, II, 236.
[2] Johnstone, Sir H. H., *A History of the Colonization of Africa by Alien Races*, p. 271.
[3] Coupland, *East Africa*, pp. 434–5.
[4] *C.H.B.E.* VIII, 453.

with her the independence of Zanzibar (1862). In the Red Sea area, however, the French occupied Obok opposite Aden (1862), where they could, if they wished, develop a port to serve the steamships of the Messageries Imperiales, which, furnished with a heavy mail subsidy, had begun in 1861 to compete with the P. and O. liners between Suez and Bombay. Meanwhile, in Farther India, the French annexed Cochin-China and Cambodia (1861–62), and, still farther afield, sent convicts to New Caledonia, to the fury of the eastern Australians who had just obliged Western Australia to forego that type of labour and were trying to forget a long chapter in their own past (1864).

The French had occupied Obok in anticipation of the speedy completion of the Suez canal. The thousands of half-hearted fellaheen supplied by the Egyptian corvée had made but slow progress, and at one stage the whole undertaking had been in jeopardy. Said had died early in 1863, and his young successor, Ismail (1863–79), professed himself willing to be guided by the new Sultan Abdul-Aziz (1861–76). In spite of the protests of Austria and the growing desire of its own business men for a canal, the British Government made up its mind to thwart what it believed were the military designs of the French. It persuaded Abdul-Aziz to impose fresh conditions on de Lesseps' company, which it must either refuse and thus forfeit all hope of the Sultan's firman, or accept and, hard pressed as it was for money, break down. However, a way was found out of the impasse. In response to the appeals of the multitudinous French investors, Napoleon presided over an arbitration commission, which deprived the Company of the corvée labour, the network of subsidiary canals and broad belts of land on either side of the main canal, but required the Egyptian Government to pay the Company some £3,360,000 for the right to resume these valuable concessions (July 1864).[1] And so the canal, France's canal, went on.

Two months before Napoleon's canal commission gave its award, Great Britain had relinquished her protectorate over the Ionian Islands. The Italian struggle for unity, and Lord Russell's justification of it on the analogy of the "Glorious Revolution" of 1688,[2] had taught the Greeks of the mainland, the Ionian Islands and Crete that they, like Englishmen and Italians, ought to be free to choose their own rulers. In October, 1862, a revolution at Athens sent King Otho packing, as he had come nearly thirty years before, in a British warship, and the Provisional Government and the three guaranteeing Powers, Great Britain, France and Russia, faced the problem of finding a successor. Early in the negotiations, Great Britain offered to strengthen Greece by handing over the Ionian Islands, provided the Greeks would accept a constitutional monarch and promise to refrain from attacking

[1] Hoskins, *British Routes to India*, p. 362; *C.M.H.* xi, 638; xii, 433.
[2] Temperley and Penson, *British Foreign Policy*, p. 222.

the Turks. Since they had agreed that the new king should not be chosen from any of their own royal or imperial houses, the Powers set aside the overwhelming vote of the Greek National Assembly in favour of Prince Alfred, Queen Victoria's second son, and by the Treaty of London (March 1864) arranged that Prince William of Denmark should become king under the style of George I. Thereupon the Ionian Islands were transferred to the Kingdom, the fortifications at Corfu were dismantled, and the islands of Corfu and Paxo were guaranteed in perpetual neutrality (May 1864).[1] But Crete remained under the rule of the Ottoman Sultan.

The abandonment of the Ionian Islands did little, if anything, to weaken Great Britain's hold upon the Mediterranean route to the East. Corfu had never been of more than secondary importance compared with Malta or Gibraltar, and now that steam had reduced distances in the Mediterranean, those two bases were amply sufficient for British needs especially as Russia no longer had a Black Sea fleet. Moreover Napoleon's star was waning visibly, and, above all, Great Britain no longer feared France's iron battleships. By 1865 she had won the race in naval armaments, in spite of the British iron— France's "great primary want", Cobden had told the sympathetic Emperor—that was pouring into France under the admirable Anglo-French commercial treaty of 1860. Her naval yards were being adapted so fast to the building of large iron ships that the day was soon coming when she need lay down no more protected wooden ships, while her merchant marine was even experimenting with vessels of the new Bessemer steel, and, by the same token, the British Government had found a new interest in Spain as a source of excellent haematite ores (1861).[2] Far-reaching improvements in the fortifications and harbour facilities at Malta had already been undertaken to meet the requirements of the new navy (May 1863). There was no need to repeat this expense at out-of-date Corfu. It seemed better to reduce it permanently to the status of an undefended port and to give it up.

Secure at sea, the British Government resigned itself to the thought that the Suez canal would sooner or later be an accomplished fact. It therefore heard with comparative equanimity that, in 1865, a small steamer had worked its way from sea to sea through the main channel and its subsidiaries,[3] and made no protest a few months later when the Sultan Abdul-Aziz, a heavy borrower in Paris and much beholden for financial aid to his spendthrift vassal at Cairo, promoted Ismail to the rank of Khedive in primogeniture[4] and, under strong pressure from Napoleon, at last issued the firman sanctioning the canal project (March–May 1866). Henceforward the British Government confined itself to ensuring that this "second

[1] *C.H.B.F.P.* II, 617.   [2] Clapham, *Economic History*, II, 225.
[3] Hoskins, *British Routes to India*, p. 367.
[4] *C.M.H.* XI, 637.

Bosporus" should be truly international. Nevertheless Lord Napier's brilliant Abyssinian campaign (1867–68) enhanced British-Indian prestige in all those parts where Africa draws near to Asia, and served as a reminder that British power stood unshaken at the far end of "the Ditch".[1]

The winning of the Sultan's firman was almost the last outstanding diplomatic success of the Second Empire. A month later Italy and Prussia went to war with Austria. The Austrians defeated the Italians by land and sea, but so crushing was their own defeat at the hands of Prussia in Bohemia that they were obliged to hand Venetia over to France for transfer to Italy (1866). The Austrian Empire, still possessed of Fiume and Trieste, reorganised itself as the Dual Monarchy of Austria-Hungary; in the background the majority of the German states coalesced round Prussia as the North German Confederation, while Napoleon was compelled to cancel his last claims on Italian gratitude for past services by helping the Papalini to drive Garibaldi back from Rome (Nov. 1867).

Meanwhile Great Britain had once more thwarted the harassed Emperor. The new Greek King, whose sister had recently married the Prince of Wales, himself married a Russian Grand Duchess, a marriage which marked Russia's tentative return to Mediterranean politics (1867). Napoleon, the third guarantor of Greece, lacking such personal links with the Athenian court, tried to earn merit there by proposing that Crete should be annexed by Greece. Great Britain, desiring no further changes in the Mediterranean *status quo*, refused her consent.

Nevertheless one more great day awaited the foundering Second Empire. On 17 November, 1869, the Suez canal was opened formally.[2] The Empress Eugenie in the imperial yacht headed the procession which picked its way down the scarcely finished channel, and everywhere the eagle-headed tricolour was much in evidence. But the first vessel which passed through de Lesseps' canal in the ordinary way of business was on the British register, and seventy-five per cent of the shipping that worked its way through during the next five years flew the Red or Blue Ensign.[3] Mehemet Ali had spoken truly when he told the British that this was their way to India, and now, to emphasise that fact, the British, after an initial failure, carried their Mediterranean-Red Sea cable through to Bombay (1870).

Napoleon's empire fell suddenly and in its fall cleared the way for a united Italy and produced a crisis in the Black Sea. As the conquering Germans poured across the frontiers of France, the French garrison was recalled from Rome to help to defend its own country. Two days after the siege of Paris had begun, the Italian troops forced

[1] *C.H.B.F.P.* III, 16 ff.
[2] Hoskins, *British Routes to India*, p. 368.
[3] *Ibid.* p. 372.

their way into Italy's predestined capital (20 Sept. 1870). A few weeks later, just after the fall of Metz, the Czar Alexander II, in collusion with Bismarck, wiped out the "blot upon his reign" by tearing up (31 Oct. 1870) the Black Sea clauses of the Treaty of Paris. Making the best of it, the Powers first signed a joint declaration that no one Power could set aside a treaty without the consent of the other signatories, and then recognised the *fait accompli* by de-neutralising the Black Sea. The Straits were still to be closed to non-Turkish warships, save when, in time of peace, the Sultan might admit the ships of friendly powers to uphold what was left of the Treaty of Paris.[1]

It remained to be seen what influence would be exerted in Mediterranean affairs by a united Italy, estranged from France but friendly to Great Britain, and perhaps by the new German Empire to which Italy was so closely bound. It was significant that Brindisi now supplanted Marseilles as the port *par excellence* for the Eastern mails (1870).[2] One thing was certain. Russia, who had employed her years of enforced abstention from Mediterranean politics since 1856 by consolidating her hold upon the western Caucasus, turning the Caspian Sea into a Russian lake, finding her way down to the warm waters of the Pacific at Vladivostok, and pushing along the road that leads to India through Tashkent and golden Samarkand, would soon have warships and fortified bases on the Black Sea. Britain must once more take up her watch upon the Dardanelles, and redouble her vigilance on the North-West Frontier of India.

For the rest, the opening of an unbroken waterway to India through Suez could not fail to diminish the importance of the alternative route by way of the Cape of Good Hope. The 'fifties had been a time of relative prosperity for the British colonies at the southern end of Africa. Merino wool and mohair, hides and skins, some wine still, copper and guano, the ivory and latterly the sugar of Natal, the growing population that went therewith and improvements in the steamship, had given Cape Town regular steamship connection with Great Britain by the Union Line since 1857. But the 'sixties had been a dangerous and depressing decade, during which the Cape Colony had watched with dread the progress of the work at Suez, lest the canal should draw away for ever the Indian and Australasian shipping that put into Table Bay. Those fears of ruin were not realised. Some loss there was; but the Suez canal, for many years to come narrow and of uncertain depth, at all times burdened with heavy tolls and offering but a relatively slight shortening of the Australian passage, by no means drained the Cape route of its accustomed shipping. On the contrary, new shipping was attracted to the Cape by the diamonds, ostrich feathers and even gold that now began to

[1] Temperley and Penson, *British Foreign Policy*, p. 331.
[2] Hoskins, *British Routes to India*, p. 411.

give the interior of South Africa an importance in the eyes of the world which it had hitherto lacked.

Nor did the completion of the Suez canal rob the Cape Peninsula entirely of its strategic importance. True, the loss of its unique position and the new-found wealth of the interior were two of the considerations, among many others, which induced the Imperial Government to press self-government on a half-unwilling Cape Colony (1871–72).[1] Nevertheless, in the course of the discussions which preceded that step, a highly placed official at the Colonial Office could affirm that "when the idea of concentrating British troops instead of scattering them among all the Colonies is more fully developed, the importance of Cape Town as...the true centre of the Empire, will be recognised. It is clear of the Suez complications, almost equally distant from Australia, China, India, Gibraltar, the West Indies and the Falklands, the best sanatorium for troops from the East, and the best depot for reliefs, a good and cheap market for provisions, and a repairing place for large ships. If all South Africa should be federated Cape Town...might possibly be retained as a small Crown Colony". His chief noted: "I don't think this is practicable".[2] Doubtless Lord Kimberley was right, but, for all that, the British Government was destined to keep a garrison in the Cape Peninsula longer than at any other station in the self-governing Empire (1914–16),[3] and to maintain there to this day the naval base of Simonstown, "clear of the Suez complications".[4]

[1] *C.H.B.E.* VIII, 442.
[2] C.O. 48/455. Minute by R. S. W. Herbert on despatch No. 53, Sir H. Barkly to Secretary of State, 31 May 1871.
[3] *C.H.B.E.* VIII, 750. [4] *C.H.B.E.* VIII, 758.

CHAPTER XVI

THE STRAITS SETTLEMENTS, 1815–1863

THE efforts of the Dutch in the seventeenth century had secured the undisputed mastery of the Eastern Archipelago. No other European power had a footing within the inner circle of the islands. The Portuguese had been completely rooted out; and the efforts of the English and the French to establish and maintain themselves within this coveted sphere of trade were brought to ruin by violence at Amboyna, by the result of war at Pulo Run, by economic pressure at Bantam and in Cochin China. At the beginning of the eighteenth century the English East India Company held only a few unimportant and ill-managed factories on the outer coast of Sumatra. The chief of these was York Fort, afterwards renamed Fort Marlborough, near Bencoolen. The purpose of this establishment was to supply the Company with pepper; but as the relative importance of the pepper trade declined, so the settlement decayed. It was villainously unhealthy; it had always been staffed with the bad bargains of the Company's service, for no one else had been willing to go. At the beginning of the nineteenth century Raffles described it as the most wretched place he had ever seen.

I cannot convey to you an adequate idea of the state of ruin and dilapidation which surrounds me. What with natural impediments, bad government, and… repeated earthquakes, we have scarcely a dwelling in which to lay our heads, or wherewithal to satisfy the cravings of nature. The roads are impassable; the highways in the town overrun with rank grass; the Government House a den of ravenous dogs and polecats.[1]

The chief evil seems to have been a culture system imitated apparently from the Dutch.[2] But it had also long been a penal settlement to which Indian criminals were sent to labour on the Company's plantations. Its principal attraction had lain in the opportunities which it offered to the Company's servants employed there for a clandestine trade in opium with the Dutch in Java.

The archipelago had always offered a profitable market for Indian opium and piece-goods; and though the Dutch company had sought to retain this trade wholly in its own hands, it was frustrated by the private interests of its own servants and the activity of English merchants. The Dutch had done their utmost, even after the treaty of 1784, to preserve the trade of the archipelago inviolate. They could not prevent the vessels of other European nations sailing through the Straits of Malacca on their way to and from Canton, but they strove hard to cut off foreign shipping from access to any port except Batavia.

[1] *Memoir of Raffles*, p. 293. [2] *Ibid.* p. 297.

Any vessel deviating from the regular China route was sure to be closely followed by Dutch cruisers, and all native traders would be severely warned to have nothing to do with the intruders. The English therefore sought to establish relations with the princes—and in this region the princes were the chief merchants of their territories—whose territories communicated indirectly with the forbidden coasts. A small company of Madras merchants, for instance, about 1770 opened relations with the princes of Achin, at the northern extremity of Sumatra, and of Kedah, on the opposite coast of the Malay Peninsula. At both these places they found the political position most unstable. At both they were offered large trading privileges on condition of providing the prince with aid against his enemies. One of their agents was Francis Light, a captain of country shipping, who was well acquainted with the Malay language and customs. He was an enterprising and able man, who was eager to see the English flag flying in the Straits of Malacca. But the East India Company would not suffer a private group of its own servants to establish themselves in semi-political power in Malaya; and the factories which the Company set up were soon abandoned as profitless.[1]

Although this ended for the moment attempts to enter into formal relations with the chiefs of the archipelago, Light and others continued to follow the trade, and Light himself used the island of Salang, then known by the name of Junk Ceylon, as his headquarters. He repeatedly urged upon the Government of Bengal the advantages of having an English harbour to the eastward of India. Such an establishment promised strategic as well as commercial advantages. Experience in the Seven Years' War and in the War of the American Revolution had shown the French disposed to concentrate their efforts on the Coromandel Coast. When in the autumn the north-east monsoon broke upon the coast, English fleets could find no shelter nearer than Calcutta with its dangerous passage up the Hugli or Bombay far away on the other side of India. A maritime post to the eastward would be not only a place of rendezvous comparatively secure from disturbance but also a place of shelter during the monsoon and a harbour from which the Coromandel Coast could be reached speedily as soon as the danger of cyclones had passed away.[2]

Light's persistency, aided by the experience of war, at last had its way. Early in 1786 the rajah of Kedah made him an offer of the island of Penang in return for an annual payment of 6000 dollars. Sir John Macpherson, the acting Governor-General, gave him permission to treat for the cession of the island. In consequence the British colours were hoisted there on 12 August 1786.[3] Within a twelvemonth

[1] Cf. Dodwell, H., *Nabobs of Madras*, pp. 130–5; also Light to Hastings, 17 January 1772 (Br. Mus. Add. MSS. 29133, f. 8).
[2] *V. infra* p. 601, also *C.H.B.E.* i, 781-2.
[3] Leith, *Short Account*, p. 2; *cf.* a MS. note of Marsden's in the copy of Leith in the library of the School of Oriental Studies.

sixty Chinese families had settled on the island. The picturesque story that the island was given to Light as the dowry of the princess whom he was said to have married seems to be nothing but a legend.[1]

The establishment of the English in the Straits led immediately to applications from various Malay chiefs for assistance against the Dutch, who had certainly been rendered more aggressive owing to the appearance of probable rivals so close to their strongholds.[2] Such complications were unwelcome to the prudent Cornwallis, at that time Governor-General; and endeavours were made to find a settlement which would secure the strategic advantages of Prince of Wales Island, as Light had called Penang, without its political entanglements. Cornwallis's brother was at that time in command of the East India squadron; and he warmly recommended a settlement on the Andaman Islands. In 1792 this was determined on; but a short experience soon showed the unsuitability of the chosen site, and the people employed there were transferred to Penang.[3] Meanwhile events in Europe drew renewed attention to the latter settlement.

As the Napoleonic War progressed, Great Britain found herself short of naval stores such as pitch and hemp, and in great want of large timber for shipbuilding. In 1804 Philip Dundas, a nephew of Henry Dundas, put forward a plan to establish a naval arsenal at Penang. He urged that the island could command unlimited supplies of timber both for building and spars, and that stores could either be obtained locally or made good by the use of local substitutes, such as dammar instead of pitch. Under the influence of Henry Dundas, the East India Company readily agreed to set up a separate government in the island. Philip Dundas was to be the Governor, assisted by a council on the pattern of the other presidencies; and Stamford Raffles was appointed assistant secretary of this new province. The instructions delivered to the Governor contemplated not only the foundation of a new naval base but also the extension of British political influence. Treaties were to be made with the princes of the Malay Peninsula, and the complete command of the Straits of Malacca was to be secured. But once more expectations were disappointed. The victory of Trafalgar and the consequences which flowed from it relieved the British dockyards of many of their difficulties. The Admiralty gave up the idea of establishing a naval station at Penang, and the Company in consequence ordered the reduction of the over-elaborate organisation which had been set up.[4] In 1806

[1] Steuart, A. F., *Francis and William Light*, pp. 25 *seqq.*

[2] Some curious letters will be found in the appendix to Marsden's *Malay Grammar*. Cf. Newbold, G., *Political and statistical account of the British settlements in the Straits of Malacca*, II, 48.

[3] Cf. Leith, *op. cit.*, p. 6; and Cornwallis-West, *Life and letters of Admiral Cornwallis*, pp. 235 *seqq.*

[4] Hammond to Liverpool, 7 April 1802 (Add. MSS. 38410, f. 1); *Parl. Pap.* 1805, x, pp. 719 *seqq.*; *Memoir of Raffles*, pp. 5, 12; Boulger, D. C., *Raffles*, p. 52; Raffles, *On the Administration of the Eastern Seas*, pp. 3–5.

Napoleon virtually annexed Holland and the British conquered the
Cape. But the years after Tilsit (1807) were still very critical for
British dock-yards and trade.

Soon after this, in 1811, Lord Minto, the Governor-General of Bengal,
resolved to root out French influence altogether from the Eastern seas
by the conquest of Java.[1] In these projects Raffles played a considerable part. He had distinguished himself by the knowledge which he
had rapidly acquired of the languages and customs of the people. He
entered into friendly understandings with various Malay and Javanese
princes, thus materially contributing to the success of the expedition.[2]
The overthrow of the Dutch proved easy. Their power had been
shaken by the assumption of authority on the part of Janssens,
Napoleon's nominee, and here, as in the other Dutch dependencies,
the Dutch were divided between detestation of French control and
hatred of their English rivals.

The project of the Indian Government had at first been limited to
the expulsion of the French and the destruction of all fortresses.
Raffles argued strongly against this plan. He pointed out that if the
Dutch were left without arms or means of defending themselves they
would be massacred by the inhabitants of the island. There was some
truth in this view; and indeed in the neighbouring island of Sumatra
the sultan of Palembang seized the opportunity of the destruction of
Dutch power to massacre the garrison at Palembang.[3] Other considerations too were at work. The immense wealth of the island, and
"the face of prosperity which every part of the island wears, even
weighed down, as it has been, by a most oppressive system", impressed Minto, who personally visited Java, with its great potential
value.[4] He decided therefore to retain posession of it at all events
until the Home Government decided what was to be done. The administration was entrusted to Raffles, of whose qualities Minto had
formed the highest opinion. After a short campaign against the sultan
of Jakakarta in 1812, British authority was completely uncontested.

This was the more remarkable because the establishment of British
power was accompanied by a great change of system. By proclamation, dated 11 September 1811, Minto declared that the Dutch law
should continue provisionally in force, except that torture and mutilation were prohibited. The Lieutenant-Governor was to have authority
to moderate sentences delivered against offenders, and to make
regulations subject to the approval or disallowance of the Governor-
General.[5] Raffles promptly made use of these powers. He found, for
instance, that the Chinese were almost monopolising the Government
contracts and farms of revenue; and took steps to prevent this in future.[6]

---

[1] See chapter III for the British policy of colonial conquest in the Napoleonic War.
[2] Lady Minto, *Lord Minto in India*, p. 249.   [3] *Memoir of Raffles*, pp. 110 seqq.
[4] *Lord Minto in India*, p. 311.   [5] *Memoir of Raffles*, pp. 103–4.
[6] *Ibid.* p. 72.

He also dealt with the delicate question of slavery, prohibiting the import of slaves, requiring all slaves to be registered, and founding a society to promote the manumission of slaves.[1] He introduced, too, sweeping changes into the general administrative system of the island. He had strongly disapproved of the policy of forced cultures which the English factories in Sumatra had borrowed from the Dutch; and naturally resolved to abolish the system of forced services which he found in Java. His aim was to replace it by a system of land revenue similar to that which existed in India. In this he was warmly supported by one of the Dutchmen who found a place on his council. Muntinge described the change as "the first, the most difficult, and certainly the most hazardous steps towards the introduction of a system of political government and regulated taxation".[2] The other members of his council, however, much disliked the proposal and predicted its failure.[3] In brief, it consisted in separating the revenue duties from judicial functions. The island was divided into districts, in which collectors were appointed to collect the revenue through village headmen, with the assistance of officials intermediate between the collectors and the headmen. The collectors were instructed to furnish the Government "with the fullest and completest view of the actual resources of the country". The minutest details were to be secured, in order to facilitate the settlement of the revenue. Survey officers were to map out each collectorate.[4] Raffles thought that a payment in money equivalent to about two-fifths of the annual gross rice produce of the soil would prove a suitable and equitable standard of assessment, the cultivator being relieved of all obligations to provide the Government with labour or produce.[5]

This scheme was obviously borrowed from the *ryotwari* system as worked by Read and Munro in the Madras Presidency. Raffles himself observed that he had completed his plan when he learnt of the Madras methods through the Fifth Report of the Select Committee of 1812. "The principles of the ryotwar system had suggested themselves without my knowing that they had been adopted elsewhere."[6] But it seems possible that information reached Raffles by other channels. He had serving with him in Java Major Colin Mackenzie, an officer of the Madras Army, who was distinguished by his interest in the customs of the South Indian peoples and his knowledge of their languages. A spirit so closely akin to Munro's, and indeed to Raffles's own, may well have suggested to the latter the revenue plan which Munro had already worked out elsewhere.

[1] Boulger, *op. cit.* p. 182.
[2] Deventer, M. L. van, *Daendels-Raffles*, pp. 86–7.
[3] Captain Travers's Journal, *ap.* Boulger, *op. cit.* p. 198.
[4] Raffles's Revenue Instructions, 11 February 1814, ap. *Review of the colony of Java*, pp. 99 *seqq.*
[5] *Memoir of Raffles*, pp. 214 *seqq.*
[6] Raffles to Minto, 13 February 1814 (*Memoir of Raffles*, p. 224).

This change involved alterations in the duties and position of the "regents", who, under the Dutch, had been ostensibly entrusted with the whole management of local administration. Raffles did not desire in any way to lower their position. He therefore visited each district, explaining the nature and object of the changes which he was introducing, and personally fixed the emoluments of each regent at a rate higher than he had claimed to be actually receiving before the introduction of the new system.[1] The net effect of the change was to remove the management of the Government lands from the native chiefs, but to leave them responsible for "the important department of the native police".[2]

The introduction of these changes inevitably provoked much criticism. Minto had urged the retention of the island on the ground that it would more than pay for its administration; but that opinion proved inaccurate. Revenues had been over-estimated, and charges under-estimated. Raffles had been obliged to draw repeatedly on the Government of Bengal; and this disappointment disturbed both the Indian Government and the Court of Directors.[3] Then Raffles found good ground to criticise the conduct of the chief military officer under him, Major-General Gillespie. Gillespie was a man of unquestioned gallantry and skill, but his judgment was more uncertain. Gillespie bitterly resented Raffles's strictures, and, on his return to Bengal, accused Raffles of financial misconduct. Lord Hastings, the Governor-General, as a soldier, was much inclined to accept the statements of his brother officer, and at first forwarded to England serious charges which he regarded as well established.[4] But Raffles was fortunately able to disprove the charges brought against him, and both the Governor-General and afterwards the Court of Directors agreed that he was free from every serious charge.[5]

The reforms which Raffles had introduced into the administration of the island had occupied all the later years of the war; and, by the time that they had been set going, peace was at hand. Raffles himself had hoped that the island might be retained by Great Britain. He had the fullest sense of its value and importance, describing it as "the other India".[6] The Home Government itself seems at one moment to have inclined in the same direction.[7] But the Anglo-Dutch Convention of 1814 restored to the Dutch all their possessions in the archipelago, in order to demonstrate the moderation of British colonial aims and to strengthen the Government of our Dutch allies.[8] The

[1] Raffles to Minto, January 1814 (*Memoir of Raffles*, p. 223).
[2] Raffles's Proclamation, 15 October 1813 (*ibid.* pp. 216–17).
[3] *Private Journal of Lord Hastings*, I, 40; and Egerton, H. E., *Raffles*, pp. 124–5.
[4] Moira to Liverpool, 27 March 1814 (Add. MSS. 38410, ff. 318 *seqq.*).
[5] Egerton, *op. cit.* pp. 111–15.
[6] Raffles to Marsden, 5 October 1811 (*Memoir of Raffles*, p. 98).
[7] Egerton, *op. cit.* 123.
[8] Napoleon thought the restoration of the Dutch East Indies very stupid. See Gourgaud, G., *Journal de Ste-Hélène*, II, 315.

question then promptly emerged whether the English were to be excluded once more from the trade of the archipelago and Cochin-China, or whether some effort was to be made to secure a share of it. Raffles at least had no two minds on the subject. In a powerful memorandum which he submitted to George Canning, then President of the Board of Control, he argued that the attitude of the Dutch remained the same as it had always been.

> Their commercial ambition and their animosity against British trade was never greater than at this moment. They are deeply impressed with the recollection of their ancient maritime and commercial grandeur, and would favour any other nation, especially the Americans, to our prejudice. Of the disposition of the mother-country the actual contemplation of a prohibitory duty on British shipping trading to their colonies is some evidence, and various incidents which took place at the moment of transferring the colonies are sufficient to prove the assuming spirit of the colonial government.[1]

With this view the Government of Bengal agreed, and, when Raffles went to take up his position as Lieutenant-Governor of Bencoolen, he was directed to provide the Home Government with the earliest and most regular information on the conduct of the Dutch Government.[2]

The remedy which Raffles recommended was the occupation of some port as yet unoccupied by the Dutch in the heart of their sphere of control.

> There are yet, at least there were when the last accounts came away, ports of which we may take possession before them and princes at liberty to make treaties with us in favour of our commerce. To their intimidation of the natives we may oppose a court of protection. To their imposition of heavy duties,...we can oppose the facility of obtaining our goods free of duty.[3]

Bencoolen and Penang were too remote, he thought, to serve the necessary purpose. Banka or Rhio were the places which he thought the best. But if anything was to be done, it must be done without delay. He desired no territorial gains as such. He sought the increase of the naval, not of the military power of Great Britain, and declared that Dutch and natives alike should be assured that dominion was not the object of any new establishment which might be made.

These words for the moment fell on deaf ears. The ministry desired no additional responsibilities, and disliked those who sought to thrust new ones upon them. Raffles, on the contrary, clung fast to his conceptions of the needs of British trade, and almost at once risked the whole of his future career. When in charge of Java, he had deposed the sultan of Palembang, in Sumatra, for his treacherous massacre of the Dutch, and had etablished a new sultan. The Dutch authorities, on resuming their possessions, would not allow this relic of British power to remain. They deposed Raffles's sultan, and restored his

---

[1] Add. MSS. 31237, f. 243.   [2] *Memoir of Raffles*, pp. 303-4.
[3] Add. MSS. *ut supra*.

predecessor, compounding for the slaughter of their countrymen by a fine of 500,000 dollars. Raffles had entered into a treaty with the sultan by which the garrison which the Dutch had maintained was withdrawn in return for the cession of the island of Banka. The Dutch occupied Banka, and reimposed their garrison on the sultan. Raffles was most indignant at the abandonment of his agreement. He held that the Dutch were in honour bound to observe the treaty which the English had made while in custody of the Dutch power. He held, too, that the English, having recognised the independence of the sultan, ought to maintain it. He therefore sent over to Palembang from Fort Marlborough a small detachment under the command of a British officer. The Dutch seized him and sent him on a man-of-war to Batavia, and Raffles drew up a protest against their proceedings.[1] When the news reached England, the ministry was much annoyed with the stand which Raffles had made. In the House of Lords Bathurst declared that Raffles had been given the title of Lieutenant-Governor as a personal concession only and that he had been invested with no political authority whatever, and Liverpool observed that the protest had been made by one with no right to issue such a document.[2] The Court of Directors instructed him that he was to refrain from any "communication with the Dutch authorities or with any of the native states, which may in any way pledge the British Government, without distinct authority to that effect from the Presidency of Fort William".[3] Once more the Home Government, looking rather to the importance of maintaining good relations with the Dutch than to the maintenance of British interests in the East, had refused to follow Raffles's lead.

He, however, had a strong sense of the urgent importance of checking the progress of Dutch colonial policy. He was convinced that it was aimed at "the annihilation of our commerce and of our intercourse with the native traders throughout the Malay archipelago". The Dutch held the Straits of Malacca and Sunda, the only passes through which ships could sail into that region. Had the late treaty been designed, he asked, to give back to the Dutch a wider authority than they had possessed before? Were they to be suffered to extend their control only in order to exclude British traders from every harbour except Batavia? Britain should declare her intention of maintaining the free navigation of the archipelago and her right of unrestricted intercourse with all independent princes. Unless she acted speedily, none would remain unhampered by Dutch treaties. "To effect the objects contemplated, some convenient station within the archipelago is necessary."[4] Fortunately the Governor-General,

---

[1] Cf. Boulger, *op. cit.* p. 275. The protest and connected papers are printed *ap. Annual Register*, 1819, pp. 216 *seqq.* See also Court, M. H., *Palembang*, pp. 62 *seqq.*
[2] Hansard, XXXIX, 155 *seqq.*
[3] Despatch to Raffles, 7 January 1819 (India Office, Sumatra, no. 41).
[4] See Raffles's important letter of 14 April 1818, *Memoir of Raffles*, pp. 305 *seqq.*

Lord Hastings, was more sensible than the ministry at London of the needs of British trade. He authorised Raffles to take precautions against the "manifest endeavours [of the Dutch] to establish an absolute supremacy to our exclusion".[1]

This was the result of a visit which Raffles had paid to Calcutta in the latter part of 1818. In December he sailed with authority to form an establishment at some place within the Straits not subject to Dutch mastery.[2] Hastings's last words were, "Sir Stamford, you may depend upon me." The object which Raffles sought was

a port which should have a commanding geographical position at the southern entrance of the Straits of Malacca, which should be in the track of our China and country trade, which should be capable of affording them protection or of supplying their wants, which should possess capabilities of defence by a moderate force, which might give us the means of supporting and defending our commercial intercourse with the Malay states, and which, by its contiguity to the seat of the Dutch power, might enable us to watch the march of its policy and when necessary to counteract its influence.[3]

Rhio had been the place on which Raffles had set his eye; but he thought that he might find that the Dutch had already anticipated him there, and, even before he sailed, he had turned to Singapore as a possible alternative.[4] The Dutch had in fact done what he supposed. They forced a treaty on Rahmat Shah which excluded all shipping but their own, established a Dutch garrison, required Rhio ships to fly the Dutch flag, and appropriated half the revenues of the island.[5] Raffles countered by making a treaty, signed on 30 January 1819, with the sultan of Johore, transferring the island of Singapore to the East India Company. "What Malta is in the West," Raffles declared, "that may Singapore become in the East."[6]

But the cession and occupation of Singapore left many difficulties still to be overcome. The Government of Penang was bitterly opposed, foreseeing that the new establishment would greatly reduce its importance. The Dutch were furiously angry at a change which threatened their monopoly. The Home Government would need great persuasion to accede to a policy which it had not inaugurated and which might involve trouble with Holland. The first of these, though of the least importance, might have led to most embarrassing consequences. The Governor of Penang, Colonel Bannerman, informed the Bengal Government that the protest which the Dutch lodged— against the occupation of Singapore—was fully justified, refused to send a single man to assist in the defence of Singapore in case it was attacked, and urged the evacuation "of the post Sir S. Raffles has so injudiciously chosen". Fortunately the Bengal Government was not

[1] *Memoir of Raffles*, p. 304. [2] *Ibid.* pp. 371, 374.
[3] *Statement of the services of Sir Stamford Raffles*, p. 54.
[4] Raffles to Marsden, 12 December 1818 (*Memoir of Raffles*, p. 374).
[5] *Ibid.* pp. 496–7.
[6] *Memoir of Raffles*, p. 379. For the progress of Singapore see chapter XI.

misled by his asseverations, and warned him that he might have difficulty in excusing himself should his conduct encourage the Dutch to attack the settlement at Singapore.[1] The Dutch protested in vigorous terms, claiming general rights which Lord Hastings could not prudently admit. He replied therefore that since the occupation was an accomplished fact, he could not "relinquish our possession without subscribing to rights which you claim and of which we are not satisfied".[2]

The news reached England when the ministry was still asserting that Raffles was a mere commercial agent. The Secret Committee of the East India Company, which was of course the mouthpiece of the President of the Board of Control, George Canning, doubted whether the Company had authority to make any new acquisitions south of the equator, also whether the chief from whom Raffles had obtained his cession of Singapore had the right to make any such grant, and was sure that Raffles had exceeded the powers conferred upon him by Lord Hastings and his council.[3] Raffles expected that his reward would be a letter of recall.[4] But the views of the Bengal Government favoured the retention of Singapore. Further, the case against the Dutch was strongly argued by pamphlets such as Assey's *On the trade to China*; a committee of the House of Lords recommended the maintenance of a depot which possessed such manifest advantages for trade; and finally negotiations with the Dutch disclosed the possibility of an amicable settlement.

The occupation of Singapore and the numerous complaints that were constantly referred home by the British and Dutch agents in the Eastern archipelago indeed finally convinced both the Home Governments that they stood to gain much by arbitration. Towards the close of 1819 Lord Clancarty, the British ambassador to the Netherlands, learnt that the Dutch Government was willing to negotiate, and it was soon decided that a Dutch Commission should travel to England. In July 1820 a series of preliminary talks was begun in London between the representatives of Britain, Castlereagh, Foreign Secretary, and Canning, President of the Board of Control, and the representatives of the Netherlands, Baron Fagel, Dutch ambassador at London, and M. Elont.[5] In January, 1820, Canning had got the Court of Directors to appoint a Secret Select Committee, consisting of four of the directors, to represent the Company in the negotiations, and, in the planning of the groundwork for the British proposals, he referred often, between January and July 1820, to this committee for advice. From the beginning this committee insisted that, whatever else was done, the passage through the Straits of Malacca must be

---

[1] Egerton, *op. cit.* pp. 184 *seqq.*
[2] *Ibid.* p. 183.
[3] *Ibid.* p. 191. Cf. Boulger, *op. cit.* p. 297.
[4] Boulger, *op. cit.* p. 312.
[5] India Office, Dutch Records, vol. xxx.

safeguarded, and that the retention of Singapore was essential for this purpose.[1]

When the commissioners met, in July 1820, each side made a statement of the points which it thought were at issue between the two countries in the East. For the Dutch M. Elont claimed Banka and Billiton as dependencies of Java, and he also asked for a settlement of the questions of Singapore, of the Dutch possessions on the mainland of India, and of the financial account between the Netherlands and Britain in the East.[2] Castlereagh and Canning based their claims on two principles: that the British were neither willing to acquiesce in the exclusion of their commerce from the archipelago, nor to expose their China trade *via* the Straits of Malacca and Sunda by leaving all the important posts on those routes in the hands of the Dutch. The Dutch immediately agreed with the first point and declared that "The Government of the Netherlands distinctly and solemnly disclaim any design on their part to aim either at political supremacy or at commercial monopoly in the Eastern Archipelago"; the merchants of each nation were henceforth to have the right to use the ports of the other in the archipelago, with the exception of the Moluccas, on the footing of the most-favoured nation.

M. Elont then pressed the Dutch claim to Billiton as a dependency of Banka, which had been transferred to the Dutch by article 2 of the Treaty of 1814. Canning denied the validity of this claim, and replied that all the instruments by which Billiton had been transferred to the British spoke of "Banka, Billiton, and their dependencies". However, Canning offered to cede Billiton to the Dutch if the latter ceased to oppose the establishment of the British factory at Singapore. M. Elont warmly opposed this proposal, on the grounds that the British claim to Singapore was invalid. Canning suggested other arrangements, and at this stage did not insist on the British retention of Singapore. Nevertheless, the dispute over Singapore threatened to bring the negotiations to an abrupt end, and, as both parties were anxious to avoid this, it was decided (August 1820) to adjourn the conference until more information had been received from the East.[3]

In March 1822 there was some prospect of a renewal of the negotiations, and Thomas Courtenay, Secretary of the Board of Control, and acting secretary to the conference, drew up a report from which it appears that Canning was then ready to admit the invalidity of British rights to Singapore and to evacuate that factory provided that the Dutch promised on the one hand not to establish themselves there and on the other to grant the British some other establishments in the archipelago as compensation. Canning was

---

[1] Board's Correspondence with Secret Commission, vol. i, pp. 93–150, 208–52.
[2] I.O. Dutch Records, vol. xxx.
[3] *Ibid.*

also willing to exchange Billiton for Fulta and Calcapore, and to buy the other Dutch establishments in India.[1]

By November 1823, when the negotiations were actually resumed, the position had changed. Castlereagh had died, and Canning, who had succeeded him at the Foreign Office, was by this time convinced that the main emphasis of the Dutch would be laid on a favourable financial settlement, and that the retention of Singapore was essential and possible. "We can agree tacitly to pay rather highly for the continental settlements in consideration of the forbearance of the Dutch in regard to Singapore."[2] On 18 November 1823 Canning and Wynn, the new President of the Board of Control, met Baron Fagel and M. Falck, the Dutch minister for the colonies, who had taken the place of M. Elont. Canning now pressed on the negotiations and within two months nine conferences were held. M. Falck soon cleared the ground by proposing that Singapore and Malacca should be set against Billiton and Bencoolen; and that the Dutch debts to Britain should be cancelled out by the cession of the Dutch continental possessions. Wynn preferred to balance Singapore, Malacca, and the continental possessions against Billiton and Bencoolen (which the Company valued and wished to retain as of strategic importance) and urged that the Dutch should pay £400,000 to clear their debts. M. Falck objected to their making any payment at all.[3] Four days later Wynn reduced the sum demanded to £200,000, but M. Falck stood firm and there was some danger of the negotiations falling through. The attitude of the Secret Select Committee also caused some trouble. Courtenay warned Canning, "It appears probable that there will be at least as much difficulty in negotiating with the India House as with M. Falck."[4] The directors objected very much to the cession of Bencoolen and they also pointed out that it was foolish to allow any pecuniary compensation for the Dutch possessions in India, which, as they said, "would in the event of a war immediately fall into our hands".[5] Canning, however, conciliated them by promising that the Company should enjoy the administration of Singapore and the new acquisitions by the treaty on the same terms as they had held Bencoolen. On February 23 M. Falck suggested that the Dutch debts should be estimated at £50,000; Canning seized the opportunity, and a compromise of £100,000 was reached.[6] On 17 March 1824 the treaty was formally signed. The merchants of both nations were given the right to trade in the archipelago. No new settlements were to be made there without the previous authority of the Home Governments. Britain ceded Ben-

[1] I.O. Dutch Records, vol. xxx, March 1822.
[2] Ibid. 10 December 1823. Memo. by Courtenay.
[3] Ibid. 9 January 1824.
[4] Ibid. 15 January 1824.
[5] Ibid. 2 January 1824.
[6] I.O. Dutch Records, vol. xxxi.

coolen and all other British establishments and interests in Sumatra, and withdrew her objections to the Dutch occupation of Billiton. Holland cleared her debts to Britain by the payment of £100,000; she ceded Malacca and her establishments in India, and withdrew her objections to the British occupation of Singapore.

The treaty was recognised both in England and in Holland as a satisfactory solution of the questions at issue.[1] It is probable that Britain could have extorted harsher terms, but, as Canning told the House of Commons, "It was the interest of this country not to press too hard upon the Dutch Government."[2] Canning himself was quite content with the retention of Singapore.

Thus Raffles triumphed at last, and Great Britain reaped the fruit of his courage and foresight.

"I cannot deny", Canning wrote in 1824, "that your extreme activity in stirring up difficult questions, and the freedom with which you committed your government without their knowledge or authority to measures which might have brought a war upon them, unprepared, did at one time oblige me to speak my mind to you in instructions of no very mild reprehension. But I was not the less anxious to retain those fruits of your policy which appeared to me really worth preserving...."[3]

Singapore had in 1819 been granted to Raffles by Sultan Husain of Johore and the local chief who was actually ruling the island when the transfer was made. The Dutch alleged that Husain was not the rightful sultan, but a younger brother whom Raffles had recognised as sultan in order to obtain a grant. This view is supported by a letter written by Husain in 1827, admitting that he had been raised to the rank of sultan by the Company. Raffles however asserted that his grantor was the elder, not the younger brother.[4] It is unlikely that either party was particularly scrupulous on such a point. Raffles considered that his action was entirely justified by the fact that neither the Dutch nor any other European power had ever had a settlement on the island of Singapore; while the chiefs themselves could easily be made to assert whatever was asked of them by the nearest power. Raffles's grantors seem in the same year to have assured the Dutch that the settlement had been made by force and without their consent, and to have informed the English that they had only done so for fear of an attack from the Dutch.[5]

The original grant of 1819 bestowed upon the English the site for a factory together with an area within range of a cannon-shot around it. Special areas were to form the "compounds" of the Chinese and Malay inhabitants respectively, in accordance with the traditional mode of arranging a city frequented by peoples of various races and customs. The general management of the island was to be considered every Monday by a council consisting of the English chief or Resident,

[1] I.O. Dutch Records, vol. XXXI.   [2] Hansard, New Series, XI, 1443; 17 June 1824.
[3] Boulger, *op. cit.* p. 276.
[4] Wilkinson, R. J., *Peninsular Malays*, p. 79; *Memoir of Raffles*, pp. 397–8.
[5] Wilkinson, *op. cit.* p. 79.

the sultan, and his local representative, the two last being allowed to attend by deputy.[1] At the same time Raffles laid down a series of "general rules...conducive to the general interests of Singapore" and defining the rights of the several parties. These provided for the payment to the sultan and his representative of a monthly sum of 2300 dollars, in lieu of all claims on port dues, tribute, and monopolies. The Resident was to advance money to build "a respectable mosque" near the residence of the sultan. The sultan and his agent were relieved from the obligation of attending at the Monday meetings, though they were to receive a seat on the bench and all due respect whenever they thought fit to attend. In all cases regarding religious ceremonies, marriages, and inheritance, Malay custom was to be followed wherever not contrary to reason, justice, or humanity; and British law was to be enforced "with due consideration to the usages and habits of the people".[2] After a settlement had been reached with the Dutch, it was thought advisable to enter into a formal treaty with the sultan for the cession of the island in full sovereignty in return for a payment of 60,000 dollars and monthly stipends of 2000 dollars.[3]

Thus at last Great Britain became entitled to a dependency within the circle of the archipelago, and the Dutch claim to a complete monopoly of the commerce of that region was broken down. This result was the work of Raffles alone. He saw that the position of the Company outside the Straits could not secure to British subjects a share in the trade of the archipelago; his administration of Java had taught him the secrets of the Dutch trade; his arguments persuaded the Government of Lord Hastings both of the need of action and of the expediency of occupying some port within the Straits from which British trading interests could be guarded; and he chose Singapore as the site best suited to his purpose. The result was the appearance of a rival to Batavia, backed not by the great territorial possessions of the Dutch, but by the naval power of Great Britain and strong in its freedom from restrictions on trade such as the merchant encountered as soon as he set foot in the Dutch possessions. Raffles had repeatedly declared that conquest and military power formed no part of his projects. Nevertheless, the establishment of a great naval power at Singapore was inevitably followed by great political changes and provoked the jealousy of the power which had sought the paramountcy of the archipelago as sedulously as Great Britain had sought the paramountcy of India.

Accordingly the treaty of 1824 failed to produce that mutual understanding which had been its professed object. It had been accompanied by "a solemn disavowal on the part of the Netherland government of any design to aim either at political supremacy or at

---

[1] Agreement dated 26 June 1819, *ap.* Newbold, *op. cit.* 1, pp. 485 *seqq.*
[2] Newbold, *op. cit.* 1, pp. 487 *seqq.*
[3] *Ibid.* 1, pp. 490 *seqq.*

commercial monopoly in the eastern archipelago".[1] But almost at once British merchants began to complain that the Dutch were levying increased duties on their trade. Their contention was supported by the Board of Trade, which urged that the Dutch ought to be desired to withdraw the ordinance complained of.[2] The Dutch, in reply to Canning's remonstrance, pointed out that the treaty limited only the rate which might be imposed on foreign vessels, leaving both parties at liberty to lay what duties they chose upon foreign goods.[3] There for a while the matter rested; but in 1831 complaints began again, and, although Palmerston, now Foreign Minister, was disposed to agree with the view of the treaty taken by the Dutch, he nevertheless invited the Dutch "to make such modifications in the present tariff at Java as will place the commercial intercourse between Great Britain and that island upon the just and liberal footing contemplated by the treaty of 1824".[4]

Great Britain would have raised the question earlier but for the Belgian crisis which had made her unwilling to raise difficulties at such a juncture.[5] When the Dutch stood fast upon their former ground, Palmerston in 1835, acting on the advice of the Board of Trade, declared that the treaty had been grossly violated, and requested not only a change in the future but also restitution "of all that has been unjustly taken from our merchants upon imports under the British flag for some time past".[6] After some pressure the Dutch minister, Verstolk, at last gave way and agreed that, so long as Dutch industry did not require a greater degree of protection, the proportional duties should be levied on woollen and cotton goods in accordance with the provisions of the treaty in regard to shipping.[7] But, ever since the occupation of Singapore, the Dutch had been busily extending their control and binding the various chiefs of the archipelago to admit their trade on special terms. In 1841 Palmerston returned to the attack.

"For several years past," he wrote, "the Dutch authorities in India have acted in a spirit of hostility to British commerce entirely inconsistent with the spirit of the said treaty; and while, on the one hand, those authorities have endeavoured by various oppressive and vexatious regulations to exclude British commerce from all places in which Netherland authority is established, they have systematically continued to establish Netherland settlements (some of which are merely nominal) at a great variety of places at which no real sovereignty could be exercised by the Netherland government, but where considerable commercial intercourse had previously been carried on between British merchants and the natives of those places; and then the Netherland authorities, pretending to apply to such places all the vexatious and prohibitory regulations which have been promulgated by them for the real Netherland possessions in India, have endeavoured step by step to curtail and destroy British commerce with the natives of those quarters."[8]

[1] Note from the British to the Dutch plenipotentiaries, 17 March 1824 (*Parl. Pap.* 1840, XLIX, p. 11). [2] *Ibid.* p. 23. [3] *Ibid.* p. 27.
[4] *Ibid.* pp. 68, 71. [5] *Ibid.* p. 71. [6] *Ibid.* p. 117. [7] *Ibid.* p. 124.
[8] *Parl. Pap.* 1842, XXX, p. 145.

When questioned on this matter, Verstolk gave the Dutch treaty with Jambi as an example of the treaties which had been made of recent years. By this treaty, which was made in 1834, the sultan placed himself under the "protection and sovereignty of the Dutch Indian government". The navigation and trade were placed under Dutch control. The customs dues were to be brought into conformity with those levied at the Dutch settlement of Palembang, and the Dutch reserved a right of levying a special duty on all foreign salt imported.[1] Palmerston commented on this document as follows:

The Netherland Government imposes on the sultan of Jambi the obligation to levy within his ports the unequal duties, as regards British and Dutch commerce respectively, which are established by the Netherland tariff, instead of the equal duties formerly levied at Jambi on the trade of both nations, and thereby manifest injury is occasioned to British trade....You will therefore distinctly intimate to the Netherland Government that if that Government perseveres in the system it has adopted in the east, such a course must lead Her Majesty's Government to consider what measures may be best calculated to afford British commerce that protection which the proceedings of the Netherland Government will have rendered necessary.[2]

These discussions show what irreconcilable, and therefore hostile, systems Raffles's action had brought into contact in the archipelago. Both nations were eager to secure the largest possible share of the trade of the area. But while British interests would be served best by liberty of trade, the Dutch aimed at limiting to the greatest possible extent the activities of the intruders into their ancient domain. The temporary destruction of the Dutch power in the later years of the Napoleonic Wars had given Great Britain an opening in a region where till then her activities had been principally clandestine; and, once such an opening had been secured, it seemed utterly unreasonable to English merchants that the Dutch should be allowed to use the restoration of their former possessions in order to extend them to the detriment of English trade. The Dutch, on the contrary, considered that the settlement of 1814 restored the *status quo ante bellum*, and regarded Raffles's efforts first of all to extend British influence in Sumatra and then to establish the English at Singapore as an unjustifiable endeavour to take away the position which had been given back to them in 1814.

These irreconcilable views preventing any real harmony between the two nations, the English proceeded to show that the Dutch could not hope to enjoy any monopoly of expansion. James Brooke, son of a servant of the East India Company, had joined the Company's army and been wounded in the first Burmese War. He had then abandoned the Company's service, but had developed a strong interest in the East, in which he was destined to wield great influence. He made a voyage to China and then, in 1839, sailed eastwards again in a private yacht, the schooner *Royalist*. He visited Sarawak; in 1840 he assisted the rajah to put down a rebellion, and, in the next

[1] *Parl. Pap.* 1842, xxx, p. 168. [2] *Ibid.* p. 178.

year, he received the government of Sarawak under agreement with the rajah. He was to some extent assisted by H.M.S. *Dido*, under the command of Captain Keppel, and he was made Consul so as to invest him with an official position under the British Crown. In 1844, on reports of the existence of coal on the little island of Labuan, off the Sarawak coast, Captain Bethune, R.N., was commissioned to undertake enquiries as to the best site for a naval station in that neighbourhood.[1] In 1848, under treaty with the sultan of Northern Borneo, the island was occupied. To the Dutch these measures bore the same appearance as their own measures had borne in English eyes. They "broke the cordial understanding established between the two authorities in the east, and the right of the stronger replaced the balance of power which the treaty [of 1824] had aimed at setting up".[2] The Dutch Government protested in 1845; but Lord Aberdeen replied:

Under these circumstances Her Majesty's Government consider that they could not be justly accused of any infraction of the Treaty of 1824 if they were to form a settlement even on the coast of Borneo itself; and that they would only be following the example set to them by the Netherlands Government which has not hesitated to extend its political relations in this and such other portions of the Indian archipelago as are not by the treaty included among those within which no other Netherland settlement can be formed.[3]

The treaty had in fact limited new British settlements to the north of the line running through the Straits of Singapore, excluding by name certain islands in which the Dutch were specially interested.[4]

These acquisitions in Borneo brought the expansion of British power in the islands to a close. But the possession of Penang, of Singapore, and Malacca involved a growing interest and influence in the Malay Peninsula. Here the main difficulty lay not in the policy of the Dutch but in the undefined claims of Siam. At first British policy was directed to avoiding all entanglements. The Malacca Report of 1809 had demonstrated the ease with which the Malay rajahs might be made dependent, and even tributary, to the power in control of that fortress.[5] But Raffles was averse from any such movement. In instructions which he issued in 1820, for instance, he prohibited the acting resident at Singapore "from all intercourse with the Malay states in general which may be beyond courtesy and civility".[6] He certainly would not have tolerated any attempts on the part of the Dutch to set up their influence in the peninsula, and to that extent he regarded Great Britain as "the protecting authority" of the Malay states; but he sought no direct control over them. "Our commercial treaties",

[1] *Parl. Pap.* 1852–3, LXI, p. 313.
[2] Temminck, C. J., *Coup d'œil*, II, p. 441.
[3] *Parl. Pap.* 1854, LXXII, p. 60.
[4] Article 12 of the treaty of 1824.
[5] Egerton, *op. cit.* p. 24.
[6] Raffles to Travers, 24 March 1820 (India Office, Sumatra, no. 50).

he wrote in 1819, "will have for their object the free and safe navigation of the coasts and rivers and the security of intercourse at the
different ports, rather on a principle of responsibility than one of
direct check and control."[1] The treaties made with Perak, Selangor,
and Johore in 1818 illustrate this attitude.[2] They all declare perpetual
peace and friendship; they confer on British subjects the privileges
enjoyed by the most favoured nations; they prohibit the revival of
obsolete or interrupted treaties should these tend to the hindrance of
British trade; and they prohibit the grant of monopolies to any person.
But they contain no phrase suggesting that the East India Company
would ever guarantee the independence of the princes in question or
take them under its protection.

At that time British relations with Siam were difficult and uncertain.
The cessions to be required from Burma at the conclusion of the first
Burmese War (1824–6) had been closely considered with a view to
their possible transference to Siam in return for Kedah and other
territory in the Malay Peninsula.[3] Crawford, the resident at Singapore, thought that the war had brought an opportunity "to arrange
all our differences with the Siamese, to place our commercial intercourse both with that nation and Ava upon a liberal footing calculated
to open a new and extensive channel to British industry, and finally
to place us in an attitude which will afford us at little risk or expense
ample security against the future aggressions or arrogance of either
power".[4]

The trouble with Siam had emerged in consequence of troubles in
Kedah, the ruler of which had made the original grant of Penang
and of the small piece of territory on the mainland opposite the island,
known as Province Wellesley. This chief, like others established in the
Malay Peninsula, was claimed by Siam as a dependent ruler. But,
as was frequent in oriental relations, the degree of dependence was
uncertain. It varied from time to time with the strength of the chiefs
and that of the overlord. Nominally these Malay chiefs were "liable
to contributions in men, money, and provisions, when the Siamese
are at war". But the only regular mark of their subjection was the
despatch every three years of a golden flower in recognition of the
supremacy of the king of Siam.[5] In strict accordance with Eastern
laxity in such matters, the Siamese had never protested against the
transfer to the East India Company of territory by one of its dependent
chiefs.[6]

It seems highly probable that the cession of Penang to the Company
had been inspired by the hope that the rajah would thus secure the

---

[1] *On the Administration of the Eastern Seas in 1819*, p. 16.
[2] Aitchison, Sir C. V., *Treaties* (ed. 1909), vol. II, part VIII.
[3] Harrington's minute, 12 July 1825 (India Office, Home Misc. 666, p. 192).
[4] Despatch of 31 May 1824 (Home Misc. 663, pp. 223 *seqq.*).
[5] Crawford, J., *Embassy to Siam*, pp. 447–8.
[6] *Ibid.* p. 160.

protection of the British against the Siamese claims. In 1787 the Siamese were pressing the states of Kedah, Patani and Trengganu, demanding the personal appearance of the chief or his heir.[1] Light had sought the instructions of the Bengal Government as to the protection which he might promise to the chief of Kedah. Cornwallis replied: "The governor-general in council has already decided against any measures that may involve the Company in military operations against any of the eastern princes. It follows of course that any act or promise which may be construed into an obligation to defend the king of Quedah is to be avoided."[2] But at the same time Light was authorised within these limits to do what he could for the security of the little state. For some years the possibility that the Company would not look on inactively at any attack on Kedah seems to have restrained the Siamese. But in 1821, after a series of threats and demands, the Siamese at last invaded and conquered Kedah. The Penang Government stood neutral, to the great indignation of naval officers called upon to prevent the inhabitants and refugees in Penang and Province Wellesley from attacking the Siamese invaders. There was, too, a sharp divergence of opinion as to the action which should have been taken. Raffles thought that if a force had been sent to Kedah before the Siamese expedition had appeared, Kedah would never have been attacked.[3] But, as a member of the Penang council pointed out, such a course was impossible when the Bengal Government had "always declined sanctioning any interference with Siam and Quedah".[4]

Underlying the whole question was a broad matter of policy. In what degree was the Company prepared to undertake the responsibility of controlling the states of the Malay Peninsula? The Governor-General in 1825, Lord Amherst, recognised the evils which an extension of Siamese power would produce on the trade of the English settlements at Penang and Singapore. But he was not willing to act on his own responsibility.[5] The question was in some degree set at rest by the treaty which Burney succeeded in arranging with Siam in 1826. Siamese authority was recognised in Kedah, but the Siamese agreed to forego claims as of right against Perak, the sultan of which might "if he desired" continue to send to Bangkok the triennial gold flowers of subjection; and they also promised not to obstruct the trade in Trengganu or Kelantan, which they had repeatedly threatened.[6] The net effect of this arrangement was to exclude Siamese influence from the parts of the Malay Peninsula to the north and east of Singapore, and to leave a group of chiefs free

[1] See the letters to Light, ap. Marsden, op. cit. p. 155.
[2] Despatch, ap. Begbie, P. J., Malay Peninsula, p. 98.
[3] Memoir of Raffles, p. 507.
[4] Newbold, op. cit. II, pp. 7 seqq. and 16 n.
[5] Despatch to the Secret Committee, 4 September 1825 (Home Misc. 666, p. 659).
[6] Articles 12–14 of the treaty, Newbold, op. cit. I, pp. 460 seqq.

from the threat of Siamese expansion and looking to the British Government as their natural protector. The East India Company refused consistently to take the step of asserting any responsibility for their well-being, but even it at times was compelled by circumstances to intervene, and thus the way was prepared for the protectorate established by the Government of the Crown after the transfer in 1867.

Apart from operations in Naning, a dependency of Malacca, in 1830, undertaken to enforce the payment of an enlarged tribute,[1] the local troubles were confined to piracy and difficulties arising with the numerous Chinese immigrants who flocked both to the English settlements and to the Malay States. Piracy was the main occupation of various tribes of the archipelago, and much difficulty was at first found in suppressing it. The men-of-war stationed in the archipelago had not the speed necessary to catch the Malay praos; but in order to encourage their efforts, a reward of £20 a head for every pirate destroyed was offered and paid. Gradually, with the advent of steamships, which found coaling bases in Singapore and Sarawak, this pest was greatly reduced. In 1852 the coast of North Borneo, which had been infested with fleets of Dyak pirates, was reported to be safe for every boat. In this connection the establishment of British rule in Sarawak and Labuan did much to facilitate the sweeping of the seas.[2]

But another cause was economic. Dutch policy had deprived the chiefs of their accustomed profits by way of trade, and had thus driven them to seek gain by encouraging their subjects to embark on piratical raids, the profits of which were mainly secured by the seizure and sale of slaves. But the second and third quarters of the nineteenth century were marked by a considerable activity against the slave trade and the institution of slavery itself. Thus in 1823 Raffles issued a regulation at Singapore, declaring that since the place had only been acquired after the passing of the act prohibiting slave trade, all persons imported, bought or sold since 26 February 1819 were entitled to claim their liberty. The personal followers of the sultan of Johore or of chiefs visiting the place were excluded from this law except that they could not be bought or sold at Singapore, and the second class also would acquire rights to liberty if they resided within the island for a year. Steps were also taken to bring to an end the ancient institution of debtor-slaves.[3] At the same time a considerable development of trade occurred. The establishment of the British at Singapore prevented the expansion of the Dutch monopolist system, opened new markets, increased the demand for

[1] Cf. Newbold, *op. cit.* i, pp. 230 *seqq.*; Begbie, *op. cit.* pp. 134 *seqq.*, and Wilkinson, R. J., *Papers on Malay Subjects*, v, pp. 26 *seqq.*
[2] Moor, J. H., *Indian Archipelago*, pp. 15 *seqq.*; *Parl. Pap.* 1852–3, LXI, pp. 345 *seqq.* Cf. Owen Rutter, *The Pirate Wind*.
[3] The regulation is printed in *Memoir of Raffles*, appendix, p. 46.

commodities such as tin, and thus increased the resources of the Malay chiefs, and indirectly contributed to the reduction of both piracy and slave trading.

This economic development was not the work of British merchants only. They were greatly assisted by a large influx of Chinese settlers. The Chinese had always taken a considerable share in the trade of the archipelago. They had settled for instance in large numbers at Batavia, in other islands such as Borneo, and in the Malay Peninsula itself, for the most part in Singapore. This foreign element brought with it difficulties as well as advantages. The Chinese always tended to escape from the regular administration of the law. The Dutch, following the custom which they found prevalent in Malaya, required the Chinese to occupy a special quarter of Batavia, and appointed a headman, the "China capitan", to administer justice according to their own laws. The Chinese immigrants, according to the practice of their countrymen at home, organised themselves into societies embracing all persons coming from particular provinces; and these societies at times came into conflict with the persons appointed by the European government to administer their affairs. The Dutch from time to time fell into panic at the rapid increase of these immigrants, sometimes, as in 1740, slaughtering them without mercy or discrimination. Happily Singapore was never disgraced by such episodes. But in the Malay Peninsula incidents occurred which showed that Chinese settlers were not always to be regarded with trust. Thus, in September, 1834, some hundreds of Chinese tin-miners in Selangor rose on their Malay employers, set fire to their houses, and massacred the Malays. At the close of the period covered by the present chapter, trouble was brewing in Larut owing to the rivalry of two different Chinese societies.[1]

The organisation of the government of the British settlements in the archipelago was at first, and long remained, exceedingly defective. Until the abandonment of Sumatra in 1824, there were two governments, Penang, with Province Wellesley and Malacca, and Fort Marlborough with Singapore. At the head of each was a Lieutenant-Governor assisted by a council and acting under the orders of the Governor-General and council of Bengal. After the cession of Fort Marlborough to the Dutch, a period of uncertainty followed, but at last Singapore was added to the Penang Government. These arrangements did not permit the consolidation of the administrative ideas on which Singapore had been founded. Raffles desired earnestly to bring the English merchants inhabiting his new settlement into an organic relation with the official government. "I am satisfied", he wrote to the Government of Bengal, "that nothing has tended more to the discomfort and constant jarrings which have hitherto occurred

[1] Cf. Newbold, op. cit. I, pp. 12–14, II, p. 33; Wilkinson, op. cit. pp. 102 seqq.; Schlegel, G., Thian Ti hwui, passim; Memorandum on Chinese immigrants, Parl. Pap. 1859, XVI, p. 73.

in our remote settlements than the policy which has dictated the exclusion of the European merchants from all share, much less credit, in the domestic regulation of the settlement of which they are frequently its most important members."[1] In a private letter of the same period he speaks of having given the place "something like a constitution" and "fashioned all my regulations more with reference to the pure principles of the British constitution than upon the half-caste or country-born regulations of our Indian administration".[2]

With this object he had introduced a system by which the principal merchants were nominated justices of the peace and sat with the Resident, as the head of the government was at first called, in the administration of justice. These magistrates were also empowered to propose such regulations as they considered necessary to the Resident for his approval.[3] But almost as soon as this had been done, the union of Penang, Malacca and Singapore placed the last-named under the Recorder's Court which had been set up at Penang in 1807. This court consisted of a professional lawyer as Recorder, but the Governor of Penang and his three councillors were also members of the court with rank superior to that of the professional judge. In this respect the court differed considerably from the courts of the like name established at Madras and Bombay, where the Recorder had sat alone. The change was probably designed to prevent the conflicts which had arisen in India between the judiciary and the executive. But in the Straits Settlements, as the Penang group came to be called, it provoked bitter criticism on the part of the unofficial inhabitants, who felt that they were improperly excluded from all voice in the administration. They were indeed placed in the same position as private merchants occupied in India; and their attitude was much the same as that of British merchants at Calcutta or Madras. But in India the interests of the great territories attached to those centres of government obviously overweighed those of the European inhabitants. In the Straits no such counterbalance existed, and the normal attitude of the merchant of Singapore was one of constant hostility to the official rulers.[4]

Singapore certainly suffered much from neglect. It complained that its bridges and other public works were allowed to fall into decay, and that no money was forthcoming for the maintenance of a flotilla for the defence of shipping against pirates.[5] It was used as a convict settlement, but required by the Government of India to bear the charges of the maintenance of the convicts.[6] The development of

[1] Raffles to the Governor-General in council, 6 June 1823 (*Memoir of Raffles*, appendix, pp. 62 *seqq.*).
[2] *Ibid.* pp. 559–60.
[3] Regulations III and VI of 1823, *ap. Memoir of Raffles*, appendix, pp. 42 *seqq.*
[4] Cf. Newbold, *op. cit.* 1, pp. 27 *seqq.*; Crawfurd, *Embassy to Siam*, pp. 559–60; Low, *Dissertation on Penang*, pp. 236 *seqq.*
[5] Earl, G. W., *Eastern Seas*, pp. 405–6.
[6] Note by J. Crawfurd, 22 July 1858 (*Parl. Pap.* 1862, XL, p. 588).

trade led to growing relations with England rather than with India. The officials on whom the Government of India relied for advice knew nothing of the Malays or the Chinese, and Lord Canning in 1859 thought that the Straits Settlements would be staffed better from the Chinese consular service than from the Indian covenanted service. He observed too that although he had been required to report on more than one difficult question, only twice had he had an opportunity of discussing such matters with "officers who had had public experience of the affairs of the Straits Settlements".[1] Consequently the abolition of the East India Company's government in 1858 opened the way to a readjustment of the position. The Company would have bitterly opposed every effort to diminish the area entrusted to its control. But when India was transferred to the management of a department of the Queen's Government, the only question was whether the Straits Settlements would be administered better under the India Office or the Colonial Office. The inhabitants of Singapore were quick to observe the change which the abolition of the Company had made. In 1858 they petitioned the House of Commons, urging the immediate need of separation from India. "Ignorant apparently", they said, "of the many circumstances in which the Straits Settlements differ so widely from continental India, the supreme government has almost invariably treated them from an exclusively Indian point of view, and shown a systematic disregard of the wants and wishes of their inhabitants."[2] Moreover, in political affairs the local government had always been restricted "from interfering with matters beyond the limits of the island. The cultivation of friendly relations with native states and chiefs has been neglected, and Government does not possess that influence in the Indian archipelago which the interests of British commerce require". After prolonged discussions between the India Office, the Colonial Office and the Treasury, the proposed transfer was at last authorised by an Act of Parliament, under which the Straits Settlements were constituted as a separate government under the authority of the Colonial Office.[3]

For many years Singapore had been the heart of British interests in Malaya. Its growth during the forty-eight years between its foundation and its transfer to the Colonial Office had been remarkable indeed. The little settlement of perhaps 5000 people in 1819 was reckoned to have doubled in size before Raffles returned to England in 1824. Eleven years later the population is said to have risen to 30,000. The census of 1849 disclosed a population of 59,000, and that of 1860 one of 80,000. Trade had expanded in a like degree. In 1840 the exports and imports of the place were valued at four millions sterling. In 1867 they were valued at ten millions.

---

[1] Minute, 7 November 1859 (*Parl. Pap.* 1862, xl, p. 594).
[2] *Parl. Pap.* 1862, xl, p. 585.
[3] 29–30 Victoria, c. 115.

CHAPTER XVII

THE EXPLORATION OF AFRICA, 1783–1870.

APART from the conquest of the Cape from the Dutch, little actual expansion of the Empire took place in Africa in the period covered by this survey, but the story of exploration cannot be neglected, as it was pregnant with important political consequences at a later period. It is perhaps more than a coincidence that the beginnings of the New Empire synchronised to some extent with a new forward movement, which in the course of a century was to reveal the broad features of the geography of the vast, previously almost unknown, interior of Africa. Before tracing in outline the story of this great outburst of activity, it is desirable to glance briefly at the state of European knowledge of Africa at the opening of the period.

A superficial study of a long succession of maps, made in the sixteenth and seventeenth centuries, in which the whole interior of the southern half of Africa is filled with geographical details, has led some to suppose that a large part had been then explored by the Portuguese who held the coasts. This is certainly a mistake, since we can trace the gradual development of the picture so presented through the addition of hearsay information, mostly relating to Abyssinia, to the framework supplied by Ptolemy's map in the second century A.D. The distortion is seen at its worst, perhaps, in a map of 1623 preserved at the Vatican, in which the Blue Nile system is brought down almost to the borders of Cape Colony. In the north the case was somewhat different, for some knowledge of the Sudan had filtered through, not only from the writings of Arab geographers, but from actual intercourse of European commercial agents, especially Genoese, as early as the fifteenth century, as has been demonstrated by the researches of M. de la Roncière.[1] In the north-east the Nile, and the problems surrounding its origin, had lured adventurers to its upper reaches, and even in Roman times Nero's agents are supposed to have pushed as far as the *Sudd* region of the White Nile.

In the rest of the continent the advance had been restricted to one or two isolated regions. In Abyssinia, Portuguese Jesuit missionaries discovered the source of the Blue Nile quite early in the seventeenth century, and they and their successors made this kingdom one of the best-known parts of the continent, the Nile route being used as a means of access as well as the shorter way from the Red Sea coast. Abyssinia too was the scene of the famous journeys of the

La Roncière, C. de, *Découverte de l'Afrique au Moyen-Age.*

Scotsman James Bruce (1769–73) at the opening of the modern period. Elsewhere the greatest advance in early days was in the region of Congo and Angola, where travellers like the Dutchman Jan van Herder (1642) and the Capuchin missionary Girolamo de Montesarchio (1659) had penetrated to the neighbourhood of Stanley Pool and the lower Kwango,[1] while others had reached the headwaters both of the Kwango and the Kwanza farther south. In the region of the Zambesi Portuguese agents had visited the country of the Kalanga chief known as the Monomotapa (in the present Mashonaland), though the grandiose scheme for the conquest of the gold region of Manika under F. Barreto in 1569 had been a miserable failure.[2] North of the Lower Zambesi information about Lake Nyasa and its outlet by the Shiré had been obtained by the Jesuit Mariana as early as 1624,[3] the lake appearing thenceforth on the best maps down to its actual discovery in 1859.

Some advance, too, had been made in the Senegal region by the French (especially La Courbe and Brue, from about 1685 on[4]), and by the Englishman Richard Jobson on the Gambia, while in South Africa Dutch exploration of the interior had been begun in the seventeenth century by the great expedition of Van der Stel (1685–86).[5] It was continued later by Coetsee, Hop, the Van Reenens, R. J. Gordon, and the Englishman, William Paterson, so that at the beginning of our period the basin of the Orange River was fairly well known, while pioneers had also pushed to the north of it. But all these explorations had hardly touched more than the fringe of the unknown, while in many parts, especially in Guinea and the region behind Zanzibar, all but the actual coast-line was still virgin ground. In the improved cartography of the eighteenth century represented by the work of the great French map-makers Delisle and D'Anville, the imaginary geography of the interior was at last swept away, it being now realised that the filling up of the centre had been due to great exaggeration of the distances covered by travellers in the neighbourhood of the coasts. The wide blank spaces in the best of the newer maps represent pretty faithfully the vast field which lay open to the pioneers of the new period.

The founding, in 1788, of the African Association (developed out of the "Saturday's Club"), which marks the beginning of systematic exploration in that continent, was itself in part the outcome of the earlier movement which led to the voyages of Captain James Cook; for Sir Joseph Banks, who had been closely concerned in those voyages, was one of the founders. The first problem attacked was

[1] Dapper, *Afrikaens. Gewesten* (Amsterdam, 1676), p. 217 and map opp. p. 184; Avelot, R., *Une Exploration oubliée* (*La Géographie*, XXVI (1912), 319–28).
[2] See *C.H.B.E.*, VIII, 96–9.
[3] Schurhammer, G., in *Stimmen der Zeit* (1920), Heft 4.
[4] Cultru, P., *Premier voyage du Sieur de la Courbe...en 1685*.
[5] Waterhouse, G., *Simon van der Stel's Journal*, 1685–6.

that of the course and termination of the Niger, which had long
exercised the minds of geographers. From quite early times the
existence, south of the Sahara, of a great river with a generally
east-and-west course, had been known, but while some held it to
flow westward to the Senegal, others correctly believed it to flow
to the east, but imagined that it must either join the Nile, or end in a
central lake or swamp. Its actual mouths had been visited from the
sea, but the network of interlacing streams and unhealthy mangrove-
swamps of the delta had been unfavourable to penetration from this
side.

The Association's first efforts were directed from the north and
north-east. It quickly enlisted the services of John Ledyard, an
enterprising American who had already traversed the whole extent
of Northern Asia, and who started for Egypt with a view to crossing
North Africa from east to west in the latitude of the supposed
course of the Niger; and of William Lucas,[1] who had gained experience of African life in Morocco, and was commissioned to cross the
desert from north to south through Fezzan. But Ledyard died at the
outset of the journey and Lucas was forced to return without even
leaving the coast of Tripoli, though not before he had gathered
valuable information on the Sudan countries. The next agent,
F. Hornemann, made a successful journey from Cairo to Murzuk in
Fezzan in 1798, and, setting out again from Tripoli in 1800, succeeded
in crossing the desert to the region between Lake Chad and the Niger,
but died in Nupe not far from that river, and the circumstances of his
death have been only partially cleared up.[2]

From the west, the problem was attacked in 1791 by Major
Daniel Houghton, who made his way some 500 miles inland through
the basins of the Gambia and Senegal in the hope of reaching the
famed emporium of Timbuktu. But being plundered of all his goods
by Moorish robbers he too came to a miserable end. Four years
later the Association secured the services of a young Scottish surgeon,
Mungo Park, destined to gain fame as the first of great African
explorers, though he too perished before his work was completed.
Following in Houghton's footsteps in 1795, he pushed into the unknown with but a few followers, and in the face of difficulties and
dangers of all kinds showed a fortitude and determination never
surpassed in the history of exploration. Robbed and made captive
by the fanatical Moors north of the Senegal, he escaped in a state of
utter destitution, but pushed stubbornly on, supported by native
charity, till at last he was rewarded by the sight of the Niger at Segu,
and once for all demonstrated its eastward flow. He advanced some
way down the river, but was then forced to turn back, reaching the

---

[1] There appears to be some doubt as to this man's Christian name.
[2] Hornemann, F., *Travels to Mourzouk* (London, 1802); Pahde, A., *Der erste Deutsche Afrikaforscher* (Hamburg, 1895); also note in *Globus*, LXXXIX (1906), 316.

coast after further adventures by a more southerly route than that previously taken, and finally landing at Falmouth in December 1797.

Park's story aroused universal interest, but for several years nothing further was done to prosecute discovery, Park marrying and settling down in Scotland. But the lure of Africa proved too strong for him. The African Association having obtained Government support for a new venture, he was put in command of a far larger and better equipped expedition than the first, the personnel being made up, unfortunately, entirely of white men (soldiers for the most part), who fell easy victims to the unhealthy climate. Park was efficiently supported by his brother-in-law, Alexander Anderson, whose death soon after reaching the Niger was a serious blow to him. From the Gambia the more direct southerly route was adopted, and for a time all went well, but with the advent of the rains many of the party fell ill and by the time the Niger was reached at Bamaku three-fourths of the escort had succumbed. Having gained Sandandig in Bambarra, Park constructed a larger vessel by joining two canoes together, and having sent home his journal by his guide Isaaco, started with his diminished party, determined to navigate the great river to its end or perish. This was in November 1805, and for several years nothing was heard of the explorer, whose fate was in the end only partially cleared up through the enquiries of the guide Isaaco. Considering the unfavourable conditions in which the voyage was begun it seems to have been surprisingly successful for a time, as the river was traced for hundreds of miles round its great northern bend and by its farther southward course as far as the Bussa rapids in about 10° N. Here disaster overtook the party, their vessel being wrecked during the attempt to pass the rapids, and all but a native slave perished.[1] The fruit of Park's heroic efforts was thus to a large extent lost, though the information which filtered through was enough to show how important a contribution he had made towards solving the problem of the Niger's course.

But the great river's ending was still a mystery. The supposed great range of the Kong Mountains was thought to bar its direct southward passage, and while some, like Major James Rennell, had believed it to end in a central lake or swamp, others (among them Park when setting out on his last journey) imagined that it must make a vast sweep to the east and south, and ultimately join the Congo, greatest of African rivers. As the African Association found it impossible to continue its efforts, the British Government took up the quest, and in 1816 organised two large expeditions, the one, under Major John Peddie, being commissioned to follow in Park's steps from the side of the Upper Niger, the other, under Capt. J. H. Tuckey, to attempt the ascent of the Congo from its mouth. Both

---

[1] On the circumstances of Park's death see *Geog. Journal*, LVII (1921), 130; LXXV (1930), 95.

proved disastrous, disease and death wrecking them before results of any value had been gained. Tuckey's advance was checked by the furious cataracts of the Lower Congo, and for over half a century his "farthest"—less than 150 miles from its mouth—marked the limit of positive knowledge of the great river. No new advance had been made towards solving the Niger problem on the ground, but by this time it had become clear to those who studied the evidence at home (e.g. Reichard in Germany in 1802 and subsequently James Macqueen in Great Britain) that its only possible termination could be the network of interlacing creeks at the head of the Gulf of Guinea.

But the British Government had become fully alive to the importance of opening up North Central Africa to legitimate commerce, and in 1818 a new attempt was made from the north, by the caravan route starting from Tripoli, where Great Britain had an energetic representative in Col. G. H. Warrington. The leader of the expedition, Joseph Ritchie, succumbed to fever on reaching Murzuk, but his companion, Capt. G. F. Lyon, went to the southern borders of Fezzan and collected useful information about the Sudan. In 1821 a large expedition was organised under the joint command of Major Dixon Denham, Capt. Hugh Clapperton and Dr W. Oudney, to try once more the passage of the Sahara by way of Murzuk. This was successfully accomplished, and when the inhospitable desert was at last left behind, the expedition (February 1823) discovered Lake Chad (then a larger body of water than at present), and entered into friendly relations with the Sultan of Bornu on its western shores. Trips to the west and south shed light on the geography of the neighbouring regions, and on one of these Denham reached the Shari, the chief feeder of the lake, finding it an imposing stream 400 yards wide—a welcome sight to one used to the arid regions of the north. Clapperton and Oudney set out together for the important commercial centre of Kano, but the latter died en route (January 1824), Clapperton going on alone and also visiting Sokoto, in which city the Fulah conquerors of this region had lately established themselves. A farther advance towards the Niger proved impossible, and the expedition started to recross the desert in September 1824, reaching Tripoli early in 1825. A large tract of unknown ground had been explored for the first time, the rumoured interior lake at last brought to light, and a virtual proof obtained that the Niger could end only in the Gulf of Guinea.

Encouraged by the success of this expedition, and by the hopes held out of opening up a profitable intercourse with the teeming countries of the Central Sudan, the Government decided to send out Clapperton once more, to attempt to trace the Niger upwards from the sea. On arriving at the Guinea coast Clapperton decided to avoid the fever-laden swamps of the delta and to start from firmer ground to the west, near Lagos, whither Hausa caravans from the Sudan often made their way, and the coast was left in December 1825. Fever soon carried off two of the Europeans of the party, but Clapperton pushed on with his servant Richard Lander through Yoruba-land, and struck the Niger near the Bussa rapids where Park had lost his life. Thence he went on to Kano and Sokoto, but, disheartened by the hostile reception now given him, he too at length succumbed to fever in April 1827. After a vain attempt to find the Niger to the south, Lander returned to the coast by the previous route. He now became fired with the ambition of completing his master's task, and prevailed on the Government to send him out once more. Starting with his brother John early in 1830, he again made his way to Bussa and, obtaining canoes with some difficulty, traced the previously unknown part of the Niger's course to its outlet in the ocean, and the main problem connected with that river was thus at last completely solved.

Further efforts were now directed to the opening up of commercial relations with the native states, but even on this side little success was attained by the expedition of Laird, Allen and Oldfield in 1832–33, or by the grandiose Government expedition of 1841, though on the former the great eastern tributary of the Niger—the Benue—was explored for some distance. Further exploration of both main river and tributary was carried out by the more successful expedition of Dr W. B. Baikie in 1854. The expeditions of 1841 and 1854 were both accompanied by Samuel Crowther, a native African convert to Christianity, who afterwards took a foremost part in establishing the Niger Mission of the Church Missionary Society, and became the first native bishop in 1864.

Meanwhile two more journeys to the upper Niger had been made from the north and west. Major Gordon Laing, who in 1822 had pushed some way inland from Sierra Leone, left Tripoli in 1825 in the hope of reaching Timbuktu from this side. He succeeded in overcoming all obstacles (though very severely wounded in the desert during an attack by Tuareg raiders) and reached his goal in August 1826. But he aroused the suspicion of the rulers and, being forced to leave, was treacherously murdered two days later.[1] His papers were not recovered, and the circumstances attending his death were not fully unravelled until the present century. Soon afterwards Timbuktu was reached from the west by the French traveller René Caillié, who attached himself, disguised as a native, to a trading caravan. After a short stay in the city he once more joined a caravan to cross the desert to the north in the most inhospitable of all its sections, reaching the southern borders of Morocco

---

[1] Mézières, B. de, "Major G. Laing and the circumstances attending his death" (*Geog. Journal*, xxxix (1912), 54–7).

after extreme sufferings from thirst, and continuing across the Atlas range to Tangier. The whole width of the Western Sahara was not again crossed by a European for a full half-century.

More than twenty years after Laing's journey the British Government once more took up the task of opening up the Central Sudan from the north. An expedition was organised under James Richardson, who had already travelled in the desert in 1845–46, and the Government arranged that he should be accompanied by the German traveller and archaeologist Dr Heinrich Barth, who had already done much work in the Mediterranean borderlands and was particularly well qualified for ethnological and geographical research in the countries to be visited. A second German, the young geologist Dr Overweg, also joined the expedition, which left Tripoli in March 1850 and reached the borders of the Hausa country early in 1851, having, from Murzuk, taken the western route *via* Aïr. The travellers separated with a view to covering more ground, intending to meet in Bornu, but Richardson, whose health had for some time been precarious, died in March without reaching the capital. After doing some useful work in conjunction with his compatriot, Overweg too fell a victim to the climate, and Barth was left eventually to continue the work alone. For this he proved himself entirely competent, his untiring researches into the geography, history and ethnology of the greater part of the Central Sudan yielding results surpassing those of any previous traveller. In the south-west he visited the Sultanate of Adamawa and struck the upper course of the great eastern tributary of the Niger; in the south-east he visited Baghirmi and explored the Shari system; and in the north-east passed round the north of Lake Chad to Kanem. Then, turning west, he crossed the Niger at Say and made his way through unknown districts within its great bend to Timbuktu, returning along the course of the river, previously followed in this section only by Park in his fatal descent to Bussa. Practically the whole course of the river from source to mouth was thus laid down on the map. When staying in the capital of Bornu before recrossing the Sahara to return to Europe, Barth encountered a young and enthusiastic compatriot in the person of Dr E. Vogel, who had been sent out by the British Government to supplement the work of the expedition by careful astronomical observations. He remained in the country some time longer, but early in 1856 was assassinated by order of the Sultan of Wadai, to whose capital he had made his way from Lake Chad.

Valuable as were the results of Barth's researches, they were not followed up by the British Government, and not till many years later did private enterprise finally establish British influence in the region between Lake Chad and the Lower Niger.

Apart from the solving of the Niger problem, little progress was made in the first three-quarters of the nineteenth century towards a better knowledge of the West African hinterland. In Senegal something was done by the French. In 1844–45 and 1846–48 A. Raffenel carried out two missions for the Minister of Marine, during the first of which he surveyed the Faleme, the southern upper branch of the Senegal, and he became deeply impressed with the importance to France of this route into the interior. Somewhat later (1863–66) M. E. Mage and C. Quentin pushed on to Segu on the Upper Niger.[1] In 1850 M. Panet attempted to cross the Western Sahara from the Senegal to Algeria, but could only reach Morocco. From the opposite direction some advance into the desert south of Algeria resulted from the journeys of H. Duveyrier.

In British territory, the Gambia was ascended almost to the Baraconda fall by Governor Ingram in 1842,[2] but this had already been passed by Richard Jobson in 1620.[3] In 1841 an agent of the Church Missionary Society, W. C. Thomson, went inland under the orders of the Governor of Sierra Leone, reaching Timbo in Futa Jallon.[4] Behind the Gold Coast, T. E. Bowdich had carried out a mission to the Ashanti capital, Kumasi, on behalf of the local authorities, as early as 1817,[5] and had been followed the next year by J. Dupuis,[6] an agent of the Home Government, but the objects of both were treaty-making rather than exploration. Farther east, the enterprising traveller John Duncan made his way through Dahomé to Adafudia in the far interior, but he seems to have somewhat exaggerated the distance covered.[7] On visiting the mouth of the Volta, the largest river of this part of Africa, he was impressed with its importance, but it was not explored till many years later. East of the Niger delta, Capt. J. Becroft ascended the Old Calabar River over 200 miles in a merchant steamer, the *Ethiope*, in 1843, but farther progress was then stopped by rapids, and nothing more was done in this direction for many years.[8] While acting as British Consul at Fernando Po in 1861 and the following years Sir Richard Burton carried out an exploration of the Cameroon Mountains and a mission to Dahomé, described in two interesting books.

Farther south, in the region of the equator, a more important advance was made in the next decade by the French-American traveller Paul du Chaillu, starting from the French settlement of the Gaboon, where his father acted as agent for a trading company. By his first important journey, begun in 1855 on behalf of the

[1] Mage, T. E., *Voyage dans le Soudan occid.* (Paris 1868).
[2] *J. R. Geog. Soc.* xvii (1847), 150.
[3] Jobson, R., *The Golden Trade* (London, 1623).
[4] *J. R. Geog. Soc.* xvi (1846), 106.
[5] Bowdich, T. E., *Mission to Ashantee* (London, 1819).
[6] Dupuis, J., *Residence in Ashantee* (London, 1824).
[7] Duncan, J., *Travels in W. Africa, 1845–46*, 2 vols. (London, 1847).
[8] *J. R. Geog. Soc.* xiv (1844), 260.

American Academy—he had gone to the United States in 1852—he shed the first clear light on the system of the great Ogowé River, besides studying the gorilla in its natural haunts and collecting much information on the native tribes. On the publication of a vivid narrative of his journey in 1861, his veracity was quite unjustly impugned, and he set out again in 1863, determined to do still better work and so silence his critics. He met with various disasters, but covered some new ground, and laid the foundation of better mapping of the region by astronomical observations.[1]

As a precursor of the many German explorers who interested themselves somewhat later in the interior south of the Congo, the ethnologist, A. Bastian, made a journey to the capital of the native kingdom of Congo in 1857.[2]

As in North-West Africa the course of exploration was closely bound up with the Niger problem, so in the north-east the ancient riddle of the Nile source was responsible in a large measure for the progress of geographical knowledge. But whereas the lower course and mouth of the Niger were the last parts to become known, the progress of exploration having been mainly down-stream, the earlier exploration of the Nile naturally started from the ancient seat of civilisation traversed by its lower course. In 1798–1800 the work of the savants attached to Bonaparte's Egyptian expedition did something to extend the knowledge of the lower parts of its basin, and the rise to power of Mehemet Ali in 1805 gave a new impulse to exploration farther inland. In 1813 John Ludwig Burckhardt, a Swiss agent of the African Association, crossed the Nubian desert from Korosko to Abu Hamad, pushing on to Berber and Shendi before striking east to the Red Sea at Suakin. West of the Nile Valley the Libyan desert and its oases were explored by a number of travellers from 1818 on. This was not altogether new ground, for it had been traversed by the Jesuit agents Poncet, Brevedent, and Du Roule in the late seventeenth and early eighteenth centuries, as well as by the Bavarian monk, Pater Krump, sent in 1700 by Pope Innocent XII to convert the Emperor of Abyssinia. Nearly a century later (1793) the Englishman, W. G. Browne, followed the desert caravan route west of the Nile on his adventurous journey to Darfur. Of the later travellers, the Frenchman F. Cailliaud made extensive journeys in this region, visiting the Great (Kharjeh) Oasis in 1818, and subsequently (1819–20), with his compatriot Letorzek, making the round of all the oases, including that of Siwa in the north. In 1819 also the Englishman, Archibald Edmonstone, struck south-west from the Nile to the Dakhla Oasis, returning by that of Kharjeh. In the north German travellers shared in the work,

---

[1] Besides his own works, see obituary by E. G. Ravenstein, *Geog. Journal*, XXI (1903), 680 with portrait.
[2] Bastian, A., *Afrikanische Reisen* (Bremen, 1859).

an expedition under Baron von Minutoli visiting Siwa in 1820, while in 1824–25 more extended journeys were made by the French traveller J. R. Pacho, who in the latter year followed the desert route through Siwa to the more western oases south of the Mediterranean coast.[1]

At the same time a distinct advance was made on the Nile itself. In 1821 Cailliaud and Letorzek reached the junction of the Blue and White Niles in the train of an Egyptian military expedition and gave the first clear intimation of the importance of the White river in the economy of the system. In 1827 Linant de Bellefonds, another emissary of the African Association, pushed up this branch almost to 13° and formed the opinion that it must take its rise in lakes rather than in a supposed east-to-west mountain range. In 1824 the German, Eduard Rüppell, had visited Kordofan, occupied the year before by the Egyptians, and between 1837 and 1839 the Austrian mining expert, Russegger, made important journeys both in Southern Kordofan and on the Blue Nile. In Abyssinia, too, explorers of various nationalities were busy, and added in detail to the knowledge gained many years before by the Portuguese Jesuits and others, and more recently through James Bruce's travels. In 1809–10 the Englishman, Henry Salt, made journeys in the northern interior on behalf of the British Government, and his narrative, published in 1814, was long the standard English book on the country. Later, the work was continued by the Frenchmen, Combes and Tamisier (1835–36), Lefebvre, Ferret, and Galinier (1839–43) and especially by the brothers D'Abbadie, who between 1837 and 1848 carried out an extensive triangulation and thus supplied the first scientific basis for the mapping of a large part of Abyssinia. The Nile watershed was crossed to the south, and the country of Kaffa, on the upper waters of the Juba, visited. The head streams of this river had been struck in the early seventeenth century by the Portuguese traveller Antonio Fernandez, but its ultimate destination remained a mystery, not finally solved till the last decade of the nineteenth century. On the English side the journeys of Dr Charles Beke (1840–43) deserve mention, while the long residence in the country of the Italian missionary, Guglielmo Massaja, permitted the collection of much valuable material, eventually embodied in a monumental work in eleven big volumes.

A further important step in Nile exploration was made in 1840–41 by two expeditions fitted out by Mehemet Ali. The second of these, in which the Frenchmen, D'Arnaud and Sabatier, and the German, Ferdinand Werne, took part, pushed south past the *Sudd* region to beyond 5°, being then stopped by the rapids at Gondokoro, which remained a hindrance to any decided further advance for some

[1] Minutoli, as his name indicates, came of an old Italian family, a member of which had settled in Germany.

covenanting thenceforward to pay the rent for the leased lands to the Ashantis instead of the Fantis. By this treaty it was acknowledged that Fanti Land, including Cape Coast Castle and all the neighbouring English posts, belonged exclusively by right of conquest to the King of Ashanti. On their side the Ashantis promised not to interfere with the English so long as they remained neutral and did not enter into native quarrels.

The steps taken to enforce the Act for the Abolition of the Slave Trade (1807) were of vital importance in the history of West Africa, since for nearly sixty years that history centres round the measures taken to suppress the oversea trade in slaves. The local slave trade between the negro tribes went on as before and nothing could be done to put it down. British efforts for many years were necessarily confined to the sea, and it was upon the shoulders of the navy that the burden of suppression was laid.

The period between the granting of a new Charter of Justice to Sierra Leone in 1800 and the coming into force of the Abolition Act in 1807 was critical in the history of that colony. The Admiralty despatched an expert officer to examine the colony as a base for the defence of the trade routes in the Atlantic against French privateers.[1] He made a very adverse report upon its condition, and it was ultimately decided that its government by a Company must be brought to an end and that the Crown must assume direct responsibility. An Act of Parliament to effect the transfer was passed in 1807 and the actual surrender took effect on 1 January 1808. The traders who had held shares in the Company went on with their own ventures individually, while the philanthropists turned to different means to carry out their schemes for the civilisation of Africa.

To what extent had the Company achieved the purposes for which it had been founded fifteen years before? As a commercial venture it had failed, for the whole of its capital had been lost and the subscribers had not even received interest on their investments. Yet much had been accomplished, and the experiment takes an essential place in the history of British enterprise in tropical Africa. It marked a new departure in the sphere of colonisation. Nowhere else had a colony been established in which negro freemen had full civil rights, and could exercise simple political rights in a way that black men had never done before. They had sat as keen and intelligent jurymen, and when given clear and steady direction they had shown that they could make good and dependable settlers on the land. Individual settlers had made new homes for themselves round Freetown under the British flag, and thus for the first time a real British settlement had been established on the coast of tropical Africa in radical contrast to the so-called West African 'settlements', which, as we have seen,

---

[1] For the naval situation see chapter III and Rose, J. H., *Man and the Sea*, pp. 245 *seqq.*

were not true settlements at all but mere trading posts surviving only by the sufferance of savages. Sierra Leone had started on an untrodden road.

During the short life of the Sierra Leone Company there appeared a new factor in the development of British enterprise in tropical Africa which has had a vital influence upon its direction—the great missionary societies. In the course of twenty years of hard fighting for the abolition of the slave trade the humanitarians acquired a special and unique knowledge of colonial problems. Untouched by motives of personal gain such as moved the merchants, they were actuated solely by religious and philanthropic principles that won them the respect of Parliament and society. The inspirers of the movement were men of wide interests and connections, but they were specially remarkable for their fervent attachment to the principles of evangelical religion, and it was among those who were filled with the zeal of the revival movement that they found their most loyal supporters. Their hatred of the slave trade was excited not only by the sufferings of its victims but by the feeling that the negroes were fellow human beings to whom the gospel had been denied. The campaigns for abolition and for the evangelisation and civilisation of the African were intimately connected because the leaders of both were drawn from the same group. While the London Missionary Society (1795) found its principal field of work in South Africa, the Church Missionary Society (1799), whose official name was "the Society for Missions to Africa and the East", from the beginning turned interest to the West Coast.[1]

One of the most serious difficulties the Society had to face was the lack of English candidates for work in the mission field, and the first mission in West Africa was established with two German "missionary catechists" on the Rio Pongas outside the colony of Sierra Leone. In the troubles between the colony and its neighbouring enemies, the slave traders, the mission was attacked and destroyed and the first effort to evangelise the native tribes thus came to a rapid end.

The first phase of the history of anti-slave-trade negotiations[2] may be said to end in 1818, when at last they seemed to have produced some tangible results in a network of treaties. Cynical observers sneered that the promises were not worth the paper they were written on, and events in African waters proved that they were right. The construction and working of practical machinery to carry out the prohibitions was the crucial test and it has left a permanent mark on the government of African dependencies.

The influence of the abolitionist group was even more powerful in this field than in that of diplomacy. In the domestic and colonial sphere their pressure was continuous, and Zachary Macaulay was

[1] Stock, E., *History of the Church Missionary Society*, I, 69.
[2] For a summary account of the diplomatic negotiations see *C.H.B.F.P.* II, 235-247.

not far from the truth when he told the Governor of Sierra Leone in 1807: "I have no doubt that Government willl be disposed to adopt almost any plan which we may propose to them with respect to Africa, provided we will but save them the trouble of thinking."[1] From the beginning it was determined to base the preventive system on Sierra Leone which lay close to the worst centres of slave trading north of the equator. Though taken over as a Crown colony on 1 January 1808, as we have seen, its affairs were still in practice largely influenced by certain of the old directors of the Company, and they planned to combine two purposes—the civilisation of the colony and the suppression of slaving.

In accordance with Macaulay's advice,[2] action was attempted along three lines, (1) naval sloops were ordered to West African waters with instructions to intercept slavers, whether sailing under British, allied or enemy flags, and to bring them into Sierra Leone for trial, (2) a Vice-Admiralty Court was set up there, for, otherwise, the captured vessels would have to be taken to England or the West Indies for adjudication, and (3) arrangements were made for landing captured slave cargoes in the colony, where the negroes might either be absorbed into its body of free labour, recruited for the West Indian regiments or restored to their original homes. At the same time instructions were issued to the naval officers on the station to get into touch with the native chiefs along the African coast, to explain to them the civilising purpose behind the Abolition Act and to demonstrate the advantages they would derive from legitimate commerce. Even thus early, plans were made to conclude treaties with the chiefs by which they would pledge themselves to put down slave trading in their territories,[3] but it was long before this policy could be attempted in earnest.

Theoretically these measures could not have been improved upon, but to carry them out satisfactorily in practice was extraordinarily difficult, and the story of the suppression of the trade in African waters resolves itself into a series of unsuccessful experiments and the difficulties they placed on the devoted shoulders of our colonial officials. The idea of effecting anything through the coast chiefs did not succeed for many years, though ultimately it proved the most effective means of all.

For the ten years preceding 1807 it was calculated that about 80,000 slaves drawn from all parts of the African coast were annually exported across the Atlantic. More than an eighth of the number came from the coast between the Senegal and Cape Palmas, near the middle of which lies Sierra Leone. Less than one-eighth came

[1] C.O. 267/25. Macaulay to Governor Ludlam, 4 November 1807.
[2] C.O. 267/24. Macaulay to Castlereagh, Col. Sec., 8 May 1807.
[3] Ad. 2/1364. 10 November 1807. Instructions to Capt. Parker of H.M.S. *Derwent*, despatched to West Africa.

in West Africa. Captured slave ships and their cargoes were brought there for trial and the resulting condemnations introduced large and increasing numbers of 'liberated Africans'[1] into the colony and presented its Governors with the most difficult problem with which they had to deal.

The erection in Africa of a Court of Vice-Admiralty with prize jurisdiction had been suggested in the early years of the European war, but it was not until 1808 that it was set up after consultation with James Stephen, the legal adviser to the Colonial Office. The letters patent named the Chief Justice of Sierra Leone as judge, and to this post Robert Thorpe was appointed. He had held high judicial office in Upper Canada and had caused much trouble there,[2] so that Macaulay was strongly opposed to his selection. Thorpe was very reluctant to leave England to take up his duties, and it was not until questions had been raised in the House of Commons as to the cause of his delay that he at length sailed for Sierra Leone in 1811. Meanwhile, the work of the Admiralty judge had been left to the Governor, a soldier by profession, or to a merchant and store-keeper in the town, neither of whom was a trained lawyer. The decisions they gave in prize cases may have done rough justice, but they were reached by roads where little attention was paid to legal propriety. When Thorpe, with his accustomed quarrelsomeness, wished to attack the actions of his predecessors and through them their patrons, the African Institution, he could find ample material.

Immediately after the assumption of direct responsibility by the Crown an Order-in-Council was issued by which the Governor of Sierra Leone was authorised to receive and protect negroes landed from slave-ships that were condemned by the Court of Vice-Admiralty.[3] They might either be enlisted in the armed forces of the Crown or apprenticed to settlers for terms not exceeding fourteen years. Their numbers soon proved too great to be dealt with in this way, and, with the approval of Lord Bathurst, Governor Maxwell began to establish them on unoccupied lands in the Sierra Leone Peninsula with an allowance from government stores for their maintenance. Thenceforward these settlements of 'liberated Africans' were a constant drain on the funds supplied from the British Exchequer towards the expenses of government.

When Senegal and Goree were returned to France under the provisions of the Treaty of Paris, the transfer was carried out under the command of Lieut.-Col. Charles Macarthy, who after its completion was appointed Governor of Sierra Leone and the chief representative of the Crown in all the West African settlements (1814). He held the appointment for ten years, a longer term of office than

---

[1] 'Liberated Africans' was a technical term much used in the subsequent discussions.
[2] Dunham, A., *Political Unrest in Upper Canada*, pp. 115, 145, 163, 168.
[3] Order-in-Council, 16 March 1808.

that enjoyed by any Governor, and he has an important place in the history of the region. Macarthy was a man of extraordinary activity and wide vision and, intensely imbued, as he was, with the spirit of philanthropy, he saw in Sierra Leone the centre from which Great Britain might spread the blessings of civilisation to the adjacent parts of tropical Africa. To suppress the contraband slave trade, which was still rampant in the regions adjacent to the colony, he was prepared to extend British territorial responsibilities in the neighbouring regions, and at first Bathurst was willing to sanction his annexations. The Isles de Los were occupied in 1818 in order to put down the activities of Portuguese slave traders who were using them as a base, but Bathurst would not consent to the military occupation of Bulama in the Bissagos Islands which was to become such a bone of contention with Portugal a few years later.[1] Under the prompting of the American Colonisation Society, which was planning grandiose schemes for the settlement of liberated negroes in West Africa, it seemed not unlikely that the United States would consent to extend their protection to philanthropic settlements on the Sherbro River to the south and to the regions between Sierra Leone and the Gambia to the north. These American schemes caused great uneasiness to Macarthy, for he believed that they would seriously affect British trade and would hamper the effective prosecution of our anti-slave trade measures. Many American slavers were active on the coast under the nominal protection of the Spanish flag, and Macarthy believed that the local agents of the American Colonisation Society were using the philanthropic designs of their subscribers as a cloak for surreptitious assistance to the slave merchants. He was not permitted by Bathurst to establish British occupation on the Sherbro River as he proposed, but he was very active in establishing new settlements of liberated Africans up the Sierra Leone River and so in effecting British control over the immediate hinterland of the colony.

The population of the colony had risen from about 4000 in 1808 to more than 10,000 in 1814, and a new accession was received in 1816 when the 3rd and 4th Battalions of the West Indian Regiments were disbanded and the discharged negro soldiers were established with gratuities on the new lands that Governor Macarthy had occupied up the river. Added to the heavy expenses for the maintenance of the liberated Africans, the establishment of these new colonists and of immigrants who came in 1817 from Jamaica and Barbados greatly increased the drain of Sierra Leone on the funds provided by Parliamentary grants. The cost of maintaining the colony rose within ten years from £24,000, at which it stood when Macarthy was appointed, to £95,000 per annum during the later years of his Governorship, and it was clear that, although his philanthropic schemes might have

---

[1] *V. infra*, p. 655.

established a fully organised system of government with proper buildings and means of communication, they had been very expensive. Bathurst had constantly urged the necessity for economy, but his protests were ineffectual, and recurrent criticism in Parliament emphasised the necessity for a fresh stocktaking in our African policy.

The Commissioners who reported in 1811 made far more serious strictures on the forts and factories under the Company of Merchants than they did upon Sierra Leone. The Committee which administered the Parliamentary grant to the Company were naturally very antagonistic to the recommendations of the Commissioners for reform, which they attributed to the partisanship of the African Institution. They stubbornly opposed the alteration of their old constitution and nothing could be done while the war in Europe continued, but in 1816 the matter was brought up in earnest in Parliament and in the following year definite plans for reform were put forward by a Select Committee.[1] The undeniable fact was that despite the legal abolition of the British trade more slaves were being exported from the vicinity of our settlements on the Gold Coast than ever before and the officers of the Company had to stand idly by while slaving went on under their very eyes. The alternatives were, either a great extension of British territorial responsibility on the Coast and the suppression of slaving by strict governmental control of the land, or withdrawal from the forts, whose expense was now ludicrously disproportionate to the amount of legitimate trade that was done. If withdrawal were carried out and effort concentrated upon naval measures based on Sierra Leone, the cost could be controlled within defined limits, but this would mean the abandonment of the hopes of opening up Guinea to legitimate trade and civilising influences on which the philanthropists had set their hearts.

The decision remained in suspense for four years while the Company used all its Parliamentary influence against reform, but ultimately in 1821 an Act was passed for its dissolution and for vesting in the Crown all its forts, possessions and property.[2] Thus the last of the long line of African Companies dating from the reign of Charles II was brought to an end and the Crown was left in direct control of all the British West African settlements with Sierra Leone as their centre of government.

The new post upon St Mary's Island in the Gambia River, whither the British merchants trading on the river and those who had been at Goree and Senegal during the war had removed, was in 1816 chosen as the seat of government in preference to the ancient James Fort. The new post was named Bathurst after the Colonial Secretary, and until 1821 it was nominally under the control of the Company of Merchants. On the abolition of the Company it passed under the

---

[1] Appointed 1816, re-appointed 1817. For report see *Parl. Pap.* 1817, VI.
[2] 1 and 2 Geo. IV, c. 28.

direct administration of the Governor of Sierra Leone, and Sir Charles Macarthy was responsible for its establishment upon a firm footing. He extended British control over various islands in the river and posts on its banks, so that he may be called the founder of the modern Gambia Colony in place of the earlier trading post. The consequent difficulties that arose over the French competition from their adjacent post at Albreda mark the beginning of the modern Anglo-French rivalry in West Africa.

Sir Charles Macarthy formally took over the government on the Gold Coast from the officials of the dissolved Company of Merchants at Cape Coast Castle in March 1822 and faced a peculiarly difficult situation owing to the breakdown of all the treaty arrangements with the menacing Ashanti power. The last of those treaties had been negotiated as recently as 1820 by Joseph Dupuis, who was sent to reside at Kumasi as British consul, and by it the Fantis on the coast were recognised as being under British protection. Many difficulties had arisen and Macarthy was convinced that they were entirely the fault of the Ashantis and that the proper policy to adopt was to crush their power by military force. During 1823, on recurrent visits to Cape Coast Castle from his base at Sierra Leone, he did his best to organise the local levies into a disciplined force and secured a nucleus of regular white troops from the Cape of Good Hope and companies of the Royal African Colonial Corps which had been raised in England. Unfortunately he entirely under-rated the strength and discipline of the Ashantis, and when he advanced against their invading army in January 1824, he had not more than 500 men, white and black, to cope with something like 10,000 Ashanti warriors well provided with munitions purchased from the Dutch and Danish trading posts. Macarthy and his men were overwhelmed and slain at Insamaarkow and their severed skulls were carried in triumph to Kumasi to serve for many years as drinking cups for the Ashanti King and his chieftains.[1] Whereas the Ashantis had previously held the power of the white men in respect, they were now convinced of their own superiority and were emboldened to new exploits of conquest against their Fanti enemies.

The news of Macarthy's disaster was greeted with consternation in England and it was realised that drastic measures would have to be taken to repair it. It was some months before the reinforcements that were sent could reach West Africa and meanwhile the Ashantis continued their triumphant course of rapine and destruction and only a terrible epidemic of smallpox among the attackers saved Cape Coast Castle itself from destruction. Not until August 1826 was the situation restored, when the Ashantis were decisively beaten at the battle of Dodowa and the remnants of their armies were driven back

---

[1] For a detailed story of Macarthy's disaster, see Claridge, W. W., *History of the Gold Coast*, I, 345-55.

to their own country, leaving the coast settlements in comparative peace. The result was of great importance; for the English now for the first time became the owners of the land on which their forts and factories stood. They no longer had to pay rents under the 'notes', and only the Dutch continued a payment to the Ashanti King for their castle of Elmina. But it was not until after the appointment of Captain George Maclean as Governor of the Gold Coast in 1830 that definitive terms of peace were arranged.[1]

It was remarked earlier that the Sierra Leone experiment as the creation of the abolitionists was a constant object of attack by their unrelenting and powerful opponents led by the West Indian Committee. The information supplied by Robert Thorpe about the deficiencies of the colony was pointed by his venomous pen in many pamphlets and letters to the press after his dismissal from the Chief Justiceship of Sierra Leone, as he believed at the instigation of Zachary Macaulay and the African Institution. The opponents of the philanthropists received aid from the African merchants when the administration of the Company of Merchants was attacked by the Select Committee in their report of 1817, and their contributions to the controversy were marked with the same bitterness of wounded self-interest as characterised the attacks of the West Indian planters. They proclaimed violently that the philanthropic plans of the leaders of the abolitionists were merely a sanctimonious cloak for self-seeking motives of gain, and they pointed out with some truth that the only mercantile firm that was making profits from the trade at Sierra Leone was the house with which Zachary Macaulay and his family were connected.[2] The heavy expense of maintaining the liberated Africans gave them an admirable target to aim at when the estimates for the West African settlements, the "white elephant of the colonial empire",[3] came before the House of Commons.

A labyrinth of assertion and counter-assertion filled the columns of the London newspapers and reviews in the early 'twenties, until, in 1824, Joseph Hume and the economic reformers took up the attack upon the expenditure in Sierra Leone on the ground of the urgent need for safeguarding the interests of British tax-payers.[4] Public uneasiness was undoubtedly growing, and it was stretching far beyond the circles that had for years been engaged in these controversies. The news of Macarthy's disaster brought matters to a head and it was clear that the Government were bound to set on foot an impartial enquiry into the whole state of affairs in the West African settlements. Some such stock-taking had been necessary in many other parts of the empire now that the haphazard arrangements of the long war

[1] 30 November 1831. Hertslet's *Treaties*, IV, 109, and supplementary convention, IV, 115.
[2] J. Macqueen in *Blackwood's Edinburgh Magazine*, May 1827, p. 622.
[3] Marryat, J., *More Thoughts Still* (1818), p. 96.
[4] *Hansard*, LXXXVII, 962.

period had to be tightened. Commissioner Bigge had been sent to New South Wales in 1819, the Commission of Eastern Enquiry to Ceylon and Mauritius in 1823 and the Commission of Enquiry to Cape Colony in the same year. The appointment of Major James Rowan and Henry Wellington as Commissioners for West Africa was therefore directly in accord with Bathurst's policy.

According to their instructions they were to investigate the state of affairs in "Sierra Leone and its dependencies", and as these now included the Gambia posts and the Gold Coast forts, the whole of West African affairs was to be taken into review. They were especially directed to enquire into the affairs of the Liberated Africans Department and its growing expenditure, and when they reported in 1827, this matter filled a prominent place in their exhaustive and well-documented Report.[1] The verdict of the Commissioners was a disheartening one, for they found that the results of eighteen years of constant and expensive effort to raise and civilise the liberated Africans fell "infinitely short" of the high hopes with which it had been undertaken. They shrewdly analysed the inherent causes of the failure and pointed to many defects due to slackness and inefficiency in the agents of government, but they were too much disillusioned to make any far-reaching suggestions for new policy. The optimistic forecasts that had been the common currency of the philanthropists had proved so worthless that the Commissioners would coin no more. The Government had taken over a thankless job and they had to carry on, because the nation had set its hand to the African task and honour forbade them to draw back.

Before the Report appeared public opinion, even among the philanthropists themselves, had settled to a mood of black pessimism about the West African settlements. The disappointment of all the hopes of rapid success in promoting African civilisation and legitimate trade was bad enough, but it was even more bitter to have to recognise that, despite all that had been done, far more negroes were being carried into slavery across the Atlantic in 1825 than in the palmiest days of the old British trade. As we have already seen, the most active abolitionists turned away from the African Institution[2] to found a new Anti-Slavery Society with different aims and a new leader. Wilberforce had resigned his functions in March 1824 to Thomas Fowell Buxton, M.P., who was thenceforward for the next eighteen years in the forefront of African controversies.

The crucial decision as to future African policy was taken by Bathurst with the approval of the Cabinet of Lord Liverpool even before the reception of the Commissioners' Report. A drastic limitation of commitments in the support of the liberated Africans and

---

[1] *Parl. Pap.* 1827, VII, Pt. 1.
[2] See chapter IX. The African Institution lingered on until 1827, but it did very little after 1820.

the Sierra Leone colony in particular was decided on. It was clear that money must be expended on the Gold Coast until the Ashantis had been driven off and some of the stain of Macarthy's disaster removed, but Parliament would not continue to supply funds to maintain philanthropic experiments as in earlier years, and the estimates for Sierra Leone were cut to the bone. Neither the Ministers nor their supporters would consent to any further assumption of territorial responsibilities, and Bathurst sent out peremptory orders to Governor Sir Charles Turner to make no more treaties with native chiefs. His successor, Lord Goderich, was just as emphatic, and in 1827 he wrote to Sir Neil Campbell, the next Governor, in terms which unmistakably mark the policy that was to be pursued for many years. "Your predecessor and yourself have been repeatedly informed that His Majesty desired no further territorial acquisitions or rights of sovereignty in Africa."[1] Again: "His Majesty's Government are unwilling to sanction arrangements involving the cession of territory to this country; for, not to mention the political objections which attach to measures of that description, it is impossible to overlook the inconvenience which must manifestly ensue from contracting obligations of alliance with...people whose extreme weakness would be perpetually urging them to claim our interference on their behalf."[2] The bearing of such a declaration of policy on contemporary action in the similar circumstances in South Africa gives it additional importance in the history of the Empire.

When Sir Neil Campbell arrived in Africa as Governor of Sierra Leone in 1826, his authority extended not only to the colony itself but also to all the forts along the Gold Coast. Interest was mainly directed to the colony, for English fortunes in the other posts had touched low-water mark. Trade was almost nil; slaving went on everywhere save under the very guns of the forts; the few civilians left were without money or occupation and only the military officers in command of the Royal African Colonial Corps and the native auxiliaries exercised some small authority. Campbell strongly urged the abandonment of all the forts with the possible exception of Cape Coast Castle. Even before this, however, some of the Ministers, including the Duke of Wellington and William Huskisson, had planned such a withdrawal,[3] and *The Times* had gone so far as to announce that this was the Government's intention.[4] But Bathurst would not agree and proposed instead to remove the Gold Coast from the direct control of the Governor of Sierra Leone and to appoint a Lieutenant-Governor there and a similar officer on the Gambia. However, this plan was not accepted, and in January 1827 R. W. Hay, the Permanent Under-

---

[1] C.O. 268/26. Goderich to Campbell, 9 June 1827.
[2] *Ibid.* Same to Same, 8 August 1827.
[3] C.O. 323/148 and C.O. 267/84.
[4] *The Times*, 20 and 27 April 1826.

Secretary for the Colonies, wrote privately to Governor Campbell to give him advance information of the instructions that had already been prepared for the abandonment.

It was intended to remove the base of the preventive squadron in African waters to Fernando Po. When the news that abandonment was on the point of being ordered reached the ears of the few African merchants still interested in the Gold Coast, they were up in arms, backed by the Birmingham manufacturers who feared the loss of their market for brass wire and trinkets. Ultimately, under this powerful pressure, it was decided that, though the grants for the maintenance of the settlements must be drastically cut and the Government would accept no further direct responsibility, the merchants might maintain their factories at their own risk, receiving a small money grant from Parliament and certain arms and munitions for their defence. The transfer of the forts to the merchants took place in 1828, and so things returned to something like the same system as had prevailed before the abolition of the Company in 1821. In reality, however, there was a change for the better. The merchants who now took charge were organised in a single Committee in London, which was not hampered by the cumbrous constitution of the old Company, riddled as it was by the antagonisms of the ex-slave-trading firms of Liverpool and Bristol.

That with these not very promising beginnings the Gold Coast was saved for the Empire to be the nucleus of our vast modern interests in West Africa was in the main due to two men, though in very different degrees. It was the London merchant, Matthew Forster, who, by his persistence with the Colonial Office, prevented the abandonment of, and, by his consistent efforts in West African commerce, restored some measure of prosperity to, English trade on the Gold Coast. In a measure he was the first of the line of mercantile pioneers which includes the more celebrated names of Macgregor Laird, Sir George Taubman Goldie and Sir Alfred Jones, but his greatest service to the Empire was that he found the right man to do the work on the spot. Lieutenant George Maclean of the 3rd West Indian Regiment went out to Africa in 1826 with the Royal African Colonial Corps, and as Military Secretary to the Governor attracted favourable notice at the time of the defeat of the Ashantis at Dodowa. When the Merchants' Committee took over the administration they needed a Governor and Forster recommended Maclean. He went out again in 1830, and, thenceforward, for fourteen years, he laboured with unremitting energy and ultimate success to raise our African settlements from the depths of destitution and fear in which he found them to the security and modest prosperity of 1843.

Maclean's first task was to arrange the long-delayed peace with the Ashantis, which had been in suspense since their defeat in 1826. His sole legal authority was a commission as Justice of the Peace from the Governor of Sierra Leone, but that did not impede his action. Though *de facto* Governor, he was usually called "President", as the first of the Council appointed by the Merchants' Committee in London. The members of his Council were all commercial employees who were only interested in trade, and they did not interfere with him in political matters. For those he was naturally well-fitted by a shrewd judgment and great will power. His capacity for hard work in the West African climate, added to his mental qualities, made him from the beginning the dominant figure on the coast. He arrived at Cape Coast Castle in February 1830 and a little more than a year later he had done what all his predecessors had failed to do. He arranged secure terms of peace with the Ashantis (April 1831), though ratification was delayed a few months longer (June 1831). The treaty was nominally concluded between the King of Ashanti and the Fanti chiefs in alliance with Great Britain, and, since it remained in force for more than twenty years, we can rightly characterise it as the principal title-deed of the Gold Coast Protectorate, as the region came later to be called.

Little documentary material exists to afford evidence of Maclean's activities. He carried out his negotiations with the Africans through personal negro agents to whom he gave his orders by word of mouth, and as he knew well that the Committee of Merchants would only be interested in an increase of trade without bothering about the way in which it had been obtained, he troubled them with few despatches and never entered into details. He took a free hand and went ahead, and this was peculiarly what was wanted in the extraordinary circumstances on the Coast. When Maclean arrived, the English and all other white men were despised and distrusted by the negroes, who would only make use of them to serve their own purposes. Five or six years later the President was looked up to by almost every chief as a just and impartial composer of quarrels. With a minimum of fuss and red tape, he set himself to understand the native mind, and by dint of unfailing tact and firmness he could do infinitely more than he could have done if obliged to keep within the strict bounds of written instructions. To the accurate legal mind of "Mr Over-Secretary" Stephen, Maclean's proceedings appeared outrageous when they came before him in the late 'thirties on the petitions of aggrieved opponents of the Committee of Merchants. Definite orders had been given to Maclean's superior officer, the Governor of Sierra Leone, to annex no territory and accept no responsibility beyond the borders of the colony or the merchants' forts. Yet here was the President of the Gold Coast Council wielding a vast power as arbiter among hundreds of thousands of negroes with whom he stood in no legal relationship whatever. Stephen and the Colonial Secretaries he served and prompted were disposed to listen to the detractors of the man who could do all this extra-legally, yet who, it could not be denied, had brought the Gold

Coast to peace and had raised English trade there from nothing to something very substantial.

Between the Gambia and Sierra Leone lies a deltaic region, threaded by creeks and rivers, and inhabited by small tribes of negroes, who for centuries had been middle-men in the disposal of slaves brought down from the interior, the Futa-Jallon region, where there were incessant tribal wars. These slaves were known to be among the best obtainable in Africa, and this region, called in the eighteenth century "the Rivers of the South", was a regular resort of slave traders. Along the sea-board ran a chain of islands called the Bissagos and within the delta were islands separated by creeks. The two most important of these were Bulama and Cacheo. Portugal claimed territorial sovereignty over the whole area, and since the late seventeenth century, when some of her merchants had attempted to exploit it under the Companhia de Cacheu é Rios de Guiné, there had been from time to time Portuguese Governors in the Bissagos.[1] Englishmen attempted to establish a slave-trading post in Bulama towards the end of the eighteenth century, and in 1792 the native chiefs made a cession of the island to a British naval officer. It was upon this treaty that later British claims were based, although the Portuguese always protested against them. In 1814 certain British merchants trading to Africa were authorised to occupy Bulama as a dependency of the colony of Sierra Leone, and in the following year the Governor proposed to send a small force of native troops to protect the trading settlement. Permission was refused by Lord Bathurst and in the 'twenties the American Colonisation Society, which was interested in the foundation of Liberia as a refuge for liberated slaves, proposed to occupy Bulama as a convenient port of call for their ships. They did not fear British opposition, for according to them the utter impossibility of maintaining the colony of Sierra Leone unless at a great expense of life would cause Great Britain to abandon it, and Bulama and Liberia might then be joined as a home for a great American-African nation.[2]

In 1830 the Portuguese again formally asserted their claim to Bulama by raising their flag in the island, but the British authorities in Sierra Leone removed it more than once in the next year or two and Palmerston protested energetically to Lisbon. Bulama was not only a convenient link between the British settlements on the Gambia and in Sierra Leone, it also commanded the entrance to the rivers down which legitimate commerce might be attracted from the interior; it might also be made to control the Portuguese slave trade in the region to the north of Sierra Leone and so give invaluable help to our preventive officers.[3]

[1] For the history of the long-drawn Bulama question, see the collection of papers relating to the Arbitration which settled it in 1870: F.O. 63/988.
[2] Pratt's *Missionary Register*, September 1828.
[3] C.O. 267/160. Governor Doherty to Russell, 1840.

Besides the general difficulties at sea with slave ships flying Spanish and Portuguese flags, there were in the eastern part of the Gulf of Guinea at this period particular questions of sovereignty which were the antecedents of much international friction in the latter part of the nineteenth century. When the Commissioners of Enquiry recommended the abandonment of the outlying English posts, the most easterly one, with a single exception, was at Accra near to the important Danish factory of Christiansborg. What has been said concerning the conditions surrounding the Gold Coast forts does not apply as a whole beyond Accra. The exceptional post was at Whydah; it was sometimes occupied by Englishmen in the eighteenth century and sometimes not, and the same is true of the French in respect of an adjacent French post. The Portuguese, however, were almost constantly at Whydah (or Ajuda as they call it), and they attached some importance to it as the port of entry to the kingdom of Dahomey, supplying such good slaves as to be known pre-eminently as the Slave Coast. Farther to the east lay the Oil Rivers, with which we are not yet concerned.

Though there were no English merchants at Whydah in 1810, we still maintained our pretensions and would not recognise complete Portuguese sovereignty. The stipulations of the anti-slave trade treaty of 1810 restricted Portuguese freedom of action beyond her own territories, but were expressly declared not to limit or restrain the commerce of Ajuda, though Britain did not resign her legitimate pretensions thereto.[1] This exception was particularly hampering for the British preventive officers, for Whydah, with its guaranteed impunity, became the most flourishing slave-trading mart in West Africa. The only way to deal with its slavers was to capture them at sea, and this was very difficult with ships based on Sierra Leone, which was a thousand miles away. Captured slavers had to be navigated thither for trial against adverse winds and currents, a voyage which took on an average some nine weeks and kept the captors off the station for all that time while other slavers were trading with impunity. The Admiralty authorities were convinced that a more convenient base must be found, and they fixed upon the lofty island of Fernando Po lying in the extreme angle of the Gulf of Guinea just where the coast turns south. With its central volcanic peak the island offered health-giving breezes at various heights and was suitable as a place of recuperation for the hard-worked men of the preventive service.

Effective propositions for the occupation of Fernando Po were first made in 1825, but they raised doubts as to the territorial rights in the island, and Canning as Foreign Secretary was reluctant to arouse suspicion that Great Britain was coveting the African territory of another power. Like all the African lands of her discovery, Portugal laid claim to Fernando Po until the eighteenth century, but she never

---

[1] Art. X of Treaty. *British and Foreign State Papers*, 1812–14, II, 556.

did anything to occupy it. Spain, on the other hand, recognised that she was debarred from Africa by the celebrated Tordesillas Agreement, and when she wished to obtain negroes for her American plantations, she purchased them from the Portuguese. But by the Treaty of Utrecht (1713) she had been compelled to cede to England the *Asiento* or contract for the supply of slaves, and this led to incessant wrangles and was bitterly detested by the Spaniards. When she was on the point of a new war against the English she saw an opportunity of getting rid of the *Asiento* and using her own merchants for slaving. In the Treaty of San Ildefonso (1778), by which Spain and Portugal composed their differences over their frontiers in South America, the old prohibition against Spain's entry into African waters was broken and Portugal ceded to her the island of Fernando Po in full sovereignty to serve as a base for her projected slave station.

Spain, however, did nothing, and Fernando Po remained derelict and unoccupied save for a few savages. In fact, so little was known about it that when Canning informed the Portuguese Minister of the plan for occupying it, he claimed it formally as in the effective possession of Portugal, forgetting the cession to Spain in 1778. However, Canning knew better, and asked Spain whether she would cede her claims in the island for a money payment or in exchange for a West Indian island. No clear or satisfactory reply was vouchsafed to this question, and the matter of a legal position for the new establishment dragged on from 1828 for many years. But meanwhile practical steps were pressed on for the occupation, and in 1827 an expedition was sent out under Captain Owen, R.N., a well-known and experienced officer in African surveys. Various experiments were tried between 1827 and 1832 to make the occupation serve its purpose, but none of them was markedly successful, and preparations were under way for the abandonment of Fernando Po when it became connected with certain events that give it a lasting place in the history of British enterprise in tropical Africa.

When individual firms of Liverpool merchants, after the proscription of the slave trade, had to seek new African commodities for which to exchange the goods the negroes desired, some of them thought of palm oil and palm kernels. They had been tried on a small scale for the manufacture of candles in the latter part of the eighteenth century, but it was not until after the Peace that such cargoes could find a ready market in London or Liverpool. The best source was found to be in the creeks and tidal rivers that came out to the sea through dense mangrove swamps in the region east of Whydah and the Slave Coast, and gradually this part of Guinea came to be known as the Oil Rivers.

We have discussed in another chapter[1] the problems afforded by the River Niger and the attempts made to trace its course to the sea

[1] See chapter XVII.

from the time of Mungo Park onwards. In 1830 the most baffling of the problems was solved by the emergence of Richard and John Lander from the Oil Rivers after their long voyage down the lower part of the Niger's course. They made their first contact with a white settlement at Fernando Po, and when some Liverpool merchants under the lead of Macgregor Laird determined to follow up the trade possibilities revealed by the explorations of the Landers, it was natural that Fernando Po should be made the base of operations of a new expedition. There was no plan to acquire territorial sovereignty, so that the Government could look upon Laird's trading scheme with a favourable eye. The African Steamship Company was founded with capital raised in Liverpool to develop commerce on the Lower Niger, and in 1832 Laird himself went out with the first expedition. It returned to Fernando Po in 1834 after suffering grievous loss, but it amply proved Laird's contention that the lands along the Niger offered good trade prospects, for they were in direct communication with the vast interior without the interposition of middlemen like those on the Gold Coast. When the news of the death of Lander from his wounds immediately after reaching Fernando Po became known in England, it attracted renewed attention to African affairs and added to the rising tide of opinion that a new start must be made in West African policy.

In each of the regions in which Englishmen were active, events were approaching a crisis in the late 'thirties, when the abolitionists were waging their last pitched battle with the planting interest over the apprenticeship system which had followed emancipation.[2] During the ten years since Sir Neil Campbell's Governorship Sierra Leone had passed into the hands of Governor after Governor, none of whom could grapple successfully with the rival claims of economy and the fifty-three thousand liberated Africans who had been poured into the colony during the period. The last of them was another Campbell, and his attempts at philanthropy were, in the opinion of Lord Glenelg, the Colonial Secretary in Melbourne's Cabinet, so injudicious that he was recalled in disgrace in 1837. It was seriously proposed to hand the colony back to the merchants and have done with it like the Gold Coast, but the proposal was greeted with a chorus of horror by the philanthropists, who pointed to what they called the infamy of Maclean's system.

There can be no doubt, however, that Maclean had done great things for the Gold Coast settlements; he had made it possible to trade where previously everything had been derelict, and he had acquired an immense influence for peace with Ashantis and Fantis alike. But he was an easy butt for slanders, for much that he did was opportunist rather than legal, and he was none too tender with the ne'er-do-weels who were shipped out to the Coast as their last chance

[1] See chapter IX.

of making a living. Their scandalous tongues accused him of dictatorship in public life and immorality in private, and by 1839, after ten years of his rule, the clamour against him rose so high among the evangelical party that, when the Marquis of Normanby succeeded Lord Glenelg as Colonial Secretary, the time for stock-taking had clearly arrived.

(II) 1839–1870

Just as the late 'thirties were marked by fundamental changes in the administration of colonial affairs in the colonies of settlement, so also were they critical in our relations with tropical Africa, and to a large extent for the same cause, the replacement of an easy-going and opportunist official[1] at the Colonial Office by a man of exceptional calibre and great determination and energy. For years the men on the spot in Africa had had to get things done as best they could and to keep things running, rather than trouble about precedents or obedience to regulations. The Secretaries of State had never had the time, or perhaps the inclination, to work out a comprehensive policy for the West African settlements, and it was notorious that their decisions were swayed by the pertinacity of the philanthropists whose judgments were sometimes warped by their ideals or their hopes.

James Stephen succeeded as Permanent Under-Secretary to Lord Glenelg in 1836 and thenceforward he strove unceasingly, and with far-reaching effects, for orderly methods of colonial administration founded on a proper legal basis of regulation and precedent. For two years his hands were too full for him to look very closely into West African affairs, but he had to do so in 1838 when preparing materials for his chief, Lord Glenelg, to defend the grants in aid of Sierra Leone in Parliament. His investigations were most disquieting.

The influence of the philanthropists of Exeter Hall on Parliament and on public opinion had passed its zenith, and where, before, their enthusiasms had been accepted at their face value, they had now to counter the piercing criticism of the hard-headed realists who were prominent in the House of Commons. Stephen knew that damaging attacks would be made on the philanthropists' favourite colonial experiment at Sierra Leone, and he could find no valid ministerial defence.

The political beliefs of Sir William Molesworth, the principal critic, were widely different from those of the West Indian interest, but they were more dangerous. He alleged that the misgovernment

R. W. Hay, Permanent Under-Secretary, 1825-36.

42-2

of Sierra Leone was proverbial. The peculation, the lavish expenditure and the public plunder for which the colony had been notorious had given it so bad a name that it might be aptly designated as one enormous job.[1] Ten years later Delane in *The Times* was even more savage. "The model colony on the coast has resulted in a hideous hot-bed of iniquity and pestilence, where even the brutish cannibal of the interior finds a lower depth of degradation—No person can now rise in Exeter Hall and deny that in every single department of the system it has been a total failure."[2] Stephen would not go so far as the politicians, but he found so much justification for their attacks upon the scandals that he was determined to have a thorough stock-taking of West African administration.

In Sierra Leone the constitutional arrangements were good enough on paper, but they were maladministered. But on the Gold Coast, as he saw it, the evils sprang from the entrusting of the government of the settlements to a Committee of Merchants which had resulted in the utterly illegal proceedings of their employee, President Maclean. "A colonial administration", he wrote, "conducted by merchants with contributions from the public Treasury was an experiment which it was obvious enough could issue in nothing but a constant attempt to encroach more and more on the part of the grantee, who would soon lose sight of the distinction between commercial factories and Government colonies and whose officers would as a matter of course aspire to the rank and consideration of Governors."[3] This crystallises the view of the Colonial Office officials concerning Maclean. Because he was merely an employee of the Merchants' Committee, they disdained what he had done to pacify the Gold Coast and to increase British trade, for it had been done without either countenance or help from the only official authorities in West Africa, the fleeting succession of Governors at Sierra Leone who were nominally responsible. To Stephen the Merchants' Committee were nothing but 'contractors'. Their contract was to supply at as cheap a rate as possible[4] the minimum of executive government that was essential, and their arrangements were deserving of as much or as little respect as those of a firm of victualling contractors. Holding such views and expressing them repeatedly in minutes to his successive political chiefs, Stephen did much to prepare for the thorough stock-taking in West African affairs which he desired. The son of one of Wilberforce's principal coadjutors among the 'Saints', it was natural that he should have a personal interest in Africa, but, as far as we can see, it did nothing to deflect him from the course his duty dictated. He was not, as his father had been, one of the 'philan-

---

[1] Molesworth, Sir W., *Selected Speeches*, p. 38.
[2] *The Times*, 6 January 1848.
[3] C.O. 267/150. Minute by Stephen, 23 April 1838, on letter from Governor Nichol of Fernando Po.
[4] C.O. 267/165. Minute by Stephen, 18 November 1841.

thropists' whose hearts led them to extravagant hopes where their heads might have given them warning. Stephen looked at West Africa as he looked at every other imperial problem, with the cool eyes of the trained lawyer and a determination to put things into systematic form where before they were merely chaotic survivals from two generations of opportunist makeshifts. Even Stephen's skill and resourcefulness in the devices of government failed to achieve order, but the bitter public controversy over them certainly affected public opinion in other directions of his colonial policy. In West Africa his efforts left a permanent mark on the administration, and they were a fundamental factor in the formation of our policy towards the natives.

Stephen was getting to work on these problems in the critical years when the last leader of the philanthropists was putting forward his supreme effort. Though they derived from the same group, the generation of Wilberforce, the ideas of Buxton and Stephen on policy were widely different. They were neither opposed nor complementary; they were different because they looked at a complex of problems from quite different points of view. Yet the ideas of each fill an essential place in the genesis of our empire in tropical Africa.

Buxton, as Wilberforce's successor in the leadership of the philanthropists, had carried his ten years of campaigning to success in the Abolition Act of 1833, and turned thence to examine the scandals that were said by colonial informers like Dr John Philip[1] to be rampant in our treatment of the aborigines within the Empire. In the session of 1835 he moved for a Select Committee to make a comprehensive survey of the whole question, and when it was appointed he became chairman. The Committee took voluminous evidence throughout the sessions of 1836 and 1837 and it reported[2] just before the dissolution on the death of William IV, when Buxton lost his seat. Attention was not confined to South Africa or even to the natives within the British Empire, who were the Committee's original concern. They ranged widely over the problem of the relations of the white men with the aborigines who dwelt beyond the borders of the lands that were definitely under the administration of the Crown, and in many respects this was the part of the Committee's work that was of the greatest importance. The Maoris of New Zealand and the tribes of West Africa were neither of them at that time British subjects, but they were in close relations with the Empire and the policy to be pursued towards them was a matter of urgent practical interest. The Report of the Aborigines Committee, which was very largely Buxton's own, was a step on the road that led to the international covenant of 1919 in regard to dealings with native races— a covenant largely based on the practice of the British Empire in its dependencies.

[1] See *C.H.B.E.* VIII, 313.
[2] For the salient points in the Report, see Bell and Morrell, *Select Documents*, pp. 545–552.

With the abandonment of the Apprenticeship System in 1838[1], Buxton was free to turn away from West Indian controversies and to devote the whole of his powers to Africa. He threw himself into the task with extraordinary vigour, and his influence over the evangelically minded public reached its zenith. *The Times*, his most critical opponent, went so far as to call this period "the era of Sir Fowell Buxton", and there is no doubt that the Whig Cabinet very largely moulded their African policy under his prompting. He set himself to the preparation of an overwhelming case to prove that all our efforts for thirty years against the slave trade had failed and that there must be a new start on different lines. When the first part of his book, *The African Slave Trade and its Remedy*, appeared in 1839, the evidence it accumulated and the passion with which it was presented created a sensation, for it was shown that, despite all the work of our preventive service, three times as many Africans were carried across the Atlantic to slavery in 1837 as in 1807.

Buxton had come to believe that the true lines of approach lay through two inter-connected policies, both devoted to the land and not to the sea on which our previous efforts had been concentrated. The first was the conclusion of treaties with African chiefs, although the Aborigines Committee had stated it as their opinion that such treaties were inexpedient as rather the preparatives and the apology for disputes than measures of security.[2] The second line of approach lay through the promotion of legitimate trade with Africa with governmental assistance. Now in neither of these suggestions was Buxton a pioneer, for each had been advocated years before, though not by persons of his distinction or influence. It will be remembered that in the middle 'twenties Governors Turner and Campbell of Sierra Leone had been strictly ordered by Bathurst to abandon their plans for treaties with native chiefs on the borders of the colony. Such treaties might put a stop to the establishment of slave factories, but they might involve us in native quarrels and so were to be avoided. Later Secretaries of State had issued similar prohibitions, so that the adoption of Buxton's proposals would mean a complete *volte face* in the policy of the Colonial Office. Nor was he more original in pressing on the promotion of legitimate trade; the only new point was the demand for governmental aid which was peculiarly obnoxious to the African merchants like Macgregor Laird and Robert Jamieson, who wished to get on with their trading ventures without official interference. Stephen also was opposed to such a plan because he believed that it would lead to fresh opportunities for peculation and extravagance.

However, Buxton had the ear both of the Cabinet and the public, and he could count on the warm support of the Church Missionary

[1] See chapter XIII.
[2] Aborigines Committee Report, Sec. VIII in Bell and Morrell, *Select Documents*, p. 551.

Society, which at last saw opportunities of pursuing its evangelising work on the Niger with more success than it had achieved in Sierra Leone in thirty years. To further the projects, a new Society for the Extinction of the Slave Trade and the Civilisation of Africa was founded in 1839 with a very distinguished membership, and it received royal patronage when the Prince Consort presided over its general meeting in Exeter Hall in June 1840. The Colonial Secretary, Lord Normanby, promised ample governmental assistance, and Palmerston set on foot new negotiations with Spain for the purchase of Fernando Po as a base of operations, although Britain had declined a previous offer from the Spanish side in 1827. But the negotiations dragged on owing to the disturbed state of Spain, and ultimately a fervid outburst of nationalism put an end to the proposal as an insult to Spanish honour and dignity by the cession of the "key to the Niger and the commerce of the interior".[1]

The preparations for a lavishly equipped expedition to the Niger went on apace during the autumn of 1840 and the spring of 1841 in spite of a rising tide of opposition to what Stephen's friend, Herman Merivale, publicly characterised as "a chimerical speculation of civilising Africa by establishing a legitimate commerce".[2] The opposition came from many sides—from academic theorists like Merivale, from the political opponents of the Whig Ministry, who saw an opportunity to make capital from the African scandals surrounding Maclean and the Sierra Leone colony, and from interested merchants who disliked government interference in what was traditionally no man's land and open to unrestricted individual enterprise. But it was all of no avail, for the Government were determined to proceed with Buxton's schemes.

Besides the material preparation for the expedition, it was necessary to draw up instructions for the commissioners who were to proceed with it. From this followed its most important results, for there was a lasting change in policy. Bathurst's prohibitions against native treaties of 1826-7 were reversed and conditions for the conclusion of such treaties, which are among the fundamental maxims of our modern native policy, were prescribed to Commissioners for the Niger expedition. They were first expressed by Lord John Russell as Colonial Secretary to Governor Doherty of Sierra Leone[3] some six months before the formal instructions were issued. There were three matters to be considered in forming any new treaty policy: (a) the tightening-up of preventive measures against the slave trade, (b) the acceptance or refusal of sovereignty over African territory, and (c) the extension of British jurisdiction into lands over which no sovereignty was claimed and which lay beyond the boundaries of our

---

[1] See Arrija, J., *La Guinea Española*, pp. 18–21.
[2] Merivale, H., *Lectures on Colonisation* (ed. of 1841), p. 303.
[3] Russell to Doherty, 23 July 1840. *Parl. Pap.* 1865, v, 452.

direct administration. It was only on the first of these that a clear and consistent line was taken up and persisted in, and this was laid down by Buxton in *The African Slave Trade and its Remedy*. Provisions pledging the chiefs to suppress all slaving activities within their territories were first inserted in treaties concluded with tribes between Sierra Leone and the Gambia, and they were so successful that, within the ten years 1841–51, it was claimed that the slave trade had been almost completely suppressed in the region to the north of Sierra Leone. During that period, twenty such treaties were concluded by the Commissioners appointed by the Governor of Sierra Leone.[1] British subjects were not to engage directly or indirectly in any native war; Great Britain might appoint agents within the territories and the chiefs guaranteed to keep open paths for trade through their lands and to grant to British subjects any commercial privileges conceded to the subjects of foreign powers.

It was not claimed that any rights of sovereignty were acquired by such treaties, and in fact Lord John Russell definitely prohibited the conclusion of any treaty which would bind Great Britain "to give military aid to African chiefs or to assume any right of sovereignty or protection over any portion of the soil or waters of Africa".[2] On the other hand, he gave definite instruction to the Commissioners of the Niger expedition to acquire in full sovereignty a site for a commercial port on the Lower Niger, and though owing to the failure of the expedition, which is mentioned elsewhere,[3] the instruction came to nothing, it marked the first attempt by Great Britain to annex territory within the limit of modern Nigeria.

Before we take up the question of the extension of British jurisdiction beyond the limits of directly administered territory, we must return to trace the progress of the agitation against the regime of George Maclean and the Committee of Merchants which was raging without intermission while Buxton was organising his new Society for the Civilisation of Africa. The Committee had to apply annually for the Parliamentary grant towards their expenses and this afforded an opportunity for focusing their attacks on the system. There were two special grounds of charge. Stephen was convinced that the national honour was being smirched by Maclean and the Committee of Merchants for their own gain, and Matthew Forster, their spokesman, practically admitted in the Commons that much of the Manchester cotton cloth and Birmingham hardware that was sent to the Gold Coast went to pay for the slaves that were exported to Cuba and Brazil. Parallel with this was the scandal of permitted domestic slavery in the settlements. If they were British colonies, this was

---

[1] For the text of these treaties see the successive volumes of *British and Foreign State Papers*.
[2] C.O. 267/165. Russell to Governor Carr 8 November 1841.
[3] *V. supra*, p. 620.

patently illegal, but if it were abolished, the settlements would become a refuge for crowds of runaway slaves from the Ashantis, and inevitably the settlements would have to fear new attacks from the interior. The complexity of these social questions was not appreciated by arm-chair critics in England, and even the better informed Colonial Office could not decide consistently as to whether the settlements were colonies or not.

The situation was difficult for the man on the spot who had to deal with facts far more intractable than the philosophic theories which were so attractive to the philanthropists. Whatever his defects, Maclean was undoubtedly a man of great courage and he took the wisest course to benefit those over whom he ruled; he went the way his long experience of Africa dictated as best adapted to serve the cause of peace and trade, and he wrote and explained as little as possible. In its ultimate results that course was justified, but it roused his critics to a fury which reached its height just as the Niger Expedition was sailing and Buxton's fame was at its zenith.

It was decided to have a new survey of affairs in West Africa made by an experienced investigator. The Commissioner chosen by Russell was Dr R. R. Madden, who had served as an official of the Mixed Commission Court in Havana, and having strong negrophile leanings was acceptable to Buxton and the philanthropic party. He was explicitly instructed to report upon political conditions in Sierra Leone and all the British establishments in West Africa and the truth of the accusations of implication in slave-trading schemes made against local officials and merchants. He spent the first part of 1841 in Africa, and though he was only on the Gold Coast for a few days, he took it upon himself to set up a proclamation that entirely overruled Maclean's reasonable contention as to the legal status of the settlements. Acting, as he gave forth, in the name of the Governor of Sierra Leone, Madden proclaimed that the settlements were undeniably British and so within the Abolition Act of 1833. All slavery was illegal. The position was an impossible one, for the Commissioner did not stay to handle the difficulties resulting from his precipitate and high-handed action, and it says much for Maclean's power and skill that he saved the settlements from falling into immediate anarchy.

Madden's highly coloured report was condemnatory of almost everyone and everything connected with West African administration, and his recommendations for reform were crude and ill-conceived. To Stephen he seemed "a very careless, inaccurate and superficial reporter of the state of things in our African colonies".[1] The influence of the report had nothing to do with Lord Stanley's important decision within a few weeks of reading Stephen's memorandum. The news of the tragic end of the Niger expedition had arrived, and, added to all the other West African difficulties, it convinced the

---

[1] C.O. 267/165. Memo. by Stephen, 30 November 1841.

Cabinet that there must be a full-dress inquiry. There had been no clear-cut line between the parties about African policy, but since 1832 the philanthropists had been mainly Whigs, and now that their schemes had come to such shipwreck some of their less reputable opponents were delighted that a Tory Ministry should set up an inquiry into African affairs. The shock broke Buxton, who never held up his head again,[1] and the Society for the Civilisation of Africa was wound up in 1843 to the triumphant applause of *The Times*, which proclaimed that its failure was a proof that "the Buxton era" was over.

A Select Committee was appointed by the House of Commons in March 1842 "to enquire into the state of the British possessions on the West Coast of Africa more especially with reference to their relations with the neighbouring native tribes". Their Report,[2] which was presented in August, marks an important stage in the history of Britain's relations with tropical Africa, and did justice to Maclean's work during the fourteen years of his administration. It fully admitted his merits and those "of the Committee under whom he acted, which with a miserable pittance of between £3500 and £4000 a year has exercised from the four ill-provided forts of Dixcove, Cape Coast, Anamaboe and British Accra, manned by a few ill-paid black soldiers, a very wholesome influence over a coast not much less than 150 miles in extent and to a considerable distance inland, preventing within that range external slave trade, maintaining peace and security, and exercising a useful, though irregular, jurisdiction among the neighbouring tribes".[3] To remedy this state of affairs and place matters upon a proper legal footing, it was therefore recommended that the Crown should resume direct control of all the forts, and that the irregular jurisdiction built up by Maclean should be placed upon a legal basis, although there was no intention to extend British sovereignty over the whole of the regions in which it was exercised.

The circumstances of Sierra Leone also demanded that the Governors should have some legal powers over the tribes beyond the limits of the colony, for criminals and rebels against British authority fled to the neighbouring savages whom they stirred up to wars among themselves and whom they strove to excite to raids against Freetown itself. To remedy this, Governor Jeremie had secured authority under an Act of the Sierra Leone Legislature to pursue suspected British subjects or liberated Africans into native territory and bring them for trial into the colony, thus exercising similar extra-territorial jurisdiction to Maclean's on the Gold Coast and to the jurisdiction exercised in South Africa under the Cape Punishment Act.[4] Jeremie's Act was closely modelled on that measure,

[1] He died on 19 February 1845. [2] *Parl. Pap.* 1842, XI (551).
[3] *Ibid.* Part I, pp. iv, v.
[4] 6 and 7 Will. IV, c. 57. See *C.H.B.E.* VIII, 383.

but the Colonial Office had to pronounce it *ultra vires*, for no Colonial Legislature could pass valid Acts dealing with territories beyond its own defined limits.

Accordingly two Foreign Jurisdiction Acts were passed by Parliament to authorise the Crown by Order-in-Council to exercise power beyond annexed territory in as ample a manner as if it had been acquired by the cession or conquest of territory.[1] It was not until 1850 that Earl Grey laid it down that the territories in which this extra-territorial jurisdiction could be exercised were those in which treaties embodying it had been concluded with the local chiefs.[2] Thus an added impetus was imparted to the progress of treaty-making with African chiefs, and rudimentary 'protectorates' began to appear along the African coasts. Meanwhile France was approaching the same result by a somewhat different road.

One of the last important acts of Maclean before his death from dysentery at Cape Coast Castle in 1847 was the negotiation of a treaty with the neighbouring Gold Coast chiefs such as was contemplated by the Foreign Jurisdiction Acts. This was known as the Bond of 1844.[3] No innovations were introduced and it conferred no new territorial rights, but it legalised and defined the jurisdiction in purely criminal matters which Maclean had gradually extended over the whole region behind the coast settlements. This was a very necessary step, for the chiefs and people were now being educated and could no longer, as in earlier years, be regarded and treated as simple savages. The extension of mission stations was in part the cause of this, though their influence was not wholly good, for the missionaries, who were mostly organised under the Swiss Basel Mission and worked from the Danish settlement at Christiansborg, were very indiscreet. In their anxiety to gain converts, they strove to sweep away all native beliefs and thus broke down the social system of the Africans. The vast majority of the converts of the Basel Mission soon fell away, but the social evils remained, and there was much disorder round the Danish forts with repercussions in British territory.

In 1850 the Gold Coast was separated from Sierra Leone and constituted a separate government with Executive and Legislative Councils for the management of its affairs, as had been recommended by the Select Committee of 1842.[4] The Danes, anxious to relieve themselves of their responsibilities in Africa which were proving very costly, offered to sell their settlements to Great Britain and indicated that another Power would be approached if she did not accept. The British Government agreed to pay £10,000, and in 1850 Christiansborg and the rest of the small Danish settlements were handed

[1] 6 Vict. c. 13 and 6 and 7 Vict. c. 94.
[2] C.O. 267/218. Grey to Governor Macdonald, 24 July 1850.
[3] For the text see Claridge, W. W., *History of the Gold Coast*, I, 452–3.
[4] Letters Patent, 24 January 1850.

over, thus leaving only the Dutch as our competitors along the Gold Coast. To the rivalry of France we will refer later.

The Legislative Assembly for all the chiefs and headmen of the countries upon the Gold Coast under British protection was constituted in 1852 by a document called the Poll Tax Ordinance[1] agreed to by a meeting of the chiefs and the Governor at Cape Coast Castle. They agreed to contribute to the expenses incurred by the Government on their behalf and were absolutely entitled to protection and the guarantee of their independence against Ashanti, so that the Ordinance was of great importance as a fundamental constitutional document. But the innovation of a parliament representing the people was not followed up and the Legislative Assembly never met again.

We must now return to the affairs of Sierra Leone and the Report of the Select Committee of 1842 concerning that colony. Its most important recommendations have already been dealt with in connection with the extension of British jurisdiction into native territories. Successive Governors had desired not only to extend their jurisdiction but also to acquire actual sovereignty over adjacent regions by annexation. To all such suggestions the Colonial Office was firmly opposed, and thus when in 1825 Sherbro Island was annexed by treaty, the annexation was disavowed and the flag hauled down.[2] Lord John Russell expressed this policy firmly in 1841 when he wrote to the Governor of Sierra Leone: "You are to consider yourself absolutely prohibited from concluding any treaty which should have the effect of binding [Great Britain] to give military aid to African chiefs or to assume any right of sovereignty or protection over any portion of the soil or waters of Africa."[3] Stephen strongly concurred in this and wrote: "If we could acquire the whole of Africa it would be but a worthless possession....Sierra Leone must have some limit inland, and fix that limit where you will, there would still be growing up among the colonists new temptations to wander beyond it, and on the part of the Government, motives...for overtaking fugitives by acquiring the country into which they have escaped";[4] and, again, Grey wrote: "The settled policy of Her Majesty's Government is not to extend the limits of the colony."[5] The renunciation was, of course, strongly supported by the members of Parliament representing the rising 'Manchester School', and Bright roundly declared: "Fresh acquisitions of territory [in West Africa] add to the burdens of the people of Great Britain and Ireland. We take the burden and we pay the charge."[6]

[1] Text in Claridge, I, 479–80.
[2] Sherbro Island was definitely acquired between 1861 and 1882.
[3] C.O. 267/165. Russell to Governor Carr, 8 November 1841.
[4] C.O. 267/169.
[5] C.O. 267/193. Grey to Governor Macdonald, October 1846.
[6] Currey, H., British Colonial Policy, p. 167.

Parliament was anxious to reduce this burden by making Sierra Leone pay its own way, and a new method was proposed to get rid of the 'liberated Africans' and at the same time supply the deficiency of labour in the sugar colonies in the West Indies, which was so seriously reported upon by a Select Committee sitting in the same session as the Select Committee on West Africa of 1842. The policy of promoting emigration of negroes under indentures from Sierra Leone to the West Indies began in 1843 and continued for nine years, but it met with little or no success. It was proposed also to obtain emigrants from the Gold Coast, but that attempt never succeeded, for the negroes there would not listen to any suggestions of the emigration agents who were sent to recruit among them. From the north about 14,000 emigrants were sent across the Atlantic in nine years, but when they arrived in the West Indies they proved unwilling to work and very refractory. The interest of the scheme from our angle lies in the fact that it aroused again in unison the opponents of the slave trade, who maintained that it was nothing but a subtle way of reviving the trade in a disguised form. The French sugar colonies were suffering as badly from labour shortage as the British, and they attempted to follow the British example and transport indentured negro labour from West Africa: they went to the Kroo Coast to the south of Sierra Leone to obtain the recruits. They persisted longer than did Great Britain, but with no better success. However, their efforts brought French ships and French merchants back to the African coast far to the south of the Senegal, where they had been rare since the abolition of the slave trade by France in 1830, and thus began a new rivalry between France and Great Britain in West Africa which was to continue until the twentieth century.

Before we trace the results of this rivalry during our period, it is necessary to note the later activities of Great Britain in Fernando Po and their bearing on the coasts adjacent to the Oil Rivers, where British trade was rapidly becoming of more importance under the enterprise of Macgregor Laird and his merchant associates. To the eastward of the Gold Coast, and intervening between it and the Oil Rivers, lies the Slave Coast with two important native towns, Whydah and Lagos, whence in the early 'forties much slaving was carried on. In earlier years England had had a trading station at Whydah, but it had been abandoned, and the West African Committee recommended that it should be re-occupied to prevent the slave trade from the native Kingdom of Dahomey which lies inland. The Wesleyan Mission on the Gold Coast was anxious to establish missionary work in the region, and its leader acted as mediator in arranging a treaty with the King of Dahomey against slave-trading. In order to supervise the carrying out of the treaty, it was proposed to appoint a British consular officer in the Bight of Biafra. Captain John Beecroft, who had remained in Fernando Po in the face of Spanish protests when the British station in that island was abandoned, was suggested for the post, but the design was not proceeded with, and Beecroft remained in an unofficial position. For several years he continued in Fernando Po as *de facto* Governor without Spanish interference, and the island was the base from which British trading activities in that region were carried on.

French merchants from their new settlement on the Gaboon were becoming very active competitors with the British for the trade of Dahomey and there were fears that France was aiming at territorial acquisitions along the Slave Coast. The Church Missionary Society allied themselves with the African merchants to press the Government to take definite action at Whydah and Lagos, for they had established a mission station at Abbeokuta on the Lower Niger and they desired some measure of protection against the undependable King of Dahomey. Palmerston, as Foreign Secretary, was willing to act and in 1849 appointed Beecroft as British consul in the Bights of Benin and Biafra, but the Colonial Office under Earl Grey was unwilling to accept fresh responsibilities in West Africa and so nothing was done. Abbeokuta was attacked by Dahomey in 1851 and suffered considerably, while the chief of Lagos, under the prompting of some Portuguese slavers, was making his town a centre for renewed slaving and a focus for anti-British activity. To remedy this, a naval blockade was attempted, but it was not successful in clearing up the recurrent disorders. France strongly protested against the extension of British interference on the coast, especially at Whydah, where she claimed to have ancient rights. Portugal, too, put forward claims under the old treaty of 1810, and the disputes dragged on through the 'fifties without any decision being reached.

Affairs became more urgent in 1859 when French merchants, especially the firm of Messrs Régis, began to use Lagos as a centre from which to recruit negroes under indentures to supply the plantations in their colony of Réunion. The negroes were ostensibly free emigrants, but it was shown with truth that they were collected in the native wars that were devastating the interior and that they were in reality slaves. When Great Britain protested, it was retorted that the system had a precedent in what she herself had done in the regions round Sierra Leone in the 'forties.[1] The arguments in favour of stricter British control at Lagos were sufficiently strong to convince Lord John Russell as Foreign Secretary that he must take action. The disorders in Lagos itself were a threat to the peace of the whole surrounding region; the palm oil trade of the Oil Rivers was of growing importance, amounting in 1860 to more than £1,000,000, and supplies of cotton were coming down in larger quantity than ever before from the interior and became an important substitute for part of the supply from the United States which had ceased with the

[1] *V. supra*, p. 669.

outbreak of the Civil War. The Colonial Office still opposed the occupation of Lagos on the ground that it would add another to the responsibilities we were finding so heavy in the Gold Coast settlements, but at length the arrival of French naval gunboats in the neighbouring lagoons between Lagos and Port Novo compelled the Duke of Newcastle to give way.[1]

A naval vessel with a detachment of the West India Regiment was sent to lie off Lagos in 1861 and demand from its king the cession of the town and port and a certain amount of territory in the immediate vicinity. In the face of this force the king gave way and Lagos was formally annexed. The Governor who was put in charge of the new colony was strictly enjoined not to take sides in the quarrels of the tribes in the interior, but it was very difficult to obey these orders for there was constant trouble with the King of Dahomey. As the Colonial Office had expected, the same sort of difficulties as those in the Gold Coast settlements were found in the government of the new colony, and the questions of domestic slavery and of jurisdiction among the neighbouring tribes were a constant source of trouble to the Governor. He was told that the colony must be as far as possible self-supporting and so he devoted great attention to fostering its trade, and Lagos saw its commerce in the products of the Lower Niger region rapidly increasing, the projects that Buxton had put forward twenty years before thus achieving at last some success. The cotton exports from the interior rose during the Cotton Famine of the early 'sixties, but the exports of palm oil surpassed them in value even during this period.

The independent Government of the Gold Coast which was established in 1850, when the settlements were separated from the nominal control of Sierra Leone, was in difficulties from the beginning. The idea of governing through a Legislative Assembly of the chiefs came to nothing, and it proved impossible to collect from the natives the Poll Tax established by the Poll Tax Ordinance,[2] for the device of employing paid collectors independent of the chiefs led to much peculation and constant local disorder. It was found that the only way in which obedience could be secured from the Fanti tribes was through their traditional leaders, the chiefs and headmen, and so a return was gradually made to the system of indirect rule which Maclean had employed. But the protected tribes would not pay taxes to the central Government, which thus was always in financial difficulties. The West India Regiments based upon Sierra Leone, which were at first employed to garrison the settlements under the Crown, proved unable to stand the West Coast climate for long,

[1] For details of these complicated disputes, see Scotter, W. H., ' 'International Rivalry in the Bights of Benin and Biafra", an unpublished dissertation in the Library of the University of London, pp. 62–104.
[2] Claridge, i, 495.

and a Gold Coast Corps was recruited from local natives to replace them. But only slaves and wastrels would take service, and from the beginning the Corps was mutinous and useless for defence.

In 1853 the Ashantis again became menacing and sent down an army of 6000 men into the territory under British protection. However, the Fantis combined together against them and with British help assembled a much more numerous force than the invaders, who were compelled to retire to Kumasi without daring to give battle. For the next seven years the settlements were in comparative peace, only disturbed by troubles with the mutinous Gold Coast Corps and irritating disputes with the Dutch at Elmina and other posts over their sale of arms and powder to the Ashantis. The general peace in the Protectorate led to a modest increase in prosperity, and some of the African merchants made fair profits on a small scale in the trade in manufactured goods with the interior through native intermediaries.

However, in 1862 the period of peace was coming to an end and once again trouble arose with the King of Ashanti, who complained that the British settlements were a refuge for runaway slaves and debtors from his dominions. He claimed that by long precedent it was customary to return such runaways on both sides. But Governor Pine believed that was only a pretext to pick a quarrel, for he knew that the Ashantis had been preparing for war for some time and had bought up all the arms and powder they could get from the Dutch. He therefore firmly refused to return the fugitives the Ashantis demanded, and in April 1863 they invaded the Protectorate in force. The Governor found himself in a very difficult position, for though he got together all the reinforcements he could from Lagos and elsewhere, he had no homogeneous force to resist the invaders, and the Gold Coast Corps, which ought to have formed the strength of it, was untrustworthy.

A long series of humiliations for the British and their native allies followed. The Ashantis beat them piecemeal in two pitched battles and for months ravaged the Fanti country at their will, plundering and slaughtering with little resistance the tribes we had promised to protect. British prestige suffered badly and especially because the Dutch Governor at Elmina openly sided with the Ashantis.

Governor Pine warned the Colonial Office that a considerable military force would be needed from oversea if the Ashantis were to be expelled from the Protectorate and the situation restored. He told the Duke of Newcastle that only an expedition to Kumasi and the decisive military overthrow of the Ashantis could ensure their future good behaviour, but his warnings were disbelieved in England, and after some months of vacillation, Newcastle would only permit Pine to advance against the invaders with a very limited force. But before anything could be accomplished, fresh orders were sent out to Cape Coast Castle that the expedition must at once be abandoned, and the force that had advanced to the Ashanti boundary recalled to the coast. The effect was calamitous. From the Battle of Dodowa to the death of George Maclean British prestige had stood very high among the natives of West Africa, but now, owing to the incompetence and indecision of the Ministers in Downing Street, it had been converted into open contempt.[1] The prosperity of the Gold Coast was ruined, and merchants and natives alike were involved in famine and bankruptcy. There have been few more scandalous episodes in our imperial history.

When the disaster was realised in London, it was generally felt by the responsible public that the hesitating policy or lack of policy of successive Governments had involved us far more deeply in the tangled problems of tropical Africa than had ever been consciously intended. The only advocates of a forward native policy were now the supporters of the Church Missionary Society who wanted to see their new missions on the Lower Niger more adequately protected from our base at Lagos. The African merchants, now that they had lost the inspiration of Macgregor Laird, who died in 1861, no longer combined together to influence governmental policy, and it was left to a group of members of Parliament, under the lead of C. B. Adderley, to demand a drastic limitation of our commitments in West Africa. The members of the group were characterised generally by a desire to limit our colonial responsibilities in every direction, and the fact that events in West Africa seemed to be involving us in a new and unwelcome colonial rivalry with France made them anxious to abandon all territorial control there save in Sierra Leone, and so to put a stop to the constant drain of the West African settlements upon the Exchequer.

Upon Adderley's motion a Select Committee of the House of Commons was appointed in 1865 to make a survey, as he put it, of the results of British rule in West Africa especially in regard to the matter of protectorates. Cardwell, as Colonial Secretary, consented to the inquiry and both Disraeli and Bright supported it, but when the Committee began to take evidence, it soon appeared that the idea of abandoning the settlements was quite impracticable. We were already far too deeply committed by our treaties with the native chiefs to contemplate it, and all that was possible was to refuse to extend our responsibilities farther and to concentrate our commitments in order to secure economy of administration and a definite statement as to what we actually intended to do. The Committee recommended that the separate Governments of the Gold Coast Settlements and of Lagos should be abolished and that they should be placed under one supreme Governor-in-Chief of the British West African Settlements whose seat should be at Sierra Leone.[2]

---

[1] Wolseley, II, 257.   [2] *Parl. Pap.* 1865, v (412).

The Prime Minister (Earl Russell) and the Colonial Secretary (Cardwell) accepted the recommendations of the Select Committee's Report and, accordingly, in February 1866, a Government-in-Chief of the West African Settlements was set up with subordinate administrations at Cape Coast Castle and Lagos. Each of the latter was under an Administrator who could not report direct to the Colonial Office, but was subject to the general control of the Governor-in-Chief at Sierra Leone. This arrangement was unfortunate and impracticable from the first. The Governor could only visit the subordinate administrations very rarely and could not be expected to understand the very specialised local conditions in each case. The whole scheme, in fact, was a flagrant example of the impossibility of drawing up in London a paper plan that would work, however logical and shapely it might seem. The Parliamentary Committee had tacitly admitted that the idea of abandoning the Settlements, with which they began, could not be carried out, but they had so little understanding of the real circumstances in West Africa and such a lack of foresight that their recommendations were for the most part still-born.

On the Gold Coast the new arrangements produced particularly unfortunate results. British prestige among the chiefs had touched low-water mark, and the recommendations of the Committee were made use of by malcontents in the hope of stirring up revolt. The semi-educated natives who had received some training in the mission schools believed that a British withdrawal was imminent and that they would soon get a chance of governing the country as they pleased despite the chiefs and the British alike. The Fanti chiefs were disquieted by the failure in the recent Ashanti campaign and their fears were increased by the official announcement that they must repel any future Ashanti invasion by their own efforts, and that they could only expect British assistance if the safety of the forts were menaced. There were serious riots at Cape Coast Castle and sporadic revolts in many parts of the Fanti country, and a complete breakdown was only averted by the fact that the Ashanti kingdom was on the brink of civil war and was in no condition to undertake a new invasion of the Coast districts.[1]

It was only by the determination of the British officials on the spot that the worst of these dangers were overcome, but one step forward was made by the Home Government in the hope of removing some of the difficulties which had made the Ashanti invasion of 1863 so perilous. The Dutch and British settlements on the Gold Coast were inextricably intermixed, sometimes side by side, as, for instance, at Accra, where the Dutch and British forts were only a mile apart. It was impossible to obtain a proper yield from the customs in the British ports because the goods could be imported free through the adjacent Dutch settlements, and this seriously affected the finances

[1] Claridge, i, 537.

of our colonial Government. Suggestions for an exchange of territory were made in 1860, but the objections of the native tribes under British protection brought the negotiations to nothing. In 1867, however, these objections were put aside under the new policy recommended by the Select Committee, and a treaty was arranged between the Netherlands and Great Britain by which the Dutch settlements in the eastern part of the coast were exchanged for the British in the west. This excited much unrest among the tribes and added greatly to the difficulties of the British administration of the Gold Coast. It was not until 1872[1] that the matter was cleared up by the cession of all the Dutch settlements in West Africa in return for the payment of a capital sum.

In this chapter our attention has been concentrated upon the West Coast because that was the only part of tropical Africa in which British enterprise was engaged upon a considerable scale before the latter half of the nineteenth century. West Africa had been the scene of European mercantile rivalry ever since the fifteenth century, but on the East Coast only Portugal had territorial possessions, and those had gradually sunk into unimportance and obscurity, leaving the Arab powers of Muscat and Zanzibar predominant almost everywhere in the waters of the Arabian Sea and along the shores of the African continent.

When Great Britain acquired Mauritius and the Seychelles at the Peace of 1816, France retained Réunion and her interests in Madagascar, and so there were rival bases round which new European interests began to grow up in East African waters in the second quarter of the nineteenth century. British activities in that region were directed from Bombay and were closely bound up with our policy round the entrance to the Red Sea and the Persian Gulf,[2] and had little in common with events in West Africa. But France first took a part in the affairs of East Africa because of her difficulties in finding a supply of labour for her sugar plantations in Réunion after emancipation. We have already spoken of the schemes of Messrs Régis for recruiting indentured labourers in the country round Sierra Leone to supply to the planters of Martinique and Guadeloupe. The same firm in 1859 began to employ Arab recruiters in the mainland territories of East Africa that were nominally part of the domains of the Sultan of Zanzibar. Their activities disturbed the trade of the coast, which was mostly carried on by Arab merchants with manufactured goods from India or Great Britain that came out *viâ* Bombay. The British firms affected protested to the Foreign Office, while the Anti-Slavery Societies, who had already agitated against the inden-

---

[1] Convention signed at The Hague, 25 February 1871, ratified at The Hague, 17 February 1872. See Volume III.
[2] See Coupland, R., *East Africa and its Invaders*, passim.

tured traffic in West Africa, moved actively against the French
extension of recruiting into a new region. They found also that many
of the old Portuguese slavers, ousted from the West Coast by our
efforts, had transferred their energies to the colony of Mozambique
whence they were carrying slaves in considerable numbers to Brazil.
The interior of East Africa was being thrown into turmoil everywhere
from the region behind Mombasa southward to the Zambesi by slave
raiders under Arab and Portuguese half-breeds, and the Foreign Office
was moved by Livingstone and others to serious action against both
the French merchants and the Portuguese. East African affairs therefore began to emerge from their long obscurity and to attract considerable attention during the 'sixties, but the important sequel of
these events must be dealt with in our next volume.

CHAPTER XIX

COLONIAL SELF-GOVERNMENT, 1852–1870

"THE normal current of colonial history is the perpetual assertion of the right to self-government."[1] So wrote Sir Charles Adderley in 1869, and such, in truth, had been the course of events in the sixteen years whose history he reviewed. Concession had followed concession; the strong current of events mastered all doubts. Lord Grey's paternalism had yielded to a genuine restoration of colonial self-government. Durham, Wakefield, Buller, Molesworth, Sydenham were long dead, but their works had followed them. When Gladstone took office in 1868, some imagined that greater changes were imminent and that the young nations of the Empire were about to leave the imperial fold.

These were the years when the British constitution was thought by some to have attained its perfect form, when the leading figures in our political life were the greatest statesmen of Victorian England, when Palmerston, Derby, John Russell, Disraeli and Gladstone held, in turn, the reins of power. It was a period of great administrations and growing prosperity. Facts had vindicated the repeal of the Corn Laws and the Navigation Acts. Taxation was reduced; exports increased; shipping prospered. England completed her passage to free trade. A new spirit of social philanthropy and religious toleration was abroad. Population had grown rapidly, the means of transport were multiplied, restrictions on the use of capital and on industry were abolished. "The genius of the age", said Disraeli in 1852, "is in favour of free exchange." Reform was in the air; it haunted the path of ministries and reached even the Universities and the Civil Service. Political life was active. Out of the confused situation of 1851 had come "the fated coalition between Whigs and Peelites", to be followed by a consolidation of the Conservative and Liberal parties. The country had confidence in its leaders; Russell was the tried champion of democracy, Palmerston upheld the British name abroad, Gladstone by wise finance had increased the wealth of the country and raised the general standard of life. Of these three it was Palmerston who dominated the earlier years of the period and, when he died, the great duel for power between Gladstone and Disraeli began.

"Peace", wrote Lord Aberdeen to Princess Lieven in 1852, "is the only great interest we have in view",[2] and after the blunder of the Crimean War England held aloof from Continental entanglements.

---

[1] Adderley, Sir C. B., *Review of the Colonial Policy of Lord J. Russell's Administration*, p. 3.
[2] Balfour, Lady Frances, *Life of George, Fourth Earl of Aberdeen*, II, 172.

The doctrine of nationality was changing the face of Europe and the balance of power. England regarded with sympathy the union of Italy, though not without apprehension the policy that founded the German Empire. Already she felt her ties with the communities of the New World no less than of the Old. But could she release herself safely and conscientiously from all responsibility for the maintenance of public right, freedom and national independence in Europe?[1] Her feelings fluctuated between pacifism and panic and this sense of her international responsibility, as the dilemma of her foreign policy, created by her imperial position, posed itself again and again.

But in these years she was in no mood for further oversea expansion. Bases of trade, coaling stations, strategic positions commanding routes of communication were not ignored. These things fell in with her desire for commercial expansion. But she had passed through half a century of colonial wars and troubles, and thoughtful men were already anxious at the magnitude of her empire.[2] Retrocession rather than expansion was her inclination, for she sought trade and not territory. So, in South Africa, she gave their independence to the Orange River Colony and the Transvaal; she would not be tempted by Napoleon III's proposal for a partition of north-west Africa; she fought shy of the Suez Canal project, lest she should be involved in Egypt, and she handed over the Ionian Islands to Greece. In Central America she came to terms with the United States: in the Pacific she refused the offer of the Sandwich Islands and Fiji and discouraged the expansionist spirit of her Australasian colonies and the arguments of missionaries. Kaffir and Maori wars made her reluctant to add to the native problems of the Empire. In West Africa her main concern was the suppression of the international slave trade, and when that was virtually ended in 1865 the abandonment of the West African colonies was proposed. Only in and around India did she continue to consolidate her power on a large scale and in China to force her trade. The political distractions of Europe and the United States left her a singular freedom oversea, and while she was watchful of France in their old fields of rivalry and of Russia's advance in Central Asia, no new competition instigated her to define new fields of interest or seek new acquisitions.

Such were the mood and temper of England and such the conditions abroad—peace for her and expanding trade—in the years which established and extended her policy of colonial self-government. No dangers disquieted or disturbed her judgment on its wisdom, or her outlook on the British communities beyond the seas, or impaired her power and will to give it full effect. Regardless of the fortunes of parties and the fate of ministries, her colonial policy

[1] See Morley, J., *Life of Gladstone*, Book VI, chap. v.
[2] Cf. Sir S. Northcote to Disraeli, 18 February 1864, in Lang, A., *Life, Letters and Diaries of Sir S. Northcote*.

remained steadfast and continuous. Like the old colonial policy, it had become a national policy. And, unconsciously, English opinion was reassessing imperial values. The conception of a possession, with all that it implied, began to be displaced by a conception of partnership on the one hand and trusteeship on the other.

"To propose", wrote Adam Smith, "that Great Britain should voluntarily give up all authority over her colonies...would be to propose such a measure as never was, and never will be, adopted by any nation in the world."[1] In that great chapter on Colonies, included in the *Wealth of Nations*, this was one of the few mistaken judgments. For what he excluded from consideration is in substance what happened. In the decade 1840–50 the new policy had been given effect in Canada and it was afterwards extended to the principal colonies of the empire. The mother country interfered no more with their administration. Within a few years almost all the reservations of power, which the Colonial Reformers and Lord Durham himself had recommended, were surrendered too—the control of their customs, of their waste lands, the form of their constitutions, the Post Office, and at last the sacred principle of free trade. Our "salutary neglect" of each other prevailed once more.

"Great agreement in the House on the subject," wrote John Bright in his journal, after Lord John Russell's speech on colonial policy in 1850, "marvellous absence of prejudice when the objects are ten thousand miles away. Should like to move that the Bill be extended to Great Britain and Ireland."[2] How many years of tragic history might have been spared could ministers have carried their new spirit across St George's Channel! Statesmen had seen before, and were to see again, that in most of its aspects the Irish question was "an imperial question",[3] but at this turning-point of imperial policy the nation at the gate of the Empire was not recognised.

In 1872 Disraeli, brooding on things past, said, "self-government, in my opinion, when it was conceded, ought to have been conceded as part of a great policy of imperial consolidation". It ought to have been accompanied by an imperial tariff, by securities for the people of England for the enjoyment of the unappropriated lands, by a military code defining mutual responsibilities for imperial defence and by the institution of a representative imperial council.[4] All of which was good criticism and showed that Disraeli had read Adam Smith on colonies to more purpose than the free traders. But was "a great policy of imperial consolidation" possible in 1850? Could the Whig statesmen have persuaded jealous and restless colonists and

[1] *Wealth of Nations*, ed. Nicholson, J. S., p. 254.
[2] Trevelyan, G. M., *John Bright*, p. 176.
[3] Morley, *Gladstone* (ed. 1908), 1, 697.
[4] Buckle, G. E., *Life of Benjamin Disraeli*, v, 195.

doubting Englishmen to take larger views? The historian cannot answer that question, but he can discern the strength of the forces which carried the new policy victoriously forward.

Adam Smith's conception of a united empire had gained little hold of the English imagination. The instinctive preference for local life which had asserted itself in our early colonial history remained pre-eminent. The current of opinion ran towards freedom. Self-government, self-help and self-development were the great political and economic panacea. Economic teaching had gained increasing influence and reputation, and as developed by Ricardo, inclined more and more to *laissez-faire*—colonists, like other people, were the best judges of their own interests. Men had grasped Adam Smith's central principle of non-interference, but they overlooked his complementary idea of imperial unity. Like other measures of reform in that age, colonial self-government originated with and was propagated by extra-Parliamentary forces and depended on the support of public opinion. The British Empire was not reshaped by a Washington or a Bismarck.

We must remember, too, the force of the American example, which had been strengthened by the colonial revolutions in Spanish and Portuguese America. The English follow experience, and experience confirmed the old idea that colonies were destined to independence. The inevitability of separation, and the need to prepare for it betimes, is the burden of much argument about the colonies in the middle of the nineteenth century. A weakening faith in the future of the Empire facilitated the grant to the colonies of the rights for which they had begun to ask. One lesson, too, of the American War was burned into the heart of England; if separation comes, let it be amicable. "If the North American colonies," said Lord Derby in the House of Lords in 1854, "increasing in wealth, in population and in importance desire to part from this country, in God's name let us part on terms of peace and friendship."[1]

Nor must we forget the opportunist character which English statesmanship so often wears. Great principles are enunciated when a particular problem calls for a solution. They are applied to the occasion and the circumstances. The Canadian rebellions produced the doctrine of colonial self-government: it proved a successful remedy and re-established itself as a general policy.

Moreover, with the adoption of free trade, the advantage of the colonial connection seemed almost to have vanished. Here again American experience had pressed the scale in favour of colonial liberty. The independence of the old colonies had not prejudicially affected our American trade. Nor had Adam Smith's idea of free trade within the Empire—of a vast internal market ringed by a common customs system—much attractive power on the mother

[1] Hansard, 29 June 1854.

country when colonial trade was small and when the universal adoption of free trade was the cherished hope of British statesmanship. What other advantages remained? The colonies had refused to take our convicts, and free emigration in any event, it seemed, would follow its natural course. While, if the advantages were fast vanishing, the dangers and burden still stayed. Colonies, it was argued, weakened rather than strengthened the Empire's defensive power. They were not likely to assist us in war, more likely to be its cause. England had passed into one of her recurring moods of pacifism and was anxious to avoid any threat to the long and profitable peace.

Economy was another watchword of the day. Colonies were expensive. Their infant years were costly and anxious. New Zealand and South Africa with their native wars had been a constant burden. The West Indies had involved us in much trouble and controversy. Why should we tax ourselves any longer for the pleasure of governing and protecting them?

Views such as these, widely held in England at this time, explain the easy acceptance of the new policy by contemporary opinion. Responsible government satisfied the colonists and suited England's interests. It was in harmony with the political philosophy of the time. It could be applied without far-reaching legislative measures, by a simple administrative act, by an instruction from the Colonial Secretary to a governor. It built on what existed. It could also be applied in successive stages, and to colony after colony, as circumstances justified, and thus gave to our imperial system a singular elasticity, appropriate to an empire of such amazing variety.

On this tide of opinion Great Britain embarked on her liberal colonial policy, and it was a policy on which there could be no return. Rather it gathered momentum from its own nature. As for combining with it measures of imperial consolidation, free trade made an imperial tariff impossible. The colonies would not submit to England's control of their unappropriated lands, and her record in this matter made it almost impertinent to suggest it. Colonial representation in Parliament was frequently discussed. In the debates on the Reform Bill Joseph Hume had excited laughter by moving to give the colonies, including India, nineteen representatives.[1] Disraeli suggested to his chief, Lord Derby, that thirty colonial members at St Stephen's would be a great element of future strength in the Conservative party: the method adopted in the election of the American Senate could be followed.[2] Molesworth urged the policy in the discussion on the Australian Government Bill (1850): "The colonies would feel that they formed with the British islands one complete body politic."[3] But no Government ever ventured on such difficult ground. Apart from the practical difficulty—"the wide

[1] Hansard, 16 August 1831. [2] Buckle III, 237.
[3] Hansard, 18 February 1850.

intervening ocean"—an imperial Parliament was inconsistent with the new policy. "The Colonies would not submit to be taxed by English votes, nor we by the Colonial." Later, Thorold Rogers rejected it with the wider argument that English and colonial life were too different to be regulated in common.[1] To the diversity of character and interest in the various parts of the Empire was added the diversity of forms of government which the new imperial system had introduced. There was no longer the uniformity of political method and spirit essential to Adam Smith's plan.

And in a more peaceful age the problem of imperial defence had lost its former prominence. Each phase of our colonial policy was shaped in relation to the mother country's changing needs. In the late eighteenth century, questions of defence and revenue loomed large and urgent and hence their importance in Adam Smith's conception of an empire. But for a large part of the nineteenth century, Great Britain, with her unchallenged command of the sea, felt secure; her colonies could not share the burden of her debt; and with the expansion of her industries, she was most intent on securing the utmost freedom for her trade. Her colonial policy, as had previously happened, was subordinated to her commercial policy. Thus the prevailing tendencies were centrifugal. Peace, prosperity and security have seldom been the promoters of unity, and a generation which enjoyed them would have looked askance on measures of consolidation.

The success of the policy sealed the decision. In the colonies to which it was applied responsible government speedily vindicated itself. Lord Elgin, reviewing the years 1848–54 in Canada, wrote that he had given the new principles full effect, and "intensely exciting questions", such as the clergy reserves and seigneurial tenure, had been settled in an atmosphere of general approval. Canada, previously unwilling to undertake any burden for defence, was now maintaining an efficient local force, and he looked prophetically forward to the day when Canadians will "desire to share with their brethren of the Mother Country the glories and sacrifices of honourable warfare". He concluded by observing that "the maintenance of the position and due influence of the Governor is one of the most critical problems that have to be solved in the adaptation of Parliamentary government to our colonial system".[2] His successor, Sir Edmund Head, pointed to the political experience self-government affords. The Canadian politician learned to "school his mind to principles of toleration".[3] And, on the other hand, the mother country was relieved of problems difficult for her to settle impartially and certain to bring her unpopularity.

[1] Rogers, J. E. Thorold, "Colonial Question", *Cobden Club Essays*, pp. 449–50.
[2] *Parl. Pap.* 1854–5, XXXVI, pp. 41–3.
[3] *Ibid.* 1857–8, XL, *Reports on Colonies*, 1856, p. 5.

From the Australian colonies came similar encouraging reports. The Canadian example had smoothed the way for Australia and it was felt impossible any longer to keep the Australians on a different political footing from that of the Canadians. Pakington had transferred the administration of the Crown lands. Successive Secretaries of State agreed that responsible government might be introduced, provided there was no injustice to individuals;[1] that the various colonies might frame their Second Chambers as each thought fit, provided they had the respect of the community and could check hasty legislation,[2] and that Van Diemen's Land might change its name to Tasmania.[3] They accepted the new constitutions with no alterations in provisions simply of a local character,[4] and though the Home Government declined to enact a federal union, it offered to consider any proposals for such from the various Legislatures.[5] The attempt to define local and imperial affairs and to limit the Royal disallowance of colonial Acts to the former, which the colonies themselves and Gladstone and Molesworth favoured, and to which it was argued the American constitution provided an analogy, was, after prolonged consideration, abandoned. The prerogative remained untouched, to be exercised according to custom.[6] Responsible government was also conceded to South Australia, in spite of the Governor's doubts,[7] and Moreton Bay was separated from New South Wales, since it seemed better to run the risk of forming into a colony an immature but promising community than to let ill-feeling grow.[8] The Colonial Office had decided to act in the spirit and not on the letter of Pakington's despatch. And so, through the four years 1852–6, and through the four administrations, Conservative, Coalition, Whig, and Conservative again, one common and increasing purpose ran. Successive Colonial Secretaries vied with each other in yielding all that the Australians asked. Never was seen such a rapid and generous transference of power. The response was immediate. The Legislative Council of New South Wales expressed "its deep sense of the conciliatory spirit evinced"[9] and the separatist party in the Australian colonies practically disappeared.

In New Zealand events took a similar course. When the General Assembly under the new constitution met for its first session in 1854, it passed a resolution in favour of ministerial responsibility. The Home Government at once concurred, and Sir George Grey wrote "that Her Majesty's Government have no objection whatever to offer to the establishment of the system known as responsible Government in New Zealand".[10] "The system", he wrote, "rests on no written law,

---

[1] *Parl. Pap.* 1854, XLIV, p. 71, *Papers relating to Constitutions*, July and August.
[2] *Ibid.* 1854–5, XXXVIII, p. 30.   [3] *Ibid.* p. 62.
[4] *Ibid.* 1856, XLIII, p. 23.   [5] *Ibid.* p. 25.
[6] See Knaplund, P., *Gladstone and Britain's Imperial Policy*, pp. 72–77.
[7] *Ibid.* pp. 60, 117.   [8] *Ibid.* pp. 14, 28.
[9] *Ibid.* 1854, XLIV, p. 8.   [10] *Ibid.* 1854–5, XXXVIII, p. 599.

but on usage only", and no legislation therefore is necessary to give it effect. The next year, "after a long struggle between contending parties", responsible government came into operation in Newfoundland. In Tasmania the first responsible ministry resigned office in February 1856.

It is hardly necessary to illustrate further the triumph of the new spirit. A great era of constitutional change throughout the Empire had begun, and the form of government was under consideration in most colonies. Where, for one reason or another, the new principle could not be applied, other constitutional concessions were made. In 1853 Newcastle granted to the Cape "one of the most liberal constitutions enjoyed by any of the British possessions", intended, he wrote, to appease the "jealousies of sometimes conflicting races" and "to promote the security and prosperity, not only of those of British origin, but of all the Queen's subjects".[1]

Responsible government wherever it was applied seemed an infallible remedy for colonial discontent. The "old irritant sores" between England and her colonies vanished and left no trace behind. The "din of indignation against Downing Street policy", which Lord Salisbury had heard in 1852, "from the Cape to New Zealand, from Bishop to potboy", died away.[2] Confidence and affection towards the 'home' superseded distrust and hostility. Loyalty became the common watchword and awoke new feelings towards the motherland. Subscriptions came from the colonies for the widows and orphans of the Crimean War, sufferers from the Indian Mutiny and the cotton famine in Lancashire. England's troubles had become the colonies' troubles. At the same time progress, which had seemed to avoid the dependent community, was apparent on all sides. A magic wand had been passed over the face of the Empire. No wonder that John Bright wrote in 1857, "now men actually abhor the notion of undertaking the government of the colonies",[3] while Gladstone triumphantly hailed the colonial generosity as the first fruits of a rational system of colonial administration. All parties and all opinions agreed. In Parliament the old acrimony no longer marked a colonial debate, and the government of the colonies, to their great advantage, ceased to be a party question.[4] Even Carlyle, who had hoped that the Australian colonies would not imitate the "national palaver" of the mother country, realised that England "must let her colonies go, in this wild manner, down the wind".[5]

Would England now renounce all right to interfere with self-governing colonies? Or was there some point where she would draw a line, some error that the colonists were not "free to commit"?

[1] *Parl. Pap.* 1852–3, LXVI, p. 364.
[2] Cecil, Lady Gwendolen, *Life of Robert Marquis of Salisbury*, I, 34.
[3] Morley, J., *Life of Richard Cobden* (12th ed.), p. 659.
[4] Cf. Hansard, 3 March 1859, and Walpole, S., *Life of Lord John Russell*, II, 302.
[5] Bodelsen, C. A., *Studies in Mid-Victorian Imperialism*, p. 31.

Would there, for example, be freedom in religious matters? It had seemed to England a worthy system of colonisation to found a Christian Church simultaneously with a civil polity. But established churches could not be acclimatised in the new colonial societies. It was soon apparent that what the colonists wanted was to substitute the voluntary principle for Church establishment. The matter was debated by Parliament in connection with the Canada Clergy Reserves Bill, when Newcastle begged the Lords "to leave the colonists of this empire to arrange their own church affairs",[1] and the Government declined to intervene. In religious as in other matters, responsible government gave the colonies freedom and they went their own way.

Thus, by the side of colonial self-government, the principle of the emancipation of the colonial churches was during these years gradually established and accepted by the Colonial Office.[2] The practice of making them grants of land and money had been discontinued: the clergy could not let their land and had no time to cultivate it. The colonial churches, following the analogy of self-government, depended upon voluntary support. But the Colonial Office was willing that temporary pecuniary assistance should be given to ministers of religion from colonial funds if that were acceptable to the colony and provided the grants were not confined to particular denominations and were governed by a general intelligible rule. Certain judicial decisions also made clearer the effect of responsible government upon the position of the colonial churches. It appeared that the ecclesiastical supremacy of the Crown was not effective in a self-governing colony, that colonial churches were more or less independent associations, and colonial Bishops, bishops of free churches. The Colonial Office gave consideration to the consequences of these decisions. While sensible of the advantage which the colonial episcopate derived from its connection with the Established Church of England, "it would, in their opinion," wrote Cardwell to the Bishop of London (25 May 1866), "be inconsistent with the settled principles of colonial policy to establish in the colonies by imperial legislation a prerogative in respect to ecclesiastical matters which the highest Court of Appeal has declared to have no existence in law".[3]

The basis for any necessary legislation was thus "the cessation of connection between the Crown and the Colonial Episcopate except in Crown Colonies; the equal freedom from the State of the Colonial English Church with that of other communions". "A simple voluntary constitution", writes Adderley, "was the inevitable destiny of the Colonial Church",[4] neither better nor worse than that of other religious communions, under which it would maintain its own

---

[1] Hansard, 22 April 1853.
[2] Marindin, G. E., *Letters of Frederick, Lord Blachford*, pp. 295–6.
[3] *Parl. Pap.* 1866, XLIX, p. 237. [4] Adderley, p. 399.

internal arrangements, as other corporate bodies, by the general law. The principle of religious liberty in England's imperial policy worked itself out in this form in this period. No colonial Legislature would establish the Anglican Church: all seemed willing to recognise it as a voluntary church. The mother country could influence, but not control, the religious life of its daughter nations. So another step was taken in shaping their future relations.

The status of the Church in the Crown Colonies was a different matter, but it was necessarily influenced by the development in the self-governing colonies. In 1869 the church settlement in the West Indies was considered. It was seldom in this period that home politics influenced decisions of colonial policy. But when the question arose whether the Anglican Church in the West Indies should be disendowed, or whether there should be equal concurrent endowment of Anglican and other Christian communities, the decision in favour of the former policy was probably determined more by the principles of Gladstone's Government than by the fitness of the negro population for the voluntary system.[1]

Lord Grey had thought that England ought to insist on Free Trade as the commercial policy of the whole Empire. He would draw the line at Protection. This vital issue arose in connection with the Canadian tariff in 1859. The Colonial Secretary hesitated about the allowance of the measure, but finally contented himself with expressing regret that "the experience of England, which has fully proved the injurious effect of the protective system...should be lost sight of". Canada resented the censure, took up the challenge, and claimed freedom in its financial policy, "even if it should unfortunately happen to meet the disapproval of the Imperial ministry". "Her Majesty cannot be advised to disallow such Acts, unless Her advisers are prepared to assume the administration of the affairs of the Colony irrespective of the views of its inhabitants."[2] So was decided the fiscal autonomy of the colonies and the sacred doctrine of free trade went by the board. But it remained a tender spot at home, and Colonial Secretaries still lectured colonies on free trade.

What about the native races? With all their giving, the Home Government were slow to give away the native. Exeter Hall was a power to be reckoned with, and English opinion was solid on the question and ready to express itself strongly. Humanitarian influences remained strong in English colonial policy. Before granting the constitution of 1853 to the Cape Colony Newcastle modified the electoral provisions of the Act in the interests of the coloured voters. "It is extremely undesirable", he wrote, "that the franchise should be so restricted as to leave those of the coloured classes who in point of intelligence are qualified for the exercise of political power practically unrepresented"; the exercise of political rights, enjoyed

[1] Taylor, Sir H., *Autobiography*, I, 219.   [2] *Parl. Pap.* 1864, XLI, p. 88.

by all alike, would prove to be one of the best methods of uniting all the Queen's subjects at the Cape, without distinction of class or colour, by one bond of loyalty and a common interest.[1] A Natal Act dealing with the natives was disallowed by Lord Lytton in 1858: he would not agree to differential legislation. On this matter "the opinion of all leading statesmen in England is so fairly pronounced (whatever be the party in power)".[2] But South Africa had not responsible government. The question was more difficult in New Zealand; yet even in self-governing colonies the native question was a stumbling-block in the path of concession, and in New Zealand control over native affairs was at first reserved. In 1856 Labouchère declined to interfere in the constitutional difficulties of the colony, but on the native question he wrote, "notwithstanding all the respect due to the principle of responsible government, the management of native affairs should remain for the present mainly in the hands of a Governor responsible for it to the Crown".[3] Three years later Carnarvon restated in similar terms the Government's policy. They "wish to give the fullest effect to the system of responsible government...but they cannot, either for the sake of the colonists or for that of the natives, or for imperial interests, surrender the control over native affairs". They have to justify to Parliament the expense of maintaining a military force in New Zealand and so "they must retain in their hands the administration of these affairs which at any moment may involve the employment of these troops".[4] The Maori Wars in New Zealand raised cardinal issues of imperial policy, the discussion of which dragged on for a decade and produced important political results. England tried to play the rôle of impartial arbitrator. But she found she could retain only the shadow of power. The Maori Wars convinced her that the colonists would treat the natives more prudently and more temperately, if they shaped their own policy and bore its consequences.

When the Hudson's Bay Territory was handed over to Canada, no conditions were made about the Indian tribes. Lord Granville preferred to rely on the "sense of duty and responsibility belonging to the Government and people of such a country as Canada" and was sure that the Indians would be treated with forethought, consideration and friendly interest.[5] The colonies, Lord Blachford told Florence Nightingale, know the wish of the mother country, but they are not very tolerant of her interference.[6]

Nor was the Government disposed to interfere in questions of constitutional change, as, for example, when, in 1854, Canada wished to establish an elective Legislative Council, or when, in 1860, Tasmania legislated on the same question. On the latter occasion

[1] *Parl. Pap.* 1852-3, LXVI, p. 363. [2] *Ibid.* 1860, XLV, p. 467.
[3] *Ibid.* XLVI, p. 479. [4] *Ibid.* XLVII, p. 179.
[5] *Ibid.* 1868-9, XLIII, p. 390. [6] Blachford, p. 251.

Newcastle explained that Tasmania could amend her constitution if she wished, and that he had declined to disallow the Act since it had been passed legally, though "in a way which we should consider in this country rather sharp practice".[1] Another Tasmanian Act was disallowed on the ground of neglect of vested interests. Newcastle thought the colonists were mistaken in sacrificing certain religious endowments, "but it was an error they were free to commit". "When vested rights were touched, however, the Crown must intervene."[2] Similarly, a Victorian law reducing the Governor's salary during his term of office was disallowed in 1862, though Newcastle did not dispute the right of the colony to fix a lower salary for future Governors.[3] The power of colonial Legislatures to amend their own constitutions was established and defined in 1865 by the Colonial Laws Validity Act, which provided that "every representative Legislature shall, in respect to the colony under its jurisdiction, have and be deemed at all times to have had, full power to make laws respecting the constitution, powers and procedure of such Legislature" and of the Courts of Justice.[4]

Thus the great matters were surrendered without serious friction. The Home Government did not always understand the colonial point of view, but they yielded to it. On the general conduct of Parliamentary government, though loath to interfere in domestic disputes, they gave at times advice, usually wise, helpful and impartial. Governors needed guidance, and in this field England's experience could generally provide principle and precedent. Nor did the Government refuse financial assistance on occasion. This, as Labouchère said, was one of the best means which the mother country possessed of assisting her colonies.[5] On the other hand was the principle, much emphasised in England in these years, that "coextensive with the right of self-government was the duty of self-support", and that insistence on economy which so much affected colonial policy and imperial development in these years. In the result, such help was only given in special circumstances. Lord Stanley, for example, favoured a loan to Prince Edward Island, as the Government was simply repairing a wrong done to the island in the disposal of its land in 1767. And Newcastle, in 1862, following the precedents of 1842 to 1851, offered an imperial guarantee of the interest on a loan to be raised by the provincial governments in British North America for constructing an Inter-Colonial Railway.[6]

In the adaptation of Parliamentary government to the colonial system the Governor held the crucial position. Lord Elgin, who had pioneered the way, in his last Report, as we have seen, laid stress on

---

[1] Hansard, 9 February 1860.
[2] *Ibid.* 21 February 1860.   [3] *Parl. Pap.* 1863, xxxviii, p. 561.
[4] Keith, A. B., *Responsible Government in the Dominions*, i, 409.
[5] Hansard, 10 May 1858.   [6] *Parl. Pap.* 1862, xxxvi, p. 657.

this. The Governor, he wrote, tends to become the link between the mother country and the colony and his influence must harmonise local and imperial authority, not by stretching his power, but by frankly accepting the Parliamentary system; it is his business to take account of the larger interest of the colony and his opinion will have weight for its impartiality.[1] Colonial Secretaries had frequently to remind the Governors of these principles—the Queen's representative must not appear the "sovereign of a party", or preclude himself from accepting as advisers any persons whom the course of Parliamentary proceedings may present, even if, as in one case on which advice was sought, they had been publicly disgraced:[2] the Governor must hold himself "as far as possible aloof from, and above, all personal conflicts", and Darling was relieved of his office in 1866 for departure from this rule:[3] he must uphold "the principle of rigid adherence to the law"—"The Queen's Representative is justified in deferring very largely to his constitutional advisers in matters of policy and even of equity. But he is imperatively bound to withhold the Queen's authority from all or any of those manifestly unlawful proceedings by which one political party...is occasionally tempted to establish its preponderance over another"; "it is always the plain and paramount duty of the Queen's representative to obey the law";[4] he "ought not to be made the instrument of enabling one branch of the Legislature to coerce the other".[5] Far from the storms of local passion, the Colonial Office, by its disinterested and impartial directions, sought to maintain the true spirit of constitutional government.

What was the extent of a Governor's discretion when he differed from his superiors at home? In 1859 Sir George Grey was recalled from the Cape for disregarding his instructions. The Cabinet held that a Governor might expound his own views when opposed to theirs and, within reasonable limits, delay acting on instructions which he deemed inexpedient, but might not leave them unnoticed or act in opposition to them.[6] Disraeli said that governing England from Balmoral doubled his work, and Colonial Secretaries had come to realise that Governors must have discretion and could not be precisely directed in distant portions of the globe. As Newcastle wrote to Gore Browne in New Zealand in 1861, it is not possible in time of war to "regulate affairs by didactic despatches which require more than two months for their transmission".[7] An interesting point bearing on a Governor's powers arose at the end of the Maori Wars when Bowen, acting on the advice of his ministers, awarded a decorative distinction, what he described as "a local honour", to

---

[1] *Parl. Pap.* 1853–4, XXXVI, p. 43.
[2] Martineau, J., *Life of the Fifth Duke of Newcastle*, pp. 311–12.
[3] *Parl. Pap.* 1866, L, p. 701.   [4] *Ibid.* pp. 695, 697.
[5] *Ibid.* 1867–8, XLVIII, p. 677 and see above pp. 370–1.
[6] Hardinge, Sir A., *Carnarvon*, I, 128–9.   [7] Martineau, p. 317.

members of the militia, etc. "for bravery on service".[1] In censuring him for this Granville states the general position of the Governor. The authority of a Governor is derived either from Acts of the Imperial Parliament or local Legislature or from the Royal Letters Patent which constitute his commission. By one or other of them the prerogative of convoking or proroguing the Legislature, dissolving the House of Representatives, pardoning criminals, appointing or dismissing officers holding during royal pleasure, is committed to the Governor. "The authority inherent in the Queen as the Fountain of Honour throughout her Empire has never been delegated to you. And you are not therefore competent as Her Majesty's Representative to create any of these titular or decorative distinctions which, in the British Empire, have their source, and are valuable because they have their source, in the grace of the Sovereign."[2]

Self-government promoted the spirit of nationality. Larger issues of policy began to arise, affecting colonial development and the imperial system. The confederation of Canada became a question of practical politics and the same possibility was foreseen in Australia and South Africa. But what would be the place of colonial nations in the British Empire? Confederation might possibly be a prelude to independence. On this large issue the mother country was chary of taking the lead. She preferred to follow the wishes of her colonies, but did not shrink from the logic of her policy.

Canadian unity became possible in the 'sixties. For various reasons the possible independence of Canada was not dreaded in England. Many thought it would improve our relations with the United States and, in any case, diminish the occasions of friction with her; and, on the general grounds of the prosperity, strength and harmony of the North American colonies, confederation was favoured and encouraged.[3] After all, it had been placed in the programme of our colonial policy by no less a person than Lord Durham himself. Nor had England in the days of her earlier Empire opposed the union of her colonies. Union gave them strength and their strength would relieve her of problems, burdens and expense. As for its effect on their ties with her, that was not a matter of anxiety. Gratified to think that with free institutions Canada had solved the problem of union, England took the risks of the future with good will. The temper and judgment displayed in the proceedings of the Quebec Conference, wrote Cardwell, "will ever remain on record as an evidence of the salutary influence exercised by the institutions under which these qualities have been so signally developed".[4]

As soon as the union was accomplished in 1867 British policy was directed towards strengthening the Dominion by the addition of other British lands in North America. Granville took up the question

---

[1] *Parl. Pap.* 1870, L, p. 42. [2] *Ibid.* 1870, L, pp. 190–1.
[3] Cf. vol. VI, p. 445. [4] *Parl. Pap.* 1865, XXXVII, p. 361.

of the Hudson's Bay territory, which Canada needed from many points of view. Moreover it was undesirable, and a danger to peaceful relations with the United States, for an inhabited territory to be without a proper Government. He suggested a settlement of the dispute with the Company and proposed terms to facilitate the transfer of its lands.[1] British Columbia followed into the union and in this case the Home Government took some initiative. In August 1869 Granville wrote to Musgrave that the Cabinet favoured its inclusion in the Dominion, since in the larger federation questions could be dealt with more comprehensively, and interests, particularly of transit, better consulted, and added that they had felt bound to give "a more unreserved expression of their wishes and judgment" in the case of British Columbia than might have been fitting elsewhere, because its constitutional connection with Great Britain was closer than that of other parts of British North America.[2] The steps taken to strengthen the new Dominion show that the desire to further colonial interests directed policy, and, whatever might be thought in some quarters at home of the possibility of Canada becoming a part of the United States, it was not the object of British statesmen to promote that result.

It is interesting to note here the manner in which British Columbia was carried through the stages of its political development, for the story is characteristic of the tendencies of colonial policy during this period. In 1858 Carnarvon thought that "at present...free institutions would be a useless gift", and Newcastle concurred—responsible government was "only applicable to colonists of the English race".[3] In 1863 the latter, then in office again, felt that economy and efficiency would be best served by the union of Vancouver Island and British Columbia under one Government, but local feeling was averse from this step. Moreover, Vancouver Island had representative institutions and could not well be deprived of them, and British Columbia was not thought ready for them. The fixed population of British Columbia was not yet large enough to form a sufficient and sound basis of representation, while the migratory element far exceeded the fixed and the aboriginal far outnumbered both together. So Newcastle conferred on the colony "a system of virtual though imperfect representation" through "the tried machinery of a Legislative Council". Two years later the Assembly of Vancouver Island for economic reasons voted for immediate union with British Columbia, expressing a desire for representative institutions, or "apparently for what is called responsible government". In these changing circumstances the Home Government took steps for the complete union of the two colonies, and, four years after, as

[1] *Parl. Pap.* 1868–9, XLIII, p. 440.
[2] *Ibid.* 1868–9, XLIII, pp. 370–1.
[3] Hansard, 26 July 1858.

we have seen, were urging the inclusion of British Columbia as a province in the Dominion.[1]

It was easier for the mother country to transfer powers than duties. In the old Empire the colonies had provided for their own local defence. After 1783 we took over the burden. But when the colonies regained self-government the question of defence arose again and became a principal issue in colonial policy. It is discussed elsewhere in this volume[2] and need be surveyed only briefly here. England's chief motive was economy. Colonial self-government ought to diminish her military expenditure; with that object, in part, it had been granted. Union for defence was pressed upon the North American colonies as a duty by the mother country although she refrained from any initiative in regard to their political union.[3]

For the same reason she was anxious to hasten South Africa's progress to responsible government.[4] The colonies were naturally reluctant to assume larger financial responsibilities. If they educated the mother country on the full meaning of self-government, she, on her side, had to awaken them to its responsibilities. You cannot "separate the blessings and benefits of freedom from its burdens", said Gladstone in 1864; in other words, the colonies should pay their own way.[5] A Committee, appointed in 1861 to consider colonial military expenditure, laid down some general principles, to which effect was given in the following decade.[6] British troops were to be gradually withdrawn from the colonies and concentrated at the heart of the Empire. Distant possessions would be defended by the Navy and otherwise as far as possible by local effort. Dependencies maintained for imperial objects would be defended at England's cost, other colonies at their own. It is noteworthy that the Committee was appointed primarily to consider the apportionment of colonial military expenditure. The broadest views of the question of defence were not taken, for the object of the reorganisation was not the strengthening of imperial defence but the relief of the English tax-payer. Moreover, the dangers seemed local—a native war, or a negro insurrection, or an American raid on Canada—and not a general war. Great Britain did not claim to control the various systems of local defence—she had never organised the local defences of her colonies in the seventeenth and eighteenth centuries—and she turned back to her old tradition. Nor did she ask the colonies to bear any part of the general cost of defending the Empire or expect their help in a European War. To guard the lines of imperial communications

[1] *Parl. Pap.* 1866, XLIX, pp. 121 ff.; 1867, XLVIII, pp. 281 ff.
[2] See chapter XXII.
[3] *Parl. Pap.* 1862, XXXVI, p. 604; 1867, XLVIII, pp. 415, 453, 473, 491 and cf. *C.H.B.E.* VI, 462.
[4] *Parl. Pap.* 1870, XLIX, Granville to Wodehouse, 9 December 1869, pp. 387–9.
[5] Morley, *Gladstone*, I, 573.
[6] *Parl. Pap.* 1861, XIII, Report of Committee.

and to protect her colonies as well as herself from external aggression remained her duty alone.

It was in the negotiations with New Zealand, faced with the dangers of the Maori Wars, that the question became most difficult and that the views of the mother country were most explicitly expressed. Writing to Gore Brown in July 1860, G. C. Lewis, then Secretary for War, defines England's conception of her obligations in the matter of defence. He "cannot silently accept what appears to be the colonial estimate of those responsibilities". "England cannot undertake the defence, against a nation of warlike savages, of a number of scattered farms or villages", or to "secure the colonists against prospective difficulties". She may be expected to punish aggression, to defend the centres of population, to hold the keys of the country. Beyond this her action depends on the demands elsewhere, on the urgency of the case, and the disposition of the colonists to share expense. "Wise government and prudent conduct on the part of the settlers will do far more than an increased military force to maintain the relations between Europeans and natives on a satisfactory footing."[1] The Colonial Secretary was not less explicit that the colony ought to bear the expense of the war. "The cost of all war and government", wrote Newcastle to Sir George Grey in February 1863, "should be borne by those for whose benefit it is carried on." "It cannot be alleged that New Zealand has at any time been governed in the interest of the inhabitants of the United Kingdom. The colonists are not compelled to give a preference to English manufacturers, or to carry their produce to an English market. They contribute no quota to the Imperial army, no money to the Imperial treasury. The British taxpayer, in short, has never derived, or endeavoured to derive from New Zealand any other advantages than those which the Colony and the mother country enjoy in common from commerce and emigration."[2]

How unsatisfactory the arrangements had become was to be seen, for example, in the financial settlement for the expenses of the wars (1868). "The winding up of accounts", writes Adderley, "was rendered intricate by the gradual and indistinct process through which imperial protective policy had been abandoned."[3] England claimed £1,500,000 from the colony for the use of ships, pay of troops, etc.; New Zealand claimed about £1,000,000 from the mother country for barrack rent, etc., including rewards for capturing deserters and postage, and suggested that the £3,000,000 the colony had spent on the war was due to England's mismanagement and ought to be refunded. No rational principle of settling the account could be found, and the Duke of Buckingham in the end thought it best to let bygones be bygones and made a clean sweep of the matter.[4]

[1] *Parl. Pap.* 1862, XXXVII, p. 262.   [2] *Ibid.* 1863, XXXVIII, p. 323.
   Adderley, p. 153.   [4] *Ibid.* pp. 153-6.

The final withdrawal of British troops was, however, much resented by New Zealand as a desertion of the colony. Granville, in his reply to Bowen (25 March 1870), absolutely disavowed any such wish; but, he argued, "the employment of British troops in a colony possessed of responsible government was objectionable in principle except in the case of foreign war and under conditions arising out of such a war". New Zealand could not be "made an exception from that rule which, with due consideration for circumstances, is in course of application to other colonies".[1] The matter gained a larger significance in imperial policy through being discussed in Parliament and leading to ministerial declarations on the question of separation.

Responsible government was not during these years extended beyond the North American and Australian colonies and New Zealand. The system seemed suitable only for colonies of English race. The Cape remained content with the representative institutions granted in 1853. But the question of military expenditure brought the constitutional question to the front and in Gladstone's first Administration the mother country was pressing the sovereign gift on its reluctant subjects in South Africa. Here accumulating difficulties complicated the question: "the relationship between Europeans and natives raised problems far more pressing than those of republican independence or colonial self-determination".[2] In some other parts of the Empire the tendency was to reverse the wheel of progress. In the early 'fifties the whole chorus of West Indian Governors was sounding a warning against extending self-government in the islands. The absence of the proprietary body and of persons of education was an insuperable obstacle.

Natal, Sir Benjamin Pine wrote in 1854, needs an "extended municipal organisation", not free institutions; local and practical matters, rather than large issues, occupy the attention of the colonists.[3] Here he touched on a central problem of colonial government. Canada, when she received self-government, wisely copied the example of the United States and created a better system of local administration. But, as a rule, colonies with responsible Legislatures tended to centralise administration, and the prospect of a colony obtaining local self-government depended on the mother country introducing it at an earlier stage of its development.

In the West Indies there was great need to retrench establishments, consolidate the services and bring about more concert between the island Legislatures. Not one of the islands was "financially healthy". England, feeling her responsibility for the welfare of the emancipated negroes, bore a heavy charge for a large ecclesiastical establishment. "In 1864", writes Adderley, "I received a letter from a West Indian

---

[1] *Parl. Pap.* 1870, L, pp. 278–9.
[2] de Kiewiet, C. W., *Imperial Factor in South Africa*, p. 6.
[3] *Parl. Pap.* 1854–5, XXXVI, p. 219.

Chief Justice informing me that an archdeacon had died, and expressing a hope that the vacant office would not be filled up again, but that 'if the House of Commons had more money to dispose of than they knew what to do with they would be so good as to send it them in any shape rather than archdeacons'."[1]

Large establishments, civil, ecclesiastical and judicial, disproportionate to the needs of the colony, were characteristic of the old system of jobbing patronage. Here was a compensation to the Colonial Secretary for some of the drawbacks of his office. In St Helena, a little watering station, for example, though there were only three clergymen, there was a Bishop for superintendence and he wanted Her Majesty to set up for him an Ecclesiastical Court of jurisdiction over them.[2] Such establishments were now being reduced and government made more efficient and economical. Some constitutions were changed and the West Indies declined to the status of Crown Colonies.

Ought we to attempt to assimilate the laws of the diverse members of the Empire to those of each other and of the mother country, even if we could not assimilate their political systems? The question was sometimes raised, and is a fundamental issue in any imperial system. In a discussion of it in 1858, Lord Stanley, while admitting the inconvenience of the diversity, said the Government would not attempt to establish a uniform system of laws throughout the British Empire. In time, with the penetration of British ideas, that might come to pass. But in some cases a pledge had been given and the colonists were attached to their own laws, and we could not purchase the advantages of uniformity at the expense of the loyalty and goodwill of any of our colonies.[3] The nature of the new Empire, the manner of its acquisition, the means by which it was held together, as well as the instincts of Englishmen, were against any compulsory assimilation. Ideas and traditions voluntarily and insensibly acquired would have more force as a means of union than such a policy.

The Crown Colonies do not concern our main theme, except as illustrating the vast and complicated system of government that had grown up throughout the Empire. Almost every colony had a unique system of government, appertaining to its population and history or the circumstances of its acquisition and life. The annual reports of the Governors presented to the Colonial Secretary a strange and diversified picture. If he ever had the industry to turn their pages, he must sometimes have thought that the sublime and the ridiculous were not far apart: in the Gold Coast Lieutenant Brownell enters the camp of 20,000 Ashanti and persuades them to leave the province without fighting;[4] in Ceylon the Ceylonese children learn the facts of English history from John to Elizabeth. We can understand why,

[1] Adderley, p. 307. [2] *Ibid.* p. 352.
[3] Hansard, 19 March 1858. [4] *Parl. Pap.* 1854-5, XXXVI, p. 202.

harassed by insoluble problems, he felt averse from further annexation, why the era was one of retrocession rather than expansion, and the Government ready, wherever circumstances would justify it, to extend responsible government. Perhaps we can also explain on this ground some of the delays which were so injurious to good administration. Free trade, the desire to extend self-government, and the humanitarian sentiment dominated policy and gave to it a larger and more generous tone. Motives of economy often cramped and perverted action, but the prevailing impression conveyed is, not of imperial greed or autocracy, but of a desire to understand the needs of the various parts of the Empire and to give to each a government, just and impartial and as nearly adjusted as might be to its particular needs and capacities.

Let us now turn from principles to persons and ask how far individuals were responsible for the general improvement in our colonial administration that marks this period. "Cabinets", it was said, "always hated colonies." Colonial questions took time, and ministers generally had matters of more immediate Parliamentary urgency and of greater interest to them nearer home. This threw the more responsibility on to the Colonial Secretary. Lord Derby, in 1855, criticising Lord John Russell's absence in Vienna, said that there was no minister whose presence in the country was more necessary than that of the Colonial Secretary, because his duties were so much apart from those of his colleagues and he alone knew them.[1] The Colonial Secretary generally meant the permanent officials. From 1794, for sixty years, the Colonial Office had been attached to the War Office—Lord Derby once wittily called it "the office at war with all the colonies"—but at the outbreak of the Crimean War the offices were separated.

There was now more ability in the colonial administration than in any preceding period. The Under-Secretaries continue to be men of intellectual mark. "The choice of a Permanent Under-Secretary", wrote Sir Henry Taylor, is "by far the most important function which it can devolve upon a Secretary of State to exercise." Its consequences extend through all the colonial empire.[2] George Higinbotham, the Australian politician, spoke in 1869 of the colonies having "been really governed during the whole of the last fifteen years by a person named Rogers".[3] Sir Frederick Rogers, Lord Blachford, succeeded Herman Merivale as Under-Secretary in 1860. He had entered the Colonial Office in 1846, early enough to be lectured by James Stephen on how to manage the colonies, and had been an Assistant Under-Secretary and a Commissioner of Land and Emigration. Taylor says that he combined "force with circumspection", that he had "a surefooted impetuosity".[4] Stephen had

[1] Hansard, 9 March 1855, p. 336. [2] Taylor, II, 131.
[3] D.N.B. article "F. Rogers". [4] Taylor, II, 134.

virtually governed the colonial empire for twenty-five years; Merivale, who succeeded him, held office from 1848 to 1859, and as Rogers remained till 1871, between them they covered the great transition. Most of the colonial business Lord Blachford described as official details and controversies even of the most petty kind, but two principles, he said, had established themselves in his time—"colonial self-government and the emancipation of the colonial churches".[1]

Though there was continuity in the permanent administration, the chief office changed hands frequently. During the years 1852–1870 there were some fourteen different Colonial Secretaries; in one year, 1855, no less than four changes; and only one long tenure of office, when the Duke of Newcastle, coming to it for the second time, held it from 1859 to 1864 in Palmerston's last ministry. But men of note did not shun the office. Lord John Russell took it in 1855, as also did Molesworth. Stanley held it for the third time in his father's administration in 1856. Bulwer Lytton, Carnarvon, Granville, all held it. It cannot be said that any Colonial Secretary of the period left his mark upon policy, for the lines were already laid down—they were common to both parties and no great and new declaration of policy was made.

It was a difficult and responsible office and the Secretary could not expect much help from his colleagues, for he was the only man who knew the business. Pakington, says Sir Henry Taylor, was "a man of sense", but "that is far from being a sufficiency for the office of Secretary for the Colonies".[2] He was Colonial Secretary in the "Who? Who?" ministry of 1852, so called because the Duke of Wellington, by that date rather deaf, kept ejaculating "Who? Who?" when Lord Derby told him the names of his somewhat obscure colleagues.[3] Pakington conciliated the Australian colonies, for which Molesworth gave him full credit, while declaring that as to Canada he remained "in Stygian darkness". Newcastle, Blachford found "painstaking, clearheaded and just", but more ambitious than able,[4] and Gladstone thought his administrative powers declining in his later years. Cardwell, who succeeded him in 1864, was "enormously safe".[5] Molesworth was one of the band who fought the battle of colonial reform and gave to the second Empire its character of a league of free communities. His keen vision saw it shaping into "a system of states clustered round the central hereditary monarchy of England".[6] When he became Colonial Secretary in July 1855 much was expected of him which his premature death disappointed. Bulwer Lytton brought imagination and an unusual knowledge to the office. The author of *The Caxtons* gloried in England's imperial destiny as mother of nations and civiliser of barbarous peoples. He

[1] Blachford, pp. 295–6.
[2] Taylor, ii, 78.
[3] Buckle, ii, 345, 348 n.
[4] Blachford, p. 225.
[5] *Ibid.* p. 226.
[6] Fawcett, M. G., *Molesworth*, p. 269.

gave a new social importance to the Crown Agents for the colonies,[1] improved the administration of the Ionian Islands, and in British Columbia laid a corner stone in the foundation of the Canadian federation. Ably supported by his Parliamentary Secretary, Lord Carnarvon, he trained and inspired him for greater work.

There was now more care in the choice of Governors. Before the Reform Act of 1832 owners of rotten boroughs put pressure on the Secretary of State in the matter of appointments. This kind of pressure had ceased, but a negligent or facile Colonial Secretary might do incalculable harm to a colony by a bad appointment.[2] Grey and Newcastle began a new practice. "Colonial government has become a profession," wrote Newcastle, and so there are not many vacancies for new men, though occasionally a place may be found for a man from India or elsewhere "who has shown a *spécialité* for the government of mankind".[3] With few exceptions colonists were not appointed; generally an aristocratic personage was chosen, if he could be found, though some of the best Governors were men tested in the colonial service. Sir Henry Taylor instances Stephenson, Walker and Wodehouse.[4] Lord Salisbury was seeking a colonial post in 1858, but declined the Governorship of Moreton Bay, which Bulwer Lytton offered him the next year, finding that the salary would be used up in the expenses of hospitality.[5]

A new spirit showed itself in our dealings with the colonies. Carnarvon saw the importance of friendly and hospitable relations with colonial delegates. Interested and well informed in colonial matters, he struck a more sympathetic note and showed a power of appeal to the feelings of the colonies to which they cordially responded. In 1860 Newcastle suggested to Palmerston that the colonies might be mentioned in the Queen's speech with "a little praise and sympathy", an innovation that would gratify them much. The Duke wished to retain the colonies "by bonds of mutual sympathy and mutual obligation", and knew nothing of the views of "some supposed theoretical gentlemen in the Colonial Office who wish to get rid of all colonies as soon as possible".[6]

The Duke's words remind us that these decades were the period when separatist opinion reached its height. It need hardly be said that it originated earlier. Adam Smith himself posed the remorseless alternative. "If the project [i.e. the project of an empire] cannot be completed, it ought to be given up."[7] In his view the Empire was a vain dream unless the colonies shared equally with the mother country in its government and its burdens as well as in its advantages. After the American War the belief in the eventual independence of colonies governed English opinion. The Colonial Reformers con-

[1] Escott, T. H. S., *Lytton*, p. 314.   [2] See Cecil, Lady Gwendolen, I, 32–3.
[3] Martineau, p. 308.   [4] Taylor, II, 242–5.   [5] Cecil, I, 65–7.
[6] Martineau, pp. 286–9.   [7] *Wealth of Nations*, p. 404.

tributed new ideas—systematic colonisation and self-government—
and restored faith in the Empire. But it was not clear whither their
ideas led, and after the concession of responsible government, more
and more the question was asked—to what end? On the surface it
seemed that the Empire was dissolving under the new policy. Much
was conceded, yet more was still asked. Lord Grey, in his *Colonial
Policy*, 1853, said that the policy of abandoning the colonies is "not
only openly advocated by one active party in the country, but is also
hardly less effectually supported by persons occupying an important
position in Parliament".[1] His political chief, Lord John Russell, had
hinted in 1850 that the colonies might go.[2]

Historians talked in the same way. To qualify our colonies "for
present self-government and eventual independence is now the
universally admitted object and aim of our colonial policy", wrote
Mills in his *Colonial Constitutions*, 1856.[3] Cornewall Lewis had provided the background of political theory for separatism, and Merivale
argued that after all it hardly mattered. Goldwin Smith, in the early
'sixties, gave eloquent advocacy to the policy in the press. He would
"retrench our Empire in order to add to our security and greatness".[4]
He did not expect Palmerston to do this, but when Gladstone came
to power he thought the time was ripening. And whatever the Duke
of Newcastle might think about his subordinates, the "theoretical
gentlemen" in the Colonial Office certainly held these views. "I
had always believed", wrote Lord Blachford, "that the destiny of
our colonies is independence; and that in this point of view the
function of the Colonial Office is to secure that our connection, while
it lasts, shall be as profitable to both parties, and our separation,
when it comes, as amicable as possible",[5] and, again, "we are, I
suppose, all looking to the eventual parting company on good terms".[6]
And Taylor, in 1864, wrote to the Duke himself that our American
possessions were a sort of *damnosa haereditas*. Ties should be slackened,
and "facilities and propensities for separation prepared".[7] He regretted that the Prince of Wales and the Duke, who had visited
Canada in the summer of 1860, had so successfully cultivated colonial
loyalty and that the American Civil War had given Canada and
ourselves a common object.

Checked for a time by the Colonial Reformers, separatism had
gained new force from the progress of events. As new liberties were
conceded, so faith in the permanence of any ties declined. The influence of the Manchester School was in the same direction. The
colonial connection was regarded as artificial and associated with
mercantilism. Free trade and *laissez-faire* biased their adherents
against it. From the point of view of profit and loss the colonies

[1] Grey, Earl, *Colonial Policy of Lord John Russell's Administration*, I, 17.
[2] Hansard, 8 February 1850. [3] Mills, A., *Colonial Constitutions*, p. lxix.
[4] Bodelsen, p. 88. [5] Blachford, pp. 299-300.
[6] *Ibid.* p. 158. [7] Taylor, II, 194.

seemed to have lost their *raison d'être*, and glory was only an "imagined advantage".

Colonies, it was argued, no longer served the ends for which they were founded. In an age of expanding trade and industry England's goal was to become the workshop of the world and colonies had no important place in it. What value was an Empire which we did not govern? Few desired the break up of the Empire, but many expected it, and some were therefore prepared to facilitate it. Bright wanted peace and thought that the independence of Canada would remove a danger of war. He welcomed Canada's first protective tariff as "the first step towards the separation of Canada from Great Britain".[1] Cobden was not always consistent, but he seems to have favoured separation. Of Canada he wrote in 1865: "I have felt an interest in this confederation scheme, because I thought it was a step in the direction of an amicable separation."[2] Trollope, whose writings appealed to a large public, argued that separation was in the interests of the colonies. They would prosper as the United States had done. Goldwin Smith, too, argued that the Colonies were injured by their state of dependency. He looked forward to "the moral federation of the whole English-speaking race throughout the world".[3] Too much must not be made of sentences torn from their context and casual judgments about colonies, but sentiments of this kind were general enough from all quarters to show the drift of opinion.

Thus the desire for economy, the feeling that the colonies would gain in wealth and dignity, the sense of inevitability and the determination to avoid a violent rupture were the motives that in different degrees promoted separatist opinion. As the colonies grew to maturity, the Empire was gradually resolving itself into a family of nations. Observers saw the tendency without correctly interpreting its significance. Was it evolution or dissolution? Who knew? They were conscious only that we were passing into a new stage of imperial development and prepared themselves to see it end, as the previous stage had ended, in a dissolution of the Empire, which this time they were resolved should be peaceable. Thus J. E. Cairnes, in a lecture on colonial government in 1864, writes: "The British Empire...has reached its natural goal.... Instead of a great political we shall be a great moral unity...in peace good friends and customers and firm allies in war."[4] In such language he expressed a general view. Canada, owing to its size and situation and leadership in self-government, was always the particular case for separation, the example of its desirability. The Canadian politicians who visited England in 1864–7 in connection with confederation returned home with the feeling that the independence of Canada would be welcome to England, which feared a war with the United States in her defence.[5]

---

[1] Bodelsen, p. 36.   [2] Morley, J., *Life of Richard Cobden*, p. 935.   [3] Bodelsen, p. 56.
[4] Cairnes, J. E., *Political Essays*, p. 58.   [5] Bodelsen, p. 45.

These feelings did not, however, imply any disposition to hasten the day of separation or any indisposition to fulfil the duties of imperial defence. At the time of the *Trent* affair England promptly sent 10,000 men to Canada. Cornewall Lewis, Secretary for War, declared in 1862 that, though he looked forward without apprehension to the independence of Canada, England must not cast Canada loose until she had sufficient strength for independence.[1] Gladstone, later in life, said that he had never been inimical to the colonial connection; and when in 1870 he spoke on the withdrawal of troops from New Zealand, he explained that the Government did not desire colonial independence, but only that, if separation came, it should be friendly. "That is the sense, the principle and the secret of our policy." The next year the Under-Secretary for the Colonies, Knatchbull-Hugessen, emphatically disavowed a separatist policy. The policy of the Government, he said, was to make the colonies feel "that there was nothing to be gained by separation"; he had the vision of "a confederation of all English speaking peoples bound together by a tie too light to be galling or oppressive, but too strong to be broken by hostile attack".[2] The uncertain future to which imperial relations tended may have had its advantages. Ministerial dealings with the colonies were probably the more helpful and conciliatory. Concessions were made without grudging. Let the colonies have the part, since they were certain one day to have the whole.

But the climate of opinion was changing. Out of the New Zealand question sprang the new imperialist movement. In 1868, too, the Royal Colonial Institute was founded as a non-political society for the discussion of colonial subjects and imperial problems. From it came in the following year a proposal for a conference of representatives of self-governing colonies to discuss imperial relations. The constitution of the Colonial Office, it was argued, was ill adapted for carrying on friendly intercourse with colonial governments, while the British Parliament was absorbed in home affairs. Granville deprecated the idea of "a standing representation of the colonial empire in London" owing to the diversity of the problems of the different colonies, and maintained that the policy of the Government had been misrepresented.[3] The proposal was rejected by the colonies themselves, but public interest was awakened and schemes for closer political union began to be discussed.

The movement of public opinion on large questions cannot be traced from year to year. Yet before closing this brief survey of colonial policy in the mid-Victorian era, it is convenient to summarise the causes which checked the influence of *laissez-faire* and placed imperial problems in a new perspective. It must be remembered that separatism was only an opinion and not a policy. It never entered into the official speech of ministers or governed their actions.

[1] Bodelsen, p. 39, n. 2.   [2] *Ibid.* p. 93.   [3] *Parl. Pap.* 1870, XLIX, p. 453.

Their policy followed steadily the revived tradition of self-government. Thus, on matters of policy there was general agreement, but forecasts of the future differed. Many, nervously apprehending the future, saw the shape of independence on the horizon and regarded separation as in the logic of history. But when history did not repeat itself, the false prophets lost their influence. Moreover, practically all the so-called separatists would have accepted imperial relations as they exist to-day as the goal of which they were thinking. As for "the man in the street", whom Disraeli called into our political life and vocabulary in 1866–7, there is no ground for thinking that he was ever separatist in feeling.

Throughout these years the people of England were becoming more conscious of Greater Britain. The immense emigration of the earlier decades created ties across the ocean with new classes in England, more sympathetic to colonial society. Power was passing to them and they had not the aristocratic or the commercial view of colonies, but saw in them their kinsmen beyond the seas. Popular writers made the colonies known: politicians, travellers and poets began to speak a different language. New notes were struck whence a new harmony might spring. Dilke wrote of "the grandeur of our race, already girdling the earth".[1] He criticised "the one-sided nature of the partnership", but he thought that the colonies should remain in the Empire if they wished. The retention of the dependencies "stands on a wholly different footing to that of the colonies". They gain by our trade, are "a nursery of statesmen and of warriors", stimulate our activity and receive benefit from English rule.[2] He defends modern imperialism as a mutual advantage. Tennyson, who was reaching the height of his influence at home and in the colonies, drew a new moral from American independence—"never more...shall we sin our fathers' sin". They "drove from out the mother's nest, that young eagle of the west". Writers who believed in the permanence of the connection felt their way to new ground. Some saw in the colonies, if generously treated, "a chain of faithful and most powerful allies".[3] Adderley wrote of the possibility of a "common partnership" as a middle course between dependence and separation.[4] The new nations might grow apart from England in their interests but closer in their sympathies as causes of friction vanished and their common heritage was realised. The importance of the Crown as a uniting factor began to appear.

The colonists on their part never viewed self-government or federation as the prelude to independence. They asked for what they thought their natural rights as Englishmen—the powers they needed to shape their lives in a new land, but they valued the connection with,

[1] Bodelsen, p. 69.
[2] Dilke, Sir C. W., *Greater Britain* (3rd ed.), pp. 393, 564.
[3] Bodelsen, p. 91.
[4] Adderley, p. 420.

and not least the protection of, the mother country. Self-government
had re-created loyalty and their real sentiment became better known.
After 1870 it was clear that feelings were changing. The arguments
for separation seemed to lose their strength, they faded out of politics.
The colonies had ceased to be a burden on the budget of the mother
country. They had not proved the occasion of war. No disruptive
event occurred. The inevitable independence had drawn no nearer.
No colonies petitioned for the freedom which was to be had for the
asking. Their growth and prosperity awoke a sense of pride, and the
development of communications brought them closer. Canada improved her relations with the United States and improved British
relations too, and her maturity did not break up the family of nations
in the Empire.

Great Britain, too, realised that the world around her was changing.
Peace seemed less secure. Her easy possession of industrial supremacy
was no longer unchallenged. The militant nationalism of Europe
isolated her, and its tariffs increased her sense of the importance of
colonial trade. A new competition for colonies awoke and put a new
value on overseas possessions. Europe had shown little disposition to
adopt her political and economic philosophy. In a changing world
she counted for less and her sympathies turned towards her own kin
over the seas. "We are bound to the communities of the New World,"
said Disraeli.[1] The current of world affairs was drifting the nations of
the Empire together and not apart. And the personality and opinions
of the Queen exerted a significant unifying influence.

All these things were signs and warnings of a new age. Out of the
old ideas, opinion was groping its way towards a conception of imperial unity which by its very nature did not naturally and inevitably
end. The colony was not a ripening fruit, but a growing branch. This
was England's reaction to the political and economic changes confronting her. The national movement which had re-created and
consolidated other nations and her own colonies stirred in her a new
sense of imperial unity. It awoke in her a responsive feeling to those
colonial communities which were heirs with her of a common culture
and institutions and still looked to her for defence. The idea of the
inevitable independence of colonies disappeared and talk of federalism
took its place. The large State was becoming the political form of the
future. Thus the imperial federation movement began. What Canada
had done, Australia and South Africa and the whole Empire might
do.

Disraeli, quick to sense the future, brought the imperial question
into the foreground of politics. We must reconstruct our colonial
Empire, he said in 1872, and respond to "those distant sympathies
which may become the source of incalculable strength and happiness
to this land". Attributing to Liberalism an attempt during forty years

[1] (In 1859), Buckle, IV, 239.

to disintegrate the Empire, he declared that the attempt had failed. "How has it failed?" he asked. "Through the sympathy of the colonies for the mother country. They have decided that the Empire shall not be destroyed."[1] There was justice in this, but it was not the whole story. Would they have so decided but for that policy of self-government in which both Conservative and Liberal statesmen had collaborated? Would they have so decided had it been accompanied by "a great policy of imperial consolidation"?

[1] Buckle, v, 195.

CHAPTER XX

THE CROWN COLONIES, 1845–1870

(i) THE SUGAR COLONIES

THE economic system of the sugar colonies down to the beginning of the nineteenth century had been supported on three main props—the slave trade, slave labour, and a highly protected market for colonial sugar in the United Kingdom. The first of these props was knocked away in 1807, the second in 1833–38, and the third was to disappear under the influence of the free trade movement which was carrying all before it in the mother country.

Already, in 1844, a considerable reduction had been made in the import duty on foreign sugar, provided that it could be certified as the produce of free labour only. A very short experience of this measure proved that the distinction thus made could not be upheld in view of commercial treaties existing between England and countries retaining the slave system.[1] The following year the duties on both colonial and foreign free-labour sugar were lowered by approximately 10s. per cwt. Then, in 1846, the famous Sugar Duties Act was passed, which swept away the prohibitory duties on refined sugar, abolished the discrimination against slave-grown sugar, and provided for a rapid reduction in the preference given to colonial sugar, until, in 1851, the duties on foreign and colonial produce should be equalised.

The colonists received the news with mingled fury and despair. In their eyes the decision of the mother country was an almost unbelievable betrayal. Even with the monopoly of the British market the freeing of the slaves had hit many of the colonies hard; their output had declined and their costs had risen. How, it was asked, could they be expected to compete on equal terms with the sugar of Cuba and Brazil, the producers of which not merely employed slave labour but also benefited by the slave trade, which the British Government had been unable to suppress? The admission of slave-grown sugar would mean, on the one hand, the irremediable ruin of the West Indies, while, on the other, it would give an immense stimulus to the prosperity of foreign countries whose produce was raised to the accompaniment of the blood and tears of hundreds of thousands of negroes still languishing under a system so abhorrent to the British people that they had utterly abolished it in their own possessions. The blow was the harder because prices had ruled re-

---

[1] Cf. Sir Robert Peel in H. of C., 1846, Hansard, Second Series, LXXXVIII, 97.

latively high in the early 'forties, and, on many estates which could still procure labour at a reasonable wage, it had been possible to show a profit. But it was precisely this rise in prices, due to the decreased output of the West Indies as a whole, that caused the population of the United Kingdom to demand the termination of the duties favouring colonial sugar. Nor can it be denied that the resulting fall in price benefited the home consumers. Over a period of ten years, 1845 to 1854, the price of sugar to the British consumer was reduced by 44 per cent., while the rate of consumption had been exactly doubled, having risen from 17 lb. per head of the population to 34 lb. per head.[1]

The Sugar Duties Act of 1846 had been in operation for less than a year when the great commercial crisis of 1847 came to a head in England. The prosperity engendered by the railway boom had stimulated over-trading in many other directions. In particular, many of the big merchanting houses engaged in the shipment and finance of produce from the East and West Indies had for some considerable period been indulging in unsound methods of finance, notably the advancing of money against sugar or other produce before ever the crop had been taken from the land.[2] The steps taken by the Bank of England to contract credit and protect its gold reserve led to the failure of a number of important firms. Between August 1847 and August 1848 thirteen West India houses and four Mauritius houses went into liquidation.[3] These disasters entailed the failure of many of their branches or agents in the colonies themselves, which were further hit by the collapse of the West India Bank, whose headquarters were in Barbados but which had branches in other islands. In 1847 the Mauritius Bank also failed, and the Planters' Bank in Jamaica in 1848. Many of the bills which were drawn by planters on their agents in England were dishonoured on their arrival and were sent back to the drawers, thus adding to their losses and to the general confusion.[4] The average price of sugar in bond, which had been 33s. 2d. per cwt. in 1846 fell to 27s. 8d. in 1847 and was as low as 22s. 6d. at the end of 1847. This was due to the general collapse of commodity values in England as a sequel to the crisis; to an exceptionally large sugar crop throughout the West Indies in 1847; and to the fact that imports of foreign sugar doubled between 1846 and 1847.

The fall in prices, coupled with the widespread belief (propagated above all by the planters themselves and by their representatives in England) that the British sugar colonies could never compete on

[1] Customs Tariffs of the United Kingdom from 1800 to 1897, Parl. Pap. 1898, LXXXV, p. 210.
[2] Committee on Sugar and Coffee Planting, Parl. Pap. 1847–48, XXIII, Part 1, Q. 2599.
[3] Evans, D. R., The Commercial Crisis, 1848–1849, Appendix, pp. lxix–lxxx.
[4] Committee on Sugar and Coffee Planting, Parl. Pap. 1847–48, XXIII, Part 1, Evidence, Q. 8092.

equal terms with slave-grown sugar, destroyed for the time their credit at home.

Unable in many cases to obtain advances from the colonial banks or to draw upon the merchants at home, the planters found themselves in a very difficult position. The higher prices ruling in the home market since emancipation had induced the planters to offer high wages and to put up with almost any conduct on the part of the negro labourers; but after 1846 preference in the home market was doomed, the crisis supervened, and prices came down to a much lower level. With costs of production, other than wages, as high as they were in 1848, it was impossible to maintain the rates of wages previously paid, even if the situation had not been complicated by the temporary financial stringency and the general shortage of liquid funds. Everywhere there was a concerted action to reduce wages, which in most cases was successful. By July 1848 it was estimated that there had been a reduction in wages in the West Indies of 25 per cent., and in some colonies, e.g. Antigua, of as much as 50 per cent.[1] In Jamaica it was found impossible to lower wages on some estates without suffering the loss of the whole of the labour supply, while in British Guiana there was a serious strike accompanied by incendiarism and much ill feeling on both sides. "With a quarter of the owners of the plantations in a state of insolvency, the wages in arrears for months, and produce destined for their liquidation seized by creditors, it was impossible but that an angry spirit should be generated."[2]

But no mere lowering of wages could suffice to maintain cultivation in the absence of credit and capital. Scores of plantations were abandoned either on the instructions of their owners at home or as a result of the ruin of the resident proprietors. Mortgages were foreclosed and estates sold at auction, but often no purchasers could be found, or the property was sold with all its plant and machinery at little more than the value of cleared land. In Jamaica proprietors gave up their estates and sold their machinery to sugar planters in Cuba.[3]

In two colonies, British Guiana and Jamaica, the wrath of the planters led to serious political consequences. In neither case, but particularly in Jamaica, were they prepared to acquiesce in the withdrawal of the protection they had enjoyed for so long in the home market, and they were willing to stake their all in a last desperate attempt to secure a reversal of the policy of the mother country.

The earlier struggles between the Combined Court and the Crown over the civil list of British Guiana have already been described.[4] The Civil List had been voted in 1841 for a period of seven years,

---

[1] Lord John Russell in H. of C., Hansard, Second Series, c, p. 363.
[2] Barkly to Grey, 21 March 1849, *Parl. Pap.* 1849, xi, p. 336.
[3] *Committee on Sugar and Coffee Planting, Parl. Pap.* 1847–48, xxiii, Part ii, Q. 12,870.
[4] *V. supra*, chapter xiii.

while in 1844, in return for a loan ordinance enabling the colony to finance the introduction of Indian coolies on a large scale, the Court of Policy had voted the continuance of the Civil List for a further seven years as from 31 December 1847. But the actual control over financial supplies was in the hands, not of the Court of Policy, in which the casting vote of the Governor always ensured an official majority, but of the Combined Court where the Governor and five official members were confronted by eleven elected members, and were therefore always liable to be outvoted. The power of the Combined Court had been greatly increased by the abolition of slavery and by the cessation of the Imperial Customs duties on the repeal of the Colonial Possessions Act in 1846, measures which had the effect of depriving the Crown of practically the whole of the revenues which it had formerly enjoyed independently of the Combined Court.[1] When supplies came to be voted for the financial year 1848, the Combined Court refused to grant them unless the Crown agreed to a reduction of 25 per cent. in the salaries guaranteed by the Civil List. The elected members contended first, that the Government had broken the implied compact in virtue of which the Civil List had been granted in 1841 and renewed in 1844, by passing the Sugar Duties Act of 1846 and so admitting slave-grown sugar to the home market; secondly, that the low price of sugar resulting from this latter measure had destroyed the financial basis of the estimates, which were now quite out of relation with the diminished resources and poor prospects of the colony; thirdly, that it was unfair that, while the planters were engaged in a desperate struggle for existence, the holders of offices should alone continue to enjoy the same emoluments as formerly. The colonists in British Guiana were further encouraged in their demands by the proposal of Lord Harris, Governor of Trinidad, for a drastic reduction of official salaries in that colony, including his own.[2] The force of this example appeared all the greater inasmuch as Trinidad was a Crown Colony, devoid of any elective element in its Legislative Council. The Colonial Office under Earl Grey was, however, determined not to concede to the Combined Court a demand which would have involved the recognition that this Court and not the Court of Policy was the real legislative body for the colony. Grey pointed out that the honour of the colony was pledged to the existing office holders by the Ordinance renewing the Civil List, passed by the Court of Policy in 1844; moreover, those in favour of this reform were really beginning at the wrong end in seeking to reduce the Civil List, which was responsible for only one-seventh of the public expenditure of the colony, instead of concentrating on the remaining six-sevenths in which there were undoubtedly large economies that could be made without either breaking faith or diminishing the efficiency of the

---

[1] First Report of the Select Committee on Ceylon and British Guiana, Parl. Pap. 1847, XI, p. 7.
[2] Harris to Grey, 19 July 1848, Parl. Pap. 1849, XXXVII, p. 574.

public administration.[1] The analogy of Trinidad broke down on closer investigation, not only because the finances of Trinidad were in a much more serious condition than those of British Guiana, but also because the revenues of the latter colony were less dependent on the prosperity or depression of the sugar industry, while in any case the bulk of the taxes in British Guiana fell on the labouring classes rather than on the planters.

The Combined Court, finding the Colonial Office could not be moved by the threat of the stoppage of supplies, proceeded to put it into execution, and refused to vote any of the tax ordinances which should normally have been renewed for the coming year. The stoppage lasted from September 1848 to August 1849 and involved the colony in a very serious double loss—on the one hand, the complete cessation of immigration, and, on the other, the blow to the public revenue resulting from the non-collection of taxes and the importation of large quantities of goods which were rushed in to take advantage of the suspension of customs duties.[2]

The conflict was finally resolved by the efforts of Sir Henry Barkly, who succeeded the very unpopular Sir Henry Light as Governor. Barkly was himself a proprietor of sugar plantations and had distinguished himself while a member of Parliament as an able and moderate supporter of the West India interests. None the less, like D'Urban twenty years earlier,[3] he met with the most bitter and uncompromising opposition from the extreme element in the Combined Court, and, sympathetic though he was to the distress of the planters, he was driven to acknowledge the complete unreasonableness of many of their representatives. "It is impossible, nevertheless, to forget that these gentlemen bore prosperity in former days as ill as they now do adversity, or to dismiss from the mind that my predecessors, without a single exception, have been forced, as the representatives of the Crown, to listen in the Court of Policy to vituperation as undignified as that which I am now called on to notice, and have been thwarted in the Combined Court by precisely the same manœuvres as I have been met with."[4] After the end of nearly a year of wrangling, during which Barkly succeeded in cutting down the estimates for 1849 (apart from the Civil List) by £80,000, or nearly 50 per cent., and in introducing a new franchise law to widen the electorate, the Combined Court gave way and voted the taxes for the coming year. This time the Government made no concessions, and its success was obtained, partly by its firmness, partly by a revulsion of feeling inside the colony against the suicidal policy of the extreme section, and partly by the arrival of the Report of the Select

[1] Grey to Walker, 17 June 1848, *Parl. Pap.* 1847–48, XLVI, p. 604.
[2] Barkly to Grey, 4 May 1850, *Parl. Pap.* 1851, XXXIX, p. 103.
[3] See above, chapter XIII.
[4] Barkly to Grey, 16 June 1849, *Parl. Pap.* 1850, XXXIX, p. 40.

Committee on Ceylon and British Guiana, which reported in May 1849 that the Crown was entitled "to insist upon an adherence to the Civil List arrangement made in 1844, for the full period for which the Civil List was granted, and that no attempt to set aside that arrangement, either by direct or indirect means can be justified."[1]

The dramatic events in British Guiana did not pass unnoticed in other colonies. In Mauritius an attempt was made to elect formally a political association to represent the views and grievances of the planters and to bring pressure to bear on the Governor and Council to reduce taxes and expenditure.[2] At a public meeting held in Port Louis on 17 October 1848 a letter from London was read "from which it appeared that the West India Colonies were resolved not to pay any taxes whatever".[3] The association was however proclaimed illegal by the Governor,[4] Sir W. M. Gomm, and the demand, which was made at the same time, for full representative institutions with an elective Assembly, was rejected by the Government. But many of the legitimate complaints of the colonies were met by a series of measures designed to reduce the administrative expenditure of the island and to relieve the financial stringency resulting from the failure of the big mercantile sugar houses and of the Mauritius Bank.

It was in Jamaica, as might be expected, that the repercussions of the admission of slave sugar and of the crisis of 1847–48 were most severely felt. The temper of the Jamaican planters was such that they were prepared to sacrifice even their own interests if they could thereby embarrass the Home Government or its chief representative in Jamaica.[5] Material for a quarrel was not far to seek. In February 1849, after months of acrimonious dispute with the Governor, during the course of which the Assembly decided to reject the Imperial Government's offer of a loan of £100,000,[6] a bill was passed and submitted to the Council providing for a reduction varying from 10 per cent. to 33 per cent. in the salaries of the Governor, judge, clergy and other officials of the island. The Council unanimously rejected this measure, to the fury of the Assembly, who accused the members of the Council (all nominated officials) of allowing their own self-interest to stand in the way of public retrenchment and economy. An open rupture between the two bodies ensued and, although part of the annual revenue was voted by the Assembly, the rum duties were allowed to lapse with a consequent loss of £50,000 to the Exchequer.[7] This dispute was temporarily composed in 1850 and supplies

[1] *Report from the Select Committee on Ceylon and British Guiana, Parl. Pap.* 1849, XI, p. 8.
[2] *Papers relating to Condition of Jamaica, Trinidad and Mauritius, Parl. Pap.* 1849, XXXVII, p. 831.
[3] *Ibid.* p. 895.
[4] *Ibid.* p. 843.
[5] Cf. *Correspondence on Mutual Abolition of Customs Duties in Canada and the West Indies, Parl. Pap.* 1856, XLIV, p. 234.
[6] The Assembly wished to use this loan to establish a bank for making advances to planters, but this purpose was excluded by the conditions imposed by Parliament.
[7] Sir C. Grey to Earl Grey, 31 December 1851, *Parl. Pap.* 1852, XXXI, p. 40.

were granted until early in 1853. The planters had cherished the hope that the new Conservative administration under the Earl of Derby, which had come into power in February 1852, would reinstate the preferential duties on colonial sugar. But the Chancellor of the Exchequer, Disraeli, refused to reverse the policy of 1846, and the colonists, feeling themselves finally forsaken by the mother country, abandoned themselves to counsels of despair. The Assembly in 1853 made a new attempt to cut down official salaries by 20 per cent. and, on its rejection by the Council, broke off all relations with the latter and refused to vote the annual supplies.[1]

The relations of the Governor, Sir Charles Grey, with the Assembly were by this time hopelessly compromised, and the Colonial Office therefore replaced him by Sir Henry Barkly. Barkly brought with him the promise of a loan of £500,000 at a low rate of interest to replace an equivalent amount of island indebtedness bearing a much higher rate of interest, and a further loan of £50,000 to enable the colony to reduce its official establishment. This offer was conditional on the introduction of important measures of constitutional and financial reform, failing which, Barkly told the Assembly, "it would be vain to expect that a body so little in harmony with the spirit of the times as the Assembly of Jamaica can be long maintained in the exercise of irresponsible power".[2] The Assembly, realising that this was no idle threat, gave way, voted supplies for the ensuing year, and, in 1854, passed an Act for the Better Government of the Island and for raising a Revenue in support thereof. The most important provisions of this Act were, first, the formation of a new and more representative Legislative Council with the power of initiating any legislative measure not involving the imposition of taxes or the appropriation of public money; secondly, the creation of an Executive Committee consisting of three members of the Assembly, one member of the Council and the Governor, to be the official organ of communication between the Governor and the Legislature, to have the sole power of originating any vote of money in the Assembly, and to control both the disbursement of public funds and the auditing of the accounts; thirdly, certain taxes, estimated to produce £50,000 annually, were earmarked for a term of thirty years to meet the interest and sinking fund on the loan of £500,000 and to make provision for the civil government. It may be noted that the first of the above provisions restored to the Council a right which it had originally possessed, but which it had been compelled to relinquish to the Assembly. The second provision was of great importance, both as a precedent for other West India colonies and as removing the main causes of the gross abuses which had characterised the Assembly's financial administration in the past, e.g. the right of every member

---

[1] Sir C. Grey to Earl Grey, 10 May 1853, *Parl. Pap.* 1852–53, LXV, pp. 169–73.
[2] Barkly to Newcastle, 16 August 1853, *Parl. Pap.* 1854, XLIII, p. 261.

to propose a money vote and its extreme laxity in regard to the collection and disbursement of public funds. The third provision gave to the Crown a fixed revenue for a long term of years and thus ended a struggle with the Assembly which had been going on ever since 1685.[1]

The apparent ruin of the colonies as a result of the passing of the Sugar Duties Act of 1846 was not allowed to pass without protest by the supporters of the sugar interests in England, who, although no longer so powerful as formerly, were still extremely vocal in the House of Commons. Their chief spokesman, Lord George Bentinck, succeeded in securing the appointment in 1848 of a Committee of Enquiry of which he himself was made Chairman. The Committee heard an enormous amount of evidence, indicating the extreme distress prevailing everywhere in the West Indies and Mauritius, but their final conclusions did not give much comfort to the colonists. They rejected the long and drastic draft report of the Chairman and adopted by a majority a report the only practical proposal of which was the retention of a differential duty of 10s. in favour of British plantation sugar for a period of six years.[2] The Government, now committed to a far-reaching free trade policy, refused to adopt this recommendation, though it made the minor concession of prolonging till 1854 the operation of the diminishing scale of preference laid down in the Act of 1846.[3] But although the Government would not yield on the one point which the colonists were unanimous in demanding—the maintenance of a substantial discrimination against slave-grown sugar—it was quite willing by administrative and other measures to give as much relief as possible to alleviate a situation which was undeniably critical. First, two long-standing grievances of the colonists were met, at least partially, by the admission of sugar for use in distilleries and by lowering considerably the duties on colonial rum in England and still more in Scotland and Ireland; secondly, the colonies were permitted to remove the differential duties which they had hitherto been compelled to levy upon foreign imported goods; thirdly, the restrictive provisions hedging round immigration were relaxed and Parliament guaranteed the interest on £500,000 to be raised by the West Indies for immigration and public works, while £155,000 was also advanced immediately by the Exchequer to Trinidad and British Guiana for the same purpose—the interest being fixed at 4 per cent., which was at least 2 per cent. below the rate at which the colonies could have borrowed on their own security; fourthly, the period of repayment of certain long outstanding loans, e.g. the slave insurrection loan to Jamaica of 1831 and the hurricane loans to Barbados, St Lucia and Tobago of 1832 and to

[1] Cf. Whitson, A. M., *The Constitutional Development of Jamaica, 1660–1729*, chap. VI.
[2] *Committee on Sugar and Coffee Planting, Parl. Pap.* 1847–48, XXIII, Part III, p. 418.
[3] Hansard, 1848, XCIX, 738.

Antigua, Montserrat and Nevis of 1843, amounting in all to nearly £800,000, was further extended; finally, steps were taken to reduce drastically the administrative expenditure of certain of the colonies which were hardest hit—notably Mauritius, British Guiana and Trinidad.

In 1849 an important measure—the abolition of the Navigation Acts—was passed by Parliament, partly on grounds of general policy and partly with special reference to the West Indies, which had clamoured for this for years. At the last, however, opinion in the sugar colonies was by no means unanimous as to the benefits to be expected from this measure, many of the witnesses before the Committee of 1847–48 holding either that its effects would be negligible or that it would do more harm than good, as any advantages gained by the lowering of freights would redound as much to the benefit of Cuba, Brazil and other foreign rival producers as of the West Indies.[1] The general results were certainly not startling: Mauritius and Trinidad, both of which islands exported a good deal of produce to France, received a temporary influx of foreign shipping, but it was soon found that the effective monopoly of British shipping was too strong to yield to the competition of foreign vessels.[2] In most of the British colonies, also, the planters were completely in the hands of the merchants and could not, if they would, sell their sugar direct to other countries. Jamaica had hoped that freedom of shipping would restore her former importance as an entrepôt for the countries of Central and South America, but the lines of trade had shifted and direct communication was being established between Europe and South America.

The abolition of the Navigation Acts was in a sense a necessary corollary of the Sugar Duties Act of 1846, but the disabilities it removed were more apparent than real and the victory turned out to be a hollow one.

The direct effects of the abolition of slavery, combined with the disappearance of the preference in the British market for colonial sugar, upon the economic system of cultivation in the West Indies were, first, the need for measures to counteract the shortage and irregularity of the labour supply, secondly, changes in the system of land tenure, and thirdly, changes in the technique of sugar cultivation and manufacture.

The shortage of labour in most of the islands which had been chronic since 1835 was enhanced by a remarkable series of epidemics which swept over them in the early 'fifties. In Jamaica cholera raged in 1850–51, destroying between 40,000 and 50,000 of the population, and was followed in 1852 by smallpox. The Bahamas were swept by cholera in 1852–55, Bermuda by yellow fever in 1853; while in 1854

---

[1] *Committee on Sugar and Coffee Planting, Parl. Pap.* 1847–48, XXIII, Part I, Q. 8177, Part II, Q. 9034.

[2] Cf. *Annual Report for Mauritius, Parl. Pap.* 1854–55, XXXVI, pp. 172–3.

most of the other islands, including Mauritius, suffered more or less from cholera; Barbados alone lost 20,000 inhabitants from this cause. These recurrent epidemics throw light on the almost complete absence of sanitation and hygiene throughout the West Indies, not altogether surprising perhaps in view of the state of most English towns at the time. Nevertheless, the conditions in the British West Indies formed a humiliating contrast with those existing in the French and Spanish West India islands. In Kingston there was neither lighting nor scavenging. "Never was a town more disgracefully neglected than the chief town of the chief island of the British West Indies", said a doctor sent out to report to the British Government, and he added: "The colonists if left to themselves will do little and that little badly."[1] The same authority described in very strong terms the wretched housing conditions of the mass of the population in Jamaica, which in his view were the cause that "in spite of 200 ministers of religion it is an acknowledged fact that the bulk of the people are retrograding both in morals and enlightenment".[2]

The problem of the scarcity of labour, especially for field work in the sugar plantations, was one which could be successfully dealt with only by the importation of additional labourers from outside. This was true in a greater or less measure of all the sugar colonies, with the single important exception of Barbados, but in a pre-eminent degree of Mauritius, British Guiana and Trinidad. In each of these colonies there was a relatively small native negro population, which seemed to be withdrawing more and more from field work of every kind, except mere subsistence cultivation; in each there was an abundance of fertile land, and the sole hope of the maintenance and expansion of the sugar industry lay in the importation of labour from outside. The main source of supply of such labour was India, though both British Guiana and Trinidad had important subsidiary sources in the Portuguese of Madeira and the Creoles of the other West India islands. But there were two formidable obstacles in the way of immigration—the problem of finance, and the restrictive provisions enforced by the Colonial Office. The first of these difficulties was largely removed for British Guiana and Trinidad by the loan of £375,000 made to these colonies by the Imperial Parliament in 1848 for immigration purposes.[3] The wealth of Mauritius was so great and her revenues expanded so rapidly with the increasing cultivation of sugar that she was able to finance the whole of her immigration from her own resources without external assistance. The second obstacle was more serious. During almost the whole of the long reign of Sir James Stephen as Permanent Under-Secretary of the Colonial

[1] *Report of Dr Milroy on the Cholera in Jamaica, Parl. Pap.* 1854, XLIII, p. 397.
[2] *Ibid.* p. 391.
[3] British Guiana used £50,000 out of the £250,000 allotted to her for the construction of a railway.

Office, there was a rigid insistence on the stipulation that no contract might be entered into with an immigrant labourer which had a longer duration than one year. But in 1846 Mr Gladstone sanctioned three-year contracts, subject to the right of cancellation after six months' service, on giving one month's notice, and on repayment being made of a fair proportion of the cost of conveying the immigrant to the colony. This concession, however, was deprived of much of its value to the planters because it did not apply to Africans or Indians, its effective scope being virtually limited to the Portuguese from Madeira, the Canaries, etc. Very slowly and only under the continual pressure of the colonists, supported by the strong recommendations of the Governors, the Colonial Office was forced reluctantly to modify the rigidity of its policy. Under Earl Grey permission was first given in 1848 for three-year contracts with Africans imported at the expense of the colonists,[1] and in 1849 with Indians, but in each case only if the contracts were made within the colony; while in 1850, for special reasons, contracts for five years with Chinese outside the colony were allowed. In 1857 Indian immigrants to Mauritius were allowed to be engaged in India under contracts of service for three years and in 1862 the term was extended to five years, the same privilege being also granted to British Guiana, Trinidad, Jamaica and to other colonies importing Indians.

At the same time other restrictions continued to hedge round immigration and to increase its cost. Only ships conforming to prescribed regulations as to size, deck-clearance, etc., might be used for conveying immigrants; Indians might not be shipped to the West Indies except in certain specified months (September 1 to March 1); it was required that a certain proportion of the immigrants should be females; and the introduction of Africans was almost wholly confined to those released from the captured slave ships of other nations. Even the limited and carefully controlled immigration of Africans, particularly those released from slave ships, involved us in difficulties with other countries such as France, and laid us open to the charge of hypocrisy and to the accusation that "our capture of slave ships and disposal of their human cargo was 'not a ruinous work of philanthropy, but very good business'".[2]

It is clear that these regulations were necessary in the interest of the immigrants, but they had the effect of increasing the cost and were therefore unpopular in the colonies. Apart from the refusal to permit the free recruitment of Africans—a policy to which the Colonial Office steadfastly and rightly adhered—the colonists resented most strongly the repeated disallowance of their local laws or ordinances, aimed at legalising contracts of longer duration than one year and at preventing vagrancy and evasion on the part of the imported labourers.

[1] In the case of Jamaica this permission was not given till 1855.
[2] Mathieson, W. L., *Great Britain and the Slave Trade, 1839–1865*, p. 154.

While the colonists at times laid themselves open to the charge that they were seeking to substitute a condition of virtual serfdom imposed on their immigrant labour for the old state of slavery, they had much to endure from the continuous misrepresentations of the missionaries and from the inability of the well-meaning but doctrinaire administrators of Downing Street to grasp the precise nature of the problem confronting the sugar colonies. Earl Grey was never tired of reiterating his faith in short contracts and the operation of economic forces. Contracts of such length as three years he declared would deaden the incentive to work hard.[1] But when in 1847 he disallowed an ordinance of Lord Harris designed to keep the coolies in Trinidad on the estates to which they had been sent, the only result was that the Indians wandered away and died by hundreds in the bush and along the roadside.[2] It was not realised by Grey that long contracts, provided that they were subject to suitable safeguards, protected the interests of the immigrants as well as those of the planters. When attempts were made to bring in Chinese, it was found that they refused to come unless they were guaranteed a long contract in advance, and it was found necessary to give permission to enter into five-year contracts with them at the port of embarcation. There was a strong consensus of opinion amongst the Governors of colonies that the well-being of the coolies was greater under long than under short contracts, and the same applied to most other categories of imported labour. Thus Lord Harris, the very able Governor of Trinidad, in pressing Grey to consent to longer contracts for liberated Africans, urged that his main object was "not to increase the industrial value of the labourer, but in the hope of accelerating the moral and social improvement of the man".[3]

It was in Mauritius, on the initiative of Earl Grey, that the first successful attempt was made, in 1847, to control the vagrant habits of the Indians and so obviate the serious loss caused by the desertion of coolies who had been introduced at great expense to work as labourers on the sugar estates. It was then provided that planters should pay a stamp duty on contracts to cover part if not the whole of the cost of immigration, and that the immigrant should pay a monthly tax whenever he was not actually working under contract. At the end of five years' industrial residence (defined as residence in the colony under an engagement to labour for hire) the cost of his passage back to India, if he wished to return, was to be paid by the colony.[4] This system proved very successful in Mauritius, and it was shortly afterwards adopted in British Guiana and Trinidad, and later in Jamaica and St Lucia. The cost of providing return passages, however, became

[1] Grey to Barkly, 15 December 1849, *Parl. Pap.* 1850, XL, p. 489.
[2] Harris to Grey, 21 February 1848, *Parl. Pap.* 1847–48, XLVI, p. 183 and Davy, J., *The West Indies before and since Emancipation* (1854), p. 309.
[3] Harris to Grey, 23 November 1850, *Parl. Pap.* 1852–53, LXVII, p. 441.
[4] Earl Grey, *The Colonial Policy of Lord John Russell's Administration* (1853), I, 71–5.

a heavy burden, and in 1853 the Colonial Office and the Government of India agreed in the case of the West Indies to the extension of the qualifying period for a free passage to ten years, of which it was required that five years should be under indenture, while in Mauritius the return passage was abrogated.[1] The immigrants were also encouraged to stay in the colony to which they had been brought, by the grant of a bonus in the form of money or land in lieu of their return passage.

Thus immigration, adopted at the outset in a haphazard manner as a means of helping the planter out of difficulties resulting from the abolition of slavery, developed finally into a regular system of indentured labour, in spite of the natural reluctance of the Colonial Office, which found it difficult to convince public opinion in England of the need of such restraints.[2] In the three colonies, Mauritius, British Guiana and Trinidad, immigration did much more than merely supplement the uncertain work of the ex-slaves and apprentices and prevent the abandonment of sugar cultivation: it led to a large expansion of the sugar industry based entirely on indentured labour imported from outside. A Governor of Mauritius, commenting on the progress of the island, described immigration as "this sheet anchor of colonial prosperity".[3] There were not wanting critics of this development, who objected to the building up of the industry on a larger scale by means of compulsion, as a retrogressive move involving a return to quasi-servile methods of cultivation.[4] But while admitting that there is much to be said for this point of view, there can be no doubt that the whole success of immigration as an economic policy depended upon the application for the first few years of some degree of constraint after the immigrants had been recruited and had arrived in the colony. Labour conditions and types of contract prevailing in England were not applicable to the tropical sugar colonies, and though the Portuguese from Madeira could work in the tropics satisfactorily without indentures, they were the only type of labour available that could be relied upon to do so; the Indian coolies could not. But whereas between 1850 and 1860 a large proportion of the Indians brought in to the colonies returned to India, this practice became increasingly rare[5] in the succeeding decade, as conditions became more familiar, arrangements for their reception were perfected, and the proportion of women of their own race increased—in 1870 there were half as many Indian females as males in Mauritius. Once the coolies had become educated to steady habits of work, there

[1] *Fourteenth Report of Colonial Land and Emigration Commissioners, Parl. Pap.* 1854, XXVIII, pp. 64–6.
[2] Grey to Harris, 15 April 1848, *Parl. Pap.* 1847–48, XLV, p. 201.
[3] Higginson to Labouchere, 31 May 1856, *Parl. Pap.* 1857, Sess. 1, X, p. 226.
[4] Hincks to Labouchere, 22 August 1857, *Parl. Pap.* 1859, Sess. 2, XXI, p. 45.
[5] It was estimated in 1870 that not more than 20 per cent. of the Indians introduced into British Guiana returned home. *Annual Report on British Guiana for 1870, Parl. Pap.* 1872, XLII, p. 56.

was little need for constraint. Thus, out of a total Indian population in Trinidad of 28,425 in 1870, 7855 were under their first five years' contract, 2330 having completed their original contracts were working under fresh engagements, leaving 18,209 residents in the colony under no form of indenture.[1] Even those who went back to India were not necessarily a loss to the colony, because "the steady return of coolies with their savings is steadily though slowly raising the reputation of Trinidad as a labour market".[2]

In Mauritius the ease with which Indians could be introduced led to considerable laxity in their treatment, in spite of the efforts of the Directors of the East India Company. The unsatisfactory conditions under which the Indians were employed were finally revealed as a consequence of an Ordinance, which was passed in 1867 under the influence of the very depressed state of the colony, due to a series of bad sugar crops, a bad epidemic of malaria and a severe hurricane. The Ordinance, which was rushed through in a moment of panic and, surprisingly, was not disallowed by the Colonial Office, was designed to compel the old immigrants (i.e. those whose indentures had expired) to re-engage themselves in regular employment, especially on the sugar plantations. The provisions of the Ordinance proved to be exceedingly oppressive, and in response to complaints a Royal Commission was appointed in 1872 to investigate the working of the immigration system. Its report in 1874 roundly condemned the innovations of 1867,[3] with the result that the objectionable features of the Ordinance were repealed, and much-needed improvements in other directions were introduced.

The native Creoles in all the islands resolutely refused to enter into any form of contract and retained their freedom to work, or not, for the plantations as they chose, with results that were generally ruinous to the industry where only their labour could be had. In the one important exception—Barbados—the over-population of the island, combined with a marked reluctance to emigrate—exercised as powerful a form of economic compulsion as was possible elsewhere by means of legislation applied to immigrant labour.[4] But it is important to recognise that in many of the islands such factors as irregularity of wage payment (often due to lack of funds), the shortage of cottages, insecurity of tenure, the abuses of absentee ownership, etc., contributed powerfully to discourage the negroes from working as labourers on the plantations.

Jamaica, alone of the major sugar colonies, not merely suffered

[1] *Annual Report on British Guiana for 1870, Parl. Pap.* 1872, XLII, p. 77.
[2] *Report on Immigration, Parl. Pap.* 1860, XLIV, p. 38.
[3] *Report of Royal Commission on Treatment of Immigrants in Mauritius, Parl. Pap.* 1875, XXXIV, pp. 577–84.
[4] Yet the pressure of population drove as many as 20,000 Barbadians to emigrate to other islands in the West Indies and to British Guiana during the decade 1861–71; nevertheless the population had increased by 10,000 at the census of 1871. *Annual Report on Barbados for 1871, Parl. Pap.* 1873, XLVIII, p. 104.

acutely from shortage of labour, but also never succeeded, in spite of many attempts, in procuring immigrants on a large scale. The total number brought in between 1845 and 1870 was only 22,034 compared with 128,259 for British Guiana and 50,279 for Trinidad, and this in spite of a very considerable expenditure. The disparity between Jamaica and other West India colonies, which were able to attract immigrants, arose from causes which were largely peculiar to the former. There was in Jamaica, far more than elsewhere, an organised opposition to immigration, which came chiefly from the missionaries and from the negro members of the Legislative Assembly, who feared that competition would lessen the dependence of the planters upon Creole labour. For this reason this party obstructed every endeavour to finance immigration out of the public revenues and sought to throw the whole burden on the proprietors of estates. Moreover, the administrative machinery in Jamaica was so inefficient and corrupt that much of the money voted for immigration purposes was merely wasted, while many of the schemes proposed were abortive because they contained provisions to which the Colonial Office refused to give its consent. But there were also economic reasons which rendered immigration to Jamaica less attractive than elsewhere, both to the immigrant and to the individual planters. The current rate of wages was much lower than in either Trinidad or British Guiana, while the extent of the island and the large number of estates necessitated a greater sub-division of such immigrants as could be brought in. Many of the estates were of small size. Barkly estimated that two-fifths of the estates each produced more than 100 hogsheads per annum and three-fifths less than 100 hogsheads, while only those producing above 100 hogsheads could pay their way.[1] Partly as a consequence of this, the medical supervision and hospital accommodation were notoriously deficient in Jamaica.[2] The island was heavily in debt, most of the planters embarrassed, and they could ill afford additional expenditure for immigration purposes. When the time came for the repatriation of coolies who had not renewed their indentures, the Jamaicans failed repeatedly to honour their obligations, with the result that further immigration from India was discouraged. As late as 1870 a "very large number of coolies" were described as being "constantly in a half starved condition, without strength to work and unable ever to obtain the means of recovering health and strength".[3]

In the smaller islands immigration was never on a large scale and was sporadic in character. Low wages made it difficult to attract Indian immigrants; the lack of continuity of immigration acted as a

[1] Barkly to Newcastle, 26 May 1854, *Parl. Pap.* 1854, XLIII, p. 130.
[2] A stipendiary magistrate in 1854 declared: "This island has literally been a charnel house to the greater number of those who have arrived." *Parl. Pap.* 1854, XLIII, p. 120.
[3] Grant to Kimberley, 19 December 1870, *Parl. Pap.* 1871, XLVII, p. 7.

deterrent factor, while financial considerations ruled out some of the more impoverished islands. It was generally easier and cheaper to bring in Portuguese from Madeira and Africans released from slave ships than Indians; and the Portuguese, who proved very satisfactory field labourers in most cases, constituted the bulk of the foreign labour imported into these colonies.

The real value of the immigrants for the sugar colonies, and it was very appreciable, did not consist in giving the planters a labour supply independent of the Creole labour, for the negroes except in Mauritius and British Guiana still formed the majority of the labourers. But even a few immigrants on an estate were sufficient to assure the planter of at least a minimum number of workers on whom he could rely; and the influence upon the Creoles of the knowledge that the planters could draw upon an alternative source of labour supply was very marked. It is noteworthy that, apart from some rioting in British Guiana in 1856, due to jealousy of the Portuguese who had ousted the Creoles from retail trading[1], there does not appear to have been friction between the immigrants and the native labourers of the colonies. A typical instance may be cited from Grenada. "They [the ex-apprentices] look with no jealous eyes upon the coolie; on the contrary they hail his arrival with joy and seem to regard him as the instrument destined eventually to redeem them from the necessity of daily manual labour."[2] There was also an additional reason for the good relations between these two classes— the immigrants provided a good market for the domestic produce of the Creoles.[3] It was estimated in Trinidad in 1862 that "the indenturing of one coolie to an estate provides means of employment for two Creole labourers".[4]

Moreover, the immigration of indentured labour gave to Mauritius, British Guiana and Trinidad a continuous flow of docile labour, which, when it had once become acclimatised to the conditions of the colony, provided an efficient and, indeed, a cheaper substitute for the slave labour of former times. It is true that the substitution was by no means complete, for large numbers of Creoles (negroes and mulattoes) continued to work on the estates in both British Guiana and Trinidad. In 1867 the Governor of British Guiana estimated that there were at least 20,000 Creoles working for the planters, while a great deal of the heaviest work on the estates was being done by them.[5] At the same time there were over 38,600 Indian and 6100 Chinese immigrants engaged on the sugar estates besides a large number of Portuguese.[6] Hence, whereas twenty years earlier, in the crisis of 1846–50, strikes

[1] Correspondence respecting the recent disturbances in British Guiana, Parl. Pap. 1856, XLIV, p. 44.
[2] Hincks to Stanley, 10 May 1858, Enclosure, Parl. Pap. 1859, Sess. 2, XXI, p. 457.
[3] Barkly to Cardwell, 26 July 1866, Parl. Pap. 1867, XLVIII, p. 118.
[4] Keate to Newcastle, 20 June 1863, Parl. Pap. 1864, XL, p. 26.
[5] Hincks to Buckingham, 31 August 1868, Parl. Pap. 1868–69, XLIII, p. 38.
[6] Scott to Kimberley, 20 October 1870, Parl. Pap. 1871, XLVII, p. 43.

which disorganised the whole work of the plantations had been of frequent occurrence, the Creoles also were now working well, although their labour remained less continuous than that of the Indians and other imported workers. In Mauritius there were 89,200 coolies and only 6000 Creoles on the estates in 1870, and the much greater degree to which this small island was able to expand its sugar production with the aid of coolie labour was mainly due to its proximity to India and to the close and uninterrupted communications that could be maintained. The mortality of the coolies on the journey to Mauritius was much lower than on the journey to the West Indies, while the cost of their introduction to Mauritius was less than half the cost to the West Indies. The Mauritian planters had immigration agents in India who did their best to divert the flow of emigrants from the West Indies and to direct it to Mauritius. They are even said in their zeal to have described British Guiana as "a great ice land".[2] Not only was the labour supply more amenable and more continuous than it had been before the introduction of immigrants, but the wages of Creole labour were also lower.[3] Although there was some rise in wages during the high prices prevailing at the time of the Crimean War, they did not reach the level which ruled before 1847, and they fell away again as prices relapsed after 1860.

The abolition of the preferential duties on colonial sugar had, amongst other results, that of stimulating the transfer of estates from absentee proprietors. Without a protected market it was difficult to meet the heavy additional expenditure on attorneys and managers, together with their secret commissions and other deductions from the net profits of the owner. Most of the former owners, moreover, were burdened with mortgages and similar liabilities which eventually they became unable to meet. Sometimes the mortgagee took possession of the estate and himself became the proprietor of it, but often it was sold for what it would fetch to a buyer who was resident in the colony. The English law of real property, however, as it was applied in the colonies, was a hindrance to such transfers because the estate when sold remained subject to the various liens which had been placed upon it, and its income as a going concern was often less than the charges to which it was subject. The estate was then placed in Chancery and abandoned, since no one could afford to run it. The first colony which attempted to deal with this problem was St Lucia, where a mortgage office had been established as early as 1829 and where an ordinance, known in the colony as the *saisie réelle*, authorising the seizure and sale of real property, was brought into operation in 1833. Under this ordinance sixty-nine sugar estates out of a total of eighty-one in the island were disposed of by judicial sale

---

[1] *Papers relating to West Indies and Mauritius, Parl. Pap.* 1859, Sess. 2, xx, p. 134.
[2] Hincks to Cardwell, 13 October 1865, *Parl. Pap.* 1866, XLIX, p. 322.

between 1833 and 1843,[1] and the new purchasers assumed possession of properties which had thus been relieved of mortgages, amounting for the whole island in 1829 to £1,189,965.[2] This measure, based on French law and precedent, proved highly beneficial to St Lucia, but it was not adopted by the other islands until long afterwards. It was not until 1854 that the first of the West Indian Encumbered Estates Acts was passed. This Act (amended in 1858) was modelled on the Irish Encumbered Estates Act of 1849 which had dealt successfully with the same sort of difficulties as prevailed in the West Indies. The West Indian Act did not come into force automatically throughout the colonies; its application depended on a vote of the local Legislature requesting the Crown to issue an Order-in-Council to that effect. St Vincent took this step in 1857, and nine other islands had placed themselves under the Act by 1867 (Jamaica in 1861 and Antigua in 1864). Four important sugar colonies—Barbados, St Lucia, Trinidad and British Guiana—refrained from subjecting themselves to the Act, holding that sufficient remedy was to be obtained under the laws already prevailing in each.[3] The essential principle of the Act was to enable an estate, which was crippled by mortgages and other liens, to be summarily sold by judicial decree; the proceeds of the sale were distributed amongst the interested parties through the medium of a specially constituted Court, and the purchaser received a parliamentary title free from any encumbrances.[4] As a result creditors of long standing obtained payment of at least part of their claims, while the estates passed from the hands of their insolvent owners into those of purchasers who were in possession of capital; thus new capital was introduced into the colonies, and estates, which in some cases had been for over forty years in Chancery, were brought again into cultivation.[5] By 1874 a total of 155 estates had been sold in the islands subject to the operation of the Acts, the purchase price of the estates sold amounting to £249,015.[6]

There was also for many years a marked diminution in the number of estates, caused mainly by the abandonment of properties which were expensive to run, either owing to their situation, the poverty of the soil, or the lack of labour. The reduction in numbers was specially great in Jamaica, where many estates, which under slavery were only profitable in years of high prices, had lingered on until free trade led to their final abandonment. On the other hand, under the stimulus of immigration, there was a considerable increase in the numbers of estates in Trinidad, British Guiana and Mauritius.

There were three main forms of land tenure prevailing on West

[1] Colebrooke to Earl Grey, 28 November 1850, *Parl. Pap.* 1850, XXXVI, p. 241.
[2] Breen, H. H., *St Lucia*, p. 284.
[3] *Report on West Indian Encumbered Estates Court*, 1884, *Parl. Pap.* 1884, LV, p. 837.
[4] Cust, R. J., *West Indian Encumbered Estates Acts* (1865), p. 65.
[5] *Annual Report on the Virgin Islands, Parl. Pap.* 1866, XLIX, p. 378.
[6] Cust, R. J., *Supplement to West Indian Encumbered Estates Acts* (1874), p. 3.

Indian sugar estates between 1845 and 1870: first, the proprietor might either cultivate the land himself or have it managed for him by an agent (an attorney or manager); secondly, he might lease out the property on an annual rental; thirdly, he might cultivate it in that form of partnership with his labourers known as *métayage*. The first of these systems, under which the labourers received only the current rate of wages for their work, was by far the most common. The second system was relatively rare, but the third was widely practised in some of the smaller islands during part or the whole of the period. The earliest adoption of *métayage* seems to have been in St Lucia, where it was put into operation soon after the abolition of slavery.[1]

During the great slump of 1846–48 *métayage* was introduced into many of the sugar colonies, and it was even tried in British Guiana and Jamaica, but although it helped, especially in the former, to tide over the worst of the crisis, it was unsuited to plantations which were conducted on a large scale, and it soon yielded place again to the older system of direct management and wage labour.[2] But in St Lucia, Montserrat, Tobago, Grenada, Nevis and one or two other islands, *métayage* came to assume a very real importance. The system differed materially in different colonies and even on different estates in the same colony; indeed, this variety of practice and the fact that, as a system, it was unknown to English and so to colonial law, constituted serious difficulties in the way of its successful adoption. The negroes' inveterate distrust of written agreements led to reliance being placed upon the existence of local, and generally ill-defined custom; but disputes were naturally liable to occur, and when they came before the courts they were settled, not in accordance with custom or practice, but according to some existing law that appeared to bear most closely upon the special case, such as laws regulating contracts, land tenancies, or relations between masters and servants.[3] The most usual practice under *métayage* was for the proprietor of the estate to supply the land, sugar-making plant, carts and horses, while the *métayer* furnished all the labour required for the cultivation of the land, for the manufacture of crop into sugar, and for carting. Of the sugar produced, the *métayer* took one half, while the other half went to the proprietor together with the skimmings and the molasses. The *métayer* also often received a small part of the rum where any was made. The portion of the sugar belonging to the *métayer*, after being cured and packed in hogsheads, which were in some cases provided by himself and sometimes by the proprietor, was carted to the shipping bay or town nearest the estate, the *métayer* supplying the carters.[4]

[1] Breen, H. H., *St Lucia*, p. 300.
[2] Barkly to Earl Grey, 11 February 1850, *Parl. Pap.* 1851, xxxix, pp. 28–9.
[3] *Annual Report on Tobago for 1874, Parl. Pap. 1874,* LI, p. 428.
[4] *Annual Report on Tobago for 1857, Parl. Pap. 1857,* Sess. 2, XXI, p. 480.

All the evidence goes to show that the effects of *métayage* upon the efficiency of management and the output of sugar estates were bad and that any progress in method was almost impossible under it. Sir Henry Barkly's phrase, "The *métairie* system is only another name for abandonment",[1] was echoed by many of the Governors of other colonies when it was tried. The system arose originally from the complete inability of a section of the proprietors to find the money to pay wages to their labourers when times were bad and prices low, and there is no question that its adoption enabled many properties to be maintained which must otherwise have been abandoned. Affording, as it did, greater freedom and, in some cases, a larger net yield to the negroes, it attracted workers to the plantations who would sooner have cultivated their own provision grounds than work for the low and uncertain wages offered by the planters. On the other hand, the latter greatly preferred the method of direct management and wage payment, and they always returned to this method as soon as it became feasible. The attitude of the planters can be seen clearly from the observations of the Administrator of St Lucia, himself a resident in the island for many years. "The system is gradually disappearing...its presence is a sure indicator of weakness and lack of resources; it encourages absenteeism; it has a tendency to disturb the social equilibrium by giving to the illiterate classes a degree of wealth and importance which should be the concomitants as well as the rewards of intelligence and education."[2] That there were compensating advantages to the negroes can be seen from the annual report of the Governor of Tobago for 1857: "It affords a revenue to non-capitalist proprietors; it tends to establish a useful middle class of yeomanry, it retains for the use of the peasantry a larger share of the soil and labour produce than the mere pittance of plantation wages."[3] In that same year one estate of 600 acres was cultivated solely by *métayers* and produced a crop of 130 hogsheads of sugar, and the Governor estimated that not less than one-third of the crop of the island was the product of *métayer* labour. The nature of the sugar industry was, however, fundamentally opposed to the general adoption of *métayage*. For a sugar estate to be profitable under European ownership, it was necessary to have a large and expensive plant, considerable working capital, and expert skill and direction. Cultivation on the share system was naturally unacceptable to the owner of machinery and equipment costing from £20,000 to £40,000, except as a last resort, preferable only to complete abandonment. Technical progress also was out of the question, while the incentive to the cultivators to give of their best was restricted, in view of the well-recognised

---

[1] Barkly to Grey, 11 February 1850, *Parl. Pap.* 1851, XXXIX, p. 29.
[2] Hincks to Newcastle, 22 June 1861, Enclosure, Report by Breen on St Lucia, *Parl. Pap.* 1862, XXXVI, p. 61.
[3] *Annual Report on Tobago for 1857, Parl. Pap.* 1859, Sess. 2, XXI, p. 468.

economic defects of a system under which both parties share equally in the gross produce.[1] With the lower costs of production achieved in the 'fifties and 'sixties, the prices ruling in most years yielded large profits to well-managed and well-placed estates, and their owners had no difficulty in financing commitments for wages. By 1870 Tobago was the only island in which *métayage* could be regarded as substantially successful, although it also existed to some extent on the rapidly decaying sugar estates of Montserrat, Grenada and Nevis. In Tobago, itself one of the comparatively unimportant sugar islands where small estates predominated, the negroes succeeded, largely owing to the absence of immigrant labour, in resisting the attempts of the planters to return to the wage system, and *métayage* was still widely in operation there as late as 1886.[2]

With the British market open after 1854 to the sugar producers of all countries on an equal footing, the only way in which British planters could maintain their hold on that market was by lowering the costs of production and improving the quality of their sugar. The first of these objects was attained by the greater use of manures, by employing machinery in the cultivation of the land, by a more efficient organisation of agricultural operations, and by the introduction of indentured labour. Prior to about 1850 the planters relied mainly upon farmyard manure[3] and, especially in Jamaica, large pens were kept for the breeding of stock, some of which were used for draught purposes on the sugar estates, while many were sold to planters in the other islands. But not the least valuable part of the product of pens was the manure which was so essential to the continued fertility of the soil. The increasing use of the steam engine as a motive power for the sugar works, however, led to a diminution in the number of horses and mules, and the discovery of the value of guano as a fertiliser in European agriculture suggested its use on the sugar plantations as a substitute for the diminishing supply of farmyard manure. The experiment was an immediate success and large quantities were imported to those islands which were in need of it and were sufficiently prosperous to meet the expense. The two chief consumers of guano were Barbados and Mauritius, both islands cultivating the sugar-cane very intensively and possessing abundant supplies of labour. In Trinidad the fertility of the soil and the practice of allowing the cane to ratoon for a number of years decreased the necessity for the use of artificial manure, and to some extent the same causes obtained in British Guiana, but there a more important factor was the shortage of labour, which could not be spared for the purpose of laying manure. In Jamaica the need for fertilisers was very great, but the planters lacked both the labour to apply them and the capital

[1] Marshall, A., *Principles of Economics*, 8th ed. pp. 643–5.
[2] *Her Majesty's Colonies (Colonial Exhibition of 1886)*, p. 337.
[3] Davy, J., *The West Indies before and after Emancipation*, p. 115.

to pay for them. The cost of manure was heavy; in 1858 Peruvian guano to the value of £80,000 was imported into Barbados, though not all of this was intended for consumption within the island, as there was an appreciable amount of re-export to other West India Islands, and it was estimated in 1860 that the average annual consumption of imported manures in Barbados was about £45,000. In the case of Mauritius the corresponding figure for 1858 was as high as £110,000. In the early days of the application of guano the effects in stimulating the fertility of the soil were very marked. "It is to the extended use of this valuable manure", said the Governor of Mauritius in 1854, "that Mauritius is chiefly indebted for her increasing produce."[1] But it was later found that the intensive use of guano, as a means of forcing crops from the land in successive years without any rotation or period of fallow, was attended by serious drawbacks; in particular, in Mauritius it fostered the cane borer pest which was doing considerable damage in the early 'sixties. Hence there arose a tendency in both Barbados and Mauritius to rely less upon guano and to recur more to farmyard manure.[2]

Another improvement was the more widespread use of the plough and of horse hoes and harrows, the employment of which became increasingly common as the memories of the methods prevailing under slavery gradually faded, and the planters adjusted their system of cultivation to the necessity for economising in labour. It is surprising how slowly this adjustment was carried out in some of the islands; thus, the Governor of St Vincent, in reporting considerable progress in this direction in 1863, stated that "three years ago there was scarcely an estate in the island where implemental husbandry was used".[3] A new development, which was only beginning to have effect towards the end of the period, was the introduction of steam ploughs. The deeper ploughing that could be carried out wherever it was feasible had a very marked effect on the yield of the soil. In 1863 the first steam plough was brought into Antigua and its success led to others being imported with the result that this "wonder working implement", as it was described in 1886,[4] was largely responsible for carrying sugar cultivation in Antigua through the period of falling prices which set in in the 'seventies.

The third way in which costs of production could be lowered was by the introduction of better plant and machinery for the manufacture of sugar. The improvements consisted in the more extensive use of the steam engine for driving sugar-mills, in more efficient machinery for expressing the juice from the sugar cane and for the subsequent stages in the making of muscovado sugar, and, also,

[1] Annual Report on Mauritius for 1853, Parl. Pap. 1854–55, xxxvi, p. 176.
[2] Annual Report on Mauritius for 1862, Parl. Pap. 1864, xl, p. 104.
[3] Annual Report on St Vincent for 1863, Parl. Pap. 1865, xxxvii, p. 54.
[4] Her Majesty's Colonies (Colonial Exhibition of 1886), p. 352.

especially in Mauritius and British Guiana, in the manufacture of refined sugar by the vacuum-pan process. This latter process produced a sugar of much better quality than the ordinary muscovado and it fetched a correspondingly better price in the market. There were, however, important difficulties in the way of the more general adoption of the vacuum pan, the centrifugal machine, and other methods of obtaining high-grade sugars. They involved a very heavy capital outlay such as few resident proprietors could command; one result of which was that the more up-to-date plant and equipment was commonly to be found on the estates of absentee rather than on those of resident owners. The capital cost was in fact so heavy that it did not pay to use the vacuum-pan process except on the large estates.[1] The running expenses were also greater—in making muscovado only the megass or refuse of the canes was burnt, while with the vacuum pan it was estimated that it required a ton of coal to make a ton of sugar.[2] But the greatest obstacle lay in the operation of the British import duties on sugar. These duties were not uniform but differential, the amount of the duty varying with the extent to which the sugar was refined. This discrimination benefited, as it was intended to do, the great bulk of the sugar produced in the West Indies, which was of inferior quality and came in at the lowest scale of duties.[3] But it hit British Guiana and Mauritius, particularly the latter, which was in any case exporting a considerable proportion of its crop in a refined state to Australia, and the Mauritian planter had "often great difficulty in keeping down his quality of sugar so as not to come up to the standard of the higher duties, which would entail loss as the market value of this sugar would not compensate for the higher duty".[4]

One of Earl Grey's favourite remedies for the economic ills of the colonies, which he was never tired of urging on the planters, was the adoption of central factories, i.e. the separation of the process of manufacture of the sugar from that of the cultivation of the sugarcane. He pointed out that it was impossible for the planter to combine efficiently the functions of an agriculturist, a manufacturer, a distiller and, at times, a merchant. In the French colony of Guadeloupe an earthquake had destroyed all the existing factories, and instead of replacing them the colonists started a central factory system;[5] it was this example which Earl Grey wished the English colonists to follow. The latter, however, objected, first, that their works were still in existence and they did not wish to abandon them; secondly, that as all the canes were harvested at the same time there would be delays involving loss, owing to the rapid deterioration of the cut canes if they

[1] *Report of Committee on Sugar Industries, Parl. Pap.* 1878–79, XIII, Q. 2835.
[2] *Ibid.* Q. 3829.
[3] *Ibid.* Q. 5694.
[4] *Annual Report on Mauritius for 1858, Parl. Pap.* 1860, XLIV, p. 116.
[5] *Committee on Coffee and Sugar Planting, Parl. Pap.* 1847–48, XXIII, Part II, Q. 10,405.

were not immediately put through the manufacturing process; thirdly, that the heavy cost of transporting the canes to a factory at a distance from the estate would more than offset any gain in the efficiency of manufacture resulting from the division of labour and the economies of large-scale production. This last was the most important practical difficulty, especially in view of the extremely bad roads in nearly all the colonies. A further objection was felt on the ground that "the new system would involve a certain loss of independence and position";[1] in other words, considerations of prestige, quite apart from their natural conservatism, made the planters opposed to the change. Finally, the evidence as to the results of the central factories established in Guadeloupe and Martinique was by no means conclusive in their favour.[2] It was not until 1874 that the first central factory to be constructed in a British sugar colony was opened in St Lucia.

Although from 1845 to 1852 the general economic condition of nearly all the sugar colonies had been critical, owing to low prices and the fear lest complete ruin should result from the loss of the preference hitherto granted to colonial sugar in the home market, the period from 1853 to 1860 saw in most cases a considerable change for the better. After a fall to £1. 1s. 5d. per cwt. (in bond) in 1854, the year of complete equalisation of the sugar duties, the price of sugar rose steadily and in 1857, owing to the Crimean war, reached £1. 15s. 7d.—the highest average price for a year since 1841—and it continued to rule high down to the end of 1860. At these prices many of the planters were able to make large profits and to pay off old mortgages on their estates. Capital was once more forthcoming for the larger properties, while the smaller estates, especially on the less important islands, tended increasingly to pass from absentee to resident owners. Unfortunately, the improvement in sugar prices also brought with it an increase in the price of land and a return to the former custom of buying estates on mortgages, thus proving that in this respect the new race of planters had learned little from the misfortunes in the past. "Destroy this fictitious value of land (the very interest money on which eats up half his crop) and teach the planter to regulate his own personal expenses and the expenses of cultivating his property by his minimum and not his maximum income, and there is an elasticity in Barbados and its resources which need create no despair."[3] Nearly twenty years later it was said that the sugar estates were "the consols of Barbados", in which residents with spare capital were accustomed to invest their money, receiving 6 per cent. on it in contrast to 4 per cent. from the banks.[4]

[1] Annual Report on St Lucia for 1870, Parl. Pap. 1872, XLII, p. 118.
[2] Committee on Coffee and Sugar Planting, Parl. Pap. 1847–48, XXIII, Part II, Q. 10,408 and Report of Committee on the Sugar Industries, Parl. Pap. 1878–79, XIII, Q. 2841.
[3] Walker to Newcastle, 27 September 1859, Parl. Pap. 1860, XLIV, p. 56.
[4] Annual Report on Barbados for 1876, Parl. Pap. 1877, LIX, p. 355.

Not only the value of the land but wages also rose appreciably in many cases with the rise in the selling price of sugar. But despite this rise in cost the higher prices stimulated production, which increased in the British West Indies and British Guiana by 15·6 per cent. for the average of the years 1858–60 compared with the average of 1853–55. Even in Jamaica Sewell found that "since 1858 as many properties have been resuscitated as abandoned; and I regard it as one of the most favourable signs of improvement that the work of regeneration...has been at least inaugurated by new men".[1]

The succeeding decade (1861–70) witnessed a remarkable consolidation of the more favourable economic condition of the sugar colonies which had prevailed since 1855, even though the average price of sugar was some 5s. less per cwt. than for 1855–60. During the 'sixties sugar failed to follow the general trend of rising gold prices owing to the great increase in world production, which grew by nearly 50 per cent. during the decade, the increased output coming mainly from Cuba and from the rapidly developing beet-sugar industries of the continent of Europe. Beet sugar, which furnished 22 per cent. of the total world production of sugar for the average of 1859–61, was 34 per cent. of the much larger total in 1868–70 while the share of British cane sugar (including India) fell from 17 to 12 per cent.[2] In spite of the relative decline, there was an absolute increase in the output of nearly all the West India Islands, due largely to the more effective regulations applied to coolie immigration and its extension to many of the lesser islands, while all the other factors making for more efficient methods of production and lower costs contributed to the same result. Under these influences Mauritius, British Guiana and Trinidad were rapidly extending their production of sugar and were enjoying increasing prosperity, tempered in the case of Mauritius during the five years preceding 1870 by bad harvests due to droughts and hurricanes, by the high price of rice in India, and by the outbreak for the first time in 1866 of a severe epidemic of malaria.

Jamaica was an exception to the general rule, so far as the expansion of sugar production was concerned, if her output for 1868–70 is compared with that for 1842–45, for she suffered most from labour difficulties and benefited least by immigration, but it must be borne in mind that her prosperity was less dependent upon sugar exports than that of most of the other islands. In 1868–70 the average value of her total export was £1,199,500, of which sugar contributed only £496,200, or 41·5 per cent., the balance being made up of rum, coffee, pimento, ginger, logwood, and other products. These latter, apart from rum, were largely produced by the small cultivators, the negroes

[1] Sewell, W. G., *The Ordeal of Free Labor in the West Indies*, p. 243.
[2] Farren, Sir T. H., *The Progress of the Sugar Trade*, Parl. Pap. 1884, LXXIV, p. 374.

The uncertainties were not so great in British Guiana and Trinidad with their favourable climates and the possibility of canes ratooning for a number of years, and a growing labour supply, as in such colonies as Antigua or Barbados, which were always liable to drought, in Jamaica with its chronic labour difficulties, or in the lesser islands, where the standards of cultivation and manufacture of sugar were generally inferior, and any falling off of price involved heavy losses.

The new economic conditions of free labour did not lead to the growth of an educated middle class, partly because educational facilities were poor and scanty, and partly because there was little scope for the formation of such a class in these colonies, such occupations as existed of a higher grade than plantation labour falling largely into the hands of the "coloured" class, i.e. those with an admixture of white and negro blood. The consequences were to be seen only too clearly in the working of the island legislatures. Moreover, the opening up of Canada, Australia and South Africa, combined with the struggling conditions of most of the sugar colonies, had diverted the flow not merely of capital but also of white emigration to other lands possessing greater attractions. In many of the islands there was a marked decline in the white population as compared with the days of slavery, and the new managers of estates who took over from former bankrupt owners had generally to be found within the colonies. The Attorney-General of St Vincent remarked significantly in 1862:[1] "The class of persons now filling the posts of attorneys, managers and overseers is without doubt greatly inferior to the same class of persons of years gone by."

The available evidence does not point to any considerable rise in the moral and social level of the negro. Little was done in most of the colonies towards his social improvement. In the often quoted words of Lord Harris: "A race has been freed, but a society has not been formed."[2] The negro peasantry in their own villages lived a most primitive existence without medical aid and with scarcely more contact with the standards of English civilisation than they would have had in Africa; but even on the plantations and in the towns the legislature made little or no contribution towards the social welfare of the Creole. Education was mostly left to the efforts of missionaries, and where public instruction was provided the low quality of the teachers deprived it of much value. Even when Governments were willing, there were serious difficulties to contend with. In such colonies as St Lucia or Trinidad, which had a predominantly Roman Catholic population, the Church threw its influence against State education. Again, the unwillingness of the negro to submit to any form of direct taxation made it difficult to raise the necessary funds. "Things were not so bad", said the Governor of

<hr>

[1] *Papers relating to St Vincent, Parl. Pap.* 1863, xxxviii, p. 639.
[2] Harris to Grey, 19 June 1848, *Parl. Pap.* 1847–48, xlvi, p. 645.

Antigua, "while the slave generation lived, but their descendants grew up without the old restraints but without any guidance to adapt them to new conditions."[1]

The most ambitious attempt at improving the social condition of the negro was made in Trinidad, where one of the ablest of West Indian Governors, Lord Harris, promulgated a Territorial Ordinance in 1846. Under this Ordinance, which was frequently amended, Trinidad was divided up into wards (there were forty-one of these in 1852) each of which was administered by a Warden who had power to levy rates on all land and houses, the proceeds of which were devoted to road-making within the wards, police, education, and assistance for the aged and destitute, etc.[2] This attempt to apply some of the principles of English local government to a West Indian colony succeeded only for a while and in part; the collection of rates from the negroes proved very difficult; the scheme for free secular elementary education broke down largely owing to the opposition of the Churches;[3] and after the initial enthusiasm of the early Wardens had waned, the roads were neglected. At a time when even the general colonial civil service was not highly efficient,[4] it was useless to expect much from a system of unpaid local administrators.[5] It was also in Trinidad that a later Governor, Sir A. H. Gordon, did much both for the moral and material improvement of the negroes by passing an Ordinance in 1868 throwing open the Crown lands to small owners. He thereby encouraged settlement and increased the production of cocoa and other crops by peasant proprietors.

In general the material progress of the negro was more apparent than his social development. The coolie immigration into British Guiana and Trinidad afforded a market for his produce while still leaving his wages relatively high, and in these colonies his prosperity was probably greatest. Elsewhere, the ease with which it was possible to squat on Crown lands or to buy up the land of derelict estates at a low price, enabled the negroes to make themselves largely independent of the planters and to sell their labour only at crop time or when it was convenient to them. The incentive to earn at least harvest money seems to have been strongly felt by the women, for there is evidence that in the later years of the period women frequently formed a majority of the field labourers. The small *métayers* of Tobago or Grenada, the Jamaican negroes who cultivated ginger or coffee, or picked pimento, the hard-working Barbadian cultivators who produced sugar cane on their own land and had it manufactured by the

---

[1] Hamilton to Labouchere, 10 May 1856, *Parl. Pap.* 1857, Sess. 1, x, p. 191.
[2] See Text of Ordinance of 1852, *Parl. Pap.* 1852–53, LXVII, pp. 661–71.
[3] Caldecott, A., *The Church in the West Indies*, p. 124.
[4] Morrell, W. P., *Colonial Policy of Peel and Russell*, pp. 255–6.
[5] After 1853 the wardens were paid and received a commission on the rates recovered by them without recourse to sales of property by a decree of the Court. Elliott to Labouchere, 20 August 1856, *Parl. Pap.* 1857, Sess. 1, x, p. 93.

planter at his mill, these and many others knew a measure of prosperity which was certainly large in relation to their former condition. Against these must be set perhaps a greater number who had relapsed into a barbarism which belied the hopes aroused by the undoubted signs of improvement observed immediately after emancipation. Miserably housed, almost devoid of medical care, neglecting education and religion, thriftless and ridden by superstition, many of them showed how little capable they were of benefiting from the freedom they had gained.[1] But effective aid would have involved some measure of constraint, and to this the spirit of the times was opposed. Some of the worst conditions were to be found in the small over-crowded island of Barbados. The skilled Barbadian artisan or house servant was the aristocrat of the West Indian negroes and was easily recognisable when found in other islands. But the poor landless negroes, who formed the bulk of the whole population of the island (161,594 in 1871), were employed at very low wages and forced to pay a high rent for the "miserable shanty" they lived in.[2] The Assembly, in a Memorial to the Governor in 1876,[3] admitted the "intense and apparently hopeless poverty which is to be found in the colony" and attributed it, as was probably just, to that over-population which made sugar estates in Barbados the "consols" of the West Indies.

The immediate effects of the period of stress, resulting from the equalisation of the sugar duties, upon the constitutional development of British Guiana and Jamaica have been described above. The Jamaican constitutional experiment of 1854—the appointment of a small salaried Executive Committee having the sole right to originate money votes in the Legislative Assembly—was widely copied in succeeding years in the other self-governing colonies in the West Indies. Thus Tobago in 1854, St Kitts in 1857, St Vincent, Nevis and Antigua in 1859 all adopted Executive Committees on the model of Jamaica, with considerable success at least at the outset.

But in truth the malady was too deep to be cured by such a device. The Executive Committee, notably in Jamaica, found itself in an impossible position, for it was responsible both to the Governor and to the Assembly. When a dispute arose between these two authorities there was no means of resolving it, and the new system eventually foundered in Jamaica on the rock of this divided allegiance. Above all, the old representative system had grown unworkable as a direct result of the emancipation of the slaves. The white residents were much reduced in numbers and ability, owing to the long-continued absenteeism and to the lessened attractiveness of the West Indies to British emigrants. The negroes, ill-educated and illiterate, formed the vast majority of the population, but only a few of them were entitled

---

[1] Cf. Mathieson, W. L., *The Sugar Colonies and Governor Eyre*, pp. 1–22.
[2] *Papers relating to the late Disturbances in Barbados, Parl. Pap.* 1876, LIII, p. 151.
[3] *Loc. cit.* p. 168.

to the franchise. In Jamaica in 1864 there were 1903 electors on the register out of a population of about 450,000, and in such conditions there was little prospect of finding sixty-eight members worthy to take their seats in the two chambers of the legislature. The result in the small colonies was apathy and stagnation, and in Jamaica partisan conflict and a "complete absence of stability".[1] The Governors were powerless to initiate the most necessary reforms, while the legislatures were too apathetic or too much dominated by self-interest and petty jealousies to carry out even those measures which were clearly in the general interest. The public buildings were everywhere a disgrace to colonies which, at least in the past, had been prosperous. Barkly wrote of Mauritius: "It would almost seem as though architecture had been prohibited under our rule—even the buildings occupied by most of the public departments were erected by the French, generally with very different objects. Thus the Governor's usual residence was destined for a College; the barracks for a prison; the civil hospital for a barracks; the Protestant cathedral for a powder magazine, and the coolie orphan asylum for a mill for the manufacture of gunpowder."[2] The roads were neglected, despite their obvious importance for the sugar industry, and colonial revenues were devoted more to keeping up an extravagant establishment than to supplying the real needs of the colonies.

In Jamaica it required a negro rising to achieve what so many Secretaries of State for the Colonies in the past had desired—the reform of the legislative system of the island. The negro population of Jamaica in the early 'sixties had not been prospering, in part owing to the high prices of provisions resulting from the American Civil War. But there were other causes of complaint: the tax system was in many ways oppressive; wages for plantation labour were not paid regularly and were often in arrears, while disputes arising out of such matters or out of questions relating to the occupation of land were dealt with by magistrates who were mostly themselves planters and therefore biased in favour of their own class; the negro peasantry wanted more land of which plenty was lying idle in large estates, but the negroes could not hold it on a secure tenure.

In 1862 Eyre was appointed Lieutenant-Governor of Jamaica and two years later was confirmed in his post as Governor. He failed to understand the economic conditions of the island or to appreciate the grievances of the people. Becoming embroiled with the chief spokesman of the negroes, a coloured member of the Assembly named Gordon, he treated the latter in such a way as to excite the resentment of the negroes, who were further exacerbated by the publication of the so-called Queen's Letter which reached the island in 1865 in answer to a petition. This Letter, written by Cardwell the Colonial

[1] Wrong, H., *Government of the West Indies*, p. 70.
[2] Barkly to Cardwell, 18 July 1864, *Parl. Pap.* XXXVI, p. 98.

Secretary, but based on Eyre's despatches, so far from expressing sympathy with the distress of the peasantry, merely advised them to work hard on the plantations for wages and assured them "that it is from their own industry and prudence, in availing themselves of the means of prospering that are before them, and not from any such schemes as have been suggested to them, that they must look for an improvement in their conditions".[1] Finally, a serious riot broke out in Morant Bay in the parish of St Thomas on 11 October 1865. After the rioters had been fired upon, they captured the Court House where the Custos (Chief Magistrate) and seventeen other occupants were killed. From there the rioting spread into the rest of the parish and for two or three days the greater part of the parish was at the mercy of the insurgent negroes led by Paul Bogle. The rioting did not extend outside the parish of St Thomas in the extreme eastern corner of the island. Governor Eyre and General O'Connor commanding the troops took prompt steps to check and localise the trouble, with the result that the situation was completely in hand by October 15. The total number killed was twenty-one white and coloured civilians and seven rioters. No women were molested throughout the rising and no resistance was offered to the troops, who did not suffer any casualties. The white population of St Thomas had been badly scared and exacted a terrible revenge. Martial law was proclaimed in the whole county of Cornwall except Kingston and the negroes were hunted down by the troops. Many were executed without trial, but the majority were tried by court martial and hanged. Gordon was captured at Kingston, illegally taken by Eyre's orders to Morant Bay, there tried by court martial as the chief instigator of the rebellion, and hanged on entirely insufficient evidence. In all 586 negroes were put to death, 1005 houses were destroyed and large numbers, including some women, were flogged. Public opinion was violently excited in England, a Commission of investigation was appointed, and while its findings largely exonerated Governor Eyre personally from responsibility for the wanton and inexcusable harshness used in putting down the rebellion, he had clearly been a failure as a Governor and was re-called to England.[2] Before his recall Eyre succeeded in persuading the frightened legislature that the time had at last arrived for constitutional reform; after attempting a compromise, which was rejected by the Colonial Office, the Assembly decided to leave the form of government to be decided by the Crown. An Order-in-Council was issued on 11 June 1866 by which a nominated Legislative Council was set up, composed of the Governor, six officials who held their seats *ex officio*, and an unspecified number of unofficial members of whom three were at first appointed. "The Assembly of Jamaica, for

[1] Olivier, Lord, *The Myth of Governor Eyre*, p. 146.
[2] Cf. Mathieson, W. L., *The Sugar Colonies and Governor Eyre, 1849–1866*, and Olivier, Lord, *op. cit.*

centuries so tenacious of its powers and privileges, had finished its career by a complete abdication of all its powers." [1]

Under an able and energetic Governor, Sir J. P. Grant, the new Legislative Council rapidly got to work, the elected vestries and road boards, which were notoriously corrupt, were abolished, the judicial system was remodelled, the police force reorganised, and, despite a severe financial crisis in 1867, the public finances of the island were put on a sound basis. By 1870 the fruit export industry was beginning to assume importance and there seemed every prospect of a rapid growth in the prosperity of Jamaica.

Once again the example of Jamaica proved decisive, and in 1865 Dominica, in 1866 Antigua, St Kitts and Nevis, and in 1868 St Vincent, adopted Crown Colony government with a single Chamber and a nominated majority. The Virgin Islands had already adopted this system in 1859. By 1875 Barbados, the Bahamas and Bermuda alone of the old colonies retained their old constitutions.

Attempts to secure a greater degree of economy and centralisation in the case of small and nearly contiguous islands were continued during the period under review in the face of the opposition and obstruction of the local legislatures. Finally, in 1870, the legislatures of the Leeward Islands passed resolutions providing for the federation of their governments under a single Governor-in-Chief, with a general Legislative Council consisting of three officials, seven members nominated by the Crown and ten elected members, all except the officials being chosen from the several local legislatures. Matters of general importance, such as the administration of justice, the control of police, immigration, education and the post office, were placed under the general legislature, while matters of local interest were retained by the separate legislatures, the scope of whose powers was thus greatly restricted.

At the end of the period under review a further constitutional change took place in most of the West India colonies—the disestablishment of the Church of England. In Jamaica the Governor had estimated in 1869 that out of a population of 500,000, the Nonconformists had charge of 200,000, the Established Church of 100,000, while no religious provision was made for 200,000, and he added that this last was the only increasing class. [2] Religious feuds had always been pronounced there, and Sir R. W. Rawson, the Governor of the Windward Islands, declared that Jamaica exhibited the lamentable spectacle of a people of whom it might be said, "see how the Christians *hate* one another". [3] In many of the colonies the Roman Catholics formed the bulk of the population, and the charges for the establishment were often a heavy burden on the finances of the islands; in

[1] Wrong, H., *op. cit.* p. 77.
[2] Grant to Granville, 23 July 1869, *Parl. Pap.* 1871, XLVIII, p. 571.
[3] Rawson to Granville, 17 April 1870, *ibid*, p. 604.

Jamaica in 1864 £38,000 out of a gross revenue of £314,000 were appropriated to the support of the Established Church.[1] The Home Government, influenced by the desire to secure religious equality, and following the example of the disestablishment of the Church of Ireland in 1869, urged on the colonies the disestablishment and disendowment or concurrent endowment of their Churches. Granville wrote to Grant "that the moral and religious culture of the subject race, and not the ascendancy of any one community ought to be the object of your Government".[2] Thus pressed, the now docile legislature of Jamaica passed (without protest from the local Church)[3] an Act in June 1870 for the disestablishment and gradual disendowment of the Church of England in Jamaica, which was in future to be supported on the voluntary principle. Similar action was taken in most of the other colonies,[4] although in Trinidad there was concurrent endowment of the Church of England and the Roman Catholic Church, while the long-standing triple endowment in British Guiana of the Anglican, the Reformed Dutch and the Presbyterian Churches was not interfered with. In Barbados, where the Church of England was very strong and there were few Nonconformists, the Legislature refused to agree to the disestablishment of the Church of England and continued to endow it on a liberal scale out of the public revenues, but made in addition small grants to Wesleyan and Moravian missions and to the Roman Catholic Church. In Mauritius the Church of England was disestablished and its endowments from public funds largely reduced.

(ii) THE BAHAMAS, BERMUDA, BRITISH HONDURAS

The Bahamas. From 1845 until the American Civil War the inhabitants of the Bahamas continued to derive a fluctuating and often illegitimate livelihood from "wrecking", i.e. the salvage of the contents of vessels wrecked on any of the 500 rocks and islands which comprise the colony. The number of wrecks was large because of the great volume of trade passing near or between the islands and because of the strong and variable currents and sudden violent gales. Much of the activity of the local Legislature was devoted to attempts to regulate the business of "wrecking" and it was gradually brought under control. Prior to 1847 "wreckers" who rescued passengers or crew had no financial claim on the vessel or cargo, but in that year an Act was passed entitling the "wrecking" vessel engaged in saving lives to be "awarded salvage on the wrecked property in equal proportions with vessels of the same size engaged in salving such property".[5] All "wrecking" vessels had to be licensed; "wreckmasters"

[1] Grant to Granville, 23 July 1869, *Parl. Pap.* 1871, XLVIII, p. 569.
[2] Granville to Grant, 1 March 1869, *ibid.* 1871, XLVIII, p. 567.
[3] Caldecott, A., *op. cit.* p. 142.
[4] See *West Indies, Ecclesiastical Grants, Parl. Pap.* 1871, XLVIII, p. 249, and *Parl. Pap.* 1873, XLVIII, p. 259.   [5] Nisbett to Pakington, 8 May 1852, *Parl. Pap.* 1852, XXXI, p. 73.

were appointed, and salvage was apportioned on a definite scale. But Rawson held in 1866 that the law required both enforcement and amendment.[1] From 1858 to 1864 as many as 313 wrecks were reported, of which 259 were total losses; out of 286 wrecks, 110 were British, 157 American, 13 French and 6 Spanish. The value of all the wrecked goods entered at the customs from 1855 to 1864 was £638,864.[2]

The outbreak of the American Civil War brought very great temporary prosperity to the Bahamas, as Nassau became a centre for blockade-running to Charleston and other ports of the Confederate States. The volume of exports rose from £196,000 in 1861 to £1,008,000 in 1862 and £4,672,000 in 1864; in the latter year 72 per cent. of the exports consisted of raw cotton shipped to the United Kingdom. But the end of 1865 saw the cessation of blockade-running and the colony relapsed into its former state, relying mainly upon its traditional products, salt, sponges and pineapples, together with a small amount of cotton (the cultivation of which received a temporary stimulus from the high prices ruling during the war) and the proceeds of "wrecking". This last business was, however, on the decline for three main reasons: first, the erection of numerous lighthouses by the Imperial Government; secondly, the increasing use of steamships, especially for the more valuable cargoes; thirdly, the tendency of trade routes to shift to the north and south of the Bahamas. The diminution of "wrecking" was not without its advantages for the colony, as this occupation, which was once described as "in turns desultory, indolent and exciting", had a demoralising effect on the population and diverted attention from agriculture. The ex-slave population of the Bahamas was certainly not more satisfactory when working for hire than that of the rest of the West Indies, and the irregularity of the supply of labour was intensified by the allurements of wrecking. Towards the end of the period the local legislature built an hotel in Nassau to provide for the increasing numbers of Americans who were coming over, especially from New York, to spend money there in the holiday season, but it was only after the establishment of regular steamship sailings to New York that this tourist traffic assumed much importance for the economic life of the colony. The period ended in great depression, owing, partly, to the reaction from the prosperity of the Civil War and, partly, to a very severe hurricane which swept the islands in 1866 and destroyed many of the fruit trees and cotton plants and tore away the sponges.

Bermuda. The Bermuda Islands remained almost to the end of the period a purely trading and maritime centre, the population devoting themselves entirely to shipbuilding and carrying by sea. Although the abolition of the Navigation Acts in 1849 deprived them

[1] Rawson to Cardwell, 20 January 1866, *Parl. Pap.* 1866, XLIX, p. 290.
[2] *Ibid.* p. 292.

of an undoubted advantage, this loss was for a time partially offset by the growth of the wealth and commerce of the adjacent continent. Possessing an abundance of resinous cedar wood and craftsmen who were skilled in the construction of small schooners and brigantines, Bermuda not only built ships for Nova Scotia and Newfoundland but owned a merchant fleet of over one hundred sail and did a considerable carrying trade between the West Indies and the United States and British North America.[1] During the American Civil War Bermuda benefited, though to a much smaller degree than the Bahamas, from the abnormal conditions then prevailing. The gain was of short duration and not without its drawbacks: "Everybody acquainted with Bermuda", said the Governor in 1867, "now feels and acknowledges that the fictitious prosperity of the Civil War was a great calamity, one of the least evil results of which was an increase of permanent burdens devolved upon the colony on account of its apparent and temporary riches."[2] Soon after the end of the Civil War the steamer ousted the sailing ship in trade between the West Indies and the American continent, and the shipbuilding and carrying trades of Bermuda were destroyed.

Bermuda, however, still had her imperial naval dockyard which brought much money to the islands, and the very cause of the final loss of her prosperity as a maritime centre was to be the basis of a new source of wealth. A former Governor, Sir William Reid, had introduced in 1839 the plough and the harrow and endeavoured to encourage agriculture in the island, and although the methods of cultivation remained very primitive there was a gradually increasing production of early potatoes, onions and arrowroot, which finally became important articles of export. In 1869 the first steamship communication between Bermuda and New York was opened up and thereafter the island was able to reap the advantage of the high prices which its *primeurs* fetched in the American market.

British Honduras. Throughout the period 1840 to 1850 the white settlers in British Honduras continued to press for legislative reform, and evidence accumulated of the unsatisfactory nature of government by public meeting. In 1848 there were more members (64) than the total number of voters (59) in the settlement: the real power was in the hands of London merchants who controlled the mahogany firms in Belize. "The bulk of the meeting consists of mahogany cutters, measurers and mechanics, ill-educated and financially dependent on the merchants."[3] In 1853 the ancient system of government was abolished and in its place a Legislative Assembly was constituted with seventeen elected and four nominated members.[4]

---

[1] *Annual Report on Bermuda for 1878, Parl. Pap.* 1878–79, L, p. 13.
[2] *Ibid. 1866, Parl. Pap.* 1867–68, XLVIII, p. 123.
[3] *Annual Report on British Honduras for 1847, Parl. Pap.* 1847–48, XLVI, p. 172.
[4] Mills, A., *Colonial Constitutions* (1856), p. 227.

The Superintendent received greater powers than he formerly possessed: the right of originating all grants and appropriations which proceeded from the Assembly; the power of nominating three members of the Assembly; the right to initiate bills in the House, and to refer back for amendment any measures that had been passed by the House and sent to him for assent. As a result of smaller numbers the Assembly gained in quality and showed a greater sense of responsibility.[1]

The northern and north-western part of the Settlement was continually disturbed over many years by fighting, which began in 1847 when the Indian inhabitants of Yucatan revolted against the domination of the Yucatecans, who were largely Spanish in origin. It was difficult for the settlers of British Honduras to preserve neutrality in the conflict, and a number of military expeditions had to be undertaken, with results which were not always satisfactory to the prestige of British arms. This border unrest not only tended to absorb both money and attention to the detriment of the development of the colony; but also many Spaniards were permanently driven out of southern Yucatan and settled in the northern parts of British Honduras, where for a time they cultivated the sugarcane on a small scale with some success. There were also boundary disputes with the contiguous State of Guatemala which were finally settled by the Convention of 1859. In 1862 the British Government drew the logical deduction from the abandonment of Spanish sovereignty in America and the final stabilisation of the frontiers of British Honduras, and decided, in response to a memorial from the inhabitants, to convert what had originally been a British settlement in Spanish territory into a colony. The Governor of Jamaica was appointed Governor of British Honduras and was represented locally by a Lieutenant-Governor, who took the place of the Superintendent. The local Assembly proved as time went on to be inefficient; there were perpetual disputes between the landed and commercial interests; and the elected members of the Assembly, who were drawn principally from the capital, were not concerned with any improvements except in Belize itself and were "to a great extent incapable of forming a correct opinion on matters of general public importance". Of Belize the Lieutenant-Governor wrote in 1867: "Well indeed may many foreigners look with wonder at a possession which after a lapse of nearly 200 years, is without one road to its capital, has no public buildings of any solidity, and gives no token of the vast fortunes which have been realised from mahogany and trade." He went on to say: "However well adapted the present constitution might have been to the circumstances of the Colony when Belize was to all intents and purposes British Honduras, when agricultural pursuits were unknown, when all was one vast forest into which labourers were sent

[1] *Annual Report on British Honduras for 1856, Parl. Pap.* 1857-58, XL, p. 31.

from Belize to bring down its valuable woods therefrom...nothing can be more prejudicial to the interests of the colony now that agriculture is making rapid strides both in the North and South... now that important townships and settlements are being established ...in the North, and now too that wealthy and intelligent electors have been to a great extent superseded by uneducated petty traders, journeymen and labourers."[1] Finally in 1870 the Legislative Assembly was abolished by its own act and was replaced by a Legislative Council composed of six official members and four unofficial members appointed by the Lieutenant-Governor.[2]

Repeated attempts were made to regulate the cutting of mahogany, especially by prohibiting the felling of undersized and immature trees, but the regulations were not properly enforced and the destruction of the forests continued.[3] In 1867 it was reported that the natural forests were becoming exhausted and that the future of the colony must lie in agriculture.[4] This prediction, it may be noted, was a frequent one throughout the history of the colony, and was not borne out by subsequent fact. Thus the average exports of mahogany and logwood for the years 1866–68 were 4,000,000 feet and 7000 tons respectively, while in 1882–84 they were 6,000,000 feet and 15,500 tons.

The economic life of British Honduras showed no considerable changes during the period under review. The chief domestic exports continued to be mahogany and logwood, the amount of which fluctuated from year to year; for the ten years 1857–66 the average annual export of mahogany was 6,835,000 feet and of logwood 7400 tons. The timber industry required a large capital and the number of proprietors was small, individual estates being in some cases over one million acres. Despite the absence of railways, mahogany cutting had been going on in British Honduras for more than two hundred years, while exports had tended to increase rather than diminish in spite of the great fall in prices. The supply of timber was to some extent kept up by natural growth, and it was the custom to cut over a part of an estate every fifteen or twenty-five years in the case of mahogany and every eight or ten years in the case of logwood.[5] The mahogany interests benefited from the large demand for furniture during the period of solid furniture making which prevailed throughout the early and middle Victorian era; from the requirements of the railways during the period of rapid construction down to 1850; and from its use in shipbuilding before the days when iron and steel replaced wood in ship construction. With the opening up of other countries, however, and with free trade in timber, supplies especially from Mexico increased, and prices fell.

[1] Parl. Pap. 1867–68, XLVIII, p. 12.
[2] Burdon, Sir J. A., Archives of British Honduras, III, 323.
[3] Ibid. II, 188 and III, 89 and 185.
[4] Ibid. III, 306.
[5] Report of Henry Fowler, Parl. Pap. 1880, XLVIII, p. 101.

In the first half of the nineteenth century Belize had a considerable importance as an entrepôt, both for British goods for export to the neighbouring countries, and for products of the Central American states. But with the establishment of direct communication between these states and Europe this entrepôt trade became less important.[1] During the American Civil War it increased considerably only to decline afterwards. The Civil War also brought a small influx of settlers from the defeated South into the southern part of the colony. These men had capital and they started a number of sugar estates on a fair scale with some success until the great fall in prices after 1875 made sugar cultivation unprofitable.

In general, British Honduras was not a progressive colony during the years 1845–70, partly because of poor government, which was reflected in the absence of any attempt to improve communications, but chiefly from lack of labour. Some attempt was made to introduce Chinese into the colony, but they did not prove a success, and the experiment was not repeated.

(iii) CEYLON

The great coffee boom, which had been in progress since 1840, reached its peak in 1845. In that year the preference given to colonial coffee in England was reduced, a step which alarmed equally the existing owners of plantations in Ceylon and the English capitalists who were contemplating investment in the colony. There was thus a sudden decrease in the import of capital and in the sales of land for coffee plantations, which was reflected in a falling off of Government revenue. During 1846 and 1847 the full effects of the financial crisis in England were experienced in Ceylon: the price of coffee slumped heavily, and not only many of the planters but also a number of important mercantile houses, which had been financing them, found themselves in difficulties. There were several large failures, many estates had to be given up, while in others mortgagees were compelled to take over properties on which they had made advances.

The new Governor of Ceylon, Lord Torrington, who arrived in the island in May 1847, found the colony in a state of acute financial difficulty and decided to institute a thoroughgoing reform of its finances. He abolished the export duties on the produce of Ceylon with the exception of the duty on cinnamon, which was lowered from 1s. per lb. to 4d. per lb., and equalised the import duties on British and foreign produce.[2] In their place he imposed taxes on guns, dogs, shops, carriages, etc., and brought in a Road Ordinance requiring all the inhabitants to work six days in the year on the road or to pay a sum of money in lieu of work. In July 1848, however, an insurrection broke out in the Kandyan Province, the immediate cause of which

[1] Chief Justice R. Temple in *Journal of the Society of Arts*, v (1857), 121.
[2] Torrington to Grey, 13 December 1847, *Parl. Pap.* 1849, xxxvi, pp. 37–43.

was the dissatisfaction caused by the new taxes. The underlying causes lay rather in the grievances cherished by the Kandyan chiefs and priests as a result of British rule, in which they had never acquiesced, and which had lessened their power and abolished many of their rights and privileges. After the Convention of 1815 the Government had assumed a number of the former duties of the Kandyan Kings, such as the nomination of lay managers for temple lands and the recognition of chief priests elected by the Buddhist community as the legal holders of these estates. It was also responsible for the custody of a relic which was held in great veneration as Buddha's tooth. Between 1844 and 1847, however, the British Government instructed its representatives in the island that a Christian administration must not be associated with the practices of an idolatrous religion, with the result that the religious susceptibilities of the Kandyans were outraged. There were also economic grounds for complaint, as a consequence of the sale of Crown lands in the interior to coffee planters and of the migration of coolies and Sinhalese from the plains into the hill country. Finally, the inefficiency of the Civil Service and the absence of an effective administration of government in Kandy were important contributing factors.[1] The insurrection was put down without much difficulty, but the action of the Governor in prolonging martial law, and the fact that several of the new taxes had to be repealed or modified, so much weakened his position that he was compelled to resign in 1850.

The years following the revolt were difficult ones for the colony. The price of coffee continued to be low, the budget showed deficits, and the new Governor, Sir George Anderson, was forced to cut down the expenditure on roads and public works, to the great dissatisfaction of the planters. As always at such times there were complaints of the cost of official salaries, and there was a strong agitation within the colony for a change in the political system, giving the unofficial members a majority on the Legislative Council. This was resisted by the Home Government and, with the revival of prosperity after 1853 and a larger expenditure on roads by the succeeding Governor, Sir H. Ward, the agitation died down. Ward also passed in 1856 an Irrigation Ordinance, attempting to revive the old form of village organisation which in the past had served to maintain and keep in use irrigation works. Depending as it did on the local co-operation of the rice cultivators and on the active supervision of the local Government Agent, which was not always forthcoming,[2] this Ordinance was not a sufficient substitute for direct Government action to improve irrigation. But the Government's funds were conditional on the state of the public revenues; and the competition of roads and bridges, and later

[1] For the Kandyan revolt see *Parl. Pap.* 1850, XII and 1851, VIII, XXII, and XXXV. Cf. also Mills, L. A., *Ceylon under British Rule*, chap. x and Morrell, W. P. *op. cit.* pp. 528–32.
[2] *Report on the District of Saffragam for 1864, Parl. Pap.* 1866, XLIX, p. 533.

of the railway, did not leave much available for irrigation, which affected the good of the people rather than the prosperity of the coffee planters and thus did not always receive the help its importance deserved. However, the Irrigation Ordinance proved very successful in securing "that combination of purpose and effort which the abolition of *rajakaria* in 1832 helped to dissolve, and without which the cultivation of paddy becomes if not impossible at least difficult and unremunerative".[1] The administrations of Ward in the 'fifties and of Sir Hercules Robinson in the late 'sixties were both noteworthy for the extent to which the Government directly encouraged and financed irrigation works.

In general the policy of the Government in regard to public works was the essential test by which the colonists assessed its efficiency, for Ceylon was a country which, before the coming of the British, had been colonised only in the maritime provinces. The discovery that coffee of fine quality could be grown in the highlands of the interior led to a pressing demand for better communications, which were also of the first importance from the standpoint of administration and military security. Down to 1861 most of the surplus revenue that the colony could afford was put into the construction of roads and bridges, progress being particularly rapid during the Governorship of Sir H. Ward, which coincided with a period of high prices and expanding public revenue. In addition to the construction of main roads out of public funds, Ward passed Ordinances in 1857 and 1858 providing for the construction of branch roads by means of grants in aid from the Government equal to half the estimated cost, the other half being contributed by the estate owners in the district who were interested in the construction of such roads.

The great weight and bulk of the coffee to be carried to the port necessitated metalled roads, and, even so, the heavy tropical rains did much damage to the roads, carried away bridges, and involved continual expense for repairs. The annual repair bill for the Colombo-Kandy road between 1848 and 1853 was £12,000, and even this expenditure only kept the road in repair during the dry season, the crop having to be pushed forward as rapidly as possible so as to get to the port of shipment before the beginning of the south-west monsoon in May. By 1855 a coffee crop of some 500,000 cwt. was being moved over the roads of Ceylon in bandies (carts drawn by oxen) and the rate of transport was both very slow and costly. "In the district of Bedulla when the Nuwera Ellia Road was most out of repair the cost of conveying a cwt. of coffee to Colombo, 155 miles, was 14s. and bandies were often three months on the road."[2]

With the extension of coffee cultivation in the 'fifties into more distant parts of the highlands, and the continual growth of the total

[1] *Report on the Western Province for 1864, Parl. Pap.* 1866, XLIX, p. 521.
[2] Ward to Labouchere, 9 June 1856, *Parl. Pap.* 1857, Sess. 1, X, p. 324.

crop, the need for a more efficient method of transport was vital. The earliest project for a railway was in 1846 and an estimate of cost was prepared, but the project was swept away like so many others by the collapse of the great railway boom in England in 1847–48. The plan was revived by the planters and merchants of Ceylon who in 1853 petitioned the Governor for a railway, with the result that a bill was introduced into the Legislative Council, and passed, authorising an agreement to be entered into with the Company which had been formed to construct the railway in 1846. The railway was estimated to cost £856,557, but unfortunately no proper surveys had been made and it soon became apparent that the estimate would be greatly exceeded. A revised estimate drawn up by the Company's engineer in Ceylon put the cost at £2,214,000; the colony in alarm abandoned the whole scheme and cancelled the contract with the Company, paying the latter £300,000 in respect of work already carried out and interest on capital.

The third attempt, however, was successful, for in 1861 the Council resolved to ask for tenders for the construction of the railway, and in 1863 accepted the tender of a London contractor, Favielle. Construction began immediately and the line from Colombo to Kandy (75 miles) was completed and opened for traffic on 1 October 1867. The railway, which was owned and operated by the Ceylon Government, proved to be immediately remunerative; indeed, its success was temporarily embarrassing, for it diverted "from the general revenue into the sinking fund large items in the shape of tolls, cart licences, arrack licences, formerly accruing from the immense cart traffic on the Kandy road".[1] Once the railway was built it meant an immense saving to the planters in costs of transport as well as the further advantages of certainty and speed.

It was estimated that before the coming of the railway the colonists were paying from £150,000 to £200,000 for the heavy traffic between the estates and the port of shipment.[2] But while it was being built the Governor drastically cut down expenditure on public works, i.e. on roads, in order to finance as much as possible of the cost of the railway out of revenue, at which the planters complained bitterly. In 1864 a long-drawn-out dispute with the Home Government over the allocation of the cost of the military forces in Ceylon ended in a decision that the whole cost should be charged to the colony,[3] with the result that there was a revolt in the Legislative Council and the unofficial members resigned in a body. In the following year the Ceylon League was formed to conduct a new agitation to amend the constitution, so as to obtain an unofficial majority in the Legislative Council and a consequent control over the raising and expenditure

[1] Robinson to Granville, 9 October 1869, *Parl. Pap.* 1870, XLIX, p. 257.
[2] Doyne, W. T., *Ceylon Railway*, p. 43.
[3] *Papers relating to Ceylon Military Expenditure, Parl. Pap.* 1865, XXXVIII.

of public funds. The agitation was fed in Ceylon by the financial crisis of 1866 which caused severe depression in the colony. The Colonial Office refused to listen to the representations of the Ceylon League; the coffee plantations expanded rapidly under the stimulus of the railway; a new and active Governor, Sir H. Robinson, pursued a vigorous policy of road building; and the whole agitation collapsed.

The policy of the Government of Ceylon in regard to public works was in striking contrast to that of any of the West Indian Islands or British Guiana. This may be ascribed in part to the influence of India and to the fact that the Ceylon Civil Service had been largely moulded on that of India. The large size of Ceylon, its recent occupation and the sudden rise of the coffee-planting industry were contributing causes, and it must be remembered too that the Governor of Ceylon was, subject to the concurrence of the Colonial Office, a very autocratic ruler of his colony, with an official majority in the Legislative Council on which he could always rely.

The economic development of Ceylon between 1845 and 1870 was dominated by the production of coffee in plantations managed by English and, especially in the early days, by Scottish planters, financed by British capital. As the industry progressed and coffee plantations became valuable properties, absentee ownership grew up very much in the same way as it had existed for centuries in the West Indies, though the extent of absenteeism was not so great in Ceylon, if only for the reason that coffee planting there was a pioneering enterprise the success of which depended essentially upon the capacity of the man on the spot. The whole of the capital for construction purposes and for plant was imported from Great Britain, while the funds needed for financing the cultivation and transport of the crop were, as in the case of the West Indies, mainly provided by drafts on London merchants to whom the crops were consigned. The extent to which the capital for financing the coffee plantations was drawn from Great Britain rendered the planters very susceptible to financial stringency at home. Thus the three great crises of 1847, 1857 and 1867 were all periods of acute difficulty and embarrassment for the Ceylon coffee planters. Although most of the fixed capital was raised on mortgage, a good deal was also found by means at first of private companies and later of limited liability companies. Of the private companies a writer said: "They have been beyond all doubt a great benefit to the Island. Their estates being represented by shares, have changed hands without being forced upon the market and have been steadily held and profitably worked. They were amongst the pioneers of coffee cultivation in Ceylon and suffered in their early investments such losses as almost always attend explorers."[1]

A peculiar feature of the coffee-planting industry of Ceylon consisted in the fact that it depended for its labour supply upon a seasonal

[1] Speculum, *Ceylon: Her present Condition* (Colombo, 1868), p. 23.

influx of Indian coolies from Malabar and Southern India in general. The vast majority of these migrated each year to Ceylon, returning to their homes after the crop season was over. It was estimated in 1880[1] that 2,250,000 Tamils had migrated from Southern India between 1839 and 1879, but the permanent settlement in Ceylon was very small. In the 'seventies about 250,000 Tamils were working annually on the coffee plantations. The organisation of this immigration proved to be a matter of some difficulty. In 1858 an Ordinance was passed constituting an Immigrant Labour Commission and setting up a Government Agent in India to organise the supply of labour to Ceylon, the expenditure being met by a levy on the coffee planters.[2] The following year an attempt was made to introduce the system prevailing in Mauritius[3] by an Ordinance giving legal validity to contracts of service up to three years made in India. The first of these Ordinances (No. 15 of 1858), however, proved a complete failure in its main object, that of encouraging the supply of labour from India, and was repealed in 1861,[4] while the second Ordinance (No. 15 of 1859) was resisted by the Government of Madras and disallowed by the Colonial Office.[5] But in 1862 (Ordinance 20 of 1861) the immigration system was put on a more satisfactory basis by a return to the earlier method of spontaneous immigration, together with the operation of private agents, by the sanction of contracts up to three years if made in Ceylon and by a number of provisions for the protection of the immigrants.[6] The Government also took steps to improve transport conditions for the immigrants and appointed a Superintendent of Immigration to look after their interests.

The rapidity with which coffee planting in Ceylon increased can be seen by the figures of imports into Great Britain, which increased from 178,603 cwt. valued at £363,260 in 1845 to 620,132 cwt. valued at £1,574,033 in 1861 and 1,054,029 cwt. valued at £2,753,004 in 1870. By this last date Ceylon had become as completely dependent upon coffee for her prosperity as the West Indian Islands were upon sugar. But, as in the case of the West Indies and Mauritius, where it was possible in 1870 to see danger ahead from the competition of bounty-fed beet sugar, so also in Ceylon one observer, at least, Dr Thwaites, the Superintendent of the Royal Botanic Gardens at Peradeniya, judged already in 1869 the seriousness of the peril confronting the coffee industry from the appearance in 1868 of the coffee blight, which was later to destroy the whole industry.[7]

Before coffee came into prominence Ceylon had been chiefly

[1] Ferguson, A. M. and J., *Summary of Information regarding Ceylon*, p. 9.
[2] *Nineteenth Report of Emigration Commissioners, Parl. Pap.* 1859, Sess. 2, p. 213.
[3] Report of Sub-Committee of Legislative Council of Ceylon, 1859, C.O. 57/26.
[4] MacCarthy to Newcastle, 30 October 1861, C.O. 54/363.
[5] Newcastle to Ward, 7 June 1860, C.O. 54/351.
[6] MacCarthy to Newcastle, 27 May 1862, C.O. 54/369.
[7] *Autobiography of Sir William Gregory*, p. 285.

famous as the source of the world's supply of cinnamon, but the cinnamon trade was severely hit in the nineteenth century by the competition of cinnamon from Java and of cassia. The price of cinnamon, which had been 5s. per lb. in 1844, fell to 1s. 3d. in 1855, and though the abolition of the export duty in 1853 increased the competing power of Ceylon cinnamon in the world market, its price was still too high, until in the 'sixties the growers (by this time almost all natives, to whom the European planters had sold their estates) met their rivals by lowering the quality and increasing the quantity of their output, and by the inclusion of chips, "the coarse and broken fragments which previously had been used in the manufacture of cinnamon oil".[1] For a time the device was successful and the import of cassia into England fell heavily, while the export of Ceylon cinnamon and chips increased from 879,361 lb. valued at £43,972 in 1859 to 2,684,367 lb. valued at £134,269 in 1869, but the deterioration of quality ultimately led to a fall in the price and damaged the reputation of Ceylon cinnamon.

The economic life of the native inhabitants of Ceylon was based essentially on agriculture—above all on the cultivation of rice, though Ceylon normally had to import large quantities of rice, owing to the presence of so many Tamil immigrants who formed the main labour supply on the plantations. In addition to rice and cinnamon there was a considerable native cultivation of coffee, which for a time expanded with the growth of the European plantations and benefited by adopting in some measure the improved methods introduced by the planters.[2] Thus the average exports for 1850–55 were, native coffee £588,452, plantation coffee £374,721, but as more and more of the best lands available fell into the hands of the planters the balance swung very heavily in favour of the latter, and from 1856 onwards plantation coffee bulked much larger than native coffee in the exports from the island. For the average of the years 1868–70 the exports of native coffee were only £331,463 in value compared with £2,249,090 for plantation coffee. However, the natives themselves benefited indirectly by the growth of coffee planting. Ferguson estimated in 1887 that "from each acre of coffee or tea land kept in full cultivation in Ceylon five natives (men, women and children) directly or indirectly derive their means of subsistence".[3] Certainly the increase in imports of cotton cloth and foodstuffs between 1850 and 1870 bore witness to rising standards of living.

Other native products of importance were coconut oil and coir from the coconut palm cultivated in the maritime province, the annual exports of which, chiefly to Europe, amounted on the average to £146,600 and £44,000, respectively, for the years 1868–70;

[1] Mills, L. A., op. cit. p. 220.
[2] Report on the Central Province for 1864, Parl. Pap. 1866, XLIX, p. 547 and Ferguson, A. M. and J., Ceylon in the Jubilee Year, p. 62.
[3] Ferguson, A. M. and J., op. cit. p. 98.

the products of the palmyra palm; and areca nuts and tobacco, which were exported to India, but also, like arrack, another product of the coconut palm, were largely consumed in the island. Finally, mention should be made of the pearl fishery of the Gulf of Manaar, which afforded a welcome but very uncertain revenue to the Government, who sold the right of fishing for pearls to speculators. There was no pearl fishing from 1837 to 1855, but in the ten years 1855–64 there were seven fisheries which yielded an aggregate gross revenue to the Government of £252,176.

The outstanding achievements of British rule in Ceylon by 1870 may be summed up (apart from the actual work of administration), as the construction of a network of good roads covering a great part of the colony; the building of the railway from Colombo to Kandy; the vast expansion of coffee planting; and the beginnings of the restoration and improvement of the ancient system of irrigation.

CHAPTER XXI

FREE TRADE AND COMMERCIAL
EXPANSION, 1853–1870

(i) TRADE AND COMMUNICATIONS

IN 1841 Sir George Cornewallis Lewis wrote in his *Essay on the Government of Dependencies*: "If a dominant country understood the true nature of the advantages arising from the relation of supremacy and dependence to the related communities, it would voluntarily recognise the legal independence of such of its own dependencies as were fit for independence; it would, by its political arrangements, study to prepare for independence those which were still unable to stand alone."[1]

For thirty years after 1840 this opinion, though with variations, was widely held in England, not merely by academic theorists, but by leading statesmen like Gladstone and Granville, and by most of the officials responsible for the execution of colonial policy.[2] Such a feeling is unique in the history of imperialism. Why was it so widespread? Why did it gather strength in the 'sixties? How far did it influence England's economic relations with her colonies?

Among anti-imperialist writers after 1846 were men who thought that England had lost the one advantage of Empire, commercial monopoly, and retained only its burdens. That consideration played an important part in Goldwin Smith's anti-imperialism. "The time was when the universal prevalence of commercial monopoly made it worth our while to hold colonies in dependence for the sake of commanding their trade. But that time has gone. Trade is everywhere free or becoming free; and this expensive and perilous connexion has entirely survived its sole legitimate cause."[3] Imperial feeling, it is implied, varies with the importance of the Empire as a market. In the world of universal free trade dominated by industrial England, the closed imperial market which had nurtured England's economic strength up to the early nineteenth century was no longer valuable; it became valuable again only in the 'seventies when the competition of the newly industrialised nations of the continent revived the importance of the imperial market and heightened Englishmen's appreciation of the advantages of Empire. These considerations are

---

[1] Lewis, G. C., *Essay on the Government of Dependencies*, p. 324 (ed. by C. P. Lucas).
[2] See Bodelsen, C. A., *Studies in Mid-Victorian Imperialism*; Schuyler, R. L., "Climax of Anti-Imperialism in England", *Political Science Quarterly*, XXXVI, 537.
[3] Goldwin Smith, *The Empire* (1863), p. 63.

more useful as an explanation of the awakening imperialism of the 'seventies, the agitation for fair trade and the imperial federation movement, than as an explanation of the anti-imperialism of the 'forties. The loss of the colonial monopoly did for some people give a keener edge to the burdens of Empire. But the point did not occupy an essential position in the general structure of "Little England" arguments because the writers who inclined most naturally to anti-imperial views had never considered the monopoly of colonial trade an advantage.

Laissez-faire economics, which since the late eighteenth century had dominated English thought on social problems, had an anti-imperialist bias because the Empire was associated with economic restriction, and no doubt the men of the 'sixties were able to entertain such anti-imperial ideas as we have quoted because of the mental climate created by economists like Adam Smith who denied that political and commercial control of colonies was profitable, and radical reformers like Molesworth who denied that it was right. But what was significant about mid-Victorian anti-imperialism was not the virulence of a few followers of "the Manchester School", but the tacit assumption among moderate and reasonable men that colonial separation was inevitable and desirable. Their attitude to empire was different in important respects from that of earlier anti-imperialists. They were compelled to reflect on the nature of the imperial tie by a specific and temporary problem and they derived their assumptions as to the inevitability of separation from its difficulties. The problem was Canada. Canada was both a burden and a danger; the maintenance of troops was a considerable expense to the United Kingdom and there was an ever present danger that Canada would involve England in war with the United States. In the 'sixties there was open talk in the United States of annexation of Canada and there was a strong American party in the Canadas. It is the peculiar urgency of the Canadian problem in the 'sixties which explains in large measure the chronology of English anti-imperialism. Similar objections, in a rather attenuated form, applied to the Australian colonies and, especially after the Maori wars, to New Zealand. But only the most determined of "Little Englanders" ever tried to bring India within the scope of their arguments.

Mid-Victorian anti-imperialism had therefore a very restricted theoretical basis. It was restricted also in the area of opinion it covered. Even in the 'sixties there were important groups who did not share the view that the Empire was a burden. Throughout most of the period *The Times* for example argued the case against the Little Englanders. Nor did English manufacturers share the anti-imperial feeling. Between 1846 and 1849 a number of Acts had placed the Empire on a free trade basis; the British Government repealed the preferences on colonial grain and timber; empowered the legislatures of the five British North American colonies to repeal the duties enacted at Westminster, which gave British manufactures an advantage in the Canadian market; and threw the carrying trade of the Empire open to the world. But these events did not mark any change in the assumptions of English manufacturers about the rôle of the colonies in British economic life. Throughout the agitation for free trade the opposition to the preferences on Canadian wheat and timber came not from the free trade industrial interests, but from their opponents, the agriculturists. After 1846, as before, the colonies were to be sources of raw materials and markets for English goods, and if necessary this character was to be maintained by legislation. In adopting free trade, Earl Grey made it clear that the British Government "did not abdicate the duty and the power of regulating the commercial policy not only of the United Kingdom but of the British Empire".[1] This was no mere academic claim. On three occasions between 1846 and 1860 various colonies attempted to establish tariffs which, in effect if not in intention, gave protection to colonial industries. On each occasion important sections of manufacturing opinion in England petitioned against them. Such opinion lies behind the section of the Australian Government Act of 1850 which prohibited the Australian legislatures enacting tariffs with differential customs duties, and delayed for twenty years the establishment of tariff reciprocity between the Australian colonies.[2]

In 1859, when Galt, the Canadian Finance Minister, laid heavy import duties on manufactures which could be produced in Canada and admitted raw materials free, the Chamber of Commerce and Manufacturers of Sheffield petitioned the Government to press for its withdrawal.[3] The Canadian Government was able to assert its fiscal independence, but in India the protests of English manufacturers were more though not consistently effective. Throughout the nineteenth century the Lancashire cotton interest petitioned against any change in the Indian tariff which seemed to give a measure of protection to the Indian cotton industry.[4] In 1859 a new Indian tariff was brought into operation, the chief feature of which was that cotton yarn paid 5 per cent and cotton manufactures, among other things, 10 per cent. The duties on British cotton piece goods were doubled and in some cases quadrupled. There was a storm of protests from both English cotton manufacturers and Bombay importers, and the next year the duties on raw cotton and cotton goods were equalised at 10 per cent. In 1861 the preference on the raw material was re-

[1] Lord Grey, *The Colonial Policy of Lord John Russell's Administration*, I, 281.
[2] Allin, C. D., *Australian Preferential Tariffs and Imperial Free Trade*, chap. III.
[3] For the Canadian Tariff see Edward Porritt, *Sixty Years of Protection in Canada, 1846–1901*, chaps. I, II, III: and for the general imperial tariff problem see *The fiscal and diplomatic freedom of the British Overseas Dominions*, (ed. D. Kinley); Fuchs, J. C., *Trade Policy of Great Britain and her Colonies since 1860*.
[4] For the Indian Tariff see Hamilton, C. J., *Trade Relations between England and India*, chaps. VII, VIII; Strachey, Sir J. and Sir R., *Finance and Public Works in India*, chap. XV.

introduced—the duty on yarn was reduced to 5 per cent while that on cotton manufactures remained at 10 per cent. In 1862 the duty on yarn was reduced to 3½ per cent and that on manufactures to 5 per cent. Throughout most of the period therefore the Indian tariff gave preferential treatment to the Indian industry; at least in the period 1861–74 it is not true that the Indian tariff was manipulated to prevent the accumulation of capital by Indians. But that was certainly not through want of effort on the part of the Lancashire industrialists. The jute manufacturers of Dundee, in a similar way, agitated against the Indian jute industry, but they were ineffective, because the Indian jute factories were owned by Scots and because Dundee was not as politically important as Manchester.

But, though in many cases the efforts of English industrialists to control colonial tariffs in the interests of English industry failed, the fact that they were made points to the persistence of certain elements of mercantilist psychology in the attitude of English manufacturers towards the colonies. Men who preached *laissez-faire* as the golden rule of domestic politics were proposing to the Government of India that all cotton lands should be exempt from land tax for a period, and that the Indian Government should guarantee a certain price to all cotton. Such attempts to control colonial economic life failed, yet the division of labour between England and the colonies at which they aimed was in fact maintained, though by forces less directly under human control than tariff policy.

In 1850 the different parts of the Empire varied considerably in their economic maturity, from India and the West Indies, which had been worked for the British market for two centuries, to the Cape, which had not yet developed an export staple and still depended for almost all its stores on the United Kingdom. Yet the Empire had certain general economic uniformities. From the economic point of view it was the best of all possible empires—a group of pioneer communities attached to a highly industrialised nation, buying the products of that nation in return for food and raw materials. In the decades after 1850 the uniformities became increasingly marked because the prime factor in the economic activity of almost all the colonies became the inflow of English capital. The urge behind economic development was the necessity to produce export crops to meet the debt and sinking fund charges. Increasing concentration upon a few staple products for export, large capital imports in the shape mainly of capital goods, a high rate of investment, full employment despite heavy immigration, profit inflation and rising property values; this was the common pattern of economic activity in the colonies.

Depending so largely on one market for the sale of their products and one source for their capital, the colonial economies were very unstable. Their exports were almost entirely raw materials and food, the prices of which on occasions fluctuated violently. Their import of goods depended mainly on their import of capital and fluctuated with business movements in England. And the colonies found it difficult to adjust themselves to these variations because they lacked the mechanism which in a fully developed monetary economy made adjustment easier. It followed, too, that the colonies tended to reflect fairly accurately the variations of English economic life. For most colonial products it was the price on the English market which determined the output; except in 1800-1 Canadian corn prices for example usually followed the English closely.

This economic immaturity of the colonies determined the organisation of their trade with the United Kingdom. The evidence for the organisation of British foreign trade in the mid-nineteenth century —the private papers of the great merchant exporters and the numerous law suits and bankruptcy cases—has not yet been thoroughly examined; but it is possible to make certain tentative generalisations on the basis of a small sample. Consignment played an important part somewhat longer in the British export trade to the colonies than in that to Europe or America. The British goods exported to Australia, South Africa and Canada (India is reserved for separate treatment) were not, as a rule, bought by merchants in the colonies on their own account: they were consigned by the British manufacturers or merchants to their agents in the colonies or to banks acting as commission houses, who sold them to colonial customers. This generalisation does not of course apply to railway material, the colonial demand for which was known: the construction firm building in the colonies usually bought direct from the British manufacturer, paying part of the price in debentures on the railway company. But most goods were consigned. Sometimes the manufacturer consigned his goods direct to the agent in the colonies, though this was not common in 1850–70. More frequently he used the services of the large merchant houses, who, on his behalf, consigned the goods to their agents in the colony; the shipping and insurance business was done by the merchant; the risk remained the manufacturer's. Alternatively, the manufacturer might sell his goods outright to the merchant firm. It is not possible to determine the relative importance of these two last methods. The goods sent to Australia in the boom years 1853–4 were generally not ordered but consigned; and consigned not by a few large merchant houses but by a large number of comparatively small shippers.[1] But whichever method was adopted, the merchant came increasingly to dominate the pattern of economic activity. "The universal custom of drawing on the merchant after consignment had been made to him placed at the disposal of the manufacturer the capital resources of the mercantile class, and so promoted continuity of operation and

---

[1] *Bankers' Magazine*, October 1855, p. 613.

concentration of effort on the part of the class which was best fitted for manufacturing."[1]

The persistence of consignment in the colonial trades arose naturally from the disparity of capital resources. Britain, with her highly developed financial machinery, inevitably took the initiative in exporting; no Australian merchant, for example, could compete in the Australian market with English merchants who were able to buy for cash and sell on long terms of credit. Colonial merchants had to buy on long credit and at the same time to give long credit terms to Australian retailers. It was a burden which very few had sufficient capital to bear. The lack in most of the colonies of a prosperous class of merchants importing on their own account is the key to many problems of colonial economic history.

This persistence of consignment, while primarily due to a disparity of capital resources, had additional causes: the distance and uncertainty of the colonial markets, and the character of England's exports to the colonies, largely miscellaneous goods which could not be sold by sample. In the 'fifties and 'sixties a number of factors were developing, removing these additional causes and systematising this trade. The proportion of commodities like steam engines for which the demand could be ascertained with exactness, and commodities like the coarse cottons which could be graded accurately, was increasing; English firms specialised in commodity and market, established branches in the colonies and traded to order; the introduction of a bond and warehouse system enabled colonial importers to hold their surplus stocks until the market could absorb them. Speedier communication —most important of all these developments which were making colonial markets less speculative and insecure—brought the colonies nearer to the home country. But none of these developments affected Britain's disproportionate control of capital resources, and consignment remained the character of the export trade to the colonies. That trade was by no means the only one in which consignment played an important part—as late as 1869, 60 per cent of the imports of cotton goods into America from Europe were consigned. But comparing it generally with other trades, it was the one in which consignment was most deeply rooted, lasted longest and where it was most extensively consignment by manufacturers.

The importance of consignment had been very clearly stated by a witness before the Committee of 1833.

"The manufacturers in England are obliged to operate on a very large scale; they have a regular demand for two-thirds or three-fourths of what they make, and the rest they ship; and their reason for shipping is that they do not choose to depreciate their own article and they do not choose to compete with their customers;

---

[1] Buck, N. S., *The Development of the Organisation of Anglo-Indian Trade*, p. 172.

they can only sell at a fit price a certain quantity, and the excess they export."[1]

Since 1833 a number of England's markets had established sufficient parity of financial resources to trade with her on something approaching an equality. But in trade with the newer parts of the world, and the most important of these were British colonies, the disproportion of financial resources remained the fundamental fact of the trade. Thus the export trade to the colonies occupied a rather peculiar rôle in the development of mid-nineteenth-century capitalism; it was more than any other branch of England's trade the channel through which the manufacturers of England continued to dispose of the surplus production necessary to obtain the full economies of large-scale production.

The organisation of the import trade from the colonies was equally immature. These imports were so varied and difficult to tabulate that, despite their greater command of capital, the English merchants were unable to take the initiative in trading. At a time when the cotton market had developed a highly specialised organisation, Canadian timber was contracted for by the importing merchant and auctioned at Liverpool or in London; and wool from Australia was consigned to a small group of London selling brokers and sold at their wool auctions. The system characteristic of the early nineteenth century whereby merchants and planters in all parts of the world consigned produce for sale in the country and drew bills in anticipation of its value remained most important in the long trades—the chief of which were the colonial trades.[2]

Though Anglo-Indian trade has been included under certain of these generalisations, the effects of the East India Company monopoly, the nature of the political connection with India and the possession of a wealthy merchant class of its own gave it certain distinguishing characteristics.

Private trade by Englishmen with India was started chiefly by the civil servants and agents of the East India Company who became agents and bankers. For many years their firms—the Great Houses— carried on most of the private trading. The capital was supplied from salaries, and as it was usual to make the partners trustees in all the settlements of their constituents, great numbers of the servants of the Government retired home leaving their fortunes in the hands of those agents and bearing high interest.

By 1850 the age of these agency houses was over; in 1835 six of them crashed for £15 million, and five or six came to grief with the collapse of the Union Bank in 1847.[3] After the crash the few better houses that could command capital in Calcutta profited by an accumulation of business in their hands and by the reduced cultivation

---

[1] *Report on Manufactures, Parl. Pap.* 1833, VI, p. 93.
[2] See Clapham, J. H., *Economic History of Modern Britain*, II, p. 315.
[3] *The Calcutta Review*, 1848, p. 163.

of indigo—the crop which had ruined so many of them. But their place as the main channel of Anglo-Indian trade was taken by private firms of Liverpool and London merchants specialising in East India trade, with branches in Bombay and Calcutta. Many of them, like Gledstones, were firms which entered the trade after the ending of the East India Company monopoly in 1813.

Unlike private firms in English domestic production, these firms very rarely adopted joint-stock organisation; they made all the extensions of their trade out of their own very large profits. From the 'fifties, when merchants were taking over trade, down to the slump after the Great War was the great period of the English merchant houses, and among them few were wealthier or more important than the East Indian. While the adoption of joint-stock organisation in domestic production was gradually dissociating the ownership of capital from its management, the great East India merchants remained at once capitalists and entrepreneurs. Together with the big Liverpool firms trading to America, to which, indeed, they were linked by capital and personal relations, they formed the *haute bourgeoisie* of mid-Victorian England. Though there was a tendency in the 'sixties for a small number of these firms to concern themselves increasingly with the financing of the trade rather than with the trade itself, most of the firms remained actively engaged in trade. In addition to these firms were the English merchants who had their headquarters in India, the most important single group of which were the merchants of Calcutta who bought tea and consigned it to an agency in London for auction in Mincing Lane; and the wealthy Parsee merchants of Bombay.

In the thirty years after the abolition of the East India Company's monopoly Anglo-Indian trade was highly speculative, conducted by firms with large liabilities and small capital resources. A vivid light on the conditions of trade is thrown by the fact that even as late as the year 1847, long after steam communication had been established, bills at 10 months' date were the ordinary medium of trade between England and India. By the 'fifties the age of growing pains was over, the trade was in the hands of large and powerful firms and the ordinary medium of trade was bills drawn four months after sight. But the developments which gave Anglo-Indian trade its strength gave it also its weakness; when one of the great firms did crash, the repercussions were widespread and disastrous. When writing on foreign exchanges Goschen contrasted the East India trade and its bills of sometimes as much singly as £10,000 with the numerous drafts which made up a continental parcel of remittances to similar amount—bills against cattle, eggs and butter, drafts of travelling Englishmen on their London banks. The Continental transactions were more petty and retail than the wholesale cargo orders of the Indian trade. But they were also much safer. "Even in the tremendous destruction of French capital, there has been no such spectacle as that which our Exchange Banks have presented of stupefaction over the failure of Gledstones."[1] Those trades which brought England the raw material for the greatest of her industries—textiles—were characterised by very large trading units—the American, the Indian and somewhat later the Australian.

Steam and iron-built vessels became important on the route to North America earlier than on any other. Down to the end of the period most of the cargo continued to be carried in sailing ships, but news went by steam, and the progress of communication was considerably accelerated by competition between the line supported by the British Government and that supported by the Canadian. In 1852 the Cunard Company, which had been carrying the mails under contract to the British Government since 1840, was running a weekly service from Liverpool to New York. The Canadian Government attempted to run a rival line from Liverpool direct to the St Lawrence ports. Their first contract with the Liverpool firm Mackeen, McHarty and Company was not successful and terminated in 1854; but in the same year they made a contract with Hugh Allan and in 1859 he started a weekly service between Liverpool and Quebec. By 1863 four-fifths of the mail between Canada and Great Britain was carried by Allan and one-fifth by Cunard.

The steam age began very early in the Atlantic. From the start Cunard used steam; from the start Allan's ships were built of iron and they adopted steam and the screw propeller very early. In this development Government support occupied a central position, for Atlantic steam lines could be made to pay only if they could obtain contracts to carry mail. These mail subventions were of profound consequence in bridging the gap between the known high costs of steamship operation and the commercial revenue obtainable. This Government aid was primarily important in the Atlantic, where in the 'forties it gave Britain a monopoly of steam navigation. But it was not confined to this area. Four years before the Allan line adopted steam the African Steamship Company was founded with a monthly contract to the West African colonies; and by 1860 the P. and O. was carrying mail from London via Alexandria to Bombay and Calcutta, Singapore, Hong Kong and Sydney.[2]

Compared with the Atlantic routes the shipping on the Indian route was, in many respects, backward; the merchant who owned his own ships to carry his merchandise was an important element in the Indian when in other trades he had disappeared; and the political exigencies of trade in Eastern waters preserved among the larger firms the semi-naval traditions of the East India Company.[3] By 1853 the British colonies and spheres of interest in the East were linked to

[1] Goschen, G. J., *The Theory of the Foreign Exchanges*, p. 63.
[2] See Smith, W., *The History of the Post Office in British North America*, chaps. XVII, XVIII.
[3] Hoskins, H. L., *The British Routes to India*, chap. X and *passim*.

each other and to the United Kingdom by a comprehensive system of steam lines. The overland route was established as the main channel of communication with India. Twice a month steamers sailed from England to Alexandria, where the passengers and mail went overland to Suez and Aden. Here the routes parted; one line, the old East Indian, going to Bombay and the other, the P. and O., to Ceylon, Madras and Calcutta. From Bombay steamers sailed twice a month to China. In the next twenty years, along these routes went the news of the Empire in the East, the letter home from the planter in Assam, the orders of the East India Directors and then of the Secretary of State, and the despatches of proconsuls. But the bulk of the commerce, and most of the passengers, continued to go by sail around the Cape. A few of the lighter and more valuable of Indian exports went overland, but the change which came with the opening of the Suez Canal was not prepared for by any general re-orientation of trade along the overland route in the years before 1869.

Closely linked with this system of routes to the East was the route to Australia and to the Cape. In 1851 the General Screw Steam Company extended their old Cape service on to Australia; and in 1852 the Australian Mail Steam Packet began a monthly service to Australia *via* Panama. It was in the commercial shipping between Britain and Australia that most of the improvements in the sailing ship were made. The new Australian trade, more than any other, formed and moulded the whole business of professional deep sea ship-owning. It was in the struggle to exploit this new and suddenly expanding trade that many important English shipping firms established themselves, small owners and export-loading brokers growing up with the trade. In 1864 three of the most notable of these lines of packets sailing from Liverpool to Melbourne—the Black Ball, the Eagle, and the White Star—amalgamated to form the Australian and Eastern Navigation Company. The Cape in the early 'fifties was mainly a port of call on the way to Australia and the East; no important independent services were started until the late 'sixties. In 1870, not only to meet the demands of the increased home trade and immigration into the diamond fields but also to serve the very considerable colonial trade, the Cape and Natal Steam Navigation Company was started to establish a powerful line of steamers to ply between London and the Cape, Algoa Bay and Natal, to sail once a month and call at Madeira and St Helena.

The great expansion of British commerce with the East and Australia caused no important change in the direction of the main trade routes. A small direct trade between India and Australia sprang up in the 'sixties when a few of the iron clippers which carried emigrants to Australia went on to India and Burma, generally with a cargo of walers[1] for the army in India, and loaded either jute home from

---

[1] Viz. horses from New South Wales.

Calcutta or rice from Rangoon; a few clippers, too, went out to Melbourne with a general cargo and then across to China and home again with tea. But no important three-cornered trade grew up; in normal periods the needs of the increase in trade were met by the adoption of larger, and to an increasing extent iron, vessels, and by experimenting with steam navigation on the Cape route. In the 'sixties the proportion of iron-built ships in all trades increased rapidly, but progress in steam was slow. Steamers were used for short trades and valuable goods because of the considerable saving in insurance and interest money; but on the long voyage they could not compete with sailing vessels. In the long Australian and Eastern routes the lack of suitable coaling stations, the large space taken by coal and a prejudice against the carriage of fragile commodities like tea in steamers, maintained the supremacy of sail. In the 'fifties the great American clippers running out of Liverpool—built in the yards of the United States and Canada—were the main traders on these routes. During the Australian boom of 1852–3 shipping was diverted from the Indian to the Australian trade; Liverpool owners hired or bought American trans-Atlantic packets and clippers, and the ship-builders of Boston and Nova Scotia were crowded with English orders. It was these large American-built ships of about 2000 tons which carried the Irish emigrants to America, and the English miners to California and Australia. But their great day was soon over. The profitableness of various types and sizes of vessel in a trade depended largely on the nature of the cargo. The soft-wood clippers which carried out the great immigration to Australia in the 'fifties were not suited to carry the wool, hides, tallow and wheat which Australia exported to Britain in small quantities. They were therefore replaced by their London rivals, British-built hardwood teaks of half the size —the Blackwall frigates—which spread from the China tea trade to the Australian and West Coast trades. The older larger ships gradually drifted into the less important trades; a favourite route was from Melbourne to Auckland and then over to the Chincas to load guano, and from this trade a few survivors descended to the Quebec timber trade. This change in the type of ship in use on the Australian and Eastern routes was of considerable importance for the British ship-building industry, for it was a change from American to British-built ships. In the late 'sixties a new type of ship began to carry a larger portion of Anglo-Australian and Anglo-Indian trade. As Australian exports to the United Kingdom became larger and more confined to wool, the small London ships were supplanted by the magnificent iron clippers of the Clyde, Liverpool and Aberdeen.

Such remained the disposition of Britain's Australian and Eastern trade routes until the opening of the Suez Canal in 1869. The voyage around the Cape to India—and in 1869 this was still the route for almost all goods—took between six and eight months. This fact contributed greatly to the fluctuations of prosperity in India and Australia; prices might change completely in the half year between production and sale. It was this fact too which concentrated the Eastern trade in Britain's hands; she became the entrepôt for Indian and Chinese commodities; in 1867, for example, 27 per cent of the cotton which she imported and 24 per cent of the tea were re-exported.[1] Large interests grew up in England which specialised in the warehousing and financing of this entrepôt trade. The immediate effect of the opening of Suez was to put a premium on the use of steam and to depreciate the value of the great amount of wealth represented in the sailing fleets. It accelerated the technical perfection of the steamer; the rate of technical progress was so rapid that the steamers built in the early 'seventies were unable to compete with those completed in the middle of the decade. The tendency to reduce freights after 1870 was, therefore, due not merely to the shortening of the time of the voyage and the consequent saving of insurance and interest, but also to the increasing quantity of steam tonnage competing for freight, an increase due to an accelerated rate of technical progress. In the ten years after 1870 very heavy investment was made in the British shipbuilding industry. On the other hand, much less capital was tied up in long-term credits on Indian trade. The long-term effect of Suez was to destroy Great Britain's large entrepôt trade in Eastern goods. Europe went direct to India; Calcutta and Bombay traded directly with Marseilles and Genoa, Venice, Trieste, Havre and Hamburg, and even with California. Ten years after the opening of the canal 40 per cent of the external trade of India was with foreign countries, and though part of this represents the trade in opium and cotton goods to China, over half was trade with European countries which before 1869 had used Great Britain as an intermediary.[2] It was of equal importance that within England itself the English manufacturer joined hands with the Indian merchant or commission agent behind the backs of the great East India importing houses of London. These houses still remained the most important among the merchant class, but they lost what had virtually been a monopoly of the importation of Indian goods.

These developments would not have been possible had it not been for the development, about the time of the opening of the Suez Canal, of telegraphic communication between the East and the markets of the West. There had been attempts after the Mutiny to establish cable communications with India, and in 1858 the Red Sea and Indian Telegraph Company was formed with a Government subsidy; but the line it eventually laid worked only for a few months. In 1865 the first overland telegraph between Europe and India was established by the completion of the Turkish line via Constantinople; another land line

[1] *Report of the Royal Commission on Depression in Trade and Industry, Parl. Pap.* 1886, XXIII, 345.
[2] Wells, D. A., *Recent Economic Changes*, 1891, p. 33.

ran out to India *via* Germany, Russia and Persia. But these land lines were badly organised and under foreign control; attention was therefore concentrated on the submarine telegraph. In 1870 the British Indian Telegraph Company laid the first successful direct cable between England and Bombay. From Bombay it continued round the south of India to Singapore, whence one line ran north to meet the Russian overland cable, and the other went to Australia, three years before the Atlantic cable was completed.

On the basis of this revolution in communication and the widening difference of time between the transport of goods and the conveyance of news there grew up new types of commercial dealings and a more highly developed market.[1] From the 'thirties onward there was a slight but increasing disparity between the speed of goods and news; news came quickly by steam and goods slowly by sail; the superior speed of news was especially important in the Indian trade where news and goods came by different routes. This disparity, increased by telegraphic communication, was the origin of dealing in futures.

For a few months in 1857 telegraphic contact was made with India, months which coincided with a fear of shortage in the American cotton supply; for the first time dealings in cotton "to arrive" became a feature of the Indian Liverpool cotton trade. The soaring cotton prices during the American Civil War developed the practice; many Liverpool brokers not only bought cotton already at sea, but bought cotton for shipment many months ahead. After the laying of the Atlantic cable in 1867 and the Indian cable in 1870, buying and selling cargoes afloat, or "to arrive", became a regular feature of the cotton market, and somewhat later of the market in other commodities easy to sample. The system of cables, along with the opening of Suez, made the first important inroad on the position of the merchant. The manufacturer was put once again in direct contact with his markets and his raw materials. English manufacturers sometimes entered into negotiations for the future delivery of their goods, and some of the less substantial firms raised part of their short-term capital in this way; it greatly increased the ease with which funds could be obtained. It has been explained how the growth of communications affected the import of Indian commodities into the United Kingdom; the great East India merchant firms of London, who since the 'thirties had imported all the Indian produce, gradually lost part of their trade, not merely the large re-export trade but the import of Indian goods for home consumption. With the growing efficiency of communication the importance of consignment in the long trades diminished; in the 'sixties English merchants, for example, consigned large amounts of commodities to their agents, the large importing houses of Bombay and Calcutta, who held stocks and sold as demand

[1] See Dumbell, S., "The Origin of Cotton Futures," *Economic History*, I, 259.

arose; already by the later 'seventies most of the goods were sold "to arrive" or bought in execution of Indian orders.

Between 1850 and 1870 maritime communication between the colonies and Britain was considerably improved. Any important general decrease in freight rates would have greatly increased the differential advantage of colonial goods on the English market, especially those from Australia and India, for transport costs constituted a very large proportion of their price. But there was, in fact, no such decrease. The abolition of the Navigation Laws in 1849 did not cause important reductions, partly because the monopoly abolished was imperfect. In 1845 half the total British seaborne trade was governed not so much by the Laws of Navigation as by exceptions to them; the most important of these was the American agreement of 1830 which allowed American ships to share in the trade between British colonies and foreign countries. Therefore, though immediately after 1849 there was a decrease in freights on certain routes, it was slight; it was, moreover, not due to the competition of foreign shipping in the colonial trades but to competition in the carrying trade between foreign countries and Great Britain.[1]

In the 'fifties and 'sixties political circumstances combined with technical improvements to give English shipping a monopoly of colonial, and indeed of other, shipping, more effective than the Navigation Laws had maintained. The United States, her main competitor, was disorganised by Civil War. The Crimean War and the Indian Mutiny and the great demand for Indian cotton between 1861 and 1864 kept freights high, gave British shipowners enormous profits and enabled them to extend their supremacy. The adoption of iron-built vessels put a premium upon the engineering skill which England had in abundance.

Steam power had not been introduced to any considerable extent even by 1870, and where it was introduced steam freights were higher than sail. Though inventions for the economic employment of steam were perfected in the early 'sixties, the conservatism of Government officials and of a class of owners drawn quite largely from men who had started as sailsmen in control of their own small shipping firm delayed their adoption; the engines actually in use consumed an uneconomically large amount of coal. Not until the 'seventies was steam power swifter than sail. The steamships of Cunard took fourteen days to make the eastward passage of the Atlantic and many clippers took less. The greater advantage of steam over sail was its regularity —the time of a passage by sail might vary 30 per cent or 40 per cent on different voyages—and this advantage did not become really decisive until the establishment about 1870 of a system of submarine cables and the growth of commercial dealings depending upon

---

[1] There is no collection of freight rates for this period, but *The Economist* gives occasional quotations.

scheduled regularity. It was this necessity, inducing technical development, rather than the technical development directly, which accelerated the adoption of steam after 1870. In 1869 some English shippers complained that the rates for steamers were being affected by the competition of sailing vessels which were accepting ruinously low freights. It was the irregularity of the sailing ship, and to an increasing extent their inferior speed and the attempt to mitigate these disadvantages by lower freights, that was the prime cause of freight reduction in the 'seventies. In this reduction the opening of the Suez Canal was important, because on the routes to India and Australia it gave the steamer the monopoly of a much quicker route at a time when steam was little if any faster than sail. But not until many years afterwards was the decline in transport costs sufficient to bring large amounts of, for example, Indian wheat to London. Not until the 'nineties was the reduction on Canadian rates sufficient to enable Canada to supply Britain with a noticeably larger proportion of her wheat.

Wherever on a particular route a tendency towards lower freights between 1850 and 1870 can be detected, it is usually to be associated, not with any change in the prime costs of transport but with changes in the character of the trade. Thus, for example, in the 'fifties Canadian exports to Britain were bulky goods, while her imports were largely miscellaneous goods which took very little room; the freights out from Quebec and Montreal had therefore to bear the burden of both voyages and were very high; as heavy capital goods came to form an increasing proportion of Canada's imports, there was a slight but perceptible decline in freight rates. In a similar way, after the Indian Mutiny, the heavy exports of coal and railway material and the lack of return cargoes from India drove up Indian freights.

Such were the organisation and routes of colonial trade. There remains a problem of vital importance—what part did English merchant firms trading to the colonies play in the economic exploitation of the Empire which was the main development in the decades after 1850?

The colonial trade routes were long and the capital resources of the colonial producers small; the capital put into production by English traders in the form of long-term credits must therefore have been considerable. The situation varied somewhat with the commodity. But it was the usual practice, e.g. in the Australian trade, for an importing firm in London—and by the 'sixties most of them had large capital resources—to make advances to the proprietor of an estate in the colonies. The Canadian timber industry before the growth of large-scale units was largely financed by advances from English shipping and importing firms.

A large amount of English short-term capital was locked up in the trade with Canada. Canada imported mainly manufactured goods on credit, while almost all her exports—grain, flour and timber—sold for cash. The exporting houses of Kingston, Montreal and Quebec were "supported" by merchants in England—a Canadian called it "a wretched and pernicious dependence"; there was a constant balance against Canada represented by stocks of imported goods in wholesale and retail stores of the country, by book debts or by real estate. In 1866 it was estimated that the mercantile indebtedness of Canada to Great Britain amounted to twenty to twenty-five million dollars.[1]

But it was not merely that English merchant firms placed their financial resources behind the colonial producer. London firms with branches in Bombay and Calcutta or English firms with their headquarters in India tended to go into production in the colonies on their own account. The great mercantile houses trading to India with branches at Bombay and Calcutta preferred on the whole to confine themselves to making advances to and buying from the natives, for their command of capital gave them a practical right of pre-emption. But when in certain localities no one else would grow the staples they required in sufficient quantity or quality, they stepped in, bought land and produced directly.[2] In general there was a distinction between the new exotic products and cotton. The bulk of the short-term capital of the cotton producers was provided by Indian firms— by the native agencies which collected the cotton and exported it to the coast. The Parsee firms of Bombay had entered the cotton trade early in the century, and it was men like Sir Jamsetjee Jeejeebhoy and Nusserwanji and Kaliandas, with large mercantile connections in the interior and renting Government dues over extensive districts, who financed a large amount of the cotton production.[3] But some of the new exotics the mercantile firms did cultivate and many of the great merchants of the Presidency towns employed agents to grow sugar and coffee and even cotton.

Of all British colonies Canada was most firmly rooted in the old colonial system, and responsible Canadian opinion thought that the withdrawal of the preference on Canadian grain and the modification in the timber preference would ruin Canadian industry and commerce and lessen Canadian consumption of British manufactures; the lumbermen of St John, Halifax, Sydney and Quebec, and the grain and flour merchants of Montreal, all protested vigorously against repeal.

The history of the next ten years belied most of these fears and showed that, even for Canada, the corpus of legal restrictions abolished between 1846 and 1849 was not of fundamental importance. For

---

[1] *Bankers' Magazine*, 1866, p. 62.
[2] Lee, W. N., *Tea Cultivation, Cotton and other Agricultural Experiments in India* (1863); Bell, E., *The Empire in India*, p. 288.
[3] Harris, F. R., *Jamsetjee Tata*, chap. I.

some ten year more, economic forces and the inertia of commercial organisation maintained the same general features of Anglo-Canadian trade.

Freightage formed so large a part of the cost of Canadian wheat in London that the opening of the colonial trades to foreign shipping might be supposed to have increased Canada's competitive power. The reduction of freights, English free traders argued, would neutralise the abolition of the preferences. There was in fact some reduction in the general level of freights. Norwegian and Prussian ships brought most of the wood from Archangel and Onega; Dutch, Danes and Finns, Swedes and Norwegians carried a part of our Baltic trade and some of these last two brought teak from India. In the Canadian carrying trade itself ships of many nationalities as well as the new vessels of the colony competed with the British. But what reduction there was, was due mainly to the competition of foreign shipping in the non-colonial trades, and it was not sufficient to increase Canada's differential advantage in the London market. "A comparison of quotations in the five years after repeal suggests that the competitive power of Montreal had not been materially improved."[1] Canadian grain freights did not approximate to those of the United States until rolling stock and heavy manufactures formed a high proportion of British exports to Canada.

Nor did the reduction of the preference on colonial timber—it was not abolished completely until 1860—make any immediate substantial difference to the position of Canada as a timber producer. The export of Canadian timber to England continued to increase until 1867. True, it formed a decreasing proportion of England's total supply, one-half in 1853 and about one-third in 1867; but what is remarkable is the rigidity of the trade and the delayed response to the change in relative prices. But by the late 'sixties Britain was drawing most of her timber supplies from the Baltic; the useful white wood of Norway replaced the North American white spruce. On the other side of the Atlantic, the demands of the United States had replaced the British demand as the basis of the Canadian timber industry. Nevertheless, although England turned elsewhere for the bulk of her timber, the products of the forest continued to form the largest single element in Canadian exports to her, accounting for about 40 per cent of the total.

British North America occupied a unique position in the Empire, for on its borders lie the United States, an alternative market for Canada's raw materials, and to some extent an alternative source of capital goods and even of capital. After the abolition of the British preferences on timber and grain it was inevitable that British North America should attempt to develop its commercial interests. Strong agitation for the lowering of the tariff between Canada and the United

[1] Burn, D. L., "The Repeal of the Navigation Laws," *Cambridge Historical Journal*, 1928, p. 268.

States culminated in the Reciprocity Treaty of 1854; until the abrogation of this treaty in 1866 Canadian grain, timber and ores found a ready market in the United States, and the United Kingdom found a market in the United States for the products of her industry, a market from which she was partially excluded by the 1859 tariff.

Even before that tariff American goods had the natural advantages of proximity. The value of the United States exports of domestic produce to British North America advanced from £1,330,000 in 1852 to about £3,930,000 in 1858—an increase of nearly 200 per cent in six years, as compared with an increase in the United Kingdom exports to British North America of only 15 per cent. The 1859 Canadian tariff placed a 20 per cent duty on the import of all manufactures. Its effect is clearly reflected in the trade figures of five leading articles of British manufacture exported to Canada.

	1856 £	1860 £	Duty
Cotton manufactures	402,111	461,909	20%
Iron, tin, cutlery, hardware	640,853	469,322	20
Leather manufactures	15,275	8,734	25
Silk manufactures	44,966	42,399	20
Woollen manufactures	410,039	379,078	20
	£1,513,244	£1,361,442	

And this decrease was at a time when British trade with the United States was increasing. Alone of the British colonies, British North America shows a relative decrease per head of population in the import of British goods. Nevertheless the extent to which the United States had made inroads on the United Kingdom's position in the Canadian market can be exaggerated. By 1870 the miscellaneous commodities, drugs, books, haberdashery, etc., which figured largely in British exports to Canada in the 'fifties, were no longer an important item, but the reason was Canadian and not American competition. In such commodities as carpets, china ware, drugs, fancy goods and hosiery, British exports to Canada were, in 1870, roughly three times those of the United States. In iron, too, Britain had still a marked predominance; in 1868 Canada imported $3,286,726 iron from the United Kingdom and only $739,137 from the United States, though it is notable that in this year Canada bought most of her rolling stock from the United States. In textiles British predominance was even more marked than in iron, and the United Kingdom had, of course, a monopoly of the very important item—commissariat and ordnance stores. Down to 1870 the financial and technical superiority of English industry was more than sufficient to neutralise the heavy cost of transporting goods to Canada.

In 1851 gold was discovered at Bathurst in New South Wales, and between 1851 and 1855 gold to the value of some £125 millions was exported from Australia. On the economic life of all the Australian colonies and on Anglo-Australian trade the effect was revolutionary. Already in 1850 Australia was the largest supplier of wool to the United Kingdom—providing her with 39 million pounds as compared with 9 million from Germany, the next most important source of supply; thus Australia supplied something over a half of her wool imports. But Australia was not a very good market for English goods: she imported from England, in 1853, £1,080,112 of goods consisting largely of miscellaneous stores. Within a year of the gold discoveries exports from the United Kingdom to Australia were trebled and what was, in effect, a new market created for British industry. The discovery of gold concentrated the bulk of Australian labour and floating capital in mining, which made many miscellaneous industries in Australia unremunerative at the very time when the great outflow of gold and the great rise in immigration increased the demand for the product of those very industries. Food and all the equipment of life for a rapidly increasing population had to be imported. Food was supplied largely by New Zealand, but the miscellaneous commodities—clothing, earthenware, plate, stationery—came from the United Kingdom. The demand in Victoria for "apparel, slops and haberdashery", which in 1851 was £243,946, leapt to £1,202,673 in 1853.[1] Australia, which in 1850 had been the seventh of Britain's markets, became for two years her second. In 1853 the handful of Australians took from the United Kingdom as much of her goods (within a few thousands) as did the whole of British India, being in the proportion of £28 per head in Australia to 1s. per head in India. The Australian diggers must have been thirsty men: in 1853 they took half the total export of wine and beer from Great Britain —200,000 barrels of strong beer and 1½ million gallons of wine, exclusive of spirits.

These high figures are not a completely accurate guide to Australian demand. Most of the goods had been consigned in the hope of probable sale and late in 1854 the plethora of goods caused a disastrous fall in price. But though Australian demand for haberdashery, clothing, hardware, etc. declined, it remained one of the characteristic features of the Australian trade down to the 'seventies; and Australia continued to be the most important market for such goods, absorbing, in 1870, £218,624 of the total £2,205,255 worth of apparel which England exported, and £117,000 worth of saddlery out of a total of £326,000.[2]

The gold discoveries did not have any important effect on the character of Australian exports to the United Kingdom. In 1870, as in 1853, the staple export was wool, with hides and tallow next, but

---

[1] *Annual Statement of trade and navigation of United Kingdom, Parl. Pap.* 1854–1855, LI, i, 251.
[2] *Ibid.* 1872, LXIII, ii, 113.

very far behind. The amount of wool exported continued to increase during the years of the gold boom, despite the concentration of labour and the high Australian prices. But a change had taken place in the basis of this export; the internal demand for meat replaced the demand of the English manufacturers as the factor controlling its volume. The quadruple rise in the price of meat in Australia, due to increased immigration, more than compensated for the rise in the price of wool and tallow.[1] Because the Australian population grew so rapidly, the growing English textile industry was able to obtain its wool; companies with large capitals were formed to exploit the new areas being opened in the 'sixties and new breeds of sheep were introduced.

The older sources of England's wool supply were stationary or declining; Europe, mainly Spain and Germany, which in 1844 had supplied 60 per cent of England's total imports, in 1858 supplied only 22 per cent. In the period 1850–70 almost all Australia's wool was sent to the quarterly sales at London, which was the centre of a great entrepôt trade. After 1870 buyers from the United States, provided with large credits, arrived at Melbourne; their demand for wool was so urgent that they sent home part of the wool not by the long sea route at cheap freight to Boston, but overland *via* San Francisco. In the late 'sixties improvement in meat preservation made it possible for Australia for the first time to export some of her meat; in 1867 the United Kingdom imported preserved meats from Australia to the value of £40,000; in 1870, 250,000 cases were imported worth £500,000. A taste for Australian preserved meat, hitherto confined to prisons and poor-houses, spread rapidly in the manufacturing districts and even among the upper classes.[2] It was the beginning of a minor revolution in the conditions of Anglo-Australian trade.

On the English clothing industry and shipping trade the sudden increase in the Australian demand had an immediate and profound effect, which communicated itself throughout the whole of English industry. Apart from this direct effect of increased demand was the more general effect of the increase in gold supplies on prices and the rate of interest. There was a rapid increase in the amount of capital available in London, due not only to the increased import of gold, but also to the large remittances from Australian bonus and investment companies; the Burra-Burra copper mines near Adelaide in one season yielded 1200 per cent profit to the proprietary.[3] The rate of interest in 1852 and 1853 fell as low as 2 per cent. Prices rose rapidly until 1864. The combined result of these factors was to give

---

[1] Cairnes, J. E., "The Australian Episode", *Essays in Political Economy* (1873), p. 20.
[2] Report of the Union Bank of Australia, *Bankers' Magazine*, 1872, p. 107. The export of *frozen* meat was later. See Clapham, J. H., *An Economic History of Modern Britain*, II, 90.
[3] *Calcutta Review*, XXVIII, 91.

English industry an immense fillip at a time when it had scarcely recovered from the depression of 1847. English manufacturers found their profits increasing and, with interest rates so low, were able to make large extensions of their industry. It is highly probable that the continued rise in prices was not due to the direct effect of the new gold supplies on circulation, but to the investment boom and the increased demand for goods which it caused. The figures of the Bank of England's gold reserve between 1847 and 1853 show only a slight increase; indeed, after 1866, when gold production began to fall off considerably, the Bank of England's reserve, and notes and deposits based upon it, began to grow more rapidly than when gold production was booming.[1]

Much of the Australian and Californian gold imported into England was re-exported, the bulk of it ultimately to the East. As to the causes of this drain of bullion to the East, and its effects on Anglo-Indian trade, there was considerable controversy; but the facts were not in doubt—the export of silver to India and China, the increased import into England of Eastern goods and the relative stability, at a low level, of the prices of such goods. Tooke and Newmarch noticed that the prices in 1857 of the main colonial and tropical commodities— tea, sugar, coffee, tobacco, raw silk, indigo and cotton—were little higher than in 1851.[2] The difficulty was to find the operative factor in these complicated changes. Did the changes start with the low prices of Indian goods, due to the hoarding habits of Indians which enabled India to absorb bullion without a rise in prices—these low prices causing an increased demand for Indian goods and therefore an export of silver to pay for them? Or did the changes begin with a change in the value of silver? It is probable that while prices rose in the gold-standard countries like Great Britain, and in the double-standard countries like France, they did not rise in countries like India which had a silver standard. The great increase in the amount of gold made the prices of goods in silver-standard countries relatively lower. There was therefore an increased demand for such goods, and gold was exported to France to buy the silver displaced from the French currency and send it in payment to the East. The increase in the import of Indian goods was sudden and large.[3]

Between 1850 and 1875 Anglo-Indian trade changed considerably in volume and to a less extent in composition. After decades of slow progress Indian exports to the United Kingdom increased rapidly from the early 'fifties until the heavy fall in the exchange value of the rupee in the 'seventies. The main cause of this increase, as of the

[1] Phinney, J. T., "Gold Production and the Price Level", *Quarterly Journal of Economics*, XLVII, 665.

[2] Tooke and Newmarch, *History of Prices*, VI, 168. See also Lees, N., *The Drain of Silver to the East* (1866).

[3] Sayers, R. S., "The Standard in the Eighteen-fifties", *Economic History*, Jan. 1933, pp. 583–5.

general increase in English import trade, lay in the rising standards and changing demand schedules of Englishmen. But in the case of India special causes reduced the element which formed so large a part of the price of Indian goods—transport costs: the abolition of internal customs in the twenty years before 1853, the gradual removal of all export duties until by 1874 only that on rice remained, the abrogation of all discrimination in favour of British shipping, and above all the extension of the great trunk roads and the creation of a railway system.

The constituents of English export trade were also changing. Even as late as 1858 it could be said that "India is chiefly known as a dealer in drugs, dyes and luxuries", and in that year the import into England of what had been the characteristic articles of the old Indian trade—drugs, dyes, spices, oils, sugar, silk, saltpetre, and silk manufactures—was 61 per cent of our total imports from India. But the export from India of almost all such articles was in 1858 either stationary or declining. With every year fewer of the cargoes which had made the Indian fortunes of the eighteenth century landed in England. Some, like spices, declined rapidly because of changing English tastes and needs. Others, like indigo, continued to figure largely in Indian exports to the United Kingdom for a long time and about half was re-exported to the Continent, but the Indians' dislike of enforced cultivation, the greater profitableness of rice and the development of synthetic dyes about the 'sixties put an end to its importance. The export of Indian sugar soon ceased completely. In 1853 India exported to the United Kingdom 44,000 tons—about 2 per cent of the United Kingdom total—and even of this small amount over a half was re-exported to the Continent. In 1863 for the first time India's imports exceeded her exports. The British West Indies and, to an increasing extent, Mauritius, where the cane industry was developed by British planters with the help of Indian labour, were England's important sources of supply.

As the old staples declined in importance, a number of circumstances acting in varying combinations—the rising standard of living in England, changed conditions in her alternative sources of supply, the decrease in freight rates and in costs of internal transport—brought to England from India either new commodities or old ones in significantly new quantities.

A small group of exotics, recently acclimatised in India by English capital and enterprise, grew rapidly in these years—tea, cinchona and coffee. With successive reductions in the tea duty and cheap sugar England was acquiring the tea habit. While the consumption of coffee was decreasing and that of spirits was stationary, the consumption of tea per head increased from 1·47 lb. p.a. in 1843 to 3·37 in 1866. China continued to supply the bulk of our tea; but the proportion of Indian to China tea was slowly increasing—from 0·3 per cent in 1853 to 8 per cent in 1874—and conditions were arising in the East and adjustments of taste being made in England which caused the rather sudden supersession of China by Indian tea. After ten years of heavy costs and no returns the plantations of Assam began in the 'fifties to produce tea at a cost which, for similar brands, was lower than the Chinese. The greater political security of India, the greater application of capital and the growth in the 'sixties of managing agencies which, by grouping together several producing units under the control of one agency, rationalised both production and marketing—all these factors increased the differential advantage of Indian tea on the English market. At the same time the English taste for tea was revolutionised. Indian tea, at first so pungent that it could be sold only by mixing small quantities of it with Chinese, became by the 'eighties the customary English tea.[1]

More important than these exotics were the large quantities of raw materials and grains which decreasing returns in English agriculture and increasing returns in English industry, as well as the paralysis at certain periods of England's normal supplies, enabled India to throw on to the London market.

Many Englishmen were acutely aware quite early in the century that the raw materials for British industry came from sources beyond England's political control which might easily be disabled: in particular they feared that political events (a slave rising was what most of them expected) would cut off their supply of cotton.

More obvious than the insecurity of England's main supplies was their inadequacy. The rapid increase in production in the 'fifties put a strain on the customary sources of supply of many of Britain's most important raw materials; the rise in their price, which probably represents the rigidity of her supply more than the effects of the new gold, was felt acutely by many English industries; in 1836, for example, Leeds had thirty-nine flax-spinning factories fully employed; in 1860, because of the high price of flax, only nine flax factories were at work.

Long before the cotton famine accentuated the inadequacy and broadcast the insecurity, British manufacturers had looked to the colonies as alternative sources of raw material—but above all to India. For India could grow—in fact did grow—most of the necessary raw materials, but some in deficient quality, and all at prices which, after paying heavy transport costs, could not compete in British markets in normal times. Attempts were made to improve the quality of Indian products; the Government botanists did a large amount of useful work; the merchants of Mark Lane, who were large importers of hemp and flax, sent out specimens to India. But proposals to encourage the cultivation of these staples directly were not very effective. The Government and the majority of English business men relied upon the improvements in transport and the operations of the

---

[1] For the cultivation of tea see below, p. 793.

price system to bring larger supplies from India whenever necessary. The improvements in transport made, in fact, little change in Indian conditions of supply, and over the whole period the proportion of raw materials which in normal times Great Britain drew from India did not increase. But the Indian supplies were extremely elastic; her export was only a small proportion of her total production. And therefore, while the normal English price brought only small quantities to England, a sharp rise in English prices due to acute shortage would divert large amounts of Indian produce from home consumption to export to the United Kingdom. Throughout this period, therefore, India remained a secondary source of supply, becoming the main source whenever events created a favourable price. On two occasions political events created such a price—during the Crimean War and during the American Civil War.

Before the Crimean War England drew almost all her tallow, flax, hemp and linseed from Russia. The blockade of the Baltic ports in 1854 reduced the usual supplies from Russia by 50 per cent and the reduction was particularly marked in hemp, reduced by over 60 per cent, and in linseed, by over 80 per cent. At the high prices prevailing for these commodities in Great Britain India turned her supplies to the London market. The large-scale import of Indian linseed into the United Kingdom did not start in 1854; three years before the war the demands of a reviving industrial machine had quadrupled the import of Indian linseed, and between 1851 and 1854 the average import was 1,415,000 bushels p.a. But the war established India for the first time as the main supply of oil seed, and though, after the war, Russia continued to send fairly large quantities, the bulk of our supplies came from India.

The American Civil War threatened the supply of a much more important raw material. Down to 1861, 80 per cent of England's cotton came from the United States; Indian cotton imported into Great Britain in 1860 formed only 7 per cent of the total quantity and $4\frac{1}{2}$ per cent in value, and although 216,832,000 lb. were actually imported and brought to the market, more than two-fifths was too poor in quality to find buyers for English consumption. A fair amount of long-stapled cotton was imported from Egypt, Brazil and the West Indian Islands, and some small amount of a very fair quality from Port Natal. The danger of depending so largely on a single foreign source for the raw material of our most important manufacture was obvious to the manufacturers in the first half of the century, and there were many attempts to develop India as an alternative supply. But at worst, what they feared was a gradual decrease through slave risings or emancipations. No one in his wildest speculations ever predicted a stoppage of the supply in consequence of a blockade of the southern ports by the federal forces. In 1861, when the stoppage came, it was comparatively sudden and complete. For the next four years, until

1864, the United States supplied only 3 per cent of England's cotton supplies and frantic efforts were made to obtain new supplies from Egypt and Turkey and even remote Pacific Islands. But to make up the bulk of the deficiency England looked naturally enough to India, and by 1864 two-thirds of our cotton came from India. But it was two-thirds of a very reduced total.

It is perhaps strange that India was not able to supply more of the deficiency, for the cotton sent to England in normal years was only a small fraction—about one-eighth—of her domestic consumption. But even the trebled prices of 1861–4 failed to draw off more than the top layers of Indian cotton. The fact shows how little Indian railway construction had altered the conditions of supply.

Nevertheless, the rapid transference of Britain's main raw material supply from the western to the eastern hemisphere, from a country where our purchases were balanced by the export of our own manufactures to sources like India and to a less extent Egypt and Turkey, which could not take payment of our purchase in kind, was a minor revolution, demanding readjustments which were the more difficult because native demand was not resilient. The profits of the increased cotton exports went mainly into demand in the Indian home market, and the increased export of cotton from India did not immediately provoke an increased demand for British goods. The large purchases of Indian cotton, which increased moderately in quantity but enormously advanced in price, led at first to a great increase in the export of bullion; between September and December 1863 the bullion stock of the Bank of England fell by over two millions and the Bank rate went up to 8 per cent. Apart from the gold supplies by California and Australia it is hard to see in what way this transference of the cotton trade could have been accomplished without producing a major commercial convulsion. The consignment of gold from Melbourne and San Francisco constantly came to hand at the most critical junctures. The immediate strain was to some extent alleviated by manipulation of Council Bills, for Sir Charles Wood brought home the balances of the Indian Government which had been accumulating in India. In the course of 1863–4 great progress was made in overcoming the tendency of the sudden import of cotton from the East to carry away excessive quantities of gold and silver. In the long run adjustment took the form of an increased import of English goods: English productions gained a footing at least in Calcutta and Bombay, and the immense wealth poured into Bombay and Bengal during 1863–4 broke down many of the barriers to the reception by Indians of thoroughly European notions of commerce.

Many Englishmen—many manufacturers among them—thought that the cotton famine would drive English capital and intelligence to exploit the cotton fields of India, and so modify English machinery that India would establish itself permanently as the main supply of cotton. These hopes were disappointed, for by 1870 the Indian supply had fallen to 10 per cent. For fifty years Indian cotton had been used in England to supplement the American in the coarser yarns and fabrics: the two qualities had been used in proportion to their relative price at the time—that price being an exact measure of their relative availability for the purpose of the manufacturer. The Orleans cotton was always worth just half as much again as the Surats.[1] During the famine, improvements made the Surats to some extent available for the finer yarns, but did not alter this proportion. Therefore the moment American cotton reappeared in Liverpool it resumed its old position of relative superiority.[2]

While the increased supply of Indian cotton failed to maintain itself after 1864, there was a permanent increase in certain other less important commodities. The consumption of rice per head in England increased from 4 lb. in 1843 to $8\frac{1}{2}$ lb. in 1866. For some purposes it was a cheaper alternative to the grains from the Baltic, the Ukraine and America—in many manufactures, for example, it replaced wheat-flour dressing; the influence of men returning from India and the spread among the upper middle classes of rice and curry as a dish also increased consumption; and it was in this period that the English working classes first took to the rice pudding. The bulk of this in-creased consumption of rice came from India. In the quality she exported she had no competitors, and supplied not only the United Kingdom but through her much of the Continent: in 1858, out of a total of 3,692,023 cwt. of Indian rice imported into the United Kingdom, 1,119,662 cwt. were re-exported to foreign countries. But important as British demand was for Indian rice, it never became the determining market; the internal and Chinese markets always took the greater part.

About the 'fifties the United Kingdom began to import from India a number of other commodities; compared with the total imports the share from India was not large, but it makes a significant increase on the total previously imported from India. India sent us quantities of teak; the large increase in wool started in 1852, and in 1857 India supplied Great Britain with 15 per cent of its wool. The Indian export of wheat began also to increase, though it did not become important until the 'seventies.

The nature of the political connections between India and the United Kingdom produced a complicating element in their economic relations. The East India Company, and after 1858 the Indian Government, had certain payments to make in London out of the Indian revenue—the Home Charges—"England's salary for ruling India". The term covered a number of payments; in this period it included dividends to the proprietors of East India Stock, interest on

[1] The Orleans fibre was much longer, cleaner and more even than the Surat cotton.
[2] On the Cotton Famine see Henderson, W. O., *The Lancashire Cotton Famine*.

debt, the expenses of the establishment in England, and the cost of civil and military stores.

At successive periods in the nineteenth century three different methods were used to remit the Home Charges to London—remittance by up-country investments, by bills of hypothecation, by London drawings upon India. Down to 1813 the East India Company bought goods directly with the proceeds of Indian taxation and consigned them "sale in London". After the withdrawal of the Indian monopoly in 1813 the Company effected its remittances by transmitting them to China to buy goods for sale in London, but partly also by bills on Indian goods direct from India to London. While in the first case the system of direct purchase continued, a new method was developed in the second. The Company was able to use the large number of merchants who had settled in the three presidency towns after 1813. Upon consignment of any of a certain seven staples consigned to London by private merchants the Government advanced about three-fifths of their value. It was by these means that merchants in India were able to finance their consignments home. This method of remittance prevailed into the early 'fifties and explains much of the character and organisation of Indian trade at this time. But with the growth of the Company's indebtedness the bills of hypothecation had frequently to be supplemented by borrowing in London upon the security of taxes in India; and out of this necessity about the time of the Punjab war arose the system of remitting by means of bills drawn in London on the Indian treasury. The East India Company, and after 1858 the Secretary of State, estimated each year the amount of the London payments for the succeeding year and then advertised from time to time at fixed rates of interest for tenders of drafts upon India, which were bid for by merchants with debts in India.

The amount of Home Charges grew steadily and there was a great rise after 1858.[1]

1856	£ 3·5 millions	
1862–3	7·5	,,
1869–70	10·5	,,

Not all this was remitted by the bills—the Secretary of State sometimes used the balances in the London Banks of the Guaranteed Railway Companies for this purpose—but the great bulk was. And they made the Secretary of State the dominating factor in trade relations with the East—an authority utterly beyond competition because he was above loss. The precise rôle of the bills in Indian commerce varied according to the extent of loans to India, but in most years the cash in hand or in immediate prospect was the most important item in any exchange calculations of European business with the East. Indeed, it determined the main outlines of Anglo-

[1] For an estimate of the annual amount of Home Charges, see Dutt, R. *Economic History of India in the Victorian Age*, pp. 212, 373.

Indian trade, for the Indian cultivators had to limit their choice of staples to such produce of their soil as would, after a long voyage, be acceptable in England or in some foreign country indebted to England.

The trade with India was an integral part of British trade with China. The peculiar difficulty of this trade was that while the English market needed the tea and silk of China, there was no Western commodity in which China would take payment. The words of the Emperor Ch'ien Lung to George III were still true half a century later. "The Celestial Empire possesses all things in prolific abundance and lacks no product within its borders. There is therefore no need to import the manufactures of outside barbarians in exchange for our own products." In the earlier part of the nineteenth century a large amount of Chinese exports to England had been paid for by the Home Charges of the Indian Government. When a less cumbersome method of remitting these charges was evolved the Chinese exports were paid for, in the main, by developing the export of opium from India to China. The opium traffic created a balance of trade in favour of India which enabled British merchants in China who exported silk and tea to England to settle their debts in China. Between 1850 and 1854 Britain exported to China and Hong Kong an annual average of goods to the value of £1·73 millions, and between 1865 and 1868 goods to the value of £7·13 millions. Much of this does not represent trade with China itself, for during these years Hong Kong was becoming the distributing centre for a vast trade in opium, cotton, tea and silk. No precise estimate of the value of this trade is possible because the port was free, but the tonnage entering rose considerably, from 625,536 tons in 1859 to 1,063,252 tons in 1866.

British exports to India consisted almost entirely of the products of the British textile or the British iron and steel industries. Textiles, cotton chiefly, made up a proportion of the total value which fluctuated between 55 and 70 per cent. The proportion of iron and steel and copper products varied rather more according to the import of capital. In the years after the Mutiny it ranged about 25 per cent. Throughout the 'sixties it was almost 20 per cent, but started to sink below that mark towards the end. This large and expanding market for the products of England's two main industries has an importance which needs no emphasis.

But even in the middle of the nineteenth century there were signs of that regrowth of the Indian cotton industry which would eventually be England's competitor in her most important market. For all types of textiles the amount exported to India increased, but the advance was conspicuously slow in those types which came into competition with the products of Indian mills.[1]

English miscellaneous goods were never an important part of India's imports, but the proportion increased during this period.

[1] Hamilton, C. J., *Trade Relations between England and India*, p. 243.

The Indian upper classes were acquiring a taste for Western dress and luxuries; the English in India were increasing in number, in particular the presence of the army was an important cause of development.

Between 1840 and 1853 British export trade to foreign countries was, on the whole, increasing more rapidly than exports to British possessions. Despite the prodigious increase of British exports to Australia in 1853, the proportion taken by British territories in that year was almost identical with the proportion taken in 1840—about 33 per cent. Between 1853 and 1870 the general trend of increase was roughly the same.[1]

Year	Value of British exports to foreign countries		Value of British exports to British possessions	
	Amount million	Per cent	Amount million	Per cent
1854	63	64·9	34	35·1
1855	69		27	
1856	83		33	
1857	85	68·5	37	31·5
1858	77		40	
1859	84		46	
1860	92		44	
1861	83		42	
1862	82	66·8	42	33·2
1863	96		51	
1864	109		51	
1865	118		48	
1866	135		54	
1867	131	72·4	50	27·6
1868	129		50	
1869	142		48	
1870	148		52	

The decrease in the five-yearly average of exports to the Empire from 33·2 per cent in 1859–64 to 27·6 per cent in the period 1865–9 was due partly to a considerable decline in the amount of British capital exported to India between 1867 and 1870, partly to a comparative decline in the Australian demand, and partly to the effect of American competition in the Canadian market. The proportion of British exports to India was 9·3 per cent in 1854; it rose to 12·1 per cent for the period 1855–9 and to 13·0 per cent for 1860–4; in the five years after it sank to 10·9 per cent. The Australian market, which absorbed 12·4 per cent of British exports in the boom period 1854–9, took only 6·9 between 1864 and 1869.

But the significance of imperial trade is greater than these general figures would suggest. Manufacturers were greatly concerned in the middle of the last century with the problem of raw materials. The urgency of that problem was accentuated by sudden shortage due to

[1] *First Report of the Royal Commission on Depression of trade and industry, Parl. Pap.* 1886, XXI, p. 189.

political events. But behind these adventitious causes lay one more profound—an economic machine working up to conditions of full employment. Tooke and Newmarch wrote of the middle years of that century that "the consumption of raw materials in this country in the production of goods for the foreign and home market has proceeded faster than the additions made to the supply of those raw materials".[1] For her essential raw materials Britain drew largely on her colonies, not merely in emergencies but as normal sources of supply; cotton came from the United States and India, wool from Australia, India and the Cape, silk from China and India, and hemp from India alone. India, exporting raw materials and food where formerly she had exported spices and drugs, had replaced the West Indies as the economically most valuable part of the Empire. "We have often remarked", wrote *The Economist* in 1870, "upon the great importance of a good supply of the raw materials of our chief manufacturing industries as lying at the foundations of our mercantile superiority; the opening up of new colonial possessions is more important from this point of view than as forming new markets for our manufactures."[2]

In the mid-nineteenth century the United Kingdom had still an actual monopoly of the trade of the Empire; there were only two important streams of trade between colonies and foreign countries: the country trade between India and China, which was an integral part of the Anglo-Indian trade, and the growing trade between Canada and the United States. For the rest, England was the colonies' main market and supply. In the last ten years of this period England began to lose her monopoly position in world markets. French industry developed; deposits in French savings banks grew enormously and French capitalists began to buy back railway securities held in Britain; French and Belgian iron manufacturers began to compete with English iron masters. English commercial and industrial supremacy was not in this period seriously challenged, but the growing pressure of competitors underlined the importance of the possession of colonial markets.

(ii) BANKING AND INVESTMENT

Until the 'fifties there was no adequate financial machinery to carry away the gradually accumulating capital of Britain to finance colonial production. Australia had three chartered banks, with headquarters in London; the West Indies had one—the Colonial Bank, which in 1850 was the largest of all the Anglo-Colonial banks; Mauritius had one bank backed by the East India House of Reid, Irving and Company; and there was the Bank of British North

---

[1] Tooke and Newmarch, *History of Prices*, iii, 361.
[2] *The Economist*, 1870, p. 1006.

America (incorporated 1836). But for most of their short-term accommodation colonial producers depended on local banks with very small capital resources or on advances from purchasers in the United Kingdom; all colonies lacked adequate machinery for financing trade and production and remitting money to England. Between 1850 and 1870 there were established in all parts of the Empire large Anglo-Colonial banks directed from London and with extensive resources of English capital.

In Australia the demand for loanable capital was much more urgent than in the other colonies, and the first important Anglo-Colonial banks were established there in the 'thirties. In 1850 there were seven banks in Australia, of which three were of English origin and had their headquarters in London: the Bank of Australasia (1834), the Bank of South Australia (1835) and the Union Bank of Australia (1837).[1] It was through these banks that most of the first gold from the new discoveries was remitted to England. Merchants by their over-trading were debarred from any control over the exchange and were unable to purchase gold for remittance to England, so that the banks were almost undisturbed possessors of the field. They were able to buy heavily before prices rose very high and they made enormous profits; the Bank of New South Wales, for example, in 1852 paid 33 per cent bonus and 10 per cent dividend. To exploit this situation the colonial banks increased their capital, the Oriental Bank established a Melbourne branch and a large number of London capitalists combined to promote new banks. Local opposition to the establishment of Anglo-Australian banks was very successful, since three out of the five largest proposed Anglo-Australian banks failed to obtain charters. Of the eight banks established between 1850 and 1858 in order to finance the gold rush, only two were Anglo-Australian—the English, Scottish and Australian Bank and the London Chartered Bank of Australia. There was a similar banking boom in the 'sixties after the Act of 1862 had given limited liability to banks and in order to finance the growing Australian trade; but the most important were of Australian origin.

Most of the banking capital of Australia was therefore raised in Australia itself by local banks. Nor was all the capital of the Anglo-Australian banks raised in England. A number of them stipulated that a portion of their capital should be held in the colonies. How far the colonists ever held their full number of shares it is not possible to say, but the probability is that they rarely did so. On its foundation in 1837 the Union Bank of Australia stipulated that half its original capital might be held in the colonies; but in 1872 only 5800 of these 12,000 shares were on the colonial register and steps had to be taken to enlarge the bank's local connections by transferring the

[1] For Australian Banking see Mackay, A. L. G., *The Australian Banking and Credit System*, pp. 1–84.

full quota to the colonies. Nor was all the capital of the Anglo-Australian banks, wherever raised, employed in Australia. In 1857, and in 1864–70, when the English rate of interest was high, the greater part of the bank's proprietary capital was kept in England available for investment. And in 1854, when Australia had a plethoric supply of capital, Anglo-Australian banks were carrying on their business exclusively on deposits.

The high rate of profit of 1852–4 did not last long; as coin from England arrived the price of rough gold tended to assimilate itself to the English mint price; many English capitalists came into the field as gold buyers and still further decreased the margin of profit. Though the banks continued to derive considerable profits from exchange dealings, it was in discounting good bills, in financing Anglo-Australian trade, that their main business lay. In all banks the amount of bills discounted rose rapidly. While the bills drawn by the branches in the colonies and accepted by the home office of the Union Bank of Australia for the second half of 1852 were £649,800, for the last six months of 1853 they were £1,028,000, and the total continued to increase rapidly. They took charge of much of the technical work and insurance for the Australian squatters and advanced them money on the security of shipments.[1] In particular they concentrated in their hands the business of the English commission houses, who transferred their business from the purely colonial banks. In the later years their work as agents of these houses became an increasing proportion of their business. The local mercantile and industrial interests of Australia tended to favour the banks of local origin which did not depend upon English capital and were not controlled by distant proprietors. There was growing up a body of purely Australian economic interests interlocked with the local banks and aided by the influence of the local governments. Between 1860 and 1868, while the four Anglo-Australian banks did little more than maintain their position, the local banks, the Colonial Bank of Australasia, the Bank of New South Wales, the Bank of Victoria and the National Bank of Australasia, more than doubled their deposits.

In any agrarian community the methods of the provision of capital control the main features of the social structure. It is therefore a question of considerable importance to determine the ways in which the Anglo-Australian banks assisted the development of sheep farming in these formative years of Australian society. The Australian farmer had two needs: he wanted, first, long-term capital to buy and stock his land; he needed also short-term credits to maintain himself until his wool was sold. The need of long-term loans varied in the different colonies, and was particularly strong in areas like South Australia, which was being opened up in the 'sixties and where squatters wished

---

[1] For the importance of the colonial banks in financing Australian sheep farming see Shann, J., *Economic History of Australia*, p. 299.

to secure their land by purchasing the freehold. But for both forms of accommodation the demand was greater among Australian agriculturists probably than anywhere else in the world. Few of them had large capital resources of their own, and the interval between clipping the wool and its sale in London was extremely long.

The provision of short-term credits by the discounting of bills of exchange drawn on a London merchant formed the traditional business of the Anglo-Australian banks, and they gradually extended the type of security upon which they would advance money; in the 'fifties they made advances on wool while it was still in the pastoralists' hands, and in the 'sixties on wool consigned for the English wool sales but not backed by a bill of exchange. But there was a substantial difference between this type of advance and lending on the security of title deeds to real estate. Large parts of Australia were up for sale, and the character of Australian pastoral farming in areas like New South Wales turned very much on the policy adopted towards such advances by the big Anglo-Australian banks.

The five Anglo-Australian banks established before 1858 were established under Royal Charter which prohibited them from lending money on the security of real estate; they were to "confine their transactions to discounting Commercial Paper and Negotiable Securities, and other legitimate banking business". Not until 1870 could a Chartered Bank, in strict law, hold a title to land as the collateral security of an advance. This prohibition did not of course apply to local colonial banks, or to Anglo-Colonial joint-stock banks established under the limited liability legislation of 1858 and 1862; and, in the case of the Chartered Banks, the actual practice of lending money on land considerably antedated the legal decisions of 1870. In colonies like New South Wales and South Australia most of the banks in all probability confined themselves to discounting good commercial bills or making advances on wool; bills still formed the bulk of the business of the Chartered Banks. But in the new areas like South Australia the English banks were forced, if they were to do any business there at all, to lend money on the security of real estates. In 1867 there were six banks operating in South Australia.

South Australian banks	31 Dec. 1867[1]
Debts due to bank	£2,559,739
Deposits	1,272,161
Notes in circulation	247,782
Bills in circulation	10,331

In the late 'sixties the increasing abundance of capital in Australia forced the English banks to lend on land, and a decade later it had become the main feature of banking in Australia.

The generalisation may therefore be hazarded that the Anglo-Australian banks up to 1870 were mainly concerned with the provision

[1] *Bankers' Magazine*, 1869, p. 11.

of short-term capital, and did not play a leading rôle in the development of new areas until after that date. During the period 1850–70 a large part of this work was done by the investment and land companies.

The privileged position of the East India Company delayed for many decades the establishment of English joint-stock banks in India, and until the 'fifties the credit conditions of the Indian trade were peculiarly inadequate; the three Presidency banks held much of the Government debt and discounted Government bills, but were excluded from foreign business; the East India Company down to about 1847 discounted bills of lading, but only sufficient to remit its Home Charges to India; the agency houses which did most of the exchange business were by their combination of trading and banking highly unstable; after 1840 a number of small Indian joint-stock banks were established. On three occasions between 1836 and 1850 attempts were made to establish Anglo-Indian banks with large capital resources, and all were prevented by the East India Company, the directors of which were closely linked with the Government banks and the agency houses. And when eventually Anglo-Indian banks were successful in obtaining charters, it was due not to any change in the East India Company's policy but to an administrative accident.

In 1851 a Royal Charter was granted to the Oriental Banking Corporation, which had evolved from a co-partnership for exchange business established in Bombay in 1842. Though it was limited to exchange business and could not issue notes, this bank soon became the most important exchange bank in the East and established branches in Mauritius, South Africa, Melbourne and Sydney. In 1853 two more Anglo-Indian banks were incorporated—the Chartered Bank of India, Australia and China, and the Bank of Asia—and a little later the Chartered Mercantile Bank of India, London and China. All four banks had large nominal capitals and were closely linked with the East India houses in London and with English banking firms. Looked at in one light they represent an attempt of these East India houses to enlist London capital in the financing of their trade. They were concerned too with financing the great extension of Eastern commerce which followed the opening of the Chinese ports in 1842. The extension of banking facilities modified the methods of trade. Down to the 'fifties the merchants at Canton paid for the Indian opium and cotton in treasure or first-class bills on London. After the establishment of banks linking India and China the Chinese branches of the banks drew drafts upon the branches in Bombay and Calcutta and sold them to the merchants, who used them to make their payments in India. The banks remitted to England the proceeds of these drafts in English exchange.

The grant of limited liability by the Acts of 1858 and the Consolidating Act of 1862 coincided in India with the boom in cotton exports. A large number of new joint-stock banks were formed; but most of them lacked that background of commercial and financial support which made the earlier Chartered Banks so successful, and few survived the collapse of 1866. In 1866 there were twenty-four banks transacting exchange business in Bombay, and twenty-two in Calcutta; a year later there were only seven.[1]

Canada, of all the colonies, had the most developed system of local banks; only two English banks were founded there—the Bank of British North America (1836) and the Bank of British Columbia, founded in 1858 to finance the gold discoveries, but extended after 1864 to all parts of North America outside the area of the Hudson's Bay Company. And, alone of all the colonies, Canada had access to an alternative money market. Even in this period small amounts of United States' capital were being invested in Canadian undertakings; a large amount of the capital of the Bank of Montreal, founded in 1822, was American.

In South Africa, Government concern with revenue excluded the English joint-stock banks in much the same way as the East India Company delayed their entry into India. The Bank of Australasia at its foundation had attempted to establish branches in South Africa and was unable to obtain Government permission. Government pressure prevented the growth of a system of inter-colonial banking, partly because of a belief in the needs of distinct capitals and distinct responsibility for each colony, partly because the Government at the Cape derived much of its revenue from the monopoly of banking by the two state banks, the Lombard Bank which specialised in lending on mortgage and the Discount Bank which discounted negotiable securities.

Until the 1862 Act almost all the English banks in the colonies were founded under Royal Charter, which gave to the bank an undefined prestige, to the shareholders a liability limited to double the value of their shares. The Charters imposed certain general conditions.[2] As a general rule notes were to be redeemable in specie on demand and the note issue was not to exceed the paid-up capital; the banks were to hold a specie reserve of one-third the note issue. Most banks departed from these rules in one particular or another, and after the passing of the Act of 1862 the need for a Charter and therefore the obligation of accepting certain restrictions no longer existed. It was often argued, too, that restrictions which generalised the experience of English banking were not suited to the developing banking system of a pioneer economy. In many respects those criticisms are just; but it remains true that this general system of regulation gave the Anglo-Colonial banks a strength which served as a valuable toughening element in the growth of colonial banking

---

[1] *Bankers' Magazine*, 1893, p. 730.
[2] These conditions are analysed in detail in Baxter, A. S. J., *The Imperial Banks*, chap. II.

systems. Hardly one of the chartered colonial banks failed in this period. They needed large capitals—their business was in many cases very hazardous and behind the majority of them was the same group of interlocking interests.

Though their precise function varied from colony to colony and from bank to bank, their general significance is clear. They played an essential rôle in the expansion of imperial trade. To an increasing extent they concentrated in their hands the financing of that trade; they took over from the great mercantile houses the highly specialised business of exchange and by separating the functions of banker from those of merchant they tended to eliminate from imperial trade the element of fantastic speculation. They were the agencies through which the large sums from Indian planters and civil servants and Australian sheep farmers were remitted to England. At times of the year when trade bills were scarce, finance bills drawn by the branch in the colonies were used to remit money. In the Australian colonies, New Zealand and to some extent India the imperial banks took charge of the colonial loans. In Canada the financial business was done by two great London houses, Barings and Glyn Mills, and in South Africa mainly by the Crown Colonies Agency. The New Zealand loan of 1859 was negotiated through the Union Bank of Australia, which converted its reserve fund of £200,000 from the funds to this investment; the remaining £325,000 was taken up by the public and the Bank of England.[1] The six associated Australian banks negotiated the Victorian Railway Loan of 1862. The assistance of these large banks, closely connected with the important English financial houses, was of great value to the colonial governments when they came on to the London money market.

In 1875 England's foreign investment was a more important element in her economic system than in 1850. It is probable that for the first ten years of this period the export of capital was increasing faster than domestic investment. Of the companies, introduced on the Stock Exchange between January and August 1856, for example, schemes involving an outlay in foreign countries and colonies accounted for £19,110,000. Certain allowances have to be made, since several of the schemes were subscribed jointly on English and Continental exchanges, and a fair amount of bank capital was not called up in full; but probably about £11,000,000 of capital were exported. The total capital of home companies for the same period was £4,380,000, of which £1,000,000 was for the Imperial Hotel Scheme. After 1865, when more reliable computations can be made, the two streams of investment seem to keep pace, domestic investment being slightly more in 1868–71 and foreign investment very slightly more in 1872–5.[2]

[1] *Bankers' Magazine*, May 1859, p. 263.
[2] Douglas, Paul H., "An Estimate of the Growth of Capital in the United Kingdom, 1865–1909", *Journal of Economic and Business History*, 1930, p. 684.

Though it is not possible to calculate the geographical distribution of England's foreign lending, there is between 1850 and 1870 a clear general trend. In 1850 about a third of England's foreign investment was in America and the remainder in Northern Europe; in 1913 nearly 50 per cent was in the Empire, 20 per cent in the United States, nearly 20 per cent in Central and South America and less than 5 per cent in Europe.[1] It is in the decades after 1850 that the geography of English foreign investment begins to assume this shape. It was in these years that the stream of English investment first moved out on a large scale to the virgin areas of the world with epoch-making results for the whole English economy. Germany and France were beginning slowly to finance their own industry; and though the impecunious European fringe and especially Turkey borrowed largely, increasing emphasis was placed on non-European borrowers. Of these, the United States, which had borrowed so largely in the late 'thirties, still suffered in the early 'fifties from the repudiations of 1841 and 1842, and the large investments in the late 'fifties were stopped by the war. It was the Empire which in these years was the principal single area of English investment.

Before 1850 English capital had flowed out to the whole world, but very little of it to the Empire; after 1875 there was a contraction in our foreign lending in which the colonies shared. About 1870 Australia started to finance more of her own developments. Between 1870 and 1872 the cash deposits of Australian banks increased by £7,000,000, being profits derived entirely from the colonial export to this country. Owing to the freedom with which the Australian banks would lend money on this basis, there was no strong inducement for Englishmen to send capital to Australia for investment. Indeed, the tendency in 1869–72 was strongly in the other direction, i.e. to withdraw money because profitable mortgages could not be found. Government loans were contracted for in Australia at lower rates than they would probably have been in the London market; at the same time former Australian loans, the bonds of which were held in the United Kingdom, were being steadily paid off by periodical drawings. In areas of pioneer economy the rate of capital increase is high, and it is very probable that the proportion of income saved is greater than in older societies. Income, which in England would have been spent on comforts and luxuries, in the colonies flowed into capital investment. But while, at least in Australia, local capital was able, to some extent, to satisfy the normal commercial demands, the loans for large-scale capital construction had to be obtained from London. In the years before 1870, therefore, England supplied the colonies with all their long-term capital; years in which many of Britain's old Continental borrowers were able to satisfy their own needs. The bonds of colonial governments took their place alongside

[1] Paish, G., *Journal of the Royal Statistical Society*, LXXIV, 167.

British Government stock as virtually gilt-edged securities. The *Bankers' Magazine* in 1869 very clearly described the attractions of colonial stock.

"The frequency with which our colonial offspring borrow money from us, the parental capitalists, and the fullhandedness of the public to supply the wants, may fairly be numbered with what is memorable of the expiring year.... They are rosy, rounded, plump; we are stiff, inelastic; offering few advantages for the present and even fewer in the future. What for example are the three per cents unless bought in under great depression and sold out afterwards? What are railways unless one is behind the scenes. Of course there are Turkish and other securities offering great temptations; but to be involved with such is accompanied by different feelings from those experienced in, for example, South Australian holdings....

These last are Anglo-Saxon; growing with the growth of the colonies, firm as the granite rocks that underlie the earth, neither to be jeopardised by revolution, nor to be impaired by suspense or repudiation."[1]

The amount of English capital invested abroad at any date is largely a matter of conjecture. It has been estimated that £300,000,000 capital was invested outside Great Britain in 1854. Down to 1860 Great Britain exported capital at an average of about £30,000,000 per annum, making a total in 1860 of about £650,000,000. Less capital seems to have been exported during the years of cotton shortage, but between 1870 and 1875, during the great inflation before and after the Franco-Prussian war, very large amounts were exported, possibly some £55,000,000 per year. This would make the total of English capital invested abroad by 1875 some £1,300,000,000. It is possible to estimate fairly accurately the proportion of this invested in colonial government stock. The amount of the British colonial debts was about £118,000,000 and of Indian and Canadian railways and canals about £125,000,000. Almost all this debt was held in England. The amount of foreign government securities held in England is difficult to calculate because a large proportion of certain loans during this period was issued on Continental markets, but it may be reckoned at the highest as £500,000,000. Investment in the colonies, other than in Government bonds, was about £150,000,000, and similar investments in non-colonial areas perhaps about £200,000,000. The sums assessed to income tax for dividends arising from British, Indian, colonial and foreign stocks suggests a similar distribution: £21,160,000 was income from British securities, £7,032,000 from Indian, £2,840,000 from colonial and £9,341,000 from foreign.[2] It may be safely estimated, therefore, that of the great increase in the amount of English capital invested abroad between 1850 and 1875 at least two-fifths had gone to the Empire.

The greatest single movement of capital in this period was to India for the construction of public works and railways. Public works were not very important; before 1850 expenditure on them hardly exceeded £250,000; four years later it had risen to £4,000,000 and a

[1] *Bankers' Magazine*, January 1869, p. 75.
[2] *Journal of the Statistical Society*, XXXVII, 168.

special Public Works Department was set up. Though the Mutiny slowed up irrigation works, it caused great expenditure on military buildings. But down to 1869 the Government persisted in its policy of paying for public works out of current revenue. That policy had many disadvantages—it meant heavy taxation and the withdrawal of capital at a time when it was insufficient for the ordinary wants of production; but from the point of view of Anglo-Indian economic relations its most important disadvantage was that it closed for the English investor a large and profitable field. It was railway construction which took most of English investment. The Indian railway system was built in a comparatively short and well-defined period; the sudden increase of construction in the 'fifties was determined not by any new economic conditions but by the assimilation by the Government of considerations of economic advantage which had been a commonplace of English commercial pamphleteers since the 'thirties. Not until Dalhousie became Governor-General in 1848 did the Indian Government really appreciate the economic significance of an Indian railway system and the desirability of employing English private enterprise to build it; and it was not until 1859 that his scheme was adopted and the construction of five thousand miles of railway by eight companies formed for the purpose was sanctioned. Until then the lines had been few and dictated purely by strategic considerations. There was no appreciation of what the railways would cost or how the capital might be raised. The Government had built some railways with capital raised directly by Government loan—they had employed Indian contractors with few resources because the English contractors demanded terms which the Government thought exorbitant. At one time the Government of India seriously considered extending that system—raising the capital and building a network of railways itself. The decision in the late 'fifties to entrust the building of Indian railways to joint-stock companies formed in England with their interest guaranteed by the Government was a fact of the first importance for the economic history of both England and India. The capital could possibly have been raised more cheaply by direct Government borrowing, but such borrowing would have drawn much more on Indian investors; as regards labour and capital equipment the Government, by employing joint-stock companies, was able to obtain the services of the great English contracting firms experienced in English and Continental railway construction.

Almost all the share capital of these railways was held in England; among ordinary English middle-class investors the shares were highly popular and especially in the early years—in 1856, for example, when £1,000,000 capital was advertised for the Eastern Bengal Railway, applications amounted to £15,000,000. Though fluctuations in the value of different classes of shares arose from sudden pressure or local political and economic disaster, Indian railway stock was, compared with ordinary shares and with other railway securities, a medium through which a fair and secure return could be obtained for surplus capital. "A guarantee of 5 per cent., combined with the advantage of participation in subsequent profits, renders this description of shares preferable in some respects to Government annuities and therefore parties desirous of securing an undisturbed income purchase largely."[1]

A large number of the shares was held by the contracting firms, who took them in part payment of their services; in some of the guaranteed companies these firms had the controlling interest, e.g. Messrs Brassey, Paxton and Wrythes, who built the East Bengal Railway. To a large extent the same people interested themselves in Indian Government stock and in the guaranteed railways. A considerable amount of the interest on Indian Government loans was straightway invested in Indian railway stock. Glynn and Company, Prescotts, Smith Payne and several other large banks had large accumulations of Indian bond interest belonging to their constituents which found their way into Indian railways.

The Indians themselves invested hardly at all in railway loans. Indian trusts, retired people, banks and unenterprising zemindars invested considerably in the loans of the Indian Government and in the 'sixties the wealthy native bankers and landowners were keen enough in availing themselves of Government security—the issue of an ordinary loan by the Government at 4 per cent or 5 per cent was eagerly competed for and all would be taken up in a few days. But though the Government did persuade some Indian princes to invest in Indian railways, there was no Indian enthusiasm for Indian railway stock, though the security was precisely the same and railway capital had the possibility of additional interest at 5 per cent. Out of the £76,000,000 railway capital raised up to the beginning of 1868 only £750,000 had been subscribed in India, and of this small sum a large proportion came from Europeans living in India. At the beginning of 1868 there were 49,690 holders of Indian railway stock, and of these 40,221 were in England, 422 Englishmen in India, and 397 Indians.[2] The contrast with the Indian Government loans is marked. In 1870, £72,989,638 of the Government of India debt was held in India— though not all by Indians—and only £35,196,700 in England.[3] These loans were raised generally at $3\frac{1}{2}$ per cent; the railway loans, which had in fact the same security, were raised at 5 per cent and attracted very few Indian investors.

Compared with English railways those of India had hardly any parliamentary costs and paid nothing for their land. The Indian Government, by the terms of the guarantee deed, bought it with its

[1] Bankers' Magazine, 1855, p. 185.
[2] Danvers, J., Indian Railways, p. 26. Danvers was Government Director of the Indian Railway Companies. Report from the Select Committee of the East Indian Railways, Parl. Pap. 1884, vol. II, 284.
[3] Financial Statement of the Government of India, 1871.

own funds. These facts and cheap labour led the early projectors to hope for great profits; but, in fact, the great cost of freight from England and the inland transport of iron work, the expense of procuring sleepers, and the very high rate of wages and salaries of European superintendents and overheads more than counterbalanced the advantages. Few railways made enough to repay the guaranteed interest of 5 per cent.[1]

Freight, of course, was an important element in Indian railway costs; but though in the early days railway constructors feared that their increased competition for freight would seriously raise the cost of railway construction, freight rates down to 1860 seem to have varied little year by year. The balance of trade was always so much against the United Kingdom that, until railways and companies started exporting dead weight to India, shippers were in the habit of sending ships to India in ballast, relying on home freights to pay for both voyages. Indian exports to the United Kingdom were growing throughout the period and bulky goods formed an increased proportion. Down to 1860–61, therefore, the average freight paid for dead weight and measurement goods varied very little—it was about 25s. per ton; after that the average rose to 31s., and during 1865 and 1866 as much as 40s. and 45s. was paid. The high cost of internal transport also helped to increase the cost of railway construction.

The transfer to India of the capital for railway construction influenced the mechanism as well as the content of Anglo-Indian trade, by its effect on the means of remitting the Home Charges. Any large payment which had to be made in India neutralised the effectiveness of the East India Company's bills, and later those of the Secretary of State, as methods of adjustment in Anglo-Indian trade. The Indian railway companies paid their subscriptions into the treasury at London and drew on it when they had to pay for railway stock in England and pay the expenses of their home office establishments; when they needed to make payments in India they drew on the East India Company's treasuries there, and later on the Indian Government. In these circumstances the amount of bills issued in London was small, and merchants had to send bullion. In the years immediately following the Mutiny, for example, when the Government's expenses in India considerably exceeded the Home Charges, rates were still advertised at which bills were issued, but were fixed so high as virtually to exclude remitters; the insignificant amounts actually drawn were obtained merely by parties not sufficiently conversant with exchange operations to prevent their incurring unnecessary loss.

In the years after the India Act (1858) both capital exports to India and the Home Charges increased very rapidly. The actual proportions between them varied from year to year. The Home Charges tended to make the balance of trade adverse to India, but in

[1] See below, p. 799.

years when there was a large export of railway capital, or when the Indian Government became a creditor of England on the exchange account for the amount raised in England to cover a famine deficit, then the exchange turned against England. The form of the alteration was a diminution of the fortnightly sales of Council drafts on India; instead of finding the usual bills to remit to Calcutta, merchants found a smaller supply than usual and the demand for gold for export to buy silver in the double-currency countries was increased.

When Edward West wrote on India in 1857 he was overwhelmed both by the vast field for profitable investment which it offered and Englishmen's ignorance of it. "There are", he wrote, "profitable investments for joint-stock companies and for emigrants who possess capital, employment for enterprising and intelligent young men, ample supplies of raw cotton, sugar, rice, tobacco and indigo...increased demand for manufactured goods...upon 100 million acres of land in British India which are now waste and unproductive."[1] There were many attempts in the twenty years after West wrote to exploit the raw materials of India. Before 1850 a large amount of British capital had been invested in the cultivation of indigo, but the difficulties of labour supply made that an unprofitable crop. But after 1850 English capital through private traders and through joint-stock enterprises was put into the cultivation of cotton, though not on a large scale, and into coffee and tea. The history of the Indian tea industry illustrates clearly the rôle of English capital and enterprise in developing the material resources of India.

In the cultivation of tea in India there were three stages.[2] For nearly twenty years after the tea plant was found growing in Assam, it was developed, at very great expense, by the Government and the East India Company's botanists. In the second stage officials of the East India Company and the military put out their money in creating new tea plantations; they played an essential part in the production of many new exotics. Production of tea requires a steady outlay of capital for four years without any return. The Government's work was mainly experimental; English capitalists declined to invest money in speculations so far removed from the great centres of European commerce. Production was taken up by a few civil and military officers who had retired to the hills and eventually, after successive relaxations of the regulations, by civil and military officers actually in employment. This Government action was of capital importance in the development of the tea, cinchona and silk of the lower Himalayan ranges, for except the savings of the services there is no capital available for investment in the North-West Provinces of India. Private

---

[1] West, E., *Emigration to British India* (1857), p. 106.
[2] On the tea industry in India see Baildon, S., *Tea in Assam* (1880); Lees, N., *Tea Cultivation, cotton and other agricultural experiments in India* (1863).

persons as well as civil servants formed plantations. Some of them remained as tea producers, but many seemed to have made their profit by selling out to new English tea companies.

How far was Indian tea production financed by English capital and how far was such capital the savings of the ordinary English investors? To both questions it is only possible to sketch an answer. Some Indian capital went into tea, but most of the plantations were English-owned, some by private planters and some by English joint-stock companies. Many of the men who bought plantations in the early days remained, and there were always Englishmen coming out as private planters working 100 to 200 acres. But as most private planters were retired servants of the East India Company their activity does not represent an investment of English capital. The conditions of marketing made production difficult for them, and most of the tea was produced on plantations owned by joint-stock companies. Most of the private planters worked their estates with advances from the banks or agencies on the security of their title deeds; the Calcutta tea agencies often borrowed money on their own security and lent it, plus money charges, to the tea estate. The rate of interest was high and many planters who made their estates in the beginning from borrowed money consumed the value of their plantations in interest; by the time the bushes bore the leaves, three years' interest would represent nearly 50 per cent additional cost of making the estate. How far the joint-stock companies in tea production tapped the general pool of English capital it is impossible to say without detailed examination of their records. In some cases the initiative in joint-stock formation came from groups of planters in India as a more convenient method of raising capital than bank advances, and in such companies planters and other Anglo-Indians took large numbers of shares. In other cases the source of capital was London capitalists, who formed companies to exploit the resources of India; the tea-importing firms held many of the shares of certain tea companies. Perhaps the companies formed after 1867, when tea was earning very high profits, drew more largely on the sources of capital which were providing capital for industrial development at home. Of the total capital employed in Indian tea production, it would seem that only a small proportion came from ordinary English savings. Many of the companies were working on too small a capital and were therefore very heavily in debt to the agents or the banks. It was a common suggestion that shareholders should raise, by debentures among themselves, money to redeem all present indebtedness, provide a working capital and save the crushing charges they had to pay.

Almost all the capital for the Indian railways had been raised in England, and largely from the great mass of undifferentiated English capital. Canada, too, in the same period laid down the main lines of her railway system, but her experience was very different. The

Grand Trunk Railway, built between 1853 and 1859, drew very little of its capital from England. The original capital was small and little was offered for public subscription. Most of the money was raised, or so it was planned, by debentures, and of these a large portion went to buy out the existing companies, a smaller part to prominent Canadians and the largest part to the contractors as part payment. In these hands most of the debentures remained, in the beginning because investors thought they would be extraordinarily remunerative, later because the general feeling that they would not be highly remunerative made it disadvantageous to sell, and because possession of them carried political power. What capital did come from England came mainly therefore from the capital resources of the contractors —Peto, Brassey, Betts and Jackson—and as events turned out it was a very small proportion. A large part of the capital for the actual construction of the railway, and all the money for the constant repairs and renewals, were provided for by the provincial governments out of revenue and loans. "The investment of British capital was reckoned in the books of the Grand Trunk in the early sixties at $12 million. The net debt of the Canadian provinces, including $20 million borrowed for canal purposes in the 'forties and guaranteed upon such smaller railways as the Great Western, amounted to $70 millions."[1]

Apart from the Grand Trunk, L. H. Jenks estimates that "lesser railway projects, mines, land and mortgage companies, banks and municipal loans" in Canada absorbed about £5,000,000 of British absentee capital in the 'fifties and 'sixties. The Federation, when the provincial debts of about £16,000,000 were taken over by the Dominion Government, enabled the Canadian Government to borrow more freely on London, but it was not until the Canadian Pacific Railway that the ordinary English investor began to invest on a large scale in Canadian railways.

The importance of British investment in Canada lay more in the political issues it involved than in its economic results. During this period there were three great concerns in London which had interests in Canada; the Hudson's Bay Company, which, until the sale of its territorial rights to the Canadian Government in 1869, had a monopoly of the Red River and Saskatchewan country; the shareholders of the Grand Trunk Railway; and the two great banking firms, Baring Brothers and Glyn Mills, who from 1837 to 1901 divided the Canadian account between them, and were also bankers and directors of the Grand Trunk.[2] All three interests had a hand in the formation of policy. Throughout this period the colonial governments of British North America were in financial difficulties, and the support on the London market of two such powerful firms was at once a source of financial strength and a danger of political control. The connection

[1] Jenks, L. H., *The Migration of British Capital to 1875*, p. 204.
[2] See *C.H.B.E.*, vol. VI, chap. XIX.

of all three groups with the Colonial Office was extremely close; many of the Hudson's Bay directors, for example, were important members of the Whig Party, and it was commonly believed by Canadian radicals that the Hudson's Bay shareholders were determined to prevent the opening up of the North-West Territory.[1]

The misfortune that attended the Grand Trunk Railway delayed for two decades investment in large capital construction in Canada. The Canadians were quickly able to supply their own needs for floating capital out of the profits of their own undertakings. In 1861 men were found to complain that "in Canada itself there is not a sufficient field for the employment of provincial capital, and therefore Canadian capitalists year after year establish themselves in Wisconsin and Illinois and engage in the American produce trade."[2] But there was great need of large amounts of capital for two works which could not reasonably be expected to make returns for another generation. One was the construction of a railroad from the Atlantic to the Pacific. The other was the improvement of the navigation of the St Lawrence and the Lakes, the provision for the produce of the frontier regions of British North America of an export route cheaper than the Erie Canal which diverted the trade down to New York. The experience of the first made it impossible in the 'sixties to raise capital for the second, and the main lines of Canadian economic development ran increasingly north and south. Already before 1870 the United States had begun to invest in a small way in Canadian industry.

Unlike India and British North America, the Australian colonies in the two decades after 1850 did not build many miles of railway, and English investment was consequently more widely dispersed. The largest single investment was in gold production or in undertakings very directly concerned with gold. For the extraction of the first alluvial gold in Victoria comparatively little capital was required— a pick-axe, a shovel and a shallow tin dish; nevertheless, in 1854 there were six large Australian gold companies quoted on the London Stock Exchange with a total capital of £720,000, almost all of which was called up. Within a few years the alluvial fields ceased to yield a remunerative amount of gold, and the reef mines which took their place required large amounts of capital; after 1855 Australian mining became an organised business run by joint-stock companies with large capitals, using expensive machinery. In 1870 it was estimated that the value of machinery in gold mining in Victoria was £2,128,896.

In the same years a large number of immigration companies were formed, and a large, but incalculable, amount brought in by the immigrants. In the 'sixties there was a group of loan and mortgage companies formed to speculate in land. In 1864 the North Australian

[1] Watkins, E. W., *Canada and the States. Recollections.* 1851–1886; "Canada's Relations with the Empire as seen by the *Toronto Globe*", *Canadian Historical Review*, x, 106.
[2] *Bankers' Magazine*, 1861, p. 345.

Company was formed with a capital of £100,000 to secure allotments of land in the northern territory annexed to the province of South Australia; and a year later a Loan and Agency Company was formed for New Zealand, in direct connection with the Bank of New Zealand; it advanced money on the mortgage of freeholds and the stocks of squatters, and made loans on the growing clip of wool and sent it to London for sale by its agency.

English capitalists were shy of Australia after the crisis of 1857.[1] The absence of any considerable projects of capital construction and the large profits from gold and wool gave Australia, in the 'sixties, large supplies of capital for all normal purposes. The boom in tin and gold late in 1872 was financed by small companies with shares of small denomination and formed in Australia itself. The Government of New South Wales, which until 1872 had raised all its loans on London at 5 per cent, was in that year able to place 4 per cent loans in the colony.

The investment of British capital in the various colonies had certain common characteristics which gave it a character of its own and determined its rôle in the evolution of English mid-nineteenth-century capitalism. A very high proportion of this investment was in the loans of colonial governments.

Colonial Government Debt in December 1870[2]

Debt of British India: Direct Liabilities	£108,186,338
Railways etc. guarantees	95,000,000
Ceylon	700,000
Dominion of Canada	21,016,904
New South Wales	9,681,130
South Australia	1,944,600
Queensland	3,509,250
Victoria	11,841,891
New Zealand	7,841,891
Cape of Good Hope	1,569,907
Natal	268,000

In the middle of the nineteenth century the number of good industrial investments, apart from railway shares, was very small. The security of the bonds of foreign governments varied considerably, but most of them were highly speculative. Until the middle of the century, therefore, the only security for people who desired a fixed income was Consols. Some wider extension of the field of gilt-edged securities was a necessary condition of the evolution of a class of rentiers. The colonial bonds which, from the 'fifties onwards, were issued on London in increasing numbers were to all intents and purposes gilt-edged securities; they returned a steady 5 or 6 per cent and they were always issued near par. People who wished to obtain a steady

---

[1] Wood, C., *The Business Cycle in Australia*, p. 41.
[2] Compiled from *Fenn on the Funds* (1874 edition).

income found a large number of new shares in which they could invest, and the number of people able to draw a large portion of their income from such sources increased. Joint-stock organisation was not widely adopted until the 'eighties, and it was upon Government stock, home, colonial and foreign, that the English rentier class developed. Another consequence flowed from this characteristic of investment in the colonies. The fact that an increased proportion of English capital was invested in gilt-edged securities held for income decreased its mobility. Throughout this period the bank rate was ineffective as a control of the long-term rate of investment. This, of course, was partly due to the fact that the bank did not have a monopoly of note issue; but in part also it was due to the fact that a large amount of capital was invested in Government stock by people who held for income and therefore did not sell when the price of their stock varied. It is arguable therefore that at certain periods in the mid-nineteenth century the increasing proportion of investment in Government stock starved English industry of capital.

English investment in the colonies was peculiar in the second place because it depended so largely on the activity of the Government. In industries where the technique and social structure allowed the employment of large amounts of cheap labour—industries like Australian mining which produced rapid returns—capital was easily and spontaneously invested; but such industries account for only a small proportion of the United Kingdom's investment in her colonies between 1850 and 1870, most of which was investment of large amounts of capital in public improvements which could produce good returns only after one or two generations. Long-term loans at low rates of interest—essential to create the conditions to attract private initiative and capital—could be provided only by some sort of Government guarantee; the most important economic movements of the great age of *laissez-faire* were evoked by Government action. Certain investment the Governments in the colonies had to undertake in order to maintain their political authority, and the most important of the loans and grants to the colonies in the 'forties were for this purpose; other investment was forced on the Government by pressure from specific economic interests, like the pressure of the Cotton Supply Association on the Indian Government to build railways. Capital flowed into colonial railway companies under the stimulus of a state guarantee of interest; without that guarantee capital would not have moved in those directions, the rate of interest in England would have been much lower and perhaps the history of the English rentier class rather different. The English Government in the mid-nineteenth century, which refused to assume economic functions, in guaranteeing the interest on colonial railway loans affected economic life in much the same way as they would have, had they planned and financed a large programme of public works in England. The political connection

manufacturers went to produce, at lower prices, raw material for her industries and food for her people.

It is from this last characteristic that the main importance of colonial investment for English economic life arises. The export of capital is not necessarily beneficial for the exporting country; it was not, for example, beneficial for France between 1890 and 1913. Its effects depend on a large number of variable factors: the organisation of the monetary system in the borrowing and lending countries, the character of the trading relations between the two and the mechanism by which the loan is translated into a transfer of actual goods. The character of the trading relations has already been analysed; England exported mainly textiles and products of heavy industry in return for food and raw materials. Capital exports can bring about movements of goods in a number of ways: through the direct expenditure of the loan by the actual borrowers on goods produced by the lending country; through a general increase in the purchasing power of the borrowing country which to some extent increases the demand for the exports of the lending country; through lower prices in the lending country due to a downward movement of exchange caused by the outward flow of gold—a decline in prices which enables the borrowing country to purchase more goods from the lender; and lastly through a change in the price levels due to a re-arrangement of demand in the two countries. A thorough examination of the problem of transfer must await a detailed analysis of banking policy and the movements of gold and short-term loans which has not yet been scientifically undertaken. But one feature of English investment in the colonies is clear: that the first of these methods, which is by no means a usual or frequent means of effecting the necessary readjustment, was the main method by which loans to the colonies were transformed into a transfer of goods. What really makes the restoration of equilibrium difficult is the fact that a considerable part of a loan may be spent by a borrowing country on its own domestic goods. There is consequently a decreased demand for the products of the industries of the capital-exporting countries, and particularly of that group of industries which works for the home market. The fact that so much English foreign investment was in the colonies and that these colonies spent a high proportion directly on the products of English industry made the process of adjustment easier and profitable. When Great Britain lent money to the colonies, there was no falling off of demand for the products of home industry. The difference between the character of demand in the capital-exporting and in the borrowing country did not exist; for England built the railway systems of the Empire at the same time as she developed her own.

The increased demand for English goods directly due to colonial investment was a demand primarily for the product of the iron and metal industries; it occurred comparatively abruptly and at a time when the plant of such industries was already working to capacity. In 1866, for example, the East Indian Railway had very considerable difficulty in obtaining rolling stock in the quantities required; *The Economist* mentioned an indenture of this railway which included a thousand new engines as a mere item.[1] This intensified demand was a primary factor in the consolidation of the mid-Victorian economic system. It is reflected clearly in the output figures for various commodities. The percentage increase in the decade 1850–60 was 65 per cent for cotton yarn, 104 per cent for cotton piece goods, 75 per cent for iron and steel and 280 per cent for machinery, including rolling stock.

The manufactures, for which as a result of the capital exports there was a greater demand, became somewhat dearer relative to other types of goods. The price of iron bars, for example, rose from 67 in 1851 to 112 in 1853 and remained in the 100's until 1857; it was high again in 1864 and very high after 1872. In the 'fifties there was no idle plant in the English engineering and metal industries and one might have expected the prices in such industries to diverge more markedly from the general level than in fact they did. It is probable that at this period the machinery of engineering was sufficiently unspecialised to be turned, without great difficulty, to the manufacture of rails and engines. There were many firms like Sharp Stewart and Company of Manchester, established in 1805, and until the late 'thirties making machines for planing, slotting and punching, which in the 'forties started to build locomotives and in the 'fifties employed all their plant in this branch. For many of the older manufacturers of locomotives the colonial demand came at a highly opportune time, for it was a demand upon private establishments at a time when the practice was increasing among English railway companies of building their own locomotives. Many companies, which in the early days of the English railway age built for the domestic demand, continued to prosper in the 'fifties and 'sixties upon the Indian demand. Robert Stephenson and Company, who sent the first locomotive to Australia in 1854, came to rely almost entirely on the colonial demand.[2]

This increased demand drew into the metal industries, and to a somewhat less extent into the textile industry, a proportionately larger amount of the national labour supply[3] and of capital. While the capital value of farm land increased by only 80 per cent and home railways by 58 per cent, the capital in mines increased by 95 per cent and in iron works by 314 per cent.[4] English capital was becoming concentrated in the exporting industries in forms which, especially

---

[1] *The Economist*, April 1866, p. 501.
[2] Ahrons, E. L., *The British Steam Railway Locomotive*.
[3] Booth, C., "Occupations of the People of the United Kingdom, 1801–1881", *Journal of the Statistical Society*, 1886, p. 416.
[4] *Ibid.* 1878, p. 16, R. Giffen, "Recent Accumulations of Capital". The figures are obtained from income tax returns capitalised at twenty years' purchase.

after the great inventions of the period, were increasingly stereotyped and immobile.

The increased demand for rails and engines had been met partly by turning unspecialised plant to produce them, and, more important, by applying new labour and capital, but in part also by inventions which economised labour and capital. In the twenty years after 1828 when Neilson introduced the hot blast there was hardly any technical progress in the primary processes of iron and steel making. In 1856 Henry Bessemer introduced in a paper before the British Association the first of the great inventions which were to transform the English iron and steel industry. It is difficult to avoid the correlation between this outburst of labour-saving inventions with the demand for iron for colonial railways. Though in the 'fifties some improvements were made in textile industry, they cannot in number or importance compare with those in iron and steel, and this significant difference may well be due to a difference in the intensity and speed of demand. The development of expensive and highly specialised plant, necessitating greater command of capital and larger aggregations of labour, was increasing the size of the unit of production considerably in the textiles and very considerably in the metal industries.

As to the general supply of capital as distinct from its form and disposition among English industries, the investment of capital in the colonies increased it considerably. The development of manufacturing industries which it stimulated raised urban rents and consequently the savings from them. It kept up the domestic rate of interest and therefore increased that considerable portion of English saving which comes from rentier incomes. More important still were the incomes which arose directly from the colonies, whether by investors or civil servants or traders in them. Even before much capital was exported to the Empire, economists who believed that English capital was increasing faster than the openings for profitable investment pointed to "the large fortunes in constant course of remittance from the colonies" as one of the most important causes.[1]

It is a convenient and natural assumption that capital moved out to the colonies in response to a relative scarcity of capital and a higher rate of interest. But it is doubtful whether in fact English investors in these twenty years obtained a substantially higher return on foreign than on domestic investment.[2] The greater part of England's imperial investments were in the form of fixed interest-bearing securities the price of which did not vary greatly; on these issues the investor obtained only a fraction more than he would have done in similar domestic investments. The position as to the return on investments

[1] Fullarton, J., On the Regulation of Currencies (1844), p. 169.
[2] On the profitability of the United Kingdom's foreign investments see Cairncross, A. K., "Did Foreign Investments Pay?" The Review of Economic Studies, III, 67; Nash, R. L., Short View of the Profitable Nature of our Investments (1881).

in private or joint-stock companies in the colonies is less clear. Some of the colonial companies paid dividends much higher than any in England; for example, the Australian Gold Companies, which in the 'fifties made enormous profits by remitting gold to England, and some of the more successful Land and Investment Companies. But mortality among such companies was also extremely high. Banks, too, fluctuated violently between considerable prosperity and bankruptcy. In 1866–7, in the recession after the great cotton boom, nineteen banks failed in India with total losses of £13 million. The conditions in India were exceptional, but even in other parts of the Empire increased competition wore down the profits of the banks. In 1863 the banks having establishments in Victoria showed a capital and reserved profits of £8 million; in 1872 these items had increased by 27 per cent; but the profits show no such increase. Notwithstanding that the total capital employed and business done were greater, the actual bank earnings were less. The total shareholders' money (i.e. paid-up capital and reserved profits) in the Australasian banks amounted in 1872 to £12,121,000, and the dividends paid to £1,471,466. The average return is about 12 per cent, but in fact the business was done by a very small group of banks—only four banks paid over 4 per cent.

It is equally difficult to decide how profitable such an important colonial investment as tea was to English investors. On the profits of the private planter there is, of course, no information. The share list of the tea companies printed in *The Economist* from 1867 onwards gives a very high rate of profit. Against this high rate has to be reckoned the very heavy mortality among the earlier tea companies; most of the companies bought their plantations at ridiculously high prices and their administrative expenses were very high. Apart from these adventitious causes of failure were certain permanent factors: tea gardens required a considerable amount of capital to start with and several years of waiting before a profitable return; moreover there was a persistent shortage of labour. Consequently the early tea companies were, almost without exception, failures. The Assam Company, for example, the earliest and most important of them, which in 1839 took over two-thirds of the Government's plantations, threw away about £200,000 of its paid-up capital.[1]

The years between 1850 and 1875 have a unity of their own, distinct, on the one hand, from the slow unspectacular progress of the decades before, and, on the other, from the great depression which set in about 1875. It is a period unique in history for rapidity and magnitude of economic expansion. The export values, which increased 40 per cent between 1840 and 1850, increased by 90 per cent in the next decade and by 47 per cent between 1860 and 1870; between 1870 and 1880 the increase was only 12 per cent. Wages, almost stationary between 1830 and 1850, rose steadily from 1850 to

[1] Lees, N. *Tea Cultivation in Assam*, p. 60.

1886, but the rise was most marked between 1850 and 1874, when wages rose 56 per cent. Whatever method of computation is used, the national income and the amount of capital were growing prodigiously during these years. The statistician Giffen found a sudden rise after 1850 both in income-tax returns and in the amount of property subject to legacy duty; and he calculated that between 1865 and 1875 the amount of capital increased by nearly 50 per cent, while between 1875 and 1885 it increased at only half this rate. The explanation of this efflorescence has been found in a great variety of circumstances: factory legislation, trade unions, the new railways, and the new gold from California and Australia. But none of these by themselves explains satisfactorily what is the most remarkable feature of the expansion—the substantial rise in real wages. The opening of the British grain market may have prevented a fall, but is unlikely to have caused a considerable rise, since England did not draw largely on foreign supplies until a decade later. The influx of new gold explains rising prices and increasing investment, but is not inevitably associated with rising real wages. An important part of the explanation is to be found in the character and extent of English overseas investment between 1850 and 1875, in the fact that it was assuming an increasing importance in English economic life, and further that so large a proportion of it was to new and undeveloped countries within the Empire. Part of their loans the colonies spent on English goods—textiles and the products of heavy industry; and since, at least in the case of the latter, the supply was inelastic under the conditions of mid-nineteenth-century industry, their relative price tended to increase. Part of their loans they spent on railway construction and on the exploitation of their natural resources; with decreasing transport costs and the operation of increasing returns, the price of their products became relatively cheaper. The movement was not steady and consistent, but between 1850 and 1875 there was a general tendency for the net barter terms of trade between the United Kingdom and the colonies to change in favour of the former, i.e. for one unit of British manufactures, and therefore one unit of British labour, to buy more units of raw materials and food from abroad. The process was helped by the greater speed of technical improvement in British industry which increased the productivity of British labour.

By 1870 Britain had become an industrial state, her rising prosperity based on the export of textiles and iron manufactures, and her food and raw materials drawn largely from foreign and colonial sources. The development of the preceding thirty years would have been less rapid and the problems of internal readjustment more difficult had not this rising industrial nation had an Empire in the undeveloped regions of the world. The first British Empire had broken on the difficulty of establishing a system of economic relations satisfactory to both the mother country and the colonies. If economic facts which drove them apart in the eighteenth century drew Great Britain and her colonies together in the nineteenth, it was due not to any change in the imperial attitude of Englishmen, but to the changed economic conditions which enabled an economic partnership to be established which was profitable to both.

CHAPTER XXII

IMPERIAL DEFENCE, 1815–1870

IN the ceaseless colonial warfare of the eighteenth century Great Britain acquired the strategic and economic framework on which her future empire was to be based. Eighteenth-century strategy was a compromise between the advocates of operations conducted exclusively in the maritime and colonial spheres and those, who, while recognising the importance of colonial expansion, also saw the need for "containing operations" in Europe and for the denial of the Rhine delta to France. After 1815 the need for military[1] operations diminished, while the responsibilities of consolidation and peaceful expansion increased. Thus new strategic problems were created, involving not only imperial defence, considered as a whole, but many lesser problems of local defence, closely related to the new developments in trade, communications and armaments. Both the general and the local problems, however, were complicated by the existence of widely differing types of colonies and by the fact that while the population of some remained stationary, that of others was increasing rapidly. All problems, moreover, which could be classed as strategic were for many years completely overshadowed by constitutional problems involving the ultimate political destiny of those colonies which became self-governing, with the result that the strategic principles governing imperial defence received little recognition until after the Crimean War. Whereas the constitutional position was subject to constant change, the machinery of imperial defence was never seriously tested, and thus problems of imperial defence were treated almost entirely from constitutional, administrative and financial standpoints. In addition, they were treated locally, as if the defence of each separate part of the Empire was a problem entirely self-contained. The phrase "imperial defence" had, of course, no currency in the early mid-nineteenth century. It was preceded by the transitional phrase "colonial defence", which was inadequate and misleading since it implied a series of purely local problems disconnected from each other and from those of the mother country.

In Parliament, during the immediate post-war period, the Tories were more alive to the strategic realities than the Whigs, but their policy was conceived very largely in a static and eighteenth-century spirit. The Whigs cared little for strategic principles, but realised that new imperial conditions demanded the readjustment of privileges and obligations. They, therefore, advocated both shifting the financial

---

[1] The word military is used in its general strategic sense, implying both naval and land operations and administration, except in cases where it obviously bears the more limited meaning.

burden of colonial defence on to the self-governing colonies and the complete overhauling of naval and military administration. The Radicals and separatists went farther and urged the drastic reduction of British military forces and even their total abolition. All parties tended to be somewhat reckless in the use of pseudo-strategic arguments in support of non-strategic plans for economy, reform and the bestowal on the colonies of responsible government, so that ministers were not infrequently engaged in pursuing the right strategic policy for the wrong reason. In attempting the reform of naval and military administration, the Whigs were actuated by the same ideas which led them in turn to seek the reform of Parliament, the Church, education and municipal government. Nor were these "rotten boroughs" of the services exclusively administrative in character, the "dockyard vote" being of direct political importance. But, just as the reformers in their zeal for the constitutional side tended to neglect the principles of strategy when dealing with imperial defence, so they tended to neglect the principles of command and administration when dealing with the service administrative departments. As a result, their reforms were in danger of losing in efficiency what they gained in simplicity and honesty.

The strategic situation immediately after 1815 was that the British peoples had acquired a number of naval bases from which British trade had suffered injury during the recent wars.[1] In Europe, Heligoland was retained from Denmark to deny its use to a future enemy. Malta and the Ionian Islands, used in company with Gibraltar, strengthened British control of the overland route to the East and more than compensated for the final cession of Minorca to Spain after it had been in British hands from 1708 to 1756, 1763 to 1782 and 1798 to 1802. On the sea route to the East the British position was greatly strengthened by the re-acquisition of Gambia and the acquisition of Ascension Island in the South Atlantic, and the Cape of Good Hope at the turning-point to the Indian Ocean. Beyond the Cape the British acquired Mauritius, with Port Louis and Grand Port, Rodriguez, and also the Seychelles and the Chagos Archipelago, with good anchorages at Mahé and Diégo Garcia respectively. In the immediate neighbourhood of India Britain retained Ceylon, with the important harbour of Trincomalee, previously ceded by the Treaty of Amiens, together with the Maldives to the south-west, and also acquired the Laccadives off the coast of Malabar and the Andamans in the Bay of Bengal. In the East Indies British gains included Province Wellesley, Malacca and trading stations in Sumatra.

In the West Indies, the British strategic position was strengthened by the final cession of St Lucia, the great strategic prize of the eighteenth century, and by the re-occupation of Tobago and Trinidad, the first two of which possessed good anchorages. On the mainland Britain also acquired a section of Honduras and the three colonies of Demerara,

[1] See chapter III.

by the withdrawal of imperial troops. No attempt had yet been made to persuade the colonists to undertake their own defence except in the form of increased money contributions.

Meanwhile the Whigs had been turning their attention to the reform of the naval and military administrative systems. Responsibility for the execution of naval policy initiated by the Cabinet, lay with the Board of Admiralty.

The whole of the administrative business of the navy, including construction, repairs, pay, food, clothing and dockyards, both at home and in the colonies, was managed by the Board of Navy Commissioners and various subsidiary Commissioners, acting under the authority of the Board of Admiralty. This system dated from the time of Henry VIII and represented the well-recognised principle of separating operations of war from administrative routine. In 1832, however, on the initiative of the then First Lord, Sir James Graham, the Navy Commissioners and the subsidiary commissioners were abolished in the supposed interests of efficiency and economy, and their work divided between the various members of the Board of Admiralty. Much jobbery and sinecurism were thus swept away, but taken as a whole the change was injudicious and retrograde. On paper the Board of Admiralty had absorbed the Navy Board, whereas in practice the Navy Board's routine had absorbed the Board of Admiralty and left it no time to attend to its real work, the planning and execution of naval operations. As, however, no major operations were undertaken until the Crimean War, the work of the Board was not immediately tested and for the time being the so-called reforms were held to have achieved their purpose.[1]

Responsibility for initiating military policy for the Empire as a whole lay, of course, with the Cabinet, but the execution of military policy by the army, both on the command and administrative sides, was curiously divided. Operations abroad were under the control of the Secretary of State for War and Colonies, at the Colonial Office, acting in conjunction with the Secretary at War, at the War Office, who was the chief link between Parliament and the army on the financial side. The Commander-in-Chief, at the Horse Guards, representing the personal authority of the sovereign, possessed wide powers over discipline, command and patronage, both in peace and war. The Master-General of the Ordnance provided all arms and stores for cavalry and infantry of the line and, in addition, was responsible for the discipline, pay and allowances of the artillery and engineers. Other special powers also existed such as those exercised by the Inspectors-General of Fortifications and Cavalry. The Commissariat department was situated at the Treasury and the militia was con-

---

[1] "As an independent and superior Board, concerned primarily with the function of command, undisturbed by details of management, the Admiralty Board, as constituted through our long series of wars at sea, disappeared." Richmond, Sir H. W., *National Policy and Naval Strength*, p. 241.

trolled by the Home Secretary. In 1837, as a result of two recent royal commissions, it was proposed to make the Secretary at War a Cabinet minister and responsible to Parliament for the general business of the army. "The Secretaries of State, however, would still continue, as at present, to signify the King's commands as to the employment of the armed forces for any specific object [operations?]; but these orders, except in the most pressing emergencies, would be conveyed through the Secretary at War to the Commander-in-Chief." "The Secretary at War thus to become responsible, not merely for the management at the financial details of the Army, but for its being kept on a proper footing with reference to the duties to be performed."[1]

Apparently the reformers made the mistake of assuming that the main division in army organisation lies between the civil and military branches, instead of between command and administration, which latter includes a good deal of what the uninitiated would class as military business. The reformers were undoubtedly right in attempting to reduce the existing chaos, but their proposals would most probably have proved unworkable and were very properly and very successfully opposed by the Duke of Wellington, on the grounds that they would have placed the command, discipline and patronage too much in the hands of Parliament.

Both in the case of navy and army administration the reformers appear to have acted without any clear appreciation of the position occupied by administration in the fighting services. Faced by sinecurism, overlapping, and service "rotten boroughs", they were too prone to apply in adulterated form solutions which were proving successful elsewhere. They failed to realise that the test of naval and military reforms is war, and as no immediate tests were forthcoming, they had no standards to judge but their own. In the case of the Navy Board, moreover, they failed to take into account the fact that, although riddled with graft and inefficiency, the system itself was sound in principle even though the army's system both of administration and command could not be justified by any principle at all. On the other hand, it must be admitted that the reformers received very little intelligent or constructive advice from service experts, who in most cases were either too ignorant to appreciate the issues at stake or too weak to withstand the general demand for reform.

The next important change in imperial defence policy took place with the accession of the Russell Whig ministry in 1846, and the appointment of Lord Grey to the Colonial Office. Grey had already held the posts of Secretary at War and Under-Secretary for the Colonies, and was anxious to reduce the garrisons in Australia where the population was increasing rapidly, undisturbed by internal or external menaces. He at once announced his intention of withdrawing the imperial troops from New South Wales and recommending the

[1] *Parl. Pap.* 1837, xxxiv (1) [78], pp. 9–10.

formation of local police for the maintenance of internal order.[1] His next step was to hand over to the care and maintenance of the colonists the fortifications at Sydney and shortly afterwards all barracks and military works throughout the colony. Provided that the colonists paid for these works, he was willing to supply a fixed number of imperial troops. Any further troops required would have to be paid for in full by the colonists, or else they might raise local forces or police of their own, in which case he was prepared to supply them with expert assistance and advice.[2] This plan became known as the Grey policy of announcing the terms on which imperial troops could be sent to a colony, and it was justly claimed that lengthy and undignified haggling with colonial legislatures was thereby avoided. It was a policy, moreover, not merely of reducing colonial military expenditure by the withdrawal of imperial troops, but also of stimulating the colonists to take active measures for their own defence. Grey next turned his attention to Canada, where he proposed to reduce the scattered garrisons and to concentrate such imperial troops as remained at Quebec and Kingston. Any further troops required by the colonists could be sent out at their own cost.[3] In addition, Grey looked to increasing the security of Canada by the settlement of pensioners and by the construction of a strategic railway from Halifax to Quebec so as to give direct access to Canada without the necessity of using the United States' railway from Portland through Maine. Owing to the fact that the Canadian rebellion was now over, the mere reduction of troops was a comparatively simple matter. In fact by 1847 the Canadian garrisons had already been reduced from 15,000 to 9000 men.[4] On the other hand, Grey's attempt to extend his policy to the Cape failed, largely owing to the Kaffir Wars continuing intermittently from 1846 to 1852, which resulted in the imperial troops at the Cape being increased from 2000 to 5000 between the years 1840 and 1847[5] and to 9000 by 1852.[6]

Both Pakington and Newcastle, the successive Colonial Secretaries in the Derby-Disraeli and Aberdeen ministries, attempted to continue Grey's policy, particularly in the West Indies, where no serious attempt had been made either to reduce the garrisons or to persuade the islanders to contribute more towards them since Lord Bathurst's attempt in 1816. The permanent decline in the prosperity of the islands had drawn attention to the need for a general reduction and concentration of their imperial garrisons which under the existing system were not only extremely expensive but so widely distributed as to be strategically unsound.[7] Naturally, however, the strategic

[1] Grey to Fitzroy, 24 November 1846, *Parl. Pap.* 1851, xxxv (123), p. 373.
[2] Grey to Fitzroy, 21 November 1849, *Parl. Pap.* 1851, xxxv (123), pp. 363–78.
[3] Grey to Elgin, 14 March 1851, *Parl. Pap.* 1851, xxxvi [1344], pp. 255–7.
[4] *Parl. Pap.* 1849, xxxii (56).   [5] *Ibid.*
[6] *Parl. Pap.* 1861, xiii (423), p. 367.
[7] Trevelyan to Merivale, 10 January 1852, W.O. 1/601, 451.

argument was only used in order to support the financial one. It was urged that the absence of danger from France and Spain, and the abolition of slavery, had "rendered it unnecessary to continue arrangements for which there may have been sufficient grounds at the time when they were first adopted".[1] The presence, moreover, of imperial garrisons was a distinct check on the initiative of the islanders in raising police and militia.

In 1853, under the joint pressure of Newcastle and the Treasury, a preliminary decision was taken to withdraw troops from St Kitt's, Dominica, Grenada, St Vincent and Tobago, and to make Barbados the station for the main garrison.[2] Here, however, immense departmental difficulties and obstruction arose, centring round the lack of extra barrack accomodation at Barbados. There seemed no hope of making a fresh strategic distribution and of saving money at the same time except by sending some of the troops home, and a regiment had to return from Jamaica in order to help accommodate the surplus at Barbados.[3] At the Cape, Newcastle was more successful. In 1853 he secured a temporary reduction of 2500 imperial troops following the temporary cessation of war with the natives, and the grant of a representative constitution to the colony.[4]

The partial execution of Grey's policy both by himself and his successors during the late 'forties and early 'fifties marks the end of the second major attempt after 1815 to reduce the Home Government's commitments as regards the numbers and expense of troops in the colonies. Only in North America, where the cessation of the rebellions had left garrisons admittedly too large, was any substantial success achieved. In the Cape the attempt proved premature owing to incessant warfare, and in the West Indies it was blocked by administrative difficulties. In the Australian colonies its success was mainly technical since the number of troops involved was small. By acquiring representative institutions these colonies had placed themselves in a position where they found it difficult to avoid the burden of defence obligations.

Of the more general aspects of strategic development one of the most important was the rapid increase in the demand for shipping. Steam propulsion was introduced, though only as an auxiliary in the first instance, and iron construction soon followed. Improvements in scientific calculations and industrial technique produced larger ships making faster voyages, and between 1827 and 1848 the total British tonnage, both sail and steam, rose from $2\frac{1}{2}$ to 4 million tons and increased by another million tons before 1860. Although the imports of food and raw material were of greater bulk than the exports of manufactured articles, the difference in cargo space was

[1] Pakington to Colebrooke, 25 August 1852, *Parl. Pap.* 1854, XLI (177), p. 1.
[2] Newcastle to Colebrooke, 21 October 1853, *ibid.* p. 113; and Newcastle to Mackintosh, 21 October 1853, *ibid.* p. 165.
[3] Colonial Secretary to Commander-in-Chief, 30 March 1854, W.O. 1/593, 517.
[4] Newcastle to Cathcart, 14 March 1853, C.O. 49/47, 261.

easily absorbed by exports of coal, while the carriage of emigrants to British colonies and the United States provided constant employment for surplus tonnage outward bound. With the gradual removal of such restrictions on sea-borne trade as the Navigation Laws, the Corn Laws and the East India Company monopolies, and with the adoption of a general policy of free trade, British shipping received progressive stimulation from year to year. Behind this movement was the invaluable support of bodies such as Lloyd's, Trinity House, the Board of Trade and the Hydrographic Department of the Admiralty, working to improve the standard of shipbuilding and navigation and to ensure the safety of life at sea.

For some years the centre of naval activity was the Mediterranean, owing to the progressive weakening of the Ottoman Government. In 1816 Lord Exmouth broke the independent power of Algiers, and in 1827 a joint British, French and Russian fleet under Sir Edward Codrington intervened to prevent the suppression of the Greek nationalists and destroyed Mehemet Ali's Turco-Egyptian fleet at Navarino. In 1833 Mehemet Ali occupied Syria with an Egyptian army under his son Ibrahim Pasha and obtained control of the Turkish fleet which deserted to his side when sent against him. The powers again intervened, and in 1840 the British Mediterranean fleet under Sir Robert Stopford captured Beyrout while Sir Charles Napier landed and defeated the Egyptian army. Stopford and Napier subsequently bombarded Acre and Ibrahim Pasha withdrew to Egypt. These events were important because behind them lay the desire of the British to prevent Russia from controlling the Bosporus and so exercising influence over Egypt and the imperial communications with India and the Far East.

Meanwhile the populations of Australia, New Zealand and Canada were increasing steadily and important strategic extensions of territory were taking place on the Eastern trade routes. In 1818 Malacca was temporarily ceded to the Dutch, but was regained in 1824 in return for our withdrawal from Sumatra. In 1819 Sir Stamford Raffles made an agreement with the ruler of Johore for a British settlement at Singapore, the island itself being ceded in 1824.[1] In connection with the suppression of piracy Sir James Brooke was appointed Rajah of Sarawak in 1841 by the former piratical Sultan of Brunei, who also ceded Labuan to the Imperial Government in 1846. With a view to securing still firmer control over the land route to India, Aden was forcibly occupied by the Government of Bombay in 1839. It was already an important trade centre and in 1850 was declared a free port, and with the materialising of projects for the Suez Canal its strategic value was greatly enhanced. In 1854 the Kuria Muria Islands were acquired from the Imam of Muscat for development as a coaling station, while three years later Perim was occupied and

[1] See chapter xvi.

used both as a coaling and a cable station. On the Australian route the Cocos-Keeling Islands had been occupied by the Ross family since 1825, and in 1857 they were placed under Admiralty control. The acquisition of bases and the action taken against pirates, particularly in the Malay archipelago, cleared the way for a further extension of the China trade which occurred after the revocation of the East India Company's monopolies in 1834. Five years later, British warships intervened in support of the traders and combined operations ensued on an extensive scale, including the capture of Canton and Amoy in the south and of Shanghai and Ningpo in the north. By the Treaty of Nanking (1842) the four cities which had been captured were declared "treaty ports" with the addition of Foochow, and the island of Hong Kong was ceded to the Imperial Government and became a Crown Colony with a Governor and legislature. In the Atlantic a very important base on the South American route to Australia was secured in 1832 by the annexation of the Falkland Islands. For some years the difficulty of administering them was so great that they were left under Admiralty control and only became a Crown Colony in 1843.

Within the Empire the rebellions in Canada and the Kaffir Wars at the Cape provided the only difficulties requiring a military solution, but in neither case were the operations of more than local character. Apart from the danger to Canada from possible invasion by the United States, only two states were causing the Imperial Government any general anxiety in the colonial field. France, the hereditary enemy, was once more becoming a colonial rival, though for some years she was too much absorbed in the conquest of Algeria to act elsewhere. Russia, on the other hand, was considered to be a more serious menace, her activities both on the east and west of the Black Sea, menacing both Turkey and Persia, and also in Turkestan, Afghanistan and China, they were regarded with the gravest suspicion. The Crimean War, therefore, not only provided a very severe test for the Imperial Government's strategic machinery and technique but it also raised the whole question of imperial defence in general terms, despite the fact that operations were practically confined to Europe and the Near East. Had the war ended in a return to general peace within the Empire, its effects would have been important enough, but followed, as it immediately was, by the Second China War (1856–60) and the Indian Mutiny (1857–8), it caused the general strategic crisis to be extended over a period of six years. In addition it had important repercussions on opinion. Colonial enthusiasm for the mother country was aroused, while separatism and the peace movement at home both lost ground. Finally, the war was directly responsible for rapid and far-reaching changes of naval armament both in England and France and for the gradual reform of British naval and military administration.

The war itself took England by surprise, the Government and the press only being convinced that war was necessary towards the end of the preliminary negotiations.[1] In consequence no serious military preparations were undertaken in advance. Nevertheless the "opening movement, both in conception and organization, was perhaps the most daring, brilliant, and successful thing of the kind we ever did".[2] The Russians having withdrawn altogether from Turkish territory before the Franco-British force reached Varna to support the Turks, the object was changed to an attack on the Crimea and the capture of Sevastopol. "Designed as the expedition was to assist an ally in its own country, it was suddenly called upon without any previous preparation to undertake a combined operation of the most difficult kind against the territory of a well-warned enemy. It involved a landing late in the year on an open and stormy coast within striking distance of a naval fortress which contained an army of unknown strength, and a fleet not much inferior in battle power and undefeated."[3] Luckily the Russians sank most of their fleet in order to block the entrance to Sevastopol and the allied landing was undisturbed. Nevertheless, the defences of Sevastopol on the sea front proved superior to the guns of the allied fleet, while the allied armies menaced by a Russian field army on their flank had great difficulties in conducting the siege by land. In the Baltic the Russian defences, consisting of "frowning casemates", electrically fired mines, and sunken battleships blocking the approaches to Kronstadt, Sveaborg, Reval and Helsingfors, also proved superior to the allied battle fleet and the army of 10,000 French troops.

The Indian Mutiny, which immediately followed, removed the last vestiges of Company control and brought about a complete reorganisation of the English and Indian troops. The Second China War was more serious than the Mutiny, involving the double capture of the Taku ports, and the final capture of Pekin, which alone required 10,000 troops. The immediate result of these operations, following on the anti-piratical operations of 1854–6, led to the establishment in 1864 of a special China Squadron separated from the East Indies command.

The serious examples of departmental inefficiency revealed by the Crimean War led to strong criticism by experienced statesmen of the existing military system.[4] In consequence the Aberdeen Ministry decided to separate the War Department from the Colonies and endow it with a fourth Secretaryship of State. The Palmerston Ministry went a step farther and not only amalgamated the office of Secretary at War with that of the new Secretary of State for War but completely abolished

[1] See Martin, B. Kingsley, *The Triumph of Lord Palmerston*, for a very important examination of public opinion at the time.
[2] Corbett, Sir Julian S., *Some Principles of Maritime Strategy*, p. 292.
[3] *Ibid.* p. 292.
[4] Hansard, Third Series, cxxiv, 741; cxxx, 62; cxxxi, 223; cxxxii, 605.

the Board of Ordnance by dividing its duties between those of the new Secretary of State and the Commander-in-Chief. As root and branch measures these reforms had much to commend them, in so far as they aimed at simplicity, unified control and the abolition of jobbery. Like most contemporary military reforms, however, both executed and projected, they failed to take sufficient account of the strategic principles governing imperial defence. In consequence new difficulties arose owing to the dual control exercised by the now separate departments of War and Colonies over troops employed on colonial service.[1] Just as in the case of the navy, moreover, there was an obvious tendency for the department of the new Secretary of State for War to become overwhelmed by masses of routine business previously conducted by the Board of Ordnance and other subsidiary departments.

Meanwhile the main problem of imperial defence, namely the determination of the number, character and distribution of the imperial forces as a whole, plus the co-ordination of governmental, naval and military technique to that end, remained very much where it had been before the Crimean War. Faced with the overwhelming need for economy, political opinion was more than ever convinced that "self-government begets self-defence". By this was meant that colonies should automatically be made responsible for their own defence on receiving the gift of representative institutions, it being further argued that unless the colonists assumed at least part of this responsibility they could not possess the moral satisfaction that resulted from exercising the full rights of citizenship. The Colonial Office, therefore, continued to bicker with the colonies over the minutiae of garrison expenditure, without always avoiding the impression that the imperial troops available for colonial purposes were being put up to the highest bidder. In such circumstances it is scarcely to be wondered at that the colonial assemblies were in general opposed both to further reductions in their existing garrisons and also to being forced to pay greater defence contributions to the Imperial Exchequer. To the Home Government's purely financial and political arguments they replied with arguments of an equally partisan character, pointing out that since the Home Government still controlled their foreign relations they could in no sense be held responsible for the consequences of imperial policy. Withdrawal would not only leave the colonies a prey to native tribes and foreign invaders but also to the disruptive and lawless elements amongst their own people, whose existence was in many cases a result of deliberate policy on the part of the Home Government.

Finally, the colonial contractors and shopkeepers were opposed to losing such large and not over inquisitive customers, while the ladies lamented the threatened exodus from their drawing rooms and

---

[1] See an interesting criticism in the *United Service Magazine*, 1 (1861), p. 528.

parlours. The colonists, moreover, could rightly claim that during the Crimean War they had shown a very different spirit from that attributed to them by the separatists at home.[1] All through 1854–5 dispatches had poured in from colonial Governors, transmitting loyal addresses and resolutions from their legislatures in support of the war, and enclosing contributions to the Patriotic Fund amounting finally to £143,000.[2] Realising also the general threat created by the Russian menace, the colonies bestirred themselves to raise or reorganise their militia forces. Nova Scotia set about raising a strong militia in 1854, and next year an Act was passed in Canada for reorganising the existing militia and for raising volunteers,[3] of whom 5000 were actually trained by 1856. The Canadians went even further and sent a body of volunteers to fight side by side with British troops in the Crimea, a new step in imperial history. At the Cape an Act was passed for internal defence in 1855, and in the same year volunteers were raised in Natal. In Australia both New South Wales and Victoria raised volunteers in 1854, and Tasmania in 1859. Considering these evident signs of "self-reliance", it is surprising that the Colonial Office continued to treat what was largely an imperial strategic problem almost exclusively from a financial and political standpoint.

In the years 1851–61 between 40,000 and 47,000 imperial troops were employed in the colonies, including Hong Kong, at an annual average cost to the Home Government of £3,500,000, the colonies contributing, in addition, sums which varied between £237,000 and £398,000. The substantial reductions already made in the garrison of British North America by 1847 were carried still farther after 1852, so that by 1861 the garrison totalled only 4200, a lower figure than that of 1835 immediately before the rebellions. The cost to the Imperial Exchequer between 1853 and 1858 thus fell from £580,000 to £470,000, while the colonists' contribution rose from £1700 to £40,000. In the Windward and Leeward Islands (excluding Jamaica) steady reductions were made from 1854 onwards, the imperial troops falling from 3800 to 2300 between 1851 and 1861, the lowest figure since 1815. Here also the Home Government's cost was reduced from £303,000 to £225,000 between 1854 and 1858 while the colonists' contribution rose from £2100 to £12,000 in 1858, and to £29,000 in 1860.[4] At the Cape the Colonial Office policy continued to be frustrated by local difficulties of political and native administration. In 1857 the imperial troops had even to be increased from 6000 to 10,000 men, the highest figure ever before reached, the cost to the Home Government rising to £935,000 against the colonists' contribution of £34,000. From that date, however,

---

[1] See C.H.B.E., II, 718; VII, pt. I, 525, pt. II, 199.
[2] Parl. Pap. 1854–5 [1871] [63], [1888] [1940] [1983], XXVI.
[3] C.O. 42/598.
[4] Parl. Pap. 1859, Sess. 2, XVII (114) and 1861, XIII (423), pp. 72–3, 367.

rapid reductions were made, so that by 1860 imperial troops at the Cape numbered only 4700, while the colonists' contribution had risen to £56,000.[1]

The policy of the Aberdeen Ministry with regard to Australia centred chiefly in the proposals of Sir William Denison, who became Governor of New South Wales in 1854. He argued that Grey's policy of making the colonists pay for everything in excess of their quota of imperial troops meant in practice that they paid for all their defence apart from guards for Government House and for the protection of stores and buildings. This, he held, was unsound, because it took no account of the difference between external and internal dangers. He himself advocated as a general policy the sharing between the mother country and the colonies of all military charges, except charges for works, stores and construction, which should be borne by the colonies alone.[2] The objection to this plan was that it would apparently give the colonists the right to fix the numbers of their own imperial garrisons instead of the Imperial Government being able to refuse to send more troops even in cases where the colonists were prepared to pay the full charge for them.[3] In 1858 the Grey policy of the imperial quota was reaffirmed despite Denison's continued advocacy of his own plan, which caused him to be regarded at home as pro-colonial.[4] During 1855 internal trouble caused a slight increase in the numbers of imperial troops in New South Wales and Victoria, but, whereas the Home Government's expenditure remained at under £100,000, the colonists' contributions rose from £88,000 in 1853 to £166,000 by 1857.[5] In New Zealand a fierce departmental struggle developed with the Colonial Office during 1856 in consequence of the colonists' desire to receive special treatment because of the internal menace created by the Maoris. Both the general and provincial legislatures were involved and strong feelings were aroused. Meanwhile the total of imperial troops rose from 1600 in 1851 to 5000 in 1861.[6]

Although, therefore, the Colonial Office policy made uninterrupted progress in North America and the West Indies, both as regards reducing the numbers of imperial troops and stimulating the colonists to increase their contributions and raise volunteers, the internal situation at the Cape and in Australia was unfavourable to its efforts. Moreover, in the case of Mediterranean ports, held purely for strategic purposes, it suffered a definite setback, the garrisons of

---

[1] *Parl. Pap.* 1859, Sess. 2, XVI (114); 1861, XIII (423), pp. 72–3, 367, and 1870, XLII (254). See also vol. VIII, chap. XVI.

[2] Denison to Labouchere, 18 April 1856, Denison, Sir W., *Varieties of Vice-Regal Life*, I, p. 347.

[3] Minute by Merivale, 8 December 1856, C.O. 201/494.

[4] C.O. 309/43 and C.O. 201/504.

[5] *Parl. Pap.* 1859, Sess. 2, XVI (114).

[6] *Parl. Pap.* 1861, XIII (423), p. 367. See also vol. VII, pt. II, chap. VII.

Gibraltar and Malta being increased from 3600 and 3300 men to 6000 and 7000 respectively between the years 1856 and 1861,[1] largely as a result of the Crimean War. The Second China War was an additional obstacle to the policy of reduction, the garrison of Hong Kong being raised to 8000 men in 1860.[2] Some success, however, was achieved in Ceylon, where the numbers fell in 1855 from 3500 men to a little over 2000,[3] although practically no saving was made on the average cost of £127,000, despite the fact that the island's contribution rose to £74,000 in 1858[4] and to £97,000 in 1860.[5]

While the Colonial Office, the War Office and the Treasury continued to regard imperial defence mainly as a series of local problems connected solely by constitutional and financial similarities, a new outlook on the general problem emerged in consequence of a recrudescence of the French invasion scare. This scare, originating during the reign of Louis Philippe, had been, alternately, allayed by the 1848 revolution, stimulated by Napoleon III's *coup d'état* and allayed once more by the Anglo-French alliance during the Crimean War. No sooner, however, was the Peace of Paris signed than Napoleon's attempt to profit by the naval lessons of the war, coupled with his occupation of Saigon and New Caledonia, roused all the old misgivings. Undoubtedly his most provocative act was the improvement and extension of the naval dockyard and shore defences at Cherbourg. This was a matter on which British opinion was extremely sensitive. It had long been a cardinal axiom in British strategic calculations that, while the French had no port in the Channel capable of accommodating battleships, they could not possibly invade England direct from their north coast, since the battle fleets necessary to cover the invading army could be blockaded in Brest, Rochefort and Toulon. Now, however, with the threat of a first-class base in the Channel itself, direct invasion loomed up, not merely as a possibility, but as an immediate probability.[6] In addition, the French press during the years 1857–8 assumed a distinctly bellicose tone, which instead of dying down was aggravated by the Orsini bomb episode of 1859. For the first time for many years the British Government found itself faced by an apparently serious French menace and by the clamours of its own press and Parliament for vigorous and immediate action.

On the naval side the chief effect was to accelerate a remarkable revolution already impending in naval architecture, armament and propulsion. Not only were radical changes made in naval *matériel* but an entirely new type of *personnel* was introduced into the service.

---

[1] *Parl. Pap.* 1861, XIII (423), p, 367.
[2] *Ibid.*
[3] *Ibid.*
[4] *Parl. Pap.* 1859, Sess. 2, XVI (114).
[5] *Parl. Pap.* 1861, XIII (423), pp. 72–3.
[6] "Heaven send Cherbourg may never be graven on the heart of Queen Victoria." *United Service Magazine*, I (1859), p. 22.

The ships which won the battle of Trafalgar and bombarded Acre in 1840 were built of wood, propelled by sails, and armed with smooth-bore, muzzle-loading guns, firing solid shot. No competition existed between the attack and the defence. Yet, within twenty-five years of the bombardment of Acre, British warships were being built of iron, protected by steel armour plating, and propelled by steam-driven screw propellers, while their guns were rifled breech-loaders, firing elongated shells fitted with high explosives. Artillery was thus matched against armour in a continuous competition necessitating further experiments and invention. The naval revolution which produced these changes must not be considered as an isolated naval phenomenon, but rather as the naval counterpart of the industrial revolution then in progress.

The introduction of steam into the British navy followed naturally on the experiments of the mercantile marine, but met with considerable opposition since "the big paddle boxes encumbered the gun deck and impaired the sailing qualities of the ship. Without producing satisfactory speed steam increased the risk of fire. Excessive coal consumption limited the radius of action; and the vulnerability of their boilers, engines, and paddle boxes confined steamers for the most part to services as tugs, transports, and despatch vessels."[1] Despite the early invention of the screw propeller it was not introduced into the British service till 1845; thus nearly all the objections levelled against the paddles were avoided. Nevertheless, steam was still regarded only as an auxiliary, and for the next twenty-five years all British warships were fully rigged with masts and spars. Under the influence of Colonel Paixhans the conversion of the French navy to steam was being carried out far more rapidly. Paixhans, moreover, was a strong advocate of shells which were adopted by the French for naval purposes in 1837. He argued that shells would soon prove destructive to wood and so upset the whole broadside principle of construction and gun-mounting on which the British fighting system was based. Steam ships mounting shell guns would be able to fight end-on and the British would thus be forced to scrap all existing *matériel* and start level. The apparently bellicose attitude of Louis Philippe's government and the popular acceptance of the theory that steam had "bridged the Channel" led to a panic in the British press. Faced by these apparent threats and dangers, the British Admiralty reluctantly followed suit in the matter of shells, while disbelieving the extreme claims made for them by French enthusiasts. Iron, for shipbuilding purposes, was already regarded as a better material than wood and far safer as regards fire, but as a result of many experiments both in England and France it was held to be less satisfactory as a means of resisting solid shot.[2] The immunity, however, of the French floating batteries at the bombardment of Kinburn, compared with the punish-

[1] Baxter, J. P., *The Introduction of the Ironclad Warship*, p. 11.
[2] *Ibid.* pp. 94–7, 101–3, 122–6.

ment inflicted on the Anglo-French wooden, steam-driven line-of-battle ships by the forts of Sevastopol, caused a considerable sensation in both navies.[1] Napoleon III, himself an artillerist, personally directed the French experiments based on the lessons of the war, with the result that in 1859 *La Gloire* was launched, a steam "frigate", built of wood, but completely surrounded by a belt of iron plating. The failure of the French to build an all-iron ship was due to lack of liaison between their metallurgical industries in eastern France and their shipbuilding centres on the coast.[2] Long before *La Gloire* was launched, however, it had become obvious that, despite the need for vigorous economy after the war, the British would be forced to make some reply to the French initiative.

Already, in 1858, anxiety with regard to the power of the French steam-driven wooden navy had become so great that the building of ironclads was considered a matter "not only of expediency but of absolute necessity".[3] After prolonged discussion as to the question of design the Admiralty, in April 1859, approved the plans of the *Warrior*, which was launched in 1861. This great revolutionary piece of ship construction was a full-rigged steam "frigate" of 9000 tons (as compared with *La Gloire's* 5600), built entirely of iron and having armour plating over the midships' section, leaving the bow and stern unarmoured, so as to lessen weight and ensure good sailing qualities. In recognition, moreover, of the tendency towards increased size and reduced numbers of naval guns the *Warrior* carried a main armament of twenty-six 68 pounders and eight 110 pounders. The cost of construction was over £350,000, a staggering sum to those who looked forward to a steady decline in naval expenditure.[4] Nevertheless, in the face of apparent French menaces, the second Palmerston Ministry suspended the building of all large wooden ships, except for the purpose of casing them with iron, and ordered eleven new sea-going ironclads (not floating batteries or monitors) to be laid down. The French had evidently hoped to discount the superiority of the British in the handling of traditional types of ships and weapons by starting a new competition in which French inventiveness and technique would gain an advantage. The result, however, was entirely contrary to their expectation, for when once the ironclad policy was accepted, it was found that Britain possessed the enormous advantage of having all her shipbuilding centres, with the exception of Southampton, Portsmouth and the Thames, close to the areas producing coal, iron, and engineering equipment. This ensured the highest degree of co-operation between all the human elements involved in warship construction. A further advantage derived from the adoption of all-metal construction was

[1] Baxter, pp. 69–91. [2] *Ibid.* pp. 98–114.
[3] *Parl. Pap.* 1861, v (438), pp. 231, 338.
[4] Baxter, pp. 154–9, 164-7, 175–8, 274–6.

that the navy was no longer dependent on America and the Baltic for timber supplies as it had been in the old wars.

The next stages in the naval revolution were chiefly connected with guns and gun-mounting, many experiments being made with turrets, barbettes and the central battery system. Under pressure of the increasing size of guns, the broadside system was seen to be doomed owing to difficulties of mounting, handling and serving. Moreover, with fewer as well as larger guns, it was desirable to obtain a wider arc of fire than that obtained by the broadside system. For some years every solution was blocked by the continued use of masts, spars and sails, but in 1869 the Admiralty laid down the *Devastation*, possessing one short mast for signalling, set amidships, and with four big guns disposed in two turrets, set on the centre line of the ship, immediately ahead and astern of the mast and funnels. The ship had no superstructures such as the poop and forecastle, so that the main armament had an uninterrupted fire ahead and astern, while all four guns could fire simultaneously on the broadside. Not only had artillery at last asserted itself, but the engines had come into their own as the sole means of propulsion.

It must not be supposed that these developments led to an immediate change in the whole character of the British navy, since, for many years to come, wooden ships, either armoured or unarmoured, were retained in commission, as were fully-rigged ironclads, with guns mounted on the broadside or in a modified and restricted system of turrets. Foreign navies, when operating far from home ports, were still compelled to reserve their steam for fighting purposes, whereas the British, through the possession of well-placed coaling stations, could rely on obtaining fresh supplies of coal at frequent intervals. A further advantage derived from continuous steaming was that it enabled warships to steer a direct course unhampered by dependence on the wind.

A closer examination of the naval problem shows that fleets based on Chatham, Portsmouth and Devonport could easily cover the home focals and terminals of British trade. In the west Atlantic, Halifax, Bermuda, Antigua and Port Royal (Jamaica) could be used to cover the routes to Canada, the United States, Honduras, Guiana and the West Indies. Under existing conditions these routes could only be threatened from the Azores, Canaries, Madeira or the mainland ports of Spain and Portugal. But both these states were presumed to be friendly. The northern section of the route for all ships bound south of the equator could be protected from Gibraltar and Sierra Leone. Possible attacks could be made from the same bases as those which menaced the western route, with the addition of the Cape Verde Islands, but for the same reason attacks were unlikely. The southern section contained Ascension Island, St Helena, Simon's Bay and the Falkland Islands. Attacks were only possible from the South American Republics and these again were assumed to be friendly. The Eastern route, from Simon's Bay, had three branches, to India, China and Australasia. Warships based on Mauritius, Aden, Trincomalee and Bombay could be used to protect the Indian branch, while Hong Kong provided a good base near the terminals of the China trade route. The Australian branch, being an open route, was practically free from interference by commerce raiders. Along the overland route to the East, Gibraltar, Malta and the Ionian Islands provided sufficient bases for the Mediterranean fleet. The Pacific routes to Australia and New Zealand from Vancouver and Cape Horn lay through open water and were in little danger of interruption. All other trade routes were covered by a chain of bases not more than 4000 miles apart, which was the maximum distance British warships could cover under steam alone, at an economic speed, without refuelling. The route between Canada and China was not as yet sufficiently developed to raise an immediate strategical problem. The main conclusion to be drawn was that Britain was in a better position to protect her trade routes than any single power was to attack them.

Thus, by 1861, Britain had not only gained the lead from France in the naval armaments' race, but was about to reap further advantages from the steam and ironclad policy. Nevertheless, the rapid and fundamental changes in naval *matériel* which were taking place so bewildered both service and civilian opinion in Britain that for some years it seemed as if the principles of war had become completely nullified. Technical achievement had outstripped strategic thought. Steam, it was held, had "bridged the Channel", whatever that phrase might mean, and the invasion scare, despite the *Warrior* and her successors, continued for some years unabated. England was no longer "safe", fleet or no fleet, and in consequence pressure was put on the Government from all sides to increase "home defence". It became known that as far back as 1847 the Duke of Wellington had stated that in future England would not be safe one week after war was declared. It was not known that he had naturally added the proviso that this statement could only be true if the fleet were beaten.[1] Since, in the case of war with France, the full statement had been true ever since the seventeenth century, it was of no particular importance, but the garbled version coming in the midst of an existing panic had a serious effect.

The invasion question was of immediate interest to the colonies, for not only did it give the Colonial Office a real strategic reason for withdrawing the garrisons, but it appeared as a threat to the lines of communication of each individual colony. On its solution, moreover, depended the action which each colony would take or might be

[1] For Wellington's letter to Burgoyne and the circumstances of its publication see Wrottesley, G., *Life and Correspondence of F.-M. Sir John Burgoyne*, I, pp. 436–44.

expected to take in case of a local threat to its own individual security. There was, of course, a good case for retaining the bulk of the imperial troops in Britain as a pool or reserve, capable of immediate transfer either to the colonies themselves or to enemy territory. It was obvious, for instance, that Britain must at all costs prevent the occupation of the Dutch or Belgian ports by any power with a strong army. The transport of the troops, the protection of imperial lines of communication, and the defence of imperial territory from invasion must depend on the existence of a navy, capable of defeating or blockading the enemy's battle fleet, safeguarding the chief focals and terminals of imperial sea-borne trade and dealing effectively with enemy commerce raiders. These were truisms established during the wars of the eighteenth century. In the eighteen-fifties and 'sixties, however, they were completely forgotten. The policy of defence by means of a strong navy was abandoned in favour of defence by troops retained in Britain to fight on British soil, regardless of the fact that, should command of home waters be lost, the British Isles could be starved into submission without the landing of a single enemy soldier. This applied equally to the colonies, for, even if self-sufficient as regards food, they would soon have been forced into submission if deprived of economic contact with the mother country.

The difference between the case of the colonies and the British Isles lay in the fact that the blockade by sea of an individual colony affected that colony alone, whereas the loss or even partial loss of control over home waters would not only reduce the British Isles to starvation but would simultaneously endanger the whole Empire. Nevertheless, during the early 'sixties the failure to co-ordinate strategic thought with technical achievement was so pronounced that the principle of defence of land by land forces alone was accepted almost without protest, not only by statesmen and publicists but even by experienced officers of the navy and army. It was admitted, however, that even if the whole of the regular army, minus the garrison of India, was concentrated at home, it would still be too weak to face a powerful foreign invasion. The first solution, therefore, was to enrol large bodies of volunteers, a special Act for this purpose being passed in May 1859. The Volunteer Movement, as developed in England, was morally bracing in its conception of civic patriotism based on the principle of "defence not defiance". Strategically, however, it was unsound, since it proposed to match large bodies of half-trained amateur infantry, devoid of artillery, engineers and ancillary services, against fully trained professional soldiers. Had an enemy once effected a successful landing, the volunteers would have been of as much use as the trained bands of 1588 would have been against Parma's Spanish veterans. Had the volunteers upon enrolment accepted an obligation to fight overseas, they could have been used as reserves for the army acting offensively according to its traditional rôle, but naturally this obligation would have been contrary to the essence of the contract. Nevertheless, the movement spread rapidly so that by 1860 there were 18,000 volunteers capable of embodiment living within 20 miles of the General Post Office,[1] and by 1861 there were 160,000 in the whole of England.[2]

While politicians were pleased by the success of a plan involving such a small drain on the Exchequer, professional soldiers were becoming increasingly sceptical as to the value of amateur reserves insufficiently supported by the technical arms. They, therefore, put forward an alternative means of discounting the numerical weakness of the army, namely forts. Regular troops, it was argued, if only they were properly protected, could withstand invading forces more than twice their strength. Apart from ignoring completely the possibility of enemy investment by sea, the advocates of fortifications apparently assumed a static position as regards military science. Forts which were impregnable in 1860 were to remain impregnable for at least fifty years, otherwise the capital outlay involved in construction would have been better expended in increasing the army's numerical strength. They also assumed a static population, since proposals were freely put forward for establishing forts at such points as Muswell Hill, Stoke Newington and Blackheath. Considered from an imperial standpoint the idea of fixed defences was equally unsound, since it tied the defenders to their fixed positions and denied them freedom of manœuvre. Nevertheless, elaborate plans were drawn up for the construction of fixed defences all over the Empire. In January 1859 Captain Astley Cooper Key reported to the Admiralty that "the defences of Portsmouth are at present totally insufficient to prevent a bombardment of the dockyard, in the absence of our fleet".[3]

In consequence of these views Cooper Key was chosen to sit on a royal commission appointed in 1859 "to consider the defences of the United Kingdom",[4] its terms of reference, however, being restricted to Portsmouth, Plymouth, Portland, Pembroke, Dover, Chatham and the Medway. The commissioners at the outset assumed the defeat or absence of the navy and asked questions of the naval witnesses in such a manner as to produce the answers required. In their report, printed in 1860, they recommended the construction of new defensive works capable of accommodating 30,000 men and mounting 3721 guns at an estimated cost of over 11 millions.[5] Luckily these recommendations were never completely carried out, chiefly on the grounds of expense, but their influence on imperial defence as a whole was

[1] Parl. Pap. 1860, XLI (452), pp. 645–6.
[2] Parl. Pap. 1871, XXXIX (171).
[3] Colomb, Vice-Admiral P. H., Memoirs of Admiral Sir Astley Cooper Key, p. 289. "Captain Key's mistake was the very common one of confusing force with the position of force. The superior force is secure because it is superior. The inferior force may be made less inferior by its position, but it is the inferior force still and cannot be secure." Ibid. p. 291.
[4] Parl. Pap. 1860, XXIII [2682].   [5] Ibid. pp. 439–87.

retrograde. The conception of forts as a means of protecting naval bases from chance raids was sound enough, but to construct fortifications for the express purpose of defending the bases of a fleet incapable of resisting an invading army, covered by an enemy battle fleet, was strategically illogical. From the standpoint of imperial defence the Volunteer Movement and the fortifications theory of defence were equally unsound since they encouraged the setting up of a series of local and self-contained defence systems. While ignoring the navy's rôle as the essential link, they encouraged the heresy that islands and isolated dependent territories can be defended by troops alone. The difference between the two theories was that the Volunteer Movement was at least inexpensive and for colonial purposes had much to commend it, provided a sufficient fleet was maintained. In colonial warfare local knowledge and local experience might counterbalance the greater military efficiency of regular troops fighting under strange conditions, a fact which was strikingly illustrated by the Boer War. The fortifications theory, apart from its enormous expense, was strategically unsound, even from a purely land conception of warfare, in that it hampered the defending forces in their power of manœuvre.

Despite the important changes in ideas about defence produced by the invasion scares and the policy of Napoleon III, little attempt had so far been made either in the United Kingdom or the Colonies to consider imperial defence problems as a whole. The War Office, Colonial Office and the Treasury continued to work in co-operation in order to secure economy and reform, but made no attempt to secure the co-operation of the Admiralty in working out a general strategic policy. In charging these Departments with neglecting the wood for the trees it must at least be admitted that the problems which they actually chose to face were both difficult and urgent in themselves. First, there was the great difference which existed between the various types of colonies; secondly, there was the difference in speed at which they were developing; and thirdly, the difference between the types of military danger, internal and external, to which they were subject. As regards the contributions made by the colonies towards their own defence, it was not so much the smallness or even the inequality of the sums that mattered as the lack of uniformity in collecting, spending and recording them. Eventually the War Office took action by suggesting that the Imperial Government should only assume obligations for defending the colonies against white aggressors and to a less extent against formidable tribes, but in no case should it bear all the expense, except in cases where the troops acted as a garrison for purely "imperial purposes". On the contrary, the Imperial Government ought to insist, in all ordinary cases, that the colonists either contributed part of the defence expenses, or raised local forces.

In consequence of this letter a departmental committee was set up in 1859, on the suggestion of General Peel, Secretary of State for War, consisting of Frederick Elliott, Under-Secretary of State for the Colonies, John Robert Godley, Under-Secretary of State for War, an original founder of the Canterbury settlement, and George Hamilton, Secretary of the Treasury.[1] Its object was to discover whether any such principle as the War Office had suggested could be generally applied. Godley and Hamilton, in a majority report,[2] found no precedent for making the colonies contribute, but thought that their failure to do so must be considered as historically unparalleled and a great obstacle to the growth of self-reliance. In 1857–8, 47,000 troops were being employed imperially at a total cost of £3,968,000, the colonies contributing £378,000. The Cape contributed only one twenty-fourth of its expenses, while the Australian colonies contributed more than one-half. Troops had been withdrawn from the colony of Victoria because she would not pay for more, although she alone contributed £94,000 out of Australia's total contribution, £170,000. Meanwhile, troops had been withdrawn from Antigua, because she would not provide barracks for them, and sent to Barbados, where the Imperial Government had to provide them in any case. The majority also expressed themselves strongly on the chaotic position of the colonial allowances paid to imperial troops.

They recommended, therefore, that a distinction should be drawn between posts, such as Malta and Gibraltar, garrisoned purely for imperial purposes, and self-governing colonies. The first class, they held, should not be expected to contribute towards defence, but the self-governing colonies should be dealt with either along the lines followed by Lord Grey or those advocated by Sir William Denison. The objections to the Grey plan were that it was strategically unsound to fix a definite number when circumstances kept altering, and that to change the numbers constantly would necessitate fresh negotiations. Moreover, it deprived the colonists of joint enterprise in the scheme and did not stimulate self-reliance. The chief objection to the Denison scheme was that it appeared to give the colonists the right to fix the number of troops required, although the objection could be avoided by specifically retaining this right for the Imperial Government. On the whole the majority report favoured the Denison scheme, but thought "self-reliance" the best defence of all, adding that garrisons were simply baits to would-be aggressors, unless strong in numbers and in first-class forts, and that the best means of defence for our widely scattered Empire was "naval superiority".[3]

Elliot, the third member of the committee, in a minority report, objected to any uniform system of colonial military contributions, arguing that war and peace were not the only reasons for the Imperial

[1] Memo. by Godley, 2 October 1858, W.O. 33/6; Hawes to Merivale, 14 March 1859, C.O. 323/255.
[2] *Parl. Pap.* 1860, XLI (282).   [3] *Ibid.* pp. 574–83.

Government assuming defence obligations, since the colonies were also economic sources of supply. Poor colonies should not be deprived of troops required for police purposes merely because they could not afford to pay for them, nor should they be forced to contribute merely because a vital strategic port lay within their boundaries. Wealthy dependencies, on the other hand, even though they were held entirely for imperial strategic purposes, ought to be made to pay substantial contributions.[1] Hearing of the existence of the report, Adderley pressed for its publication,[2] which was eventually agreed to in March 1860[3] and produced further discussion.[4] In March 1861 Arthur Mills moved for a select committee of the House of Commons on colonial military defence and expenditure. Palmerston took the line that little good could be expected from such a committee which would be usurping the functions of the executive. As it was known, however, that Gladstone was in favour of the motion, it was carried,[5] and on 13 March 1861 the committee was set up "to enquire and report whether any and what alterations may be advantageously adopted in regard to the defences of the British dependencies, and the proportion of the cost of such defence as now defrayed from imperial and colonial funds respectively". The debate was very ably criticised by an anonymous writer, who pointed out that the existing difficulties dated from the separation of the departments of War and Colonies in 1854, and who also criticised the dual control of the army by the War Office and the Horse Guards.[6] The writer agreed with Palmerston that the committee could never succeed in tackling what was really a Cabinet question involving important questions of foreign policy as well as adjustments of spheres of activity with colonial legislatures. The select committee of 1861, however, had the advantage over all its predecessors appointed for similar purposes in that by its terms of reference "the defence of the British dependencies", and not finance only, were to be its concern. On the other hand, the fact that nothing was said or implied about naval defence shows clearly that the committee was constituted in a somewhat illogical manner and set only a limited task. As regards *personnel* it contained some of the ablest men in the House, all of whom were experts on colonial affairs, but they were experts almost exclusively on the colonies' constitutional, administrative and financial problems and not on strategy. Their outlook, moreover, was so dominated by the idea of self-reliance that it is difficult in some cases to distinguish the desire for imperial co-operation from the desire for imperial disintegration. Inevitably, and perhaps wisely, the committee practically ignored all aspects of defence except constitutional and

[1] *Parl. Pap.* 1860, XLI (282), pp. 583–91. [2] Hansard, Third Series, CLVI, 2220–1.
[3] *Ibid.* CLVII, 1637–40. [4] *Ibid.* CLVIII, 1826–33.
[5] *Ibid.* CLXI, 1399–1421 *seqq.*
[6] *United Service Magazine*, I (1861), p. 528.

colonies, no accounts being rendered to the War Office or Treasury.[1] After commenting on this want of system, the report stated that it was impossible to lay down any rule for "communities so various as those which compose the British Empire", but that the responsibility for and main cost of defence of the imperial posts "properly devolves on the Imperial Government".[2] Colonies proper ought to undertake the main burden of their own defence. Negotiations with colonial legislatures were deprecated, and Lord Grey's policy approved.[3]

Considering the application of these principles in detail, the report recommended that imperial troops should be reduced still further in the self-governing colonies of Australia, and that the New Zealanders should rely chiefly "on their own resources".[4] In South Africa, local effort against the warlike tribes should be stimulated and the settlers asked for a larger contribution.[5] Ceylon, which already contributed £97,000 out of a total of £110,000 spent on its defence, should make an even larger contribution. The West Indian garrisons should be withdrawn, being useless for defence, and unsuitable as police.[6]

Expenditure on colonial fortifications was disapproved, naval defence being preferred, the commissioners in conclusion submitting, "that the tendency of modern warfare is to strike a blow at the heart of the hostile power; and that it is, therefore, desirable to concentrate the troops required for defence of the United Kingdom as much as possible, and to trust mainly to naval supremacy for securing against foreign aggression the distant dependencies of the Empire".[7]

By advocating naval defence, the committee sought to obtain strategic authority for the withdrawal of the garrisons and for demanding further colonial contributions. Had they declared for a stronger sea-going battle fleet with adequate cruiser and flotilla protection, their recommendations would have been reasonable, for in many cases there were good strategic grounds for withdrawing the garrisons. But it is clear from the questions asked and the evidence given, that they tended to over-emphasize the value of floating batteries and coast-defence ships, in other words, cheap substitutes for forts and troops. Despite the great mass of evidence called, which involved the asking of nearly 4000 questions, the report had little to offer beyond the ordinary expressions of parliamentary opinion then current. As Palmerston had prophesied, it had merely confirmed a large number of members in their preconceived ideas about the constitutional and financial aspects of land defence in the self-governing colonies. The problems of combined defence for the whole Empire were scarcely considered.

In March 1862, in a debate in the Commons on the report of the select committee, Arthur Mills, who had been its chairman,

[1] Parl. Pap. 1861, XIII (423), p. 73.   [2] Ibid. p. 74.
[3] Ibid. p. 73.   [4] Ibid. p. 74.
[5] Ibid. p. 74.   [6] Ibid. pp. 74–5. [7] Ibid. p. 75.

moved a resolution that the self-governing colonies ought to bear the main responsibility for their internal order and defence. The resolution was eventually carried with the addition of the words "and ought to assist in their own external defence".[1] Although the resolution did not actually mention the raising of land forces by the colonies, such a development was naturally implied. As a matter of fact certain colonial land forces were already in being, the Royal Canadian Regiment of Foot having come into existence with an effective strength of 1000 men as far back as 1858.[2]

The situation, however, caused by the Civil War in America was considered so serious that immediate reinforcements were sent out to Canada in 1862, thus raising the imperial garrison to 12,000.[3] At the same time the Colonial Office urged the Canadian legislature to make every possible effort to increase their own defence beyond the existing force of 18,000 volunteers,[4] with the result that there was a general spread of the militia movement in addition to the volunteers. Nevertheless, the defence of Canada against well-organised aggression from the United States had long been recognised as impracticable, owing chiefly to its relative disparity in population and the tremendous length of frontier involved. The only direct access to the interior of Canada from England was by the St Lawrence river which, in winter, was blocked by ice, so that until the completion of the strategic railway from Halifax to Quebec the only line of communication left open in winter was by the Grand Trunk Railway running from Portland (Maine) through United States territory.[5] The result of further enquiries into the ultimate possibilities of Canadian defence led to the conclusion that in case of serious trouble the Canadians must look after themselves.[6]

With the close of the Civil War and the reduction of the United States army to 54,000, tension was somewhat eased and the number of imperial troops employed was reduced to 8000.[7] In 1866 imperial reinforcements were again asked for owing to the danger from Fenians, and by 1868 the numbers had risen once more to 11,000,[8] costing the Imperial Government £741,000[9] as against £470,000 in 1858,[10] while the Canadian volunteers had increased to over 30,000. Nevertheless, it was decided to withdraw all imperial troops from Canada with the exception of garrisons to be retained for purely imperial purposes at the naval bases of Halifax and Esquimalt, a

1 Hansard, Third Series, CLXV, 1032–60.
2 Stacey, C. P., *Canada and the British Army*, 1846–1871, pp. 105–6.
3 *Parl. Pap.* 1870, XLII (254).
4 *Parl. Pap.* 1862, XXXVI [3061].
5 An interesting letter on this subject appeared in *The Daily News* of 16 October 1862.
6 *Parl. Pap.* 1865, XXXVII [3434] and Hansard, Third Series, CLXXVI, 373–8.
7 *Parl. Pap.* 1870, XLII (254).
8 *Ibid.*
9 *Parl. Pap.* 1867–8, XLII (62), p. 359.
10 *Parl. Pap.* 1859, sess. 2, XVII (114).

policy which after consideration was carried to completion in 1871.[1]

As regards the Australian colonies the Colonial Office achieved better success for the policy of the select committee.[2] In 1863 the Duke of Newcastle informed them all except Western Australia, that in future they must pay £40 for each officer and man of the 1300 imperial infantry which the Home Government proposed to allot them. Extra troops, if available, must be paid for at the rate of £70 per man.[3] The execution of this policy, however, was somewhat retarded by the recrudescence of trouble with the Maoris in New Zealand, which not only involved considerable fighting during the years 1862–9 but led to an acute imperial crisis. Ever since the first serious fighting with the Maoris the New Zealand legislature had been demanding the right to control the imperial troops allotted to them. These troops were paid for by the Imperial Government, which refused to acknowledge this claim and in 1864 went a step farther by claiming to direct and control the operations of all forces engaged in the Maori War including those raised locally. From a strategic point of view this claim was incontestable, since it involved the principle of the unity of command, but it was resisted on the same principle by Sir George Grey, the Governor, who counter-claimed for himself the control over all the forces, including the imperial forces, on the grounds that he already controlled all native and internal affairs and that his status as governor included that of commander-in-chief. This placed the military commander-in-chief appointed by the Imperial Government in a very awkward position.[4] Naturally under such conditions the military operations did not make satisfactory progress and Sir George Grey assumed command in person by way of substantiating his claim on behalf of the colony. The Imperial Government thereupon decided to withdraw the imperial troops altogether and Sir George Grey resigned. At the end of 1868 Lord Granville, the new Colonial Secretary, informed New Zealand that the Gladstone ministry, which had just come into power, would proceed with the withdrawal, despite the fact that some of the Maori chiefs were still in arms.[5] This policy was sharply criticised at home, and when in March 1869 Lord Granville refused the New Zealand Government's request for a loan wherewith to organise its own defence, a controversy broke out in the English press, and the Government was charged with creating a feeling of exasperation in order to promote secession. Only one battalion of regulars now remained, and in 1870 this was ordered to Australia and then sent home, the final stages of

[1] See *C.H.B.E.* VI, 717. [2] *Ibid.* VII, pt. I, 526–8.
[3] *Parl. Pap.* 1863 [459], pp. 2–3.
[4] Keith, A. B., *Responsible Government in the Dominions*, pp. 1248–57, 1869–97; see also *ibid.* (1928), pp. 966–74.
[5] *Parl. Pap.* 1868–9, XLVIII (307).

the war being conducted by militia volunteers, both white and Maori, and with Australian assistance.[1]

In consequence of a decision taken in 1867, which was to have general application, the Derby-Disraeli and Gladstone Ministries had been withdrawing other imperial garrisons. Imperial troops had already been withdrawn from Australia and Tasmania[2] and sent to New Zealand, their places being taken by volunteers. The battalion which passed through on its way home from New Zealand was the last to serve in Australia.

In 1869 the policy of withdrawing imperial troops was applied to South Africa, with the idea of reducing the garrison to a single battalion stationed at Simon's Bay, but continued difficulties with the natives, increasing friction with the Boers, and the general unrest caused by the opening up of the diamond mines, prevented this policy from being carried into effect.

Nevertheless, the Cape Mounted Rifles were disbanded in company with the African Artillery, the Canadian Rifle Regiment and the 3rd West Indian Regiment. In the Mediterranean a saving of 4000 troops at an annual cost of £200,000 to the Imperial Government had already been achieved in 1864 by the withdrawal of the garrison from the Ionian Islands, on their cession to Greece. By 1870 all imperial troops had left Australia, New Zealand and Tasmania, only untoward circumstances preventing immediate withdrawal from Canada and South Africa. Army estimates for colonial military expenditure in 1870 dropped from the standard sum of 3 millions or over, which had prevailed since 1854, to £2,237,000,[3] and declined still further in succeeding years. It is clear, however, from the persistence with which the policy of withdrawal was pursued and the satisfaction with which its final success was achieved, that it held a position in parliamentary thought quite out of proportion to its strategic interest or merit.

A more interesting and constructive development took place in 1865 with the passing of the Colonial Naval Defence Act,[4] authorising the commissioning of colonial warships and the raising of colonial naval personnel, including volunteers. By arrangement with the Imperial Government personnel might be borrowed from the Royal Navy, of which all colonial warships and personnel would in any case form part. Legal and constitutional matters connected with enrolment and service and the use of colonial ships and personnel outside territorial waters were to be decided by the Crown in Council. No charge for the creation of such forces was to fall on the imperial revenue. Although carefully framed so as to include naval development in the widest sense, the possibilities of the Act were hardly apparent at the time, and there is reason to believe that to contem-

[1] See *C.H.B.E.* VII, pt. II, 139–41, 215–7.
[2] *Parl. Pap.* 1868–9, XLVIII (307).
[3] *Parl. Pap.* 1870, XLII [38].   [4] 1865, I, 189, Bill 51.

poraries it represented little more than a scheme for colonial "coast-defence ships" and floating batteries. Obviously the colonies were not yet in a position to build large sea-going warships for themselves, and, even supposing they bought ships from Britain, they would have had few dockyards capable of maintaining them permanently in colonial waters. In the first instance the Act was clearly meant to apply to the Australian colonies, whose external trade was entirely oceanic, conducted, for the most part, over very great distances. The internal physical conditions of Australia, moreover, had tended to produce settlements on the coast and, therefore, a desire for naval defence both of trade and pastures. In 1867 Victoria commissioned a sloop in connection with the Maori war in New Zealand, which was the germ of the future Royal Australian Navy.

Considering the emphasis placed on the purely political conception of self-reliance, of which the Colonial Naval Defence Act was intended to be a further extension, it is remarkable that during the period 1815 to 1860 there was such a poverty of constructive thought on matters of imperial strategy. There seems little doubt that the apparent disregard and even contempt with which politicians treated naval and military opinion during this period was due to the lack of intellectual distinction in service circles for which the services themselves were largely to blame. In default of receiving useful and constructive advice from service experts, ministers and parliaments, faced with urgent problems, were bound to act for the best according to their own lights. No one could accuse the navy, with its well-known conservative traditions, of lethargy during the great transition of naval architecture, but its activity was confined almost entirely to changes in *matériel*. In the army, conditions of service were so closely bound up with social and economic affairs that under peace conditions it was extremely difficult for serving officers to advocate changes in policy and outlook. First and subsequent commissions were still matters of purchase, and the infantry were still armed with muzzle-loaders. In Parliament, moreover, the spectacle displayed by retired officers of both services wrangling over technicalities of *matériel* and administration must have confirmed the civilian reformers in the opinion that little help could be expected from them on wider issues. Looking through the military literature of the period one is struck by the absence of interest in the problems of imperial strategy. An isolated instance to the contrary is a crude but intelligent pamphlet published as early as 1848 advocating the seizure of strategic posts with a view to strengthening our commercial supremacy at sea which other nations were beginning to challenge. The Suez and Panama canals would be cut in the near future and we must hasten to consolidate our position both at Singapore and Labuan.[1]

[1] Faddy, Lt.-Col., *Essay on the Defence and Military System of Great Britain at Home and Abroad.*

One of the first requisites of progressive strategic thought is the existence of some medium for the exchange and discussion of opinions apart from the ordinary resources of the press. This was provided for in a certain measure by the *United Service Magazine*, which, from 1859 onwards, published some extremely stimulating articles on imperial defence problems. A more important and official development, however, was the appearance in 1857 of the *Journal of the United Service Institution*,[1] giving reports of its lectures and discussions as well as containing original articles. This was of special value, since it not only provided an official medium for the dissemination of new ideas about imperial strategy but also lessened the extraordinary intellectual barrier then existing between the services. In 1859, too, a step of the most far-reaching significance was taken by the creation of the Staff College for the army. For some years, however, the lectures and discussions at the United Service Institution tended to avoid major policy and to concentrate unnecessarily on purely technical matters. But considering that exalted personages were generally present in the chair as well as in the body of the meeting, it was obviously inadvisable for serving officers who valued their professional security to advance controversial opinions touching the higher direction of service policy. In fact, in view of the conditions governing the services at the time, it is surprising that any individual opinions were advanced at all. The existence of the invasion scare, however, stimulated discussion. Unlike the problems of *matériel*, then in process of solution by the navy, the various proposals for volunteers and fortifications directly touched the lives of the people and, therefore, achieved a wider publicity. In addition, it was beginning to be realised that recent advances in artillery would influence operations on land just as much as they were influencing operations at sea. Finally, there was the immediate prospect of the application of the breech-loading and rifling system to small arms, which would have an even greater influence on infantry tactics than that exerted by changes in artillery. From the point of view of the raising and training of volunteers and militia, consisting almost entirely of infantry, both at home and in the colonies, the small arms question was of paramount importance.[2]

In 1867 the report of a select committee on the army, including India and the colonies, was published, in which some interesting points arose concerning the strategic distribution of the imperial land forces.[3] Conflicting evidence was given as to the expediency of concentrating troops at home in order to be able to reinforce any particular colony.[4] The Duke of Cambridge, in opposing this sug-

[1] Now the Royal United Service Institution. The *United Service Magazine* was an entirely separate and unofficial production; see Bibliography.
[2] It is impossible within the scope of this chapter to discuss the important strategic issues raised by the increased power of land weapons.
[3] *Parl. Pap.* 1867, VII (478).
[4] *Ibid.* pp. 301–2, 344–5, 382–3, 391.

gestion, quoted the example of the Indian Mutiny when reinforcements were sent to India from the garrisons of the Cape, Mauritius and Ceylon, in much shorter time than sending them from home would have required. Substantial garrisons distributed throughout the Empire would, he claimed, form a better system for inter-imperial transfer and reinforcement than a single force concentrated at home, "so long as we have the command of the sea".[1] No emphasis, however, was laid on the fact that command of the sea was essential to *any* scheme involving the strategic movement of troops from one part of the Empire to another.

Meanwhile statesmen were considering the imperial possibilities arising from a European war in which the mother country might be engaged. "Nobody", wrote Lord Thring in 1865, "expected Canadian regiments to storm the Redan side by side with the English soldiers. Nobody hopes to see Australians or New Zealanders volunteer for service out of their own country."[2] "Nobody", wrote Morley, "believes that the presence of Australian representatives in the imperial assembly that voted funds would reconcile their constituents at the other side of the globe to paying money for a war, say, for the defence of Afghanistan against Russia or for the defence of Belgian neutrality."[3] "It is not likely, however, nowadays," wrote Dilke, in 1868, "that our colonists would, for any long stretch of time, engage to aid us in our purely European wars. Australia would scarcely feel herself deeply interested in the guarantee of Luxembourg, nor Canada in the affairs of Servia."[4] It would be difficult to find a less fortunate group of prophecies uttered by responsible men.

The first satisfactory and comprehensive statement of the problems of imperial defence was made by Sir John Colomb, an officer in the Royal Marine Artillery, who in 1867 published a remarkable pamphlet in which he laid down those general principles of imperial strategy which guide British defence policy to-day.[5] Ignoring local and technical issues, he treated the problems of imperial defence as a whole, both as regards territory and services. Seeking for some common essential on which to build his argument, he found it in commerce. Commerce, he asserted, is the link of empire; and the paralysis or even the interruption of it would bring us to our knees before a single foreign soldier landed on our soil. The navy and the army are intimately connected, and cannot be considered as being in separate strategic compartments. The navy is our shield; it is the first-line defence, and the last line of defence. The army is the spearhead of attack. In war, the navy's function must be to blockade the

[1] *Parl. Pap.* 1867, VII (478), 344–5.
[2] Thring, H., *Suggestions for Colonial Reform*, p. 23.
[3] Morley, J., *Critical Miscellanies*, III, 315.
[4] Dilke, C. W., *Greater Britain* (1868), II, 151.
[5] Colomb, J. *The Protection of our Commerce and the Distribution of our War Forces considered.*

enemy's ports, defeat his main forces, and thus hold the sea routes connecting the naval commercial bases of the Empire. In this way our own commerce can be automatically protected and the enemy's prevented. The rôle of the army must be to garrison India, and to protect naval bases and home ports from cruiser raids and small landing parties. But, in addition, the army must be used to reinforce imperial strategic bases lying along the lines of communication, and to act offensively from them against enemy territory. In this way the army can develop its attack under cover of the navy's defence of the bases and sea communications. It is utterly useless, therefore, to rely on land defence for isolated sections of imperial territory, unless their sea communications can be kept open, as, otherwise, not being self-sufficient, they would be starved out by blockade without ever being invaded. India alone, he considered, should be garrisoned in force; as regards Canada, our only other colony with a great land frontier, Britain would restrict her help to the protection of Canada's sea communications. The invasion of the United Kingdom must, therefore, be considered as possible only after we had already been defeated at sea, isolated, blockaded and starved into complete surrender. It would be an occupation rather than an invasion; not even the last act of the tragedy, but rather an epilogue.

It must not be supposed from this summary of his ideas that Colomb was in any way a fanatic. He was the founder of the "blue water school", but he recognised the army as the equal partner of the navy in a general system which should co-ordinate the work of both. It was chiefly his insistence on a correct appreciation of the proper function and distribution of the two forces which gave the false impression that he belittled the function of the army and led some of his supporters in after years to over-emphasise the function of the navy. In reality, his clear appreciation of the problem of function enabled him to allot the army a much more important rôle than had been suggested hitherto. As regards peace distribution, he laid down that it should depend on war possibilities with reference to the general welfare of the Empire.

Our system of maintaining strong forces in the Indian, Pacific and South Atlantic Oceans was such, he argued, that, in case of war with the United States, our peace distribution would merely require expansion. In case of a European war, however, it would require radical alteration and a concentration in home waters and the Mediterranean. Politically, we must seek alliance with the smaller maritime powers, so that even as neutrals the full use of their ports and coaling stations might be denied to an enemy. These arguments he developed and repeated in a subsequent series of lectures and pamphlets which formed the basis and inspiration for *Essays on Naval Defence*, written by his brother, Admiral Philip Colomb.

One of the most interesting points about the writings of the brothers Colomb is that they did not really say anything that was new. They merely disinterred the traditional doctrines of British strategy, as understood by such masters as Chatham, Spencer, St Vincent, Barham and Wellington, and presented them in terms of the mid-nineteenth century. By insisting on the vital character of imperial sea communications they showed the sea in its true relation to imperial affairs, that is to say, as a highway and not merely as a barrier, whereas in land warfare communications mean military communications and nothing more. In war the preservation of the imperial sea routes for purposes of commerce was to be coupled with the denial of the use of sea communications to the enemy, involving the defeat of the enemy's main forces in battle or the negation of their action by blockade. In addition to the battle fleet this would necessitate a cruiser force, capable, not only of preventing enemy commerce, but also of dealing with enemy raiders, especially in cases where the enemy refused action with his battle fleet and adopted a strategical defensive, as Germany did in the Great War. As we have shown in discussing the British adoption of steam, the strategy involved in executing such a policy presented no technical difficulties. It was neither necessary nor practicable, any more then than now, to ensure absolute command over all sea communications at all times, since normally the sea is uncommanded and in war the command is often in dispute.

As regards numerical and fighting strength the principle which gradually gained acceptance after the Crimean War was that the British fleet at its "average moment" should be superior to any possible combination of two other fleets at their "selected moment". This was known as the "two power standard" and was accepted as sufficient until the Naval Defence Act of 1889. As regards distribution, Sir John Colomb's observation that a European war would necessitate a concentration of force in home waters and the Mediterranean was clear enough and again presented no technical difficulties.

Thus, by the year 1870, the British Empire was equipped not only with a fleet and bases adequate for the main purposes of imperial defence, but also with a doctrine of imperial strategy suitable for its needs. With the exception of the garrison of India, the imperial army was now mainly concentrated at home, an arrangement which, with increased powers of steam, was becoming more suitable for imperial purposes and absolutely essential in case of a European war. The policy of the withdrawal of the garrisons, which bulked so large in the story, was not in itself unsound, and, as time advanced, certainly became sounder, although it was constantly advocated on grounds which were either unstrategic or strategically unsound. The reformers of naval and military administration, though often wrong in the practical application of their ideas, were certainly correct in principle and did much to keep the services in line with the changes taking place in other departments of government. In 1868 the accession to power of the Gladstone Ministry paved the way for the complete reorganisation of the army undertaken by Cardwell and the abolition of the purchase of commissions. As in the case of the navy, Colomb showed the army its true rôle in the system of imperial defence and so helped to produce a "common doctrine". As an advocate of the closest possible relations between the various parts of the Empire for purposes of defence, he became a keen supporter of the political conception of an imperial conference at which defence might be discussed. Russia, France and the United States continued to be cited as the chief sources of possible danger, but mercantile and industrial changes were still favouring the British Empire. In 1869 the Suez Canal was opened and a new phase in imperial strategy began, but one in which the principles laid down by Colomb remained unchanged.

CHAPTER XXIII

INTERNATIONAL LAW AND THE GROWTH OF THE EMPIRE, 1783–1870

I

THE termination of the American War of Independence left many outstanding questions to be settled between Great Britain, France and the United States. These questions involved boundary disputes and the rights of navigation and fishing off the coasts of British North America, and some of them were not finally disposed of for more than a century after the Treaty of Paris of 1783. Though relations between Great Britain and the United States were often strained almost to breaking point over these questions,[1] from 1814 war was avoided and an era of arbitration for the settlement of international disputes was inaugurated by the treaty of 1794 between the two countries. This treaty, known as the Jay Treaty, referred several matters to joint commissions, of which the one of chief interest related to the boundary between the possessions of Great Britain and the United States in the area described in the treaty of 1783 as the "St Croix river".[2] This matter the Commissioner settled and fixed a boundary. But other questions of a similar nature remained and the Treaty of Ghent, 1814, appointed Commissions to deal with the disputed sovereignty of islands in the Bay of Fundy and also the north-eastern boundary between the United States and Canada. The first of these was settled in 1817, but the second, known as the Maine Boundary question, proved much more troublesome. The two Commissioners appointed by the treaty could not agree and in 1828 the King of Holland was appointed arbitrator. The dispute raised an important question regarding the rights of the two countries where the boundary was in dispute. The boundary between Maine and British North America had been inadequately fixed by the treaty of 1783 and part of the territory in question was unoccupied in 1827 when the parties agreed to choose an arbiter. The United States contended, it would seem correctly, that such part of the territory as was only constructively in possession of Great Britain before 1783 could not be brought under its actual sovereignty so long as the validity of the title was in question.[3] In 1831 the King of Holland made an award, but as it was in the nature of a recommendation and not of a definite award, the United States resolved not to accept it and Great Britain did not insist. This case is often cited as an illustration of the rule

[1] See *C.H.B.E.* vi, 202, 203. [2] See *C.H.B.E.* i, 776 *seqq.*
[3] Hall, W. E., *International Law*, § 27; *British and Foreign State Papers*, 1827–8, pp. 490–585.

that an arbitral award is not obligatory if the arbitrator exceeds his jurisdiction.[1] The boundary question was not finally settled till 1842.

The famous dispute regarding the Oregon territory was settled by diplomacy and not by arbitration. Questions regarding the disputed matters of discovery, occupation and settlement were involved.[2] The Oregon territory was of vast extent, embracing some 600,000 square miles lying between the Rocky Mountains and the Pacific Ocean, and between 42° and 54°·40 N. Lat. The United States laid claim to the whole, and feeling in the United States ran so high that the slogan "Fifty-four forty or fight" was heard constantly. The grounds of the claim were prior discovery and settlement, the virtual recognition of the title of the United States by the restoration by Great Britain of Astoria under the Treaty of Ghent, 1814, and the acquisition under the treaty of 1819 of Spanish rights derived from discovery. These grounds were controverted by the British Government who, besides relying on discovery and settlement, pointed out that the treaty of 1814 made an express reservation of British claims. The controversy ended in a compromise, the Treaty of Washington, 1846, providing that the boundary should follow the 49th degree of north latitude to "the middle of the channel which separates the continent from Vancouver's Island" and should proceed thence southerly "through the middle of said channel". A difference of views then arose regarding the channel referred to, there being two channels, between which lay the island of San Juan and other islands. The matter was finally settled by the Treaty of Washington, 1871, by which the question was referred to the arbitration of the German Emperor, whose decision was given in favour of the United States.[3]

The claim of Spain to territories on the north-west of America and to the exclusive rights of sovereignty, navigation and commerce in the territories, coast and seas in that part of the world was raised in relation to the Nootka Sound in 1790.[4] A lengthy controversy ensued in which Spain limited the claim to continents and islands which belong to the King "so far as discoveries have been made and secured by treaties and immemorial possession and uniformly acquiesced in". The claims were thus based not only on discovery but on immemorial possession. The facts were disputed by the British Government, especially that of valid occupation of the great extent of territory claimed, namely Vancouver Island and British Columbia. The Spanish claim to block British colonisation in territories beyond those occupied and settled on the Pacific coast was strongly resisted

[1] Lauterpacht, H., *The Function of Law in the International Community* (1933), pp. 127–30.
[2] See *C.H.B.E.* I, 185; VI, 549.
[3] Moore, J. B., *International Arbitration*, vol. I, chap. VII. On the Oregon controversy in general see Twiss, Sir Travers, *The Oregon Question*; Hall, W. E., *International Law*, § 33; Moore, J. B., *Digest of International Law*, §§ 80, 81, 104, 835.
[4] *V. supra*, pp. 29–31.

by Pitt. Under the Convention finally signed between Great Britain and Spain on 28 October 1790, navigation and fishing in the Pacific were declared open to British subjects, except within 10 leagues of the coast occupied by Spain, and existing settlements of Spaniards on the Pacific coast were to be respected. Thus another and almost final blow was given to Spanish claims over unoccupied territories in America.[1]

Before leaving these legal questions relating to the boundaries of British territories in North America reference must be made to the controversy regarding the navigation of the River St Lawrence. The development of the modern law of nations governing the navigation and use of international rivers may be said to date from the peace settlement of 1814–15. The Scheldt and the Rhine were opened to international navigation by the Treaty of Paris, 1814 (Art. 5) and the Powers represented at the Congress of Vienna, 1815, declared that "those States which are separated or traversed by the same navigable river engage to regulate by common consent all matters relating to the navigation of this river" (Art. 108 of the Final Act of the Congress of Vienna). Great Britain and the United States have contributed to the development of the law of fluvial navigation, but the policies of the two countries have been based on different principles. To-day it is generally recognised that apart from express agreement there is no legal right of navigation of an international river by other states, but the upper riparian state may be said to have an "imperfect" right to such navigation, which requires a treaty to regulate its exercise. The British standpoint has been the insistence of the right of navigation as a conventional right, i.e. one requiring a definite agreement; the United States has claimed that the upper riparian has a natural or moral right to freedom of navigation to the sea. The latter also urged that one nation has a right to trade with another with its consent, thus opening the way for freedom of navigation of international rivers to non-riparians.[2] These principles were to be seen in the claim by the United States to navigate the St Lawrence to the sea. Great Britain controlled the land on both sides of the lower part of this river and refused to open the river to the United States unless satisfactory compensation was forthcoming. Jefferson had used the argument with regard to the Mississippi that the basis of the "natural" right was "a sentiment written in deep characters on the heart of man" and that the closing of the river by a lower riparian to an upper riparian was an act of force by a stronger society against a weaker, condemned by the judgments of mankind. Similar arguments were used in regard to the St Lawrence towards Great Britain

[1] C.H.B.F.P. I, 197–201; Phillimore, Sir R., International Law, vol. I, §§ 176, 188; Halleck, H. W., International Law (4th ed.), I, 498.
[2] See Bacon, R., "British and American Policy and the Right of Fluvial Navigation", British Year Book of International Law, 1932, pp. 76–92.

whose Government was only prepared to concede the right of navigation by express agreement on terms. By Article 4 of the Reciprocity Treaty of 5 June 1854 freedom of navigation was granted to the inhabitants of the United States to navigate the River St Lawrence and the canals in Canada used as a means of communicating between the Great Lakes and the Atlantic Ocean on payment of the same tolls as British subjects. This treaty was terminated in 1866, but by the Treaty of Washington, 1871 (Art. 26) complete freedom "for the purposes of commerce" was granted to the citizens of the United States, subject to laws and regulations of Great Britain and Canada, and at the same time freedom of navigation for purposes of commerce of the rivers Yukon, Porcupine and Stikine in Alaska, which had just been acquired by purchase from Russia, was granted to British subjects.[1] Great Britain had acquired rights of navigation of the Columbia River by treaty of 1846.

The Great Lakes of North America, Ontario, Erie, Huron and Superior, were divided between the contracting parties by the Treaty of Paris, 1783, the boundary being fixed as running through the middle of the lakes and of the waterways connecting them. The water on either side of the boundary is under the exclusive jurisdiction of the respective countries. Navigation on these lakes, excepting the coasting trade, is open to British and American citizens. Lake Michigan lies wholly within the territory of the United States but by the Treaty of Washington 1871 (Art. 28) the navigation of this lake was open to British subjects.

During the war of 1812–14 the Great Lakes were the theatre of naval warfare and captures thereon were held to be governed by the law of naval prize.[2] After the war was over the British Government was considering an increase of naval forces on the Great Lakes, but was approached by the Government of the United States with a view to limiting the naval armaments which each state should keep on them. After some negotiations Lord Castlereagh instructed the Hon. Charles Bagot, the British Minister at Washington, to enter into such an agreement. This was effected by exchange of notes on 28 and 29 April 1817 between Mr Bagot and Mr Rush. The agreement provided that the naval forces to be maintained upon the American Lakes by the two Powers should be henceforth confined to the following vessels on each side, on Lake Ontario one vessel, not exceeding 100 tons burden and armed with one 18-pound cannon, on the upper lakes two vessels of the same size and armament and on Lake Champlain to one vessel of the same size and armament. That is, four small vessels on the whole of the Great Lakes. All other armed vessels were to be at once dismantled and no other vessel

---

[1] See VI, 645, 647.
[2] See cases cited by Lord Sterndale, P., in his judgment in *Craft captured on Victoria Nyanza*, 3 *Brit. and Col. Prize Cases*, p. 295.

of war to be built or armed there. The agreement to cease to be binding after six months notice given by either party. President Monroe communicated the agreement to the Senate in 1818, which approved and consented to it, and it was formally proclaimed by the President on 28 April 1818. During the American Civil War (1861–5) the United States gave notice to terminate the agreement, but before the six months had elapsed the notice was withdrawn.

Agreements between states are made by means of treaties or conventions, though sometimes, as in the present case, the less formal exchange of notes is resorted to. It is unusual for a subject of so great importance to be settled in this way and for the settlement to remain for so long as that under consideration. The Rush-Bagot agreement is in harmony with, and was the precursor for, the management of the frontier between British North America and the United States, which, for the whole of its 3000 miles, has no fortresses or military works. The arrangement of 1817 still holds good, though, since the making of the canals connecting the Great Lakes with the sea, one of the reasons for the prohibition to build and arm vessels of war on the lakes has disappeared.[1] The Rush-Bagot Convention is sometimes, but erroneously, stated to have neutralised the Great Lakes. The legal position resulting from the agreement is rather in the nature of a negative servitude, though it must be admitted that the conception of international servitudes is a controversial one.[2] Neutralisation as applied to waterways is best illustrated by the provisions relating to the Suez Canal whereby no act of war may take place in the Canal or within three miles from either end,[3] and there is nothing of this nature in the agreement between Great Britain and the United States. The Rush-Bagot agreement is an admirable example of how armaments may be reduced where there is good-will on both sides. By a somewhat similar arrangement to the Rush-Bagot agreement Lord Palmerston, in 1850, acceded to the request of the United States for the cession of a portion of Horseshoe Reef near the outlet of Lake Erie for the erection of a lighthouse on the condition that the Government of the United States engaged to erect such a lighthouse and maintain a light therein, and that no fortifications were erected on the Reef. The lighthouse was erected in 1856.[4]

When a portion of a state secedes from the parent state and obtains recognition of independence, the rights of the inhabitants of the new state as regards the parent are those only which belong to any other

---

[1] Callahan, J. M., *The Neutrality of the American Lakes*; Moore, J. B., *Digest*, § 143; Hunt, H. E., "How the Great Lakes became high seas", *Am. Journ. of Int. Law*, v, 285; *C.H.B.F.P.* II, 223.

[2] See Judgment of the Permanent Court of International Justice in the case of *Wimbledon* (Series A, No. 1, p. 24).

[3] Suez Canal, 1888, Arts. 1, 4, 5, 6. Westlake points out that the term "neutralisation" is not strictly apposite, since neutrality does not admit the passage of belligerent forces across the territory. (*Peace*, p. 347.) "Demilitarisation" is more appropriate.

[4] Moore, J. B., *op. cit.* 1, 554.

independent state, except in so far as they may be modified or enlarged by conventional stipulation between the parent and the newly recognised state. We have seen how far this proposition was borne out in the relations between the United States and Great Britain in regard to the navigation of the St Lawrence, but disputes between the two states regarding fishery rights off the coasts of Newfoundland, which arose out of concessions made by Great Britain in the Treaty of Paris 1783 raised this and other difficult questions of international law.[1] By that treaty the inhabitants of the United States were granted rights of fishing on the Grand Bank and other banks of Newfoundland and the coasts of Newfoundland, in the Gulf of St Lawrence and on the coasts, bays and creeks of other British possessions in North America as well as the right to land and dry nets and cure fish in unsettled bays, creeks and harbours of Nova Scotia, the Magdalen Islands and Labrador so long as they remained unsettled. After the war of 1812–14 a dispute arose as to whether these concessions had been abrogated by the war. Great Britain contended that this was the result of the war and the inhabitants of the United States were forbidden to exercise the privileges specified in the Treaty of Paris. After several years of discussion[2] a new treaty was made in 1818 conceding to the inhabitants of the United States liberty to fish off the southern coast of Newfoundland and on the western and northern coasts within defined limits, also on the shores of the Magdalen Islands and the southern coast of Labrador to and through the Straits of Belle Isle (saving the rights of the Hudson's Bay Company). Further, they gained the right to land and dry nets and cure fish on unsettled bays, but, after they were settled, only with the consent of the inhabitants and owners of the soil. The position taken up by the United States was legally indefensible and the rights of fishing were accepted as having been acquired by agreement.[3]

Negotiations for further extension of these rights, but on a mutual basis, were begun in 1849 at the instance of Canada, and in 1854 the Reciprocity Treaty of that year was signed. Further concessions were granted to United States citizens and to British subjects along the eastern coast of the United States north of 36° N. Lat., certain kinds of fishing (e.g. salmon) being excepted. This treaty expired in 1866 and the parties were sent back to that of 1818. The Treaty of Washington, 1871, again regulated the matter with further concessions by the United States. The privileges granted by Great Britain were found by a Commission to be considerably greater than those conceded by the United States and a sum of five and a half million dollars was awarded to Great Britain in compensation.[4] Newfound-

---

[1] See *C.H.B.E* I, 264, 542–3, 778, and VI, 134–8, 673–9.
[2] *B.F.S.P.*, VII (1818–19), 79–97.
[3] Hall, W. E., *op. cit.* § 27.
[4] See *C.H.B.E.* VI, 672–3.

land had received the grant of responsible government in 1855, and difficulties constantly arose under its municipal regulations with respect to the exercise of the rights granted to American fishermen. The whole matter was finally referred to the Hague Tribunal which settled the dispute by an award in 1910 which was, with some modifications, embodied in a treaty of 20 July 1912.[1]

Another fishery dispute between Great Britain and France arose out of the provisions of the Treaty of Utrecht, 1713, whereby Newfoundland was recognised as belonging to Great Britain. The French then gained certain rights of fishing off the coasts of New-foundland and of landing for the purpose of drying their nets and curing the fish. These privileges were renewed by the Treaties of Paris, 1763, and Versailles, 1783. By the latter treaty Great Britain undertook to prevent competition with the French and to cause any settlements erected within the "French shore" in Newfoundland to be removed. After 1855 the Newfoundland Government raised considerable difficulties as to the meaning of the Articles in the treaty of 1783 both as regards the kinds of fish to be caught and the pro-hibition of settlements within the area. The dispute was only finally settled by the Anglo-French Convention of 1904 whereby the French abandoned these exclusive rights and retained rights of fishing on terms of equality with the Newfoundland fishermen.[2]

A state is under a primary duty of respecting the independence of other states and of refraining from doing any act which violates them. But if its safety is gravely imperilled by acts done within the territory of another state, whose government either does not or is unable to prevent them, it is recognised that the threatened state may take such action as may be necessary to protect itself even though in so doing the independence of the other state may be compromised. Such action is not hostile in its character as it is not directed against the state itself. The rebellion in Canada in 1837 gave rise to such an incident in the case of the *Caroline*.[3] A body of insurgents collected in American territory, forcibly seized arms from an American arsenal and seized an island in American territory above the Falls of Niagara and fired shots into Canadian territory. They also made preparations to cross over to Canada in a small steamer, the *Caroline*. A party of British troops crossed the river and cut her out from her moorings and sent her adrift down the Falls of Niagara. The Government of the United States complained of this violation of territory and a discussion ensued. Lord Ashburton, the British Minister, tendered an apology. Mr Webster, the United States Secretary of State, admitted that while "exceptions growing out of the great law of self-defence do exist, these exceptions should be confined to cases in which that

---

[1] Wilson G. G., *The Hague Arbitration Cases*, pp. 135–205; Scott, J. B., *Hague Court Reports*, pp. 195–225; Pitt Cobbett, *Leading Cases in International Law* (5th ed.), i, 152–8. [2] *C.H.B.F.P.* iii, 312.   [3] See *C.H.B.E.* vi, 269.

necessity of self-defence is instant, overwhelming, and leaving no choice of means, and no moment for deliberation". It is now generally admitted that the facts in this case satisfied these requirements.[1] The British operations against Denmark in 1807, resulting from the demand of the British Government for the surrender into British custody of their fleet, are also defended on the same principle.[2]

The nineteenth century witnessed the first application of principles of international law to interoceanic artificial waterways necessitated by the opening of the Suez Canal in 1869. Great Britain took a leading part in formulating those rules which, however, did not become incorporated in an international convention until 1888. Meantime, the possibility of the making of an interoceanic canal connecting the Atlantic and Pacific Oceans either across the Isthmus of Panama or through Nicaragua was under discussion between Great Britain and the United States. The latter involved British interests, not only because of the proximity of Jamaica and other British islands in the West Indies, but also by reason of the fact of British claims over the Moskito territory, through which the river San Juan, the proposed Atlantic end of the Canal, enters the Caribbean Sea. The Moskito Coast was under the general supervision of the British authorities at Belize in British Honduras and was organised as a Colonial Government in 1836. The story of the Moskito Coast[3] and of the relations between Great Britain and Spain whereby the former acquired a territorial possession in Central America is a complicated one and the negotiations with the United States were frequently jeopardised by the political situation in that country and by fear of British violation of the Monroe Doctrine as it had been set forth in somewhat exaggerated terms by President Polk. Meantime, the United States negotiated a treaty in 1848 with New Granada (afterwards the Republic of Colombia) whereby the latter granted the former exclusive right of transport across the Isthmus of Panama while the United States guaranteed to New Granada her possessions in the Isthmus. One means of working the traffic across the Isthmus was thus guaranteed to the United States, and a railway was built by American capital and opened in 1855. The negotiations for a treaty with Great Britain took a more favourable turn when Palmerston acceded to the American proposals that Great Britain should join in guaranteeing the neutrality of the projected canal, at the same time he quieted the fears of the Americans by disclaiming any intention of forming British Colonies in Central America. Sir Henry Bulwer had recently been appointed British Minister at Washington and he and John M. Clayton, the Secretary of State, negotiated and on 19 April

[1] Hyde, C. C., *International Law*, vol. I, § 66; Hall, W. E., *op. cit.* § 83; Westlake, J., *Peace*, p. 313; Moore, J. B., *Digest*, II, 409–11.

[2] Hall, W. E., *op. cit.* § 83 and authorities cited; Rose, J. H., article in *Transactions of R. Hist. Soc.* (1906).

[3] See *C.H.B.E.* I, 383–4; and *Archives of British Honduras*, ed. Sir J. Burdon, vol. II.

1850 signed a treaty which is generally cited as the Clayton-Bulwer Treaty.[1] The object of the treaty as stated in the preamble was to set forth the views and intentions of the parties "with reference to any means of communication by ship canal which may be constructed between the Atlantic and Pacific Oceans by way of the river San Juan de Nicaragua and either or both of the Lakes of Nicaragua and to any port or place on the Pacific Ocean". The Governments of the contracting parties declared that neither of them would ever obtain or maintain for itself exclusive control over such ship canal or erect or maintain fortifications commanding the same or occupy or fortify or colonise or assume or exercise any dominion over Nicaragua, Costa Rica, the Moskito Coast or any part of Central America (Art. i). It was also agreed that vessels of the contracting parties in case of war between them should be exempt from blockade, detention or capture by either of the belligerents and that this provision should extend to such distance from the ends of the canal as might be established. Furthermore they agreed to protect the canal from interruption, seizure or unjust confiscation and to guarantee its neutrality "so that the said canal may for ever be open and free" (Art. v). Other states were to be invited to enter into stipulations with the contracting parties similar to those entered into with each other (Art. vi). Article viii contained a general stipulation stating that as the contracting parties not only desired to accomplish a particular object, but also to establish a general principle, they thereby agreed to extend their protection by treaty stipulations to any other practicable communications whether by canal or railway across the isthmus and especially to the interoceanic communications then proposed to be established by the way of Tehuantepec or Panama.

It was unfortunate that so many of the treaties between Great Britain and the United States seemed fated to give rise to further disputes owing to differences of construction, and this was the case with the Clayton-Bulwer Treaty. Though Clayton definitely accepted Bulwer's reservation that renunciation of territorial interests did not apply to British Honduras, he declined to affirm or deny the British title in their settlement or its alleged dependencies.[2] Considerable discussion took place during the following years as to the Moskito Coast, and as to a group of islands in the Bay of Honduras known as the Bay Islands which, in the eighteenth century, had from time to time been occupied by British forces. The situation was further exacerbated by the bombardment in 1852 by a warship of the United States navy of Greytown, then held by a force of Nicaraguan filibusters.[3] The whole matter was finally settled by a series of

---

[1] See *C.H.B.F.P.* ii, 265–9.

[2] See Moore, J. B., *op. cit.* iii, 137, for text of declaration of Sir H. Bulwer and letter of Mr Clayton.

[3] For cases arising out of the bombardment of Greytown see Wheaton, H., *International Law* (Dana's edition), p. 145 note; and *Archives of British Honduras*, vol. ii.

treaties negotiated by Sir Charles Lennox Wyke with the Central American Republics. That with Honduras was signed on 28 November 1859, whereby Great Britain recognised the sovereignty of the Republic of Honduras over the Bay Islands and the Moskito Coast and provision was made for a mixed commission to investigate the claims of British subjects arising out of grants, leases or otherwise. The Clayton-Bulwer Treaty was replaced on 5 February 1900 by the Hay-Pauncefote Treaty without impairing the general principle of neutralisation established in Art. viii of that Convention. This general principle had been adopted in the Suez Canal Convention of 1888.[1]

It is now admitted that the right of visit and search is essentially a belligerent right and can only be exercised in time of peace in exceptional cases under the provision of treaty stipulations or for the suppression of piracy or in self-defence. The claim of Great Britain during the Napoleonic wars to visit and search for British seamen on board neutral vessels, both public and private, for the impressment of seamen of British birth found on such vessels was a cause of serious friction with the United States, and was one of the factors which contributed to the outbreak of war in 1812 between the two countries. The principle of the English Common Law as regards nationality was summed up in the maxim *nemo potest exuere patriam* and the rule that naturalisation in a foreign country without the King's consent did not effect a change in the nationality of a British subject was the law until 1870.[2] This doctrine of the inalienability of British allegiance led to the questionable claims of the British Government during the Napoleonic wars to search neutral vessels, public and private, and to remove from them British seamen for service in the British Navy even though such persons had been naturalised in the United States. The accidental killing of an American seaman by a British warship off New York in 1806 while performing the duty of search and impressment raised a ferment in the United States and while negotiations for settlement of the case were taking place in England and a treaty had been agreed upon the whole situation was further aggravated by another serious incident. Seamen having deserted from H.M.S. *Leopard* and enlisted on the U.S.S. *Chesapeake*, the former cruised off the American coast and awaited the *Chesapeake*. Having met the latter outside American waters the captain of the *Leopard* demanded the surrender of the seamen; this was refused. The *Leopard* fired two broadsides and the American vessel yielded and several deserters were removed and the *Chesapeake* returned to port with a loss of three

---

[1] Moore, J. B., *op. cit.* p. 181. On the whole subject of the Clayton-Bulwer Treaty and subsequent events, see *C.H.B.F.P.* II, 265–78; Moore, J. B., *op. cit.* pp. 130–209; Arias, H., *The Panama Canal* (1911).

[2] The Law of the United States at this time was similar (*The People* v. *Isaac Williams*, 1799; Scott, J. B., *Leading Cases in International Law*, pp. 134, 158). In 1868 Congress passed an Act declaring expatriation to be "a natural and inherent right of all people".

killed and eighteen wounded. The British Government at once expressed regret, offered immediate reparations, and recalled the Admiral in command of the station. At the same time it issued a proclamation recalling all British seamen from foreign service and, while maintaining the right to remove them from foreign merchant ships, limited the right of British commanders to making a requisition to the commanders of foreign warships for the delivery of British sailors on board and failing compliance therewith they were ordered to report the matter to the Government or to British ministers in neutral courts. A special British mission was sent to America to endeavour to arrange matters, but as the United States Government was desirous of obtaining at the same time the removal of various hardships on their commerce due to the enforcement of the British Orders-in-Council issued in reply to Napoleon's Milan and Berlin decrees, and the British Government was slow in making concessions, the United States declared war in June 1812, before news of the concessions reached Washington.

The Treaty of Ghent, which ended the war in 1814,[1] is silent on its causes, but shortly afterwards negotiations on the subject of impressment were opened between the two Governments. A draft treaty was prepared in which the British Government gave up the right of impressment on the seas. The British proposed that all seamen who were to be considered Americans were to be naturalised before the signature of the treaty, the United States delegates pressed for the date of the ratification of the treaty. The negotiations broke down in 1818 on this trivial difference, but it may be asserted that no English jurist will be found to-day to assert the right of search for British sailors on foreign ships of war or merchant ships. From the point of view of international law the British claim was indefensible, though there were analogous cases in which the removal of alien enemies from neutral merchant ships was a common practice; this was subsequently limited by treaties to the removal of persons in the service of the enemy.[2] The British claim was based on municipal law and was an assertion of a right to exercise jurisdiction on board ships of another nation outside its territorial limits. It could not be justified on the ground that neutral vessels carrying British seamen were violating their neutrality, for none of these vessels was captured and taken before a Prize Court for condemnation on that ground. The only extenuation possible for this action was that the rules of maritime international law were not so well settled as now and that the need for men for the British navy had never been greater. The British authorities were also exasperated by the inducements held out to

---

[1] On the subject of impressment of seamen see Walker, T. A., *Science of International Law*, pp. 124–30; Manning, W. O., *Law of Nations*, p. 456; Wheaton, H., *International Law* (Dana's edition), §§ 108, 9, and note on p. 175; Moore, J. B., *Digest*, ii, §§ 317–20; *C.H.B.F.P.* i, 522–6, 540–2.

[2] See the case of *The Trent, infra*, p. 869.

British sailors to desert and take service on American vessels on more favourable terms, a practice which was not wholly extinct a century later.[1] But these excuses cannot be accepted as justification for the British claims, which were not based on the custom of nations, and in the case of search of neutral warships involved the violation of the flag of a friendly power. Such claims have now been abandoned and the King's Regulations and Admiralty Instructions state that "His Majesty's Officers are not authorised to send on board a foreign ship to take from her any British seamen against the will of the foreign commander". (1906 ed., Art. 404.)

Another subject of great importance in international law which was a source of friction between Great Britain and the United States and other states was the suppression of the slave trade which involved the right of search by warships of foreign vessels suspected of being engaged in this trade. The public conscience of the world for a long time both permitted and encouraged this ignoble traffic, but towards the end of the eighteenth century public opinion was moving towards its suppression. Between 1792 and 1815 Denmark, Great Britain, the United States, Portugal, Holland, Sweden and France prohibited the traffic. A Declaration signed on 8 February 1815 at Vienna by the Plenipotentiaries of the eight signatory Powers of the Treaty of Paris, 1814 (Annex xv) condemned the slave trade and stated the desire of the signatories to take steps to put an end to its existence. But these exalted sentiments are somewhat chilled by the following pronouncement that such steps can only be taken having regard to the interests and customs of their subjects and that the date for the final termination of the trade should be a matter of negotiation between the Powers.[2] This declaration was not reached without considerable difficulty, Spain, for example, urging that the abolition of the slave trade would ruin her colonies.

The chief difficulty in the way of enforcing the abolition of the slave trade lay in the need for a maritime police to supervise the sea-traffic in the affected areas. This could not be successfully carried out unless the right of visit and search were conceded to cruisers engaged in this work. A case which came before Lord Stowell in 1817[3] in which a British naval officer seized a French ship off the coast of West Africa and sought to obtain condemnation of the vessel on the ground that she was engaged in the slave trade against French laws was decided against the officer. Lord Stowell held that the slave trade was not piracy by international law and that the right of visit and search was essentially a war-right, apart from piracy, and could only be exercised by a warship over a foreign merchant ship by treaty. The Supreme Court of the United States delivered a judgment on the same lines in 1825.[4] Except on the part of Great Britain attempts

---

[1] Walker, T. A., *Science of International Law*, p. 124.   [2] *B.F.S.P.*, III, 971.
[3] *The Le Louis*, 2 Dodson, 210.   [4] *The Antelope* (10 Wheaton, 66).

to suppress the slave trade were of a very half-hearted character. Nothing but the right of search would avail and this was difficult to obtain. Between 1833 and 1839 Great Britain negotiated treaties giving her the right of search with Spain, Hayti, Uruguay, Venezuela, Bolivia, Argentina, Mexico, Texas and the Hanse Towns. In 1841 the Quintuple Treaty with France, Austria, Prussia and Russia gave each state a mutual right of search. The British policy was to assimilate the slave trade to piracy, but other states were unwilling to accept the consequences of this treatment. The United States and France were especially strong in their opposition to this point of view, and, though France had signed the Quintuple Treaty, the opposition in the Chamber of Deputies was sufficiently strong to prevent its ratification. As regards the other signatory and ratifying Powers the treaty was a success for British diplomacy, though it did not go so far as to assimilate the slave trade to piracy, and vessels captured on suspicion of being engaged in the trade were sent before the Courts of their respective countries. Portugal conceded the right of search in 1842. Negotiations with the United States were less successful, the British desire for visit and search, though on a mutual basis, was felt to be a menace to the freedom of the seas as understood in the United States. The fact that slaves who in any way managed to reach British territory were free was a further source of friction, as slavery was still lawful in the Southern States of the Union. Though the slave trade was condemned by American Law, it continued to flourish under the United States flag until after the outbreak of the Civil War in 1861, though by the Webster-Ashburton Treaty of 1842 provision was made for the joint operations of British and American cruisers off the coast of Africa and Cuba for the suppression of the trade (Arts. viii and ix). By an additional convention (17 February 1863) the area of operations was extended to the coasts of Madagascar, Porto Rico and Santo Domingo. But these articles were not in practice enforced and it was not till after the abolition of slavery in the United States in 1863 that co-operation became possible. A treaty of 7 April 1862 provided for the trial of suspected vessels by mixed tribunals at Sierra Leone, the Cape of Good Hope and New York.[1] These Courts were replaced by those of the respective tribunals of the contracting powers by a treaty of 30 June 1870.

The chief difficulty in reaching an agreement with the United States was the opposition of the latter to the exercise of the right of visit and search in peace time by British cruisers. The renunciation of this claim was made by Great Britain in 1858.[2] One result of the agreement was that between 1859-60 and 1864-5 the slave trade of Cuba dwindled from 30,000 in the former year to 143 in the latter. Meantime negotiations between Great Britain and France continued

---

[1] *C.H.B.F.P.* II, 514.
[2] For text of Lord Malmesbury's statement see Moore, J. B., *op. cit.* II, 945.

and a Convention was entered into on 29 May 1845, which, while not recognising the right of visit, allowed ships of the two squadrons to notify the presence of suspicious vessels to warships of the other which were flying their flag. The right provided for was that of verification of the flag which did not include the further right of search. The Anglo-French Treaty of 1845 was not renewed at the expiration of ten years when it terminated, and the proceedings of the British and French vessels engaged in the suppression of the slave trade were regulated by confidential instructions given by the naval authorities to their respective naval commanders. But the jealousy of France for the rights of their flag was a considerable drawback to the suppression of this nefarious trade. After the General Act of the Conference of Berlin concerning the Congo (1884–5) and the Anti-slavery Act of Brussels, 2 July 1890, more serious concerted action was taken by the Signatory Powers, though France still maintained her traditional attitude as regards her flag and did not ratify the Convention of 1890.[1] The slave trade, since these treaties, now stands condemned by the conventional law of nations.

The chief means by which Powers have acquired territory occupied by aboriginal inhabitants have been occupation, conquest and cession. Thus Spain and Portugal conquered and annexed vast territories in the American continent and the Spice Islands. In North America British acquisitions were made in a similar manner, the rights of the natives being ignored with certain honourable exceptions as that of Penn. In Asia, where the peoples were in a more advanced state of civilisation, it will be found that colonial acquisitions had been generally made by conquest or cession from native rulers. In Africa treaties with native rulers were not infrequently made, the purport of which very frequently was unknown or unintelligible to the native chiefs. Australia was considered a *res nullius* and acquired by occupation, having no settled inhabitants or settled law when it was annexed.[2] The acquisition of New Zealand was based on cession by the chiefs; Queen Victoria disclaimed every pretension to seize the islands of New Zealand or to govern them as part of the dominions of Great Britain, unless the free and intelligent consent of the natives, expressed according to their established usages, was first obtained.[3]

The treatment of the aboriginal inhabitants of the newly discovered countries and of territories subsequently opened up to colonisation has been already mentioned,[4] but the later development of the relationship of civilised states with the primitive inhabitants of the

[1] Gidel, G., *Le Droit international public de la Mer*, I, 989–410 (with bibliography); C.H.B.F.P. II, 220, 235, 244; Moore, J. B., *Digest*, II, 914–51; C.M.H. x, 19.
[2] *Cooper* v. *Stuart* (1889), 14 App. Ca, at p. 291.
[3] See despatch of 1839 in *Parl. Pap.* 1840, xxxiii (238), cited by Lindley, M. F., *The Acquisition and Government of Backward Territory*, p. 41; C.H.B.E. vii, pt. ii, 25, and *Naval Miscellanies* (Navy Rec. Soc. Pubns lxiii), iii, 348, 353.
[4] See C.H.B.E. i, 191, 544.

American and African Continents calls for further examination and is closely connected with the attempts to suppress the slave trade. To Great Britain is due the greatest credit for the movement which, though slow in its action, led to international co-operation in the later years of the nineteenth century to deal with the problems arising from the contact of civilised and uncivilised peoples. In England the names of William Wilberforce, Thomas Clarkson, Zachary Macaulay and Thomas Fowell Buxton will always be honourably associated with the early stages of the movement. The abolition of slavery throughout the British Empire was effected in 1833.[1] In 1835 there was formed in England a British and Foreign Aborigines Protection Society which worked in union with an anti-slavery society. Largely through the influence of Thomas Fowell Buxton, M.P., a select Committee of the House of Commons on Aboriginal Tribes was appointed in 1835. The scope of the Committee was to consider what measures ought to be adopted with regard to the native inhabitants of countries where British settlements are made, and to the neighbouring tribes, in order to secure to them the observance of justice and the protection of their rights. The Committee reported in 1837.[2] The disastrous consequences to uncivilised peoples of intercourse with Europeans were portrayed in striking language and the Committee urged that Great Britain should take the lead in a movement to make the contact between the civilised and uncivilised races a benefit to both and a means of increasing their mutual welfare. The Committee made a series of proposals by which British policy regarding aborigines should be governed in the future, based on a principle of trusteeship, a principle which was also enunciated by Chief Justice Marshall in 1831 regarding the relations of the United States to the Indians in their territory.[3] It is not too much to say that these principles have been those which have guided the British Government during the nineteenth century. The difficulties in protecting native races from demoralising influences such as the importation of alcoholic liquors and firearms have been largely due to lack of international co-operation, remedies for which only began to be found by international conferences such as those of Berlin and Brussels in 1885 and 1890.[4]

Two factors, totally unconnected with each other, played important parts in the formulation of principles of American policy which were enunciated by President James Monroe in his message to the United States Congress on 2 December 1823, and which have become known as the Monroe Doctrine. The first was a claim advanced by Russia, then in occupation of Alaska, to exclusive rights over parts of North

[1] *Vide supra*, chapter IX.   [2] *Parl. Pap.* 1837, VII (425), 82.
[3] *Cherokee Nation and The State of Georgia*, 5 Peters 17.
[4] Snow, A. H., *The Question of Aborigines in the Law and Practice of Nations*, A Report to the U.S. Dept. of State, 1919; Lindley, M. F., *The Acquisition and Government of Backward Territory in International Law*.

America and the Behring Sea down to the 51st degree of North latitude. This position was contested by the United States and by Great Britain, and the United States claimed that the American continents were no longer subjects for any new European establishments. The second factor was that the Holy Alliance was known to be considering the question of intervening in South America on behalf of Spain against her revolted colonies.

On the first subject Monroe's message stated that "the American continents...are henceforth not to be considered as future subjects for colonisation by any European Power" and that "with the existing colonies or dependencies of any European Power we have not interfered, and shall not interfere". The former proposition which involved the consequence that the whole of the continents of America was actually in the possession of civilised Powers was demonstrably incapable of proof, the matter was one of political geography. The doctrine was unacceptable to Great Britain. "We cannot acknowledge the right of any power to proclaim such a principle; much less to bind other countries to the observance of it" said Canning[1] in conversation with the American Minister. Later, on 20 June 1824, in a formal protocol the British Government said: "The British Plenipotentiaries assert in utter denial of the above principle, that they considered the unoccupied parts of America just as much open as heretofore to colonisation by Great Britain, as well as by other European Powers, agreeably to the Convention of 1790 between the British and Spanish Governments, and that the United States would have no right whatever to take umbrage at the establishment of new colonies from Europe in any such parts of the American continent."[2] This part of the message has become known as the Non-colonisation principle. The second part of Monroe's doctrine, which has been called the Non-intervention principle, was as follows: "With the Governments who have declared their independence and maintained it, and whose independence we have, on great consideration and on just principles acknowledged, we could not view any interposition for the purpose of oppressing them or controlling in any other manner their destiny, by any European Power, in any other light than as the manifestation of an unfriendly disposition toward the United States." This doctrine of non-intervention of European Powers in American affairs was preceded in the message by a doctrine of non-intervention by the United States in European affairs: "In the wars of the European Powers, in matters relating to themselves, we have never taken any part, nor does it comport with our policy so to do", which is the embodiment of the policy of no "entangling alliances" laid down by Washington and Jefferson. With this latter part of the message we have no further concern, but the non-colonisation and non-intervention doctrines relating to America were invoked by the

[1] See Perkins, Dexter, *The Monroe Doctrine, 1823–1826*, p. 33. [2] *Ibid.* p. 38.

United States on numerous occasions, the two principles not always being kept separate. If the non-colonisation principle was distasteful to the British Government, the non-intervention principle was not, and Monroe's message hastened the decision of the British Government to recognise the new republics in South America. In its original form it is certain that the use of such expressions as "manifestation of an unfriendly disposition towards the United States" was not intended, as is frequently the case when states use similar expressions, to indicate that the United States was prepared to fight in support of Monroe's doctrine. It was essentially a pronouncement of policy, not necessarily a rule of action to be enforced by the sword. It was and remains a unilateral declaration and does not form part of international law, it is not even part of the law of the United States, it is not legally binding on any American Government for it has never been enacted by Act or Resolution of Congress.[1] Its subsequent development has supported the phrase used by Señor Madariaga that, as English liberty has dwindled down from precedent to precedent, the Monroe Doctrine may be said to have widened out from President to President.[2] A very important extension of the Doctrine was promulgated by President Polk in his message of 2 December 1845. In this message Polk extended the armed intervention which Monroe had in view to diplomatic intervention in the North American continent. It was understood as being aimed at the advisory policy of England and France in Texas and possibly Anglo-French intervention in the Argentine and was strongly resented both in England and France. He further emphasised the non-colonisation doctrine of Monroe by stating that no future European colony or dominion shall with our consent be planted or established on any part of the North American continent.[3]

The authorities in Yucatan having offered the dominion and sovereignty to Great Britain and Spain President Polk in a special message to Congress of 29 April 1848 again reiterated the Monroe message that there was no room for future European colonies in America. Mr Calhoun, in an able speech, denied the application of the principle to Yucatan.[4] The alleged encroachment of Great Britain on Venezuela was also referred to in the same discussion. In the negotiations for the Clayton-Bulwer Treaty for a ship canal across the Isthmus of Panama Lord Palmerston disclaimed any intent to occupy, fortify or colonise or assume or exercise any dominion over Nicaragua, Costa Rica, the Moskito Coast or any part of Central America and this was embodied in the first Article of the Convention. It is "the first, and indeed the only formal treaty assurance in history by a European state with regard to colonising activities in the New

---

[1] See Dana's note 36 in Wheaton's *International Law*.
[2] *Problems of Peace* (Fourth Series), p. 63.
[3] Perkins, Dexter, *The Monroe Doctrine, 1866–1867*, p. 89.
[4] Clark, J. Reuben, *Memorandum on the Monroe Doctrine*, p. 123.

World".[1] Though the treaty was afterwards attacked as a violation of the Monroe Doctrine, the plans for the making of the Canal jointly with the United States were clearly not within its scope, but it is argued that acceptance of the British position in Central America was. The treaty left open the question of recognition of British sovereignty in Belize and the renunciation of British claims in that area was rather a recognition of Monroe's principles. But the British Government claimed that the clause related only to future acts and did not embrace places at the time in their possession. It was in the discussion in Congress on Honduras and the Bay Islands in 1853 that most was heard of the violation of the Monroe Doctrine, and it was in the discussion on a motion by Mr Cass to affirm the non-colonisation principle that we hear for the first time of the Monroe Doctrine which had hitherto been referred to as "Declaration" or "principles".[2] Thereafter the expression became universal to denote the growing dogma of American policy. Disraeli's speech on Anglo-American relations in 1856 is a sound statement of the British view of the policy embodied therein.[3]

II

Between the years 1763 and 1815 there were only short periods during which Great Britain was not at war and in nearly all these cases her foes were not single states but combinations of states. A study of these wars which were waged both on land and on sea demonstrates that the influence of sea power was a decisive factor. Just as in the long drawn-out conflict between Rome and Carthage victory ultimately rested with the power which had the control of the sea, so during the period under consideration the same results are noticeable. This is particularly so in the Napoleonic era which ended with Waterloo and the Treaties of Paris and Vienna.

It is, therefore, with the rules of maritime international law which were developed during that period that we are chiefly concerned, for it was then that they assumed a form which was the basis on which the modern superstructure has been built. In a previous chapter[4] we have traced the beginnings of most of the doctrines which were elaborated during this period such as Contraband and Blockade. The rules relating to maritime war are, in the main, the resultant of two forces, those of the belligerent and neutral Powers, each asserting opposing rights. The belligerent demanded in the name of self-preservation that his operations against his adversary should not be interfered with by non-belligerent states or persons. He asserted the right to prevent his adversary from receiving aid by the carriage

---

[1] Perkins, *op. cit.* p. 204. [2] Perkins, *op. cit.* p. 223.
[3] Cited in *C.H.B.F.P.* II, 277. On the Monroe Doctrine see Reddaway, W. F., *The Monroe Doctrine*; Alvarez, A., *La Doctrine de Monroe*.
[4] See *C.H.B.E.* I, chap. XIX.

to him in neutral vessels of articles which would assist him in his military operations or would prolong his resistance. The neutral contended that he was entitled to continue his peaceful relations with the belligerents with whom he had no quarrel. It will be seen that there is thus a collision of interests between the two parties and the rules which were developed are a compromise between them, at times leaning to one side or the other according to the respective strength of the parties. The result, however, has doubtless been that the rules which have received the most general acceptance have been those which supported belligerent claims. This was to be expected as one of the parties to the dispute was armed and in a position to enforce his claims, unless the other party considered them so detrimental as to compel him to take up arms in defence of his interests.[1] The neutral has had to concede the right to a belligerent to interfere with his merchant vessels by visit and search to ascertain if they were carrying contraband goods, and he has had to admit the legality of capture of his merchant vessels attempting to enter a blockaded port or area.

In considering the growth of the law of neutrality it will be found that territorial sovereignty is at the same time a source of neutral responsibility as well as its measure. While a state must, as a neutral, be reasonably expected to show more watchfulness over occurrences within its territory than when peace reigns in the world, it is also clear that for occurrences outside its borders it cannot be held responsible.[2] Since a neutral's responsibility ceases with the three mile limit from its territory, belligerents have established the right to interfere with neutral commerce on the high seas which is injurious to their operations, because for grave and obvious reasons the neutral state has declined to set bounds to the activities of its citizens in this respect. Any such interference with neutral shipping must be justified before a Prize Court, and only if the state is of opinion that the decisions of that Court are not in accord with international law will it intervene diplomatically. The law of neutrality, therefore, has two branches: (1) that affecting states in their relations to each other, and (2) that affecting states in their relations to individuals. The rules of international law under the first head, as they developed by the middle of the nineteenth century, were on the basis of the neutral state observing complete impartiality between the belligerents and refraining from aiding either of them and, within certain limits, restraining persons within its territorial jurisdiction from assisting either of the belligerents—the belligerent being under the obligation to respect the neutral state's sovereign rights by refraining from any acts in violation of its neutrality. As regards neutral individuals, they are only responsible to their own states, and the belligerent's attitude towards them is limited by the duty which he owes to the

---

[1] See Westlake, J., *War*, p. 194.   [2] Hall, W. E., *Digest*, §§ 21, 22.

neutral state of which they are members. There has sometimes been a confusion between these two branches of law so that belligerent states have sometimes sought to make neutral states responsible for acts of their citizens in carrying on contraband trade with their enemies as if that were a violation of the state's neutral duty. The French statement of the law in 1777, that it will be found, whether by consulting usage or treaties, not that trade in articles contraband of war is a breach of neutrality, but that the persons engaged in it are exposed to the confiscation of their goods,[1] represents the practice which states have since maintained. When, as has been the case, a belligerent state finding itself at a disadvantage compared with its enemy in obtaining supplies from neutral traders, has sought to blame the neutral state for unneutral conduct, the answer has invariably been on the basis of the French statement above cited. The neutral state, in effect, says, our merchants are entitled to carry on trade with your adversary as well as with you and if the trade is in contraband goods it is for you to prevent them from reaching your enemy.[2]

During the eighteenth century opinions of writers and the practice of states were moving towards a position on which the modern principles regarding the relations between belligerent and neutral states were ultimately based. The former, in advance of the practice of states, abandoning the doctrine of *justum bellum* of Grotius, taught the doctrine of complete impartiality on the part of a neutral state regardless of the justice of the case of the belligerent. But exemption was made of acts done under treaties made before war broke out. Various examples might be given of troops furnished by a neutral state to a belligerent under such treaties without involving the neutral state in the war. Under such treaties Great Britain both in the Seven Years' War and in the War of American Independence drew large bodies of troops from German princes.[3] The protest of Sweden in 1788 against Danish troops being sent to Russia was in advance of the current practice, but treaties were coming into being providing against such conduct, and the Neutrality Edicts issued by the Two Sicilies and the Papal States forbade the enlistment by a belligerent in the territories of neutral states of their subjects for service in foreign states. Privateers were, however, still being fitted out by neutrals for service with belligerents. The Neutrality Edicts issued by several of the Italian States and by Holland during the American War of Independence prohibited such a procedure on behalf of their subjects, and when M. Genêt in 1792 granted commissions to American citizens to prey on English commerce the United States took a firm stand by prohibiting such action as being an infringement of its sovereignty.[4] The subsequent prosecution and acquittal of an American citizen, Stephen Henfield, for violating the

[1] Cited by Hall, W. E., *Digest*, § 24.
[2] Cf. Bismarck's complaint to Great Britain in 1870, *B.F.S.P.* LXX, 73.
[3] For example, see Hall, W. E., *op. cit.* §211.
[4] Moore, J. B., *Digest*, VII, § 1295.

law of the United States in cruising in a privateer commissioned by
M. Genêt showed that the existing law was not sufficient to support the
view of the Government. Consequently in 1794 Congress passed an
Act making it a penal offence for citizens or inhabitants of the United
States to accept commissions or enlist in the service of a foreign state
and prohibiting the fitting out or arming of vessels to be employed
by a foreign belligerent or the reception of any increased force by
such vessels when armed. "The policy of the United States in 1793
constitutes an epoch in the development of the usages of neutrality"
and though it represented notions in advance of existing opinions,
it is in the main identical with the standard of conduct which is now
adopted by the community of nations.[1] The American Act was
enlarged and re-enacted in 1818, and in 1819 Great Britain passed
a Foreign Enlistment Act which was based on it; in 1870 a new
statute on the subject was passed which in several respects exceeds
the requirements of international law and which is still in force.

One interesting fact emerges from the disputes between states
during the period under consideration, namely, that their policies
have never been consistent. States when neutral have adopted a
different attitude from that which they assumed when belligerent
and *vice versa*. The change of view of Russia, a party to the Armed
Neutralities, when she became a belligerent, may be cited as an
example, and the assertion by the United States of extreme belligerent
rights during the Civil War, 1861–5, was in contrast with the condemnation of commercial blockades by Mr Secretary Cass in 1859.
Other examples could be given, and, whether it be a question of the
lists of contraband articles or of freedom of neutral goods on enemy
ships or of enemy goods on board neutral ships, the history of the
period attests the influence of policy rather than a consistent application of settled rules of international law.

The trial of all cases of maritime capture, whether of ships or goods,
was conducted by the Prize Courts of the captors, but these Courts
in continental countries were under the direct control of the executive
government. In England it was claimed for these Courts that "they
decide not by the laws of England, with regard to ships or cargoes
detained as prize of war, any farther than those laws coincide with
the principles of law acknowledged by all nations...but are entirely
independent and remote, as are all other English Courts of Justice,
from the immediate direction of the Throne in particular cases, unless
where there are instructions previously existing, before such cases
came before them; and which instructions are in consequence of an
Act of Parliament".[2]

[1] Hall, W. E., *op. cit.* § 213. The foregoing sketch is largely based on Hall's masterly
exposition.
[2] *The Case of the Dutch Ships*, 1758, p. 36 (published anonymously but believed to be
written by Sir James Marriott). See also Sir W. Scott in *The Maria* (1799), 1 C. Rob.
p. 340, and Lord Parker in *The Zamora* (1916), 2 Brit. and Col. Prize Cases, 1 at p. 12.

The opening up to the Dutch of the trade between France and her colonies in 1756, a trade hitherto confined to French flags, led to the British Prize Courts condemning the Dutch ships engaged in the trade as being, in effect, enemy ships; the doctrine was known as the "rule of the war of 1756".[1] During the War of American Independence the Rule was not enforced, possibly because before hostilities commenced France had thrown open her colonial trade to all neutrals and this was represented as a permanent change in her policy. Events showed that this was not so, as the trade was again closed to neutrals at the conclusion of the war. In 1793 France threw open to all flags her colonial trade and neutral merchants at once rushed in to take advantage of the trade. In November of that year commanders of British warships and privateers were ordered "to stop and detain for lawful adjudication, all vessels laden with goods the produce of any French colony, or carrying provision or other supplies for the use of any such colony"—an extension beyond the original object of the Rule. This time it was the young and growing mercantile marine of the United States which took up the trade. The United States and other neutral Powers protested and in 1794 instructions were issued whereby direct trade between the United States and French West Indian colonies was left unmolested and in 1798 the rule of capture was further relaxed in favour of European neutrals carrying the produce of enemy countries (France, Spain or Holland) to their own countries or to England. But these relaxations were strictly construed by the Prize Courts and what the Instructions to naval officers did not permit was held to be prohibited. The justice of the British Rule of the War of 1756 in its original form has been much disputed. It was defended at the time, not only in the judgments of the Prize Courts of England, and especially in those of Sir William Scott (Lord Stowell), but also in an able pamphlet by Mr James Stephen, *War in Disguise*, first published in 1805, which went through three editions in four months.[2] Mr Justice Storey in the United States supported the Rule in its original form, but dissented from its extension in 1793, and Chancellor Kent, another great American lawyer, pointed out the possibility that the United States with increased maritime power and influence might in some future war feel more sensibly the weight of argument in favour of the policy and equity of the Rule.[3] Among modern writers, Admiral Mahan, whose knowledge of the effect of the possession of sea-power in war was unrivalled, wrote that the principle of the Rule of 1756 was not only strictly just but wisely expedient. "The gist of the Rule was that the intervention of a neutral for the commercial benefit of a belligerent was as inconsistent with neutrality as it would be to help him with

[1] See *C.H.B.E.* I, 551.
[2] Edited and reprinted by Sir Francis Piggott in 1917.
[3] Kent's *Commentaries* (Abdy's edition), p. 229.

men or arms. The neutral was not to suffer: what he did habitually in peace was open to him in war—except the carriage of contraband and of cargoes hostile in ownership: but what was closed to him in peace it was contrary to neutrality to undertake in war for the belligerent's easement."[1]

The effect of the Rule of the War of 1756 was further emphasised by the application to it of the doctrine of "Continuous Voyage". Neutrals having obtained a relaxation of the Order of 1793 enabling them to trade between enemy colonies and their own ports, proceeded to elude the principle of the Rule of 1756 by exporting colonial produce to France and Spain and exporting the manufactures of France and Spain to their colonies. By these means trade between the mother countries in Europe and their colonies was secured. American vessels took cargoes from French and Spanish colonies to American ports, all the documents relating to the voyage were destroyed, new documents relating only to the voyage from the neutral to the enemy port were procured and thus a ship was able to produce complete evidence showing the innocence of the voyage. Sometimes by accident the evidence of the earlier voyage came to light and the Prize Court held that the whole voyage from the colony to the mother country was a "continuous voyage" and rendered the ship and cargo liable to condemnation.[2] If the landing of the cargo at the neutral port were proved to be a fictitious landing, as in cases where the payment of import duties was followed by re-export and payment of a drawback, condemnation was decreed. The question whether the goods imported into the neutral country had in fact become part of the "common stock" of that country was regarded as vital to ensure the release of the captured neutral ship and cargo. The evidence to support such a claim was carefully scrutinised by the Court. "The truth may not always be discernible, but when it is discovered, it is according to the truth and not according to the fiction that we are to give to the transaction its character and denomination" said Sir William Grant in delivering the most elaborate opinion on the subject.[3]

The principle of continuous voyage was applied to other subjects than the colonial trade. It was applied to the French coasting trade which had been opened to neutrals,[4] to the Retaliatory Order in Council of 7 January 1807 in a case where the cargo was transhipped from one vessel to another[5] and to cases of trading with the enemy.[6] The United States Supreme Court also applied it to trading with the

---

[1] *Some Neglected Aspects of War*, p. 191. See on the whole question "The opening by belligerents to neutrals of closed trade" in Higgins, A. Pearce, *War and the Private Citizen* (1912), pp. 169–92.

[2] See *The Mercury* referred to in *The William* (5 C. Rob. p. 385).

[3] *The William*.   [4] *The Ebenezer*, 6 C. Rob. 250.

[5] *The Thomyris*, Edwards, 17.

[6] An early case in 1760, *The Constantia* (Burrell, 208), applied the principle, and in *The Jonge Pieter* (4 C. Rob. 79) Sir William Scott applied it to goods which were to be transhipped and forwarded by land or canal navigation.

enemy in a case during the War of 1812–14.[1] In a case during the Mexican War in which the captured vessel and cargo were condemned for the carriage of contraband the Supreme Court of the United States recognised that the effect of interposing a neutral port between the home port and that of the enemy did not prevent it from proceeding to condemnation.[2] The English Court had applied the doctrine of "Continuous Voyage" to absolute contraband even before its application to colonial trade,[3] but there are few cases on contraband in these courts during the Napoleonic wars and they are not always consistent with each other.[4] The same is true as regards the service of ships for breach of blockade, but the balance of opinion was against the application of the doctrine to blockade. Thus, before the outbreak of the American Civil War it had been applied in a large variety of cases in Great Britain, and the United States and in at least one case in France during the Crimean War.[5] During the American Civil War several important cases in the American Prize Court carried the doctrine further into blockade and contraband; this time it was chiefly British vessels and the owners of the cargo who were the sufferers by such decisions.

The methods of contrabandists and of blockade-runners tend to repeat themselves in different wars. During the Seven Years' War and the War of American Independence the West India islands of St Eustatius and Curaçoa formed a base to cover trade in the produce of the French colonies and for blockade-runners, whilst in the American Civil War Nassau in the Bahamas and Cardenas and other ports in Cuba became entrepôts for the transhipment of goods intended for the Confederate forces, or were used as intermediate ports by vessels whose ultimate purpose was to break the blockade of the southern ports of the United States then in the occupation of the Confederates. The Judges both of the District Courts and of the Supreme Court of the United States at once appreciated the importance of the doctrine of "Continuous Voyage" and in the first case of the period condemned ship and cargo by applying the doctrine to a vessel whose ostensible destination was Havana, but whose real destination the Court found to be New Orleans then under blockade. The vessel was captured while *en route* for Havana.[6] This was a clear case of applying the doctrine to blockade, uncomplicated by questions of contraband. Subsequent cases confirmed the application of the doctrine to blockade,[7] though in one of them (*The Dolphin*) the decision might have been based on the carriage of contraband. In the case of

---

[1] *The Joseph*, 8 Cranch, 451.
[2] *Jecker v. Montgomery* (1851), 18 Howard (U.S. Rept. p. 111, at p. 115).
[3] *The Jesus* (1761), Burrell, 164; *The Hendric and Alida* (1776), Hay and Marriott, 96.
[4] See Briggs, H. W., *The Doctrine of Continuous Voyage*, p. 36.
[5] *The Frau Howina*—Calvo, *Le Droit International* (5th ed.), IV, 87.
[6] *The Circassian*, 2 Wallace Rep. 135.
[7] *The Dolphin*, 7 Fed. Cases, 868; *The Pearl*, 5 Wall. 574.

The Bermuda attempted breach of blockade and carriage of contraband were both present and the fact of the goods being consigned "to order" together with the spoiling of papers on board justified the condemnation of the ship and cargo, ostensibly destined for Nassau, but whose real destination was Charleston.[1] Cargo on vessels destined for Matamoras on the Rio Grande River in Mexico, were held not to be liable to condemnation as it was decided that the blockade of the river was not legitimate, the river being partly neutral. But as part of the cargo consisted of stores and the evidence showed that they were destined for the Confederate forces it was condemned.[2] The importance of this case lies in the application of the doctrine of "Continuous Voyage" to conditional contraband with an ulterior inland destination.[3] The case of *The Springbok* did not carry the principle any farther, but was much criticised on the ground that the contraband goods on board the vessel whose ostensible destination was Nassau were condemned on evidence which was only grounds of suspicion and did not afford clear proof of enemy destination. Such criticism does not appear to be justified, and the Court had reasonable grounds for the decision at which it arrived.

As has invariably been the case the neutral ship and cargo-owners who had suffered from the condemnation of their property invoked the aid of their government on the ground that the American Prize Courts were violating international law. The decisions were received with almost unanimous disapproval by English international lawyers at the time, but the Government of the day, acting on the advice of the Law Officers, refused to intervene. Claims for compensation in several of the cases were brought before the International Commission set up under the Treaty of Washington, 1871, but they were only successful in one case, which was a claim for compensation for the detention of the *Springbok*.[4]

If the decisions of the American Courts are to be criticised, it is chiefly on the ground that the judges were unfamiliar with the law of prize and not infrequently confused contraband and blockade; but as regards the justice of their decisions it is believed, that notwithstanding the contrary views of many eminent international lawyers, at the time and subsequently, that they represented an honest attempt to hold the balance between neutrals and belligerents. That they went beyond previous decisions on the subject is certain, but they were the application of "old principles to new circumstances", and so long as the continuity of the original and established principle is unbroken, the practice cannot be condemned as being an innovation on the ancient law.[5] The fact that the British Government refrained

---

[1] 3 Wall. 514: there were similar facts in *The Stephen Hart* (3 Wall. 559) though here the ostensible destination was Cardenas, in Cuba.

[2] *The Peterhoff*, 5 Wall. 28.

[3] 5 Wall. 1.

[4] Moore, J. B., *Digest*, VII, 725–6.

[5] See *The Atalanta*, 6 C. Rob. 440.

from protests is evidence that it realised that the American Courts were justified, notwithstanding the neutral tradition of the Government, in asserting its belligerent rights to the uttermost legitimate limits. The American cases were strongly relied upon in the decisions of the British Prize Courts during the War of 1914–18.[1]

Contraband lists have in the past formed a fruitful source of dispute between belligerent and neutral states and afford another example of the inconsistency of states.[2] The list issued by the United States during the Civil War dealing apparently with absolute contraband of war contained a final clause of a sweeping character so as to include "goods and commodities which might be useful to the enemy in war". The continental nations during the period strove to limit the list of articles of contraband to munitions of war, naval stores and materials for use in shipbuilding. England considered contraband to be of two sorts, absolute and conditional. The former consisted of articles of primary use in war which were condemnable if shown to be destined for the enemy territory; conditional contraband consisted of articles of use both in war and in peace (*ancipitis usus*) such as foodstuffs and coal, which were condemnable only if shown to have a destination to the armed forces or a base of supply of those forces.

The doctrine of the English Courts was, therefore, that provisions were not generally contraband but might become so in circumstances arising out of the particular situation of the war, or the conditions of the parties engaged in it. Accordingly, the important feature is the characteristic of essentiality, and in determining in what circumstances seizure of merchandise of double use can be justified the main difficulty is either to find a general test of essentiality or to secure proof that delivery of particular articles would be essential to the prosecution of the war.[3] In 1793 and 1795 the British Government ordered the seizure of all vessels carrying provisions to France in retaliation for a decree of the National Convention of 1793 ordering the seizure of all neutral vessels carrying foodstuffs to England.[4] The United States protested, and by treaties between the two countries Lord Stowell's test of the contraband character of goods was adopted.[5] The American Courts in 1816[6] and again in 1866 adopted a similar test. The divergence between Anglo-American and Continental doctrine on the subject of contraband continued until the end of the nineteenth century.[7]

---

[1] On the subject of Continuous Voyage see Briggs, H. W., *The Doctrine of Continuous Voyage*; Gantenbein, J. W., *The Doctrine of Continuous Voyage*.
[2] See *C.H.B.E.* I, 554.
[3] Hall, W. E., *op. cit.* § 241.
[4] Heckscher, E. F., *Continental System*, ch. III.
[5] Pyke, H. R., *The Law of Contraband of War*, p. 122.
[6] *The Commercen*, 1 Wheaton 382.
[7] *The Peterhoff*, 5 Wall. 28, 58.

The early history of the law of blockade has already been dealt with:[1] divergencies of practice between England and the United States on the one hand and Continental countries on the other manifested themselves during this period. Napoleon complained in 1806 that Great Britain resorted to commercial blockade against ports and harbours without taking military steps against them. This complaint was made, says Westlake, "with a lofty disregard of more than a century of intervening history".[2] After the Napoleonic wars there was a movement for abolishing commercial blockades which received support from Cobden and others in England and in the United States from Secretary Cass in 1859. It was part of the movement in favour of neutrals, and for the abolition of the right of the capture of private property at sea. But on the outbreak of the American Civil War a commercial blockade of the whole of the southern coast of the United States was declared. A blockade, whether strategic, that is accompanied by military operations, or commercial, in order to be binding on neutrals must be effective in contradistinction to the mere declaration unaccompanied by naval power to enforce it ("paper" blockade). The Continental view required the presence of the blockading ships in the immediate vicinity of the blockaded port as was laid down in treaties of the Armed Neutralities of 1780 and 1800. Great Britain and later the United States acted on the principle that the danger to the blockade-runners was sufficiently ensured thereby making the blockade effective by the presence of cruisers on different stations "so communicating with each other as to be able to intercept all vessels attempting to enter the ports" of the blockaded area.[3] By Article 4 of the Declaration of Paris, 1856, it is agreed that "blockades, in order to be binding must be effective, that is to say, maintained by a force sufficient really to prevent access to the coast of the enemy". When once a blockade is established it must be maintained continuously, and the temporary removal of the blockading squadron necessitates a new notification to neutrals on its resumption. The Anglo-American practice differed from the Continental as regards notification. In the former a vessel remained liable to capture from the time it sailed for a port blockade of which had been notified and of which the master had knowledge, if the blockade existed at the moment of capture. The Continental practice required that warning should be given to each individual ship which was only liable to capture on a second attempt to break blockade.

Besides the carriage of contraband or breach of blockade which render neutral vessels liable to capture, another means of assistance to the enemy consisted in the carrying of despatches which relate to

---

[1] See *C.H.B.E.* I, 555. [2] Westlake, *War*, p. 227.
[3] See *The Nancy* (1809), 1 Acton, 57. In this case the Prize Court held that the blockade was insufficiently enforced by warships and restored the captured ship.

the operations of war.[1] British Prize Courts also condemn neutral vessels carrying combatants or intending combatants for purposes connected with the war where the carriage was undertaken on behalf of the belligerent state.[2] This liability to seizure and confiscation did not exist where persons with a military character were travelling as private persons at their own expense.[3] In all these cases the offending ship is taken in for adjudication by the Prize Court, but there was a question as to the right of a belligerent to remove enemy persons from a neutral ship without taking the ship in for adjudication. This seems at one time to have been a common practice, but states began to regulate it as early as 1675 by treaties limiting the right of removal to persons in the military employ of the enemy.[4] The question of the removal of enemy reservists may be said still to remain an open one, but a question of a somewhat different character arose between Great Britain and the United States during the American Civil War. *The Trent*, a British mail-steamer, was stopped on 6 November 1861 on a voyage between Havana and the Island of St Thomas in the West Indies by the U.S.S. *San Jacinto* commanded by Captain Wilkes who removed from her Messrs Mason and Slidell and their two Secretaries. Messrs Mason and Slidell were commissioned by President Jefferson Davis of the Confederate States to go to Europe to secure aid by diplomatic means. *The Trent* was allowed to proceed and the captured envoys were landed in America. When the news of Captain Wilkes' exploit was known in the United States it was hailed with enthusiasm, but when the news reached England on 27 November the greatest indignation at what was popularly held to be a violation of the British flag was universally manifested. In the correspondence between the two Governments which followed and which ultimately led to the release of Messrs Mason and Slidell the British Government had a strong case. *The Trent* was under no contract with the Confederate Government for the carriage of its envoys, and was therefore in no sense engaged in an act of unneutral service. The envoys were not military or naval officers or members of the belligerent armed forces who were the only persons whom it had ever been lawful to seize and remove from a neutral ship. They were engaged in a diplomatic mission to neutral states and were travelling in a neutral ship. Lord Russell rested the immunity which he claimed for the envoys very largely on the ground of their diplomatic character and on the privilege accorded to neutral states to receive such agents from belligerent states. Persons in the military service of a belligerent state are sometimes referred to as "analogues of contraband". Not always a happy expression as the analogy is far from complete. Contraband

---

[1] *The Atalanta* (1808), 6 C. Rob. 440.
[2] *The Orozambo* (1807), 6 C. Rob. 430.
[3] See dictum of Sir W. Scott in *The Friendship* (1807), 6 C. Rob. 420.
[4] Wheaton, H., *International Law*, Dana's edition, note 228, p. 656.

must have an enemy destination and the ulterior destination of the envoys was neutral. It was also pointed out to Mr Secretary Seward by some of the Great Powers of Europe that the American action was in contradiction to the principles for which the United States had stood in their assertion of neutral rights. The incident was closed by the release of Messrs Mason and Slidell though Mr Seward contended that the mistake made by Captain Wilkes was in his not having taken in *The Trent* for adjudication by the Prize Court.[1]

The long-continued struggle over the question of the liability to capture of enemy goods under a neutral flag was terminated by the Declaration of Paris, 1856, in favour of the neutral claim for "free ships, free goods".[2] The English and French rules on the subject were different, the English Prize Court, following the principles of the *Consolato del Mare*, condemned enemy goods on neutral ships but released neutral goods in an enemy ship, while the French Courts condemned neutral goods on an enemy ship but did not capture enemy goods under a neutral flag; the English test was the nationality of the goods, the French test the nationality of the ship. Before war was declared on Russia by Great Britain and France on 28 March 1854 it became obvious that an agreement was essential as to the rules that the two Powers would apply. Sweden and Denmark as probable neutrals notified the rules of neutrality they proposed to observe in the event of war, these rules included the admission to their ports of all belligerent ships of war, but not of privateers.[3] Simultaneously with the declaration of war the Queen's Declaration was issued in which it was stated: "To preserve the commerce of neutrals from all unnecessary obstruction, H.M. is willing, for the present, to waive a part of the belligerent rights appertaining to her by the law of nations." The Declaration then stated that seizure of contraband goods, prevention of carriage by neutrals of enemy despatches and of breach of blockade would be maintained. "But H.M. will waive the right of seizing enemy's property taken on board a neutral vessel, unless it be contraband of war. It is not H.M.'s intention to claim the confiscation of neutral property, not being contraband of war, found on enemy's ships; but H.M. further declares, that being anxious to lessen as much as possible the evils of war, and to restrict its operations to the regularly organised forces of the country, it is not her present intention to issue letters of marque for the commissioning of privateers." The Emperor of the French made a similar declaration with the difference in wording necessitated

[1] Hall, W. E., *op. cit.* § 253; Westlake, J., *op. cit.* 304 and *C.M.H.* xii, 18; *C.H.B.F.P.* ii, 501; Moore, J. B., *op. cit.* § 1264; Bernard, M., *Neutrality of Great Britain during the American Civil War*, p. 322; Malkin, Sir H. W., "*The Trent* and *The China*", *British Year Book of International Law*, v, 66.

[2] See *C.H.B.E.* i, 548–51.

[3] Malkin, Sir H. W., "The inner history of the Declaration of Paris", *British Year Book of International Law*, 1927, p. 5.

by the fact that the claims the two countries were waiving were different. The reaction of the United States to the communication of this declaration was favourable to the acceptance of the doctrine of "free ships free goods" for which the United States had long contended and which they had embodied in many treaties. Apart, however, from treaties, their Courts applied the British rules of prize law. Mr Marcy, the American Secretary of State, urged that the rule should become a permanent one in international law and that the immunity from capture of enemy goods other than contraband should also be adopted. The United States was not, however, favourable to the abolition of privateering unless it was coupled with the adoption of the rule of immunity from capture of private enemy property. The right to commission privateers was, it was urged, the only way in which a weak naval power could in any way defend itself in a war against a powerful naval adversary. The privateer had, undoubtedly, in the past been the important weapon of a weak naval power, and the French privateers after Trafalgar and the American privateers during the war of 1812–14 inflicted very grave losses on British commerce. The privateers had a bad reputation, their discipline was bad and the incentives to action were mainly selfish, viz. the prize money which was the reward of their activities. Queen Victoria, in a minute on the proposal for the abolition of privateers, wrote: "Privateering is a kind of Piracy which disgraces our civilisation, its abolition throughout the world would be a great step in advance."[1] At the conclusion of the Peace Conference at Paris in April 1856, the British delegates proposed a declaration embodying the principles on which the Allies had acted during the war with a statement as to the necessity for the effectiveness of blockades. The Declaration of Paris contains four Articles: (1) Privateering is and remains abolished. (2) The neutral flag covers enemy goods with the exception of contraband of war. (3) Neutral goods, with the exception of contraband of war, are not liable to capture under the enemy's flag. (4) Blockades, in order to be binding, must be effective; that is to say, maintained by a force sufficient really to prevent access to the enemy's coast. A Protocol was appended to the Declaration in which it was agreed that "the Powers which have signed it or which shall have acceded to it, cannot hereafter enter into any arrangement in regard to the application of the right of neutrals in time of war which does not at the same time rest on the four principles which are the object of the said Declaration".[2]

This Declaration has now received almost universal acceptance; it is the most important international instrument regulating the right of belligerents and neutrals at sea. The only maritime state which

[1] Malkin, Sir H. W., *op. cit.* p. 30.
[2] For texts see Higgins, A. Pearce, *The Hague Peace Conferences*, p. 1 and Malkin, Sir H. W., *op. cit.* p. 1.

has not acceded to it is the United States, but that State in all wars in which it has been engaged has acted on its principles. The two great changes which it effected as regards British naval practice were the abolition of privateering and the adoption of the principle that "free ships make free goods" and these two principles are linked together. It now appears that the Government of the day thought that the *quid pro quo* for the abolition of privateering was substantial and in the best interests of Great Britain. Whether in modern conditions of warfare the old and long established practice of seizing enemy goods under a neutral flag could have been enforced is pure speculation, but there have not been wanting many authorities who believe the price paid for the concession to neutrals was too high. The third and fourth rules of the Declaration call for no comment, the third represented the long practice of British Prize Courts and the fourth represented the doctrine, if not always the practice, of Great Britain.[1]

The Declaration of Paris is important as representing the beginning of written rules of international law relating to warfare. The practice of Great Britain and France at the beginning of the Crimean War in allowing days of grace to Russian merchant ships in their ports at the outbreak of war is also noteworthy as showing a mitigation of the severity of the existing rule under which such vessels were liable to seizure and condemnation. Turkey in 1853 had also allowed Russian merchant ships to leave her ports: the concession was mutual. Prussia and Austria made a similar concession in 1866 and France and Germany in 1870. The practice was continued and formed the basis of the Sixth Hague Convention, 1907.

It has now become one of the recognised duties of belligerents that they must respect the territorial waters of neutral states and not commit any warlike act within them, such as visit, search or capture of suspected vessels. We have seen that though the principle had long received recognition, it was often more honoured in the breach than in the observance.[2] Cases of violation occurred less frequently during the latter part of the eighteenth and the early years of the nineteenth century, but British warships were sometimes the offenders. In 1793 a French frigate was captured in Genoa harbour and was not restored nor any apology made for violation of Genoese neutrality,[3] but the United States compelled the return of a vessel captured by a British cruiser in Delaware Bay.[4] In 1801 a British frigate captured some Swedish vessels in Norwegian waters, but though it was admitted

---

[1] Important new and hitherto unpublished material relating to the origin of the Declaration of Paris is to be found in Sir H. W. Malkin's article already referred to: see also Piggott, Sir Francis, *The Declaration of Paris*, 1856 (1919).

[2] See *C.H.B.E.* I, 190.

[3] Westlake points out this was not due to British disregard of the law of neutrality, but was part of a policy to force Genoa to take the part of the allies (*War*, p. 232).

[4] Hall, W. E., *op. cit.* § 220.

by the British Government that the violation of Danish sovereignty
called for and produced an apology, it referred the question to the
Prize Court. The ships were restored.[1] Modern British practice has
supported the views then advanced by the British Government that
the legality of the capture must as a rule first be dealt with by the
Court. Sir William Scott emphasised the sanctity of neutral waters
when he released a vessel captured off the mouth of the Mississippi
within three miles from the nearest land, though these were unin-
habitable mud islands,[2] and in another case he restored a ship that
had been captured by boats sent from a British cruiser lying within
neutral waters, though the captured ship was outside the territorial
limit. He pointed out that an act of hostility is not to take its commencement on neutral ground: "You are not to avail yourself of
a station in neutral territory, making as it were a vantage ground of
the neutral country, a country which is to carry itself with perfect
equality between both belligerents, giving neither the one nor the
other any advantage."[3] But mere passage through neutral waters
is not enough to invalidate a subsequent capture.[4] Several cases
occurred during the wars of 1812–14, and during the American Civil
War the Federal naval forces sometimes overstepped the neutral
border line. The *Florida*, for example, was captured by the U.S.S.
Wachusett in the Brazilian harbour of Bahia in 1864. Brazil protested
and demanded reparation which was at once forthcoming.[5] The
sanctity of neutral waters is clearly a rule of international law, but
it is evident that in the stress of warfare it is not always observed.
Where the violation of these waters has been proved, the duty of the
belligerent state to restore the captured property, where possible,
and to make satisfactory reparation is also fully recognised. Sometimes
a belligerent vessel attacked by its enemy in neutral waters, instead
of relying on the protection of the neutral state has actively defended
itself. In such a case it was held by the Arbitrator in a case between
the United States and Portugal where the *General Armstrong*, an
American privateer was attacked by a British squadron in Fayal
harbour in 1814, that Portugal was not responsible for the consequences.[6] It is and was recognised in this case that the neutral state
is under a duty to do what it can to prevent a violation of its sovereignty and to demand reparation. If it does not do so, its inaction
may be viewed as compromising its neutrality.

It has been already remarked that the rules of neutrality are the
resultant of the opposing forces of neutrals and belligerents. The

---

[1] Hall, W. E., *op. cit.* § 25. [2] *The Anna* (1805), 5 C. Rob. 373.
[3] *The Twee Gebroeders* (No. 1), 1800, C. Rob. 162.
[4] *The Twee Gebroeders* (No. 2), 1801, 3 C. Rob. 336.
[5] See Wheaton, H., *op. cit.* Dana's edition, notes 207, 208, 209. The case of the *Chesapeke*,
seized in a Nova Scotian harbour by a United States warship in 1863 is of considerable
interest and it involved questions of belligerent rights as well as of piracy.
[6] Hall, W. E., *op. cit.* § 228; Westlake, J., *War*, p. 232.

force of the neutral operated in different ways at different times. Sometimes combinations of neutral states were formed to curb the claims of a powerful belligerent, at others a belligerent was prepared to make concessions to a neutral whom he was desirous of conciliating; at others a powerful neutral who was aggrieved and who felt he had more to gain than to lose by the operation would resort to something in the nature of the modern boycott by issuing a decree of non-intercourse; at others a neutral took up arms against the belligerent either by becoming an ally of his enemy or by using forcible means in the nature of reprisals.

When Great Britain was in the throes of the War of American Independence in which the thirteen colonies were being assisted by France and Spain, neutrals were feeling the pressure of her assertion of her belligerent rights. In 1778 Sweden and Denmark approached the Empress Catharine of Russia for the formation of a combined fleet for the protection of the trade of the Northern Powers. The Empress was personally inclined to favour the British side, but Panin, her Chancellor, was unfavourable and by flattery and an appeal to her vanity obtained the issue on 28 February 1780 of a Declaration of principles to be communicated to the belligerent Powers for the security of Russian commerce, and to neutral Powers, as the basis of a league to be formed between them for the protection of neutral rights. The declaration formed the basis of the First Armed Neutrality of 1780. The rules laid down are as follows: (1) All neutral vessels may freely navigate from port to port and on the coasts of nations at war. (2) Enemy goods on board neutral ships, except contraband of war, to be free. (3) Contraband goods to be limited to those contained in the treaty of commerce of 1766 with Great Britain which restricted them to munitions of war as therein defined. (4) That a port should only be considered to be blockaded where the attacking Power has stationed its vessels sufficiently near and in such a way as to render access thereto clearly dangerous. (5) That these principles shall serve as a rule for proceedings and judgments as to the legality of prizes.[1] Though this declaration is generally referred to as due to a desire to improve the rules of maritime law for the benefit of neutrals, "it was", says Wheaton, "the accidental result of a mere court intrigue and of the rivalry of two candidates [Panin and Potemkin] for the favour of a dissolute, ambitious and vainglorious woman" who was so ignorant of what she had done that she was under the impression that she had issued a declaration favourable to Great Britain.[2]

---

[1] Text of Declaration in Martens, *Recueil des Traités*, 2nd ed. III, 158; and Scott, J. B., *The Armed Neutralities of 1780 and 1800*, pp. 273, 641, a valuable collection of excerpts from numerous text-writers and also the texts of the various diplomatic documents relating to the subject.

[2] Wheaton, H., *History of the Modern Law of Nations*, p. 298.

The first of these Articles was a denial of the British principles as embodied in the Rule of the War of 1756 that trade opened to neutrals in time of war but closed in time of peace rendered them liable to capture. The second Article embodied the rule of "free ships, free goods" which was contrary to that observed by English Prize Courts whose practice was based on the *Consolato del Mare*. The limitation of contraband to "munitions of war" was also a restriction on British practice, while the rule as to blockade that the blockading ships must be stationary (*arrêtés*) and near to the blockaded port was opposed to the British practice whereby the effectiveness only was emphasised and this might be maintained by cruisers.

Hard pressed though Great Britain was by the revolted colonies, France, Spain and Holland, she returned a dignified answer refusing acceptance of the proposals, which, however, were accepted by her enemies as well as by Denmark, Sweden, Prussia, Austria, Portugal and the Two Sicilies. The accession of the enemies of Great Britain was valueless as indicating a settled policy or their views of existing international law, while the secondary naval Powers were naturally prepared to accommodate their views to their interests. The results of the first Armed Neutrality bear out the principles already expressed of the inconsistency of states and their subordination of practice to policy. Phillimore expresses these results as follows: "The most remarkable fact connected with the Armed Neutrality of 1780 remains to be stated, namely, that *everyone* of the Powers composing this hallowed league for the maintenance of international justice upon the principles of the Russian Edict departed from the obligation which they had contracted as *neutrals* as soon as they became *belligerents*."[1] Meantime, except where otherwise provided by treaty, the principle of "free ships, unfree goods", remained the general rule. Treaties for "free ships, free goods" were made during the latter part of the eighteenth century and in 1800 the principle reappeared in a re-issue of the Declaration of 1780 when the Second Armed Neutrality between Russia, Sweden, Prussia and Denmark was formed in 1800. The cause of the formation of this new league was not the enforcement of this principle, but the assertion by the Northern Powers of an alleged right of convoy. We have already seen that the question whether neutral merchant ships sailing under the convoy of one or more of their national warships were exempt from visit and search by English cruisers was raised in an acute form in the middle of the seventeenth century.[2] For more than a century the English practice appears to have remained unquestioned, but in 1798 a Swedish warship convoying merchant vessels, after a slight resistance, was brought in for adjudication by the British Prize Court

[1] Phillimore, Sir R., *Commentaries upon International Law*, vol. III, § cxci; see also *Diaries ...of Lord Malmesbury*, I, 355, 362.
[2] See *C.H.B.E.* I, 557.

warships and privateers in the war with Great Britain, such as seizing American merchant ships carrying neutral property to English ports, and those carrying enemy goods, were pressing heavily on American commerce. The relations between the United States and Great Britain were also greatly improved by the signature of Jay's treaty in 1794, which owing to French jealousy did not tend to make the Franco-American relations any easier. French complaints were met with denials of the allegations, but France reiterated them and emphasised the feeling of chagrin with which she had viewed the application of the law of neutrality for which the United States was making a firm stand. The Government of the latter was pressing France for a settlement of claims for spoliation and maltreatment of vessels at sea, for losses by an embargo laid on their ships in Bordeaux, and for illegal seizure and condemnation of her merchant ships. The proceedings of French privateers and Prize Courts, especially those sitting in the West Indies, and the absence of any settlement of their claims, together with the order issued under circumstances of great indignity by the French Government for the United States representative to quit France, led to diplomatic intercourse between the two countries being suspended in 1798. The position was aggravated by the French decree of 18 January 1798 ordering the capture of vessels carrying merchandise the production of England or her possessions.[1] In 1798 Congress passed various statutes authorising the arming of merchant ships to defend themselves against French depredation[2] and to "subdue and capture" any French vessels offending and to bring them in for condemnation by the Prize Court, commercial intercourse between the two countries was suspended and all treaties were denounced. Captured vessels were to become the property of the United States, or of the captors or to be divided between the Government and the captors according to circumstances. A proviso was inserted in the Statute authorising armed resistance to the effect that whenever the Government of France should cause their armed vessels to refrain from lawless depredations and outrages against American merchant vessels instructions should be issued to such vessels to submit to search by the commanders of French vessels. A period of maritime hostilities followed, the first prize being taken from the French in June 1798. There was no declaration of war. This condition of affairs lasted till 30 September 1800 when a truce of peace and commerce was signed by the two Powers and ratified in the following July.[3]

The action of the United States was a protest by a neutral against

---

[1] Moore, J. B., op. cit. v, 608.

[2] The United States took a similar course in 1917 before declaring war on Germany, see chapter on "Defensively armed merchant ships" in Higgins, A. Pearce, International Law and Relations, p. 290.

[3] Text in Scott, J. B., op. cit. p. 487.

the violation of its rights by a belligerent, and in this case it was successful. The nature of the relationship which existed between the two Powers during this period is disputed. In cases[1] which came before the American Courts arising out of the operations at sea some of the judges characterised the position as "limited, partial war" and "a qualified state of hostility", while Webster, in his speech on French spoliation, considered that the situation did not amount to open and public war. The situation was anomalous, as reprisals were not ordered against French vessels in general and the American courts remained open to French citizens. Force was authorised to be used for certain objects and in certain circumstances against French vessels. The position is generally described as America's "partial" war with France, but it appears rather to fall under the heading of reprisals limited to such acts only as are the best for enforcing redress in the circumstances of the particular case. The acts of the American vessels were acts of war though not in intention and it was for France to determine whether they set up a state of war or not. The treaty of 1800 contains no reference to a state of war between the parties, but recites that they were "desirous to terminate the differences which have arisen between the two states". Similar anomalous conditions have obtained since 1800 and international lawyers are still debating a definition of war.[2]

It was as a preliminary to more forcible actions to assert neutral rights that the non-intercourse Act of 1790 was passed by the United States legislature, and it was as an answer to belligerent claims made by both belligerents, whereby neutral rights were seriously affected, that the United States passed non-intercourse legislation in 1807.[3] It was not followed immediately by stronger measures and after being in force till 1809 was repealed.

The treaty of 1794 between Great Britain and the United States expired in 1806 and American traders were suffering from the acts of both belligerents. The defence of the British Orders-in-Council were based on the justice of retaliation and on these grounds were supported by judgment of the Prize Court. Sir William Scott in *The Fox*[4] said: "Retaliatory measures they are. I have no hesitation in saying they would cease to be just if they ceased to be retaliatory, and they would cease to be retaliatory from the moment the enemy retracts in a sincere manner from those measures of his which they are intended to retaliate...neutrals are prohibited to trade with France because they are prohibited by France from trading with England." It was further contended by the British Government

---

[1] *Bas* v. *Tingy* (1800), 4 Dall. 37.
[2] McNair, A. D., *Transactions of the Grotius Society*, 1925, p. 25; Brierly, J. L., *Cambridge Law Journal*, 1932, p. 308; Williams, Sir J. F., *ibid.* 1933, vol. 1; Wright, Quincy, *Am. Journ. of Int. Law*, XXVI, 362.
[3] See *C.H.B.F.P.* I, 366–7.   [4] *The Fox* (1807) Edwards, 314.

that as neutrals had taken no steps to resist the illegalities of the French they must submit to inconvenience from the acts of a belligerent government greater in degree than would be justified if no cause for retaliation had arisen.[1] The United States then put in force in 1807 a non-importation Act and an embargo was laid on all shipping in American ports. This state of affairs lasted until March 1809 when an Act was passed prohibiting all friendly intercourse between the United States and Great Britain and France until their decrees were revoked. In 1811 the United States accepted Napoleon's version that the offending decrees had been revoked so far as concerned American vessels and on 23 June 1812 British Orders-in-Council were rescinded as regards American property. But meantime American sympathy with France, coupled with indignation at the action of the British in impressing seamen on American ships and continued enforcement of the British Orders-in-Council, resulted on 19 June 1812 in President Madison declaring that a state of war existed with Great Britain.

The employment of acts of force against a state which fall short of war has already been noticed.[2] These took the form of reprisals which often were the preliminary to war, and were usually accompanied by embargo of such ships of the offending state as were in the port of the state making the reprisal. Such ships were detained until the dispute was settled, when they were released, or if the dispute ended in war they were condemned.[3] A modern example of reprisal is the Proclamation of 1854 which preceded the declaration of war against Russia, but in that case by mutual arrangement the merchant ships in the ports of the belligerent states were given "days of grace" wherein they could leave. Pacific blockade has also been employed since the beginning of the nineteenth century as a measure of restraint short of war. An earlier example, the blockade of Porto Rico by England in 1725, has already been noted,[4] but the modern instances have been generally against small Powers, either as a form of reprisals or by way of intervention or an act of international police. One of the earliest examples in modern times was the blockade in 1827 of the coasts of Greece, at that time under Turkish dominion, by the combined fleets of Great Britain, France and Russia while all the powers professed to be at peace with Turkey. This was followed by the untoward event of Navarino, where the whole of the Egyptian fleet was destroyed. War subsequently broke out between Russia

[1] For a discussion of "Retaliation in Naval Warfare", see Higgins, A. Pearce, *Studies in International Law and Relations*, chap. XII.

A very similar situation arose in 1915–18 and the arguments on which the judgments of the British Prize Court justified the Orders-in-Council of 1915 and 1917 were on similar grounds.

[2] *C.M.H.* VII, chaps. IX, X; Manning, W. O., *The Law of Nations*, chap. X; Walker, T. A., *The Science of International Law*, pp. 415–26; Moore, J. B., *op. cit.* VII, § 1099; *C.H.B.F.P.* vol. II, chap. III. [3] See *C.H.B.E.* I, 546.

[4] See *C.H.B.E.* I, 547.

and Turkey which was concluded by the Treaty of Adrianople, 1829, but England and France remained at peace with Turkey. Other similar blockades followed in which England or France was chiefly concerned. The offending vessels were not confiscated and the modern rule was developed that there should be no interference with ships belonging to third Powers.[1]

The humanitarian spirit was at work in other directions than the abolition of slavery and, in 1864, thanks to the philanthropic efforts of MM. Moynier and Dunant, both Swiss citizens, who had been horrified by the sight of the sufferings of the sick and wounded at Magenta and Solferino, was instrumental in obtaining the summons by the Swiss Government of a Conference to consider the subject of the sick and wounded in land warfare. In 1864 the Geneva Convention on this subject was signed and has been ratified by the majority of the states in the world. An attempt made in 1868 to extend its humane principles to naval warfare was unsuccessful, but the work done at Geneva was of value during the succeeding years and subsequent Conventions signed at Geneva in 1906 and 1929 have enlarged the scope of the original Convention, while the Hague Conferences of 1899 and 1907 applied the same principles to naval warfare.[2]

In another direction, with a view of endeavouring to prohibit the use of weapons which needlessly aggravate the sufferings of men in warfare or render their death inevitable, a Conference was summoned at St Petersburg in 1868 by Alexander II when a Declaration was signed by a large number of states in which the Contracting Powers renounced, in a war between themselves, the employment by their naval or military forces of any projectile of a weight below 400 grammes (about 14 ounces avoirdupois) which is either explosive or charged with fulminating or inflammable substances. This Declaration is the first formal agreement restricting the use of weapons of war. The reasons given for the restriction are marked by a high feeling of humanity; the Contracting Powers were agreed that the "necessities of war ought to yield to the requirements of humanity and that it is inhuman to aggravate uselessly the sufferings of disabled men". The application of the principle made at the time was limited and appears to be practically obsolete to-day, but the principle itself was incorporated into the Hague Convention on the laws of war adopted in 1899. The recent practices in war suggest that the standard set in 1868 has not been maintained.

[1] Hall, W. E., *op. cit.* § 121; Hogan, A. E., *Pacific Blockade*.
[2] For texts see Higgins, A. Pearce, *op. cit.* p. 8.

BIBLIOGRAPHY

Part I. Collections of Manuscripts in Public and Private Archives and Official Papers and Publications

1. Public Record Office.
2. Other Collections.
3. Select List of Parliamentary Papers.
4. Select List of Parliamentary Debates.

Part II. Other Works

1. General Bibliography.

    (a) Bibliographies and Guides.
    (b) Periodicals.
    (c) Collected Historical Records.
    (d) General Histories and Descriptive Works.
    (e) Biographies.

2. Special Bibliographies.

    A. Colonial Policy and Administration.
        i. Colonial Policy in general.
        ii. The Colonies in the Revolutionary and Napoleonic Wars.
        iii. The Humanitarian Movement.
        iv. Transportation.
        v. Emigration and Land Policy.
        vi. Economic Policy and History.
        vii. International Law and Relations.
        viii. Imperial Defence.

    B. The History of the Colonies (other than the Dominions).
        i. Gibraltar, Malta and the Ionian Islands.
        ii. The West Indies, Bermuda, British Honduras and British Guiana.
        iii. Tropical Africa.
        iv. Ceylon, British Malaya and Hong Kong.
        v. Mauritius and Seychelles.
        vi. Falkland Islands, St Helena and Ascension.

BIBLIOGRAPHY

For the history of the Dominions reference should be made to the bibliographies of vols. VI–VIII. Attention is here mainly confined to general matters of imperial policy and to the colonies and protectorates of the Dependent Empire. The pamphlet literature of the nineteenth century is so extensive that only a few representative works have been included.

PART I

COLLECTIONS OF MANUSCRIPTS IN PUBLIC AND PRIVATE ARCHIVES AND OFFICIAL PAPERS AND PUBLICATIONS

By Professor A. P. NEWTON and A. TAYLOR MILNE

1. PUBLIC RECORD OFFICE

(a) COLONIAL OFFICE

In 1782 by Burke's Sinecure Act (22 George III, c. 82), the Secretaryship of State for the American, or Colonial, Department, which had been established in 1768, and the Commissioners for Trade and Plantations were abolished, and the functions of the latter were entrusted to a Committee of the Privy Council. Pending the appointment of the Committee, colonial affairs were dealt with by a subordinate branch of the Home Department, styled the Plantations Branch. By Order-in-Council of 5 March 1784 the Committee of Trade and Foreign Plantations was appointed in accordance with Burke's Act. It was re-organised by further Orders-in-Council in 1786 and the business of the Plantations Branch was transferred to it. In 1794 Henry Dundas, who had dealt with colonial affairs as Secretary for the Home Department, was made Secretary for War and also nominally Secretary of State for the Colonies, but the Departments of War and the Colonies were not actually united until 1801, when Lord Hobart (afterwards Earl of Buckinghamshire) was created Secretary of State for the War and Colonial Departments. By that date the Committee for Trade and Foreign Plantations (the predecessor of the modern Board of Trade) had ceased to deal with colonial affairs, which had gradually been concentrated in the hands of the Secretary of State.

Between 1815 and 1854 the Secretary of State for War and the Colonies was mainly concerned with colonial affairs and he was usually called the Secretary of State for the Colonies. In 1854 a fourth Secretaryship of State was created for War and the functions of the third Secretary of State were confined to colonial affairs.

SECRETARIES OF STATE WHO ADMINISTERED THE AFFAIRS
OF THE COLONIES BETWEEN 1782 AND 1794

1782, July 10.	Thomas Townshend (afterwards Lord Sydney).
1783, April 2.	Frederick, Lord North (afterwards Earl of Guilford).
December 19.	George, Lord Temple (afterwards Marquess of Buckingham).
December 23.	Thomas, Lord Sydney.
1789, June 5.	William Wyndham Grenville (afterwards Lord Grenville).
1791, June 8.	Henry Dundas (afterwards Viscount Melville).
1794, July 11.	William Henry, Duke of Portland.

CEYLON

C.O. 54. Original Correspondence. 1798–1919. 828 volumes. These include the Reports and Papers of the Commissioners of Eastern Inquiry, 1830–5. See also C.O. 416 below.
C.O. 337. Register of Correspondence. 1849–1910. 22 volumes.
C.O. 55. Entry Books. 1794–1872. 121 volumes.
C.O. 56. Acts. 1835–1916. 17 volumes.
C.O. 57. Sessional Papers. 1831–1919. 200 volumes.
C.O. 58. Government Gazettes. 1813–1919. 197 volumes.
C.O. 59. Miscellanea. 1795–1919. 130 volumes.
C.O. 416. Commissioners of Eastern Inquiry. 1829–30. 32 volumes. Papers supplementary to those in C.O. 54 above.

CURAÇOA

C.O. 66. Correspondence, etc. 1800–16. 4 volumes.

DOMINICA

C.O. 71. Original Correspondence. 1730–1872. 144 volumes.
C.O. 72. Entry Books. 1770–1872. 18 volumes.
C.O. 73. Acts. 1768–1900. 22 volumes.
C.O. 74. Sessional Papers. 1767–1919. 39 volumes.
C.O. 75. Government Gazettes. 1865–1919. 13 volumes.
C.O. 76. Miscellanea. 1765–1887. 77 volumes.

FALKLAND ISLANDS

C.O. 78. Original Correspondence. 1831–1919. 153 volumes.
C.O. 339. Register of Correspondence. 1846–72. 2 volumes.
C.O. 399. Entry Books. 1832–70. 7 volumes.
C.O. 79. Acts. 1846–1917. 3 volumes.
C.O. 80. Sessional Papers. 1845–1912. 7 volumes.
C.O. 81. Miscellanea. 1846–1919. 74 volumes.

FERNANDO PO

C.O. 82. Original Correspondence and Entry Books. 1828–43. 12 volumes. After 1842 see SIERRA LEONE.

FIJI

C.O. 83. Original Correspondence. 1860–1919. 149 volumes.
C.O. 419. Register of Correspondence. 1860–1909. 7 volumes.
C.O. 400. Entry Book. 1859–62. 1 volume.
C.O. 84. Acts. 1875–1916. 5 volumes.
C.O. 85. Sessional Papers. 1875–1919. 25 volumes.
C.O. 86. Government Gazettes. 1874–1919. 21 volumes. For papers before 1874 see also NEW SOUTH WALES.[1]

GAMBIA

C.O. 87. Original Correspondence. 1828–1919. 210 volumes.
C.O. 341. Register of Correspondence. 1849–1907. 10 volumes.
C.O. 401. Entry Books. 1827–72. 16 volumes.
C.O. 88. Acts. 1843–1916. 6 volumes.
C.O. 89. Sessional Papers. 1843–1913. 11 volumes.
C.O. 90. Miscellanea. 1822–1919. 93 volumes. See also SIERRA LEONE.

GIBRALTAR

C.O. 91. Original Correspondence. 1705–1919. 472 volumes.
C.O. 342. Register of Correspondence. 1850–1907. 15 volumes.

[1] See Vol. VII, Pt. i, p. 648.

C.O. 92. Entry Books. 1803–72. 33 volumes.
C.O. 93. Acts. 1832–1915. 5 volumes.
C.O. 94. Government Gazettes. 1839–1919. 108 volumes.
C.O. 95. Miscellanea. 1704–1919. 102 volumes.

GOLD COAST

C.O. 96. Original Correspondence. 1753–6 and 1843–1919. 609 volumes.
C.O. 343. Register of Correspondence. 1849–1910. 22 volumes.
C.O. 402. Entry Books. 1843–72. 13 volumes.
C.O. 97. Acts. 1852–1915. 6 volumes.
C.O. 98. Sessional Papers. 1854–1919. 32 volumes.
C.O. 99. Government Gazettes. 1872–1919. 34 volumes.
C.O. 100. Miscellanea. 1845–1919. 69 volumes. See also SIERRA LEONE.

GRENADA

C.O. 101. Original Correspondence. 1747–1873. 135 volumes. From 1874 see WINDWARD ISLANDS.
C.O. 102. Entry Books. 1763–1872. 25 volumes.
C.O. 103. Acts. 1766–1918. 24 volumes.
C.O. 104. Sessional Papers. 1766–1919. 40 volumes.
C.O. 105. Government Gazettes. 1834–1919. 23 volumes.
C.O. 106. Miscellanea. 1764–1919. 113 volumes.

GUADELOUPE

C.O. 110. Original Correspondence, Entry Books, etc. 1758–1816. 25 volumes.

GUIANA, BRITISH

C.O. 111. Original Correspondence. 1781–1919. 627 volumes. Demerara, Essequibo and Berbice.
C.O. 345. Register of Correspondence. 1850–1908. 18 volumes.
C.O. 112. Entry Books. 1801–72. Including also Surinam, 1812–16, for which see below.
C.O. 113. Acts. 1837–1918. 14 volumes.
C.O. 114. Sessional Papers. 1805–1919. 172 volumes.
C.O. 115. Government Gazettes. 1838–1919. 129 volumes.
C.O. 116. Miscellanea. 1686–1919. 288 volumes, including the papers of the Dutch Association, 1686–1792.

HELIGOLAND

C.O. 118. Original Correspondence. 1807–94. 61 volumes.
C.O. 346. Register of Correspondence. 1850–1910. 6 volumes.
C.O. 347. Register of Out-Letters. 1874–90. 2 volumes.
C.O. 119. Entry Books. 1807–77. 7 volumes.
C.O. 120. Acts. 1883–9. 1 volume.
C.O. 121. Sessional Papers. 1881–90. 1 volume.
C.O. 122. Miscellanea. 1834–90. 36 volumes.

HONDURAS, BRITISH

C.O. 123. Original Correspondence. 1744–1919. 298 volumes.
C.O. 348. Register of Correspondence. 1855–1907. 13 volumes.
C.O. 124. Entry Books. 1630–1872. 15 volumes.
C.O. 125. Acts. 1855–1916. 10 volumes.
C.O. 126. Sessional Papers. 1848–1917. 21 volumes.
C.O. 127. Government Gazettes. 1861–1919. 18 volumes.
C.O. 128. Miscellanea. 1807–1917. 98 volumes.

St Croix

C.O. 244. Entry Books. 1808–15. 10 volumes.

St Domingo

C.O. 245. Original Correspondence and Entry Books. 1693–1801. 10 volumes and bundles.

St Eustatius

C.O. 246. Miscellaneous in-letters. 1779–83. 1 bundle.

St Helena

C.O. 247. Original Correspondence. 1805–1919. 187 volumes.
C.O. 366. Register of Correspondence. 1849–65. 4 volumes.
C.O. 248. Entry Books. 1815–1872. 18 volumes.
C.O. 249. Acts. 1837–1911. 5 volumes.
C.O. 250. Sessional Papers. 1836–1913. 7 volumes.
C.O. 251. Government Gazettes. 1845–1907. 3 volumes.
C.O. 252. Miscellanea. 1836–1919. 84 volumes.

St Lucia

C.O. 253. Original Correspondence. 1709–1873. 150 volumes. After 1873 see Windward Islands.
C.O. 367. Register of Correspondence. 1850–69. 4 volumes.
C.O. 254. Entry Books. 1794–1872. 19 volumes.
C.O. 255. Acts. 1818–1918. 15 volumes.
C.O. 256. Sessional Papers. 1820–1918. 25 volumes.
C.O. 257. Government Gazettes. 1857–1919. 38 volumes.
C.O. 258. Miscellanea. 1722–1919. 115 volumes.

St Thomas

C.O. 259. Entry Books of Correspondence, etc. 1808–15. 6 volumes.

St Vincent

C.O. 260. Original Correspondence. 1668–1873. 118 volumes. From 1873 see Windward Islands and Register thereof.
C.O. 261. Entry Books. 1776–1872. 24 volumes.
C.O. 262. Acts. 1768–1919. 27 volumes.
C.O. 263. Sessional Papers. 1769–1919. 38 volumes.
C.O. 264. Government Gazettes. 1831–1918. 30 volumes.
C.O. 265. Miscellanea. 1763–1919. 99 volumes.

Sierra Leone

C.O. 267. Original Correspondence. 1691–1919. 584 volumes and bundles.
Under Sierra Leone are included the West African Settlements, Senegambia, Goree, Cape Coast Castle, Gambia, Gold Coast, etc. at certain periods.
C.O. 368. Register of Correspondence. 1849–70. 7 volumes.
C.O. 268. Entry Books. 1672–1872. 57 volumes.
C.O. 269. Acts. 1801–1915. 8 volumes.
C.O. 270. Sessional Papers. 1776–1919. 48 volumes.
C.O. 271. Government Gazettes. 1817–1919. 25 volumes.
C.O. 272. Miscellanea. 1819–1919. 96 volumes. Blue books.

Straits Settlements

C.O. 273. Original Correspondence. 1838–1919. 497 volumes.
C.O. 426. Register of Correspondence. 1867–1911. 18 volumes.
C.O. 425. Entry Books. 1867–73. 8 volumes.

C.O. 274. Acts. 1867–1919. 14 volumes.
C.O. 275. Sessional Papers. 1855–1919. 101 volumes.
C.O. 276. Government Gazettes. 1867–1919. 86 volumes.
C.O. 277. Miscellanea. 1867–1919. 70 volumes. Blue books.

Surinam

C.O. 278. Original Correspondence and Entry Books. 1667–1832. 28 volumes.
See also Guiana, British.

Tobago

C.O. 285. Original Correspondence. 1700–1873. 91 volumes. After 1873 see
Windward Islands.
C.O. 286. Entry Books. 1793–1872. 11 volumes.
C.O. 287. Acts. 1768–1898. 15 volumes.
C.O. 288. Sessional Papers. 1768–1898. 30 volumes.
C.O. 289. Government Gazettes. 1872–98. 7 volumes.
C.O. 290. Miscellanea. 1766–1893. 73 volumes. See also Trinidad.

Trinidad

C.O. 295. Original Correspondence. 1783–1919. 525 volumes.
C.O. 372. Register of Correspondence. 1850–65. 6 volumes.
C.O. 296. Entry Books. 1797–1872. 31 volumes.
C.O. 297. Acts. 1832–1918. 22 volumes.
C.O. 298. Sessional Papers. 1803–1919. 114 volumes.
C.O. 299. Government Gazettes. 1833–1919. 97 volumes.
C.O. 300. Miscellanea. 1804–1919. 131 volumes. Blue books.

Turks and Caicos Islands

C.O. 301. Original Correspondence. 1848–82. 66 volumes. For period 1799–
1848 see Bahamas.
C.O. 409. Entry Books. 1849–72. 5 volumes.
C.O. 302. Acts. 1849–1916. 8 volumes.
C.O. 303. Sessional Papers. 1849–1905. 7 volumes.
C.O. 304. Miscellanea. 1852–1919. 67 volumes. Blue books.

Virgin Islands

C.O. 314. Original Correspondence. 1711–91. 1 volume. 1854–72. 23 volumes.
From 1816–53 see St Christopher and after 1872 Leeward Islands.
C.O. 315. Acts. 1774–1899. 10 volumes.
C.O. 316. Sessional Papers. 1773–1880. 10 volumes.
C.O. 317. Miscellanea. 1784–1896. 67 volumes.

West Indies

C.O. 318. Original Correspondence. 1624–1919. 352 volumes. Military and
naval despatches, reports, etc. of Commissioners of legal enquiry, of enquiry into
the state of the captured negroes and correspondence relating to the West
Indies generally.
C.O. 375. Register of Correspondence. 1849–1914. 8 volumes.
C.O. 319. Entry Books. 1699–1872. 56 volumes.
C.O. 320. Miscellanea. 1820–40. 10 volumes. Memoranda on military matters,
the slave trade, etc.
C.O. 441. West Indies Incumbered Estates Commission. 1857–92. Journals and
entry books. 25 boxes.

Windward Islands

C.O. 321. Original Correspondence. 1874–1919. 37 vols. For earlier correspondence see Barbados, Grenada, St Lucia, St Vincent and Tobago.
C.O. 376. Register of Correspondence. 1850–1907. 19 volumes. The earlier
original correspondence to which reference is made will be found under the
separate islands.

COLONIES (GENERAL)

C.O. 323. 1689–1919. 819 volumes.

This class comprises the series, down to 1782, formerly known as "Plantations General", amongst the records of the old Board of Trade.[1] It also includes Law Officers' reports on Colonial Acts, applications for colonial appointments, circulars and the correspondence relating to the colonies generally in the Secretary of State's Office. Between 1801 and 1854 much of the correspondence concerns both the War and Colonial Departments which were then under the same Secretary of State.

C.O. 432. Register of Correspondence. 1861–70. 3 volumes.

C.O. 378. Register of General Miscellaneous Correspondence. 1852–1919. 19 volumes.

C.O. 324. Entry Books. 1662–1872. 175 volumes.

C.O. 325. Miscellanea. 1744–1858. 46 volumes.

C.O. 326. Register of In-Letters. 1810–49. After 1849 see the separate registers under each colony.

EMIGRATION

C.O. 384. Original Correspondence. 1817–94. 190 volumes.

C.O. 428. Register of Correspondence. 1850–72. 5 volumes.

C.O. 385. Entry Books. 1814–71. 30 volumes.

C.O. 386. Colonial Land and Emigration Commission. Original Correspondence and Entry Books. 1833–94. 193 volumes.

PATRONAGE

C.O. 429. Original Correspondence relating to applications for appointments. 1861–70 and 1881–1919. 131 volumes. See also COLONIES (GENERAL).

C.O. 430. Register of Correspondence. 1867–70 and 1887–1909. 11 volumes.

(b) FOREIGN OFFICE

The records now classified as belonging to the Foreign Office date, with certain exceptions, from March 1782 when the re-arrangement of the business of the Office of the Secretaries of State left the Secretary for the Northern Department with matters relating to foreign countries. The records are listed on the public shelves of the Public Record Office in a comprehensive MS List which supersedes all previous lists. The papers are generally open to public inspection down to 1885. They contain many documents of importance relating to colonial affairs, but cannot here be more particularly described. The classes of most importance for our purpose are the following: GENERAL CORRESPONDENCE. Original despatches, reports, etc. from British ambassadors, consuls, etc. arranged chronologically under countries. The following may be especially noted:

AFRICA. F.O. 2. Papers relating to expeditions, correspondence of consuls. 1825–1905. 983 volumes. F.O. 97/433–8. Niger Expedition, etc.

BORNEO (F.O. 12); COMORO (F.O. 19), 1848–67, 9 volumes; CORSICA (F.O. 20), 1793–8, 22 volumes; HELIGOLAND (F.O. 36), 1808–17, 11 volumes; IONIAN ISLANDS (F.O. 42), 1778–1820, 17 volumes; LIBERIA (F.O. 47); MOSKITO (F. O. 53); PACIFIC ISLANDS (F.O. 58); SULU (F.O. 71); ZANZIBAR (F.O. 107).

SLAVE TRADE PAPERS. (F.O. 84), 1816–99, 2276 volumes; and F.O. 97/430–2.

This immense collection contains the correspondence in connection with the various measures for suppression of the slave trade and includes many documents of direct importance to the history of our African settlements and treaties with native chiefs. There are detailed MS lists on the shelves of the Public Record

---

[1] See List of 1876.

Office. Many of the more important documents have been printed in the volumes of *British and Foreign State Papers* published annually and in the papers presented to Parliament, for which see our list below.

See also SIERRA LEONE (F.O. 315), 1819–68, 96 volumes and bundles.

(c) WAR OFFICE

These records consist of official papers of the Secretary at War, the Secretary of State for War and Colonies (see above) and the Commander-in-Chief. They contain many papers of interest for our purpose, which can most readily be found by reference to the *Alphabetical Guide to War Office Records in the Public Record Office* (P.R.O. *Lists and Indexes*, No. LIII, 1931). In that list the subjects with which the documents deal are arranged alphabetically and thus it is easy to ascertain what particular documents contain important references to colonial affairs.

(d) ADMIRALTY

For a description of the classes of Admiralty records which are likely to contain material of importance in relation to our subject see *C.H.B.E.* vol. VIII, p. 879.

(e) TREASURY

For a description of the classes of Treasury records proper see Giuseppi, M., *Guide to the Public Records*, vol. II, pp. 142–52. They relate to financial matters, and since Treasury sanction had to be obtained for arrangements involving financial commitments, there are constant references to the colonies. See especially:

T. 7. Letters on Colonial Affairs. 1849–89. 26 volumes.

T. 28. Letters to the Secretaries of State for the Colonies, etc. 1796–1856. 34 volumes.

T. 28. Letters to America. 1763–1838. 4 volumes. These include correspondence with the West Indies.

T. 38. Departmental Accounts and papers relating to the Colonies. 1685–1838.

T. 38. Supply Books. 1700–1855. These show the grants of supplies for the several public services. They afford the readiest means of tracing expenditure on any particular object.

T. 39. Accounts of Foreign and Colonial Stations. 1846–76.

T. 64. Colonies. 1680–1867. Shipping and trade returns. Correspondence, despatches, etc.

The Treasury records also now include those of various abolished offices and expired Commissions of Inquiry, etc. Among these the following are of direct interest for the history of the Colonies.

T. 70. AFRICAN COMPANIES. 1693 volumes and bundles. This class comprises the records of the Royal African Company and its predecessor to 1750, and of the Company of Merchants trading to Africa, 1750–1821. They include:—
For the history of the Companies: Minute books, letter books and papers.
For the business of the Companies: Ledgers, Journals, etc. Together with many documents relating to personnel.

T. 71. SLAVE REGISTRATION and COMPENSATION RECORDS. 1812–46. 1630 volumes.
These comprise the records of the SLAVE REGISTRATION DEPARTMENT, 1813–34, 650 volumes; and the SLAVE COMPENSATION COMMISSION, 1833–46, 94 volumes. These records are very detailed, but are disappointing in their content of historical material.[1]

---

[1] For a description of them see Wastell, R., "The Slave Compensation Commission", an unpublished thesis in the Library of the University of London.

(f) HOME OFFICE

There is much information about the colonies in the correspondence of the Home Office with other departments. H.O. 10 and H.O. 11 are essential for the study of transportation and many other subjects of colonial interest; H.O. 30 and H.O. 50 contain correspondence with the Colonial Office; H.O. 76 has shipping statistics; and other important material is to be found in the series H.O. 28, H.O. 35, H.O. 48, H.O. 100 and H.O. 252.

(g) BOARD OF TRADE

The series B.T. 1 and B.T. 3 contain much material on colonial trade. The Minutes of the Committee for Trade and Plantations are in the series B.T. 5, and other papers of the Committee in B.T. 6. Other series also contain trade and shipping returns, as do the Audit Office Papers (A.O. 3 and A.O. 6).

(h) CUSTOMS HOUSE

Customs House Accounts (in particular Customs 3, 5 and 10) contain the ledgers of imports into and exports from Great Britain, including her colonial trade. There are many gaps in the earlier papers owing to the fire at the London Customs House in 1814.

(i) PRIVY COUNCIL OFFICE

The Privy Council Registers (P.C. 2) and the Unbound Papers (P.C. 1) contain much material for colonial history. For instance, P.C. 1/67–92 concern "Convicts and Prisons, 1819–44".

(j) GIFTS AND DEPOSITS IN THE PUBLIC RECORD OFFICE

G.D. 8 (Chatham Papers), G.D. 22 (Russell Papers) and G.D. 29 (Granville Papers) are all valuable for colonial policy and administration.

2. OTHER COLLECTIONS

(a) IN GREAT BRITAIN

For the study of this period the papers of the following statesmen in the British Museum, Department of Manuscripts, are indispensable: Liverpool Papers (Add. MSS. 38190–489), Huskisson Papers (Add. MSS. 38734–770), Peel Papers (Add. MSS. 40181–617), Aberdeen Papers (Add. MSS. 43039–358), Wellesley Papers, 2nd series (Add. MSS. 37274–318), Windham Papers (Add. MSS. 37842–935), Melville Papers (Add. MSS. 40100–2, supplemented by those at Rhodes House, Oxford, in the National Library of Scotland and in private hands), Gladstone Papers, Napier Papers and Ripon Papers.

In addition there are many small groups of papers in the British Museum relating to the history of the colonies, which may be found by consulting the published catalogues and indexes of the collection. Some account of West Indian material there is given in L. J. Ragatz, *Guide for the Study of British Caribbean History* (Washington, 1932). For Ceylon, St Helena and East Africa the records of the East India Company in the India Office are indispensable.

Among papers in private hands which are essential for the study of this period are the Howick Papers at Howick Hall and the Palmerston Papers at Broadlands. Other sources are indicated in the "Special Bibliographies" below. For a summary account of the principal collections of philanthropic and other societies see *C.H.B.E.* vol. VII, pt. I, pp. 654–5, and vol. VIII, pp. 883–85.

(b) IN THE COLONIES

A fuller account of colonial archives will be printed in volume III of this *History*. As regards the West Indies the most complete collections of manuscripts are at Kingston, Jamaica. In the Record Office there are letters patent, deeds, wills and various court records. The Admiralty Court and the Colonial Secretary's Office also contain papers of value, and official records collected in the West India Reference Library of the Institute of Jamaica are noted in the *Bibliographia Jamaicensis* and its *Supplement*. In the offices of parochial boards in the island are records of the old slave courts. The records of other West Indian islands are less well preserved. Some account of them may be found in the following:—H. C. Bell and others, *Guide to British West Indian Archive Materials, in London and in the Islands, for the History of the United States* (Washington, 1926); L. J. Ragatz, *Guide for the Study of British Caribbean History*, 1763–1834 (Washington, 1932); R. Pares, "Public Records in British West India Islands", *Bull. Inst. Hist. Research*, VII (1930), 149–57; A. M. Butterfield, "Records of the Supreme Court, the Chancery and the Vice-Admiralty Courts of Jamaica," *Bull. Inst. Hist. Research*, XVI (1938), 88–99; and V. L. Oliver, "Records of Barbados, Demerara and the Leeward Islands", *Caribbeana*, Oct. 1934. Selections from the records of British Honduras have been published in *Archives of British Honduras*, ed. Sir J. A. Burdon (3 vols. 1931–5), where full lists of local records are given.

Until well into the nineteenth century the Legislative Papers of the colonies were not printed, but they are to be found in manuscript in the Public Record Office, London (see Part I, 1 (a) above). For later printed journals W. Gregory, *List of the Serial Publications of Foreign Governments*, 1815–1931 (New York, 1932), which includes the British colonies, should be consulted.

For archives of the Dominions see Bibliographies in vols. VI, VII and VIII.

3. SELECT LIST OF PARLIAMENTARY PAPERS

The following list includes the most important papers presented to the Houses of Parliament relating to colonial affairs in general and the dependent empire in particular during the period 1783 to 1870. The papers are arranged chronologically under broad headings with a brief indication of their contents, and form a much more comprehensive list than has yet appeared. For papers relating to Canada and Newfoundland, Australia and New Zealand, and South Africa, see the Bibliographies of vols. III, VII and VIII respectively.

House of Commons' Papers issued before 1800 were collected in two series: *Parliamentary Reports*, 1715–1801 (4 vols. issued in 1773 and 11 vols. issued in 1803), known as the "First series", and *Papers printed by Order of the House of Commons from the year 1731 to 1801* (110 vols. of Speaker Abbott's Collection as bound for the House of Commons Library), known as the "Second series". There are imperfect indexes to both collections. From 1801 onwards details can be obtained from the sessional indexes and from the following consolidated indexes published by the House of Commons: *Indexes to the Reports of Commissioners on Colonies* (1812–40) *and Emigration* (1812–47), *Parl. Pap.* 1847, LVIII (710–IV); *General Index to the Bills*, 1801–52, *Parl. Pap.* 1854, LXX (O. 8); *General Index to the Reports of Select Committees*, 1801–52, *Parl. Pap.* 1854, LXX (O. 9); *General Index to the Accounts and Papers, etc.*, 1801–52, *Parl. Pap.* 1854; *General Index to the Bills, Reports, Estimates, and Accounts and Papers, etc.*, 1852–99, *Parl. Pap.* 1909.

House of Lords' Papers, many of which are duplicates of those of the Commons, can be traced in a *General Index to the Sessional Papers printed by Order of the House of Lords, or presented by Special Command*, 1801–37, *Parl. Pap.* 1859, Sess. 2, H.L., XXXI; 1859–70, *Parl. Pap.* 1872, H.L., LXVIII.

The following annotated guides to the papers of both Houses cover part of the field: M. I. Adam, J. Ewing and J. Munro, *Guide to the Principal Parliamentary Papers relating to the Dominions*, 1812–1911 (Edinburgh, 1913) and L. J. Ragatz,

A Guide for the Study of British Caribbean History, 1763–1834, *including the Abolition and Emancipation Movements* (Washington, 1932).

The references given below indicate in each case the session during which a paper was printed, the volume for that session into which it has been bound by the House of Commons, or House of Lords, and the Sessional ( ) or Command [ ] number of the paper. It should be noted that the sessional numbers of *Bills* are a separate series from those of *Accounts and Papers*, also that, in the case of House of Lords' Papers, the sessional numbering of volumes did not begin until 1834 and papers before that date constitute a single series. References to House of Commons Papers printed before 1800 are to the "2nd series", as described above.

Unless otherwise indicated references given below are to House of Commons' Papers.

COLONIAL POLICY AND ADMINISTRATION

1810, II (362). Report from Select Committee on Sinecures.
1810–11, III (246). 2nd Report from Sinecures Comm.
1810–11, X (94). Estimate for colonial establishments. [Thereafter annually.]
1812, II (181). 3rd Report from Sinecures Comm.
1813–14, H.L., LXIX (33). Bill *re* patents for colonial appointments.
1813–14, II (308). Bill *re* examining colonial revenues.
1813–14, XI (87), (114). Papers *re* colonial appointments.
1814–15, VII (81), (82), (83). Accounts *re* colonial trade with Ireland, 1800–13.
1814–15, VII (353). Names of colonial Governors, Lieutenant-Governors, etc.
1814–15, IX (224). Estimates for colonial establishments.
1816, VII, Pt. I (501). Report from Sel. Comm. on Roman Catholics in Colonies.
1816, XIII (216). Papers *re* civil and military offices in colonies.
1817, XIV (497). Value of colonial trade.
1817, XV (174). Report from Sel. Comm. on Roman Catholics in Colonies. [Reprinted 1851, XX (42).]
1817, XVII (129). Colonial offices held.
1819–20, IV (85), (86). Colonial civil and military establishments.
1820, III (269). Report from Lords' Sel. Comm. on Timber Duties.
1820, XII (62). Progress in auditing colonial accounts.
1821, VI (186). Report from Sel. Comm. on Foreign Trade.
1821, XIV (64). Colonies in possession of Britain.
1821, XIV (485). Corresp. *re* colonial military defence.
1821, XV (119), (362). British troops stationed in colonies.
1822, H.L., CXXVIII (65). Bill to regulate colonial trade.
1822, XIX (21). Colonial estimates.
1822, XX (377). Names of colonial agents, and dates.
1823, IV (411). Report from Sel. Comm. on Commerce.
1823, XIII (192). Colonial estimates.
1823, XIV (167). Colonial absentee officials.
1823, XIV (343). Colonial receipts and disbursements.
1824, XVI (17). Colonial estimates.
1824, XVI (116). Colonial receipts and disbursements.
1824, XVI (440). Colonial absentee officials.
1825, H.L., CLXXV (133). Bill for further regulating colonial trade.
1825, H.L., CLXXVI (186). Bill consolidating customs laws.
1825, III (431). Bill for salaries of Colonial Clergy.
1825, XVIII (30). Colonial estimates.
1825, XIX (231). Colonial receipts and disbursements.
1825, XIX (363). Colonial absentee officials.
1826, I (45). Bill to amend Colonial Clergy Act.
1826, IV (404). 1st Report from Sel. Comm. on Emigration.
1826, XX (156). Colonial estimates.
1826, XXII (388). Colonial absentee officials.
1826, XXVI (332). Instructions to Colonial Commissioners.
1826–7, V (88), (237), (550). Further Reports from Sel. Comm. on Emigration.

1826–7, xv (161). Colonial estimates.
1826–7, xviii (187). Colonial absentee officials.
1828, xvii (122). Colonial estimates.
1828, xxi (191). Lists of colonial Acts and Proceedings.
1828, xxi (266). Colonial absentee officials.
1829, xvi (41). Colonial estimates.
1829, xxi (167). Colonial absentee officials.
1830, xviii (89). Colonial estimates.
1830, xxi (212), (352). Corresp. re colonial finance.
1830, xxi (351). Colonial land grants.
1830, xxi (353). Colonial absentee officials.
1830, xxix (650). Number of emigrants, 1820–30.
1830–1, iv (64), (194). Reports of Commission on Colonial Revenues.
1830–1, ix (235). Colonial absentee officials.
1831, xiii (31). Colonial estimates.
1831, xix (260). Date of capture of each colony, population, trade, shipping, etc.
1831–2, H.L., ccxcvi (103). Bill for auditing colonial accounts.
1831–2, iv (627). Exchequer Bills Bill.
1831–2, xxvii (362). Colonial estimates.
1831–2, xxxii (164). Colonial absentee officials.
1831–2, xxxii (210). Colonial pensions granted since 1815.
1831–2, xxxii (724). Report from Emigration Commissioners.
1833, vii (650). Fees charged on colonial appointments.
1833, xxiv (169). Colonial estimates.
1833, xxvi (140). Colonial absentee officials.
1833, xxvi (141). Corresp. with Governors re emigration.
1833, xxvi (434). Papers re colonial offices abolished or salaries reduced, 1830–33.
1833, xxvi (696). Number of emigrants, 1825–32.
1834, vi (570). Report from Sel. Comm. on Colonial Military Expenditure, 1834.
1834, xlii (184). Colonial estimates.
1834, xliv (151). Colonial absentee officials.
1834, xliv (323). Colonial charters of justice.
1835, vi (473). Report from Sel. Comm. on Colonial Military Expenditure, 1835.
1835, xviii (507). Report from Sel. Comm. on Sinecures.
1835, xxxvii (212). Colonial absentee officials.
1835, xxxviii (146). Colonial estimates.
1835, xxxviii (374), (408), (586). British expenditure on colonies, 1832–4.
1835, xxxix (49). Circular to Governors re protecting native interests.
1835, xxxix (87). Corresp. re emigration.
1836, vii (538). Report from Sel. Comm. on Aborigines, 1836.
1836, xi (512). Report from Sel. Comm. on Colonial Lands, 1836.
1836, xxxvii (573). Vote of £5400 for Colonial Office, 1835.
1836, xxxviii (160). Colonial estimates.
1836, xxxix (537). Circular re duration of Governorships, 1828.
1836, xxxix (598). Colonial accounts.
1836, xl (76). Corresp. re emigration.
1836, xlv (298). Imports from Colonies.
1837, vii (425). Report from Sel. Comm. on Aborigines, 1836.
1837, vii (516). Report from Sel. Comm. on Colonial Accounts.
1837, xl (149). Colonial estimates.
1837, xlii (132). Report from Canadian emigration agent.
1837, xlii (442). Acts passed by colonial legislatures re demise of crown.
1837, xliii (358). Report of Emigration Commissioners.
1837–8, xxii (669). Report from Sel. Comm. on Transportation.
1837–8, xxxvii (314). Colonial estimates.
1837–8, xl (388). Report of Agent-General for Emigration, 1838.
1837–8, xl (389). Report on emigration.
1837–8, xlvii [137]. Number of emigrants, 1832–6.
1839, H.L., ii (95). Bill to prevent abuse of colonial legislative authority.

1839, XXXI (142). Colonial estimates.
1839, XXXIX (536–I), (536–II). Reports on emigration.
1839, XXXIX (580). Emigrant ships, 1837–9.
1839, XLI (55). Clergy maintained by public money in Colonies.
1840, H.L., X (85). Colonial imports and exports, 1828–38.
1840, H.L., XXVII (295). British plantation sugar imported, 1814–40.
1840, VIII (527). Report from Sel. Comm. on East Indian Products.
1840, XXX (179–v). Colonial estimates.
1840, XXXIII (35). Commissions for Colonial Land and Emigration Commissioners, 1840.
1840, XXXIII (113), (613). Papers and corresp. re emigration.
1840, XXXIV (596). Pensions for colonial service.
1840, XXXIV (632). Colonial expenditure.
1841, III (236). Bill re colonial import duties.
1841, VI (333). Report from Sel. Comm. on Emigration (Scotland).
1841, XIV (224–v). Colonial estimates.
1841, XXI (294). Emigration of female paupers.
1842, H.L., II (164). Bill to amend colonial trade laws.
1842, I (219). Bill to amend colonial trade laws.
1842, XXV [355]. Passenger Acts.
1842, XXV (567). Land and emigration reports.
1842, XXVII (130). Colonial estimates.
1842, XXVII (173). Order re colonial barracks.
1842, XXXI [373], (301). Papers re emigration.
1842, XL (O. 11), (O. 30). Colonial trade bill.
1843, H.L., III (88). Bill re colonial unsworn testimony.
1843, IV (164). Bill re colonial unsworn testimony.
1843, XXIX (261). Emigration reports.
1843, XXXI (91–v). Colonial estimates.
1843, XXXIV (109), (291), (323). Papers re emigration.
1843, LII (605). Colonial trade and shipping.
1844, H.L., II (183). Bill to regulate colonial posts.
1844, IV (438). Bill to regulate colonial posts.
1844, XXXI (178). Emigration reports.
1844, XXXIII (108–v). Colonial estimates.
1844, XXXIV (179), (608). Colonial accounts, 1842–3.
1844, XXXV (181), (503). Papers re emigration, emigrant ships.
1845, VI (534). Colonial Trade Bill.
1845, VIII (530). Report from Sel. Comm. on Colonial Accounts.
1845, XXVII [617]. Emigration reports.
1845, XXIX (257–v). Colonial estimates.
1845, XXXI (49). Date of capture of each colony, population, trade, shipping, etc.
1845, XXXI (589). Legislative Councils in colonies without Assemblies, 1836–44.
1845, XXXI (623). Colonial agents in Britain.
1845, XXXV (356). Colonial bishops, religious instruction, etc.
1846, H.L., III (282). Customs Duties Bill.
1846, H.L., III (290). Colonial Copyright Laws Bill.
1846, H.L., XIX (185). Value of British exports, 1830–45.
1846, I (612). Customs Duties Bill.
1846, XXIV [706]. Emigration reports.
1846, XXVI (266–v). Colonial estimates.
1846, XXVII (168). Order in Council, 1838, re masters and servants in colonies.
1846, XXVII (455). Corresp. re Colonial Office establishment since 1833.
1846, XXVII (679). Return of colonial duties.
1846, XXVII (680). Colonial accounts, 1843–4.
1846, XXIX (400). Applications for representative govt. and answers.
1846, XXIX (702). Provision for destitution in colonies.
1846, XXIX [728]. Annual reports of colonial Governors for 1845. [Continued yearly.]

1846, XLV (83), (97). Corresp. *re* colonial-built ships.
1846, XLV (170). Corresp. *re* loss of emigrant ship *Cataraque*.
1847, H.L., III (290). Colonial Copyright Bill.
1847, VI (737), (737–II). Report from Lords' Sel. Comm. on Colonization from Ireland.
1847, XXXIII [809]. Emigration reports.
1847, XXXV (299–v). Colonial estimates.
1847, XXXVII (119). Colonial representations *re* differential duties.
1847, XXXVII (696). Return *re* colonial shipping, trade, etc., 1835–44.
1847, XXXVII (740). Colonial accounts.
1847, XXXVII [869]. Annual reports by colonial Governors.
1847, XXXIX [777], [824]. Papers *re* emigration.
1847, LVIII, Pt. IV (710–IV). Index to Reports of Commissioners (Colonies), 1812–40.
1847–8, H.L., VII, p. 131. Colonial laws repealing customs duties.
1847–8, H.L., XXI (191). Return *re* Colonial Office establishment.
1847–8, VI (703). Colonial Loans Bill.
1847–8, XVII (415), (593). Reports from Lords' Sel. Comm. on Colonization from Ireland.
1847–8, XXIII, Pt. I (123), (137), (167), (409); XXIII, Pt. II (184), (206), (230); XXIII, Pt. III (245), (361–II); XXIII, Pt. IV (361), (361–II, Supp. No. 1). Reports from Sel. Comm. on Sugar and Coffee.
1847–8, XXVI [961], [961–II]. Emigration reports.
1847–8, XXVII (455). Grey's letter *re* additional Under-Secretary for Colonies.
1847–8, XL (327–v). Colonial estimates.
1847–8, XLII (42). Appt. of additional Under-Secretary for Colonies.
1847–8, XLIII (371). Corresp. *re* co-operation between Colonial Office and Board of Trade.
1847–8, XLVI [1005]. Annual reports by colonial Governors.
1847–8, XLVII [932], [964], [971], [985], [986], (50), (50–II), (345). Papers *re* emigration.
1847–8, XLIX (568). Circular *re* Roman Catholics.
1847–8, LI (473), (473–II). Legal officers in colonies since 1832.
1847–8, LI (586). Memorial of mill-owners *re* deportation of operatives.
1849, H.L., III (120). Bill for trial of Admiralty cases in colonies.
1849, H.L., V (224). Colonies Postal Bill.
1849, I (549). Bill for trial of Admiralty cases in colonies.
1849, III (473). Colonies Postal Bill.
1849, XI (86). 3rd Report from Lords Sel. Comm. on Colonization from Ireland.
1849, XXX (165). Public Works Loans Commissioners—sums for emigration.
1849, XXXI (268–v). Colonial estimates.
1849, XXXII (56). Colonial garrisons, 1829, 1835, 1840, 1847.
1849, XXXIV [1126]. Annual reports by colonial Governors.
1849, XXXIV (3). Names of colonial Governors, salaries, etc.
1849, XXXIV (224). Colonial expenditure, 1843–7; and military expenditure since 1835.
1849, XXXIV (239). Return *re* colonies, date of acquisition, govt., troops, etc.
1849, XXXVIII [1025], (593), (593–II). Papers *re* emigration.
1849, LI (90), (90–II). Communications with colonies *re* Navigation Acts.
1849, LI (476). Colonial postage rates.
1850, XXXIV (256–v). Colonial estimates.
1850, XXXVI [1231], [1287]. Annual Reports by colonial Governors.
1850, XXXVI (180), (498). Colonial postal rates.
1850, XXXVI (352). Colonial duties.
1850, XXXVI (536). Legal officers in colonies since 1848.
1850, XL [1163], (173), (734). Papers *re* emigration.
1851, XIX (632). Report from Sel. Comm. on Passenger Act.
1851, XX (42). Report from Sel. Comm. on Roman Catholics in Colonies. [Reprint of 1816, VII, Pt. I (501).]

1851, XXI (372), (605). Reports from Sel. Comm. on Steam Communications with East.

1851, XXXII (211–v). Colonial estimates.

1851, XXXIV [1421]. Ann. reports by colonial Governors.

1851, XXXIV (11). Return *re* capital punishment in colonies.

1851, XXXIV (627). Colonial expenditure, 1847–9.

1851, XXXIV (667). Return *re* colonial duties.

1851, XL (198). Corresp. *re* emigrant ship *Washington*.

1851, XL (347), (347–II). (379), (429), (680). Papers *re* emigration.

1852, H.L., II (83), (109), (122). Colonial Bishops Bill.

1852, H.L., III (199). Colonial Crown Revenues Bill.

1852, I (103), (384), (530). Colonial Bishops Bill.

1852, II (382). Colonial Crown Revenues Bill.

1852, XXIX (238–v). Colonial estimates.

1852, XXX [1515]. Reports of Treasury Comm. on colonial naval, ordnance and commissariat establishments.

1852, XXXI [1539]. Ann. Reports by colonial Governors.

1852, XXXI (144). Value of colonial imports and exports.

1852, XXXI (200). Return *re* colonial accounts.

1852, XXXI (391). Return *re* colonial Governors.

1852, XXXI (566). Troops employed in colonies, 1848–50.

1852, XXXII (355–I), (355–II), (355–III), (355–IV), (355–V), (355–VI), (355–VII). Petitions, etc. *re* colonial churches since 1845.

1852, XXXII (458). Colonial Bishops—number, salaries, etc.

1852, XXXIII [1474]. Papers *re* emigration.

1852, XXXIV [1489]. Papers *re* emigration.

1852, XLIX (245), (542). Papers *re* emigrant ships, 1847–52.

1852–3, H.L., III (246). Colonial Bishops Bill.

1852–3, H.L., III (301), (324), (335). Colonial Churches Bill.

1852–3, H.L., III (309). Colonial Coining Bill.

1852–3, I (724). Colonial Coining Bill.

1852–3, I (750). Colonial Bishops Bill.

1852–3, I (831). Colonial Churches Bill.

1852–3, V (841). Colonial Bishops (Consecration) Bill.

1852–3, V (914). Bill to amend Passenger Act, 1852.

1852–3, LIX (92). Return *re* troops in colonies.

1852–3, LIX [1595], [1693]. Colonial Reports for 1851 and 1852.

1852–3, LXII (84), (836). Returns *re* colonial customs duties.

1852–3, LXII (396), (1000). Colonial expenditure by Britain, 1849, 1851–2.

1852–3, LXII (929). Colonial accounts.

1852–3, LXII (1004). Number of letters of Emigration Commissioners, 1852.

1852–3, LXVIII [1627], [1650], (23). Papers *re* emigration and emigrant ships.

1852–3, XCV (204), (793). Corresp. *re* colonial postage rates.

1852–3, XCVIII (113), (205). Reports *re* mortality on emigrant ships.

1852–3, XCVIII (299). Return *re* colonial shipping. [Thereafter annually.]

1854, I (28). Bill *re* colonial clergy.

1854, XIII (163), (349). Reports from Sel. Comm. on Passenger Ships.

1854, XLI (46). Return *re* troops in colonies, 1851–3.

1854, XLIII (487). Return *re* colonial Governors, etc.

1854, XLVI [1763], (436), (436–1). Papers *re* emigration, 1852–4.

1854, XLVI (178), (255), (492). Papers *re* emigration and emigrant ships.

1854–5, I (247). Colonial Appeals Bill.

1854–5, IV (188), (231). Colonial Lighthouses Bill.

1854–5, V (17), (75). Bill to amend Passenger Acts.

1854–5, XVII (523). Report of Emigration Commissioners *re* Bristol.

1854–5, XXXII (72). Return *re* staff appts. in colonies, 1822 and 1853.

1854–5, XXXVI [1919]. Colonial Reports for 1853.

1854–5, XXXVI (164). Return *re* colonial Governors, etc.

1854–5, XXXVI (295). Return *re* colonial customs duties.

1854–5, XXXVI (444). Return *re* colonial Bishops.
1854–5, XXXVI (503). Colonial expenditure by Britain, 1854.
1854–5, XXXIX (42), (464). Papers *re* emigration.
1854–5, L (355). Corresp. *re* colonial lighthouses.
1856, XLII [2050]. Colonial Reports for 1854.
1856, XLIV (36). Papers *re* emigrant ships.
1856, XLIV (285). Return *re* colonial customs duties.
1856, XLIV (431). Corresp. *re* Canadian and West Indian goods.
1857 Sess. 1, X [2198]. Colonial Reports for 1855.
1857 Sess. 1, X (14), (144), (147). Papers *re* emigration and emigrant ships.
1857 Sess. 1, XII [2166]. Corresp. *re* registration of colonial vessels at Hong Kong.
1857 Sess. 1, XVI (120). Return *re* customs changes abroad.
1857 Sess. 2, H.L., III (117). Bill *re* colonial courts.
1857 Sess. 2, XXVIII (125), (306). Papers *re* emigration.
1857 Sess. 2, XXVIII (237). Return *re* colonial Governors, etc.
1857 Sess. 2, XXVIII (238). Names and salaries of Emigration Commissioners and staff.
1857 Sess. 2, XXVIII (303). Return *re* copyright in colonies.
1857 Sess. 2, XXVIII (307). Returns *re* colonial govts.
1857–8, XL [2403]. Colonial reports for 1856.
1857–8, XLI (165). Papers *re* emigration.
1857–8, XLI (378). Return *re* colonial customs duties.
1857–8, XLIII (392). Return *re* colonial judicial offices.
1857–8, XLIII (521). Papers *re* Chinese emigrant ships.
1857–8, LIII (131). Return *re* customs changes.
1859 Sess. 1, XVII (239). Return *re* colonial judicial offices.
1859 Sess. 1, XVII (240). Return *re* cost of colonies, 1853–7.
1859 Sess. 2, I (79). Bill *re* colonial legislatures.
1859 Sess. 2, XVII (114). Return *re* colonial military forces, 1853–7.
1859 Sess. 2, XXI [2567]. Colonial Reports for 1857.
1859 Sess. 2, XXII (218), (228). Papers *re* emigration.
1859 Sess. 2, XXIII (32). Return *re* colonial judicial offices.
1860, V (327). Bill *re* offences abroad.
1860, XLI (282). Report of Comm. on Colonial Military Defences.
1860, XLIV [2711], [2711–1]. Colonial Reports for 1858.
1860, XLIV (606). Papers *re* emigration.
1860, XLV (569). Return *re* colonial Governors.
1860, XLV (598). Return *re* customs changes.
1860, LX (350). Number of emigrant ships since 1853.
1861, XIII (423). Report from Sel. Comm. on Colonial Military Expenditure, 1861.
1861, XL [2841], [2941–1]. Colonial Reports for 1859.
1861, XL (186). Papers *re* emigration.
1861, XL (296). Return *re* colonial forces, 1858–9.
1861, XLIII (264). Copy of Act *re* Law of Evidence (1843).
1861, LVIII (513). Lighthouses accounts, 1856–61.
1862, V (62). Bill *re* Writs of Habeas Corpus abroad.
1862, XXXVI [2955], [2955–1]. Colonial Reports for 1860.
1862, XXXVI (73). Return *re* troops in colonies, 1835 and 1858.
1862, XXXVI (355). Papers *re* emigration.
1862, XXXVI (396). Return *re* public officers.
1862, XXXVI (474). Return *re* colonial customs changes.
1862, XXXVI (475). Return *re* colonial Governors.
1863, I (237). Bill *re* Letters Patents in colonies.
1863, I (250). Bill to confirm certain colonial acts.
1863, I (251). Bill *re* clergy ordained abroad.
1863, V (129). Vice-Admiralty Courts Bill.
1863, XXXII (173). Numbers of troops in colonies.
1863, XXXVIII (147). Return *re* colonial accounts, 1860–1.
1863, XXXVIII (430). Return *re* numbers of emigrants, 1815–63.

1854–5, XXXVI (463). Malta—Portions of criminal code.
1854–5, XLV [1869]. Malta—Report on plague in 1813.
1856, XLIV (139). Ionian Islands—Acts re pensions.
1857 Sess. I, I (2). Ionian Islands—Bill re military and naval commissions.
1857 Sess. I, I (149). Malta—Corresp. re jury law.
1860, III (281). Ionian Islands—Bill re marriages.
1861, XXXVI (11). Gibraltar—Number of wine rooms.
1861, LII (535). Malta—Return re murders etc., 1840–60.
1861, LVIII [2891]. Ionian Islands—Gladstone's mission.
1861, LXVII (185). Ionian Islands—Papers re Legislative Assembly.
1863, XXXVI (350), (537). Malta—Corresp. re new dock.
1863, XXXVIII (329). Ionian Islands—Memorials of Marcoras and Xydras.
1863, XXXVIII (484). Ionian Islands—Salaries and pensions.
1863, LXXIV [3113]. Malta—Corresp. re Italian extradition.
1863, LXXIV [3185]. Ionian Islands—Despatch re Union with Greece.
1863, LXXIV (485). Ionian Islands—Contributions to Great Britain.
1864, II (197). Ionian Islands—Bill to amend acts.
1864, XXXVII (144), (355), (432), (432–1). Malta—Papers re new dock.
1864, XXXVII (220). Malta—Letter re French Creek property.
1864, XL (243), (531). Malta—Petitions for reforms.
1864, LXVI [3247]. Ionian Islands—Treaty with Austria, France, Prussia and
    Russia, 14 Nov. 1863.
1864, LXVI [3322]. Ionian Islands—Treaty with Greece, 29 March 1864.
1864, LXVI [3323]. Ionian Islands—Treaty of Britain, France and Russia with
    Greece, 29 March 1864.
1864, LXVI (54). Ionian Islands—Corresp. re occupation.
1865, XXXV, Pt. II (59). Malta—Papers re French Creek Dock.
1865, LVII [3462]. Gibraltar—Anglo-Spanish Declaration re merchant ships.
1865, LVII [3471]. Ionian Islands—Corresp. re pensions.
1865, LVII [3571]. Ionian Islands—Accession of Turkey to Treaty of 29 March
    1864.
1866, XLI (328). Gibraltar, Malta—Return re mortality of garrisons.
1867, XXXVII [3921], [3921–1]. Gibraltar, Malta—Papers re sanitation.
1867, LXXIV [3827]. Ionian Islands—Despatches re state since withdrawal of
    British Protection.
1867–8, I (202). Ionian Islands—Bill re Lord High Commissioner.
1868–9, XLIII (217). Malta—Papers re administration.
1870, XLIX (251). Malta—Papers re Clergy in Council.
1871, XLVIII (208). Gibraltar—Statement re local revenues.

WEST INDIES, BERMUDA, BRITISH HONDURAS AND BRITISH GUIANA

(See also the Annual Reports of Colonial Governors, 1846–70, noted under
COLONIAL POLICY above, and SLAVERY AND THE SLAVE TRADE below.)

1783, XIII (426), (428). Anglo-American Trade Bill.
1784, V (59). Evidence re distressed state of Sugar Colonies.
1785, IX (112), (113), (114), (115), (116), (117), (118), (119). Jamaica—Lists of
    vessels, 1783–4.
1788, XVIII (548). Bill regulating trade between America and West Indies.
1789, XXVII (648), (649), (650), (651), (652). Sugar colonies—Exports and imports.
1789, XXVII (670). Troops sent to West Indies.
1790, XXXI (705). Account re West Indian shipping.
1790, XXXI (706). Expenses of fortifying Grenada.
1792, XXXV (770). Minutes on the Sugar Bill.
1794–5, XV (119). Grenada and St Vincent—Report from committee on mer-
    chants' petitions.
1794–5, XL (810), (811), (812), (813). West Indies—Grey-Jervis Expedition.
1795–6, XLII (840). West Indies—Grey-Jervis Expedition.

1796–7, XLIII (867), (868), (869). St Domingo—Papers *re* occupation.

1799–1800, XXVIII (171), Grenada and St Vincent—Report on McDowall's Petition.

1801, H.L., I, p. 649. West Indies—Bill to regulate prize courts.

1801, III (98). Grenada—Report from Sel. Comm.

1801–2, H.L., II, p. 171. West Indies—Sugar Bounties Bill.

1801–2, II (25). Grenada—Report from Sel. Comm.

1801–2, IV (86). Trinidad—State of cultivation.

1805, H.L., XIII (44). West Indies—Bill to consolidate import and export laws.

1806, H.L., I (18). West Indies—Foreign Shipping Bill.

1806, H.L., I (26), (80). West Indies—Neutral Shipping Bill.

1806, H.L., I (50). Tortola Imports and Exports Bill.

1806, H.L., I (61). West Indies—Public Accounts Bill.

1806, H.L., VII (22). Jamaica—Exports of sugar to Great Britain, 1792–1806.

1806, H.L., VI (56). Report, 31 May 1784, on intercourse between West Indies and North America.

1806, I (169). Bill *re* neutral trading in West Indies and South America.

1806, I (182). West Indies—Public Accounts Bill.

1806, XII (37), (65). Tortola—Exports and imports.

1806, XII (118). Papers *re* colonies lately belonging to the Batavian and French Republics.

1806, XIII (225). West Indies—Intercourse with America.

1806–7, II (83). Report from Sel. Comm. on Distillation and on Distress in Sugar Colonies.

1807, III (65). West Indies—Report from Sel. Comm. on Commercial State.

1807, III (73). Dominica—Report from Comm. on Fire at Roseau.

1808, H.L., XV (101). West Indies—Commissioners of Accounts Bill.

1808, H.L., XVIII (99). West Indies—Report from Sel. Comm. on Commercial State, 1807.

1808, I (291). West Indies—Public Accounts Bill.

1808, IV (178), (278), (300), (318). Four Reports from Sel. Comm. on Distillation.

1808, IX (195). Prizes prosecuted in Vice-Admiralty Courts, Jamaica, etc.

1808, XX (9). West Indies—Imports of provisions and lumber, 1804–6.

1809, H.L., XXIII (77). Bill imposing duty on sugar and coffee from Martinique and Mariegalante.

1809, V (141). West Indies—Report from Comm. on Army Expenditure.

1810–11, II (225). West Indies—Report from Sel. Comm. on Free Labourers from East.

1810–11, XI (184). Trinidad—Papers *re* constitution and laws.

1811, H.L., XLV (46). Prices of brown sugar, 1807–11.

1811, XLVI (112). Trinidad—Papers *re* capitulation, population, etc.

1812, H.L., XLVII (40). Bill to prohibit intercourse between Jamaica and St Domingo.

1812, I (346). West Indies—Crown Revenues Bill.

1812, X (279). Jamaica—Petition to Prince Regent.

1812, X (355). Berbice—Commissioners for Crown Estates.

1812, X (356), (372), (373). West Indies—Report of Commissioners of Revenue Inquiry.

1812–13, III (182). St Vincent—Report from Sel. Comm. on Losses by Eruption.

1813–14, XI (87), (114). West Indies—Papers *re* colonial appointments.

1814–15, VII (353). West Indies—Names of Governors, etc.

1814–15, VII (478). West Indies—Population and clergy.

1814–15, IX (100), (224). West Indies—Accounts and estimates.

1816, II (466). Bill for regulating trade of Demerara, Berbice and Essequibo.

1816, VIII (509), (528). Berbice—Report of Commissioners *re* Crown Estates.

1816, XIII (216). Civil and military offices in St Lucia, Tobago, Berbice, Demerara, Essequibo and Ile de France.

1816, XIV (172), (266), (274). Colonial produce consigned from West Indies.

1816, XIV (392). Bahamas—Exports and imports.

1816, xix (213). West Indies—Places held by non-residents.
1817, xvii (129). West Indies—Colonial offices held under Crown.
1817, xvii (170). Trinidad—Neutrality in contest on Spanish continent.
1820, H.L., cxiv (52). Barbados—Bill to permit import of coffee from America.
1820, xii (293). Tobago—Corresp. re administration of justice.
1821, xiv (684). Leeward Islands—Return re Governors.
1822, H.L., cxxviii (64), (65). Bills to regulate West Indian and American trade.
1822, i (181), (346). Bill to regulate West Indian and American trade.
1822, ii (229), (361). Bill to regulate West Indian and American trade.
1822, xx (178). West Indies—Persons holding office.
1823, xiv (343). Trinidad—Accounts.
1823, xvii (16), (17). Trinidad—Various papers, immigrants from Spanish Main.
1824, xvi (116). Trinidad—Accounts.
1825, H.L., clxxvi (168). West Indies—Bishops' Salaries Bill.
1825, i (219), (352). West Indies—American Trade Bill.
1825, i (365), (444). Bill regulating trade of British possessions abroad and repealing customs laws.
1825, xv (517). West Indies—1st Report of Commissioners on Administration of Justice.
1825, xix (231). Trinidad—Accounts.
1825, xx (351). West Indies—Clergy.
1826, i (45). Jamaica—Bill to amend Clergy Salaries Act.
1826, xxii (328). Papers re sugar duty, 1776–1826.
1826, xxvi (174). Anguilla—Report of Commission.
1826, xxvi (276). West Indies—2nd Report on Administration of Justice.
1826, xxvi (332). Instructions to Colonial Commissioners.
1826–7, xv (37). British Honduras—Papers re appt. of Col. Arthur, 1814.
1826–7, xv (159). West Indies—Grants in aid for building churches and Bishops' residences. [See also 1828, xvii, p. 396; 1829, xvi (65) 1830, xvii (85).]
1826–7, xviii (126). Jamaica and Leeward Islands—Salaries of officials.
1826–7, xviii (276). West Indies—Eight returns of British and foreign shipping, 1814–26.
1826–7, xviii (500). Accounts of shipping, West Indies and North America, 1816–26.
1826–7, xviii (554). Jamaica—Attack on Wesleyan meeting house.
1826–7, xxiii (478), (551). Trinidad—Reports of Commissioners on land titles and state of colony.
1826–7, xxiv (559). West Indies—1st Report, 2nd ser., of Commissioners on Administration of Justice.
1826–7, xxv, p. 21. West Indies—Corresp. between Britain and U.S.A. re American commercial intercourse.
1826–7, xxvi (36). West Indies—3rd Report on Administration of Justice.
1828, xix (573). West Indies—Crown Lands.
1828, xxi (191). West Indies—Acts and proceedings of Legislative Assemblies printed.
1828, xxiii (525). Trinidad—Huskisson's despatch re land grants.
1828, xxiii (577). West Indies—2nd Report, 2nd ser., of Commissioners on Administration of Justice.
1829, xv (340). Papers re coffee and sugar duties since 1789.
1829, xvii (319). Papers re imported sugar, 1819–29.
1829, xxiv (334). West Indies—3rd Report, 2nd ser., on Administration of Justice.
1830, H.L., cclxxxviii (159). West Indies—Treasury Minute remitting duties, 15 April 1828.
1830, xviii (426). Jamaica—Troops stationed in.
1830, xxi (212), (352). Trinidad—Corresp. re revenue and expenditure.
1830, xxi (349). Jamaica—Sums voted for Army.
1830, xxi (673). Jamaica—Persons confined in gaols and workhouses.
1830, xxii (454). West Indies—Rum and molasses exported to U.S.A. and Canada, 1812–29.

1830, XXV (466). Yearly produce of duties on cotton-wool, coffee and sugar, 1792–1829.

1830, XXVII (268). Molasses imported from West Indies, 1820–30, and re-exported.

1830, XXVII (452). Duties levied on West Indian products imported into Canada, 1829.

1830, XXVII (481). Duties on West Indian goods imported into Britain.

1830, XXVII (O. 52), (O. 53). Proposed resolutions *re* sugar duties.

1830–1, II (26). Bill amending Act of 6 Geo. IV regulating colonial trade.

1830–1, II (334). Corresp. *re* state of gaols in West Indies, British Honduras and British Guiana.

1830–1, IX (120). Statement to Board of Trade *re* state of West Indies.

1830–1, XVI, p. 263. West Indies—Corresp. between Great Britain and U.S.A. *re* commercial intercourse with U.S.A.

1831, H.L., CCXCIV (80). West Indies—Statement *re* state of colonies.

1831, XIX (260). West Indies—Papers *re* date of capture, etc., population, govt., trade, shipping.

1831–2, IV (371). Barbados, St Vincent, St Lucia—Bill to allow import of lumber and provisions duty free.

1831–2, XX (381). West Indies—Report from Sel. Comm. on Commercial State.

1831–2, XXVII (362). West Indies—Estimate for official salaries.

1831–2, XXX (382). Protest of West India merchants, 6 April 1832.

1831–2, XXXI (58). Jamaica—Establishment and revenue, 1822–31.

1831–2, XXXI (59). Jamaica—Laws passed for relief of Catholics, Jews and free persons of colour, 1827–32.

1831–2, XXXI (197). West Indies—Papers *re* hurricanes.

1831–2, XXXI (211). West Indies—Names of persons apptd. to judicial offices since 1801.

1831–2, XXXI (212). Trinidad—Memorials, expenditure, answers.

1831–2, XXXI (213). St Lucia—Memorials and corresp. *re* expenditure.

1831–2, XXXI (363). West Indies—Laws for relief of persons of various persuasions.

1831–2, XXXI (432). Orders-in-Council *re* administration of justice in Guiana, Trinidad, etc.

1833, IV (155). Bill to regulate colonial trade.

1833, XXIV (169). West Indies—Estimate for official salaries. [Thereafter annually.]

1833, XXVI (540). Jamaica—Memorial of Baptist missionaries, 1832.

1833, XXVI (544). Jamaica—Offices held by members of Council.

1833, XXVI (736). Amount advanced under 2 & 3 Will. IV, c.-125, for assistance of West Indian proprietors.

1833, XXXIII (590). Report on Ure's sugar experiments.

1834, XLII (311), (476). Jamaica—Estimates for grant to Baptist Missionary Society and others.

1835, XXXIX (71). British Guiana—Despatch to Governor, 29 Nov. 1834.

1835, XXXIX (418). British Honduras—Commissions by which officers have commanded.

1836, XXXIX (135), (607). British Honduras—Authority of officers, expense of govt. from 1824.

1836, XLVIII (174). Jamaica—Statement by Agent *re* proceedings of Governor and Assembly.

1836, XLVIII (O. 44). Jamaica—Proceedings under Abolition Act.

1837, XLIII (332). British Honduras—Corresp. *re* Col. Arthur.

1837, XLIII (353). Jamaica—Abstracts *re* schools and education.

1837–8, XL (138). West Indies—Statistics of health of troops since 1803.

1837–8, XLVII [137]. Bermuda, British Honduras—Statistical returns *re* population, education, commerce.

1837–8, XLVIII (113), (520). West Indies—Reports from Latrobe on negro education.

1837–8, LII (180), (232). British Guiana—Orders-in-Council regulating employment.

1838, H.L., xiv (24). Jamaica—Return *re* church establishment and schools, 1831–6.

1838, H.L., xviii (70). Jamaica—Return of exports for 53 years ending 31 Dec. 1836.

1838, H.L., xviii (358). Jamaica—Return of exports from Great Britain since 1828.

1839, H.L., ix (136). Jamaica—Various papers and corresp.

1839, H.L., xvi (268). Sugar from foreign states.

1839, xxxv (107–i), (107–ii), (107–iii), (200), (217), (288), (290), (304), (581). Jamaica—Papers *re* state of colony.

1839, xxxv (107), (107–iii), (523). British Guiana—Papers, circular instructions.

1839, xxxvii (107–v), (107–vi). Leeward Islands—Papers *re* state of colony.

1839, xxxvii (107–vi). Bahamas, British Honduras—Papers *re* state of colony.

1839, xxxix (463). British Guiana—Corresp. *re* hill coolies.

1839, xli (541). Jamaica—Number of schools and scholars.

1840, H.L., xvii (308). West Indies—Statistical reports on health of navy, 1830–6.

1840, viii (in 537). Jamaica—Exports for 55 years, 1782–1836.

1840, xxxiv (77). British Guiana—Corresp. *re* hill coolies.

1840, xxxiv (82). Trinidad—Despatch *re* immigration.

1840, xxxiv (141). Jamaica—Corresp. *re* barracks at Maroon Town.

1840, xxxiv (151). British Guiana—Corresp. *re* immigration of labourers.

1840, xxxiv (154). West Indies—Corresp. *re* health of troops.

1840, xxxiv (238). Jamaica—Annual imports, 1835–9.

1840, xxxiv (288). British Guiana—Memorial to Schomburgk, explorer.

1840, xxxiv (404). British Guiana—Papers *re* Civil List.

1840, xxxiv (595). Leeward Islands—Corresp. *re* convention of General Council and Assembly.

1840, xxxiv (616). British Guiana—Treasury Minutes, 1836 and 1840, *re* relief advances.

1840, xxxv [212]. Jamaica—Papers *re* state of colony.

1841, xvi [321]. West Indies and British Guiana—Various papers.

1841, xvi (411). Jamaica—Accounts, 1838–9.

1841, xxvi (290). Sugar imported into Britain, 1815–40.

1841 Sess. 2, iii [344]. Jamaica—Papers *re* state of colony.

1841 Sess. 2, iii [346]. Demerara and Berbice—Report on state of labourers.

1841 Sess. 2, xiii (479). West Indies—Report from Sel. Comm. on Employers and Labourers.

1842, xxvi (49). Sums spent on West Indian Relief, 1831–41, 1842–6.

1842, xxix [374]. Jamaica—Papers *re* state of colony.

1842, xxix [376]. West Indies and British Guiana—Various papers.

1842, xxix [379]. Trinidad—Papers *re* state of colony.

1842, xxxix (64). Sugar imported into Britain, 1831–41.

1842, xxxix (293). West Indies—Imports into Britain of sugar, molasses, rum, coffee and cocoa, 1831–41.

1843, xxxiii (136). West Indies—Immigrants since 1834.

1843, xxxiii (142), (489). St Kitts—Corresp. *re* conduct of Governor.

1843, xxxiii (292). Jamaica—Corresp. *re* customs duties.

1843, xxxiv [438]. Papers *re* emigration from West Africa to West Indies.

1843, xxxv (404). British Guiana—Corresp. *re* return of coolies to India.

1843, lii (439). Coffee and cocoa imported into Britain, 1820–42.

1844, xxxiv (266). Jamaica—Memorial from House of Assembly.

1844, xxxv [530]. West Indies—Corresp. *re* immigration of labourers.

1844, xxxv (284). West Indies—Projected immigration of hill coolies.

1844, xlv (153). Sugar imported into Britain, 1830–43.

1844, xlv (250). West Indies, British Guiana—Imports of sugar, molasses, rum, coffee and cocoa into Britain from 1832.

1844, xlv (392). West Indies—Coffee imported, 1820–43.

1845, xxxi (66). Jamaica—Memorial from House of Assembly.

1845, xlvi (80). West Indies—Sugar imported into Britain, 1820–44.

1846, XXVII (303). Jamaica—Memorial from Chamber of Commerce *re* sugar question.

1846, XLIV (196). West Indies—Sugar imported into Britain, 1815-40.

1846, XLIV (700). Jamaica—Memorial from Kingston Chamber of Commerce *re* sugar question.

1847, XXXVII (287). British Guiana—Subscriptions for Irish and Scottish Highlands Relief.

1847, XXXVII (713). Barbados—Corresp. *re* lighthouse.

1847, XXXIX (325), (496). West Indies, British Guiana—Corresp. and papers *re* immigration of labourers since 1834.

1847, LIX (in 3). Rum duties, 1800-45.

1847, LX (717). West Indies—Exports and imports, shipping, 1840-6.

1847, LXIII (716). British Guiana—Corresp. *re* railways.

1847-8, XXIII, Pt. 2 (184). 4th Report from Sel. Comm. on Sugar and Coffee.

1847-8, XXIII (in 206). Jamaica—Average cost of sugar and net proceeds of seven estates, 1831-46.

1847-8, XL (327-VII). Barbados—Estimate for lighthouse.

1847-8, XLIV [927]. Papers *re* hurricane in Tobago, loans to Tobago and British Guiana to encourage immigration.

1847-8, XLIV (62). Trinidad—Corresp. *re* supply of labour, etc.

1847-8, XLIV (193). Trinidad—Petition *re* sugar cultivation.

1847-8, XLIV (370). British Guiana, Trinidad—Despatches *re* coolies, 1844-7.

1847-8, XLIV (684). Trinidad—Scheme for bank.

1847-8, XLIV (685). Jamaica—Despatches from Grey.

1847-8, XLV (399). West Indies—Promotion of immigration.

1847-8, XLVI (749). Corresp. *re* distress in sugar-growing colonies.

1847-8, LVIII (400). Sugar imported into Britain.

1849, XXXVII [1065]. Jamaica—Papers *re* state of colony, 1793-1847.

1849, XXXVII (280). Jamaica—Corresp. *re* general condition.

1849, XXXVII (280-II). Trinidad—Corresp. *re* general condition.

1849, XXXVII (594). British Guiana—Papers *re* dispute over Estimates.

1849, L (178), (351). West Indies, British Guiana—Imports of sugar, molasses, rum, coffee and cocoa into Britain, 1831-48.

1849, LI (121). Trinidad—Despatch *re* Navigation Laws.

1850, XXXVI (541). St Kitt's, Anguilla—Act to repeal customs.

1850, XXXIX [1139]. Jamaica—Papers *re* affairs.

1850, XXXIX (21). British Guiana—Papers *re* dispute over Estimates.

1850, XL (643). West Indies—Corresp. *re* emigration from Sierra Leone and St Helena.

1850, LII (280). Sugar imported into Britain, 1793-1849.

1851, XXXVII (104). Jamaica—Papers *re* cholera outbreak.

1851, XXXVI (154). British Guiana—Papers *re* dispute over Estimates.

1851, XXXIX (624). British Guiana—Papers *re* state of colony, growth of sugar.

1851, XL (243). Corresp. *re* emigration of children to Bermuda.

1851, LIII (264). Sugar imported into Britain, 1800-50.

1852, XXXI (405). British Guiana—Despatches from Barkly, 1851-2.

1852, LI (442). Sugar imported into Britain, 1800-51.

1852, LXVIII (986). Corresp. *re* Chinese immigrants into British Guiana and Trinidad.

1852-3, VII (20). West Indian Loan Bill.

1852-3, LVIII (861). Jamaica—Estimate for Governor's salary.

1852-3, LX (457). Jamaica—Report on yellow fever on *Highflyer*.

1852-3, LXV [1655]. Jamaica—Papers *re* legislative proceedings.

1852-3, LXV (260). Barbados—Despatches *re* yellow fever.

1852-3, LXV (268). West Indies—Corresp. *re* circulation of British coins.

1852-3, LXV (894). West Indies—Statement *re* loans.

1852-3, LXV (938). Antigua—Corresp. *re* black regiment.

1852-3, LXVII (76), (936). Jamaica—Despatches *re* sugar-growing.

1854, III (202). Jamaica Loan Bill.

1854, XXXIX (380). West Indies—Account of loans.
1854, XL [1806]. Jamaica—Corresp. *re* legislative proceedings.
1854, XLI (177). West Indies—Corresp. *re* removal of troops.
1854, XLIII [1848]. Jamaica—Papers and corresp.
1854, XLIII (235). Jamaica—Report and corresp. *re* cholera epidemic.
1854, XLIII (362). Bahamas—Report and corresp. *re* seizure of packages.
1854, XLIII (428). Bermuda—Papers *re* temporary administration since 1 Jan. 1853.
1854, LXV (15). West Indies—Accounts of trade, shipping, etc., 1846–52.
1854–5, III (266). Tobago Loan Bill.
1854–5, VI (205). Bills *re* loans to Antigua, Nevis and Montserrat.
1854–5, XXXVII (16). Bermuda—Papers *re* cholera epidemic.
1854–5, XXXVII (159), (241), (470). West Indies—Corresp. *re* loans.
1854–5, XXXIX (O. 7). Corresp. *re* Chinese immigrants into British Guiana and Trinidad.
1856, VI (121), (148). West Indies Loans Bill.
1856, XLIV (108). Jamaica—Report and corresp. *re* Evelyn (Customs Dept.).
1856, XLIV (230). Jamaica—Papers *re* church affairs.
1856, XLIV (431). Corresp. *re* customs duties on West Indian and Canadian products.
1856, XLIV (432). British Guiana—Corresp. *re* recent disturbances.
1856, LV (351). West Indies—Account of imports and exports, 1850–5.
1857 Sess. 1, XIV (154). Bermuda—Dietaries of convicts.
1857 Sess. 2, XXVIII (305). British Guiana—Corresp. *re* registration tax.
1857 Sess. 2, XLIII [2271]. British Honduras—Convention with Honduras, 27 Aug. 1856.
1857–8, II (221). West Indies—Bill to amend Incumbered Estates Act, 1854.
1857–8, XII [2429]. Antigua—Despatches *re* forming volunteer corps.
1857–8, XLI (105). Bermuda—Papers *re* yellow fever.
1857–8, XLI (286). West Indies—Statement *re* guaranteed loans.
1857–8, XLI (525). Corresp. *re* Chinese immigrants into British Guiana and Trinidad.
1857–8, XLIII (481). Corresp. *re* Chinese emigration to West Indies, etc.
1859 Sess. 1, XV (202). Trinidad—Corresp. *re* health of troops.
1859 Sess. 1, XVI [2452]. West Indies—Papers *re* immigration.
1859 Sess. 2, I (80). Bill *re* Antigua laws.
1859 Sess. 2, XX (31), (31–1). West Indies—Corresp. *re* labour.
1859 Sess. 2, XXII (209). Trinidad—Corresp. *re* health of troops.
1860, III (219). Dominica—Bill *re* loan.
1860, XLV [2700]. Bermuda—Papers *re* convict establishment.
1860, XLV (250). West Indies—Return of immigration loans.
1860, XLV (600). St Lucia—Letter from West India Committee *re* taxation and expenditure.
1860, XLV (616). Jamaica—Report of House of Assembly on Vere Case.
1860, XLV (617). Jamaica—Despatch of Governor *re* newspapers.
1860, LX (68). Account of loans to Antigua, St Kitts, Nevis, Dominica, Montserrat.
1860, LXVIII [2590]. British Honduras—Convention with Guatemala *re* boundary.
1860, LXVIII [2703]. British Honduras—Treaty with Honduras *re* Bay Islands, etc.
1861, XL (43). West Indies—Account of loans.
1862, II (190). Jamaica Loan Bill.
1862, V (148). West Indies—Bill to amend Incumbered Estates Acts, 1854, 1858.
1862, XXXVI [3012]. Jamaica—Corresp. *re* debt settlement.
1862, XXXVI (72). West Indies—Account of loans.
1862, XXXVI (113). West Indies—Immigrants since 1843.
1863, XXXVIII (69). West Indies—Account of loans.
1863, XXXVIII (115). West Indies—Return *re* salaries.
1863, XXXVIII (509). St Vincent—Corresp. *re* riots.
1863, LXVII (272). Imports into Britain of sugar, molasses, rum, coffee, cocoa and cotton from West Indies.

1863, LXXII [3231]. Bahamas—Corresp. *re* New York trade.
1864, IV (215). West Indies—Bill to amend Incumbered Estates Act.
1864, XLI (205), (478). Return *re* sales under West Indian Incumbered Estates Act, 1862, and corresp.
1865, XXXVII (44). West Indies—Account of loans.
1866, III (17). Jamaica Govt. Bill.
1866, XXX [3682], [3683], [3683–1]. Jamaica—Report of commission on disturbances.
1866, XLIX (477). Bermuda—Report on yellow fever, 1864.
1866, L (55). West Indies—Account of loans.
1866, LI [3594], [3594–I], [3594–II], [3594–III], [3595], [3681], [3749]. Jamaica—Corresp. *re* disturbances.
1866, LI (88). Jamaica—Corresp. *re* Gordon.
1866, LI (380). Jamaica—Papers from missionaries and corresp. *re* disturbances.
1866, LI (504). Jamaica—Corresp. *re* conduct of naval officers.
1867, II (291). Dominica—Bill *re* loan repayment.
1867, VII (126). West Indies—Clergy Salaries Bill.
1867, XLII (33). Jamaica—Corresp. *re* conduct of military officers.
1867, XLII (183). Jamaica—Courts martial on Cullen and Morris.
1867, XLIX [3859], [3903]. Jamaica—Papers and corresp.
1867, XLIX (39). West Indies—Account of loans.
1867, XLIX (60), (282), (283). West Indies—Returns *re* ecclesiastical establishment.
1867, LXIV (485). St Vincent—Return *re* quarantine regulations, etc.
1867–8, V (124), (249). West Indies—Clergy Salaries Bill.
1867–8, XLVIII (142). West Indies—Account of loans.
1867–8, XLVIII (355). Jamaica—Costs of proceedings against Governor Eyre.
1867–8, LXIII (204). St Vincent—Corresp. *re* quarantine.
1868–9, III (200). Jamaica Loan Bill.
1868–9, XLIII (55). West Indies—Account of loans.
1868–9, XLIII (240). West Indies—Return *re* ecclesiastical establishment.
1868–9, XLIII (407). Bahamas—Act for disendowing Church of England.
1870, XLIX (232). West Indies—Immigrants and liberated Africans, 1843–56, and each year, 1857–69.
1870, L (49). West Indies—Advances and repayments.
1870, L (196). West Indies—Return *re* ecclesiastical funds.
1870, L (450). Trinidad—Papers on state of education.

TROPICAL AFRICA

(See also the Annual Reports of Colonial Governors, 1846–70, noted under COLONIAL POLICY above, and SLAVERY AND THE SLAVE TRADE below)

1801–2, II (100). Report from Sel. Comm. on Sierra Leone.
1803–4, V (24). Report on petition of Sierra Leone.
1806, XII (195). Account of grants to Sierra Leone Company.
1806–7, H.L., IX (40). Sierra Leone Company Bill.
1806–7, II (55). Report from Sel. Comm. on Sierra Leone.
1810–11, X (101), (102). Grants to Sierra Leone Co., appt. of Chief Justice.
1812, X (101). Report of Commissioners on African Settlements.
1812, X (370). Papers *re* recruiting on coast of Africa.
1813–14, XI (233). West Africa—Estimates for British forts.
1814–15, VII (400), (415). African Co.—Accounts and papers.
1816, IV (470). West Africa—Report from Sel. Comm. on Settlements and Forts. [See also 1816, VII (506) and 1817, VI (431).]
1820, XI (95). West Africa—Estimates for forts.
1820, XII (90). Sierra Leone—Papers *re* state.
1821, XV (119), (362). West Africa—British troops.
1821, XVI (155). West Africa—Estimates for forts.
1821, XXI (724). West Africa—Letter to Treasury *re* Estimates.

1823, XIII (192). Gold Coast—Estimates.
1823, XV (327). African Company—Return *re* officers.
1824, XVI (17). Gold Coast—Estimates.
1824, XVII (269). Sierra Leone—Accounts *re* trade.
1825, XVIII (30). Gold Coast—Estimates.
1825, XIX (503). Sierra Leone—Civil establishment.
1825, XXV (520). Sierra Leone—Duties, exports, population, schools, churches, etc.
1826, XX (156). Gold Coast—Estimates.
1826–7, VII (312), (552). Sierra Leone—Report of Commissioners of Inquiry.
1826–7, XV (7). West Africa—Return of Europeans sent since 1815.
1826–7, XV (161). Gold Coast—Estimates.
1828, XVII (122). Gold Coast—Estimates.
1829, XVI (41). Gold Coast—Estimates.
1829, XXV (236). Sierra Leone—Papers *re* population.
1830, X (66). Report from Sel. Comm. on Sierra Leone and Fernando Po.
1830, XVIII (89). Gold Coast—Estimates.
1830, XXI (57). Sierra Leone—Expenditure, 1812–28, treatment of captured negroes, vessels on West African station since 1815, etc.
1830–1, VI (323). Gold Coast—Estimates.
1831, XIII (31). Gold Coast—Estimates.
1831–2, XXVII (157). Gold Coast—Estimates.
1831–2, XXVII (362). West Africa—Civil Estimates.
1831–2, XLVII (364). Sierra Leone—Mr Justice Jeffcot's charge and corresp.
1833, XXIV (169). West Africa—Civil Estimates.
1834, XLII (184). West Africa—Civil Estimates.
1835, XXXVIII (144). West Africa—Civil Estimates.
1836, XXXVIII (160). West Africa—Civil Estimates.
1837, XL (149). West Africa—Civil Estimates.
1838, XXXVII (314). West Africa—Civil Estimates.
1838, LII (728). Two Orders-in-Council *re* indentured Africans.
1839, XXXI (142–v). West Africa—Civil Estimates.
1840, XXX (179–v). West Africa, Niger Expedition—Estimates.
1840, XXXIII (57). Niger Expedition—Corresp.
1840, XXXIV (224). Orders-in-Council *re* liberated Africans.
1841, XIV (224–v). West Africa, Niger Expedition—Estimates.
1841 Sess. 2, II (14–v). West Africa, Niger Expedition—Estimates.
1842, XI (551). Report from Sel. Comm. on West Africa.
1842, XXVI (494). Niger Expedition—Cost of outfitting.
1842, XXVII (130–v). West Africa—Civil Estimates.
1842, XXXVIII (289). Africans brought to Britain, 1840–2.
1843, XXXI (83). Niger Expedition—Mortality.
1843, XXXI (91–v). West Africa—Civil Estimates.
1843, XXXIII (622). Sierra Leone, Gambia—Acounts, 1835–42.
1843, XXXIV (438). West Africa—Papers *re* emigration to West Indies.
1843, XLVIII [472]. Niger Expedition—Papers.
1843, LII (268). Sierra Leone, Gambia—Duties and expenditure.
1844, XXXIII (108–v). West Africa—Civil Estimates.
1844, XXXIV (504). Sierra Leone—Patients in Kissy Hospital, 1835–42.
1845, XXIX (257–v). West Africa—Civil Estimates.
1845, XXXI (158). Sierra Leone—Despatches and Proclamation of Lt.-Gov. Ferguson, 1844.
1846, XXXVI (266–v). West Africa—Civil Estimates.
1847, XXXV (229–v). West Africa—Civil Estimates.
1847, XXXIX (191). West Africa—Papers *re* emigration to West Indies.
1847–8, XL (327–v). West Africa—Civil Estimates.
1847–8, XLIV (732). Sierra Leone—Report by Butts and Guppy on emigration.
1849, XXXI (417). West Africa—Civil Estimates.
1850, XXXIV (256–v). West Africa—Civil Estimates.

1850, XL (643). Sierra Leone, St Helena—Corresp. *re* emigration of labourers to West Indies.
1851, XXXII (211–v). West Africa—Civil Estimates.
1852, XXIX (238–v). West Africa—Civil Estimates.
1852, XLIX (284). West Africa—Corresp. *re* mails.
1852, LIV [1455]. Lagos—cost of reduction.
1852–3, IV (913). Sierra Leone—Bill *re* Liberated Africans.
1852–3, LXV [1680]. Sierra Leone—Papers *re* Liberated Africans.
1852–3, LXV (703). Gold Coast—Despatches *re* war between Fantees and Ashantees.
1854–5, XXXVI (456). Gold Coast—Papers *re* Fantees and Ashantees.
1854–5, XXXVII [1997]. Sierra Leone—Corresp. *re* Moriah Expeditions.
1854–5, XXXVII (383). West Africa—Copies of Acts, Orders-in-Council, etc.
1856, XLII [2111]. Sierra Leone—Further corresp. *re* Moriah Expeditions.
1856, XLII (433). Gold Coast—Return *re* Fitzpatrick's appt.
1857 Sess. 2, XXVIII (245). Gold Coast—Corresp. *re* Fitzpatrick's appt.
1859 Sess. 2, XXII (182). Gold Coast—Further return *re* Fitzpatrick's appt.
1861, III (177). Sierra Leone—Offences Bill.
1863, XXXVIII (284). Sierra Leone—Papers *re* dismissal of Fitzjames.
1864, XLI [3364], [3364–I], (385), (393). Gold Coast—Corresp. and papers *re* Ashantee War.
1865, V (412). Report from Sel. Comm. on West African Settlements.
1865, XXXII (171). Gold Coast—Corresp. *re* troops, etc., 1863–4.
1865, XXXVII (70). Gold Coast—Corresp. *re* Ashantee War.
1865, XXXVII (170). West Africa—Ord's Report.
1867, XLIX (197). Sierra Leone—Ordinances of 1866, petitions and corresp.
1867, XLIX (198). West Africa—Corresp. *re* arrest of King Aggery.
1867, LXXIV [3900]. Gold Coast—Convention with Holland, 1867.
1870, L (444). Gambia—Petition *re* proposed cession to France.
1870, LXI [C. 140]. Corresp. *re* West Coast of Africa.

SLAVERY AND THE SLAVE TRADE

(Excluding correspondence with foreign powers)

1788, XVIII (547). Slave Ships Bill.
1788, XXII (565). Dimensions of slave ships.
1789, XIX (585). Bill to amend Slave Ships Act.
1789, XXIV (622) to (625). Papers *re* negroes in Jamaica.
1789, XXIV (626) to (634). Various papers *re* slave trade.
1789, XXV (635) to (645). Minutes of evidence on slave trade.
1789, XXVI (646), (646*a*). Report from Comm. for Trade and Plantations on slave trade.
1790, XX (605). Bill to continue Slave Ships Act.
1790, XXIX (697). Report of Barbados Comm. and other papers *re* slave trade.
1790, XXIX (698). Sel. Comm. on Slave Trade, 29 Jan. 1790—Evidence.
1790, XXIX (699). Sel. Comm. on Slave Trade, 23 April 1790—Evidence.
1790–1, XXXIV (745) to (748). Slave trade—Minutes of evidence.
1791, IX (98). Report from Comm. of Whole House on Slave Trade.
1792, XXXV (766) to (769). Slave trade—Vessels engaged, slaves imported into West Indies, propositions.
1793, XXIII (680). Bill to abolish foreign slave trade.
1794, XXIV (715). Bill to abolish foreign slave trade.
1795–6, XXVI (790), (791). Bill for abolition of slave trade.
1795–6, XLII (848). Jamaica—Acts imposing duties on slave importation.
1795–6, XLII (849). West Indies—Slaves imported from 1789.
1797–8, XXVIII (872). Bill regulating shipping of slaves.
1797–8, XXVIII (873). Bill to prohibit slave trade within certain limits.

1797–8, XLV (931). Corresp. with West Indian Governors *re* slave trade.
1797–8, XLV (932). Slave trade—Two acts of St Kitts.
1798–9, XXIX (904). Bill to explain act regulating shipping of slaves.
1798–9, XXIX (905), (906). Bill to prohibit slave trade within certain limits.
1798–9, XLVIII (964), (965), (966). Papers *re* slaves and slave trade.
1798–9, XLVIII (967 *a*). Further corresp. with Governors *re* slave trade.
1798–9, XLVIII (967 *b*). Tobago—Report of Legislature on slave trade.
1801–2, IV (88). Vessels employed in slave trade.
1803–4, I (110). Bill for abolition of slave trade.
1803–4, X (119). Papers *re* slave trade.
1805, I (35). Abolition Bill.
1805, X (39). Papers and corresp. *re* abolition.
1806, H.L., I (76). Bill to prohibit new ships engaging in slave trade.
1806, I (91), (124). Bill to prevent importation of slaves.
1806, I (213). Bill to prohibit certain ships clearing out to Africa for negroes.
1806, XII (84). Orders-in-Council prohibiting importation of slaves.
1806, XIII (265). Slave trade—Accounts.
1806–7, H.L., XIV, p. 165. Slave trade—Papers.
1806–7, I (68), (92). Bill for abolition of slave trade.
1810, XIV (204). Orders-in-Council *re* slave trade.
1810, XIV (353). Condemnation of *Commercio de Rio*.
1810–11, I (57). Bill to render Abolition Act more effectual.
1810–11, XI (203). Slave ordinances in Spanish colonies.
1811, H.L., XLVI (114). Papers *re* trial of Hodge, Tortola.
1811, H.L., XLVI (117). Papers *re* prosecution of Huggins, Nevis.
1812, X (180). Observations by W. Dawes on slave trade.
1812–13, II (322). Bill *re* prosecutions under Abolition Acts.
1812–13, XIII (41), (50). Orders-in-Council *re* slave trade.
1813–14, H.L., LXIX (34). Bill to allow British registration of condemned ships.
1813–14, H.L., LXXI, p. 157. Address to Prince Regent on slave trade.
1813–14, XII (289), (342). Returns *re* slave ships condemned in British colonies.
1813–14, XII (354). Papers *re* captured negroes at Sierra Leone.
1813–14, XII (356). Papers *re* captured negroes enlisted.
1814–15, H.L., LXXIII (70), (80), (84). Bill prohibiting British subjects assisting foreign slave trade.
1814–15, I (229). Bill for preventing slave trade.
1814–15, II (378). Bill for supporting captured slaves.
1814–15, II (458). Bill for preventing slave trade.
1814–15, VII (455). Orders-in-Council *re* slave trade.
1816, XIX (508). Jamaica—Acts *re* poll tax on slaves.
1817, H.L., LXXXVII (18), (26). Slave trade—Papers.
1817, XVII (338). Colonial slave laws.
1817, XVII (477). Orders-in-Council *re* slave trade.
1818, I (151), (325). Bill to explain Abolition Acts.
1818, XVII (247), (251), (374), (433). Papers *re* treatment of slaves in Nevis, Dominica, St Kitts; colonial acts; corresp.
1819, XV (192). Estimates for Slave Trade Commissioners' salaries and expenses. [Thereafter annually.]
1819, XVIII (414). Colonial slave laws.
1819, XVIII, p. 427. Slave trade conferences at London and Aix-la-Chapelle.
1819, XCVII (159). Bill to extend Act for more speedy trial of offences at sea to Abolition Laws.
1820, XI (95). Estimates for London Slave Trade Commission awards.
1821, XXII (165). Orders-in-Council *re* slave trade.
1821, XXII, p. 641. Despatch from Sierra Leone Commissioner.
1821, XXIII (347), (366). Orders-in-Council *re* slave trade.
1821, XXIII (589). Act of Antigua against export of slaves.
1822, I (169), (356). Bill to amend and consolidate Abolition Laws.

1822, XIX (21). Estimate for London Slave Trade Commission awards.
1822, XXII (127). Slave vessels captured and condemned.
1823, III (276). Bill to amend Abolition Laws.
1823, XIII (275). Estimate for London Slave Trade Commission awards.
1823, XVIII (68). Acts of colonial legislatures for registry of slaves.
1823, XVIII (89), (347), (537). Papers re slave population of West Indies.
1823, XVIII (348). Papers re trials of slaves in Berbice for obeah and murder.
1823, XVIII (457). Corresp. re treatment of slaves in Honduras.
1823, XIX, p. 311. Corresp. with British Commissioners at Sierra Leone, etc.
1824, H.L., CLIX (28). Bill for more effectual suppression of Slave Trade.
1824, H.L., CLXXIV, p. 39. Papers re amelioration of slavery.
1824, III (225). Bill to amend Abolition Laws.
1824, XXIII (158), (333), (338). Demerara—Papers re trial of Joseph Smith.
1824, XXIII (160). Colonial acts re treatment of slaves.
1824, XXIV (439). Letter re slaves in Honduras.
1824, XXIV, p. 215. Corresp. with British Commissioners at Sierra Leone, etc.
1824, XXIV, p. 427. West Indies—Papers re measures for amelioration of slavery.
1825, XXV (66). West Indies—Slave population, manumissions, etc.
1825, XXV (74). Papers re Lescesne and Escoffery.
1825, XXV (113), (127). Papers re Shrewsbury Case, Barbados.
1825, XXV (235). Papers re slaves in Tortola.
1825, XXV (310). Demerara—religious worship of slaves.
1825, XXV (476). Demerara, Berbice—proceedings of fiscals.
1825, XXVII, p. 281. Corresp. with Commissioners at Sierra Leone, etc.
1826, XXVI (214). Titles of colonial acts re slavery from 1823.
1826, XXVI (333), (351). Antigua—Grace Jones Case; slave insubordination.
1826, XXVI (400). Abstracts of returns re slave populations since 27 June 1825.
1826, XXVI (401). Berbice, Demerara—Proceedings of fiscals. [See also 1826, XXIX, p. 587.]
1826, XXVIII (353). Returns re slave population in West Indies.
1826, XXIX, pp. 1 and 131. Religious worship of slaves.
1826, XXIX, p. 299. Corresp. with commissioners at Sierra Leone, etc.
1826, XXIX, p. 607. Abstracts of colonial slave acts.
1826–7, XVIII (127). Coloured population of West Indies in 1820 and at last census.
1826–7, XVIII (554). Jamaica—Corresp. re attack on Wesleyan Meeting House.
1826–7, XXI (42). Disposal of prize slaves at Cape of Good Hope.
1826–7, XXII (68), (14), (5), (376). Corresp. with Governor of Mauritius re slave trade.
1826–7, XXII (111), (146). Public functionaries owning or employing slaves.
1826–7, XXII (128). Number of slaves manumitted, for last five years.
1826–7, XXII (129). Return re colonial slaves.
1826–7, XXII (462). Captured negroes at Tortola.
1826–7, XXII (463). Report on captured negroes at St Kitts, Nevis and Tortola.
1826–7, XXII (464). Report on captured negroes at Demerara.
1826–7, XXIII (465). Slave laws and regulations re labour.
1826–7, XXIII (497). Extracts from Trinidad Inquiry into negro character.
1826–7, XXV, pp. 53 and 347. Papers re measures for amelioration of slavery.
1826–7, XXV, p. 1. Papers re measures of amelioration.
1828, I (527). Bill to continue Act amending Abolition Laws.
1828, XXIV (125). Abstracts of corresp. with East India Co. re slavery and slave trade.
1828, XXV (204). Returns from West India colonies re slaves, from 1 Jan. 1821.
1828, XXV (206). Corresp. re slaves at Seychelles.
1828, XXV (261). Minutes of Privy Council evidence re Berbice and Demerara manumissions.
1828, XXV (570). Slave population in West Indies.
1828, XXVI (522). British Honduras—Report on Indian claims to freedom.
1828, XXVI (523). Jamaica—Letter re slave laws and missions.

1828, XXVI (524). Jamaica—Return *re* slaves sold for debt since 1808.
1828, XXVI (535). Tortola—Report on captured negroes.
1828, XXVII, p. 89. Papers *re* measures of amelioration.
1829, XXV (227). Abstract *re* slave population in each colony.
1829, XXV (292). Report of Comm. on slave trade in Mauritius.
1829, XXV (301). Demerara, Berbice—Orders-in-Council *re* manumissions.
1829, XXV (333). Papers *re* measures of amelioration.
1829, XXV (335). Reports from protectors of slaves.
1829, XXV (336). Trinidad—Returns *re* manumitted slaves and free labourers.
1830, III (475). Bill to reduce bounties for rescuing slaves.
1830, III (539). Bill to amend Abolition Acts.
1830, XV (262). Reports from protectors of slaves.
1830, XVIII (88). Estimates *re* captured negroes.
1830, XXI (582). Return *re* population of slave colonies—white, free black and
    coloured, and slaves.
1830, XXI (583), (672), (674), (676). Slavery in West Indies—Various papers.
1830-1, VI (273). Estimates for slave registry.
1830-1, VI (280). Estimates *re* captured negroes.
1830-1, XVI (121). Disposal of slaves escheated to Crown since 1821.
1830-1, XVI (230). Orders-in-Council for consolidating slave laws.
1830-1, XVI (301). Corresp. *re* slave laws in St Vincent, Dominica, St Kitts, Nevis,
    Tobago and Virgin Islands.
1830-1, XVI (302). Manumissions, 1817–26.
1830-1, XVI (305). Abstract of slave population in each colony.
1831, XIII (28). Estimates for slave registry.
1831, XIII (30). Estimates *re* captured negroes.
1831, XIX (304). Reports from governors *re* treatment of captured negroes.
1831, XIX (305). Papers *re* emancipation of Crown slaves.
1831-2, H.L., CCCVI (239). Report from Sel. Comm. on Slave Laws. [See also
    CCCVII (127).]
1831-2, H.L., CCCVIII (7), (93), (253). Papers *re* amelioration of slavery.
1831-2, H.L., CCCVIII (183). Papers *re* Swiney trial.
1831-2, H.L., CCCVIII (184), (185), (228), (254). Various reports and papers.
1831-2, XX (721). Report from Sel. Comm. on Measures for Extinction of Slavery.
1831-2, XXVII (158). Estimates for slave registry.
1831-2, XXVII (278). Estimates *re* captured negroes.
1831-2, XLVI (279), (649), (733). Papers *re* consolidation of slave laws.
1831-2, XLVII (285). Jamaica—corresp. *re* slave rebellion.
1831-2, XLVII (365). Jamaica—manumissions granted, 1825–30.
1831-2, XLVII (480). Jamaica—Ancle case.
1831-2, XLVII (481). Jamaica—Report and corresp. *re* religious instruction.
1831-2, XLVII (482). Jamaica—Papers *re* slave insurrections and trials of mission-
    aries.
1831-2, XLVII (561). Jamaica—Report on injury sustained during slave rebellion.
1831-2, XLVII (660), (737). Slaves imported, manumissions, runaways, Jackson
    case, and other papers.
1831-2, XLVII (738). Jamaica—Corresp. *re* Act of 1774, *re* slave import duties.
1831-2, XLVII (739). Barbados—Slave population.
1831-2, XLVII (743). Antigua—Report *re* apprenticed Africans liberated in 1828.
1833, IV (492), (593), (688). Bill for abolition of slavery.
1833, XXIV (166), (168). Estimates for slave registry and captured negroes.
1833, XXVI (539), (540), (541), (542). Slavery—Various papers: slaves registered,
    Baptist missionaries' memorial, Williams case, slaves liberated.
1833, XXVI (699). Orders-in-Council *re* transportation of slaves, etc.
1833, XXVI (700). West Indies—Papers *re* slave population.
1833, XXVI (736). Amount advanced to West Indian proprietors under 2 & 3 Will.
    IV, c. 125.
1833, XXVI (O. 52). Stanley's Resolutions for abolition of slavery.
1834, XLIV (152). Orders-in-Council *re* abolition.

1835, L (177), (278–I), (278–II). Papers *re* measures under Emancipation Act.
1835, LI (561). British Honduras—Orders-in-Council *re* slavery.
1836, XV (560). Report from Sel. Comm. on Apprenticeship System.
1836, XLVIII (166, Pt. III, 1). Papers *re* West Indian emancipation.
1836, XLVIII (174), (O. 44). Jamaica—Proceedings under Emancipation Act.
1836, XLIX (166, Pt. III, 2). Papers *re* West Indian emancipation.
1836, XLIX (330). Tobago—Orders-in-Council under Emancipation Act.
1837, VII (510). Report from Sel. Comm. on Apprenticeship System.
1837, LIII (521). Papers *re* emancipation measures.
1837–8, XLVIII (113), (520). West Indies—Report from Latrobe on negro education.
1837–8, XLIX (154–I), (154–II). Papers *re* emancipation.
1837–8, LII (688). Jamaica—Memorial on foreign slave trade.
1839, XXXIX (467). Ceylon—Corresp. *re* slavery.
1842, XXXVIII (289). Return *re* Africans brought to Britain, 1840–2.
1842, XLV [363]. Quintuple Slave Trade Treaty, 1841.
1843, LVIII (568). Ceylon—Corresp. *re* slavery.
1845, XLIX (73), (212). Slaves landed in West Indies and America, 1815–43.
1845, XLIX (471). Various returns *re* slave trade.
1847, XXXV (229–VII). Sums voted for services in suppression.
1847–8, XXII (272), (366), (536), (623). Reports from Sel. Comm. on Slave Trade.
1847–8, LXIV [970]. Papers *re* engagements with King Pepple and other African chiefs.
1849, XIX (308), (410). Reports from Sel. Comm. on Slave Trade.
1850, IX (53), (590). Reports from Lords' Sel. Comm. on Slave Trade.
1850, LV (149). Memorials from West Indies on slave trade, 1848–9.
1852–3, XXXIX (920). Report from Sel. Comm. on Slave Trade Treaties.
1854–5, VI (236). Bill for carrying into effect Sherbro engagements.
1854–5, LVI (406). Treaties with Sherbro chiefs.
1857–8, LXI (454). West Africa—Return *re* ships, men, health, slaves freed, etc., 1854–7.
1862, XXXVI [3064]. Return *re* slave trade cases tried in Mixed Commission Courts at Cape of Good Hope, 1843–62.
1865, LVI [3490]. Return *re* slave trade cases tried at Sierra Leone, Havana, Loanda, Cape of Good Hope and New York.
1867–8, LXIV (158). West Africa—Return *re* ships, men, health, slaves freed, etc., 1858–67.
1870, LXI [C. 140]. Corresp. *re* West Coast of Africa.
1870, LXI [C. 209]. Report from Comm. on East African Slave Trade.

CEYLON

(See also the Annual Reports of Colonial Governors, 1846–70, noted under COLONIAL POLICY above)

1819, XVIII (319). Papers *re* war in Ceylon.
1819–20, IV (56), (88). Account of revenue, civil officers.
1821, XIV (653). Abstract of revenue.
1821, XVI (622). Return of pensions and allowances.
1825, XXIV (513). Papers *re* government.
1828, XXIII (593). Colonial debt, corresp. *re* cinnamon trade.
1829, XXIII (344). Civil and military establishments, 1796–8.
1830, XXI (212), (352). Corresp. *re* finances.
1831–2, XXXII (274). Reports of Colebrooke and Cameron.
1833, XXVI (332). Charter for improving administration of justice.
1833, XXVI (698). Instructions referred to in Goderich's despatch to Horton.
1834, XLIV (228). Letter from Horton *re* salt monopoly.
1843, LVIII (568). Corresp. *re* abolition of slavery.
1845, XXXI (640). Minutes and corresp. *re* Civil Service.

1847, LIX (657). Imports of sugar, molasses, rum and coffee from Ceylon, 1831–46.

1847, XLI (93). Existing tariff, revenue, imports and exports.

1847, XLI (495). Corresp. re dismissal of Langslow.

1847, LXIII (716). Corresp. re railways.

1847–8, XLII [933]. Reports and corresp. re finance and commerce.

1847–8, XLII (41). Abstracts of imports and exports, duties.

1847–8, XLII (369). Despatch re commercial difficulties.

1847–8, XLVI [1005]. Corresp. re condition.

1849, XI (297), (573), (591). Reports from Sel. Comm. on Ceylon.

1849, XXXVI [1018]. Papers re affairs.

1850, XII (66), (106), (605). Reports from Sel. Comm. on Ceylon.

1851, VIII, Pts. I and II (36). 3rd Report from Sel. Comm.

1851, XXII (99), (634). Report of Commission and Evidence.

1851, XXXV (414). Expense of military establishments, 1849.

1851, XXXV [1301]. Papers re affairs.

1851, XXXV [1413]. Corresp. re court martial of Capt. Watson.

1851, XXXV (303). Memorial from Cingalese Episcopalians.

1852, XXXI (571). Instructions re cinnamon duty.

1852, XXXII (355–IV). Corresp. re Church.

1852, XXXVI (568). Report of Finance Comm.

1852–3, LXV (88). Account re Ceylon Commission.

1852–3, LXV (410), (927), (985). Corresp. re idolatry.

1852–3, LXV (919). Corresp. re Basses Rock lighthouses.

1857, Sess. 2, XXVIII (45). Corresp. re state.

1860, XLV (457). Report and papers re Ceylon Railway.

1860, XLV (527). Report and corresp. re Galle Harbour.

1862, XXXVI (440). Return re charges paid by Imperial Exchequer, 1856–60.

1863, LXIII (491). Further corresp. re Basses Rock lighthouses.

1865, XXXVIII (215). Corresp. re military expenditure.

1866, XLIX (183). Corresp. re treatment of a prisoner.

1867, XLVIII [3904]. Petition re Legislative Council.

1867–8, XLVIII (39). Corresp. re Legislative Council.

1868–9, I (224). Great Basses Rock Lighthouse Bill.

1868–9, II (250). Galle Harbour Bill.

BRITISH MALAYA

(See also the Annual Reports of Colonial Governors, 1846–70)

1831–2, IX (735–I). Corresp. re govt. of Prince of Wales's Island, Singapore and Malacca.

1831–2, X, Pt. II (735–II). Corresp. re Prince of Wales's Island.

1846, XXVII (323). Rules re immigration of labourers from Straits of Malacca into British Guiana, Trinidad and Jamaica.

1854–5, I (246). Bill to amend Malaya Acts.

1857, Sess. 2, XXIX (322). Corresp. re Singapore port dues.

1857–8, XLIII (254). Corresp. re Malacca.

1862, XL (259). Corresp. re Straits Settlements.

1866, V (176). Straits Settlements Govt. Bill.

1868–9, V (259). Bill to separate Straits Settlements from Calcutta diocese.

HONG KONG

(See also the Annual Reports of Colonial Governors, 1846–70)

1844, XXXIII (484). Estimates for establishment at Hong Kong and Five Treaty Ports. [Thereafter annually.]

1844, LI [521], [534]. Papers re Treaty of Nanking.

1844, LI [570]. Statement of foreign trade with China.

1846, XXVII (264). Annual receipts and expenditure.
1847, XL (347), (497), (743). Papers re opium trade, resignation of Montgomery Martin.
1847, LX (in 717). British trade with China, 1840–6.
1849, XXXIX [1119]. British trade with China, 1847–8.
1850, XLI [1286]. British trade with China, 1848–9.
1851, XXII [1383]. Progress of the colony.
1852, XVIII [1499]. Statement re land sales.
1852, XXXII (355–IV). Church affairs.
1857, Sess. 1, XII [2166]. Corresp. re registration of colonial vessels.
1857, Sess. 1, XII (148). Reports and papers on British position and prospects.
1857, Sess. 2, XLIII (101). Corresp. re Legislative Council.
1857–8, XLIII (115), (388), (481). Papers re defence, Chapter of Justice, emigration.
1860, XLVIII (44), (161). Corresp. re opium, Anstey and others.
1862, XXXVI (427). Corresp. re Anstey.
1863, XXXVIII (113). Anstey Inquiry.
1864, XLII (281). Exports to Hong Kong, 1833–63.
1865, XXXVIII (214). Corresp. re garrison.
1866, XLI (59), (60), (93), (149,), (181), (182). Papers re garrison.
1866, L (120). Papers re execution of Mo-Wong.
1867–8, XLVIII [3987]. Ordinance re maintenance of order.
1868–9, XLIII (409). Corresp. re gambling houses.
1868–9, LXIV [4097–X]. Abstracts re Chinese trade, 1864–8.

MAURITIUS

(See also the Annual Reports of Colonial Governors, 1846–70, and SLAVERY AND THE SLAVE TRADE above)

1826, III (430). Report from Sel. Comm. on Slave Trade.
1826–7, VI (90). Minutes of Slave Trade Committee.
1826–7, XVIII (283), (346). Papers re sugar exported, 1812–25.
1830, XXI (212), (352). Corresp. re finances.
1830, XXVII (354), (393). Accounts re sugar exported, 1825–30.
1844, XXXV (356). Corresp. re Indian labourers.
1847, LIX (657). British imports of sugar, molasses, rum and coffee, 1831–46.
1847–8, XLIV (527). Papers re finances.
1849, XXXVII (280–II). Corresp. re general condition.
1849, L (in 351). British imports of sugar, rum, coffee and cocoa, 1831–48.
1854, VI (139). Vice-Admiral Const. Bill.
1856, XLIV (181). Corresp. re removal of Brownrigg.
1857–8, XLI (371), (523). Papers re education revenue and grants.
1859, Sess. 2 (31–I). Corresp. re labourers.
1862, XXXVII (435). Exports to Australia.
1863, LXVIII (148). Memorials and corresp. re sugar duties.
1864, XLI (100). Corresp. re sugar duties.

SEYCHELLES

(See also SLAVERY AND THE SLAVE TRADE and MAURITIUS above)

1826, XXVII (295), (352). Papers re slave trade.
1826–7, XVIII (284). Quantity of cotton exported since capture.
1828, XXV (205). Slaves shipped and landed since capture.

FALKLAND ISLANDS

(See also the Annual Reports of Colonial Governors, 1846–70)

1841, XIV (224–V). Estimates for establishment. [Thereafter annually.]
1841, Sess. 2, III (3). Papers re state.
1843, XXXIII (160). Corresp. since Aug. 1841.
1845, XXXI (129). Corresp. re currency.

1845, XXXI (193). Return *re* govt. grants since 1840.
1851, XXXIV (in 667). Customs duties.
1852, XVIII [in 1499]. Papers *re* Falkland Islands Co., etc.
1857–8, XLI (285). Memorials and corresp. *re* W. P. Snow.

ST HELENA
(See also the Annual Reports of Colonial Governors, 1846–70)

1816, XII (220). Account of transports sent.
1831–2, X, Pt. I (735–II). Revenue and expenditure, 1814–29.
1834, XLI (311). Estimates. [Thereafter annually.]
1837–8, XLI (737). Reports of Commissioners *re* E.I.C. servants.
1851, XXXVI (163), (435). Papers *re* revenue, 1848–50.
1851, XXXIV (in 667). Customs duties.
1852, XXXII (355–1). Church affairs.
1857–8, XLIII (388). Charter of Justice.

4. SELECT LIST OF PARLIAMENTARY DEBATES

Summaries of British Parliamentary Debates previous to 1803 may be found in Cobbett's *Parliamentary History* (36 vols., London, 1806–20), supplemented by *Jordan's Parliamentary Journal* (9 vols., London, 1792–95), *The Senator, or Clarendon's Parliamentary Register* (32 vols., London, 1790–1802) and Woodfull's *Impartial Report of the Debates* (12 vols., London, 1794–6). From 1803 onwards much fuller summaries were given in the *Parliamentary Debates*, known until 1813 as *Cobbett*, thenceforward as *Hansard*. This publication has run through four series and a fifth is current. The figures given in the references below indicate the series, volume and column in which may be found the more important debates on colonial affairs in keneral, and the dependent empire in particular, during the period 1803 to 1870. The debates are given in chronological order and unless otherwise indicated, were in the House of Commons.

For debates relating to Canada and Newfoundland, Australia and New Zealand, and South Africa, see the bibliographies of vols. III, VII and VIII respectively.

War in Ceylon; 14 March 1803. I, 855.
Slave trade; 13 Feb. 1803. I, 1080.
Slave trade; 30 May, 6, 7, 8, 11, 13, 19, 25, 27 June 1804. II, 440, 519, 543, 561, 613, 649, 669, 779, 848, 863.
Lords. Slave trade; 28 June, 23 July 1804. II, 871, 889, 926.
Sierra Leone Company; 29 June, 9 July 1804. II, 883, 965.
Slave trade; 15, 28 Feb. 1805. III, 521, 641.
State of West Indies; 5 April 1805. IV, 222.
Lords. West Indian accounts; 26 April 1805. IV, 428.
Lords. West Indian accounts; 21, 28 May 1805. V, 34, 124.
Lords. Colonial intercourse with America; 25 June, 4 July 1805. V, 558, 731.
Lords. American Intercourse Bill; 31 March, 17, 21, 24 April, 6 May 1806. VI, 592, 767, 808, 909, 1031.
Slave Importation Bill; 31 March, 18, 21, 25 April, 1, 2 May 1806. VI, 597, 805, 839, 917, 1021, 1027.
American intercourse; 21 April 1806. VI, 834.
Lords. Slave Importation Bill; 7, 16 May 1806. VII, 32, 227.
Lords. American Intercourse Bill; 12 May, 17 July 1806. VII, 94, 1189.
American Intercourse Bill; 19, 22, 23 May, 3, 13, 17 June, 8 July 1806. VII, 252, 336, 349, 507, 668, 686, 969.
Tortola Free-Port Bill; 19, 23 May 1806. VII, 253, 364.
West India Accounts Bill; 21 May, 11, 13, 16 June 1806. VII, 295, 608, 661, 676.
Slave trade; 3, 10 June 1806. VII, 508, 580.

Lords. Tortola Free-Port Bill; 20 June 1806. VII, 778.
Lords. Slave trade; 24 June 1806. VII, 801.
Grenada and St Vincent Loan Bill; 11 July 1806. VII, 1092.
Lords. Slave Ship Restriction Bill; 15 July 1806. VII, 1143.
Distillation of sugar; 30 Dec. 1806. VIII, 238.
Lords. Slave Trade Abolition Bill; 2, 12, 21 Jan., 2, 4, 5, 6, 9, 10 Feb. 1807. VIII, 257, 431, 468, 601, 612, 657, 677, 691, 701.
Slave Trade Abolition Bill; 10, 17, 20, 23, 27 Feb. 1807. VIII, 717, 829, 939, 945, 1040.
Sugar drawbacks; 17, 18 Feb. 1807. VIII, 840, 849.
Slave Trade Abolition Bill; 6, 9, 16 March 1807. IX, 59, 63, 114.
West Indian Planters' Petition; 12 March 1807. IX, 85.
Abolition of slavery; 17 March 1807. IX, 142.
Lords. Slave Trade Abolition Bill; 18, 23 March 1807. IX, 146, 168.
State of West Indies; 10 Aug. 1807. IX, 1151.
African Company's Petition; 24 Feb. 1808. X, 710.
Distillation from sugar; 24 Feb. 1808. X, 712.
Sugar Distillation Committee; 28 March 1808. X, 1256.
Sugar Distillation Bill; 13 April, 12, 18, 23, 27 May, 3, 13 June, 2 July 1808. XI, 55, 160, 404, 493, 702, 816, 867, 1130.
State of West Indies; 21, 24 June 1808. XI, 973, 1056.
Lords. Sugar Distillation Bill; 23 June 1808. XI, 998.
State of the Empire; 24 June 1808. XI, 1042.
West Indian produce; 14 April 1809. XIV, 33.
Martinique Trade Bill; 26 April, 15 May, 6 June 1809. XIV, 258, 581, 897.
Lords. Slave trade; 12 Feb. 1810. XV, 374.
Lords. Slave trade; 12 March 1810. XVI, 11 ****.
Slave trade; 12 March 1810. XVI, 12 ******.
Slave trade; 15 June 1810. XVII, 658.
Lords. Slave trade; 18 June 1810. XVII, 747.
Slave Trade Felony Bill; 5 March 1811. XIX, 233.
Free labour in West Indies; 4 April 1811. XIX, 708.
Petition re Trinidad; 5 April 1811. XIX, 714.
Sierra Leone; 8 April 1811. XIX, 739.
Justice in Trinidad; 14 May, 13 June 1811. XX, 134, 610.
Sierra Leone; 6, 11 June 1811. XX, 461, 570.
Malta, Vice-Admiralty Court; 6 June, 18 July 1811. XX, 464, 1017.
Barbados and sugar trade; 22 Jan. 1812. XXI, 278.
Leeward Island duties; 11 Feb. 1812. XXI, 742.
Tobago Planters' Petition; 9 March 1812. XXI, 1213.
West Indian produce; 19 March 1812. XXII, 92.
West Indian Revenues Bill; 14, 20 July 1812. XXIII, 1058, 1099.
Lords. Slave trade, West Indies; 23 July 1812. XXIII, 1187.
West Indies; 29 July 1812. XXIII, 1272.
Slave trade; 7 Dec. 1812. XXIV, 198.
Lords. Slave trade; 18 Dec. 1812. XXIV, 318.
Martinique sugar; 13 May 1813. XXVI, 106.
Slave trade; 14 July 1813. XXVI, 1211.
Lords. Slave trade; 6 Dec. 1813, 4, 5 May 1814. XXVII, 243, 647, 656.
Colonial Offices Bill; 22, 28 March, 18, 25 April, 6 May 1814. XXVII, 339, 365, 434, 522, 731.
Colonial appointments; 29 March 1814. XXVII, 375.
Leeward Islands; 18 April 1814. XXVII, 431.
Governor Ainslie of Grenada; 25, 27 April 1814. XXVII, 522, 575.
Sugar Drawback Bill; 27, 28 April 1814. XXVII, 559, 582.
Slave trade; 28 April, 2 May 1814. XXVII, 576, 637.
West Indies—Le Marchant; 13, 22 June 1814. XXVIII, 62, 121.
Slave trade; 15, 27, 28 June, 20, 26 July 1814. XXVIII, 92, 268, 372, 384, 802, 846.

Lords. Slave trade—Grenville's Motion; 27, 28, 29, 30 June, 11, 14 July 1814. xxviii, 299, 362, 417, 466, 655, 700.
Lords. Slave trade—Quaker petition; 6 July 1814. xxviii, 609.
Slave trade; 24 Nov. 1814, 23 Feb. 1815. xxix, 511, 1005.
Malta trade; 10 Feb. 1815. xxix, 713.
Emigration; 8 March 1815. xxx, 52.
Slave trade; 14, 18, 24 April 1815. xxx, 607, 657, 794.
Foreign Slave Trade Bill; 18 April 1815. xxx, 657.
Foreign Slave Trade Bill; 5 May 1815. xxxi, 168.
Lords. Foreign Slave Trade Bill; 1, 5, 8, 16, 21, 30 June 1815. xxxi, 557, 606, 848, 912, 1062.
Governor Ainslie of Grenada; 2 June 1815. xxxi, 596.
Slave trade; 5, 29 June 1815. xxxi, 609, 1040.
Importation of Slaves Bill; 13 June, 5 July 1815. xxxi, 772, 1127.
Ionian Islands; 14 Feb. 1816. xxxii, 540.
Lords. Ceylon; 26 Feb. 1816. xxxii, 830.
Lords. Slave trade; 22 March 1816. xxxiii, 522.
Slave trade; 26 March 1816. xxxiii, 599.
Ionian Islands; 21 May 1816. xxxiv, 636.
West Indian slavery; 22 May, 19 June 1816. xxxiv, 719, 1151.
Lords. West Indian slavery; 30 May, 27 June 1816. xxxiv, 908, 1271.
Missionaries in colonies; 25, 26 June 1816. xxxiv, 1260, 1266.
Berbice; 26 June 1816. xxxiv, 1267.
Lords. West Indian religious instruction; 28 June 1816. xxxiv, 1278.
Trinidad; 18, 20 March 1817. xxxv, 1190, 1206.
Lords. West Indian slavery; 20 March 1817. xxxv, 1204.
Slave trade; 9 July 1817. xxxvi, 1321.
Lords. Slave trade; 10 July 1817. xxxvi, 1366.
Slave Trade Treaty with Spain; 28 Jan., 9, 11 Feb., 18 March 1818. xxxvii, 67, 232, 332, 1164.
Lords. Slave trade; 23 Feb. 1818. xxxvii, 575.
West Indies Indemnity Bill; 9 March 1818. xxxvii, 880.
Slave Trade Bill; 3 April 1818. xxxvii, 1185.
Colonial slavery; 22 April 1818. xxxviii, 294.
Slaves in Dominica; 22 April 1818. xxxviii, 298.
Slaves in Nevis; 20 May 1818. xxxviii, 841.
Lords. Slave trade; 21 May 1818. xxxviii, 856.
Portuguese Slave Trade Treaty Bill; 28 May 1818. xxxviii, 996.
Slave trade; 10 June 1818. xxxviii, 1317.
Slave trade; 15, 19 Feb., 19 March 1819. xxxix, 433, 541, 1105.
Lords. Slave trade; 19 Feb. 1819. xxxix, 510.
Lords. West Indian slavery; 4 March 1819. xxxix, 848.
Sierra Leone; 19 March 1819. xxxix, 1105.
Netherlands Slave Trade Bill; 19 March 1819. xxxix, 1105.
Ceylon; 11 May 1819. xl, 330.
Lords. Ordination in colonies; 26 May 1819. xl, 800.
Slave Registry Bill; 8 June 1819. xl, 976.
Colonial establishments; 10 June 1819. xl, 1077.
Slave trade; 7 July 1819. xl, 1542.
Lords. Slave trade; 9 July 1819. xl, 1547.
Colonial revenues; 29 Nov. 1819. xli, 355.
Gibraltar; 4 May 1820. New ser. i, 96.
African Company; 30 May, 16 June 1820. New ser. i, 634, 1124.
Lords. Ionian Islands; 17 July 1820. New ser. ii, 485.
Slave trade; 6 Feb. 1821. New ser. iv, 428.
African Co. Abolition Bill; 20 Feb. 1821. New ser. iv, 823.
Ionian Islands; 23 Feb. 1821. New ser. iv, 933.
African Co. Bill; 9 April 1821. New ser. v, 90.
Barbados Fund; 21 May 1821. New ser. v, 858.

Maxwell's Slave Removal Bill; 1 June 1821. New ser. v, 1068.
Justice in Tobago; 6 June 1821. New ser. v, 1119.
Ionian Islands—Maitland's conduct; New ser. v, 1128.
Lords. Slave trade; 25 June 1821. New ser. v, 1285.
Slave trade; 26 June 1821. New ser. v, 1325.
Slave Trade Laws Consolidation Bill; 12 Feb. 1822. New ser. VI, 278.
Distress in Grenada—Petition; 22 March 1822. New ser. VI, 1200.
Ionian Islands—Maitland; 14 May 1822. New ser. VII, 562.
West Indian and American Trade Bill; 17 May 1822. New ser. VII, 674.
Slave trade and slavery; 27 June, 25 July 1822. New ser. VII, 1399, 1783.
Piracy in West Indies; 23 July 1822. New ser. VII, 1725.
State of Trinidad and other colonies; 25 July 1822. New ser. VII, 1801.
Colonial revenues and expenditure; 25 Feb. 1823. New ser. VIII, 248.
Leeward Islands duties; 14 March 1823. New ser. VIII, 590.
Abolition of slavery; 18, 27 March 1823. New ser. VIII, 624, 766.
Distress in Tobago; 27 March 1823. New ser. VIII, 754.
Abolition of slavery; 15 May 1823. New ser. IX, 255, 257.
Duties on East and West Indian sugar; 22 May 1822. New ser. IX, 444.
Leeward Island duties; 9 June 1823. New ser. IX, 819.
Quarantine at Malta; 10 July 1823. New ser. IX, 1526.
Lords. Abolition of slavery; 4, 16, 18 March 1824. New ser. X, 703, 1046, 1215.
Sugar duties; 8 March 1824. New ser. X, 782.
Sierra Leone; 12 March 1824. New ser. X, 962.
Gold Coast Settlements; 12 March 1824. New ser. X, 962.
S.P.G. in colonies; 12 March 1824. New ser. X, 964.
Abolition of slavery; 15, 23 March 1824. New ser. X, 1011, 1331.
West Indies—Slave population; 16 March 1824. New ser. X, 1064, 1091.
Slave Trade Piracy Bill; 29 March 1824. New ser. X, 1424.
Lords. Slave Trade Piracy Bill; 30 March 1824. New ser. XI, 1.
Demerara—Smith Case; 13 April, 1, 3, 10, 11 June 1824. New ser. XI, 400, 961, 1079, 1167, 1206.
West Indian Company Bill; 10 May 1824. New ser. XI, 609.
Sugar bounties; 13 May 1824. New ser. XI, 730.
Arrests in Jamaica; 21 May 1824. New ser. XI, 796.
Abolition of slavery; 10, 15 June 1824. New ser. XI, 1167, 1406.
Colonial policy; 21 March 1825. New ser. XII, 1097.
West Indian Company Bill; 29 March 1825. New ser. XII, 1278.
Sierra Leone; 14 April 1825. New ser. XII, 1349.
West Indian Company Bill; 16 May 1825. New ser. XIII, 605.
Slave trade in Mauritius; 17 May 1825. New ser. XIII, 781.
Mauritius Trade Bill; 3 June 1825. New ser. XIII, 1039.
Lords. Colonial Intercourse Bill; 14 June 1825. New ser. XIII, 1132.
Deportations from Jamaica; 16 June 1825. New ser. XIII, 1173.
Abolition of slavery; 28 Feb., 1, 3 March 1826. New ser. XIV, 918, 968, 1076.
Slave trials in Jamaica; 1 March 1826. New ser. XIV, 1007.
Lords. Abolition of slavery; 7, 14 March 1826. New ser. XIV, 1139, 1343.
Emigration; 14 March 1826. New ser. XIV, 1360.
Lords. Antigua; 14 April 1826. New ser. XV, 202.
Lords. West Indian slavery; 14, 17 April 1826. New ser. XV, 202, 248.
Slavery in Antigua; 14 April 1826. New ser. XV, 219.
Lords. Property in West Indies; 20 April 1826. New ser. XV, 385.
West Indian property; 20, 25 April 1826. New ser. XV, 489, 577.
Slavery in Demerara and Berbice; 20 April 1826. New ser. XV, 502.
Justice in West Indies; 25 April 1826. New ser. XV, 587.
Mauritius—Slave trade; 9 May 1826. New ser. XV, 1014.
Slavery in colonies; 19 May 1826. New ser. XV, 1284.
Emigration; 27 Nov., 5, 7 Dec. 1826, 15, 26 Feb. 1827. New ser. XVI, 142, 227, 298, 475, 653.
Lords. Emigration; 8 Dec. 1826. New ser. XVI, 317.

Case of Col. Bradley; 8 Dec. 1826, 14 Feb. 1827. New ser., XVI, 321, 460.
Mauritius—Slave trade; 21 Feb. 1827. New ser. XVI, 605.
Missionaries in Jamaica; 13 March 1827. New ser. XVI, 1166.
Emigration; 5 April 1827. New ser. XVII, 241, 927.
Coloured people in West Indies; 12 June 1827. New ser. XVII, 1242.
Emigration to colonies; 4 March, 17 April 1828. New ser. XVIII, 938, 1547.
Slave trade; 5, 6 March 1828. New ser. XVIII, 975, 1023.
West Indian slavery; 6 March 1828. New ser. XVIII, 1023.
Lords. S.P.G. in colonies; 18, 21 March 1828. New ser. XVIII, 1161, 1236.
West Indian produce, sugar duty; 1 April 1828. New ser. XVIII, 1422.
Sugar duties; 9, 16 June 1828. New ser. XIX, 1206, 1373.
Lords. West Indian slavery; 23 June 1828. New ser. XIX, 1463.
Emigration; 24 June 1828. New ser. XIX, 1501.
S.P.G. in colonies; 6 April 1829. New ser. XXI, 455.
Sierra Leone; 19 May 1829. New ser. XXI, 1461.
Sugar Duties Bill; 25 May 1829. New ser. XXI, 1565.
Slavery in Mauritius; 3 June 1829. New ser. XXI, 1696.
Slavery in West Indies; 4 June 1829. New ser. XXI, 1741.
West Indies and United States; 5 Feb. 1830. New ser. XXII, 133.
Lords. West Indian slavery; 8 Feb. 1830. New ser. XXII, 180.
Slave trade; 16 Feb. 1830. New ser. XXII, 568.
West Indian trade; 23 Feb., 1 March 1830. New ser. XXII, 848, 1066.
Justice in colonies; 23 Feb., 4 March 1830. New ser. XXII, 856, 1264.
Slavery; 11 March 1830. New ser. XXIII, 177.
West Indian produce; 19 March 1830. New ser. XXIII, 622.
Colonial expenditure; 22 March 1830. New ser. XXIII, 714.
Emigration; 23 March 1830. New ser. XXIII, 782.
Mauritius—Sugar and slavery; 13, 17 May 1830. New ser. XXIV, 672, 774.
West Indies; 18 May 1830. New ser. XXIV, 829, 834.
Ceylon; 27 May 1830. New ser. XXIV, 1155.
Ceylon—Habeas Corpus; 7 June 1830. New ser. XXV, 27.
West Indian planters; 14 June 1830. New ser. XXV, 307.
Sugar duties; 14, 21, 30 June, 1 July 1830. New ser. XXV, 314, 525, 828, 858.
Supply—Colonial expenses; 14 June 1830. New ser. XXV, 323.
S.P.G. and colonies; 14 June 1830. New ser. XXV, 340.
Sierra Leone; 14, 15 June 1830. New ser. XXV, 340, 394.
Emigration petition; 15 June 1830. New ser. XXV, 366.
Rum duties—Petition; 17 June 1830. New ser. XXV, 428.
Colonial slavery; 1, 13, 16 July 1830. New ser. XXV, 857, 1171, 1226.
West Indian Spirits Duties Bill; 5 July 1830. New ser. XXV, 952.
Mauritius—Delavale Case; 7 July 1830. New ser. XXV, 1071.
West Indian slavery; 8, 9, 10, 23 Nov., 13, 20 Dec. 1830. 3rd ser. I, 296, 330, 349,
      359, 649, 1047, 1352.
West Indian-American intercourse; 8, 12 Nov., 17 Dec. 1830. 3rd ser. I, 299,
      471, 1311.
Justice at Gibraltar; 19 Nov. 1830. 3rd ser. I, 590.
Lords. Slavery; 30 Nov., 10, 16 Dec. 1830. 3rd ser. I, 691, 964, 1204.
Colonial Acts Validity Bill; 2 Nov. 1820. 3rd ser. I, 746.
Emigration Bill; 23 Dec. 1830, 22 Feb. 1836. 3rd ser. II, 115, 875.
West India Interest—Sugar duties; 3, 21 Feb. 1831. 3rd ser. II, 126, 784.
Lords. Slavery; 10 Feb. 1831. 3rd ser. II, 348.
West Indian trade with America; 11, 14, 18 March 1831. 3rd ser. III, 345, 430, 535.
Sugar duties; 11 March 1831. 3rd ser. III, 373.
West India Interest; 25 March 1831. 3rd ser. III, 938.
Slavery and compensation; 29 March 1831. 3rd ser. III, 1135, 1144.
West Indian slavery; 27 June 1831. 3rd ser. IV, 372.
Slave Registry office; 8 July 1831. 3rd ser. IV, 994.
Lords. Slavery petition; 15 July 1831. 3rd ser. IV, 1302.
Expense of captured negroes; 18 July 1831. 3rd ser. IV, 1439.

Colonial expenditure; 25 July 1831. 3rd ser. v, 280.
Supply—Sierra Leone; 25 July 1831. 3rd ser. v, 291.
Colonial representation; 16 Aug. 1831. 3rd ser. vi, 110.
Sugar Refining Bill; 18 Aug., 5, 12 Sept. 1831. 3rd ser. vi, 216, 1166, 1317.
Deportations from Jamaica; 18 Aug. 1831. 3rd ser. vi, 218.
Sugar Refining Bill; 14, 22, 28 Sept. 1831. 3rd ser. vii, 27, 490, 728.
West Indian Relief; 30 Sept. 1831. 3rd ser. vii, 893.
West India Interest; 6 Oct. 1831. 3rd ser. viii, 176.
Sugar Refining Bill; 7, 13 Oct. 1831. 3rd ser. viii, 347, 358, 758.
Barbados and St Vincent Importation Bill; 13 Oct. 1831. 3rd ser. viii, 694.
Lords. British factory at Canton; 13 Dec. 1831. 3rd ser. ix, 207.
Lords. French Slave Trade Treaty; 19, 23 Jan. 1832. 3rd ser. ix, 587, 772.
French Slave Trade Treaty; 24 Jan., 6 Feb. 1832. 3rd ser. ix, 810, 1351.
Lords. Emigration; 2 Feb. 1832. 3rd ser. ix, 1146.
Insurrection in Jamaica; 20 Feb. 1832. 3rd ser. x, 535.
Lords. Jamaica; 27 Feb. 1832. 3rd ser. x, 724.
Sugar Duties Bill; 29 Feb. 1832. 3rd ser. x, 966.
West Indian Relief; 29 Feb. 1832. 3rd ser. x, 973.
Sugar duties, West Indies; 7 March 1832. 3rd ser. x, 1236.
West Indian colonies; 9, 15 March 1832. 3rd ser. xi, 34, 290.
Sugar duties; 9, 23 March 1832. 3rd ser. xi, 63, 807.
Emigration; 14 March 1832. 3rd ser. xi, 205.
Colonial slavery; 4 April 1832. 3rd ser. xi, 1276.
Lords. West India Interest; 17 April 1832. 3rd ser. xii, 596.
Lords. Colonial slavery; 24 May, 1 June, 2 July 1832. 3rd ser. xiii, 6, 285, 1180.
Colonial slavery; 24 May 1832. 3rd ser. xiii, 34.
West Indian distress; 30 May 1832. 3rd ser. xiii, 190.
Colonial policy; 4 June 1832. 3rd ser. xiii, 387.
West Indian loan; 29 June 1832. 3rd ser. xiii, 1172.
Produce of slave labour; 2 July 1832. 3rd ser. xiii, 1242.
Colonial estimates; 23 July 1832. 3rd ser. xiv, 648.
Lords. West Indian Relief Bill; 14 Aug. 1832. 3rd ser. xiv, 1361.
West Indian Relief Bill; 3, 8, 9 Aug. 1832. 3rd ser. xiv, 1104, 1250. 1295.
Abolition of slavery; 19, 27 Feb. 1833. 3rd ser. xv, 948, 1178.
Lords. Slave trade; 26 Feb. 1833. 3rd ser. xv, 1142.
Lords. State of West Indies; 26 Feb. 1833. 3rd ser. xv, 1143.
Lords. Abolition of slavery; 6, 28 March 1833. 3rd ser. xvi, 281, 1184.
Sugar duties; 6, 7 March 1833. 3rd ser. xvi, 324, 387.
Abolition of slavery; 18, 19 March 1833. 3rd ser. xvi, 729, 826.
Sugar refining; 3 April 1833. 3rd ser. xvii, 74.
Lords. Abolition of slavery; 22 April, 2, 17 May 1833. 3rd ser. xvii, 373, 837, 1339.
Abolition of slavery—Stanley's Motion; 14, 15, 17 May 1833. 3rd ser. xvii, 1193, 1263, 1346.
Slavery—Petitions; 24 May 1833. 3rd ser. xviii, 67.
Lords. Abolition of slavery; 30 May, 7 June 1833. 3rd ser. xviii, 102, 360, 446.
Abolition of slavery—Govt. proposals; 30, 31 May, 3, 7, 10, 11 June 1833. 3rd ser. xviii, 112, 204, 308, 458, 515, 573.
China trade; 5 June 1833. 3rd ser. xviii, 377.
Sugar refining; 17 June 1833. 3rd ser. xviii, 909.
Lords. Conference with Commons on slavery; 20 June 1833. 3rd ser. xviii, 1014.
Lords. Govt. Motion on slavery; 25 June 1833. 3rd ser. xviii, 1163.
Sugar refining; 17, 24 July 1833. 3rd ser. xix, 791, 1164.
Abolition of slavery—Govt. proposals; 22, 24, 25 July 1833. 3rd ser. xix, 1056, 1184, 1234, 1252.
Lords. Slavery—Govt. proposals. 8, 14, 15, 19, 20 Aug. 1833. 3rd ser. xx, 502, 503, 587, 628, 753, 783.
China Trade Bill; 12 Aug. 1833. 3rd ser. xx, 562.
Lords. China Trade Bill. 16, 19, 20 Aug. 1833. 3rd ser. xx, 713, 751, 786.
Sugar duties; 28 Feb. 1834. 3rd ser. xxi, 943.

Results of Slavery Abolition Act; 17 March 1834. 3rd ser. XXII, 280.
Emigration agents; 18 April 1834. 3rd ser. XXII, 963.
Aboriginal tribes in colonies; 1 July 1834. 3rd ser. XXIV, 1061.
Slavery Abolition Compensation Fund; 4 Aug. 1834. 3rd ser. XXV, 919.
Lords. Effects of abolition; 11 Aug. 1834. 3rd ser. XXV, 1132.
Abolition in Jamaica; 27 Feb. 1835. 3rd ser. XXVI, 416.
Slave trade—Buxton's Motion; 12, 19 May 1835. 3rd ser. XXVII, 1039, 1233.
Lords. Slave trade; 27 May 1835. 3rd ser. XXVIII, 168.
Slave trade—Royal message; 10 June 1835. 3rd ser. XXVIII, 587.
Berbice—Mr Walker; 10 June 1835. 3rd ser. XXVIII, 633.
Slaves in Mauritius; 12 June 1835. 3rd ser. XXVIII, 726.
Abolition of slavery; 19 June 1835. 3rd ser. XXVIII, 918.
Sugar duties; 19 June 1835. 3rd ser. XXVIII, 960.
Coffee duties; 23 June 1835. 3rd ser. XXVIII, 1053.
Aborigines in colonies; 14 July 1835. 3rd ser. XXIX, 549.
Compensation to slave owners; 3, 13 Aug., 4 Sept. 1835. 3rd ser. XXX, 13, 474, 1381.
Slave trade—Sardinia; 28 Aug. 1835. 3rd ser. XXX, 1091.
Justice in Mauritius; 15 Feb., 1 March 1836. 3rd ser. XXXI, 390, 1140.
Lords. Justice in West Indies; 11 March 1836. 3rd ser. XXXII, 189.
Apprenticeship in colonies; 22 March 1836. 3rd ser. XXXII, 450.
Mauritius—Borthwick's Motion; 22 March 1836. 3rd ser. XXXII, 490.
East Indian sugar; 25 March 1836. 3rd ser. XXXII, 591.
Slavery Abolition (Jamaica) Bill; 15 April 1836. 3rd ser. XXXII, 1106.
East and West Indian sugar; 29 April 1836. 3rd ser. XXXII, 471.
Cape Coast Castle trade; 30 May 1836. 3rd ser. XXXIII, 1141.
Lords. Slavery Abolition (Jamaica) Bill; 31 May 1836. 3rd ser. XXXIII, 1168.
Lords. East Indian sugar; 2 June 1836. 3rd ser. XXXIII, 1332.
Malta—Petition; 7 June 1836. 3rd ser. XXXIV, 161.
Slave trade; 5 July 1836. 3rd ser. XXXIV, 1266.
Female emigration; 5 July 1836. 3rd ser. XXXIV, 1268.
Female emigration; 8, 11 July, 5 Aug. 1836. 3rd ser. XXXV, 12, 96, 944.
Slave Compensation Bill; 10 Aug. 1836. 3rd ser. XXXV, 1055.
Colonial banks; 17 Feb. 1837. 3rd ser. XXXVI, 634.
Trade with Java; 7 March 1837. 3rd ser. XXXVII, 6.
Sugar duties; 23 June 1837. 3rd ser. XXXVIII, 1608.
Slavery treaties; 6 July 1837. 3rd ser. XXXVIII, 1822.
Slavery in India; 10 July 1837. 3rd ser. XXXVIII, 1853.
Lords. Colonial slavery; 23 Nov., 11, 22 Dec. 1837. 3rd ser. XXXIX, 132, 938, 1423.
Negro apprenticeship; 14 Dec. 1837. 3rd ser. XXXIX, 1081.
Slave Compensation Bill; 16 Dec. 1837. 3rd ser. XXXIX, 1183.
Lords. Negro emancipation; 23 Jan., 20 Feb. 1838. 3rd ser. XL, 352, 1284.
Lords. Slave trade; 29 Jan. 1838. 3rd ser. XL, 596.
Slave trade; 1, 2 March 1838. 3rd ser. XLI, 321, 364.
Lords. Slave trade; 2 March 1838. 3rd ser. XLI, 345.
Lords. Hindoos in Guiana; 6 March 1838. 3rd ser. XLI, 416.
Colonial Administration; 6, 7 March 1838. 3rd ser. XLI, 476, 571.
Lords. Negro apprenticeship; 9, 23 March 1838. 3rd ser. XLI, 705, 1166.
Lords. Slavery Abolition Act Amendment Bill; 13, 15, 22, 27 March 1838. 3rd ser. XLI, 802, 899, 1124, 1310.
British Honduras; 16 March 1838. 3rd ser. XLI, 951.
Lords. Abolition of slavery; 29 March, 2, 3 April 1838. 3rd ser. XLII, 1, 261, 344.
Negro apprenticeship; 29, 30 March, 3, 6, 7 April 1838. 3rd ser. XLII, 40, 156, 360, 465, 474.
Lords. Negro apprenticeship; 9 April 1838. 3rd ser. XLII, 475.
Lords. Malta Commission; 3 May 1838. 3rd ser. XLII, 799.
Foreign slave trade; 10 May 1838. 3rd ser. XLII, 1122.
Lords. Negro apprenticeship; 22 May, 15 June 1838. 3rd ser. XLIII, 84, 744.

Foreign slave trade; 22 May, 18 June 1838. 3rd ser. XLIII, 86, 128, 793.

Negro apprenticeship; 22, 24, 25, 28 May 1838. 3rd ser. XLIII, 87, 149, 279, 383.

Sugar duties; 15, 25 June 1838. 3rd ser. XLIII, 771, 1075.

Lords. Apprenticeship in Crown Colonies; 16 July 1838. 3rd ser. XLIV, 203.

Lords. West Indian Prisons Bill; 19 July 1838. 3rd ser. XLIV, 319.

Captured Slave Vessels Bill; 26 July 1838. 3rd ser. XLIV, 636.

Foreign slave trade; 7, 15 Aug. 1838. 3rd ser. XLIV, 1012, 1313.

Lords. Slavery in Mauritius; 8 Feb. 1839. 3rd ser. XLV, 183.

Slave trade; 8 March 1839. 3rd ser. XLVI, 145.

Lords. Capture of Aden; 11 March 1839. 3rd ser. XLVI, 207.

Lords. West Indian labourers, 10 March 1839. 3rd ser. XLVI, 790.

Lords. Mauritius; 26 March 1839. 3rd ser. XLVI, 1219.

Jamaica Bill; 9 April 1839. 3rd ser. XLVI, 1243.

Lords. Malta—Press; 18, 19, 30 April, 4 June 1839. 3rd ser. XLVII, 225, 311, 639, 1305.

Malta; 22 April 1839. 3rd ser. XLVII, 458.

Jamaica—Suspension of Constitution; 22, 23, 26 April, 3, 6, 30 May 1839. 3rd ser. XLVII, 459, 497, 573, 765, 871, 1105.

Lords. Slavery in Mauritius; 29 April 1839. 3rd ser. XLVII, 624.

Lords. Slave trade in Antigua; 2 May 1839. 3rd ser. XLVII, 715.

Lords. Jamaica Petition; 2 May 1839. 3rd ser. XLVII, 719.

Trade with Africa; 2 May 1839. 3rd ser. XLVII, 721.

Slave trade; 3 June 1839. 3rd ser. XLVII, 1253.

Govt. of Jamaica Bill; 7, 10, 19 June 1839. 3rd ser. XLVIII, 81, 97, 508.

Lords. Mauritius—Orders in Council; 10 June 1839. 3rd ser. XLVIII, 92.

Sugar Duties Bill; 12, 28 June 1839. 3rd ser. XLVIII, 163, 1021.

Lords. Emigration of free negroes; 14 June 1839. 3rd ser. XLVIII, 220.

Colonial Waste Lands; 25 June 1839. 3rd ser. XLVIII, 841.

Lords. Malta; 27 June 1839. 3rd ser. XLVIII, 923.

Lords. Govt. of Jamaica Bill; 28 June, 1, 2, 4, 5 July 1839. 3rd ser. XLVIII, 1005, 1029, 1096, 1183, 1233.

Lords. Church in colonies; 25 July 1839. 3rd ser. XLIX, 744.

Lords. Chinese opium trade; 1 Aug. 1839. 3rd ser. XLIX, 1052.

Lords. Portuguese Slave Trade Bill; 1, 2 Aug. 1839. 3rd ser. XLIX, 1058, 1128.

Portuguese Slave Trade Bill; 8, 9, 20, 27 Aug. 1839. 3rd ser. L, 119, 157, 438, 604.

Lords. West African trade; 15 Aug. 1839. 3rd ser. L, 294.

Lords. Slave Trade Bill; 15, 16, 19 Aug. 1839. 3rd ser. L, 300, 365, 381.

Colonial mails; 23 Aug. 1839. 3rd ser. L, 584.

Coolies in colonies; 4, 6 Feb. 1840. 3rd ser. LI, 1247, 1310.

China trade; 13, 18, 21 Feb., 6, 12, 19 March 1840. 3rd ser. LII, 178, 344, 454, 978, 1155, 1221.

Lords. African trade; 17, 28 Feb. 1840. 3rd ser. LII, 314, 745.

Lords. China; 20, 21 Feb. 1840. 3rd ser. LII, 425, 433.

Lords. East and West Indian produce; 12 March 1840. 3rd ser. LII, 1151.

Coolies in colonies; 12 March 1840. 3rd ser. LII, 1157.

Chinese trade and war; 24 March, 2, 7, 8, 9, 10, 11 April, 4 May 1840. 3rd ser. LIII, 6, 430, 669, 749, 986, 995, 996, 1182.

Emigration to South Australia; 27 March 1840. 3rd ser. LIII, 219.

Lords, Chinese War and trade; 10 April, 4, 5 May 1840. 3rd ser. LIII, 966, 1158, 1208.

Lords. Chinese trade and war; 12 May 1840. 3rd ser. LIV, 1.

Lords. Transportation; 19 May 1840. 3rd ser. LIV, 246.

Emigration; 2 June 1840. 3rd ser. LIV, 832.

Colonial Passengers Bill; 4, 22 June 1840. 3rd ser. LIV, 930, 1386.

Ionian Islands; 23 June 1840. 3rd ser. LV, 62.

Lords. Colonial Passengers Bill; 25 June 1840. 3rd ser. LV, 70.

Sugar Duties Bill; 25, 29 June 1840. 3rd ser. LV, 76, 196.

China—Orders in Council; 6 July 1840. 3rd ser. LV, 455.

Lords. Colonial labourers; 28 July 1840. 3rd ser. LV, 1067.

Lords. Mauritius; 7 Aug. 1840. 3rd ser. LV, 1379.

East and West Indian rum; 2, 12, 15, 26 Feb. 1841. 3rd ser. LVI, 204, 586, 626, 1145.

Slavery in East Indies; 8 Feb. 1841. 3rd ser. LVI, 456.

Niger Expedition; 11, 16 Feb. 1841. 3rd ser. LVI, 510, 692.

Highland emigration; 11 Feb. 1841. 3rd ser. LVI, 514.

Emigration; 11, 25 March 1841. 3rd ser. LVII, 134, 596.

Colonial customs duties; 12, 31 March, 2 April 1841. 3rd ser. LVII, 148, 752, 883.

Colonial appointments; 18 March 1841. 3rd ser. LVII, 359.

Transportation; 23 March, 23 April 1841. 3rd ser. LVII, 527, 1055.

Emigration to New South Wales; 22 April 1841. 3rd ser. LVII, 974.

Lords. West Indian mails; 27 April 1841. 3rd ser. LVII, 1147.

West Indian mails; 27 April 1841. 3rd ser. LVII, 1153.

Slave Compensation Bill; 27 April 1841. 3rd ser. LVII, 1165.

Lords. China—Petition from Bombay; 29 April 1841. 3rd ser. LVII, 1243.

Lords. Sugar duties; 7 May 1841. 3rd ser. LVIII, 1.

Sugar duties; 7, 10, 11, 12, 13, 17, 18, 20, 24 May 1841. 3rd ser. LVIII, 16, 97, 188, 259, 351, 505, 562, 676, 709.

West Indian Mails; 8 June 1841; 3rd ser. LVIII, 1350.

Lords. Slave trade; 20 Sept., 5 Oct. 1841. 3rd ser. LIX, 608, 1114.

Emigration, colonial lands; 4 Feb. 1842. 3rd ser. LX, 76.

Colonial duties; 7, 8, 22 Feb. 1842. 3rd ser. LX, 104, 150, 803.

Slave trade treaty; 8, 21 Feb. 1842. 3rd ser. LX, 145, 721.

West Indian bishops; 8, 15 Feb. 1842. 3rd ser. LX, 148, 442.

Sugar colonies; 14 Feb. 1842. 3rd ser. LX, 329.

Riots in Jamaica and Demerara; 24 Feb. 1842. 3rd ser. LX, 1002, 1006.

Colonial Passengers Bill; 28 Feb. 1842. 3rd ser. LX, 1179.

Colonial produce; 28 Feb. 1842. 3rd ser. LX, 1184.

Emigration of coolies; 1 March 1842. 3rd ser. LX, 1321.

Colonial Passengers Bill; 11 March 1842. 3rd ser. LXI, 419.

West Indian clergy; 11 March 1842. 3rd ser. LXI, 420, 490.

West Indian immigration; 22 March 1842. 3rd ser. LXI, 1092.

Colonial Passengers Bill; 14 April 1842. 3rd ser. LXII, 497.

Colonial duties; 15 April 1842. 3rd ser. LXII, 519, 539.

Colonial emigration; 19 April 1842. 3rd ser. LXII, 811.

Colonial Passengers Bill; 20 May 1842. 3rd ser. LXIII, 582.

Sugar duties; 3 June 1842. 3rd ser. LXIII, 1155.

Captured slave vessels; 16 June 1842. 3rd ser. LXIII, 1639.

Colonial Customs Duties Bill; 28 June 1842. 3rd ser. LXIV, 742.

Colonial Passengers Bill; 5 July 1842. 3rd ser. LXIV, 983.

Colonial Passengers Bill; 26 July 1842. 3rd ser. LXV, 644.

Lords. Slave trade; 2 Aug. 1842. 3rd ser. LXV, 935, 936.

Portuguese Slave Trade Bill; 8 Aug. 1842. 3rd ser. LXV, 1177.

Lords. Right of Search; 7 Feb. 1843. 3rd ser. LXVI, 214.

Lords. Chinese War; 14 Feb. 1843. 3rd ser. LXVI, 525.

Chinese War; 14 Feb. 1843. 3rd ser. LXVI, 547.

Right of Search; 16 Feb. 1843. 3rd ser. LXVI, 703.

Trade with Ceylon; 27 Feb. 1843. 3rd ser. LXVI, 1339.

Lords. Slave trade; 28 Feb. 1843. 3rd ser. LXVII, 4.

Lords. China trade; 17 March 1843. 3rd ser. LXVII, 1077.

Coast of Africa Bill; 17, 20 March 1843. 3rd ser. LXVII, 1095, 1143.

Suppression of opium trade; 4 April 1843. 3rd ser. LXVIII, 362.

Systematic colonization; 6 April 1843. 3rd ser. LXVIII, 484.

Indian slavery; 10 April 1843. 3rd ser. LXVIII, 749.

Lords. Slavery and slave trade; 11 April 1843. 3rd ser. LXVIII, 820.

Colonial clergy, West Indian magistrates; 24 April 1843. 3rd ser. LXVIII, 865.

Expense of colonies; 22 June 1843. 3rd ser. LXX, 205.

Sugar Duties Bill; 22 June 1843. 3rd ser. LXX, 213.

Lords. Slave Trade Suppression Bill; 7, 21 July 1843. 3rd ser. LXX, 735, 1293.

West Indian Relief; 21 July 1843. 3rd ser. LXX, 1291.
China—Opium compensation; 4 Aug. 1843. 3rd ser. LXXI, 241.
Lords. Chinese Intercourse Bill; 7 Aug. 1843. 3rd ser. LXXI, 316.
West Indian Relief Bill; 7 Aug. 1843. 3rd ser. LXXI, 358.
Slave Trade Suppression Bill; 18, 21, 22 Aug. 1843. 3rd ser. LXXI, 930, 983, 1002.
Lords. Slave trade; 5 Feb. 1844. 3rd ser. LXXII, 209.
Lords. Chinese treaty; 6 Feb. 1844. 3rd ser. LXXII, 263.
Chinese trade; 10 Feb. 1844. 3rd ser. LXXII, 472.
Colonial corn; 2 March 1844. 3rd ser. LXXIII, 1553.
Expense of colonial establishments; 19 April 1844. 3rd ser. LXXIV, 117.
Lords. Slave-grown sugar; 26 April 1844. 3rd ser. LXXIV, 272.
Sugar Duties Bill; 3, 10, 14, 17, 20, 21 June 1844. 3rd ser. LXXV, 154, 420, 907, 987, 1113, 1212.
Lords. Slave Trade Treaties Bill; 18 June 1844. 3rd ser. LXXV, 1089.
Sugar Duties Bill; 27 June 1844. 3rd ser. LXXVI, 21.
Lords. Sugar Duties Bill; 2 July 1844. 3rd ser. LXXVI, 169.
Slave trade—Palmerston's Motion; 16 July 1844. 3rd ser. LXXVI, 922.
Lords. Instructions for Slave trade suppression; 25 July 1844. 3rd ser. LXXVI, 1372.
Emigration—Dr Rolph; 13 Feb. 1845. 3rd ser. LXXVII, 444.
Ionian Islands—The Bandieras; 20 Feb. 1845. 3rd ser. LXXVII, 827.
Lords. Sugar duties; 21 Feb. 1845. 3rd ser. LXXVII, 924.
Sugar duties; 24, 26 Feb. 1845. 3rd ser. LXXVII, 1043, 1234.
Liberated Africans; 25 Feb. 1845. 3rd ser. LXXVII, 1173.
Hong Kong; 25 Feb. 1845. 3rd ser. LXXVII, 1203.
Lords. Sugar duties; 28 Feb. 1845. 3rd ser. LXXVIII, 119.
Sugar duties; 28 Feb., 3, 14 March 1845. 3rd ser. LXXVIII, 210, 238, 907.
Colonial accounts; 1 April 1845. 3rd ser. LXXVIII, 1321.
Lords. Sugar Duties Bill; 11 April 1845. 3rd ser. LXXIX, 460.
Slave trade; 7, 16 May 1845. 3rd ser. LXXX, 239, 466.
Ionian Islands—the Bandieras; 8 May 1845. 3rd ser. LXXX, 289.
Slave trade; 13 June 1845. 3rd ser. LXXXI, 478.
Hong Kong; 16 June 1845. 3rd ser. LXXXI, 600.
Slave trade—Hutt's Motion; 24 June 1845. 3rd ser. LXXXI, 1156.
Lords. Brazil Slave Trade Bill; 7 July 1845. 3rd ser. LXXXII, 59.
Slave trade—Palmerston's Motion re right of search; 4 July 1845. 3rd ser. LXXXII, 223.
Brazil Slave Trade Bill; 24, 31 July, 4 Aug. 1845. 3rd ser. LXXXII, 1043, 1286, 1371.
Ceylon; 25 July 1845. 3rd ser. LXXXII, 1120.
Malta—Education; 30 July 1845. 3rd ser. LXXXII, 1199.
Colonial Office; 28 May 1846. 3rd ser. LXXXVI, 1420.
Sugar Duties Bill; 22, 23 June, 20, 24 July 1846. 3rd ser. LXXXVII, 811, 904, 1304, 1404.
Troops in Colonies; 17 July 1846. 3rd ser. LXXXVII, 1231.
Captured negroes; 17 July 1846. 3rd ser. LXXXVII, 1267.
Transportation; 20 July 1846. 3rd ser. LXXXVII, 1347.
Sugar Duties Bill; 27 July, 3, 10 Aug. 1846. 3rd ser. LXXXVIII, 32, 287, 465.
Malta—Carnival; 3 Aug. 1846. 3rd ser. LXXXVIII, 318.
Colonial Office; 6 Aug. 1846. 3rd ser. LXXXVIII, 366.
Lords. Sugar Duties Bill; 10, 13 Aug. 1846. 3rd ser. LXXXVIII, 467, 648.
British Possessions Bill; 13, 15 Aug. 1846. 3rd ser. LXXXVIII, 678, 738.
Colonies—Representative Govt.; 14 Aug. 1846. 3rd ser. LXXXVIII, 714.
Lords. Emigration of Irish paupers; 29 Jan. 1847. 3rd ser. LXXXIX, 597.
Lords. Sugar bills; 16, 19 Feb. 1847. 3rd ser. XC, 19, 212.
West Indies—Immigration; 19 Feb. 1847. 3rd ser. XC, 248.
Voluntary emigration; 4 March 1847. 3rd ser. XC, 837.
West Indian produce; 13 May 1847. 3rd ser. XCII, 784.
Passengers Act Amendment Bill; 21 May 1847. 3rd ser. XCII, 1237.
Hong Kong; 1 June 1847. 3rd ser. XCII, 1365.
Irish colonization; 1 June 1847. 3rd ser. XCII, 1369.

Lords. Irish emigration; 4 June 1847. 3rd ser. XCIII, 96.
Colonization—Godley's plan; 7, 14 June 1847. 3rd ser. XCIII, 187, 471.
Emigrant ships; 28 June 1847. 3rd ser. XCIII, 972.
Slave-trading vessels; 9 July 1847. 3rd ser. XCIV, 125.
Hong Kong, Ningpo; 9 July 1847. 3rd ser. XCIV, 141.
Lords. Irish emigrants; 12 July 1847. 3rd ser. XCIV, 180.
Ceylon—Langslow's Case; 13 July 1847. 3rd ser. XCIV, 278.
Passengers Bill; 20 July 1847. 3rd ser. XCIV, 597.
Effects of negro emancipation; 23 July 1847. 3rd ser. XCIV, 692.
Navigation laws; 20 Dec. 1847. 3rd ser. XCV, 1421.
Sugar and coffee plantations; 3, 4 Feb. 1848. 3rd ser. XCVI, 7, 80, 84.
Lords. West Indian petitions; 7 Feb. 1848. 3rd ser. XCVI, 171.
Lords. Slave trade suppression; 22 Feb. 1848. 3rd ser. XCVI, 1037.
Slave trade—Hutt's Motion; 22 Feb. 1848. 3rd ser. XCVI, 1091.
Slave trade—Baillie's Motion; 24 March 1848. 3rd ser. XCVII, 971.
Tobago Relief Bill; 1 May 1848. 3rd ser. XCVIII, 538.
Navigation Laws; 15 May 1848. 3rd ser. XCVIII, 988.
Slave Trade Committee; 17, 18 May 1848. 3rd ser. XCVIII, 1167, 1197.
Commercial policy; 23 May 1848. 3rd ser. XCVIII, 1265.
Navigation laws; 29 May, 1, 8, 9, 16 June 1848. 3rd ser. XCIX, 9, 179, 251, 510,
    573, 792.
Lords. Tobago Relief Bill; 6 June 1848. 3rd ser. XCIX, 422.
West Indian distress; 16 June 1848. 3rd ser. XCIX, 729.
Colonial Office and West India Committee; 19 June 1848. 3rd ser. XCIX, 809.
Sugar duties; 19, 22, 23, 26, 29, 30 June 1848. 3rd ser. XCIX, 811, 1012, 1089,
    1217, 1314, 1317, 1416.
Lords. West Indian distress; 27 June 1848. 3rd ser. XCIX, 1243.
Colonial Office—Questions; 29 June 1848. 3rd ser. XCIX, 1308.
Sugar duties; 3, 7, 10, 15, 21, 31 July, 3, 4 Aug. 1848. 3rd ser. C, 4, 242, 310, 501,
    642, 1042, 1113, 1159.
Colonial govt.—Molesworth's Motion; 25 July 1848. 3rd ser. C, 816.
Lords. Emigration to Australia; 10 Aug. 1848. 3rd ser. CI, 1.
Navigation laws; 10 Aug. 1848. 3rd ser. CI, 56.
Colonies—Omitted corresp.; 14 Aug. 1848. 3rd ser. CI, 127.
Lords. Slave trade—Denman's Motion; 22 Aug. 1848. 3rd ser. CI, 365.
Sugar Duties Bill; 22 Aug. 1848. 3rd ser. CI, 376.
Mauritius—Questions; 24 Aug. 1848. 3rd ser. CI, 496.
Lords. Sugar Duties Bill; 28 Aug. 1848. 3rd ser. CI, 568.
West India Colonies Bill; 28 Aug. 1848. 3rd ser. CI, 584.
Tobago Petition; 29 Aug. 1848. 3rd ser. CI, 630.
Lords. Emigration tax; 9 Feb. 1849. 3rd ser. CII, 457.
Navigation laws; 14 Feb. 1849. 3rd ser. CII, 680.
Colonial system—Ceylon and British Guiana; 20 Feb. 1849. 3rd ser. CII, 938.
Lords. Slave trade; 22 Feb. 1849. 3rd ser. CII, 1078.
Lords. Convict establishments; 23 Feb. 1849. 3rd ser. CII, 1171.
Convict system, Transportation; 8 March 1849. 3rd ser. CIII, 383.
Navigation Bill; 9, 12, 23, 26 March 1849. 3rd ser. CIII, 464, 625, 1196, 1295.
Transportation to South Africa; 27 March 1849. 3rd ser. CIII, 1371.
Condition of colonies; 4 April 1849. 3rd ser. CIV, 288.
Passengers Bill; 4 April 1849. 3rd ser. CIV, 299.
Colonial administration; 16 April 1849. 3rd ser. CIV, 313.
Navigation Bill; 18, 23 April 1849. 3rd ser. CIV, 462, 622.
Lords. Navigation Bill; 7 May 1849. 3rd ser. CIV, 1316.
Lords. Navigation Bill; 8, 24 May 1849. 3rd ser. CV, 1, 875.
Emigration from Ireland; 15 May 1849. 3rd ser. CV, 500.
Colonial possessions—Roebuck's Motion; 24 May 1849. 3rd ser. CV, 928.
International arbitration—Cobden's Motion; 12 June 1849. 3rd ser. CVI, 53.
Navigation Bill; 14 June 1849. 3rd ser. CVI, 187.
Colonial govt.—Molesworth's Motion; 26 June 1849. 3rd ser. CVI, 937.

British Guiana—Hume's Motion; 24 July 1849. 3rd ser. CVII, 920.
Slave trade (Persian Gulf) Bill; 27 July 1849. 3rd ser. CVII, 1030.
Ceylon—Address; 28 July 1849. 3rd ser. CVII, 1079.
Lords. West Indian distress; 30 July 1849. 3rd ser. CVII, 1101.
Ceylon—Hawes's Motion; 6, 11 Feb. 1850. 3rd ser. CVIII, 417, 641, 643.
Colonial policy—Russell's Resolutions; 8 Feb. 1850. 3rd ser. CVIII, 535.
Transportation—Adderley's Motion; 14 Feb. 1850. 3rd ser. CVIII, 777.
Lords. Emigrant ships; 15 Feb. 1850. 3rd ser. CVIII, 809.
Lords. Emigrant ships; 26 Feb., 5, 15, 22 March 1850. 3rd ser. CIX, 7, 354, 954, 1247.
Slave trade treaties—Hutt's Motion; 19 March 1850. 3rd ser. CIX, 1093.
Emigration of orphan children; 28 May 1850. 3rd ser. CXI, 433.
Sugar duties—Buxton's Motion; 31 May 1850. 3rd ser. CXI, 528.
Coffee—Anstey's Motion; 9 July 1850. 3rd ser. CXII, 1186.
British Guiana—Motion; 22 July 1850. 3rd ser. CXIII, 88.
Ionian Islands—Hume's Motion; 23 July, 9 Aug. 1850. 3rd ser. CXIII, 175, 976.
Ceylon Committee; 26 July, 12 Aug. 1850. 3rd ser. CXIII, 335, 339, 1043.
Passengers Act Amendment Bill; 17 Feb. 1851. 3rd ser. CXIV, 768.
Lords. Transportation; 4 March 1851. 3rd ser. CXIV, 1086.
Ceylon; 17 March 1851. 3rd ser. CXV, 23.
Lords. Ceylon; 18 March, 1 April 1851. 3rd ser. CXV, 109, 843.
Colonial military expenditure; 10 April 1851. 3rd ser. CXV, 1364.
Lords. British Guiana; 14 April 1851. 3rd ser. CXVI, 128.
Coffee and timber duties; 14 April 1851. 3rd ser. CXVI, 179.
Lords. Transportation to Tasmania; 9 May 1851. 3rd ser. CXVI, 740.
Transportation to Tasmania; 20 May 1851. 3rd ser. CXVI, 1168.
Ceylon—Baillie's Resolution; 27, 29 May 1851. 3rd ser. CXVII, 6, 130.
Lords. Transportation to Tasmania; 6 June 1851. 3rd ser. CXVII, 543.
Lords. Navigation laws; 17 June 1851. 3rd ser. CXVII, 847.
Armaments—International arbitration; 17 June 1851. 3rd ser. CXVII, 916.
Borneo—Sir James Brooke; 10 July 1851. 3rd ser. CXVIII, 436.
Navigation laws; 24 July 1851. 3rd ser. CXVIII, 1395.
Sugar refining; 1 Aug. 1851. 3rd ser. CXVIII, 1824.
Ionian Islands; 5 April 1852. 3rd ser. CXX, 718.
East India Company's charter; 19 April 1852. 3rd ser. CXX, 806.
Passengers Act Amendment Bill; 19 April 1852. 3rd ser. CXX, 869.
Colonial Bishops Bill; 28 April 1852. 3rd ser. CXX, 1263.
Lords. Emigration to South Australia; 17 May 1852. 3rd ser. CXXI, 672.
Colonial Bishops Bill; 19 May 1852. 3rd ser. CXXI, 738, 742.
Passengers Act Amendment Bill; 4 June 1852. 3rd ser. CXXII, 67.
West Indian distress; 7 June 1852. 3rd ser. CXXII, 101.
Lords. West Indies; 10 June 1852. 3rd ser. CXXII, 378.
Colonial Church—Gladstone's Motion; 23 June 1852. 3rd ser. CXXII, 1204.
Ionian Islands—Hume's Motion; 2 Dec. 1852. 3rd ser. CXXIII, 826.
Sugar duties; 9 Dec. 1852. 3rd ser. CXXIII, 1156.
Lords. Transportation; 17 Feb., 1 March 1853. 3rd ser. CXXIV, 165, 782.
Transportation; 24 Feb. 1853. 3rd ser. CXXIV, 554.
Lords. Colonial Church—Petition; 18 March 1853. 3rd ser. CXXV, 419.
Canada. Clergy Reserves Bill; 18 March 1853. 3rd ser. CXXV, 450.
Lords. Transportation; 28 April 1853. 3rd ser. CXXVI, 664.
Lords. Transportation—Grey's Motion; 10 May 1853. 3rd ser. CXXVII, 1.
Lords. Slave trade—Petition; 23, 30 May 1853. 3rd ser. CXXVII, 488, 762.
Lords. Affairs of Jamaica; 30 June 1853. 3rd ser. CXXVIII, 947.
Lords. Transportation Bill; 18 July 1853. 3rd ser. CXXIX, 348.
Lords. Colonial Church Regulation Bill; 21 July 1853. 3rd ser. CXXIX, 512.
Transportation Bill; 11, 12 Aug. 1853. 3rd ser. CXXIX, 1600, 1682.
Malta—Criminal code; 15 Aug. 1853. 3rd ser. CXXIX, 1732.
Lords. Withdrawal of troops from West Indies; 23 Feb. 1854. 3rd ser. CXXX, 1137.
Emigrant ships; 2 March 1854. 3rd ser. CXXXI, 203.

Colonial Clergy Disabilities Bill; 20 March 1854. 3rd ser. CXXXI, 998.
Slave trade—Pechell's Motion; 4 April 1854. 3rd ser. CXXXII, 426.
Lords. Justice at Singapore; 12 June 1854. 3rd ser. CXXXIII, 1354.
Lords. Transportation; 4 Aug. 1854. 3rd ser. CXXXV, 1293.
West Indian Incumbered Estates Bill; 7, 9 Aug. 1854. 3rd ser. CXXXV, 1376, 1499.
Slave Trade Treaties Bill; 9 Aug. 1854. 3rd ser. CXXXV, 1483.
Lords. Ticket-of-Leave System; 9 March 1855. 3rd ser. CXXXVII, 322.
Lords. Colonial Secretary; 9 March 1855. 3rd ser. CXXXVII, 336.
Lords. Secretaries and Under-Secretaries Bill; 12 March 1855. 3rd ser. CXXXVII, 384.
Colonial Dept.; 12 March 1855. 3rd ser. CXXXVII, 419.
China trade; 27 March 1855. 3rd ser. CXXXVII, 1243.
Lords. Slave trade and West Indies; 26, 28 June, 20 July 1855. 3rd ser. CXXXIX, 113, 271, 1196.
Transportation—Scott's Motion; 3 April 1856. 3rd ser. CXLI, 387.
Lords. International maritime law; 22 May 1856. 3rd ser. CXLII, 481.
Lords. West India Loans Bill; 12 June 1856. 3rd ser. CXLII, 1388.
Lords. Brazilian slave trade; 21 July 1856. 3rd ser. CXLIII, 1070.
Transportation Bill; 9 Feb. 1857. 3rd ser. CXLIV, 352.
Lords. Chinese War; 24, 26 Feb., 12, 17 March 1857. 3rd ser. CXLIV, 1155, 1310, 2196, 2383.
Chinese War; 26, 27 Feb., 2, 3 March 1857. 3rd ser. CXLIV, 1391, 1495, 1589, 1726.
Lords. Opium trade with China; 9 March 1857. 3rd ser. CXLIV, 2027.
Transportation Bill; 15, 22 May 1857. 3rd ser. CXLV, 338, 773.
Slave trade—Cuba; 22 May 1857. 3rd ser. CXLV, 748.
Honduras Treaty; 29 May 1857. 3rd ser. CXLV, 1003.
Lords. Transportation Bill; 12 June 1857. 3rd ser. CXLV, 1641.
British Guiana—Immigration; 3 July 1857. 3rd ser. CXLVI, 885.
Slave trade—Buxton's Motion; 14 July 1857. 3rd ser. CXLVI, 1492.
Lords. Slave trade—Brougham's Resolution; 17 July 1857. 3rd ser. CXLVI, 1661.
Chinese War; 20 July 1857. 3rd ser. CXLVII, 49.
Lords. British Guiana—Immigration; 24 July 1857. 3rd ser. CXLVII, 349.
Lords. Slave trade—Petition; 17 June 1858. 3rd ser. CL, 2195.
Slave trade and U.S.A.; 18 June 1858. 3rd ser. CLI, 41.
Lords. Hong Kong—Coolie emigration; 21 June 1858. 3rd ser. CLI, 70.
Slave trade—Hutt's Resolution; 12 July 1858. 3rd ser. CLI, 1286.
Hudson's Bay Co.—Roebuck's Motion; 20 July 1858. 3rd ser. CLI, 1788.
Lords. Jamaica immigration; 8 Feb. 1859. 3rd ser. CLII, 169.
Lords. Slave trade and right of search; 14, 15 Feb. 1859. 3rd ser. CLII, 314, 387.
Lords. Ionian Islands; 21 Feb. 1859. 3rd ser. CLII, 596.
Colonial and foreign wood; 3 March 1859. 3rd ser. CLII, 1189.
West Indies—Immigration; 3 March 1859. 3rd ser. CLII, 1219.
Lords. Slave trade—*Charles et Georges*; 8 March 1859. 3rd ser. CLII, 1415.
Slave trade—*Charles et Georges*; 8 March 1859. 3rd ser. CLII, 1478.
Lords. Singapore—Petition; 10 March 1859. 3rd ser. CLII, 1602.
Lords. Ionian Islands; 11 March 1859. 3rd ser. CLIII, 1.
Hong Kong; 12 July 1859. 3rd ser. CLIV, 1057.
Lords. Malta; 21 July 1859. 3rd ser. CLV, 150.
Relations with China; 13, 24 Feb. 1860. 3rd ser. CLVI, 919, 1714.
Lords. China—Elgin's statement; 21 Feb. 1860. 3rd ser. CLVI, 1461.
East India indentured labourers; 8 March 1860. 3rd ser. CLVII, 111.
Lords. China expedition; 30 March 1860. 3rd ser. CLVII, 1586.
Colonial military defence; 31 March 1860. 3rd ser. CLVIII, 1810, 1826.
Lords. Slave trade—Mozambique; 25 June 1860. 3rd ser. CLIX, 908.
China war; 12, 13, 16 July 1860. 3rd ser. CLIX, 1808, 1879, 1947.
Lords. Bermuda convicts; 26 July 1860. 3rd ser. CLX, 181.
China expedition; 14 Feb. 1861. 3rd ser. CLXI, 400.
Lords. China—Yangtse Expedition; 19 Feb. 1861. 3rd ser. CLXI, 546.

Slave trade—Cave's Resolutions; 26 Feb. 1861. 3rd ser. CLXI, 950.
Transportation—Childers's Motion; 1 March 1861. 3rd ser. CLXI, 1233.
Colonial military expenditure—Miles's Motion; 5 March 1861. 3rd ser. CLXI, 1400.
Relations with China; 12, 14 March 1861. 3rd ser. CLXI, 1960.
Lords. Ionian Islands; 21 March 1861. 3rd ser. CLXII, 133.
Lords. Hulks at Bermuda; 23 April 1861. 3rd ser. CLXII, 976.
Brazilian slave trade; 26 April 1861. 3rd ser. CLXII, 1186.
Ionian Islands—Pigott's Motion; 7 May 1861. 3rd ser. CLXII, 1654.
Lords. Colonial cotton; 28 May 1861. 3rd ser. CLXIII, 149.
Lords. East African slave trade; 15 July 1861. 3rd ser. CLXIV, 855.
Slave trade; 26 July 1861. 3rd ser. CLXIV, 1641.
Ceylon—Expenses; 6 May 1862. 3rd ser. CLXVI, 1282.
Lords. Slave trade, Anglo-American treaty; 20 May 1862. 3rd ser. CLXVI, 1957.
Lords. Slave trade treaty with U.S.A.; 27 May 1862. 3rd ser. CLXVII, 1.
Slave Trade Treaty Bill; 24 June 1862. 3rd ser. CLXVII, 964.
Lords. Jamaica—Finances; 14 July 1862. 3rd ser. CLXVIII, 260.
Jamaica Loan Bill; 14 July 1862. 3rd ser. CLXVIII, 313.
Lords. Jamaica Loan Bill; 22 July 1862. 3rd ser. CLXVIII, 659.
Transportation Acts; 9 March 1863. 3rd ser. CLXIX, 1229.
Lords. Cession of Ionian Islands; 16, 17 April 1863. 3rd ser. CLXX, 178, 275.
Lords. Seizure of British vessels by U.S. cruisers; 23, 24 April 1863. 3rd ser. CLXX, 554, 653.
Trent Case, seizure of British vessels; 23, 24 April 1863. 3rd ser. CLXX, 576, 579, 703.
Ionian Islands; 12 May 1863. 3rd ser. CLXX, 1586.
Lords. U.S. Prize Courts; 18 May 1863. 3rd ser. CLXX, 1818.
Lords. British commerce and American cruisers; 15 June 1863. 3rd ser. CLXXI, 874.
Lords. Ionian Islands; 30 June 1863. 3rd ser. CLXXI, 1719.
Lords. Relations with China; 6 July 1863. 3rd ser. CLXXII, 270.
Lords. Cession of Ionian Islands; 9, 27 July 1863. 3rd ser. CLXXII, 412, 1440.
Lords. *Alabama* Case; 11 Feb. 1864. 3rd ser. CLXXIII, 427.
Anglo-American relations; 12, 25 Feb., 14 March 1864. 3rd ser. CLXXIII, 501, 1475, 1917.
Malta—Admiralty dock; 22 Feb. 1864. 3rd ser. CLXXIII, 889.
Lords. Anglo-American relations; 2, 5 Feb. 1864. 3rd ser. CLXXIII, 1053.
Ionian Islands; 18 March 1864. 3rd ser. CLXXIV, 343.
Sugar duties; 14, 15 April 1864. 3rd ser. CLXXIV, 972, 1142.
Lords. Anglo-American relations—Prize law; 26, 29 April 1864. 3rd ser. CLXXIV, 1595, 1861.
Anglo-American relations; 28 April 1864. 3rd ser. CLXXIV, 1777.
Pensions to colonial governors; 29 April 1864. 3rd ser. CLXXIV, 1944.
Anglo-American relations; 13 May 1864. 3rd ser. CLXXV, 467.
Lagos—Question; 9 June 1864. 3rd ser. CLXXV, 1456.
Pensions to colonial governors; 28 June 1864. 3rd ser. CLXXVI, 426.
Ionian Islands; 15 July 1864. 3rd ser. CLXXVI, 1575.
Emigration to America; 28 July 1864. 3rd ser. CLXXVI, 2161.
West Africa—Adderley's Motion; 21 Feb. 1865. 3rd ser. CLXXVII, 535.
Lords. Transportation to Australia; 27 Feb. 1865. 3rd ser. CLXXVII, 737.
Lords. Anglo-American relations; 23 March 1865. 3rd ser. CLXXVIII, 68.
Ionian Islands—Pensions; 24 March 1865. 3rd ser. CLXXVIII, 202.
Lords. Belligerent rights; 15 May 1865. 3rd ser. CLXXVIII, 886.
Defence of colonies; 26 May 1865. 3rd ser. CLXXVIII, 905.
Lords. Belligerent rights; 12 June 1865. 3rd ser. CLXXIX, 1.
Colonial Governors' Pensions Bill; 22 June 1865. 3rd ser. CLXXIX, 663.
Lords. Colonial Governors' Pensions Bill; 30 June 1865. 3rd ser. CLXXIX, 964.
Jamaica Govt. Bill; 15, 22, 26, 28 Feb. 1866. 3rd ser. CLXXXI, 581, 918, 1173, 1264.
Colonial Governors Act Amendment Bill; 27 Feb. 1866. 3rd ser. CLXXXI, 1200.
International maritime law; 2 March 1866. 3rd ser. CLXXXI, 1407.

(b) PERIODICALS

The following periodicals are those which have most frequently dealt with colonial affairs in general. For British newspapers *The Times Tercentenary Handlist of English and Welsh Newspapers, Magazines and Reviews* [1620–1920], 2 vols. 1920, should be consulted.

American Historical Review. New York, etc. 1895– . In progress.
Annual Register for 1758– . London, 1761– . In progress.
Board of Trade Journal. London, 1877– . In progress.
Bulletin of the Imperial Institute. London, 1903– . In progress.
Bulletin of the Institute of Historical Research. London, 1923– . In progress.
Cambridge Historical Journal. Cambridge, 1924– . In progress.
Colonial Gazette. Nos. 1–424. London, 1838–47.
Colonial Office Journal. London, 1907–10. Continued as the *Colonial Journal,* 1913– . In progress.
Colonial Office List. London, 1862– . In progress. Unofficial annual.
Colonial Review. London, 1824–29.
Contemporary Review. London, 1866– . In progress.
Crown Colonist. London, 1931– . In progress.
Dublin Review. London, 1836– . In progress.
Edinburgh Review. Edinburgh and London, 1802–1932.
Empire Review. London, 1923– . In progress.
English Historical Review. London, 1886– . In progress.
Fortnightly Review. London, 1865– . In progress.
Fraser's Magazine. 106 vols. London, 1830–82.
Gentleman's Magazine. 303 vols. London, 1731–1907. Index, 4 vols. 1789–1821.
History, new series. Historical Association, 1916– . In progress.
Irish Historical Studies. Dublin, 1937– . In progress.
Journal of Modern History. Chicago, 1929– . In progress.
National Review. London, 1883– . In progress.
Notes and Queries. London, 1849– . In progress.
Politica. London School of Economics, 1934– . In progress.
Political Science Quarterly. Boston, New York, 1886– . In progress.
Quarterly Review. London, 1809– . In progress.
Revue d'histoire des colonies. Paris, 1913– . In progress. Current title, *Revue d'histoire coloniale.*
Round Table. London, 1910– . In progress.
Scottish Historical Review. 25 vols. Glasgow, 1903–28. Indexes, 2 vols., 1918, 1933.
Statesman's Yearbook. London, 1864– . In progress.
Statistical Abstract for the several British Overseas Dominions and Protectorates. London, 1865– . In progress.
Transactions of the Royal Historical Society. London, 1871– . In progress.
United Empire. London, 1909– . In progress. Supersedes the *Journal* and *Proceedings of the Royal Colonial Institute* (1869–1909).
Westminster Review. 181 vols. London, 1824–71.

(c) COLLECTED HISTORICAL RECORDS

For fuller lists of printed sources relating to particular subjects, see the bibliographies in *C.H.B.E.* vols. IV–VIII, and the Special Bibliographies below.

BELL, K. N. and MORRELL, W. P. (Ed.). *Select Documents on British Colonial Policy,* 1830–60. Oxford, 1928.
BIRD, J. (Ed.). *The Annals of Natal,* 1495–1845. 2 vols. Pietermaritzburg, 1888.
BLADEN, F. M. and BRITTON, A. (Eds.). *Historical Records of New South Wales.* 7 vols. in 8. Sydney, 1892–1901.
CANADA. PUBLIC ARCHIVES. *Reports.* Ottawa, 1872– . In progress.
EGERTON, H. E. (Ed.). *Federations and Unions within the British Empire.* 1911. 2nd edn. Oxford, 1924.

EYBERS, G. W. (Ed.). *Select Constitutional Documents illustrating South African History,* 1795–1910. 1918.

KEITH, A. B. (Ed.). *Selected Speeches and Documents on British Colonial Policy,* 1763–1917. 2 vols. Oxford, 1918.

KENNEDY, W. P. M. (Ed.). *Statutes, Treaties and Documents of the Canadian Constitution,* 1713–1929. 2nd edn. Oxford, 1930.

McNAB, R. (Ed.). *Historical Records of New Zealand.* Vols. I–II. Wellington, N.Z., 1908–14.

MORISON, S. E. (Ed.). *Sources and Documents illustrating the American Revolution,* 1764–88. Oxford, 1923.

WATSON, J. F. (Ed.). *Historical Records of Australia.* Sydney, 1914– . In progress.

(d) GENERAL HISTORIES AND DESCRIPTIVE WORKS

BRIDGE, J. S. C. *From Island to Empire: a short history of the expansion of England by force of arms.* 1908. Also pubd. in French, Paris, 1910.

BRODRICK, Hon. G. C. and FOTHERINGHAM, J. K. *History of England,* 1801–37. 1919. Longman's *Political History of England,* ed. by W. Hunt and R. L. Poole, vol. XI.

CHEVALLIER, J. J. *L'Évolution de l'Empire britannique.* 2 vols. Paris, 1930.

DILKE, Sir C. W. *Greater Britain, a record of travel in English-speaking countries during* 1866–7. 2nd rev. edn. 1876.

DOMVILE-FIFE, C. W. *Encyclopaedia of the British Empire.* 3 vols. Bristol, 1924.

EGERTON, H. E. *Origin and Growth of Greater Britain.* Oxford, 1908. 2nd edn. 1920.

FAIRGRIEVE, J. and YOUNG, E. *Growth of Greater Britain.* 1924. Historical geography.

FAWCETT, C. B. *A Political Geography of the British Empire.* New York, 1933.

FORBES, A. H. *History of the British Dominions beyond the Seas,* 1558–1910. 1919. Embodies Clough's *Expansion of the British Empire* (1858).

GEORGE, H. B. *Historical Geography of the British Empire.* 7th edn. Revised by R. W. Jeffery. 1924.

GRESSWELL, W. P. *The Growth and Administration of the British Colonies,* 1837–97. 1898.

GUNN, H. (Ed.). *The British Empire. A survey.* 12 vols. 1924. Includes sections by A. Berriedale Keith, E. Lewin, Sir C. P. Lucas, A. P. Newton and J. A. Williamson.

HALEVY, É. *History of the English People.* Vols. I–III, 1815–41. London, 1924–7. Translation of *Histoire du peuple anglais au XIX siècle,* 3 vols. Paris, 1912–23.

HALL, W. P. and ALBION, R. G. *History of England and the British Empire.* Boston, 1937.

HERBERTSON, A. J. and HOWARTH, O. J. R. (Eds.). *Oxford Survey of the British Empire.* 6 vols. Oxford, 1914.

HERBERTSON, A. J. and THOMPSON, R. L. *Geography of the British Empire.* 1912. 3rd edn., rev. by O. J. R. Howarth. Oxford, 1918.

HUGHES, E. A. *Britain and Greater Britain in the 19th century.* Cambridge, 1920.

KIRKMAN, F. B. B. *Growth of Greater Britain.* 1909.

LECKY, W. E. H. *History of England in the eighteenth century.* 8 vols. 1878–90.

—— *History of Ireland in the eighteenth century.* 5 vols. 1892.

LOW, S. and SANDERS, L. C. *The History of England during the Reign of Victoria,* 1837–1901. 1913. Longmans' *Political History of England,* ed. by W. Hunt and R. L. Poole, vol. XII.

LUCAS, Sir C. P. *Historical Geography of the British Colonies.* Introduction and vols. I–VII. 15 vols. Oxford, 1887–1923.

MAGNAN DE BORNIER, J. *L'Empire britannique: son évolution politique et constitutionelle.* Paris, 1930.

MANNING, H. T. *British Colonial Government after the American Revolution,* 1782–1820. New Haven, Conn., 1933.

MARRIOTT, Sir J. A. R. *The Evolution of the British Empire and Commonwealth.* 1939.

MARTIN, R. M. *History of the British Colonies.* 5 parts. 1834–5.
—— *The British Colonies.* 6 vols. 1851–7. A different work from the preceding.
MARTINEAU, A. and MAY, L. PH. *Tableau de l'expansion européenne à travers le monde.* Paris, 1935.
MARTINEAU, HARRIET. *History of England during the Thirty Years' Peace,* 1816–46. 2 vols. 1844–50. Rev. edn. 4 vols. 1877–8.
MATHIESON, W. L. *England in Transition,* 1789–1832. 1920.
MAXWELL, Sir H. *A Century of Empire,* 1801–1900. 3 vols. 1909–11.
MORLEY, JOHN, Lord. "The Expansion of England." *Macmillan's Magazine,* vol. XLIX (1884), pp. 241–58.
MUIR, RAMSAY. *Short History of the British Commonwealth.* Vol. II, *The Modern Commonwealth,* 1763–1919. 2nd ed. 1934.
NEWTON, A. P. and EWING, J. *The British Empire since 1783: its political and economic development.* New edn. 1939.
PAUL, H. *History of Modern England* [1845–95]. 5 vols. 1904–6.
ROBERTSON, C. G. and BARTHOLOMEW, J. G. *Historical and Modern Atlas of the British Empire.* New edn. 1924.
ROBINSON, H. *Development of the British Empire.* New edn. Boston, 1936.
ROBINSON, H. J. *Colonial Chronology. A chronology of the principal events connected with the English colonies and India.* 1892.
SANDERSON, E. *The British Empire in the Nineteenth Centnry.* 6 vols. 1898–29.
SEELEY, Sir J. R. *The Expansion of England.* 1883. New edn. 1925.
SOMERVELL, D. C. *The British Empire.* 1930.
TILBY, A. WYATT. *English People Overseas.* 6 vols. 1908–14. 2nd edn. of vols. I–II. 1910.
TREVELYAN, G. M. *British History in the Nineteenth Century,* 1782–1901. 2nd edn. 1937.
TROTTER, R. G. *The British Empire-Commonwealth. A study in political evolution* [*since 1783*]. New York, 1932.
WALPOLE, Sir SPENCER. *History of England from the Conclusion of the Great War in 1815.* Rev. edn. 6 vols. 1910–13.
WALPOLE, Sir SPENCER. *History of Twenty-Five Years,* 1856–80. 4 vols. 1904–8.
WILLIAMS, B. *The British Empire.* 1928. Home University Library.
WILLIAMSON, J. A. *A Short History of British Expansion.* 2nd edn. 2 vols. 1930.
WOODWARD, E. L. *The Age of Reform,* 1815–70. Oxford, 1938. *Oxford History of England,* ed. by G. N. Clark.
WOODWARD, W. H. *A Short History of the Expansion of the British Empire.* 6th edn. Cambridge, 1931.
ZIMMERMANN, A. *Die europäischen Kolonien.* 5 vols. Berlin, 1896–1903. Vol. II and III deal with the colonies.

(e) BIOGRAPHIES

For biographies relating to particular subjects see *C.H.B.E.*, vols. IV–VIII, and the Special Bibliographies below.

COLLECTED BIOGRAPHY

BOASE, F. *Modern English Biography.* 6 vols. 1892–1921. Brief biographies of persons, not in the *D.N.B.*, who died after 1850.
GIBB, A. D. *Scottish Empire.* 1937. Scottish Empire-Builders.
GUNN, H. *Makers of the Empire.* 1924. British Empire Survey, vol. VIII.
STEPHEN, L. and LEE, Sir S. (Eds.). *Dictionary of National Biography.* Rev. edn., including 1901 Supplement. 22 vols. 1908–9.
STRIDE, W. K. *Empire-Builders: a course of lectures.* 1906.
WARD, T. H. (Ed.). *Men of the Reign.* A biographical dictionary of eminent persons of British and Colonial birth [who died 1837–84]. 1885.
Who's Who, an annual biographical dictionary. 1849– . In progress.
Who was Who, 1897–1916. 1920.

WILLIAMSON, J. A. *Builders of the Empire.* Oxford, 1925.
  Valuable obituaries are also to be found in the *Annual Register,* the *Gentleman's Magazine* and *The Times.*

INDIVIDUAL STATESMEN

ASHLEY, Hon. E. *Life of Palmerston,* 1846–65. 2 vols. 1876.
ASPINALL, A. *Lord Brougham and the Whig Party.* 1927.
BALFOUR, Lady FRANCES. *Life of Lord Aberdeen.* 2 vols. 1922.
BEACH, Lady V. *Life of Sir Michael Hicks-Beach.* 2 vols. 1932.
BEATTY, R. C. *Lord Macaulay, Victorian Liberal.* Norman, 1938.
BELL, H. C. *Life of Palmerston.* 2 vols. 1936.
BENSON, E. F. *Queen Victoria.* 1935.
BRADY, A. *William Huskisson and Liberal Reform.* 1928.
BRIGHT, P. (Ed.). *Diaries of John Bright.* 1930.
BROUGHAM, HENRY, Lord. *Life and Times of Henry, Lord Brougham.* 3 vols. Edinburgh, 1871.
BUTLER, Sir W. *Autobiography.* 1911.
CECIL, Lady GWENDOLEN. *Life of Lord Salisbury.* 2 vols. 1921.
CHILDE-PEMBERTON, W. S. *Life of Sir Charles Adderley, Lord Norton.* 1909.
CHILDERS, E. S. C. *Life and Correspondence of H. C. E. Childers.* 2 vols. 1901.
CLARK, G. KITSON. *Peel and the Conservative Party.* 1929.
COLLIER, J. *Sir George Grey.* Christchurch, N.Z., 1909.
COUPLAND, R. *Raffles.* 2nd edn. 1934.
DALLING, Lord, and ASHLEY, E. *Life of Palmerston, with Selections from his Diaries and Correspondence.* 5 vols. 1870–6.
DENISON, Sir W. T. *Varieties of Vice-Regal Life.* 2 vols. 1870.
DISRAELI, B., Earl of Beaconsfield. *Lord George Bentinck.* 1852. Later edn. 1874.
DUFFY, Sir C. G. *My Life in Two Hemispheres.* 2 vols. 1898.
DUNCOMBE, T. H. *Life and Correspondence of T. S. Duncombe.* 2 vols. 1868.
EGERTON, H. E. *Sir Stamford Raffles.* 1900.
ELLIOTT, A. R. D. *Life of Lord Goschen.* 2 vols. 1911.
ESCOTT, T. H. S. *Edward Bulwer, first Baron Lytton.* 1910.
ESHER, Lord. *The Girlhood of Queen Victoria.* 2 vols. 1912.
FAWCETT, M. G. *Life of Sir William Molesworth.* 1901.
FITZMAURICE, Lord EDWARD. *Life of the second Earl of Granville.* 3rd edn. 2 vols. 1905.
GARNETT, R. *Edward Gibbon Wakefield.* 1898.
GWYNN, S. and TUCKWELL, G. M. *Life of Sir Charles W. Dilke.* 2 vols. 1917.
HARDCASTLE, M. S. *Life of Lord Campbell.* 2 vols. 1881.
HARDINGE, Sir A. H. *The fourth Earl of Carnarvon.* 3 vols. 1925.
HARROP, A. J. *The Amazing Career of Edward Gibbon Wakefield.* 1928.
HENDERSON, G. C. *Life of Sir George Grey.* 1907.
HERRIES, E. *Memoir of J. C. Herries.* 2 vols. 1880.
KEBBEL, T. E. *Life of Lord Derby.* 1890.
KENNEDY, W. P. M. *Lord Elgin.* Oxford, 1926. Makers of Canada, vol. VI.
LANG, A. *Life, Letters and Diaries of Sir Stafford Northcote.* 2 vols. Edinburgh, 1891.
LEADER, R. E. *Life and Letters of J. A. Roebuck.* 1897.
LEE, Sir S. *Queen Victoria.* Rev. edn. 1904.
LE MARCHANT, Sir D. *Memoir of Lord Althorp.* 1876.
LYALL, Sir A. *Life of the Marquis of Dufferin and Ava.* 2 vols. 1905.
MARTIN, A. P. *Life and Letters of Robert Lowe, Viscount Sherbrooke.* 2 vols. 1893.
MARTIN, Sir T. *Life of the Prince Consort.* 5 vols. 1875–80.
MARTINEAU, J. *Life and Correspondence of Sir Bartle Frere.* 2 vols. 1895.
—— *Life of Henry Pelham, fifth Duke of Newcastle,* 1811–64. 1908.
MAXWELL, Sir H. *Life and Letters of the fourth Earl of Clarendon.* 2 vols. 1913.
MERIVALE, C. *Memoir of Herman Merivale.* 1884.
MONYPENNY, W. F. and BUCKLE, G. E. *Life of Benjamin Disraeli, Earl of Beaconsfield.* 6 vols. 1910–20.
MOORE-SMITH, G. C. *Life of Sir Harry Smith.* 1901.

MORISON, J. L. *The eighth Earl of Elgin.* 1928.
MORLEY, JOHN, Lord. *Life of Gladstone.* 3 vols. 1903.
—— *Richard Cobden.* 1881. 10th edn. 1903.
MORRIS, E. E. *Memoir of George Higginbotham.* 1895.
NEW, C. W. *Lord Durham.* Oxford, 1929.
PARKER, C. S. *Sir James Graham, 2nd Baronet.* 2 vols. 1907.
PELLEW, G. *Life and Correspondence of Lord Sidmouth.* 3 vols. 1847.
POPE, J. *Memoirs of Sir John A. Macdonald.* 2 vols. Ottawa, London, 1894.
RAFFLES, S. *Memoir of Sir Stamford Raffles.* 1830.
RAMSAY, A. A. W. *Sir Robert Peel.* 1928.
REES, W. L. *Life of Sir George Grey.* 2 vols. 1892.
REID, S. J. *Life and Letters of Lord Durham.* 2 vols. 1906.
REID, T. WEMYSS. *Life of W. E. Forster.* 2 vols. 1888.
ROSE, J. HOLLAND. *William Pitt.* 2 vols. 1911–12.
ROY, J. A. *Joseph Howe.* Toronto, 1935.
ST JOHN, Sir S. R. *Life of Sir James Brooke, Rajah of Sarawak.* 1879.
SAINTSBURY, G. *The Earl of Derby.* 1892.
SCROPE, G. P. *Memoir of the Life of Lord Sydenham.* 1843.
SHORTT, A. *Lord Sydenham.* Toronto, 1911.
STANHOPE, Lord. *Life of Pitt.* 4 vols. 3rd edn. 1867.
STANMORE, Lord. *Sidney Herbert.* 2 vols. 1906.
STEPHEN, C. *The first Sir James Stephen.* 1906.
STEPHEN, L. *Life of Sir J. F. Stephen.* 1895.
THOMPSON, E. *Life of Lord Metcalfe.* 1937.
TORRENS, W. M. *Memoirs of Viscount Melbourne.* 2 vols. 1878.
TREVELYAN, G. M. *Life of John Bright.* New edn. 1925.
—— *Lord Grey of the Reform Bill.* 2nd edn. 1929.
TREVELYAN, Sir G. O. *Life and Letters of Lord Macaulay.* 1876. Rev. edn. 1908.
TURNER, R. E. *James Silk Buckingham.* 1934.
TWISS, H. *Life of Lord Eldon.* 3 vols. 1844.
VILLIERS, G. *A Vanished Victorian* [Fourth Earl of Clarendon]. 1938.
WALPOLE, S. *Life of Lord John Russell.* 2 vols. 1891.
WOLF, L. *Life of Lord Ripon.* 2 vols. 1921.
WORSFOLD, W. B. *Sir Bartle Frere.* 1913.
WRONG, G. M. *Charles Buller and Responsible Government.* 1926.
—— *The Earl of Elgin.* 1905.
YONGE, C. D. *Life of Lord Liverpool.* 3 vols. 1868.

2. SPECIAL BIBLIOGRAPHIES

A. COLONIAL POLICY AND ADMINISTRATION, 1783–1870

i. *COLONIAL POLICY IN GENERAL*

(a) MANUSCRIPT SOURCES

See Part I, 1 and 2, particularly the following series in the Public Record Office: Colonial Office Papers, C.O. 48, C.O. 49, C.O. 54, C.O. 55, C.O. 111, C.O. 136, C.O. 158, C.O. 159, C.O. 188, C.O. 201–18, C.O. 323; Board of Trade Papers, B.T. 5 and 6; Home Office Papers, H.O. 28, H.O. 35–8 and H.O. 100; Treasury Papers, T. 29 (Treasury Board Minutes), T. 64/50 (Papers of T. Bradshaw); Chatham Papers, G.D. 8; and Russell Papers, G.D. 22. For chapter IV the correspondence of George III and George IV in the Royal Archives, Windsor, and the Windham Papers in the British Museum were also used. For chapter VIII, W. E. Gladstone's Black Leather Book of Political Memoranda among the Gladstone Papers in the British Museum and the Howick Papers at Howick Hall were used. For the study of Canadian self-government the Durham Papers, Elgin-Grey Papers, Howe Papers, Macdonald Papers and Tupper Papers, all in the Public Archives of Canada, Ottawa, are indispensable.

(b) OFFICIAL PUBLICATIONS

See Part I, 3 and 4, and the following additional Parliamentary Papers:—
Australia, Rept. on Conduct of Gov. Darling, *Parl. Pap.* 1889, VI (580); Rept. on South Australia, *Parl. Pap.* 1841, IV (119), (394); Papers *re* alterations to constitution, *Parl. Pap.* 1849, XXXV [1074]; Corresp. *re* Govt. Bill, *Parl. Pap.* 1850, XXXVII [1160]; Papers *re* Alterations to Constitution, *Parl. Pap.* 1850, XXXVII [1182], [1183], [1190], *Parl. Pap.* 1851, XXXV [1303], *Parl. Pap.* 1852, XXXIV [1534], *Parl. Pap.* 1852–3, LXIII [1611], *Parl. Pap.* 1854, XLIV [1827], *Parl. Pap.* 1854–5, XXXVIII [1866], [1902], [1915], [1927], *Parl. Pap.* 1856, XLIII [2135]; corresp. *re* Federal Assoc., *Parl. Pap.* 1857 Sess. 2, XXVIII (239). *Canada*, Rept. on Civil Govt., *Parl. Pap.* 1828, VII (569); Rept. on Lower Canada, *Parl. Pap.* 1834, XVIII (449), Rept. of Commissioners in Lower Canada, *Parl. Pap.* XXIV (50); Durham's Rept., *Parl. Pap.* 1839, XVII (3), (3–II), (3–III), (139), (303); Corresp. with Governors on Responsible Govt., 1839–48, *Parl. Pap.* 1847–8, XLII (621); Rept. on Hudson's Bay Co., *Parl. Pap.* 1857 Sess. 2, XV (224), (260); Corresp. *re* confederation, 1867, *Parl. Pap.* 1867, XLVIII [3769], [3770]. *New Zealand*, Rept. on State of Islands, *Parl. Pap.* 1837–8, XXI (680); Rept. on Colonization, *Parl. Pap.* 1840, VII (582); Rept. on New Zealand Co., *Parl. Pap.* 1844, XIII (556); Corresp. *re* Responsible Govt., *Parl. Pap.* 1854–5, XXXVIII (160); *Parl. Pap.* 1857 Sess. 2, IX (171). *South Africa*, Repts. on Administration, 1826–7, XXI (282), (371), (406); Corresp. *re* Representative Assembly, *Parl. Pap.* 1846, XXIX (400), *Parl. Pap.* 1850, XXXVIII [1137], [1234], *Parl. Pap.* 1851, XXXVII [1362], *Parl. Pap.* 1852, XXXII [1427].

(c) COLLECTED HISTORICAL RECORDS

BELL, K. N. and MORRELL, W. P. (Eds.). *Select Documents on British Colonial Policy, 1830–60.* Oxford, 1928.

DOUGHTY, Sir A. G. (Ed.). *The Elgin-Grey Papers.* 4 vols. Ottawa, 1937. Public Archives of Canada Special Pubn.

EGERTON, H. E. (Ed.). *Federations and Unions within the British Empire.* 2nd rev. edn. 1924.

EGERTON, H. E. and GRANT, W. L. (Eds.). *Canadian Constitutional Development.* 1907.

EYBERS, G. W. (Ed.). *Select Constitutional Documents illustrating South African History.* 1918.

KEITH, A. BERRIEDALE. *Selected Speeches and Documents on British Colonial Policy, 1763–1917.* 2 vols. Oxford, 1918.

KENNEDY, W. P. M. (Ed.). *Statutes, Treaties and Documents of the Canadian Constitution, 1713–1929.* 2nd edn. Oxford, 1930.

NEWTON, A. P. (Ed.). *Federal and Unified Constitutions: a collection of constitutional documents for the use of students.* 1923.

SHORTT, A. and DOUGHTY, (Sir) A. G. (Eds.). *Documents relating to the Constitutional History of Canada, 1759–91.* 2nd edn. Ottawa, 1918. Public Archives of Canada Pubn.

(d) CONTEMPORARY WRITINGS

ADDERLEY, Sir C. B. (Lord Norton). *Letter to Mr Disraeli on Present Relations with the Colonies.* 1861. 2nd edn. 1862.

—— *Our Relations with the Colonies and Crown Colonies.* 1870.

—— *Review of "The Colonial Policy of Lord John Russell's Administration" by Earl Grey, 1853.* 1869.

—— *Some Reflections on the Speech of Lord John Russell on Colonial Policy.* 1850.

ADOLPHUS, J. *The Political State of the British Empire.* 4 vols. 1818.

BAGEHOT, WALTER. *The English Constitution.* 1867. 2nd edn. rev. 1872.

BELL, S. S. *Colonial Administration of Great Britain.* 1859.

BLISS, H. *The Colonial System.* 1833.

BRITISH TRAVELLER, A. *The Colonial Policy of Great Britain considered.* Philadelphia, 1816.

BROUGHAM, HENRY, Lord. *An Inquiry into the Colonial Policy of the European Powers.* 2 vols. Edinburgh, 1803.

—— *Speeches on Social and Political Subjects, with Historical Introductions.* 2 vols. 1857. Part of his *Works.* 11 vols. 1855–61.

BULLER, CHARLES. *Mr Mother-Country, of the Colonial Office.* 1840.

—— *Responsible Government for Colonies.* 1840. Reprinted in E. M. Wrong, *Charles Buller* (1926).

BURY, Viscount (Earl of Albemarle). *The Exodus of the Western Nations.* Vol. II (1865), pp. 459–63.

CAIRNES, J. E. *Political Essays.* 1873.

CARLYLE, THOMAS. *Latter Day Pamphlets.* 1850.

CHAPMAN, M. S. *Parliamentary Government, or Responsible Ministries for the Australian Colonies.* 1854.

CLOWES, W. (Publishers). *Rules and Regulations for Her Majesty's Colonial Service.* 1837.

Considerations on Colonial Policy. 1813.

DALRYMPLE, Sir J. *Queries concerning Foreign Politics.* 1789.

DANSON, J. T. *Observations on the Speech of Sir William Molesworth on Colonial Expenditure and Government.* 1848.

Dialogues of the Living. 1845. Satires on the Colonial Office.

DILKE, Sir C. W. *Greater Britain.* 1868. 2nd rev. edn. 1876.

DURHAM, Lord. *Lord Durham's Report on the Affairs of North America.* Ed. by Sir C. P. Lucas. 3 vols. Oxford, 1912.

FLETCHER, R. *England and her Colonies.* 1857.

FORSTER, W. E. *Our Colonial Empire.* Edinburgh, 1875.

FOXBOURNE, H. R. *Story of our Colonies.* 1869.

GLADSTONE, W. E. *Our Colonies.* 1855.

GODLEY, J. R. *Extracts from Letters to C. B. Adderley.* 1863.

GREY, H. G., 3rd Earl. *The Colonial Policy of Lord John Russell's Administration.* 2nd edn. 2 vols. 1853.

HEAD, Sir F. B. *A Narrative.* 2nd edn. 1839.

HORTON, Sir R. J. WILMOT. *Exposition and Defence of Earl Bathurst's Administration of the Affairs of Canada.* 1838.

KNOX, W. *Extra Official State Papers, by a late Under Secretary of State.* 2 vols. 1789.

LEWIS, Sir G. CORNEWALL. *An Essay on the Government of Dependencies,* 1841. Ed. by Sir C. P. Lucas. Oxford, 1891.

MACFIE, R. A. *Papers on Colonial Questions.* 1871.

MERIVALE, HERMAN. "The Colonial Question in 1870." *Fortnightly Rev.* Feb. 1870.

—— *Lectures on Colonization and Colonies, delivered before the University of Oxford in 1839, 1840 and 1841, and reprinted in* 1861. Ed. by K. Bell. Oxford, 1928.

MILL, JOHN STUART. "Colonies." *Westminster Rev.,* vol. XXXII (Dec. 1838).

MILLS, A. *Colonial Constitutions.* 1856.

—— *Colonial Military Expenditure.* 1863.

—— *Colonial Policy and New Zealand.* 1864.

—— *Systematic Colonization.* 1847.

Question of Federation of the British Provinces in America. 1858. Confidential official pamphlet.

ROEBUCK, J. A. *The Colonies of England, a plan.* 1849.

ROGERS, T. *The Colonial Question.* 1872.

ROSCHER, W. G. F. *Kolonien, Kolonialpolitik und Auswanderung.* 1848. 3rd edn., rev. by R. Jannasch. Leipzig, 1885.

RUSSELL, Lord JOHN (Earl Russell). *An Essay on the History of the English Government and Constitution.* 1823.

SEWELL, H. *The Case of New Zealand and our Colonial Policy.* 1869.

SMITH, GOLDWIN. *The Empire. A Series of Letters published in the "Daily News".* 1863.

STEPHEN, Sir J. *Address on British Colonies and Colonization.* 1858.

—— "On Colonization as a Branch of Social Economy." *Trans. Nat. Assoc. Promotion Social Sciences,* 1858.

THRING, H. (Baron). *Colonial Reform.* 1865.

WAKEFIELD, E. G. *England and America.* 1833.

—— *A Letter from Sydney.* 1829. Reprinted in Everyman's Library, 1929.

—— "Sir Charles Metcalfe in Canada." *Fisher's Colonial Mag.* July 1844. Reprinted in E. M. Wrong, *Buller* (1926).

—— *A View of Sir Charles Metcalfe's Government of Canada.* 1844.

—— *A View of the Art of Colonization.* 1849. New edn. by J. Collier. Oxford, 1914.

WRAXALL, Sir N. *A Short Review of the Political State of Great Britain.* 1787.

(e) DOCUMENTS, MEMOIRS AND CORRESPONDENCE

AUCKLAND, WILLIAM, Lord. *Journal and Correspondence.* 4 vols. 1861–2.

BLACHFORD, FREDERIC, Lord. *Letters of Lord Blachford.* Ed. by G. Marindin. 1896.

BOWEN, Sir G. F. *Thirty Years of Colonial Government,* 1859–88. Ed. by S. L. Poole. 2 vols. 1889.

BROUGHTON, Lord. *Recollections of a Long Life.* 6 vols. 1909–11.

CANADA. PUBLIC ARCHIVES. *Calendar of Durham Papers.* Ottawa, 1924. Rept. of the Public Archives for 1923.

COBDEN, RICHARD. *Political Writings.* 2 vols. 1867.

—— *Speeches on Questions of Public Policy.* 3rd edn. 2 vols. 1908.

ELLENBOROUGH, Lord. *A Political Diary,* 1828–30. Ed. by Lord Colchester. 1881.

GLADSTONE, W. E. *Gladstone's Speeches.* Ed. by A. Tilney Bassett. 1916.

GLAZEBROOK, G. P. DE T. (Ed.). *The Hargrave Correspondence,* 1821–34. Toronto, 1938.

GREVILLE, C. C. F. *The Greville Memoirs.* (i) *A Journal of the Reigns of King George IV and King William IV.* 3 vols. 1874. (ii) *A Journal of the Reign of Queen Victoria* [to 1860]. 5 vols. 1880. Reeve's edn., 1896, is less complete. New edn. ed. by L. Strachey and R. Fulford. 8 vols. 1938.

GUEDALLA, P. (Ed.). *Gladstone and Palmerston.* 1928. Their correspondence.

—— (Ed.). *The Queen and Mr Gladstone.* Vol. I, 1845–79. 1933. Correspondence.

HAMILTON, Sir W. A. B. "Forty-four years at the Colonial Office." *Nineteenth Century,* April 1909.

HINCKS, Sir F. *Reminiscences of his Public Life.* 1884.

HISTORICAL MANUSCRIPTS COMMISSION. *Report on the Knox Manuscripts.* H.M.S.O., 1909. Various Collections, vol. VI.

—— *Report on the Manuscripts of J. B. Fortescue preserved at Dropmore.* 10 vols. H.M.S.O., 1892–1927.

—— *Report on the Manuscripts of Earl Bathurst preserved at Cirencester Park.* H.M.S.O., 1923.

HUSKISSON, WILLIAM. *The Huskisson Papers.* Ed. by L. Melville. 1931.

—— *Speeches.* 3 vols. 1831.

JENNINGS, L. T. (Ed.) *The Croker Papers.* 3 vols. 1884.

KAYE, Sir J. W. *Life and Correspondence of Charles, Lord Metcalfe.* Rev. edn. 2 vols. 1858.

—— (Ed.) *Selections from the Papers of Lord Metcalfe.* 1885.

KNAPLUND, P. (Ed.). *Letters from Lord Sydenham to Lord John Russell.* 1931.

LEWIS, Sir G. CORNEWALL. *Letters to Various Friends.* Ed. by Sir G. F. Lewis. 1870.

LONDONDERRY, Lord (Ed.). *Memoirs and Correspondence of Viscount Castlereagh.* 12 vols. 1847–53.

MALMESBURY, Lord. *Memoirs of an ex-Minister.* 2 vols. 1884.

MELBOURNE, WILLIAM, Lord. *Lord Melbourne's Papers.* Ed. by L. C. Sanders. 1890.

MILL, JOHN STUART. *Autobiography.* 1873.

MOLESWORTH, Sir W. *Selected Speeches on Questions relating to Colonial Policy.* Ed. by H. E. Egerton. 1903.

NAPIER, M. *Selections from Correspondence.* 1879.

PARKER, C. S. (Ed.). *Sir Robert Peel, from his private papers.* 3 vols. 1891–9.

PARKES, Sir H. *Fifty Years in the Making of Australian History.* 2 vols. 1892.

PEEL, Sir ROBERT. *Memoirs.* Ed. by Earl Stanhope and E. Cardwell. 2 vols. 1857.

RUSSELL, Lord JOHN (Earl Russell). *Early Correspondence of Lord John Russell,* 1805–40. Ed. by R. Russell. 2 vols. 1913.
—— *Later Correspondence of Lord John Russell,* 1840–78. Ed. by G. P. Gooch. 2 vols. 1925.
—— *Recollections and Suggestions,* 1813–73. 1875.
—— *Selections from Speeches.* 2 vols. 1870.
SELBORNE, Lord. *Personal and Political Memoirs.* 1899.
SMITH, GOLDWIN. *Reminiscences.* Ed. by A. Haultain. 1910.
—— *A Selection from Goldwin Smith's Correspondence.* Ed. by A. Haultain [1913].
STANHOPE, Lord (Ed.). *Correspondence between William Pitt and Charles, Duke of Rutland,* 1781–7. 1840.
STANMORE, Lord. *Records of Private and of Public Life.* 4 vols. Privately printed, 1897.
TAYLOR, Sir H. *Autobiography.* 2 vols. 1885.
—— *Correspondence.* Ed. by E. Dowden. 1888.
VICTORIA, Queen. *Letters,* 1837–61. Ed. by A. C. Benson and Viscount Esher. New edn. 3 vols. 1907.
—— *Letters.* 2nd series, 1862–85. Ed. by G. E. Buckle. 3 vols. 1927.
WALPOLE, HORACE (3rd Earl of Orford). *Letters.* 1820. New edn. by Mrs P. Toynbee. 16 vols. Oxford, 1903–5. *Supplement.* 2 vols. Oxford, 1918. Another edn. is now being published, 1938– .
WELLINGTON, Lord. *Despatches, Correspondence and Memoranda.* 8 vols. 1867–80.
WEST, Sir A. E. *Private Diaries.* Ed. by H. G. Hutchinson. 1922.
—— *Recollections,* 1832–86. 2 vols. 1899.
WINDHAM, WILLIAM. *The Windham Papers.* Introd. by Lord Rosebery. 2 vols. 1913.

(*f*) LATER WORKS

For other biographies, see Section 1 (*e*) above

ADAMS, G. B. "The Origin and Results of the Imperial Federation Movement in England." *Proc. Wisconsin State Hist. Soc.* 1899, pp. 93–116.
BATTYE, J. S. *Western Australia.* Oxford, 1924.
BEAGLEHOLE, J. C. *Captain Hobson and the New Zealand Company: a study in colonial administration.* Northampton, Mass., 1928.
—— "The Royal Instructions to Colonial Governors, 1783–1854: a study in British Colonial Policy." *Bull. Inst. Hist. Research,* vol. VII (Feb. 1930), pp. 184–7. Summary of thesis in University of London Library.
BELL, Sir H. *Foreign Colonial Administration in the Far East.* 1928.
BERTRAM, Sir A. *The Colonial Service.* 1930.
BODELSEN, C. A. *Studies in Mid-Victorian Imperialism.* Copenhagen, London, 1924.
BOURINOT, Sir J. G. *Canada under British Rule,* 1760–1900. Cambridge, 1900.
BRADSHAW, F. *Self-Government in Canada.* 1903.
BRADY, A. *William Huskisson and Liberal Reform.* Oxford, 1928.
BRUCE, Sir C. *The Broad Stone of Empire.* 2 vols. 1910. Crown Colony administration.
BUTLER, J. R. M. "The Origins of Lord John Russell's Despatch of 1839 on the Tenure of Crown Offices in the Colonies." *Cambridge Hist. Jour.* vol. II (1928); pp. 248–51.
COUPLAND, R. *The American Revolution and the British Empire.* 1930.
CREIGHTON, D. G. "The Victorians and the Empire." *Canadian Hist. Rev.* vol. XIX (June 1938), pp. 138–53.
CROMER, Lord. *Ancient and Modern Imperialism.* 1910.
CURREY, C. H. *British Colonial Policy,* 1783–1915. Oxford, 1916.
DAVIS, H. W. C. *The Age of Grey and Peel.* Oxford, 1929.
DAWSON, R. M. *The Civil Service of Canada.* 1929.
—— "Canadian Civil Services before Confederation." *Canadian Hist. Rev.* vol. V (June 1924), pp. 118–31.
DE KIEWIET, C. W. *British Colonial Policy and the South African Republics,* 1848–72. 1929. Royal Empire Society Imperial Studies, No. 3.

DE KIEWIET, C. W. *The Imperial Factor in South Africa*. Cambridge, 1937.

DUBOIS, M. *Systèmes coloniaux et peuples colonisateurs*. Paris, 1895.

DUNHAM, A. *Political Unrest in Upper Canada, 1815–36.* 1927. Royal Empire Society Imperial Studies, No. 1.

EGERTON, H. E. "The Colonial Reformers of 1830." *King's College Lectures* (1913), pp. 141–80.

—— *Short History of British Colonial Policy.* 9th edn. rev. by A. P. Newton. 1932.

—— "The System of British Colonial Administration of the Crown Colonies in the seventeenth and eighteenth centuries compared with the System prevailing in the nineteenth century." *Trans. Royal Hist. Soc.*, 4th ser., vol. 1 (1918), pp. 190–217.

FIDDES, Sir G. V. *The Dominions and Colonial Offices.* 1926. Whitehall Series.

FOSTER, Sir W. "The India Board, 1784–1858." *Trans. Royal Hist. Soc.*, 3rd ser., vol. XI (1917), pp. 61–85.

GLAZEBROOK, G. P. DE T. *Sir Charles Bagot in Canada.* Oxford, 1929.

HALL, H. L. *Australia and England.* 1934.

—— *The Colonial Office: a History.* 1937. Royal Empire Soc. Imperial Studies Series, No. 13.

HARROP, A. J. *England and New Zealand.* 1926.

—— *England and the Maori Wars.* 1937.

HERTZ, G. B. *British Imperialism in the Eighteenth Century.* 1908.

HIGHAM, C. S. S. (Ed.). "Sir Henry Taylor and the Establishment of Crown Colony Government in the West Indies." *Scottish Hist. Rev.* vol. XXIII (1926), pp. 92–6.

HOLLAND, B. H. *Imperium et Libertas. A Study in History and Politics.* 1901.

IRELAND, A. *Far Eastern Tropics: a Study in the Administration of Tropical Dependencies.* Boston, 1905.

—— *Tropical Colonization.* 1899.

JENKYNS, Sir H. *British Rule and Jurisdiction beyond the Seas.* Oxford, 1902.

KEITH, A. BERRIEDALE. "Development of Colonial Self-Government in the 19th century." *Royal Soc. of Arts Jour.*, vol. LVI (1908), pp. 332–47.

—— *Responsible Government in the Dominions.* New edn. 2 vols. 1928.

KENNEDY, W. P. M. *The Constitution of Canada.* Oxford, 1931.

KIDD, B. *The Control of the Tropics.* 1898.

KILPIN, R. *The Romance of a Colonial Parliament.* 1930.

KITSON CLARK, G. S. R. *Peel and the Conservative Party.* 1929.

KNAPLUND, P. "The Buller-Peel Correspondence regarding Canada, 1841." *Canadian Hist. Rev.* vol. VIII (March 1927), pp. 41–50.

—— (Ed.). "E. G. Wakefield on the Colonial Garrisons, 1851." *Canadian Hist. Rev.* vol. V (June 1924), pp. 228–36.

—— *Gladstone and Britain's Imperial Policy.* New York, 1927.

—— "Gladstone's View on British Colonial Policy." *Canadian Hist. Rev.* vol. IV (1923), pp. 304–15.

—— "Sir James Stephen and British North American Problems, 1840–7." *Canadian Hist. Rev.* vol. V (March 1924).

—— "Mr Over-Secretary Stephen." *Jour. Mod. Hist.* vol. I (1929), pp. 40–66.

LANGSTONE, R. W. *Responsible Government in Canada.* 1931.

LEROY-BEAULIEU, P. *De la colonisation chez les peuples modernes.* Paris, 1874. 6th rev. edn. 2 vols. Paris, 1908.

LIVINGSTON, W. R. "The First Responsible Government in British North America." *Canadian Hist. Rev.* vol. VII (June 1926), pp. 115–36.

—— *Responsible Government in Nova Scotia.* Iowa City, 1930.

LOWER, A. R. M. "The Evolution of the Sentimental Idea of Empire." *History*, vol. XI (Jan. 1927), pp. 289–303.

MACDONNELL, U. N. "Gibbon Wakefield and Canada subsequent to the Durham Mission, 1839–42." *Bull. Dept. Hist. Queen's Univ. Kingston*, No. 49 (1924–5).

MANNING, H. T. *British Colonial Government after the American Revolution, 1782–1820.* New Haven, Conn., 1933.

MARTIN, C. (Ed.). "The Correspondence between Joseph Howe and Charles Buller, 1845–8." *Canadian Hist. Rev.* vol. VI (Dec. 1925), pp. 310–31.

MARTIN, C. *Empire and Commonwealth.* Oxford, 1929.
MARTIN, K. L. P. "Influence of the Crown in the Evolution of Responsible Government." *Canadian Hist. Rev.* vol. XXXI (1922), pp. 334–42.
MELBOURNE, A. C. V. *Early Constitutional Development in Australia. New South Wales,* 1788–1856. 1934.
MORISON, J. L. *British Supremacy and Canadian Self-Government.* 1919.
—— "Imperial Ideas of Benjamin Disraeli." *Canadian Hist. Rev.* vol. I (1920), pp. 267–80.
MORRELL, W. P. *British Colonial Policy in the Age of Peel and Russell.* Oxford, 1930.
MORRIS, G. W. and WOOD, L. S. *English-Speaking Nations: a Study in the Development of the Commonwealth Ideal.* Oxford, 1924.
MUNRO, W. B. *Canada and British North America.* Philadelphia, 1905.
PENSON, L. M. "The Origin of the Crown Agency Office." *Eng. Hist. Rev.* vol. XL (April 1925), pp. 196–206.
PETTY DE THOZÉE, C. *Théories de la colonisation au XIXe siècle.* Brussels, 1902.
PHILPOTT, W. E. "The Origin and the Development of the Protectorate System" [1800–48]. *Bull. Inst. Hist Research,* vol. XII (Feb. 1935), pp. 199–201. Summary of thesis in University of London Library.
REEVES, W. P. *The Long White Cloud* [New Zealand]. 1898.
REINSCH, P. S. *Colonial Administration.* 1905. Comparative study.
SCHUYLER, R. L. "The Climax of Anti-Imperialism in England." *Polit. Science Quart.* vol. XXXVI (1921), pp. 537–61.
—— *Parliament and the British Empire: some constitutional controversies concerning imperial legislative jurisdiction.* New York, 1929.
—— "The Recall of the Legions: a phase in the decentralization of the British Empire." *Amer. Hist. Rev.* vol. XXVI (Oct. 1920), pp. 18–36.
—— "Rise of Anti-Imperialism in England." *Polit. Science Quart.* vol. XXXVII (1922), pp. 440–71.
SMILLIE, E. A. *Historical Origins of Imperial Federation: a comparative historical and political study of the various schemes for the reconstruction of the relations of Great Britain and her colonies,* 1754–1867. Montreal, 1910.
SMITH, W. "Canada and Constitutional Development in New South Wales." *Canadian Hist. Rev.* vol. VII (June 1926), pp. 95–114.
SNOW, A. H. *Administration of Dependencies: a study of the evolution of the federal empire.* 1902.
STOYE, J. *The British Empire: its Structure and its Problems.* 1936. First pubd. in German, 1935.
SWEETMAN, E. *Australian Constitutional Development.* Melbourne, 1925.
TEMPERLEY, H. W. V. Great Britain and her Colonies: (1) The new colonial policy (1840–70). In *Cambridge Modern History,* vol. XI (1909), pp. 754–66.
TODD, A. *Parliamentary Government in the British Colonies.* 2nd edn. 1894.
TYLER, J. E. *The Struggle for Imperial Unity,* 1868–95. 1938. Royal Empire Society Imperial Studies, No. 16.
WEDDERBURN, Sir D. *British Colonial Policy.* 1881.
WHITELAW, W. M. "Responsible Government and the Irresponsible Governor." *Canadian Hist. Rev.* vol. XIII (Dec. 1932), pp. 364–86.
WRONG, E. M. *Charles Buller and Responsible Government.* 1926.
—— "The Growth of Nationalism in the British Empire." *Amer. Hist. Rev.* vol. XXII (Oct. 1916), pp. 45–57.
WRONG, H. *The Government of the West Indies.* 1923.
ZIMMERMANN, A. *Die europäischen Kolonien.* 5 vols. Berlin, 1896–1903.

ii. *THE COLONIES IN THE REVOLUTIONARY AND NAPOLEONIC WARS*

(a) MANUSCRIPT SOURCES

See Part I, 1 and 2, particularly the following series in the Public Record Office:
Colonial Office Papers, C.O. 25, C.O. 28, C.O. 54, C.O. 59, C.O. 71, C.O. 111,

C.O. 117, C.O. 137, C.O. 138, C.O. 152, C.O. 167, C.O. 253, C.O. 285, C.O. 295, C.O. 296; Board of Trade Papers, B.T. 1, B.T. 3 and B.T. 5; Foreign Office Papers, France, F.O. 27; Holland, F.O. 37; Ionian Islands, F.O. 42; Russia, F.O. 65; Turkey, F.O. 78; Home Office Papers, H.O. 30 and H.O. 253; War Office Papers, W.O. 6 and W.O. 70; Admiralty Papers, Adm. 1; Chatham MSS., G.D. 8. See also the Paoli MSS. in the British Museum, B.M. Add. MSS. 22688.

(b) OFFICIAL PUBLICATIONS

See Part I, 3 and 4, for Parliamentary Papers and Debates of the Period, also the summaries in the *Annual Register* and Cobbett's *Political Register*.

(c) BIBLIOGRAPHIES

BOURNE, H. E. "A Decade of Studies of the French Revolution." *Jour. Mod. Hist.* vol. 1 (June 1929), pp. 256–79.
HÜFFER, H. *Quellen zur Geschichte des Zeitalters der französischen Revolution.* Ed. by F. Luckwaldt. Innsbruck, 1907.
KIRCHEISEN, F. M. *Bibliographie du temps de Napoléon.* 2 vols. Paris, 1902–12.

(d) CONTEMPORARY WRITINGS

BOSANQUET, C. *Thoughts on the value to Great Britain of Commerce in General and...the Colonial Trade in Particular.* 1808.
Considerations on Colonial Policy. 1813.
EDWARDS, B. *The West Indies.* 6 vols. 1818–19.
FISHER, R. B. *The Importance of the Cape of Good Hope.* 1814.
McKINNEN, D. *Tour through the British West Indies, 1802–3.* 1804.
MALTHUS, T. R. *Essay on the Principle of Population.* Edn. of 1803.
MILL, J. *Commerce Defended.* 1807. 2nd edn. 1808.
Naval Chronicle (The). 40 vols. 1798–1818.
ODDY, J. J. *European Commerce.* 1805.
PERCIVAL, R. *An Account of the Cape of Good Hope.* 1804.
PHILLIMORE, J. *Reflections on the Licence Trade in London.* 1811.
SOCIETY OF SHIPOWNERS. *Collection of Papers and Reports on Navigation and Trade.* 1807.
SPENCE, W. *Britain Independent of Commerce.* 1807.
STEPHEN, J. *War in Disguise: or the Frauds of the Neutral Flag.* 1806.
TORRENS, R. *The Economists Refuted.* 1808.
WEST, Sir E. *Letter on the Licence Trade.* 1812.

(e) DOCUMENTS, MEMOIRS AND CORRESPONDENCE

ADAMS, J. Q. *Memoirs.* Ed. by C. F. Adams. 12 vols. 1874–7.
AUCKLAND, Lord. *Journal and Correspondence.* 4 vols. 1861–2.
COLLINGWOOD, Lord. *Correspondence.* 2 vols. 1828.
CORBETT, Sir J. (Ed.). *Private Papers of George, 2nd Earl Spencer.* 4 vols. 1913–24. Navy Records Soc. Pubns, vols. XLVI, XLVIII, LVIII, LIX.
CROKER, J. W. *Correspondence and Diaries.* 3 vols. 1884.
DESVERNOIS, B. *Mémoires, 1789–1815.* Paris, 1898.
DOUBLET, P. L. J. O. *Mémoires sur l'invasion de Malte en 1798.* Paris, 1883.
GALLATIN, Count (Ed.). *A Great Peace Maker. The Diary of James Gallatin.* New edn. New York, 1916.
GOURGAUD, G. (Baron), *Journal de Sainte-Hélène.* Paris, 1899.
HARDMAN, W. and ROSE, J. HOLLAND (Eds.). *Documents relating to the History of Malta in 1798–1815.* 1909.
HISTORICAL MANUSCRIPTS COMMISSION. *Report on the Manuscripts of Earl Bathurst.* H.M.S.O., 1923.
—— *Report on the Manuscripts of J. B. Fortescue preserved at Dropmore.* 10 vols. H.M.S.O., 1892–1927.

Rose, J. Holland. "British West Indian Commerce as a Factor in the Napoleonic War." *Cambridge Hist. Journ.* vol. iii (1929), pp. 34–46.
—— "Canning and the Spanish Patriots in 1808." *Amer. Hist. Rev.* vol. xii (Oct. 1906), pp. 39–52.
—— *The Indecisiveness of Modern War and other Essays.* 1927. Especially Essays v–x.
—— *Life of Napoleon I.* 11th edn. 2 vols. 1935.
—— *Life of Pitt.* 2 vols. 1911.
—— *Man and the Sea.* 1936.
—— "Napoleon and Sea Power." *Cambridge Hist. Jour.* vol. i (1924), pp. 138–57.
—— "The Political Reactions of Bonaparte's Eastern Expedition." *English Hist. Rev.* vol. xliv (Jan. 1929), pp. 48–58.
Saintoyant, J. *La colonisation française pendant la période napoléonienne,* 1799–1815. Paris, 1931.
Silberling, N. J. "Financial and Monetary Policy of Great Britain during the Napoleonic Wars." *Quart. Jour. Economics,* Feb.–May 1924.
Sorel, A. *L'Europe et la Révolution française.* 4 vols. Paris, 1904.
Theal, C. McG. *History of Africa South of the Zambesi,* 1795–1802. 2 vols. 1919.
Updyke, F. A. *The Diplomacy of the War of 1812.* Baltimore, 1915.
Van Loon, H. W. *The Rise of the Dutch Kingdom,* 1795–1813. New York, 1915.
Walker, E. A. *History of South Africa.* 1935.
Webster, C. K. "The American War and the Treaty of Ghent, 1812–14." *Cambridge History of British Foreign Policy,* vol. i, chap. v. Cambridge, 1922.
—— *British Diplomacy,* 1813–15. 1921.
—— *The Congress of Vienna,* 1814–15. New ed. 1934.
—— *The Foreign Policy of Castlereagh,* 1812–15. 1931.

iii. *THE HUMANITARIAN MOVEMENT*

(a) Manuscript Sources

See Part I, 1 and 2 above, particularly the following series in the Public Record Office: Colonial Office Records, Sierra Leone, C.O. 267; West Indies, General, C.O. 318, C.O. 320 and C.O. 441. The most important source for the anti-slavery movement is the papers of the Slave Trade Department of the Foreign Office, F.O. 84, supplemented by F.O. 97/430–2. The Archives of the Mixed Commissions at Cape Town, Havana, Jamaica, Sierra Leone and New York are in the series F.O. 312–15. In the British Museum there are many scattered manuscripts relating to slavery and the slave trade, including B.M. Add. MSS. 18272, "Collections relating to the Slave Trade, consisting of Evidence of Merchants given in the Years 1775–88"; Add. MSS. 21254–6, "Fair Minute Books of the Committee for the Abolition of the Slave Trade, 1786–9"; Add. MSS. 27970, "Capt. J. H. Archer's Memoranda and Accounts"; Add. MSS. 38416, "Lord Liverpool's Papers relating to the Slave Trade, 1787–1823"; Add. MSS. 38578, "Slave Trade, 1811, 1822, Letters and Papers"; Add. MSS. 40862–3, "Ripon Papers, correspondence with Goderich and Mulgrave".

The Anti-Slavery and Aborigines Protection Society, London, has the archives of earlier anti-slavery societies and much unsorted correspondence; the West India Committee, London, has the "Minutes of the Society of West India Merchants", "the Minutes of the Standing Committee of West India Planters and Merchants" and Minutes of other *ad hoc* committees formed to oppose abolition. The Diary of Frederick White, a magistrate in Jamaica, is in Rhodes House Library, Oxford. The Wilberforce, Clarkson and Buxton Papers are still chiefly in private hands.

(b) Official Publications

See Part I, 3 and 4, particularly the Parliamentary Reports on Slavery of 1829, 1832, 1836 and 1837; and the Debates of 1807, 1823, 1833–4 and 1838.

(c) BIBLIOGRAPHIES

RAGATZ, L. J. *A Guide for the Study of British Caribbean History*, 1763–1834, *including the Abolition and Emancipation Movements*. Washington, 1932.

WORK, M. N. *A Bibliography of the Negro in Africa and America*. New York, 1928.

(d) PERIODICALS

AFRICAN INSTITUTION. *Reports*. London, 1807–24. *Anti-Slavery Monthly Reporter*. London, 1825–33. Continued as *Anti-Slavery Reporter*. In progress.

British Emancipation. London, 1837–40. Continued as *British and Foreign Anti-Slavery Reporter*.

Christian Observer. London, 1802–74. The organ of the Clapham Sect.

Edinburgh Review. Articles on slavery appeared in vols. XXV, XXXIX–XLIII, XLV, XLVI, LV, LIX, LX and LXVI (1815–38).

Journal of Negro History. Washington, 1916– . In progress.

Quarterly Review. Articles on Slavery appeared in vols. XXIX–XXXIII, XLIII, L and LVIII (1823–37).

West Indian Reporter. London, 1827–32. The organ of the West India Committee. Published intermittently.

Westminster Review. Articles on slavery by the Utilitarians appeared occasionally, 1824–36.

(e) CONTEMPORARY WRITINGS

For a comprehensive list of the pamphlet literature, see Ragatz's *Guide*, pp. 405–572.

ANTI-SLAVERY SOCIETY. *Report of the Agency Committee*. 1832.

Antigua and the Antiguans...with an impartial view of the Free Labour system. 2 vols. 1844.

BANDINEL, J. *Some Account of the Trade in Slaves from Africa*. 1842. Bandinel was Chief Clerk in the Slave Trade Dept. of the Foreign Office.

BANNISTER, S. *British Colonization and Coloured Tribes*. 1838.

—— *Humane Policy, or Justice to the Aborigines*. 1838.

BARCLAY, A. *A Practical View of the Present State of Slavery in the West Indies*. 1826.

BEAUMONT, A. H. *Compensation to Slave Owners fairly considered*. 1826.

BECKFORD, W. *A Descriptive Account of Jamaica*. 2 vols. 1790.

BEVAN, W. *The Operation of the Apprenticeship System in the British Colonies*. 1838.

BICKELL, R. *The West Indies as they are, or a Real Picture of Slavery*. 1825.

BISSET, R. *The History of the Negro Slave Trade*. 2 vols. 1805.

BRIDGES, G. W. *A Voice from Jamaica in reply to William Wilberforce*. 1823.

BROUGHAM, HENRY, Lord. *A Concise Statement of the Question regarding the Abolition of the Slave Trade*. 1804. *Appendix to the Concise Statement*. 1804.

BURNLEY, W. H. *Observations on Trinidad and Negro Emancipation*. 1842.

BUXTON, C. *Slavery and Freedom in the British West Indies*. 1860.

BUXTON, Sir T. FOWELL. *The African Slave Trade*. 1839. 2nd edn. 1840.

CLARK, R. *Sierra Leone. A Description of the Manners and Customs of the Liberated Africans*. 1843.

CLARKSON, T. *An Essay on the Slavery and Commerce of the Human Species*. 1788.

—— *The History of the Rise, Progress and Accomplishment of the Abolition of the African Slave Trade*. 2 vols. 1808. 2nd edn. 1839.

—— *Thoughts on the Necessity of improving the Condition of the Slaves*. 1823.

COLERIDGE, H. N. *Six Months in the West Indies in 1825*. 1826.

CROPPER, J. *Letters addressed to William Wilberforce*. Liverpool, 1822.

DE LA BECHE, Sir H. T. *Notes on the Present Condition of the Negroes in Jamaica*. 1825.

DENMAN, Hon. J. *Practical Remarks on the Slave Trade*. 1839.

—— *The Slave Trade, the African Squadron, and Mr Hutt's Committee*. 1849.

DWARRIS, Sir F. W. L. *The West India Question plainly stated*. 1828.

Extracts from the Evidence taken before Committees of the two Houses of Parliament relative to the Slave Trade. By a Barrister. 2nd edn. 1851.

FRANCKLYN, G. *Answer to Clarkson's Essay on Slavery.* 1789.
—— *Observations occasioned by the Attempts at Abolition of the Slave Trade.* 1789.
GLADSTONE, Sir J. *Correspondence between John Gladstone and James Cropper on Slavery.* Liverpool, 1824.
HODGSON, S. *Truths from the West Indies.* 1838.
HORTON, Sir R. J. WILMOT. *First Letter on Negro Slavery.* 1830. *Second Letter.* 1830.
—— *The West Indian Question practically considered.* 1826.
HUNTLEY, Sir H. V. *Seven Years' Service on the Slave Coast of Western Africa.* 2 vols. 1880.
Immediate not Gradual Abolition. 1824.
INNES, J. *A Letter to Lord Glenelg on the Working of the New System in the British West Indies.* 1835.
JEREMIE, J. *Four Essays on Colonial Slavery.* 1831.
MACAULAY, Z. *East and West India Sugar.* 1823.
—— *Negro Slavery.* 1823.
MACDONNELL, A. *Considerations on Negro Slavery.* 1824.
—— *The West India Legislatures Vindicated.* 1826.
MCMAHON, B. *Jamaica Plantership.* 1839.
MACQUEEN, J. *The West India Colonies: the Calumnies and Misrepresentations circulated against them.* 1825.
MARRYAT, J. *A Reply to Various Publications recommending an Equalization of Duties on East and West India Sugar.* 1823.
MARTIN, Sir H. W. *A Counter-Appeal in Answer to William Wilberforce.* 1823.
PALMER, A. L. *Official Correspondence relating to Removal from the Special Magistracy.* 1837.
Progress of Colonial Reform (The). 1826. Continued by *Further Progress of Colonial Reforms,* 1827.
RAMSAY, J. *An Essay on the Treatment and Conversion of African Slaves.* 1784.
—— *Objections to the Abolition of the Slave Trade.* 1788.
Review of the "Quarterly Review" on Colonial Slavery. 1824.
SELLS, W. *Remarks on the Condition of the Slaves in the Island of Jamaica.* 1823.
SHARP, GRANVILLE. *A Representation of the Injustice and Dangerous Tendency of tolerating Slavery in England.* 1769.
Slave Law of Jamaica, with Proceedings and Documents relative thereto. 1828.
SLIGO, Lord. *Jamaica under the Apprenticeship System.* By a Proprietor. 1838.
SMEATHMAN, H. *Plan of a Settlement to be made near Sierra Leone.* 1786.
SOCIETY FOR THE MITIGATION AND GRADUAL ABOLITION OF SLAVERY. *The Slave Colonies of Great Britain.* 1825.
STEPHEN, J. *England enslaved by her own Slave Colonies.* 1826.
—— *Reasons for Establishing a Registry of Slaves in the Colonies.* 1825.
—— *Review of Colonial Slave Registration Acts.* 1820.
—— *The Slavery of the British West Indian Colonies delineated.* 2 vols. 1824.
—— *Second Letter to Wilberforce in defence of Registry Bill.* 1816.
STURGE, J. and HARVEY, T. *The West Indies in 1837.* 1838.
Substance of Three Reports of the Commissioners of Inquiry into the Administration of Civil and Criminal Justice in the West Indies. 1827.
THOME, J. and KIMBALL, H. *Emancipation in the West Indies: Six Months' Tour in Antigua, Barbados and Jamaica, 1837.* New York, 1838.
THORPE, R. *View of the Present Increase of the Slave Trade.* 1818.
WALKER, J. *Letters on the West Indies.* 1818.
WATSON, R. *A Defence of the Wesleyan Methodist Missions in the West Indies.* 1817.
WEST INDIA COMMITTEE. *British Colonial Slavery.* 1833. Extracts from documents.
WHEATON, H. *Enquiry into the British Claim to a Right of Visitation and Search.* Philadelphia, 1842.
WHITELEY, H. *Three Months in Jamaica in 1832.* 1833.
WILBERFORCE, W. *An Appeal...on behalf of the Negro Slaves in the West Indies.* 1823.
WILLIAMS, JAMES. *A Narrative of Events since 1st August, 1834.* 1838.
WILSON, J. L. *The British Squadron on the Coast of Africa.* 1851.

Winn, T. S. *A Speedy End to Slavery in our West India Colonies.* 1827.

Wright, W. *Slavery at the Cape of Good Hope.* 1831.

Young, Arthur. "On the Abolition of Slavery in the West Indies." *Annals of Agriculture,* vol. IX (1788), pp. 82 *seqq.*

—— "Abolition of the Slave Trade." *Annals of Agriculture,* vol. XVII (1792), pp. 523 *seqq.*

Yule, Sir H. *The African Squadron vindicated.* 1850.

(*f*) Biographies, Memoirs and Correspondence

Auckland, Lord. *Journal and Correspondence.* 4 vols. 1861–2.

Booth, C. *Zachary Macaulay.* 1934.

Buxton, C. *Memoirs of Sir Thomas Fowell Buxton.* 1848. New edn. 1872.

Coupland, R. *Wilberforce.* Oxford, 1923.

Griggs, E. L. *Thomas Clarkson.* 1936.

Harford, J. S. *Recollections of Wilberforce.* 1864.

Hinton, J. H. *Memoirs of William Knibb.* 1847.

Hoare, P. *Memoirs of Granville Sharp.* 1820.

Knutsford, Viscountess. *Life and Letters of Zachary Macaulay.* 1900.

Lascelles, E. C. P. *Granville Sharp and the Freedom of Slaves in England.* 1928.

Lewis, M. G. *Journal of a West India Proprietor.* Ed. Mona Wilson. 1929.

Livingstone, D. *The Last Journals of David Livingstone.* 2 vols. 1874.

—— *Missionary Travels and Researches in South Africa.* 1858.

Richard, H. *Memoirs of Joseph Sturge.* 1864.

Romilly, W. and others (Eds.). *Memoirs of the Life of Sir Samuel Romilly, with a Selection from his Correspondence.* 1840.

Roscoe, H. *Life of William Roscoe.* 2 vols. Boston, 1833.

Rosebery, Lord. *Pitt and Wilberforce.* Edinburgh, 1897. Letters.

Stephen, Sir G. *Anti-Slavery Recollections.* 1854.

Stephen, Sir J. "The Clapham Sect." *Essays in Ecclesiastical Biography.* 4th edn. 1860.

Taylor, T. *Biographical Sketch of Thomas Clarkson.* 1839.

Wilberforce, A. M. (Ed.). *Private Papers of William Wilberforce.* 1897.

Wilberforce, R. I. and S. (Eds.). *Correspondence of William Wilberforce.* 2 vols. 1840.

—— *William Wilberforce.* 5 vols. 1838.

(*g*) Later Works

Abel, A. H. and Klingberg, F. J. *A Side-light on Anglo-American Relations, 1839–58, furnished by the Correspondence of Lewis Tappan and others with the British and Foreign Anti-Slavery Society.* Washington, 1927.

Adams, J. E. "The Abolition of the Brazilian Slave Trade." *Jour. Negro Hist.* vol. X (Oct. 1925), pp. 607–37.

Banaji, D. R. *Slavery in British India.* Bombay, 1934.

Bleby, H. *Death Struggles of Slavery.* 1853.

Burn, W. L. *Emancipation and Apprenticeship in the British West Indies.* 1937.

Cairnes, J. E. *The Slave Power.* 1861.

Campbell, P. C. *Chinese Coolie Emigration to Countries within the British Empire.* 1923.

Clarkson, T. *History of the Abolition of the Slave Trade.* 2 vols. 1808. New edn. 1839.

Coupland, R. *The British Anti-Slavery Movement.* 1933. Home University Library.

Davy, J. *The West Indies before and since Slave Emancipation.* 1854.

Du Bois, W. E. B. *The Suppression of the African Slave Trade to the United States of America.* New York, 1896.

Erickson, E. L. "The Introduction of East Indian Coolies into the British West Indies." *Jour. Mod. Hist.* vol. VI (June 1934), pp. 127–46.

Hattersley, A. F. "The Emancipation of Slaves at the Cape" [of Good Hope]. *History,* vol. VIII (Oct. 1923), pp. 181–6.

HERRINGTON, E. I. "British Measures for the Suppression of the Slave Trade upon the West Coast of Africa, 1807–33." *Bull. Inst. Hist. Research*, vol. II (Nov. 1924), pp. 53–7. Summary of thesis in University of London Library.

HOCHSTETTER, F. *Die Abschaffung des britischen Sklavenhandels im Jahre 1806, 1807*. Berlin, 1911.

HUTCHINSON, E. *The Slave Trade of East Africa, 1769–1874*. 1874.

INGHAM, E. G. *Sierra Leone after a hundred years*. 1894. Contains extracts from Lieut. Clarkson's Diary and Correspondence.

JOHNSTON, Sir H. H. *The Negro in the New World*. 1910.

KLINGBERG, F. J. *The Anti-Slavery Movement in England*. New Haven, Conn., 1926.

LINDSEY, A. G. "Diplomatic Relations between the United States and Great Britain bearing on the Return of Negro Slaves, 1783–1828." *Jour. Negro Hist.* vol. V (Oct. 1920), pp. 391–419.

LIVINGSTONE, W. P. *Black Jamaica*, 2nd edn. 1900.

MACINNES, C. M. *England and Slavery*. Bristol, 1934.

—— *The Gateway of Empire*. Bristol, 1939.

MARTIN, E. C. *The British West African Settlements, 1750–1821*. 1927.

MARTIN, T. P. "Some International Aspects of the Anti-Slavery Movement, 1818–23." *Jour. Econ. and Business Hist.* vol. I (Nov. 1928), pp. 137–48.

MATHIESON, W. L. *British Slavery and its Abolition, 1823–38*. 1926.

—— *British Slave Emancipation, 1838–49*. 1932.

—— *Great Britain and the Slave Trade, 1839–65*. 1929.

—— *The Sugar Colonies and Governor Eyre, 1849–66*. 1936.

MILNE, A. T. "The Slave Trade and Anglo-American Relations, 1807–62." *Bull. Inst. Hist. Research*, vol. IX (Nov. 1931), pp. 126–9. Summary of thesis in University of London Library.

—— "The Lyons-Seward Treaty of 1862." *Amer. Hist. Rev.* vol. XXXVIII (1933), pp. 511–25. With documents.

OLIVIER, Lord. *The Myth of Governor Eyre*. 1933.

PHILLIPS, U. B. "A Jamaica Slave Plantation [1791–1811]." *Amer. Hist. Rev.* vol. XIX (April 1914), pp. 543–58.

—— "An Antigua Plantation, 1769–1818." *North Carolina Hist. Rev.* vol. III (July 1926), pp. 439–45.

—— "Plantations with Slave Labour and Free." *Amer. Hist. Rev.* vol. XXX (July 1925), pp. 738–54.

PITMAN, F. W. "Slavery on the British West India Plantations in the Eighteenth Century." *Jour. Negro Hist.* vol. XI (Oct. 1926), pp. 584–668.

ROSE, J. HOLLAND. "The Royal Navy and the Suppression of the West African Slave Trade." *Mariner's Mirror*, vol. XXII (1936), pp. 54–64, 162–71.

—— "Steam Power and the Suppression of the Slave Trade." *Man and the Sea* (1936), chap. XII.

RUSSELL, Mrs C. E. B. *General Rigby, Zanzibar and the Slave Trade*. 1935.

SCHUYLER, R. L. "The Constitutional Claims of the British West Indies. The Controversy over the Slave Registry Bill of 1815." *Polit. Science Quart.* vol. XL (March 1925), pp. 1–36.

SEWELL, W. G. *Ordeal of Free Labour in the West Indies*. New York, 1861.

SOULSBY, H. G. *The Right of Search and the Slave Trade in Anglo-American Relations*. Baltimore, 1933.

TIMPSON, G. F. *Jamaican Interlude*. 1939. Slave Emancipation.

TREPP, J. "The Liverpool Movement for the Abolition of the Slave Trade." *Jour. Negro Hist.* vol. XIII (1928) pp. 268–85.

VAN ALSTYNE, R. W. "The British Right of Search and the African Slave Trade." *Jour. Mod. Hist.* vol. II (March 1930), pp. 37–47.

WASTELL, R. E. P. "History of Slave Compensation, 1833–45." *Bull. Inst. Hist. Research*, vol. XI (June 1933), pp. 48–50. Summary of thesis in University of London Library.

WESLEY, C. H. "The Abolition of Negro Apprenticeship in the British Empire." *Jour. Negro Hist.* vol. XXIII (April 1938), pp. 155–99.

WESLEY, C. H. "The Emancipation of the Free Coloured Population in the British Empire." *Jour. Negro Hist.* vol. XVIII (April 1934), pp. 137–70.
—— "The Neglected Period of Emancipation in Great Britain, 1807–23." *Jour. Negro Hist.* vol. XVI (April 1932), pp. 156–79.
WILLIAMS, G. *History of the Liverpool Privateers…with an Account of the Liverpool Slave Trade.* Liverpool, 1897.
WYNDHAM, Hon. H. A. *The Atlantic and Slavery.* 1935.
—— *The Atlantic and Emancipation.* 1937.

IV. TRANSPORTATION

(a) MANUSCRIPT SOURCES

See Part I, 1 and 2 above, and the relevant sections in vols. VI and VII of the *C.H.B.E.* The papers of the Home Office, Privy Council Office and Treasury contain much material on this subject, particularly the series H.O. 10, H.O. 11 and P.C. 1/67–92, "Convicts and Prisons, 1819–44."

(b) OFFICIAL PUBLICATIONS

See Part I, 3 and 4 above, and the lists in *C.H.B.E.* vol. VII, Pt 1 (*Australia*), pp. 666 *et seq.* The three reports of the Commissioner, J. T. Bigge, are of primary importance: *Parl. Pap.* 1822, XX (448) and 1823, X (33), (136). The following papers contain valuable evidence printed as appendices, especially the Rept. of 1837–8: Rept. of Sel. Comm. on Transportation, *Parl. Pap.* 1812, II (241); Rept. of Sel. Comm. on Gaols, *Parl. Pap.* 1819, VII (579); Rept. of Sel. Comm. on Secondary Punishments, *Parl. Pap.* 1831, VII (276); Instructions *re* Convict Vessels, *Parl. Pap.* 1834, XLVII (81); Corresp. on Secondary Punishments, *Parl. Pap.* 1834, XLVII (82), (614); Rept. of Sel. Comm. on Darling, *Parl. Pap.* 1835, VI (580); Rept. on Prison Discipline in Van Diemen's Land, *Parl. Pap.* 1837, XL [121]; Rept. of Sel. Comm. on Transportation, *Parl. Pap.* 1837–8, XXII (669); Papers *re* Transportation, *Parl. Pap.* 1839, XXXIV (76), (534); Bishop of Tasmania's Communication on Transportation, *Parl. Pap.* 1847, XXXVIII (741); Corresp. *re* Norfolk Island, *Parl. Pap.* 1847, XLVIII [785]; Copies of Petitions *re* Transportation since 1838, *Parl. Pap.* 1851, XLV (130); Corresp. with Governor of Tasmania *re* Transportation, 1856, XLIV (140); Rept. of Sel. Comm. of House of Lords on Transportation, *Parl. Pap.* 1856, XXIV (124); Repts. of Sel. Comm. on Transportation, *Parl. Pap.* 1856, XVII (244), (296), (355), (355 I.); Rept. of Sel. Comm. on Transportation, *Parl. Pap.* 1861, XIII (286).
The following papers printed in New South Wales are also indispensable: Minutes of Evidence taken before the Committee of the Legislative Council on Policy, 1835; Two Repts. of Comm. on Gaols, 1835. See also the *Historical Records of Australia* (35 vols., Sydney, 1914–23) and the *Historical Records of New South Wales* (vols. I–VIII, Sydney, 1892–1901).

(c) CONTEMPORARY WRITINGS

ADDERLEY, Sir C. B. (Lord Norton). *A Century of Experiments on Secondary Punishments.* 1863.
ALLISON, W. R. *Remarks on the Transportation System.* 1847.
ARTHUR, Sir G. *A Defence of Transportation.* 1835.
ATKINSON, J. B. *Penal Settlements and their Evils.* 1847. Examines Maconochie's reforms.
BANNISTER, S. *On abolishing Transportation and reforming the Colonial Office.* 1837.
BARRINGTON, G. *History of New South Wales.* 1810.
BEAUMONT, G. DE and TOCQUEVILLE, A. COMTE DE. *On the Penitentiary System in the United States.* 1833.
BENNETT, H. G. *Letter to Viscount Sidmouth on the Transportation Laws and Colonies.* 1819.
—— *Letter to Earl Bathurst.* 1820.

BENTHAM, J. *Panopticon versus New South Wales*. 1812. Reprinted in his collected *Works* (11 vols, 1837), together with other writings on convicts and transportation.

BLOSSEVILLE, B. E. P., Marquis de. *Histoire des colonies pénales de l'Angleterre dans l'Australie*. Paris, 1831. A defence of transportation.

BROWNING, C. A. *Convict Life and England's Exiles*. 1847.

BURN, D. *Vindication of Van Diemen's Land*. 1840.

CHISHOLM, C. *Transportation and Emigration relatively considered*. 1847.

COLQUHOUN, P. *Treatise on the Police of the Metropolis*. 1800.

COMBE, G. *Remarks on the Principles of Criminal Legislation and Prison Discipline*. 1854.

CROFTON, Sir W. *A Few Remarks on the Convict System*. 1847.

—— *The Convict System and Transportation*. 1863.

DALRYMPLE, A. *A Serious Admonition to the Publick on the Intended Colony at Botany Bay*. 1786.

DU CANE, Sir E. F. *Convict System in the Colonies*. 1870.

—— *Punishment and Prevention of Crime*. 1885.

FRY, H. P. *Systems of Penal Discipline*. 1850.

GIBSON, C. B. *Life among Convicts*. 2 vols. 1863. A clergyman's experiences.

GRELLET, H. R. *Case of England and Western Australia in respect to Transportation*. 1864.

HALE, M. B. *Transportation Question, or Why Western Australia should be made a reforming Colony instead of a Penal Settlement*. 1857.

HASLEM, J. *Convict Ships: Narrative of a Voyage to New South Wales in 1816*. 1819.

HENDERSON, A. *Scraps and Facts of Convict Ships*. 1845.

HOWITT, W. *Letters on Transportation as the only means of effectual convict reform*. 1863.

INNES, F. M. *Secondary Punishments, the Merit of a Home and a Colonial Process*. 1841.

JEBB, Sir J. *Report on the Discipline and Management of the Convict Prisons and Disposal of Convicts*. 1852.

KINGSMILL, J. *Prisons and Prisoners*. 1849.

—— *Common Sense View of the Treatment of Criminals, especially those sentenced to Transportation*. 1850. By an experienced clergyman.

LACKLAND, J. *Common Sense, an Enquiry into the Influence of Transportation on the Colony of Van Diemen's Land*. 1847.

LANG, J. D. *History of New South Wales*. 1834.

—— *Transportation and Colonisation*. 1837. By a Presbyterian clergyman.

LA PILORGERIE, J. *Histoire de Botany Bay*. Paris, 1836. Opponent of Transportation.

LILBURNE, E. *Complete Exposure of the Convict System*. n.d.

MACARTHUR, J. *New South Wales*. 1837.

MACONOCHIE, A. *General View regarding the Social System of Convict Management*. 1837.

—— *Report on the State of Prison Discipline in Van Diemen's Land*. 1838.

—— *Thoughts on Convict Management*. Hobart, 1838. *Supplement*, 1839.

—— *On the Management of Transported Criminals*. 1845.

—— *Crime and Punishment, the Mark System*. 1846.

—— *Norfolk Island*. 1847.

MACQUEEN, T. P. *Australia as she is and as she might be*. 1840.

MELVILLE, H. *Australasia and Prison Discipline*. 1851.

MERRUAU, P. *Les Convicts en Australie*. Paris, 1853.

MUDIE, J. *The Felony of New South Wales*. 1836. Scandal.

MURRAY, P. J. *Not so base as they seem; the Transportation, Ticket-of-Leave and Penal Servitude Questions plainly stated*. 1857.

PATERSON, G. *History of New South Wales*. Newcastle upon Tyne, 1811.

POCOCK, Z. P. *Transportation and Convict Discipline*. 1847.

REEVE, H. *Australia and the Penal Colonies*. 1837.

REID, T. *Two Voyages to New South Wales and Van Diemen's Land, including Facts and Observations relative to the State and Management of Convicts of both Sexes*. 1822.

RITCHIE, D. *Voice of our Exiles, or Stray Leaves from a Convict Ship*. Edinburgh, 1854.

ROSS's *Van Diemen's Land Annual*. Hobart, 1829 et seq.

SMITH, SYDNEY. *Works.* 3 vols. 1848. Contains three essays on transportation contributed to *Edinburgh Review.*

TAILLANDIER, A. H. "De la transportation." *Reflexions sur les lois pénales de France et d'Angleterre.* Paris, 1824.

TORRENS, Sir R. R. *Transportation considered as a Punishment and as a Mode of founding Colonies.* 1863.

ULLATHORNE, W. M. (Bishop). *Horrors of Transportation.* Dublin, 1838.

—— *On the Management of Criminals.* 1866.

WAKEFIELD, E. G. *View of the Art of Colonisation.* 1844.

WHATELEY, R. (Archbishop). *Thoughts on Secondary Punishments.* 1832.

—— *Remarks on Transportation and on a Recent Defence of the System.* 1834.

WILKINSON, W. M. *What England should do with her Convicts.* 1864.

ZELUT, H. F. *Mémoire sur la déportation.* Paris, 1855.

(d) BIOGRAPHIES, MEMOIRS AND CORRESPONDENCE

ASTLEY, W. *Tales of the Convict System.* Sydney, 1892.

BALLIÈRE. *La déportation de 1871. Souvenirs.* Paris, 1889. New Caledonia.

BUTLER, C. *Life and Times of Bishop Ullathorne.* 1926.

ELDERSHAW, M. B. *Phillip of Australia.* 1938.

GRIFFITHS, A. *Memorials of Millbank.* 1875.

LLOYD, G. T. *Thirty-three Years in Tasmania and Victoria.* 1862.

LOVELESS, G. *Victims of Whiggery.* 1837. By a Tolpuddle Martyr.

MITCHEL, J. *Jail Journal.* 1854. By the transported Irish leader.

MONCELON, L. *La Bague, et la colonisation pénale à la Nouvelle Caledonie. Par un témoin oculaire.* Paris, 1886.

MORTLOCK, J. F. *Experiences of a Convict transported for Twenty-one Years.* 1864.

O'BRIEN, E. M. *Life of Archpriest Thierry.* Sydney, 1922.

PRAETOR, J. *Souvenirs d'un déporté en Nouvelle Caledonie.* Paris, 1871.

RASHLEIGH, R. *The Adventures of Ralph Rashleigh, a Penal Exile in Australia.* 1936.

REILLY, J. T. *Reminiscences of Fifty Years in Western Australia.* 1903.

ROCHEPORT, H. *Adventures of my life.* 1896. New Caledonia.

THIERCELIN, L. *Aventures d'une Parisienne à la Nouvelle Caledonie.* Paris, 1872.

THIERRY, B. *Reminiscences of Thirty Years' Residence in New South Wales and Victoria.* 1863.

WHITE, C. *Convict Life.* Bathurst, 1889.

WRIGHT, S. S. *Narrative and Recollections of Van Diemen's Land.* 1840.

The following were written by Canadian political exiles (*cf.* TIFFANY, O. E. *The Relations of the United States to the Canadian Rebellion of 1837–8,* Buffalo, 1905):

DUCHARME, L. *Journal d'un exile politique aux Terres Australes.* Montreal, 1845.

GATES, W. *Recollections of Life in Van Diemen's Land.* Stockport, U.S.A., 1850.

MARSH, R. *Seven Years of my life, or a Narrative of a Patriot Exile.* Buffalo, 1847.

MILLER, L. B. *Notes of an Exile to Van Diemen's Land.* New York, 1846.

PRIEUR, F. X. *Notes d'un condamné politique.* Montreal, 1864.

SNOW, S. *The Exile's Return.* Cleveland, O., 1846.

WAIT, J. *Letters from Van Diemen's Land, written during Four Years' Imprisonment for Political Offences.* Buffalo, 1843.

WRIGHT, S. *Narrative and Recollections during a Three Years' Captivity.* New York, 1844.

(e) LATER WORKS

BARTON, G. B. *History of New South Wales.* Vol. I, 1783–9. Sydney, 1889.

BATTYE, J. S. *History of Western Australia.* Oxford, 1914.

BRITTON, A. *History of New South Wales.* Vol. II, 1789–94. Sydney, 1894.

CAMPION, E. *Étude sur la colonisation par les transportés anglais, russes et français.* Rennes, 1901.

COGHLAN, Sir T. A. *Labour and Industry in Australia, 1788–1901.* 4 vols. 1918.

COLLINS, D. *Account of the English Colonies in New South Wales.* 2 vols. 1798–1802. Ed. by J. Collier, 1910.

FENTON, J. *History of Tasmania*. Hobart, 1884.
FINN, E. *Chronicles of early Melbourne*. Melbourne, 1888.
FORSYTH, W. D. *Governor Arthur's Convict System. Van Diemen's Land*, 1824–36. 1935.
IVES, G. *History of Penal Methods*. 1914.
McCORMACK, E. I. *White Servitude in Maryland*, 1634–1820. Baltimore, 1904.
MOLESWORTH, Sir W. *Selected Speeches*. 1903.
O'BRIEN, E. M. *The Foundation of Australia*. 1937.
OLDHAM, W. "The Administration of the System of Transportation of British Convicts, 1763–93." *Bull. Inst. Hist. Research*, vol. XI (Nov. 1933), pp. 126–7. Summary of thesis in University of London Library.
PHILLIPS, M. *A Colonial Autocracy. New South Wales under Macquarie*. 1909.
RUTTER, O. *The First Fleet. The Record of the Foundation of Australia*. 1937.
SCOTT, E. "The Resistance to Convicts in Victoria, 1844–53." *Victoria Hist. Mag.* vol. I (1911).
THOMAS, J. *Convicts and Convict Systems*. 1886. Chiefly New Caledonia.
WEST, J. *History of Tasmania*. 2 vols. Launceston, 1852.
WHITE, C. *Old Convict Days in Australia*. Sydney, 1906.
WOOD, G. A. "Convicts." *Jour. and Proc. Royal Australian Hist. Soc.* vol. VIII (1922), pp. 177–208.

v. *EMIGRATION AND LAND POLICY*

(a) MANUSCRIPT SOURCES

See Part I, 1 and 2 above, and the relevant sections of *C.H.B.E.* vols. V–VIII. The papers of the Colonial Land and Emigration Commissioners are among the Colonial Office records in the Public Record Office, series C.O. 384, C.O. 385, C.O. 386 and C.O. 428. The accounts of emigration agents are in the Audit Office series, A.O. 3. A wealth of material in letters from emigrants to their friends at home remains practically untouched.

(b) OFFICIAL PUBLICATIONS

See Part I, 3 and 4 above, and the lists in *C.H.B.E.* vols. VI–VIII, particularly the following Parliamentary Papers: Repts. from the Sel. Comm. on Emigration, *Parl. Pap.* 1826, IV (404) and 1826–7, V (88), (237), (550); Rept. of Cockburn, *Parl. Pap.* 1828, XXI (109), (148); Rept. of the Commissioners for Emigration, *Parl. Pap.* 1831–2, XXXII (724); Rept. from the Sel. Comm. on Disposal of Lands, *Parl. Pap.* 1836, XI (512); Repts. of the South Australian Commissioners, *Parl. Pap.* 1836, XXXVI (491); 1837–8, XXIX (97); 1839, XVII (255); 1840, XXVIII (556); Rept. from Sel. Comm. on New Zealand, *Parl. Pap.* 1840, VII (582); Rept. from Sel. Comm. on South Australia, *Parl. Pap.* 1841, IV (119), (394); Rept. from Sel. Comm. on Passenger Acts, *Parl. Pap.* 1851, XIX (632); and the Annual Reports of the Colonial Land and Emigration Commissioners, 1842–73.

The principal Parliamentary Debates on Emigration were in the Sessions 1826–7, 1828, 1831, 1842, 1843 and 1847–8.

(c) CONTEMPORARY WRITINGS

BOWIE, J. *Notes on Australia*. 1837.
BREES, S. C. *A Key to the Colonies*. 1851.
BUCKINGHAM, J. S. *Canada, Nova Scotia* [etc.]. 1843.
BUCKTON, T. J. *Western Australia*. 1840.
BURN, J. I. *Familiar Letters on Population, Emigration and Home Colonization*. 2nd edn. 1838.
BUTLER, S. *The Emigrant's Handbook*. 1843. New edn. 1858.
CAPPER, H. *South Australia*. 1837.
COBBETT, W. *The Emigrant's Guide*. 1829.
DUNCUMB, J. *The British Emigrant's Advocate*. 1837.

FERRIE, A. *Letter to Earl Grey.* Montreal, 1847.

FITZROY, R. *Remarks on New Zealand.* 1846.

FOX, Sir W. *The Six Colonies of New Zealand.* 1851.

GOUGER, T. *Emigration for the Relief of Parishes.* 1833.

GOURLAY, R. *General Introduction to a Statistical Account of Upper Canada.* 3 vols. 1822.

HALE, E. E. *Letters on Irish Emigration.* Boston, 1852.

HEAD, Sir F. B. *The Emigrant.* 1846.

HORTON, Sir R. J. WILMOT. *The Causes and Remedies of Pauperism.* 1829.

—— *A Letter to Sir Francis Burdett.* 1826.

MACARTHUR, J. *New South Wales.* 1837.

MACTAGGART, J. *Three Years' Residence in Canada.* 2 vols. 1829.

MATTHEW, P. *Emigration Fields.* 1839.

MILLS, A. *Systematic Colonization.* 1847.

NASH, R. W. *Stray Suggestions on Colonization.* 1849.

PICKEN, A. *The Canadas as they at present commend themselves to Emigrants.* 1832.

ROLPH, T. *Emigration and Colonization.* 1844.

SELKIRK, Lord. *Observations on the Present State of the Highlands.* 1806.

SIDNEY, S. *The Three Colonies of Australia.* 1852.

SMITH, S. *The Settler's New Home.* 1849.

STEPHENS, J. *South Australia.* 2nd ed. 1839.

SWAINSON, W. *New Zealand and its Colonization.* 1859.

WAKEFIELD, E. G. *The British Colonization of New Zealand.* 1837.

—— *England and America.* 2 vols. 1833.

—— *A Letter from Sydney.* 1829. New edn. 1929.

—— *The New British Province of South Australia.* 1834.

—— *A View of the Art of Colonization.* 1849. New edn. by J. Collier. Oxford, 1914.

WENTWORTH, W. C. *A Statistical Description of the Colony of New South Wales.* 1819.

WILLCOCKS, J. B. *Emigration, its Necessity and Advantages.* 1848.

WILSON, E. *A Scheme of Emigration on a National Scale.* 1869.

(d) BIOGRAPHIES, MEMOIRS AND CORRESPONDENCE

ARNOLD, T. *Passages in a Wandering Life.* 1900.

BECKE, L. and JEFFERY, W. *Admiral Phillip.* 1899.

COYNE, J. H. (Ed.). *The Talbot Papers.* Royal Soc. of Canada, 1909.

GALT, J. *Autobiography.* 2 vols. 1833.

GARNETT, R. *Wakefield.* 1898.

GOUGER, R. *The Founding of South Australia as recorded in the Journals of Mr R. Gouger.* Ed. by E. Hodder. 1898.

HARROP, A. J. *The Amazing Career of Edward Gibbon Wakefield.* 1928.

HENDERSON, G. C. *Sir George Grey.* 1907.

JONES, H. F. *Samuel Butler.* 2 vols. 1919.

O'CONNOR, I. *Edward Gibbon Wakefield.* 1928.

PARKES, Sir H. *Fifty Years in the Making of Australian History.* 2 vols. 1892.

SEELEY, R. B. *Memoir of the Life and Writings of M. T. Sadler.* 1842.

SKELTON, O. D. *Life and Times of Sir A. T. Galt.* Toronto, 1920.

STRICKLAND, S. *Twenty-Seven Years in Canada West.* 2 vols. 1853.

SWAINSON, W. *New Zealand and its Colonization.* 1859.

WAKEFIELD, E. G. *The Founders of Canterbury.* 1868. Letters, ed. by E. J. Wakefield.

—— *Adventures in New Zealand from 1839 to 1844.* 2 vols. 1845.

WHITINGTON, F. T. *William Grant Broughton, Bishop of Australia.* Sydney, 1936.

(e) LATER WORKS

ADAMS, W. F. *Ireland and Irish Emigration to the New World from 1815 to the Famine.* New Haven, 1932.

BATTYE, J. S. *Western Australia.* Oxford, 1924.

BONWICK, J. *The Port Phillip Settlement.* 1883.

CARROTHERS, W. A. *Emigration from the British Isles, with Special Reference to the Development of the Overseas Empire.* 1929. Valuable bibliography.

COWAN, H. I. *British Emigration to British North America*, 1783–1837. Toronto, 1928.

EDWARDS, I. E. *The 1820 Settlers in South Africa.* 1934.

EPPS, W. *Land Systems of Australasia.* 1894.

FORD, H. J. *The Scotch-Irish in America.* 1915.

GISBORNE, W. *The Colony of New Zealand.* 1888.

GUILLET, E. C. *The Great Migration.* New York, 1937. British emigration across the Atlantic. Valuable bibliography.

HARROP, A. J. *England and New Zealand.* 1926.

HITCHINS, F. H. *The Colonial Land and Emigration Commission.* Philadelphia, 1931.

HODDER, E. *History of South Australia.* 2 vols. 1893.

HOGAN, J. F. *The Gladstone Colony.* 1898.

JENKS, E. *History of the Australasian Colonies.* 1912.

JOHNSON, S. C. *History of Emigration from the United Kingdom to North America,* 1763–1912. 1913.

JOHNSTON, Sir H. H. *History of the Colonization of Africa by Alien Races.* Cambridge, 1899.

JOURDAIN, W. R. *History of Land Legislation and Settlement in New Zealand.* 1925.

LANGLOIS, G. "L'Immigration britannique au Canada." *Actualité économique,* vol. x (1935), pp. 626–39.

MACDONALD, N. *Canada, 1763–1841. Immigration and Settlement.* 1939.

McKENZIE, N. R. *The Gael fares forth. The Romantic Story of Waipu and Sister Settlements.* Auckland, 1935.

MADGWICK, R. B. *Immigration into Eastern Australia, 1788–1857.* 1937.

MARAIS, J. S. *The Colonization of New Zealand.* 1927.

MILFORD, G. D. *Governor Phillip and the Early Settlement of New South Wales.* 1935.

MILLS, R. C. *The Colonization of Australia, 1829–42.* 1915.

MOREHOUSE, F. "The Irish Migration of the 'Forties." *Amer. Hist. Rev.* vol. xxxiii (April 1928), pp. 579–92.

—— "Migration from the United Kingdom to North America, 1840–50." Unpublished thesis in the Library of Manchester University.

MORRELL, W. P. *New Zealand.* 1935.

MORRISON, H. M. "The Crown Land Policies of the Canadian Government, 1838–72." Unpublished thesis in the Library of Clark University, U.S.A.

—— "The Principle of Free Grants in the Land Act of 1841." *Canadian Hist. Rev.* vol. xiv (Dec. 1933) pp. 392–407.

O'BRIEN, E. M. *The Foundation of Australia.* 1937.

PATERSON, G. C. *Land Settlement in Upper Canada, 1783–1840.* Toronto, 1921.

PRICE, A. GRENFELL. *The Foundation and Settlement of South Australia, 1829–45.* Adelaide, 1924.

RANKEN, G. *The Squatting System in Australia.* 1875.

RATHGEN, C. *Die englische Auswanderung im neunzehnten Jahrhundert.* Leipzig, 1896.

REEVES, W. P. *State Experiments in Australia and New Zealand.* 2 vols. 1902.

REYNOLDS, L. G. *The British Immigrant: his Social and Economic Adjustment in Canada.* Toronto, 1935.

RIDDELL, R. G. "A Study in the Land Policy of the Colonial Office, 1762–1855." *Canadian Hist. Rev.* vol. xviii (Dec. 1937), pp. 385–405.

ROBERTS, S. H. *History of Australian Land Settlement, 1788–1920.* Melbourne, 1924.

—— *The Squatting Age in Australia, 1835–47.* 1935.

RUSDEN, G. W. *History of Australia.* 3 vols. 1883.

—— *History of New Zealand.* 3 vols. 1883. 2nd edn. 1895.

SIEGFRIED, A. *Edward Gibbon Wakefield et sa doctrine.* Paris, 1904.

TUCKER, G. "The Famine Immigration to Canada, 1847." *Amer. Hist. Rev.* vol. xxxvi (April 1931), pp. 533–49.

TURNER, F. J. *The Rise of the New West.* New York, 1906.

TURNER, H. G. *History of the Colony of Victoria.* 2 vols. 1904.

WALPOLE, K. A. "Emigration to British North America under the early Passenger Acts, 1803–42." *Bull. Inst. Hist. Research,* vol. vii (Feb. 1930), pp. 187–9. Summary of thesis in University of London Library.

—— "The Humanitarian Movement of the Early Nineteenth Century to remedy Emigrant Vessels to Canada." *Trans. Royal Hist. Soc.* 4th ser., vol. xiv (1931), pp. 197–224.

vi. *ECONOMIC POLICY AND HISTORY*

(a) MANUSCRIPT SOURCES

See Part I, 1 and 2 above, particularly the records of the Board of Trade (B.T. 1–6), the Audit Office (A.O. 3 and 6) and the Treasury (T. 64). There are trade statistics in the series "Home Office Departmental, War and Colonial Office, 1794–1840" (H.O. 30 and H.O. 50). Two bundles of Shipping Returns, 1791–7 are in H.O. 76/1–2.

(b) OFFICIAL PUBLICATIONS

See Part I, 3 and 4, particularly the following Parliamentary Papers: Rept. from Comm. E.I.C., China Trade, *Parl. Pap.* 1830, v (644), (655); Rept. from Sel. Comm. on E.I.C. Petition, *Parl. Pap.* 1840, VII (359); Rept. from Sel. Comm. on New Zealand, *Parl. Pap.* 1840, VII (582); Rept. from Sel. Comm. on Export of Machinery; Rept. from Sel. Comm. on West Indian Labour, *Parl. Pap.* 1842, XIII (479); Repts. from Sel. Comm. on Navigation Laws, *Parl. Pap.* 1847, x (232), (246), (392), (556), (678). The Official *Year Books* of the Dominions and India have also a retrospective value.

(c) BIBLIOGRAPHIES

BEALES, H. L. *A Select List of Books on Economic and Social History*, 1700–1850. 1927.

HEADICAR, B. M. and others. *A London Bibliography of the Social Sciences*. London School of Economics, 1931–7. 7 vols.

MANN, J. DE L. "List of Books and Articles on British Economic History, 1925." *Economic Hist. Rev.* 1927– . In progress.

MARWICK, W. H. "A Bibliography of Scottish Economic History." *Economic Hist. Rev.* vol. III (Jan. 1931), pp. 117–37.

POWER, E. *The Industrial Revolution, 1750–1850. A Select Bibliography.* 1927. Economic History Society Bibliographies, No. 1.

PRENDEVILLE, P. L. "A Select Bibliography of Irish Economic History. Part III. The Nineteenth Century." *Economic Hist. Rev.* vol. IV (Oct. 1932), pp. 81–90.

WILLIAMS, J. B. *A Guide to the Printed Materials for English Social and Economic History,* 1750–1850. 2 vols. New York, 1926.

(d) PERIODICALS

Board of Trade Journal. London, 1877– . In progress.

Economic History (Supplement to the *Economic Journal*). London, 1926– . In progress.

Economic History Review. London, 1927– . In progress.

Economica. London, 1921– . In progress.

Economist. London, 1843– . In progress.

Quarterly Journal of Economics. London, 1887– . In progress.

ROYAL STATISTICAL SOCIETY. *Journal.* London, 1838– . In progress.

(e) CONTEMPORARY WRITINGS

COLQUHOUN, P. A. *Treatise on the Wealth, Power and Resources of the British Empire.* 1814.

CRAIK, G. L. *Annals of Commerce.* 3 vols. 1844.

DIBBS, J. *Three Letters to Lord John Russell on the Navigation Laws.* 1848.

EVANS, D. M. *The Commercial Crisis, 1847–8.* 1848.

HARLE, W. L. *The Total Repeal of the Navigation Laws discussed.* Newcastle upon Tyne, 1848.

HUSKISSON, W. *Speeches.* 3 vols. 1831.

LASALLE, H. *Les Finances de l'Angleterre.* 1803.

LINDSAY, W. S. *Letters on the Navigation Laws.* 1849.

McCULLOCH, J. R. *A Descriptive and Statistical Account of the British Empire.* 2 vols. 1837. 4th edn. 1854.

MACDONNELL, A. *Colonial Commerce.* 1828.

MARRYAT, J. *A Reply to various Publications recommending an Equalisation of the Duties on East and West Indian Sugar.* 1823.

MARTIN, R. M. *The Sugar Question in Relation to Free Trade and Protection.* 1848.

MASSON, J. P. *A Letter to Ministers suggesting Improvements in the Trade of the West Indies.* 1825.

MEARES, J. *Voyages from China to North-West America,* 1788–9. 1799.

MILL, J. S. *Principles of Political Economy.* 1848.

NORTHCOTE, Sir S. H. (Lord Iddlesleigh). *A Short Review of the History of the Navigation Laws.* 1849. Published anonymously.

—— *Our Free Trade Policy Examined.* 1846.

PARNELL, Sir H. B. (Lord Congleton). *On Financial Reform.* 1830.

—— *Preferential Interests (The).* 1841.

PORTLOCK, N. *A Voyage to the North-West Coast of America.* 1789.

REINHARD, C. *Observations on British Commerce.* 1804.

RICARDO, D. *Anatomy of the Navigation Laws.* 1847.

ROGERS, T. "Cobden and Modern Political Opinion. The Colonial Question." *Cobden Club Essays,* 2nd ser. (1862), pp. 452–58.

ROOKE, J. *An Enquiry into the Principles of National Wealth.* 1824.

SENIOR, N. W. *Industrial Efficiency and Social Economy.* Ed. by S. L. Levis. 2 vols. 1929.

SMITH, ADAM. *The Wealth of Nations.* 2 vols. 1776. Ed. by E. Cannan. 2 vols. 1922.

Statement (A) of the Claims of the West India Colonies to a Protecting Duty against East India Sugar. 1823.

Statistical Illustrations of the British Empire. 1827.

TALLEYRAND, Prince de. "Les États-Unis et l'Angleterre en 1795: lettre de M. de Talleyrand." *Rev. hist. diplomatique,* vol. III (1889), pp. 64–77.

—— *Mémoire sur les relations commerciales des États-Unis avec l'Angleterre.* Paris, 1809. American edn. Boston, 1809.

TAZEWELL, L. W. *A Review of the Negotiations between the United States of America and Great Britain respecting the Commerce of the two Countries.* 1829.

TOOKE, T. and NEWMARCH, W. *History of Prices.* 6 vols. 1838–57.

(*f*) LATER WORKS

ALBION, R. G. *Forests and Sea Power.* Cambridge, Mass., 1926.

ALLIN, C. D. and JONES, G. M. *Annexation, Preferential Trade and Reciprocity.* Toronto, 1912.

ANSTEY, V. *The Economic Development of India.* 1929.

ASHTON, T. "Overseas Competition and Commercial Policy." *Iron and Steel in the Industrial Revolution* (1924), chap. v.

BABCOCK, F. L. *Spanning the Atlantic.* New York, 1931.

BARNES, D. G. *A History of the English Corn Laws,* 1660–1846. 1930.

BELL, H. C. "British Commercial Policy in the West Indies, 1783–93." *Eng. Hist. Rev.,* vol. XXXI (1916), pp. 429–41.

BEMIS, S. F. *Jay's Treaty, a Study in Commerce and Diplomacy.* New York, 1923.

BENNS, F. L. *The American Struggle for the British West India Carrying-Trade,* 1815–30. Bloomington, 1923.

BOWEN, P. C. *A Century of Atlantic Travel,* 1830–1930. [1930.]

BOWLEY, A. L. *England's Foreign Trade in the Nineteenth Century.* Rev. edn. 1905.

BRADY, A. *William Huskisson and Liberal Reform.* 1928.

BREDON, J. *Life of Sir Robert Hart.* 1909.

BROODBANK, Sir J. G. *History of the Port of London.* 2 vols. 1921.

BURN, D. L. "Canada and the Repeal of the Corn Laws." *Cambridge Hist. Jour.* vol. II (1928), pp. 252–72.

BUXTON, S. *Finance and Politics, an Historical Study,* 1783–1885. 2 vols. 1888.

—— *Mr Gladstone. A Study.* 1901.

CADY, J. F. *Foreign Intervention in the Rio de la Plata,* 1838–50. 1929.

CAMPBELL, P. C. *Chinese Coolie Emigration to Countries within the British Empire.* 1923.

CHAPMAN, G. J. *The Lancashire Cotton Industry.* 1904.

CHAPMAN, S. J. *The History of Trade between the United Kingdom and the United States.* 1899.

CLAPHAM, J. H. *Economic History of Modern Britain.* Vols. I and II. 1930, 1932.

—— "The Last Years of the Navigation Acts." *Eng. Hist. Rev.* vol. XXV (1910), pp. 480–501, 687–707.

COSTIN, W. C. *Great Britain and China, 1833–60.* 1937.

CUNNINGHAM, W. *Growth of English Industry and Commerce.* 1882. 6th rev. edn. 2 vols in 3. Cambridge, 1915–21.

DAVIDSON, J. *Commercial Federation and Colonial Trade Policy.* 1900.

—— "England's Commercial Policy towards her Colonies since the Treaty of Paris" [1783–1897]. *Polit. Science Quart.* vol. XIV (1899), pp. 39–68, 211–39.

DOUGLAS, Sir R. K. *Europe and the Far East.* 2nd edn. Cambridge, 1913. New York, 1924.

ELLISON, T. *The Cotton Trade of Great Britain.* 1886.

EVANS, G. H. *British Corporation Finance, 1775–1850.* Baltimore, 1936.

FARRER, T. H. *Free Trade and Fair Trade.* 3rd edn. 1886.

FAY, C. R. *Great Britain from Adam Smith to the Present Day.* 1928.

—— *Imperial Economy, 1600–1932.* Oxford, 1934.

FAYLE, C. E. *A Short History of the World's Shipping Industry.* 1933.

FUCHS, C. J. *Die Handelspolitik Englands und seiner Kolonien seit 1860.* Leipzig, 1893. English trans. by C. H. M. Archibald, 1905.

GIFFEN, Sir R. *Essays in Finance.* 2nd series. 1880–6.

GOEBEL, D. B. "British Trade to the Spanish Colonies, 1796–1823." *Amer. Hist. Rev.* vol. XLIII (Jan. 1938), pp. 288–320.

GRAHAM, G. S. *British Policy and Canada, 1774–91. A Study in Eighteenth Century Trade Policy.* 1930.

GREGORY, T. E. (Ed.). *British Banking Statutes and Reports, 1832–1928.* 2 vols. 1929.

HILL, H. A. "The Navigation Laws of Great Britain and the United States." *Jour. Social Science,* vol. IX (1878), pp. 101–16.

HIRST, F. W. *Free Trade and the Manchester School.* 1903.

HOBSON, J. A. *Imperialism. A Study.* 1902.

HOLLAND, B. H. *The Fall of Protection, 1840–50.* 1913.

HORNBY, Sir E. *An Autobiography.* Boston, 1929.

HOSKINS, H. L. *British Routes to India.* 1928.

HUGHES, E. R. *The Invasion of China by the Western World.* 1937.

HUNT, B. C. *The Development of the Business Corporation in England, 1800–67.* Cambridge, Mass., 1936.

HUNTER, W. C. *The "Fan Kwae" at Canton before Treaty Days, 1825–44.* 2nd edn. Shanghai, 1911.

HYDE, F. E. *Mr Gladstone at the Board of Trade.* 1934.

JACKSON, G. G. *The Ship under Steam.* 1927.

JENKS, L. H. *The Migration of British Capital to 1875.* New York, 1927.

JEUDWINE, J. W. *Studies in Empire and Trade.* 1923.

KEENLEYSIDE, H. L. *Canada and the United States.* New York, 1929.

KNOWLES, L. C. A. *Industrial and Commercial Revolutions in Great Britain in the Nineteenth Century.* 4th edn. 1926.

KNOWLES, L. C. A. and C. M. *The Economic Development of the British Overseas Empire.* 3 vols. 1924–36.

KUO, P. C. *A Critical Study of the First Anglo-Chinese War.* Shanghai, 1935.

LAWSON, W. *Pacific Steamers.* Glasgow, 1927.

LEVI, L. *History of British Commerce, 1763–1878.* 1880.

LINGELBACH, A. L. "The Inception of the British Board of Trade." *Amer. Hist. Rev.* vol. XXX (July 1925), pp. 701–27.

—— "William Huskisson as President of the Board of Trade." *Amer. Hist. Rev.* vol. XLIII (July 1938), pp. 759–74.

LUBBOCK, B. *The Colonial Clippers.* Glasgow, 1921.

MacINNES, C. M. *An Introduction to the Economic History of the British Empire.* 1935.

MANTOUX, P. *La révolution industrielle au XVIIIᵉ siècle.* Paris, 1906.

MASTERS, D. C. *The Reciprocity Treaty of 1854.* 1937.

MICHIE, A. *The Englishman in China during the Victorian Era.* Edinburgh, 1900.

MORSE, H. B. (Ed.). *Chronicles of the East India Company trading to China, 1635–1834.* 5 vols. 1926–9.

—— *The International Relations of the Chinese Empire, 1834–60.* 1910.

MURRAY, M. *Ships and South Africa.* Oxford, 1933.

OWEN, D. E. *British Opium Policy in China and India.* New Haven, Conn., 1934.

PAGE, W. (Ed.). *Commerce and Industry.* 2 vols. 1919. Vol. I, "A Historical Review of the Economic Conditions of the British Empire, 1815–1914." Vol. II, "Tables of Statistics."

PARES, R. "The Economic Factors in the History of the Empire." *Economic Hist. Rev.* vol. VII (May 1937), pp. 119–44.

PARKINSON, C. N. *Trade in the Eastern Seas, 1793–1813.* Cambridge, 1937.

PERRIS, G. H. *Industrial History of Modern England.* New York, 1914.

PORRITT, E. *The Fiscal and Diplomatic Freedom of the British Oversea Dominions.* Ed. by D. Kinley. 1922.

PORTER, G. R. *Progress of the Nation.* 1836. Rev. edn. brought up to date by F. W. Hirst, 1912.

PRITCHARD, E. H. *The Crucial Years of Early Anglo-Chinese Relations, 1750–1800.* Pullman, Wash., 1936.

RAFFLES, Sir STAMFORD. *Report on Japan to the Secret Committee of the English East India Company.* 1930.

RAGATZ, L. J. *The Fall of the Planter Class in the British Caribbean, 1763–1833.* New York, 1928.

REDFORD, A. *The Economic History of England, 1760–1860.* 1931.

REES, J. F. *A Survey of Economic Development, with Special Reference to Great Britain.* 1933.

SARGENT, A. J. *Anglo-Chinese Commerce and Diplomacy (mainly in the Nineteenth Century).* Oxford, 1907.

SCHOLEFIELD, G. H. *The Pacific, its Past and Future, and the Policy of the Great Powers from the Eighteenth Century.* 1919.

SCHUYLER, R. L. "British Imperial Preference and Sir Robert Peel." *Polit. Science Quart.* vol. XXXII (Sept. 1917), pp. 429–49.

—— "The Abolition of British Imperial Preference, 1846–60." *Polit. Science Quart.* vol. XXXIII (March 1918), pp. 77–92.

SEE, C. S. *Foreign Trade of China.* New York, 1919.

SHANN, E. *An Economic History of Australia.* Cambridge, 1930.

SMART, W. *Economic Annals of the Nineteenth Century.* 2 vols. 1910–17.

SMITH, C. A. M. *The British in China and Far Eastern Trade.* 1920.

SMITH, W. *The History of the Post Office in British North America, 1639–1870.* Cambridge, 1920.

SOOTHILL, W. E. *China and England.* Oxford, 1928.

TANSILL, C. C. *The Canadian Reciprocity Treaty of 1854.* Baltimore, 1922.

TSIANG, T. F. "China and European Expansion." *Politica,* vol. II (1936), pp. 1–18.

—— "New Light on Chinese Diplomacy, 1836–49." *Jour. Mod. Hist.* vol. III (1931), pp. 578–91.

TURNER, R. E. *James Silk Buckingham.* 1934.

WAGNER, D. O. "British Economists and the Empire." *Polit. Science. Quart.* vol. XLVI (1931), pp. 248–76; vol. XLVII (1932), pp. 57–74.

WALLACE, F. W. *In the Wake of the Windships.* Toronto, 1927.

—— *Wooden Ships and Iron Men.* Toronto, n.d.

WILLIAMS, J. B. "The Development of British Trade with West Africa, 1750–1850." *Polit. Science Quart.* vol. L (June 1935), pp. 195–213.

WILLOUGHBY, W. W. *Foreign Rights and Interests in China from 1842.* Baltimore, 1920.

WRIGHT, A. *Romance of Colonisation: Economic Development.* 1923.

vii. *INTERNATIONAL LAW AND RELATIONS*

(a) MANUSCRIPT SOURCES

See Part I, 1 and 2, for lists of Colonial Office and Foreign Office Records, the papers of Lord John Russell, Palmerston, Grey, Peel, Aberdeen, Gladstone and Ripon.

(b) COLLECTED HISTORICAL RECORDS

See Part I, 3 and 4, for Parliamentary Papers and Debates.

COBBETT, W. PITT (Ed.). *Leading Cases in International Law.* 5th edn. 2 vols. 1924–31.

HERTSLET, Sir E. and others (Eds.). *British and Foreign State Papers.* London, 1841–. In progress. Including Papers from the year 1800 onwards.

—— *Treaties between Great Britain and Foreign Powers.* 31 vols. 1835–1927. Incorporated, 1928, in *British and Foreign State Papers.*

MANNING, W. R. (Ed.). *Diplomatic Correspondence of the United States concerning the Independence of the Latin American Nations.* 3 vols. New York, 1925.

—— *Diplomatic Correspondence of the United States: Inter-American Affairs,* 1831–60. Vol. VI, *Great Britain.* Washington, 1936.

MARTENS, G. F. von, and others. *Nouveau Recueil général des traités.* 37 vols. Gottingen, 1817–75. *Table générale.* 1875–6.

MOORE, J. B. *History and Digest of the International Arbitrations to which the United States has been a Party.* 6 vols. Washington, 1898.

—— *Digest of International Law.* 8 vols. Washington, 1908.

—— *International Adjudications.* New York, 1929–. In progress.

SCOTT, J. B. (Ed.). *Cases on International Law.* New edn. 1922.

—— (Ed.). *Hague Court Reports.* 2 vols. New York, 1916, 1932.

SMITH, H. A. (Ed.). *Great Britain and the Law of Nations. Select Documents.* Vols. I and II. 1932–5.

TEMPERLEY, H. W. V. and PENSON, L. M. (Eds.). *A Century of Diplomatic Blue Books,* 1814–1914. Cambridge, 1938.

—— *Foundations of British Foreign Policy from Pitt (1792) to Salisbury (1902).* Cambridge, 1938.

WEBSTER, C. K. (Ed.). *Britain and the Independence of Latin America. Select Documents from the Foreign Office Archives.* 2 vols. 1938.

(c) BIBLIOGRAPHIES

The bibliographies in the *Cambridge Modern History,* vols. X and XI (1907–9), and in the *Cambridge History of British Foreign Policy,* vols. II and III (1922–3), should be consulted for more detailed lists of works on British Foreign Policy.

ABBOTT, W. C. *An Introduction to the Documents relating to the International Status of Gibraltar,* 1704–1934. New York, 1934.

BEMIS, S. F. and GRIFFIN, G. G. *Guide to the Diplomatic History of the United States,* 1775–1921. Washington, 1935. Valuable for Anglo-American relations.

FOREIGN OFFICE. *Catalogue of Printed Books in the Library of the Foreign Office.* 1926.

HEADICAR, B. M. *Catalogue of the Edward Fry Library of International Law.* 1923. At the London School of Economics and Political Science.

HEATLEY, D. P. *Diplomacy and the Study of International Relations.* Oxford, 1919.

MAXWELL, L. F. *A Bibliography of English Law.* Vol. III, 1801–1932. 1933. *Supplement,* 1936.

WINFIELD, P. H. *The Chief Sources of English Legal History.* Cambridge, Mass., 1925.

(d) PERIODICALS

American Journal of International Law. New York, 1907–. In progress.

British Year-Book of International Law. London, 1920–. In progress.

GROTIUS SOCIETY. *Publications.* London, 1928–. In progress. *Transactions.* London, 1915–. In progress.

(e) CONTEMPORARY WRITINGS

ADAMS, JOHN QUINCY. "British Colonial and Navigation System." *Amer. Quart. Rev.* vol. II (1827), pp. 267–306.

BURGE, W. *Commentaries on Colonial and Foreign Laws generally.* 4 vols. 1838. New edn. 4 vols. in 5. 1907–28.

CASS, L. *An Examination of the Question concerning the Right of Search.* By An American. Paris, 1842.

CHIPMAN, W. *Remarks upon the Disputed Points of Boundary under the Fifth Article of the Treaty of Ghent.* St John, N.B., 1838.

CLARK, C. *Summary of Colonial Law.* 1834.

FALCONER, T. *The Oregon Question.* 1845.

GALLATIN, A. *A Memoir on the North-Eastern Boundary.* New York, 1843.

GREEN, DUFF. *The United States and England.* 1842.

HOSACK, J. *Rights of British and Neutral Commerce.* 1854.

LAWRENCE, W. B. *Visitation and Search.* Boston, 1858.

—— *The Treaty of Washington.* Providence, 1871.

OUSELEY, Sir W. G. *Reply to An American's Examination of the Right of Search.* 1842.

PRITCHARD, G. *Queen Pomare and her Country.* 1878.

PRITCHARD, W. T. *Polynesian Reminiscences.* 1866.

STURGIS, W. *The Oregon Question.* Boston, 1845.

THOM, A. *The Claims to the Oregon Territory.* 1844.

TWISS, Sir TRAVERS. *The Oregon Question examined.* 1846.

—— *Two Introductory Lectures on the Science of International Law.* 1856.

WHEATON, H. *Enquiry into the Validity of the British Claim to a Right of Visitation and Search.* Philadelphia, 1842.

(f) LATER WORKS

For biographies, see Section 1 (e) above

ADAMS, E. D. "The Ashburton-Webster Negotiations." *Amer. Hist. Rev.* vol. XVII (1912), pp. 764–82.

—— *Great Britain and the American Civil War.* 2 vols. 1925.

ALVAREZ, A. *La doctrine de Monroe.* 1924.

ARIAS, H. *The Panama Canal.* 1911.

BACON, R. "British and American Policy and the Right of Fluvial Navigation." *Brit. Yearbook Internat. Law* (1932), pp. 76–92.

BALDWIN, J. R. "England and the French Seizure of the Society Islands." *Jour. Mod. Hist.* vol. X (June 1938), pp. 212–31.

BAXTER, J. P. "The British Government and Neutral Rights, 1861–5." *Amer. Hist. Rev.* vol. XXXIV (1928), pp. 9–29.

—— "Some British Opinions as to Neutral Rights, 1861–5." *Amer. Jour. Internat. Law,* vol. XXIII (1929), pp. 517–37.

BELL, H. C. F. *Life of Palmerston.* 2 vols. 1936.

BEMIS, S. F. *A Diplomatic History of the United States.* 1937.

BENNS, F. L. *The American Struggle for the British West India Carrying-Trade,* 1815–30. Bloomington, 1933.

BERNARD, M. *Neutrality of Great Britain during the American Civil War.* 1870.

BIGELOW, J. *Breaches of Anglo-American Treaties.* New York, 1917.

BIXLER, R. W. "Anglo-Portuguese Rivalry for Delagoa Bay." *Jour. Mod. Hist.* vol. VI (Dec. 1934), pp. 425–40.

BOWLES, T. G. *Declaration of Paris of 1856.* 1900.

BRIGGS, H. W. *The Doctrine of Continuous Voyage.* 1926.

BURROWS, M. *History of the Foreign Policy of Great Britain.* 1895. New edn. 1897.

BUTLER, Sir G. and MACCOBY, S. *The Development of International Law.* 1928.

CALLAHAN, J. M. *The Neutrality of the American Lakes and Anglo-American Relations.* Baltimore, 1898.

CECIL, A. *British Foreign Secretaries,* 1807–1916. 1927.

CLARK, J. R. *Memorandum on the Monroe Doctrine.* 1930.

CLARKE, R. C. "British and American Tariff Policies and their Influence on the Oregon Boundary Treaty." *Proc. Pacific Coast Branch Amer. Hist. Assoc.* (1926), pp. 32–50.

COBDEN, R. *Speeches on Questions of Public Policy.* 2 vols. 1908.

COLERIDGE, E. H. *Life and Correspondence of Lord Coleridge.* 2 vols. 1904.

COMMASTER, H. "England and the Oregon Treaty of 1846." *Oregon Hist. Quart.* vol. XXVIII (1927), pp. 18–38.

CORBETT, P. C. *The Settlement of Canadian-American Disputes.* New Haven. 1937.

CRUTTWELL, C. R. M. *A History of Peaceful Change in the Modern World.* 1937.

CUSHING, C. *The Treaty of Washington.* New York, 1873.

DARCY, J. *France et Angleterre, cent années de rivalité coloniale, l'Afrique.* Paris, 1904.

DOUIN, G. *L'Angleterre et l'Égypte.* 2 vols. Paris, 1928–30.

DOYLE, J. A. (Ed.). "The Papers of Sir Charles R. Vaughan, 1825–35." *Amer. Hist. Rev.* vol. VII (1902), pp. 500–3.

DRIAULT, E. *L'Égypte et l'Europe: la crise de 1839–41.* 2 vols. Cairo, 1930.

DUNNING, W. A. *The British Empire and the United States* [1814–1914]. New York, 1914.

ELLIOTT, C. B. "The Doctrine of Continuous Voyages." *Amer. Jour. Internat. Law,* vol. I (1907), pp. 60–104.

FRIEDMANN, W. *Contributions of English Equity to the Idea of an International Equity Tribunal.* 1935.

GANTENBEIN, J. W. *The Doctrine of Continuous Voyage.* 1929.

GUIZOT, F. P. G. *An Embassy to the Court of St James in 1840.* 1862.

—— *Mémoires pour servir à l'histoire de mon temps.* 8 vols. Paris, 1858–67.

HALL, Sir J. R. *The Bourbon Restoration.* 1909.

—— *England and the Orleans Monarchy.* 1912.

HALL, W. E. *International Law.* 8th edn. by A. P. Higgins. Oxford, 1924.

HALLBERG, C. W. *The Suez Canal: its History and Diplomatic Importance.* New York, 1931.

HALLECK, H. W. *International Law.* 1878. New ed., 2 vols., 1908.

HARDY, G. *Histoire de la Colonisation française.* Paris, 1928.

HICKSON, G. F. "Palmerston and the Clayton-Bulwer Treaty." *Cambridge Hist. Jour.* vol. III (1931), pp. 295–303.

HIGGINS, A. P. *Studies in International Law and Relations.* 1928.

HOBSON, J. A. *Richard Cobden, the International Man.* 1919.

HOGAN, A. E. *Pacific Blockade.* 1908.

HOSACK, J. *Rise and Growth of the Law of Nations.* 1882.

HOSKINS, H. L. *British Routes to India.* New York, 1928.

HOWE, G. F. "The Clayton-Bulwer Treaty." *Amer. Hist. Rev.* vol. XLII (April 1937), pp. 484–90.

HUNT, H. E. "How the Great Lakes became High Seas." *Amer. Jour. Internat. Law,* vol. V (1911), pp. 285 *et seq.*

HYDE, C. C. *International Law.* 2 vols. Boston, 1922.

JORDAN, D. and PRATT, J. W. *Europe and the American Civil War.* New York, 1931.

KNAPLUND, P. *Gladstone's Foreign Policy.* 1935.

LAUTERPACHT, H. *The Function of Law in the International Community.* 1933.

LAWRENCE, T. J. "The Colonies in International Law." *King's College Lectures on Colonial Problems,* ed. by F. J. C. Hearnshaw, 1913.

—— *A Handbook of Public International Law.* 11th edn. 1938.

LAWSON, L. A. *The Relation of British Policy to the Declaration of the Monroe Doctrine.* New York, 1922.

LINDLEY, M. F. *The Acquisition and Government of Backward Territory.* 1926.

LONG, M. H. "Sir John Rose and the Informal Beginnings of the Canadian High Commissionership." *Canadian Hist. Rev.* vol. XII (March 1931), pp. 23–43.

MALKIN, Sir W. H. "The Inner History of the Declaration of Paris." *Brit. Year Book Internat. Law,* vol. XXI (1927).

—— "*The Trent* and *The China.*" *Brit. Yearbook Internat. Law,* vol. V (1911), pp. 66 *et seq.*

MALMESBURY, Lord. *Memoirs of an ex-Minister.* 2 vols. 1884.

MANNING, W. O. *Commentaries on the Law of Nations.* New edn. 1875.

MANNING, W. R. "The Nootka Sound Controversy." *Amer. Hist. Assoc. Ann. Rept. for* 1904 (1905), pp. 279–478.

MARTIN, T. P. "Free Trade and the Oregon Question, 1842–6." *Facts and Factors of Economic History.* E. F. Gay Memorial Volume. Cambridge, Mass., 1932.

—— "The Influence of Trade (in Cotton and Wheat) on Anglo-American Relations, 1829–46." *Louisville Courier-Journal,* 1923. Series of articles.

—— "The Upper Mississippi Valley in Anglo-American Anti-Slavery and Free-Trade Relations, 1837–42." *Miss. Valley Hist. Rev.* vol. xv (1928), pp. 204–20.

MERK, F. "British Government Propaganda and the Oregon Treaty." *Amer. Hist. Rev.* vol. xl (Oct. 1934), pp. 38–62.

—— "British Party Politics and the Oregon Treaty." *Amer. Hist. Rev.* vol. xxvii (July 1932), pp. 653–77.

—— "The Oregon Pioneers and the Boundary." *Amer. Hist. Rev.* vol. xxix (1924), pp. 681–99.

—— "The Snake River Expedition, 1824–5. An Episode of Fur Trade and Empire." *Miss. Valley Hist. Rev.* vol. xxi (1934), pp. 49–62.

MILLS, D. "British Diplomacy and Canada—the Ashburton Treaty." *United Empire,* new ser. vol. ii (1911), pp. 683–712.

MORROW, R. L. "The Negotiation of the Anglo-American Treaty of 1870." *Amer. Hist. Rev.* vol. xxxix (July 1934), pp. 663–81.

MOWAT, R. B. *The Diplomatic Relations of Great Britain and the United States.* 1925.

NEWTON, Lord. *Lord Lyons.* New edn. 2 vols. 1916.

NEWTON, A. P. "United States and Colonial Developments, 1815–46." *Cambridge History of British Foreign Policy,* vol. ii (Cambridge, 1923), chap. vi, pp. 220–83.

—— "The West Indies in International Politics, 1550–1850." *History,* vol. xix (1934–5), pp. 193–207, 302–10.

OPPENHEIM, L. F. L. *International Law.* New edn. 2 vols. 1935–7.

PERKINS, D. *The Monroe Doctrine, 1823–6.* 1927.

—— *The Monroe Doctrine, 1826–67.* 1933.

PHILLIMORE, Sir R. *Commentaries on International Law.* 3rd edn. 4 vols. 1875–89.

PIGGOTT, Sir F. T. *The Declaration of Paris, 1856.* 1919.

PRATT, J. W. "The British Blockade and American Precedents." *U.S. Naval Inst. Proc.* vol. xlvi (1920), pp. 1789–1802.

PURYEAR, V. J. *International Economics and Diplomacy in the Near East, 1834–53.* 1935.

PYKE, H. R. *The Law of Contraband of War.* 1915.

RAIKES, T. *A Portion of a Journal, 1831–47.* 4 vols. 1856–7.

RAMSAY, A. A. W. *Idealism and Foreign Policy.* 1925.

REDDAWAY, W. F. *The Monroe Doctrine.* 1898.

REEVES, J. S. *American Diplomacy under Tyler and Polk.* Baltimore, 1907.

RIDDELL, W. R. "Settlement of International Disputes by and between English-speaking Nations." *Yale Law Jour.* vol. xxii (1913), pp. 543–53, 583–9.

RIPPY, J. F. *The Rivalry of the United States and Great Britain for Latin America, 1808–30.* 1929.

ROBERTS, S. H. *History of French Colonial Policy, 1870–1925.* 2 vols. 1929.

SCHAFER, J. "The British Attitude towards the Oregon Question, 1815–46." *Amer. Hist. Rev.* vol. xvi (1911), pp. 273–99.

SCHUYLER, R. L. "Polk and the Oregon Compromise of 1846." *Polit. Science Quart.* vol. xxvi (1911), pp. 443–61.

SETON-WATSON, R. W. *Britain in Europe, 1789–1914: a Survey of Foreign Policy.* 1937.

SIOUSSAT, St G. L. "Duff Green's *England and the United States.*" *Amer. Antiq. Soc. Proc.* new ser. vol. xl (1931), pp. 175–276.

SMITH, E. *England and America after Independence: a Short Examination of their International Intercourse, 1783–1872.* 1900.

SNOW, A. H. *The Question of Aborigines in the Law and Practice of Nations.* 1902.

SOULSBY, H. G. *The Right of Search and the Slave Trade in Anglo-American Relations.* Baltimore, 1933.

TARRING, Sir J. C. *Chapters on the Law relating to the Colonies.* 1906.

TEMPERLEY, H. W. V. *The Foreign Policy of Canning,* 1822–7. 1925.

TWISS, Sir TRAVERS. *The Law of Nations.* 2nd edn. 2 vols. 1875–84.

VAN ALSTYNE, R. W. "American Filibustering and the British Navy: a Caribbean Analogue of Mediterranean Piracy." *Amer. Jour. Internat. Law,* vol. XXXII (1938), pp. 138–42.

—— "Anglo-American Relations, 1853–7. Documents." *Amer. Hist. Rev.* vol. XLII (April 1937), pp. 491–500.

—— "The British Right of Search and the African Slave Trade." *Jour. Mod. Hist.* vol. II (March 1930), pp. 37–47.

—— "British Diplomacy and the Clayton-Bulwer Treaty, 1850–60." *Jour. Mod. Hist.* vol. XI (June 1939), pp. 149–83.

—— "The Central American Policy of Lord Palmerston, 1846–8." *Hispanic Amer. Hist. Rev.* vol. XVI (1936), pp. 339–59.

—— "Great Britain, the United States and Hawaiian Independence, 1850–5." *Pacific Hist. Rev.* vol. IV (1935), pp. 15–24.

WALKER, T. A. *History of the Law of Nations.* 1899.

—— *Science of International Law.* 1893.

WARD, Sir A. W. and GOOCH, G. P. (Eds.). *Cambridge History of British Foreign Policy,* 1783–1919. 3 vols. Cambridge, 1922–3.

WEBSTER, C. K. "Castlereagh and the Spanish Colonies." *Eng. Hist. Rev.* vol. XXVII (Jan. 1912), pp. 78–95; vol. XXX (Oct. 1915), pp. 631–45.

WEBSTER, C. K. *The Foreign Policy of Castlereagh,* 1815–22. 2nd edn. 1934.

—— "The Study of British Foreign Policy (Nineteenth century)." *Amer. Hist. Rev.* vol. XXX (1925), pp. 728–37.

WELLESLEY, Hon. F. A. (Ed.). *The Paris Embassy during the Second Empire: Selections from the Papers of the Earl of Cowley,* 1852–67. 1928.

WESTLAKE, J. *International Law.* 2 vols. 1910–13.

WHEATON, H. *Elements of International Law.* New edn. 1936.

WILLIAMS, M. W. *Anglo-American Isthmian Diplomacy,* 1815–1915. Washington, 1916.

WILLSON, B. *American Ambassadors to England,* 1785–1928. 1929.

—— *Friendly Relations. A Narrative of Britain's Ministers and Ambassadors to America,* 1791–1930. 1934.

—— *The Paris Embassy,* 1814–1920. 1927.

WILSON, G. G. *The Hague Arbitration Cases.* 1915.

viii. *IMPERIAL DEFENCE*

(a) MANUSCRIPT SOURCES

See Part I, 1 and 2 above, particularly the records of the Admiralty and War Office in the Public Record Office. The papers of the Secretary to the Navy Board include a series of "Letters relating to the Colonies, 1697–1839" (Adm. 1/3814–24). Among the War Office papers are "In-Letters, Colonies and Dependencies" (W.O. 1/430–601) and "Out-Letters, Secretary-at-War, General, Colonies, etc. 1783–1858" (W.O. 4/120–343) and "Out-Letters, Secretary of State, Colonies, etc." (W.O. 6/1–213). Ordnance Office papers are in W.O. 55, Warrants in W.O. 24, and Staff Returns in W.O. 25.

(b) OFFICIAL PUBLICATIONS

See Part I, 3 and 4, particularly the following Parliamentary Papers: Corresp. *re* Colonial Military Defence, *Parl. Pap.* 1821, XIV (485); Rept. from Sel. Comm. on Colonial Military Establishments and Expenditure, *Parl. Pap.* 1834, VI (570); Rept. of Commissioners on Consolidating Army Depts., *Parl. Pap.* 1837, XXXIV, Pt. I [78]; Return *re* Military Expenditure, 1843–4 and 1846–7, *Parl. Pap.* 1849, XXXIV (224); Return *re* Colonies, Troops, Commissariat, etc., *Parl. Pap.* 1849, XXXIV (239); Return *re* British Troops in Colonies, 1829, 1835, 1840 and 1847,

Parl. Pap. 1849, XXXII (in 56); Corresp. with New South Wales *re* reduction of troops, *Parl. Pap.* 1851, XXXV (123); Corresp. *re* civil list and military expenditure in Canada, *Parl. Pap.* 1851, XXXVI [1344]; Number of troops in Colonies, 1848–50, *Parl. Pap.* 1852, XXXI (566); Corresp. with West India Colonies *re* removal of troops, *Parl. Pap.* 1854, XLI (177); Return *re* numbers of troops in Colonies, 1851–3, *Parl. Pap.* 1854, XLI (46) Despatches of Governors *re* War with Russia, *Parl. Pap.* 1854–5, XXXVI [1871], (63), [1888], [1940], [1983]; Rept. of Treasury Comm. on Naval Estimates and State of Navy, 1852–8, *Parl. Pap.*, 1859, XIV (182); Return *re* expense of military forces in Colonies, *Parl. Pap.* 1859 Sess. 2, XVII (114); Rept. of Comm. on Expense of Colonial Military Defences, *Parl. Pap.* 1860, XLI (282); Rept. of Commissioners on Defences of U.K., *Parl. Pap.* 1860, XXIII [2682]; Dept. of Sel. Comm. on Colonial Military Expenditure, *Parl. Pap.* 1861, XIII (423); Rept. from Sel. Comm. on Board of Admiralty, *Parl. Pap.* 1861, V (438); Number of Proposals *re* Shot-Proof Ships, *Parl. Pap.* 1862, XXXIV (392); Iron-Cased Ships, *Parl. Pap.* 1862, XXXIV (432); Return *re* Cost of *Warrior*, *Parl. Pap.* 1862, XXXIV (68); Rept. from Sel. Comm. on Ordnance, *Parl. Pap.* 1863, XI (487); Rept. from Sel. Comm. on Army (India and Colonies), *Parl. Pap.* 1867, VII (478); Statements of amounts in Army Estimates for Colonies, *Parl. Pap.* 1866, XLI (61), 1867, XLI (63), 1867–8, XLII (62); Corresp. with New Zealand Governors, *Parl. Pap.* 1868–9, XLVIII (307); Return of Effectives in Colonies for last ten years, 1870, XLII (254).

(c) PERIODICALS

Army Quarterly. London, 1920– . In progress.
Brassey's Naval Annual. London, 1886– . In progress.
Canadian Defence Quarterly. London, 1923– . In progress.
Cavalry Journal. London, 1906– . In progress.
Journal of the Royal United Service Institution. London, 1857– . In progress. The R.U.S.I. was founded in Paris in 1815. The *Journal* becomes valuable for strategy with J. C. R. Colomb's first lecture pubd. in 1869.
Journal of the Society for Army Historical Research. London, 1921– . In progress.
Mariner's Mirror. London, 1911– . In progress.
Naval and Military Magazine. London, 1857– . Title varied. Now incorporated in *Army Quarterly*.
Naval Chronicle. 40 vols. London, 1799–1818.
Naval Review. London, 1911– . In progress.
NAVY RECORDS SOCIETY. Publications. London, 1894– . In progress.
Royal Engineers' Journal. London, 1870– . In progress.
United Service Magazine. 236 vols. London, 1829–1920. Incorporated *Army and Navy Magazine* and *Naval and Military Journal*. See especially vols. for 1859, Pt. I, p. 22, and 1861, Pt. I, p. 528.

The Libraries of the Royal United Service Institution, the Admiralty and War Office contain good collections of early service journals as well as other works.

(d) CONTEMPORARY WRITINGS

BUSK, H. *The Navies of the World.* 1859.
CLODE, C. M. *The Military Forces of the Crown: their Administration and Government.* 2 vols. 1869.
COLOMB, Sir J. C. R. *The Protection of our Commerce and the Distribution of our War Forces considered.* 1867. For later works of Colomb, see below under LATER WORKS.
DILKE, Sir C. W. *Greater Britain.* 1868.
DUNDONALD, Lord. *Observations on Naval Affairs.* 1847.
EDDY, C. W. *Suggestions on Colonial Means of Defence from Naval Attack.* 1865.
FADDY, P. *Essay on the Defence and Military System of Great Britain at Home and Abroad.* 1848.
GREY, Lord. *The Colonial Policy of Lord John Russell's Administration.* 2 vols. 1853. Contains Russell's Despatches on the reduction of the garrisons in New South Wales, 1846–50.

HEAD, Sir F. B. *The Defenceless State of Great Britain.* 1850.
MERIVALE, H. *Lectures on Colonization and the Colonies.* 1861.
MILLS, A. *Colonial Military Expenditure.* 1861.
NAPIER, Sir C. *The Navy: its past and present State.* 1851.
THRING, H. (Baron). *Suggestions for Colonial Reform.* 1865.

(e) LATER WORKS

ALBION, R. G. *Forests and Sea Power: the Timber Problem of the Royal Navy,* 1652–1862, Cambridge, Mass., 1926.
BALLARD, G. A. "The Navy." *Early Victorian England,* vol. I (1934).
BAXTER, J. P. *The Introduction of the Ironclad Warship.* Cambridge, Mass., 1933.
BIDDULPH, Sir R. *Lord Cardwell at the War Office,* 1868–74. 1904.
BODELSEN, C. A. G. *Studies in Mid-Victorian Imperialism.* 1924.
CHAPPELL, M. G. "The Select Committee of 1861 on Colonial Military Expenditure and its Antecedents." 1933. Unpublished thesis in the University of London Library.
CLOWES, Sir W. LAIRD. *History of the Royal Navy.* Vol. VII. 1903.
COLOMB, J. C. R. *Imperial Strategy.* 1871.
—— *The Defence of Great and Greater Britain.* 1880.
—— "British Defence," 1800–1900. *British Dangers.* 1900.
COLOMB, P. H. *Essays on Naval Defences.* 1899.
—— *Memoirs of Admiral Sir Astley Cooper Key.* 1898.
CORBETT, Sir J. S. *Some Principles of Maritime Strategy.* 1911.
D'EGVILLE, Sir H. *Imperial Defence....Sir John Colomb.* 1913.
DILKE, Sir C. W. and WILKINSON, S. *Imperial Defence.* 1892.
FORTESCUE, Hon. Sir J. W. *History of the British Army.* Vols. XI–XIII (1815–70). 3 vols. 1923–30.
HAMILTON, C. F. "The Canadian Militia." *Canadian Defence Quart.,* Oct. 1928, Jan. 1929.
LUCAS, Sir C. P. *The Empire at War.* Oxford, 1921. Vol. I reviews defence policy, 1815–70.
MARTIN, B. KINGSLEY. *The Triumph of Lord Palmerston.* 1924.
MORLEY, JOHN, Lord. *Critical Miscellanies* (1871–7), vol. III, p. 315.
MURRAY, Sir O. A. R. "The Admiralty." *Mariner's Mirror,* vol. XXIV (1938), pp. 329–52, 458–78. Naval administration, 1763–1904.
NAPIER, Sir C. *The Navy: its past and present State.* 1851.
RICHMOND, Sir H. W. *National Policy and Naval Strength.* 1928.
ROBERTSON, F. L. *The Evolution of Naval Armament.* 1921.
ROSE, J. HOLLAND. *Man and the Sea.* 1936.
SENIOR, W. *Naval History in the Law Courts.* 1927.
STACEY, C. P. *Canada and the British Army,* 1846–71. 1936.
THURSFIELD, Sir J. R. *Nelson and other Naval Studies.* 1909.

B. THE HISTORY OF THE COLONIES

For the history of the Dominions, see the bibliographies in vols. VI–VIII

i. *GIBRALTAR, MALTA AND THE IONIAN ISLANDS*

For Manuscript Sources and Official Publications, see Part I above

GIBRALTAR

(a) BIBLIOGRAPHY

ABBOTT, W. C. *An Introduction to the Documents relating to the International Status of Gibraltar,* 1704–1934. New York, 1934.

(b) Contemporary Writings

Ancell, S. *Circumstantial Journal of the Long and Tedious Blockade and Siege oj Gibraltar.* Liverpool, 1785.

Blake, C. *How to Capture and Govern Gibraltar.* 1856.

Cairns, A. *Historic Sketches of Gibraltar and its Neighbourhood.* Melbourne, 1854.

Cockburn, Sir G. *Voyage to Cadiz and Gibraltar.* 2 vols. 1815.

Drinkwater, J. *History of the Late Siege of Gibraltar.* 1790.

Gardiner, Sir R. *Report on Gibraltar considered as a Fortress and a Colony.* 1856.

Heriot, J. *An Historical Sketch of Gibraltar.* 1792.

Le Michaud d'Arçon, J. C. E. *Mémoire pour servir à l'histoire du siège de Gibraltar.* Cadiz, 1783.

Lopez de Ayala, I. and Bell, J. *History of Gibraltar.* 1845.

Martin, R. M. *Gibraltar, its condition, importance.* 1853.

Montero, F. M. *Historia de Gibraltar y de su campo.* Cadiz, 1860.

St Clair. *Propriety of retaining Gibraltar impartially considered.* 1783.

Sayer, F. *History of Gibraltar.* 2nd edn. 2 vols. 1865.

Urquhart, D. *The Pillars of Hercules.* 2 vols. 1848.

(c) Later Works

Garratt, G. T. *Gibraltar and the Mediterranean.* 1938.

History of Gibraltar and its Sieges. 1873.

Kenyon, E. R. *Gibraltar under Moor, Spaniard and Briton.* 1938.

Lord, W. F. *England and France in the Mediterranean, 1660–1830.* 1901.

Lucas, Sir C. P. *Historical geography of the British colonies:* Vol. I, *The Mediterranean and Eastern Colonies;* 2nd edn. rev. by R. E. Stubbs. Oxford, 1906.

Macmillan, A. (Ed.). *Malta and Gibraltar Illustrated.* 1915.

Spilsbury, J. *Journal of the Siege of Gibraltar, 1779–83.* Ed. by B. H. T. Frere. Gibraltar, 1908.

Whitton, F. E. "The Great Siege of Gibraltar, 1779–83." *Blackwood's Mag.,* July, 1937.

MALTA

(a) Contemporary Writings

Bigelow, A. *Travels in Malta and Sicily.* Boston, 1831.

Boisgelin, L. de. *Ancient and Modern Malta.* 2 vols. 1805.

Christophoro d'Avalos, F. A. de. *Tableau historique et politique de Malte et de ses habitants.* 1818.

Cockburn, Sir G. *Voyage to Cadiz and Gibraltar, up the Mediterranean to Sicily and Malta, in 1810 and 1811.* 2 vols. 1815.

Dillon, J. J. *Memoir concerning the Political State of Malta.* 1807.

Eton, W. *Authentic Materials for a History of the People of Malta.* 1802–7. Reprinted 1927.

Mitrovich, G. *The Cause of the People of Malta.* 1836.

Mustoxidi, A. *Al dispaccio dei 10 Aprile 1840 da Sir Howard Douglas…Confutazione.* Malta, 1841.

Penn, G. *The policy and interest of Great Britain with respect to Malta.* 1805.

Porter, W. "History of the fortress of Malta." *Royal United Service Inst. Mag.* vol. v (1861), pp. 19–30.

Seddall, H. *Malta, Past and Present.* 1870.

Tallack, W. *Malta under the Phoenicians, Knights, and English.* 1861.

Webster, W. B. *English Governors and Foreign Grumblers, or Malta in 1864.* 1864.

Wilkinson, C. *Epitome of the History of Malta and Gozo.* 1804.

Wood, Sir M. *Importance of Malta considered in the Years 1796 and 1798.* 1803.

(b) Later Works

Badger, G. P. *Historical Guide to Malta and Gozo.* Malta, 1878.

Bartolo, Sir A. *Admiral Troubridge: a page of Maltese history retold.* [Valetta], 1913.

BARTOLO, Sir A. "History of the Maltese Islands," in A. Macmillan, *Malta and Gibraltar* (1915), pp. 9–172.
—— *Sovereignty of Malta and the Nature of its Title.* Malta, 1909.
BUSUTTIL, V. *Summary of the History of Malta.* Valetta, 1903.
Daily Malta Chronicle. Special Number dealing with Malta past and present, ed. by Sir A. Bartolo. [Valetta], 1913.
DIXON, C. W. *The Colonial Administrations of Sir Thomas Maitland.* 1940.
HARDMAN, W. *History of Malta,* 1798–1815, ed. by J. H. Rose. 1909.
LAFERLA, A. V. *British Malta.* Vol. I. 1800–72. Malta, 1938.
—— *Gleanings from the history of Malta,* June–Sept. 1798. Malta, 1908.
—— "Malta in the diplomatic history of the Napoleonic Wars." *Melita,* vol. I (1921), pp. 1–8 *et seq.*
—— "Sir Thomas Maitland." *Archivum Melitense,* vol. I (1911), pp. 50–57.
LORD, W. FREWEN. *Sir Thomas Maitland.* 1897.
MACMILLAN, A. (Ed.). *Malta and Gibraltar Illustrated.* 1915.
RUTTER, J. G. *Illustrated Guide to Malta and Gozo, with a Short History of the Maltese Islands.* Valetta, 1930.
RYAN, F. W. "*The House of the Temple*": *a Study of Malta and its Knights in the French Revolution.* 1930.
SCHERMERHORN, E. W. *Malta of the Knights.* [1929.]
SCICLUNA, H. P. (Ed.). *Documents relating to the French occupation of Malta in* 1798–1800. Valetta, 1923.
TENISON, E. M. *Short History of the Order of St John of Jerusalem.* 1922.
VIVIANI, L. *Storia di Malta.* 3 vols. 1934.
WINTERBERG, A. *Malta: Geschichte und Gegenwart.* Leipzig, 1879.
ZAMMIT, Sir T. *Malta: the Islands and their History.* 2nd edn. Valetta, 1929.
The following periodicals contain valuable articles and documents: *Archivum Melitense* (Valetta, 1910–). *Bulletin of the Institute of Historical Research, Malta* (Valetta, 1931–); *Archivio Storico di Malta* (Rome, 1929–).

IONIAN ISLANDS

(a) BIBLIOGRAPHIES

LEGRAND, E. L. J. *Bibliographie Ionienne.* 2 vols. Paris, 1910. See also the occasional bibliographies by W. Miller of recent work in Modern Greek History in *Cambridge Historical Journal,* vols. II and VI, and *American Historical Review,* vols. XXXVII and XL.

(b) CONTEMPORARY WRITINGS

ANSTED, D. T. *The Ionian Islands in the year 1863.* 1863.
BOWEN, G. F. *The Ionian Islands under British Protection.* 1851.
Constitutional Chart of the United States of the Ionian Islands as passed on 2nd May 1817. 1818.
DAVY, J. *Notes on the Ionian Islands and Malta.* 2 vols. 1842.
GIFFARD, E. *A Short Visit to the Ionian Islands.* 1837.
HOLLAND, Sir H. *Travels in the Ionian Isles.* 1815.
ILENOS, S. *East and West (The Annexation of the Ionian Islands to the Kingdom of Greece).* 1865.
KIRKWALL, Lord. *Four Years in the Ionian Islands.* 1864.
LAUDERDALE, 8th Earl of. *Substance of the Earl of Lauderdale's Speech in the House of Lords on moving for Despatches, etc., explanatory of Sir Thomas Maitland's Conduct as Lord High Commissioner of the Ionian Islands.* 1820.
NAPIER, Sir C. J. *The Colonies...of the Ionian Islands in particular.* 1833.
PAPANICOLAS, G. D. *The Ionian Islands: what they have lost.* n.d.
—— *Usque adeo? or, What may be said for the Ionian People.* 1853.
SMITH, G. *The Empire.* 1863. Pp. 232–56 deal with the Ionian Islands.
TURNER, W. *Journal of a tour in the Levant.* 3 vols. 1820. Part of Vol. I deals with the Ionian Islands.
VAUDONCOURT, F. G. DE. *Memoirs of the Ionian Islands.* 1816.

(c) LATER WORKS

BUTLER, L. "Minor expeditions of the British Army: XI. Capture of the Ionian Islands." *United Service Mag.* XXXII (1906), pp. 295–302.
DIXON, C. W. *Sir Thomas Maitland.* 1940.
HIDROMENOS, A. M. *Political History of the Seven Islands, 1815–64.* 2nd edn. Corfu, 1935.
HILLS, N. L. *Life of Sir Woodbine Parish.* 1910.
LAFERLA, A. V. "Sir Thomas Maitland." *Archivum Melitense,* vol. I (1911), pp. 50–7.
LORD, W. FREWEN. *Lost possessions of England.* 1896.
—— *Sir Thomas Maitland.* 1897.
MILLER, W. *History of the Greek People, 1821–1921.* 1922.
—— (Ed.). "Three Letters on the Ionian Islands, 1850–3." *Eng. Hist. Rev.* vol. XLIII (April 1928), pp. 240–6.
MINOTTO, S. D. *Les forts de Corfou et leur démolition.* Athens, 1937.
MORLEY, Lord. "The Ionian Islands." *Life of Gladstone* (1903), vol. I, pp. 594–620.
TEMPERLEY, H. W. V. (Ed.). "Documents illustrating the Cession of the Ionian Islands to Greece, 1848–70." *Jour. Mod. Hist.* vol. IX (March 1937), pp. 48–55.
THEOTOKES, Count S. [Gladstone's Mission to the Ionian Islands.] Corfu, 1924. In Greek.
WARD, Sir A. W. "Greece and the Ionian Islands." *Cambridge History of British Foreign Policy,* vol. II, chap. XIV. Cambridge, 1923.

ii. *WEST INDIES, BERMUDA, BRITISH HONDURAS AND BRITISH GUIANA*

For Manuscript Sources and Official Publications see Part I above, particularly the following Parliamentary Papers: Rept. from Sel. Comm. on Commercial State of West Indies, *Parl. Pap.* 1807, III (65); Rept. from Sel. Comm. on Commercial State of West Indies, *Parl. Pap.* 1831–2, XX (381); Rept. from Sel. Comm. on State of West Indies, *Parl. Pap.* 1842, XIII (479); Rept. from Sel. Comm. on Sugar Duties, *Parl. Pap.* 1862, XLIII (390); Repts. from Sel. Comm. on Late Disturbances in Jamaica, *Parl. Pap.* 1866, XXX [3602], [3683], XXI [3683–1]. The Annual Reports of the Governors printed as Parliamentary Papers from 1849 onwards and the Annual Reports of the Colonial Land and Emigration Commissioners from 1842 are invaluable.

WEST INDIES

(a) BIBLIOGRAPHIES AND GUIDES TO MATERIALS

BELL, H. C., PARKER, D. W. and others. *Guide to the British West Indian Archive Materials, in London and in the Islands, for the History of the United States.* Washington, 1926.
CUNDALL, F. *Bibliographia Jamaicensis.* Kingston, 1902. *Supplement,* 1908.
—— *Bibliography of the West Indies, excluding Jamaica.* Kingston, 1909.
LEWIN, E. *Subject Catalogue of the Library of the Royal Empire Society.* Vol. III. 1932.
LINCOLN, W. "List of Newspapers of the West Indies and Bermuda in the Library of the American Antiquarian Society." *Proc. Amer. Antiq. Soc.* vol. XXXVI (1926), pp. 130–55.
NEW YORK PUBLIC LIBRARY. *List of Works relating to the West Indies.* New York, 1912.
PARES, R. "Public records in British West India Islands." *Bull. Inst. Hist. Research,* vol. VII (1930), pp. 149–57.
RAGATZ, L. J. *A Guide for the Study of British Caribbean History, 1763–1834.* Washington, 1932.
—— *A Guide to the Official Correspondence of the British West India Colonies with the Secretary of State, 1763–1833.* 2nd edn. 1929.
WEST INDIA COMMITTEE. *Catalogue of the Library of the West India Committee.* 1912.

(b) CONTEMPORARY WRITINGS

For works on Slavery and the Slave Trade, see Part II, A. iii,
"Humanitarian Movement," above

Antidote to West India Sketches, drawn from Authentic Sources..., Nos. 1–6. 1816.
[BAYLEY, F. W. N.] *Four Years' Residence in the West Indies.* 1833.
BUXTON, C. *Slavery and Freedom in the British West Indies.* 1860.
COKE, T. *A History of the West Indies. With an Account of the Missions.* 3 vols. 1811.
COLERIDGE, H. N. *Six Months' Residence in the West Indies in 1825.* 1826.
"Colonial Policy; West India Distress." *Edinburgh Rev.* (1831), pp. 330–51.
CUST, R. J. *Treatise on the West Indian Encumbered Estates Acts.* 1859. 2nd edn. 1865. Supplement, 1874.
DAVIS, W. D. *Remarks on the Constitution of the Judicatures, with Comments on the Administration of Justice in the West Indies.* Grenada [1833].
DAVY, J. *The West Indies, before and since Slave Emancipation.* 1854. Valuable and reliable.
DAY, C. W. *Five Years' Residence in the West Indies.* 2 vols. 1852.
DESSALLES, A. *Histoire générale des Antilles.* 5 vols. Paris, 1847–48.
EDWARDS, B. *History, Civil and Commercial, of the British Colonies in the West Indies.* 2 vols. 1793. 5th edn. 5 vols. 1819.
—— *Thoughts on the Late Proceedings of Government respecting the Trade of the West Indian Islands with the United States of North America.* 1784.
EDWARDS, B. & YOUNG, Sir W. *Historical Survey of the Island of Saint Domingo...and a History of the War in the West Indies in 1793 and 1794.* 1801.
Extracts from Papers printed by Order of the House of Commons, 1839, re the West Indies. 1840.
Facts Relative to the Conduct of the War in the West Indies Collected from the Speech of the Rt Hon. Henry Dundas. 1796.
GURNEY, J. J. *A Winter in the West Indies.* 1840. 3rd edn. 1841.
HALLIDAY, Sir A. *The West Indies.* 1837.
HELPS, Sir A. *Conquerors of the New World and their Bondsmen.* 2 vols. 1848–52.
INNES, J. *Thoughts on the Present State of the British West India Colonies.* 1840.
LOWE, J. *Inquiry into the State of the British West Indies.* 1807.
MACDONNELL, A. *Colonial Commerce.* 1828.
MADDEN, R. R. *Twelve Months' Residence in the West Indies during the Transition from Slavery to Apprenticeship.* 2 vols. 1835.
M'QUEEN, J. *The West Indian Colonies.* 1825.
PINCKARD, G. *Notes on the West Indies.* 3 vols. 1806.
PRINGLE, J. W. *Remarks on the State and Prospects of the West India Colonies.* 1839.
RAYNAL, G. T. F. *Philosophical and Political History of the Settlement and Trade of the Europeans in the East and West Indies.* 4 vols. 1776. Also 1788 edn. in 8 vols. and 1818 edn. in 3 vols.
REGNAULT, E. *Histoire des Antilles.* Paris, 1844.
SAINT CLAIR, T. S. *Residence in the West Indies.* 2 vols. 1834.
SEWELL, W. G. *Ordeal of Free Labor in the British West Indies.* New York, 1861. A sympathetic but critical account of the progress of the colonies after emancipation.
SOUTHEY, T. *Chronological History of the West Indies.* 3 vols. 1827.
STEPHEN, J. *Crisis of the Sugar Colonies.* 1802.
—— *The Opportunity: or Reasons for an Immediate Alliance with St Domingo.* 1804.
STURGE, J. and HARVEY, T. *The West Indies in 1837.* 1838.
TAZEWELL, L. W. *Review of Negotiations between the U.S. and Great Britain on Commerce, especially...the West Indies.* 1829.
TROLLOPE, ANTHONY. *The West Indies and the Spanish Main.* 1860.
UNDERHILL, E. B. *The West Indies.* 1862.
WALKER, J. *Letters on the West Indies.* 1818.
WENTWORTH, T. *West India Sketch Book.* 2 vols. 1835.
West India Reporter. London, 1827–32. Organ of the West India Committee.

West India Sketches drawn from Authentic Sources. 1816–17. Series of pamphlets issued by the African Institution.

WILLIAMSON, J. *Medical and Miscellaneous Observations relative to the West India Islands.* 2 vols. Edinburgh, 1817.

WILLYAMS, C. *Account of the Campaign in the West Indies in the Year* 1794. 1796.

WINTERBOTHAM, W. *Historical, Geographical, and Philosophical View of the American United States, and of the European Settlements in America and the West Indies.* 4 vols. 1795.

WOODCOCK, H. I. *The Laws and Constitution of the British Colonies in the West Indies having Legislative Assemblies.* 1838.

YOUNG, Sir W. *West India Common-place Book, compiled from Parliamentary and Official Documents.* 1807.

(*c*) LATER WORKS

ARCHER, J. H. LAWRENCE. *Monumental Inscriptions of the British West Indies.* 1875.

ASPINALL, Sir A. E. *British West Indies: their History, Resources, and Progress.* 1912.

—— *West Indian Tales of Old.* 1912.

BELL, H. C. "British commercial policy in the West Indies, 1783–93." *Eng. Hist. Rev.* vol. XXXI (1916), pp. 429–41.

CALDECOTT, A. *The Church in the West Indies.* 1898. Valuable for the history of disestablishment in the West Indies.

Colonial and Indian Exhibition. 1886. A great deal of detailed official information about the different islands in the West Indies, with some historical retrospect.

CUNDALL, F. *Political and Social Disturbances in the West Indies.* Kingston, 1906.

DAVIS, N. D. *Westward Ho! with Nelson in* 1805. Demerara, 1896.

EDEN, C. H. *The West Indies.* 1880.

FISKE, A. A. *The West Indies.* 1899. Story of the Nations Series.

FROUDE, J. A. *The English in the West Indies.* 1888. Strongly biased in favour of the planters.

HANNAY, D. "Spanish Trade with the Indies." *Edinburgh Rev.* vol. CCXXVIII (1918), pp. 247–64.

HART, F. R. *Admirals of the Caribbean.* 1923.

HIGHAM, C. S. S. "Sir Henry Taylor and the Establishment of Crown Colony Government in the West Indies, 1871." *Scot. Hist. Rev.* vol. XXIII (1926), pp. 92–6.

JOHNSTONE, R. "Nelson in the West Indies." *Jour. Inst. Jamaica*, vol. II (1897), pp. 380–412 *et seq.*

KENNEDY, A. *Story of the West Indies* (1898). Story of the Empire.

LANG, J. *Outposts of Empire.* 1908. Romance of Empire.

LUCAS, Sir C. P. *Historical Geography of the British Colonies.* Vol. II, *West Indies.* Oxford. 1890. 2nd edn. revised by C. Atchley, 1905.

MARTINEAU, A. and MAY, L. PH. "Trois siècles d'histoire Antillaise." *Rev. Hist. Coloniale*, vol. XXIII (1935), pp. 205–48.

NEWTON, A. P. "The West Indies in International Politics, 1550–1850." *History*, vol. XIX (1934–5), pp. 197–207, 302–10.

OLIVER, V. L. *Caribbeana, being Miscellaneous Papers relating to the History, Genealogy, Topography and Antiquities of the British West Indies.* Vols. I–VI, pt. 4, 1910–19.

PENSON, L. M. *Colonial Agents of the British West Indies.* 1924.

—— "The London West India Interest in the 18th Century." *Eng. Hist. Rev.* vol. XXXVI (1921), pp. 373–92.

PITMAN, F. W. "The West Indian Absentee Planter as a British Colonial Type." *Proc. Pacific Coast Branch Amer. Hist. Assoc.*, 1927, pp. 113 *et seq.*

RAGATZ, L. J. "Absentee Landlordism in the British Caribbean, 1750–1833." *Agricultural History*, Jan. 1931, pp. 7–24.

—— *Les Antilles dans l'histoire coloniale anglaise de l'Amérique du Nord.* Paris, 1935.

—— *Fall of the Planter Class in the British Caribbean, 1763–1833.* New York, 1928. A mine of information.

—— *Statistics for the Study of British Caribbean Economic History.* 1928.

—— *The West India approach to the Study of American Colonial History.* 1935.

RODWAY, J. *West Indies and the Spanish Main.* 1896. Story of the Nations Series.

SIEBERT, W. H. *Legacy of the American Revolution to the British West Indies and Bahamas.* Columbus, O., 1913.

TILBY, A. W. "Britain in the Tropics, 1527–1910." 1912. *English People Overseas,* vol. IV. Pp. 23–65 relate to the West Indies.

WRONG, H. *Government of the West Indies.* Oxford, 1923. A good account of constitutional development in the West Indies.

Jamaica

(a) BIBLIOGRAPHIES

CUNDALL, F. *Bibliographia Jamaicensis:* a list of Jamaica books and pamphlets, magazines, articles, newspapers, and maps, most of which are in the Library of the Institute of Jamaica. Kingston, 1902. *Supplement,* 1908.

(b) CONTEMPORARY WRITINGS

Addresses to His Excellency Edward John Eyre. 1866.

BECKFORD, W. *Descriptive Account of the Islands of Jamaica.* 2 vols. 1790.

BIGELOW, J. *Jamaica in 1850.* 1851.

BLEBY, H. *The Reign of Terror: a Narrative of Facts concerning Ex-Governor Eyre, George William Gordon, and the Jamaica Atrocities.* 1868.

BRIDGES, G. W. *Annals of Jamaica.* 2 vols. 1828.

BROWNE, P. *Civil and Natural History of Jamaica.* 1789.

BURGE, W. *Reply to the Letter by the Marquis of Sligo to the Marquis of Normanby, relative to the Present State of Jamaica.* 1839.

—— *Speech of W. Burge, Esq., Q.C., Agent for Jamaica, at the bar of the House of Commons, against the Bill intituled "an Act to make Temporary Provision for the Govt. of Jamaica",* Monday, April 22nd, 1839. 1839.

DALLAS, R. C. *History of the Maroons.* 2 vols. 1803.

DROUIN-DE-BERCY, M. *Histoire civile et commerciale de la Jamaïque.* Paris, 1818.

EDWARDS, B. *Proceedings of the Governor and Assembly of Jamaica in regard to the Maroon Negroes.* 1796.

Farewell Address of the Inhabitants of Jamaica to the Rt Hon. Sir Charles Theophilus Metcalfe. Kingston, 1842.

FINLASON, W. F. *Commentaries upon Martial Law, with an introduction containing Comments upon the Jamaica Case.* 1867.

—— *History of the Jamaica Case.* 1869.

—— *Justice to a Colonial Governor: or, Some Considerations on the Case of Mr Eyre.* 1868.

—— *Report of the Case of the Queen v. Edward John Eyre.* 1868.

FOULKS, T. *Eighteen Months in Jamaica, with Recollections of the Late Rebellion.* 1833.

LEWIS, M. G. *Journal of a West India Proprietor.* 1834.

[LUCKOCK, B.] *Jamaica: Enslaved and Free.* [1846.]

M'MAHON, B. *Jamaica Plantership.* 1839.

Marly: or the Life of a Planter in Jamaica. 1828.

MARTIN, B. *Jamaica, as it was, as it is, and as it may be.* 1835.

MILNER, T. H. *Present and Future State of Jamaica considered.* 1839.

NUGENT, Lady M. *Journal of a Voyage to, and Residence in, the Island of Jamaica from 1801 to 1805.* 2 vols. 1839. New edn. by F. Cundall. 1934.

PHILLIPPO, J. M. *Jamaica, its Past and Present State.* Philadelphia, 1843.

PRICE, G. E. *Jamaica and the Colonial Office: Who Caused the Crisis?* 1866.

PRINGLE, H. *The Fall of the Sugar Planters of Jamaica.* 1869. A former stipendiary magistrate in the island, with first-hand knowledge of the conditions.

RENNY, R. *A History of Jamaica.* 1807.

SLIGO, Lord. *Letter to the Marquess of Normanby relative to the Present State of Jamaica.* 1839.

STEWART, J. *An Account of Jamaica and its Inhabitants.* 1808.

—— *A View of the Past and Present State of Jamaica.* 1823.

UNDERHILL, E. B. *Letter addressed to the Rt Hon. E. Cardwell.* 1865.
WILLIAMS, B. T. *The Case of George William Gordon.* 1866.
WILLIAMS, C. R. *Tour through the Island of Jamaica.* 1826.
The following local periodicals contain valuable material: *Jamaica Despatch,* 1832– ; *Kingston Chronicle,* 1805– ; *Royal Gazette,* 1780– ; *Watchman,* 1829–32, continued as *Jamaica Watchman,* 1832–65.

(c) LATER WORKS

CROFTON, W. C. *A Brief Sketch of the Life of Charles Baron Metcalfe.* Kingston, Ontario, 1846.
CUNDALL, F. *Biographical Annals of Jamaica.* Kingston, 1904.
—— "Governors of Jamaica." *West India Circular,* vol. XXXIV (1919), pp. 8–9 *et seq.* Biographical accounts of the Governors of Jamaica, commencing with Edward Doyley. Two volumes, dealing with 17th and 18th century Governors, have been published in book form.
—— *Historic Jamaica.* 1915.
—— "Jamaica in the Past and Present." *Soc. Arts Jour.* vol. XLIV (1896), pp. 104–30.
—— *Studies in Jamaica History.* 1900.
DELANY, F. X. *A History of the Catholic Church in Jamaica.* New York, 1931.
GARDNER, W. J. *History of Jamaica.* 1873. New edn. by A. W. Gardner. 1909. The standard history of Jamaica.
GAUNT, M. *Where the Twain Meet.* 1922.
GRANT, Sir J. P. *Jamaica and its Governor during the Last Six Years.* 1871.
HUME, A. H. *The Life of Edward John Eyre.* 1867.
INSTITUTE OF JAMAICA. *Journal.* 2 vols. Kingston, 1891–9.
KAYE, Sir J. W. *The Life and Correspondence of Charles, Lord Metcalfe.* 2 vols. 1858.
MATHIESON, W. L. *The Sugar Colonies and Governor Eyre,* 1849–66. 1936. See also the same author's works on slavery and the slave trade.
MUSGRAVE, Sir A. "Jamaica: Now and Fifteen Years since." *Jour. Royal Colonial Inst.* vol. XI (1879–80), pp. 225–70.
OLIVIER, Lord. *Jamaica, the Blessed Isle.* 1936.
—— *The Myth of Governor Eyre.* 1933. A re-examination of the case against Governor Eyre in respect of the Jamaica rebellion of 1865.
STEPHENS, J. E. R. (Ed.). *Supreme Court Decisions of Jamaica and Privy Council Decisions from 1774 to 1923.* 2 vols. 1924.
THOMPSON, E. J. *The Life of Charles, Lord Metcalfe.* 1937.
UNDERHILL, E. B. *The Tragedy of Morant Bay: a Narrative of the Disturbances in the Island of Jamaica in 1865.* 1895.
—— *Life of J. M. Phillippo.* 1881.
WYNDHAM, Hon. H. A. "The case of Governor Eyre." *Chambers's Jour.* Feb. 1925, pp. 105–7.

Bahamas

(a) CONTEMPORARY WRITINGS

HARVEY, T. C. *Official Reports of the Out Islands of the Bahamas.* 1858.
McKINNEN, D. *Tour through the British West Indies in the Years* 1802 *and* 1803, *giving a Particular Account of the Bahama Islands.* 1804.
Review of that Portion of Sir Charles B. Adderley's Review of Earl Grey's Colonial Policy and Lord J. Russell's Administration, and the subsequent Colonial History, which relates to the Bahamas. Nassau, 1870.

(b) LATER WORKS

CARTER, Sir G. T. *General Descriptive Report of the Bahama Islands.* 1902.
HASSAN, J. T. (Ed.). *Bahama Islands.* 1899.
MALCOLM, H. G. (Ed.). *Historical Documents relating to the Bahama Islands.* Nassau, 1910.
—— *History of the Bahamas House of Assembly.* Nassau, 1921.

MALCOLM, H. G. (Ed.). *List of Documents relating to the Bahama Islands in the British Museum and Record Office, London.* Nassau, 1910.
MOSELEY, M. *The Bahamas Handbook.* Nassau, 1926.
POWLES, L. D. *Land of the Pink Pearl: or Recollections of Life in the Bahamas.* 1888.
SHATTUCK, G. B. *The Bahama Islands.* New York, 1905.
SIEBERT, W. H. *Legacy of the American Revolution to the British West Indies and Bahamas.* Columbus, O., 1913.
STARK, J. H. *Stark's History and Guide to the Bahama Islands.* Boston, 1891.
WRIGHT, J. M. "History of the Bahama Islands." Shattuck's *Bahama Islands* (1905), pp. 419–588.

Barbados
(a) CONTEMPORARY WRITINGS

ORDERSON, J. W. *Creolana: or Social and Domestic Scenes and Incidents in Barbados in Days of Yore.* 1842.
POYER, J. *History of Barbados.* 1808.
SCHOMBURGK, Sir R. H. *History of Barbados.* 1847.

(b) LATER WORKS

BARRAUD, C. W. *The Records of Barbados.* 1902–4.
DAVIS, N. D. *Westward Ho! with Nelson in 1805.* Georgetown, 1896.
HAYNES, R. *The Barbadian Diary of Gen. Robert Haynes, 1787–1836.* Medstead, 1934.
REECE, J. E. and CLARK-HUNT, C. G. (Eds.). *Barbados Diocesan History* [1825–1925]. 1928.
SINCKLER, E. G. *The Barbados Handbook.* 1912.
STARK, J. H. *Stark's History and Guide to the Barbados and the Caribbee Islands.* Boston, 1893.
STARKEY, O. P. *The Economic Geography of Barbados.* New York, 1939.

Leeward Islands
(a) CONTEMPORARY WRITINGS

ATWOOD, T. *History of the Island of Dominica.* 1791.
FLANAGAN, Mrs. *Antigua and the Antiguans.* 2 vols. 1844.
JOHNSON, J. *Historical and Descriptive Account of Antigua.* 1830.
Letters from the Virgin Islands illustrative of Life and Manners in the West Indies. 1843.
LUFFMAN, J. *Brief Account of the Island of Antigua.* 1789.

(b) LATER WORKS

BERKELEY, T. B. H. "Leeward Islands: their Past and Present Condition." *Proc. Royal Colonial Inst.* vol. XII (1880–1), pp. 9–50.
BURDON, Lady K. J. *Handbook of St Kitts-Nevis.* 1920.
[DAVIS, N. D.] *One Hundred Years Ago: or the Battle of Dominica.* Darnell Davis's *Pamphlets*, vol. I, no. 2. Demerara, 1882.
HIGHAM, C. S. S. "The General Assembly of the Leeward Islands." *Eng. Hist. Rev.* vol. XLI (1926), pp. 190–209, 366–88.
KING, G. H. *The Gibraltar of the West Indies.* Brimston Hill, St Kitts, 1933.
MORRIS, Sir D. "Colony of the Leeward Islands." *Proc. Royal Colonial Inst.* vol. XXII (1890–1), pp. 226–63.
OLIVER, V. L. *History of the Island of Antigua.* 3 vols. 1894–9.
ST JOHNSTON, Sir T. R. *French Invasions of St Kitts-Nevis.* Antigua, 1931.
—— *Leeward Islands during the French Wars.* Antigua, 1932.
WATKINS, F. H. *Handbook of the Leeward Islands.* 1924.

Trinidad and Tobago
(a) CONTEMPORARY WRITINGS

BURNLEY, W. H. *Observations on the Present Condition of the Island of Trinidad.* 1842.
CARMICHAEL, Mrs A. C. *Five Years in Trinidad and St Vincent.* 2 vols. 1834.
DE VERTEUIL, L. A. A. *Trinidad.* 1858.

DRAPER, E. A. *Address to the British Public on the Case of Brig.-Genl. Picton, late Governor and Capt.-Genl. of the Island of Trinidad.* 1806.

FULLARTON, W. *A Statement, Letters and Documents respecting the Affairs of Trinidad.* 1804.

GAMBLE, W. H. *Trinidad, Historical and Descriptive.* 1866.

HART, D. *Trinidad and the Other West India Islands and Colonies.* 2nd edn. 1866.

JOSEPH, E. I. *History of Trinidad.* Port-of-Spain, 1838.

LAVAYSSE, J. F. D. *Statistical, Commercial and Political Description of Venezuela, Trinidad, Margarita, and Tobago.* 1820.

—— *Voyage aux Iles de Trinidad, Tobago....* 2 vols. Paris, 1813.

M'CALLUM, P. F. *Political Account of the Island of Trinidad.* 1807.

—— *Travels in Trinidad.* 1805.

MARRYAT, J. *Substance of a Speech delivered in the House of Commons upon Mr Hume's Motion for Appointing a Commission of Inquiry to Report on the State of the Island of Trinidad.* 1823.

PICTON, Sir T. *Letters Addressed to the Rt Hon. Lord Hobart.* 1804.

ROBINSON, H. B. *Memoirs of Lt.-Genl. Sir Thomas Picton.* 2 vols. 1836.

VINDEX [i.e. WILMOT HORTON, HYDE VILLIERS, and Major MOODY]. *Considerations Submitted in Defence of the Orders in Council for the Melioration of Slavery in Trinidad.* 1825.

WOODCOCK, H. I. *History of Tobago.* 1867.

(b) LATER WORKS

BODU, J. M. *Trinidadiana: being a Chronological Review of Events which have occurred in the Island from the Conquest to the Present Day.* Port-of-Spain, 1890.

BORDE, P. G. L. *Histoire de l'île de la Trinidad sous le gouvernement espagnol (1498 à 1797).* 2 vols. Paris, 1882.

CARDEW, F. G. *Taking of Tobago, 1793. Jour. Royal United Service Inst.* vol. LXX (1925), pp. 411–15.

COLLENS, J. H. *Handbook of Trinidad and Tobago.* Port-of-Spain, 1912.

FRASER, L. M. *History of Trinidad from 1781 to 1839.* 2 vols. Port-of-Spain, 1891–96.

Handbook of Trinidad and Tobago. Port-of-Spain, 1924.

HAY, L. G. *Handbook of the Colony of Tobago.* 1884.

INNISS, L. O. *Trinidad and Trinidadiana: a Collection of Papers, Historical, Social, and Descriptive.* Port-of-Spain, 1910.

REIS, C. *The Government of Trinidad.* 2nd. edn. 1931. A history.

STARK, J. H. *Stark's Guide Book and History of Trinidad.* 1897.

WISE, K. S. *Historical Sketches of Trinidad and Tobago.* 4 vols. Trinidad Hist. Soc., 1936–8.

Windward Islands

Grenada

Brief Inquiry into the Causes of, and Conduct pursued by, the Colonial Government for quelling the Insurrection in Grenada. 1796.

DAVIS, W. D. *Practical Summary of the Constitution of the Colony of Grenada.* Grenada, [1877].

GARRAWAY, D. G. *Short Account of the Insurrection of 1795–6.* St George's, [1877].

HAY, J. *A Narrative of the Insurrection in the Island of Grenada, 1795.* 1823.

TURNBULL, G. *Narrative of the Revolt and Insurrection of the French Inhabitants of the Island of Grenada.* Edinburgh, 1795.

WELLS, S. *Historical and Descriptive Sketch of the Island of Grenada.* Kingston, 1890.

St Lucia

BREEN, H. H. *St Lucia: Historical, Statistical, and Descriptive.* 1844.

McHUGH, R. F. *Handbook and Guide to St Lucia.* 1890.

WILLYAMS, C. *Account of the Campaign in the West Indies in the year 1794...with the reduction of the Islands of Martinique, St Lucia...* 1796.

St Vincent

ANDERSON, R. M. *St Vincent Handbook, Directory, and Almanac.* Kingston, 1909, 1911, 1914.
MORRIS, V. *A Narrative of the Official Conduct of Valentine Morris, Esq., late Capt. Genl., Governor in Chief, etc., of the Island of St Vincent.* 1787.
MUSGRAVE, T. B. C. *Historical and Descriptive Sketch of the Colony of St Vincent.* [St Vincent], 1891.
SHEPHARD, C. *Historical Sketch of the Island of St Vincent.* 1831.
YOUNG, Sir W. *Account of the Black Charaibs in the Island of St Vincent's.* 1795.

BERMUDA

(*a*) CONTEMPORARY WORKS

COTTER, R. *Sketches of Bermuda.* 1828.
GODET, T. L. *Bermuda.* 1860.
LLOYD, S. H. *Sketches of Bermuda.* 1835.
[WHITTINGHAM, F.] *Bermuda, a Colony, a Fortress and a Prison.* 1857.
WILLIAMS, W. F. *Historical and Statistical Account of the Bermudas.* 1848.

(*b*) LATER WORKS

GREENE, J. M. "Bermuda, alias Somers Island: historical sketch." *Jour. Amer. Geog. Soc.* vol. XXXIII (1901), pp. 220–42.
HAYWARD, W. B. *Bermuda, Past and Present.* [1923.]
KERR, W. B. *Bermuda and the American Revolution.* Princeton, 1936.
OGILVY, J. *An Account of Bermuda, Past and Present.* Hamilton, 1883.
STARK, J. H. *Stark's Illustrated Bermuda Guide.* 1897.
STRODE, H. *The Story of Bermuda.* 1932. Reissue, 1935.
TUCKER, A. T. *Correspondence and Letters of a Bermuda Merchant, 1779–99.* St George's Hist. Soc. [Hamilton], 1930.
VERRILL, A. E. "Relations between Bermuda and the American Colonies during the Revolutionary War." *Connecticut Acad. Trans.* vol. XIII (1907), pp. 47–64.

BRITISH HONDURAS

(*a*) CONTEMPORARY WORKS

Defence of the Settlers of Honduras against the Unjust and Unfounded Representations of Col. George Arthur. Jamaica, 1824.
HENDERSON, G. *An Account of the British Settlements of Honduras.* 1811.
Honduras Almanac, 1828. Belize, 1828.
TEMPLE, R. "On British Honduras, its History, Trade, and Natural Resources." *Jour. Soc. Arts,* vol. V (1857), pp. 113–30.

(*b*) LATER WORKS

BRISTOWE, L. W. and WRIGHT, P. B. *Handbook of British Honduras for 1888–9.* 1888, 1889–90, 1890–1, 1891–2, 1892–3.
BURDON, Sir J. A. *Archives of British Honduras.* 3 vols. 1931–5. A very useful series of extracts and summaries of archives, many of which have since been destroyed by fire or flood.
—— *Brief Sketch of British Honduras.* 1928.
FOWLER, H. *Narrative of a Journey across the Unexplored Portion of British Honduras.* 1879.
GIBBS, A. R. *British Honduras.* 1883.
JOHNSTON, Sir H. H. *Pioneers in Tropical America.* Pioneers of Empire. 1914.
METZGEN, M. S. and CAIN, H. E. C. *Handbook of British Honduras.* 1925.
MORRIS, D. *The Colony of British Honduras.* 1883.
WILLIAMS, E. W. *The Baymen of Belize and how they wrested British Honduras from the Spaniards.* 1914.

BRITISH GUIANA

(a) BIBLIOGRAPHIES

NIJHOFF, M. *Livres anciens et modernes...les Guyanes néerlandaises, anglaises et françaises, et les Antilles néerlandaises.* La Haye, 1907.

NOUVION, V. DE. *Extraits des auteurs et voyageurs qui ont écrit sur la Guyane, suivis du catalogue bibliographique de la Guyane.* Paris, 1844. (Soc. d'Études pour la colonisation de la Guyane française, No. 4.) Paris, 1844.

(b) CONTEMPORARY WORKS

BOLINGBROKE, H. *Voyage to the Demerary.* 1809.

BRYANT, J. *Account of an Insurrection of the Negro Slaves in the Colony of Demerara.* Georgetown, 1824.

COUSINERY, M. *Voyage fait à Demerary et à Surinam.* Paris, 1831.

DALTON, H. G. *History of British Guiana.* 2 vols. 1855.

HILHOUSE, W. *Indian Notices.* 1825.

Local Guide of British Guiana, containing Historical Sketch, Statistical Tables, and the Entire Statute Law of the Colony in force January 1, 1843. Demerara, 1843.

M'DONNELL, A. *Considerations on Negro Slavery.* 1824.

MARRYAT, J. *Examination of the Report of the Berbice Commissioners and an answer to the Letter of James Stephen respecting the Crown Estates in the West Indies.* 1817.

New Local Guide of British Guiana, with Appendices to the same, containing together Historical Sketch, Chronological List, etc., and the Ordinances in daily use up to date. Demerara, 1864.

PREMIUM, B. *Eight Years in British Guiana.* 1850. An intelligent and moderate-minded planter.

Report of the Trials of the Insurgent Negroes before a General Court-Martial, held at Georgetown, Demerara. Georgetown, 1824.

SCHOMBURGK, Sir R. H. *Description of British Guiana.* 1840.

—— "Journey from Esmeralda, on the Orinoco, to San Carlos and Moura on the Rio Negro, and thence by Fort San Joaquim to Demerara, in the spring of 1839." *Royal Geog. Soc. Jour.* vol. x (1840), pp. 248–67.

—— "Report of the Third Expedition into the Interior of Guayana." *Royal Geog. Soc. Jour.* vol. x (1840), pp. 159–90.

SOLEAU, A. *Notes sur les Guyanes françaises.* Paris, 1835.

"Survey of the English possessions in America and in particular that of Guiana." *Colonial Essays* (1864), pp. 31–158.

VENESS, W. T. *El Dorado: or British Guiana as a Field for Colonisation.* 1867.

(c) LATER WORKS

BENNETT, G. W. *History of British Guiana.* Georgetown, 1875.

British Guiana: Arbitration with the U.S. of Venezuela: Appendix to the Case on behalf of the Govt. of Her Britannic Majesty. 7 vols. 1898. Contents: Vol. I: Documents, etc., 1593–1723. Vol II: Documents, etc., 1724–63. Vol. III: Documents, etc., 1763–8. Vol. IV: Documents, etc., 1769–81. Vol V: Documents, etc. 1781–1814. Vol. VI: Documents, etc., 1815–92. Vol. VII: Mr Schomburgk's memo. of 1839 on the boundary of British Guiana: Sir R. Schomburgk's reports and letters on his survey of the boundary of British Guiana: Diplomatic correspondence: Dutch posts and post-holders: Dutch grants of land: evidence by affidavit: British Commissions to Indian captains: Administrative reports since 1886: Chronological list of the principal maps of Guiana.

British Guiana Boundary: the Case on Behalf of the Govt. of Her Britannic Majesty. 1898.

British Guiana Boundary: Arbitration with the U.S. of Brazil. 1903; *the case on behalf of the Govt. of His Britannic Majesty.* 1903.

British Guiana Boundary: the Counter-Case. 1903.

British Guiana Boundary: Notes to the Counter-Case. 1903.

BRONCKHURST, H. V. P. *The Colony of British Guiana.* 1883.

CHAMBERLAIN, D. *Smith of Demerara, Martyr-Teacher of the Slaves.* 1924.

CLEMENTI, Sir C. *A Constitutional History of British Guiana.* 1937.

CLEVELAND, S. G. *Venezuelan Boundary Controversy.* Princeton, 1913.

DE VILLIERS, Sir J. A. J. "The Foundation and Development of British Guiana." *Geog. Jour.* vol. XXXVIII (1911), pp. 8–25.

EDMUNDSON, G. C. "The Relations of Great Britain with Guiana." *Trans. Roy. Hist. Soc.* 4th ser., vol. VI (1923), pp. 1–21.

IM THURN, Sir E. F. "Essequibo, Berbice, and Demerara under the Dutch." *Timehri,* vol. II (1883), pp. 33–80, 327–47; vol. III (1884), pp. 15–47.

JENKINS, J. E. *The Coolie, his Rights and Wrongs: Notes of a Journey to British Guiana.* 1871.

NETSCHER, P. M. *Geschiedenis van de Koloniën Essequebo, Demerary en Berbice.* The Hague, 1888.

Official History of the Discussion between Venezuela and Great Britain on their Guiana Boundaries. Atlanta, 1896.

PENSON, L. M. "The Making of a Crown Colony: British Guiana, 1803–33." *Trans. Roy. Hist. Soc.* 4th ser., vol. IX (1926), pp. 104–34.

Question de la frontière entre la Guyane Britannique et le Brésil. 4 vols. 1903–4.

—— *Contre-mémoire.* 1903.

—— *Annexe au contre-mémoire.* 1903.

—— Vol. II: *Traduction française de certains extraits des rapports rédigés par Robert Hermann Schomburgk.* 1903.

RODWAY, J. *Guiana: British, Dutch, and French.* 1912.

—— *History of British Guiana.* 3 vols. Georgetown, 1891–4.

RODWAY, J. and STARK, J. H. *Stark's Guide-Book and History of British Guiana.* [c. 1901.]

RUGG, R. *Anglo-American Boundaries Question.* 1896.

SCHOMBURGK, R. *Richard Schomburgk's Travels in British Guiana, 1840–4.* 2 vols. Georgetown, 1922–3.

SEIJAS, R. F. *Venezuelan International Law: British Boundaries of Guayana.* Paris, 1888.

STRIKLAND, J. *Documents and Maps on the Boundary Question between Venezuela and British Guiana.* Rome, 1896.

Timehri: the Journal of the Royal Agricultural and Commercial Society of British Guiana. 24 vols. Demerara, 1882–1921.

UNITED STATES OF AMERICA. *Commission on Boundaries between Venezuela and British Guiana. Report.* 3 vols. Washington, 1897.

WATT, H. *British Guiana.* 1887.

WEBBER, A. R. F. *Centenary History and Handbook of British Guiana.* Georgetown, 1931.

iii. *TROPICAL AFRICA*

(a) MANUSCRIPT SOURCES

See Part I, 1 and 2. In the library of the Royal Geographical Society, London, there are the following papers of explorers: "Original Journals and other MSS. relative to the Expedition of Denham and Clapperton"; "Original Maps drawn by Livingstone, Speke, etc."; "Original Journals of St Vincent-Erskine in South Africa, 1868–76"; "Observations on the West Coast of the Morocco State, 1830, with an Account of the Death of Major Laing."

(b) OFFICIAL PUBLICATIONS

See Part I, 3 and 4, particularly the following Parliamentary Papers: Rept. from Sel. Comm. on Sierra Leone, *Parl. Pap.* 1801–2, II (100) and 1st ser. x; Rept. of Commissioners on African Settlements, *Parl. Pap.* 1812, x (101); Rept. from Sel. Comm. on African Ports *Parl. Pap.* 1817, VI (431); Rept. of Commission on Sierra Leone, *Parl. Pap.* 1826–7, VII (312), (552); Rept. from Sel. Comm. on Sierra Leone, *Parl. Pap.* 1830, x (661); Rept. from Sel. Comm. on West Africa, *Parl. Pap.* 1842, XI (551); Papers *re* Niger Expedition, *Parl. Pap.* 1843, XLVIII [472]; Rept. from Sel. Comm. on West African Settlements, *Parl. Pap.* 1865, v (412).

(c) BIBLIOGRAPHIES AND GUIDES TO MATERIALS

LEWIN, E. *Subject Catalogue of the Library of the Royal Empire Society.* Vol. 1, *The British Empire generally, and Africa.* 1930.

WOODSON, C. G. *The African Background Outlined, or Handbook for the Study of the Negro.* Washington, D.C., 1936.

WORK, M. N. *A Bibliography of the Negro in Africa and America.* New York, 1928.

EXPLORATION

(a) CONTEMPORARY WRITINGS

ABBADIE, ANTOINE D'. *Géodésie de l'Ethiopie.* Paris, 1860–73.

ABBADIE, ARNAULD D'. *Douze ans dans la Haute Ethiopie.* Paris, 1868.

ALEXANDER, Sir J. E. *Expedition into the Interior of [South] Africa.* 2 vols. 1838.

ALLEN, W. and THOMSON, T. R. H. *Expedition to the River Niger in 1841.* 2 vols. 1848.

BAIKIE, H. W. B. *Exploring Voyage up the Rivers Kwo'ra and Binue.* 1856.

BAINES, T. *Explorations in South-West Africa.* 1864.

BAKER, Sir R. F. *Albert Nyanza...and Explorations of the Nile Sources.* 2 vols. 1866.

BARTH, H. *Travels and Discoveries in North and Central Africa.* 5 vols. 1857.

BROWNE, W. G. *Travels in Africa, etc.* 1799, 1806.

BRUCE, JAMES. *Travels to discover the Source of the Nile.* 5 vols. Edinburgh, 1790.

BURCKHART, J. L. *Travels in Nubia.* 1819.

BURTON, Sir R. F. *The Lake Regions of Central Africa.* 2 vols. 1860. Narrative of the Expedition with Speke, embodying a mass of information on the country traversed and its peoples, given in another form in *Jour. Royal Geog. Soc.* vol. XIX (1859), pp. 1–464.

—— *Wanderings in West Africa.* 2 vols. 1863.

—— *A Mission to Gelele, King of Dahome.* 2 vols. 1864.

CAILLIÉ, R. *Journal d'un Voyage à Temboctu.* 3 vols. Paris, 1830.

CAMERON, V. L. *Across Africa.* 2 vols. 1877.

CAMPBELL, JOHN. *Travels in Southern Africa.* 1815.

—— *Second Journey.* 2 vols. 1822.

CHAPMAN, J. *Travels in...Southern Africa.* 2 vols. 1868.

CLAPPERTON, H. *Journal of a Second Expedition.* 1829.

DENHAM, D., CLAPPERTON, H. and OUDNEY, W. *Travels and Discoveries in North and Central Africa.* 3rd edn. 2 vols. 1828.

DU CHAILLU, P. B. *Explorations...in Equatorial Africa.* 1861.

—— *Journey to Ashango-Land.* 1867.

DUNCAN, J. *Travels in Western Africa.* 2 vols. 1847.

DUVEYRIER, H. *Les Touareg du Nord.* Paris, 1864.

GALTON, Sir F. *Explorer in Tropical South Africa.* 1853.

GRAY, W. and DORCHARD, Staff-Surgeon. *Travels in Western Africa.* 1825.

HEUGLIN, T. VON. *Reisen in Nord-Ost-Afrika.* Gotha, 1857. Followed by other narratives published in 1868, 1869 and 1877.

HORNEMANN, F. *Travels from Cairo to Mourzouk, 1797–8.* 1802.

HUISH, R. (Ed.). *The Travels of Richard and John Lander.* 1836.

HUTCHINSON, T. J. *Narrative of the Niger, Tshadda and Binuë Exploration.* 1855.

HUTTON, W. *A Voyage to Africa.* 1821.

JAMIESON, R. *A Further Appeal against the proposed Niger Expedition.* 1841.

KRAPF, J. L. *Travels, Researches...in Eastern Africa.* 1860. Includes a useful summary of other work in East Africa, by E. G. Ravenstein.

LAING, A. G. *Travels in...Western Africa.* 1825.

LAIRD, M. and OLDFIELD, R. A. K. *Expedition...by the River Niger in 1832–4.* 2 vols. 1837.

LANDER, R. L. *Records of Captain Clapperton's Last Expeditions.* 1830.

LANDER, R. L. and LANDER, J. *Journal of an Expedition to explore the...Niger.* 3 vols. 1833.

LEDYARD, J. *Voyages de MM. Ledyard et Lucas en Afrique.* Paris, 1804.

LIVINGSTONE, DAVID. *Missionary Travels and Researches in South Africa.* 1857. New edn. 1899.
—— *Last Journals.* 2 vols. London, 1874.
LIVINGSTONE, DAVID and LIVINGSTONE, CHARLES. *Expedition to the Zambesi*...1858–64. 1865.
MASSAJA, G. *I Miei Trentacinque Anni...nell' alta Etiopia.* 11 vols. Rome, 1885–93.
MAUCH, K. *Reisen im...Süd-Afrika.* Gotha, 1870. Also *Petermanns Mitt.* Ergänzgsh. 37. Gotha, 1874.
OWEN, Capt. W. F. W. *Voyage to explore the Shores of Africa, etc.* 2 vols. 1833.
PARK, MUNGO. *Travels into the Interior Districts of Africa.* 1799. New edn. 1816.
—— *Journal of a Mission to the Interior of Africa...in 1805.* 1815.
PETHERICK, J. *Egypt...and Central Africa, etc.* 1861.
RAFFENEL, A. *Nouveau Voyage dans le Pays des Nègres.* 2 vols. Paris, 1856.
READ, P. *Lord John Russell and the Niger Expedition.* 1840.
ROHLFS, G. *Reise durch Nord-Afrika...(Petermanns Mitt.* Ergänzgsh. 25, 34). Gotha, 1868, 1872.
—— *Reise durch Marokko...nach Tripoli.* Bremen, 1868.
RICHARDSON, J. *Narrative of a Mission to Central Africa.* 2 vols. 1853.
SALT, H. *Voyage to Abyssinia...in 1809–10.* 1814.
SCHÖN, J. F. and CROWTHER, S. *Journals* [of the Niger Expedition]. 1842.
SCHWEINFURTH, G. A. *The Heart of Africa.* 2 vols. London, 1873. Translation of *Im Herzen von Afrika.* Admirable account of pioneer journeys in the South-west Nile basin, and beyond, begun in 1868.
SIMPSON, W. *A Private Journal kept during the Niger Expedition.* 1843.
SPEKE, J. H. *Journey of the Discovery of the Source of the Nile.* 1863.
THOMPSON, G. *Travels...in S. Africa.* 2 vols. 1827.
TUCKEY, J. H.[1] *Expedition to explore the river Zaire or Congo.* 1818.
VON DER DECKEN, Baron C. C. *Reisen in Ost-Afrika....* 1859–65. 4 vols. in 6. Leipzig, 1869–79.
WERNE, F. *Expedition zur Entdeckung des Weissen Nil.* Berlin, 1848.
—— *Reise durch Senaar, etc.* Berlin, 1852.

The following contemporary periodicals are essential for studying exploration during the period:

Bulletin de la Société de Géographie. Paris, 1822 *passim.* Contains many original accounts of journeys of French explorers on the White Nile, etc.
Journal of the Royal Geographical Society. Vols. I–L. London, 1832–80, *passim.* Nearly all the more important explorations during the period are summarily described.
Proceedings of the Association for...Discovery of the Interior Parts of Africa. London, 1790–1810. Original records of the explorations of the Association's agents.

(b) LATER WORKS

BAKER, J. N. L. *History of Geographical Discovery, etc.* [1931]. The best comprehensive summary of the history of exploration in general.
BEKE, C. T. *The Sources of the Nile.* 1860. Takes stock of the knowledge existing at the time.
BLAIKIE, W. G. *Personal Life of David Livingstone.* 1888.
BOVILL, E. W. *Caravans of the Old Sahara.* 1933. Mainly political history, but gives a good concise view of Saharan exploration.
BROWN, R. *The Story of Africa and its Explorers.* 5 vols. London, 1892–5. 4 vols. New York, 1911. A popular, but detailed and comprehensive account of the subject.
BURTON, Lady ISABEL. *Life of Sir R. F. Burton.* 2 vols. 1893.
BURTON, Sir R. F. (Ed.) and others. *The Lands of Cazembe.* Royal Geog. Soc., 1873.
CAMPBELL, R. J. *Livingstone.* 1929.
COOLEY, W. D. *Inner Africa laid open.* 1852. Based on the reports of travellers, old and recent.

[1] Printed erroneously as 'TUCKEY, J. K.' in the work itself.

DEHÉRAIN, H. *Le Soudan Egyptien sous Mehemet Ali.* Paris, 1898.
EVANS, I. L. *The British in Tropical Africa: an Historical Outline.* Cambridge, 1929.
GIBBON, L. G. (Pseud.). *Niger. The Life of Mungo Park.* Edinburgh, 1934.
HERTSLET, Sir E. *Map of Africa by Treaty.* Rev. edn. 3 vols. 1909.
HEWITT, W. H. *Mungo Park.* 1923.
HITCHMAN, F. *Richard F. Burton.* 2 vols. 1887.
HUTCHINSON, T. J. *Impressions of Western Africa.* 1858.
JOHNSTON, Sir H. H. *Livingstone and the Exploration of Central Africa.* 1891.
—— *The History of the Colonisation of Africa by Alien Races.* 1913.
—— *The Nile Quest.* 1903. A readable account of Nile exploration, but not altogether accurate in detail.
KELTIE, Sir J. S. *The Partition of Africa.* 2nd edn. 1895. Exploration receives full attention as a factor in the partition.
KINGSLEY, M. H. *West African Studies.* 1899.
MACQUEEN, J. *Geographical Survey of Africa.* 1840.
—— "Geography of Central Africa." *Jour. Royal Geog. Soc.* XXVI (1856). Learned discussions, largely theoretical, based on historical research.
MOCKLER-FERRYMAN, A. F. *Imperial Africa.* Vol. I, *British West Africa.* 1898.
MOSSMAN, S. *Livingstone, the Missionary Traveller.* London, 1882.
MURRAY, A. *Life and Writings of James Bruce.* Edinburgh, 1808.
MURRAY, H. *Historical Account of Discoveries in Africa.* 2 vols. Edinburgh, 1818. (Later edns., 1830, 1840.)
MURRAY, T. D. and SILVA WHITE, A. *Sir Samuel Baker: A Memoir.* 1895.
SCHONFIELD, H. J. *Richard Burton, Explorer.* 1936.
SUPAN, A. *Ein Jahrhundert der Afrika-Forschung.* Gotha, 1888. (*Petermanns Mitt.* vol. XXXIV (1888), pp. 161–88.) Perhaps the best concise summary of African exploration in the century after the founding of the African Association.
THOMSON, J. *Mungo Park and the Niger.* 1890. A comprehensive account of exploration in the Niger region, with Park as the central figure.

SIERRA LEONE

(a) BIBLIOGRAPHY

LUKE, C. H. *A Bibliography of Sierra Leone.* 1925.

(b) CONTEMPORARY WRITINGS

AFRICAN INSTITUTION. *Reports of the Committee of the African Institution.* I–XVIII. London, 1807–24.
BEAVER, P. *African Memoranda.* 1805.
BRYSON, A. *Account of the Origin, Spread, and Decline of the Epidemic Fevers of Sierra Leone.* 1849.
[CHURCH, M.] *Sierra Leone: or, the Liberated Africans.* 1835.
CORRY, J. *Observations upon the Windward Coast of Africa.* 1807.
CLARKE, E. *Sierra Leone.* 1843.
CLARKSON, T. *History of the Rise, Progress, and Accomplishment of the Abolition of the African Slave Trade by the British Parliament.* 2 vols. 1808. 2nd edn. 1839.
DALLAS, R. C. *History of the Maroons.* 1803.
DAVIES, W. *Extracts from the Journal of the Rev. W. D. when a Missionary at Sierra Leone.* Llanidloes [1835].
FALCONBRIDGE, Mrs A. M. *Narrative of Two Voyages to the River Sierra Leona.* 1802.
HORTON, J. A. B. *West African Countries and Peoples.* 1868.
KILHAM, Mrs H. *Present State of the Colony of Sierra Leone.* Lindfield, 1832.
—— *Report on a Recent Visit to the Colony of Sierra Leone.* 1828.
KOELLE, S. W. *Narrative of an Expedition into the Vy Country of West Africa.* 1849.
LAING, A. G. *Travels in Timannee, Kooranko, and Soolima Countries in West Africa.* 1825.
MACAULAY, K. *The Colony of Sierra Leone vindicated from the Misrepresentations of Mr MacQueen of Glasgow.* Edinburgh, 1827.

MacQueen, J. *The Colonial Controversy.* Glasgow, 1825.
—— *Fourth Letter to R. W. Hay, Esq., in reply to Mr K. Macaulay's "Sierra Leone vindicated."* Glasgow, 1827.
Madden, R. R. *Slave Trade and Slavery.* 1843.
Matthews, J. *A Voyage to the River Sierra Leone.* 1788. New edn. 1791.
Norton, Mrs C. E. S. *Residence at Sierra Leone.* 1849.
Poole, T. E. *Life, scenery, and customs in Sierra Leone and the Gambia.* 2 vols. 1850.
Rankin, F. H. *White Man's Grave: a Visit to Sierra Leone in 1843.* 2 vols. 1836.
Ricketts, H. T. *Narrative of the Ashantee War, with a View of the Present State of Sierra Leone.* 1831.
Sharp, G. *Memoirs Composed from his own Manuscripts... by Prince Hoare.* 1820.
Shreeve, W. W. *Sierra Leone: a Freed British Colony on the West Coast of Africa.* 1847.
Sierra Leone Company. *Account of the Colony of Sierra Leone.* 1795.
—— *Substance of the Report of the Court of Directors* [1791–1801]. 1792–1801.
Smeathman, H. *Plan of a Settlement to be made near Sierra Leone.* 1786.
Thorpe, R. *Letter to William Wilberforce.* 1815.
Wadström, C. B. *An Essay on Colonisation particularly applied to the Western Coast of Africa.* 1794.
Winterbottom, T. *Account of the Native Africans in the Neighbourhood of Sierra Leone.* 1803.

(c) Later Works

Alldridge, T. J. *The Sherbro and its Hinterland.* 1901.
—— *A Transformed Colony: Sierra Leone as it was, and as it is.* 1910.
Banbury, G. A. L. *Sierra Leone: or, White Man's Grave.* 1888.
Butt-Thompson, F. W. *Sierra Leone.* 1926.
—— F. W. *Sierra Leone in History and Tradition.* 1926.
Clarkson, J. "Diary of Lieutenant J. Clarkson, R.N., Governor, 1792." *Sierra Leone Studies* (1927), vol. VIII.
Crooks, J. J. *Historical Records of the Royal African Corps.* Dublin, 1925.
—— *A History of the Colony of Sierra Leone.* Dublin, 1903.
Davies, J. A. S. "The annexation of Sulima, Lavana, and Mano Salija." *Sierra Leone Studies*, vol. XVII (1932), pp. 34–9.
Edwards, F. A. "The French and Sierra Leone." *Gentleman's Mag.* (Nov. 1898), pp. 446–69.
George, C. *The Rise of British West Africa.* 1904.
Goddard, T. N. *The Handbook of Sierra Leone.* 1925.
Griffith, T. R. "Sierra Leone: past, present, and future." *Proc. Royal Colonial Inst.* vol. XIII (1881–2), pp. 56–98.
Ingham, E. G. *Sierra Leone after a Hundred Years.* 1894.
Kingsley, M. H. *West African Studies.* 1899.
Lucas, Sir C. P. *A Historical Geography of the British Colonies.* Vol. III, West Africa. 3rd edn. rev. by A. B. Keith. Oxford, 1913.
—— *Partition and Colonisation of Africa.* 1922.
McPhee, A. *The Economic Revolution in British West Africa.* 1926.
Martin, E. C. *The British West African Settlements, 1750–1821.* 1927. R. Col. Inst. Imperial Studies Series, No. 2.
Mellor, G. R. "British Policy in Relation to Sierra Leone, 1808–52." *Bull. Inst. Hist. Research*, vol. XIV (Nov. 1936), pp. 122–4. Summary of an unpublished thesis in the University of London Library.
Migeod, F. W. H. *A View of Sierra Leone.* 1926.
Mockler-Ferryman, A. F. *Imperial Africa.* Vol. I, British West Africa. 1898.
Newland, H. O. *Sierra Leone: its Peoples, Products, and Secret Societies.* [? 1916.]
Pierson, A. T. *Seven Years in Sierra Leone.* 1897.
Prothero, Sir G. (Ed.). *West Africa.* 1920. Peace Handbooks, No. 90.
Quilliam, A. "A Chapter in the History of Sierra Leone." *African Soc. Jour.* vol. III (1903), pp. 83–99.
Trotter, J. K. *Niger Sources and the Borders of the New Sierra Leone Protectorate.* 1898.

UTTING, F. A. J. *The Story of Sierra Leone.* 1931.
WILLIAMS, G. W. *History of the Negro Race in America from* 1619 *to* 1880. New York, 1883. Pp. 85–94 relate to Sierra Leone.
WILLIAMS, J. B. "The Development of British Trade with West Africa, 1750–1850." *Polit. Science Quart.* vol. L (June 1935), pp. 194–213.

GAMBIA

(a) CONTEMPORARY WRITINGS

BOWDICH, T. E. *Excursions in Madeira and Porto Santo.* 1825.
FOX, W. *A Brief History of the Wesleyan Missions on the Coast of Africa.* 1851.
HUNTLEY, Sir H. V. *Seven Years' Service on the Slave Coast of Western Africa.* 2 vols. 1860.
MOLLIEN, G. *Travels in the Interior of Africa.* 1820.

(b) LATER WORKS

ARCHER, F. B. *The Gambia Colony and Protectorate: an Official Handbook.* [1906.]
ARMITAGE, Sir C. H. "Gambia Colony and Protectorate." *Royal Soc. Arts Jour.* vol. LXXVI (1928), pp. 810–18.
CARNARVON, 4th Earl of. "Negotiations with France as to Gambia." *Speeches on the Affairs of West Africa, etc.* (1903), pp. 48–67.
FITZGERALD, C. *The Gambia and its Proposed Cession to France.* 1875–6.
GEORGE, C. *The Rise of British West Africa.* 1904.
GRAY, J. M. *A History of the Gambia.* Cambridge, 1940.
HAMLYN, W. T. *A Short History of the Gambia.* Bathurst, 1931.
LEGRAND, G. "La Gambie: notes historiques et géographiques." *Bulletin du Comité d'Études Historiques et Scientifiques de l'Afrique Occidentale Française,* vol. XI (1928), pp. 432–84.
MARTIN, C. "Gambie." *Renseignements Coloniales* (1917), pp. 121–30.
MITCHINSON, A. W. *The Expiring Continent.* 1881.
MOCKLER-FERRYMAN, A. F. *Imperial Africa.* Vol. I, *British West Africa.* 1898.
PROTHERO, Sir G. (Ed.). *Gambia.* 1920. Peace Handbooks, No. 91.
REEVE, H. F. *The Gambia: its History, Ancient, Mediaeval and Modern.* 1912.
YOUNG, Sir F. "Report on the Gambia question." *Proc. Royal Colonial Inst.* vol. VII (1875–6), pp. 68–83, 122–4.

GOLD COAST

(a) BIBLIOGRAPHIES AND GUIDES TO MATERIAL

CARDINALL, A. W. *A Bibliography of the Gold Coast.* [Accra], 1932.
FULLER, Sir F. C. *Bibliography of the Gold Coast.* [1924.]

(b) CONTEMPORARY WRITINGS

BEECHAM, J. *Ashantee and the Gold Coast.* 1841.
BOWDICH, T. E. *Mission from Cape Coast Castle to Ashantee.* 1819.
—— *The British and French Expeditions to Teembo.* Paris, 1821.
"British Settlement on the Gold Coast." *United Service Jour.* vol. XXVI (1838), pp. 346–53 *et seq.*
CRUICKSHANK, B. *Eighteen Years on the Gold Coast of Africa.* 2 vols. in 1. 1853.
DALZEL, A. *History of Dahomey.* 1793.
DUPUIS, J. *Journal of a Residence in Ashantee.* 1824.
FREEMAN, T. B. *Journal of Two Visits to the Kingdom of Ashantee.* 1843.
—— *Journal of Various Visits to the Kingdom of Ashanti.* 1844.
HORTON, J. A. B. *Letters on the Political Condition of the Gold Coast.* 1870.
HUTTON, W. *Voyage to Africa.* 1821.
JEEKEL, C. A. *Onze Bezittingen op de Kuste van Guinea.* Amsterdam, 1869.
MEREDITH, H. *Account of the Gold Coast of Africa.* 1812.
—— "Description de la Côte-d'or." Eyrie's *Abrégé des voyages modernes,* vol. XI (1824), pp. 157–213.
RICKETTS, H. I. *Narrative of the Ashantee War.* 1831.

(c) Later Works

Bell, Sir H. H. J. *The History, Trade, Resources and Present Condition of the Gold Coast Settlement*. Liverpool, 1893.

Boyle, F. *Through Fanteeland to Coomassie*. 1874.

Brackenbury, Sir H. *Ashanti War*. 1874.

Brackenbury, Sir H. and Huyshe, G. L. *Fanti and Ashanti*. 1873.

Butler, Sir W. F. *Akim-foo: the History of a Failure*. 1875.

Cardinall, A. W. *In Ashanti and Beyond*. 1927.

Claridge, W. W. *A History of the Gold Coast and Ashanti*. 2 vols. 1915.

Danquah, J. B. *Gold Coast*. 1928.

Ellis, A. B. *A History of the Gold Coast*. 1893.

—— *Tshi-Speaking Peoples of the Gold Coast*. 1887.

Fuller, Sir F. C. *A Vanished Dynasty, Ashanti*. 1921.

George, C. *The Rise of British West Africa*. 1904.

Glover, Lady C. *Life of Sir John Hawley Glover*. 1897.

Hardy, J. "Captain George Maclean; a Centenary Study." *United Empire*, vol. xxii (1931), pp. 191–4.

Hastings, A. C. G. *The Voyage of the* Dayspring: *being the Journal of the late Sir J. H. Glover*. 1926.

Hay, Sir J. D. *Ashanti and the Gold Coast*. 1874.

Hayford, J. E. C. *Gold Coast Native Institutions*. 1903.

Henty, G. A. *The March to Coomassie*. 1874.

James, P. G. "British Policy in Relation to the Gold Coast from 1815 to 1850." *Bull. Inst. Hist. Research*, vol. xiv (Nov. 1936), pp. 124–7. Summary of an unpublished thesis in the University of London Library.

Larsen, K. *De Danske i Guinea*. Copenhagen, 1918.

Lilley, C. C. "A Short History of the Nkonya Division of the Ho District." *Gold Coast Rev.* vol. i (1925), pp. 108–26.

Macdonald, G. *Gold Coast, Past and Present*. 1898.

Macdonnell, Sir R. G. "Our relations with the Ashantees." *Proc. Royal Colonial Inst.* vol. v (1873–4), pp. 71–102.

Martin, E. C. *The British West Africa Settlements, 1750–1821*. 1927.

—— "The English Establishments on the Gold Coast in the Second Half of the Eighteenth Century." *Trans. Royal Hist. Soc.*, 4th ser., vol v (1922), pp. 167–208.

[Maurice, Sir J. F.] *Ashantee War*. 1874.

Migeod, F. W. H. "A History of the Gold Coast and Ashanti." *Jour. African Soc.* vol. xv (1916), pp. 234–43.

Mockler-Ferryman, A. F. *Imperial Africa. Vol. i, British West Africa*. 1898.

Nathan, Sir M. "Historical Chart of the Gold Coast and Ashanti." *Jour. African Soc.* vol. iv (1904), pp. 33–43.

Orgle, T. K. "Pre-British Gold Coast." Cunard's *Negro Anthology* (1934), pp. 634–6.

Prothero, Sir G. (Ed.). *Gold Coast*. 1920. Peace Handbooks, No. 93.

Reade, W. W. *Story of the Ashantee Campaign*. 1874.

Redmayne, P. *The Gold Coast, Yesterday and Today*. 1938.

Reindorf, C. C. *History of the Gold Coast and Ashanti*. Basel, 1895.

Rogers, E. *Campaigning in West Africa and the Ashantee Invasion*. 1874.

Rouard de Card, M. M. E. *Les territoires Africains et les conventions franco-anglaises*. Paris, 1901.

Sanderson, R. W. "History of Nzima up to 1874." *Gold Coast Rev.* vol. i (1925), pp. 95–107.

Sarbah, J. M. *Fanti Customary Laws*. 1897. 2nd edn. 1904.

Saxton, S. W. "Historical Survey of the Shai People." *Gold Coast Rev.* vol. i (1925), pp. 127–45.

Smith, E. W. *The Golden Stool: Some Aspects of the Conflict of Cultures in Modern Africa*. 1926.

Southon, A. E. *Gold Coast Methodism*. 1934.

STANLEY, Sir H. M. *Coomassie and Magdala.* 1874.

SWANZY, A. *Trade on the Gold Coast.* 1874.

—— "Civilisation and Progress on the Gold Coast of Africa, as affected by European contact with the native inhabitants." *Jour. Royal Soc. Arts,* vol. XXIII (1875), pp. 415–26.

WARD, W. E. "Problems in Gold Coast History." *Gold Coast Rev.* vol. II (1926), pp. 37–52.

—— *A Short History of the Gold Coast.* 1935.

WELMAN, C. W. *The Native States of the Gold Coast.* 1930.

NIGERIA

(a) CONTEMPORARY WRITINGS

BAIKIE, W. B. "Notes of a Journey from Bida in Nupe, to Kano in Haussa, performed in 1862." *Royal Geog. Soc. Jour.* vol. XXXVII (1867), pp. 92–109.

BURTON, Sir R. F. *Abeokuta and the Cameroons Mountains.* 2 vols. 1863.

CAMPBELL, R. *Pilgrimage to My Motherland: an Account of a Journey among the Egbas and Yorubas of Central Africa in* 1859–60 [*c.* 1861].

COLE, W. *Life in the Niger.* 1862.

CROWTHER, S. A. and TAYLOR, J. C. *Gospel on the Banks of the Niger.* 1859.

MAY, D. J. "Journey in the Yoruba and Nupe countries in 1858." *Royal Geog. Soc. Jour.* vol. XXX (1860), pp. 212–33.

TUCKER, S. *Abbeokuta.* 1856.

(b) LATER WORKS

AJISAFE, A. K. *Laws and Customs of the Yoruba People.* 1924.

ARNETT, E. J. "A Hausa Chronicle." *African Soc. Jour.* vol. IX (1910), pp. 161–7.

—— *The Rise of the Sokoti Fulani.* Kano, 1929.

BAILLAUD, E. *La politique indigène de l'Angleterre en Afrique occidentale.* Paris, 1912.

BOVILL, E. W. *Caravans of the Old Sahara: an Introduction to the History of the Western Sudan.* 1933.

BOYLE, C. V. "Historical Notes on the Yola Fulanis." *African Soc. Jour.* vol. X (1910), pp. 73–92.

BURDON, (Sir) J. A. *Historical Notes on Certain Emirates and Tribes.* 1909.

BURNS, A. C. *History of Nigeria.* 1929.

ELLIS, A. B. *Yoruba-Speaking Peoples of the Slave Coast of West Africa.* 1894.

GEARY, Sir W. N. M. *Nigeria under British Rule.* 1927.

GEORGE, C. *The Rise of British West Africa.* 1904.

GOLDIE, H. *Calabar and its Mission.* 1890.

HASTINGS, A. C. G. *The Voyage of the* Dayspring: *being the Journal of the late Sir John Hawley Glover.* 1926. The papers of Sir John Hawley Glover are in the Library of the Royal Empire Society.

HAZZELDINE, G. D. *White Man in Nigeria.* 1904.

HINDERER, Mrs A. *Seventeen Years in the Yoruba Country.* 1873.

HOGBEN, S. J. *The Muhammadan Emirates of Nigeria.* 1930.

HOUDAS, O. V. *Documents arabes relatifs à l'histoire du Soudan.* Paris, 1901.

JOHNSON, O. "Lagos past." *Lagos Institute Proceedings.* 1901.

JOHNSON, S. *History of the Yorubas.* 1921.

JOHNSTON, Sir H. H. *Britain across the Seas, Africa.* [1910.]

LIVINGSTONE, W. P. *Mary Slessor of Calabar, Pioneer Missionary.* 1918.

LUGARD, Lord. *The Dual Mandate in British Tropical Africa.* 3rd edn. 1926.

—— "England and France on the Niger: the Race for Borgu." *Nineteenth Century* (June 1895), pp. 889–903.

LUGARD, Lady. *A Tropical Dependency.* 1905.

MACLEOD, O. *Chiefs and Cities of Central Africa.* 1912.

MARTIN, E. C. *The British West African Settlements, 1750–1821.* 1927.

MAXSE, F. I. "Acquisition of British Nigeria." *National Rev.* (Jan. 1904), pp. 783–98.

—— "The Story of Nigeria." *National Rev.* (Dec. 1903), pp. 607–23.

MEEK, C. K. *Northern Tribes of Nigeria.* 2 vols. Oxford, 1925.
MOCKLER-FERRYMAN, A. F. *British Nigeria.* 1902.
—— *Imperial Africa.* Vol. I, British West Africa. 1898.
MOLONEY, Sir C. A. "Notes on Yoruba and the Colony and Protectorate of Lagos." *Royal Geog. Soc. Proc.* vol. XII (1890), pp. 596–614.
MOORE, W. A. *History of Itsekiri.* 1936.
MOREL, E. D. *Affairs of West Africa.* 1902.
—— *Nigeria: its Peoples and Problems.* 1911.
NIVEN, C. R. *A Short History of Nigeria.* 1937.
ORR, C. W. I. *Making of Northern Nigeria.* 1911.
PALMER, H. R. "Kano Chronicle: translated with an Introduction by H. R. P." *Jour. Royal Anthrop. Inst.* vol. XXXVIII (1908), pp. 58–98.
—— *Sudanese Memoirs.* 3 vols. Lagos, 1928. Translated from the Arabic.
PAYNE, J. A. O. *Table of Particular Events in Yoruba History.* Lagos, 1893.
PERHAM, M. *Native Administration in Nigeria.* 1937.
PROTHERO, Sir G. (Ed.). *Nigeria.* 1920. Peace Handbooks, No. 94.
ROBINSON, C. H. *Nigeria, our Latest Protectorate.* 1900.
ROTH, H. L. *Great Benin: its Customs, Art, and Horrors.* Halifax, 1903.
SCHULTZE, A. *Sultanate of Bornu.* 1913. Trans. from German by P. A. Benton.
SCOTTER, W. H. "International Rivalry in the Bights of Benin and Biafra, 1815–85." *Bull. Inst. Hist. Research,* vol. XII (June 1934), pp. 63–6. Summary of unpublished thesis in London University Library.
TALBOT, P. A. *Peoples of Southern Nigeria.* 4 vols. Oxford, 1926.
TEPOWA, A. "A Short History of Brass and its People." *Jour. African Soc.* vol. VII (1907), pp. 32–88.
THOMAS, N. W. *Anthropological Report on the Edo-Speaking Peoples of Nigeria.* 2 vols. 1910.
TREMEARNE, A. J. N. *The Niger and the West Sudan.* [1910.]
—— "Notes on the Origin of the Hausas." *Jour. Royal Soc. Arts* (1910), pp. 767–75.
VIARD, E. *Au Bas-Niger.* Paris, 1886.
WELLESLEY, Lady. *Sir George Goldie, Founder of Nigeria.* 1934.
WOLF, L. *Letzte Reise nach der Landschaft Barbar (Bariba) oder Borgu, etc.* Berlin, 1890.

EASTERN AND CENTRAL AFRICA

(a) CONTEMPORARY WRITINGS

BAKER, Sir S. W. "Account of the Discovery of the Second Great Lake of the Nile, Albert Nyanza." *Royal Geog. Soc. Jour.* vol. XXXVI (1866), pp. 1–18.
—— *Albert Nyanza: Great Basin of the Nile and Exploration of the Nile sources.* 2 vols. 1866.
BURTON, Sir R. F. *Lake Region of Central Africa.* 2 vols. 1860.
—— "On Lake Tanganyika, Ptolemy's Western Lake Reservoir of the Nile." *Royal Geog. Soc. Jour.* vol. XXXV (1865), pp. 1–15.
BURTON, Sir R. F. and SPEKE, J. H. "Coasting voyage from Mombasa to the Pangani River." *Royal Geog. Soc. Jour.* vol. XXVIII (1858), pp. 188–226.
—— "Exploration in East Africa." *Royal Geog. Soc. Proc.* vol. III (1858–9), pp. 348–58.
GUILLAIN, C. *Documents sur l'histoire, la géographie, et le commerce de l'Afrique orientale.* 3 vols. Paris [1856].
LIVINGSTONE, D. *Cambridge Lectures.* 1858.
—— *Despatches addressed by Dr Livingstone...in 1870, 1871, and 1872.* 1872.
—— "Expedition to Lake Nyasa in 1861–3." *Royal Geog. Soc. Jour.* vol. XXXIII (1863), pp. 251–76.
—— "Extracts from the Despatches of Dr David Livingstone to Lord Malmesbury." *Royal Geog. Soc. Jour.* vol. XXXI (1861), pp. 256–96.
—— *Last Journals of David Livingstone in Central Africa.* 2 vols. 1874.
—— *Missionary Travels and Researches in South Africa.* 1857.
—— *Popular Account of Dr Livingstone's Expedition to the Zambesi and its Tributaries.* 1875.

MacQueen, J. "Kilimandjaro and the White Nile." *Royal Geog. Soc. Jour.* vol. XXX (1860), pp. 128–36.

Petherick, J. "Journey up the White Nile to the Equator, and travels in the Interior of Africa, in the years 1857–58." *Royal Geog. Soc. Proc.* vol. IV (1859–60), pp. 39–44; vol. V (1860–1), pp. 27–39.

Petherick, J. and Petherick, B. H. *Travels in Central Africa.* 2 vols. 1869.

Speke, J. H. "Captain Speke's Discovery in Central Africa." *Cape Monthly*, vol. VII (1860), pp. 159–67.

—— *Journal of the Discovery of the Source of the Nile.* 1864.

—— "Upper Basin of the Nile." *Royal Geog. Soc. Jour.* vol. XXXIII (1863), pp. 322–46.

—— *What Led to the Discovery of the Source of the Nile.* 1864.

Wakefield, T. "Routes of Native Caravans from the Coast to the Interior of Eastern Africa." *Royal Geog. Soc. Jour.* vol. XL (1870), pp. 303–39.

(b) Later Works

Baker, F. G. "Sir Richard F. Burton as I knew him." *Cornhill*, vol. LI (Oct. 1921), pp. 411–23.

Baker, J. A. "Geographical Notes on the Khedive's Expedition to Central Africa." *Royal Geog. Soc. Jour.* vol. XLIV (1874), pp. 37–73.

—— "Khedive of Egypt's Expedition to Central Africa." *Royal Geog. Soc. Proc.* vol. XVIII (1873–4), pp. 50–69.

Beccari, G. B. *La questione del Nilo e la Società Geografica Italiana.* Florence, 1875.

Bell, N. *Heroes of South African Discovery.* 1884.

Blaikie, W. G. *Life of David Livingstone.* 1911.

Cameron, V. L. "Journal of Lieut. V. L. C., Commander of the Livingstone East Coast Aid Expedition." *Royal Geog. Soc. Proc.* vol. XIX (1874–5), pp. 136–55.

—— "On his Journey across Africa from Bagamoyo to Benguela." *Royal Geog. Soc. Proc.* vol. XX (1875–6), pp. 304–28.

Campbell, R. J. *Livingstone.* 1929.

Chiesi, G. *La colonizzazione europea nell' Est Africa.* Turin, 1909.

Coupland, R. *East Africa and its Invaders, from the Earliest Times to the Death of Seyyid Said in 1856.* Oxford, 1938.

—— *The Exploitation of East Africa, 1856–90.* 1939.

—— *Kirk on the Zambesi.* 1928.

Dawson, R. B. *Livingstone.* 1918.

Dearden, S. *The Arabian Knight: a Study of Sir Richard Burton.* 1936.

Douglas, M. *In Lionland. The Story of Livingstone and Stanley.* 1900.

Fraser, A. Z. *Livingstone and Newstead.* 1913.

Geddie, J. *Lake Regions of Central Africa.* 1883.

Grant, J. A. "Summary of Observations on the Geographical Climate, and Natural History of the Lake Region of Equatorial Africa." *Royal Geog. Soc. Jour.* vol. XLII (1872), pp. 243–342.

Gregory, J. W. *Livingstone as an Explorer.* Glasgow, 1913.

Hitchman, F. *Richard F. Burton.* 2 vols. 1887.

Horne, C. S. *David Livingstone.* 1912.

Johnston, Sir H. H. *Livingstone and the Exploration of Central Africa.* 1891.

—— *Uganda Protectorate.* 2 vols. 1902.

Lugard, Lord. *Rise of our East African Empire.* 2 vols. 1893.

Penzer, N. M. *An Annotated Bibliography of Burton.* 1923.

Schonfield, H. J. *Richard Burton, Explorer.* 1936.

Schweinfurth, G. A. *Heart of Africa.* 2 vols. 1878.

Smith, G. W. *David Livingstone.* 1913.

Speke, J. H. *Journal, 1859–63.* 1922.

Stanley, H. M. *How I found Livingstone.* 1872.

Thomas, H. B. and Scott, R. *Uganda.* 1935.

Wright, T. *Life of Sir Richard Burton.* 2 vols. 1906.

Young, E. D. *The Search after Livingstone.* 1868.

BRITISH SOMALILAND

(a) CONTEMPORARY WRITINGS

ISENBERG, K. W. and KRAPF, J. L. *Journal of the Rev. Messrs Isenberg and Krapf, Missionaries.* 1843.

WILKINSON, Sir J. G. "Accounts of the Jimma Country." *Royal Geog. Soc. Jour.* vol. XXV (1855), pp. 206–14.

(b) LATER WORKS

BARTON, J. "Origins of the Galla and Somali Tribes." *Jour. East Africa Uganda Nat. Hist. Soc.* No. 19 (1924), pp. 6–11.

BOURNE, H. R. F. *Story of Somali.* 1904.

BURTON, Sir R. F. *First Footsteps in East Africa.* 2 vols. 1894 [1856].

CATO, C. "British Somali." *Empire Rev.* vol. XXXIII (1919), pp. 368–77.

DRAKE-BROCKMAN, R. E. *British Somaliland.* 1912.

HAMILTON, J. A. L. M. *Somaliland.* 1911.

LUCAS, Sir C. P. *Historical Geography of the British Empire.* Vol. I, *Mediterranean and Eastern Colonies.* Oxford, 1906. Pp. 84–94 deal with British Somaliland.

KENYA

(a) CONTEMPORARY WRITINGS

CHRISTOPHER, W. "Extract from a Journal by Lieut. W. Christopher, commanding the H. C. Brig. of War *Tigris*, on the East Coast of Africa." *Royal Geog. Soc. Jour.* vol. XIV (1844), pp. 76–103.

KRAPF, J. L. *Travels, Researches, and Missionary Labours, during an Eighteen Years' Residence in East Africa.* 1860.

Slave Trade of East Africa. 1868.

(b) LATER WORKS

ADMIRALTY. *Handbook of the Kenya Colony.* 1920.

AINSWORTH, J. "British East African Protectorate: Early History and Development. The Native Tribes and their Progress." *Jour. Manchester Geog. Soc.* vol. XXIX (1913), pp. 10–22.

BEECH, M. W. H. *The Suk: their Language and Folklore.* Oxford, 1911.

CHIESI, G. *La colonizzazione europa nell' Est Africa.* Turin, 1909.

CORSI, A. *Colonie Inglesi.* Rome, 1913.

CRANWORTH, 2nd Baron. *A Colony in the Making.* 1912.

DUNDAS, C. C. F. "Native Laws of Some Bantu Tribes of East Africa." *Jour. Royal Anthrop. Inst.* vol. LI (1921), pp. 217–78.

"East African Slave Trade." *Quart. Rev.* vol. CXXXIII (1872), pp. 521–57.

GREGORY, J. W. *Foundations of British East Africa.* 1901.

—— *Great Rift Valley.* 1896.

HINDE, S. L. and HINDE, Mrs H. *Last of the Masai.* 1901.

HOBLEY, C. W. *Bantu Beliefs and Magic.* 1922.

—— *Ethnology of A-Kamba and other East African Tribes.* Cambridge, 1910.

—— *Kenya, from Chartered Company to Crown Colony.* [1929.]

—— "Romance of the Foundation of Uganda and Kenya Colony." Weinthal's *Cape to Cairo Railway,* vol. I (1923), pp. 501–15.

HOLLIS, Sir A. C. *The Masai.* Oxford, 1905.

—— *The Nandi.* Oxford, 1909.

HORNELL, J. "Indonesian Influence on East African Culture." *Jour. Roy. Anthrop. Inst.* vol. LXIV (1934), pp. 305–32.

HUTCHINSON, E. *Slave Trade in East Africa.* 1874.

JACKSON, Sir F. J. *Early Days in East Africa.* 1930.

JOHNSTON, Sir H. H. *Britain Across the Seas.* [1910.]

LEYS, N. *Kenya.* 1924. 3rd edn. 1926.

Luck, C. C. "Origin of the Masai and Kindred African Tribes and of Bornean
    Tribes." *East African Hist. Soc. Jour.* No. 26 (1926), pp. 91–193.
Lugard, Lord. *Rise of our East African Empire.* 2 vols. 1893.
McDermott, P. L. *British East Africa, or Ibea: a History of the formation and work
    of the Imperial British East African Company.* 1893. 2nd edn. 1895.
Macdonald, Sir J. R. L. *Soldiering and Surveying in British East Africa.* 1897.
Mackenzie, Sir G. S. "Uganda and the East African Protectorate." *Fortnightly
    Rev.* (Dec. 1894), pp. 882–94.
Maugham, R. C. F. "Early History of the East African Coast." *United Empire*,
    vol. v (1914), pp. 733–44.
New, C. *Life, Wanderings, and Labours in Eastern Africa.* 1873.
Orde-Browne, G. St J. *Vanishing Tribes of Ken.* 1925.
Playne, S. and Gale, F. H. *East Africa, British.* 1908–9.
Ross, W. McG. *Kenya from Within: a Short Political History.* [1927.]
Routledge, W. S. and Routledge, Mrs K. *With a Pre-historic People: the Akikuyu
    of British East Africa.* 1910.
Salvadori, M. *La colonisation Européenne au Kenya.* Paris, 1938.
Smith, A. D. *Through Unknown African Countries.* 1897.
Stigand, C. H. *Land of Zinj.* 1913.
Tate, H. R. "First Footsteps in British East Africa." *East African Annual* (1938),
    pp. 13–18.
Thomson, J. *Through Masai Land.* 1885.
Tilby, A. W. "Britain in the Tropics, 1527–1910." *English People Overseas*, vol. IV.
    1912. Pp. 147–95 relate to East Africa.

ZANZIBAR AND THE EAST AFRICAN COAST

(*a*) Contemporary Writings

Boteler, T. *Narrative of a Voyage of Discovery to Africa and Arabia.* 2 vols. 1835.
Deckan, Baron K. von der. "Geographical Notes of an Expedition to Mount
    Kilimandjaro." *Royal Geog. Soc. Jour.* vol. XXXIV (1864), pp. 1–6.
Grant, J. A. *A Walk across Africa.* 1864.
Guillain, C. *Documents sur l'histoire, la géographie, et le commerce de l'Afrique orientale.*
    3 vols. Paris [1856].
Kirk, Sir J. "Notes on Two Expeditions up the River Rovuma." *Royal Geog.
    Soc. Jour.* vol. XXXV (1865), pp. 154–67.
Owen, W. F. W. *Narrative of Voyages to explore the shores of Africa* [etc.]. 2 vols. 1833.

(*b*) Later Works

Admiralty. *Handbook of German East Africa.* 1916.
—— *Handbook of Kenya Colony.* [1920.]
Burton, Sir R. F. *Zanzibar.* 2 vols. 1872.
Calendar for 1927: showing Important Events in Zanzibar History. Supplement to the
    Zanzibar Official Gazette, 12 Feb. 1927.
Cameron, V. L. *Across Africa.* 1877.
—— "Zanzibar, Its Past, Present, and Future." *Revue des Col. Intern.* vol. I (1885),
    pp. 417–30.
Chiesi, G. *La colonizzazione europea nell' Est Africa.* Turin, 1909.
Colomb, P. H. *Slave-Catching in the Indian Ocean.* 1873.
Coupland, R. *East Africa and its Invaders.* Oxford, 1938.
—— *The Exploitation of East Africa.* 1939.
Craster, J. E. E. *Pemba, the Spice Island of Zanzibar.* [1913.]
Crofton, R. H. *The Old Consulate at Zanzibar.* 1935.
Elton, J. F. "On the Coast Country of East Africa, South of Zanzibar." *Royal
    Geog. Soc. Jour.* vol. XLIV (1874), pp. 227–52.
Firminger, W. K. *Protectorate of Zanzibar.* British Empire Series, vol. II (1899),
    pp. 259–78.
Frere, Sir H. B. E. "Zanzibar and its Sultan." *Macmillan's Mag.* (1875), pp. 183–92.
—— "Zanzibar, a Commercial Power." *Macmillan's Mag.* (1875), pp. 275–88.

GRIMM, C. VON. *Der wirthschaftliche Werth von Deutsch-Ostafrika.* Berlin, 1886.
HOLLINGSWORTH, L. W. *A Short History of the East Coast of Africa.* 1929.
INGRAMS, W. H. *Chronology and Genealogies of Zanzibar Rulers.* Zanzibar, 1926.
—— "Ethnology, History and Native Industry and Occupations." *Zanzibar: An Account of its People, Industries, and History* (1924), pp. 1–22, 35–76, 80–4.
—— *Zanzibar, its History and its People.* 1931.
JOHNSTON, Sir H. H. "British Interests in Eastern Equatorial Africa." *Royal Soc. Arts Jour.* vol. XXXIII (1885), pp. 605–15.
LEWIN, P. E. *Germans and Africa.* 1915.
LYNE, R. N. *Zanzibar in Contemporary Times.* 1905.
NEWMAN, H. S. *Banani: the Transition from Slavery to Freedom in Zanzibar and Pemba.* [c. 1898.]
PEARCE, F. B. *Zanzibar.* 1919.
PLUMON, E. *La colonie allemande de l'Afrique orientale.* Rennes, 1905.
PROTHERO, Sir G. (Ed.). *Kenya, Uganda and Zanzibar.* 1920. Peace Handbooks, No. 96.
REUTE, R. S. *Said Bin Sultan (1791–1856).* 1929.
RUSSELL, Mrs C. E. B. *General Rigby, Zanzibar, and the Slave Trade.* 1935.
SALIL-IBN-RAZIK. *History of the Imâms and Seyyids of 'Oman, from A.D. 661–1856...* Ed. by G. P. Badger. 1871. Hakluyt Soc. Pubn. vol. XLIV.
SWANN, A. J. *Fighting the Slave-Hunters in Central Africa.* 1910.
THOMSON, J. "East Africa as it was and is." *Contemp. Rev.* (Jan. 1889), pp. 41–51.
VAUGHAN, J. H. *The Dual Jurisdiction in Zanzibar.* 1935.
WOOLF, L. *Empire and Commerce in Africa.* [1919.]

NYASALAND

(a) CONTEMPORARY WRITINGS

LIVINGSTONE, D. "Expedition to Lake Nyassa in 1861–3." *Royal Geog. Soc. Jour.* vol. XXXIII (1863), pp. 251–76.
—— "Exploration to the West of Lake Nyassa in 1863." *Royal Geog. Soc. Jour.* vol. XXXIII (1864), pp. 245–51.
ROWLEY, H. *Story of the Universities' Mission to Central Africa.* 2nd edn. 1867.

(b) LATER WORKS

COTTERILL, H. B. "Nyasa—with Notes on the Slave Trade." *Soc. Arts Jour.* vol. XXVI (1878), pp. 678–85.
—— "Opening out of the District to the North of Lake Nyassa." *Soc. Arts Jour.* vol. XXVII (1879), pp. 242–7.
COUPLAND, R. *The Exploitation of East Africa.* 1939.
—— *Kirk on the Zambesi.* Oxford, 1928.
DRUMMOND, H. *Tropical Africa.* 1888.
Handbook of Nyasaland. 2nd edn. 1910. Another edn. by S. S. Murray, 1922.
JACK, J. W. *Daybreak in Livingstonia: the Story of the Livingstonia Mission to British Central Africa.* 1900.
JOHNSTON, Sir H. H. *British Central Africa.* 1897.
MORSHEAD, A. E. M. ANDERSON. *History of the Universities' Mission to Central Africa, 1859–96.* 1897. 4th edn. 1905.
NORMAN, L. S. *Nyasaland without Prejudice.* 1934.
PROTHERO, Sir G. (Ed.). *Nyasaland.* 1920. Peace Handbooks, No. 95.
STEVENSON, J. *Arabs in Central Africa and at Lake Nyassa.* Glasgow, 1888.
—— *Civilisation of S. E. Africa.* Glasgow, 1877.
SWANN, A. J. *Fighting the Slave-Hunters in Central Africa.* 1910.
TOZER, W. G. *Letters of Bishop Tozer and his Sister.* 1902.
YOUNG, E. D. *Nyassa: a Journal of Adventures whilst exploring Lake Nyassa.* 1877.
—— "Recent Sojourn at Lake Nyassa." *Royal Geog. Soc. Jour.* vol. XXI (1877), pp. 225–33.

iv. *CEYLON, BRITISH MALAYA AND HONG KONG*

CEYLON

(a) MANUSCRIPT SOURCES

See Part I, 1 and 2.

(b) OFFICIAL PUBLICATIONS

See Part I, 3 and 4, particularly the Repts. from Sel. Comm. on Ceylon, *Parl. Pap.* 1850, XII (66), (106), (605) and 1851, VIII, Pts. 1 and 2 (36); and corresp. on Ceylon Military Expenditure, *Parl. Pap.* 1865, XXXVIII (215).

(c) CONTEMPORARY WRITINGS

BENNETT, J. W. *Ceylon and its Capabilities.* 1843.

BOYD, H. *Miscellaneous Works of Hugh Boyd.* Vol. II. 1800. Boyd was sent on a mission to the Kingdom of Kandy.

BUSSCHE, L. DE. *Letters on Ceylon.* 1826.

CORDINER, J. *Description of Ceylon.* 1807.

DAVY, J. *Account of the Interior of Ceylon and of its Inhabitants.* 1821.

DEGRANDPRÉ, Le Comte. *Voyage in the Indian Ocean.* 2 vols. 1803.

D'OYLY, Sir J. *A Sketch of the Constitution of Kandyan Kingdom.* 1832.

[FELLOWES, R., *pseud.* PHILALETHES.] *History of Ceylon.* 1817.

FORBES, J. *Eleven Years in Ceylon.* 1840.

HAAFNER, J. *Voyages dans la péninsule occidentale de l'Inde et dans l'Ile de Ceilan.* 2 vols. Paris, 1811.

HENDERSON, J. M. *History of the Rebellion in Ceylon.* 1868.

HOFFMEISTER, W. *Travels in Ceylon.* Edinburgh, 1848.

HORTON, Sir R. J. WILMOT. *Letters on Colonial Policy, particularly as applicable to Ceylon.* Colombo, 1833. New edn. 1839.

HUNTER, W., WOLF, J. C. and ESCHELSKROON, A. *Description du Pégu et de l'île de Céylon.* Paris, 1793.

JOHNSTON, Sir A. *Correspondence to and from Sir Alexander Johnston regarding the Abolition of Slavery in Ceylon.* 1818.

—— *Narrative of the Operations of a Detachment in an Expedition to Candy.* 1810.

KNIGHTON, W. *History of Ceylon.* 1845.

MARSHALL, H. *Ceylon.* 1846.

Narrative of Events which have recently occurred in the Island of Ceylon. 1815.

PENNANT, T. *The View of Hindoostan.* 4 vols. 1798–1800.

PERCIVAL, R. *Account of the Island of Ceylon.* 1803.

PETER, W. *Appeal to the British Government in behalf of the British Colony and Province of Ceylon.* Frankfort, 1836.

PRIDHAM, C. *Historical, Political, and Statistical Account of Ceylon and its Dependencies.* 2 vols. 1849.

SABONADIÈRE, W. *The Coffee Planter of Ceylon.* 2nd edn. 1870.

SIRR, H. C. *Ceylon and the Cingalese: their History, Government, and Religion.* 2 vols. 1850.

SPECULUM (pseud.). *Ceylon: Her Present Condition.* Colombo, 1868.

STEUART, J. *Notes on Ceylon and its Affairs.* 1862.

TENNENT, Sir J. E. *Ceylon.* 2 vols. 1860.

VALENTIA, 9th Viscount. *Voyages and Travels to India, Ceylon... in the years 1802–6.* 3 vols. 1809.

WARD, Sir H. G. *Speeches and Minutes of the late Sir Henry George Ward.* Colombo, 1864.

(d) LATER WORKS

BASSETT, R. H. *Romantic Ceylon, its History, Legend and Story.* 1929.

BLAZE, L. E. *History of Ceylon.* Colombo, 1900.

BURROWS, Sir S. M. "Conquest of Ceylon, 1795–1815." *Cambridge History of India,* vol. V (1929), pp. 400–408.

CLARENCE, L. B. "One Hundred Years of British Rule in Ceylon." *Proc. Royal Colonial Inst.* vol. XXVII (1895–6), pp. 314–49.
CLEGHORN, H. *The Cleghorn Papers*. Ed. by W. Neil. 1927.
CODRINGTON, H. W. *Short History of Ceylon*. 1926.
DE SILVA, C. R. "Ceylon under the British Occupation, 1795–1833." 1931. An unpublished thesis in the library of the University of London. A very detailed history based on original sources.
DIXON, C. W. *Colonial Administration of Sir Thomas Maitland*. 1940.
D'OYLY, Sir J. *Diary of Mr John D'Oyly*. Colombo, 1917.
DOYNE, W. T. *Ceylon Railway*. 1860.
ENRIQUÉZ, C. M. D. [*pseud.* THEOPHILUS]. *Ceylon, Past and Present*. [c. 1927.]
FERGUSON, A. M. and J. *Summary of Information regarding Ceylon*. 1880.
GREGORY, Lady A. (Ed.). *Sir William Gregory. An Autobiography*. 2nd edn. 1894.
HALE, B. *Travels in India, Ceylon, and Borneo* [1831]. 1931.
HIGGINS, M. MUSAEUS-. *Stories from the History of Ceylon*. 2 vols. Colombo, 1913–16.
[JENKINS, R. W.] *Ceylon in the Fifties and the Eighties*. Colombo, 1886.
LA THOMBE, — DE. "A Collection of Notes on the Attack and Defence of Colombo." *Jour. Royal Asiatic Soc., Ceylon Branch* (1888), pp. 365–414.
LEWIS, F. "Johnston's Expedition to Kandy in 1804." *Jour. Royal Asiatic Soc., Ceylon Branch*, vol. XXX (1925), pp. 43–65.
LEWIS, J. P. "Andrew's Journal of a Tour to Candia in the year 1796." *Jour. Royal Asiatic Soc., Ceylon Branch*, vol. XXVI (1918), pp. 6–52.
—— *Ceylon in Early British Times*. Colombo, [1915].
LUCAS, Sir C. P. *Historical Geography of the British Colonies*. Vol. I, *The Mediterranian and Eastern Colonies*. Oxford, 1906. Pp. 95–124 deal with Ceylon.
METHLEY, V. M. "The Ceylon Expedition of 1803." *Trans. Royal Hist. Soc.*, 4th ser., vol. I (1918), pp. 92–128.
MILLIE, P. D. *Thirty Years Ago: or Reminiscences of the Early Days of Coffee Planting in Ceylon*. Colombo, 1878.
MILLS, L. A. *Ceylon under British Rule*, 1795–1932. Oxford, 1933. A scholarly work based on original sources, with an excellent bibliography.
OBEYESEKERE, D. *Outlines of Ceylon History*. Colombo, 1912.
PERERA, E. W. "Ceylon under British Rule." *Wright's Twentieth Century Ceylon* (1907), pp. 60–84.
PIERIS, P. E. *Ceylon and the Hollanders*, 1658–1796. Tellippalai, 1918. 2nd edn. 1924.
—— (Ed.). *Letters to Ceylon*, 1814–24, *being Correspondence addressed to Sir John D'Oyly*. Cambridge, 1937.
SKINNER, Major T. *Fifty Years in Ceylon, an Autobiography*. 1891.
[SUCKLING, H. J.] *Ceylon: a General Description of the Island*. 2 vols. 1876.
TERRY, A. "Expedition against Kandy in 1804." *United Service Mag.* vol. XXXVI (1907–8), pp. 279–86.
TURNER, L. J. B. "British Occupation of the Maritime Province of Ceylon, 1795–6." *Ceylon Antiquary*, vol. III (1918), pp. 237–57.
—— "Civil Govt. of the Maritime Province of Ceylon, 1798–1805." *Ceylon Antiquary*, vol. IV (1919), pp. 123–34.
—— "Madras Administration of the Maritime Province of Ceylon, 1795–8." *Ceylon Antiquary*, vol. IV (1919), pp. 36–53.
—— "The Maritime Province of Ceylon, 1798–1805: General History of the Hon. Frederick North's Administration." *Ceylon Antiquary*, vol. VI (1920), pp. 18–26.
—— "Military Establishments in the Maritime Province of Ceylon, 1798–1805." *Ceylon Antiquary*, vol. V (1919), pp. 59–69.
—— "Pilama Talawuwe, Maha Adigar: his Political Intrigues, 1798–1803." *Ceylon Antiquary*, vol. III (1918), pp. 219–25.

BRITISH MALAYA

BAKER, A. C. "Some Account of Anglo-Dutch Relations in the East at the Beginning of the Nineteenth Century." *Jour. Royal Asiatic Soc., Straits Branch*, No. 64 (1913), pp. 1–68.

BELL, Sir H. *Foreign Colonial Administration in the Far East.* 1929.

BLAGDEN, C. O. "Notes on Malay History." *Jour. Royal Asiatic Soc., Straits Branch,* No. 53 (1909), pp. 139–62.

BUCKLEY, C. B. *An Anecdotal History of Old Times: from the Foundation of the Settlement ...1819, to the transfer to the Colonial Office...1867.* 2 vols. Singapore, 1902.

COOK, T. A. B. *Raffles, founder of Singapore.* 1918.

COUPLAND, R. *Raffles.* 2nd edn. 1934.

EGERTON, H. E. *Sir Stamford Raffles: England in the Far East.* 1900.

EMERSON, R. *Malaysia: a Study in Direct and Indirect Rule.* New York, 1937.

LUCAS, Sir C. P. *Historical Geography of the British Colonies.* Vol. 1, *The Mediterranean and Eastern Colonies.* 2nd edn. rev. by R. E. Stubbs. Oxford, 1906. Pp. 197–207 deal with the Straits Settlements.

MAKEPEACE, W., BROOKE, G. E. and BRADDELL, R. St J. *One Hundred Years of Singapore.* 2 vols. 1921.

MAXWELL, Sir P. B. *Our Malay Conquests.* 1878.

MAXWELL, Sir W. G. and GIBSON, W. S. (Eds.). *Treaties and Engagements affecting the Malay States and Borneo.* 1924.

MILLS, L. A. *British Malaya, 1824–61.* Singapore, 1925.

SKINNER, A. M. "Outline History of the British Connection with Malaya." *Jour. Royal Asiatic Soc., Straits Branch,* No. 10 (1882), pp. 269–80.

SWETTENHAM, Sir F. A. *British Malaya: an Account of the Origin and Progress of British Influence in Malaya.* 1907.

—— "The Straits Settlements and Beyond." *The Empire and the Century* (1905), pp. 827–34.

WARD, A. B. *Outlines of Sarawak History, 1839–1917.* Kuching, 1927.

WINSTEDT, R. O. *A History of Malaya.* 1935.

WRIGHT, A. "Singapore and Sir Stamford Raffles." *Quart. Rev.* vol. CCXXXII (1919), pp. 265–83.

WRIGHT, A. and REID, T. H. *The Malay Peninsula.* 1912.

HONG KONG

CURREY, E. H. "Boat Actions and River Fights: The Opium War, 1840–1; Capture of the Forts at Bocca Tigris, Canton River; Cession of Hong-Kong to Great Britain; and Operations in and around Canton, Feb. to May, 1841." *United Service Mag.* vol. XLIX (1914), pp. 569–80; vol. L (1915), pp. 11–22.

EITEL, E. J. *Europe in China: the History of Hongkong.* 1895.

ELGIN, Lord. *Letters and Journals.* 1872.

HERTSLET, Sir E. *Treaties, etc., between Great Britain and China and between China and Foreign Powers.* 2 vols. 1896.

Historical and Statistical Abstract of the Colony of Hongkong, 1841–1930. Hongkong, 1932.

Hongkong (Descriptive and Historical Leaflet). Hongkong, 1924.

Hongkong: a Short History of the Colony. [c. 1928.]

LANE-POOLE, S. *Sir Harry Smith Parkes.* 1894.

LUCAS, Sir C. P. *Historical Geography of the British Colonies.* Vol. 1, *The Mediterranean and Eastern Colonies.* Oxford, 1906. Pp. 275–84 deal with Hongkong.

MACMURRAY, J. V. A. *Treaties and Agreements with and concerning China.* 2 vols. New York, 1921.

MORSE, H. B. (Ed.). *Chronicles of the East India Company trading to China, 1634–1834.* 5 vols. Oxford, 1926–9.

—— *International Relations of the Chinese Empire, 1834–60.* 1910.

OLIPHANT, L. *Narrative of the Earl of Elgin's Mission.* 1859.

PARKER, E. H. *China: her History, Diplomacy and Commerce.* 1901.

SAYER, G. R. *Hongkong, Birth, Adolescence, and Coming of Age.* 1937.

v. *MAURITIUS AND SEYCHELLES*

For Manuscript Sources and Official Publications, see Part I above.

MAURITIUS

(a) BIBLIOGRAPHIES

LEWIN, E. *Subject Catalogue of the Library of the Royal Empire Society*, vol. IV (1937).

MAURITIUS INSTITUTE. *Catalogue of English Works in the Mauritius Public Library.* Mauritius, 1904.

—— *Catalogue of French Works in the Mauritius Public Library.* Mauritius, 1904. Supplement, 1911.

(b) CONTEMPORARY WRITINGS

Archives de l'Ile de France: journal littéraire et politique. 4 vols. Mauritius, 1818–19. 74 nos., of which Nos. 6–7 are in manuscript in the Royal Empire Society Library.

Arrêts administratifs et règlements du Conseil Provincial et du Conseil Superieur de l'Ile de France sous le régime de la compagnie des Indes, contenant les Actes de la colonisation de l'Ile Maurice, 1722 à 1767. Lille, 1859.

BILLIARD, A. *Voyage aux coloniaux orientales.* Paris, 1822.

BOLTON, W. D. *Almanach de Maurice.* 1854.

BORY DE ST VINCENT, J. B. G. M. *Voyage to, and Travels through, the Four Principal Islands of the African Seas.* 1805.

BRUNET, P. *Voyage à l'Ile de France.* Paris, 1825.

"Earl Grey and the Mauritius." *Colonial Mag.* vol. XVI (1849), pp. 169–79.

GRANT, C. (Baron de Vaux). *History of Mauritius.* 1801.

JEREMIE, Sir J. *Short Appeal to the House of Commons in Answer to the Charges brought against the Inhabitants of Mauritius.* [1835.]

[MAURE, A.] *Souvenirs d'un vieux colon de l'Ile Maurice.* [La Rochelle], 1840.

MILBERT, J. G. *Voyage pittoresque à l'Ile-de-France.* 2 vols. Paris, 1812.

PRIDHAM, C. *England's Colonial Empire.* Vol. I, *The Mauritius and its Dependencies.* 1846.

SAINT-PIERRE, J. H. B. DE. *Voyage to the Isle of France.* 1800.

(c) LATER WORKS

AUSTEN, H. C. M. *Sea Fights and Corsairs of the Indian Ocean: being the Naval History of Mauritius from 1715–1810.* Port Louis, 1935.

BIRT, H. N. *Benedictine Pioneers in Australia.* 2 vols. 1911. Chapter II deals with Mauritius.

BOUTON, L. "Les célébrités mauriciennes: esquisses biographiques." Boucherville's *Revue des Coloniaux*, vol. I (1871–2), pp. 35–57.

BOWEN, Sir G. F. "Thirty Years of Colonial Government." *Rev. Hist. et Litt. de l'Ile Maurice*, vol. III (1890), pp. 523–6; vol. IV (1890), pp. 4–8 et seq.

BRUCE, Sir C. "Evolution of the Crown Colony of Mauritius." *Scot. Geog. Mag.* vol. XXIV (1908), pp. 57–78.

CANIVET, C. *Les colonies perdues.* 1884.

COQUEVAL, H. "Précis de l'histoire de l'Ile Maurice." *Rev. Hist. et Litt. de l'Ile Maurice*, vol. VI (1893), pp. 234–40.

CREPIN, P. "Iles de France et de Bourbon." *Histoire des colonies françaises*, ed. by G. Hanotaux and A. Martineau, vol. VI. Paris, 1933.

DAVIDSON, Sir W. E. *Notes on the Naval Operations in the Indian Ocean, 1800–10.* Mahé [1909?].

DUCRAY, F. *Le contre-coup de 89 à l'Ile de France.* Port Louis, 1883.

DUPLOMB, CH. "L'Ile de France (île Maurice): rapport du Contre-Amiral de Kerguelen au Comité de Salut Public au sujet des mesures prendre pour la défense de l'Ile de France, 25 Avril, 1794." *La Géographie*, vol. XLIV (1925), pp. 109–15.

EDWARDES, S. B. DE B. *L'histoire de l'Ile Maurice*. Paris, 1910.
——— *History of Mauritius* (1507–1914). 1921.
EPINAY, A. *Renseignements pour servir à l'histoire de l'Ile de France jusqu'à l'année* 1810. Mauritius, 1890.
FIELD, A. G. "The Expedition to Mauritius in 1810 and the Establishment of British Control." *Bull. Inst. Hist. Research*, vol. x (Nov. 1932), pp. 126–9. Summary of unpublished thesis in University of London Library.
FROBERVILLE, F. DE. *Souvenirs de l'Ile de France*. Mauritius, 1874.
GRANT, C., Baron de Vaux. *Letters from Mauritius in the Eighteenth Century*. Mauritius, 1886.
HITIÉ, E. *Histoire de Maurice*. Port Louis, 1897.
HUET DE FROBERVILLE, L. *L'Ile de France: le combat du Grand-Port et la fin de l'occupation française*. Port Louis, 1910.
INGRAMS, W. H. *A School History of Mauritius*. 1931.
LUCAS, Sir C. P. *Historical Geography of the British Colonies*. Vol. I, *The Mediterranean and Eastern Colonies*. Oxford, 1906. Pp. 131–68 deal with Mauritius.
MACQUET, A. "Étude historique sur les commencements de l'administration de l'Ile de France." *Rev. Hist. et Litt. de l'Ile Maurice*, vol. IV (1890), pp. 193–9.
MAGON DE SAINT-ELIER, F. "Les origines de l'Ile Maurice." *Hist. et Litt. de l'Ile Maurice*, vol. I (1887), pp. 95–6 *et seq.*
——— "L'Ile de France sous le gouvernement du roi." *Rev. Hist. et Litt. de l'Ile Maurice*, vol. I (1888), pp. 521–6 *et seq.*
——— "L'Ile de France sous la Compagnie des Indes." *Rev. Hist. et Litt. de l'Ile Maurice*, vol. I (1888), pp. 373–9 *et seq.*
MALLESON, G. B. "Isle of France and Her Privateers." *Rev. Hist. et Litt. de l'Ile Maurice*, vol. III (1890), pp. 358–60 *et seq.*
PITOT, A. "History." Macmillan's *Mauritius* (1914), pp. 11–70.
——— *L'Ile de France: esquisses historiques*, 1715–1810. Port Louis, 1899.
——— *L'Ile Maurice: esquisses historiques*, 1810–28. 2 vols. Port Louis, 1910–12.
POYEN-BELLISLE, I. H. DE. *La guerre aux îles de France et Bourbon*, 1809–10. Paris, 1896.
Revue historique et littéraire de l'Ile Maurice. 7 vols. Port Louis, 1887–94.
SOCIÉTÉ ROYALE DES ARTS ET DES SCIENCES DE L'ILE MAURICE. *Centenaire*, 1829–1929. Port Louis, 1932.
[TELFAIR, C.] "Account of the Conquest of Mauritius." *Rev. Hist. et Litt. de l'Ile Maurice*, vol. VI (1893), pp. 267–70 *et seq.*
WALTERS, A. *The Sugar Industry of the Mauritius*. 1910.

SEYCHELLES

(a) CONTEMPORARY WORKS

DEGRANDPRÉ, L. M. J. O'H., Le Comte. *Voyage in the Indian Ocean*. 2 vols. 1803.
PRIOR, Sir J. *Voyage in the Indian Seas*, 1810–11. 1820.

(b) LATER WORKS

ANASTAS, C. *Histoire et description des Iles Séchelles*. Mauritius, 1897.
BRADLEY, J. T. *History of the Seychelles Islands*. Port Victoria, 1936.
DAVIDSON, Sir W. E. *Notes on the Naval Operations in the Indian Ocean*, 1800–10. Mahé [1909?].
FAUVEL, A. A. *Unpublished Documents on the History of the Seychelles Islands anterior to* 1810. Mahé, 1909.
"French in the Seychelles." *Colonial Office Jour.* vol. III (1910), pp. 302–5.
HAWTREY, S. H. C. *Handbook of Seychelles*. Mahé, 1928.
LUCAS, Sir C. P. *Historical Geography of the British Colonies*. Vol. I, *The Mediterranean and Eastern colonies*. Oxford, 1906. Pp. 169–79 deal with Seychelles.
SAUZIER, TH. "Contributions à l'histoire et à la géographie de l'archipel des Seychelles." *Rec. Hist. et Litt. de l'Ile Maurice*, vol. VII (1894), pp. 65–72, 81–92.

vi. *FALKLAND ISLANDS, ST HELENA AND ASCENSION*

FALKLAND ISLANDS

(*a*) CONTEMPORARY WRITINGS

HADFIELD, W. *Brazil, the River Plate, and the Falkland Islands.* 1854.
MACKINNON, L. B. *Some Account of the Falkland Islands.* 1840.
SULLIVAN, B. J. *Description des Iles Malouines ou Falkland.* Paris, 1850.
WHITINGTON, G. T. *Falkland Islands.* 1840.

(*b*) LATER WORKS

ALLARDYCE, Sir W. L. "Falkland Islands and its Dependencies." *United Empire*, vol. I (1910), pp. 334–5.
—— "Falkland Islands in History." *Dalhousie Rev.* vol. III (1923), pp. 291–302.
—— *Story of the Falkland Islands.* Falkland Islands, 1909.
BOYSON, V. F. *Falkland Islands.* Oxford, 1924.
DICKSON, J. Q. "The Empire's Outpost in the South Atlantic." *United Empire*, vol. VII (1916), pp. 161–72.
PROTHERO, Sir G. (Ed.). *Falkland Islands: Kerguelen.* 1920. Peace Handbooks, No. 138.
GOEBEL, J. *The Struggle for the Falkland Islands.* New Haven, Conn., 1927.
GOMEZ, LANGENHEIM. *La tercera invasion inglesa.* Buenos Aires, 1934.
GROUSSAC, P. *Les Iles Malouines.* Buenos Aires, 1910.
HOBLEY, C. M. *Falkland Islands, South America.* 1917.
MACDONALD, F. C. *Bishop Stirling.* 1929.
ST JOHNSTON, T. R. *Falkland Islands.* Stanley, 1920.

ST HELENA

(*a*) BIBLIOGRAPHY

St Helena Bibliography. St Helena [1937].

(*b*) CONTEMPORARY WRITINGS

BARNES, J. *Tour through the Islands of St Helena.* 1817.
BEATSON, A. *Tracts relative to the Island of St Helena.* 1816.
BROOKE, T. H. *History of the Island of St Helena.* 1808. 2nd edn. 1824.
Description of the Island of St Helena. 1805.
ELWOOD, Mrs A. K. *Narrative of a Journey Overland.* 2 vols. 1830. Vol. II, pp. 338–57, relate to St Helena.
STUART, R. "St Helena in 1838." *United Service Jour.* vol. XXVIII (1839), pp. 68–77.

(*c*) LATER WORKS

DEHERAIN, H. *Dans l'Atlantique: Saint Hélène aux XVIIe et XVIIIe siècles.* Paris, 1912.
ELLIS, A. B. *West African Islands.* 1885. Pp. 1–27 relate to St Helena.
FOSTER, Sir W. "Acquisition of St Helena." *Eng. Hist. Rev.* vol. XXXV (1919), pp. 281–9.
GOSSE, P. *St Helena, 1502–1938.* 1938.
HARE, R. H. A. *Voyage of the Caroline.* 1927.
HAUTERIVE, E. D. *Sainte Hélène,* Paris, 1933.
JACKSON, E. L. *St Helena: The Historic Island.* 1903.
JANISCH, H. R. (Ed.). *Extracts from the St Helena Records.* Jamestown, 1885. 2nd edn. 1908.
MATHIAS, O. L. "St Helena under the East India Company." *Fortnightly Rev.* vol. CXXIII (1928), pp. 738–46.

MELLISS, J. C. *Saint Helena.* 1875.
RENTY, E. DE. "L'Angleterre en Afrique: les îles africaines." *Questions Diplomatiques,* vol. XXX (1910), pp. 29–46.

ASCENSION

ELLIS, A. B. *West African Islands.* 1885. Pp. 28–52 relate to Ascension.
ELWOOD, Mrs A. K. *Narrative of a Journey Overland from England.* 2 vols. 1830. Vol. II, pp. 367–71, relate to Ascension.
FORD, E. H. *History and Postage Stamps of Ascension Island.* 1933.
MUNDY, G. C. *Pen and Pencil Sketches.* 2 vols. 1833.

INDEX

CAMBRIDGE: PRINTED BY W. LEWIS, M.A., AT THE UNIVERSITY PRESS